NOVELL'S

CNE® Study Guide
IntranetWare™/NetWare® 4.11

NOVELL'S

CNE® Study Guide
IntranetWare™/NetWare® 4.11
• • • • • • • • • • • • • • • • •

D A V I D   J A M E S   C L A R K E ,   I V

Novell Press, San Jose

Novell's CNE® Study Guide IntranetWare™/NetWare® 4.11

Published by
Novell Press
2180 Fortune Drive
San Jose, CA 95131

Library of Congress Catalog Card No.: 96-078781

ISBN: 0-7645-4512-4

Printed in the United States of America

10 9 8 7 6 5 4 3 2 1

1QBCM/RV/QR/ZX/FC

Distributed in the United States by IDG Books Worldwide, Inc.

Distributed by Macmillan Canada for Canada; by Contemporanea de Ediciones for Venezuela; by Distribuidora Cuspide for Argentina; by CITEC for Brazil; by Ediciones ZETA S.C.R. Ltda. for Peru; by Editorial Limusa SA for Mexico; by Transworld Publishers Limited in the United Kingdom and Europe; by Academic Bookshop for Egypt; by Levant Distributors S.A.R.L. for Lebanon; by Al Jassim for Saudi Arabia; by Simron Pty. Ltd. for South Africa; by Pustak Mahal for India; by The Computer Bookshop for India; by Toppan Company Ltd. for Japan; by Addison Wesley Publishing Company for Korea; by Longman Singapore Publishers Ltd. for Singapore, Malaysia, Thailand, and Indonesia; by Unalis Corporation for Taiwan; by WS Computer Publishing Company, Inc. for the Philippines; by WoodsLane Pty. Ltd. for Australia; by WoodsLane Enterprises Ltd. for New Zealand. Authorized Sales Agent: Anthony Rudkin Associates for the Middle East and North Africa.

For general information on IDG Books Worldwide's books in the U.S., contact our Consumer Customer Service department at 800-762-2974. For reseller information, including discounts and premium sales, contact our Reseller Customer Service department at 800-434-3422

For information on where to purchase IDG Books Worldwide's books outside the U.S., contact our International Sales department at 415-655-3078 or fax 415-655-3281.

For information on foreign language translations, contact our Foreign & Subsidiary Rights department at 415-655-3018 or fax 415-655-3281.

For sales inquiries and special prices for bulk quantities, contact our Sales department at 415-655-3200 or write to the address above.

For information on using IDG Books Worldwide's books in the classroom or for ordering examination copies, contact our Educational Sales department at 800-434-2086 or fax 817-251-8174.

For press review copies, author interviews, or other publicity information, please contact our Public Relations department at 415-655-3000 or fax 415-655-3299.

For authorization to photocopy items for corporate, personal, or educational use, contact the Copyright Clearance Center, 222 Rosewood Drive, Danvers, MA 01923, or fax 508-750-4470.

For general information on Novell Press books in the U.S., including information on discounts and premiums, contact IDG Books at 800-434-3422 or 415-655-3200. For information on where to purchase Novell Press books outside the U.S., contact IDG Books International at 415-655-3021 or fax 415-655-3295.

John Kilcullen, *President & CEO, IDG Books Worldwide, Inc.*
Brenda McLaughlin, *Senior Vice President & Group Publisher, IDG Books Worldwide, Inc.*
The IDG Books Worldwide logo is a trademark under exclusive license to IDG Books Worldwide, Inc., from International Data Group, Inc.

Rosalie Kearsley, *Publisher, Novell Press, Inc.* Novell Press and the Novell Press logo are trademarks of Novell, Inc.

Welcome to Novell Press

Novell Press, the world's leading provider of networking books, is the premier source for the most timely and useful information in the networking industry. Novell Press books cover fundamental networking issues as they emerge — from today's Novell and third-party products to the concepts and strategies that will guide the industry's future. The result is a broad spectrum of titles for the benefit of those involved in networking at any level: end-user, department administrator, developer, systems manager, or network architect.

Novell Press books are written by experts with the full participation of Novell's technical, managerial, and marketing staff. The books are exhaustively reviewed by Novell's own technicians and are published only on the basis of final released software, never on prereleased versions.

Novell Press at IDG Books Worldwide is an exciting partnership between two companies at the forefront of the information and communications revolution. The Press is implementing an ambitious publishing program to develop new networking titles centered on the current versions of IntranetWare, GroupWise, and Novell's ManageWise products. Select Novell Press books are translated into 14 languages and are available at bookstores around the world.

Rosalie Kearsley, Publisher, Novell Press, Inc.
Colleen Bluhm, Associate Publisher, Novell Press, Inc.

Novell Press

Publisher
Rosalie Kearsley

Associate Publisher
Colleen Bluhm

Acquisitions Editors
Anne Hamilton
Jim Sumser

Managing Editor
Terry Somerson

Development Editor
Kevin Shafer

Copy Editor
Kevin Shafer

Technical Editor
Gamal Herbon

Production Director
Andrew Walker

Pre-Press Coordination
Tony Augsburger
Theresa Sanchez-Baker

Media/Archive Coordination
Leslie Popplewell
Michael Wilkey

Project Coordinator
Phyllis Beaty

Graphics Coordination
Shelley Lea

Production Staff
Renée Dunn
Stephen Noetzel

Quality Control Specialist
Mick Arellano

Proofreader
Christine C. Langin-Faris

Indexer
Ty Koontz

Illustrator
David Puckett

Cartoonist
Michael Kim

Cover Design
Archer Design

Cover Photographer
Jim Kranz

I dedicate this book to the human race for never ceasing to amaze me . . .
and since you're a human, I guess in some strange way, I dedicate this book to you!

About the Author

David James Clarke, IV is the original creator of the CNE study guide phenomenon. He is the author of numerous #1 best-selling books for Novell Press, including *Novell's CNE Study Guide, Novell's CNE Study Guide for NetWare 4.1,* and the new IntranetWare Study Guide series. Clarke is a technical advisor for *CyberState University,* an on-line network training institute, and developer of *The Clarke Tests v3.0,* an interactive learning system. He is also the producer of the best-selling video series *So You Wanna Be a CNE?!* Clarke is a Certified Novell Instructor (CNI), a CNE, and a CNA. He speaks at numerous national conferences and currently serves as the president and CEO of Clarke Industries, Inc. He lives and works on a white sandy beach in California.

Foreword

Novell recognized very early that networking calls for a different kind of company and a different type of approach to dealing with computer systems. We know we need partners, and we regard the CNEs as being among the most important partners of all. The CNE program creates the pervasive expertise that will be needed to be of service to pervasive computing as it develops. Intelligent networking requires trained technicians on the spot, who can deal with the myriad configurations and platforms that Novell networking seeks to seamlessly connect. That in turn fosters openness, fosters freedom of choice. None of that would be well served if Novell tried to impose a one-size-fits-all networking system. So the CNE is essential right there on the ground. CNEs can go for the best answers, including those produced by other companies. They are practical, expert, and creative in fitting the technology to particular business needs. We are proud to be their partners in this unfolding enterprise.

The opportunities for CNEs have never been greater. Networking is more and more in demand; it is the solution virtually every company is turning to. A CNE understands business issues and networking capabilities, and combines them in such a way as to create and deliver effective solutions.

From a broader perspective, networking is also becoming ever more pervasive in the activities of our daily lives. The whole thing is exploding and will continue to explode in the foreseeable future. Change is happening, and the technician's skills will also need to evolve at a rapid rate. The CNE program is very conscious of the need to keep up with real world developments and future directions. So much more innovation is in store; so much more is going to be connected to computer networks — we have only begun to imagine the possibilities! All that change spells growing opportunities for everyone who participates in moving to better, more powerful solutions for our customers. In all of this, it is the CNE who will be on the front lines of progress.

Novell's CNE Study Guide for IntranetWare/NetWare 4.11 by David James Clarke, IV is a great example of the Novell partnership philosophy: human, open, precise, and expert. It is an extraordinarily welcome resource to help students join with Novell in the amazing and ever-changing future of computer networking.

Drew Major
V.P. & Chief Scientist, Operating Systems
Novell, Inc.

Acknowledgments

Wow, this was fun! Even though the pace was fast and furious, we all had a great time exploring IntranetWare, writing about the CNE program, and inventing ACME — A Cure for Mother Earth. I emphasize the word *"we."* I know it sounds corny, but I couldn't have written this book without the help and support of numerous friends and family. Let me introduce them to you.

Family is everything. I gained a new respect for them while writing this book, mostly because I continued to test the envelope of sanity. Crazy hours, crazy requests, crazy trips. Mary, my wife, deserves the most credit for supporting my work and bringing a great deal of happiness into my life. She is my anchor. Then there's Leia, my daughter. Somehow she knew just when I needed to be interrupted — daughter's intuition. Most of all, they both have brought much needed perspective into my otherwise one-dimensional life. For that, I owe them everything.

I also owe a great deal to my parents for their unending support and devotion. They are the architects of my life and I couldn't have accomplished anything without their guidance and love. In addition, my sister Athena and her family (Ralph and Taylor) deserve kudos for standing by me through thick and thin. In addition, thanks to my second family for opening their hearts to me. Don and Diane have been wonderfully generous to me, Mary, and their precious granddaughter, Leia. Also, Keith and Bob have been great brothers to me, and Lisa and Pam have been great sisters to Mary. Finally, Jessica has been a creative and fun influence on Leia.

Before I close my family circle, I must thank two important "extended family" members — Dr. James Buxbaum and Virginia Zakoor. They are life-friends who have always supported my writing. Together we are works-in-progress — a screenplay with James and a novel with Virginia. Someday we'll finish . . . .

ZEN

What no wife of a writer can ever understand is that he's working when he's staring out of the window.

Burton Rascoe

Now let's meet the true architect of this book — my partner Cathryn Ettelson. She has been instrumental in all aspects of this book — research, the Mad Scientist's laboratory, exercises, midnight phone calls, and the list goes on. I owe a great deal to this brilliant woman, and I truly couldn't have written this book without her. This is who I'm talking about when I say "*we.*" Thanks Cathryn. Now you can have that week-long vacation I've been promising you for years.

Next, I would like to thank Lori Ficklin, who was responsible for bringing my words to life — literally. Also, her husband, Richard, deserves a lot of credit for making sure I didn't ramble on forever. And, of course, there's Mike Kim. He's the collective funny bone of our group. Not only is Mike a gifted cartoonist, but he comes from the other side of Cyberspace — where most of the world lives. For that, he gives this book unique perspective and readability. I've been blessed to have such wonderful friends who stick with me through good times and bad. This is our eleventh book together, and I couldn't have done it without all of them.

Behind every great book is an incredible production team. It all starts with Kevin Shafer — legendary editor. His flawless organization, quick wit, and patience were instrumental in bringing this book to life. I can say with 100 percent certainty, he is the best editor I've ever worked with. Next, David Puckett deserves a great deal of praise for creating the beautiful illustrations in this book. I've always believed a picture is worth a thousand words. But his pictures are worth a few thousand more. And, of course, Jim Sumser for keeping me up to speed on all the exciting adventures at IDG Books Worldwide. He is our Robin Hood, our Knight in Shining Armor, our Hans Solo . . . . you get the idea.

Phyllis Beaty, Renée Dunn and Stephen Noetzel deserve a lot of the credit for finishing this book on time. They all performed above and beyond the call of duty in every aspect of production. Thanks to Gamal Herbon for being our technical eyes and ears — what a smart guy! I would also like to thank Mick Arellano, Christine Langin-Faris, Rebecca Plunket and all the proofreaders, typesetters, artists, and management who made this book possible, especially Andrew Walker and Terry Somerson. Finally, thanks to IDG Books Worldwide's sales, marketing, and bookstores for putting this book in your hands. After all, without them I'd be selling books out of the trunk of my car.

ZEN

You can tell a lot about a person by the way he eats jelly beans.

Ronald Reagan

Now, let's talk about Novell Press. What an amazing organization. They are truly the future of network publishing. It all starts with Rose Kearsley. She *is* Novell Press. Rose has been a wonderful friend and supportive publisher throughout the past five years. I can only hope for greater things in the future. And the dramatic revolution of these Study Guides is due in part to her almost clairvoyant insight — not to mention her uncanny ability to convince people they need to give us stuff. Then there's Colleen Bluhm who has been a wonderful friend through thick and thin — always e-mailing, calling, or popping up just at the right time. Colleen has also been my eyes and ears to Novell Education, an invaluable resource. She's a rock at Novell Press that I always count on for quick and accurate answers. Together, these great people bring Novell Press books to life. Give them a "thanks" next time you see them.

Life is not one-dimensional. Every now and then, when I leave my cave, I appreciate the support from numerous friends and colleagues. First, I'd like to thank my partner Paul Wildrick. He has been a constant source of excitement, business, and chaos. It seems like everyday he has a bright new idea for forging a new "frontier" for computing. Let's see, so far we've "frontiered" CyberState University, *LANimation*, World Wire, a dozen videos, *The Clarke Tests v3.0*, and more. My life would be so relaxing without you.

Speaking of CyberState University, I'd also like to say "Thanks" to David and Michael for doing such an amazing job. You bring "Synergy" to the Synergy Learning System®. And speaking of *The Clarke Tests v3.0*, I'd like to thank my other great friends, Lisa and Brian Smith, for keeping the ship afloat. Fulfillment and Tech Support: a match made in administrative heaven.

Next, I'd like to thank all of my NetWare Users International (NUI) friends for being there with me "on the road." You're all wonderful people and you're doing great things for NetWare users everywhere. The most thanks go to Ted Lloyd for spearheading the whole thing. He's a business genius with a great, big heart. What a rare combination these days. And thanks to all my extraordinary friends at Diablo Valley College (DVC): Leslie Leong, Dan McClellan, and Matt Anderson, for being there for me in the very beginning. And to my good friend Rich Rosdal of Clarity Technologies for always believing in me.

Finally, thanks to golf courses everywhere for giving me a reason to live; Tears for Fears for inspiration; The Tick for being a superhero role model; and Babs and Buster Bunny for teaching me everything I know about people.

ACKNOWLEDGMENTS

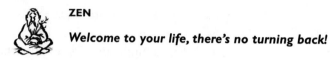

ZEN

Welcome to your life, there's no turning back!

Tears for Fears

I saved the best for last. Thanks to *YOU* for caring enough about IntranetWare and your education to buy this book. You deserve a great deal of credit for your enthusiasm and dedication. Thanks again, and I hope this education changes your life. Good luck, and welcome to your new exciting life! Enjoy the show.

Contents at a Glance

Contents

Introduction

Hi! I'm baaaaack!

It seems like just yesterday we were frolicking through the life of a CNE in the original *Novell's CNE Study Guide*. Well, the world's changed and CNEship has entered a new frontier — IntranetWare! It's unlike anything you've ever seen. There are clouds, trees, gardeners, and leaf objects. It's a plethora of permaculture; a virtual cornucopia of chlorophyll. And that's not all. IntranetWare introduces a whole new dimension in networking — NDS. You're in for the ride of your life. Green thumb required.

So, do you still want to be a CNE? The "007" of cyberworld? Good. Don't worry, you still get to traverse the obstacle course of unpredictable network challenges. It's just that the course has gotten a little bigger and the obstacles have gotten a little more unpredictable. The good news is the rewards still greatly outweigh the pain. You'll be more competitive in today's job market and maybe even save the world along the way. Life as a CNE has never been more exciting! Ready, set, go.

Life as a CNE!

ZEN

"Anything I've ever done that ultimately was worthwhile . . . initially scared me to death."

Betty Bender

By picking up this book, you've just shown that you are interested in taking steps toward furthering your career. Congratulations! That puts you a notch higher than a lot of your competition. Becoming an IntranetWare CNE demonstrates that you can hold your own as a network administrator. As a CNE, you're in prime position to help your users get the most out of your network, to help management get the most out of your users, and to help yourself get the most out of your career opportunities.

SO WHO NEEDS CNES, ANYWAY?

The whole world does, that's who. NetWare networks are, hands-down, the most popular network in the world. According to various surveys, 70 percent of all networks in the world are running some version of NetWare networking software. All other networking companies combined (including Microsoft, IBM, Banyan, and LANTastic) only account for the other 30 percent.

By early 1997, there were an estimated 5.7 million NetWare servers in the world. If you conservatively estimate an average of 10 users per server, you're looking at 55 million users. And those numbers are growing rapidly every month. Just imagine how many users will be out there by the time you read this paragraph. That's a significant number of people who need help with their networks. Lucky thing for them that you're interested in becoming a CNE.

ZEN

"A lot of prizes have been awarded for showing that the universe is not as simple as we might have thought!"

Stephen Hawking

HOW MUCH TROUBLE IS IT?

Achieving CNE status can be one of the best ways you'll find to enhance your position in the computer industry. To become certified, you must prove that you know the fundamentals of networking and can handle the daily needs of designing, installing, managing, and troubleshooting IntranetWare WANs. To prove this knowledge, you must pass seven computer-based exams.

Taking a test is one thing, but how do you get ready for the test? You must learn all this stuff first, right? Of course. But it may not be nearly as difficult to learn the networking ropes as you may think.

Understanding how IntranetWare networks run consists of learning some fundamental principles and a few key tools, then building on those. Once you know the fundamentals, you can begin to see how other aspects of the network fit in, how and where problems might occur, and how to solve those problems.

To learn about IntranetWare and prepare for the tests, you can take seven courses, study books like this one, or go the "real world" route and learn IntranetWare on the job. Even better, you can combine these methods. Most people will tell you that nothing beats actual experience when learning new things. This is true with IntranetWare, too. You can learn a lot from books and from classes, but until you get your hands into the network yourself, some concepts will still be a little foggy.

On the other hand, the "sink-or-swim" method of real-world learning can be relatively slow and painful by itself. Using a good Study Guide (such as this book) or taking an IntranetWare course can give you a terrific jump-start on the way to knowledge. A few days spent in class or with this book can save you several months of trial-and-error.

So, if you're like most people, the best approach is to combine as much "hands-on" experience as possible with as much "book learning'" as you can stand. This book was designed to help you out, without driving you crazy. No promises.

So, where do we go from here? A magic carpet ride, of course. A journey down the path to enlightenment — IntranetWare Nirvana. Don't worry. You don't have to travel alone. I'll be by your side every step of the way — your trusted CNE tour guide. And, I've brought along a few other friends to help. Heroes from our unspoiled history — before instant popcorn, talking cars, and daytime television. There's Albert Einstein, Sherlock Holmes, Gandhi, and Mother Teresa, just to name a few — the IntranetWare dream team. With friends like these, you can't do anything but succeed. Ready, set, go.

▶ . . . . ◀

Magic Carpet Ride

ZEN

"I don't pretend to understand the universe; it's a great deal bigger than I am."

Thomas Carlyle

The journey begins with a "seed of thought." Before you know it, you'll have a huge NDS tree growing out of your head. Chapter 1 explores the next generation of Netware. . . . *Intranet*Ware. That's right, Novell has expanded the LAN to include the "Intranet." And you'll learn everything about it in Chapter 1. It's also a preview of the entire book. The main new feature is NDS (Novell Directory Services) — that's covered in Chapter 2. Next, you'll learn the basic fundamentals of NDS — it's a whole new ballgame. Once you're done with NDS, it's time to attack the IntranetWare CNE obstacle course — design, installation, and management.

IntranetWare CNEs have three main tasks — design, installation, and management. First, you design the NDS tree — as a superhero. Second, you install the servers using an established design — as a doctor. And, third, you get to configure and manage it — as an NDS gardener. Talk about your split personalities! CNEs must excel in all three jobs, although each is very different. Fortunately, this book will help you every step of the way.

In Chapter 3, we introduce the pseudo-fictitious organization ACME. ACME is a group of world-famous heroes from the past who have banded together to save the world. We will be using them throughout the book in examples, exercises, and case studies. In Chapter 3, we will create the team responsible for ACME's NDS tree design and provide a large list of design inputs, including WAN layouts, an organization chart, and a workflow diagram. Good luck, and by the way, thanks for saving the world!

Then, you're in for the ride of your life. Chapter 4 explores the nuts and bolts of NDS design — a very important CNE task. Once again, we'll use ACME as an example. You will learn about tree design, partitioning, time sychronization, and most important, accessibility design. This is where the fun begins! Finally, in Chapter 5 you get to start NDS implementation. It all starts with a small seed. Then with water, sunlight, and love, the seedling grows into a fruitful, majestic tree. In Chapter 5 we learn how to bring our design to life and provide a transition to the next part — IntranetWare installation.

In Chapter 6, the network is born. This is the true implementation of NDS design. During IntranetWare installation, you follow six stages and 23 steps toward IntranetWare Nirvana. It's a great place to start. Next, in Chapter 7, you will explore the miracle of IntranetWare migration. IntranetWare is so different from earlier versions, upgrading is really migrating. It's a whole new frontier of networking. This chapter outlines the steps of migrating from NetWare 2, 3, or 4 all the way to IntranetWare. It seems like a breeze next to installation.

Once the tree has been designed and installed, it's time to take care of it. Chapter 8, NDS Management, deals with the daily tasks of gardening. We cover object naming, NWADMIN, object types, and Bindery Services. Try to keep the dirt out from under your fingernails. As we learn in Chapter 9, the tree also needs to be pruned periodically. This provides better health and efficiency (distributed databases) as well as tree stability and longevity (fault tolerance). Also, we'll explore time synchronization for better access to sunlight.

ZEN

"Some books are to be tasted, others swallowed, and some few to be chewed and digested."

Sir Francis Bacon

In Chapter 10, we learn that the file system represents NetWare life "within" the server. All of our focus so far has been "above" the server. Now we get a chance to work with a big, electronic filing cabinet. Chapter 11 continues this journey with a look at security. Information is now the new commodity — more valuable than money. We need to take new measures to protect our information. IntranetWare includes a five-layered security model including login/password authentication, login restrictions, NDS rights, file system access rights, and attributes. Think of it as your impenetrable network armor.

Once the LAN has been installed (born) it enters the second and third phases of its lifespan — configuration (childhood) and management (adulthood). In Chapter 12, the first of two related chapters, I'll walk you through the five steps of configuration using Leia as an example. Then, in Chapter 13, we're introduced to the final phase of LAN life span — adulthood. Here the network gets married, joins a bowling league, has children of her own, plans for retirement, and finally retires.

That leaves the last two topics: printing and optimization. Printing (Chapter 14) is "the great challenge." IntranetWare printing is simple and works great until . . . you add users. It's their fault. In this chapter, we will explore some proven methods for successful IntranetWare printing installation, management, and troubleshooting. In addition, we'll get a peek at printing's future — NDPS. Then we complete the journey with Chapter 15 — the final frontier. Once you've lived through the LAN life span and set up IntranetWare printing, only one task is left — optimization. Put the pedal to the metal and enter the new frontier at the speed of light. Your life will never be the same.

That pretty much sums it up — five courses in one book. Wow! These chapters cover everything there is to know about IntranetWare, life as a CNE, and saving the world. Of course, we couldn't survive our journey without four great appendices. Appendix A is an overview of Novell Education. Appendix B is a great cross-reference of CNE course objectives. It points you in the right direction — course by course. Appendix C has all the answers — literally. It has answers for case studies, exercises, and quizzes. Finally, Appendix D provides all the help you'll need to survive in the "real world."

Speaking of answers, I have a few life puzzles I could use answered. How about you?

Life Puzzles

ZEN

"Next, when you are describing,
A shape, or sound, or tint;
Don't state the matter plainly,
But put it in a hint;
And learn to look at all things,
With a sort of mental squint."

Lewis Carroll

There is a difference between puzzles and problems. Life puzzles allow you to stretch your mind and explore parts of your brain you didn't even know you had. Also, they usually have one answer — or so it seems. Life problems, on the other hand, arise through the everyday process of getting out of bed and putting on your clothes. Also, there is never a "right" answer — just shades of gray. We cover both in this book:

> ▸ *Life Puzzles* — Any fun book would be incomplete without crossword and word search puzzles. Take a crack at 20 doozies and don't blow a brain cell.

▶ *Life Problems* — Concepts are important, but the real test is in the doing. There are almost 50 original exercises and case studies in this book. Some are written, but most are hands-on. These labs are designed to provide you with "real life" experience in managing local and global IntranetWare WANs. And as an extra bonus, you get to save the world in the process.

So, the moral is — read this book in bed, and enjoy the life puzzles.

In addition to life puzzles and problems, there are a myriad of other informational tidbits scattered throughout the book. These quips provide instant information in the form of Zen, Quizzes, Tips, Real World, The Brain, and SmartLinks. Check them out:

ZEN

Words of wisdom from people more enlightened than I am. Plus, they make you look really smart in front of your friends.

QUIZ

These brain puzzlers help bring much needed perspective into your difficult and absorbing journey. It's a great idea to come up for "mental air" every now and then. And these quizzes will appear at just the right time — before you mentally suffocate.

TIP

Highlights time-proven management techniques and action-oriented ideas. These tips are great ways of expanding your horizons beyond just CNEship — they're your ticket to true nerdom.

REAL WORLD

Welcome to the real world. I don't want you to be a two-dimensional CNE in a three-dimensional world. These icons represent the other dimension. In an attempt to bring this book to life, I've included various real-world scenarios, case studies, and situational walk-throughs.

THE BRAIN

In case yours turns to Jell-O. These are great context-sensitive references to supplemental brains. Brains-for-hire, like IntranetWare documentation, Application Notes, Albert Einstein, and so on. Enjoy them, and give yours a rest.

SMART LINK

We live in a "virtual" world: surfing the net, online dating, cyber children, and talking toasters. So, I thought it was only fitting to include these virtual Smart Links in my book. All you have to do is click on the URL code with your pencil and you will be instantaneously transported to a great, cool site on the Web. You're welcome.

WHAT'S NEW

WHAT'S
NEW

Life's always a 'changin! And we have the latest and greatest from Novell and IntranetWare.

Are We Having Fun Yet?!

ZEN

"All the animals except man know that the principle business of life is to enjoy it."

Samuel Butler

Inevitably, at some point you're going to want to apply all this great IntranetWare knowledge to some physical structure — a WAN perhaps. One assumes you will *act* on this book's CNE concepts, theories, exercises, and examples. One assumes at some point, you'll need to scream! That's OK, I'm here for you. I care.

The main goal of this book is to take you on a magic carpet ride through the next generation of NetWare — IntranetWare. Nobody said it couldn't be fun! As a matter of fact, I've worked overtime to make this the most painless, and even enjoyable, IntranetWare experience of your life. I've even included a life-size poster of Lola Bunny — just kidding.

It would be irresponsible of me to abandon you at the very moment you need the most help — real life! I'm here for you — every step of the way. I'm only a cybercall away. Also, in an effort to provide you with the most complete education possible, we have developed a special CNE Study Guide version of *The Clarke Tests v3.0* and placed it on the CD-ROM in the back of this book. See Appendix D for complete details on the CD-ROM contents.

In addition, I spend most of the year traveling around the globe — meeting you! I speak at NetWare Users International conferences, Networld + Interop, Networks Expo, and others. But if none of that works for you, I'm always available to chat. Really! I'm sitting by the cyperphone waiting for it to "cyberring." Find me:

- ▶ Internet: dciv@garnet.berkeley.edu

- ▶ The Web: http://www.cyberstateu.com/clarke.html

- ▶ CompuServe: 71700,403 or DAVID_IV

- ▶ CyberState University: 1-888-GET-EDU*Cated*

- ▶ World Wire: DAVID CLARKE, IV

  - • Sign up at 1-510-254-1194 (on-line)

  - • Phone: 1-510-254-7283

- ▶ The *Clarke Tests v3.0*: 1-800-684-8858

- ▶ NUI Conferences: 1-800-228-4NUI

So, get prepared for a magic carpet ride through IntranetWare administration. Fasten your seat belt, secure all loose objects, and keep your arms inside the ride at all times. There's no limit to where you can go from here!

Ready, set, go!

IntranetWare CNE — A New Frontier

 ZEN

"As knowledge increases, wonder deepens."

Charles Morgan

There's a whole galaxy of IntranetWare knowledge nuggets out there — and we will explore every last one of them. Our mission is to boldly go where no one has gone before — or at least get through this book without losing our marbles. Our first stop — the twilight zone. Take a quick look at this mind-twisting crossword puzzle. Welcome to your life! Scary, huh? Whatever you do, don't attempt the puzzle now, it could cause irreparable damage to your brain cells. On second thought — go ahead! You'll like it — really. And when you've had enough, the answers are in Appendix C. Cheers!

INTRANETWARE CNE — A NEW FRONTIER

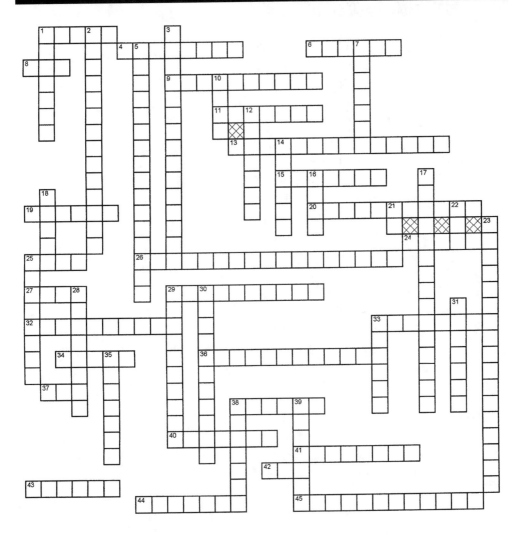

Across

1. Where the World Health Index is calculated
4. NetWare 4.11 server startup directory
6. Default server installation method
8. A "global village"
9. Prehistoric file sharing

11. Perpetuating the filing myth
13. Scrawling signatures
15. Just do it!
19. Dynamic bad block remapping
20. Most reliable external time source
24. The rules of NDS
25. Not up
26. The MONITOR.NLM washing machine
27. Top of the world
29. Where orphan files go to live
32. Characteristics of each network resource
33. ASCII, by default
34. A whole new world above the WAN
36. Dinosaur of NDS security
37. When lightening strikes
38. Mobile users
40. Etch-a-Sketch for NDS
41. More than 64 entries
42. First IntranetWare volume
43. Defines country code, character code set, and keyboard mapping
44. The new server superhero
45. Layout of the LANd

Down

1. Your friend for NDS gardening
2. Are you really AEinstein?
3. Storing and forwarding MHS messages
5. A measure of our future
7. Pruning in the non-GUI world
10. A Cure for Mother Earth
12. General layout of NDS tree design
14. "Elder" partitions
16. They turn colors in the fall
17. "On," by default
18. The new home of Sherlock Holmes and Dr. Watson
21. IntranetWare context navigation tool

22. The goal
23. Gathering unused RAM in IntranetWare
25. The new BINDFIX
28. I'm just not your _____
29. Virtual reality ACME
30. Physical network resources in the NDS tree
31. "I've deleted my file and can't get up!"
33. Server installation with all the bells and whistles
35. _____ comic, paper bag optional
38. Your friend for NDS gardening
39. IntranetWare in German

See Appendix C for answers.

IntranetWare CNE Basics

▶ · ◀

To IntranetWare, or not to IntranetWare — that is the question.
Whether tis nobler in the mind to suffer
The slings and arrows of previous NetWare versions,
Or to take arms against a sea of troubles, and by opposing end them.

To Upgrade, To Migrate.
No more bindery — and by a migration to say we end the heartache,
And the thousand natural shocks that the bindery is heir to!
Tis a consummation devoutly to be wished.

To Upgrade, To Migrate.
To Migrate — perchance to plan poorly.
Aye, there's the rub.
For in that poor planning, what problems may arise.
When we have shuffled off this earlier version, must give us mortal pause.
There's the respect that makes calamity of staying with an earlier version.

William Shakespeare (as told by Richard Rosdal)

Welcome to IntranetWare — the next generation of computing. Not since *Romeo and Juliet* has there been so much network synergy. Not since *Hamlet* has a company been so driven. Not since *The Tempest* has a product been so compelling. Even William Shakespeare saw it coming.

You are in for the ride of your life. Like a roller coaster, it starts with a deep breath and seatbelt (Chapter 1). Then, you make the nerve-racking ascent toward the sky (Chapter 2). Finally, in Chapter 3, we'll let you loose on the most exhilarating 1,600 pages you've ever read. Truly an "E" ticket ride!

The portal to a new frontier has been opened up for you today . . . warp speed ahead.

Introduction to IntranetWare

"We've come halfway across the galaxy to see IntranetWare!"

So you think you know NetWare. Well, I have a surprise for you! Not even Bo knows this version — IntranetWare. Novell's fifth generation of the NetWare operating system is a completely new ball game — and fortunately nobody is on strike.

Welcome to IntranetWare!

IntranetWare is the big kahuna. It represents Novell's tenth try at the NetWare network operating system. The original architects of NetWare — Drew Major and Superset — returned to the proverbial drawing board and completely redesigned the interface, communications, and functionality. The result is a powerful, flexible, and fast wide area network operating system. There's a mouthful.

IntranetWare epitomizes transparent connectivity. It unobtrusively provides the user with simultaneous access to multiple network resources from one login — whatever that means. Simply stated, users no longer belong to servers — they belong to the *network* as a whole. All resources of the wide area network (WAN) are created as objects in a hierarchical tree, much like files in a directory structure. Users, servers, printers, volumes, and groups are treated equally and given simultaneous access to each other's resources. It's been a long and winding road, but we've finally achieved NetWare Nirvana in true form. This is all made possible through IntranetWare's great wonder — Novell Directory Services (NDS).

NDS is an object-oriented database that organizes network resources into a *hierarchical* tree — there's that fancy word again. The global NDS tree is fully replicated and distributed throughout the network, providing efficient connectivity and network fault tolerance — which is easier said than done. NDS also features a single login and hidden security system that makes access to any server, volume, or network resource completely transparent to the user. NDS takes care of the complexities of network topology, communications, protocol translation, and authentication in the background far away from the user.

Think of NDS as a friendly cloud of joy overlooking your network! NDS is simplicity through sophistication.

TIP

NDS enables you to manage network resources (such as servers, users, and printers) and services, but it does not control the file system (directories and files). IntranetWare provides a variety of non-NDS utilities for managing the file system.

In addition to Novell Directory Services, IntranetWare offers myriad additional features and benefits. We will explore them in just a moment.

SMART LINK

For an introduction to Novell Directory Services, consult the on-line IntranetWare documentation at http://www.novell.com/manuals.

IntranetWare is not an upgrade of NetWare 3.1 — it requires a system *migration*. IntranetWare is a completely different way of approaching networking. It splits the role of networking into halves — logical and physical. The logical half defines organizations and workgroups. The physical half defines users and servers. The beauty of this approach is that IntranetWare can be as simple or complex as you want it to be. In addition, it includes a feature called *bindery emulation* that enables an IntranetWare server to look like a NetWare 3.12 server. This is a whole new twist on backward compatibility. All in all, IntranetWare is a great solution for small-, medium-, and large-size local area networks (LANs), metropolitan area networks (MANs), and wide area networks (WANs). Also, you better get used to it, because IntranetWare is the foundation of Novell's new Enterprise approach to networking. Before you know it, NetWare 3 will be long gone and you'll be reading *Novell's CNE Study Guide for IntranetWare 3*.

TIP

NetWare 3.12 is actually more similar to IntranetWare than you might think. NetWare 3.12 was originally developed because users of NetWare 3.11 were complaining that NetWare 4.0 had all the cool features. To satisfy these users, Novell released a special version of NetWare 3.11 that included some of the new advanced NetWare 4.0 features (such as VLMs, SMS, a new menu system, on-line documentation, and better Windows support). In reality, NetWare 3.12 is a subset of IntranetWare without NDS.

THE FOUNDATION OF NETWARE 3.12

If all of this seems a little overwhelming, have no fear, Uncle David is here. IntranetWare actually isn't as alien as you might think. As a matter of fact, Novell hasn't made any dramatic changes to the fundamental architecture of the core operating system (OS). The Novell designers simply built on top of what exists in NetWare 3.12. As you can see in Figure 1.1, NetWare 3.12 consists of the core OS and some supplemental services. All the services shown in this figure are mostly unchanged in IntranetWare. These services include:

- ▸ *Core OS* — Of course, the core operating system has been "tweaked" a little in IntranetWare, but the fundamental 32-bit architecture remains unchanged from NetWare 3.12. IntranetWare still relies on the console prompt and uses NetWare Loadable Modules (NLMs) to provide additional functionality.

▸ · ◂

FIGURE 1.1

The Foundation of NetWare 3.12

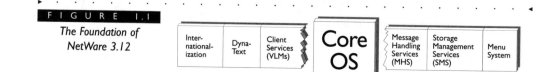

| Inter-national-ization | Dyna-Text | Client Services (VLMs) | **Core OS** | Message Handling Services (MHS) | Storage Management Services (SMS) | Menu System |

WHAT'S NEW

WHAT'S NEW

I would like to interrupt this book for an emergency broadcast message from Novell. As you know, the latest release of NetWare isn't NetWare at all — it's "IntranetWare." So, what happened to NetWare? Fortunately, it's still here. As a matter of fact, the IntranetWare solution uses "NetWare 4.11" as its primary operating system. Confusing? Yes.

So, here's the bottom line: IntranetWare the network-centric WAN solution and NetWare 4.11 is the server-centric LAN OS it uses. Throughout this book, we will refer to "IntranetWare" as the product, and "NetWare 4.11" as the core OS. Now, I will return you to your regularly scheduled programming.

- ▸ *Internationalization* — Both NetWare 3.12 and IntranetWare are designed to support a variety of international languages and utilities. In IntranetWare, the operating system, error message files, and documentation are available in the following languages: Chinese (simplified and traditional), French, German, Italian, Japanese, Korean, Portuguese, Russian, and Spanish.

THE BRAIN

For further information on using IntranetWare in languages other than English, refer to the "International Use of NetWare 4" section of the *Novell NetWare 4.11 Concepts* manual or surf the Web at http://www.novell.com/manuals.

▶ *DynaText* — The DynaText viewer included with IntranetWare offers all the functionality of the Novell DynaText viewer provided in NetWare 3.12, plus a quicker response time, enhanced graphical user interface (GUI), Macintosh and UnixWare support, and compatibility for public or private notes in on-line manuals.

▶ *Client services (VLMs)* — Both NetWare 3.12 and IntranetWare offer better workstation connectivity through the NetWare DOS Requester. The Requester uses Virtual Loadable Modules (VLMs) to provide enhanced workstation support for NDS, NCP packet signing, and advanced user authentication. The latest version also supports connection timeout optimization, auto-reconnect, and much better extended memory management. In addition, IntranetWare includes an optional 32-bit Client for advanced workstations.

▶ *Message Handling Services (MHS)* — Novell now includes a sophisticated e-mail engine with NetWare 3.12 and IntranetWare. In NetWare 3.12 this engine is implemented as Basic MHS; in IntranetWare, it is termed MHS Services for IntranetWare. Both versions provide a background engine for storing and forwarding IntranetWare messages. In addition, they provide a starter e-mail application called FirstMail, which includes both DOS and Windows versions. The IntranetWare version of MHS also provides full integration with NDS and IntranetWare administration utilities. It takes advantage of specific mail-oriented NDS objects and includes SFT III compatibility. Furthermore, Enterprise customers can benefit from the comprehensive messaging features of GroupWise.

▶ *Storage Management Services (SMS)* — Like MHS, both NetWare 3.12 and IntranetWare include a background engine for backing up and restoring server data. SMS enables data to be stored and retrieved by using a variety of front-end applications. Also, these applications can call on numerous independent storage devices attached directly to the IntranetWare server. In addition, SMS can back up a variety of file systems-including DOS, OS/2, Macintosh, MS Windows, and UNIX. Another exciting feature of SMS is workstation backup. This might seem a little backward for those of you who are used to backing up servers from the workstation — now we're backing up workstations from the server. IntranetWare's SMS adds support for NDS backup and the System Independent Data Format (SIDF).

▸ *Menu System* — Since NetWare 3.11, Novell has dedicated itself to providing a better integrated menu system. NetWare 3.12 and IntranetWare use the new Saber-like menu system for building a consistent user interface. It includes better memory management, a higher level of workstation security, and user input options.

ZEN

"The guy who invented headcheese must have been really hungry."

Jerry Seinfeld

THE EVOLUTION OF INTRANETWARE

As I mentioned earlier, IntranetWare builds on the foundation of NetWare 3.12. Now, let's take a look at the evolution of NetWare from a server-centric OS to a network-centric OS. As you can see in Figure 1.2, there are five main features that make NetWare 4.11 the operating system of the next generation. These features build on top of the NetWare 3.12 foundation and reach to the sky. The most pervasive of these features is NDS:

▸ *Novell Directory Services (NDS)* — NDS is also known as the "Cloud." It oversees all facets of network operation — from logging in to multiprotocol routing. In short, IntranetWare is NetWare 3.12 with NDS. It's that simple — or not. Life in the NDS universe is a little more complicated than you might think. The price for user transparency is your blood, sweat, and tears. NDS generates a great deal more administrative overhead than you might be used to. But all of your hard work is worth it. NDS will ultimately increase user productivity and add more value to the network. Some customers are projecting a 300 percent return on their IntranetWare investment. We'll take a much closer look at NDS in just a moment, then spend all of Chapter 2 learning its hidden secrets. Welcome to the X-Files.

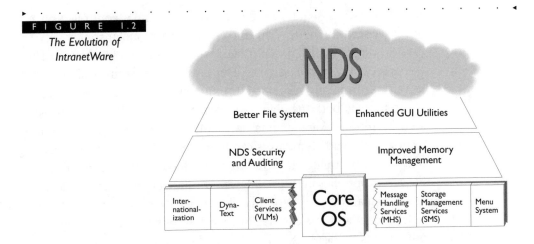

FIGURE 1.2

The Evolution of IntranetWare

▶ *Better File System* — IntranetWare optimizes the server disk with three new features: file compression, data migration, and block suballocation. File compression automatically reduces the size of infrequently used files by up to 63 percent. Data migration offloads these files to near-line storage devices. Finally, block suballocation decreases storage inefficiencies by allowing multiple files to share a single disk block. More details to come.

▶ *Enhanced GUI Utilities* — IntranetWare has vastly improved the interface for both user and administrator utilities. At the forefront of the new utility revolution is NetWare Administrator (NWADMIN) — a fully integrated Windows-based graphical administrator tool. The NetWare Administrator centralizes all IntranetWare tasks in one graphical NDS window. IntranetWare also offers a text-based menu version of NetWare Administrator (called NETADMIN), enhanced console commands, server NLMs, and new user command line utilities (CLUs). Also, don't miss the new integrated partition management tool — NDS Manager. All in all, IntranetWare not only works better, it also looks better.

ZEN

"Image is everything."

Andre Agassi

▸ *NDS Security and Auditing* — IntranetWare security is controlled by a five-layer security model. This model looks very similar to the NetWare 3.12 four-layer model, except that it includes an additional layer of access security — NDS security. This layer defines security above the server by controlling movement throughout the NDS tree. NDS access rights apply at both the object and property levels. In addition to NDS security, IntranetWare includes a comprehensive and powerful auditing feature. Independent auditors can track network transactions according to a variety of strategies, including logins/logouts, trustee modifications, file access and modification, NDS activity, queue management, and object management. The beauty of IntranetWare auditing is that independent auditors can track network resources without having any other rights to the WAN. All these features allow IntranetWare to satisfy the strict requirements of C-2 level security. You will learn more about IntranetWare NDS security later in this chapter.

▸ *Improved Memory Management* — IntranetWare manages file server RAM in a completely different way than NetWare 3.12 did. Earlier versions of NetWare allocated memory to multiple pools that served specific purposes. These pools were so inefficient that server applications could run out of RAM even if there was plenty of memory available in the main pool. IntranetWare has consolidated all server RAM into one central pool, and memory is reallocated as needed. In addition, IntranetWare includes memory protection that allows NLMs to run in a protected area of RAM. This ensures the safety of the core OS while you are testing third-party NLMs. Shields up!

As you can see from this discussion, IntranetWare represents the peak of OS evolution. It builds on the foundation of NetWare 3.12 to create a more powerful platform for the next generation of networking. For an even more detailed comparison of the NetWare 3.12 and IntranetWare features, refer to Table 1.1.

TABLE 1.1
*IntranetWare and NetWare
3.12 Features Comparison*

FEATURE	INTRANETWARE	NETWARE 3.12
ARCHITECTURE		
Maximum number of user connections per server	1,000	250
Nondedicated server	Yes (IntranetWare for OS/2)	No
Single login to network	Yes	No
Additive licensing	Yes	No
Memory protection	Yes	No
Global directory services	Yes	No
FILE SYSTEM AND STORAGE		
File compression	Yes	No
Data migration	Yes	No
Block suballocation	Yes	No
NETWORK SECURITY		
RSA public/private key encryption	Yes	No
Restrict login to specific Macintosh addresses	Yes	No
Security auditing	Yes	No
GUI utility with view of entire network	Yes	No
Remote console session security	Yes	No
Remote console modem callback	Yes	No
Maximum shared printers	256 per print server	16 per print server
RAM used with remote printer	4.6K to 5.4K	4K to 20K
Integrated messaging	Yes	No
Network Link Services Protocol (NLSP)	Yes	Yes (add-on required)

(continued)

FEATURE	INTRANETWARE	NETWARE 3.12
CLIENT SUPPORT AND INTEROPERABILITY		
LPT ports on client	LPT-1 to LPT-9	LPT-1 to LPT-3
IntranetWare Macintosh user licenses included	Matches the number of IntranetWare user licenses	5
GUI user tools	Yes	Yes
NetWare DOS Requester support	Yes	Yes

SMART LINK

For an quick overview of new features in IntranetWare, consult the on-line IntranetWare documentation at http://www.novell.com/manuals.

All the new features we've just discussed are included in both IntranetWare and the previous version in NetWare 4.1. In addition, some new features have been introduced with NetWare 4.11. Let's take moment to explore the newest features of NetWare's fifth-generation operating system.

WHAT'S NEW IN INTRANETWARE

With each release of NetWare 4, Novell improves a number of basic and Enterprise services. With IntranetWare, ten major advancements have been made, beginning with Novell Directory Services. Let's briefly review each.

1. Novell Directory Services

The major improvement in IntranetWare NDS is a philosophical one. Novell is moving toward an OS-independent version of Directory Services. Therefore, the name is no longer NetWare Directory Services, but Novell Directory Services.

To support this enhanced Enterprise approach, the new NDS includes a variety of additional leaf objects, one of which is the User template. This object is now in a "class" by itself instead of being relegated to a type of User object. In addition, audit log files are now represented by, and managed as, Directory objects. This enables you to control access to audit log files by using Directory rights assignments. Finally, the new NDS supports a connection to multiple Directory trees. As we'll learn later, Novell has just started the creation of a new "federation." Look out Star Fleet.

In addition to these structural improvements, IntranetWare includes enhanced NDS utilities. For starters, a Windows 95 version of NetWare Administrator has been added and the interface has been improved with a configurable tool bar, a configurable status bar, and the ability to hide and sort property pages for individual Directory objects. In addition, you can manage multiple trees simultaneously within the same NWADMIN window and set property values for multiple objects with the "Details on Multiple Users Option." Finally, you can print the Directory tree from within NetWare Administrator.

In addition to improved NWADMIN and NETADMIN utilities, IntranetWare includes a new graphical hierarchical browser for partition management — called NDS Manager. NDS Manager runs as a stand-alone application or as an integrated part of NWADMIN. It provides partitioning and replication services, as well as context-sensitive help for synchronizing errors detected by the "Partition Continuity Option." NDS Manager also includes the ability to repair the Directory database from a client workstation, and an update compatibility so that any or all IntranetWare servers on a network can be updated to a newer version of the DS.NLM file. We'll be spending plenty of time with Novell Directory Services in the next chapter and later in the book in Chapters 8 and 9.

2. Server Operating System

IntranetWare is based on the same stable, secure core OS as NetWare 4.1. In addition, it has been enhanced to provide improved ABEND recovery, UPS connectivity, and CLIB.NLM support. NetWare Web Server and NetWare Symmetric MultiProcessing (SMP) features have been added, as well. Let's take a closer look.

With IntranetWare, the server operating system has improved recovery options for handling an ABnormal END (ABEND). For starters, additional information about the source of the ABEND is displayed on the server console. This information identifies the NLM or hardware problem that caused the ABEND, so an administrator can take corrective actions. Also, when an ABEND occurs, information about the ABEND is automatically written to a text file (ABEND.LOG). Finally, two new SET parameters have been added that enable the server to automatically recover in various ways — "Auto Restart After ABEND" and "Auto Restart After ABEND Delay Time."

With IntranetWare, the core operating system now supports an uninterruptible power supply (UPS) connection through a serial port. This functionality is provided by the UPS_AIO.NLM module. In addition, the IntranetWare SFT III system has been enhanced with two new SET parameters and improvements in the PROTOCOLS command. Also, the server OS includes some hardware platform-related enhancements such as server memory management routines that take advantage of the Global Page attribute in Intel's Pentium Pro microprocessor and better support for the Peripheral Component Interface (PCI) bus architecture.

With IntranetWare, the CLIB.NLM file has been modularized into several NLMs. The functionality of the previous CLIB.NLM is now available in the following modules:

▸ *CLIB.NLM* — ANSI-compliant run-time interface for old CLIB functions.

▸ *FPSM.NLM* — floating-point support library

▸ *THREADS.NLM* — IntranetWare standard NLM THREADS package

▸ *REQUESTR.NLM* — standard Requester package

▸ *NLMLIB.NLM* — POSIX and other basic NLM run-time support

▸ *NIT.NLM* — old NetWare interface tools which are being replaced by interfaces in CALN32.NLM

In addition to these core OS improvements, IntranetWare adds two new products — NetWare Web Server and NetWare Support for Symmetric MultiProcessing. The NetWare Web Server technology enables you to publish documents on internal corporate networks and on the World Wide Web. Because the software runs on a standard NetWare platform, you can establish an Internet presence without using UNIX and the expensive hardware that UNIX requires. The NetWare Web Server consists of a set of NLMs that are easy to install and configure. It includes support for forms, the Remote Common Gateway Interface (R-CGI) specification, access logging, BASIC and PERL script interpreters, and the ability to easily control access to the server and its file system by using standard NDS security features. In addition, you can control access to HTML documents based on IP address, username, host name, directory structure, filename, and/or group membership.

The NetWare Symmetric MultiProcessing (SMP) technology enables the NetWare 4.11 operating system to run on a multiprocessor server. NetWare SMP enables the server to run resource-intense services (such as large databases, document management software, and multimedia applications) on a NetWare server. As I'm sure you can imagine, it provides increased processing power and better network performance to the Enterprise. In addition, there's support for up to 32 processors, depending on the hardware platform and Advanced Programmable Interrupt Controllers (APICs).

3. Installation

To make the installation process easier in IntranetWare, the INSTALL utility autodetects hardware devices installed in the server. In addition, Novell has partnered with Preferred Systems to develop and provide an additional upgrade utility with IntranetWare: DS Migrate (see Chapter 7).

During an IntranetWare installation, the INSTALL utility automatically detects the hardware devices in a server (including hard drives, CD-ROM devices, LAN cards, and so on). It then scans for and selects applicable device drivers (.DSK and .HAM files) for the hardware.

To provide IntranetWare customers with a complete upgrade solution, Novell has partnered with Preferred Systems to develop and deliver two additional upgrade utilities in IntranetWare — DS Migrate and the NetWare File Migration Utility:

> ▶ *DS Migrate* — This is a new migration and modeling solution that is built into the graphical NWADMIN utility. DS Migrate enables you to upgrade a NetWare 2.1x or NetWare 3.1x server bindery by migrating modeled bindery information to an existing IntranetWare tree. DS Migrate migrates only bindery information. Data files are migrated using either the new graphical NetWare File Migration utility or the DOS menu-based MIGRATE utility (see Chapter 7).

> ▶ *NetWare File Migration Utility* — This is a new utility for migrating files from NetWare 3.1x file systems to IntranetWare file systems. The NetWare File Migration Utility is used in conjunction with the new DS Migrate utility after NetWare 3.1x bindery migration. This facility is also incorporated into the new NWADMIN tool (see Chapter 7).

You'll get an opportunity to explore all 23 steps of the IntranetWare installation in Chapter 6.

4. NetWare Licensing Services

With IntranetWare, Novell is introducing NetWare Licensing Services (NLS). NLS is a distributed Enterprise network service that enables administrators to monitor and control the use of licensed applications on a network. It is tightly integrated with NDS technology and is based on an Enterprise service architecture. This architecture consists of client components that support different platforms and system components that reside on IntranetWare servers. NLS also provides a basic license metering tool and libraries that export licensing service functionality to developers of other licensing systems.

5. Connectivity Services

IntranetWare is fully multiprotocol-compliant. This means IntranetWare servers can communicate over the network using the traditional IPX protocol or new integrated support for TCP/IP. NetWare/IP enables you to extend IntranetWare services and applications to nodes on an existing IP network in a manner that is transparent to users. It also allows you to interconnect TCP/IP and IPX networks, enabling users on both platforms to access IntranetWare resources on either network. You can easily manage TCP/IP addresses using the Dynamic Host Configuration Protocol (DHCP) and provide access to network printers attached to UNIX hosts using the "LPR" protocol.

To use NetWare/IP in an IP-only environment, you must use network client software that supports the TCP/IP protocol. This includes the new IntranetWare Client 32, the NetWare/IP version of VLMs, or the NetWare Client for Mac OS. In addition, the new NetWare Client for Mac OS allows Macintosh workstations to access IntranetWare servers using traditional IPX or new IP protocols. Previous connectivity required the AppleTalk protocol. For more information on NetWare/IP and Macintosh connectivity, refer to Chapter 13.

6. File Services

With IntranetWare, the NetWare file system more effectively supports extended name spaces and can hold 8 million files per volume (16 million on DOS-only volumes). In addition, IntranetWare volumes mount much faster and the file system automatically monitors volume space.

With IntranetWare, the LONG.NAM module provides extended name space to Windows 95, Windows NT, and OS/2 workstation platforms. LONG.NAM is a special type of NLM that enables non-DOS file names on an IntranetWare volume.

Because extended name spaces are used more often now, LONG.NAM is loaded as part of the default server configuration.

In addition to the improvements discussed earlier, the IntranetWare file system responds more efficiently to the new 32-bit IntranetWare client architecture, delivering a higher level of performance to workstations using the new 32-bit IntranetWare client. We'll explore the IntranetWare file system in much more depth in Chapter 10.

7. Application Services

Novell has introduced two new advancements in the network application arena — the NetWare Application Manager (NAM) and NetWare Application Launcher (NAL).

The NAM utility enables you to represent applications as objects in the Directory tree. As NDS objects, you can manage applications the same way you manage other objects using NWADMIN. In addition, you can define an application directory, icon, command line parameters, and other attributes in one place; use trustee assignments to manage access to applications; and define startup scripts that establish the appropriate network environment for the application.

The NAL utility (available in both 16-bit and 32-bit versions) enables network users to launch applications represented by Application objects. When started, NAL displays a desktop that contains Application object icons. When the network user clicks on an icon, NAL sets up the workstation and starts the associated application as defined in the Application object's properties. As a CNE, you can control to what applications the network user has access and the user's ability to adjust the NAL desktop. This is just another example of how IntranetWare and NDS are working together to integrate all Enterprise services. You'll get a chance to work with the new IntranetWare application management products in Chapter 12.

8. Storage Management Services (SMS)

In IntranetWare, the enhanced Storage Management Services (SMS) feature includes a better backup utility, more effective backup and restore capabilities for the Directory, and new Target Service Agents (TSAs). Probably the most impressive improvement involves the SBACKUP utility itself:

- ▸ You can create session files from tape.

- ▸ You can search log files for specific character strings.

▸ Backup sessions can be verified with CRC values.

▸ SBACKUP now displays a running count for up to 4.2 terabytes of data as it is backed up.

When data is restored, information about the restoration target is written to the error file.

In previous versions of NetWare 4, Directory schema extensions and the mechanisms that enable you to manage file trustee assignments from NDS were not effectively backed up. This meant key security information was lost. With IntranetWare, a server's private key, User object IDs, and file trustee assignments and replica information are effectively maintained throughout the backup-and-restore process — very good news.

In addition, IntranetWare ships with new Target Service Agents (TSAs) for Windows 95 and Macintosh workstations. The IntranetWare file system TSA has also been updated. We'll take a much closer look at SMS and all of its new IntranetWare enhancements in Chapter 13.

9. Security Services

With IntranetWare, Novell introduces NetWare Enhanced Security (NES). NetWare Enhanced Security is designed to meet the Controlled Access Implementation Class C-2 requirements. This is the minimum security specification for high-security corporate and government networks.

To facilitate NES and Class C-2 compliance, the following features are provided:

▸ The AUDITCON utility has been significantly improved to enable C-2-compliant auditing.

▸ Audit log files are now represented by and managed as Directory objects. This enables you to control access to audit log files by using Directory rights assignments.

▸ A network server can be configured as an "Enhanced Security Server" by using an updated group of SET parameters.

▶ The SECURE.NCF file provides a script that configures the server as an Enhanced Security Server. You can run this script at any time from a NetWare 4.11 server system prompt, or use the following SET parameter to enable it automatically at bootup: "Enable SECURE.NCF."

As you'll learn later in the book, we live in an Information Age. Because of this, network data has taken on a greater importance than ever before. IntranetWare and the NetWare Enhanced Security System allows you to sleep easily at night, knowing that everything is secure. Don't worry — if you don't feel fully secure yet, you will get a chance to break into IntranetWare Fort Knox in Chapter 11.

10. Print Services

In IntranetWare, traditional NetWare print services have been improved and Novell has introduced the next generation of network printing — IntranetWare Distributed Print Services (NDPS). With the introduction of NDPS, traditional print services are frequently referred to as "queue-based printing." With IntranetWare, queue-based printing has been integrated into NWADMIN. In addition, you can use the new graphical NPRINTER Manager to enable network users to share a printer attached to a Windows 95 workstation. NPRINTER Manager provides the same functionality that NPRINTER.EXE used to provide on a DOS or OS/2 workstation.

NDPS is Novell's next-generation printing system. It is designed for complex print management and production requirements. It is an ideal printing solution for users in diverse environments ranging from small workgroups to Enterprise WANs.

NDPS is a distributed service consisting of client, server, and connectivity components that seamlessly link and share network printers with applications. It eliminates the need to create and configure Print Queue, Printer, and Print Server objects. In fact, NDPS doesn't require you to manage print queues at all. With NDPS, a single graphical administration utility (NWADMIN) provides comprehensive management and control for all major brands and models of printers. If this all sounds too good to be true, check out Chapter 14. If it all seems too complex for you, remember that NDPS is *optional* in IntranetWare. As a matter of fact, it probably won't be available until the *next* release of IntranetWare.

Well, that completes our brief overview of the ten most exciting enhancements to IntranetWare. For a complete summary of these features, check out Table 1.2. Wow, there's so much to learn and so little time.

ZEN

Nothing in life is to be feared. It is only to be understood.

Marie Curie

T A B L E 1.2

What's New in IntranetWare

SERVICE	FEATURE	NETWARE 4.1	INTRANETWARE
1. Novell Directory Services	NetWare Administrator	Windows 3.1*x* version only	Windows 3.*x* and Windows 95 versions
		Limited customization capabilities	Configurable tool bar, status bar, and property pages
		Supports connection to a single Directory tree only	Supports connection to multiple Directory trees
	Partition Management	Managed by PARTMGR and Partition Manager	Managed by the new NDS Manager utility
2. Server operating system	ABEND recovery	Limited options	Improved ABEND recovery options
	UPS connections	Limited to MAU support only	Serial port connection supported
	CLIB.NLM	A single module	Six related modules
	NetWare Web Server	Unavailable	Included
	NetWare Symmetric MultiProcessing	Available from OEM	Included partners only
3. Installation	Hardware detection	Limited	Substantially improved
	Upgrade utilities	Limited	Existing utilities improved and two additional migration utilities provided
4. NetWare Licensing Service	Integrated license management	Unavailable	Included

T A B L E   1 . 2

What's New in IntranetWare
(continued)

SERVICE	FEATURE	NETWARE 4.1	INTRANETWARE
5. Connectivity Services	NetWare/IP	Available, but not integrated	Fully integrated
	NetWare Client for Mac OS	Requires AppleTalk	Can communicate using IPX or IP, doesn't require AppleTalk
6. File Services	Support for long filenames	OS2.NAM for OS/2 platform	LONG.NAM supports extended name spaces for the Windows 95, Windows NT, and OS/2 platforms
	Volume capacity	Limited to 2,000,000 directory entries	Each IntranetWare volume can handle up to 16,000,000 directory entries
7. Application Services	NetWare Application Manager	Unavailable	Included
	NetWare Application Launcher	Unavailable	Included
8. Storage Management Services	SBACKUP	Limited backup services for NDS	Improved backup services for NDS
	Target Service Agents (TSAs)	Available for DOS, Windows 3.1x, and OS/2	Windows 95 and Mac OS TSAs included
9. Security Services	C-2 compatibility	Unavailable	Included
	AUDITCON	Limited events audited	Can audit many additional events
10. Print Services	NPRINTER Manager for Windows 95	Unavailable	Enables you to manage printers attached to Windows 95 workstations
	Quick Setup option	PCONSOLE only	NWADMIN and PCONSOLE
	Novell Distributed Services (NDPS)	Unavailable	Future (*optional*)

So, you bought IntranetWare and now what do you do with it? How do you design your NDS tree? Where do you put your user accounts? What steps should you take to optimize performance, transparency, and system fault tolerance? Who shot Mr. Burns? What did you get yourself into? Don't panic — these are good questions.

This book is dedicated to *you*. I hope to get you through IntranetWare with the least amount of pain. Who knows — you might even enjoy yourself along the way. We're going to start this first chapter with a brief snapshot of what IntranetWare is all about.

You will get a glimpse of the features and benefits that make Novell's fifth-generation operating system the *next generation* of networking. Here's what's in store:

- ▸ Novell Directory Services

- ▸ IntranetWare Enhanced File System

- ▸ IntranetWare Security

- ▸ IntranetWare Utility Management

- ▸ IntranetWare Configuration

- ▸ IntranetWare Management

- ▸ IntranetWare Printing

In Chapter 2, we'll expand on the heart of IntranetWare — NDS. But this is only the beginning. Once you've been introduced to the technology, you must learn what to do with it. Imagine what could happen if this power falls into the wrong hands. Imagine what Napoleon could have done with a turbocharged water cannon! No, we must harness the power of IntranetWare by learning how to design, install, and manage it. That's the true focus of *Novell's CNE Study Guide IntranetWare/NetWare 4.11*. Aah, but let's not get ahead of ourselves. It all begins with an introduction to IntranetWare, and I can't think of a better place to start than with Novell Directory Services.

SMART LINK

For a quick glimpse of *Novell's CNE Study Guide IntranetWare/NetWare 4.11*, surf to http://corp.novell.com/programs/press/hot.htm.

QUIZ

I'm in a giving mood; it must be your birthday. I have three gifts for you — small, medium, and large. Each gift is wrapped with a different color paper that is red, green, or silver. In addition, I've placed a different color bow on each package, either red, green, or gold. In order to earn your gifts, describe the wrapping and bow combination for each present. Here are some clues:

> ▸ *The small gift has a green bow.*

> ▸ *The large gift is the only one that matches.*

Remember, puzzles help stretch your imagination. But whatever you do, don't pull a frontal lobe!

(Q1-1)
(See Appendix C for all quiz answers.)

▸ . . . . ◂

Novell Directory Services

The most significant feature of IntranetWare is the introduction of Novell Directory Services (NDS). NDS is a distributed hierarchical database of network information that replaces the bindery in earlier versions of NetWare. NDS is a combination of features from OSI X.500, Banyan StreeTalk, and some other stuff no one has ever heard of. The result is an object-oriented hierarchical directory structure with complex access rights and distributed WAN partitions. Wow! Just think of it as a huge network phone book.

NDS classifies all network resources into objects. These objects can be organized by function, location, size, type, or color — it doesn't matter. The point is that the NDS tree organizes objects independently from their physical locations. When users log into the network, they can access any object in the tree to which they have rights, regardless of its location. This type of openness, however, does not come without a price. One obvious problem is security — which is why user access to network resources is controlled by a complex system of NDS security.

So, what does this all mean? The bottom line is this — users don't access physical resources anymore. Instead, they access logical objects in the NDS tree.

This means users don't need to know which IntranetWare server provides a particular resource. All they need to know is where it exists in the logical NDS world. We're going to start our discussion of NDS by introducing its fundamental components. We'll talk about NDS objects, NDS management, and Bindery Services. Then, in Chapter 2, we will delve more deeply into the NDS world, learning all there is to know before Part II ("IntranetWare Design"). Let's start with a brief peek inside the NDS Cloud.

THE CLOUD

NDS has many names:

▸ The Directory

▸ The Tree

▸ The Cloud

▸ The StayPuff Marshmallow Man

In reality, it's all of these things. But the best description is the "Cloud." NDS oversees physical network resources and provides users with a logical world to live in. This differs dramatically from what we're used to in NetWare 3.12. As you can see in Figure 1.3, the NetWare 3.12 bindery is server-centric. This means that every physical resource exists within or around the server. If user Guinevere wants to access files or printers on multiple servers, she must have a login account and security access on each one. This system makes access and management both repetitive and time-consuming. Also, note that nothing exists *above* the server. The server itself represents the highest level of the network organizational structure. Users, volumes, files, and printers all exist on each server.

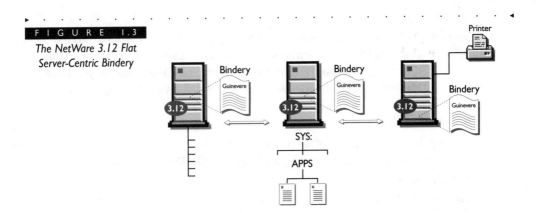

FIGURE 1.3

The NetWare 3.12 Flat Server-Centric Bindery

NDS, on the other hand, creates a whole new world *above* the server. As you can see in Figure 1.4, each network resource exists only once as a logical object above the server. Suddenly, the server has gone from being at the top of the network organizational chart to being a physical object in the NDS tree. The beauty of this system is that Guinevere only logs in once and has instant access to all network resources. She doesn't log into each server; she logs into the NDS tree and it tracks where her files and printers are. All logins, attaches, and access rights are handled in the background by NDS.

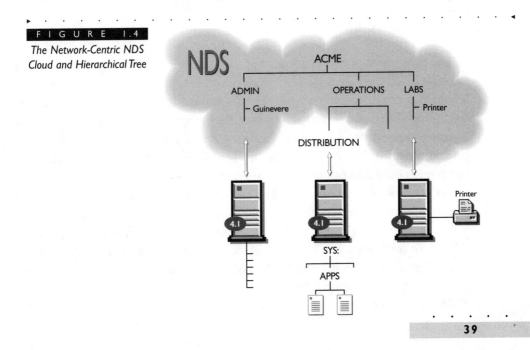

FIGURE 1.4

The Network-Centric NDS Cloud and Hierarchical Tree

TIP

NDS epitomizes user transparency. To the user, resource access seems like magic. To the administrator, it requires hours of IntranetWare design, installation, and management work. Fortunately, you have Novell's *CNE Study Guide IntranetWare/NetWare 4.11* to guide the way.

The main lesson to learn from the accompanying graphics is the direction of the arrows. In Figure 1.3, the arrows of communication are horizontal. This means that all communication exists within and among NetWare 3.12 servers. If Guinevere wants access to another resource, she must follow the horizontal communication path to another server, and either re-log in or attach. In contrast, Figure 1.4 shows the communication arrows running vertically. This means that communication occurs within and between the NDS Cloud and physical resources. The NDS Cloud handles the problem of locating resources and transparently grabs whatever Guinevere needs. This vertical communication structure makes finding and using network resources much easier for the user. In addition, it provides a single point of central network management for administrators.

ZEN

"Never keep up with the Joneses. Drag them down to your level. It's cheaper."

Quentin Crisp

The NDS tree is stored in a fully replicated, globally distributed, object-oriented database called the Directory. The Directory consists of multiple hidden system files in a hidden directory in the root of the SYS: volume on each server. These files can be replicated and distributed throughout the LAN to provide fault tolerance and increased connectivity. Although all IntranetWare servers use NDS, they don't have to contain their own Directory database. If a server contains a portion of the database, that portion is called a *partition*. If a server doesn't have a copy of the database, it must access it from some other server. The bottom line is, an IntranetWare server can contain the entire Directory database, pieces of it (partitions), or none at all.

In addition, Novell Directory Services requires a temporal assurance system called *time synchronization*. This means that everyone must agree on what time it is. Time is critical to NDS because IntranetWare uses *time stamps* for synchronization, auditing, and NDS security. Time synchronization is implemented using a variety of time server types.

Finally, Novell Directory Services is fully backward compatible. That is to say, it supports bindery emulation, so that previous versions of NetWare can peacefully coexist with IntranetWare NDS. In addition, a new feature called NETSYNC allows NetWare 3.12 binderies to be uploaded and distributed with IntranetWare NDS to other NetWare 3.12 binderies. We'll take a closer look at these features in the next chapter. For now, let's continue our discussion of NDS with a brief look at objects and properties.

NDS OBJECTS

The Directory consists of objects, properties, and values. Even though NDS replaces earlier NetWare binderies, it is organized in much the same way. NDS objects define logical or physical entities that provide organizational or technical function to the network. NDS objects come in three flavors: *[Root], container objects,* and *leaf objects.* As you can see, the tree analogy is alive and well. The [Root] is the very top of the NDS tree. Container objects define the organizational boundaries of the NDS tree and house other container objects and/or leaf objects. Leaf objects are the logical and/or physical network resources that provide technical services and WAN functionality. Leaf objects define the lowest level of the NDS structure.

Each NDS object consists of categories of information called *properties.* Properties are similar to fields in a database record that categorize types of information. User objects, for example, have properties such as Login name, Password, Postal Address, and Description. Although the same type of object may have the same properties, the information within those properties may change. For example, two User objects both have a Login Name property, but one has a value of Guinevere and the other has a value of Gilligan.

As you learned earlier, NDS objects come in three flavors: [Root], container objects, and leaf objects. Now let's take a closer look.

[Root]

The [Root] object defines the top of the NDS organizational structure. Each Directory can only have one [Root]; it is created during the installation of the first IntranetWare server in the Directory tree. The [Root] cannot be deleted, renamed, or moved. The NDS [Root] object is exceptional in that it begins the boundaries of the NDS world. It behaves much like a container object, in that it houses other container objects. The main difference is that the [Root] cannot contain leaf objects.

TIP

Each NDS object has a specific icon that graphically depicts its purpose. The [Root] object's icon is particularly interesting. Because it represents the opening porthole to the NDS world, its icon is, appropriately, a picture of the Earth.

Container Objects

Container objects are logical organizers. They are the Tupperware™ bowls of our NDS kitchen. Actually, the analogy works well — work with me here. The nature of storing Tupperware is that larger containers enclose smaller containers, which, in turn, house even smaller ones. Of course, the biggest Tupperware container in the world is the [Root]. Also, Tupperware containers are used to store fruits and vegetables. In NDS, our Tupperware containers store lettuce "leaf" objects. Sorry.

Here's a quick list of the three types of IntranetWare NDS container objects available as of this writing:

- ▶ *Country* — Designates the country where certain parts of the organization reside.

- ▶ *Organization* — Represents a company, university, or department. NDS only supports one layer of Organization objects. Therefore, these containers can only hold Organizational Units and leaf objects.

- ▶ *Organizational Unit* — Represents a division, business unit, or project team. Organizational Units hold other Organizational Units or leaf objects.

Leaf Objects

Leaf objects are logical or physical network resources. Most of your life will be spent designing, installing, and managing leaf objects — you'll quickly become a vegetarian. These are the ultimate entities that IntranetWare users seek. Because leaf objects reside at the bottom of the NDS tree, they cannot hold other leaf objects. They represent the proverbial end of the road. Here's a brief list of some of the most common NDS leaf objects. A more comprehensive list can be found in Chapter 2.

▶ *User* — Represents any user in the NDS tree (such as Guinevere).

▶ *IntranetWare Server* — Represents any IntranetWare server providing file or other services.

▶ *Volume* — Exists as a logical pointer to any physical volume on a IntranetWare server. This object enables administrators to organize volumes independently from the physical servers they are attached to.

▶ *Group* — Defines an NDS-unrelated list of users with similar network needs for the purpose of assigning access rights and other management strategies.

▶ *Print Server* — Represents any network print server.

▶ *Printer* — Represents any physical printing device on the network.

▶ *Computer* — Represents any network computer that is not providing file or print services, such as gateways, routers, and workstations.

THE BRAIN

For an overview of NDS objects (including a list of the most common container and leaf objects), refer to the Object section of the *Novell NetWare 4.11 Concepts* manual or surf the Web at http://www.novell.com/manuals.

This completes our brief discussion of NDS objects. You'll want to get to know them well because all future discussions center around how to organize and manage these cute little logical network entities. Speaking of which, let's take a quick look at some general strategies for NDS management.

ZEN

"I was a vegetarian until I started leaning towards the sun."

Anonymous

NDS MANAGEMENT

Once you understand the relationships of NDS objects, it's time to start building your tree. As in nature, it starts with the [Root] and builds from there. Figure 1.5 represents each container object as a specific graphical icon. Here's a quick summary:

▸ 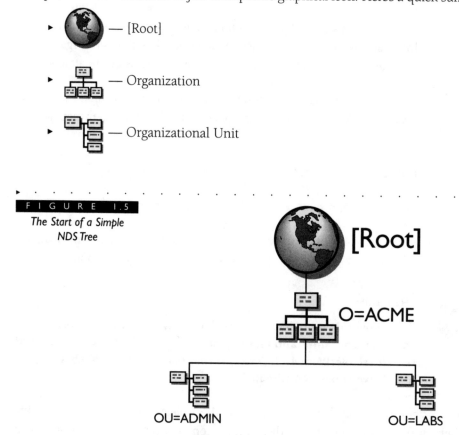 — [Root]

▸ — Organization

▸ — Organizational Unit

FIGURE 1.5

The Start of a Simple
NDS Tree

Each leaf object is represented by a graphical icon that depicts its purpose. For example, printers are represented by printer icons, servers are represented by computer icons, and users by people icons. Refer to Chapter 2 for a more detailed list of NDS object icons.

These icons are used throughout this book and in graphical NDS utilities. NetWare Administrator (NWADMIN), for example, uses icons to provide a snapshot of the entire NDS tree. This feature makes it easier for administrators and users to locate and use IntranetWare resources.

Once you've begun your tree by planting container objects, it's time to organize the physical and logical resources — leaf objects. Remember, leaf objects are stored in specific IntranetWare Tupperware containers. From there, they can either be managed, accessed, or eaten — it's your choice. Later in Part II ("IntranetWare Design") you'll find a variety of guidelines for designing and building NDS trees. For now, it's important to understand how the tree is organized and what it looks like once it's been built.

Once the NDS tree has been designed and installed, you get to move on to the third phase of CNE life — management. NDS management consists of three topics:

▶ NDS naming

▶ NDS partitioning

▶ Time synchronization

NDS naming defines rules for locating leaf objects. One of the most important aspects of a leaf object is its position in the NDS tree. Proper naming is required when users log in, access NDS utilities, print, and perform most other management tasks, as well. We'll explore naming in great depth in Chapters 2 and 4.

The next management topic is NDS partitioning. Because the Directory tree houses all your network resources, it can grow large very quickly. As with any database, size can decrease performance and reliability. For this reason, IntranetWare has a built-in database distribution feature called *partitioning and replication*. Partitioning breaks the database tree into small pieces, and replication places those pieces on multiple servers. This strategy increases database performance and provides distributed fault tolerance. You have a lot to look forward to in Chapters 2, 4, and 9.

The final management topic is time synchronization. As you learned earlier, this is a temporal assurance scheme that forces all IntranetWare servers to agree on the time. This is particularly important because all NDS background operations and security strategies rely on *time stamps*. Time synchronization is accomplished through the use of four time server types, as you'll quickly learn in Chapters 2, 4, and 9.

QUIZ

A statistician is someone who can put his head in an oven and his feet in the freezer, and then tell you, "On Average: I feel fine!" Let's see if you have what it takes.

A roulette wheel has the numbers 0 to 36. From the information below, which number have I bet on?

1. *It is divisible by 3.*
2. *When the digits are added together, the total lies between 4 and 8.*
3. *It is an odd number.*
4. *When the digits are multiplied together, the total lies between 4 and 8.*

(Q1-2)

Now, take a moment to wallow in your ignorance and enjoy the simplicity of IntranetWare in its infancy. Because later in the book, you'll be thrust — kicking and screaming — into the complex glory of NDS management.

Welcome back. I wonder how IntranetWare coexists with bindery-based servers like NetWare 3.12's? Check it out.

BINDERY SERVICES

One of the biggest concerns with IntranetWare's radical new approach is compatibility with earlier stuff — that is, bindery-based servers. Fortunately, IntranetWare contains a sophisticated *bindery emulation* system. Bindery emulation provides backward compatibility with bindery-based servers by making the IntranetWare Directory look like a flat-file bindery to NetWare 2.2 and 3.12 servers in the correct context. Because the bindery database is a flat-file structure, bindery emulation can only exist within one container at a time. Think of it as taking a two-dimensional slice of a three-dimensional object. For example, if you sliced a three-dimensional orange in half and took a two-dimensional view of it, the orange would appear to be a circle. In much the same way, if you isolate a particular container in the three-dimensional NDS tree, the objects in that container will appear to be a flat-file bindery.

The lucky container object where you set a server's bindery emulation is called the *bindery context*. You can change a server's bindery context by using the SET command at the server console. For example, in Figure 1.6, the bindery context for SALES-SRV1 is

OU=SALES.OU=MARKETING.O=ACME

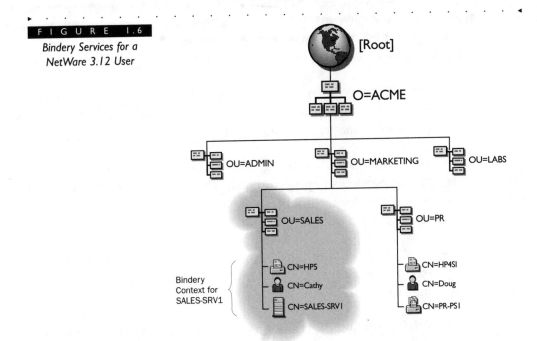

FIGURE 1.6

Bindery Services for a
NetWare 3.12 User

In this case, any user logging into SALES-SRV1 with NETx will have access to only Cathy and HP5. This user will not see any other objects in the NDS tree, including PR-PS1 and Doug.

TIP

Although IntranetWare Bindery Services may seem a little restricting, consider that you're asking a highly evolved operating system to emulate an unsophisticated flat bindery. There is one consolation, however. IntranetWare enables you to define up to 16 bindery contexts for each server. This means users logging into a specific server from a NetWare 3.12 server can, in fact, see the objects in up to 16 containers. This is because the objects are all clumped together into one *superbindery*.

By default, bindery services is enabled during installation. The bindery services context is automatically set to the context in which the IntranetWare server is installed. If you find that additional clients outside of this context need resources through bindery services, determine where access is needed and set the bindery context for those containers. Objects and properties that are unique to NDS are not available through bindery services. These include container login scripts, profile login scripts, some print services, and messaging.

Bindery services will work for you if any of the following is true:

▸ *TRUE:* You need to provide a migration period for users who have not upgraded their workstation software yet. This means that VLMs have not been loaded and users are still using the old NETx software.

▸ *TRUE:* If you are still running applications and utilities that rely on Bindery Services to operate properly. This includes many printer-based print server chips, old versions of NetWare for Macintosh, and old versions of NetWare SAA.

▸ *TRUE:* If you need to administer IntranetWare user accounts, group accounts, and print services from a NetWare 3.12 client using SYSCON and PCONSOLE.

▸ *TRUE:* If you just can't take the three-dimensional world anymore, and you want to live in a two-dimensional picture world. Or, if you like circles better than oranges.

In addition to bindery emulation, IntranetWare Bindery Services includes an advanced NDS management tool known as *NetSync*. NetSync is an NLM that enables you to copy the binderies of multiple NetWare 3.1x servers into an NDS container on a IntranetWare server. You can then manage the users, groups, and print services of the NetWare 3.1x servers as part of the NDS Directory tree using NWADMIN or NETADMIN.

Another exciting aspect of NetSync is that it enables you to integrate existing NetWare 3.1x objects without having to upgrade all their host servers to IntranetWare. In addition, NetSync enables you to create a "cluster" of NetWare 3.1x servers that can be updated any time a change is made inside the IntranetWare container. This feature enables administrators to centrally manage multiple binderies (known as a *superbindery*) and synchronize those changes to a cluster of servers. It may sound fascinating, but NetSync is not very easy to use. We'll discuss it in more detail in Chapter 8.

ZEN

"If a man wishes to be sure of the road he treads on, he must close his eyes and walk in the dark."

Anonymous

Well, that does it for Novell Directory Services — for now. This section was designed to simply whet your appetite for the 12-course meal to come. Obviously, NDS has a lot more complexity and internal features. But, of course, there's no reason to start with the entree. I've provided you with a general overview of the "Cloud," NDS objects, NDS management, and finally, Bindery Services. Although this represents NDS in a nutshell, it's not an easy nut to crack. As you'll learn in Chapter 2, NDS has many idiosyncrasies that can make it challenging to deal with on a daily basis. Then, we'll design our NDS tree in Chapter 4. In Chapter 8 you'll learn about NDS management, and finally, in Chapter 9, we'll discuss partition management and synchronization.

On the other side of the coin, the beauty of NDS is that it can be as simple or complex as you make it. I think there's a life lesson in there somewhere. In the meantime, let's take a look at the rest of IntranetWare and see what else it has to offer, starting with its enhanced file system.

IntranetWare Enhanced File System

When IntranetWare was rolled out, one of its key selling points was *improved disk management*. As a matter of fact, Novell still uses complex ROI (return on investment) calculations to justify your investment in IntranetWare. These ROI formulas are based on two major assumptions:

> ► You will save hundreds of hours managing IntranetWare because of its centralized NDS administration format.

▸ You will save thousands of dollars in disk storage because of block suballocation, file compression, and data migration.

So, here we are: the major file system enhancements in IntranetWare. These three impressive disk usage strategies were designed to solve serious disk space management problems in earlier versions of NetWare. Once again, they are

▸ Block suballocation

▸ File compression

▸ Data migration

Block suballocation solves the problem of wasted space with medium to large block sizes. *Data migration* solves the problem of disk cram by providing an efficient method for near-line storage. *File compression* eases the pain of purchasing expensive on-line disks by automatically compressing inactive files. All of these features are exciting and new, but they probably shouldn't be the basis for purchasing IntranetWare. Take a long, hard look at NDS before you make a life-changing decision like that.

Let's take a closer look at IntranetWare's file system enhancement strategies.

BLOCK SUBALLOCATION

A *block* is a discrete allocation unit of disk space. In less technical terms, it's a chunk of hard disk. A file is made up of one or more chunks of data, as needed. Each IntranetWare volume has a predefined block size. These blocks range in size from 4K all the way up to 64K. The problem arises when you use medium to large block sizes and store numerous small files. As you can see in Figure 1.7, a 64K block is fully occupied by a 5K or 63K file — it can't tell the difference. The problem is that the 5K file results in 59K of unusable wasted disk space. A couple thousand 5K files later, and you've wasted more than 100 MB of internal server disk — not a good thing.

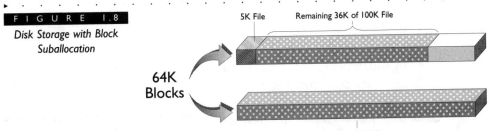

Disk Storage Without Block Suballocation

5K File   59K Wasted Space

Unusable

64K
Blocks

63K File   1K Wasted Space

TIP

A friend of mine thought it would be cool to install NetWare 3.12 on a 120 MB hard disk using a 64K block size. (I have strange friends.) Much to his surprise, the server ran out of disk space before the SYSTEM and PUBLIC files were ever loaded! IntranetWare's block suballocation feature would have solved this problem.

Block suballocation solves the problem of wasted disk space by dividing partially used disk blocks into 512-byte suballocation blocks. These suballocation blocks can be used by multiple files. For example, a 5K file would still take the first 5K of a 64K block — as shown in Figure 1.8. But the remaining 59K becomes available for leftovers from other full blocks. A second 100K file, for example, would take up another 64K block and send the remaining 36K over to the first block (as shown in Figure 1.8). Without block suballocation, the remaining 36K would occupy another entire 64K block — therefore wasting another 28K of space in addition to the 59K already wasted from the 5K file.

Disk Storage with Block Suballocation

5K File   Remaining 36K of 100K File

64K
Blocks

First 64K of 100K File

Bottom line:

▸ Without block suballocation — The two files totaling 105K would occupy three 64K blocks and waste 87K of server disk space.

▸ With block suballocation — The two files totaling 105K would occupy two suballocated blocks, leaving 23K of server disk space to be used by a third file.

The most important thing to remember about block suballocation is that it only works when files exceed the block size. Files always start at the beginning of a new block. You cannot start a new file within an already-occupied suballocation block. You can, however, store the remainder of large files within the suballocation area. Finally, block suballocation is activated at the volume level within IntranetWare. You'll learn more about how to optimize it in Chapter 15.

FILE COMPRESSION

One of the flashiest sales features of IntranetWare is file compression, mainly because most people can relate to it. The idea of more than doubling your server disk space is exciting and easy to grasp. Unfortunately, many early users ignored the true value of IntranetWare — NDS. The idea of improving your network by adding a big nebulous cloud didn't excite too many users. Of course, now that you understand the internal workings of NDS, its value becomes more apparent.

File compression enables IntranetWare volumes to hold more on-line data by automatically compressing inactive files. Users can save up to 63 percent of the server's disk space by activating file compression — that's 1 GB of files in 370 MB of space. File compression is activated in one of two ways:

▸ By flagging directories and files as IC (Immediate Compress)

▸ By using the SET command at the server console to configure various inactivity delay parameters

By default, file compression is turned ON and the inactivity delay is set to seven days. This means that if a file is not accessed within seven days, it will automatically be compressed. Users can avoid having their files compressed by flagging specific files as DC (Don't Compress). Finally, files are automatically decompressed when users access them. Decompression occurs much faster than compression, at a rate of 100K per second.

Compressing files on IntranetWare server disks occurs in five steps:

1 • A timer goes off and file compression begins. By default, all files are compressed just before midnight on the day at which the inactivity delay expires. Once file compression is activated, IntranetWare reads and analyzes each file.

2 • IntranetWare builds a temporary file describing the original file. This feature ensures that the original file is not at risk if data is corrupted during the compression process. In addition, if a disk error or power failure occurs during compression, the original, uncompressed file is retained.

3 • IntranetWare determines whether any disk sectors can be saved by compressing the file. A gain of at least 2 percent (by default) is required before a file is compressed. This parameter is configurable using the SET console command.

4 • IntranetWare begins creation of the compressed file.

5 • IntranetWare replaces the original with the compressed file after an error-free compressed version has been created.

THE BRAIN

For more information on file compression, refer to the "File Compression" section of the _Novell NetWare 4.11 Concepts_ manual.

There are ten SET parameters for managing file compression. In addition, CNEs can use the IC and DC attributes to activate and deactivate compression on specific files. Both of these strategies will be discussed as part of optimization in Chapter 15.

DATA MIGRATION

Data migration solves the problem of disk cram by providing an efficient method for "near-line" storage. "What is near-line?" you ask. Near-line storage is somewhere between on-line (hard disks) and off-line (tape backup) — I know you probably saw that coming.

As you can see in Figure 1.9, on-line storage is provided by fast, internal server disks. The problem with on-line storage is that it's finite in capacity. On the other extreme, we have off-line storage in the form of tape backups. This storage is infinite in size because multiple tapes can be used. In addition, off-line storage can be placed off-site for disaster recovery and better system fault tolerance. The problem with off-line storage is human intervention — someone must stroll over to the backup device and place the tape in the correct place, which takes time and effort. As I'm sure you've already figured out, these are two luxuries CNEs don't have.

So, what are our options? Fortunately, IntranetWare includes a form of near-line storage that solves both problems. Near-line storage is much faster than off-line tape but has the potential for infinite storage capacities, and, therefore, outperforms on-line disks. Data migration provides near-line storage by automatically transferring inactive data to a tape drive or optical disk without actually removing the data's entries from the server volume's Directory Table (DET) or file allocation table (FAT). The data still appears to be on the volume and users can transparently access the data without having to worry about which tape it's on or where the file exists.

Data migration is part of a new IntranetWare storage system known as the High Capacity Storage System (HCSS). HCSS extends the storage capacity of a IntranetWare server by integrating an optical disk library or *jukebox*. HCSS uses rewritable optical disks to move files between faster low-capacity storage devices (the server's hard disk) and slower high-capacity storage devices (jukebox). HCSS is fully integrated into IntranetWare and activated using special drivers on the server. Once it has been activated, migration is performed on a file-by-file basis, according to two criteria:

- *Capacity threshold* — The percentage of the server's hard disk that can be used before HCSS starts migrating files from the hard disk to the jukebox.

- *Least Recently Used (LRU)* — A series of guidelines that determines which files are moved from the server's hard disk to the jukebox. These guidelines move the least active files first.

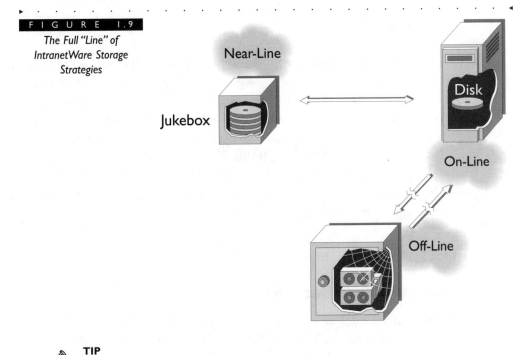

*The Full "Line" of
IntranetWare Storage
Strategies*

Near-Line

Disk

Jukebox

On-Line

Off-Line

TIP

Near-line data migration is still much slower than on-line disks, so the system must have a way of informing users that the file is on its way. Many near-line tape manufacturers provide terminate-and-stay-resident programs (TSRs) that display a message while IntranetWare is searching for the near-line file, something like, "Hold your horses, we're working over here!"

Data migration and HCSS are exciting parts of IntranetWare and should be looked at closely. Because there are performance sacrifices for installing HCSS, you should only consider it if you need real-time access to archived files. Some sample implementations include law libraries, financial information, and medical records. For a more detailed discussion of optimizing data migration, refer to Chapter 15.

QUIZ

This time we're looking for a common arithmetic symbol, which, when it is placed between 4 and 5, results in a number that is greater than 4, but less than 6. Hmmmm, I bet you thought you had escaped math in high school — nope. You're gonna need it for IntranetWare security.

(Q1-3)

Well, that completes our discussion of the IntranetWare enhanced file system. As you can see, Novell has added some pretty exciting disk management strategies to an already impressive 32-bit file system. The good news is that nothing else has changed. IntranetWare still uses a DOS-like command line and drives are mapped in exactly the same way as they were in NetWare 3.12. After all, there's no reason to fix something that isn't broken. If this section just tantalizes your appetite for more, have no fear, we'll return to the IntranetWare file system in Chapter 10. For now, let's continue our introduction with a quick look at a new and improved IntranetWare security model.

IntranetWare Security

Security in the Information Age poses an interesting challenge. Computers and communications have made it possible to collect volumes of data about you and me — from our last purchase at the five-and-dime to our detailed medical records. Privacy has become a commodity that is exchanged on the open market. Information is no longer the fodder of afternoon talk shows; it has become *the* unit of exchange for the 21st century — more valuable than money.

I'll bet you thought you left cops and robbers behind in childhood. Well, this is a variation on the game and the stakes are quite high. As a CNE, it is your responsibility to design, install, and manage the IntranetWare network. But most important, you must protect it. You need a brain filled with sophisticated security strategies and a utility belt full of advanced protection tools. Think of these as your impenetrable network armor.

IntranetWare security, in general, is pretty good. But for many of today's WANs, it's not good enough. A truly *secure* network protects more than just user data; it protects everything! So, what is "everything"? The definition of everything has changed in IntranetWare. Now the world exists in a nebulous cloud full of Tupperware containers and User objects. As the IntranetWare universe becomes more open and interconnected, security becomes more and more important. Fortunately, IntranetWare has a dramatically improved security model for creating and maintaining your impenetrable network armor.

TIP

IntranetWare is fully C-2 compatible when it comes to access and authentication security. This means it does a great job of securing your "shared" IntranetWare data. If that sounds hard to do . . . it is!

IntranetWare improves on the earlier security model by adding supplemental front-end barriers for filtering unauthorized users. Once again, the same security principle applies:

Goal — Let the good guys in and keep the bad guys out!

As you can see in Figure 1.10, the IntranetWare security model consists of five layers. They are:

1 • Login/Password Authentication

2 • Login Restrictions

3 • NDS Security

4 • File System Access Rights

5 • Directory/File Attributes

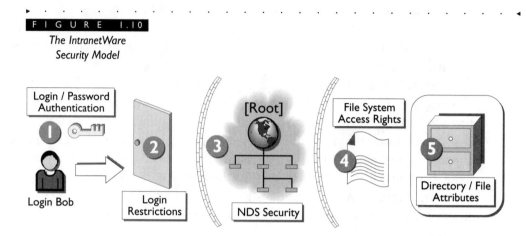

F I G U R E   1.10

The IntranetWare
Security Model

It all starts with *Login/Password Authentication*. Remember, users don't log into IntranetWare servers anymore; they log into the "Cloud." Once Bob issues his login name, the network authenticates it and asks for a password. IntranetWare uses the password to decrypt a session-specific private key. Once this has been accomplished, the system matches the username against a list of global and personal login restrictions. These *Login Restrictions* allow for conditional access according to a variety of criteria, including password expiration, time of day, station restrictions, and intruder lockout.

Now that Bob has passed layers one and two, he is officially logged into the NDS tree. His ability to access any object in the tree is determined by a complex NDS security structure. At the heart of *NDS Security* is the Access Control List (ACL). The ACL defines who can access an object and what the user can do with it. In other words, Bob can only use objects that he has rights to.

The fourth layer of the IntranetWare security model involves *File System Access Rights*. If Bob has the Supervisor right to any IntranetWare server object, he is granted unlimited access to the file system. File system security is almost identical to previous versions of NetWare and includes access rights, the Inherited Rights Filter (IRF), and effective rights. Finally, directories and files themselves are protected via *Directory/File Attribute* security. IntranetWare uses many of the same attributes as NetWare 3.12, as well as some additional attributes for file compression and data migration. Attribute security is the final line of defense and should be implemented only as a last resort.

QUIZ

So, you think you're good at math? Here's a doozy. Using the figure 7 seven times, write out a calculation that gives the answer 7777.

(Q1-4)

Well, there you go. That's IntranetWare security in a nutshell. Remember:

Goal — Let the good guys in and keep the bad guys out!

This is accomplished by creating a series of barriers and trap doors. Also, a full set of impenetrable network armor couldn't hurt. Fortunately, IntranetWare gives you all the tools you need to create a maximum security network.

Speaking of tools. . .

ZEN

"An elephant — a mouse built to government specifications."

Robert Heinlein

IntranetWare Utility Management

To do the job right, you have to use the correct tool. Just ask Batman what life would be like without his utility belt. Well, now it's your turn to explore a personalized network utility belt — thanks to IntranetWare.

One of the most dramatic improvements in IntranetWare utility management is the introduction of GUI (graphical user interface) utilities. These cute little graphical guys provide a friendly user interface for one consolidated utility — NWADMIN. In addition, the supervisor functionality and user functionality have been separated into two distinct utilities — NWADMIN and NWUSER.

In addition to GUI utilities, many of the command line and menu utilities from NetWare 3.12 have been integrated and consolidated into new IntranetWare DOS-based tools. Also, the number of command line utilities (CLUs) has dropped dramatically, even with the introduction of four or five completely new CLUs.

Finally, at the server, new NLMs and console commands have been integrated to support NDS and the enhanced file and memory management of IntranetWare. The most dramatic improvement has been the integration of all SET parameters into one central management NLM — SERVMAN, a new Saturday-morning superhero rivaling The Tick.

Let's take a closer look at all the cool toys included in IntranetWare. After all, remember:

Motto — To do the job right, you have to use the correct tool.

GUI UTILITIES

The IntranetWare GUI utilities are supported by Microsoft Windows (version 3.*x* or 95) or OS/2's Presentation Manager. These utilities provide a central Windows interface for consolidated management tasks. In addition, IntranetWare has separated the supervisor functionality from the user functionality. Supervisors use the NetWare Administrator (NWADMIN) and NDS Manager utilities; while users hang out with NWUSER. IntranetWare also offers DOS-based versions of these utilities that we'll look at in just a moment. For now, let's concentrate on the GUI tools — and we're not talking cookie dough here.

NWADMIN

NWADMIN, the NetWare Administrator, runs as a multiple document interface (MDI) application. The primary NWADMIN window is a browser that displays the NDS tree from your current context down. You can switch the tree view to the [Root] by using the Set Context choice from within NWADMIN's Options menu. In addition, you can view the complete file system within any server by double-clicking on the appropriate volume object. All in all, administrators can open a total of nine Browser windows at one time.

Figure 1.11 shows a sample of the NWADMIN browser. This utility integrates functions from four main menu tools — FILER, NETADMIN, PARTMGR, and PCONSOLE. With NetWare Administrator, you can perform a variety of tasks. Check out Chapter 8.

We will explore all the intricacies of NWADMIN throughout this book. Who knows? You might even learn to like it.

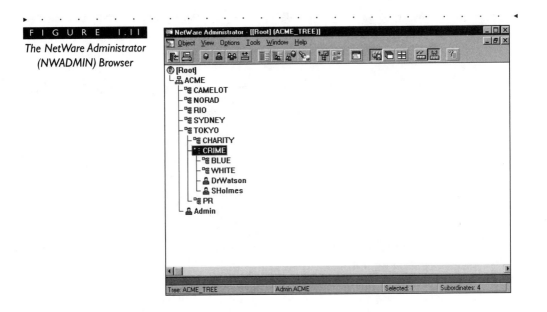

F I G U R E   1.11

*The NetWare Administrator
(NWADMIN) Browser*

TIP

If you break out in hives every time you use Windows, you had better see a doctor. Unfortunately, it's not going away anytime soon. As a matter of fact, the DOS-based equivalent of NWADMIN is an inadequate substitute, to say the least. I suggest some anti-Windows ointment — distributed freely by Novell.

NDS Manager

In IntranetWare, NDS Manager replaces the Partition Manager utility that was used in previous versions of NetWare Administrator (NWADMIN). NDS Manager performs all the management tasks of Partition Manager and it also incorporates many DSREPAIR and DSTRACE maintenance and repair procedures. We'll explore NDS Manager in great detail in Chapters 9 and 13.

NWUSER

In addition to the Supervisor utilities, IntranetWare also includes a graphical user utility — NWUSER. This GUI tool runs under Microsoft Windows or OS/2 Presentation Manager and enables users to perform simple network tasks by using a consolidated friendly interface. NWUSER consists of icons across the top of two split Browser windows. The left window lists connected servers; the right lists NDS resources available in your current context.

Icons across the top of NWUSER enable users to perform five tasks:

- ▸ *Printing* — Users can capture ports to printers and manage print jobs after they've been sent.

- ▸ *Attachments* — Users can manage network attachments, access a specific file server, and view configuration information about it.

- ▸ *Drives* — Users can manage network and search drive mappings, as well as view effective rights on selected drives.

- ▸ *Messages* — Users can send and receive messages, as well as disable incoming notes.

- ▸ *Configuration* — Users can customize their NWUSER settings.

That completes our discussion of GUI utilities. Now let's take a closer look at their boring DOS-based counterparts.

DOS-BASED UTILITIES

For those of you who just can't deal with the GUI universe, IntranetWare includes DOS-based versions of all the GUI utilities. In the case of NWADMIN, it takes four DOS-based menu utilities to cover the same features. NWUSER, on the other hand, has an identical counterpart — NETUSER. In addition to these menu utilities, IntranetWare uses command line utilities for quick-and-dirty management tasks. Let's take a quick look at some of the key DOS-based menu utilities.

NETADMIN

NETADMIN is the DOS-based version of NWADMIN. Well, that's not entirely true, because NETADMIN only covers a portion of the administrative capabilities of our GUI friend. Some of the things NETADMIN can't do include partition management, file system management, and printing services. Some of the things NETADMIN *can* do include manage objects, search the tree, change context, and implement simple security.

NETADMIN includes a browser with the same functionality as the main NWADMIN screen. The key difference is that NETADMIN browses one container at a time. As you can see in Figure 1.12, the NETADMIN browser doesn't give you the same graphical NDS snapshot that NWADMIN does. You'll find this to be pretty annoying over time.

FIGURE 1.12

The NETADMIN Browser

```
NetAdmin  4.64                        Monday  November  22, 1999  9:35am
Context: LABS.NORAD.ACME
Login Name: Admin.ACME

                          Object, Class

                                              (parent)
    ..                                        (current context)
    .
    +R&D                                      (Organizational Unit)
    +WHI                                      (Organizational Unit)
    AEinstein                                 (User)
    HP5                                       (Printer)
    LABS-SRV1                                 (NetWare Server)
    LABS-SRV1_NW411                           (Volume)
    LABS-SRV1_SYS                             (Volume)
    LABS-SRV1_VOL1                            (Volume)




Press <F10> to select the parent object, <Enter> to change the context.

Enter=Change context/Select   F10=View or edit   F5=Mark   Ins=Add   Alt+F1=More
```

PARTMGR

DOS-based partitioning and replication management are accomplished using the PARTMGR menu utility. In the GUI world, this functionality is integrated into NDS Manager. In the less-flashy DOS world, PARTMGR enables administrators to create and merge partitions and add, delete, modify, and synchronize replicas. Once again, you can only view one container at a time. Also, PARTMGR doesn't provide the same graphical icon look that NDS Manager does. As with most DOS-based utilities, you really need to know what you're doing in order to be productive with PARTMGR. Take a tip from Uncle David — use NDS Manager.

TIP

Working in NETADMIN and PARTMGR is like being in a two-dimensional ship traveling through three-dimensional space. All you get are small snapshots of the whole picture. Earlier, we used the analogy of slicing through an orange to reveal a circle. This is how it works in the DOS-based menu world. Although these tools are not for everybody, some administrators find them to be quick and efficient. Others think they're confusing and clumsy. It's your call. Warp speed ahead.

PCONSOLE

DOS-based administrators can create, configure, and manage printing services using the PCONSOLE utility. In the GUI world, these tasks are integrated into NWADMIN. They can also monitor, modify, pause, and delete print jobs. Finally, PCONSOLE includes a Quick Setup option that allows you to avoid time-consuming customization.

That concludes our quick trip through the DOS-based utility universe. It's not as pretty and cheery as GUI happyland, but many users find the DOS-based world to be more efficient and down-to-earth. Now, let's complete our discussion of IntranetWare utility management with a look inside the server.

QUIZ

How far in the future does the Star Wars saga take place?

(Q1-5)

SERVER UTILITIES

Look out, there's a new superhero in Gotham. He is faster than a speedy processor, has more storage than a CD-ROM, and is able to search huge databases in a single second. He's SERVMAN!

SERVMAN is at the core of IntranetWare's new server utility strategy. In addition to SERVMAN, IntranetWare provides numerous powerful console commands and a variety of improved NLMs. The goal is to create a sophisticated administrative platform without making it too difficult to use. The most important thing to note about IntranetWare server utilities is that they can cause serious damage if not handled correctly. As a CNE, it is your responsibility to ensure that these tools are kept out of the reach of small children and IntranetWare users. Fortunately, they're protected with a "childproof cap" in the form of Supervisor rights and file server access protection.

Let's take a quick look at what IntranetWare has to offer at the server console.

Console Commands

Console commands enable CNEs to interact directly with the IntranetWare operating system core. These commands are internal to SERVER.EXE and do not require any other support commands. Console commands enable you to perform various administrative tasks, including controlling file servers, printers, and disk drives; sending messages; setting the server clock; performing general LAN maintenance; managing external optical drives; and setting international languages.

One of the most powerful IntranetWare console commands is SET. Using this utility, you can customize the OS core with almost 100 advanced parameters. These parameters are organized into 11 categories, ranging from communications to file system to time synchronization. Warning: Don't mess around with SET unless you've been adequately trained and you're wearing protective gloves.

NetWare Loadable Modules

NLMs are Lego™ pieces that attach to the core OS and provide additional functionality. The modular architecture of NLMs enables you to load and unload them without adversely affecting the WAN. IntranetWare NLMs provide internal disk communications, protocol support, name space, and management capabilities. The management tasks are what we're interested in.

Of course, at the heart of the new IntranetWare NLM management strategy is SERVMAN — our superhero. Let's take a closer look.

▸ *SERVMAN* — IntranetWare's new SERVer MANager is the most exciting and versatile new server utility. SERVMAN provides a menu interface for SET parameters and displays valuable IntranetWare configurations. As you can see in Figure 1.13, SERVMAN includes two windows — Server General Information and Available Options. Of course, this is only the beginning.

▸ *DSREPAIR* — This is a new server NLM utility used to repair and correct problems in the NDS database. When you run DSREPAIR, all NDS database files are locked until you exit the utility. DSREPAIR runs from the SYS:SYSTEM directory and checks all NDS objects and their property references. Only run DSREPAIR as a last resort and definitely keep it out of the reach of children and IntranetWare users.

ZEN

"Wait 'till they get a load of me!"

The Joker (Batman)

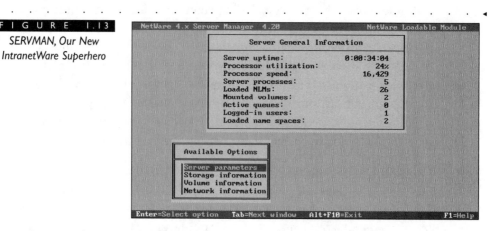

SERVMAN, Our New
IntranetWare Superhero

This completes our discussion of IntranetWare utility management. As you can see, you've only tried on your new IntranetWare utility belt for size. As times get tougher, we must acquire new tools to take on the world. Fortunately, IntranetWare is chock full of exciting new utilities. We will be exploring these tools in greater depth throughout the book. Also, refer to Chapter 13 for a more detailed discussion of server-based utilities. Be forewarned — you never know when SERVMAN might pop into your life.

Speaking of life, do you remember when yours started? Have you ever experienced the miracle of birth? How about the birth of a LAN? After all, networks are alive, aren't they?

IntranetWare Configuration

The birth of a LAN. If you take a close look at the definition of life, your IntranetWare LAN might just be alive. With this in mind, your LAN must also evolve from infant to adult. As you and I have grown (or are still growing) from childhood to adulthood, so must the IntranetWare LAN. In simple terms, there are three phases of life — birth, childhood, and adulthood.

During birth, the IntranetWare server is installed. In the grand scheme of things, this event is quick and painless (although I don't know about that latter part). Once the server has been installed, you are left with a simple directory structure, some workstations, and a cute little baby — um, I mean Admin user.

Over time, this adorable little baby will learn to walk, talk, and start getting along with others. He or she will go to school and learn some very valuable skills. Finally, at some point, he or she will make an abrupt transition into adulthood.

In IntranetWare, childhood is dominated by the LAN configuration. Your server undergoes five important modifications during configuration:

Step 1 • Workstation connectivity

Step 2 • Login scripts

Step 3 • Menu system

Step 4 • Network applications

Step 5 • E-mail

The third and final phase of life is adulthood. At this point, your LAN is secure and pretty well established in its new purpose. The goal shifts from guiding the infant to "keeping it going." These are the golden years. During adulthood, your LAN will get married, join a bowling league, have children, plan for the future, and finally retire. This phase of LAN adulthood is controlled by IntranetWare management. It goes like this:

▶ Server management

▶ Intranet management

▶ Workstation management

▶ Storage Management Services (SMS)

▶ Remote Management Facility (RMF)

Wow, I bet you didn't think becoming a CNE would be such a life-changing experience. In Chapter 12, we'll take a closer look at the five steps of IntranetWare configuration. Next, in Chapter 13, we'll break down the five components of LAN adulthood. But for now, let's take a quick peek at these two critical phases of life development — starting with IntranetWare configuration. IntranetWare management will be covered in the next section. Also, don't forget IntranetWare installation (birth!) — that's covered in Chapters 6 and 7.

STEP 1: WORKSTATION CONNECTIVITY

Workstation connectivity is where it all begins. During this step, the client computer boots and activates a variety of configuration files. These configuration files establish the client environment and attach users to the network. All this magic occurs with the help of four simple files:

- ▸ CONFIG.SYS — The first configuration file loaded during the boot process.

- ▸ AUTOEXEC.BAT — This autoexecuting batch file is modified to call the STARTNET.BAT file.

- ▸ STARTNET.BAT — A IntranetWare connectivity file that automates the workstation connection process.

- ▸ NET.CFG — The final workstation configuration file. It is used to customize ODI and VLM settings.

Once the first step of configuration has been completed, each user is well on the way to IntranetWare Nirvana. The next step is login scripts.

STEP 2: LOGIN SCRIPTS

IntranetWare supports four types of login scripts that are executed in systematic progression. These scripts automate critical user configurations. Here's a quick look:

- ▸ *Container Login Scripts* — Properties of Organization and Organizational Unit containers. They replace the System login scripts found in earlier versions of NetWare.

- ▸ *Profile Login Scripts* — Properties of Profile objects. These scripts customize environmental parameters for groups of users.

- ▸ *User Login Scripts* — Properties of User objects. They provide a tool for user-specific login customization.

▸ *Default Login Script* — Executed for any user who does not have an individual user script.

WHAT'S NEW

WHAT'S NEW

IntranetWare has introduced a new exciting workstation connectivity alternative for 32-bit clients — "Client 32." Client 32 for Windows 95 and DOS enables computers to access network resources quickly and reliably. It is easy to install and maintain, and provides many new and enhanced features that make it faster, more reliable, and more usable than previous network client software. In summary, it's a 32-bit protected mode workstation shell.

Client 32 for Windows 95 doesn't require any of the above workstation connectivity files. Instead, it loads directly from within Windows 95 and provides customizable parameters in GUI dialog boxes. Client 32 for Windows 3.1, however, does rely on AUTOEXEC.BAT, STARTNET.BAT, and NET.CFG. Keep in mind that Client 32 configuration is much different from ODI drivers and the NetWare DOS Requester. Check out Chapters 12 and 13 for more information on Client 32 workstation connectivity.

Once the Container, Profile, and/or User login scripts have been executed, the system automatically loads a user menu — Step 3. Hmmm, this childhood thing is moving along soooo smoothly — something must be wrong.

STEP 3: MENU SYSTEM

Junior goes to preschool.

In order for your users to get anything done, they need a friendly menu interface. The menu should act as a central access point for user applications and e-mail. Fortunately, IntranetWare has a built-in menu system that provides custom NetWare-looking menus. The system uses a simple script format and is versatile enough to support large groups of users with a single menu file.

The IntranetWare menu syntax is based on two simple command types:

▶ *Organizational commands* — They provide the menu's look and feel: MENU and ITEM.

▶ *Control commands* — They execute menu instructions and allow branching to submenus: EXEC, SHOW, LOAD, and GET*x*.

Once you have established a central, caring menu system, it's time to develop some applications and e-mail to go with it. Let's take a look.

STEP 4: NETWORK APPLICATIONS

IntranetWare provides excellent support for network applications. Their configuration is accomplished through a seven-step approach for installation and customization. It goes something like this:

1 • Make sure the application is IntranetWare compatible *before* you buy it.

2 • Make sure the software is truly multiuser.

3 • Determine an appropriate directory structure for the program files and all their support components.

4 • Install the software.

5 • Assign file attributes for the sharable or nonsharable network application.

6 • Grant user rights for access to network application directories.

7 • Configure the workstations for specific application needs.

Once the application software has been installed and users have proper access rights, the menu environment can be used as a friendly front end. All of this extra effort really pays off by dramatically increasing network transparency and user productivity. It's amazing how far you can get with a little TLC (tender loving computing).

WHAT'S NEW

IntranetWare introduces two fascinating tools for managing network applications: NetWare Application Manager (NAM) and NetWare Application Launcher (NAL).

NAM allows users to run network applications from within their native Windows or DOS environment. The Application Manager consists of Application objects and the NetWare Application Launcher (NAL). The Application Setup Information is stored as an Application object in the Directory tree. This eliminates the need for users to have a drive mapping or path to an applications directory in order to use the application. NAM Application objects currently support Windows 95, Windows 3.x, and DOS workstation platforms.

Once Application objects have been created, users can rely on the NetWare Application Launcher (NAL) to access network applications. NAL displays icons for all available applications in a window at the workstation, and allows users to double-click on the icon to launch the application. NAL can also replace the normal Windows 95 or Windows 3.x interface, so that users only have access to those applications that have been associated with their User object. This provides more security and unclutters the user's desktop.

IntranetWare application management provides another way of automating the user environment. NAM and NAL work together to provide simple, uncluttered, and secure access to network applications. For more information, check out Chapter 12.

STEP 5: E-MAIL

The final step in IntranetWare configuration focuses on tying all the other components together. E-mail has become one of the most critical LAN components, next to file and printing services. That's because it improves communication, increases productivity, and maximizes the use of existing resources.

E-mail in IntranetWare relies on an integrated messaging platform called *MHS Services for IntranetWare*. MHS (Message Handling Service) stores, forwards, and routes user messages. These messages include text, binary, graphics, digitized video, and audio data. MHS services is integrated with NDS and uses various NDS objects to accomplish these messaging tasks.

IntranetWare MHS services relies on three important pieces:

▸ *MHS engine* — Accepts data from a variety of user e-mail software packages and delivers it to any type of mailbox.

▸ *Mailboxes* — Physical locations on a messaging server where messages are delivered.

▸ *MHS applications* — Provide the user interface for creating and reading IntranetWare messages.

This completes the final step of IntranetWare configuration. That wasn't so bad. During this phase, we struggled through LAN childhood together, and we'll do it again in Chapter 12. You learned about the five steps of IntranetWare configuration and prepared the network for its final and most difficult challenge-adulthood.

QUIZ

David Letterman once said, "Fall is my favorite season in Los Angeles, watching the birds change colors and fall from the trees." Along those lines, here's a little mind bender for you:

There is a field with a number of trees in it. There are a number of birds (more than one) in each tree. There is more than one tree in the field, and each tree has the same number of birds in it. If you knew the total number of birds in the field, you would know the total number of trees. If there are between 200 and 300 birds, how many trees are there?

(Q1-6)

IntranetWare Management

So, you have a new car, a new job, and a new apartment. Welcome to adulthood. It's funny how we continually yearn for these days during childhood. Now that we're here, we just want to be young again. Go figure.

Once you reach adulthood, your focus shifts from "getting started" to keeping things going. As a CNE, your system moves right from childhood into LAN adulthood with a focus on IntranetWare management. Now your focus shifts to the long term. Suddenly, your mind is filled with thoughts of a family (servers and workstations), a pension (SMS), and retirement (RMF). Aah, adulthood!

IntranetWare management is the most time-consuming aspect of being a CNE. If you figure that configuration occurs only once, management dominates your life forever. In IntranetWare, this is accomplished through five strategies:

- ▸ Server management

- ▸ Intranet management

- ▸ Workstation management

- ▸ Storage Management Services (SMS)

- ▸ Remote Management Facility (RMF)

In Chapter 13 we're going to take a detailed look at these five strategies for IntranetWare management. But for now, let's take a quick look at some of the key components of LAN adulthood — starting with marriage.

ZEN

"Oh, oh, oh . . . the things you've got to know."

Anonymous

SERVER MANAGEMENT

Eventually you will find Mr. or Ms. Right. Your eyes will meet across a crowded dance floor, you will feel that wonderful flutter in the pit of your stomach. Your knees will buckle and then bang — you're married! Marriage changes everything. Suddenly, your focus shifts from "me, me, me" to "the family." Your spouse becomes the center of your life. It's like sharing a lifeboat with that "special someone" while careening down the whitewater rapids of love. Yuck.

Similarly, the IntranetWare server is at the center of your LAN. At some point, your focus shifts from "users, users, users" to "the server." After all, the entire WAN will crumble if your servers aren't running correctly.

IntranetWare server management consists of three components:

▶ Console commands — keep the server running at peak performance

▶ NetWare Loadable Modules — everything else

▶ Server protection — keep users away from the server console

It all begins at the colon prompt. The colon (:) prompt is the server console. This is where you'll spend most of your server management time. It's a comforting feeling seeing the server running smoothly — seeing the familiar "WORM" prance around the screen (assuming that MONITOR.NLM is loaded), hearing the constant hum of IntranetWare workstations, and following the IntranetWare packets as they bounce merrily along the cabling segment.

The colon prompt accepts two kinds of commands — console commands and NLMs. IntranetWare includes numerous console commands for various server management and maintenance tasks (including NDS management, time synchronization, bindery services, sending messages, activating NLMs, server protection, and network optimization). This chapter explores most of the IntranetWare console commands and gives you some hints on how to use them.

All remaining server activity is accomplished using NLMs. NLMs are modular Legos that provide supplemental functionality to the IntranetWare server. There are four kinds of NLMs: disk drivers, LAN drivers, name space modules, and management utilities. In this chapter, we'll explore each of these and some key server management tools — INSTALL.NLM, MONITOR.NLM, SERVMAN.NLM, and DSREPAIR.NLM. You can think of NLMs as network management applications at the server.

Finally, we'll learn how to protect our precious IntranetWare server. This includes locking up the physical server machine, preventing access to the keyboard with MONITOR.NLM, using the SECURE CONSOLE command, and adding a password for RMF. Also, don't forget to use The Club™. Server protection is a serious management task because of the vulnerability of the console — users can cause a lot of damage there. Many times, this security feature is overlooked and CNEs discover their inadequate security measures when it's too late — in the unemployment line.

INTRANET MANAGEMENT

Just when you were beginning to get comfortable with marriage, the *Intranet* came along. From a technical standpoint, the Intranet is simply a Web server that is confined to a private internal network and publishes files to a private audience such as the employees of a corporation. A true WWW server is connected to the Internet and publishes files to the world. From a less technical standpoint, the Intranet is nosy neighbors, bowling leagues, and poker on Saturday night.

IntranetWare is Novell's comprehensive platform for a modern, full-service intranet. It starts with IntranetWare, then adds the following intranet and Internet features:

- ▸ *IPX/IP Gateway* — This gateway enables administrators to allow IPX-based workstations to access TCP/IP-based resources, such as FTP and the World Wide Web, without having to install or configure TCP/IP on those workstations. The gateway also lets you implement access control — you can limit users by TCP port number, IP address or the target host, and the time of day.

- ▸ *NetWare MPR* (MultiProtocol Router 3.1) — This feature provides WAN (wide area network) connectivity, routing multiple protocols over leased lines, frame relay, or ISDN lines. This capability allows you to connect network users to an Internet Service Provider (ISP).

- ▸ *The NetWare Web Server* — This full-feature Web server allows you to publish HTML pages over the intranet and Internet. It also includes the Netscape Navigator browser, which enables you to locate and read information stored on the Web.

- ▸ *FTP Services for IntranetWare* — These FTP services let you configure FTP access for your intranet.

Later, in Chapter 13, we are going to expand our understanding of the IntranetWare server to the "collective whole" — *intranet*. We will explore each of the above four solutions in excruciating detail. In addition, we will add two more enterprise topics:

▸ *NDS Maintenance* — Novell Directory Services is the heart of IntranetWare's enterprise solution. Keeping it running smoothly should be your number one priority. In the next section, we will explore some time-proven techniques for NDS maintenance and troubleshooting. Also, review Chapters 4, 8, and 9.

▸ *Internationalization* — IntranetWare allows diverse users to "speak different languages" and transport messages across different communication protocols. This is accomplished with the help of built-in IntranetWare internationalization. Language-enabling and special keyboard support ensure that international users can access resources in their native languages.

There's only one guarantee in marriage — anything goes! I have a feeling there's a lot of fun ahead for us.

WORKSTATION MANAGEMENT

So, you're cruising along through life, minding your own business, and wham — it hits you. Suddenly, your family is twice as big as it was a few years ago. It's an abrupt wake-up call when you finally realize *you're* not the child anymore. A strange thing happens when children have children. Even though Leia is 27 years old — firmly planted in adulthood — she's still our little baby. We were there through the rough years — login scripts, menu system, and e-mail. Now Leia's having children of her own. Suddenly her focus shifts from marriage to her baby.

Now is a good time for your focus to shift as well — from the server to your IntranetWare children (workstations). As a CNE, you will spend just as much time managing the workstations as you will managing the server — probably more. In addition, managing workstations can be even more challenging because it encompasses a much more diverse collection of users, applications, and operating systems. And we all know users can act like babies sometimes. In order to fully optimize the client connection and keep things running smoothly, you'll have to employ a stern, yet caring, workstation management strategy.

 ZEN

"If my heart can become pure and simple like that of a child, I think there probably can be no greater happiness than this."

Kitaro Nishida

Of all the places you'll go in your life, few will be as interesting as the IntranetWare client. There you'll find fun, adventure, and NetWare (or Virtual) Loadable Modules (NLMs). The client is one of the most important aspects of an IntranetWare system because it's where the users meet the network. Someday, I guarantee you'll get the question, "Where's the ANY key?" In order to help you sleep at night, the interface should be as transparent as possible — avoid confusion and unnecessary support calls. In order to achieve client transparency, IntranetWare breaks the workstation into two key components:

> ▸ *NIC* — The internal network interface card that provides communications between the local workstation operating system (WOS) and the IntranetWare server. This hardware device is managed by a series of workstation connectivity files called ODI (Open Datalink Interface). We use LAN drivers and NLMs in the Client 32 world, and simple COM files on 16-bit workstations.

> ▸ *Workstation operating system* (WOS) — The WOS manages all local workstation services. It coordinates among local applications (word processing, spreadsheets, and databases) and local devices (file storage, screens, and printers). All of these local activities must be somehow orchestrated with network services. In the Client 32 universe, this is accomplished using CLIENT32.NLM. On the other hand, Client 16 uses relies on complex suite of workstation Legos called VLMs (Virtual Loadable Modules).

Here's a quick history lesson. Previous versions of NetWare relied on less-integrated client connectivity files. NetWare 3.11 and earlier versions used programs such as WSGEN or SHGEN to generate an IPX.COM file that implemented the IPX/SPX stack and provided the link between the workstation and internal NIC. In addition, most of the DOS Requester functionality was accomplished using one rigid file — NET.EXE.

More recent versions of NetWare (NetWare 3.12 through 4.1) relied on Client 16 connectivity files. They introduced ODI (Open Datalink Interface) drivers that provided a more flexible way of binding the IPX/SPX protocol stack. In addition, the DOS Requester functionality was expanded to include a suite of 16-bit Virtual Loadable Modules (VLMs). These VLMs together form the "NetWare DOS Requester," which provides support for DOS and MS Windows client workstations in the 16-bit environment.

Now, in IntranetWare, Novell has introduced a more integrated 32-bit client. It uses an enhanced version of ODI and 32-bit NetWare Loadable Modules at the workstation. The 32-bit solution provides graphical access to NetWare 2.2, 3.12, and 4.11 servers. It is the new and preferred way of networking from Windows 95, Windows 3.1, and/or DOS workstations.

Regardless of the way you go, you must be intimately familiar with *both* platforms. After all, CNEs should always be prepared. Later, in Chapter 13, we'll learn to play in the 32-bit and 16-bit sandboxes.

ZEN

"So near, and yet . . . so what?"

Anonymous

Children aren't so bad. Once you get the hang of it, I think you might even enjoy parenthood. Having servers and workstations enables you to relive a little bit of your own childhood and adds years to your life. Of course, all the while, you need to be thinking about the future and what happens when your children get children of their own. Planning for the future and retirement are important aspects of adulthood. Let's take a closer look.

STORAGE MANAGEMENT SERVICES

Fortunately, IntranetWare includes a versatile new backup feature called Storage Management Services (SMS). SMS is a combination of related services that enables you to store and retrieve data from various targets — using Target Service Agents (TSAs). SMS is a backup engine that operates independently from the front-end application and back-end device. As you can see in Figure 1.14, SMS supports a variety of TSA front-ends, including IntranetWare file systems, NDS, and BTRIEVE databases. In addition, the SMS server can back up four different workstation platforms: DOS, Windows 95, OS/2, and Macintosh. Any or all of these resources can be backed up to a variety of back-end devices, including DOS Read/Write disks, and tape and optical drives.

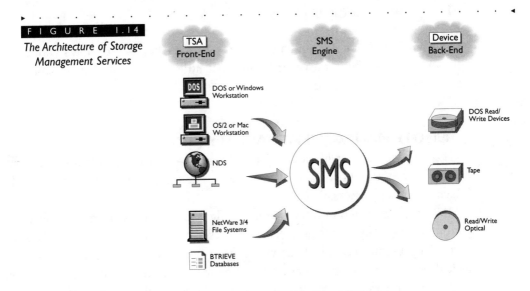

F I G U R E   1.14

The Architecture of Storage Management Services

The Architecture of Storage Management Services

So, how does it work? At the heart of the SMS model is the backup application. IntranetWare includes a starter program called SBACKUP. SBACKUP is an NLM that operates at the IntranetWare server and communicates directly with the host backup device. SBACKUP works within the SMS architecture to route data requests among TSAs and the backup device. This process consists of seven simple steps:

1 • Load the backup device driver on the host server.

2 • Load TSA software on all target devices. This includes the host server, if you plan to back it up.

3 • Load SBACKUP.NLM at the host server.

4 • Select a target to be backed up from the menu. The available options within SBACKUP should reflect all devices that have loaded the appropriate TSA.

5 • Select the backup device from an available options list. This list should reflect all devices attached to the host server.

6 • Back up the data from all loaded targets.

7 • Unload SBACKUP files in reverse order.

This completes our discussion of IntranetWare backup — so, how's your nest egg doing? Remember, you never know what little surprises life has in store for you; it's best to be prepared.

REMOTE MANAGEMENT FACILITY (RMF)

The final step in our life journey is retirement — RMF. Our life's been a very exciting adventure and now it's time to kick back and put it in cruise control. Welcome to Happy Acres!

RMF is the final step in IntranetWare configuration and management. It enables you to manage all your IntranetWare file servers from one location. This is particularly useful because file server security states that the machine should be locked away in a room or cabinet with no monitor and keyboard. Also, IntranetWare prides itself on multiple servers spanning wide geographic boundaries. In both cases, you'll spend more time trying to access the servers than doing the important stuff — maintaining and managing them.

So, how does it work? RMF supports CNE access from both a workstation and a modem. In either case, it consists of two main components:

▶ REMOTE.NLM

▶ RCONSOLE.EXE

The RMF server NLMs are broken into two functions — REMOTE facility and connection services. The REMOTE facilities are provided by one NLM — REMOTE.NLM. This module manages the information exchange to and from the workstation and the server. In addition, REMOTE.NLM enables you to specify an RMF password.

Connection services are a little bit trickier. As you remember from our earlier discussion, RMF supports access from both a direct workstation and a modem. In either case, the connection NLM is different. When you access RMF from a direct workstation, the connection NLM is RSPX.NLM. This module provides communication support and advertises the server's availability for remote access. On the other hand, when you're accessing RMF from an asynchronous modem, the connection NLM is RS232.NLM. This module initializes the server modem port and transfers screen and keystroke information to REMOTE.NLM.

Whether you're accessing RMF from a direct workstation or asynchronous modem, you're going to need RCONSOLE.EXE. RCONSOLE is a supervisor utility stored in the SYS:SYSTEM subdirectory. RCONSOLE provides direct access to the IntranetWare server console screen and enables you to perform any task as if you were sitting right in front of it. In addition, RCONSOLE provides an Available Options menu with supplemental tasks, including changing screens, scanning server directories, and performing a remote install. All in all, RCONSOLE is your friend, because it enables you to enjoy the good life without having to run around like a chicken with your head cut off.

ZEN

"Finally, science has discovered a cure for baldness, although it's not quite what you'd think. Instead of growing hair, they shrink your head to fit what hair you've got left."

Anonymous

Well, that does it. Your life in a nutshell. We've brought our LAN from birth through childhood and the rewards of adulthood. Through IntranetWare configuration and management, we've transformed a relatively limp and lifeless LAN into a powerful and productive business tool. Remember, as a CNE, you can't just set up the server and walk away. Your life is irrevocably bound to the childhood and adulthood of your LAN.

IntranetWare Printing

The final major topic of IntranetWare is printing. We always save printing for last because it's the most troublesome aspect of the LAN. Not that printing is inherently flawed; it actually works quite well under "normal conditions." The problem is that you rarely experience normal conditions. IntranetWare printing breaks down pretty quickly when things get hairy. And as I'm sure you know, things are always hairy!

SMART LINK

IntranetWare introduces a new and exciting printing model called "Novell Distributed Print Services". Check it out in "NetWare 4 Product Information" at http://www.netware.com.

Like previous versions of NetWare, IntranetWare does not have built-in printing services. These services are not available until you add them. In order to add IntranetWare printing, you work with all three main NDS printing objects:

- ▸ Print queues

- ▸ Print servers

- ▸ Printers

So, how does it work? As you can see in Figure 1.15, it all starts at the IntranetWare workstation. Somehow, users print their documents from a client application to a print queue. A print queue is a shared directory on the file server disk that stores print jobs in the order in which they are received. The print queue then lines up the various users' documents and sends them to the appropriate printer when the time is right. The print server keeps track of print job priority and directs them from the queue to the appropriate network printer. Voilà!

In a transparent IntranetWare printing environment, users print directly from their network application and the output magically appears on the printer down the hall. While this level of magic seems trivial to them, it's a nightmare for you, the CNE. In earlier versions of NetWare, it was worse, because users had to be aware of which print queue serviced "their" printer. Redirection commands were complex, and they had to redirect print jobs from local workstation ports to specific network print queues. Now you can see why it all breaks down.

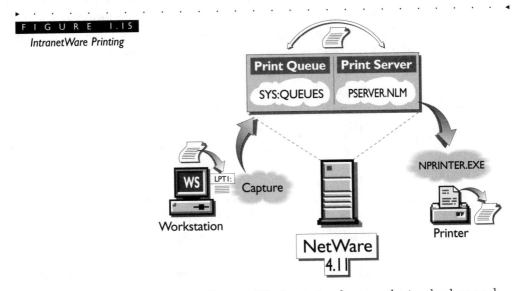

FIGURE 1.15

IntranetWare Printing

IntranetWare has dramatically simplified printing by introducing background queue management. This means users no longer have to print to queues; they can print directly to printer objects. As a matter of fact, they don't even need to know where the objects are stored, just the ones to which they want to print. Wow!

ZEN

"You think printing is bad? I know a guy with a really bad office job. He cleans windows — not the big ones — the little ones inside envelopes. Count your blessings."

Anonymous

So, everything's working fine and your users are happily printing along. Then zowie — the printer breaks! Oops, what now? Printing management is your life. More than any other network resource, printing services requires constant attention. You'll need to learn how to manage print queues, print servers, and printers. Fortunately, IntranetWare provides a variety of powerful tools for just this type of emergency. Here's how printing management works:

▶ *Managing Print Queues* — During your stint as a CNE, you'll have to learn to manage a variety of print queue tasks, including controlling print queue workflow, managing print jobs in the queue, and controlling access to the print queue. Many of these tasks can be accomplished by using NWADMIN or PCONSOLE. I recommend NWADMIN, because it enables you to manage queues from within a graphical utility. One of the most important aspects of print queue management is what you do with the jobs once they're there. NWADMIN provides two windows for this task — Print Queue Job List and Print Job Detail. More to come in Chapter 14.

▶ *Managing the Print Server* — While dealing with the print server on a daily basis, you'll have to perform a variety of tasks, including viewing print server status, bringing down the print server, and assigning print server users and operators. Once again, these tasks can be accomplished using NWADMIN or PCONSOLE. Be careful when you assign print server operators, because they're given power to control things any mortal user shouldn't have access to.

▶ *Managing the Printer* — Logically, the printer is at the end of the road. When you perform routine printer management tasks, consider viewing and controlling the printer status and responding to printer error messages. The Printer Status window in NWADMIN or PCONSOLE enables you to perform numerous maintenance tasks, including changing service mode, mounting forms, stop/starting printers, selecting form feed, and stopping jobs. I predict you'll spend a lot of time here.

So, there you have it — IntranetWare printing. That wasn't so bad, was it — YES! Wouldn't life in the IntranetWare universe be great without printing? Of course, without printers, there wouldn't be paperwork, and without paperwork, you wouldn't be reading this book. And without this book, you wouldn't be a great CNE. Without "CNE-ship," you would be stuck in a musty office somewhere generating copious paperwork. So, after all, printing is a good thing. I guess in some strange way, printing conquers bureaucracy.

I have a treat in store for you in Chapter 14 when we get to spend much more time scouring every detail of IntranetWare printing. For now, just be glad you're using IntranetWare because its printing architecture has been dramatically improved.

We sure could learn an important lesson from the following quote. Take a moment to relax. Unwind. Go for a peaceful walk. Clear your mind.

ZEN

"The trouble with life in the fast lane is that you get to the end in an awful hurry!"

Anonymous

Welcome back. This completes our discussion of the major IntranetWare technologies. So far, we've introduced NDS, the IntranetWare enhanced file system, security, utility management, client services, IntranetWare configuration, management, and finally printing. Wow, that's quite an introduction. Of course, IntranetWare is quite an impressive operating system. Remember, we're talking the peak of OS evolution here. I bet you can't wait to dive into the nitty gritty of IntranetWare design, installation, and management. But, wait, before I let you get away, we need to take a quick look at a few additional IntranetWare features — namely, memory management, internationalization, and DynaText.

Other IntranetWare Features

At the beginning of this chapter, we outlined the two types of services in IntranetWare — the "core" services and the "evolved" services. The core services of IntranetWare establish a foundation upon which to build. These services are relatively unchanged from NetWare 3.12. Two important core services we haven't discussed yet are internationalization and DynaText.

Evolved services, on the other hand, build on the foundation of IntranetWare and define the evolution of this amazing OS. At the forefront of evolved services is NDS. Additional services include a better file system, enhanced GUI utilities, NDS security and auditing, and improved memory management. It's the latter we're interested in now.

Let's take a moment to explore these three services and see what impact they'll have on your life as a CNE and your journey through the IntranetWare universe.

MEMORY MANAGEMENT

IntranetWare manages file server RAM more efficiently than did NetWare 3.12. Earlier versions of NetWare allocated memory to multiple pools that served specific purpose. In NetWare 3.12, these pools expanded as needed, but rarely returned unused memory. Occasionally, a server application ran out of RAM even if there was plenty of memory in the main pool.

IntranetWare has consolidated all server RAM into one main pool and memory is reallocated as needed. The server operates much more efficiently and applications rarely run out of valuable file server RAM. In addition, IntranetWare includes memory protection. Memory protection defines the OS's ability to run NLMs in a protected memory area on the server. IntranetWare memory protection provides CNEs with a tool to test NLMs within a protected ring of memory without bringing down the server or corrupting other applications.

Protected rings of memory are less efficient than nonprotected rings, but shield the operating system core from harmful NLMs. Ring protection provides a logical means to segment memory and provide protection for processes such as disk/LAN drivers and the operating system. These segments are limited in size and are granted privilege levels. As you can see in Figure 1.16, ring zero maintains the highest privilege level and includes the NetWare 4.11 OS files. In addition, the proven disk drivers and LAN drivers hang out there.

Ring three, on the other hand, is the lowest privilege and is defined as the protected ring. Even though it appears as though rings one and two are available, only two rings can coexist at one time-typically ring zero (OS) and ring three (protected).

IntranetWare's memory management features are made possible through a new management scheme that uses the Intel-based paging mechanism. This strategy provides the foundation for memory protection and efficient memory allocation. In addition, IntranetWare includes server console commands and NLMs for managing memory protection. At the heart of this strategy is the DOMAIN server NLM utility. For more detail regarding IntranetWare memory management, refer to Chapter 15.

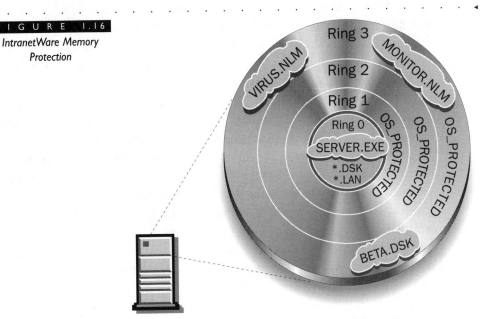

F I G U R E   1.16

IntranetWare Memory
Protection

ZEN

"The search is what anyone would undertake if he were not sunk in the everydayness of his own life. To become aware of the possibility of the search is to be onto something. Not to be onto something is to be in despair."

Walter Percy

INTERNATIONALIZATION

IntranetWare's internationalization strategy offers support for multiple languages. IntranetWare provides utility and installation capability for a variety of simultaneous languages. By default, English is used for the operating system NLMs and all utilities. Other languages can be set at installation and when utilities and services are requested. Differences in date, time, and number formats are also supported.

The most amazing of IntranetWare's international features is the ability for multiple workstations to access the same resources while simultaneously using different languages. This is made possible through the use of the NetWare DOS Requester and client SET parameters. By default, IntranetWare supports English, French, German, Italian, and Spanish languages.

Keep in mind that although most languages support the standard microcomputer hardware, some languages require special consideration. To use Japanese, for example, the keyboard must support double-byte characters. If a user with this hardware sends a message to a user with a single-byte character language, the recipient will see garbage characters on the screen. There's an important lesson here. The hardware cannot interpret the double-byte characters. In addition, software will not act as a translator, either. It will simply display the information in the native workstation language. This means if you send a German message to someone working in English, it will appear as German. IntranetWare is not yet intelligent enough to translate from German to English — nor does it want to.

DYNATEXT

IntranetWare provides electronic versions of all its product documentation. The DynaText utility enables you to choose a manual, browse its contents, search for topics, and print. As you can see in Figure 1.17, the DynaText window is broken into two halves. The left half provides an outline of all the major topics while the right half provides the book text and graphics. Scroll bars and menu icons round out the interface. DynaText supports any of the major client operating systems: Microsoft Windows 95, OS/2, and Macintosh. In addition, it supports two operating modes: stand-alone or networked. Wait, that's not all. Novell on-line documentation is also available in several languages. All you have to do is set the NWLANGUAGE parameter at the workstation and voilà, different users are viewing on-line documentation in different languages — simultaneously! What will they think of next?

To install on-line documentation on the IntranetWare server, simply use the INSTALL.NLM utility and NetWare 4.11 DynaText CD-ROM. Later in the book, we'll take a closer look at on-line documentation and provide some exercises for practicing with it on your own.

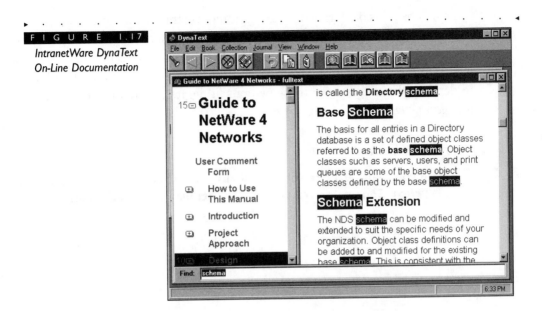

FIGURE 1.17

*IntranetWare DynaText
On-Line Documentation*

Well, there you have it. IntranetWare *is* the big kahuna. If you're not in awe by now, you must be a very hard person to impress. As we mentioned earlier, the goal of IntranetWare is transparent connectivity. The NDS Cloud surely helps the situation by enabling us to represent physical network devices as logical objects. Also, this NDS Cloud concept permeates all aspects of IntranetWare configuration, management, and printing.

QUIZ

Let's say you're going for a Sunday drive to Podunk and back. I don't know why, let's just say that you are! It's 120 miles from here, and you average 60 mph on the trip out. On the return trip, you take it easy and average 40 mph. What was your average speed for the round-trip? Don't worry, it's not as easy as it sounds.

(Q1-7)

On the other hand, I hope you've come to appreciate that IntranetWare can also be down-to-earth. It's not quite as alien as you might think. Many of IntranetWare's dramatic changes have been built on top of NetWare 3.12. Both the core and evolved services work together to provide a cohesive, cool WAN architecture.

Remember, this book is dedicated to getting you through IntranetWare with the least amount of pain. Who knows, you might even enjoy yourself along the way. In this first chapter, we've given you a brief snapshot of what IntranetWare is all about. In the remaining 14 chapters, we'll round out your education with some in-depth understanding. Get those neurons firing. It's time to dive deeper into the *next generation* of networking.

SMART LINK

If you really want to see the Next Generation of networking, surf to "Next Generation Networking" at http://www.netware.com.

Match each of the following NDS terms with its description:

1. ___ DynaText	A.	Maximum number of connections per server
2. ___ GUI	B.	E-mail engine
3. ___ SMS	C.	Holds print jobs waiting to be printed
4. ___ File compression	D.	On-line documentation
5. ___ Internationalization	E.	Rights flowing down from above
6. ___ MHS	F.	Increases disk space up to 63 percent
7. ___ Ring zero	G.	Modular programs that run on the workstation
8. ___ Data migration	H.	Maximum number of printers per print server
9. ___ VLMs	I.	NetWare OS runs here
10. ___ AUDITING	J.	Type of user interface
11. ___ 1000	K.	Useful with large disk allocation blocks
12. ___ Block suballocation	L.	Transfers inactive data to near-term storage
13. ___ 256	M.	LAN driver written to ODI specifications
14. ___ IRF	N.	Allows protocols to coexist on same network board
15. ___ Inheritance	O.	Backup engine
16. ___ Profile	P.	Type of login script
17. ___ ODI	Q.	Filters inherited rights
18. ___ MLID	R.	Provides choice of language
19. ___ IPX	S.	Security feature that can be activated at the volume or container level
20. ___ Print queue	T.	Default NetWare 4.11 communications protocol

See Appendix C for answers.

EXERCISE 1-2: GETTING TO KNOW NDS

PART I:

Write C for container or L for leaf next to each of the following objects:

1. ___ Volume
2. ___ Country
3. ___ User
4. ___ Group
5. ___ Organizational Unit
6. ___ Server
7. ___ Print Queue
8. ___ Organizational Role
9. ___ Computer
10. ___ Organization

See Appendix C for answers.

PART II:

Indicate whether you think each item below would be a container or a leaf object. If you think it would be a Container object, indicate what type of container (that is, Country, Organization, or Organizational Unit).

1. _____ The Human Resources department
2. _____ Leia
3. _____ A database server
4. _____ The PAYCHECK print queue
5. _____ ACME, Inc.
6. _____ The Administrator Organizational Role
7. _____ UK (that is, United Kingdom)
8. _____ A dot matrix printer
9. _____ The Tokyo office
10. _____ The SYS: volume

See Appendix C for answers.

EXERCISE 1-3: THE CLOUD

Circle the 20 IntranetWare CNE Basics terms hidden in this word search puzzle using the hints provided.

```
N  B  X  E  T  X  E  T  N  O  C  Y  R  E  D  N  I  B  E  S  L
G  D  I  R  E  C  T  O  R  Y  G  Y  R  W  N  N  R  I  X  L  O
Y  I  S  I  N  G  L  E  R  E  F  E  R  E  N  C  E  N  E  B  L
N  S  D  X  V  J  R  B  F  P  K  S  T  E  C  X  Y  D  J  T  C
T  T  G  S  B  Q  P  X  V  E  L  E  A  F  O  B  J  E  C  T  F
B  I  D  U  X  M  L  D  L  T  E  E  N  U  B  Q  C  R  O  K  I
H  N  U  U  E  E  I  X  U  E  S  R  Z  E  T  T  E  Y  N  Z  L
G  G  A  U  T  H  E  N  T  I  C  A  T  I  O  N  U  Z  T  V  H
I  U  O  W  T  I  M  E  S  E  R  V  E  R  F  R  M  N  A  F  B
S  I  H  Y  D  C  O  L  M  U  F  X  E  Q  G  B  C  F  I  W  R
S  S  U  B  O  R  D  I  N  A  T  E  R  E  F  E  R  E  N  C  E
Y  H  Y  R  N  F  J  M  I  L  X  B  J  T  C  O  N  T  E  X  T
T  E  F  V  Z  S  U  O  O  Y  T  R  E  P  O  R  P  G  R  T  J
K  D  D  F  C  F  C  L  F  O  D  C  H  V  M  O  A  B  K  P  G
Z  N  G  C  D  V  U  J  M  D  X  H  B  S  M  N  R  L  B  Q  H
C  A  T  W  P  H  Z  W  U  J  X  W  P  L  O  E  T  W  W  L  E
J  M  K  C  Q  V  I  K  P  G  K  K  G  S  N  V  I  T  L  P  E
F  E  E  R  M  S  J  V  X  I  F  O  G  W  N  D  T  H  Y  H  O
T  I  M  E  S  Y  N  C  H  R  O  N  I  Z  A  T  I  O  N  K  L
S  W  V  I  N  E  X  J  Y  W  H  E  G  E  M  D  O  P  E  W  V
E  O  N  Q  S  G  R  S  I  G  M  J  Q  Z  E  N  N  O  E  E  Y
```

Hints:

1. Background process that verifies authorization.
2. Flat file database found in earlier version of NetWare.
3. List of Directory tree contexts whose objects are available to users logged into a server using a NETX shell.
4. Object's leaf name.
5. Object that can hold other objects.
6. Describes an object's location in the database.
7. Distributed NDS Database.

8. Complete name of an object.
9. Object that cannot contain other objects.
10. Provides global access to network resources.
11. Item in the Directory tree that holds information about a resource.
12. Logical division of the NDS database.
13. Characteristic of an object.
14. Topmost object in the NDS tree.
15. Default type of time server.
16. Created if the parent partition exists, but no children.
17. Provides time to other servers.
18. Ensures that all network servers report the same time.
19. Hierarchical representation of the NDS structure.
20. Formerly called Greenwich Mean Time (GMT).

See Appendix C for answers.

Understanding NDS

Every cloud has a silver lining. Even Daisy-Head Mayzie had 15 minutes of fame. But she let it go to her head — literally. Let me explain.

One sunny afternoon, sweet little Mayzie sprouted a Daisy out of her head! How odd. After she got over the initial shock, Mayzie got a "big head." She left her family and friends to become a star in Hollywood. But all the money and fame didn't change the fact that she had a plant growing out of her cranium. And what's money worth anyway without somebody to share it with? So, Daisy-Head Mayzie realized her mistake and left the afternoon talk shows to return home. Yes, HOME. Not a SYS:USERS directory, not a base in baseball. No, this home is where everyone loves her for who she is, not what she has growing out of her head. Everyone lived happily ever after.

SMART LINK

For more Dr. Seuss fun, visit "Seussville" at http://www.seussville.com.

This could happen to you. You could become "NDS-Head Fred!" As a matter of fact, you can probably feel a slight "twinge" even as you read this. You knew that your new life as a CNE would be exciting, but no one prepared you for this. The more you learn about NDS, the faster your tree will sprout — until one day you'll be as rich and famous as Daisy-Head Mayzie. But don't make the same mistakes that she did. Don't abandon the people who got you here — your family, your friends, Novell, and Ortho Weed Killer. Keep your head out of the clouds and your two feet planted firmly *in* the ground.

ZEN

"Congratulations! Today is your day. You're off to great places! You're off and away!"

Dr. Seuss

I'm here to help you deal with this whole cranial gardening thing. As we learned in the last chapter, NDS is a virtual tree structure that helps you organize network resources. It's also referred to as the "Cloud" because it floats above physical resources — servers, printers, and users. In the next chapter, we begin our examination of the three phases of life as a CNE with a discussion of NDS design. But before we get there, you'll need an NDS tree growing out of your head to make sense of it all. That's the goal of this chapter. We hope to generate enough neurokinetic energy to stimulate cranial growth. In other words, we're going to make you think until it hurts. So, without any further adieu, let's start at the beginning — with the NDS database.

THE BRAIN

As a CNE, you'll have two main NDS responsibilities — design and management. NDS design focuses on the structural organization of objects, partitions, and time servers. This material is covered in excruciating detail in Chapter 4. NDS management takes over from there. It deals with sophisticated utilities and daily management tasks, including naming context, troubleshooting, partition management, and time synchronization. These topics are tackled in Chapters 8 and 9. So, what are we doing here? In this chapter, we're going to build a conceptual framework for all the fun to come. This is just a general introductory discussion. The real meat-and-potatoes happens later. So, open your mind and have fun. It'll be easier on you if you don't fight it.

Getting to Know NDS

NDS is your friend. It may seem a little intimidating at first, but when you get to know NDS, it's actually pretty fun. Really. NDS is a big Sta-Puff marshmallow man that keeps track of your network's resources. In more technical terms, it's a distributed object-oriented hierarchical database of physical network objects. Huh? Just think of it as a huge WAN phone book. NDS classifies all network resources into 29 different objects. These objects can be organized by function, location, size, type, or color — it doesn't matter. The point is, NDS organizes network resources independently from their physical locations. When a user logs into the network, he/she can access any object in the tree regardless of its location. This type of openness, however, does not come without a price. One obvious problem is security — which is why NDS is controlled by a complex, impenetrable armor known as *NDS access rights*.

So, what does NDS look like? From the outside, it looks like a big cloud hovering over your network. On the inside, however, it's a hierarchical tree similar to the DOS file system. As you can see in Figure 2.1, NDS organizes resources into logical groups called *containers*. This is like Tupperware gone mad. In Figure 2.1, servers are organized according to function. Then users are placed in the appropriate containers to simplify connectivity. In addition, productivity increases because users are near the resources they use. NDS also creates a global method of interconnectivity for all servers, users, groups, and other resources throughout the WAN. The bottom line is this — users don't access physical resources anymore. Instead, they access logical objects in the NDS tree. This means they don't need to know which IntranetWare server provides a particular resource. All they need to know is where the server exists in the logical NDS world.

▶ · ◀

F I G U R E   2.1

A Tree in a Cloud

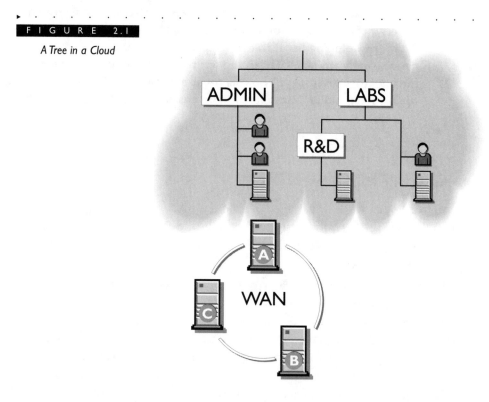

So, is NDS worth it? Well, you'll have to make that decision for yourself. But here are some of its benefits:

▶ Global database providing central access to and management of network information, resources, and services.

▶ Standard method of managing, viewing, and accessing network information, resources, and services.

▶ Logical organization of network resources that is independent of the physical characteristics or layout of the network.

▶ Dynamic mapping between an object and the physical resource to which it refers.

So, what do you think? Is NDS for you? Before you answer, let's take a moment to get to know NDS. Who knows — you might even like it.

THE "CLOUD"

NDS has many different names — the Directory, the tree, the "Cloud," the Sta-Puff marshmallow man. In reality, it's all of these things. But the most appropriate description is the "Cloud." NDS oversees physical network resources and provides users with a logical world to live in. This differs dramatically from what you're used to — NetWare 3.12. As you can see in Figure 2.2, the NetWare 3.12 bindery is *server-centric*. This means that every physical resource exists within and/or around the server. If Leia wants to access files or printers on multiple servers, she must have a login account and security access on every one. This system makes access and management both repetitive and time consuming. Also, note that nothing exists *above* the server. The server itself represents the highest level of the network organization structure. Users, volumes, files, and printers all exist within each server.

NDS, on the other hand, creates a whole new world *above* the server. As you can see in Figure 2.3, each network resource exists only once as a logical object in the "Cloud." NDS is *network-centric* in the sense that everything happens in the NDS hierarchy. Suddenly the server has gone from being at the top of the network organizational chart to being a physical object at the bottom. The beauty of this system is that Leia only logs in once and has instant access to all network resources. She doesn't log into each server — she logs into the NDS tree, and it tracks where her files and printers are. All logins, attaches, and access rights are handled in the background by NDS. This is the epitome of user transparency. The beauty is that users don't need to see inside the "Cloud"; all they need to know is that their stuff is there.

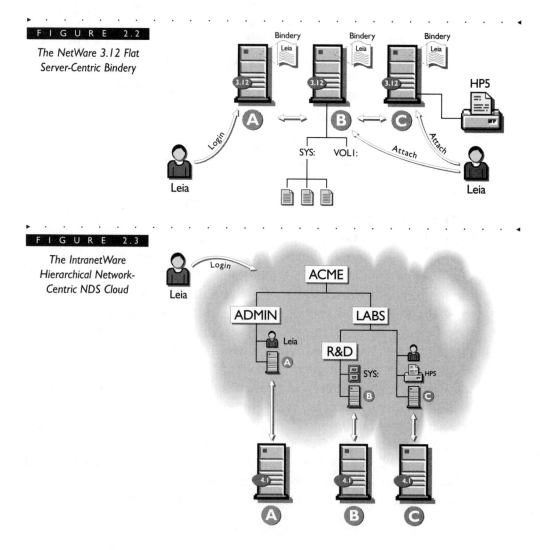

FIGURE 2.2

The NetWare 3.12 Flat Server-Centric Bindery

FIGURE 2.3

The IntranetWare Hierarchical Network-Centric NDS Cloud

The main lesson to learn from the accompanying graphics is the direction of the arrows. In Figure 2.2, the arrows of communication are horizontal. This means that all communication exists within and between NetWare 3.12 servers. If Leia wants access to another resource, she must follow the horizontal communication path to another server by either re-logging in or attaching. In contrast, Figure 2.3 shows the communication arrows running vertically. This means that communication occurs from within and between the NDS Cloud and its physical resources. The NDS Cloud handles the problem of locating resources and transparently grabs whatever Leia wants. This vertical communication structure makes finding and using network resources much easier for the user. In addition, and this is the part you'll like, it provides a single point of central network management for CNEs.

Let's take a closer look at the differences between NDS and the NetWare 3.12 bindery.

NDS VERSUS THE BINDERY

The bindery found in earlier versions of NetWare is a flat-file database that tracks network resources on each server. It's stored as the files NET$OBJ.SYS, NET$PROP.SYS, and NET$VAL.SYS in the SYS:SYSTEM directory. The bindery uses these three files to track network objects, properties, and values. When users need to access a server's resources, they must log in and register with its respective bindery. If the server doesn't recognize them, it disallows access. Then the administrator must create a special entry with different access security for this user. This is painstaking and dumb.

NDS, on the other hand, stores information about network resources in a global database, called the Directory. This database is distributed on all servers in the WAN so that users can instantly get access to what they need. Suddenly, you've been escalated from a lowly bindery user to the top of the NDS food chain. As an object, you exist at the same level as the IntranetWare server. How does it feel?

QUIZ

Let me tell you a little story. Maybe you've heard it before. It's about this little girl named Alice, who traveled through the "looking glass." Are you with me, here? When Alice entered the Forest of Forgetfulness, she didn't forget everything — only certain things. She often forgot her name, and the one thing she was most likely to forget was the day of the week.

*Now, the Lion and the Unicorn were frequent visitors to the forest —
strange creatures. The Lion lies on Mondays, Tuesdays, and Wednesdays
and tells the truth on the other days of the week. The Unicorn, on the
other hand, lies on Thursdays, Fridays, and Saturdays, but tells the truth
on the other days of the week. One day Alice met the Lion and the
Unicorn resting under a tree. They made the following statements:*

Lion: Yesterday was one of my lying days.

Unicorn: Yesterday was one of my lying days.

*From these two statements, Alice (who was a very bright girl) was able to
deduce the day of the week. Can you?*

(Q2-1)
(See Appendix C for quiz answers.)

Following is a brief comparison of NDS and the IntranetWare bindery. In each case, focus on NDS's network-centric approach.

▸ *Database* — The bindery is a flat-file database consisting of three files in the SYS:SYSTEM directory. Each server retains its own database. NDS, on the other hand, is an object-oriented hierarchical database, called the Directory. The Directory encompasses all objects in the WAN and is distributed across servers. It also consists of database files on the SYS: volume. These files are, however, protected in a special system-owned directory.

▸ *Server* — In NetWare 3.12, the server is king of the hill. It houses the bindery and controls all network resources. In IntranetWare, however, the server's importance diminishes quite a bit. It's simply another logical object in the global NDS tree. Network resources are accessed through the "Cloud" — independently from the physical server. But don't get caught up in the logical insignificance of the IntranetWare server. In the physical realm, it's still king of the hill. After all, IntranetWare has to be installed somewhere, files have to be stored somewhere, and users have to log into something.

▶ *Users* — In NetWare 3.12, users are defined as objects in the server-based bindery. You must create a User object for that user on every server on which the user needs access. In NDS, however, users are logical objects in the NDS Cloud. Each user is defined only once. The system takes care of tracking the resources to which they need access. This is made possible using a concept called context, which we'll explain a little bit later.

▶ *Login* — Bindery logins are server-centric. This means that users must log in or attach to every server they use a resource from — files, printing, or applications. NDS logins are network-centric. This means that users issue one login statement for access to the entire "Cloud." Once they're in, the world is at their fingertips.

REAL WORLD

The Sta-Puff marshmallow man has to come down to Earth sometimes. With all this flowery talk of clouds and trees, this simple fact remains — NDS is a database stored on the SYS: volume of every IntranetWare server. More specifically, the database is made up of four protected files in the SYS:_NETWARE directory:

▶ BLOCK.NDS

▶ ENTRY.NDS

▶ PARTITIO.NDS

▶ VALUE.NDS

All these files are very hard to find. Take my word for it, they are there. If you need to see them yourself, use the Directory Scan option of RCONSOLE. See Chapter 13 ("IntranetWare Management") for more details.

TIP

In order for NDS to identify you, you must provide your "full NDS name" at context. This includes your login name and user "context." There's that word again. A user's full name is a combination of who they are and where they live. My login name, for example, would be DAVID in California in the USA. We'll talk about this later in the NDS naming section of this chapter.

▸ *Network Resources* — In a bindery network, resources are owned by the server. Volumes and printers, for example, are tracked according to the server to which they're attached. User access to these resources requires login or attachment to the host server. NDS, on the other hand, distributes network resources independently from the server to which they're attached. It might seem strange, but volumes can be organized across the tree from their host servers. It's possible for users to have access to the IntranetWare file system without logical access to its host server. Very cool. But don't get too carried away. Physical volumes still reside inside IntranetWare servers. We haven't figured out how to separate the two yet — that's IntranetWare 3!

SMART LINK

For more information on the architecture of the NDS database, surf to the Novell Knowledgebase at http://support.novell.com/search/.

As you can see, NDS is a huge improvement over the NetWare 3.12 bindery. NDS is actually not even an improvement — it's a complete revolution. Nothing is as it appears. So if NDS isn't what you think it is, what is it? Let's take a closer look.

ZEN

"The truth is out there."

The X-Files

COMPOSITION OF THE TREE

Plant a tree in a "Cloud" — it's good for the environment.

As in nature, the NDS tree starts with the [Root] and builds from there. Next, it sprouts container objects, which are branches reaching toward the sky. Finally, leaf objects flutter in the wind and provide network functionality to users, servers, and the file system. As you can see in Figure 2.4, the tree analogy is alive and well.

. . . . ◄

FIGURE 2.4

The Figurative NDS Tree

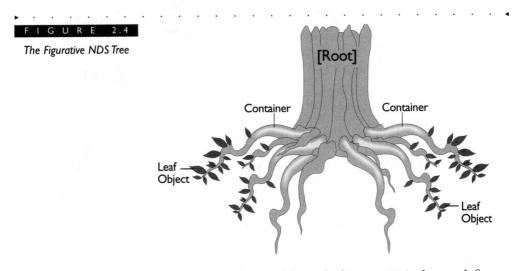

The real NDS tree is made up of special logical objects. NDS objects define logical or physical entities that provide organizational or technical function to the network. As you can see in Figure 2.5, they come in three different flavors:

- [Root]

- Container objects

- Leaf objects

The [Root] is the very top of the NDS tree. Because it represents the opening porthole to our NDS world, its icon is appropriately a picture of the Earth. Container objects define the organizational boundaries of the NDS tree and house other container objects and/or leaf objects. In Figure 2.5, we use container objects to define the ACME organization and its two divisions — ADMIN and LABS. Finally, leaf objects are the physical or logical network resources that provide technical services and WAN functionality. Leaf objects define the lowest level of the NDS structure. In Figure 2.5, leaf objects represent users, a printer, a server, and a group. NDS supports 24 different leaf object types. We'll discuss these types in detail in the next section.

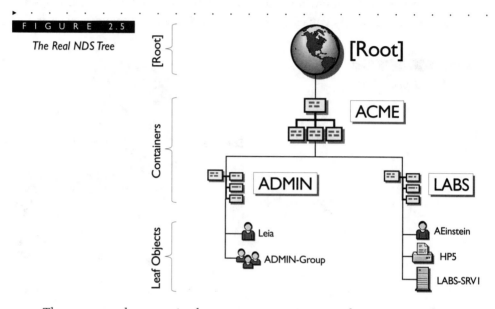

FIGURE   2.5

The Real NDS Tree

The tree can be organized any way you want, as long as it makes sense. AEinstein, for example, is placed near the resources he uses — the HP5 printer and LABS-SRV1 file server. In Chapter 4 ("NDS Design"), we'll learn more about the ACME organization and rules for tree design. For now, just focus on the conceptual framework of NDS and its tree structure.

On a more fundamental level, the NDS tree is stored in a fully replicated, globally distributed object-oriented database, called the Directory. The Directory consists of multiple hidden system files in the SYS:_NETWARE directory on each server. These files are replicated and distributed throughout the WAN to provide fault tolerance and increased connectivity. Although all IntranetWare servers use NDS, they don't have to contain their own directory database. If a server contains a portion of the database, that portion is called a *partition*. If a server doesn't have a copy of the database, then it must access it from some other server — which is less efficient. The bottom line is that IntranetWare server can contain the entire directory database, pieces of it (partitions), or none at all.

In addition, NDS requires a temporal assurance system, called *time synchronization*. This means that everyone must agree on what time it is. Time is critical to NDS because IntranetWare uses time stamps for synchronization, auditing, and NDS security. Time synchronization is implemented by using a variety of different time server types, as you'll see later in this chapter.

Typically, a single network has only one directory. Although it's possible for a WAN to have multiple NDS trees, users can only be logged into one at a time. Also, resources cannot be shared between multiple trees. For this reason, Novell is pushing toward a single tree for the whole world. We'll see, but it sure explains the world icon for the [Root].

ZEN

"So be sure when you step, step with care and great tact. And remember that life's a great balancing act. Just never forget to be dexterous and deft. And never mix up your right foot with your left."

Dr. Seuss

Now that you understand the fundamental architecture of NDS, let's take a closer look at its different container and leaf objects. Remember, plant a tree in a Cloud — it's good for the environment.

NDS Objects

When you sprout a cranial conifer and become NDS-Head Fred, leaf objects and the [Root] will become important to you. I'd like to take this opportunity to help you out a little and explain them more. After all, even Daisy-Head Mayzie studied botany.

As we just learned, the NDS tree consists of three different types of objects — [Root], container, and leaf objects. What we didn't learn is that these objects have specific properties and values. Remember, NDS is, after all, a database. An object is similar to a record or row of information in a database table. A property is similar to a field in each database record. For example, the properties of a Sales database may be Name, Phone Number, and Last Item Purchased. Finally, values are data strings stored in each object property. These values define the information around which the database is built. Let's take a closer look.

UNDERSTANDING NDS OBJECTS

As we learned earlier, NDS objects define logical or physical entities that provide organizational or technical functionality to the network. They come in three different flavors:

▶ [Root]

▶ Container objects

▶ Leaf objects

As you can see, the tree analogy is alive and well. Figure 2.5 shows that objects come in many different shapes and sizes. They can be physical resources (printers and servers), NDS resources (groups), users or logical tree organizers (containers). We'll take a closer look at each of IntranetWare's 29 different object types in just a moment.

Each NDS object consists of categories of information called *properties*. Properties are similar to fields in a database record that categorize types of information. User objects, for example, have properties such as Login Name, Password, Postal Address, and Description. While the same type of object may have the same properties, the information within those properties can be different. For example, two User objects both have a Login Name property but one has a value of Leia and the other has a value of AEinstein.

In addition, a unique collection of properties define the class of an object. For example, a Printer object differs from a User object in that it has different properties. The Printer object needs to track the default queue, for example, whereas users are more interested in generational qualifiers. NDS uses two different types of properties:

▶ *Required properties* — The NDS object cannot be created until these properties are supplied. When creating an object, you are prompted for required values (for example, last name for users and host server/host volume for the Volume object).

▸ *Multivalued properties* — These properties support more than one entry. For example, the user property called Telephone Number can hold multiple numbers that apply to a single user. Other user multivalued properties include Location and Fax Number.

Finally, values are the data stored in object properties. Refer to Table 2.1 for an illustration of the relationship between NDS objects, properties, and values.

T A B L E 2.1	OBJECT	PROPERTY	VALUE
NDS Objects, Properties, and Values	User	Login Name	AEinstein
		Title	Super smart scientist
		Location	NORAD
		Password	Relativity
	Printer	Common Name	HP5
		Default Queue	HP5-PQI
		Print Server	LABS-PSI
	NCP Server	Full Name	LABS-SRVI
		Version	IntranetWare
		Operator	Admin
		Status	Running just fine

Now let's explore each of the 29 NDS objects in detail, starting with [Root]. You never know which objects you're going to have sprouting from your cerebellum.

[ROOT]

The [Root] object defines the top of the NDS organizational structure. Each Directory tree can only have one [Root], which is created during installation of the first server in that tree. The [Root] cannot be deleted, renamed, or moved. The NDS [Root] object is exceptional in that it begins the boundaries of your NDS world. It behaves very much like a container object in that it houses other container objects. The main difference is that the [Root] cannot contain leaf objects.

> **TIP**
>
> **The NDS Directory tree is sometimes confused with the [Root] object. Unlike [Root], the tree name *can* be changed.**

Each NDS object has a specific icon that depicts its purpose graphically. The [Root] object's icon is particularly interesting. Because the [Root] object represents the opening porthole to the NDS world, its icon is appropriately a picture of the Earth. As you can see in Figure 2.6, the [Root] defines the top of our tree and houses the ACME container object.

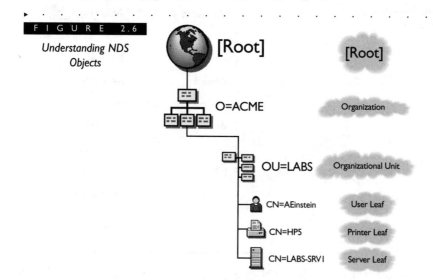

FIGURE 2.6

Understanding NDS Objects

The [Root] can hold only these specific container objects:

- *Country* — An optional container object that designates the country where your network resides.

- *Organization* — A one-dimensional container that typically represents your company.

- *Alias* — A logical NDS pointer to any other object existing elsewhere in the tree. In this case, the Alias can only point to Country and Organization objects.

The [Root] object is exceptional in one other way. It's the only NDS object without any properties. It simply exists as a placeholder for the top of the tree structure. It can have trustees, however. As we'll see in Chapter 11 ("IntranetWare Security"), any rights you assign to the [Root] are ancestrally inherited by all objects in the tree — which is a bad thing. All in all, the [Root] is a cool object, but you can't do much with it. Most of your design and management tasks will involve container and leaf objects.

REAL WORLD

You might notice the square brackets ([ ]) surrounding the [Root] object. These brackets designate the object as a special NDS entity. IntranetWare supports two other such entities — [Public] and [Supervisor]. [Public] is a special trustee that applies security to all other objects in the tree. Users can inherit the rights of [Public] without having to log in. They simply need to attach. As we'll see in Chapter 11, this creates a serious NDS security loophole.

[Supervisor] is a special superuser for bindery emulation. Users from the NetWare 3.12 world can log into NDS using [Supervisor] and inherit all its special rights. [Supervisor] has other important properties that allow you to manage NetWare 3.12 and IntranetWare coexistence.

CONTAINER OBJECTS

Container objects are logical organizers. They are the Tupperware bowls of our NDS kitchen. Actually the analogy works well — work with me here. The nature of Tupperware is that larger containers enclose smaller containers, which in turn house even smaller ones. Of course, the biggest Tupperware container in the world is the [Root]. Maybe in the future, when NDS takes over the world, we'll all be enclosed in a pale green, airtight, plastic bowl. Finally, Tupperware containers are used to store fruits and vegetables. In NDS, our Tupperware container objects store lettuce "leaf" objects. Sorry.

Here's a quick list of the three types of IntranetWare NDS container objects:

► *Country* — Designates the country where certain parts of the organization reside.

- *Organization* — Represents a company, university, or department. NDS only supports one layer of Organization objects, hence, the term "one-dimensional."

- *Organizational Unit* — Represents a division, business unit, or project team within the Organization. Organizational Units hold other Organizational Units or leaf objects. They are multidimensional.

Refer to Figure 2.6 for an illustration of the relationship between the [Root] and container objects. The ACME Organization houses other Organizational Units (including LABS), which in turn house leaf objects (like AEinstein). Let's take a closer look at these three different container objects.

ZEN

"I yelled for help. I screamed. I shrieked. I howled. I jowled. I cried, 'Oh save me from these pale green pants with nobody inside!'"

Dr. Seuss

Country Objects

The Country object is *optional*. It designates the country where your network resides and organizes other objects within the country. You can use a Country object to designate the country where your organization headquarters is or, if you have a multinational WAN, to designate each country that is part of your network. The Country object is also useful if you plan on cruising across the information superhighway. As a matter of fact, many Internet global directory providers are using the Country object as an entry point to their systems.

As I said a moment ago, the Country object is optional. It is not created as part of the default IntranetWare installation. If you want a Country object, you'll need to specifically configure it during installation of the very first server. Otherwise, adding a Country later can be a real pain. Also, this object must be a valid two-character country abbreviation. These abbreviations are defined as part of the ISO X.500 standard. Most trees don't use the Country object. Finally, Country objects can only house Organization containers and/or Organization Aliases. They cannot support leaf objects. Leafs must be stored within Organization or Organizational Unit containers.

TIP

If you don't have any compelling reasons to use the Country object, stay away from it. It only adds an unnecessary level of complexity to your WAN.

REAL WORLD

NDS supports a secret fourth container object type — Locality. The Locality object is like the Country object in that it's optional and not created as part of the default IntranetWare installation. You can use a Locality object to designate the region where your organization headquarters resides. Unlike Country objects, Locality objects can reside either under the [Root], Country, Organization, or Organizational Unit containers.

TIP

IntranetWare utilities don't recognize the Locality object.

Organization Objects

If you don't use a Country object, the next layer in the tree is typically an Organization. As you can see in Figure 2.6, ACME is represented as an "O." You can use the Organization object to designate a company, a division of a company, a university or college with various departments, and so on. Every Directory tree must contain at least one Organization object. Therefore, it is required. Many small implementations use only the Organization object and place all their resources directly underneath it. Organization objects must be placed directly below the [Root], unless a Country or Locality object is used. Finally, Organizations can contain all objects except [Root], Country, and Organization.

Earlier we defined the Organization as a one-dimensional object. This means the tree can only support one layer of Organization objects. If you look closer at the icon, you'll see a box with multiple horizontal boxes underneath. Additional vertical hierarchy is defined by Organizational Units — they are multidimensional. We'll describe them in just a moment.

Figure 2.7 illustrates the Details screen of the ACME Organization from NWADMIN. On the right side are the many page buttons, which identify categories of NDS properties. Associated with each page button is an input screen for a specific set of information. The Identification page button (shown here) allows you to define the following Organization properties:

- ▸ Name

- ▸ Other Name

- ▸ Description

- ▸ Location

- ▸ Telephone

- ▸ Fax Number

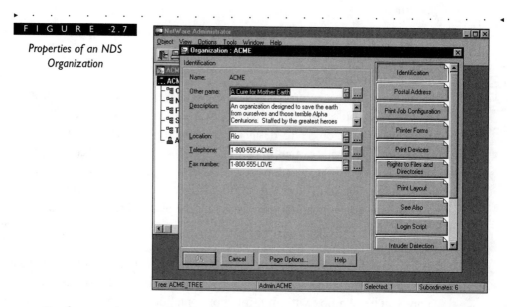

*Properties of an NDS
Organization*

Similar page buttons allow you to configure important Organization parameters, including postal information, print job configurations, trustee assignments, and so on. As far as ACME is concerned, the Organization container defines the top of the functional tree.

Organizational Unit Objects

The Organizational Unit object is a "natural group." It allows you to organize users with the leaf objects they use. You can create group login scripts, a user template for security, trustee assignments, security equivalences, and distributed administrators. All in all, Organizational Units are your friends.

Organizational Units represent a division, a business unit, or a project team. In Figure 2.6, the LABS OU represents a division within the ACME Organization. In this container, AEinstein works with his printers and servers. Organizational Units use the exact same properties as Organizations but in a slightly different way (see Figure 2.7). Organizational Units are multidimensional in that you can have many hierarchical levels of containers within containers. Remember, the Organization can only exist at one level.

Organizational Units are the most flexible Tupperware containers because they contain other OU's or leaf objects. As a matter of fact, Organizational Units can contain any NDS object type except the [Root], Country, or Organization containers (or Aliases to any of these). Now let's take a look at the real stars of our NDS world — the leafs.

LEAF OBJECTS

Leaf objects represent logical or physical network resources. Most of your CNE life will be spent designing, installing, and managing leaf objects — you'll become a vegetarian very quickly. These are the ultimate entities that IntranetWare users seek. Because leaf objects reside at the bottom of the NDS tree, they cannot hold other leafs. They represent the proverbial "end of the road." As we learned earlier, each type of leaf object has certain properties associated with it. This collection of properties differentiates the various leaf object classes. IntranetWare supports seven different categories for leaf object functionality:

- ▶ User leaf objects

- ▶ Server leaf objects

- ▶ Printer leaf objects

- ▶ Messaging leaf objects

- ▸ Network Services leaf objects

- ▸ Informational leaf objects

- ▸ Miscellaneous leaf objects

QUIZ

Look, there's that mischievious Alice again. She's trying to figure out when to believe the Lion. He says he'll help her escape from this crazy world. On what days of the week is it possible for the Lion to make the following two statements:

1. **I lied yesterday.**

2. **I will lie again tomorrow.**

Please help Alice find her way home.

(Q2-2)

In this section, we'll explore each of these seven categories and identify the key properties of all 24 NDS leaf objects. So, what's stopping you? Let's get going.

User Leaf Objects

Users are the center of your universe. After all, they are the ones that "use" the network. NDS supports five different leaf objects that help users do what they do. Let's check them out:

- ▸ *User* — Represents a person who uses the network. The user can be a beginner, a gardener, or NDS-Head Fred. The only requirement is that every person who logs into the WAN must be represented by a unique User object. When you create a User object, you can create a home directory for that user, who then has default rights to the file system. In addition, you can define default login restrictions using the special User Template object. In Figure 2.6, AEinstein is a User object in the LABS Organizational Unit. Notice the name designator — "CN." This represents Albert's login name or *common name*. As you can see in Figure 2.8, AEinstein has a plethora of user-related properties — 55, to be exact. The page buttons on the right-hand side identify property categories such as Identification, Security Restrictions, Mailbox, Print Job Configurations, Login Script, and so on.

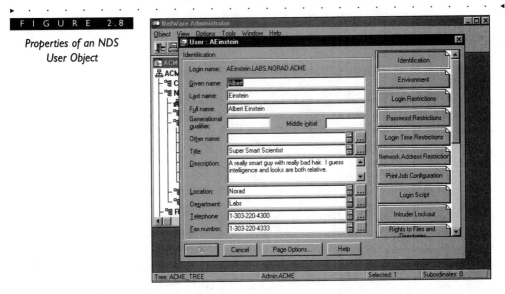

FIGURE 2.8

*Properties of an NDS
User Object*

▶ *User Template* — A new type of object available in IntranetWare that can be used to create User objects. It's similar in function to the User Template found in earlier versions of NetWare 4, except that it's now a specific type of object rather than a User object named "User_Template," which contains particular attributes. When you define a User Template object, you can designate default values for User object creation, including NDS rights and file system rights, and a setup script for copying files to each new user's home directory. This object can only be used for setting up new users; it can't be used for modifying existing User objects.

TIP

NDS is a very powerful database with a lot of valuable user information. Consider using it as a central company database of employee data. If you can't find what you need in the 55 default properties, you can always create your own. The IntranetWare SDK (Software Developers Kit) provides interface tools for modifying and adding NDS properties.

▸ *Group* — Defines an unrelated list of users for the purpose of assigning access rights and other management strategies. Remember, containers create "natural groups" for objects within the same Organization or Organizational Unit. The Group object, on the other hand, allows you to organize users from anywhere in the NDS tree. This is a great management strategy for assigning unrelated trustee rights or login restrictions.

 ▸ *Organizational Role* — Defines a position or role within the organization. If you want to assign security to a "position" instead of an "employee," consider creating an Organizational Role. The occupant can change frequently, but the responsibilities of the position will not. Whenever a user occupies the Organizational Role, they "absorb" its security. Some sample Organizational Roles include Postmaster, Chief Scientist, Administrative Assistant, and Coffee Jockey.

▸ *Profile* — IntranetWare's group login script. The Profile object contains a login script that can be shared by a group of unrelated users. If you have users who need to share common login script commands but are not located in the same portion of the tree, consider assigning them to a profile. As we'll see in Chapter 12, the Profile login script executes after the Container login script and before the User login script.

Server Leaf Objects

The IntranetWare server is still king of the physical hill. Even though it loses a lot of its significance in the logical realm, IntranetWare still resides on it, users still log in to it, and printers still attach to it. NDS supports three different leaf objects that apply to the logical server. Let's take a closer look:

▸ *NetWare Server* — Represents any server running NetWare or IntranetWare on your network. The server can be running NetWare 2, 3, 4, or IntranetWare. The NDS Server object is created automatically during installation. The only way to insert a server object is to actually install IntranetWare on the server and place it in the tree. You can, however, create virtual servers using the Alias object. We'll take a look at this strategy a little later. If you create a bindery-based server (NetWare 2 or 3), you'll need to manually create a logical NetWare server object to make its file systems available. Some of the Server object properties can be seen in Figure 2.9. The page buttons provide some interesting informational categories including Identification, Error Log, Blocks Read, Blocks Written, Connect Time, and other dynamic statistics.

▶ *Volume* — Points to a physical volume installed somewhere on the WAN. A logical Volume object is created automatically for every physical volume installed during server creation. NWADMIN will allow you to browse the file system using an NDS Volume object. You can create other volumes as logical pointers from different parts of the tree. Otherwise, consider using the Alias object. In the Volume object's properties, you can store identification information such as the host server, volume location, and so on. You can also set restrictions for use of the volume such as disk space restrictions and attribute security. Interestingly, the NDS logical volume is stored independently from the physical server to which it's attached.

▶ *Directory Map* — Represents a logical pointer to a physical directory in the IntranetWare file system. Directory Map objects are an excellent tool for centralizing file system management. Instead of creating drive mappings to physical directories, you can create them to logical

Directory Map objects. Then when the physical location changes, you only have to change the one central object. All drive mappings will then be updated immediately. Pretty cool, huh?

ZEN

*"We see them come. We see them go.
Some are fast, and some are slow.
Some are high, and some are low.
Not one of them is like another.
Don't ask us why; go ask your mother."*

Dr. Seuss

Printer Leaf Objects

Like previous versions of NetWare, IntranetWare printing relies on three main elements — print queue, print server, and printer. Each of these printing elements is represented in the NDS tree as a leaf object. Users print to print queues where jobs are stored until the printer is ready. Once a job gets to the top of the queue, the print server redirects it to the appropriate printer. Sounds pretty simple to me — you be the judge. Here's a quick look at these three critical NDS printer objects:

▸ *Printer* — Represents a physical printing device on the network. This logical object allows users to find the printers they need. Every printer must be represented by a corresponding NDS object and should be placed in the same container as the users who print to it. Some of the critical printer properties can be seen in Figure 2.10. These include Location, Department, Organization, Assignments, Configuration, Notification, and Features.

▸ *Print Queue* — Represents a logical print queue on the WAN. Every print queue must have a corresponding NDS object. Also, the location of the object in the tree directly impacts users' ability to print. Typically, the queues are stored in the same container as the users and printers to which they relate. IntranetWare gives you the flexibility to assign print queues on any volume, not just SYS:. It's about time.

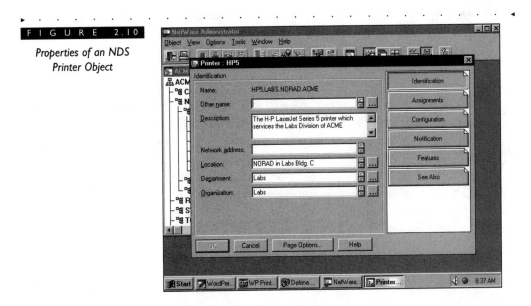

*Properties of an NDS
Printer Object*

▶ *Print Server* — Represents an IntranetWare or third-party print server. Once again, the print server should be placed in the same container as the printers and print queues with which it is associated. Also, make sure your third-party print server software is NDS compatible. If not, you'll need to create Print Server objects manually for each of your different machines. This is especially important if your users are accessing the network through bindery emulation.

TIP

Although IntranetWare introduces a new, optional priority system (called NDPS), it's important to note that it still relies on these three critical printing objects: Printer, Print Queue, and Print Server.

Messaging Leaf Objects

IntranetWare includes an impressive messaging engine called MHS Services for IntranetWare. It utilizes the Message Handling Service (MHS) standard. When you install and configure MHS, a variety of messaging objects are created. These objects allow you to control communications between users throughout the WAN. For a complete discussion of MHS Services, consult Chapter 12 ("IntranetWare Configuration"). For now, here's what they look like:

▸ *Messaging Server* — Represents a messaging server residing on any IntranetWare server. This object is created automatically during MHS Services installation. The messaging server sends, receives, and manages user e-mail.

▸ *Message Routing Group* — Represents a group of messaging servers that can transfer e-mail directly among each other. If users need to send e-mail to opposite sides of the tree, a Message Routing Group will bridge the gap.

▸ *Distribution List* — Represents a list of mail recipients for MHS Services. Instead of sending a message to every user individually, you can send it to the Distribution List. The MHS will then copy the message to each member individually. Using a Distribution List increases sending efficiency and cuts down on WAN traffic.

▸ *External Entity* — Represents a non-native NDS object that is imported for e-mail purposes. MHS Services uses this object to represent users from bindery-based directories or external e-mail. This way, other non-MHS users can participate in e-mail Distribution Lists and other NDS activities.

Network Services Leaf Objects

IntranetWare includes several exciting new object types that are designed to allow a network administrator to manage the network more easily and efficiently — saving both time and effort. In addition to the User Template object (which was discussed in the "User Leaf Objects" section earlier in this chapter), these objects include the Application object, which allows you to manage applications as objects in the NDS tree; the Auditing File object (AFO), which allows you to manage auditing file logs as objects in the tree; and the LSP (License Service Provider) object, which is used by NLS (NetWare Licensing Services) to monitor and control the use of licensed applications on the network. Let's take a closer look:

▸ *Application* — Allows network administrators to manage applications as application objects in the NDS tree. It requires NDS, which means that you can't run an application associated with such an object if you are using a Bindery Services connection. A new IntranetWare utility that utilizes this object is the NetWare Application Launcher (NAL) — which allows users to view available applications and double-click on an icon to launch the associated application. The advantage of this object for users is that they don't have to worry about drive mappings, paths, or rights when they want to execute an application.

▶ *Auditing File* (AFO) — Represents an auditing log file that can be managed as an NDS object. This object is created by an auditing utility such as AUDITCON when auditing is enabled and is used to manage an auditing trail's configuration and access rights.

▶ *LSP* (License Service Provider) — Represents an IntranetWare server with the NLS (NetWare Licensing Services) NLM loaded. NLS is a distributed, enterprise network service that enables administrators to monitor and control the use of licensed applications on a network. An LSP object is created when you register a License Service Provider (LSP) with NDS by loading NLS.NLM with the -r option.

Informational Leaf Objects

Most of the leaf objects so far have performed an obvious network function. Two other objects, however, exist for one purpose only — to store information. The AFP Server and Computer objects allow you to categorize information about non-critical physical resources such as AppleTalk servers and workstations. Let's take a closer look:

▶ *AFP Server* — Represents an AFP-based server running the AppleTalk file protocol. This service can be running on a NetWare server or native Macintosh machine. The point is that this object provides NetWare services to Apple Macintosh workstations. The AFP Server object has no effect on network operations — it only stores information about the AFP server including Description, Location, and Network Address.

▶ *Computer* — Represents a non-server network computer, including workstations, routers, and notebooks. Once again, this object has no effect on network operations; it only stores information about computers. This is, however, an excellent opportunity to integrate NDS and your inventory database. A plethora of computer properties are available to you, including Description, Network Address, Serial Number, Server, Owner, and Status.

Miscellaneous Leaf Objects

No list would be complete without the final category — miscellaneous. There are four NDS leaf objects that don't fall into any other category. They're dominated by the Alias object, which points to any of the other 28 resources. In addition, there are Bindery objects, Bindery Queues, and, of course, the Unknown leaf object — whose icon, interestingly enough, is a user with a paper bag over its head. Let's check them out:

► *Alias* — A logical pointer to any other leaf or container object in the NDS tree. Think of it as an NDS "chameleon." When you create an Alias, it assumes the icon form of its host object. Although it may look like there are two AEinstein users, only one really exists in the tree. The other is a fake pointer. The beauty of the Alias is that it allows you to distribute objects outside of their parent container. If, for example, users in Admin need access to information about AEinstein, you can place an Alias of him in the Admin container. This way, he appears to live there, but in reality it's simply a logical pointer to the real Albert Einstein in OU=LABS (see Figure 2.11). Be very careful with the Alias object. In many cases, you can't tell an Alias from the real Albert Einstein. If you delete or rename an Alias, nothing happens to the host. But if you accidentally mistake the host for the Alias and delete it, all of its Alias objects disappear into Never-Never Land. Actually, they become Unknown leaf objects.

► *Unknown* — Represents an NDS object that has been invalidated or cannot be identified as belonging to any of the other 28 classes (for example, when an Alias becomes invalidated because the user deleted the Alias's host). If you have any Unknown objects, you may want to research where they came from: It's probably a bad sign.

► *Bindery* — Represents an object placed in the NDS tree by an upgrade or migration utility. Bindery objects are used by NDS to provide backward compatibility with bindery-based utilities. This way users can access the resource from NetWare 3.12 workstations.

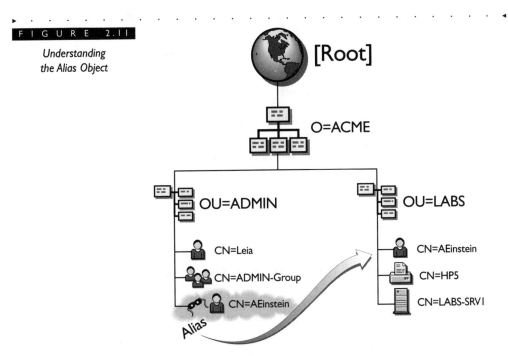

*Understanding
the Alias Object*

[Root]

O=ACME

OU=ADMIN

OU=LABS

CN=Leia

CN=ADMIN-Group

CN=AEinstein

Alias

CN=AEinstein

CN=HP5

CN=LABS-SRV1

▶ *Bindery Queue* — Represents a print queue placed in the NDS tree by an upgrade or migration utility. This is a special type of Bindery object that points to older NetWare 3.12 print queues. Users accessing the tree through Bindery Services can print to bindery-based queues. Otherwise, you'll need to create a true NDS print queue object for everybody else.

SMART LINK

For a larger dose of NDS objects, surf to the Novell Knowledgebase at http://support.novell.com/search/.

That's all of them. We've discussed every NDS object supported by IntranetWare. You'll want to get to know them well because all future discussions center around how to organize, design, and manage these cute little network entities. Once you understand the relationships between NDS objects, you can start building your tree. As you've seen in this discussion, every leaf and container object is represented by an icon graphic that depicts its purpose. For example, printers are printers, servers are computers, and users are people. These icons are used throughout this book and in graphical NDS utilities. NWADMIN, for example, uses icons to provide a snapshot of the entire NDS tree in a hierarchical structure. This feature makes it easier for administrators and users to locate and use IntranetWare resources.

ZEN

"Look what we found in the park in the dark. We will take him home, we will call him Clarke. He will live at our house, he will grow and grow. Will our mother like this? We don't know."

Dr. Seuss

Overview of NDS Design and Management

Now that you understand what the NDS tree is made of, we need to explore how it works. Three main topics dominate NDS design and management:

- NDS naming

- NDS partitioning

- Time synchronization

NDS naming defines rules for locating leaf objects. One of the most important aspects of a leaf object is its position in the NDS tree. Proper naming is required when logging in, accessing NDS utilities, printing, and for most other management tasks.

NDS partitioning deals with database performance and reliability. Since the tree houses all your network resources, it can grow large very quickly. As with any database, size can decrease performance and reliability. For this reason, IntranetWare has a built-in database distribution feature called *partitioning and replication*. Partitioning breaks the database tree into small pieces and replication places those pieces on multiple servers. This strategy increases database performance and provides distributed fault tolerance.

Time synchronization is a temporal assurance scheme that forces all IntranetWare servers to agree on what time it is. This is particularly important because all NDS background operations and security strategies rely on a time stamp. Time synchronization is accomplished through the use of four different time server types. We'll explore these types a little later in this chapter.

In Part II ("IntranetWare Design") we're going to explore naming, partitioning, and time synchronization from a design point of view. There's a lot you need to understand about how these concepts work *before* you install the very first server. Then, in Part IV ("IntranetWare Management"), we'll dedicate two chapters (Chapters 8 and 9) to managing these key NDS elements. But, for now, let's take an introductory look at how NDS naming, partitioning, and time synchronization work. Keep in mind that the real meaningful discussion of these concepts will occur in later parts of this book.

NDS Naming

Your name identifies you as a truly unique individual. Let's take NDS-Head Fred, for example. This name says "Hi, I'm Fred, and I have an NDS tree growing out of my head!" In much the same way, an NDS object's name identifies its location in the hierarchical tree. NDS naming impacts two important IntranetWare tasks:

▶ *Login* — You need to identify your exact location in the NDS tree in order for IntranetWare to authenticate you during login.

▶ *Resource Access* — NDS naming exactly identifies the type and location of NetWare 4.11 resources including file servers, printers, login scripts, and files.

The whole IntranetWare NDS naming scheme is much more complicated than "Hi, I'm Fred." It requires both your name and location. For example, a proper NDS name would be "Hi, I'm Fred in the ADMIN division of ACME." As you can see in Figure 2.12, Fred's NDS name identifies who he is and where he works. This naming scheme relies on a concept called *context*.

O=ACME

"...of ACME"

OU=ADMIN

"... in the Admin division ..."

CN=Fred

"I'm Fred ..."

CN=ADMIN-SRV1

Context defines the position of an object within the Directory tree structure. When you request a particular network resource, you must identify the object's context so that NDS can find it. IntranetWare uses very specific naming guidelines for creating an object's context, and we'll review these in just a moment. For now, let's explore why naming standards are so important.

ZEN

"Who am I? My name is Ned. I do not like my little bed. This is no good. This is not right. My feet stick out of bed all night."

Dr. Seuss

Novell recommends that before you implement NDS, you create a document that describes your naming standards. The NDS naming rules we're going to learn here only work if object names are consistent across the WAN. A naming standards document provides guidelines for naming key container and leaf objects, including users, printers, servers, volumes, print queues, and Organizational Units. In addition, it identifies standard properties and value formats. Consistency, especially in the naming scheme used for objects, provides several benefits:

> ► Consistent naming schemes provide a guideline for network administrators who will add, modify, or move objects within the Directory tree.

> ► Having the naming standards eliminates redundant planning. The standards give CNEs an efficient model to meet their needs, but leave implementation of resource objects open and flexible.

> ► Consistent naming schemes help users identify resources quickly, which maximizes users' productivity.

> ► Consistent naming allows users to identify themselves easily during login.

In Chapter 4 ("NDS Design") we'll explore NDS naming standards in great detail. In addition, you'll get an opportunity to create a naming standards document for ACME. For now, let's focus on IntranetWare rules for using NDS names. I can't think of a better place to start than context.

CONTEXT

As we learned earlier, the whole NDS naming strategy hinges on the concept of context. Context defines the position of an object within the Directory tree structure. When you request a particular network resource, you must identify the object's context so that NDS can find it.

In Figure 2.12, Fred's context is " . . . in the ADMIN division of ACME." This context identifies where Fred lives in the NDS tree structure. It identifies all container objects leading from him to the [Root]. In addition to context, Figure 2.12 identifies Fred's common name (CN). A leaf object's common name specifically identifies it within a given container. In this example, the User object's common name is "Fred."

Two objects in the same NDS tree may have the same common name — provided, however, that they have different contexts. This is why naming is so important. As you can see in Figure 2.13, our NDS tree has two "Freds," but each has a different context.

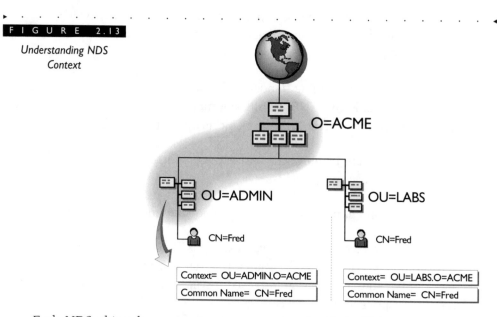

Understanding NDS
Context

Each NDS object has a naming type associated with it. This naming type is identified with a one- or two-character abbreviation:

- O=Organization container

- OU=Organizational Unit container

- CN=common name of leaf object

Also notice the syntax used to create an object's context. In Figure 2.13, Fred's context is created by identifying each of his containers in reverse order leading to the [Root]. Each container is separated by a period.

There are two types of NDS context:

- Current context

- Object context

Let's take a closer look.

Current Context

Current context defines "where you are" in the NDS tree at any given time. It is *not* "where you live." This is a very important distinction. In Figure 2.13, for example, Fred "lives" in OU=ADMIN.O=ACME. But at any given time, he can hang out in O=ACME or OU=LABS.O=ACME.

This is all made possible by *tree walking*. Tree walking allows users to navigate anywhere within the NDS tree structure. Fred's current context impacts the utilities he uses and the resources he can access. In technical terms, *current context* is a logical pointer in the NetWare DOS Requester or 32-bit Client, which identifies the NDS default container for your workstation. Simply stated, it's where you are, not where you live.

A user's current context can be set in one of the following ways:

▸ During login, using the NAME CONTEXT statement in NET.CFG.

▸ With the CONTEXT login script command.

▸ At any time, using the CX utility.

As we'll see in just a moment, current context also impacts how you approach object naming. As a matter of fact, it is the foundation of *distinguished naming*.

Object Context

In contrast to current context, *object context* defines "where you live." In Figure 2.13, for example, Fred's object context is OU=ADMIN.O=ACME or OU=LABS.O=ACME, depending on which Fred you're talking about. Context is identified by listing all containers starting from Fred and moving back toward the [Root]. Object context is used for two important purposes:

▸ Logging in

▸ Accessing resources

When logging in, users must provide their complete object context. In Figure 2.13, for example, Fred would type:

```
LOGIN .CN=FRED.OU=ADMIN.O=ACME
```

In addition to logging in, you'll need a resource's object context when trying to access it. This is particularly important for file servers, printers, Profile login scripts, Directory Map objects, volumes, and groups. The server in Figure 2.12, for example, has the same object context as Fred (that is, OU=ADMIN.O=ACME). Since Fred and the server have the same object context, they can refer to each other by their common names. Isn't that friendly?

You can view information about an object's context or change your own current context by using the CX command line utility. Let's take a closer look.

Using CX

CX is the key IntranetWare utility for dealing with NDS context. It allows you to perform two important tasks:

▶ Change your workstation's current context

▶ View information about any resource's object context

CX is a relatively straightforward command with a great deal of versatility. As a matter of fact, it's similar to the file system CD command in its general approach. If you type CX by itself, the system displays your workstation's current context. This is marginally interesting, at best. CX really excels when you combine it with one or more command line switches. Here are some of the more interesting ones:

▶ CX — View your workstation's current context.

▶ CX /T — View the Directory tree structure below your current context.

▶ CX /A /T — View all objects in the Directory tree structure below your current context.

▶ CX /R /A /T — Change your current context to the [Root] and view all objects in the Directory tree.

▶ CX /CONT — List containers only below the current context in a vertical list with no directory structure.

▶ CX /C — Scroll continuously through output.

▶ CX .OU=ADMIN.O=ACME — Change your current context to the ADMIN container of ACME.

▶ CX /? — View on-line help, including various CX options.

▶ CX /VER — View the version number of the CX utility and the list of files it executes.

Probably the most useful CX option is

▶ CX /R /A /T

I'm sure there's a hidden meaning somewhere in the rodent reference. Regardless, the CX /R /A /T option displays the relative location of all objects in the NDS tree (see Figure 2.14).

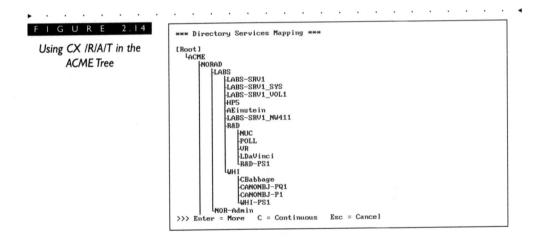

FIGURE   2.14

Using CX /R/A/T in the ACME Tree

```
*** Directory Services Mapping ***

[Root]
  LACME
      NORAD
         LABS
           LABS-SRU1
           LABS-SRU1_SYS
           LABS-SRU1_VOL1
           HP5
           AEinstein
           LABS-SRU1_NW411
           R&D
              NUC
              POLL
              UR
              LDaVinci
              R&D-PS1
         WHI
           CBabbage
           CANONBJ-PQ1
           CANONBJ-P1
           WHI-PS1
         NOR-Admin
>>> Enter = More   C = Continuous   Esc = Cancel
```

ZEN

"My alphabet starts with this letter called YUZZ. It's the letter I use to spell YUZZ-A-MA-TUZZ. You'll be sort of surprised what there is to be found once you go beyond 'Z' and start poking around!"

Dr. Seuss

If you don't remember where you live, the CX utility can be your guide. You can use it before logging in to find your home context if you are in the F:\LOGIN directory. It can also be used by administrators to print out the complete NDS tree structure every Friday afternoon. Of course, this can be a valuable asset to your IntranetWare log book. All in all, CX is a very useful utility for dealing with NDS navigation and object naming.

Now that you've discovered the importance of context, it's time to review how it impacts NDS naming rules. Knowing where you live is only half of the equation. Now we have to discover exactly who you are.

NAMING RULES

Home is where the heart is. Similarly, your network productivity is defined by the container you live in — your context. To access resources efficiently, you must be in close proximity to them. Otherwise, security and naming gets more difficult. Context is the key.

Now that we understand how NDS context works, let's review the naming rules associated with it:

▶ Current context defines your workstation's current position in the Directory tree.

▶ An object's context defines its home container.

▶ Each object has an identifier abbreviation that defines it for naming purposes (O=Organization, OU=Organizational Unit, and CN=common name of leaf objects).

▶ Context is defined by listing all containers from the object to the [Root], in that order. Each object is separated by a period.

▶ Context is important for logging in and accessing NDS resources.

So, there you have it. That's how context works. With this in mind, it's time to explore the two main types of NDS names:

▸ Distinguished names

▸ Typeful names

Distinguished Names

An object's *distinguished name* is its complete NDS path. It is a combination of common name and object context. Each object in the NDS tree has a distinguished name that uniquely identifies it in the tree. In Figure 2.12, Fred's distinguished name would be "I'm Fred in the ADMIN division of ACME."

Notice how the distinguished name identifies Fred as an individual, as well as the context in which he lives. Similarly, in Figure 2.13, Fred's NDS distinguished name would be .CN=Fred.OU=ADMIN.O=ACME. Once again, Fred's distinguished name is a combination of his common name and his context.

Here's another example (refer to AEinstein in Figure 2.15). AEinstein's context is OU=R&D.OU=LABS.O=ACME. His common name is CN=AEinstein. Therefore, his distinguished name is a simple mathematical addition of the two:

```
.CN=AEinstein.OU=R&D.OU=LABS.O=ACME
```

▸ · · · · · · · · · · · · · · · · · · · ◂

F I G U R E   2.15

Building AEinstein's Distinguished Name

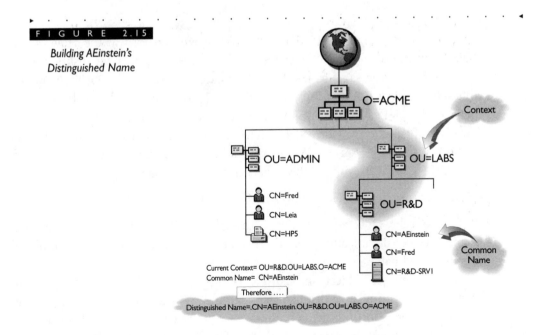

Elementary, my dear Einstein, elementary. There's no "new math" here; only simple addition. If you want complex calculations, refer to Chapter 11 ("Intranet-Ware Security").

Notice the use of periods. Neither the context nor the common name started with a period, but the distinguished name did. The leading period identifies the name as a (complete) distinguished one. Otherwise, it is assumed to be an incomplete, or *relative*, distinguished name. A relative distinguished name lists an object's path from itself up to the current context — not the [Root]. The relativity part refers to how NDS builds the distinguished name. Remember, all objects must have a unique distinguished name. The relative distinguished name is simply a shortcut.

It seems appropriate to demonstrate the relative distinguished name concept with the help of Albert Einstein.

ZEN

"The Scientific Theory I like best is that the rings of Saturn are composed entirely of lost airline luggage."

Mark Russell

Again, refer to Figure 2.15. If AEinstein's current context was the same as his object context, OU=R&D.OU=LABS.O=ACME, then his relative distinguished name would be the same as his common name, CN=AEinstein. But life is rarely this simple. What if Albert Einstein used the CX command to change his current context to OU=LABS.O=ACME? What would his relative distinguished name be now? See Figure 2.16. Correct! His relative distinguished name would become "CN=AEinstein.OU=R&D". When you add this to his current context of OU=LABS.O=ACME, you get the correct distinguished name:

.CN=AEinstein.OU=R&D.OU=LABS.O=ACME

Piece of cake. Once again, notice the use of periods. The relative distinguished name does not use a leading period. This identifies it as a relative (not complete) distinguished name.

As you can see, object and current context play a very important role in distinguished and relative distinguished naming. Whether it's fair or not, you are defined by the place you live. Of course, it can get even weirder. NDS supports trailing periods, which allow you to change the current context while using relative distinguished naming . . . as if that wasn't hard enough already. The bottom line is that each trailing period moves the current context up one container.

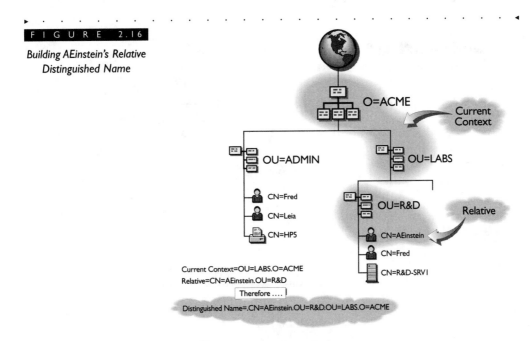

F I G U R E   2 . 1 6

Building AEinstein's Relative Distinguished Name

It seems simple at first, but it can get crazy very quickly. Let's take Leia, for example. She lives in the ADMIN container. If we were in LABS, she couldn't use a relative distinguished name to identify herself — or could she? A single trailing period would move her current context up to O=ACME. Then she could use a relative distinguished name to move down the ADMIN side of the tree (see Figure 2.17). Her current context would be OU=LABS.O=ACME, and her relative distinguished name would be

CN=Leia.OU=ADMIN.

The resulting distinguished name would be Leia's relative name plus her new current context (remember, the trailing period moved the current context from OU=LABS.O=ACME up to O=ACME). That is, her distinguished name would be

.CN=Leia.OU=ADMIN.O=ACME

Piece of cake. It gets even weirder if Leia's current context is

OU=R&D.OU=LABS.O=ACME

In this case, her relative distinguished name would be

CN=Leia.OU=ADMIN.

FIGURE 2.17

Using Trailing Periods

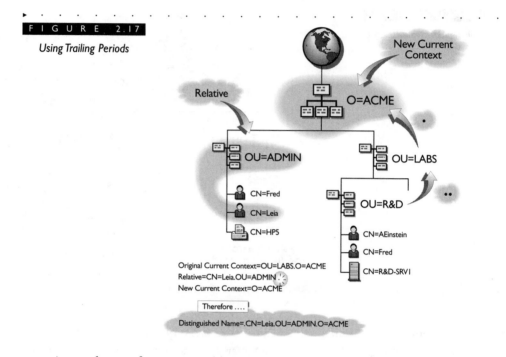

Are we having fun yet? Just like anything in life, it's very important where you place your dots. Here's a quick summary:

▸ All objects in the NDS name are separated by dots.

▸ Distinguished names are preceded by a dot. This identifies them as complete.

▸ Relative distinguished names are not preceded by a dot. This identifies them as incomplete.

▸ Trailing dots can only be used in relative distinguished names, and they modify the current context. Each dot moves the context up one container.

For a complete summary of NDS distinguished naming rules, refer to Table 2.2. Now let's step back in reality for a moment and explore the other NDS naming category — typeful names.

T A B L E 2 . 2 *Getting to Know* *Distinguished Naming*		DISTINGUISHED NAMES	RELATIVE DISTINGUISHED NAMES
	What it is	Complete unique name	Incomplete name based on current context
	How it works	Lists complete path from object to [Root]	Lists relative path from object to current context
	Abbreviation	DN	RDN
	Leading period	Leading periods required	No leading periods allowed
	Trailing periods	No trailing periods allowed	Trailing periods optional

Typeful Names

Typeful names use attribute type abbreviations to distinguish between the different container types and leaf objects in NDS names. In all the examples to this point, we've used these abbreviations to help clarify context, distinguished, and relative distinguished names. The most popular abbreviations are

- ▶ *C:* Country container

- ▶ *O:* Organization container

- ▶ *OU:* Organizational Unit container

- ▶ *CN:* common name of leaf objects

These attribute types help to avoid confusion that can occur when creating complex distinguished and relative distinguished names. I highly recommend that you use them. Of course, like most things in life — they are optional! You can imagine how crazy NDS naming gets when you choose not to use these attribute abbreviations. This insanity is known as *typeless naming.*

Typeless names operate the same as typeful names, but they don't include the object attribute type. In such cases, NDS has to "guess" what object types you're using. Take the following typeless name, for example:

.Admin.ACME

Is this the ADMIN Organizational Unit under ACME? Or is this the Admin user under ACME? In both cases, it's a valid distinguished name, except that one identifies an Organizational Unit container and the other identifies a User leaf object (see Figure 2.18). Well, here's the bottom line — which one is it? It's up to NDS.

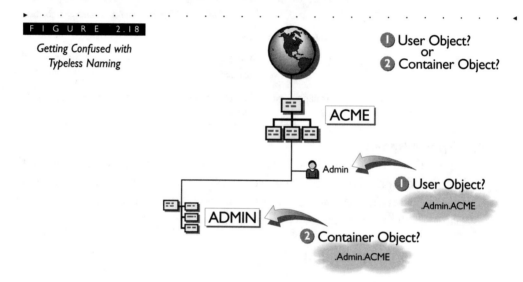

FIGURE 2.18

Getting Confused with Typeless Naming

Fortunately, IntranetWare has some guidelines for "guessing" what the object type should be.

1 • The leftmost object is a common name (leaf object).

2 • The rightmost object is an Organization (container object).

3 • All middle objects are Organizational Units (container objects).

QUIZ

Once again, we return to the Land of Forgetfulness and find Alice in cranial combat with the Lion. She still hasn't figured him out. Here's the question on the table: When can the Lion say, "I lied yesterday and I will lie again tomorrow."? Warning! The answer is not the same as that of the preceding problem!

Hmmm

(Q2-3)

Although this works for most cases, it's only a general guideline. Many times, typeless names are more complex. Take our example in Figure 2.18, for instance. We know now that the rightmost object is an Organization, but what about "Admin?" Is it a common name or an Organizational Unit? We still don't know. Fortunately, IntranetWare includes numerous exceptions to deal with complex typeless scenarios. Here's how it works:

▸ Exception Rule 1: Container objects — Many IntranetWare utilities are intelligent enough to resolve their own typeless names depending on what they are trying to accomplish. CX, for example, is used primarily for changing context. If you apply the CX command to a typeless name, it assumes the leftmost object is an Organization or Organizational Unit. This is because you can't change context to a leaf object. Other utilities that allow you to change context include NETADMIN and NWADMIN. In summary, here's how our example from Figure 2.18 would look with the CX utility:

CX .ADMIN.ACME — .OU=ADMIN.O=ACME

▸ Exception Rule 2: Leaf objects — Similarly, resource-based utilities recognize the leftmost object of a typeless name as a leaf object. Many of these utilities are expecting to see a common name. The most prevalent are LOGIN, MAP, and CAPTURE. Here's how it works for our example in Figure 2.18:

LOGIN .Admin.ACME — .CN=Admin.O=ACME

▸ Exception Rule 3: Mixed naming schemes — It is possible to generate an NDS name that mixes both typeless and typeful naming. In this case, the typeful abbreviation is used as a reference point for resolving the typeless portion of the name. NDS simply focuses on the typeful portion and moves to the left. All subsequent typeless objects are assigned one less abbreviation. Here's an example from Figure 2.18:

.ADMIN.O=ACME — .OU=ADMIN.O=ACME

Of course, this mixed NDS name would be resolved differently if CX or LOGIN were involved. Some exception rules take precedence over others.

▸ Exception Rule 4: Using current context — If all else fails, NDS uses the current context as an example of NDS naming. If your typeless name has the same number of objects as the current context, it assigns attribute abbreviations accordingly. For example, if your current context was .OU=LABS.O=ACME, the typeless name in Figure 2.18 would become .OU=ADMIN.O=ACME.

In another example, let's assume the Country object is involved. If your current context was OU=LABS.O=ACME.C=US, then .ADMIN.ACME.US would become .OU=ADMIN.O=ACME.C=US.

If, however, the typeless name has a different number of objects as the current context, the default NDS naming rules apply. That is, rightmost is an Organization, leftmost is a common name, and all intervening objects are Organizational Units.

▸ Exception Rule 5: Country object — The Country object messes up NDS defaults in almost all cases. Naming is no exception. The Country object is a special circumstance and is assumed not to exist. If you introduce the Country object in either the current context or a typeful portion of the name, you'll run into trouble. In this case, NDS tries to resolve the name using any of the previous exception rules. If they don't apply, it isolates the Country object and applies the defaults to the rest of the typeless name. Pretty weird, huh?

There you have it. This completes our discussion of typeless names and NDS naming in general. As you can see, this is a very important topic because it impacts all aspects of NDS design, installation, and management. No matter what you do, you're going to have to use the correct name to log in or access NDS resources. As we've learned, an object's name is a combination of "who they are" (common name) and "where they live" (context).

SMART LINK

If NDS naming is still a great mystery to you, join us for a special course at CyberState University: http://www.cyberstateu.com.

Congratulations! You are now a professor of NDS nomenclature. And nomenclature is important. After all, where would we be without names for all of our stuff? Here are a few important ones:

▶ *Biochip* — A computer chip that relies on the biological function of proteins and enzymes to send signals rather than on the flow of electrons, theoretically producing faster computers, often called biocomputers or organic CPUs. Also, the foundation of IntranetWare NDS.

▶ *Butterfly effect* — The major impact resulting from a minor force left unchecked over a long time such as the multiplying of a draft from a butterfly's wings in Beijing to a hurricane in Rio. This is the foundation of chaos theory. And we all know that chaos theory impacts a CNE's existence more than anything.

▶ *Cocktail diplomacy* — Verbal persuasion and discussion rather than warfare, terrorism, or other forceful tactics of international political procedure. Also, the preferred way of dealing with IntranetWare users.

▶ *Cyberphilia* — The love of computers and anything to do with computers. In extreme cases, this is said to lead to "CNE widow" — a person who has lost a spouse to the fascinations of IntranetWare.

▸ *Electropollution* — Excessive amounts of electromagnetic waves in the environment resulting from the increasingly widespread use of electricity and the electronic equipment it powers. Many believe it will eventually lead to EMI overload and an innate propensity to feel blades of wet grass between one's toes.

▸ *Faddict* — A person who compulsively follows a temporary fashion. This condition has been described as faddiction. Of course, we know the latest fad is IntranetWare CNE-ism.

As you can see, there's a lot to NDS nomenclature. Stay tuned throughout the book for more fascinating "neo-words." For now, let's shift our focus from naming to partition management. NDS partitioning is the second of our three NDS management concepts. Don't forget your seat belt.

NDS Partitioning

As you will quickly come to appreciate, the NDS tree grows and grows and grows. Before you know it, you'll have a huge monstrosity on your hands — the size of Jupiter. Fortunately, IntranetWare includes a segmentation strategy known as NDS partitioning. *Partitioning* breaks up the NDS tree into two or more pieces that can be separated and distributed, which makes dealing with NDS objects more manageable.

Since the NDS tree is stored in a database, pieces of the database can be distributed on multiple file servers. This strategy is known as *replication*. NDS replicas provide two important benefits to the "Cloud":

▸ Replicas increase network performance by decreasing the size of database files and placing resources closest to the users who need them.

▸ Replicas increase fault tolerance because extra copies of the database are distributed on multiple servers throughout the WAN.

NDS partitions have nothing to do with the logical disk partitions you're used to on the server disk. NDS partitions are logical pieces of the "Cloud," which can be distributed on multiple servers. Hard disk partitions are physical divisions of the internal disks that separate the IntranetWare operating system from DOS. Although these two concepts are unrelated, they work together in an odd way — one is stored on top of the other. To really mess up your mind, note that logical NDS partitions are stored on internal disk partitions — brain drain!

As you can see in Figure 2.19, NDS partitioning simply breaks the ACME organization into two pieces:

> ▸ *Partition A* — Known as the [Root] Partition because it is the only one that contains the global [Root] object.

> ▸ *Partition B* — Known as the LABS Partition because OU=LABS is the highest container object in that segment. In addition, Partition B is termed a child of Partition A, because LABS is a subset of the ACME Organization.

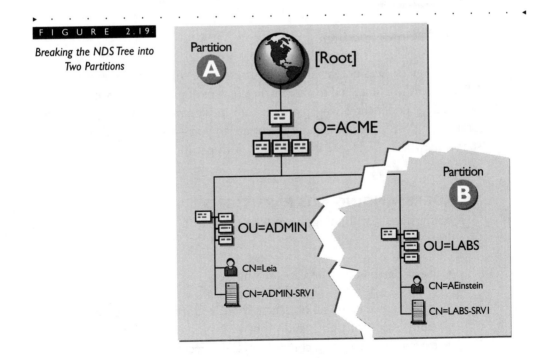

FIGURE 2.19

Breaking the NDS Tree into Two Partitions

ZEN

"Oh, the thinks you can think up if only you try!"

Dr. Seuss

Partitioning has many advantages because it allows you to separate the tree into smaller segments. Since 90 percent of all the resources accessed by users are within their own partitions, CNEs can increase efficiency by locating users near the resources they use the most. We can also increase network fault tolerance by placing copies of other partitions on local servers. This is known as replication. IntranetWare allows you to create four different types of NDS replicas:

- ▸ Master

- ▸ Read/Write

- ▸ Read-Only

- ▸ Subordinate Reference

But I digress. Let's not get ahead of ourselves. To understand the distribution of NDS replicas, we first need to explore the concept of partitioning. More specifically, we need to understand why partitions are important and what they do for us. Granted, NDS replication is more important to you — as a CNE. But you have to start somewhere. And we're going to start with partitions.

UNDERSTANDING NDS PARTITIONS

To understand partitioning, we need to review the characteristics of our NDS Cloud:

- ▸ It is a database that replaces the bindery.

- ▸ It contains data on all objects in the Directory tree, including their names, security rights, and property values. All network information except the file system comes from the Directory.

▶ It is network-centric, not server-centric, like the older bindery. This allows the Directory to track all network resources throughout the WAN.

▶ NDS uses the Directory for access control to other objects in the WAN. NDS checks the Directory to make sure that you can view, manipulate, create, or delete resource objects.

▶ NDS uses the Directory for authentication — an important part of logging in.

· ▶ Except for Server and Volume objects, the Directory does not contain information about the file system. IntranetWare data is still restricted to internal server volumes.

Partitioning is the process of dividing the Directory into smaller, more manageable pieces. These pieces can then be distributed near the users that need them. As you can see in Figure 2.19, the ACME tree has been partitioned into two segments — the [Root] partition and the LABS partition. Notice that partitioning occurs along the boundaries of container objects. All the leaf objects in a container are included in the same partition as their parent. Also notice that a partition is named for the container closest to the [Root]. In the case of Partition B, this would be OU=LABS. The topmost container object in the partition is termed the *partition root object*. I know this is confusing, but it serves an important purpose. This partition is the parent of all other child partitions in this segment of the tree. And, as we all know, parents know best. If you get confused, remember this one simple rule: [Root] with square brackets ([Root]) describes the top of the world. There is only one [Root] partition. On the other hand, root without square brackets (root) simply describes the topmost container in a given partition. Every partition must have a partition root object; therefore, there can be many of them.

Once again, returning to Figure 2.19, Partition A is the [Root] partition and Partition B is the LABS partition, with OU=LABS as the partition root object. No sweat.

As a CNE, you have total control over NDS partitioning. You can decide how, when, and where they are created. To simplify things, NDS gives you two simple choices:

▸ Centralized

▸ Distributed

ZEN

"Did I ever tell you how lucky you are?
Thank goodness for all the things you are not!
Thank goodness you're not something someone forgot
and left all alone in some punkerish place.
Like a rusty tin coat hanger hanging in space."

Dr. Seuss

In small network environments, centralizing the Directory makes it easier to manage the information in its database. The response time for users is adequate as long as the number of users and devices in the partition remains small. In this context, the term *small* means a network with roughly 1 to 10 servers or 100 to 5,000 objects, all in the same location and not connected by WAN links. If your network meets this criteria, you probably will not partition the NDS database at all. Instead, you'll leave the tree as a single database and replicate it on each of your servers. This strategy is simple and employs the IntranetWare defaults.

On the other hand, if your network is large or has several sites with many servers, you may want to partition the Directory. Partitioning also implies distributed replication. By distributing the database, you will increase the availability of the information and provide quicker access for users. In addition, distributed replication increases fault tolerance because extra copies of the database are available throughout the WAN.

Assuming you choose the distributed approach, NDS partitioning is inevitable. Unfortunately, IntranetWare doesn't help you out at all. By default, only the [Root] partition is created during initial server installation. All subsequent servers are added to this partition. It's up to you, as a CNE, to create a new partition for each new server. In partitioning, the server is the key. Remember, partitions are replicated as portions of the database on distributed IntranetWare servers. For this reason, you want to create new partitions for each new server. Well, maybe not every new server. Here are a few guidelines to think about:

▸ At the time the first server is installed in a new container, consider creating a partition at that container level. All subsequent servers in the same container should then receive replicas of the existing partition.

▸ Every time you add a new location to the NDS WAN, consider creating a container for the new location and defining a partition around it. It's assumed that new locations will bring along their own servers.

▸ For organizational purposes, consider creating a partition for each new container object even if it doesn't have its own server. This helps segment Organization-based NDS information. Also, it allows you to plan ahead in case servers are ever added to the new container.

▸ Try to create a pyramid shape when creating NDS partitions. The top level of the tree should have fewer partitions than the lower layers. This triangular design allows you to distribute the partitions relatively close to leaf objects (particularly users). This encourages you to create small partitions and distribute them closer to the users who access resources. In addition, it also increases fault tolerance by distributing many multiple segments of the database.

Keep in mind, though, that size and number of partitions can significantly affect the synchronization and responsiveness of your network. Avoid creating partitions that are too large (greater than 5,000 objects) or with too many servers (more than 10) because they take too long to synchronize, and managing replicas becomes more complex. On the other hand, avoid partitions that are too small (fewer than 100 objects). If a partition contains only a few objects, the access and fault tolerance benefits may not be worth the time you invest in managing it.

As you can see in Figure 2.20, we've installed a new server (R&D-SRV1) in the new OU=R&D subcontainer of OU=LABS. By default, this container and all its objects (particularly the server) will be added to the existing LABS partition. According to our new philosophy, we should create an additional partition for the new container and its objects (particularly the server). Using PARTMGR or NWADMIN, we create Partition C at the OU=R&D container. This becomes the R&D partition. Now we can distribute replicas of each of the three partitions to each of the three servers in our ACME NDS tree.

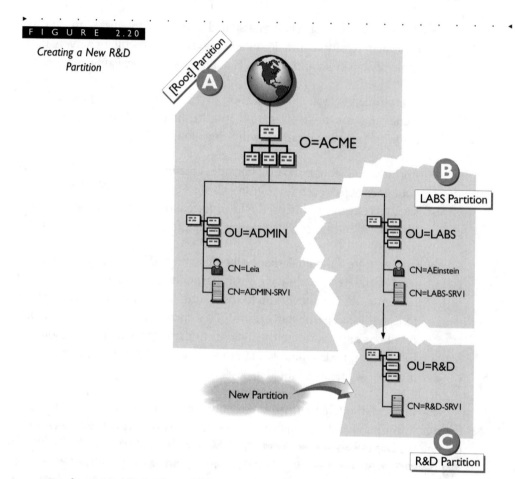

F I G U R E   2.20

Creating a New R&D
Partition

Replicas are good! They allow us to increase resource access and fault tolerance by distributing copies of partitions to multiple servers throughout the WAN. Now that we've created our partitions, it's time to distribute copies (replicas) of them to strategic servers. That's NDS replication. Don't worry — this is only an appetizer. We will revisit NDS partitioning in much more detail later in Chapter 4 ("NDS Design") and Chapter 9 ("Partition Management and Synchronization"). For now, let's introduce replication.

NDS REPLICATION

If you build the partitions . . . they will come!

Earlier we learned that NDS partitioning provides two key advantages — resource access and fault tolerance. Well, actually partitioning doesn't do anything. It only breaks up the database into little pieces. It's how we distribute these pieces to IntranetWare servers that provides the advantages. So, it's more accurate to say that NDS replication provides two key advantages:

▶ *Resource access* — Replication allows you to place resources closest to the users who access them. This decreases the time needed for authentication, modification, and information queries. It also increases the probability that information will be retrieved from the nearest available server. This limits the amount of traffic sent over slow and expensive WAN links. In addition, replication allows for faster name resolution. Name resolution is an NDS process that allows you to access information outside your current partition. Every partition stores pointers to servers containing parent and child information. An organized replication strategy allows NDS to find remote objects more quickly.

▶ *Fault tolerance* — Replication distributes exact copies of database segments to multiple servers throughout the WAN. If your local copy becomes unavailable or corrupted, another copy can be used for authentication or resource access. With replication, users can access the network even when their local server, router, or WAN link goes down. The goal is to never have a single point of failure in the IntranetWare Cloud.

It sounds too good to be true. Well, in many cases, it is. There's a cost associated with replication — synchronization delays. Since replicas need to be updated constantly, synchronization becomes an important issue. As you add more replicas, you create more synchronization traffic. This background overhead slows down critical data traffic — especially over WAN links. Also, replica management can be a nightmare as you continue to build up and modify the NDS tree. So, the real trick becomes, "How do I optimize replica distribution and minimize synchronization delays?" Just like any puzzle, the solution is staring you in the face. You just need to figure out where all the little pieces go. Fortunately, IntranetWare includes four different replica types for dealing with this crazy puzzle. Let's take a closer look.

ZEN

"My shoe is off, my foot is cold.
I have a bird, I like to hold.
My hat is old, my teeth are gold.
And now my story is all told."

Dr. Seuss

Replica Types

As we learned earlier, IntranetWare includes four different replica types. Each has its own advantages and disadvantages. Some are created by default, and others apply only to specific circumstances. Before you get excited about distributing NDS replicas, let's learn what each of the four types can do. Here's a quick look:

▸ *Master* — A read/write copy of the original partition. Each partition has only one Master replica. When you first define a partition, the Master is created by default. If you would like to redefine a partition boundary or join it with another, you must be able to access the server that holds the Master replica of that partition. This is the key difference between the Master and other replica types. If the Master replica becomes unavailable for any reason, you can upgrade any Read/Write replica using PARTMGR or NWADMIN.

▸ *Read/Write* — A read/write copy of any partition. Each partition may have multiple Read/Write replica copies. When you change objects in a Read/Write replica, those changes are propagated to all other replicas of the same partition. This process, known as replica synchronization, creates background traffic over WAN communication lines. Both Master and Read/Write replicas generate synchronization traffic. Be careful how many of these replicas you distribute. Finally, Read/Write replicas cannot be used to redefine partition boundaries — that requires a Master.

▸ *Read-Only* — A read-only copy of any partition. These replicas are used for searching and viewing objects only. You cannot make any changes to a Read-Only replica. These replicas receive synchronization changes from Read/Write and Master copies. They do not generate any replica synchronization traffic.

▶ *Subordinate References* — A special type of replica created and maintained by NDS. A Subordinate Reference is created automatically on a server when it contains a parent replica, but not any of the children. In simpler terms, Subordinate References are created on servers "where parent is but child is not." Think of it as NDS baby-sitting. The key difference is that Subordinate References do not contain object data — they point to the replica that does. This facilitates tree connectivity. The good news is that if you eventually add a child replica to the server, the Subordinate Reference is removed automatically.

There you have it: The four NDS replica types. In general, Read/Write replicas are the most popular for CNE management. Master replicas are created automatically during partitioning, and Subordinate References flourish throughout the tree as needed. Read-Only replicas, however, can be very effective if you have many servers and few containers. Now that you understand the different replica types, it's time to distribute and manage them.

Before we learn how to manage these four different replica types, let's revisit Subordinate References. I sensed a blank stare when we came across that bullet. The bottom line is, that Subordinate References increase tree connectivity by providing bridges to partitions you don't have. In Figure 2.20, for example, the ADMIN-SRV1 server gets a Master replica of the [Root] Partition. That's all! Initially it is cut off from all other portions of the tree — namely Partitions B and C. This is where Subordinate References come in. IntranetWare bridges the gap by placing a Subordinate Reference of Partition B on the ADMIN-SRV1 server. This way, Leia can access information about AEinstein by pointing to the OU=LABS container. In turn, LABS-SRV1 has a Subordinate Reference of Partition C. This allows AEinstein to manage the R&D Group. Hopefully, you can see how Subordinate References bridge the gap by providing pointers to partitions you don't have. Without them, you'd be isolated in your own little private Idaho.

Now that we've cleared that up, let's take a closer look at managing default and new NDS replicas.

Managing NDS Replicas

As we learned earlier, partitioning itself doesn't accomplish anything productive. It simply breaks the NDS database into little pieces. Replication is where the real action is. Replication allows us to distribute these pieces among strategically placed servers. We also learned that IntranetWare doesn't partition by default. It does, however, include a simple default replication strategy: *Every partition should be replicated at least three times.*

When you install a new IntranetWare server, its host partition expands. No new partition is created. Replication of the partition depends on how many servers already exist. The first server in a partition gets the Master replica. The second and third new servers receive a Read/Write replica. All other servers in the same partition are replica-deprived. Remember, the basic premise is that every partition should be replicated at least three times.

When you merge Directory trees, source servers with [Root] replicas receive Read/Write replicas of the new [Root] Partition. They also receive Subordinate Reference replicas to the [Root]'s child partitions. Next, target servers with [Root] replicas receive Subordinate References of the top-level partition of the source tree. This allows both source and target servers to share information about one another's objects — both new and old. Finally, a NetWare 3 server upgraded to IntranetWare receives a Read/Write replica of all partitions containing the server's bindery context.

So, those are the defaults. It's a great place to start, but don't think of it as the end-all. As a matter of fact, it's only the beginning. As a CNE, you should take NDS partitions and replication very seriously. Once a new server has been installed, you should consider creating a new partition around its parent container. This strategy is illustrated in Figure 2.20 with the addition of R&D-SRV1.

Also consider placing Read/Write replicas of other partitions on the new server. In Figure 2.21, we've demonstrated a strategy known as *saturated replication*. This means that every server has either a Master or Read/Write replica of every partition in the tree.

Saturated replication works fine when you have a small number of servers. In large environments, however, it's not very practical because of synchronization delays. Replica updates take place automatically at specific intervals. Some updates, such as changing a user's password, are immediate (within 10 seconds). Other updates, such as login updates, are synchronized every five minutes. Changes made to Figure 2.21, for example, would generate 27 replica updates — that's 3^3. This is manageable. But consider what background traffic would look like with 50 servers and 20 different partitions — that's 9,536,743,164,062,000,000,000,000,000,000,000 updates every few minutes. Wow!

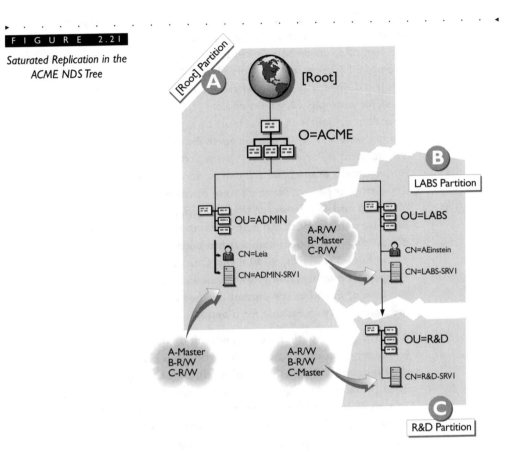

F I G U R E   2.21

Saturated Replication in the ACME NDS Tree

[Root] Partition

A

[Root]

O=ACME

B

LABS Partition

OU=ADMIN

A-R/W
B-Master
C-R/W

OU=LABS

CN=Leia

CN=AEinstein

CN=ADMIN-SRV1

CN=LABS-SRV1

OU=R&D

A-Master
B-R/W
C-R/W

A-R/W
B-R/W
C-Master

CN=R&D-SRV1

C

R&D Partition

QUIZ

Numbers can be challenging, fascinating, confusing, and frustrating, but once you have developed an interest in them, a whole new world is opened up as you discover their many characteristics and patterns. Numbers can be divided into many different categories, including amicable, abundant, deficient, perfect, and delectable numbers.

Amicable numbers are pairs that are mutually equal to the sum of all their aliquot parts: for example, 220 and 284. The aliquot parts of 220 are 1, 2, 4, 5, 10, 11, 20, 22, 44, 55, and 110, the sum of which is 284, while the aliquot parts of 284 are 1, 2, 4, 71, and 142, the sum of which is 220. There are seven known pairs of amicable numbers, the largest of which are 9,437,056 and 7,363,584.

Abundant, deficient, and perfect numbers can be linked together because all numbers fit into these categories. An abundant number is one such that the sum of all its divisors (except itself) is greater than the number itself: for example, 12, because its divisors (1, 2, 3, 4, and 6) total 16. The opposite of this is a deficient number, where the divisors total less than the number itself: for example, 10, whose divisors (1, 2, and 5) total 8. If a number is not abundant or deficient, then it must be a perfect number, which means that it equals the sum of its aliquot parts: for example, 6, where its divisors (1, 2, 3) also total 6. Perfect numbers were first named in Ancient Greece by the Pythagoreans around 500 BC and to date, only 30 have been discovered. The first four perfect numbers were discovered before AD 100, and they include 6 and 496. However, the next (33,550,336) was not found until the fifteenth century. With the help of computer technology, the process of discovering new perfect numbers has been speeded up and the latest to be found has no fewer than 240 digits. One fact that has emerged is that all the perfect numbers now known are even numbers. However, no one from the time of Euclid to the present day has been able to prove that it is mathematically impossible for a perfect odd number to exist.

So, having dealt with amicable, abundant, deficient, and perfect numbers, what, may you ask, is a delectable number? The answer is that a nine-digit number is delectable if (a) it contains the digits 1 to 9 exactly once each (no zero) and (b) the numbers created by taking the first n digits (n runs from 1 to 9) are each divisible by n, so that the first digit is divisible by 1 (it always will be), the first two digits form a number divisible by 2, the first three digits form a number divisible by 3, and so on. Only one delectable number is known. Can you find out what it is?

Matching:

A) Abundant	1) 10
B) Perfect	2) 220
C) Deficient	3) 381654729
D) Amicable	4) 12
E) Delectable	5) 8128
	6) 284
	7) 386451729
	8) 28

(Q2-4)

All this synchronization magic is accomplished within a group of servers known as a *replica ring*. A replica ring is an internal system group that includes all servers containing replicas of a given partition. In Figure 2.21, the replica ring for Partition A includes:

▸ Master: CN=ADMIN-SRV1.OU=ADMIN.0=ACME

▸ R/W: CN=LABS-SRV1.OU=LABS.0=ACME

▸ R/W: CN=R&D-SRV1.OU=R&D.OU-LABS.0=ACME

All synchronization takes place within the replica ring. The synchronization delay is greater when servers within a replica ring are separated by slow WAN links. Therefore, you'll want to keep track of replica rings and organize their distribution accordingly.

We will explore some time-proven replica distribution strategies in Chapter 4 ("NDS Design"). Then, in Chapter 9 ("Partition Management and Synchronization"), we'll delve more deeply into key facets of replication management, including fault tolerance, traffic efficiency, unsynchronized replicas, and DSTRACE. But first, let's finish off with a few general guidelines for managing NDS replicas:

▸ *Fault tolerance* — To meet fault tolerance needs, plan for three or more strategically placed replicas of each partition. You should also plan for possible WAN link failures whenever necessary. Don't place the entire replica ring in a single portion of the global network. This creates a single point of WAN link failure.

▸ *Traffic efficiency* — Generally only the information that's updated (delta) gets sent across the network. However, when you place a new replica, the entire file is copied. Each object takes up roughly 3K of space, large replicas can be in excess of 10 MB in size. Consider placing large replicas during low-traffic time periods.

▸ *Workgroups* — Create partitions that follow the boundaries of functional workgroups, then place replicas of each partition on the servers that are physically close to the users within that workgroup. This balances productivity and traffic efficiency.

▸ *Logging in* — Users need access to a Master or Read/Write replica for login authentication. In addition, NDS updates all appropriate replicas when the user logs in. For these reasons, consider distributing local Read/Write replicas closest to the servers users attach to. Let's return to Figure 2.21 as an example. Consider what happens when all ACME directors return to ADMIN headquarters for the annual meeting. AEinstein attaches to the ADMIN-SRV1 server. Since this server is part of his home partition's replica ring, he can authenticate locally. This increases login speed and decreases background synchronization traffic.

▸ *[Root]* — The [Root] partition is the most important segment of the entire NDS tree. Replicate it often. Consider creating a Read/Write replica of the [Root] partition on all geographically distributed servers. If you lose this partition, the entire network becomes inaccessible. There is a caveat, however. In the pyramid replica design, the [Root] partition has many children. Each server that receives replicas of the [Root] partition also receives Subordinate References for all of its child partitions. This may create more synchronization traffic than you initially intended. Be careful.

▸ *Bindery Services* — Be sure to follow a server's *bindery context* when distributing replicas. As we'll learn a little later, a server's bindery context lists all containers available to non-NDS users from this server. To work properly, the bindery server must have a Master or Read/Write replica of all containers in its bindery context. Don't worry — we'll revisit this topic multiple times later in the book.

▸ *Moving containers* — Because moving a container object directly affects partitions, it is considered a partitioning operation. You'll have to use the Partition Manager tool in NWADMIN to move a container. Before you do so, the container must be the highest object in its local partition. As you remember from our earlier discussion, this is called the partition root object. If you try to move the container without making it a partition root, an error message will appear. Once you've moved the container, give NDS a few minutes to resynchronize itself and update all objects with their new distinguished names. In addition, you may have to change the NAME CONTEXT statement in NET.CFG to reflect name changes.

Finally, remind your users that they now have a new identity — since their home has moved.

Well, there you have it. That's partitioning and replication in a nutshell. In Chapter 4 ("NDS Design"), we'll explore partitioning design in more detail. And you'll get a chance to create a replication strategy for ACME. Then we'll carry our discussion further in Chapter 9 ("Partition Management and Synchronization"), where we'll explore IntranetWare partitioning tools and some special strategies for managing and troubleshooting NDS replicas.

For now, sit back, relax, and wallow in your newfound knowledge. There's time for only one more NDS management topic — time synchronization.

ZEN

"Waiting for the fish to bite or waiting for wind to fly a kite. Or waiting around for Friday night or waiting perhaps for their Uncle Jake or a pot to boil or a better break or a string of pearls or a pair of pants or a wig with curls or another chance. Everyone is just waiting."

Dr. Seuss

Time Synchronization

"Does anybody really know what time it is; does anybody really care?"

NDS does. As a matter of fact, NDS has to! Every aspect of NDS existence relies on time. Sound familiar? Time synchronization is a method of ensuring that all NDS objects report the same *time stamp*. Time stamps are important for

▸ Replica synchronization

▸ Messaging

▸ Login authentication and time-based security

▸ File and directory operations

Time stamps report time according to the Universal Time Coordinated (UTC) equivalent. This is a time system that adjusts to the local time zone and Daylight Savings Time. It is also equivalent to Greenwich Mean Time (GMT). UTC is calculated using three values for each time server:

▸ Local time

▸ +/− time zone offset from UTC

▸ − Daylight Savings Time offset

For example, in San Francisco, California, the time is eight hours behind GMT. Therefore, if the time in San Francisco is 12:00 noon and there is no Daylight Savings Time, UTC is 20:00.

All of this fancy temporal footwork is accomplished during server installation with the Time Configuration Parameters Worksheet (see Figure 2.22). With this worksheet, you can define your new IntranetWare server as one of four different *time servers*. Time servers provide a consistent source for the time stamps that NDS and other features use. Each time you install an IntranetWare server, you must provide it with specific time configuration parameters, including time server type and the previous three UTC values.

F I G U R E   2.22

Time Configuration Parameters Worksheet in INSTALL.NLM

Let's explore the four different time server types and discuss the advantages and disadvantages of each.

TIME SERVER TYPES

All IntranetWare servers are *time servers* of some type. Time servers create and manage time stamps. There are two general categories of time servers: time providers and time consumers. *Time providers* provide time and are categorized as Primary, Reference or Single-Reference servers. *Time consumer servers* request their time from a provider and are categorized as Secondary servers.

Regardless, all time servers have the same fundamental responsibilities. First, they provide time to any requesting time provider, time consumer, or workstation. Second, they manage time synchronization and make sure everyone agrees what time it is. And, finally, they all adjust their internal clocks to correct discrepancies and maintain a consistent time across all IntranetWare servers.

QUIZ

If my three were a four,
And my one were a three,
What I am would be nine less
Than half what I'd be.
I'm only three digits,
Just three in a row,
So what in the world must I be?
Do you know?

Hint: Synergy.

(Q2-5)

So, which time server are you?

▶ *Single-Reference* — A time provider. This is the default configuration for most small WANs. It provides time to Secondary servers and cannot coexist with Primary or Reference servers.

▶ *Reference* — A time provider. These servers act as a central point of time control for the entire network. They get their time from an external source such as the Internet or an atomic clock.

▸ *Primary* — A time provider or time consumer. These servers work together with other Primary servers to "vote" on the correct time. This voting procedure determines network UTC in combination with values received from Reference servers.

▸ *Secondary* — A time consumer. This is part of the default configuration. These servers do not participate in voting and are told what the time is by time providers.

Let's take a closer look.

Single-Reference Time Servers

As we learned earlier, this is the default configuration for most small WANs. If used, it stands alone as the only time provider on the entire network. Therefore, it cannot coexist with Primary or Reference time providers (see Figure 2.23). All other IntranetWare servers in the same tree default to the Secondary time server type.

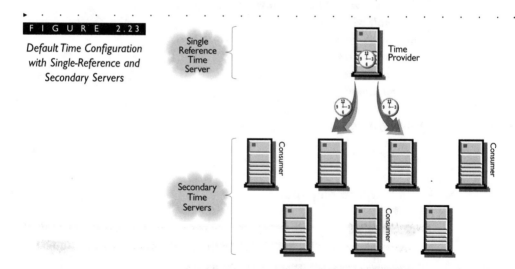

Default Time Configuration with Single-Reference and Secondary Servers

It's important to note that time servers never send out their time automatically. They must be asked to report their time. This only happens when a server's *synchronization flag* has been activated. The synchronization flag occurs when the server is confident that its internal clock is within a *synchronization radius* of accepted time. The synchronization radius defaults to 2,000 milliseconds (2 seconds). You can adjust this value through SERVMAN. The key point here is that Single-Reference servers always activate their synchronization flag because they're the only ones on the network that matter.

Finally, Single-Reference time servers typically get their time from their own internal clock. You can, however, connect the server to a more reliable external time source such as the Internet, a radio clock, or atomic time provider.

REAL WORLD

It is possible for a Single-Reference time server to coexist with other time providers, although it's not recommended. The Single-Reference time server will not check with the other time providers when sending out NDS time stamps. As far as it's concerned, it's always right.

Reference Time Servers

Reference time servers are like Single-Reference servers in that they provide a central point of time control for the entire network. These time providers almost always get their time from an external source (such as the Internet, radio clocks, and/or atomic providers).

Reference time servers differ from Single-Reference servers in one important area — they *can* coexist with Primary servers. As you can see in Figure 2.24, Reference time servers provide time to Primary servers. Primaries then vote on what time they think it should be and eventually provide time to Secondary time consumers. Even though voting occurs with Reference time servers, it's important to note that *Reference servers always win!* No matter what time the primaries decide it is, they eventually agree with the Reference server. It's like saying, "Go ahead and argue about the time as long as your answer eventually matches mine." The Reference server is given higher priority because it's thought to be more reliable. This is because it typically uses an external time source. If you use the internal server clock, you're defeating the purpose of Reference and Primary voting.

If you have a Reference server, why bother with primaries at all? It's simple — fault tolerance. If the Reference server ever goes down, the primaries can take over and negotiate time for all the Secondary time consumers.

*Custom Time Configuration
with Reference and
Primary Servers*

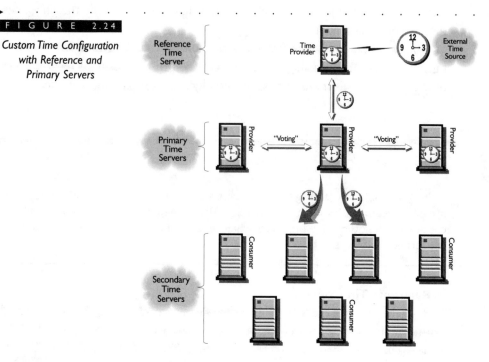

ZEN

*"Today you don't have to be tidy or neat. If you wish, you may eat with
both hands and both feet. So get in there and munch. Have a big
munch-er-oo! Today is your birthday! Today you are you!"*

Dr. Seuss

Primary Time Servers

Primary time servers work together to vote on the correct time. This voting
procedure can operate with or without the help of a Reference server. In either case,
Primary servers vote every 5 minutes and adjust their internal time 50 percent of
the time value discrepancy. They do not correct 100 percent because of oscillation
errors. The 50 percent correction allows all the time servers to eventually converge
on a single time stamp. This convergence is made easier with the presence of a
Reference server, since it provides an ultimate goal. Without a Reference server,
multiple primaries continue to vote until two of them agree. At this point, both
synchronization flags are set and Secondary servers receive the new time stamp.

There are a few important configurations in this scenario. First, there's the *polling interval*. This is the waiting period between votes. By default, it's five minutes. Next, there's the question of who votes with whom. In one configuration method, all primaries vote with everybody, whereas in another, you can specify exactly who votes with whom. We'll explore these options a little later. Finally, there's the *offset threshold* — that is, by how much should a Primary be allowed to change its clock during voting? The default is 2 seconds. The offset threshold is also a configurable parameter. Refer to Chapters 4 and 9 for more detailed information concerning Primary time server configuration.

Refer to Figure 2.24 for a review of Primary and Reference server voting. Notice that Secondary consumers ultimately get their time stamp from Primary servers. Again, this increases fault tolerance by creating redundant time providers.

Secondary Time Servers

Secondary time servers are part of the default configuration. They are the ultimate *time consumers*. They do not participate in voting and are told exactly what time it is by any of the other three types of time providers. Remember, time providers only give time stamps when they're asked for them. This puts the responsibility on the shoulders of Secondary time servers. Every 5 minutes they poll a specific time source for the correct time. If there's a discrepancy, the Secondary server changes its internal clock by 100 percent. By default, this time polling occurs every five minutes. (Of course, this is configurable.)

Probably more than 90 percent of your IntranetWare servers will be Secondary time consumers. In a generic configuration with 100 servers, you may have seven primaries, a Reference, and 92 Secondary time servers. It sure puts things in perspective.

For a summary of these four different time server types, refer to Table 2.3. Now that you're a time-server pro, let's take a closer look at the two different methods for accomplishing time synchronization — default and custom.

TIME CONFIGURATION

IntranetWare provides you with two methods for accomplishing time synchronization:

▸ Default

▸ Custom

TABLE 2.3

*Getting to Know
IntranetWare Time Servers*

FIRST SERVER TYPE	TIME PROVIDER	DESCRIPTION	GETS TIME FROM	ADJUSTS CLOCK	GIVES TIME TO
Single-Reference	Yes	Default configuration. Only services Secondary time servers	Internal clock mostly	No	Secondary
Reference	Yes	Same as Single-Reference except it participates in Primary voting	External source mostly	No	Primary and Secondary
Primary	Yes	Participates in voting to determine correct time stamp	Voting procedure or Reference server	Yes (50 percent correction per polling interval)	Secondary
Secondary	No	Default configuration; consumes time stamp from other time providers	Single-Reference, Reference, or Primary	Yes (100 percent correction per polling interval)	Clients only

The default method assumes that only two types of time servers are necessary — Single-Reference time providers and Secondary time consumers. This method is simple and efficient, but does not provide the flexibility required by large NDS implementations. The custom method, on the other hand, requires administrative planning. It uses Reference, Primary, and Secondary servers to minimize a single point of failure. In addition, the custom configuration method cuts down on network traffic by minimizing unneeded synchronization chatter. This is accomplished with the help of TIMESYNC.CFG — a custom time configuration file. Let's take a quick look at how it works. Remember, there will be a lot more time for in-depth design issues in Chapter 4 and detailed management issues in Chapter 9.

Default Time Configuration

The default IntranetWare installation assumes only two types of time servers are necessary — Single-Reference and Secondary. This default method is simple and efficient. It also doesn't require any special time synchronization reconfiguration when new servers are added to the network. They're simply defined as Secondary time consumers.

The default method uses the Service Advertising Protocol (SAP) to advertise time from Single-Reference to Secondary servers. Although SAP is fast over a single network segment, it can overburden slow WAN links. Be careful not to set up too many time providers (no more than two) on either side of a slow link. Otherwise, the time synchronization traffic might adversely affect network performance. Also ensure that SAP filters around the network do not impede SAP traffic. Remember, NDS doesn't require SAP, and many administrators choose to turn it off. If this is the case, you'll have to use TIMESYNC.CFG and the custom method.

The default method may not be ideal for large NDS implementations with many sites connected by WAN links. If you decide to add Primary servers, the voting process could involve more network traffic than necessary. All in all, the default time configuration method is a good choice for small to medium implementations. It has the following advantages:

▶ It is easy to understand and requires no planning.

▶ It does not require a special custom configuration file. You don't have to provide any configuration information to time providers because the default method relies on SAP for time stamp advertisement.

▶ SAP is fast and dynamic. If you add or delete services from the server, the updates happen quickly.

▶ The chance of synchronization error is reduced because time consumers only talk to a specific time provider. They never negotiate with other Secondary servers.

On the other hand, the default time configuration has its shortcomings — it's not the cat's meow. Here're some disadvantages:

▸ The Single-Reference server must be contacted by every Secondary server on the network. If a WAN link goes down, Secondary time servers are left wandering in temporal space. This can cause a time/space continuum anomaly — that's bad.

▸ Using SAP means that a misconfigured server may disrupt the network. Some of the Secondary servers may synchronize to an unsynchronized time provider rather than to the authorized Single-Reference server. If NDS events occur with improper time stamps, you'll run into real trouble.

▸ One time source means a single point of failure. However, should a Single-Reference server go down, a Secondary time consumer can easily be set as the Single-Reference server using SERVMAN.

Custom Time Configuration

The custom configuration method is not difficult, but it requires some planning. It uses Reference and Primary servers as time providers to minimize a single point of failure. You'll need to know the physical layout of your network before using the custom configuration method. This helps you to distribute time providers (see Chapter 4). To use the custom configuration method, you'll need to determine which servers are time providers and where Secondary servers should go for synchronization.

For the custom configuration method to work, each server is given a special configuration file — TIMESYNC.CFG. This file provides an internal listing for time-server guidance. For Reference and Primary servers, TIMESYNC.CFG provides a voting list; for Secondary servers, TIMESYNC.CFG defines a *time provider group*.

The custom configuration method cuts down on network traffic, but requires a great deal of administration. For this reason, it is appropriate for networks with more than 30 servers in distributed geographic locations. Here are some of its advantages:

▸ As a CNE, you have complete control of the time-synchronization hierarchy. You can control who votes with whom and tell Secondary servers where to get their time.

▸ You can optimize network traffic and distribute time sources around the world.

▸ You can provide redundant time-synchronization paths and alternate time providers in case of network failures.

But the custom configuration method is not the cat's meow, either. There are many circumstances when its additional administrative overhead is not justified. Here are a couple of disadvantages:

▸ Customization requires careful planning, especially on a large network. Imagine reconfiguring numerous TIMESYNC.CFG files when the tree has changed or the company moves locations. No thanks!

▸ Network expansion involves too much work and reconfiguration.

It's pretty easy to see that the default configuration works well for small networks (fewer than 30 servers), and the custom configuration method works well for large networks (more than 30 servers). If you choose the custom configuration method, try to create a pyramid hierarchy structure for time providers and time consumers (see Figure 2.24). Also, keep the number of time providers as small as possible to reduce network traffic. You can further enhance network performance by making sure time consumers get their time stamp from local servers — not over WAN links.

We're all out of time! (Pun intended.)

ZEN

"Oh! The places you'll go! You'll be on your way up! You'll be seeing great sights! You'll join the high fliers who soar to high heights!"

Dr. Seuss

That's everything you need to know about the "Cloud." Well, not really, but it's a very good start. Remember, every cloud has a silver lining and this chapter has been yours. Can you feel the *twinge* in the crown of your cranium? Has your NDS tree begun to sprout? Pretty soon, you'll be NDS-Head Fred!

The goal of this chapter was to make you think until it hurt — to generate enough neurokinetic energy to stimulate cranial growth. Have we succeeded? You be the judge. It all started with an NDS getting-familiar period. Once you were comfortable with the concept of a tree in a cloud, we learned about the 29 different objects that live there — including the [Root] and leaves. We learned that NDS objects come in two different flavors: Tupperware containers and physical leaf resources. We learned about Country objects, users, Distribution Lists, and the Alias object (if that's what it's really called).

With objects come names. Names uniquely identify "who we are" and "where we live." It works much the same way in NDS. NDS naming was the first of three important management topics we covered. We learned about the common name (who) and context (where). And we learned how these two are combined to create the distinguished name.

Then we explored partitioning — the second NDS management topic. NDS partitions are small pieces of the larger IntranetWare puzzle. We can distribute these pieces on servers throughout the WAN for increased fault tolerance and better resource access. This process is known as replication. We learned about the four different NDS replica types and how and when they can be used. By now, the [Root] should have been forming around your cerebellum.

The final NDS management topic was time synchronization. NDS has to know what time it is: Time stamps are required for logging in, NDS replication, and many other important network tasks. This is accomplished with the help of three different time providers (Single-Reference, Reference, and Primary) and one special time consumer server (Secondary). We not only learned about servers, we explored two different configuration methods (default and custom). That's just about when we ran out of time!

So, here we are — NDS-Head Fred! So far, we've explored the basics of IntranetWare and the intricacies of Novell Directory Services. That completes our discussion of IntranetWare CNE basics. Now you're ready to start the *real* journey:

- ▶ IntranetWare Design

- ▶ IntranetWare Installation

- ▶ IntranetWare Management

Don't be scared — I'll be with you every step of the way. And we'll return to these topics many times again. This is only the beginning and I can't wait for you to become a full-fledged superhero. . . .

ZEN

"Today is gone. Today was fun. Tomorrow is another one. Every day from here to there funny things are everywhere."

Dr. Seuss

SMART LINK

If you really want to get to know Dr. Seuss, check out another great site at http://www.afn.org/~afn15301/drseuss.html.

To complete this exercise, you will need Admin-level access to an IntranetWare NDS tree. You will explore the NDS tree structure using three different utilities: NetWare Administrator (NWADMIN), NETADMIN, and CX. Before beginning this exercise, you'll need to make sure that your network administrator has set up the NetWare Administrator icon in MS Windows on your workstation.

NETWARE ADMINISTRATOR

The NetWare Administrator (NWADMIN) utility is undoubtedly the most versatile utility available in IntranetWare. It can be used to perform a variety of functions, including the type of network administrator tasks that are available in FILER, NETADMIN, PARTMGR, and PCONSOLE.

During IntranetWare installation, the files for the MS Windows version of this utility are stored in the SYS:PUBLIC directory. The files for the OS/2 version are stored in the SYS:PUBLIC\OS2 directory. Before you run the NetWare Administrator in MS Windows or OS/2 on a workstation for the first time, you'll need to create an NWADMIN icon. From then on, you can select the icon to activate the utility. As stated earlier, this exercise assumes that your network administrator has already set up the NetWare Administrator icon for you in MS Windows on your workstation.

In this exercise, we are going to use NWADMIN to explore the NDS tree.

1. Exploring the browser window. Execute the NetWare Administrator (NWADMIN) utility in MS Windows or Windows 95. At least one NDS container object should be displayed. If not, select the Browse option from the Tools menu to open a browser window.

   a. What container and its objects are displayed when you activate the NetWare Administrator utility? How can you determine what your current context is? How was your current context determined? Is it the same current context that would be displayed using the CX command at the DOS prompt?

   b. How many containers are displayed? What type of containers are represented? How many leaf objects, if any, are displayed? What type of leaf objects are represented?

2. Changing context

   a. Keying in a new context. Keying in the name of a new context is one of the two methods available for changing your current context. Change your context to the [Root] by selecting Set Context . . . from the View menu. Type **[Root]** and press Enter. The [Root] icon should then be displayed at the top of the screen.

   b. Walking the tree. Next, let's try the "walking the tree" method to change your current context. Select Set Context . . . from the View menu.

     1) Click on the Browser button to the right of the New Context field to display the Select Object window.

     2) To navigate the tree, double-click on a container in the Directory Context list box on the right side of the screen to move down one level in the tree or double-click on the double-dot (..) to move up one level in the tree. The objects that are located in each container that you select will be displayed in the Objects list box on the left side of the screen. Practice walking up and down the tree. When you are finished, walk all the way up the tree, so that the [Root] icon is displayed at the top of the Object list box on the left side of the screen.

     3) The Name Filter field in the middle of the main NWADMIN browser screen allows you to restrict the objects that are listed in the Object list box on the left side of the screen by using wildcard characters or object names. The Directory Context filter field allows you to restrict the containers that are displayed on the right side of the screen by using wildcard characters or container names. Practice using these filters to limit what is displayed on the screen. When you are finished, delete any filters in either field.

4) When the container you want to select as the current context is displayed in the Objects list box (which in this case is the [Root] object), click on it, then click on the OK button at the bottom of the window. The container that you have selected will appear in the New Context field in the Set Current Context window. Click on the OK button at the bottom of the Set Current Context window to return to the main NWADMIN browser screen.

3. Opening a container object and viewing its contents. There are two methods available for opening a container and viewing its contents:

   a. Double-clicking on the container's object name or icon.

   b. Clicking on the container object to select it, then selecting the Expand option from the View menu.

      Practice using both of these methods to view the contents of various containers. Determine the type of containers that are in each container, as well as the type of leaf objects.

4. Viewing the object dialog (object details) of a container object. The object dialog lets you display and edit information relating to an object's properties. When you open an object dialog, you'll notice that there is a column of page buttons along the right side of the screen. You can click on each button, one at a time, to view the category of information indicated on the button. There two methods available for viewing the information relating to a container object:

   a. Clicking on the container object with the left mouse button to select it, then selecting the Details option from the Object menu.

   b. Clicking on the container object with the right mouse button to select it, then selecting Details from the menu pull-down that appears on the screen.

Practice using both of these methods to look at the information available for various types of container objects, including the [Root], a Country object (if one exists), an Organization object, and Organizational Unit objects.

5. Viewing the object dialog (object details) of a leaf object. There are three methods for viewing the information relating to a leaf object:

    a. Double-clicking on the leaf object.

    b. Clicking on the leaf object with the left mouse button to select it, then selecting the Details option from the Object menu.

    c. Clicking on the leaf object with the right mouse button to select it, then selecting Details from the menu that appears on the screen.

    Practice using all three of these methods to look at the information available for various types of leaf objects (including Users, Groups, Print Servers, Printers, Print Queues, and so on).

    When you are ready to exit the NetWare Administrator utility, select the Exit option from the File menu.

NETADMIN

The NETADMIN utility is a menu utility that can be used to manage NDS objects and their properties. It is much more limited in scope than the NetWare Administrator Utility.

1. Changing context. In order to change your current context for purposes of the NETADMIN utility, choose the Change context option from the NetAdmin Options menu. There are two methods of changing your context for the purposes of this utility. (When you exit the utility, you will return to the current context that was set before you ran the utility.) One is keying in the name of a new context in the field provided; the other is pressing the Insert key and walking the tree.

a. Press Insert. The contents of the current directory will be displayed, as well as a dot (.) representing the current directory and a double-dot (..) representing the parent directory. You will not need to select the dot (.) for purposes of this exercise.

b. Practice walking up and down the tree by double-clicking on the double-dot (..) to move up one level in the tree and double-clicking on a container to move down one level in the tree. You'll notice that the current context is displayed at the top of the screen. Go ahead and walk all the way up the tree by double-clicking on the double-dot (..) until the [Root] is listed as your current context, then walk down the tree by double-clicking on a container object, then double-clicking on a container object below that container object, and so on. When the current context you want is selected, press F10 to return to the NetAdmin Options menu.

2. Managing objects. In order to view and manage objects and their properties, select the Manage objects option from the Netadmin Options menu. You'll notice that you can walk the tree from this screen as well.

a. In order to display information about an object, select the object using the up-arrow key and down-arrow key, then press F10 to select it. You'll notice that the name and type of the object that you selected will be listed at the top of the menu that appears. Select the View or edit properties of this object menu option and press Enter. A list of categories will be displayed. Select the category desired and press Enter. Review the information displayed for this category, then press Esc to return to the previous menu. Use this method to display the various properties of this object, then press Esc to return to the Object, Class menu.

b. Practice using this technique to display the properties of various types of container and leaf objects. When you're ready to exit the NETADMIN utility, press Esc twice when the Object, Class menu is displayed, then select Yes and press Enter when asked if you want to exit.

CX

The IntranetWare CX command line utility can be used to display or modify your context, or to view containers and leaf objects in your Directory tree. Open a DOS window in MS Windows or Windows 95, or perform the following steps at the DOS prompt:

1. Change to the F: drive:

   ```
   F:
   ```

2. Display your current context:

   ```
   CX
   ```

3. Display on-line help for the CX command.

   ```
   CX /?
   ```

4. Display containers in the current context.

   ```
   CX /CONT
   ```

5. Display containers and objects in the current context.

   ```
   CX /A /CONT
   ```

6. Display containers at or below the current context.

   ```
   CX /T
   ```

7. Display containers and objects at or below the current context.

   ```
   CX /A /T
   ```

8. Display all the containers and objects in the Directory tree, starting at the [Root], without changing your current context.

   ```
   CX /R /A /T
   ```

9. Create and display a file that contains a visual representation of the NDS tree structure.

```
CX /R /A /T > TREE.NDS
TYPE TREE.NDS
```

10. Change your current context to the [Root].

```
CX /R
```

11. Display containers in the [Root].

```
CX /CONT
```

12. Move down one level in the NDS tree.

```
CX context
```

(where context is the name of a container that was listed in Step 11)

13. Move up one level in the NDS tree (which, in this case, happens to be the [Root]).

```
CX .
```

14. Display all containers below the [Root].

```
CX /T
```

15. Move to a container several levels below the [Root].

```
CX context
```

(where context is a context such as .WHITE.CRIME.TOKYO.ACME)

16. Move up four levels in the NDS tree.

```
CX ....
```

(where you indicate one dot for each level you want to move up in the NDS tree)

See Appendix C for answers.

EXERCISE 2-2: UNDERSTANDING NDS NAMING

Answer the following questions using the directory structure shown in Figure 2.25.

▶ · ◀

F I G U R E   2.25

*Understanding NDS
Naming for Tokyo*

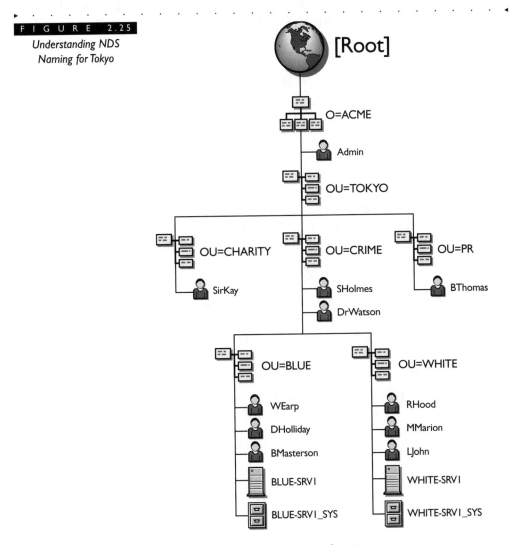

1. Indicate a typeless distinguished name for BMasterson.
2. Provide a typeful distinguished name for RHood.

3. List a typeless relative distinguished name for the CRIME Organizational Unit, assuming that your current context is the [Root].

4. Show a typeful relative distinguished name for the BLUE-SRV1 server object from the default current context.

5. If your current context is .CRIME.TOKYO.ACME, what is the shortest name that accurately references the SHolmes User object?

6. Assume your current context is .TOKYO.ACME. Indicate a typeless relative distinguished name for the LJohn User object.

7. If your current context is .PR.TOKYO.ACME, what would be a typeful relative distinguished name for SirKay?

8. Assume your current context is .WHITE.CRIME.TOKYO.ACME. Provide a typeless relative distinguished name for Admin.

9. If your current context is .BLUE.CRIME.TOKYO.ACME, what would be a typeful relative distinguished name for BThomas?

10. Assume your current context is .WHITE.CRIME.TOKYO.ACME. What is the longest possible typeful relative distinguished name for the SYS: volume on the BLUE-SRV1 server?

11. If DHolliday attaches to the BLUE-SRV1 server by default, what's his current context after login? Give two LOGIN commands for DHolliday.

12. How would MMarion visit SirKay?

13. How can you make sure that SirKay's workstation drops him into his home context when he attaches to the "Cloud"?

14. Provide ten login commands for SHolmes from .BLUE.CRIME.TOKYO.ACME:

15. What is the easiest way to move above ACME from the .PR.TOKYO.ACME context?

See Appendix C for answers.

EXERCISE 2-3: PLANT A TREE IN A CLOUD

Circle the 20 NDS terms hidden in this word search puzzle using the hints provided.

```
G  L  E  A  D  I  N  G  P  E  R  I  O  D  N  X  G  X  T  Q  W
Y  C  O  U  N  T  R  Y  R  F  T  I  O  V  S  I  H  R  R  I  Q
M  U  X  C  P  S  K  V  O  O  U  N  K  N  O  W  N  E  L  M  F
G  R  S  W  A  K  S  K  F  B  U  D  A  L  I  A  S  K  A  X  J
E  R  N  H  T  L  W  Y  I  N  J  P  V  M  M  U  U  A  I  I  N
R  E  G  A  J  R  I  B  L  U  Z  E  C  E  P  C  W  B  E  Q  H
Y  N  L  S  N  H  P  T  E  H  D  W  C  E  Y  X  V  Q  X  Q  O
L  T  X  P  B  F  H  R  Y  H  H  O  R  T  A  W  V  E  S  C  T
I  C  B  B  F  H  I  R  X  D  N  V  G  H  R  Q  K  E  B  Q  E
B  O  R  G  A  N  I  Z  A  T  I  O  N  A  L  R  O  L  E  T  K
V  N  Y  T  L  Y  B  X  E  S  E  R  H  F  K  F  W  G  U  Y  K
J  T  D  Y  V  R  N  X  O  T  V  G  E  E  B  T  L  Y  E  P  X
K  E  T  P  S  J  T  R  W  I  L  A  N  C  S  E  J  V  B  E  U
R  X  F  E  H  E  S  F  G  V  H  N  A  M  T  F  B  D  Y  L  L
M  T  W  F  A  S  Q  L  H  A  Q  I  D  K  R  O  D  Q  I  E  R
T  I  N  U  L  A  N  O  I  T  A  Z  I  N  A  G  R  O  W  S  Z
M  Y  D  L  H  S  W  N  C  X  D  A  U  Q  I  S  N  Y  V  S  S
O  D  B  N  L  R  C  G  T  J  O  T  O  O  Y  D  A  E  M  N  M
R  J  P  A  A  T  J  X  N  G  F  I  T  B  V  H  J  Y  F  A  B
Q  O  H  M  H  D  I  R  E  C  T  O  R  Y  S  C  A  N  P  M  P
W  U  N  E  Z  T  R  A  I  L  I  N  G  P  E  R  I  O  D  E  V
```

Hints:

1. Object that represents a logical NDS pointer to another object in the tree.
2. Container object that uses predetermined two-character names.
3. The context that would be displayed if you issued the CX command with no options.
4. Command line utility used to view or change your current context.
5. Object that represents a logical pointer to a physical directory in the IntranetWare file system.

6. RCONSOLE menu option that can be used to display the four main files that comprise the IntranetWare NDS database.
7. An object that represents a set of users and is used for assigning rights.
8. Identifies a name as a distinguished name.
9. Similar to a Country object, except that it can exist in the [Root], Country, Organization, or Organizational Unit container.
10. Command that can be used in NET.CFG to set the current context.
11. Item that represents a resource in the NDS database.
12. Container object that is often used to represent a company, university, or association.
13. Object that represents a position or role with an organization.
14. Container object that is considered a "natural group."
15. Object that represents a login script that is used by a group of users who reside in the same or different containers.
16. Special superuser used for bindery emulation.
17. Allows you to change the current context while using relative distinguished naming.
18. Name that contains object attribute abbreviations.
19. Name that does not contain object attribute abbreviations.
20. NDS object that has been invalidated or cannot be identified as belonging to any of the other object classes.

See Appendix C for answers.

PART 1: INTRANETWARE CNE BASICS

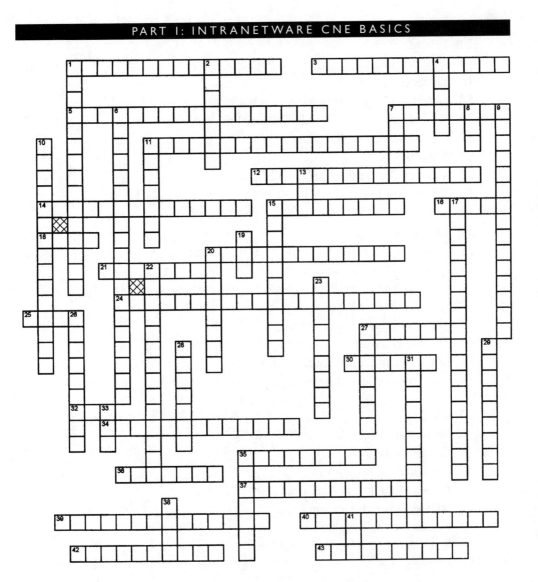

Across

1. A two-dimensional slice of 3-D NDS
3. No more wasted space
5. Your name and address combined
7. A two-dimensional tool in a three-dimensional world
11. Multiple layers of Tupperware

12. It's time to vote
14. Where am I?
15. Tupperware
16. Entrance to the "Cloud"
18. Getting to know the workstation NIC
20. Off-loading out-of-date files to near-line
21. The mysterious object class
24. A global view
25. You, me, Albert Einstein
27. Where you live
30. Everybody
32. The "Cloud"
34. Only one per partition, the king of replication
35. A piece of the "Cloud"
36. The old way of storing users
37. ACME in the NDS tree
39. The new IntranetWare approach
40. The old NetWare 3 approach
42. The other IntranetWare Directory tree
43. The time keepers of IntranetWare

Down

1. Backward compatibility to NetWare 3
2. Creating a superbindery
4. IntranetWare incognito
6. Does anyone know what time it is?
7. NDS details at the command line
8. The new e-mail engine
9. Somewhere between "off" and "on"
10. Saving space
11. You, me, printers
13. A small town in the IntranetWare global village
15. Who you are, not where you live
17. A revolving job
19. Also GMT
20. "Red books" in electronic form

22. Login interrogation in IntranetWare
23. A beginner MHS application
26. The last word in time voting
27. A two-letter container
28. They "haggle" over the time
29. When
31. Security flows down the tree
33. The new backup engine
35. A Group login script object
38. Really big hard drives
41. Life at the new IntranetWare workstation

See Appendix C for answers.

IntranetWare Design

▶ · · · · · · · · · · · · · · · · · ◀

I am MIGHTY!

I have a glow you cannot see,
I have a heart as big as the moon . . .
as warm as bath water.

We're superheroes, man
We don't have time to be charming.
The boots of good were made for walking.
We're watching the big picture, friend.
We know the score.

We are a public service, not glamor boys!
Not captains of industry,
Not makers of things.
Keep your vulgar monies.

We are a justice sandwich,
no toppings necessary.
Living rooms of America,
do you catch my drift?

Do you dig?!!!

The Tick

You are a superhero.

You are a doctor.

You are a gardener.

As an IntranetWare CNE, you are three people in one.

Today, you are a superhero. Probably the most exciting experience for anyone is the realization of a dream. For some, a dream may be as simple as more money, a better job, or pickles on ham and cheese. For others, dreaming is serious business — to be President of the United States, a cure for cancer, peace on Earth. Reality should never get in the way of your dreams. Do you have any?

Superheroes are in the dream-making business. As an IntranetWare superhero, you have one simple task — build an NDS tree and save the world. No pressure. It all starts with NDS design. You'll learn about naming standards, tree design, partitioning, replication, and time synchronization. And as if that's not enough, you'll have to implement them in a testing lab and pilot program first. Steps you take today could decide the fate of humanity. No pressure.

Wow! NDS design is serious business. Is the world in very good hands? Sure, you can handle it — you're an IntranetWare superhero!

Step 1: NDS Preparation

The world is in a lot of trouble. If we keep abusing the Planet Earth at our current pace, there'll be nothing left in a few decades.

As a matter of fact, the Alpha Centurions have discovered this and decided to do something about it. As it turns out, they are great fans of the Planet Earth and would hate to see us destroy it. They have given us until January 1, 2000, to clean up our act — or else. It's safe to say the fate of the human race is in your hands.

To save the world, we have created an organization called ACME (A Cure for Mother Earth). ACME is staffed by the greatest heroes from our unspoiled history. They are the founding mothers and fathers of Earth's Golden Age — before instant popcorn, talking cars, and daytime television. It's clear that somewhere along the human timeline, progress went amuck.

We've used the OTO (Oscillating Temporal Overthruster) prototype to vortex back in time and grab the ACME management. They're a little disoriented but more than happy to help. Now it's your turn to step up to the plate — as ACME's MIS department. You will build a pervasive internetwork for ACME using IntranetWare. The clock is ticking and connectivity is the key.

 ZEN

"Knock on the sky and listen to the sound."

M'Tau Zen

As an IntranetWare CNE, you come highly recommended. Your mission — should you choose to accept it — is to build the ACME WAN and NDS tree. You will need courage, design experience, NDS know-how, and this book. If you succeed, you will save the world and become a CNE! All in a day's work.

Actually, you have a daunting task ahead of you. A project of this magnitude requires sharp thinking and a very organized approach. All the fancy footwork and LAN lexicon in the world isn't going to help you if you don't have a game plan. That's where Figure 3.1 comes in — it's your ACME game plan. As you can see, saving the world falls into four simple steps:

▸ Step 1: NDS Preparation

▸ Step 2: Design

▸ Step 3: Implementation

▸ Step 4: Management

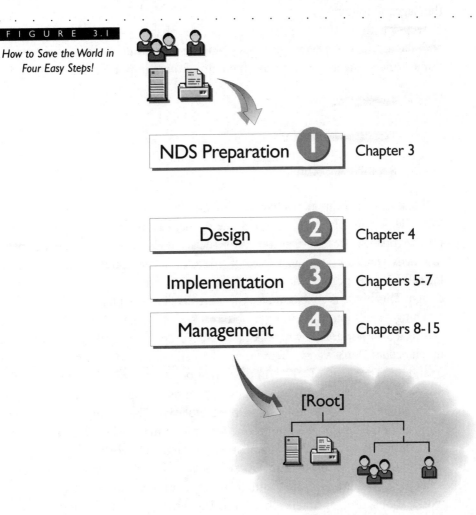

FIGURE 3.1

How to Save the World in Four Easy Steps!

NDS Preparation **①**   Chapter 3

Design **②**   Chapter 4

Implementation **③**   Chapters 5-7

Management **④**   Chapters 8-15

[Root]

In Step 1, the project starts rolling with NDS preparation. The primary focus of this phase is the project team. These are the men and women who will carry you through the triumphs and pitfalls of saving the world. The project team consists of many networking experts, including management, server specialists, NDS experts, and connectivity specialists. The team's first task is systems analysis and data gathering. Once you've gathered all pertinent project information, you can develop a project scope and move on to Step 2. All of this fun will be outlined in the pages to follow.

Step 2 is the first of the three main project phases — design, implementation, and management. NDS design begins with the formation of a tree framework. This framework is further refined with the help of three important NDS concepts:

▸ Partitioning

▸ Time synchronization

▸ Resource accessibility

These design components have a dramatic effect on the success or failure of your WAN. Unfortunately, NDS design is one of the least understood of the three main project phases. Design is especially crucial in IntranetWare because network productivity relies on the availability of resources. These resources must be organized logically. Please don't underestimate the importance and sophistication of NDS design. This phase is covered in excruciating detail in Chapter 4.

Things really start hopping in Step 3 — implementation. You're probably getting a little stir-crazy by now because NDS preparation and design don't involve much *action*. Don't worry, there's more than enough action to go around in Steps 3 and 4. The goal of NDS implementation is IntranetWare installation and migration. But before you can get there, you must get all your ducks in a row. This is the purpose of a testing lab and pilot program. The testing lab allows you to implement the design in a nonproduction environment. Then you can further test your design in a controlled segment of the larger network — a pilot program. Once all the kinks have been worked out, you can create an implementation schedule and start installing and migrating IntranetWare resources — servers, workstations, users, printers, and so on. The testing portions of Step 3 are covered in Chapter 5 ("NDS Implementation"). The real action takes place in Chapter 6 ("IntranetWare Installation") and Chapter 7 ("IntranetWare Migration"). I bet you can't wait.

Once your network's in place, it's time to make it shine. Welcome to Step 4. Management is the ongoing process of fiddling with and tweaking your IntranetWare WAN. This is where we get to earn our money as ACME superheroes!

IntranetWare management hinges on NDS. It involves partitioning, the file system, security, printing, and optimization. But none of this is useful without configuration and management. Configuration is a five-step process that brings the users on-line and offers them a productive networking environment. Additional management allows you to keep the servers running, make daily backups, and perform routine maintenance tasks from remote locations. This is where you'll spend most of your life as a CNE. Fortunately, we've devoted half of this book to IntranetWare Management (Chapters 8 through 15). Boy, do we have fun in store for you!

ZEN

"Don't Panic!"

The Hitchhiker's Guide to the Galaxy

That's all it takes to save the world and become an IntranetWare CNE. Don't hyperventilate — breathe slowly. It's going to be all right. I'm here to walk with you every step of the way. And there's a great poster in the back of this book that outlines your mission. But be careful not to let these facts fall into the wrong hands. Believe it or not, there are forces at work that do not share our love for the human race — especially the Alpha Centurions. Let's start our life-or-death journey with a closer look at the "Process."

The Process

There's more to saving the world than you might think — as we just saw. When a company makes an investment in an IntranetWare network, someone has the responsibility of implementing it. Similarly, when the Alpha Centurions decide to destroy the human race, someone has the responsibility of stopping them — you!

You weren't born with this responsibility — it was given to you. Do you feel lucky? As the director of the Labs division, Albert Einstein chose you as the head MIS consultant. In this scenario, Albert Einstein takes on the role of Information Services (IS) Manager. The IS Manager starts your project with three simple questions:

▸ What is the Process you will use for implementing IntranetWare in our organization?

▸ What resources (such as people, computers, and money) will the Process require?

▸ How much time will planning and implementation take?

Your answers to these questions set you on a path of wonder, intrigue, and very late nights. Your ability to complete the project (and save the world) depends entirely on the Process.

So, what is the Process? The Process is a systematic methodology for designing, implementing, and managing IntranetWare. In most cases, it consists of the four simple steps shown in Figure 3.1:

▸ Step 1: NDS Preparation

▸ Step 2: Design

▸ Step 3: Implementation

▸ Step 4: Management

Having a systematic approach like this reduces the time it takes to design the network, which gives you a head start on implementation and management. It also ensures that the needs of Albert Einstein are met and all critical requirements are addressed. This results ultimately in an efficient IntranetWare WAN for today and tomorrow (assuming there is a tomorrow).

Let's take a closer look at the Process and learn a little more about "saving the world."

TIP

Programmers and IS professionals sometimes call the Process a System Design Life Cycle (SDLC); others call it an Information Systems Development Methodology; or better yet, a Software Engineering Process Model. Regardless of what you call it, the Process is a structured approach toward designing, implementing, and managing an information system.

In addition to different names, there are many different approaches to the Process, including linear, structured, incremental, and/or spiral:

▸ The *linear* approach handles each step one at a time in order. It is used in traditional bottom-up software and systems development efforts.

▸ The *structured* model, on the other hand, allows all activities to take place simultaneously. This approach is used in top-down development that involves nonlinear efforts.

▸ The *incremental* approach is a variation on the structured model used with rapid prototyping.

▸ Finally, the *spiral* model allows you to modify certain requirements during the life of the project. This approach is used in inherently risky, costly, or unstable environments — kind of like saving the world.

The Process is an interesting mix of all four approaches.

NDS PREPARATION PHASE

It all begins with NDS preparation. During this phase, we create the project team and outline the Process. As you can see in Figure 3.2, we're just getting things started.

Your project team is the center of attention. It consists of nine different specialists who fall into three categories:

▸ Management

▸ Hardware Specialists

▸ Software Specialists

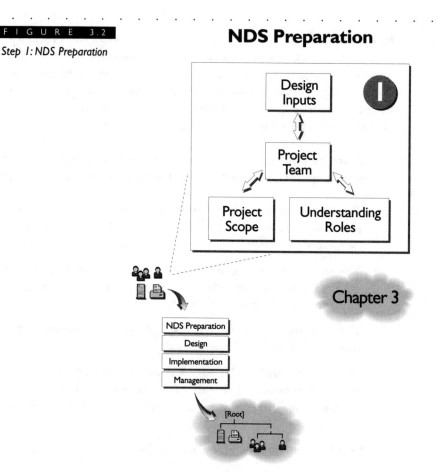

NDS Preparation

Each project team member has a specific role that must be outlined clearly. Once you've assembled the team, you must train them — not in the technological aspects of IntranetWare, but in the intricacies of the Process. Once you've trained the team members, they can begin the two most important tasks of Step 1: gathering NDS information and determining the project scope.

Data gathering is the process of determining *who* is doing *what* to *whom* and *why*. In other words, it's "just the facts, ma'am." Objectivity is crucial in data gathering. All sorts of distortion effects have been found to alter data as it is gathered. The *Hawthorne Effect* states that individuals who know they are part of a study behave differently from those who are not part of a study, or who don't know they are part of a study. In addition, the *Learning Curve* shows that data gathered early in an experiment is not always as accurate as data gathered later. The members of your project team can use a variety of methods for data gathering: observation, conversation, research, questionnaires, and random sampling. Eventually they will settle on a few key design inputs:

- The Company's Organizational Chart

- Physical WAN Layout Map

- Network Resource Lists

- A World Location Map

- Background Information and a Workflow Diagram

Later in this chapter, we will explore data gathering for ACME. We will discover each of these design inputs and learn the role they play in the Process and NDS design.

Once you've established your project team and gathered all of ACME's information, it's time to determine the project's scope. Establishing the scope of a project is critical for keeping things under control. Scope provides physical boundaries for the network as well as financial and personnel limitations. After defining the problem accurately, you must explore the system resources and determine how far they can be stretched. In many cases, the scope acts as a restraint to keep unworkable solutions from expanding too far. If the scope is too broad, the network will never be finished. If the scope is too narrow, the network surely will not meet ACME's needs. Albert Einstein is looking for the bottom line — "How much will it cost me and how long will it take?" These questions can be answered by determining the project's scope.

That's the gist of NDS preparation. With your team all fueled up and ready to go, it's time to launch into the three main phases of the Process:

- Design

- Implementation

- Management

QUIZ

Part of NDS preparation is "seeing what isn't there." Use the following rhyme to test your perceptivity skills:

A CNE came to the riverside,
With a donkey bearing an obelisk,
But he did not venture to ford the tide,
For he had too good an *.
What is the missing word?

(Q3-1)
(See Appendix C for all quiz answers.)

DESIGN PHASE

It has been my experience that all the factors, details, and lexicon in the world of networking can be narrowed down into two very important classifications: people and performance. During the design phase, you only have to concern yourself with these two categories. Analyze the ACME information and prioritize the results with respect to their influence over the people in the office and the performance of the network. It's that simple. The ultimate goal is to develop an effective balance of NDS components that creates a design synergy.

Yes, there's that word again — *synergy*. Synergy states that "the whole is greater than the sum of its parts." Synergy in networking is the product of well-orchestrated software and hardware components. In the best scenario, these resources complement each other to create a WAN that exceeds the productivity and performance of individual systems. In IntranetWare, these resources must be designed according to three important criteria (see Figure 3.3):

▸ *NDS tree* — Designing the upper and lower layers of the Directory tree. This design helps you optimize NDS so that it's productive for users and easy to manage. It also lays the foundation for partitioning and time synchronization.

▸ *Partitioning* — Next, your design must outline partition boundaries and replica placement. These procedures help provide scaleability, fault tolerance, and resource access.

▶ *Time synchronization* — The design must include guidelines for both default and customized time synchronization strategies. For customized trees, you'll need to offer setup models for TIMESYNC.CFG and efficient guidelines for time-server placement. These procedures help provide accurate synchronized time to all servers on the ACME WAN. Remember, time stamps are critical to all NDS events.

▶ . . . . ◀

Design

Step 2: Design

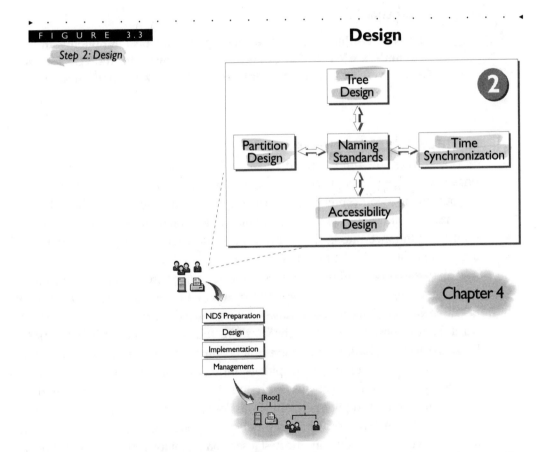

These design criteria rely on a *naming standards document* as a central point of control. After all, if you're going to save the world, everybody must speak the same language. The NDS tree relies on naming standards for container organization, partitioning, and replica placement. Time servers also rely on standardization for both default and custom configurations.

The final step in the design phase deals with accessibility. This is where synergy comes in. The system must be designed so that both physical and logical resources are easily accessible to users. Once again, this step impacts all three design criteria — NDS tree, partitioning, and time synchronization. Accessibility design should also account for the needs of non-IntranetWare users — Bindery Services.

Okay, with the ACME design in place, you're ready for *action* — literally!

SMART LINK

The NDS Design phase is the most important task in building an IntranetWare WAN. You can learn more about it in the NDS Design CNE course at CyberState University: http://www.cyberstateu.com.

IMPLEMENTATION PHASE

This is where the fun begins. If you're feeling a little restless from the first two phases, you'll get plenty of action in the final two. As you can see in Figure 3.4, all of your initial action centers around the implementation schedule. This schedule outlines the rollout of IntranetWare installation and migration. But before you can implement IntranetWare in the ACME production environment, we'll need to test it in more controlled pilot programs.

It all starts in your off-line testing lab. Here you can be creative and brave without causing system-wide crashes. While you are in the lab, you should consider installing IntranetWare multiple times and creating diverse NDS trees. Then test partitioning, replication, time synchronization, and common network applications. Finally, make sure backup and restore procedures operate correctly. All this extra work should help you avoid major pitfalls during the pilot program.

Once you're comfortable with each individual piece, consider putting them together in a controlled pilot program. The pilot system involves installing your first production IntranetWare server. Each production application can be tested in a more real-life environment. You can also test user compatibility with NDS and Bindery Services. A pilot system is your bridge between the lab and a full implementation of IntranetWare across the entire ACME WAN. You might consider the Labs division in NORAD as your pilot implementation. The scientists who work there are more likely to understand what you're going through.

FIGURE 3.4

Step 3: Implementation

Implementation

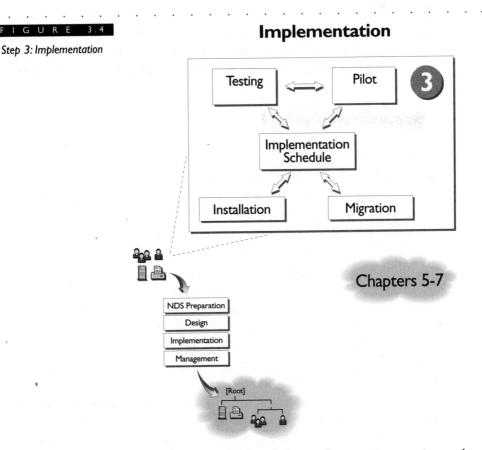

Once you've scheduled, tested, and piloted the implementation, you're ready for Prime Time!

- ▸ IntranetWare Installation

- ▸ IntranetWare Migration

IntranetWare Installation creates new servers and places them in the existing NDS tree. The very first installation is significant because it outlines the boundaries of NDS. Furthermore, IntranetWare Migration allows you to integrate NetWare 3 servers into the new system. Migration retains the existing file system and translates the bindery into NDS objects.

During this entire phase, you should always keep design *synergy* in mind.

ZEN

Wogging — Jogging interspersed with periods of walking at a brisk pace especially as a form of aerobic exercise. Also used to describe the dizzying feeling most CNEs experience prior to NDS management.

MANAGEMENT PHASE

Welcome to the "Real World." The first three phases of the Process were packed with questions, answers, intrigue, mystery, knowledge, decisions, and shopping. Here's where the adventure begins. IntranetWare management is the adventure of dealing with the WAN once it has been built. The project team has gathered a plethora of ACME information and prioritized it into a synergistic design. The implementation team has spent plenty of time and money fusing network components into a functional skeleton — now it's your turn.

In IntranetWare management, it is your responsibility to take this unsophisticated network skeleton and develop a thriving, dynamic, breathing NetWare WAN. It is your system to configure, manage, maintain, and troubleshoot. In addition, it is your responsibility to work in conjunction with other CNEs to expand this WAN into the realm of interconnectivity — *if you build it, they will come.*

Your role, as a CNE, is probably the most excruciating and the most rewarding. The project team dissembles at this point, but you stay around to keep things running on a daily basis. You are the ruler of your own kingdom — mapping out boundaries, filling it with users, adding security, and laying down the laws. This is a huge responsibility, and your success or failure hinges on three important characteristics: network knowledge, management skills, and fire containment. To be successful, you must fully understand the intricacies of your WAN, be sensitive to the needs of your users, and develop precautionary guidelines for network crashes. Nobody said it was going to be easy, but then again, the rewards will greatly outweigh the pain.

As you can see in Figure 3.5, IntranetWare management centers around NDS. Five key management components directly impact the success or failure of ACME:

▸ Security — laying down the law

▸ Partitioning — breaking the kingdom into functional regions

▸ File system — currency

▸ Printing — your kingdom's industry

▸ Optimization — keeping things running smoothly

FIGURE 3.5

Step 4: Management

Management

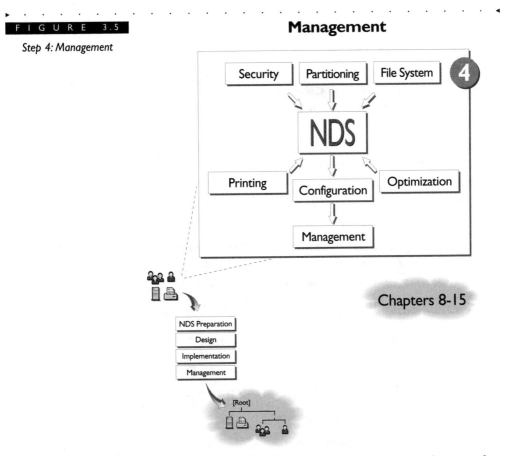

Chapters 8-15

Of course, to keep peace in your kingdom, you must have a military and bureaucratic government — that's NDS. These management aspects rely on IntranetWare configuration and management. During configuration, you establish a productive user environment with workstation connectivity, login scripts, a menu system, network applications, and e-mail. In addition, a series of management tasks help you proactively maintain file servers, the intranet, workstations, backup, and the Remote Management Facility (RMF). This is a snapshot of your daily life. This is what you signed up for!

IntranetWare management dominates the majority of your life as a CNE. The first three phases typically occur once. Management occurs every day. That's why we've dedicated more than half of this book to the final phase of the Process. As a matter of fact, this book is a road map to saving the world. Refer to Table 3.1 for more details.

SMART LINK

You can find another road map for saving the world in the on-line CNE course catalog. Surf the Web to http://netpub.com/education/x/scatlog.

Now that you understand the overall Process, let's get started with Step 1 (NDS preparation). Fortunately, you don't have to do it alone. Let's get some help. Let's build a project team.

QUIZ

Just another example of "seeing what isn't there." The same hero claims all these famous phrases. As a matter of fact, his or her name is an anagram of one of them. Who is our hero?

"The world's mine oyster."

"The better part of valor is discretion."

"Be to yourself as you would to your friend."

"If money go before, all ways do lie open."

"I'll make a wise phrase."

"All that glisters is not gold."

"Ill blow the wind that profits nobody."

(Q3-2)

	PHASE	TASK	NOVELL'S CNE STUDY GUIDE FOR INTRANETWARE
TABLE 3.1 *A Road Map for Saving the World*	NDS Preparation	Project team	Chapter 3
		Understand roles	Chapter 3
		Design inputs	Chapter 3
		Project scope	Chapter 3
	Design	Naming standards	Chapter 4
		Tree design	Chapter 4
		Partition design	Chapter 4
		Time synchronization	Chapter 4
		Accessibility design	Chapter 4
	Implementation	Testing lab	Chapter 5
		Pilot program	Chapter 5
		Implementation schedule	Chapter 5
		Installation	Chapter 6
		Migration	Chapter 7
	Management	NDS	Chapter 8
		Partitioning	Chapter 9
		File system	Chapter 10
		Security	Chapter 11
		Configuration	Chapter 12
		Management	Chapter 13
		Printing	Chapter 14
		Optimization	Chapter 15

The Project Team

Never underestimate the value of a friend — especially when you're trying to save the world. That's why we've used the OTO (Oscillating Temporal Overthruster) prototype to go back in time and recruit heroes from our unspoiled past. These heroes will not only fill the roles of ACME management — a few lucky ones will become members of your project team. It doesn't matter how many people are on the team as long as the concerns and tasks for each role are represented. You can have members performing multiple roles or specific subtasks within a role. It all depends on the size of your organization. Typically, the most efficient balance employs a one-to-one relationship. That is, one team member for each design role. So, how do you find these people? Just like any scientific method — draw straws. Asking yourself the following questions might help, too:

▶ Does ACME have an IS organization? If so, how is it organized?

▶ Who manages ACME servers? Who manages ACME workstations?

▶ Who understands the complexities of internetworking protocols? Does anyone within ACME have a handle on the physical WAN layout?

▶ Who will train the network administrators and users?

▶ Who handles software upgrades and network management?

▶ Who manages other network resources such as printers and file storage?

▶ Who can help test the networking software and applications? Do they use valid scientific methods?

As you can see, these are primarily technical questions. The majority of the project team should be made up of scientists and technically minded individuals. This isn't to say, however, that you should ignore bureaucrats. It's always a good idea to balance scientists with managerial expertise. That's also part of your job as the team leader.

Once you've established the team, make sure each member has a clear understanding of his or her responsibilities and priorities. They should also have clear expectations of how to interact with each other. Each team member has specific expertise and comes from a different area of management. Make sure that they understand the interdependency between team members. Try to avoid fostering hierarchy. Each team member has a job to do and no one member is more important than another — except you, of course. You're the most important! Finally, be sensitive to team member concerns. Everyone has something unique to add, and you should keep an open mind to their input. You never know when they might teach you something.

Most project teams are separated into three functional areas:

- ▶ Management

- ▶ Hardware Specialists

- ▶ Software Specialists

Management includes ACME's IS Manager, the Testing Lab Coordinator, the Education/Training Coordinator, and you (aka the MIS department). Hardware Specialists focus on servers, workstations, and IntranetWare printing. Finally, Software Specialists deal with NDS concerns, network applications, and general connectivity. Let's take a closer look at each of these nine ACME team members and focus on their priorities, expectations, and concerns.

SMART LINK

One of the most important aspects of building a Project Team is cost justification. Spend a moment to perform your own Return On Investment (ROI) calculations with "Cost of Networking" at http://www.netware.com.

MANAGEMENT

Of course, *you* are running the show. It's a good thing you're a CNE, or the world wouldn't have any chance at all. But you can't do everything alone. Three specialized managers can help you keep the Hardware and Software Specialists in line. They are

- ▸ IS Manager

- ▸ Testing Lab Coordinator

- ▸ Education/Training Coordinator

IS Manager

The IS Manager is the central contact point for ACME staff and management. He or she is most likely the head of the IS department and understands the ramifications of the Process. ACME's IS Manager is Albert Einstein. Following is a list of his responsibilities and concerns:

- ▸ Coordinate with the NDS Expert to ensure an efficient transition from NetWare 3 to IntranetWare

- ▸ Acquire the appropriate resources and funding to proceed with all phases of the Process

- ▸ Act as a liaison between the project team and ACME management

- ▸ Give direction to the project

- ▸ Manage costs and estimates; organize and schedule management meetings

- ▸ Create an efficient and effective network design

- ▸ Coordinate evaluation of software and licensing issues

- ▸ Coordinate design, implementation, and management timelines

- ▸ Ensure user productivity and adequate training

- ▸ Oversee the testing lab, pilot implementation, and ACME-wide rollout

Testing Lab Coordinator

The Testing Lab Coordinator performs tests on the new IntranetWare operating system with current applications. He or she should run diagnostics, provide statistics on performance, and ensure network hardware and software stability. The Testing Lab represents the first aspect of implementation. The Coordinator must be precise and systematic in his or her testing methodologies. For this reason, we've chosen Sherlock Holmes as the ACME Testing Lab Coordinator. Following is a list of his responsibilities and concerns:

- ▶ Test the compatibility between IntranetWare and current applications

- ▶ Create network performance benchmarks

- ▶ Set up the Lab environment to emulate ACME production

- ▶ Provide test results about network performance and software compatibility

- ▶ Obtain current versions of application software

- ▶ Get resources for the Lab from the IS Manager

- ▶ Coordinate pilot rollout with the IS Manager

Education/Training Coordinator

The Education/Training Coordinator analyzes the new skills required by team members. He or she then arranges for training sessions and materials to help the team attain a high level of network proficiency. In addition, the Education/Training Coordinator deals with training issues for distributed administrators and users. He or she ensures that all administrators get the opportunity to become CNEs and that ACME users feel comfortable with the new global WAN. He or she must be wise yet firm, sensitive yet diligent. For these reasons, we've chosen Buddha as the ACME Education/Training Coordinator. Following is a list of his responsibilities and concerns:

- ▶ Identify and provide implementation and administration guidelines

- ▶ Train the project team

- Train network administrators

- Train users

- Work closely with you and the IS Manager to continually evaluate team members

- Research information affecting users and administrators, then provide on-the-job training

- Lobby the IS Manager for education and training budgets

- Set up the education and training lab with the help of the Testing Lab Coordinator and other specialists

- Identify appropriate timing for training sessions and integrate sessions into the overall project time line

- Get members prepared for meetings and serve cafe latte

As you can see, the project management staff has a lot on their plate. Albert Einstein, Sherlock Holmes, and Buddha work closely with you to foster team synergy and keep the project on course.

ZEN

Karmarker's algorithm — a technique of solving a complex mathematical problem quickly by eliminating groups of possible solutions with the aid of solid geometry. Also thought to be a method of choosing the ACME Project Team.

Now let's take a look at the non-management team members: Hardware and Software Specialists.

HARDWARE SPECIALISTS

The ACME Hardware Specialists tweak computers all day. They are the ultimate gigabyte gurus who purchase, set up, and troubleshoot the network hardware. The

Hardware Specialists are an important part of the project team because they understand the intricacies of LAN-based computers. They also understand the strain IntranetWare can place on servers and workstations.

There are three Hardware Specialists on our team:

▸ Server Specialist

▸ Workstation Specialist

▸ Printing Specialist

Server Specialist

In earlier versions of NetWare, the server was the heart and soul of the LAN. Even though it takes a logical back seat in IntranetWare, its importance should never be underestimated. Regardless of what the tree looks like, it exists as three or four database files within your network server. In addition, the server plays an important role in system-wide time synchronization. As I'm sure you can imagine, the Server Specialist is invaluable in choosing the correct hardware initially and then keeping it running. We've chosen Marie Curie as the Server Specialist because of her excellent reputation as a nuclear scientist. Just draw your own conclusions. Following is a list of her responsibilities and concerns:

▸ Determine and plan the pilot implementation.

▸ Install, upgrade, and migrate all IntranetWare servers.

▸ Ensure effective time synchronization strategies.

▸ Assist the Testing Lab Coordinator.

▸ Develop an effective management strategy for centralized and distributed administrators.

▸ Establish protocol standardization. This includes standards for frame type usage. Don't forget to register your IPX addresses.

▸ Design server placement in the NDS tree. This should be coordinated with the NDS Expert.

▸ Calculate needed disk space and memory for new and existing servers.

▸ Plan and implement an IntranetWare–compatible data backup system.

▸ Establish disaster recovery options.

▸ Determine backward compatibility.

▸ Identify and install appropriate Bindery Services technology for non-IntranetWare users.

▸ Determine performance overhead created by new operating system utilities and additional NLMs.

Workstation Specialist

The Workstation Specialist spends his or her day working with users and their workstations. This is probably the most challenging job because it entails "user interface." We all know what a hurdle that can be. For this reason, the Workstation Specialist should be a counselor as well as a technical innovator. The goal here is to keep both the workstations and users "humming" with minimal fuss. The challenge is great but not insurmountable. For this reason, we've chosen Sir Isaac Newton as ACME's Workstation Specialist. He's never been the same since that apple incident. Maybe it will help him understand the user's plight. Following is a list of his responsibilities and concerns:

▸ Upgrade all workstations to Client 16 or Client 32

▸ Automate workstation connectivity as outlined in Step 1 of IntranetWare configuration (see Chapter 12)

▸ Identify and solve problems with workstation hardware

▸ Determine and implement changes to existing client procedures, as well as perform any necessary client updates

▸ Create an efficient implementation schedule for upgrading workstations

▸ Determine memory requirements to run client software and existing network applications

▸ Maintain consistent configuration files across all workstations

▸ Identify performance overhead related to the new VLMs

▸ Investigate and solve possible storage issues (for example, the 10 MB necessary for client software installation)

▸ Work with the Testing Lab Coordinator to determine the compatibility of VLMs with existing Windows 95 environments

▸ Coordinate Profile and User login scripts with the NDS Expert

▸ Determine and solve problems with specialized bindery and traveling users

▸ Determine a method for user login and connection — establishing correct name context

Printing Specialist

Aah, printers. They can be even more challenging than workstations. The Printing Specialist provides access to printers, determines printer location, and upgrades printing software. Of course, all users want their own printers — but this defeats the purpose of a network. It's also an ineffective use of ACME's resources. After all, we're trying to save the world here. The Printing Specialist must understand the needs of his or her users and their "evolution" as IntranetWare users. For his unique and overwhelming understanding in this area, we've chosen Charles Darwin as ACME's Printing Specialist. Following is a list of his responsibilities and concerns:

▸ Provide users with access to appropriate printers (this is the tricky part)

▸ Work with the IS Manager to determine budgets for printer acquisition

▸ Upgrade printing software and workstation drivers

▸ Create a well-defined migration strategy for existing and new printers

▸ Enable Bindery Services for direct connection to non-IntranetWare printers

▸ Configure and administer new printing utilities

▸ Coordinate CAPTURE statements in Profile and User login scripts with the NDS Expert

▸ Provide interconnectivity for printing for Macintosh and UNIX machines, as well as provide user access to specialized Macintosh- and UNIX-type printers

The Hardware Specialists are the true *geeks* of your project team. But they have important responsibilities with the users as well. Both the Workstation and Printing Specialists have their own user challenges to deal with. As the CNE, consider supporting them as they try to foster a productive user environment.

ZEN

"It's a well-known fact that any man would rather drill a hole in his hand than admit, especially to his wife, that he cannot handle a hardware problem by himself. Put an ordinary husband on the Space Shuttle, and within minutes he'll be attempting to repair the retro thruster modules himself. After all, if you call in NASA, they'll charge you an arm and a leg!"

Dave Barry

Now let's take a look at the final three members of our project team — the Software Specialists.

SOFTWARE SPECIALISTS

On the outside, the Software Specialists may appear to be a little less nerdy than their hardware counterparts. Don't let that fool you! The Software Specialists are just as technical as the Hardware Specialists but in a slightly different way. Software Specialists deal with the *inner* workings of the system, not the outer hardware. These heroes have a very important role in ensuring a smooth transition from NetWare 3 LANs to a global IntranetWare WAN.

There are three Software Specialists on the ACME project team. They are

- NDS Expert

- Application Specialist

- Connectivity Specialist

NDS Expert

If you thought NDS was strange, wait until you meet the NDS Expert. In order to truly understand NDS, you have to think like a "cloud" — a scary proposition. Since NDS impacts all facets of the system, this expert needs to have a firm grasp on the big picture. This is one of the most valuable members of your project team. For his intellectual spark and wizardry, we've chosen Merlin as the ACME NDS Expert. Somehow, it seems appropriate. Following is a list of his responsibilities and concerns:

- Lead the project team through most of the NDS design phase.

- Create Directory tree design, and organize the upper and lower portions of the tree.

- Design and implement NDS security.

- Design and implement NDS management components, including partitions, replica placement, time synchronization, and accessibility.

- Participate in choosing the team members. Also, communicate NDS concerns to both the IS Manager and you.

- Ensure that the design is thorough and meets all department needs at key points throughout the Process. Also ensure that each project team member participates in data gathering, and that the design phase meets established time lines.

- Coordinate System, Profile, and User login scripts with other team members, including Workstation and Printing Specialists.

▸ Oversee the creation and maintenance of a detailed design and implementation log book. This will be the cornerstone of WAN expansion.

▸ Know NDS inside and out.

Application Specialist

The Application Specialist maintains network and user applications. He or she also oversees software upgrades and coordinates the installation of specialized database and application servers. He or she also participates in certain aspects of IntranetWare configuration, including menu systems, e-mail, and workstation connectivity (see Chapter 12). Since network applications are the true productivity tools of the WAN, this specialist must be fully aware of the impact of all WAN influences on them — including NDS, synchronization, name context, distributed printers, and security. For this reason, we've chosen Gandhi as ACME's Application Specialist. He also seems to have a grasp on the big picture. Following is a list of his responsibilities and concerns:

▸ Migrate existing applications into the new IntranetWare WAN

▸ Install new applications

▸ Ensure stability of existing and new applications

▸ Provide user access to applications through connectivity and security

▸ Update menu systems

▸ Work with the Testing Lab Coordinator to ensure application compatibility with IntranetWare

▸ Coordinate System, Profile, and User login scripts with the NDS Expert

▸ Work with the Server Specialist to ensure availability of specialized application servers

Connectivity Specialist

The Connectivity Specialist works with the physical network, Internet backbone, telecommunications, WAN design, and router placement. He or she must understand the technical aspects of internetworking. In addition, the Connectivity Specialist must understand traffic concerns caused by replicas, time synchronization, and NDS overhead. For this reason, he/she must work very closely with the other project team members to optimize router placement. Maid Marion is the best woman for the job. She understands connectivity. Following is a list of her responsibilities and concerns:

▸ Determine the effect of routing, protocols, telecommunications, and WAN structure on the Directory tree design.

▸ Make decisions regarding single or multiple protocols on the network. Also coordinate with the Server Specialist to ensure protocol compatibility.

▸ Deliver better internetwork traffic throughput.

▸ Advise the project team about routing, protocols, and WAN structure.

▸ Determine the efficiency of LAN/WAN bandwidth issues. This involves determining which protocol to use on the LAN versus the WAN.

▸ Determine the need to include specialized products, including NetWare/IP and so on. This should include identifying current utilization figures.

▸ Maintain seamless connectivity to hosts and other non-IntranetWare operating systems.

There you have it. That's your project team. Nine of the greatest minds in history — plus *you*! It's nice to know the world is in such good hands.

Now that you have the team in place, you can get them rolling. The first task is data gathering — and it's a doozy! In the next section, we'll learn everything there is to know about ACME and discover some very detailed NDS design inputs. It's amazing what you can find when you go digging around. So, without any further adieu, let's get to know ACME.

ZEN

"Peanuts and pineapples. Noses and grapes. Everything comes in different shapes."

Dr. Seuss

Gathering NDS Information

As we learned earlier, data gathering is the process of determining *who* is doing *what* to *whom* and *why*. In other words, "just the facts, ma'am." In our case, it breaks out like this:

- Who — ACME

- What — Trying to make the world a better place and increase the *World Health Index*

- Whom — All living creatures on the Earth

- Why — To save the human race from Alpha Centurion annihilation

Objectivity is crucial in data gathering. Sometimes it's harder than you might think — like now. All sorts of distortions have a profound effect on the data as it is gathered. The *Hawthorne Effect* states that individuals who know they have to save the earth shrivel up and crawl into caves under the influence of immense pressure. But that's not going to happen to us, because we are CNE superheroes!

The process of gathering data for NDS design is interesting. You have a specific purpose — building a WAN infrastructure using IntranetWare and NDS. With this purpose in mind, you need to view the company through *rose-colored glasses*. This means seeing things from a specific point of view, that is, Novell's point of view. As I'm sure you've experienced, data changes as you draw it into focus. When you approach ACME, view the data from two unique points of view:

- Organizational — How does the company operate and what's its purpose?

▸ Technical — What technical devices are in place to facilitate the exchange of information?

It's a pretty tricky balancing act. Organizational design inputs are more subjective in nature. They deal with the company as a business unit and ignore the means for exchanging information. Technical design inputs, on the other hand, are objective in nature. They involve the physical WAN infrastructure and ignore the content of the message. Obviously, both are equally important, but since we're designing an NDS infrastructure, you may want to give more weight to the technical inputs (see Figure 3.6).

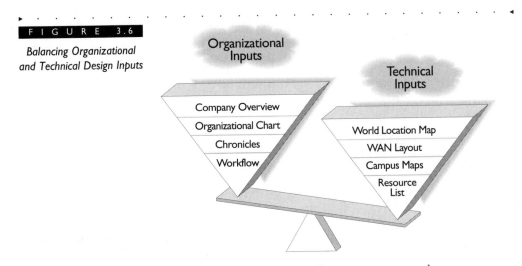

FIGURE 3.6

Balancing Organizational and Technical Design Inputs

There are four organizational design inputs. They are represented as a reverse pyramid in Figure 3.6 because information narrows as you move down the model. Here's a quick list:

▸ Company overview

▸ Organizational chart

▸ *Chronicles*

▸ Workflow

Organizational design inputs start with a company overview and snapshot of its mission statement. These items are usually detailed in the organizational chart, which also helps you identify the players and their relationships to each other. The *Chronicles* is a detailed study of each division and its key players. A careful study of the in-depth *Chronicles* will help you to create a workflow diagram. The workflow document and its accompanying diagram describe the daily operations of the company and each key player's task-oriented responsibilities. It also describes the daily or weekly movement of data from one location to another. Along with the organizational chart, the workflow document is probably the most important organizational design input.

There are also four technical design inputs. These inputs concentrate more on the delivery of information than its content. Technical inputs typically are already in place and need to be redesigned to accommodate IntranetWare and NDS. Here's a quick list:

- ▶ World Location Map

- ▶ WAN Layout

- ▶ Campus Maps

- ▶ Resource Lists

Technical design inputs start with the world location map — a global view of the company's geography. From a connectivity point of view, the world location map quickly becomes a WAN layout. The WAN layout is one of the most important technical design inputs because it summarizes the movement of data between company locations. Next, you should zero in on each location and create detailed campus maps. Each campus map identifies the distribution of buildings, LANs, routers, and existing WAN backbones. Finally, the resource list, which is the most nerdy technical design input, breaks out each campus into its physical network resources — users, file servers, print servers, print queues, and printers.

Each of these organizational and technical design inputs will play a key role in saving the world. As you'll learn in following chapters, technical design inputs help define the upper layers of the NDS tree. They also play an important role in NDS naming, partitioning, replica distribution, and time synchronization. Finally, in Chapter 8 ("Managing NDS"), we'll use the resource list to create a plethora of

NDS objects and place them in the new ACME tree. It's important to note that object placement plays a key role in resource accessibility and WAN productivity.

The organizational design inputs, on the other hand, define the bottom layers of the NDS tree. With them, we can add flexibility and purpose to the WAN infrastructure. Organizational inputs play an important role in security, configuration, management, and application design. They also help us refine our NDS objects and ensure their productive placement in the tree.

We have a lot to look forward to in the next 12 chapters. But before we can go anywhere, we need to explore ACME in depth and develop our eight critical design inputs. It's a good thing we have our project team to help. On the count of three, let them loose. 1, 2, ...

GETTING TO KNOW ACME

In the social hierarchy of needs, the world is pretty screwed up. The Pyramid of Needs states that basic fundamental needs (such as food and shelter) preclude us from enjoying higher needs (such as art, education, and corn dogs). This pyramid exists at many different levels throughout the world. Almost two-thirds of our population doesn't have sufficient resources to satisfy the lowest basic needs — medicine, food, shelter, and peace — while a smaller percentage takes higher needs — like digital watches — for granted. Something needs to change.

As a matter of fact, the Alpha Centurions have discovered this and have decided to do something about it. As it turns out, they are great fans of the Planet Earth and would hate to see us destroy it. The good news is they are a benevolent and intelligent race. They understand the Pyramid of Needs and recognize that everyone should be able to enjoy digital watches. They have discovered that the top 1 percent of the Earth's population is destroying the world at an alarming pace, while the other 99 percent are just trying to survive. In an effort to save the world, they have issued an ultimatum:

Clean up your act or find another planet to exploit!

They have given us until January 1, 2000, to clean up our act — or else! It's safe to say that the fate of the human race is in your hands. To help measure our progress, the Alpha Centurions have developed a World Health Index (WHI). The WHI is a balanced calculation of seven positive and seven negative factors that determine how good or bad we're treating the Earth. They've decided that 100 is a good number to shoot for. It represents a good balance between basic and higher needs. Once the world achieves a WHI of 100, almost everyone will be able to afford a digital watch. Here's a quick list of the 14 positive and negative WHI factors:

WHI Positive	_WHI Negative_
Charity	Crime
Love	Pollution
Birth	Starvation
Education	Disease
Health	War
Laughing	Poverty
Sports	Corruption

Bottom line: The Alpha Centurions have given us a little less than three years to increase our WHI from its current level (–2) to 100. We have until January 1, 2000. If we don't clean up our act by then, they will mercifully eradicate all humans and let the animals and plants live peacefully on the Planet Earth.

ZEN

"This magnificent butterfly finds a little heap of dirt and sits still on it. But man will never on his heap of mud keep still."

Joseph Conrad

ACME has been designed as "A Cure for Mother Earth." It is staffed by the greatest heroes from our unspoiled history. These are the founding mothers and fathers of Earth's Golden Age — before instant popcorn, talking cars, and daytime television. It's clear that somewhere along the human timeline, progress went amuck. We need help from heroes before that time. In order to vortex back in history and grab the ACME management, we've used a prototype of the Oscillating Temporal Overthruster (OTO). We've hand-chosen only the brightest and most resourceful characters, then meticulously trained each one of them for special tasks. They're a little disoriented, but more than happy to help.

These historical heroes have been placed in an innovative organizational structure. As you can see in Figure 3.7, ACME is organized around five main divisions. They are:

▸ *Human Rights* (Gandhi) — Taking care of the world's basic needs, including medicine, food, shelter, and peace. These tasks are handled jointly by Albert Schweitzer, Mother Teresa, Florence Nightingale, and Buddha. This division's work has the most positive impact on the WHI.

▸ *Labs* (Albert Einstein) — Putting technology to good use. This division is the technical marvel of ACME. In addition to research and development (R&D) efforts, the Labs division is responsible for the WHI tracking center in NORAD. This division is staffed by the wizardry of Leonardo da Vinci, Sir Isaac Newton, Charles Darwin, Marie Curie, Charles Babbage, and Ada, "The Countess of Lovelace."

▸ *Operations* (King Arthur) — Saving the world can be a logistical nightmare. Fortunately, we have King Arthur and the Knights of the Round Table to help us out. In this division, ACME routes money from caring contributors (Charity) to those who need it most (Financial) — there's a little Robin Hood in there somewhere. Also, with the help of Merlin, we will distribute all the Human Rights and Labs material to the four corners of the globe.

▸ *Crime Fighting* (Sherlock Holmes and Dr. Watson) — Making the world a safer place. This division tackles the almost insurmountable task of eradicating world crime. It's a good thing we have the help of Sherlock Holmes and some of our greatest crime-fighting superheroes, including Robin Hood, Maid Marion, Wyatt Earp, and Wild Bill Hickok. These heroes deal with the single most negative factor in WHI calculations — crime. This is very important work.

▸ *Admin* (George Washington) — Keeping the rest of ACME running smoothly. It's just like a well-oiled machine with the help of America's Founding Fathers — George Washington, Thomas Jefferson, Abraham Lincoln, FDR, and James Madison. Their main job is public relations under the command of one of our greatest orators, Franklin Delano Roosevelt (FDR). In addition to getting the word out, Admin tracks ACME activity (auditing) and keeps the facilities operating at their best.

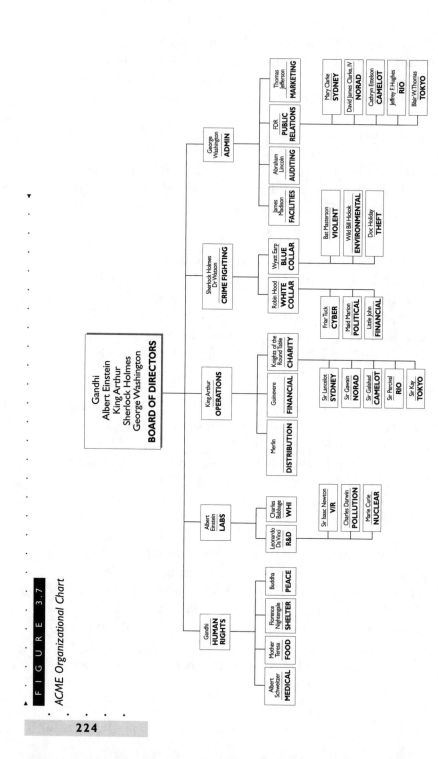

FIGURE 3.7

ACME Organizational Chart

224

SMART LINK

If you want to meet all the great ACME heroes in cyberperson, surf the Web to http://www.cyberstateu.com/clarke/acme.htm.

Now it's your turn. You are the final piece in our globe-trotting puzzle. You are ACME's MIS department. We have recruited you as the architect of our communications strategy. As an IntranetWare CNE, you come highly recommended. Your mission — should you choose to accept it — is to build the ACME WAN. You will need courage, design experience, NDS know-how, and this book. If you succeed, you will save the world and become a CNE! All in a day's work.

ACME has a daunting task ahead of it, so we don't have any time to mess around. I'd like to begin by thanking you for choosing to accept this mission. Now you'll find some design inputs included with this book. They are *for your eyes only*. Once you have read the inputs, eat them! There's other good news — you don't have to save the world alone. The project team is here to help you. Following is a list of our eight ACME design inputs and the respective roles of each project team member. Remember, we're counting on you. Be careful not to let these facts fall into the wrong hands. Believe it or not, there are forces at work that don't share our love for the human race.

ACME Overview

▶ IS Manager — Provide an in-depth tour of the ACME facilities.

▶ All project team members — Absorb ACME's mission and integrate it into everything they do.

ACME Organizational Chart

▶ IS Manager — Identify upper management.

▶ Education/Training Coordinator — Determine which groups need training and who to contact for scheduling.

▶ NDS Expert — Identify major divisions and potential ACME workgroups.

ACME Chronicles

▸ IS Manager — Identify ACME management tasks and the relationships between employees.

▸ Education/Training Coordinator — Identify individuals for managerial and technology training. Determine who will be the most affected by updated technology.

▸ All project team members — Grasp the daily routine of ACME and identify communications paths.

ACME Workflow

▸ IS Manager — Learn how ACME's workflow affects the big picture. Determine better communication paths.

▸ Testing Lab Coordinator — Identify what applications are being used and test them with IntranetWare and NDS.

▸ Education/Training Coordinator — Discover how ACME can make the most of updated networking technology to better facilitate workflow.

▸ NDS Expert — Learn how information flows throughout the company. Isolate data flow to help design the bottom layers of the NDS tree. Finally, associate workflow tasks with new NDS objects.

▸ Application Specialist — Identify what new and existing applications are needed to facilitate work and data flow.

▸ Connectivity Specialist — Follow the flow of data over the existing network communications path. Determine whether to include remote sites in the Directory tree.

ACME World Location Map

▸ Server Specialist — Determine how many servers are at each location. Track which version of NetWare each of the servers is running, and then document these servers in a Global Location Map to help the NDS Expert build the top levels of the tree.

▸ NDS Expert — Use server information to plan the upper layers of the NDS tree. Begin to sketch partitioning and replication strategies. Finally, decide whether regional containers are necessary.

▸ Connectivity Specialist — Determine how information is flowing throughout the main ACME locations.

ACME WAN Layout

▸ Testing Lab Coordinator — Determine a method of simulating typical bandwidth scenarios over existing ACME WAN links.

▸ Server Specialist — Identify key servers performing routing functions in the ACME WAN topology.

▸ Connectivity Specialist — Identify the fastest and slowest WAN links. Determine a need for remote dial-in.

▸ NDS Expert — Count the WAN sites and measure throughput across all WAN links. This will help define the upper layers of the NDS tree. It also impacts replication and time synchronization.

ACME Campus Maps

▸ Testing Lab Coordinator — Learn to simulate typical LAN traffic.

▸ Server Specialist — Determine how many servers are in each LAN segment. Identify requirements for special services such as NetWare for Macintosh and supplemental protocols.

▶ NDS Expert — Determine the major resources in each LAN. Discover how they are grouped, and build appropriate NDS objects.

▶ Application Specialist — Learn where applications are stored and how they are used. Discover more efficient alternatives.

▶ Connectivity Specialist — Learn how data is routed within LAN segments. Discover more efficient alternatives.

ACME Resource List

▶ IS Manager — Identify the resources that will require special management. Budget for upgrading existing hardware and buying new equipment.

▶ Testing Lab Coordinator — Obtain samples of all physical resources and test them under the stresses of IntranetWare and NDS.

▶ Education/Training Coordinator — Determine the need for specialized training for particular workstations and/or printers.

▶ Server Specialist — Track NetWare 3 and IntranetWare servers in each location. Determine the diversity of clients and special networking products (such as SAA, NFS, Macintosh, and TCP/IP). Plan for expansion.

▶ Workstation Specialist — Identify the status of existing clients and determine how many workstations need to be upgraded.

▶ NDS Expert — Convert existing and new resources to the new NDS naming standard, then use this list to create and place NDS objects in the tree.

▶ Application Specialist — Determine how many software licenses need to be supported for each platform. Explore the prospect of upgrading user applications.

▶ Connectivity Specialist — Identify existing protocols and plan for the addition of new ones. Propose a strategy for connecting these physical resources in local- and wide-area environments.

There you have it. The eight ACME design inputs and all of your helpers. There's a lot more to this design stuff than meets the eye. Now let's take a closer look at the remaining six ACME inputs and begin sketching out a strategy for saving the world. Sounds like fun!

QUIZ

One last time, let's test your ability to "see what isn't there." The man from the country at the top of the Himalayas came by plane to meet the man from the Far East who was wearing a chain around his neck. What was the weather when they met the man from the Middle East?

(Q3-3)

ACME CHRONICLES
A day in the life . . .

What you're about to read is for your eyes only. This is extremely confidential information. The ACME *Chronicles* is a detailed look at the life and times of ACME. This is an exceptional organization created for a singular purpose — to save the world. As you can see in Figure 3.7, ACME is organized around five main divisions:

- ▸ Human Rights

- ▸ Labs

- ▸ Operations

- ▸ Crime Fighting

- ▸ Admin

Let's go inside and see what makes them tick.

Human Rights — Gandhi in Sydney
This is the "heart" of ACME's purpose. Human Rights has the most profound positive effect on the WHI. Efforts here can save lives and increase our chances of surviving into the next century. The goal of Human Rights is to raise people from

the bottom of the Pyramid of Needs. By satisfying their basic needs (medicine, food, shelter, and peace), we hope to give humans the strength to fight for higher needs (equality, justice, education, and digital watches). This makes the world a better place and dramatically improves the WHI.

All Human Rights materials developed here are distributed every day through ten different distribution centers around the world. This is ACME's manufacturing facility for food, shelter, and medical aid. In addition, the peacekeepers use any means necessary to thwart global wars. Let's take a closer look at the four different departments of Human Rights.

- *Medical* (Albert Schweitzer) — This department is collecting basic medical materials and training doctors and nurses for field work. Also, ACME is eagerly developing vaccines and working overtime to cure serious diseases. Finally, the medical staff is taking steps to clean up the sanitation of "dirty" countries. This is all accomplished with the help of Albert Schweitzer and his dedicated staff.

- *Food* (Mother Teresa) — With the help of her country-trained culinary heroes, Mother Teresa will determine how much Opossum Stew the whole world can eat. In addition, they are developing a series of genetically engineered organisms that will transform inedible materials into food stock. Finally, ACME's Food department has teamed up with R&D to create virtual reality (V/R) programming that teaches people how to grow food of their own. After all, if you give a person a fish, they eat for a day; but if you teach them to fish, they eat for a lifetime (and get a guest spot on ESPN's *Outdoor World*).

- *Shelter* (Florence Nightingale) — With all the new healthier and happier people in the world, our attention shifts to shelter. Fortunately, Florence Nightingale and her crack construction team have developed a cheap recyclable, geodesic dome called a Permaculture. It has central heating, air conditioning, water, plumbing, and computer-controlled maid service. The most amazing thing about the dome is that it can be constructed from any native materials — that's cacti and sand in the desert, lily pads in the marsh, and snow in the Arctic. If all else fails, they're edible.

▶ *Peace* (Buddha) — One of the most overlooked basic needs is peace. All the other stuff doesn't mean a hill of beans if you're living in a war zone. Buddha's job is to somehow settle the 101 wars currently plaguing our Earth. He relies on a combination of wisdom, diplomacy, military presence, and fortune cookies.

That completes our discussion of Human Rights. Now let's take a look at the ACME Labs division.

Labs — Albert Einstein in **NORAD**

Albert Einstein is one of the greatest minds in our history, but how far can he push technology? The U.S. Military has loaned us the NORAD facility in Colorado as a base for technical wizardry. In addition to Research & Development (R&D), this is the central point of a vast WHI data-collection network.

ACME's R&D efforts are controlled by Leonardo da Vinci and his dream team of scientists. They use technology and a little bit of magic to save the Earth. Current projects include alternative power sources, V/R programming, anti-pollutants, NDS, and a cure for bad hair days. Let's take a closer look:

▶ *V/R* (Sir Isaac Newton) — V/R programming is being developed to convince the world that a cure is necessary. The V/R devices will be sold as video games and will help ACME tap the minds of the world. This borders on mind control, but in a good way (if that's possible). There's nothing that brain power and a little bit of magic can't cure.

▶ *Pollution* (Charles Darwin) — This department is developing anti-pollutants and methods of transforming garbage into fuel. Also, this group is working to eradicate the world's largest scourge — ElectroPollution. Currently Leonardo da Vinci and Charles Darwin are working on airplanes powered by pencil erasure grit.

▶ *Nuclear* (Marie Curie) — Cybernetic soldiers (Nuclear Disarmament Squads or NDS) are being designed to infiltrate and neutralize nuclear weapons facilities. Finally, somebody's splitting atoms for good.

In addition to R&D, NORAD is the central point of a vast WHI data-collection network. This network is the pulse of ACME. Collection of world data and calculation of the WHI occur here every day. Currently, the WHI sits at –2. And, as we all know, it must climb to more than 100 by January 1, 2000. Charles Babbage and Ada diligently guard the computers and make daily adjustments to WHI calculations. Ada's sacrifice is particularly notable because she used to be the "Countess of Lovelace." But fortunately for us, she has a soft spot in her heart for mathematics and Mr. Babbage.

Distributed world data-collection centers are scattered to all four corners of the Earth. There are ten ACME WHI hubs — one in every divisional headquarters — and five more scattered to strategic points around the Earth. From each of these sites, world data is sent to NORAD and calculated on a daily basis. The results are distributed to every major newspaper so the world can chart ACME's progress. In addition to the ten WHI hubs, there are hundreds of collection clusters distributed around each hub. Each cluster sends data directly to the closest hub (via dial-up lines) and eventually back to the central site at NORAD.

ZEN

Techno-hip — comfortable with the use of the modern jargon of computers and other recent technological developments. Just think — all you have to do is memorize all the CNE nomenclature in this book and you will be a "techno-hipster." An unexpected side effect of becoming a CNE.

That completes our journey through ACME technology. Now let's take a look at the Operations division.

Operations — King Arthur in Camelot

King Arthur and his court will keep ACME financed through charity drives and financial spending. After all, "money makes the world go 'round." Never before has it been more true. In addition, the Operations division handles the arduous task of distributing ACME aid to all the people who need it. Here's how it works:

▶ *Distribution* (Merlin) — We're going to need all the magic we can get. This department handles the distribution of human rights materials, medical supplies, doctors, nurses, food, hardware, building supplies, and pre-fabricated geodesic domes. No guns! It also handles implementation of WHI devices from R&D, such as anti-pollutants, Nuclear Disarmament Squads (NDS), anti-hacking viruses, and V/R programming. The latter is handled through satellite TV transmissions and video games. ACME distribution takes place through the same ten hubs as WHI. Think of it as data in (WHI) and aid out (Distribution).

- *Financial* (Guinevere) — This is the money-out department. Guinevere handles the distribution of charity contributions, including the purchase of human rights material, bailing-out of bankrupt nations, and the funding of internal ACME activities. For a more detailed discussion of Financial operations, refer to the ACME Workflow section later in this chapter.

- *Charity* (Knights of the Round Table) — This is the money-in department. The Knights collect charity from world organizations and distribute it to the Financial department for disbursement. Each of the five major Knights oversees one of five charity centers — in each of the divisional headquarters. Sir Lancelot is in Sydney, Sir Gawain is in NORAD, Sir Galahad handles Camelot, Sir Percival oversees Rio, and Sir Kay is in Tokyo. I haven't seen such dedication since the medieval ages.

Well, that's how ACME's Operations work. Now let's take a look at Crime Fighting.

Crime Fighting — Sherlock Holmes in Tokyo

Crime has one of the most negative effects on the WHI. Fortunately, we have history's greatest crime-fighting mind to help us out — Sherlock Holmes. With the help of Dr. Watson, he has identified two major categories of world crime:

- White Collar

- Blue Collar

White-collar crimes include cyberhacking and political espionage. Robin Hood and his Band of Superheroes direct white-collar crime-fighting efforts from Tokyo. Here are some of the different types of crimes they're concerned with:

- *Cyber* (Friar Tuck) — With the help of the Cyberphilia underground, Friar Tuck attempts to thwart cyber crime. Most cyber crimes occur on The Net, so ACME must constantly monitor global communications. Tuck also has the help of an off-shoot group of guardian angels known as the Cyber Angels.

▸ *Political* (Maid Marion) — She can charm her way through any politically tense situation. Political crimes are especially rampant in emerging nations, so Maid Marion enlists the help of the United Nations.

▸ *Financial* (Little John) — With some creative financing and the help of ex-IRS agents, Little John thwarts financial crimes throughout the world. These crimes especially hurt the middle class, so he has recruited some key Yuppies as undercover agents.

Blue-collar crimes are a little more obvious — such as violence and theft. This is familiar ground for Wyatt Earp and his band of western heroes. They're not glamorous, but they're effective. Here's a look at ACME Crime Fighting from the blue-collar point of view:

▸ *Violent* (Bat Masterson) — This cowboy is in his element. He thwarts violent crime by getting inside the criminal's mind — literally.

▸ *Environmental* (Wild Bill Hickok) — A great fan of the environment, Mr. Hickok uses his country charm to thwart environmental crimes such as excessive deforestation, toxic waste, whaling, oil spills, ElectroPollution, and forced extinction.

▸ *Theft* (Doc Holliday) — With his legendary sleight of hand, Doc Holliday stays one step ahead of the world's thieves.

So, that's what's happening on the crime fighting front. Now let's take a close look at the final ACME division — Admin.

Admin — George Washington in Rio

Ever since the beginning of time, humans have quested for wisdom and knowledge. Now we'll need to put all of our enlightenment to good use — or else. A few centuries ago, the United States' Founding Fathers joined a growing group of men and women called Illuminoids. These people were dissatisfied with everyday life on Planet Earth and began to reach above, within, and everywhere else for a better way. The Illuminoids formed a variety of organizations dedicated to creating a New World Order including the Masons, the Trilateral Commission, the Council on Foreign Relations (CFR), and the Bilderberg Group.

Regardless of their ultimate motivation, the Illuminoids' hearts were in the right place — "let's make the world a better place." The founder of the Trilateral Commission has always claimed they are just *a group of concerned citizens interested in fostering greater understanding and cooperation among international allies.* Whether or not it's true, it sounds like a great fit for ACME. Once again, we've used the OTO to grab some of the earliest Illuminoids and solicit their help for ACME administration.

George Washington keeps the ACME ship afloat. Along with FDR, he keeps things running smoothly and makes sure the world hears about our plight. In addition, James Madison keeps the facilities running, while Abraham Lincoln makes sure ACME is held accountable for all its work. For years, the Trilateral Commission has been rumored to covertly run the world. Now they get a chance to overtly save it!

Now let's take a look at the four departments that make up ACME's administration:

- *Public Relations* (Franklin Delano Roosevelt) — This department solicits help from the rest of the world by enlisting the help of heroes from our own age — the 1990s. We're not going to be able to save the world alone. The PR department is responsible for communicating our plight to the four corners of the Earth. Department members inform everyday citizens about the Alpha Centurion ultimatum, daily WHI quotes, and requests for charity. There is a local PR office in each major location. See the organizational chart earlier in Figure 3.7 for more details.

- *Marketing* (Thomas Jefferson) — Educating the rest of the world and soliciting help is another Marketing department responsibility. In addition to advertising, this department develops materials for distributed PR offices. Its goal is to rally all nations around ACME and our cause in order to save the Earth. They also bake really good apple pies and chocolate chip cookies.

- *Auditing* (Abraham Lincoln) — They make sure that everyone stays in line. Financial trails for all charity moneys and complete records of all changes to the WHI are tracked by the Auditing department. Although it's part of the internal ACME organization, Auditing is an independent tracking company that generates bonded reports.

▸ *Facilities* (James Madison) — This department keeps everyone working, happy, and fed. The Facilities department also organizes field trips and ACME parties. Imagine the doozy they're going to have when we finally succeed!

Well, there you have it. That's everything there is to know about ACME. I hope these Chronicles have helped you and the project team to better understand what ACME is up against. This is no normal organization. If ACME goes out of business, the world is either lost or saved — it's up to you.

ACME WORKFLOW

Although it may look complicated, the daily grind at ACME is really pretty simple. It's a combination of workflow and dataflow. *Workflow* describes the daily operations of ACME staff and their task-oriented responsibilites. *Dataflow* describes the daily or weekly movement of data from one location to another. Although the two are not always the same, they should be compatible. This is the goal of ACME synergy.

In this section, we're going to take a detailed look at how work and data flow through the ACME organization. This data has a dramatic impact on NDS design. After all, work and data flow over the WAN infrastructure. Refer to Figure 3.8 as you follow along.

▸ · ◂

F I G U R E   3 . 8

ACME Workflow Diagram

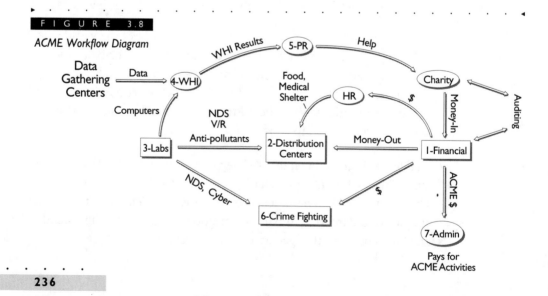

I — Financial

Of course, money makes the world go 'round! The Financial department has two main responsibilities:

- Money-in

- Money-out

Money-in focuses on funding ACME activities and distributing charities to needy people. With *Money-out*, Guinevere pays for Human Rights materials, Admin work, and Crime Fighting tools. Next, she disburses charity money through distribution centers. Money-in comes from the various Charity activities. All financial activity is audited by the internal Auditing organization.

Technically, this is accomplished from a central database at the Financial headquarters in Camelot. No money changes hands. Quarterly budgets are developed in Camelot and distributed to local banks for Human Rights, Crime Fighting, Distribution, and Admin. Each of these distributed sites sends weekly updates to the central database with the help of local servers.

2 — Distribution Centers

The Distribution department is the hub of ACME achievements. Distribution centers disburse three kinds of aid:

- Human Rights materials (such as food, medicine, and shelter)

- Money from the Financial department

- Exciting inventions from Labs

Each of the ten distribution centers maintains its own distributed database. They move material to local warehouses for delivery to needy people. Weekly summary updates are sent to the central inventory management database in Camelot. The central database oversees the big picture of aid distribution.

If a center runs out of a particular resource, one of two things happens:

1. Camelot updates the center's budget, and they purchase the resource locally.

2 •   Camelot orders the movement of resources from another distribution center. This option makes sense for finite materials such as special inventions from Labs or medical supplies.

3 — Labs and Their Inventions

This is where the brainiacs hang out. Scientists in the Labs division develop world-saving toys for:

▸ Crime Fighting — NDS and cyberviruses

▸ Distribution — V/R programming and anti-pollutants

The Labs division supports WHI and all its technical needs. New product updates are sent to Distribution and Crime Fighting for internal consumption. This is secure information.

4 — WHI Calculations

Labs is also where the WHI (World Health Index) is calculated. Charles Babbage and Ada collect data from data-gathering centers (DGCs) throughout the world. These DGCs are housed in divisional headquarters and distribution centers throughout the ACME WAN. They are

NORAD	Seattle
Rio	Cairo
Camelot	New York
Sydney	Moscow
Tokyo	St. Andrews

Ironically, the distribution centers send aid *out* and the DGCs pull data *in* — from the same ten locations. Daily WHI summary calculations are sent to NORAD each day so the final WHI calculation can be made. Results are distributed to PR daily for inclusion in global periodicals — including the ACME *Chronicles* (an hourly interactive newsletter).

5 — Public Relations

This is the voice of ACME. In addition to distributing daily WHI reports, Public Relations (PR) educates the world and helps solicit money for Charity. PR pulls the daily WHI results from NORAD twice a day. They're also the on-line editors of the ACME *Chronicles,* which gives them some great financial leads for Charity.

Charity — Money-In

Charity is ACME's open door. It is the funnel for ACME contributions. There is a charity center in each of the five divisional headquarters. This is how the top 1 percent helps the rest of us. Their motto is:

Spread the Wealth, or the Alpha Centurions will eat you!

All money collected by Charity is sent to the Financial department for disbursement. Two of the most important uses for this money are Crime Fighting and Admin. Note that the money doesn't actually change hands. It is deposited in local divisional banks, and daily updates are sent to the central financial database in Camelot.

6 — Crime Fighting

Remember, crime has one of the greatest negative effects on the WHI. The Crime Fighting department relies on the following sources:

- Labs' inventions (NDS and cyberviruses)

- Money from the Financial department

- The guile of Robin Hood, Wyatt Earp, and their respective heroes

7 — ACME Administration

The ACME staff has to eat. Admin relies on money from Financial to keep things running smoothly. You can't fight bureaucracy. In addition, the Auditing department needs audit-level access to the central financial database in Camelot. They are responsible for tracking money-in from Charity and money-out from Financial.

ZEN

Chaos theory — the systematic approach to describing very complex events in mathematics and science by rounding off numerical data to reveal very general patterns. This theory can be used to describe the irregular patterns of a dripping water faucet, fluctuations in insect populations, stock-market price changes, or the daily grind of a CNE. In all cases, chaos theory relies on the strange attractor, which is a complex and unpredictable pattern of movement — much like a user's interface with IntranetWare workstations or your understanding of ACME.

That's all there is to it. No sweat. As you can see, ACME runs like a well-oiled machine. Someone sure put a lot of effort into designing its organizational structure — and it shows! We're in good hands with ACME.

Now let's shift gears from organizational inputs to technical design inputs. These include:

- ► ACME World Location Map

- ► ACME WAN Layout

- ► ACME Campus Maps

- ► ACME Resource List

Remember, you need to create a design synergy that properly balances organizational and technical design inputs. Think *balance!*

ACME WAN MAPS

The world is a pretty big place. It takes a truly global organization to save it. ACME is this organization. Now we shift our focus from organizational design inputs to more technical data. These four inputs play an important role in designing the upper layers of the NDS tree. In addition, they affect NDS naming, partitioning, replica distribution, time synchronization, and object placement. In this section, we'll explore the first three technical design inputs:

- ► ACME World Location Map

- ► ACME WAN Layout

- ► ACME Campus Maps

ACME World Location Map

ACME's global structure is shown in Figure 3.9. This structure includes the five main divisional headquarters and five more distribution/WHI data-collection centers. The ACME organization has been distributed to all four corners of the globe to ensure cultural diversity. Five different continents are represented as well as most of the world's major countries. This is truly an organization for the world.

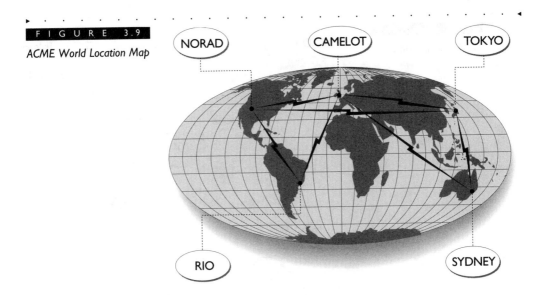

FIGURE 3.9

ACME World Location Map

ACME WAN Layout

As you can see in Figure 3.10, ACME organizes its five main hubs in a ring/star redundant design. This structure provides multiple redundant paths from each location. Even if the center of the star (Camelot) goes down, all other sites remain connected. This is accomplished with the help of sophisticated WAN hubs and high-bandwidth lines.

Note the bandwidth measurements on each WAN link. These values are important to the NDS Expert when attempting to design the upper layers of the tree. It also affects replica placement and the distribution of time providers. Refer to Chapter 4 ("NDS Design") for a more detailed discussion.

In addition to the ACME organizational chart, WAN layout is probably one of the most important design inputs. The WAN layout represents how ACME shares network resources. Your NDS tree should model it very closely.

ACME Campus Maps

The ACME campus maps allow you to zero in on specific details about primary WAN hubs. You'll need to better understand ACME's local area networks in order to refine the NDS tree. The campus maps show server distribution, router placement, remote access points, and the backbone topology. Each location within the hub provides more insight into how ACME uses its existing network resources. These campus maps can be further enhanced by adding newer technology.

FIGURE 3.10

ACME WAN Layout

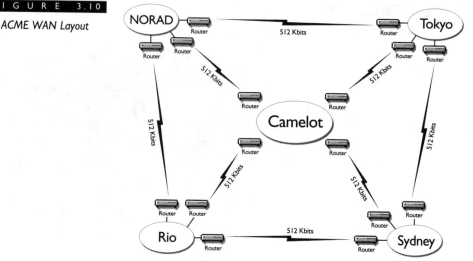

In this case, we've identified three important campuses:

▸ Tokyo — headquarters for the Crime Fighting division (see Figure 3.11)

▸ Camelot — headquarters for ACME Operations (see Figure 3.12)

▸ NORAD — headquarters for ACME Labs and technical wizardry (see Figure 3.13)

Study these campus maps very closely because they represent a graphical organization of ACME's network resources. This should help you better understand the final technical design input — ACME's resource list.

ACME RESOURCE LIST

Resources are the life-blood of your network. Let's be honest. A network is simply a bunch of resources connected together. Although this oversimplifies your work at ACME, it is a fair summary of your purpose. As a CNE, you are chartered with the role of connecting ACME's resources — both old and new.

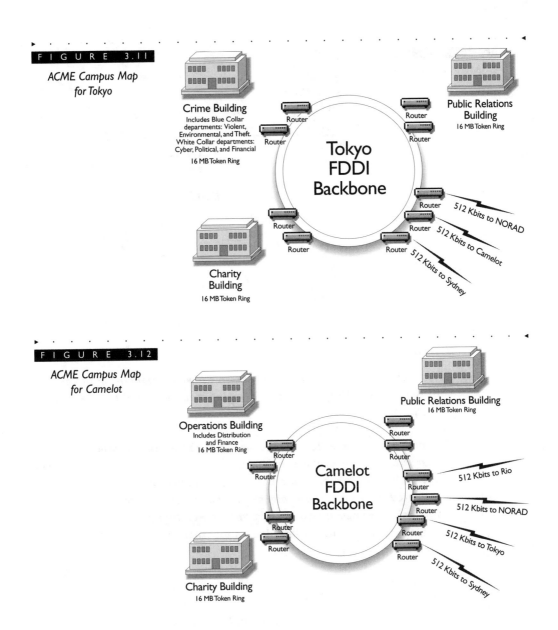

FIGURE 3.11

ACME Campus Map for Tokyo

FIGURE 3.12

ACME Campus Map for Camelot

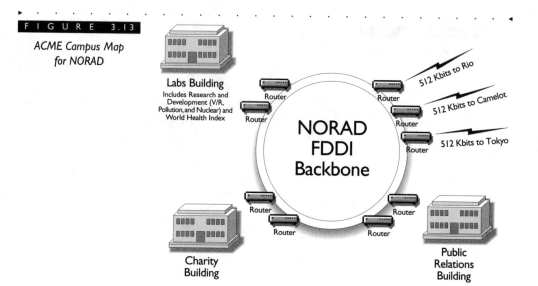

FIGURE 3.13

ACME Campus Map
for NORAD

Labs Building

Includes Research and
Development (V/R,
Pollution, and Nuclear) and
World Health Index

NORAD
FDDI
Backbone

512 Kbits to Rio

512 Kbits to Camelot

512 Kbits to Tokyo

Router

Charity
Building

Public
Relations
Building

QUIZ

The value of certain NDS resources isn't always apparent until you look at them very closely. Study the following statement and tell me what it spells:

"Three straight lines joined together so that they are rotated symmetric; four straight lines of three different lengths joined together so that they are vertically symmetric and then repeated later on; a semi-circle repeated later on; three straight lines joined together so that they are vertically symmetric; two straight lines joined together to form a right-angle; and three straight lines joined together so that they are laterally symmetric."

(Q3-4)

Before you connect the resources, you must bring them all up to the same level. This involves upgrading NetWare 3 servers to IntranetWare, installing the NetWare DOS Requester client software, testing and upgrading network applications, and improving printer hardware. In addition to upgrading, you'll need to buy some new equipment.

The upgrade process should be reflected in your resource lists. The first list you'll get is existing equipment. Once you've analyzed it, you should create a resource wish list. This list includes all the equipment (old and new) that you'll need to accomplish your goal. The wish list can become your road map. It identifies all the areas where you'll need to upgrade or purchase new equipment. Of course, you'll need help from the IS Manager and Guinevere to make this happen.

When you're creating ACME's wish list, focus on these key resources:

- Administrators

- File servers

- Print servers

- Print queues

- Printers

A naming standard is critical to resource organization. Typically, existing naming standards are haphazard at best. Few organizations use naming standards at all. You'll find even less continuity when you attempt to connect dissimilar LANs from geographically separated organizations. In Chapter 4, we'll create a naming standards document and reorganize our resource list. But for now, let's take a look at the resources you'll need in each ACME division.

Human Rights Division

In the Human Rights division, there's one main user (Gandhi) and three department heads. The main division has two file servers, a global print server, and one HP4SI printer. The Medical department is run by Albert Schweitzer. He also has two file servers and one HP4SI printer. Next, the Food department relies on Mother Teresa and her network resources: one file server and one HP4SI printer. The Shelter department has Florence Nightingale at the helm and uses two file servers and an HP4SI printer. Finally, the Peace department is managed by Buddha, who has one file server and an HPIII printer.

Labs Division

The Labs division is under the quality tutelage of Albert Einstein. He relies on one main division-oriented file server. In the R&D department, Leonardo da Vinci shares one file server with his three departments. The main print server is also located in the R&D building. Charles Darwin (Pollution), Sir Isaac Newton (V/R), and Marie Curie (Nuclear) each have their own HP4SI printers.

The WHI department is run by Charles Babbage and Ada. They need three file servers for index calculations and data storage. They also rely on a print server for output to their Canon BubbleJet printer.

Operations Division

King Arthur runs the Operations division with one file server and a lot of guile. He uses a single print server to service his Canon BubbleJet printer. The Financial department, however, is a lot more technically demanding. Guinevere needs three file servers, two print servers, and two HP4SI printers. In addition, Merlin runs the Distribution department with the help of two file servers, a print server, and an HP III LaserJet printer.

Network resources for the Charity department are much more difficult to track because they're spread across the five global hubs. Each charity center is different, depending on the needs of its network administrator. Here's a quick breakdown:

▸ *NORAD* — Sir Gawain uses one file server, a print server, and one HP4SI printer.

▸ *Rio* — Sir Percival also uses one file server, one print server, and an HP4SI printer.

▸ *Camelot* — Sir Galahad relies on one file server, a print server, and a new HP5 LaserJet printer.

▸ *Sydney* — Sir Lancelot needs one file server, a print server, and one HP4SI printer.

▸ *Tokyo* — Sir Kay is a little busier than the other locations. He needs two file servers, a print server, and an HP4SI LaserJet printer.

ZEN

Flexiplace—a place at home set aside for working that is connected by computer to an office, thereby enabling the worker to avoid commuting to an office. Also called an "electronic cottage," which allows for telecommuting. This is the preferable way of dealing with troubled IntranetWare users and ACME Operations.

Crime Fighting Division

Sherlock Holmes and Dr. Watson rely on the latest technology to help their crime-fighting efforts. They use two file servers, a print server, and an HP5 LaserJet printer. Each of their Crime Fighting departments follows suit and takes advantage of new technology.

The Blue-Collar department is run by Wyatt Earp. He needs one file server, a print server, and a single HP III LaserJet printer. In addition, each of his crime-fighting units needs its own file server and HP4SI printer. As a matter of fact, Bat Masterson needs two file servers for the Violent Crimes Unit.

Robin Hood runs the White-Collar Crime Fighting department. His criminals are a little more sophisticated. Therefore, he needs two file servers, a print server, and a Canon BubbleJet printer. In addition, each of his crime-fighting units requires its own file server and LaserJet printer. Friar Tuck uses an HP LaserJet III, Maid Marion has an HP4SI, and Little John needs two HP4SI printers to fight financial crime.

Admin Division

George Washington heads up the Admin division. He uses two file servers, a print server, and a Canon BubbleJet printer. Each of his department heads uses a similar configuration. James Madison of Facilities uses one file server, a print server, and an HP4SI printer. Abraham Lincoln has a file server and an HP4SI printer for the Auditing department, and Thomas Jefferson uses a file server and two HP III LaserJet printers.

Network resource tracking for the PR department is a bit trickier because the department is spread across all five ACME locations. Here's a quick breakdown:

▶ *NORAD* — David James Clarke, IV, uses one file server, a print server, and two printers: an HP4SI and a Canon BubbleJet.

▶ *Rio* — Jeff Hughes uses one file server and two printers: an HP4SI and a Canon BubbleJet.

▶ *Camelot* — Cathy Ettelson doesn't print as much as do David and Jeff. She uses a file server, a print server, and one HP4SI printer.

▶ *Sydney* — Mary Clarke requires the same configuration as Cathy, that is, a single file server, a print server, and an HP4SI printer.

▶ *Tokyo* — Blair Thomas follows suit with a single file server, a print server, and an HP4SI printer.

In addition to these resources, ACME has a special NDS file server in each of its five main locations: NORAD, Tokyo, Sydney, Rio, and Camelot.

That completes our detailed discussion of the ACME resource wish list. For a complete summary, refer to Table 3.2. In Chapter 4 ("NDS Design"), we'll develop a naming standards document and rename these resources. Then in Chapter 8 ("Managing NDS"), we'll learn all about object placement and create associated NDS objects.

This completes our discussion of gathering NDS information. In this section, we put ACME under the NDS microscope. This is a critical part of Step 1. All the information you've gathered here will act as raw material for ACME design, installation, and management. It's impossible to create a WAN for ACME until you get inside its collective heads and see what makes them tick. Remember, this is highly confidential information, so please make sure it doesn't fall into the wrong hands. Once you've memorized the facts that appear here, you must eat the pages!

I'm ready for NDS design now — how about you? But before we can move on to Step 2, we'll need to explore the final aspect of NDS preparation — the project scope.

	DIVISION	DEPARTMENT	RESOURCES
TABLE 3.2 *The ACME Resource* *Wish List*	Human Rights	Headquarters	Gandhi Two file servers One print server One HP4SI printer
		Medical	Albert Schweitzer Two file servers One HP4SI printer
		Food	Mother Teresa One file server One HP4SI printer
		Shelter	Florence Nightingale Two file servers One HP4SI printer
		Peace	Buddha One file server One HPIII printer
	Labs	Headquarters	Albert Einstein One file server
		R&D	Leonardo Da Vinci Charles Darwin Sir Isaac Newton Marie Curie One file server One print server Three HP4SI printers
		WHI	Charles Babbage Ada Three file servers One print server One Canon BubbleJet printer
	Operations	Headquarters	King Arthur One file server One print server One Canon BubbleJet printer
		Distribution	Merlin Two file servers One print server One HPIII LaserJet printer

(continued)

TABLE 3.2	DIVISION	DEPARTMENT	RESOURCES
The ACME Resource Wish List (continued)	Operations (continued)	Financial	Guinevere Three file servers Two print servers Two HP4SI printers
		Charity	Sir Percival Sir Lancelot Sir Gawain Sir Galahad Sir Kay Six file servers Five print servers Three HP4SI printers Two HP5 printers
	Crime Fighting	Headquarters	Sherlock Holmes Dr. Watson Two file servers One print server One HP5 printer
		Blue Collar	Wyatt Earp Bat Masterson Wild Bill Hickok Doc Holliday Five file servers One print server Three HP4SI printers One HPIII LaserJet printer
		White Collar	Robin Hood Friar Tuck Maid Marion Little John Five file servers One print server Three HP4SI printers One HPIII LaserJet printer One Canon BubbleJet printer
	Admin	Headquarters	George Washington Franklin Delano Roosevelt Two file servers One print server One Canon BubbleJet printer

TABLE 3.2	DIVISION	DEPARTMENT	RESOURCES
The ACME Resource Wish List (continued)	Admin (continued)	Facilities	James Madison One file server One print server One HP4SI printer
		Auditing	Abraham Lincoln One file server One HP4SI printer
		Marketing	Thomas Jefferson One file server Two HPIII LaserJet printers
		Public Relations	Mary Clarke David James Clarke, IV Cathy Ettelson Jeff Hughes Blair Thomas Five file servers Five print servers Five HP4SI printers Two Canon BubbleJet printers

The Project Scope

The final task in NDS preparation is establishing the project scope. This task is critical for keeping the WAN under control. Scope provides physical boundaries for the network as well as financial and personnel limitations. After gathering the information, you must explore the system resources and determine how far they can be stretched. In many cases, the scope acts as a restraint to keep unworkable solutions from expanding too far. If the scope is too broad, the WAN will never be finished. If the scope is too narrow, the WAN will surely not meet ACME's needs.

It is critical to establish a WAN scope early in the Process. This is because it has a strong influence on costs, expectations, environment, and implementation time. ACME management is always looking for the bottom line:

How much will it cost us and how long will it take?

In our example, it's important to establish scope right away. How many locations are there? What's it going to take to improve the WHI from −2 to 100? How do my current resources match up with the resource wish list? All of these are good questions that need to be answered before you move on to NDS design. Three components help you establish a project scope. Here's how they work:

- Determine project complexity — You will need to analyze certain aspects of the project to determine whether it calls for a simple or complex network. If there are 15 or more servers, for example, you'll need to design custom partitions. If there are 30 or more servers, you'll need to use the customized time configuration method. You'll also need a test lab. Other criteria that impact a project's complexity include multiple sites connected by a WAN, and expected network growth. Further analysis of ACME tells me it's going to be a very complex project.

- Developing a schedule — You'll need to develop a process time line in order to coordinate project team activities. This time line also helps ACME management assess the WAN's impact on daily business operations. Once you've developed a schedule, make sure to reevaluate it at key points along the way.

- Implementation check points — This component fits with the implementation schedule by providing a mechanism for reevaluating progress. You'll need to use a proactive approach toward keeping the project on time.

 ZEN

"I have one last request. Don't use embalming fluid on me. I want to be stuffed with crabmeat."

Woody Allen

If that doesn't sum it up, I don't know what does. On that note, we've completed our discussion of project scope and NDS preparation in general. It has been a wild ride, and the fun has only just begun. In this chapter, we learned about the Process and its four important steps:

- Step 1: NDS Preparation

- ▸ Step 2: Design

- ▸ Step 3: Implementation

- ▸ Step 4: Management

In Step 1, we created the project team and gathered filing cabinets full of ACME information. This information will become the foundation of Steps 2, 3, and 4. And who's going to accomplish them? The project team.

As you can see, preparation is crucial. If you think like a Boy Scout, you'll be okay. Please don't try to approach a project of this magnitude without being prepared. Study the information in this chapter carefully, and when you're ready, move on to Step 2 — NDS Design.

Good luck; and by the way, thanks for saving the world!

EXERCISE 3-1: ACME — A CURE FOR MOTHER EARTH

Circle the 20 NDS Preparation terms hidden in this word search puzzle using the hints provided.

```
U  C  I  T  S  D  E  U  G  U  S  O  R  M  Y  G  D  F  X  E  W
Y  C  O  M  P  A  N  Y  O  V  E  R  V  I  E  W  D  E  T  A  N
O  O  T  W  O  R  K  S  T  A  T  I  O  N  M  B  C  C  N  C  W
X  N  O  O  B  N  I  B  N  D  C  H  R  O  N  I  C  L  E  S  T
N  N  R  R  Q  R  D  N  E  G  A  P  P  L  I  C  A  T  I  O  N
G  E  F  K  M  S  P  S  T  C  Y  B  X  N  W  Y  M  I  W  I  J
M  C  X  F  X  A  I  Q  M  I  P  X  G  L  O  N  P  D  Z  N  R
Y  T  G  L  I  G  J  E  X  A  N  X  W  U  I  K  U  S  C  E  E
V  I  U  O  N  V  F  A  N  K  N  G  T  U  W  J  S  N  P  C  G
G  V  X  W  O  R  L  D  L  O  C  A  T  I  O  N  M  A  P  S  A
E  I  V  D  P  I  L  O  T  P  R  O  G  R  A  M  A  S  P  P  N
J  T  Q  I  L  S  P  U  R  V  V  L  Y  E  A  Z  P  R  F  B  A
P  Y  L  A  R  L  H  M  G  X  D  C  H  N  R  Q  Y  C  C  C  M
F  B  L  G  J  E  O  P  E  H  S  N  A  K  S  C  K  B  I  Y  S
G  M  G  R  R  R  V  M  N  L  D  G  L  F  W  G  U  H  L  T  I
W  G  J  A  Q  O  O  R  O  B  E  U  U  G  C  V  L  C  L  D  R
P  O  Z  M  I  M  P  L  E  M  E  N  T  A  T  I  O  N  O  P  S
E  L  E  R  X  P  M  R  E  S  O  U  R  C  E  L  I  S  T  S  I
A  L  P  H  A  C  E  N  T  U  R  I  O  N  S  B  D  O  W  R  X
J  W  K  K  Z  B  T  Y  V  P  T  S  K  R  E  R  I  V  L  U  D
```

Hints:
1. Short for "A Cure for Mother Earth".
2. Aliens who have discovered the planet Earth.
3. Type of specialist who maintains network and user applications.
4. Technical input that includes a detailed map of each location.
5. Organizational design input that identifies the key players at ACME and their relationship to each other.
6. Organizational design input that provides an overview of the company and its mission statement.

7. Type of specialist who works with the physical network, Internet backbone, telecommunications, WAN design, and router placement.

8. Phase I of "The Process". Analysis occurs during this step.

9. Phase II of "The Process". Installations and /or migrations occur during this step.

10. Person who is the central contact point for the ACME Staff and Management.

11. Phase III of "The Process". Involves maintaining the LAN after it's been installed.

12. Person who truly understands the "Cloud".

13. Test installation.

14. Type of specialist who manages access to printers, determines printer location, and upgrades printing software.

15. Technical input that breaks out each campus into its physical network resources — such as users, file servers, print servers, etc.

16. Type of specialist who selects hardware and keeps it running.

17. Technical input that summarizes the movement of data between company locations.

18. Organizational design input that describes the daily operations of the ACME staff and their task-oriented responsibilities.

19. Type of specialist who is responsible for upgrading connection files on clients.

20. Technical input that provides a global view of the company's geography.

See Appendix C for answers.

Step 2: NDS Design

The most fascinating thing about roller coasters is the dramatic *ups* and *downs* — literally. Not just the exceptional vertical transitions, but the emotional highs and lows, as well. It all starts with a slow, gentle climb to the highest peak of the ride. Your stomach churns as you anticipate the mind-shattering thrill that awaits. Then, as if for centuries, you pause at the apex, contemplating certain doom.

The fall is the best part. You know you're going to survive, of course, but that doesn't seem to diminish the altitude of the experience. No matter how you slice it — it's straight down, and you love it!

The rest of the ride is great, but nothing compares to the initial thrill. It transcends the rest of the experience. Each new surprise, each hairpin turn, each gut-wrenching twirl is enhanced by the dizzying effect of the very first fall. The ups make the downs that much better.

SMART LINK

Ride your own NDS roller coaster at http://mosaic.echonyc.com/~dne/RollerCoaster!/.

Welcome to the Apex of IntranetWare. I don't know if you noticed, but the first three chapters were setups — for this very moment. The slow, gentle ascension of NDS and ACME have brought you to the brink of the greatest ride of your CNE life — NDS design.

ZEN

"The greatest thrill known to man isn't flying — it's landing!"

Anonymous

NDS design is one of the most remarkable (and misunderstood) aspects of IntranetWare. You can't really understand it until you've done it, but you can't do it until you understand it — I think this is called a paradox. Fortunately, my friends and I have done *a lot* of design all over the world (and throughout time), so we'll teach you everything you need to know. It starts with four key tree (that rhymes) components:

▶ NDS Naming Standards

▶ NDS Tree Design

▶ Partition and Replica Design

▶ Time Synchronization Design

Objects and their names are the foundation of NDS. A complete naming standard is important so that you can design an NDS database that is flexible, easy to use, and meets your business needs. Also, there's so much diversity in NDS "object-ology" that a naming standard is required for most design and management tasks.

Once you've created a naming standards document, it's time to roll up your sleeves and get to work. NDS tree design is a great place to start. At this point, you convert the design inputs into a "rough" NDS tree. The *top* layers of the tree are geographic and the *bottom* layers are organizational. In addition, the container structure should resemble a pyramid in design. It's important to note that most object placement occurs later — during the NDS management phase (see Chapter 8). NDS tree design is primarily concerned with the branches of the tree and a few key leaves, such as servers and administrators.

Next, you get to partition the new tree into small little pieces and scatter them around the world (replica placement). At this point, you don't actually perform any partitioning operations, you simply *design* the partition boundaries. Once the boundaries have been designed, you must give serious thought to where they'll go — *replica placement*. Replica placement is one of the most important aspects of NDS design because it directly affects your network's performance, accessibility, and fault tolerance. Remember, you won't actually *place* anything until later — during the Partition Management phase (see Chapter 9).

Finally, Time Synchronization Design ensures that all of our servers agree on the time. You can choose to accept the IntranetWare defaults, or institute a customized time synchronization strategy of your own. The important thing is that you consider WAN performance and synchronization traffic when you build your design. Time is of the essence.

What next? Well, that completes the four main aspects of NDS design, but it doesn't end our lesson. One related topic remains, and it almost always gets overlooked — Accessibility Design. Accessibility transcends everything you do in IntranetWare. It is the sole purpose for the WAN's existence — so users can have access to stuff! If you ignore accessibility during the NDS design phase, some users will invariably get left out in the cold. You'll need to address special NDS accessibility considerations (such as mobile users, remote users, login scripts, Bindery Services, connections, and non-DOS workstations). Believe me, it'll make your life much easier if you try to be a little more accessible to your users. Give it a try.

So much to learn, and so little time. Let's start with a closer look at the fundamentals of object naming, and explore a naming standards document for ACME. Ready, set, go.

ZEN

"What's in a name? A rose by any other name would smell as sweet!"

William Shakespeare

NDS Naming Standards

Naming is very closely tied to everything we do. It uniquely identifies us ("Hi. I'm Bob"), it describes our stuff ("I have lots of computers"), and it helps us classify the diversity of mankind ("Bob's a Nerd"). Similarly, NDS naming is fundamental to the "Cloud," because it describes the interrelationships between network resources. In addition, resource searching, a key function of the NDS database, relies on naming for objects *types* and *locations*. Good naming implies improved search capabilities now and in the future when more applications take advantage of the Directory's capabilities. You must always think to the future.

IntranetWare uses a mechanism called the *schema* to define the NDS naming structure for all network resources. The schema is distributed to all IntranetWare servers, and follows very specific rules. Unlike the NetWare 3.12 Bindery, NDS is a special-purpose naming service that stores objects in a hierarchical format and services up to 16 million objects per server. Your understanding of the schema will help you manage the internal structure of NDS naming. Also, it will help you plan for the future through supplemental object types, add-on products, or third-party applications. After all, once you understand the schema, nobody says you can't change it.

Let's start our discussion of NDS naming standards with a brief stroll through the land of the IntranetWare schema. Then, we'll take a quick-and-dirty look at NDS naming rules, distinguished names, relative distinguished names, context, typeful, and finally, typeless naming. Refer to Chapter 2 for a more comprehensive discussion of these critical naming concepts. Then, the *pièce de résistance* — ACME's NDS Naming Standard. In the final section, we'll explore naming standards in general, and build a doozy for ACME.

So, sit tight, hold onto the person next to you, and enjoy this gut-wrenching, heart-in-your-throat, spine-tingling roller coaster. Truly, an "E" ticket ride.

SMART LINK

For a more in-depth discussion of NDS and to download the latest database improvements, surf to "Novell Directory Services" at http://www.netware.com.

NDS SCHEMA

Novell Directory Services (NDS) is an object-oriented name service, and all objects and properties are defined by a set of rules called the *schema*. The schema rules dictate the relationships of all objects and their associated properties. It is automatically stored on every IntranetWare server, even if it doesn't contain NDS replicas. The schema consists of the following three major components:

▸ Object Class

▸ Property Definitions

▸ Property Syntaxes

These three components work together to establish the set of rules that control the creation of a particular object class in the Directory. In Figure 4.1, you can see the relationship between these components. For instance, each object class is defined in terms of its property definitions. The property definitions, in turn, are defined in terms of certain property syntaxes. The property syntaxes determine data types for property values.

F I G U R E   4.1

Relationship Between the
Three Components of the
NDS Schema

Object Class

Property Definitions

Property Syntaxes

TIP

Probably the coolest thing about the NDS schema is its flexibility. With special tools, you can enhance and modify the object classes and their definitions. This allows you to create a myriad of exciting new NDS objects (including Picture ID, Credit Card Number, Voice Recognition Pattern, and/or Hat Size). You can even cross-link NDS to the World Wide Web by altering certain aspects of the schema. Of course, these modifications should be performed by professionals. Whatever you do, don't try this at home. Also, be sure to account for new object types when you're building your naming standards document.

However, the IntranetWare utilities will not allow you to add or modify objects in your new class. You will need to create your own utlities that manage these new NDS objects.

The *object class* defines the types of NDS objects that can be stored in the Directory. The object class is used as the template for creating individual objects and determining their set of characteristics. This means that every object in the tree belongs to an object class that specifies what properties it can use. This is how NDS tracks the different sets of properties for each object. As you can see in Figure 4.1, object classes are constructed from property definitions.

The default IntranetWare Schema contains almost 50 object classes. We discussed 29 of them in Chapter 2. These object classes cannot be removed or deleted. Each of the object classes in the Schema is defined by its relationship to other objects. This relationship is based on the object's name type.

Every NDS object is defined by its *name type* (also referred to as its naming property) and a *value*. The value is assigned by you (the CNE) during the object's creation. As we learned previously, an object's name type determines how it is used in the tree. Some objects are containers, while others are leaf objects. Table 4.1 lists the object name types that are assigned to many of the object classes.

	NAME TYPE	NAME VALUE
T A B L E 4.1 *Getting to Know Object Name Types*	C	Country
	L	Locality
	S	State or Province Name
	O	Organization
	OU	Organizational Unit
	CN	Common Name (includes all leaf objects)

The first five name types (C=Country, L=Locality, S=State, O=Organization, and OU=Organizational Unit) are all container objects. The final name type, CN=Common Name, includes all leaf object classes. This is how NDS deals with non-containers — users, printers, servers, and so on. Table 4.2 lists most of the leaf object classes that use CN as their name type.

T A B L E 4.2 *Leaf Object Classes and CN*	CN=AFP Server	CN=Organizational Role
	CN=Bindery	CN=Print Queue
	CN=Bindery Queue	CN=Print Server
	CN=Computer	CN=Printer
	CN=Directory Map	CN=Profile
	CN=Group	CN=User
	CN=Server	CN=Volume

TIP

As you may have noticed, not all of the container name types are available to you when building the NDS tree. For example, L=Locality and S=State do not show up in the current versions of IntranetWare utilities. These name types are found in the schema, but have not been implemented in the utilities. The name type L=Locality was placed in the schema for compatibility with the X.500 standard. When building the structure of your NDS tree, you will use the other container name types (namely, O=Organization and OU=Organizational Unit), which provide you with all the functionality you will need. The L=Locality may be implemented in future releases of IntranetWare and NDS.

SMART LINK

For more information regarding the NDS Schema and it's internal structure, surf over to the Novell Knowledgebase at http://support.novell.com/search/.

That's enough schema for now. We'll revisit this concept throughout the remainder of the book. Also, you'll undoubtedly run across in-depth schema discussions at cocktail parties and other social gatherings. Remember, you saw it here first.

ZEN

"Frankly, I don't believe people think of their office as a workplace anymore. I think they think of it as a stationery store with Danish. You want to get your pastry, your envelopes, your supplies, your toilet paper, six cups of coffee, and then go home."

Jerry Seinfeld

Now, let's continue our naming discussion with a quick review of the NDS naming rules. Then, we'll dive into the real meat and potatoes of NDS design — the naming standards document.

NDS NAMING RULES

Your name identifies you as a truly unique individual. In much the same way, an NDS object's name identifies its object class and location in the hierarchical tree. As we learned in Chapter 2, NDS naming impacts two important IntranetWare tasks:

▸ *Login* — You must identify your exact location in the NDS tree in order for IntranetWare to authenticate you during login.

▸ *Resource Access* — NDS naming exactly identifies the type and location of IntranetWare resources, including file servers, printers, login scripts, and files.

Before we create ACME's naming standards document, we must learn a few more things about NDS naming rules. In Chapter 2, we discussed a variety of naming issues, including:

▸ Distinguished Names

▸ Relative Distinguished Names

▸ Typeful Names

▸ Typeless Names

▸ Context

▸ Leading Periods

▸ Trailing Periods

In this section, we will review these concepts and provide some additional insight on how they affect NDS design. Then, we'll jump into a naming standards document for ACME. So, without any further adieu, let's start with distinguished names.

Distinguished Names

Each object in the tree is given a distinguished name during creation. This determines the object's name type and its location in the NDS tree. Distinguished names provide a global, complete, and unique identity for objects in the tree. In summary, it consists of three things:

▸ The name type

▸ The object's name value

▸ A list of each container between itself and the [Root]

For example, in Figure 4.2, the distinguished name for George Washington is his object name plus the names of all the containers between him and the [Root]. It begins with his common name, CN=GWashington, followed by each of his containers, OU=ADMIN.OU=RIO.O=ACME.

Here's what it looks like together:

```
.CN=GWashington.OU=ADMIN.OU=RIO.O=ACME
```

TIP

The proper order for writing an object's distinguished name is *least-significant* **(object deepest in the tree) to the** *most-significant* **(object closest to the [Root]). The distinguished name is written left-to-right. NDS will resolve distinguished names regardless of their case. For instance, in the previous example, the use of GWashington's distinguished name could also be written as "cn=gwashington.ou=admin.ou=rio.o=acme". We are, however, using uppercase/lowercase for User objects as part of our NDS naming standard.**

Figure 4.3 illustrates another example of NDS distinguished naming. It includes two NDS server objects:

```
.CN=LABS-SRV1.OU=LABS.OU=NORAD.O=ACME
```

```
.CN=WHITE-SRV1.OU=WHITE.OU=CRIME.OU=TOKYO.O=ACME
```

George Washington's Distinguished Name is .CN=GWashington.OU=ADMIN.OU=RIO.O=ACME

Relative Distinguished Names

A *relative distinguished name* (RDN) makes assumptions about an object's location in the tree — its context. It must be unique only in relation to the object's parent container. It is cumbersome to use distinguished names all the time, because they are long and redundant. You should become familiar with the use of the relative distinguished name because it allows you to identify objects in relation to their context. These names are shorter and easier to deal with.

FIGURE 4.3

*More NDS Distinguished
Names (LABS-SRV1 and
WHITE-SRV1)*

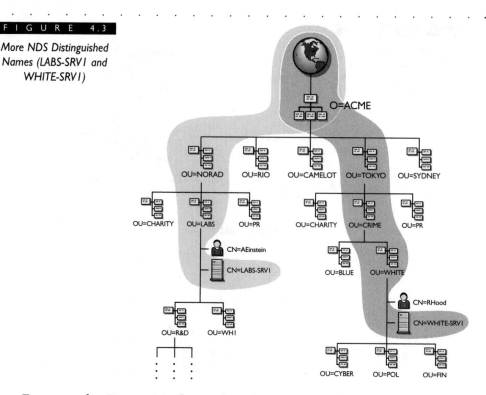

For example, Figure 4.4 shows that objects in the PR department in the NORAD location of the ACME tree have unique relative distinguished names in relation to their parent object — OU=PR. Some of the objects are CN=DClarke (user), CN=NOR-PR-SRV1 (server), CN=NOR-PR-SRV1_SYS (volume), and CN=HP4SI-P1 (printer).

A relative distinguished name must be unique, but only in the object's parent container. Two objects can share the same name, as long as they live in different containers. This is because objects in different containers are said to be distinguished relative to their parents. Check out the two HP4SI-P1 printers in Figure 4.4. Even though they share the same *relative* name, they each have a unique *distinguished* name:

```
CN=HP4SI-P1 (in container OU=PR.OU=NORAD.O=ACME)

CN=HP4SI-P1 (in container OU=CHARITY.OU=TOKYO.O=ACME)
```

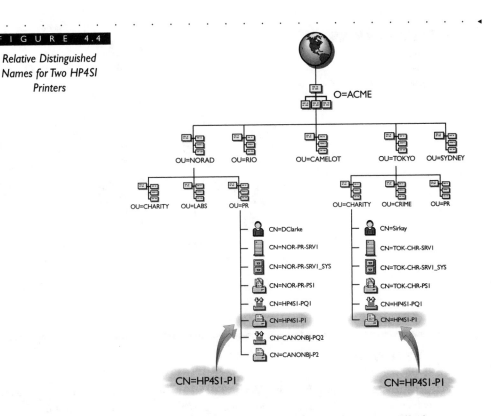

FIGURE 4.4

Relative Distinguished Names for Two HP4SI Printers

CN=HP4SI-PI

CN=HP4SI-PI

Relative distinguished names are not just reserved for leaf objects. All objects in the NDS tree have relative distinguished names in relationship to their parents. For example, you can't create two OU=NORAD containers under the O=ACME Organization. On the other hand, you can create containers with the same name, provided that they occur in different parts of the tree. For example, in Figure 4.5, notice that there is a container called CHARITY and PR under each of the locations. This is legal because each instance of the OU=CHARITY and OU=PR containers is unique within each of the location OU's.

Remember, combining each of the relative distinguished names with its parent container creates a distinguished name. Also, both relative distinguished names and distinguished names can be referenced with (*typeful*) or without (*typeless*) name types. Let's see how that works.

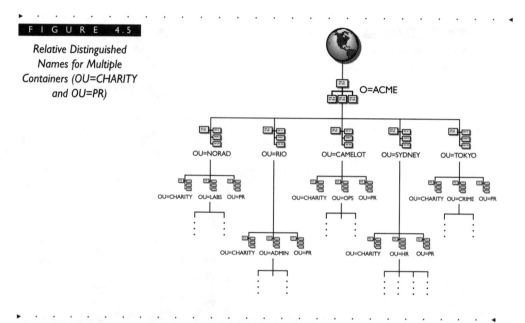

REAL WORLD

If you are migrating from NetWare 3.12, then you must create a unique relative distinguished name for each of the objects that you are passing to IntranetWare and NDS. The NetWare 3.12 bindery permits you to create the objects with the same name, as long as the object types are different. This rule does not apply to IntranetWare and NDS.

For example, it is very common for an administrator in NetWare 3.12 to create a Print Queue object and the group that will use the print queue with the same name. This is an easy method to administer the printing setup, and it is legal in the bindery. However, in IntranetWare, each leaf object is treated the same and must have a unique relative distinguished name within its home container.

During the preparation of your migration from NetWare 3.12 to IntranetWare, you must clean up or resolve any of these duplicate names. If you do not resolve the naming conflicts, then the migration program will migrate the first object, but not the second object with the same name. For more complete information about migration, refer to Chapter 5 ("Step 3: NDS Implementation") and Chapter 7 ("IntranetWare Migration").

TIP

Although users *can* share relative distinguished names in different containers, we highly recommend that you create a naming standard for usernames that makes them unique across the entire NDS tree. Having a global naming standard for users reduces the chance of a name conflict when the users are created or moved. Also, it simplifies NDS management, login, and resource access for you. These are all good things.

Typeful Names

When you place an object's name type in its name, it's referred to as *typeful naming*. Here are a couple of examples:

```
.CN=SirKay.OU=CHARITY.OU=TOKYO.O=ACME
```

```
.CN=TOK-CHR-PS1.OU=CHARITY.OU=TOKYO.O=ACME
```

You can also refer to each of these objects independently as CN=SirKay, CN=TOK-CHR-PS1, OU=CHARITY, OU=TOKYO, and O=ACME. Each object has its own object type plus a unique object name. This type of naming allows NDS to resolve the object's identity in a segmented fashion — one piece at a time. You're not required, however, to provide the name type for each segment (or at all). However, if you start mixing typeful and typeless segments, you're asking for trouble.

TIP

Using typeful names can get cumbersome for users. Consider using typeless naming at the command line, and especially for LOGIN.EXE.

Typeless Names

Typeless names are simply names without types. Makes sense. In these cases, NDS has to "guess" what object types you're using. Here are typeless versions of the names shown previously:

```
.SirKay.CHARITY.TOKYO.ACME
```

```
.TOK-CHR-PS1.CHARITY.TOKYO.ACME
```

Notice that we removed the object name type from each segment. You can now refer to the Knight as simply SirKay instead of CN=SirKay. The other leaf and container objects are similarly stripped of their typeness — TOK-CHR-PS1, CHARITY, TOKYO, and ACME. Like the typeful naming method, typeless naming is not case-sensitive. Again, using the previous examples, you can see that .siRKay.charITY.Tokyo.ACME is equivalent to .SIRKAY.ChaRIty.TOKyo.ACMe.

TIP

Typeless names are easier to use for both administrators and users because they are shorter and more intuitive. You should use typeless naming during your day-to-day operations, and become very familiar with it. You can also use this method of typeless naming for indicating either a relative distinguished name or a distinguished name.

The real tricky part of typeless names is guessing which name type to attribute to each object segment. Fortunately, IntranetWare has some guidelines for determining this. Typically:

1 • The leftmost object is assumed to be a common name (leaf object).

2 • The rightmost object is assumed to be an Organization (container object).

3 • All middle objects are assumed to be Organizational Units (container objects).

ZEN

"Diplomacy is the art of saying 'Nice Doggie' until you can find a stick!"

Will Rogers

While this works for most cases, it's only a general guideline. Many times, typeless names are more complex. Things get especially crazy when you mix typeless and typeful names, such as .SirKay.OU=CHARITY.TOKYO.O=ACME. IntranetWare uses five exception rules for resolving complex typeless names:

1. • *Container Objects* — Context utilities such as CX are intelligent enough to assume the leftmost object in a typeless name is an OU.

2. • *Leaf Objects* — Similarly, resource-based utilities such as CAPTURE recognize the leftmost object of a typeless name as a leaf object.

3. • *Mixed Names* — If both naming schemes are used in the same name, the typeful abbreviation is used as a reference point for resolving the typeless portion of the name.

4. • *Current Context* — If all else fails, NDS uses the current context to resolve typeless names.

5. • *Country Object* — If you introduce the Country object in either the current context or a typeful portion of the name, all heck breaks loose. In this case, NDS tries to resolve the name by using any of the previous exception rules. If they don't apply, it isolates the Country object and applies the defaults to the remainder of the typeless name.

Context

Context defines an object's position in the NDS tree. If two objects are in the same container, they have the same context. In NDS design terms, *context* is defined as the name of an object's parent container. As you can see in Figure 4.6, Charles Darwin (CDarwin) is working on Pollution research (OU=POLL), in the R&D department (OU=R&D) of LABS (OU=LABS) located at the NORAD office (OU=NORAD) of ACME (O=ACME). His context is

```
OU=POLL.OU=R&D.OU=LABS.OU=NORAD.O=ACME
```

TIP

The best analogy for context in NDS is the DOS PATH command. The path statement in DOS helps you quickly and automatically find files stored in specific subdirectories. In the same fashion, the context in NDS helps you quickly and automatically find resources in specific NDS containers.

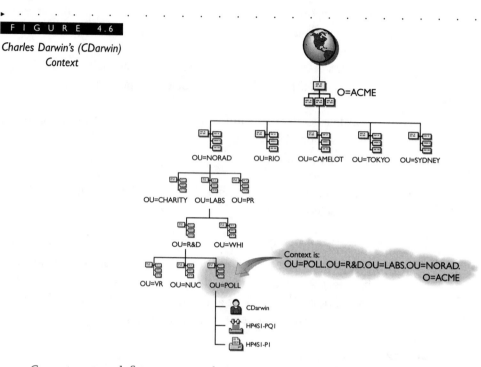

FIGURE 4.6

Charles Darwin's (CDarwin) Context

Current context defines your workstation's current position in the NDS tree. By controlling your users' current contexts, you can make resource access and tree navigation much easier. From there, they only must reference an object's relative distinguished name — which is much shorter. For example, Figure 4.7 shows several contexts within the ACME tree. If you're current context was OU=OPS. OU=CAMELOT.O=ACME, then you could reference the BubbleJet printer as CN=CANNONBJ-P1 — much easier than the long distinguished name.

There are many different ways to set a user's current context. The three most popular are

▸ NAME CONTEXT statement in the NET.CFG file

▸ CX

▸ Windows 95 Registry in Client 32 (see Chapter 12)

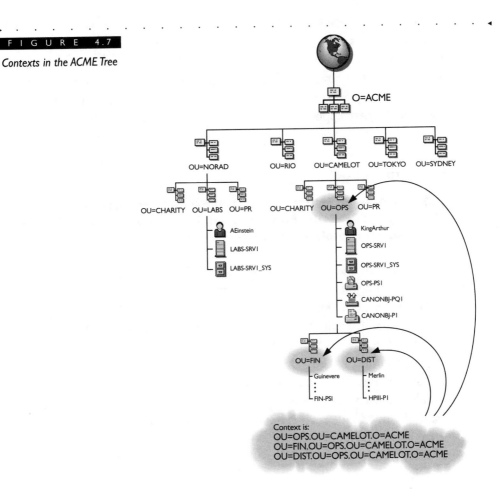

Contexts in the ACME Tree

The NAME CONTEXT statement in NET.CFG allows you to set a user's context before logging in. For example, KingArthur could log in with his relative distinguished (LOGIN KingArthur) if you put the following statement in his NET.CFG configuration file:

```
Name Context = "OU=OPS.OU=CAMELOT.O=ACME"
```

He could also use the CX (Change conteXt) command to manually set his current context prior to logging in. It goes something like this:

```
CX OU=OPS.OU=CAMELOT.O=ACME
```

Context does one other thing for you. It allows you to support users from previous versions of NetWare (NetWare 2 and/or NetWare 3). IntranetWare includes a backward-compatibility feature called Bindery Services. This feature allows bindery users and bindery-based applications to access the NDS tree as if it were a bindery. Bindery Services relies on a special context known as the *bindery context*. Users and bindery applications can only see the NDS objects in their server's bindery context. It's a two-dimensional view of the three-dimensional NDS universe.

TIP

In order to set the bindery context on a server, you can enter **SET BINDERY CONTEXT = OU=OPS.OU=CAMELOT.O=ACME** at the server console, or use **SERVMAN.NLM.**

Stop for a moment and ask yourself one simple question: "What if I were King Arthur?" Among other things, you'd live in the OU=OPS division of OU=CAMELOT. If you were a bindery user and you attached to the OPS-SRV1 server, your view of the NDS world would be severely diminished (see Figure 4.7). All King Arthur would see is a server (OPS-SRV1), its volume (OPS-SRV1_SYS), a print server (OPS-PS1), a print queue (CANONBJ-PQ1), and a printer (CANONBJ-P1).

A server's default bindery context is set to the container where it was originally installed. The context can be changed to include up to 16 different containers in a sort of "superbindery." It is important to note that previous versions of NetWare 4 (up to and including NetWare 4.02) only allowed you to set a single bindery context for your server. How restricting.

TIP

In terms of bindery context on the server, **NDS** will only see the objects that previously existed in a NetWare 3 bindery. These objects are limited to User, Group, Print Queue, and Print Server. In addition, IntranetWare has added the Profile object to assist with migrations from NetWare Name Services (NNS).

Leading Periods

A period (.) is used to separate individual name segments in distinguished names, relative distinguished names, and context. IntranetWare also supports leading and trailing periods.

A name with a leading period instructs the client software to ignore the current context and start the search at the [Root]. This means that any object name with a leading period will be treated as a distinguished name starting at the [Root].

The leading period is simply a shortcut for navigating the tree, and there can be only one leading period in the object name. Trailing periods, on the other hand, are a completely different kettle of fish.

Trailing Periods

Trailing periods alter the current context. Weird, huh? A single trailing period will move the current context up one container in the tree. For instance, you can use the following CX command to switch to the parent container:

```
CX  .
```

Unlike leading periods, you can have as many trailing periods as you want. If you want to move up two layers in the tree, simply supply two trailing periods. Simple. For example, in Figure 4.7, if you were King Arthur and you wanted to move to the O=ACME container, you would type:

```
CX  ..
```

Trailing periods can only be used with relative distinguished names — that is, names without leading periods. For example, in Figure 4.7, if King Arthur were at home and he wanted to access the LABS server, he would reference it as:

```
LABS-SRV1.LABS.NORAD..
```

In the previous example, NDS bounced King Arthur's current context one layer for each trailing period. He starts at OU=OPS and ends up at O=ACME. This resolves the server's distinguished name as .LABS-SRV1.LABS.NORAD.ACME. Piece of cake!

> **ZEN**
>
> *"If a wheel turns, and nothing else moves with it, I should say it was not a part of the machinery."*
>
> **Ludwig Wittgenstein**

OK, that's eNough Naming NoNsense for Now — lots of N's. If you need more explanation, refer to the "NDS Naming" section of Chapter 2. Our focus here is

NDS design. Now that we've explored the fundamentals of NDS naming, and discovered some name-related design caveats, it's time to dive into the real star of this show — the NDS naming standards document. I promise that we'll put all of your naming knowledge to good use.

NDS NAMING STANDARD GUIDELINES

An NDS naming standards document is crucial. It provides guidelines for naming key container and leaf objects (including Users, Printers, Servers, Volumes, Print Queues, and Organizational Units). In addition, it identifies standard properties and value formats. Consistency (especially in the naming scheme used for objects) provides several benefits, including the following:

▸ Consistent naming schemes provide a guideline for network administrators who will add, modify, or move objects within the Directory tree.

▸ Naming standards eliminate redundant planning. The standards give CNEs an efficient model to meet their needs, but leave implementation of resource objects open and flexible.

▸ Consistent naming schemes help users identify resources quickly, which maximizes user productivity.

▸ Finally, consistent naming allows users to easily identify themselves during login.

As I previously stated, the naming standards document is required — but it doesn't have to be difficult or time-consuming to create. The first step is to ask yourself a few questions:

▸ How can I provide a Directory structure for my employees that is flexible, easy to use, and meets today's business needs?

▸ How can I ensure that I provide a consistent Directory structure within all our divisions, locations, and, perhaps, operating companies?

> ▸ How can I communicate and implement a consistent standard across an entire company, one that will be followed by everyone?

The answers can be found in your naming standards document. The process of creating naming guidelines forces you to deal with these critical issues and tackle them head-on. Before you can do anything, however, you'll need to create some naming standards guidelines. And, even more importantly, you'll want to do it before installing your very first IntranetWare server. Once an installation has begun, it becomes more difficult to implement a standard. At a minimum, you should define how Organizational Unit, Server, and User objects are going to look. These are the most popular NDS objects.

So, where do you start? Many companies already have some standard in place for defining their users. This is usually based on an e-mail standard. Review the standard and make modifications where necessary to improve the current standard. If your company's network is small, you still should create naming guidelines, because it will most likely grow to include more users and resources — at which point naming becomes *very* important.

Your naming guidelines must be global in nature. You should strive to implement your naming standards consistently across the entire network so that all users and all departments can readily and easily access resources anywhere on the WAN. Global naming guidelines can also help you and your distributed administrators by clarifying the identity and purpose of all objects in the tree.

ZEN

"When you look at actual children, no matter how they are raised, you notice immediately that little girls are, in fact, smaller versions of real human beings, whereas little boys are Pod People from the Planet Destructo!"

Dave Barry

You will probably need the input from others at ACME in order to create effective naming guidelines. This may include input from e-mail administrators, network administrators, and mainframe personnel. Also, you'll need information from each division. Don't forget the Project Team.

Usually, an established host environment has user naming standards in place. Review these standards as a basis for your IntranetWare user naming guidelines. Some customers prefer to maintain their host usernames on the LAN rather than create a new standard at the network level. Others can't wait to change their host usernames.

Consider all other naming guidelines that are in place from a NetWare 3 environment when creating your NDS standard. Your NetWare 3 printers and servers may already have names defined that will work just fine after migration to the IntranetWare tree. If you have sufficient or acceptable guidelines (for your organization), then there is no need to change them.

OK, that's enough advice. Now get off the couch and let's take a closer look at the five main objectives in creating NDS naming guidelines:

1 • Make browsing and navigation of the NDS tree easier for the users.

2 • Make maintenance of the NDS tree easier for the network administration staff.

3 • Make merging separate NDS trees easier.

4 • Keep NDS object names unique as required by certain services.

5 • Avoid special characters reserved by the WAN's many operating systems.

NDS Browsing and Navigation

Your primary objective for creating naming guidelines is to provide your users with a simple view of their network resources. You may not see the immediate need for good naming guidelines. However, as more applications are written to take advantage of NDS and its searching capabilities, you'll quickly change your tune. Soon, an uncomplicated naming standard will be required.

Objects should be named with purpose and consistency. This will eventually provide you with a solid foundation for NDS browsing, navigation, and resource access. Other dividends will be recognized as applications make more use of the Directory and its services. Soon, you will see that the system is much more efficient and the users can quickly identify the network resources they need.

You should also keep the names of all the objects short and simple. These names should be descriptive enough, however, so that users can easily identify what the object is and the services it provides. For example, the object name HP4SI-P1 is short yet descriptive and lets the user know that this object is an HP4SI LaserJet printer. Another example, HP4SI-PQ1, is also short, yet descriptive. In this case, the PQ1 suffix lets the user know that the object is the print queue that supports the HP4SI printer (P1).

Throughout this book, there have been countless cases when we've relied on efficient ACME naming. In all cases, it has been helpful to have clear and simple names. Some examples of the naming guidelines for ACME are shown in Table 4.3.

TABLE 4.3	OBJECT	NAME	STANDARD
Examples of Naming Guidelines for ACME	[Root]	Tree Name	ACME_TREE
	O=Organization	A Cure for Mother Earth	ACME
	OU=Organizational Unit	Rio de Janeiro, Brazil	RIO
		Tokyo, Japan	TOKYO
		Sydney, Australia	SYDNEY
		Research and Development	R&D
		World Health Index	WHI
		Facilities	FAC
		Public Relations	PR
	CN=Users	George Washington	GWashington
		Thomas Jefferson	TJefferson
		Leonardo DaVinci	LDaVinci
		Albert Einstein	AEinstein
	CN=Servers	Server in Labs	LABS-SRV1
		Server in White	WHITE-SRV1
		Server in NORAD/PR	NOR-PR-SRV1
	CN=Printers	HP4SI in NORAD/PR	HP4SI-P1
	CN=Print Queues	Queue in NORAD/PR	HP4SI-PQ1

Easier Administration

Consistent naming also provides a framework for IntranetWare administration, monitoring, and optimization. You and your distributed administrators will be installing file servers, creating users and printers, modifying existing objects, and moving objects throughout the NDS tree. You will also set up numerous workstation configuration files, and control the user's friendly WAN interface. In all these cases, your job is going to be much easier if efficient naming guidelines are in place.

Merging NDS Trees

The ability to merge multiple NDS trees together is a dominant feature of IntranetWare. This is pruning at its finest. This miracle relies on a shared naming standard between the two trees being merged. The tree merge will be seamless to the users because their workstation configuration files will not change, even though the NDS trees are merged.

Naming has the largest negative impact on merging two disparate NDS trees. It impacts every facet of NDS management and resource accessibility. The effort to reconfigure each affected workstation and printer, for example, could slow down the overall process or may be prohibitive altogether.

QUIZ

Now's a good time for another little "brain stretcher." Try this one on for size:

Eight bingo balls numbered from one to eight are placed into a bag then drawn out at random, one by one, and the numbers written down to form an eight-figure number. What are the odds that the eight-figure number will divide by nine exactly?

(Q4-1)
(See Appendix C for quiz answers.)

Unique NDS Object Names

Some NDS objects have unusual requirements for naming exclusivity. File and Print servers, for example, broadcast their services using the Service Advertising Protocol (SAP). SAP and RIP (Routing Information Protocol) will not tolerate two different devices "SAPing" the same name. Therefore, your naming standard must identify these devices and handle them appropriately.

STEP 2: NDS DESIGN

Also, you'll want to distribute the naming guidelines to all administrators on the WAN, which will ensure object naming exclusivity where appropriate. In addition, we recommend that user objects have unique names throughout the tree. This way, users can be moved or added without conflict. Keep in mind, though, that not all objects in the NDS tree need naming exclusivity — just the finicky ones.

Avoid Special Characters

"Special" is good, but in NDS it's reserved for the tree only. NDS needs a slew of special characters for its own operations. Avoid using any of the following characters in your naming standards document:

▸ Period (.) — Used by NDS to separate the name segments of distinguished names. For example, the distinguished name for the user George Washington is CN=GWashington.OU=ADMIN.OU=RIO.O=ACME. Wow, check out all those periods.

▸ Plus (+) — Used by NDS to represent objects with multiple naming attributes (such as bindery objects). A common use of the plus sign is for bindery object naming. For example, a bindery object with the plus sign in the name is seen as CN=Bindery Name + Object. In the case of an AppleTalk print server it might appear as CN=AtpsQuser+83.

▸ Equals (=) — Used by NDS to tie name types and object names together. For example the object type O=Organization would appear as O=ACME.

▸ Backslash (\) — Precedes the previous special characters, if they are used as part of an object name. For example, if you want to use the name "ACME Inc." (which has a period at the end), you would need to type ACME Inc\.

Here's another tip from Uncle David: Avoid using spaces in any object names. You should use the dash (-) or underscore (_) characters instead. Spaces are used as delimiters for all command line parameters. If you use spaces in an NDS object name, you'll need to enclose it in quotation marks — too much work. For example, if the user George Washington is named "George Washington" in NDS with a space separating the first and last name, when George logs in, he would have to type

```
LOGIN "George Washington"
```

If he was required to provide the full distinguished name during login, he would type

```
LOGIN "George Washington.ADMIN.RIO.ACME"
```

If he used the underscore instead, it would be a little easier:

```
LOGIN George_Washington
```

You should also avoid the forward slash (/) in naming container or leaf objects. The Windows-based NWUSER utility, for example, will fail if you map permanent drives to, or CAPTURE a print queue to, an object with a forward slash in it. This is a Windows issue — figures.

ZEN

"Your children need your presence more than your presents."

Jesse Jackson

Well, there you go. That's everything you need to know about NDS naming guidelines. Now, I think we're ready to attack the ACME naming standards document. I can barely contain my excitement. How about you?!

ACME'S NAMING STANDARDS DOCUMENT

Here we are — finally. The first 10 feet of "the Great Drop." We've reached the Apex of IntranetWare, and we're looking straight down at a 100-foot drop. The first 10 feet are the most interesting, because you still don't know what to expect. Your stomach has not quite reached your throat yet. Wait until you get to NDS tree design. Producing ACME's naming standards document is not very glamorous work, but it's critical — and you would realize this if you'd been awake during the last 25 pages or so. Fortunately, it's not brain surgery. Once you understand the impact of the previous NDS naming guidelines, the rest is a piece of cake. As a matter of fact, it's as easy as 1-2-3:

> ▶ Step 1: Document the naming standard for each object class in the ACME tree.

▸ Step 2: Provide an example for each object class.

▸ Step 3: Specify properties for each object class selected.

ACME's naming standards document is simply a manifestation of these guidelines. Now that you understand the rules, you just have to apply them to ACME (or some other organization). Let's take a closer look at these three simple steps, and build a naming standard for ACME. Cool.

Step 1: Document the Naming Standard for Each Object Class in the ACME Tree

It all starts here — *review*. Begin by taking a long hard look at ACME and the network resources it uses. Consider the impact of naming on these resources, and come up with some simple guidelines for standardizing the names. This review will also help prepare you for the second phase of NDS design — NDS tree design. But let's not get ahead of ourselves.

The good news is that most of your effort is focused on a few leaf and container objects, namely:

▸ Users

▸ Organization

▸ Organizational Units

▸ Servers

▸ Printers and Print Queues

Object Class: Users   When creating a naming standard, the first step is to decide what to do with the users. IntranetWare allows usernames up to 64 characters long. However, a 64-character username is ridiculous. Consider limiting it to eight characters or less. This is appropriate in many cases, but not ACME. The eight-character rule makes file system management much easier, but it hinders the identity and exclusivity of key users. It is very important to ensure that each username is unique company-wide. Even though NDS doesn't require it, exclusivity aids messaging management.

In our case, we're going to use the first character of the first name and the *entire* last name. This helps differentiate people and simplifies identity. Also, if there are duplicate names within a single container, then the middle initial is added to resolve the name conflict.

> **TIP**
>
> IntranetWare supports single object names up to 64 characters in length. However, a limitation of the DOS command line utilities imposes a maximum context length of 255 characters. Finally, remember that bindery rules restrict object names to 47 characters for previous versions of NetWare.

As I said previously, some companies choose to limit the username to eight characters. This naming convention matches the username to the DOS home directory. Since DOS subdirectories are limited to just eight characters, this design will automatically match the name of the DOS subdirectory to the appropriate username. For example, Thomas Jefferson, becomes

    TJEFFERS

In other cases, you may want to use the first six characters of a user's last name and the first two characters of the user's first name. This name would appear as

    JEFFERTH

> **TIP**
>
> Remember, object names within the same container must be unique. Duplicate names are only allowed if objects are distributed to different containers. However, it is recommended that you keep object names unique across the entire tree.

Object Class: Organization   Your Organization name should reflect your company name. In our case, "A Cure for Mother Earth" becomes ACME, and the Organization name becomes O=ACME. With the Organization restricted to the company's name, it frees up the Organizational Units to become the true Tupperware containers of NDS logic. In addition, you may consider adding a location to the Organization name and accommodate future tree merging.

Object Class: Organizational Units   Organizational Units can span multiple container depths. With this flexibility, they can be used for "geography" and "organization." As you'll learn in the next section, geography defines the upper layers of the NDS tree. So, the first few layers of Organizational Units should be reserved for locations — OU=SYDNEY and OU=TOKYO. They could have been abbreviated to SYD and TOK, but their names are already short. Remember, the names must be *both* short and descriptive ("SYD" isn't very descriptive).

The next OU layers are dedicated to divisions and departments — OU=R&D for the Research and Development department and OU=MRKT for Marketing. Remember, be short, but descriptive. This allows for much easier tree searching and navigation.

> **TIP**
>
> **The tree name should be a combination of a shortened version of the company name plus "_TREE". You should not use the same name that you used for the O=Organization. In our case, we are using ACME_TREE for our tree name and O=ACME as the name of the Organization object. Also, keep in mind that you can't use duplicate tree names within NDS. It just wouldn't stand for it.**

Object Class: Servers   Servers are very finicky. Their names must be unique across the entire WAN because of SAP and RIP broadcasting. You may wish to consider a server name that incorporates both its location and department. For ACME, an IntranetWare server in the CHARITY department of NORAD is called NOR-CHR-SRV1 and a print server is called NOR-CHR-PS1. On the other hand, a file server in the R&D department of NORAD is called R&D-SRV1. Why?

You may wonder why the naming standards seem different for different departments — let me explain. R&D is a unique department within the ACME tree and, therefore, it doesn't need any special location designator. However, the CHARITY and PR departments are not unique departments — they exist in each location throughout the ACME tree. Therefore, the servers in those containers should use the location designator to uniquely identify them.

TIP

A printer that connects directly to the network cable and services a print queue on the file server is called a *Queue Server*. A Queue Server is a special-purpose print server that must have a unique name to broadcast using SAP. All Queue Servers use SAP to advertise their services on the network. The HP JetDirect card is an example of a Queue Server device.

Object Class: Printers and Print Queues   Unlike servers, printers and print queues don't require naming exclusivity. The department and location information is obtained through the object's NDS context. This means that an HP LaserJet 4SI in R&D can share the same name as an HP LaserJet 4SI in WHITE — they have different distinguished names because they have different parent containers. In summary, a printer's distinguished name identifies its location and department. Therefore, printer and print queue names should reflect functionality, not location.

For example, an ACME HP4SI printer is named HP4SI-P1 and its associated print queue is called HP4SI-PQ1 — regardless of where they live. A Canon BubbleJet printer is named CANONBJ-P2 and its print queue is named CANONBJ-PQ2. This type of naming provides the user with fundamental information about the printer and its associated print queue. Remember, function over location.

This completes our discussion of the main NDS object classes. In addition, you might want to consider naming standards for Group, Organizational Role, Directory Map Object, and Profile objects.

ZEN

"Do what you do best; if you're a runner, run; if you're a bell, ring."

Ignas Berstein

Naming standards for ACME's object classes are outlined in Table 4.4. Check it out.

Step 2: Provide an Example for Each Object Class

A picture is worth a thousand words. So far, ACME's naming standard is relatively one-dimensional — that is, all rules and no application. As a matter of fact, you'll find Table 4.4 is only marginally useful. That's because it doesn't have any examples. One example can convey the meaning of an entire written page. Therefore, include some brief examples in your naming standards document. It helps illustrate your reasoning. Examples also ensure that distributed administrators will stay on track.

TABLE 4.4	NDS OBJECT CLASS	STANDARD
Naming Standards for ACME Object Classes	Users	First character of the first name, plus the entire last name. All titles are spelled out.
	Organization	Abbreviation of the company name.
	Organizational Unit	Location, division, or department name. Abbreviate the name if there are more than eight characters.
	Server	Department-SRV#. Exception for the CHARITY and PR departments which require geographic information as well (that is, Location-Department-SRV#).
	Volumes	ServerName_VolumeName.
	Print Server	Department-PS#. Exception for the CHARITY and PR departments as above (that is, Location-Department-PS#).
	Printer	PrinterType-P#.
	Print Queue	PrinterType-PQ#.
	Computer	No standard because it is not used at ACME.

Table 4.5 is simply a reprint of Table 4.4, but with examples for each of the object classes. Notice how everything suddenly falls into place — just like magic. Now all you need are some property guidelines, and the naming standard is done!

TABLE 4.5

Using Examples in Your NDS Naming Standard

NDS OBJECTS	STANDARD	EXAMPLES
Users	First character of the first name, plus the entire last name. All titles are spelled out.	GWashington, SirGawain
Organization	Abbreviation of the company name which is "A Cure for Mother Earth."	ACME
Organizational Unit	Location, division, or department name. Abbreviate the name if there are over eight characters.	NORAD, R&D, ADMIN
Server	Department-SRV#. Exception for the CHARITY and PR departments, which is Location-Department-SRV#.	LABS-SRV1, NOR-CHR-SRV1
Volumes	ServerName_VolumeName.	LABS-SRV1_SYS, NOR-CHR-SRV1_SYS
Print Server	Department-PS#. Exception for the CHARITY and PR departments, which is Location-Department-PS#.	FAC-PS1, TOK-PR-PS1
Printer	PrinterType-P#.	HP4SI-P1, CANONBJ-P2
Print Queue	PrinterType-PQ#	HP4SI-PQ1, CANONBJ-PQ2
Computer	No standard because it is not used at ACME.	

REAL WORLD

In addition to NDS logical objects and resources, you should establish a naming standard for IPX internal and external network numbers. Although this makes implementation more difficult, it can simplify troubleshooting and packet filtering.

The IPX EXTERNAL network number consists of up to eight hexadecimal digits (number 0 through letter F) that identify the external cable segment. An additional IPX external network number is assigned for each new segment, additional protocol, or frame type. This number is specified in the server's AUTOEXEC.NCF file using the BIND parameter "NET=". When you use INETCFG to configure protocols, the number is called the *ID string*.

You can set standards for the IPX external network number by assigning codes for the digits. For example, you can specify that all cable segments in Camelot begin with the digits "01". The remaining digits could identify the location of the cable segment or the type of protocol. Use the following standard for external IPX network numbers:

LLDDXXXP

LL — Location
DD — Division
XXX — Identifier
P — Protocol type

The IPX INTERNAL network number is also an eight-digit hexadecimal address. But in this case, it uniquely identifies the server on the network. The IntranetWare installation program normally generates a random unique IPX internal network number, although it does allow you to specify one of your own. If you do, make sure to register your IPX internal network numbers with the Novell Network Registry at (408) 321-1506 or e-mail registry@novell.com.

Like the external number, you should set standards for the internal IPX network number. This helps locate the source of packets during troubleshooting. Use the following standard for internal IPX network numbers:

LLSSXXXX

LL — Location
SS — LAN segment
XXXX — Identifier

Some CNEs prefer to use the server's license number as the IPX internal network number. This ensures exclusivity and provides licensing documentation.

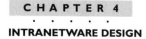
Step 3: Specify Properties for Each Object Class Selected

The final step is to put your naming guidelines under the microscope. Now, you must focus in on each object class and provide rules for Required, Optional, and System properties.

First, determine which properties should be required. Start with the mandatory NDS properties and expand from there. For example, NDS won't allow you to create a User object without Login Name and Last Name properties. In ACME's case, we're also requiring Given Name, Full Name, Middle Initial, Title, Location, Telephone Number, Fax Number, Home Directory, and Require Password.

Next, determine which properties will be optional. Finally, identify system properties (such as Network Address and so on). In addition, you'll want to provide naming rules for how the properties look. Refer to Table 4.6 for an example of ACME's User Class property standard.

TABLE 4.6		
NDS Property Standards of the ACME User Class		
PROPERTY	**REQ/OPT/ SYSTEM**	**STANDARD**
Login Name	Required	First character of the first name, plus the entire last name. Add a middle initial to resolve name conflicts.
Given Name	Required	First name of the user.
Last Name	Required	Last name of the user.
Full Name	Required	First and last name of the user.
Generational Qual.	Optional	
Middle Initial	Required	Middle initial of the user, if known.
Other Name	Optional	
Title	Required	Job title.
Description	Optional	
Location	Required	City or site location (NORAD, RIO, and so on)
Department	Optional	
Telephone Number	Required	Business phone number with area code.

	PROPERTY	REQ/OPT/ SYSTEM	STANDARD
T A B L E 4.6 *NDS Property Standards of* *the ACME User Class* *(continued)*	Fax Number	Required	Fax phone number with area code.
	Language	Optional	Preferred language of the user.
	Network Address	System	
	Default Server	Optional	Enter the same server as the home directory.
	Home Directory	Required	Enter the volume: subdirectory\user path.
	Require Password	Required	Force the user to have a password.
	Account Balance	Optional	
	Login Script	Optional	Determined by site administrators.
	Print Job Config.	Optional	Determined by site administrators.
	Post Office Box	Optional	
	Street	Optional	
	City	Optional	
	State or Province	Optional	
	Zip Code	Optional	
	See Also	Optional	

TIP

Currently, IntranetWare utilities can't be configured to enforce additional required properties. The User object, for example, is only required to have a Login Name and Last Name. Your standard, however, may be different. You will need to enforce required user properties at the management level — in your naming guidelines. Also, it helps if you explain the reasoning for including the property. This helps distributed administrators buy into it.

Once you've completed the naming guidelines and examples, there's only one more set of rules to complete your naming standards document — Syntax. Table 4.7 shows a simple, but effective, syntax standard. Notice that we've also included examples. In the most basic sense, this is a summary of the entire naming standards document. As a matter of fact, small organizations could probably get away with just the Naming Syntax guidelines.

	OBJECT TYPE	SYNTAX	EXAMPLE
T A B L E 4.7	[Root] or Tree Name	AAAA_TREE	ACME_TREE
ACME's Naming Standard Syntax	Organization	AAAA	O=ACME
	Organizational Units	XXXXX or YYYYY	OU=NORAD, OU=LABS
	Servers	XXX-YYYYY-SRV#	LABS-SRV1
	Print Servers	XXX-YYYYY-PS#	NOR-CHR-PS4
	Printers	<Prn Type>-P#	HP4SI-P1
	Print Queues	<Prn Type>-PQ#	HP4SI-PQ1
	Volume Names	<Server>_<Volume>	LABS-SRV1_SYS

The legend:
AAAA = Company Name
XXX = Location (NOR, RIO, CAM, TOK, SYD)
YYYYY = Department (LABS, CHR, PR, ADM, OPS, FIN)
SRV = File Server
PS = Print Server
CS=Communications Server
# = Quantity (1, 2, 3, . . . , 9)

(Volumes are SYS, VOL1, DATA, USERS, SHARE)
Note: File and print servers only use a location code if the parent container is not unique (that is, OU=CHARITY or OU=PR). Also, printers and print queues increment according to their print server, not container.

SMART LINK

If you need more help with your corporate naming standards, get help at http://support.novell.com/sitemap.

Whatever you do, don't skimp on naming standards — they're too important to the productivity and survival of your NDS design. More is better in this case.

Congratulations! You've completed the ACME naming standards document. What an accomplishment. It wasn't easy, but now you should feel much more comfortable about the future of ACME's design. At the very least, we know what to call stuff.

The next step is Tree Design. This is when you get a chance to show off your famous CNE creativity. But don't get too creative. There are established rules for tree design, just as there are for naming standards. Sorry, sometimes I can be such a stick in the mud — not!

ZEN

"Philosophy begins in Wonder."

Aristotle

▶ • ◀

NDS Tree Design

Somewhere near the top of the fall, you'll begin to feel your stomach in your throat. This is probably the most popular roller coaster sensation — it epitomizes The Fall. Then, the wind grabs your hair (real or otherwise) with great force and tugs it in the opposite direction. Your face turns to rubber, and your knees buckle under the force of 3Gs. Aren't roller coasters a blast?

With the naming standards document in place, you're halfway down the "Great NDS Dipper." Now it's time to shift gears and begin accelerating to full speed (3Gs). In ACME's case this means it's time to come up with the

- ▶ NDS Tree Design

- ▶ Partition and Replica Design

- ▶ Time Synchronization Design

If you build it (NDS tree design), they will come. Then, we can break the tree into little pieces (partition design), and scatter the pieces around (replica placement). Once they're there, we'll buy them all digital watches (time synchronization design). So, what are you waiting for? Let's build the NDS tree.

DESIGN GOALS

Before you get too excited about designing ACME's tree, we must review some important NDS design benefits and goals. After all, what are we trying to accomplish here?

We're trying to build the best darned tree we can. As a matter of fact, this is probably one of the most important procedures you'll ever come across in building an IntranetWare Enterprise WAN. A proper Directory tree design provides the following benefits:

▸ Partitioning and replication can be designed successfully.

▸ The network can accommodate growth without complicating revisions.

▸ Directory trees can be merged more easily.

▸ Other network services and network accessibility can be designed more easily.

▸ The Directory tree can be navigated more intuitively.

To accomplish all of these great benefits, you should have specific design goals in mind before you start. In short, your design should be organized, structured, and flexible. Here's a list of the three main design goals we'll discuss in detail:

▸ Organize the network resources in your company.

▸ Provide a blueprint for the rollout of IntranetWare.

▸ Be flexible to allow for corporate changes.

If your tree doesn't accomplish these three goals, then it's not a well-designed tree. Let's take a closer look.

Organize the Network Resources in Your Company

The primary goal of your NDS tree is *to organize network resources*. Your NDS tree structure should reflect the location and placement of network resources throughout your WAN. It should also provide easy resource access to both users and distributed administrators. To accomplish this, you must focus on both the location of resources and their purpose — balance is the key. Figure 4.8 shows how the OPS resources are grouped near the users who need them. This increases accessibility.

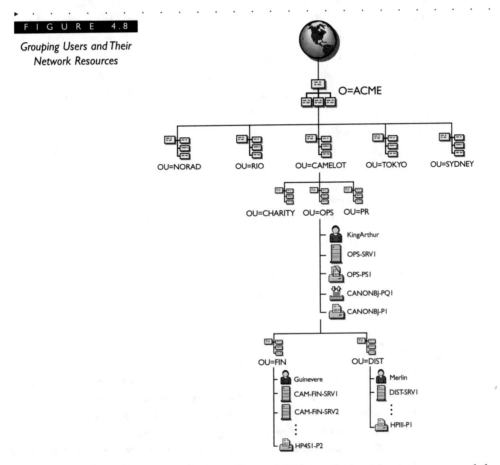

F I G U R E   4 . 8

Grouping Users and Their Network Resources

For example, some users may need access to a particular printer or server, while a larger group may need access to an e-mail server. The e-mail server would be located higher in the tree so that all users needing the resource have common access. In Figure 4.8, for example, Guinevere is placed in the same container as her CAM-FIN-SRV1 server. But her printer (HP4SI-P2) may rely on a print server (OPS-PS1) higher in the tree — a different container. We'll revisit this strategy later. The bottom line is that department-specific resources should be placed lower in the tree, and shared resources should be placed higher in the tree.

Provide a Blueprint for the Rollout of IntranetWare

After the NDS tree has been designed, it will provide a blueprint for the installation of all your IntranetWare servers. For example, the tree design will give you the location where an NDS server should be installed. Also, some companies may be forced to implement multiple trees during the rollout of IntranetWare. This is because of geographical or political pressures. Regardless, they should share the same basic tree design. This will make merging much easier when the time comes — and it will.

Additionally, your NDS blueprint provides a clear map of how to migrate the entire corporation to IntranetWare. Initially, your migration will begin with a few servers and may eventually involve hundreds of machines (52 for ACME). After you gain the experience of tree design, naming standards, lab testing, and server installation, you'll be ready to repeat this process at all locations throughout the WAN. You will be successful at each installation because your blueprint will be well understood.

Be Flexible to Allow for Corporate Changes

The final goal is flexibility. Your tree design must be flexible enough to allow for future corporate changes. This simply means that, as the corporation changes both organizationally and physically, you will be able to represent those changes easily without large modifications to the tree structure. This objective can be met by designing a tree that is rigid at the top and flexible at the bottom. You'll see what I mean in just a second.

TIP

Today's corporations are constantly shifting and changing. Some are being purchased by others, while others are undergoing mergers. The likelihood that this will decrease is very slight. Therefore, you can make your job easier by planning ahead and building in enough flexibility to anticipate these changes. How do you do that? You must not only learn, but truly understand, the rules for successful tree design. Once you understand the rules, every design question and circumstance has an answer and can be factored into your design.

These goals may seem obvious, even trivial, but don't underestimate them. You will always encounter other "forces" that want to gravitate the tree in wrong directions. *Political pressure* is one classic example. Certain individuals want the tree to reflect their personal needs (power, or whatever). The best way to deal with these individuals is to ask them one simple question, "How does this help us organize our network resources?" In other words, if you have specific goals that you can fall back on, you can deal with the political design issues by applying each issue against your design goals. Keep in mind that the network is installed to serve a business purpose, and that the tree is not a mechanism for displaying superiority in your company. If you design with this intent in mind, many of the political pressures can be easily dissipated.

Now that we've got that straight, you're ready to design ACME's NDS tree. Fortunately, I have a simple four-step plan for you — don't I always. Ready, set, design.

SMART LINK

Surf to http://www.netware.com for a comparative look at IntranetWare and its impact on small businesses.

▶ . . . . ◀

REAL WORLD

Politics should not get in the way of your tree design, but sometimes they do. Not long ago, an agency was in the process of designing its IntranetWare tree. During the design, some individuals insisted that they should be represented as their own Organizational Units in the tree because of where they appeared organizationally in their agency. They incorrectly assumed that managerial positions or positions of authority should receive special attention in the design of the tree. As important as these individuals were, they were not containers for the organization of network resources. Regardless of their titles, they were users nonetheless, and shared resources with other individuals on the same floor or building. Sorry, power mongers, you're the same as everyone else in the eyes of NDS.

QUIZ

Things are not always as they appear. What's the next logical number in this sequence?

3, 7, 10, 11, 12, ?

Where's my naming standard when I need it?

(Q4-2)

ACME'S NDS TREE DESIGN

Here we are — tree design. You're prepped and ready to begin organizing ACME's resources. Just don't get any dirt under your fingernails. Today we start down a path that irrevocably defines the future of ACME, and the fate of humanity. But there's no pressure. Decisions you make here, today, will form the foundation of ACME's network, and the platform for their purpose — sounds heavy. In other words, don't mess up the tree design.

The four-step process to follow looks something like this:

▸ *Step 1: Design Inputs* — Gather your company's design inputs (WAN layout, organizational chart, and so on).

▸ *Step 2: Pyramid* — Design the NDS tree in the shape of a pyramid.

▸ *Step 3: Top Layers* — Design the top layers of the tree according to geography.

▸ *Step 4: Bottom Layers* — Design the bottom layers of the tree according to organization.

It starts with the design inputs you gathered in the last chapter. These will help identify ACME's geography, resources, and organizational structure. Next, sketch the tree in the shape of a pyramid using geography (WAN layouts) at the top and departments (organizational chart) at the bottom. Once you have a rough design, fill it in with all the organizations and resources identified in the ACME Resource List. But don't get too carried away. Remember, tree design focuses on branches, servers, administrators, and printers. All the other resources will be placed in the tree in the "NDS Management" section of Chapter 8.

SMART LINK

If you feel the need to jump ahead, check out ACME's complete NDS tree at http://www.cyberstateu.com/clarke/acme.htm.

This four-step model is the best way to proceed, but it's certainly not the only way. The methods presented here have been developed by Novell Consulting Services and have been implemented by hundreds of their large and small customers with great success. Although each company's network will have different requirements, the tree design guidelines in this section will give you a great head start, regardless of the size of your company.

So, what does size have to do with it? It does make a difference. The line between "small" and "large" companies is very subjective, so we must establish a distinction between the two. The easiest approach is to define what we mean by a "small" company. In most cases, a small company is 5 servers or less, with no wide area network (WAN) connections, and less than 500 users. Certainly there is no written law that this is true. However, a network of this size has many less design ramifications than a network with thousands of users and a very complicated network infrastructure.

A "large" network, then, is anything greater than 5 servers *with* a WAN connection, *and* greater than 500 users. As you follow through this chapter, you will be able to determine into which category (small or large) you fall. So, let's begin the design.

STEP 1: DESIGN INPUTS

In chapter 3, we explored the first step of NDS design — NDS Preparation. One of the most important preparation tasks was Data Gathering. We discovered eight different design inputs in two different categories (organizational and technical). In this section, NDS tree design, we're very interested in five of those ACME inputs, namely:

▸ ACME WAN Layout

▸ ACME Campus Maps

▸ ACME World Map

▸ ACME Resource List

▸ ACME Organizational Chart

Notice that all four technical inputs are represented here and only one organizational input. That's because NDS tree design is primarily a technical activity. After all, what are we organizing — technical resources, not people. However, we can't totally ignore people, either. They sneak in toward the bottom.

Now, let's review these five design inputs and learn a little more about their roles in NDS tree design.

ACME WAN Layout

Figure 4.9 shows ACME's WAN layout map. The WAN layout consists of all your major hub locations and their interconnected routers and bridges. Notice in ACME's WAN layout map that all five main sites are shown with their router connections and the speed of these links in kilobits (Kbits) per second. Your WAN layout map may look similar and it may additionally include the link speeds of your satellite offices (or distribution centers in our case).

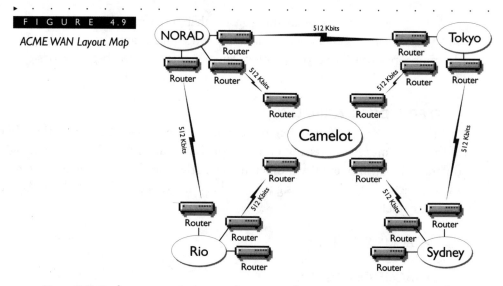

FIGURE 4.9

ACME WAN Layout Map

Your WAN documentation may be more than one, nice, compact diagram. Don't worry if your documentation consists of several pages of information. The key here is to understand how your infrastructure is organized and where the major locations are. These documents are necessary for the upper layer design of your tree, as we will explain in Step 3. Most companies have some sort of WAN map, but you may have to draw a new one. Try to consolidate all of the important interconnectivity information in a single overview.

ACME Campus Maps

The WAN layout provides a great interconnectivity overview, but it's not enough. You'll need campus maps for each major hub site. This type of documentation varies from company to company. Some companies show the entire hub and campus diagrams together, while others separate the information because of its complexity. Regardless, the campus maps should show the type of information illustrated in Figure 4.10. This is ACME's campus map for the CAMELOT hub.

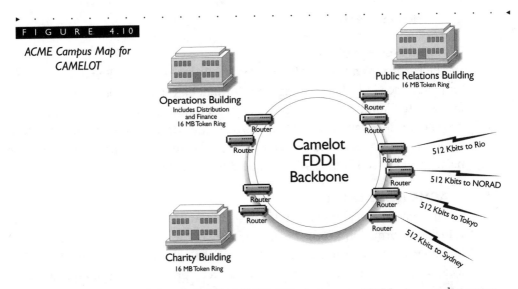

FIGURE 4.10

ACME Campus Map for CAMELOT

The ACME campus map for CAMELOT shows an FDDI ring and routers connecting the distributed buildings. The campus diagram may also show building structures and their addresses. For example, the ACME WAN layout shows a network in CAMELOT. Further research however produces a list of sites within the Camelot area, such as an operations center (OPS) located at the south end of the city and a public relations office (PR) located in the downtown district. An office for charitable contributions (CHR) is also found at the north end of the city. Figure 4.10 shows a list of these sites.

Campus maps are important because they refine ACME's WAN/LAN infrastructure. We need the campus maps to organize the second tier of ACME's top layers — that's Step 3.

ZEN

"Flying doesn't make me nervous. Driving to the airport can make me nervous. Because, if you miss that plane, there's no alternative. On the ground, you have options. You have buses, you have taxis, you have trains. But when you're taking a flight, if you miss it — that's it. No airline goes, 'Well, you missed the flight. We do have a cannon leaving in about ten minutes. Would you be interested in that?'"

Jerry Seinfeld

ACME World Map

The last map is a big one. It provides a global view of ACME and its distributed locations. Each hub site, building, and distribution center should be integrated into one ACME World Map. This provides a snapshot of the ACME geography and becomes the foundation of the top layers of ACME's tree. In addition, this information combines with the ACME WAN layout to determine if regional containers are necessary. Refer to Figure 3.9 in Chapter 3 for a picture of ACME's World Map.

ACME Resource List

The final technical input is a doozy — the ACME Resource List. This list gives valuable information about the servers and printers found in each region, site, building, or department. Table 4.8 shows the resource list for ACME with its locations, organizations, administrators, servers, printers, and print queues. These are the only resources we're interested in during NDS tree design. Later, in Chapter 8, we'll focus on all the ACME resources and place them in appropriate containers. Today, we're more interested in the branches of the tree.

Also, notice that the ACME Resource List has undergone a significant change. The original wish list can be found in Table 3.2 in Chapter 3. This list has been updated to include the naming standards discussed previously. Additionally, appropriate administrator, servers, and printers have been distributed to their proper locations — as per the WAN layout and campus maps. Don't you just love it when a plan comes together?

T A B L E   4 . 8

*ACME's Updated
Resource List*

LOC	ORG	ADMIN	SERVERS	PRINTER/QUEUES
NORAD			NOR-SRVI	
	CHARITY	SirGawain	NOR-CHR-SRVI	HP4SI-PI/PQI
			NOR-CHR-PSI	
	PR	DClarke	NOR-PR-SRVI	HP4SI-PI/PQI
			NOR-PR-PSI	CANONBJ-PI/PQI
	LABS	AEinstein	LABS-SRVI	
	WHI.LABS	CBabbage	WHI-SRVI	CANONBJ-PI/PQI
		Ada	WHI-SRV2	
			WHI-SRV3	
			WHI-PSI	
	R&D.LABS	LDaVinci	R&D-SRVI	
			R&D-PSI	
	POLL.R&D.LABS	CDarwin		HP4SI-PI/PQI
	NUC.R&D.LABS	MCurie		HP4SI-P2/PQ2
	VR.R&D.LABS	INewton		HP4SI-P3/PQ3
RIO			RIO-SRVI	
	CHARITY	SirPercival	RIO-CHR-SRVI	HP4SI-PI/PQI
			RIO-CHR-PSI	
	PR	JHughes	RIO-PR-SRVI	HP4SI-PI/PQI
			RIO-PR-PSI	CANONBJ-PI/PQI
	ADMIN	GWashington	ADMIN-SRVI	CANONBJ-PI/PQI
		FDR	ADMIN-SRV2	
			ADMIN-PSI	
	FAC.ADMIN	JMadison	FAC-SRVI	HP4SI-PI/PQI
			FAC-PSI	

(continued)

ACME's Updated
Resource List (continued)

LOC	ORG	ADMIN	SERVERS	PRINTER/QUEUES
RIO	*AUDIT.ADMIN*	ALincoln	AUD-SRV1	HP4SI-P2/PQ2
	MRKT.ADMIN	TJefferson	MRKT-SRV1	HPIII-P1/PQ1
				HPIII-P2/PQ2
CAMELOT			CAM-SRV1	
	CHARITY	SirGalahad	CAM-CHR-SRV1	HP5-P1/PQ1
			CAM-CHR-PS1	
	PR	CEttelson	CAM-PR-SRV1	HP4SI-P1/PQ1
			CAM-PR-PS1	
	OPS	KingArthur	OPS-SRV1	CANONBJ-P1/PQ1
			OPS-PS1	
	FIN.OPS	Guinevere	CAM-FIN-SRV1	HP4SI-P1/PQ1
			CAM-FIN-SRV2	HP4SI-P2/PQ2
			CAM-FIN-SRV3	
			CAM-FIN-PS1	
			CAM-FIN-PS2	
	DIST.OPS	Merlin	DIST-SRV1	HPIII-P1/PQ1
			DIST-SRV2	
			DIST-PS1	
SYDNEY			SYD-SRV1	
	CHARITY	SirLancelot	SYD-CHR-SRV1	HP5-P1/PQ1
	PR	MClarke	SYD-PR-SRV1	HP4SI-P1/PQ1
			SYD-PR-PS1	
			SYD-CHR-PS1	
	HR	Gandhi	HR-SRV1	HP4SI-P1/PQ1
			HR-SRV2	
			HR-PS1	

T A B L E   4.8

*ACME's Updated
Resource List (continued)*

LOC	ORG	ADMIN	SERVERS	PRINTER/QUEUES
SYDNEY	*MEDICAL.HR*	ASchweitzer	MED-SRV1	HP4SI-P2/PQ2
			MED-SRV2	
	FOOD.HR	MTeresa	FOOD-SRV1	HP4SI-P3/PQ3
	SHELTER.HR	FNightengale	SHELT-SRV1	HP4SI-P4/PQ4
			SHELT-SRV2	
	PEACE.HR	Buddha	PEACE-SRV1	HPIII-P1/PQ1
TOKYO			TOK-SRV1	
	CHARITY	SirKay	TOK-CHR-SRV1	HP4SI-P1/PQ1
			TOK-CHR-SRV2	
			TOK-CHR-PS1	
	PR	BThomas	TOK-PR-SRV1	HP4SI-P1/PQ1
			TOK-PR-PS1	
	CRIME	SHolmes	CRIME-SRV1	HP5-P1/PQ1
		DrWatson	CRIME-SRV2	
			CRIME-PS1	
	BLUE.CRIME	WEarp	BLUE-SRV1	HPIII-P1/PQ1
			BLUE-PS1	
	VIO.BLUE.CRIME	BMasterson	VIO-SRV1	HP4SI-P1/PQ1
			VIO-SRV2	
	ENV.BLUE.CRIME	WBHickok	ENV-SRV1	HP4SI-P2/PQ2
	THEFT.BLUE.CRIME	DHoliday	THEFT-SRV1	HP4SI-P3/PQ3
	WHITE.CRIME	RHood	WHITE-SRV1	CANONBJ-P1/PQ1
			WHITE-SRV2	
			WHITE-PS1	

(continued)

	TABLE 4.8			
	ACME's Updated			
	Resource List (continued)			

LOC	ORG	ADMIN	SERVERS	PRINTER/QUEUES
TOKYO	CYBER.WHITE.CRIME	FrTuck	CYBER-SRV1	HPIII-P1/PQ1
	POL.WHITE.CRIME	MMarion	POL-SRV1	HP4SI-P1/PQ1
	FIN.WHITE.CRIME	LJohn	TOK-FIN-SRV1	HP4SI-P2/PQ2
				HP4SI-P3/PQ3

Wow! That's quite a list. Study it carefully, because everything we do from now on will center around these critical resources. Our sole purpose in life is to organize these network resources productively — well maybe not our *sole* purpose for living, but a pretty important one. Anyway, keep this list handy, you'll need it during Steps 3 and 4.

ACME Organizational Chart

That brings us to the final design input — ACME's organizational chart (see Figure 4.11). Some companies have pages of organizational charts. Try not to get too wrapped up in them. Your main purpose here is to identify divisions, departments, or other organizational workgroups. Also, use the Work Flow Diagram (see Figure 3.8 in Chapter 3) to identify auxiliary workgroups throughout the WAN. These divisions, departments, and workgroups will become the foundation of ACME's bottom layers — that's Step 4.

TIP

Resist the temptation to design your tree around the organizational chart. This is more common than you think, mostly because it's the only design input people understand. It's also the *only* design input available in many cases. I know it's more work, but develop technical inputs for your organization and use them for your tree design. You'll thank me in the long run, especially when it comes time to design partitions and replica placement.

That completes Step 1. Many times it's the most difficult of the four steps. Very few companies document their WAN to this extent. You might even have to create a few inputs yourself. But it's worth it. Nothing's harder than trying to design the tree without them. These documents are the driving forces of the entire NDS design process.

Speaking of the process, let's move on to Step 2 — Pyramid.

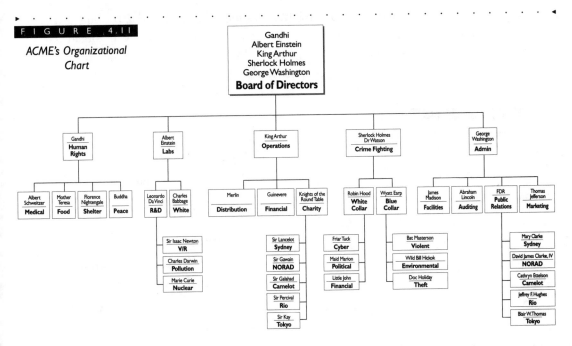

FIGURE 4.11

ACME's Organizational Chart

ZEN

"Make your plans as fantastic as you like, because 25 years from now they will seem mediocre. Make your plans 10 times as great as you first planned, and 25 years from now you will wonder why you did not make them 50 times as great."

Henry Curtis

STEP 2: PYRAMID

Now that you've gathered all the design inputs, it's time to put them to good use. The overall tree design should take the shape of a pyramid, or inverted tree. This places most of the objects at the bottom of the structure with the fewest containers at the top. Furthermore, the pyramid design should be split into two sections:

▸ Top

▸ Bottom

First, you will design the top of the tree. It should be organized according to the geography of ACME. Then, the bottom layers can rest on top. They are organized according to ACME's organization. Figure 4.12 illustrates how the pyramid design splits the top and bottom sections of the tree.

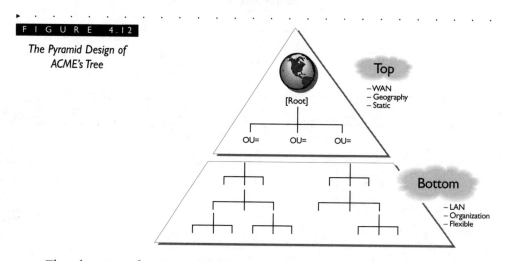

The Pyramid Design of
ACME's Tree

The advantage of a pyramid design is that the top layers become the foundation (or static layers) where upon the bottom layers can be established. The bottom layers of the tree are the layers that will be more dynamic and give your tree the flexibility it requires to change when your company changes.

Another advantage of the pyramid design is *natural partitioning*. This means that partition boundaries flow naturally and Subordinate Reference replicas are minimized. We'll discuss this later.

An alternative to our pyramid design is a flat tree that places all NDS objects in the top layers (see Figure 4.13).

With all NDS objects at the top of the tree, our ACME design becomes rigid and inefficient. A flat tree is not recommended because of the way it must be partitioned and replicated. Synchronization traffic is increased considerably, and a very large number of Subordinate Reference replicas may appear.

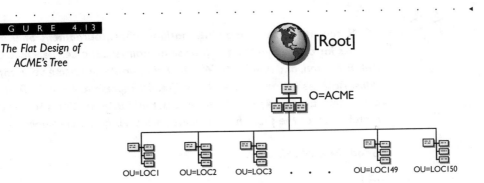

FIGURE 4.13

The Flat Design of
ACME's Tree

[Root]

O=ACME

OU=LOC1   OU=LOC2   OU=LOC3   . . .   OU=LOC149   OU=LOC150

TIP

An efficient NDS tree will have more Organizational Units at the bottom layers of the tree. No matter what, try not to exceed 50–70 Organizational Units per layer. Even the largest companies with many branch offices can meet this requirement.

As seen in Figure 4.12, the tree always starts with the [Root] object on top, followed by the O=Organization container. After the O=ACME Organization, we start distributing OU=Organization Unit(s). The top of the tree should reflect the physical structure of your WAN. This top section builds a solid foundation for the bottom layers. Typically, only a selected set of users and network resources are located in the top layers of the tree. For example, the Admin user is located in the O=ACME Organization because INSTALL automatically put it there. He or she is also the central administrator for the entire WAN, so he or she belongs there. As we stated previously, place only globally shared resources in the top layers.

The bottom of the tree is defined by the local area network (LAN) and is based on the functional organization of your company (see Figure 4.12). This can be accomplished by using the divisions, departments, workgroups, and teams in the corporation. These bottom layer OU's will hold the majority of ACME's objects, including users, file servers, printers, queues, and other network resources.

SMART LINK

Explore the true power of the Pyramid at http://www.teleport.com/~metamor/.

QUIZ

ACME recently sponsored an international chess tournament. Sherlock Holmes introduced you to the four semifinalists: Zena Le Vue, Dr. A. Glebe, Rob E. Lumen, and Ann Ziata. Was he being polite or testing your cognitive skills? Both. As it turns out, each semifinalist represented one of four continents: Europe, Africa, the Americas, and Australia. Can you correctly match each of the four chess masters with their home continent?

Good show Mr. Holmes.

(Q4-3)

Now that we understand the rough pyramid shape of ACME's tree, let's take a closer look at the top and bottom layers. Remember, each half serves a unique and special purpose.

STEP 3: TOP LAYERS

As in most things, the top is the most important half. It is the foundation of ACME's NDS tree design. The rest of the tree branches downward from there.

The top layer starts at the [Root]. Then, the O=Organization defines the company — ACME. And finally, the first tier of OU=Organization Units defines distributed WAN hubs. As you can see in Figure 4.14, ACME's top layers are organized around three main container objects:

- ► [Root]

- ► O=Organization

- ► OU=Organizational Units

Let's explore these three containers and learn how they "magically" appeared in ACME's top layers. Also, we'll throw in the C=Country object for good measure.

[Root] Object

First, you must name the tree itself. The tree name is represented by the [Root] object and is placed at the very top of the pyramid. Your tree name should represent the company name plus _TREE. For example, our company is called ACME so we chose to name the tree ACME_TREE. Check out Figure 4.14.

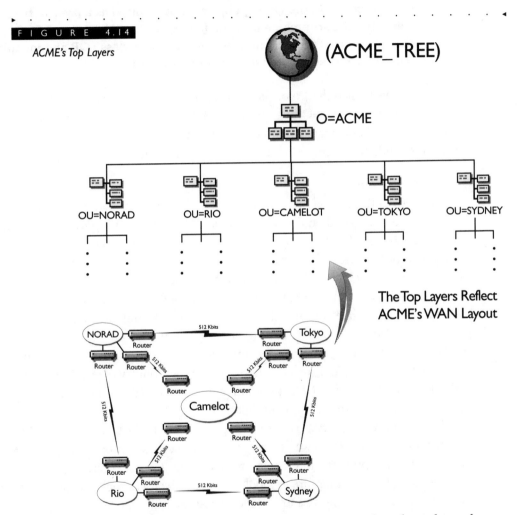

F I G U R E   4.14

ACME's Top Layers

(ACME_TREE)

O=ACME

OU=NORAD   OU=RIO   OU=CAMELOT   OU=TOKYO   OU=SYDNEY

The Top Layers Reflect ACME's WAN Layout

NORAD   512 Kbits   Tokyo
Router   Router
Router   Router   512 Kbits   Router   Router
Router   Router
                Camelot
512 Kbits   512 Kbits
            Router   Router
Router   Router
Router   512 Kbits   512 Kbits   Router
Rio   512 Kbits   Sydney
Router   Router

The tree name must be unique, because trees use SAP to broadcast themselves. SAP enables all applications requiring NDS to find the database very efficiently. If you must install more than one logical tree on the same physical WAN, be sure that the trees have different names. The company name plus _TREE guideline works because it clearly identifies the SAP broadcast as an NDS tree. Otherwise, we'll get an identity crisis where tree SAPs are confused with server SAPs. Bad news.

> **TIP**
>
> The **NDS** tree always starts with the [Root] container object. In most discussions, the [Root] object is not counted as a layer in the tree. Also, the schema defines the [Root] as the object class TOP. The [Root] object is the only instance of the object class TOP, and for this reason, TOP is known as an *effective* class. Cool.

Once you've named the [Root], it's time to move on. The next container can be either a C=Country or O=Organization. Novell Consulting Services recommends that you use the O=Organization next. The C=Country object causes all sorts of problems. And, of course, we're going to talk about it next.

C=Country Object

The C=Country designator is based on the X.500 standard and used to specify a particular country based on the X.500 standard. Public network providers, such as NetWare Connect Services (NCS), will make use of the Country object. The question is often asked, "If a company wants to connect to a public service provider, must I use the C=Country object?" Fortunately, the answer is "no." But they will add it for you. Also fortunately, the gateways that establish the connection between your private corporate tree and the public trees will be able to translate country codes as needed. So, you don't have to worry about it.

Of course it's a free country (pun intended) and you can use the C=Country container if you wish to. If you do choose to use the Country object, it will add an additional layer to your NDS tree and create some rather interesting naming problems. Consider the example in Figure 4.15.

If we add a C=Country object to the ACME tree, the first question is, "Which country do we choose?" Do we use multiple country codes? For our example, ACME is headquartered primarily in Camelot; therefore, our Country object will be C=UK (United Kingdom). Just for fun, let's look at some of the user's contexts that would be created in other locations. Abraham Lincoln resides in the RIO location, and so his name would be

```
.CN=ALincoln.OU=AUDIT.OU=ADMIN.OU=RIO.O=ACME.C=UK
```

In addition, Sherlock Holmes in the TOKYO location would have the following name:

```
.CN=SHolmes.OU=CRIME.OU=TOKYO.O=ACME.C=UK
```

FIGURE 4.15

ACME Gets a C=Country Object

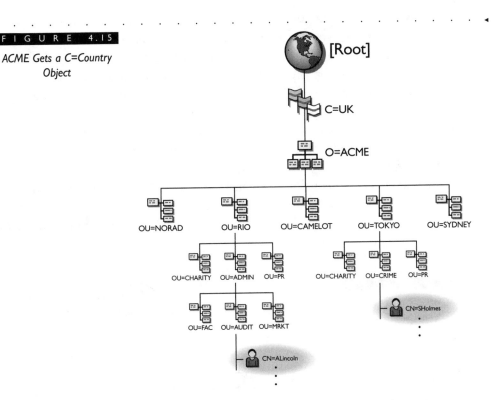

Now, these are some ugly names. In addition to being longer, these names are confusing. If Mr. Lincoln resides in RIO, why is his C object "UK"? Also for users who work in both the UK and the United States, it is difficult (if not impossible) to determine where they belong in the tree. Finally, consider the problems that will be created with typeless or relative distinguished names. Now everybody will have to specify whether they're using the C=Country attribute.

Nah, too much work. But, if you've already implemented the C=Country object in your tree, don't worry. It doesn't cause any serious connectivity problems. It's just a pain in the neck. For the rest of us, the second container under [Root] should be O=Organization.

SMART LINK

For more information regarding the perils of the Country object, surf over to the Novell Knowledgebase at http://support.novell.com/search/.

O=Organization Object

After the [Root], you can start your "real" tree with at least one O=Organization object. This tier defines the company and its purpose. All other geographic and organizational function is provided by lower OU=Organizational Units.

You should name the O=Organization the same as your company. Most companies use an abbreviation to alleviate long object names. For example, our company is named "A Cure for Mother Earth," which is abbreviated to ACME. In almost every case, this layer contains only a single O=Organization container, with all other structure handled below — with OU's. Sometimes, however, this is not the case. Some multinational conglomerates include many different companies, where each operates independently. In this case, you may want to create an O=Organization for each corporation. In Figure 4.16, we've combined ACME and the UN into a single NDS tree.

▶ · ◀

F I G U R E   4.16

ACME and the UN Share an NDS Tree

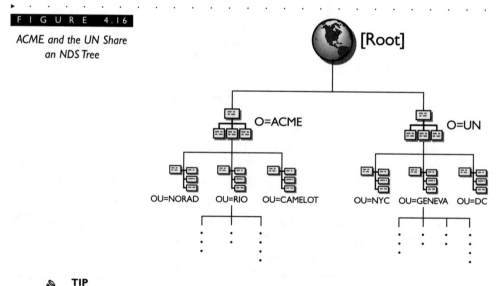

TIP

It is not recommended that you name the O=Organization the same as the [Root]. The **ACME** tree, for example uses the company name plus **_TREE** for the tree name. Our corporation would therefore be named **O=ACME**, with a tree name of **ACME_TREE**.

TIP

A single NDS tree with two or more O=Organization objects is extremely rare and not usually recommended. The reason that this configuration is not often used is because there would not be a single object at the top of the tree that represents the entire conglomerate company. This makes merging and partition management a little bit trickier. On the other hand, you may want multiple organizations if your corporation has very distinct business units that operate as separate companies with separate administration stratagies.

On the other extreme, some companies are so small that they only need a single O=Organization and no other containers. In Figure 4.17, for example, we've created a "smaller" ACME with all the users, servers, volumes, and printers in a single O=ACME container. This design is simple, easy to use, and very easy to manage.

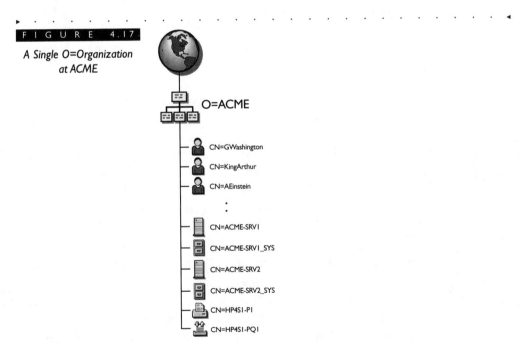

FIGURE 4.17

A Single O=Organization at ACME

O=ACME

CN=GWashington

CN=KingArthur

CN=AEinstein

CN=ACME-SRV1

CN=ACME-SRV1_SYS

CN=ACME-SRV2

CN=ACME-SRV2_SYS

CN=HP4SI-P1

CN=HP4SI-PQ1

Chances are, you don't fall into either of these extreme categories. Chances are, you're just like the rest of us and you need OU=Organizational Units to define the majority of your tree. Now, let's explore the final tier of the top layers — Organizational Units.

ZEN

"Be what you wish to seem."

Socrates

OU=Organizational Units

The final top layers are defined by Organizational Unit containers. These are the most important layers in the tree, because they represent a transition point between the inflexible upper layers and the flexible bottom layers. These OU's also define the layout of the rest of the tree. In summary, this is where your tree begins to take shape.

You can choose one of three approaches for the final tier of the top layers:

▸ *Geographical* — Organize the upper layers according to ACME's WAN Layout Map and distributed sites.

▸ *Regional* — Insert regional containers to further organize numerous distributed sites.

▸ *Departmental* — Organize the upper layers according to ACME's organizational chart and departmental workgroups.

These three top layer strategies should be prioritized in the order shown. Try the geographical approach first, it's the best one — trust me. OK, so you don't trust me. Well, at least give me a chance to convince you. Here's a detailed discussion of each of the three approaches, and an explanation of why ACME chose the geographical approach.

Geographical Top Layers   The first OU=Organizational Unit approach is based on the geographic boundaries of your WAN. Remember, the sole purpose of the NDS tree is to productively organize network resources. These resources are geographically distributed and rely on slow WAN links for interconnectivity. To optimize partitioning, replica placement, and time synchronization, you should design the first layer of OU's along these WAN boundaries.

As a matter of fact, the dynamic nature of Novell Directory Services really forces you to design the top layers of the tree according to geography. Here are some compelling reasons why:

▸ Reflects the WAN infrastructure

▸ Minimizes WAN traffic and related costs

▸ Facilitates partitioning because the WAN design provides a structure for partitions

▸ Reduces significant future changes to the Directory tree because locations are fairly permanent

▸ Places the physical network resources near the users and groups that need them

The geographical approach relies on your WAN Layout Map. As you can see in Figure 4.9, ACME is organized around five main hubs — CAMELOT, RIO, SYDNEY, TOKYO, and NORAD. These hubs become the foundation of ACME's OU structure, as shown in Figure 4.14. Once you've established the geographic top of the tree, you can zero in on each location with an organizational design — at the bottom layers.

Of course, life is full of exceptions. And the geographical approach is not *always* the answer (just most of the time). Here are two exceptions:

▸ **Exception 1** — Companies with a single site or local campus network are not dependent upon the geographical design approach. Since there's very little geography with which to work, you should skip the geographical layers and go straight to organization. Some companies with few servers and users may not need to create additional containers at all. Rather, they can place all of the NDS objects under a single O=Organization (see Figure 4.17).

▸ **Exception 2** — Companies with WAN sites or local campuses connected with very high speed links (such as T-3 or greater). In this type of situation, the location OU's are less important because the limiting slow WAN links have been removed. In this case, the very high bandwidths nullify geographic considerations.

REAL WORLD

Many companies still choose to use geographical designators even though they have very high speed WAN links. One such company, for example, has a metropolitan area network (MAN) running FDDI between 12 buildings across a city. The basis of their decision to stick with geographic sites was twofold. First, for administrative purposes, they wanted to have each building supported by a single administrator. The distributed OU sites gave the tree a good place to break out security administration. Second, certain local applications worked best with the geographic design at the top of the tree.

If you're using a campus layout (such as a research park or university), first consider the speed of the links between buildings or floors. The geographical approach could still be used with buildings representing minor OU sites within the network infrastructure. Even in ACME's case, the distributed campus buildings could be useful second-tier container objects — as long as they help organize the network resources.

As a matter of fact, the second-tier OU's in NORAD serve *both* purposes. As you can see in Figure 4.18, the NORAD campus connects three buildings — Labs, Charity, and PR. It just so happens that these are also the organizational workgroups located there. Interestingly, regardless of how we design the second-tier NORAD OU's (geographical or organizational), they will turn out the same — OU=LABS, OU=CHARITY, and OU=PR. What an interesting coincidence. This type of design overlapping occurs only in special circumstances. It's also a sign of a wonderfully designed WAN infrastructure.

Regional Top Layers The second OU=Organizational Unit approach relies on the introduction of regional containers above the geographic OU's. This is necessary if the total number of locations is high — 60 to 80 subcontainers per location, for example. Adding an intermediate "regional" layer helps to ensure a balanced pyramid design.

Consider what happens when ACME decides to expand. Let's say they decide to integrate more offices throughout the world. In this example only, ACME's WAN infrastructure would look something like Figure 4.19. Notice that the distributed offices connect together via 56-Kbit links, while the hubs still use 512-Kbit lines. Also, each city is added to the WAN layout through their appropriate regional hub.

▶ F I G U R E   4.18

ACME Campus Map for
NORAD

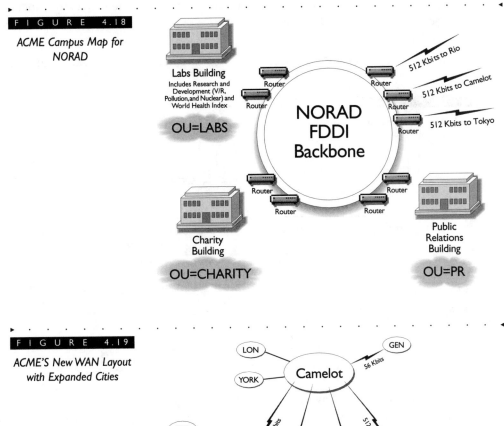

► F I G U R E   4.19

ACME'S New WAN Layout
with Expanded Cities

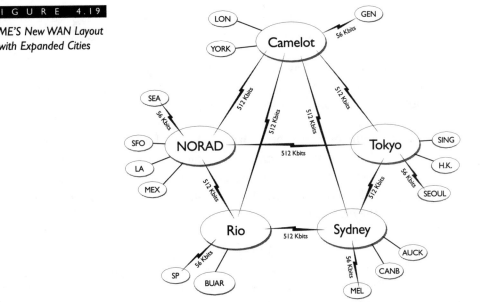

Using the WAN infrastructure, we have designed a new tree that includes regional OU's named North America (NA), South America (SA), Europe (EUR), Asia(ASIA), and Australia (AUST). These regional OUs group the appropriate cities and help keep the NDS tree design looking like a pyramid (see Figure 4.20).

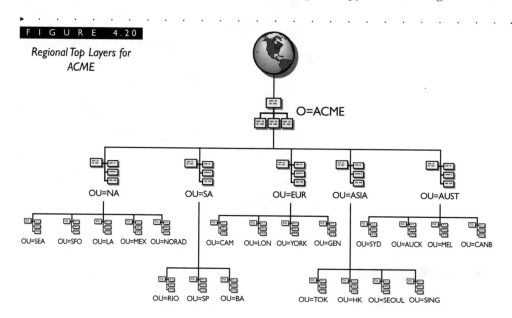

Regional Top Layers for ACME

Departmental Top Layers   The final OU=Organizational Unit option is based on the organizational workgroups throughout your company. This departmental approach should only be used in two cases:

I • Your company doesn't have a WAN infrastructure or other locations to consider. If your company operates over a LAN or high-speed WAN, then you can skip the geographical design and go directly to the organizational bottom layer design. This approach is based solely on the organizational chart.

2 • If you're a rebel, and you really want to design your tree according to the company's organizational chart. This approach is justified if there is something "very special" about your company — all resources are organized according to workgroup function. It happens.

In either of these cases, you can place your departments, divisions, and work-groups at the top of the tree and physical locations at the bottom. This is a little less efficient because any change to the organizational structure ripples down the entire NDS tree design.

Consider the example in Figure 4.21. We have swapped the ACME design and put their workgroups at the top. The first question is, "Where do most network changes occur?" Most changes occur at the organizational level. That's not to say that changes don't occur to geographic sites as well, but they are less frequent. Therefore, when you make changes to the tree, you want to impact the least number of people. Not in this case. Remember, flexibility at the bottom, rigidity at the top. Also, when considering other design requirements (such as administration, partitions, replicas, network resource placement, login scripts, and Bindery Services), it is apparent that the organization layers of the NDS tree more adequately consider these elements.

F I G U R E   4.21

ACME's Alter-Ego Tree —
Departmental Top Layers

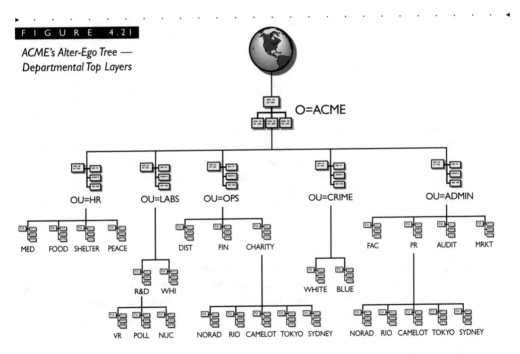

That completes Step 3. We're well on our way to NDS Nirvana. There's only one step left, and it's a doozy. But before you go on to Step 4, take a moment to review Table 4.9, which is a critical comparison of the two most popular tree-design approaches — geographical and departmental.

*Comparison of Geographical
and Departmental Design
Approaches*

FEATURE	GEOGRAPHICAL	DEPARTMENTAL
Location of objects in a partition	All objects in a partition exist at the same location.	Objects in a partition exist at multiple locations separated by WAN links.
Authentication	All users login and are authenticated locally, not across the WAN link.	Authentication takes longer and ties up the WAN links for those who must log in to a remote partition.
Administration	Changes to objects are generally made by local administrators so updates to the Directory are faster.	An administrator of departmental Organizational Units must manage objects long distance, which increases cost and complexity.
Replication	All replicas can be stored on local servers producing the synchronization costs of updating events.	To make authentication and administration faster, Read/Write replicas of all partitions must be stored throughout the WAN. Because of this, replica synchronization consumes the WAN link bandwidth and Directory updates are slow.
Sharing of network resources	Users tend to share resources locally. Administration of security and access is easier because rights can be granted at a higher level in the Directory tree.	Users tend to share resources locally. However, access to those resources is complicated because separate branches of the Directory tree contain those resources.

ZEN

Three o'clock syndrome — The tendency of office employees to become drowsy in the mid-afternoon. Or, the tendency on the part of working mothers to feel guilty about being away from home when their children arrive there from school. Or, finally, the tendency of anyone to feel anything at 3:00 a.m. or p.m.

STEP 4: BOTTOM LAYERS

With ACME's top layers in place, it's time to add organizational functionality to our tree. Then, we'll begin resource placement with the administrators, servers, printers, and print queues. These are the two functions of the bottom layers:

▸ Organizational Function

▸ Resource Placement

Organizational Function

Throughout the book, we've been harping on the tree as a framework for network resources. It's true. But what *is* ACME doing with the resources? Working! And how does ACME work? According to their organizational chart! So, it looks as though organizational function matters after all.

The bottom layers should be designed according to the organizational boundaries of your company. The bottom OU=Organizational Units should be based on ACME's divisions, departments, and workgroups. This information is detailed in Figure 4.11 (ACME's organizational chart). Further refinement can be found in ACME's WorkFlow analysis (see Chapter 3).

Another interesting thing happens as you move down the tree — resources get closer to users. Also, the communication lines shorten. Most bottom layer OU's are separated by LAN links, not slow WAN lines. This means synchronization isn't such a problem, and the design becomes very flexible. Refer to Figure 4.22 for an illustration of ACME's bottom layers.

During the design of the bottom layers, ensure that there's a place for every user and network resource. Also, distribute shared departments, if necessary. For example, ACME's Charity and PR departments have an office in each major location. Furthermore, each office has at least one server and shares information with a central database in CAMELOT. For this reason, we've decided to create an OU=CHARITY and OU=PR container in every location. This might seem repetitive, but it's the only way to handle distributed shared departments.

Also, notice in Figure 4.22 that the top layers of the ACME tree are based completely on the WAN infrastructure — they will remain fairly stable. Once the WAN infrastructure has been taken care of, your design effort should switch to the bottom of the tree. The bottom of ACME's tree is based on its organizational chart. Almost all of ACME's network resources will be placed in the bottom of the tree — close to its users.

ACME's Bottom Layers

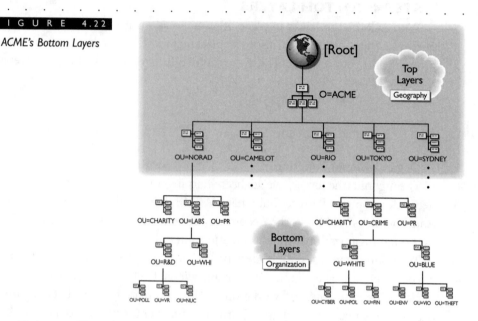

Resource Placement

Resource placement considerations also will affect how you design the bottom layers of your tree. At this point you may want to consider the networking needs of your users. How are they organized? If the resources are organized according to workgroups, they should be placed in the same container as users. However, if the network resources offer services to multiple departments, you should place the resources higher in the tree — possibly at the location container.

Remember, there should be a logical place for every network resource and user. At this point you should review ACME's updated resource list (see Table 4.8). It includes functional containers, servers, administrators, printers, and print queues. These are the only resources that will have any significant design impact. All other NDS resources (such as groups, login scripts, and directory map objects) will be placed during the NDS Management phase (see Chapter 8).

Congratulations! You're the proud parent of a baby NDS tree. It may seem innocent now, but wait until your users get hold of it. Now, wasn't that easy? Let's review — pyramid, geography, organization — all done. Well, at least with the rough draft. Next, there are a few external design factors you should consider before finalizing the design. It's time for some fine-tuning.

Let's play a game. You, me, and Albert Einstein will each toss a coin in succession. The winner will be the first to throw a head. What are each of our respective chances?

(Q4-4)

DESIGN CONSIDERATIONS

Some CNEs try to design the NDS tree all in one step — simultaneously juggling five design inputs and four external pressures. Not a good idea. First, create the top layers according to geography. Next, create the bottom layers according to organization. Now you're finished with the rough draft.

Next, fine-tune the tree with any of the following design considerations:

- ▸ Administration

- ▸ NDS partitions and replicas

- ▸ Login scripts

- ▸ Bindery Services

Interestingly, these design considerations only affect the bottom layers of the tree. Fortunately, it's the flexible half. This is because they mostly deal with user resources, and most of them live in the bottom layers of the tree — although this is not a social commentary. Let's explore these four external design pressures in a little more depth.

Administration

Tree Administration is one of the most important design considerations — mostly because it involves *you*! There are two choices: centralized and distributed. *Centralized administration* relies on a single IS (Information Services) staff for all portions of the tree. *Distributed administration*, on the other hand, distributes branch control to container administrators — typically at the departmental or geographic level. Here's how it works.

Centralized Administration In this case, the entire NDS tree is controlled by one IS group. This group manages all of the additions and deletions of NDS objects, partitioning, replication, and everything else related to the NDS database. In Chapter 11 we'll learn how to create central administrators by giving them Supervisor rights to the top of the tree — [Root].

If the NDS tree is to be managed centrally, the IS staff will build the entire tree, and will have control over all NDS objects throughout the tree. This also helps standardize naming and object placement.

Another unique approach for centralized administration is to place all servers in one NDS container. This provides easier server access and simpler tracking of server activity for network administrators. It works for smaller LANs or MANs (Metropolitan Area Network environments), but isn't a good approach for large Enterprise WANs. On the downside, it limits all your servers to one partition and it involves more serious setup and design considerations. Because of this, you'll be forced to devise a fault tolerance strategy for replica placement within and between these centralized servers. This is probably not the best way to go. If you want true NDS management, control, and efficiency, consider a distributed administration strategy.

Distributed Administration With distributed administration, on the other hand, control over portions of the NDS tree is delegated to individuals or independent groups. These individuals may be departmental administrators, or they may be responsible for all of the network resources in a particular location. In this scenario, you'll still need a central IS staff to handle the top layers of the tree. We'll also explore decentralized administration in Chapter 11.

If the NDS tree will be decentrally managed, each container administrator will decide independently how that portion of the tree is organized. The IS department handles the top layers and then relinquishes control to distributed individuals. This is difficult for many IS managers, especially with the higher learning curve associated with NDS. Just make sure your container administrators know what they're doing. If you care, you'll give them each a copy of this book (hint, hint).

SMART LINK

For an on-line gift, consider the other Novell Press study guides at http://corp.novell.com/programs/press/hot.htm.

In addition to this book, here are a few more gifts for container administrators:

1 • They should have sufficient security over their containers to create, delete, or change all their objects.

2 • They should carefully determine (and justify) if more levels must be created beneath their containers before making changes.

3 • They should actively participate in creating and using the naming standards document.

4 • They should not partition their OU's without the assistance of the central IS department.

5 • They should inform the central IS staff before adding a new server into the corporate tree.

The depth of the tree can also impact your administration choices. Remember, the recommendation is to build the NDS tree like a pyramid with fewer layers at the top and more layers at the bottom. Centralized administration dictates that a flat and wide tree is easier to administer. If your company has only a few servers and users, you can build a shallow tree that is good for centralized administration.

On the other hand, distributed administrators can determine the depth of their portion of the tree. But don't let them go wild. The NDS tree is much easier to deal with if it's three to five layers deep. Even the largest companies can design a productive NDS tree with five layers or less. Check out ACME, they use five — and that includes the [Root].

> **TIP**
>
> There is no physical limit to the number of layers in the NDS tree. There is, however, a logical limit to the total number of layers you can access. For instance, NDS has a limit of 255 characters for a distinguished name. Thus, the actual limit for the number of layers is dependent on the number of characters in the name of each container. If your OU names are long, you will not be able to have as many layers as with shorter names. For example, if all the OU names are just two characters long, then you can have 127 layers. But, if your OU's average 20 characters in length, you can only have 12 layers.

NDS Partitions and Replicas

The next external pressure comes from NDS partitions. The tree design should reflect a variety of partitioning factors, including the size of the partition (total number of objects), the total number of replicas, and where in the tree the partitions are created.

A container object is required for the creation of a partition. In addition, it is designated the "root-most" object of the partition. Figure 4.23 shows a number of partitions, and in two cases we've identified the partition root — the NORAD partition and the TOKYO partition.

Partitioning ACME's Locations

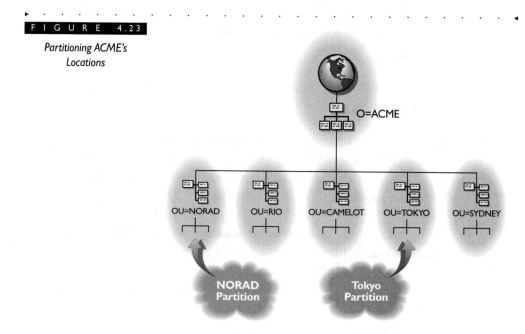

When you're creating NDS partitions, always follow the physical network infrastructure. Like the top layers of the tree, partitions typically follow the WAN layout map — creating a partition at each location. This strategy has many advantages, but the most apparent is accessibility. Network resources are always available to local users. In Figure 4.23, we've partitioned all five ACME hubs.

The size of your partitions and the total number of replicas is a design consideration for the bottom of the tree. Typically, partitions range in size from 100 to 3,500 objects. If the partition grows to be significantly larger than 3,500 objects, you should probably split the partition in two. Therefore, in Figure 4.24

we create a new partition called OPS under CAMELOT because that location's partition has grown beyond the 5,000-object limit. More partitions, in the right places, provide greater efficiency in your tree design. Remember, a partition contains information about all the objects in a specific subtree, not just the objects in a single container.

The New OPS Partition

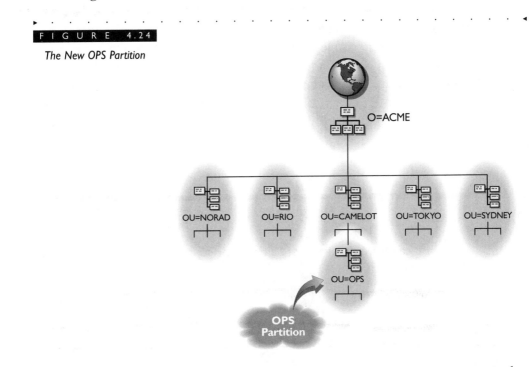

REAL WORLD

We are not suggesting that NDS will not work in partitions with more than 5,000 objects. However, based on experience, partitions work most efficiently in the 100- to 5,000-object range. Therefore, when your partitions reach this size, begin assessing the need to split the partition. Check your user's performance and synchronization performance, and use that as a guide. Also note that partitions with less than 100 objects cause more management overhead than they are worth. See Chapter 9 for more information on NDS partitioning and replication.

The next design consideration is the total number of replicas of a partition. If the number of replicas is greater than 10 to 15, consider splitting the partition to reduce the total number of replicas. Novell recommends three replicas for each partition. The primary reason you would need more than a couple of replicas for any partition is Bindery Services. As you'll learn in just a moment, IntranetWare servers require a Master or Read/Write replica of all containers within their bindery context. This number can grow very quickly.

Decide who is responsible for the partitioning of the NDS tree. If you manage the tree centrally, then all the partitioning decisions should be made by the central IS department. If tree administration is distributed, then you may turn over local partitioning control to each container administrators. Whichever way you handle partitioning make sure that you decide who's going to do it *before* you start installing servers.

REAL WORLD

If you are considering a distributed partitioning strategy, remember to grant NDS rights accordingly:

▸ Create partitions — [S] object right to partion root object

▸ Add replicas — same as for creating partitions and [S] to the host server

We will discuss partitioning design in greater depth later in this chapter and in Chapter 9 ("NDS Partition Management and Synchronization").

ZEN

"My children always had an unusual diet .... In general, they refused to eat anything that hadn't danced on TV."

Erma Bombeck

Login Scripts

The third NDS tree design consideration deals with login scripts. Login scripts impact the bottom layers of the tree and indirectly control how users access certain resources. In general, users need login scripts to map network drives, capture print queues, and set other environmental variables. Therefore, the login scripts become a very important design consideration.

Typically, users needing the same login script will be grouped together in the same OU container. You can then use the Container login script to provide access to NDS resources. Figure 4.25 shows two Container login scripts — one for OU=FIN (shared by Guinevere, *et al.*) and one for OU=DIST (shared by Merlin, *et al.*). You should separate the users who need different login scripts for the same reason. As you design the login scripts for your users, you are, in fact, designing the organizational structure of the bottom level of the tree.

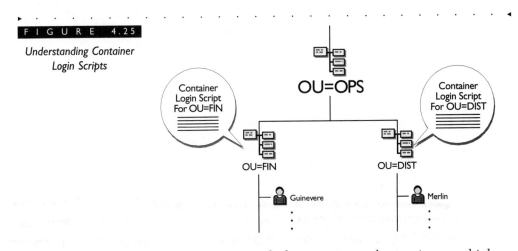

FIGURE 4.25

Understanding Container Login Scripts

Another approach is to create a single login script and copy it to multiple containers. In this case, user placement is not affected. However, this strategy requires that you (the CNE) keep track of all the scripts and make sure they're the same. Too much work. I have a solution.

You can also make use of the Profile login script. It enables you to span a single login script across multiple OU containers. For example, the SYDNEY location has a profile script for the HR department. It spans across the following three OU's: OU=MEDICAL, OU=FOOD, and OU=SHELTER. Check out Figure 4.26.

We'll discuss login scripts in much greater depth in Chapter 12. For now, let's explore the final tree design consideration — Bindery Services.

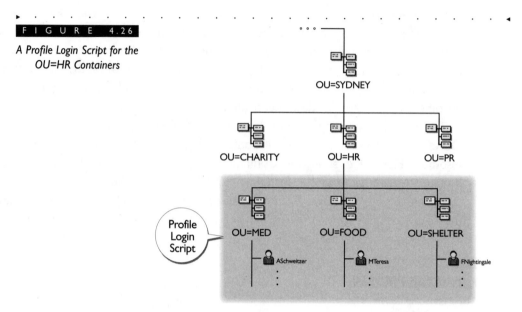

A Profile Login Script for the OU=HR Containers

Bindery Services

NDS provides backward compatibility to NetWare 2 and NetWare 3 users with a feature called *Bindery Services*. This feature allows bindery versions of NetWare and other third-party software to access the NDS database as if it were the bindery. For example, a client can use the NETx shell (NetWare 3 client) to login to an IntranetWare server and run any bindery-based application that exists there.

Bindery Services can be enabled on any IntranetWare server using the SET BINDERY CONTEXT command. You can select from 1 to 16 OU containers as the bindery context. The *server bindery context* is simply the containers the bindery user sees as the bindery. Only the leaf objects in bindery context container(s) appear to bindery users. In Figure 4.27, we've used SERVMAN.NLM to create a bindery context for the LABS-SRV1—OU=LABS.OU=NORAD.O=ACME. This means that bindery users in Labs will only see the NDS objects within the OU=LABS container.

If you're concerned about your server's bindery context, use the SET BINDERY CONTEXT command as shown in Figure 4.28. It tells you what's going on. If you want to change your server's bindery context, use the SET BINDERY CONTEXT command at the file server console.

F I G U R E 4.27

Setting Bindery Context in SERVMAN.NLM

F I G U R E 4.28

Understanding the SET BINDERY CONTEXT Command

IntranetWare Bindery Services allows you to select up to 16 OU containers as a "superbindery." Here's the kicker: In order for Bindery Services to work, the host server must have a Master or Read/Write replica of each bindery context partition. If the server has 16 bindery containers, it must hold 16 separate replicas.

As you can see, placing bindery replicas can increase the total number of replicas for each partition. This will affect the tree design because you may be forced to split a partition to reduce the number of replicas. Bindery Services is one of the main reasons you would want to maintain more than a few replicas of any partition.

Finally, what about bindery resource placement? You must place all bindery users and their appropriate users in the same bindery context container. If you plan on using many NetWare 3 users, this can get quite cumbersome. It will also affect your NDS tree design because it requires that you combine users and resources from multiple departments into a single OU — which defeats the purpose of bottom layer organization. I don't like it. Only use Bindery Services if you have to, and refer to the "NDS Accessibility Design" section at the end of this chapter for more details.

> **TIP**
>
> **Before you change the bottom of your tree design to accommodate Bindery Services, determine whether you even need Bindery Services at all. Remember, Bindery Services is an optional feature that does not have to be enabled at each server. You should determine if the clients are using NETx or applications that require Bindery Services. You could also identify the users and key applications, and force them to use Bindery Services on specific servers.**

REAL WORLD

Here is a brief list of some the applications you may encounter that make bindery calls. This is a brief list, and you need to check all your applications to determine if they require the bindery.

- ▶ Print services
- ▶ Menuing systems
- ▶ Backup utilities
- ▶ Host connectivity products
- ▶ Network management utilities
- ▶ Other NetWare 3-based applications and utilities

Congratulations again! The tree has been built *and* refined. Now we're really finished. As you can see, there are many more external design pressures to consider than just geography and organization. It's a good thing you stayed awake during those last few pages.

ZEN

"Are you having trouble in saying this stuff? It's really quite easy for me. I just look in my mirror and see what I say. And then I just say what I see."

Dr. Seuss

Now it's time to move forward. The tree has been designed, and we're ready for more. You are ready for more — aren't you? Good, because partition and replica design are next. I wonder how the roller coaster ride is going . . . .

Partition and Replica Design

"whooooa!"

"aaaaaah!"

"heeeelp!"

These are all great examples of how the roller coaster ride is going — it's going *fast*! We're halfway down "The Great Fall" now, and my stomach is officially in my throat. The exhilaration can only be eclipsed by free-falling from an airplane (now, there's an idea). We can't do that yet. That's IntranetWare 3 — Novell hasn't announced it yet.

SMART LINK

Ride your own NDS roller coaster at http://mosaic.echonyc.com/~dne/RollerCoaster!/.

Our third stop along the NDS design tour is partition and replica design. Once the tree has been designed, we get to break it into small little pieces (partitioning) and scatter them around the WAN (replica placement). At this point, you don't actually perform any partitioning operations, you simply *design* the partition boundaries. Once the boundaries have been designed, you must give serious thought to where they'll go — replica placement.

Replica placement is one of the most important aspects of NDS design because it directly affects your network's performance, accessibility, and fault tolerance. Remember, you won't actually *place* anything until later — during the NDS Partition Management phase (Chapter 9).

In the next few pages we're going to explore ACME's partition boundaries and replica placement design. But before we do, we should take a moment to review NDS partitioning and replication. We discussed these topics in depth previously in Chapter 2. Now we'll take the story a little bit farther — into the realm of design. Here's what's in store for us in this section:

▸ Understanding NDS Partitions

▸ Designing ACME's Partitions

▸ Understanding NDS Replicas

▸ Placing ACME's Replicas

Think of this discussion as Genetics 101, and we're learning how to clone NDS containers. Ready, set, clone.

UNDERSTANDING NDS PARTITIONS

NDS partitions are logical pieces of the NDS tree (see Figure 4.29). This process effectively splits the NDS database into subtrees. The subtrees can then be distributed to IntranetWare servers throughout your WAN. Partitioning the NDS tree provides you with the ability to selectively distribute the NDS tree information to the areas in your network that need the information — near the users.

The purpose of partitioning is to give you the ability to scale the NDS database across IntranetWare servers. Splitting up the database and storing its pieces on separate servers distributes the workload for both NDS and the server. In addition, IntranetWare partitioning tools allow you to choose which partitions go on which servers.

For example, in Figure 4.29, you can see that the NORAD partition and its object information is placed on the NOR-SRV1 server in NORAD. The same is true for all the other locations. By partitioning the NDS tree, you can keep the local information in each location, and yet still have access to the rest of the global database. Life is good.

Partitioning is hierarchical — meaning that the root-most partition is parent to its subordinate children. When all partitions are taken together, they form a hierarchical map back to the [Root] object. Figure 4.30 illustrates the hierarchical partition map formed by ACME's distributed locations. It also shows the parent/child relationship between OU=CAMELOT and its subcontainers.

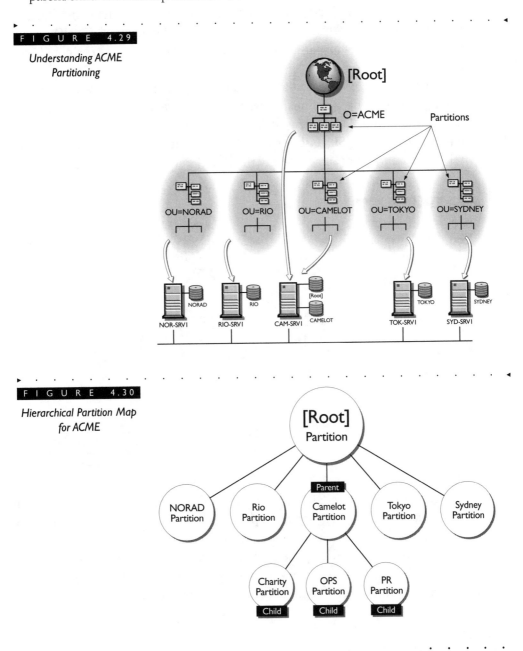

FIGURE 4.29

Understanding ACME Partitioning

FIGURE 4.30

Hierarchical Partition Map for ACME

As in life, partition parents must manage their subordinate children. This is ensured in NDS through a concept known as *Subordinate References*. When new partitions are created under an existing container, their parent must maintain pointers to the new partitions. This concept is shown in Figure 4.31. NDS requires these pointers so that all partitions are linked together to form a common database of information.

Subordinate References create and maintain the fragile link between parent and child partitions. Therefore, any server holding a parent partition can end up with a large number of Subordinate Reference pointers to its children. For example, check out the CAM-SRV1 server in Figure 4.31. It gets a copy of every location OU, because they are all children of the [Root] Partition.

Understanding Subordinate References

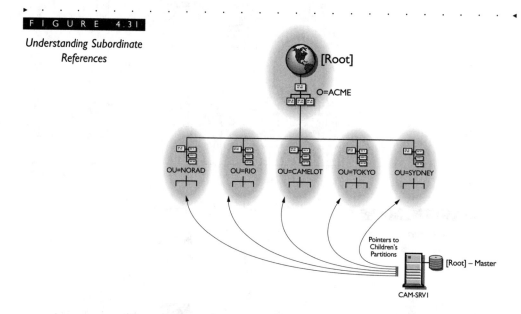

As a matter of fact, the [Root] is a very sensitive partition. Let us emphasize that NDS creates a Subordinate Reference pointer automatically when a server holding a parent partition creates a link to its child partitions. However, for greatest efficiency we recommend that you keep the number of separately partitioned containers to 50 to 70 per layer. For these reasons, we also recommend that the [Root] partition be kept small with only the [Root] and an Organization container below it.

THE BRAIN

Subordinate Reference replicas are tricky and important. You must understand them to succeed as a CNE. For a more thorough discussion and some great exercises, see Chapter 9.

With all of this "family tree" stuff in mind, let's explore some more important partitioning rules. Then, we'll learn how to create partition boundaries. Cool.

Partitioning Rules

NDS partitioning follows these simple rules:

1 • Each partition must be named and requires a single container object as the top (or root) of the partition (not to be confused with the [Root] partition). The container object that is used as the start of the partition is called the *partition root object*. Only one partition root object exists for each partition, and it is the topmost container object. Check out Figure 4.32.

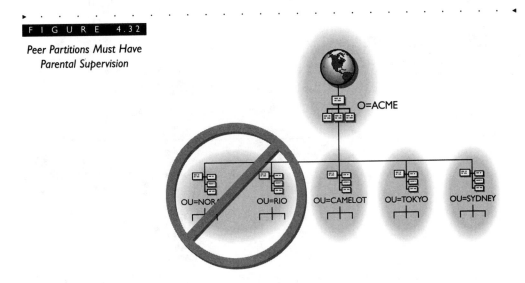

F I G U R E   4.32

Peer Partitions Must Have Parental Supervision

2 • Two containers at the same level cannot share a partition without a parent watching over them. Play nicely children. This rule is illustrated in Figure 4.32.

3 • Partitions cannot overlap with any other part of the NDS tree. This means that one object will never reside in two partitions.

4 • Each partition contains all the information for the connected subtree, unless another subordinate partition is created underneath.

Now that we know the rules, let's get busy creating partition boundaries. Here's a quick lesson.

Creating Partition Boundaries

During installation of the very first IntranetWare server in your Directory tree, the [Root] partition is created and a Master copy (replica) of it is placed on this server. In IntranetWare, the [Root] partition is the only partition the installation program creates. There is no default partitioning beyond this — it's all up to you. See Figure 4.33 for an illustration of the [Root] partition. Since this [Root] partition is the only partition that is created during installation, it is often called the *default partition*. The [Root] partition cannot be removed unless you remove NDS from all of the IntranetWare servers — which is really removing the entire tree.

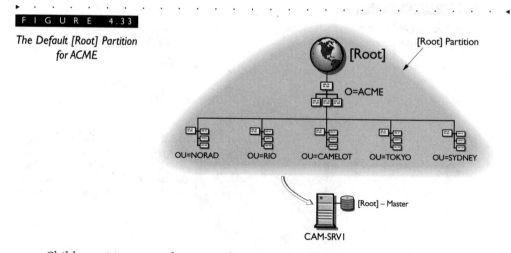

FIGURE 4.33

The Default [Root] Partition for ACME

Child partitions can be created under the [Root] partition by selecting a subordinate container object (typically an OU) as the top of the new partition. A partition can only have one topmost container object (referred to as the *partition root object*).

When the partition is created, it takes its name from the topmost container object. All of the objects in the tree that are under the partition root container are contained within the new partition. This is always true, unless there is a previously defined partition lower in the tree. The partition defined previously is not affected. Figure 4.34 shows how the NORAD partition is created underneath and to the side of the [Root] partition. All the NDS objects in the NORAD location are suddenly part of the NORAD partition.

FIGURE   4.34

The New NORAD Partition

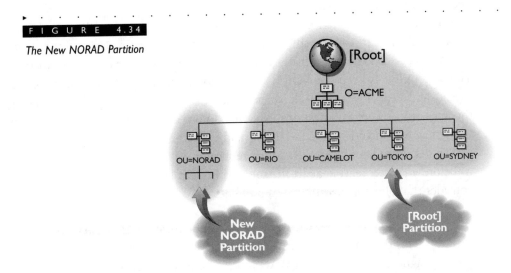

Creating a new partition under an existing parent is sometimes referred to as a *partition split*. This is because the child simple splits away from underneath the parent's control. In Figure 4.34, the NORAD child simply splits away from the [Root] partition. This operation is extremely fast because it doesn't generate any traffic on your WAN. We're simply dividing one database into two with all the information staying on the same server that contained the original partition. This split operation will create a new child Subordinate Reference pointer on all the servers that had a copy of the parent partition.

ZEN

"One of the disadvantages of having children is that they eventually get old enough to give you presents they make at school."

Robert Byrne

Now you're ready for ACME. This has been a great preview, but I want to get my hands dirty. I want to feel mud under my fingernails. I want to prune the ACME tree! (I really need to get a hobby.)

DESIGNING ACME'S PARTITIONS

Where do we start? Partition design is very simple if you follow this one cardinal rule: Partition to distribute the NDS database across ACME servers — if it doesn't need to be partitioned, then don't!

The number one design criteria for partitioning is the physical layout of your network infrastructure — mostly the location of network servers. Using this criteria, your main task is to partition the NDS database so that it localizes NDS information. The bottom line is keep the NORAD information in NORAD, the RIO information in RIO, and so on. Figure 4.29 shows how the ACME tree has been partitioned along the lines of WAN communications. Note that in our example the [Root] partition is very small and includes only the [Root] and O=ACME. This is recommended and will be discussed later when we address replication.

Before you start tearing apart the top and bottom layers of ACME's tree design, consider the following partitioning guidelines:

I • **Don't span a WAN link or physical locations with a partition** — This design guideline rule is very important and should not be ignored. If you span a WAN link, it creates unnecessary NDS synchronization traffic between two or more locations. Spanning a WAN link is shown in Figure 4.35 and should be avoided. Notice how three locations have been combined into one [Root] partition.

▶ . . . . ◀

FIGURE 4.35

Don't Span WAN Links with Partitions

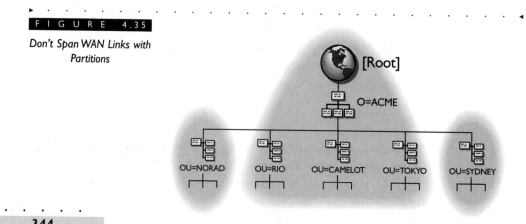

2 • **Keep the [Root] partition small** — Typically, this should include only the [Root] object and the O=Organization container. Do not include any other subordinate container OU's in the partition with the [Root] object — this creates unnecessary Subordinate References.

3 • **The top layers of the tree should be partitioned according to location** — Again, remember guideline number 1, do not span a WAN link with the same partition. Partition locally wherever possible.

4 • **The bottom layers of the tree should be partitioned in special cases only** — The bottom layers of the tree should be partitioned only if there is a special requirement. The special requirements are either size of the partition (total number of objects is greater than 3,500), too many replicas of the same partition, or the need to break out an administrative domain.

5 • **Use the pyramid design for partitioning as well** — You will want a small number of partitions at the top layers of the tree and possibly more partitions as you move toward the bottom. If you have designed the tree based on a pyramid shape, as recommended, then your partition design will naturally follow the tree design. Remember, one of the advantages of the pyramid tree design is natural partitioning. Now you know what we were talking about.

6 • **Do not create a partition unless there's a local server** — Do not create a partition (even if it includes a WAN link) if there is not a server locally on which to store it. This situation is common only with small remote offices that do not have servers at their local sites. The users would currently access all the network services across the WAN infrastructure anyway. The access to NDS is not any different. Figure 4.36 shows how the remote users in the OU=DIST container would still be part of its partition even though they don't have a server of their own.

TIP

These guidelines do not suggest that you partition every Organizational Unit in your tree. There is also such a thing as overpartitioning. Partition locally, and further partition at that site only if necessary.

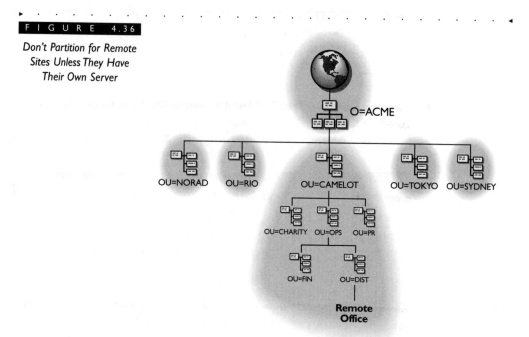

O=ACME

OU=NORAD   OU=RIO   OU=CAMELOT   OU=TOKYO   OU=SYDNEY

OU=CHARITY   OU=OPS   OU=PR

OU=FIN   OU=DIST

**Remote
Office**

REAL WORLD

No new partitions are created by IntranetWare automatically. Keeping the default of a single partition is recommended for networks with all the following characteristics:

- ► No WAN links
- ► 15 or fewer servers holding replicas
- ► Fewer than 3,500 objects

Partitioning the Top Layers of ACMEs Tree

It all starts at the top. As I'm sure you've guessed by now, the top layers should be partitioned according to the WAN infrastructure. What a surprise! Since the top layers have already been designed according to the WAN layout, the partition boundaries should follow naturally.

The NDS database will not scale as well if you try to combine multiple geographical sites into one partition. If you try to span more than one location in a partition, then the information in the partition will synchronize with the other copies across the slower WAN links. This reduces the efficiency of the network and destroys the purpose of trying to create a partition in the first place.

If you have implemented regional OU containers, then you should create a partition for each of the regional OU's and store that partition on a server separate from its parent partition. After the regional partitions are defined, you'll need to create a child partition at each location. This will distribute Subordinate References to location-based servers.

That was easy. Now for the tricky part. Let's see what's going on at the bottom layers of ACME's tree.

Partitioning the Bottom Layers of ACMEs Tree

As I'm sure you remember, the bottom layers are designed according to ACME's organizational structure. Does organization have a big impact on partitioning? Not really. We've already partitioned ACME according to location, so what do we do with the bottom layers? Nothing . . . in most cases. But, of course, the world is full of exceptions, and here are three:

▶ Partition size

▶ Number of replicas

▶ Partition administration

Partition Size   As the partition size grows, you should consider creating another partition to help distribute the workload to other servers. A normal-sized partition is approximately 3,500 objects. If the partition grows to be significantly larger, you might consider splitting it into new children. Remember, a partition contains all the objects in a defined subtree, not just the objects in a single container. But don't get carried away. A partition with less than 100 objects may not be worth the adminstrative overhead.

Figure 4.37 shows how the CAMELOT partition is split into two partitions — one parent and one new child. The OU=OPS container object becomes a new child partition to CAMELOT. We created the new OPS Partition, because CAMELOT got too big — more than 3,500 objects. Those Knights sure are busy!

F I G U R E   4.37

Splitting the CAMELOT
Partition in Two

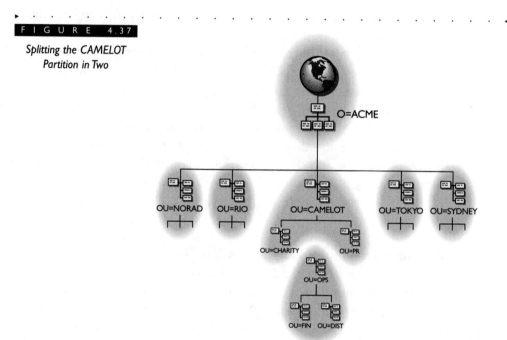

Number of Replicas   Another exception revolves around the total number of replicas of a single partition. If the total number of replicas goes beyond 10 to 15, then you should consider splitting the partition just to reduce the number of replicas that must be synchronized. Again, that's too much work for the server. The only reason you'll want more than three replicas of any partition is to support Bindery Services.

Also, keep in mind that more replicas mean more management — especially if a partition breaks and needs repairing. Replica repair can be difficult if you have a large number of replicas because each one may need to be repaired separately.

Partition Administration   NDS allows you to distribute partition administration as well. Lucky you. If a department manager wants the responsibility of managing his or her own partitioning, then you must plan the superior partitions accordingly. For example, the rights needed to partition the NDS tree are either the Supervisor object right at the OU, or the Write right to its ACL. Also, if there is a need to create a new partition from the parent, then the individual creating the child also needs full rights to the parent. For more information on NDS security, refer to Chapter 11.

This completes our partition design for ACME. If you follow these partitioning guidelines at both the top and bottom layers, the NDS information always will remain close to the user and other leaf objects. Remember, location is the key when creating partition boundaries. Review Table 4.10 for a complete picture of NDS partition design.

TABLE 4.10	WHY CREATE MORE PARTITIONS	WHY CREATE LESS PARTITIONS
When to Create an NDS Partition	They decrease administrative overhead.	They create additional Subordinate References for the child and parent partitions.
	They reduce the size of the NDS database for a given server.	They increase network complexity.
	They improve performance by placing resources near users.	They increase the time needed to navigate the Directory tree.
	They reduce network traffic caused by user access over WAN lines.	They increase traffic over WAN links caused by synchronization.
	They distribute and replicate important information and reduce the dependency on a single server.	

THE BRAIN

For more information about creating NDS partitions refer to Chapter 9 ("Partition Management and Synchronization"). In that chapter, you'll get an opportunity to create "real" ACME partitions using IntranetWare's NDS Manager. Design is theory, management is *action* **or surf the Web at http://www.novell.com/manuals.**

Very good. Now that we have ACME's partition design in place, it's time to spread them out — replica placement. This is the fun part. We get to distribute all the little pieces to ACME servers everywhere. And why do we do this? Because we can!

ZEN

Designer genes — Genetic material that has been altered through genetic engineering for use in agricultural, medical, and networking experiments. Thought to be the foundation of IntranetWare replication.

UNDERSTANDING NDS REPLICAS

The next step in NDS design is *replica placement*. Once the pieces have been created, you can distribute them. Why?

- Because replicas increase NDS fault tolerance.

- Because replicas enhance network performance.

- Because replicas simplify name resolution.

First of all, replication increases the availability of partitions — it spreads them around. This also increases reliability. For example, if a server holding a replica of your partition goes down, then you can simply use another copy for authentication and updates.

Second, distributed replicas increase NDS and client performance. Replication enables you to distribute partition copies to local servers throughout the WAN. Having a local replica decreases the time needed for certain client tasks (such as authentication, NDS changes, searches, and data gathering). This does not imply that replicas should be used for mobile users. Having a replica locally means on the server where the majority of the users need the information.

Finally, replication enhances name resolution, because users requesting NDS information first must locate a server with the data's information on it. Replication spreads the data around. If the requested information is not found on the server to which the user is already authenticated, then NDS automatically will connect the user to the proper server through the process of name resolution. This connection process is simplified when there are more replicas from which to choose. It also happens faster and more reliably.

TIP

For improved speed, you can replicate the [Root] partition in strategic locations (such as hub sites). This allows users to walk the tree faster. The [Root] partition should be kept small for the purpose of keeping NDS traffic to a minimum.

In order to truly understand replica placement, you must learn what makes them tick. Here's a list of some basic replica rules:

1 • **A partition can have multiple replicas** — Multiple copies of a partition are known as *replicas* and can be stored on separate servers across the WAN.

2 • **Only one master replica per partition** — A partition can only have one replica designated as the Master. The other partitions will have Read/Write and/or Read-Only replicas. Refer to Chapters 2 and 9 for more detail.

3 • **Only one replica of a given partition can be stored on an single server** — An IntranetWare server can hold replicas from different partitions. It cannot hold two replicas of the same partition.

4 • **All replicas will participate in the replica synchronization for a partition** — All replicas (regardless of their type) are part of their partition's synchronization list (or replica ring) and, therefore, participate in synchronization operations. Most NDS changes are sent to the replica ring immediately, but other less-critical changes are queued locally and sent in 5- and 10-minute intervals. Again, refer to Chapters 2 and 9 for more details.

TIP

With all of this in mind, remember that there's a delicate balance between NDS replication and performance. In many cases, too many replicas will *decrease* network performance because of background synchronization traffic. Bottom line: Don't go hog wild!

These rules are important because they describe the characteristics of replication. You must understand how replicas behave before you start copying ACME's partitions. If you feel you're ready, we'll move on to "Placing ACME's Replicas." If not, refer to Chapter 2 for a more detailed replica review. Ready, set, replicate.

PLACING ACME'S REPLICAS

Welcome to phase 2 of partition design — replica placement. The partitions we created in the previous section aren't going to do us any good until we clone them. As a matter of fact, replica placement is one of your most important design responsibilities — for the many reasons outlined previously. Here's how it works:

- ▸ *Fault Tolerance* — Eliminate any single point of failure in ACME's NDS tree.

- ▸ *Local Distribution* — Place replicas on local servers for efficiency and speed.

- ▸ *Bindery Services* — Bindery users and applications need Master or Read/Write replicas of their server's bindery context.

- ▸ *Improved Name Resolution* — Distribute replicas strategically to create "bridges" between separated containers.

Let's take a closer look at replica placement for ACME. And, who knows, we may learn a thing or two along the way.

Fault Tolerance

The primary goal of replication is to eliminate any single point of failure in the entire NDS tree. Distributing multiple replicas of a partition increases the availability of object information if one of the servers should become unavailable. In Figure 4.38, the NORAD and CAMELOT partitions have been replicated to multiple servers within their locations. This provides fault tolerance for each partition. If one of the servers in the partition goes down, the information isn't lost — it's available from the other server.

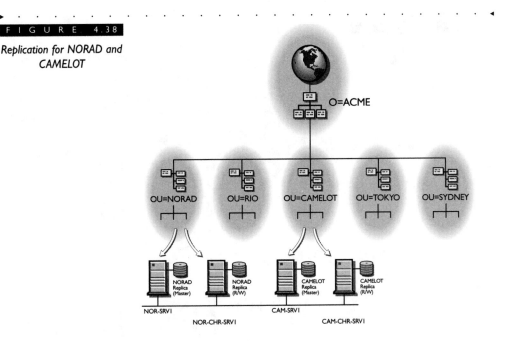

FIGURE 4.38

Replication for NORAD and CAMELOT

The IntranetWare server installation program automatically creates up to three NDS replicas for each partition — for fault tolerance. When you install additional servers into the NDS tree, IntranetWare places a replica of the server's home partition on the first three servers — a Master and two Read/Write replicas. After that, you're on your own.

For example, in Figure 4.39, the NORAD partition is automatically replicated as new servers are added. It starts with NOR-SRV1, then NOR-CHR-SRV1, and finally LABS-SRV1. Also, notice that NOR-SRV1 gets a Master replica. That's because it was the first server installed into the NORAD partition. The others receive Read/Write replicas. Then, one sunny day in June, you decide to install a fourth server (R&D-SRV1) into the NORAD partition — and nothing happens! Remember, by default, IntranetWare only replicates the partition on the first *three* servers. The first thing you should do is place a Read/Write NORAD replica on the new R&D-SRV1 server. Check out Chapter 9 for the correct procedures.

This strategy only applies to the new server's home partition. It doesn't have any affect on other partitions in the tree. This is done for one simple purpose — fault tolerance of the NDS database. If you are comfortable with where the three automatic replicas are placed, then you don't need to place any of your own.

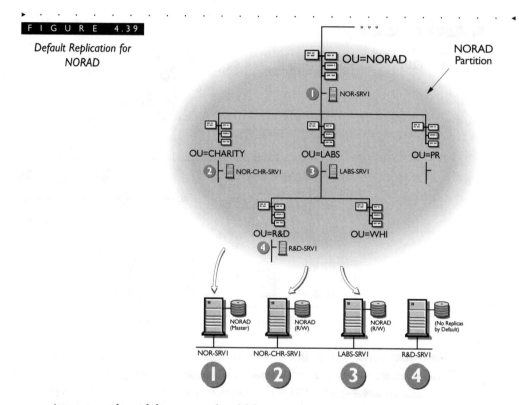

FIGURE   4.39

Default Replication for
NORAD

As a general guideline, you should have at least a Master and two Read/Write replicas of every partition, but never more than ten replicas of any partition, except the [Root]. If you don't have three servers in the same site, replicate the partition elsewhere. Just make sure the NDS information is available somewhere, but never more than ten replicas of any partitions, except the [Root].

Local Distribution

Always replicate locally — if you can. It makes your life much easier if you place all replicas of a partition on local servers. Local to who? Local to the users who need the resources defined in the host partition. Don't place replicas on servers across the WAN if a local one is available. If you follow this guideline, you can be guaranteed that the users will retrieve their personal information from the nearest available server. This is faster, more efficient, and more reliable.

ZEN

"Design globally; replicate locally."

Anonymous

Ideally, you should place the replica that contains a user's NDS information on the same server that stores the user's home directory. This may not always be possible, but it does improve the user's access to NDS objects and the file system. For example, during login, any given user will map drives to volumes, capture to print queues, and access several of their user properties. NDS will execute each of these requests regardless of where the replicas are stored. The login speed for the user will be increased, however, if the user finds the requested information on the first attached server — the local one.

TIP

Always try to place at least one replica of any given partition on a remote server — across the WAN hub. If you are forced to place all these replicas at one location, consider using a daily backup for fault tolerance. Never rely on Subordinate Reference replicas as your only copy.

Here's the $64,000 question: "What happens if the site only has one server? Do I still partition and replicate locally? How do I replicate for fault tolerance?" In the case of a remote site with just one server, you should still partition at that site and place the Master replica on that server. A second Read/Write replica should be placed at the nearest WAN location.

Figure 4.40 illustrates how a small remote office should be replicated. For this example only, assume that there is a small remote site called OU=SLC connected to the NORAD hub. There is only one server in the remote site — it's called SLC-SRV1. You should create a small partition and Master replicate it to SLC-SRV1. You should also place a Read/Write replica of OU=SLC in the NORAD location — possibly on the Master NOR-SRV1 server.

Typically, remote sites contain a small number of user objects anyway. Therefore, replicating across the WAN doesn't become such a big deal. You really don't have any choice. It's better to replicate a small partition across a WAN than to lose the NDS information altogether if the server ever goes down. And, by the way, the server *will* go down — it's the way of life.

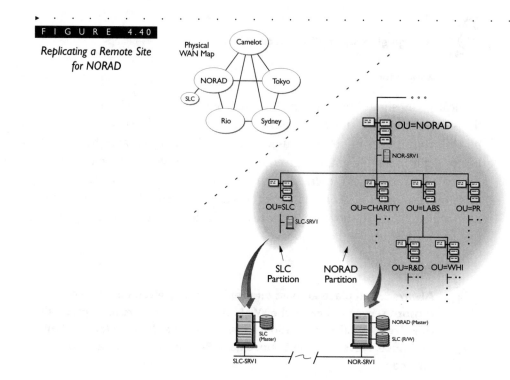

FIGURE 4.40

Replicating a Remote Site for NORAD

ZEN

"Prehistory was a very difficult time for humans. Hostile, vicious, person-eating predators roamed the Earth. Disease was rampant. Mortality rates were horrific. The automatic bank teller was still only a dream."

Dave Barry

Bindery Services

As mentioned previously, Bindery Services has a big impact on replica placement. Each bindery user or application requires a Master or Read/Write replica of its server's bindery context in order to work. The server bindery context can be set at the server console by typing the following:

```
SET BINDERY CONTEXT = OU=PR.OU=NORAD.O=ACME
```

In Figure 4.41, the bindery users attached to NOR-PR-SRV1 only see the NDS objects in the OU=PR.OU=NORAD.O=ACME container. Actually, they can't see *all* the NDS objects, just the bindery-equivalent objects (such as servers, users, groups, printers, print queues, print servers, and profiles). In case you were wondering, the Profile NDS object was added to IntranetWare as a bindery-equivalent. Unfortunately some really cool, new NDS objects aren't available to bindery users (such as Directory Maps, Organizational Roles, Computers, and Aliases).

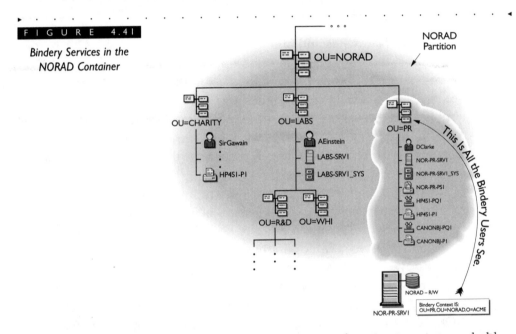

FIGURE 4.41

Bindery Services in the NORAD Container

In order for a IntranetWare server to support Bindery Services, it must hold either a Master or Read/Write replica of the partition in which the users are interested. In our case, the OU=PR users are OK, because the NOR-PR-SRV1 server has a Read/Write replica of the NORAD Partition. And, it just so happens that the OU=PR container exists within the NORAD Partition. Did I mention that the bindery context doesn't need to be its own partition? True.

REAL WORLD

Bindery Services is also required during a NetWare 3.12 to IntranetWare server upgrade. For example, when you upgrade a NetWare 3.12 server, a Read/Write replica of its home partition is placed on the new IntranetWare server. This happens regardless of whether there are already three replicas of the partition. Interesting.

Improved Name Resolution

Name resolution is the mechanism NDS uses to find object information not stored on the local server. It is also referred to as *tree walking*. If the NDS information you need is not stored locally, the server must walk the Directory tree to find a server with a replica. Every replica maintains a set of pointers to all the other replicas of the same partition — this is called a *replica ring*. Using these pointers NDS can locate the partitions that are above and below any container in the tree. Think of them as logical bridges between containers.

The [Root] is probably the most troublesome name resolution replica because it stores information about everybody. Replicas of the [Root] partition bridge to every container in the tree. For this reason, you should replicate the [Root] partition to all major hub sites in your WAN. But remember, the [Root] partition must be small. You don't want the Subordinate References getting out of hand.

Figure 4.42 illustrates replica placement for ACME's [Root] partition. In this case, we've distributed this small partition to three strategic locations — in NORAD on the NOR-SRV1 server, in CAMELOT on the CAM-SRV1 server, and in TOKYO on the TOK-SRV1 server. Don't go hog-wild on [Root] replication — three or four replicas are fine. Finally, you probably don't need to replicate any other partitions for name resolution. The [Root] partition should take care of all your tree walking needs.

THE BRAIN

Tree walking and name resolution are important parts of NDS replica design. If you don't adequately address these topics, IntranetWare and NDS will do it for you — also know as Subordinate References. Check out Chapter 9 for an in-depth discussion of Subordinate Reference replicas.

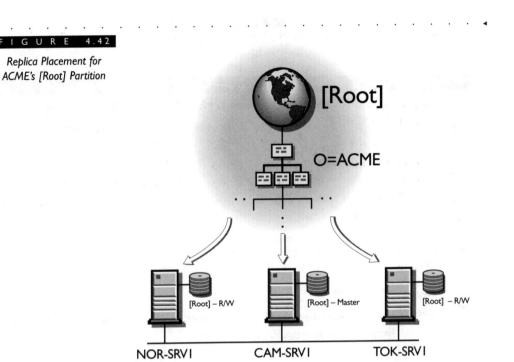

FIGURE 4.42

Replica Placement for ACME's [Root] Partition

[Root]

O=ACME

[Root] – R/W   [Root] – Master   [Root] – R/W

NOR-SRV1   CAM-SRV1   TOK-SRV1

This completes our discussion of NDS partition and replica design. In review, we can organize most network designs into two different classifications:

▶ *Quick Design* — Most network designs with minimal special needs. They use a conservative approach to replica design.

▶ *Advanced Design* — A few special network designs where the CNE fully understands the impact of aggressive replica placement.

Refer to Table 4.11 for a summary of replica design guidelines for Quick and Advanced designs.

That's it! You've taken another step toward NDS Nirvana. Three down, and only one more design step to go. So far, we've created a naming standards document, designed the top and bottom layers of the tree, and outlined partition boundaries. In the last section, we scattered the partitions to all four corners of ACME. So what's left? Time!

T A B L E   4.11

*Quick and Advanced Replica
Design Guidelines*

GUIDELINE	QUICK DESIGN	ADVANCED DESIGN
Minimum Server Requirements	486/66 MHz with 32 MB RAM	Pentium 90 MHz with 64 MB RAM
Partition Size	Up to 1,000 objects; never more than 1,500 objects	Up to 3,500 objects; never more than 5,000 objects
Number of Subordinate References	Up to ten	Never more than 35 to 40
Replicas per partition	At least two to three; never more than five	At least two to three; never more than ten
Replicas per server	Up to seven	Up to 20

SMART LINK

If you need more help placing your NDS replicas, get some help at http://support.novell.com/sitemap.

▶ · ◀

Time Synchronization Design

Time is an interesting phenomenon. Albert Einstein learned that time changes in relation to your speed. This is especially true when you're rocketing down a Big Dipper at Mach 3. Some moments seem to last forever (pausing at the Apex), while others occur in the blink of an eye (The Fall). Which of these choices describes your experience with this chapter — eternity or the blink of an eye?

No matter how you look at it, time controls everything. This is especially true in NDS. Time impacts every aspect of your IntranetWare life — NDS operations, the file system, messaging, printing, resource access, network applications, and security, just to name a few. For this reason, time synchronization becomes a priority. And it only works properly if it's been designed efficiently.

The final step in NDS design focuses on time synchronization. Time synchronization coordinates and maintains consistent time for all of the servers in your NDS tree. Time synchronization design relies on one of two time configuration strategies: default (small trees) and custom (large trees).

The *default* time synchronization option works best for small networks with only a few servers in a single location. This configuration is commonly referred to as the *single reference* configuration because it uses a Single Reference time provider.

The *custom* time synchronization option provides more flexibility for larger networks with multiple servers in distributed locations. It uses a special time provider group. The *time provider* group is designed to provide greater fault tolerance and efficiency for communicating time across multiple servers and wide area networks.

Once IntranetWare time has been configured, there's very little left to do. It simply runs. Later we'll explore both of these configuration options in detail. But before we do, let's start with a quick review of IntranetWare time synchronization in general.

QUIZ

I need a vacation, how about you? Let's take a little train trip ....

A train traveling at the speed of 50 m.p.h. enters a tunnel which is 1 1/2 miles long. The length of the train is 1/4 mile. How long does it take for all of the train to pass through the tunnel, from the moment the front enters to the moment the rear emerges?

(Q4-5)

UNDERSTANDING TIME SYNCHRONIZATION

Time synchronization provides IntranetWare servers with a mechanism for coordinating NDS time stamps. IntranetWare uses the TIMESYNC NLM to coordinate time stamps between all servers on the WAN. TIMESYNC.NLM maintains each server's Universal Time Coordinated (UTC) — a fancy name for Greenwich Mean Time (GMT).

TIP

The TIMESYNC NLM is automatically loaded each time the server is started. Time synchronization is active only when the TIMESYNC NLM is loaded. You should not unload this module.

Local time for each server is calculated by applying (adding) the time zone and daylight savings time settings to the server's UTC value. For example, if a server is located in the Mountain Standard Time zone (NORAD), its UTC offset would be +7. This value is applied (along with subtracting one hour for Daylight Savings Time, if in effect) as an offset to standardize the server's time to UTC. Therefore, each server regardless of its geographic location can be standardized to UTC time. Once again, the calculation is:

Local time +/- *time zone offset from UTC-* Daylight Savings Time offset

As you can see in Figure 4.43, you can type TIME to display these time statistics at the IntranetWare file server console.

F I G U R E   4.43

The IntranetWare TIME
Command

```
LABS-SRU1:TIME
    Time zone string: "MST7MDT"
    DST status:   OFF
    DST start:    Sunday, April 2, 2000    2:00:00 am MST
    DST end:      Sunday, October 29, 2000    2:00:00 am MDT
    Time synchronization is active.
    Time is synchronized to the network.
Thursday, December 2, 1999    4:42:36 am UTC
Wednesday, December 1, 1999    9:42:36 pm MST
LABS-SRU1:
```

The TIME command displays the time zone string, status of Daylight Savings Time (DST), if time synchronization is active, time synchronization status (synchronized or not), and the current server time (in both UTC and local format). Use this command periodically to check the status of your time servers. They must be synchronized in order to maintain accurate time stamps.

All NetWare 4.11 servers are time servers of some type — either *providers* or *consumers*. Time providers provide time to time consumers — makes sense. As you can see in Figure 4.44, IntranetWare supports three different types of time providers — *Primary server*, *Reference server*, and *Single Reference server*. On the other hand, there's only one type of time consumer: *Secondary server*. The majority of your IntranetWare servers will be time consumers.

TIME PROVIDERS	TIME CONSUMERS
Primary Reference Single Reference	Secondary

All IntranetWare time servers perform three functions in relation to time synchronization:

1 • Provide UTC time to any NLM or requesting client workstation.

2 • Provide status information regarding the synchronization of UTC time.

3 • Adjust their clock rate to correct for time discrepancies and maintain UTC synchronization.

Now, let's take a closer look at each of the four time server types. In this section, we will expand on what you learned in Chapter 2 — we're mostly interested in time design issues. You may want to review time synchronization in Chapter 2 before proceeding. See you on the other side.

Secondary Time Servers

Secondary time consumers rely on other sources to provide them with network time. A Secondary server can contact a Single Reference, Reference, or Primary server for the network time. The Secondary server will be the most prevalent type of time server on your network because most servers do not need to participate in time providing. By default, all servers except the first server are designated as Secondary servers when they're installed. The first server is defined as a Single Reference time provider.

The Secondary server will try to make up any difference between its clock and the time it receives from the network. The network time comes from any of the time providers during each polling interval. Therefore, any discrepancies in the Secondary's time will be resolved during each polling interval. Secondary servers can provide time to requesting clients or server applications.

> **TIP**
>
> **Secondary time servers do not participate in time providing. These servers do not vote with any other time server. They simply get the network time from other time providers.**

Primary Time Servers

Primary time servers are the first time providers. They are time providers because they distribute time to requesting Secondary servers. The interesting part is how they determine the time.

Primary servers poll. This voting process determines the "official time" for your WAN. Polling is accomplished by contacting all other time providers and identifying any discrepancies between the Primary server's local clock and the calculated network time. If there is a difference, then the Primary server adjusts its clock to 50 percent of the discrepancy during each polling loop.

Like all time servers, Primary time providers are obsessed with their internal *synchronization radius*. This is the allowable timing discrepancy within each server. If the Primary server is within its synchronization radius, it raises its time synchronization flag. This indicates that synchronization has occurred and everything is fine.

During the polling process, each Primary time server has one vote. This could be a problem if Primaries are your only time providers. In this case, there will never be a single source of time convergence. This problem is resolved by integrating a Reference server into your time provider group.

Reference Time Server

A Reference time server adds important stability to a Primary time provider group. Both types of time providers vote on network time, but Reference servers get the last word. During each polling interval, all the Primary time servers converge their internal clocks to the time of the Reference server. On the other hand, the Reference time server will never adjust its clock. This naturally makes the Reference time server the point of reference for convergence — hence the name.

In this scenario, the Primary servers provide fault tolerance. If the Reference server should fail, multiple Primary servers can average their time together to provide consistent network time. Therefore, the Reference server is the supreme authority of time except when it is not accessible.

TIP

During the voting process, the Reference time server has 16 votes and the primary servers only get one vote apiece. This means that the Reference server will always win the vote. Typically, you should only have one Reference server in your tree. The best balance is one Reference server and a few Primary servers. This is called a *time provider group*, and it's the topic of discussion in the next section.

REAL WORLD

Primary time servers don't immediately coverge to the Reference server's time. Since they are only capable of adjusting 50 percent of the discrepancy, total convergence takes a little time. Don't worry, though, it takes only a few minutes for most small discrepancies!

The most significant difference between Primary and Reference servers is that the Reference server does *not* adjust its internal clock. As long as it's operational, it is the center of the temporal universe. All other time servers converge to the Reference server's time. Because the Reference server is the only server that does not adjust its internal clock, you should connect it to an external time source.

SMART LINK

If you want to know what time it *really* is, check out the U.S. Government's atomic clock in Boulder, Colorado, at http://www.bldrdoc.gov/doc-tour/atomic_clock.html.

External clocks accomplish several important things. First, they provide an accurate and automated mechanism to check time. Some of your applications may require accurate time of day, if they initiate a process (such as a backup) in the middle of the night. Second, automated time sources fight temporal drift — it happens to the best of us. They ensure that the Reference server's clock stays within its synchronization radius by constantly updating it. There are various products available that connect PCs to external time sources (such as a radio clock, modem, the Internet, or the atomic clock in NORAD).

Only one Reference time server is usually needed on the network. Multiple Reference servers can be placed on the network, but they will not synchronize with each other. Some companies with large, worldwide networks prefer to use multiple Reference servers to provide fault tolerance or have a Reference closer to a particular group of servers.

Single Reference Time Servers

The Single Reference time server is a stand-alone time provider for the entire network. This is the default configuration and requires no intervention during installation. The main difference between a Reference server and a Single Reference server is that the Single Reference server can raise its synchronization flag without confirming its time with any other time sources — it has *total* control. The Single Reference server should only be used in small sites with less than 30 servers and no WAN connections.

TIP

Regardless of the size of your network, you can initially accept the Single Reference default until your installation grows beyond 30. Also, if you choose the Single Reference server option, do not use any other time providers. A Single Reference is the only time source required under this configuration.

With the Single Reference time configuration, all other servers are Secondaries. This means they all converge to the Single Reference's time during each polling cycle. A Single Reference time server can be connected to an external source, or use its own internal clock, it doesn't matter. Occasionally, it may be necessary to check the server's time against a reliable source (for example, try dialing "POPCORN") just to make sure.

ZEN

Minibang — An explosion involving much smaller amounts of energy and matter than that of the Big Bang — thought to be the origin of the universe in its current state. Also, the sound heard from a user's head when he or she finally logs in to NDS.

This completes our general time synchronization overview. Now it's time to explore two critical time synchronization design issues:

- Time Configuration

- Time Communication

Time configuration design outlines a strategy for time server definitions and placement. There are two options: default and custom. Then, *time communication design* deals with how the time servers talk to each other — SAP or Configured Lists. Let's start with time configuration design.

TIME CONFIGURATION DESIGN

Time configuration defines how your time servers are distributed. In addition, it outlines which servers are providers and which servers are consumers. As we learned previously, IntranetWare supports two basic time configuration designs:

- Default: Single Reference

- Custom: Time Provider Group

Whatever you do, be sure to choose the correct configuration method for your WAN. First, ask yourself, "Is my network distributed over multiple sites? Are there WAN links to consider?" If so, definitely use the custom method. A time provider group gives your network greater fault tolerance by distributing the time servers to multiple locations. Next, determine if your network has less than 30 servers. If so, use the default configuration method.

This sounds simple, and it is. However, these are just a few of the many factors you must consider in choosing a time configuration approach. Let's take a closer look at each.

Default: Single Reference Time Server

The first IntranetWare server is automatically configured as a Single Reference server. All other servers are Secondary time servers.

On the up side, the default configuration method is simple and requires absolutely no advanced planning. Additionally, no configuration files are needed and the possibility of errors during time synchronization is considerably minimized. This works best if you have less than 30 servers in your tree and no distributed locations. Refer to Figure 4.45 for an example of the default time configuration method.

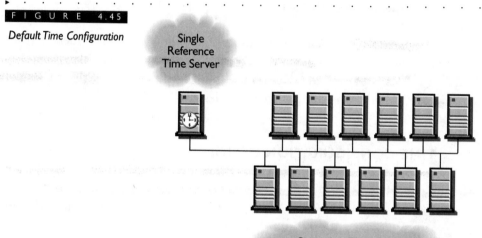

FIGURE 4.45

Default Time Configuration

The default configuration method relies on a central file server with a trusted hardware clock. Because it is the sole time provider, you should monitor its time frequently. If you're unhappy with your first time provider, you can always redesignate another server as the Single Reference using the SERVMAN utility.

On the down side, the default time configuration creates a single point of failure. If the Single Reference time server fails, all network time is lost. Even if this happens for a short period of time (a day or less), it can have a dramatic effect on NDS synchronization and security. When the sole time provider drops off, all Secondary servers continue to maintain their own time. Even worse, they continue to stamp NDS events — with the wrong time! Fortunately, they all resynchronize when the time provider wakes up.

If the default time configuration method isn't for you, consider using a time provider group. That's the other option — custom.

Custom: Time Provider Group

The custom time configuration method provides more fault tolerance, efficiency, and flexibility to large interconnected WANs. The time provider group requires one

Reference time server and a minimum of two other Primary time servers. These three or more time providers form a *time provider group* that in turn provides time to the rest of the IntranetWare servers — Secondaries.

As you can see in Figure 4.46, ACME organizes its time providers according to geography — one in each WAN hub. This configuration requires simple adjustments to the servers in the time provider group. One server will be designated as the Reference and two to seven servers may be designated as Primary time servers.

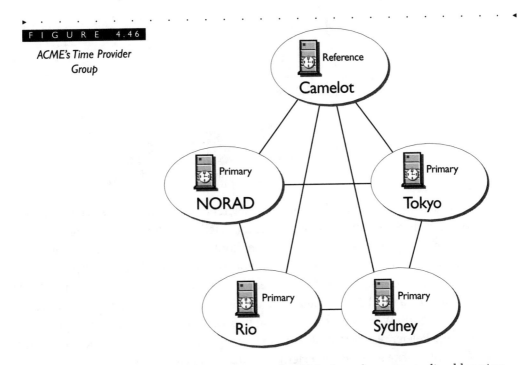

F I G U R E   4.46

*ACME's Time Provider
Group*

The selection of your Reference server should be based on a centralized location within your WAN infrastructure. For example, the ACME WAN uses a hub and spoke design. CAMELOT is the central hub, so it will be the home of the Reference server. The Primary servers are then distributed across the WAN links to each of the spoke locations. If your network is a large WAN, place a few extra Primary servers in strategic locations. The remainder of the installed file servers will be Secondary servers — by default. Figure 4.47 illustrates the placement of ACME time providers and time consumers. This design maximizes traffic efficiency and temporal fault tolerance.

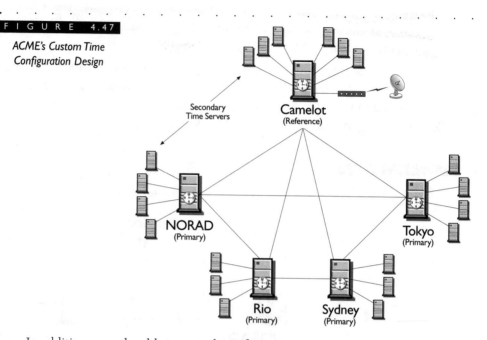

FIGURE   4.47

ACME's Custom Time
Configuration Design

Secondary
Time Servers

Camelot
(Reference)

NORAD
(Primary)

Tokyo
(Primary)

Rio
(Primary)

Sydney
(Primary)

In addition, you should connect the Reference Server to an external time source to ensure highly accurate time. Notice the satellite configuration in Figure 4.47.

Some companies may consider using multiple time provider groups. This increases redundancy in worldwide operations. For example, ACME could implement this approach by creating three independent time provider groups — one in NORAD, CAMELOT, and RIO, for example. This way, time is determined locally, instead of traversing the WAN links every polling interval. There's one caveat though. Be sure that the Reference server in each group is using the same external clock as the others. This will ensure a single (yet external) source of time convergence.

QUIZ

When I was a kid in school I memorized the following phrase in math class. Why?

"Now I know a super utterance to assist maths."

(Q4-6)

That's all there is to know about time configuration design. Once you've configured time, you have to decide how the time servers are going to communicate with each other. That's phase two — time communication design.

TIME COMMUNICATION DESIGN

With the time providers and time consumers in place, it's time to decide how they're going to talk to each other. Once again, you have two choices:

▶ Default: SAP Method

▶ Custom: Configured Lists

Time communication occurs in two instances. First, when time providers "vote" with each other about the network's correct time. And second, when Secondary time servers "poll" time providers for the correct time. This occurs at regular polling intervals. Let's take a closer look at each of the two time communication designs — starting with the default method.

Default: SAP Method

The SAP method is the default time communication design and it requires no intervention. Both time providers and time consumers communicate using the Service Advertising Protocol (SAP) by default. You should be aware that SAP causes a small amount of additional traffic on your WAN lines during time synchronization polling cycles. Also, SAP is self-configuring. This means there's no protection against a misconfigured time server. If someone messes up a local time server, everyone will feel it in a matter of minutes. This could disrupt your entire NDS time synchronization system.

Custom: Configured Lists

Configured Lists provide much more flexibility for your time synchronization communications. A Configured List allows you to specify exactly who talks to whom. You can tell time providers where to vote, and time consumers from whom to get their time. I love control.

For ACME, we've decided to use the Configured Lists design in coordination with our time provider groups. The communication design is distributed to all time servers using the TIMESYNC.CFG file.

REAL WORLD

SAP traffic is not required for NDS. It is, however, the communications protocol of choice for NetWare 3 servers. As a matter of fact, you can turn SAP off in IntranetWare with the help of built-in multiprotocol tools — called *SAP Filtering*. Refer to Chapter 13 for more details.

If you decide to filter SAP, be sure not to filter time synchronization packets. They use type "h26B."

Each server's Configured List is created using the Time Parameters option of SERVMAN. The first step is to enable the Configured List option as shown in Figure 4.48. Once you've turned it ON, you can start customizing the list.

F I G U R E   4.48

Activating Time Configured Lists in SERVMAN

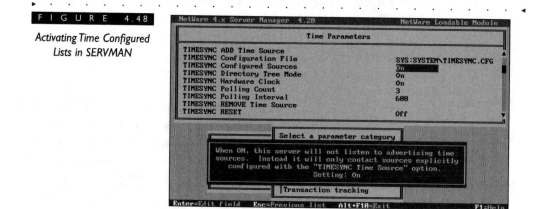

The Configured List is primarily a tool for defining with which providers this server interacts. Figure 4.48 is the Time Parameters screen for NOR-SRV1. The next step is to list all the Time Providers with whom NOR-SRV1 will vote. Remember, CAMELOT is ACME's Reference server, and all other locations have at least one Primary time server. The Configured List entries shown in Figure 4.49 include CAM-SRV1, RIO-SRV1, SYD-SRV1, and TOK-SRV1. With this design, NOR-SRV1 will always communicate with the CAMELOT Reference server first.

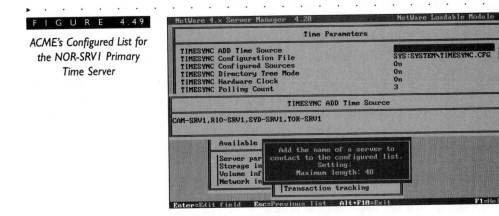

ACME's Configured List for the NOR-SRV1 Primary Time Server

The Configured Lists time communication design provides you with complete control of the time synchronization hierarchy. It also reduces SAP traffic on your network and provides direct server-to-server contact. Refer to Chapter 9 for more details about using SERVMAN as a time-management tool.

Aill in all, Configured Lists is the best time-communication method because it gives you ultimate control. However, you can combine it with SAP for control and fault tolerance. In this design, time providers will call back to SAP if anything goes wrong. Great cooperation!

ZEN

Joygerm fever — A mental condition characterized by happiness, kindness, and courtesy. Also attributed to CNEs at the point just before mental breakdown.

You're time is up! Congratulations, you've really finished ACME's NDS design. Wow, it's been a long and tough journey, but we made it to the end. Let's review.

It all started with ACME's naming standards document. A complete naming standard is important so that you design an NDS database that is flexible, easy to use, and meets your business needs. Also, there's so much diversity in NDS "object-ology," that a naming standard is required for most design and management tasks. As a matter of fact, ACME's naming standard is the center of the NDS design.

After we created the naming standards document, we moved on to the real action — NDS tree design. We started with a rough pyramid design outlining the geographic top and organizational bottom layers of the tree. Then, we further refined the design with respect to administration, partitioning, login scripts, and Bindery Services.

With the tree in place, we moved on to partitioning and replication. We started by breaking the tree into small little pieces (NDS partitioning). This occurred along the geographic boundaries of the ACME. Then, we scattered the pieces around the world (replica placement). Replica placement is one of the most important aspects of NDS design because it directly affects your network's performance, accessibility, and fault tolerance.

Finally, Time Synchronization Design ensures that all our servers agree on the time. We explored the four different time server types and learned how to design them according to two important factors: time configuration and time communication. We determined that ACME needs five Time Providers (one in each location) with a Reference server in CAMELOT. In addition, all time servers will communicate with each other using custom Configured Lists.

So, what's next? Well, that completes the four main aspects of NDS design, but it doesn't end our lesson. There's one related topic remaining and it almost always gets overlooked — NDS Accessibility Design. NDS accessibility transcends everything you do in IntranetWare. It is the sole purpose for the WAN's existence — so users can have access to stuff! If you ignore accessibility during the NDS design phase, some users will invariably get left out in the cold.

In the next section, we will explore NDS accessibility with respect to diverse clients, connection types, login scripts, and nomads. Yes, nomads. So, without any further adieu, let's end this "Fall" and get on with the rest of the Roller Coaster.

QUIZ

A hand in bridge in which all 13 cards are a 9 or below is called a Yarborough, after the Second Earl of Yarborough (d. 1897), who is said to have bet 1,000 to 1 against the dealing of such a hand. What, however, are the actual odds against such a hand? Was the noble Lord onto a good thing?

(Q4-7)

NDS Accessibility Design

Users use resources. Their life depends on it. A user's accessibility to resources hinges on your NDS design. Therefore, each user's life balances on the accessibility of your NDS design. But there's no pressure.

NDS accessibility is important because it defines all access points to IntranetWare resources. The following access points make or break user productivity:

▸ Diverse Clients

▸ Connection Types

▸ Login Scripts

▸ Administration

▸ Nomads

NDS accessibility starts at the client workstation. IntranetWare supports a variety of clients, including DOS, Windows 95, Windows NT, OS/2, Macintosh, and UNIX. The IntranetWare client accesses the NDS tree in one of two ways: through an NDS connection or Bindery Services. Either way, this connection is managed by IntranetWare and distributed servers.

When users finally attach to the tree, their productivity is controlled by a series of automatic configuration files called *login scripts*. These are your tools for ensuring productive NDS accessibility. In addition, there's a slew of accessibility *Administration* resources available to you: Groups, Profiles, IRFs, and Directory Maps, just to mention a few. Finally, there's *nomads* — those crazy migrating users who travel around the world each day, logging in from the strangest places, and always demanding resources. Nomads are the biggest challenge in NDS accessibility design.

So, you wanna be a CNE? OK, let's see what kind of Accessibility Engineer (AE) you are.

DIVERSE CLIENTS

NDS accessibility design starts at the client. This is the user's interface to our NDS world. And there are many different types of users — diverse clients.

Desktop support is key to IntranetWare. A server cannot serve the user community unless access is provided for the client. This access requires speed and reliability for all users and must make good use of limited memory at each workstation. Following is a discussion of IntranetWare's currently supported clients.

Client 32

Client 32 is the newest and most versatile workstation connectivity software in IntranetWare. It supports three different versions: Windows 95, Windows 3.1, and DOS. Client 32 is easy to install and maintain, and provides many new and enhanced features that make it faster, more reliable, and more usable than previous NetWare client software. But probably the most exciting thing about Client 32 is that it's the first true 32-bit protected mode client available for NetWare. It provides seamless GUI-integrated access to NetWare 2.2, 3.12, and IntranetWare servers. Client 32 supports both an NDS and bindery connection, and is explained in detail in Chapter 13.

Client 16

Older workstations can use the 16-bit NetWare DOS Requester for access to NetWare 2.2, 3.12, and IntranetWare servers. It supports two versions: Windows 3.1 and DOS. The NetWare DOS Requester is an older replacement for the NETx.EXE shell. This 16-bit connectivity software doesn't support the same GUI-integrated facilities as Client 32, but it is a good NDS solution for older 16-bit workstations. Client 16 supports both an NDS and bindery connection, and is explained in detail in Chapter 13.

SMART LINK

You can download the new Client 32 connectivity files for free at http://www.novell.com.

NetWare Client for OS/2

The NetWare Client for OS/2 supports a connection from an OS/2 workstation to an IntranetWare server. With this client software, an OS/2 user can connect and log into an IntranetWare server with full NDS capability, file and print, management, and security. Additionally, the NetWare Client for OS/2 will allow you to run enhanced mode MS-Windows applications in an IntranetWare environment. The NetWare Client for OS/2 supports connectivity to IntranetWare through IPX/SPX, NetBIOS, and Named Pipes.

NetWare Client for Windows NT 4.0

The NetWare Client for Windows NT 4.0 provides an NDS connection from a Windows NT workstation to an IntranetWare tree. Also provided with this client is an NT workstation version of Novell's NWADMIN utility. With these two products, you can manage your IntranetWare network with an NT workstation running NT version 4.0 and Novell's NetWare Client for Windows NT version 4.0.

You can access IntranetWare services and browse authorized NDS information including files and directories through mapping drives, configuring print queues, and attaching to other servers. The NetWare Client for Windows NT 4.0 supports services over IPX or IP transport protocols. IP services are offered through NetWare/IP over Microsoft's Windows NT TCP/IP protocol stack. This client also provides synchronized login to the Microsoft Windows NT desktop and the IntranetWare network with use of a single username and password.

Windows NT does have its moments, and here are a few to consider:

▶ Autoreconnect service for client-side fault tolerance.

▶ 32-bit ODI or NDIS drivers for a greater degree of protocol and network adapter choices.

▶ Windows NT long file names support through the IntranetWare server HPFS name space.

▶ Win32 application and backward-compatibility support for running 16-bit applications.

▶ DOS box support for running many standard IntranetWare utilities such as NETADMIN.

However, keep in mind that all of these features are now supported by IntranetWare through Client 32 and Windows 95.

NetWare Client for Mac

The NetWare Client for Mac is supported as an NDS connection to an IntranetWare server. The current version allows Mac clients to communicate via IPX to IntranetWare. File and print services, as well as NDS connections, are provided with this client — known as MacNDS. We'll learn more about Macintosh support in Chapter 13.

NetWare UNIX Client

The NetWare for Unix Client (NUC) supports a bindery-based connection to an IntranetWare server. Users running UnixWare clients can connect and access IntranetWare file and print services, as well as attach to other servers on the WAN. Each IntranetWare server that supports UnixWare clients must load the NUC.NLM. One important note: UnixWare clients don't run a login script.

The state of the client lightly impacts NDS accessibility design. For the most part, you must ensure two things. First, be sure the client software supports NDS. Second, be sure the client software provides all the IntranetWare services in a native environment. If you can accomplish these two goals, you're well on your way to achieving cultural diversity.

ZEN

"You cannot step in the same river twice, for new waters are ever flowing in upon you."

Heraclitus

Next, let's learn how these clients attach to the tree and explore the two different connection types that IntranetWare supports.

SMART LINK

For a more complete review of Novell's many diverse clients, surf to "NetWare Clients" at http://www.netware.com.

CONNECTION TYPES

Next, we must understand the different ways of accessing NDS. Remember, the user's life depends on it. If the user can't get a report out on time, it could be curtains. So, be sure you manage the user connection types so nobody gets kicked off the WAN.

IntranetWare supports two different types of network connections:

▸ NDS connections

▸ Bindery Services connections

The basic difference between these types of connections is the fact that the Bindery Services connection is server-centric. This means that multiple connections require multiple user names and passwords, and the login process must be repeated on every server the user needs access to.

On the other hand, the NDS connection provides you with the ability to have a single login to multiple IntranetWare servers. A single login allows the user to enter the username and password once. Any additional drive mappings to other NetWare 3 and IntranetWare servers will be handled in the background.

In addition, IntranetWare supports *additive licensing*. This is the ability to increase the total number of licenses on any given IntranetWare server. This enhancement allows administrators the opportunity to more closely match the number of licensed users to their actual needs. A company that currently has a 100-user license can add a 25-user license to the IntranetWare server to accommodate increased growth. IntranetWare supports 5-, 10-, 25-, 50-, 100-, 250-, 500-, and 1,000-user versions in any combination.

Let's explore the two IntranetWare connection types — starting with NDS connections.

NDS Connections

An NDS connection requires the NetWare DOS Requester or Client 32 for authentication to an IntranetWare server. An NDS connection provides a security mechanism known as RSA encryption between the client and server, and also provides background authentication. We'll explore these concepts later in Chapter 11. NDS supports three connectivity states:

▸ Connected, but not logged in

▸ Authenticated

▸ Licensed

Connected, But Not Logged In In this state, the user is attached to an IntranetWare server either through the NET*x* shell, 16-bit VLM client, or GUI Client 32. A "connected, but not logged in" state can exist for either NetWare 3 or IntranetWare users to the first attached server. You're standing on the front porch. The good news is that this is not a "licensed" connection. A IntranetWare attachment doesn't decrement your server license count as it did in NetWare 3.12. In IntranetWare, only authenticated connections are licensed.

Authenticated This type of connection indicates that an IntranetWare server has established a user's identity and he or she is in the door. Authentication occurs for both NetWare 3 and IntranetWare users, but IntranetWare offers much more security. In either case, the Authenticated connection is also licensed. This means the host server's license count drops by one. Also, the authenticating server tracks the user whether he or she uses any local resources. All other servers only count the user while he or she is using the resources. For this reason, you'll want to pay attention to which servers are authenticating which users.

Authentication is invisible to the user. During the login sequence, the user will enter a password when prompted, and the remaining process occurs behind the scenes. All sensitive data (including the password) is stored locally and is never transmitted across the wire (for security purposes). Authentication relies on encryption algorithms based on a public/private key system.

After successful authentication has occurred, a process known as *background authentication* is activated. This maintains a level of security for all activites during this session. In addition, it transparently controls user access to protected resources. A connection to another IntranetWare server, for example, does not require the user to reenter his or her password.

Licensed A connection is said to be licensed when a user has mapped a drive or captured to a printer. Each user will decrement the user license by one after a connection has been licensed. Only an authenticated connection can be licensed. Also, the license count returns to its previous level when the user stops accessing the resource (that is, "unmaps" the drive or "uncaptures" the printer).

A combination of these states determines what level a user currently has in IntranetWare connectivity. For example, when a connection is neither authenticated or licensed, the user can navigate the NDS tree through use of the CX (Change conteXt) command. This doesn't cost anything. The user has attached to a server, but has not yet authenticated. If a user is licensed and authenticated, he or she can access NDS and file system information to the extent allowed by his or her rights. This costs licenses on all servers the user accesses.

That was enlightening. Now, what about Bindery Services connections? They're much simpler.

Bindery Services Connections

NDS provides compatibility to previous versions of NetWare through the use of Bindery Services connections. This type of connection does not provide the capability of a single login to the network. For example, a client using the NETx shell to log in to an IntranetWare server must enter a username and password for each server. Additional connections to other IntranetWare servers would require the user to enter another username and password for each one.

Bindery Services can be enabled on any IntranetWare server through the SET Server Bindery Context command. You can select from 1 to 16 containers as the server's bindery context. All the leaf objects in the NDS container(s) that are also objects in the NetWare 3 bindery (that is, users, groups, queues, and print servers) are seen as the bindery.

Bindery Services in IntranetWare enable you to select up to 16 OU containers as the server bindery context. The requirement for Bindery Services is that the server stores at least a Read/Write replica of the partition where the bindery context is set.

I feel "connected" to you in some way. This NDS accessibility stuff must be going to my head. Login scripts are next.

SMART LINK

If you really want to feel "connected," surf to the Novell Knowledgebase at http://support.novell.com/search/.

LOGIN SCRIPTS

The next step in accessibility design involves login scripts. These are special NDS configuration files that are executed automatically when users log into the tree. They can save you hours of work and increase NDS accessibility — if done right.

Traditionally, login scripts were used to establish the users' network environment. The login scripts for IntranetWare are used to map network drives, map to applications, capture to printers and print queues, and set other important environment variables. The login scripts become the center of user access and need careful consideration. Fortunately, we explore them in excruciating depth in Chapter 12. For now, let's explore some important login script design considerations.

IntranetWare supports two types of login scripts:

- Bindery-based login scripts

- NDS login scripts

TIP

If you are using the older 16-bit clients, it is recommended that you execute login scripts before launching Windows. If there are users who go into Windows immediately after they boot their workstations, then you must have them log into the network and let it run the login scripts before launching Windows. This problem has been solved for Windows 95 users with the new Client 32 software.

Bindery-Based Login Scripts

Bindery-based login scripts in IntranetWare operate in the same manner as System, User, and Default scripts in NetWare 2 and NetWare 3. These login scripts should be preserved on IntranetWare servers to provide Bindery Services to NETx clients. For example, a bindery user attaching to an IntranetWare server will need bindery login scripts from specific places on the server file system. In addition, NDS clients using the /B option also attach with a bindery connection.

The System login script supports commands that affect all the bindery-based users on that server. These commands display messages, map network drives, map search drives, and set environmental variables. The System login script is the best place to manage the mapping and CAPTURE statements for all the bindery users. After a user successfully attaches to the server, the System login script executes from SYS:PUBLIC\NET$LOG.DAT, if it exists. If a User login script is present, it will execute from the SYS:MAIL\USERID subdirectory. If the User login script does not exist, then the Default login script is executed. The Default login script is hard-coded into the LOGIN.EXE program.

Figure 4.50 shows the order of execution for bindery-based login scripts. If you are familiar with NetWare 3, notice that the bindery-based login scripts for IntranetWare are executed in the same order.

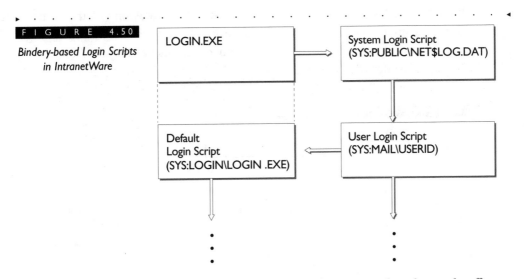

FIGURE 4.50

Bindery-based Login Scripts in IntranetWare

Bindery-based login scripts are server-centric. This means that they only affect bindery users who attach to a specific server. They have no impact on the NDS tree. Since these login scripts are server-centric, there aren't a lot of design issues. However, you should try to move all your users to NDS login scripts as soon as possible.

You can make changes to both the System and User login scripts by using the NetWare 3 SYSCON.EXE utility. You can also edit the NET$LOG.DAT file directly with any ASCII text-editor. Although the bindery-based login scripts can be edited, any changes made are not automatically synchronized to the corresponding NDS login scripts. Speaking of NDS scripts — let's see what they have in store for us.

ZEN

Barbecue mode — A maneuver that slowly rotates a spacecraft in order to distribute the sun's heat evenly over the craft's surface. Or, the state of a CNE when the network is broken.

NDS Login Scripts

NDS login scripts are properties of container, Profile, and User objects. They are only accessible through an authenticated NDS connection. Users execute Container scripts from their parent container only. This is roughly equivalent to the NetWare 3 System login script. After the Container login script, a Profile login script can be used. If no Profile exists, the User script is executed. As in the bindery-based scenario, the Default login script activates only if there's no User script. Again, the Default login script is hard-coded into the LOGIN.EXE program.

Refer to Figure 4.51 for an illustration of IntranetWare's NDS login scripts. Notice the order of execution.

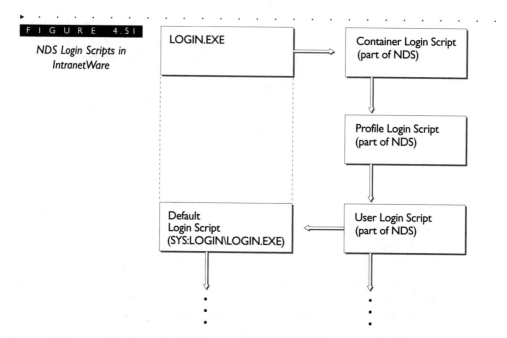

FIGURE 4.51

NDS Login Scripts in IntranetWare

As we've seen, IntranetWare supports four different NDS login scripts. We will discuss each of them in depth in Chapter 12. For now, let's discover how they impact your NDS accessibility design:

- *Container Login Script* — A property of O=Organization or OU=Organizational Unit containers. Users *only* execute their parent's container script. If one doesn't exist, tough. This is an important accessibility issue. Make sure the Container scripts exist at the bottom layers of the tree — where the users are.

- *Profile Login Scripts* — A property of the special Profile leaf object. These login scripts can be shared by any group of users, anywhere in the tree. Typically, the Profile script provides three accessibility advantages: login script sharing for the entire company, login script sharing for each location, or login script sharing for a special group. This special object solves the accessibility problem created by restricting container scripts.

▶ *User Login Script* — A property of each User object. Don't use them. It's too much work. Accomplish all accessibility configurations in the Container or Profile scripts.

▶ *Default Login Script* — Hard-coded into LOGIN.EXE. It only runs if there's no User script. You don't want it to run, and you don't want User scripts — oops! Now what? Simple, use the NO_DEFAULT command in the Container or Profile scripts.

That's enough of that. Are you ready for some fun? Well, this might qualify — nomads! But first, let's review some great accessibility Administration resources. Ready, set, access!

ADMINISTRATION

In addition to diverse clients, connection types, and login scripts, IntranetWare includes a myriad of accessibility administration resources. Here are some guidelines you may consider when implementing in your NDS design:

▶ *Groups* — Use group objects for accessibility only when all the group members exist in the same physical location. If you use global groups that span a WAN link, you will create considerable background synchronization traffic.

▶ *Profile Login Scripts* — If users with similar needs exist in separate containers, consider linking them with a Profile login script. These scripts create an additional level of maintenance over container scripts, but they're still easier to manage than user login scripts.

▶ *User Login Scripts* — Consider user login scripts in special cases only (mobile users, for example).

▶ *Organizational Roles* — Use Organizational Roles for administrative fault tolerance. Whenever you create a specific container administrator, use an OR and assign two members: the Administrator user object and a backup administrator (just in case).

▶ *IRFs* — Use IRFs to create exclusive distributed container administrators. See Chapter 11 for more details.

▶ *Drive Mappings* — Implement drive mapping naming conventions and standards for company-wide applications. For example, Drive "M:" always points to e-mail, "W:" to word processing applications, and "L:" to the company database.

▶ *Security Precautions* — Identify company-wide security practices and educate distributed administrators. For example, make sure users always authenticate to a local replica (Chapter 9) and avoid granting the [S] Supervisor NDS right to Server objects (Chapter 11).

These simple guidelines will save you hours of accessibility frustration. Remember: Time you spend early in the design is time saved a hundred-fold in the Management phase. Now, let's complete our NDS design discussion with an in-depth look at nomads. Don't get any crazy ideas . . . stay where you are!

NOMADS

Finally, there's *nomad* — the greatest challenge to accessibility design. Nomads are remote or mobile users who insist on logging in from "other places." You must make certain adjustments to your design to accommodate nomadic users. You can do it, you're a CNE.

IntranetWare allows the user to access resources from anywhere in the tree. Isn't that nice? This feature helps you manage nomadic users, but it also encourages user migration. Let's face it, we live in a TV-dinner, drive-through world. Users are on the go, and you must accommodate them. Start by asking yourself a few simple questions:

▶ "Self, does this user carry a laptop computer?"

▶ "Self, where is the user geographically located?"

▶ "Self, what is the user's home office?"

As users wander throughout the WAN, they access the network and its resources in different ways. Knowing what kind of access each user wants will help you set up the user environments. For example, some users just want dial-in access to the network from remote locations. These locations can range from their homes to hotel rooms — and even airplanes. This type of user, typically, dials in to the network from a laptop or home computer.

Some users may travel from one office to another and need full access to all the local network resources of the office they are visiting. Although the users need full access to the local resources, they still want the data from their home directory and server. Essentially, the definition of a traveling user is broken into two types:

▸ *Remote users* access the tree through dial-in connections.

▸ *Mobile users* access the tree from a variety of distributed locations and from a variety of different machines.

Remote Users

Remote users travel a lot and need network access from their laptop computer through dial-in lines. These Road Warriors are usually self-contained (that is, their laptops are configured with all the necessary applications software). The user can continue to work when on the road and merely dials into the network to transfer e-mail messages, download files, or access other resources.

The remote user requires less accessibility design considerations than a mobile user because he or she only accesses the tree for login authentication. There's very little NDS browsing and management going on. Fortunately, remote users will not impact the tree design or force you to create any special NDS objects. They simply dial into specific predetermined access points in the WAN and use their normal NDS context.

Some remote users dial in just to transfer their e-mail messages. Typically, there are special phone lines dedicated for just the remote e-mail users. These lines may have their own security and access methods and do not affect the Directory tree design.

If a remote user travels to another office and plugs a laptop computer into the network, he or she suddenly becomes a mobile user. Now that's a completely different kettle of fish. Check it out.

ZEN

"The fly that was buzzing around the house had once been her loving husband."

From the movie *The Fly*

Mobile Users

Mobile users are a more challenging breed. They travel from one office to another and from computer to computer. They don't care, they're just cyber-scavangers. Even worse, they expect full access to all local resources while maintaining the ability to get data from their home server. Yeah, right!

Mobile users may not carry laptops with them. Instead, they expect to have a computer available at the other site. Some mobile users, however, carry laptops and plug them into the network when they arrive. Thus, the best definition of a mobile user is "a nomadic individual who uses someone else's computer at someone else's site — a cyber-scavenger."

Whether the user travels thousands of miles or across the building, the issues are the same. The users want simultaneous access to local network applications and remote personal data. It's your job to make this as seamless as possible.

TIP

Users who carry laptop computers to a new location are not considered mobile users if they do not need access to the local network resources. If the users are content to access their home resources across the network, then they are simply remote users. There are no special considerations for remote users. Remember, IntranetWare will let the users log in from anywhere in the ACME world.

In order to support mobile users, you must answer two of the previous three questions: "Where is the user geographically located?" and "What is the user's home office?" There are several mechanisms for supporting mobile users, and here's a list of the most useful ones:

- ▸ Manually changing the NDS name context

- ▸ Using an Alias object to change the NDS name context

► Using workstation configuration files to change the NDS name context

► Special nomadic login scripts

Most of these mechanisms focus on the user's name context. The name context helps identify who the user is and where the user should be. While a mobile user's physical location may change, the user's context won't.

If the mobile user has traveled without a laptop computer, he or she expects to use any available computer in the office to log into the network. The main issue with this scenario is how to determine the user's name context for login purposes. There are several ways to work around this problem. The mobile user can manually enter the context at the computer console before login, you can create Alias objects that point to the user in his or her normal context, and/or the name context can be set in the workstation configuration file. Let's check them out.

Manually Changing the NDS Name Context   The first option requires user intervention. This can be troublesome to say the least. In this case, the mobile user manually enters his or her name context into the computer before login. This implies that the user understands how to use the CX (Change conteXt) command. For example, the ACME user JMadison would need to set his/her name context by typing:

```
CX .FAC.ADMIN.RIO.ACME
```

Notice the leading period. It forces NDS to start at the [Root] and resolves JMadison's name from there. This overwrites any effect from the local current context. You never now what it's going to be.

Using an Alias Object to Change the NDS Name Context   The second option doesn't require user intervention. This is a good thing. In this case, the mobile user's context can be changed automatically with the help of an Alias User object. If you have a small number of mobile users, you can create an Alias object below the O=Organization for each mobile user. The Alias would point to the user's primary object in his or her parent container.

The value of this strategy is that it creates a simple context for each of the mobile users. The users do not need to know what their context is, or even how to set it. The user simply would enter the name of the Alias during the login process.

For example, there has been an Alias object created for the user JMadison in the ACME tree. As you can see in Figure 4.52, the Alias object (called JMadison) was created directly under O=ACME. The Alias object points to the real object in the OU=FAC department at RIO. When JMadison wants to log into the network from any site, he uses the name of the Alias object as follows:

```
LOGIN .JMadison.ACME
```

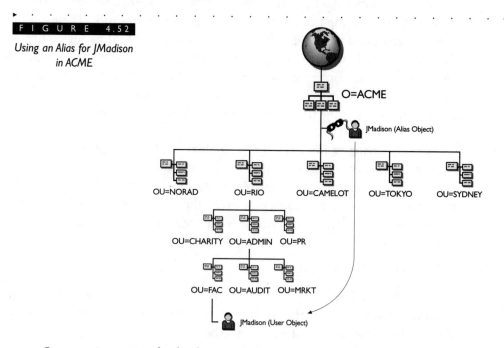

FIGURE 4.52

Using an Alias for JMadison in ACME

O=ACME

JMadison (Alias Object)

OU=NORAD   OU=RIO   OU=CAMELOT   OU=TOKYO   OU=SYDNEY

OU=CHARITY OU=ADMIN OU=PR

OU=FAC OU=AUDIT OU=MRKT

JMadison (User Object)

Once again, notice the leading period. It forces LOGIN to start at the [Root] object, and, therefore, ignores the workstation's unpredictable current context. This method works well if you have a small number of mobile users — less than 20. This method may not work if your nomad population is high.

REAL WORLD

To increase accessibility for a large group of users who often log into a remote Master replica, consider placing a local Read/Write replica of their home container on a local server. On the up side, this increases login speed and NDS accessibility. On the down side, it increases background synchronization traffic.

In addition, you can identify a user's network segment by using the NETWORK_ADDRESS login script identifier variable. This allows you to make sure nomads map drives to local servers. This increases performance and accessibility of the IntranetWare file system.

Using Workstation Configuration Files to Change the NDS Name Context The third option also doesn't require any user intervention. In this case, we can set the user's name context with a special workstation configuration file called NET.CFG. The NET.CFG file is read during the loading of the 16-bit workstation client. Following is an example of JMadison's NET.CFG. Notice the section called "NetWare DOS Requester," and the line where the NAME CONTEXT ="OU=FAC.OU=ADMIN.OU=RIO.O=ACME".

In order for this to work, the user must run his or her own NET.CFG file. This could exist on a laptop, or a special login diskette. When the user arrives on site and connects to the network, the user's name context is resolved from the setting in his or her personal NET.CFG file. Here's an example of JMadison's configuration file:

```
Personal NET.CFG for JMadison

LINK SUPPORT
    MEMPOOL 6192
    BUFFERS 10 1580
    MAX STACKS 8

LINK DRIVER NE2000
    INT 5
    PORT 300
    MEM D0000
    FRAME Ethernet_802.2
```

```
NETWARE DOS REQUESTER
    NAME CONTEXT = "OU=FAC.OU=ADMIN.OU=RIO.O=ACME"
    PREFERRED SERVER = FAC-SRV1
    FIRST NETWORK DRIVE = F
    NETWARE PROTOCOL = NDS,BIND
    SHOW DOTS = ON
    USE DEFAULTS = ON
    PB BUFFERS = 10
```

You can also use the PREFERRED SERVER variable in NET.CFG to connect JMadison to his bindery context server. This provides support for both older and newer clients.

REAL WORLD

Remember that NET.CFG configurations apply to the 16-bit client only (ODI and the NetWare DOS Requester). Client 32 uses special property sheets in the Windows 95 Registry to accomplish the same thing. See Chapter 12 for more information.

Special Nomadic Login Scripts   The final nomadic configuration option deals with special login scripts. Once the name context issue has been resolved, it's time to turn our attention toward drive mappings and CAPTURE statements. Remember, mobile users want simultaneous access to local applications and remote data. This can only be accomplished with sophisticated login script variables and a special environment variable called NW_SITE.

The following is JMadison's special mobile login script. With this script, he can log in from any of ACME's five major sites. The script demonstrates how he can be mapped to the local e-mail and application server, while maintaining a background connection to his home file system. This is his Container login script in .OU=FAC.OU=ADMIN.OU=RIO.O=ACME. (Note: It also requires the NW_SITE DOS environment variable be set in his personal CONFIG.SYS workstation file.)

```
;**********************************************************
; MOBILE CONTAINER LOGIN SCRIPT
; for OU=FAC.OU=ADMIN.OU=RIO.O=ACME
; Creation Date: 11/8/99
; Revisions:
;**********************************************************
REM Do not execute default script
NO_DEFAULT
Write "Good %GREETING_TIME, %LOGIN_NAME"
REM Map PUBLIC drive to local server
MAP S16:=SYS:PUBLIC
REM  Map F: drive to the user's home server
MAP F:="HOME_DIRECTORY"
REM Map NetWare Drives according to the NW_SITE variable
IF <NW_SITE> == "NORAD" THEN BEGIN
  MAP ROOT M:= NOR-SRV1\SYS:MAIL
  MAP ROOT W:= NOR-SRV1\SYS:APPS\WP
  MAP ROOT Q:= NOR-SRV1\SYS:APPS\QPRO
  END
IF <NW_SITE> == "RIO" THEN BEGIN
  MAP ROOT M:= RIO-SRV1\SYS:MAIL
  MAP ROOT W:= RIO-SRV1\SYS:APPS\WP
  MAP ROOT Q:= RIO-SRV1\SYS:APPS\QPRO
  END
IF <NW_SITE> == "CAMELOT" THEN BEGIN
  MAP ROOT M:= CAM-SRV1\SYS:MAIL
  MAP ROOT W:= CAM-SRV1\SYS:APPS\WP
  MAP ROOT Q:= CAM-SRV1\SYS:APPS\QPRO
  END
IF <NW_SITE> == "TOKYO" THEN BEGIN
  MAP ROOT M:= TOK-SRV1\SYS:MAIL
  MAP ROOT W:= TOK-SRV1\SYS:APPS\WP
  MAP ROOT Q:= TOK-SRV1\SYS:APPS\QPRO
  END
IF <NW_SITE> == "SYDNEY" THEN BEGIN
  MAP ROOT M:= SYD-SRV1\SYS:MAIL
```

```
     MAP ROOT W:= SYD-SRV1\SYS:APPS\WP
     MAP ROOT Q:= SYD-SRV1\SYS:APPS\QPRO
     END
  EXIT
```

The End.

Wow, what a chapter! Wow, what a ride! No matter how you slice it, NDS design is a wild time. And just think, this is just the first part of the IntranetWare Roller Coaster. There's more gut-wrenching, spine-tingling, hair-tugging fun to come. In Chapter 5, we'll explore Step 3: NDS Implementation (*swoosh!*). Then, in Chapters 6 and 7, we'll dive into IntranetWare installation (*whoooa!*). But the real fun begins with Chapter 8 — NDS management (*heeeeelp!*).

Look, if you can make it through The Fall, then you can accomplish anything. There's an exciting world of IntranetWare out there — waiting for you. Let's attack it together . . . .

EXERCISE 4-1: THE RIDE OF YOUR LIFE

Circle the 20 NDS tree design terms hidden in this word search puzzle using the hints provided.

```
H  X  B  F  I  V  E  T  H  O  U  S  A  N  D  N  J  Q
G  T  H  Z  N  A  M  I  N  G  S  T  A  N  D  A  R  D
R  E  P  L  I  C  A  T  I  O  N  A  W  G  H  Z  E  W
A  N  A  M  E  R  E  S  O  L  U  T  I  O  N  N  D  H
D  E  C  E  N  T  R  A  L  I  Z  E  D  V  E  M  E  L
I  G  O  J  D  O  V  E  R  L  A  P  M  T  N  H  Z  F
O  T  N  E  L  Y  E  I  F  X  P  O  W  H  J  R  I  V
C  B  F  S  F  W  L  H  O  E  Y  O  Y  V  A  R  L  X
L  B  I  N  D  E  R  Y  S  E  R  V  I  C  E  S  A  J
O  S  G  W  I  K  H  Q  J  K  A  E  Q  Q  S  N  R  V
C  C  U  V  O  G  P  L  T  R  M  H  N  E  J  U  T  P
K  M  R  P  O  L  L  I  N  G  I  Y  C  C  M  R  N  K
H  P  E  R  G  L  M  F  T  D  D  O  R  Y  E  H  E  M
I  G  D  I  G  E  X  T  E  R  N  A  L  C  L  O  C  K
R  T  L  M  D  H  Q  T  R  D  I  K  V  N  T  T  E  O
P  J  I  A  I  M  E  A  A  A  M  E  H  C  S  N  T  Y
B  F  S  R  M  R  I  R  O  J  N  X  Q  O  U  T  M  J
T  V  T  Y  M  S  Y  R  E  I  D  G  R  Q  S  W  O  N
```

Hints:
1. Allows objects in a container to be accessed by bindery-based servers and clients, as well as NDS objects.
2. Type of management where entire NDS tree is controlled by one individual or group in the company.
3. Allows you to specify exactly which servers should be contacted for a time provider group, and to make requests for time consumers.
4. Type of management where portions of the NDS tree are delegated to individuals or independent groups for management.
5. Provides an accurate and automated mechanism for checking time.

6. Number of objects in a partition that would cause you to consider splitting it into multiple partitions.

7. Mechanism that NDS utilizes to locate a particular IntranetWare server in the replica.

8. Guidelines document used for creating NDS objects.

9. Time maintained by all servers in an IntranetWare network.

10. Shell used by NetWare 2 or 3.11 clients to log into an IntranetWare server and run bindery-based applications.

11. Something that partitions cannot do.

12. Voting process that is accomplished by contacting all other time sources to determine any discrepancies between its local clock and the calculated network time.

13. Type of time server that synchronizes time with at least one other Primary or Reference time server.

14. Typical shape of an NDS tree design.

15. Type of external time source.

16. Type of time server that provides time to which all other time servers and workstations synchronize.

17. Process of creating copies of partitions for fault tolerance purposes.

18. Used to define the NDS naming structure for the entire IntranetWare network.

19. Type of time server that gets time from a Single Reference, Primary, or Reference time server and provides time to workstations.

20. New type of NDS container object.

See Appendix C for answers.

Step 3: NDS Implementation

As a CNE, you come highly recommended. Your mission — should you choose to accept it — is to build the ACME WAN and NDS tree. You will need courage, design experience, NDS know-how, and this book. If you succeed, you will save the world and become a CNE! All in a day's work.

SMART LINK

Speaking of work . . . NOVELL NEEDS YOU!! Get a job at http://corp.novell.com/job/.

Actually, you have a daunting task ahead of you. A project of this magnitude requires sharp thinking and a very organized approach. All the fancy footwork and LAN lexicon in the world isn't going to help you if you don't have a game plan. That's where Figure 5.1 comes in — it's your ACME game plan. As you can see, saving the world falls into four simple steps:

- Step 1: NDS Preparation

- Step 2: Design

- Step 3: Implementation

- Step 4: Management

Welcome to Step 3! This is Prime Time.

If you're feeling a little restless from the first two steps, you'll get plenty of action in Steps 3 and 4. As you can see in Figure 5.2, all your initial action centers around the implementation schedule. This schedule outlines the rollout of NetWare 4.11 installation and migration. But before you can implement NetWare 4.11 in the production ACME environment, you'll need to test it in a more controlled pilot program.

It all starts in your off-line testing lab. Here you can be creative and brave without causing system-wide crashes. While you are in the lab, you should consider installing NetWare 4.11 multiple times and creating diverse NDS trees. Next, test partitioning, replication, time synchronization, and common network applications. Finally, make sure backup and restore procedures operate correctly.

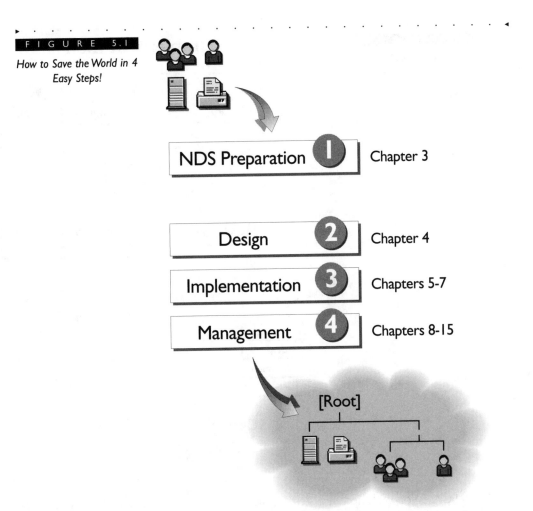

FIGURE 5.1

How to Save the World in 4 Easy Steps!

NDS Preparation ① Chapter 3

Design ② Chapter 4

Implementation ③ Chapters 5-7

Management ④ Chapters 8-15

[Root]

Once you're comfortable with each individual piece, consider putting them together in a controlled pilot program. The pilot system involves installing your first production IntranetWare server and then testing each production application in a realistic environment. You can also test user compatibility with NDS and Bindery Services. A pilot system is your bridge between the lab and a full implementation of IntranetWare across the entire ACME WAN. You might consider the Labs division in NORAD as your pilot implementation because the scientists who work there are more likely to understand what you're going through.

FIGURE 5.2

Step 3: NDS
Implementation

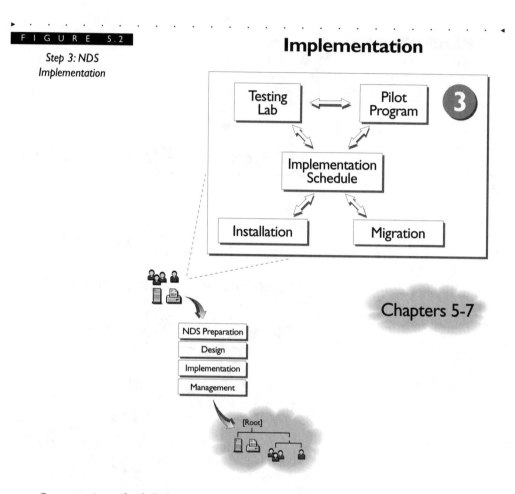

Once you've scheduled, tested, and piloted the implementation, you're ready for prime time — IntranetWare installation and migration — but not today. That's for tomorrow (Chapters 6 and 7). So, let's see where we're going today:

▸ ACME testing lab — Involves five different experiments, including hardware installation, NDS implementation, testing login scripts, testing applications, and testing backup and restore procedures.

▸ ACME pilot program — A bridge between the controlled testing lab and uncontrolled production environment. Remember, take it slowly.

▶ ACME implementation schedule — The heart and soul of NDS implementation. The implementation schedule defines ten important tasks and becomes a blueprint for ACME success. Remember, the whole world is counting on you — no pressure.

That's Step 3 in a nutshell. So, without any further adieu, let's get on with Step 3 — NDS implementation: Let's build a testing lab.

ZEN

Quipstering — Using clever or witty remarks in one's conversation or writing . . . like in this book! Oh, I'm such a "quipster."

ACME Testing Lab

It all starts in the mad scientist's laboratory. This is where all great science is made. The testing lab is a completely open environment where you can get comfortable and creative with NDS implementation. For example, you can:

▶ Install NetWare 4.11 a bunch of times

▶ Design and build the ACME NDS tree

▶ Test the NDS compatibility of existing and new applications

▶ Run login scripts

▶ Invent a new hair dryer/PDA device

This kind of experience is invaluable — and it can't be taught. The lessons you learn in the lab will help you avoid major mistakes during the pilot and full-blown implementations. The lab experience allows you to learn how IntranetWare operates within a subset of ACME. More important, the lab is a safe haven where you can experiment with strange modifications and view the impact of these changes on the NDS tree. Let's start our whirlwind tour of NDS implementation with a view inside ACME's Lab, and a hands-on demonstration of their strange new experiments. Remember to wear your protective clothing.

UNDERSTANDING THE LAB

The decision to have a lab depends entirely on your circumstances. Even though most small sites don't have the resources to install a lab, they can still benefit by getting some hands-on experience at their local education center. If you're responsible for a small site and plan to use the default configuration, the lab isn't as crucial, but it can provide you with some valuable administrative experience. And if your site is small and you *do* have a lab, you really should consider a brief testing period in the lab to familiarize yourself with IntranetWare — especially from an administrative standpoint. Besides, setting up a lab and installing IntranetWare in this environment will instill confidence in your project team as they learn about the features and capabilities of IntranetWare. Also, it will give you time to work with the operating system, perform diagnostics, and test utilities and applications.

If your site will install or migrate more than 30 NetWare 4.11 servers, an implementation of an IntranetWare lab is strongly recommended. Many customers will move from the default settings of IntranetWare to configurable parameters at approximately this number of servers. The lab gives you the opportunity to adjust and test the configuration parameters you're likely to change.

For larger sites with a wide area network (WAN) in place, we recommend that you follow, where applicable, the lab procedures presented throughout this book. Network administrators of large sites should be completely familiar with the functions and features of IntranetWare before beginning a full-scale migration to IntranetWare.

For the ACME site, lab testing is being handled at the NORAD facility in the Labs division. This facility evaluates all new software and hardware before deploying it onto the production network, so the new operating system being deployed in the ACME tree has already gone through the lab process.

Many large organizations have a permanent lab for testing new software and hardware at their site. Others may consider creating a temporary lab for this project. Either way, you will need to dedicate some hardware for use as IntranetWare servers and workstations during your lab project.

Your lab should consist of at least four nodes: two NetWare 4.11 servers and two workstations. The servers and adapter cards should be similar to the hardware that will be used in your network environment. If you're planning to upgrade your hardware, then use the new hardware in your lab environment. Each NetWare

4.11 server should exceed, if possible, the minimum hardware requirements recommended by Novell. The bottom line is that you want to duplicate your LAN topology and your actual environment as closely as possible.

Figure 5.3 shows the ACME lab being used for testing IntranetWare for the entire ACME tree installation. This lab has four dedicated NetWare 4.11 servers and three workstations for running the Novell and third-party utilities. Also, because the ACME network is primarily Token Ring, we have a Token Ring concentrator in the lab to connect the servers and workstations. All file servers have a CD-ROM drive as well as sufficient disk and memory capacity. The lab ring also has a connection to the corporate backbone located in the Labs division at NORAD.

Your lab can be smaller, but should contain at least three nodes. A three-node network would consist of two NetWare 4.11 file servers and a single workstation. One of the servers must have a CD-ROM device for installing IntranetWare. You should also try to have a network connection to your backbone so that you have access to any servers currently in operation on your network. Figure 5.4 shows a minimal configuration.

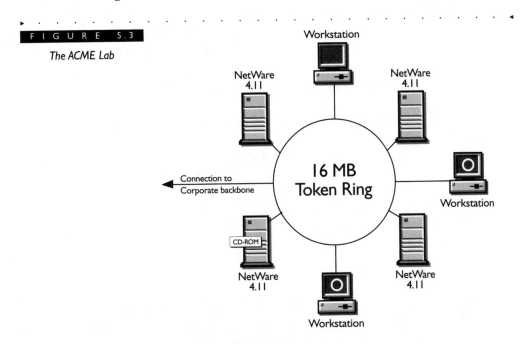

FIGURE 5.3

The ACME Lab

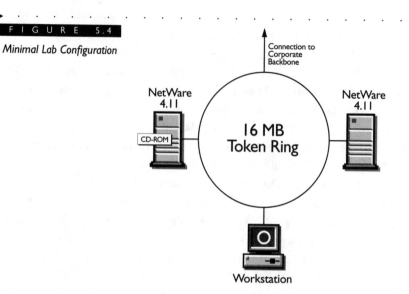

FIGURE 5.4

Minimal Lab Configuration

UNDERSTANDING THE EXPERIMENTS

The purpose of any lab is to run experiments. ACME's testing lab is no different. There are five interesting new experiments going on even as we speak:

▸ Experiment 1 — Hardware Installation

▸ Experiment 2 — NDS Implementation

▸ Experiment 3 — Testing Login Scripts

▸ Experiment 4 — Testing Applications

▸ Experiment 5 — Testing Backup and Restore Procedures

ZEN

Hawking radiation — The telltale particles that in theory escape the gravity of a black hole in space. Also thought to orbit the IntranetWare NDS tree during periods of high activity.

Experiment 1 — Hardware Installation

If your site already has a lab in place, you can simply designate a group of servers and workstations for your test. If not, be sure to meet the following minimum hardware requirements in building your lab:

▸ An IBM-compatible architecture with an 80386, 80486 (SX or DX), or Pentium processor

▸ A minimum of 20 MB of RAM for the basic IntranetWare operating system, regardless of whether it's installed from CD-ROM or across the network

▸ For a basic installation, a minimum of 90 MB of free space on the hard disk: 15 MB for the DOS partition plus 75 MB for the NetWare disk partition and SYS: volume

▸ For more features, you might need as much as 60 MB of free space on the hard disk

▸ For the DynaText viewer and the IntranetWare documentation (one language), another 60 MB of free disk space on the hard disk

▸ One network interface card (NIC)

▸ The appropriate network cabling and related components (hubs, UPS, and so on)

▸ A CD-ROM drive that can read ISO9660-formatted CD-ROM disks (if IntranetWare is being installed from CD-ROM)

Remember, these hardware requirements are just listed as minimums. They are *not* recommended standards. Realistically, you'll need a faster processor, more RAM, and a larger hard disk. Finally, check out Chapter 6 for the detailed simple and custom installation procedures for NetWare 4.11.

SMART LINK

For a detailed list of Novell-certified network hardware, consult the Novell Lab's Bulletins at http://support.novell.com/sitemap.

Experiment 2 — NDS Implementation

Refer to the section "Task 6 — Server Migration" for detailed information on installation procedures. To continue with the lab exercise, install the NetWare 4.11 operating system on each of your lab servers. Although loading the software isn't difficult, you should become familiar with install options such as the Simple install and Custom Install.

Practice removing NDS from the server, too. Occasionally, you may have to remove a server from the tree to allow for hardware repairs or shipment to another location, and you should follow the appropriate steps for removing a server from the tree.

Familiarize yourself with the install utility and its features. You may have to add new NLMs or additional licenses, and the INSTALL utility handles these procedures.

If you are migrating from NetWare 3 to IntranetWare and you have the hardware, you can perform an Across-the-Wire migration of a current NetWare 3 server to a IntranetWare lab server. This approach allows you to upgrade your hardware to a new platform for IntranetWare and without endangering your current NetWare 3 server.

Refer to Chapter 4 for valuable design strategies. For modeling you can use Preferred Systems' DS Standard product to simplify the experimentation process.

Whether you use DS Standard or Novell's NWADMIN utility, the lab tree you design will eventually become your production tree, so take your time defining the appropriate levels and placement of resources. If you have a successful and functioning lab tree, you do not need to create another tree unless you want to maintain separate trees for testing purposes.

The first partition you'll create will contain the [Root]. After your lab servers are up and running, you can use the NWADMIN or PARTMGR utilities to make additional partitions. Each of your sites should be separate partitions subordinate to [Root]. Use your lab to learn how to create replicas as well. Although your lab may be somewhat limited in size, you should still become familiar with how the partition utilities place replicas on servers.

Initially, time synchronization on your lab servers will be set up using the defaults. In other words, your first IntranetWare server will be installed as a Single-Reference server and all others as Secondary servers.

Check out the timesync parameters available through the various SET commands and the SERVMAN utility. Use the SERVMAN utility if you want to change the defaults. For example, you can create a small time provider group by changing your Single-Reference server to a Reference server, and then changing the other two or three lab servers to Primary servers. Using a LANalyzer or other equipment, you can view the packets sent and received during your timesync interval.

You can use other commands such as SET TIMESYNC DEBUG=7 to enable the time synchronization screen on your IntranetWare server. This screen will show you the status of time synchronization, as well as the adjustments that are being made if this server's time is not synchronized.

Experiment 3 — Testing Login Scripts

The lab is a great place to design and test your Container login scripts. Populate one of your containers with User objects from your company. Test the Container login script for errors and to verify that all necessary environment variables have been defined.

If you are planning to use Profile login scripts, the lab is the perfect place to test the functionality of these scripts.

Experiment 4 — Testing Applications

Not all applications need to be tested for IntranetWare compatibility. However, some applications, especially those written by internal staff, may require some testing. Here are a few important questions to ask yourself:

1 • Is the application bindery-based? Bindery-based applications require Bindery Services to be enabled on that server as well as a Read/Write replica of the defined context.

2 • Were these applications written for the NETx client of some other operating system? If so, they should be tested on a workstation with VLMs loaded. Some basic, easy tests you can perform are

   a. Run the application to completion or proper termination.

   b. Print a document with the application.

   c. Use the application to save your work onto the IntranetWare server.

   d. Test your tape backup system support for IntranetWare and NDS.

Last, but not least, consider using the new NetWare Application Manager (NAM) and NetWare Application Launcher (NAL) to integrate applications with Novell Directory Services (NDS).

You should try to keep your application testing short and simple. You will never be able to test every feature and function of every product. Concentrate your efforts on the specialty applications that are not in the mainstream.

Experiment 5 — Testing Backup and Restore Procedures

Perform a full backup and restore of an IntranetWare server. This backup should include files as well as NDS tree information. Always have a clear understanding of how your planned backup procedures work with the specific backup product you're using. The lab is the best place to gain experience in backup and recovery procedures.

ZEN

Permaculture — An alternative life-style based on agriculture in which each of the related activities is located to help conserve energy. Many members of ACME believe we should gravitate toward permaculture to help save the planet Earth. Of course, I'm doing my part by making this book only 1,600 pages long.

ACME Pilot Program

Now, you're almost ready for prime time. Before you can attack the ACME implementation head-on, you should consider testing your lab results on a small segment of the overall tree. The pilot program serves as a dress rehearsal before you move into full-scale migration. In ACME's case, the pilot program will accomplish the following:

▶ Give the project team a chance to practice its implementation procedures.

▶ Provide a "live" blueprint for full-scale client and server migration.

▶ Provide more accurate feedback for application compatibility.

▶ Give insight into how users react to NDS and the "new" logical network resources.

▶ Gather valuable performance data for fine-tuning partitioning, replica, and time synchronization designs.

We will start in the OU=LABS container, because the scientists are more sympathetic to our experiments. Who knows? They might even offer to help. In this case, we will migrate three pilot servers (LABS-SRV1, R&D-SRV1, and WHI-SRV1), two HP4SI printers, a print server (R&D-PS1), and all the administrative users under OU=LABS. This includes AEinstein, LDaVinci, CDarwin, MCurie, INewton, CBabbage, and Ada.

Refer to Task 9 of the ACME implementation schedule for more details. Speaking of schedules, let's stay on track and move forward to the center of NDS implementation — the schedule!

ACME Implementation Schedule

The ACME implementation schedule is where all the action is. It is the center of attention, a blueprint for success-another road map for saving the world. More important, it's your friend. Make one, learn it, use it.

The implementation schedule should provide detailed, measurable tasks that you can perform during the life of the ACME implementation. The main focus of the implementation schedule is the tasks and their associated subtasks. You should also include a detailed timeline with key milestones. In addition, the schedule will establish the proper timing and help to organize all the NDS implementation tasks.

The schedule also helps you track the status of the project, and can provide immediate feedback to your staff and management. A well-planned implementation schedule will not only help you manage and track the status of the IntranetWare project, but it can be used to set deadlines for each task. Let's be honest, these things can go on forever.

The implementation schedule consists primarily of a set of charts — each with a task description, its subtasks, guidelines, duration, start and end dates, percent completion, and task lead (person). If possible, the schedule should also show the interdependencies of the tasks, measure the progress, review the work, and produce reports for management. Finally, be sure to update the chart daily, weekly, and monthly-until the project is finished.

Here's a quick preview of the ten tasks in ACME's implementation schedule:

- ▶ Task 1 — Project Scope

- ▶ Task 2 — Training

- ▶ Task 3 — NDS Implementation

- ▶ Task 4 — Security and Auditing

- ▶ Task 5 — Client Migration

- ▶ Task 6 — Server Migration

- ▶ Task 7 — Printing Migration

- ▶ Task 8 — Application Migration

- ▶ Task 9 — Pilot Program

- ▶ Task 10 — Rollout

Now, let's build ACME's implementation schedule together. We will discuss each task in depth, and create a task-oriented timing chart. Remember, these charts are the road maps for ACME's success. Please take them very seriously — we have!

ZEN

Pi wars — The competition among computer experts to refine the value of the mathematical constant pi (3.14159 . . .). As we all know, it is the number expressing the constant relationship of the diameter of any circle to its circumference — or the number of CNEs it takes to screw in a lightbulb.

TASK 1 — PROJECT SCOPE

It all starts with the project scope. This establishes the boundaries of ACME's NDS implementation. This is strictly a planning stage — it doesn't involve any action. It does, however, continue throughout the first half of the project.

You need to continually assess the scope of your implementation and make subtle adjustments as needed. This involves scheduling, task orientation, documentation, and acceptance testing. ACME's project scope implementation schedule is shown in Table 5.1. But, before we explore this first schedule, let's review some of its key components:

▸ Task and Description — A detailed description of each task and its associated subtasks, usually in outline form.

▸ Duration — The actual time it takes to complete the task. The duration is calculated according to an 8-hour workday and 5-day workweek and is always less than the difference between the start and end dates. This is because of organizational concerns, scheduling conflicts, and Murphy's Laws.

▸ Start Date — When the task begins, according to the calendar. This shows interdependencies between tasks because some tasks start after others. But most are staggered (that is, they happen at the same time).

▸ End Date — When the task finishes. This is usually greater than the start date plus duration.

▸ %Complete — An ongoing meter of task progress.

▸ Person — Whoever is in charge of the task and accountable for the schedule.

Table 5.1 is a template for your implementation schedule. Fill in the information as needed.

ZEN

Croissantization — The popularization of croissants as part of peoples' diet in a trendy society. This is an example of junk-food imperialism. The aggressive international marketing of food that is high in calories but low in nutritional value, such as candy and most fast foods. Typically, the only nourishment allowed for busy CNEs.

TASK 2 — TRAINING

"Knowledge is nourishment for the mind," and it's never been more obvious than with ACME and NDS implementation. Please don't skimp on training. This is one of the most critical tasks in the entire process. Like project scope, training occurs throughout the life of the project. As a matter of fact, training occurs before, during, and after the ACME implementation.

T A B L E   5.1

ACME's Project Scope Schedule

TASK	DESCRIPTION	DURATION	START DATE	END DATE	%COMPLETE	PERSON
Main Task: Project Scope		**12 weeks**	**1/1/97**			
1.1 Determine Milestones						
1.2 Determine Critical Path						
1.3 Determine Success Factors						
1.4 Risk Analysis						
1.5 Establish Reporting and Tracking						
1.6 Documentation						
1.7 Acceptance Testing						

Because some of the later tasks are dependent on training, we will start this task first — on January 1, 1997. During the training phase, you need to train your administrators, users, and the project team. The training task also involves lab testing.

Here are some excellent sources for IntranetWare training:

▶ Novell Authorized Education Centers — Eight courses are available for IntranetWare alone. Surf the Web to
`http://netpub.com/education/x/scatlog`.

▸ NetWare Users International (NUI) — This users group offers regular meetings and conferences. Surf the Web to `http://www.nuinet.com`.

▸ Novell Press books — *Novell's CNE Study Guide IntranetWare/NetWare 4.11* and *Novell's CNE Study Guide for Core Technologies* are just a few of the titles you'll find useful. Surf the Web to `http://corp.novell.com/programs/press/hot.htm`.

▸ Vendor Workshops — These workshops are often held at NUI meetings and conferences.

▸ *Novell Application Notes* — Novell's monthly technical journal for network design, implementation, administration, and integration. Surf the Web to `http://support.novell.com/sitemap`.

▸ Colleges and Universities — Many of these institutions now offer certified IntranetWare training courses, including CyberState University (a CNE training center on the Web). Surf the Web to `http://www.cyberstateu.com`.

Refer to Table 5.2 for ACME's training schedule.

TABLE 5.2

ACME's Training Schedule

TASK	DESCRIPTION	DURATION	START DATE	END DATE	%COMPLETE	PERSON
Main Task: Training		**20 weeks**	**1/1/97**			
2.1 Determine Training Needs						
2.2 Training Strategies						
2.3 Obtain Training						
2.4 Set Up the Lab						

ZEN

Language pollution — The use of many new expressions, slang terms, or foreign words when viewed as unnecessary. Otherwise known as NDS nomenclature. Get the hint?

TASK 3 — NDS IMPLEMENTATION

NDS implementation transcends all the other tasks in the sense that it occurs continually. Once you have designed the NDS tree (see Chapter 4), you must install the servers (Chapters 6 and 7), and finally, put the resources in place and manage the tree (Chapters 8 and 9).

Following are some estimated time frames for each of ACME's NDS implementation subtasks:

1 •   Create NDS Naming Standard — 4 days

2 •   Design NDS Tree — 2 days

3 •   Design and Implement Partitions and Replicas — 3 days

4 •   Design and Implement Time Synchronizaton — 2 days

5 •   Develop NDS Accessibility Plan — 7 days

Remember, these aren't consecutive calendar days — they are actual duration. The real calendar time will be much longer. Refer to Chapter 4 for an in-depth discussion of these subtasks. For now, refer to Table 5.3 for ACME's NDS implementation schedule. Notice that it occurs one month after training begins. You'll have to learn this stuff before you can schedule it.

ZEN

Offenders' tag — An electronic device worn by a person under house arrest that monitors his/her movements and alerts police to violations of restrictions of movement. Or, the second layer of IntranetWare's five-layered security model — login restrictions.

TABLE 5.3

*ACME's NDS Implementation
Schedule*

TASK	DESCRIPTION	DURATION	START DATE	END DATE	%COMPLETE	PERSON
Main Task: NDS Implementation		**5 weeks**	**2/1/97**			
3.1 NDS Naming Standard (4 days)						
3.11 Identify Existing Standards						
3.12 Create NDS Naming Documents						
3.13 Deliver NDS Naming Documents						
3.2 NDS Tree (2 days)						
3.21 Gather Corporate Documents						
3.22 Review WAN Maps						
3.23 Review Campus Maps						
3.24 Design Top of Tree						
3.25 Review Organization						
3.26 Review Resource List						
3.27 Design Bottom of Tree						

(continued)

T A B L E   5.3

*ACME's NDS Implementation
Schedule (continued)*

TASK	DESCRIPTION	DURATION	START DATE	END DATE	%COMPLETE	PERSON
Main Task: NDS Implementation		**5 weeks**	**2/1/97**			
3.28 Place Resources in Containers						
3.29 Design Considerations						
3.29.1 Administration						
3.29.2 Partitioning						
3.29.3 Login Scripts						
3.29.4 Bindery Services						
3.29.5 Test NDS Tree Design						
3.3 Design and Implement Partitions and Replicas (3 days)						
3.31 Review WAN Map						
3.32 Partition Top of Tree						
3.33 Replica Strategy						
3.33.1 Replicate Locality						

TABLE 5.3

ACME's NDS Implementation
Schedule (continued)

TASK	DESCRIPTION	DURATION	START DATE	END DATE	%COMPLETE	PERSON
Main Task: NDS Implementation		**5 weeks**	**2/1/97**			
3.33.2 Replicate for Fault Tolerance						
3.34 Partition Bottom as Needed						
3.35 Develop Partition and Replica Guidelines						
3.36 Test Partitions and Replica Strategy						
3.4 Design and Implement Time Synchronization (2 days)						
3.41 Evaluate TimeSync Options						
3.41.1 Single-Reference (Default)						
3.41.2 Time Provider Group						
3.42 Choose Option Based on WAN						
3.43 Evaluate TimeSync Communications						

(continued)

TABLE 5.3

ACME's NDS Implementation
Schedule (continued)

TASK	DESCRIPTION	DURATION	START DATE	END DATE	%COMPLETE	PERSON
Main Task: NDS Implementation		5 weeks	2/1/97			
3.43.1 Service Advertising Protocol (SAP)						
3.43.2 Configured List						
3.44 Develop Time Synchronization Strategy						
3.45 Test Time Synchronization Strategy						
3.5 NDS Accessibility Plan (7 days)						
3.51 Analyze Existing Login Scripts						
3.52 Move System Login Script to Container Login Script						
3.53 Test Login Scripts						
3.53.1 Container Login Scripts						
3.53.2 Profile Login Scripts						
3.54 Develop Mobile User Strategy						

T A B L E   5 . 3

ACME's NDS Implementation
Schedule (continued)

TASK	DESCRIPTION	DURATION	START DATE	END DATE	%COMPLETE	PERSON
Main Task: NDS Implementation		**5 weeks**	**2/1/97**			
3.55 Test Mobile User Access						
3.56 Deliver Accessibility Plan						

TASK 4 — SECURITY AND AUDITING

Security and auditing are very important parts of the NDS implementation. Once you've established the tree guidelines, you'll need to concentrate on securing it. See Chapter 11 for more details.

Note that migrating users don't have to worry about file system security — it should already be in place. You should, however, test it first. Refer to Table 5.4 for ACME's security and auditing schedule.

T A B L E   5 . 4

ACME Security and Auditing Schedule

TASK	DESCRIPTION	DURATION	START DATE	END DATE	%COMPLETE	PERSON
Main Task: Security and Auditing		**1 week**	**3/1/97**			
4.1 Server Security						
4.11 Server Settings						
4.2 NDS Security						

(continued)

ACME Security and
Auditing Schedule (continued)

TASK	DESCRIPTION	DURATION	START DATE	END DATE	%COMPLETE	PERSON
Main Task: Security and Auditing		**I week**	**3/1/97**			
4.21 Object Security						
4.22 Property Security						
4.23 Develop NDS Security Strategy						
4.24 Test Security Strategy						
4.3 File System Security						
4.31 Develop File System Strategy						
4.32 Test File System Strategy						
4.4 Audit						
4.41 Define Audit Procedures						
4.42 Understand Audit Utilities						
4.43 Develop Audit Strategy						
4.44 Test Audit Strategy						

ZEN

Sniglet — A word made-up for something without a name or concise description. It is based on a pun or a clever combination of existing words. I guess it's safe to say this book is one big "sniglet."

The next two tasks represent the Big Two of the implementation tasks: client migration and server migration. After all, users depend on IntranetWare clients and the NDS tree depends on IntranetWare servers. In these two sections, we explain the details of client and server migration in a little more depth. Remember, these are two critical phases.

TASK 5 — CLIENT MIGRATION

Client migration is the first of two critical implementation tasks: client migration and server migration. Later in Chapters 7 and 13, we'll get a chance to install and migrate NDS client resources. But now let's take a moment to learn IntranetWare's five-step client migration strategy:

- ▶ Step 1: Assess existing network clients.

- ▶ Step 2: Determine migration strategy.

- ▶ Step 3: Share new client software with administrators.

- ▶ Step 4: User training.

- ▶ Step 5: Upgrade clients.

SMART LINK

You can download the new Client 32 connectivity files for free at http://www.novell.com.

Step 1: Assess Existing Network Clients

During the first step of client migration, you'll need to assess the current state of clients throughout your network. Survey the client operating systems (including version numbers) and determine whether they are compatible with NDS and

IntranetWare. If most of your users are using the NETx shell for connectivity, you will need to upgrade them to Client 16 or Client 32 immediately. This step usually precedes server migration because the newer shells support connectivity to both NetWare 3.12 and IntranetWare.

Next, survey client login batch files (AUTOEXEC.BAT or others). Determine if connectivity occurs within standard files (like AUTOEXEC.BAT) or special network-specific files (like STARTNET.BAT). Finally, assess each user's level of networking expertise. Determine the impact of new client software on their daily routine. The most important goal of this step is to gain an appreciation for the client diversity within your network. One of your most important tasks as a CNE is to standardize connectivity throughout the WAN.

Step 2: Determine Migration Strategy

The next step is to determine your overall client migration strategy. This involves a number of client compatibility issues from protocol to performance. Here are a few things to think about when developing a client migration strategy:

▶ Protocols — List all the protocols needed for each workstation. In response, prepare PROTOCOL and FRAME statements for NET.CFG (Client 16) or Registry (Client 32) files.

▶ Workstation Management — Will you manage workstations using SNMP tools? These tools provide information to network administrators about workstations connected to the WAN. If SNMP is necessary, be sure to include the following VLMs: MIB2IF.VLM, WSASNI.VLM, WSREG.VLM, WSSNMP.VLM, WSTRAP.VLM, and NMR.VLM (optional).

▶ Workstation Backup — If the workstation will be backed up using a central SMS-compliant backup system, be sure to load the TSASMS.COM utility.

▶ Security — If you plan on using RSA encryption or NetWare-enhanced security, be sure to include the following VLMs: RSA.VLM and SECURITY.VLM.

▶ Backward Compatibility — Will the workstation connect to bindery-based servers? Do applications running at this workstation require NETx compatibility? If so, be sure to include the following VLMs: BIND.VLM (for logging into bindery-based servers) and NETX.VLM (for backward compatibility to NETX.EXE).

▶ Performance — If the workstation requires enhanced performance, consider including parameters for large Internet packets (LIP) or packet bursting.

Once you've addressed all these issues, you can start to formulate a client migration strategy. During the migration or installation of the new client software, test different methods for the best efficiency. Try INSTALL.EXE over the network or from a batch file at your workstation. Also consider an automated strategy for upgrades from the server. For instance, when the user logs into an IntranetWare server, the automated program could download the required programs to the user's workstation. This is accomplished using WSUPDATE or WSUPGRD. Finally, consider upgrading other system software for the workstation while you're there. For example, you could take this opportunity to upgrade the workstations to the latest version of Windows or perform other necessary upgrades.

QUIZ

A friend of yours is tossing a coin and you are betting him on the outcome. You bet on heads every time. Your unit stake is one dollar per toss. You begin by betting one dollar on the first toss. If you win, you again place one dollar on the second toss. But if you lose, you double the stake to two dollars, then four dollars, and continue to double after every loss. After every win, you revert to the one dollar stake. After 100 tosses of the coin, heads has come down 59 times. How much profit are you making assuming that the 100th toss was heads?

(Q5-1)
(See Appendix C for all quiz answers)

Step 3: Share New Client Software with Administrators

Once you have determined what your client migration strategy will be, be sure to share the results with distributed administrators. If you have a lab, train the administrators on migrating typical workstation configurations. In the case of

Client 16, this means you'll need to prepare some sample INSTALL.CFG files. Also assign administrators to upgrade their own workstations to get them familiar with the different client architecture.

This brings me to an important point. During client migration, consider moving the entire client team and other IS staff members to the new software first. This will enable them to become familiar with the technology. Then when you migrate the users, your administrators will already have personal experience with the system. Once the administrators are comfortable with the new client migration strategy, you're well on your way to IntranetWare nirvana.

REAL WORLD

Client 16 migration is much easier to automate than Client 32. This is because there are very few GUI files involved. Because INSTALL.EXE copies and modifies specific files, this utility can be replaced by your own custom-designed batch files to install the client based on your specific needs.

For large installations with many workstations that are currently running NETx this is the recommended approach. Their automated process basically gives a Container login script to query the workstation for the existence of the NetWare DOS Requester. If the current DOS Requester is not found, the Container script can be designed to launch a set of batch files that will perform the functions of INSTALL.EXE on any given workstation. A scripting language such as Novell's Navigator can be used to simplify this process.

Step 4: User Training

Now it's time to review Step 1 again. Go back to your user assessment and break the users into three different categories: Really Smart, Average, and Clueless. Based on these different levels, you can customize a user training strategy. Really Smart users can be left alone while Average and Clueless clients require a great deal more attention. Also consider the workstation as the main point of network interface for users. Sometimes training doesn't stop with Client 16 or Client 32 connectivity. Most of the time you'll need to review some basic Windows 95 topics before they understand the concepts of logging in or name context. Be careful, though, you're beginning to waiver outside the realms of your CNE responsibility.

During the training process, consider all types of training — e-mail messages, paper handouts, quick-reference cards, classroom training, and on-line courses via CyberState University. Once you have trained your users, you're ready for Step 5.

Step 5: Upgrade Clients

Schedule the migration of your workstations during a period that is long enough to migrate a given selected set of users. You may need to schedule this process during a weekend. Obviously, the more people involved in the migration, the faster it will go.

The client team should plan for about 15 minutes per workstation to complete the installation of the latest client software. The team should also combine all necessary changes into a single visit to each workstation. Earlier, in Chapter 4, we learned there are a variety of different client types supported by IntranetWare, including Windows 95, Windows 3.1, DOS, OS/2, Windows NT, UNIX, and Macintosh. For the most part, IntranetWare supports three different client migration methods:

- ▸ Diskette method

- ▸ Server method

- ▸ CD-ROM method

Whichever method you choose, be sure to follow the steps precisely as outlined in Chapters 7 and 13.

QUIZ

What is the five-digit number, no zeroes, in which the last digit is five times the first, the second digit is twice the first, the third is the sum of the first and second, and the fourth is the sum of the first, second, and third?

(Q5-2)

Refer to Table 5.5 for ACME's client migration schedule. You will need a little training to get the client migration started, so you'll see that we're waiting a month after the training time line. This process could start at the same time as NDS implementation, because the Client 16 and Client 32 support supports both NetWare 3.12 and IntranetWare. It's a great place to start.

T A B L E 5.5
ACME's Client Migration
Schedule

TASK	DESCRIPTION	DURATION	START DATE	END DATE	%COMPLETE	PERSON
Main task: Client Migration		12 weeks	2/1/97			
5.1 Functional testing for each desktop						
5.2 Evaluate Client Migration Options						
5.3 Determine Client Migration Strategy						
5.4 Test Client Migration Strategy						

So, how long will it take? Consider the following calculation for ACME:

2,000 workstations (15 minutes per workstation = 30,000 minutes
30,000 minutes = 500 hours = 62.5 workdays = 12.5 weeks

Even though we've calculated a duration of 12.5 weeks, it could take up to 4 calendar months to visit every workstation.

ZEN

Hundredth-monkey phenomenom — A controversial theory proposed as an explanation for the supposed spontaneous spread of behavior when a population of animals reaches a certain high number. In one experiment, the hundredth monkey learned to wash sweet potatoes. In another experiment, the hundredth user learned how to use VLMs.

TASK 6 — SERVER MIGRATION METHODS

The second of the Big Two implementation tasks focuses on the NetWare 4.11 server. This is the *big kahuna!* The server houses NDS, stores the users' files, and provides a gateway to the cyber frontier. For all these reasons, you should take great care in server migration. Remember: IntranetWare uses the NetWare 4.11 operating system as the foundation of its servers.

Following is a detailed introduction to the four main NetWare 4.11 server migration methods. Follow this discussion closely, and then refer to Chapters 6 and 7 for more excrutiating details. Ready, set, serve!

In general, IntranetWare supports the following four different server migration methods:

▸ File Copy Method

▸ In-place Method

▸ Across-the-Wire Method

▸ Same-Server Method

Each of these options has its own advantages and disadvantages. The method you use will depend on your current operating system, available hardware, and available time. Some methods are faster than others, and some offer more configuration options. Let's take a closer look.

SMART LINK

For more information regarding the details of NetWare 4.11 server migration, study the on-line documentation at http://www.novell.com/manuals/.

File Copy Method

Perhaps the simplest migration method you can use is copying the files and data from your current operating system to the NetWare file system. This is a very dynamic migration method because you can choose which files and subdirectories you want to move. You can move an entire volume, a group of subdirectories, or a single file.

There are a few requirements you'll need to meet before you can perform a File Copy:

▸ Your new NetWare 4.11 server must be installed and running on the network along with the server you intend to migrate.

▸ You will need to choose a workstation and establish a concurrent connection to both servers.

▸ You'll need to use login accounts with rights that allow you to read and write the data to and from the appropriate source and destination servers.

▸ Your workstation must have enough memory to support the concurrent login to both servers.

▸ In a mixed operating system environment, the workstation performing the migration must be loaded with two protocols to support both operating systems.

▸ Both the source and destination servers must be visible to the workstation performing the copy.

Check out Figure 5.5 to see how the File Copy method works. In this figure, a user logs into a NetWare 3.12 server called NETWARE_312 and a NetWare 4.11 server called NETWARE_410. After connecting to both servers from a DOS workstation, the user maps drives to the source server and to the destination server. Then the user issues an XCOPY command with appropriate parameters and copies the data from the VOL1 volume to the DATA directory, or a similar volume, on the destination server.

The drive mappings for the workstations are as follows:

```
MAP F:=SERVER_312\VOL1:
```

```
MAP G:=SERVER_410\VOL1:DATA
```

The copy command would appear as

```
XCOPY F:*.* G: /S /E
```

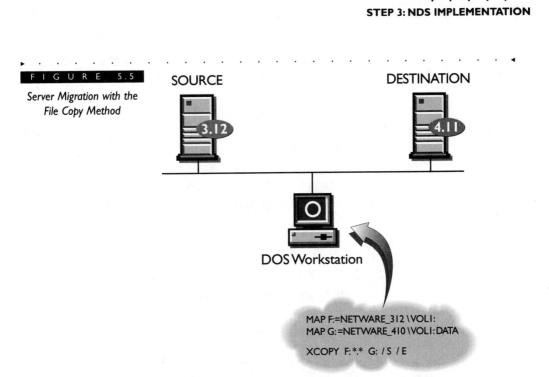

FIGURE 5.5

Server Migration with the File Copy Method

This command copies all files from the F: drive to the G: drive, including all subdirectories (/S) even if empty (/E).

Although the File Copy migration method is the simplest and quickest way to move information from one server to another, it may not be practical for those who require information other than just data (for example, trustee assignments). But for some migrations, it is currently the only option. For example, migrating a network from DEC Pathworks users to NetWare 4.11 requires the COPY command. There is no other mechanism currently available. The advantages and disadvantages of the File Copy migration method are listed as follows.

Advantages:

▶ Restricts the copy of the source server to read-only on the data files. The copy procedure provides fault tolerance because the source server is only being read and not altered in any way.

▶ Selects volumes, directories, or files that you wish to be moved. For example, the entire drive does not need to be copied to the other server, which means you can do migrations in stages.

- Supports file transfers between popular network operating systems. For example, DEC Pathworks or LANtastic files can be copied.

- Allows you to move different types of name spaces. This method supports Macintosh, NFS, and other native desktops if the workstation is already attached with active name space.

- Data files can be moved at any time because the procedure is nondisruptive to the user. However, the increased network traffic may affect users' performance.

- You can use several utilities to perform the File Copy (for example, COPY, XCOPY, NCOPY, File Manager in Windows, Norton Utilities, XTREE, and other third-party products).

Disadvantages:

- Does not move the bindery from NetWare 2 and NetWare 3. This means that users, groups, and print services are not migrated to the new server.

- Does not maintain existing source file trustee assignments. After the migration, these assignments must be redefined.

- Requires additional server hardware. Both the source and destination server must be installed and running on the network. This method also requires availability of a workstation.

- Requires a concurrent connection to both the source and destination server. Both servers must be visible to the workstation. The only way around this is to attach to the source server to move the data files to a temporary storage device, and then move the files to the destination server in stages.

- Could be slow because it moves the data files across the network from one server to another.

TIP

If the servers are not visible or you have problems communicating with the network, you should check to see if your workstation is set up with the same frame types as the servers. With the release of NetWare 4, Novell changed the default Ethernet frame type from Ethernet 802.3 to Ethernet 802.2.

The File Copy migration method is valuable to companies that are performing file server data restructuring. If you must change the layout of the server significantly or apply large changes in naming, then you may choose to simply copy the files from server to server.

In-Place Method

The In-place method uses the NetWare 4.11 installation program called INSTALL.EXE, which loads the corresponding INSTALL.NLM as the server boots. In-place migration provides you with a path to upgrade from a NetWare 3 server to NetWAre 4.11 — all in the same box. Figure 5.6 illustrates how you can upgrade a NetWare 3.12 server to NetWare 4.11 within the same physical machine.

FIGURE 5.6

Server Migration with the In-Place Method

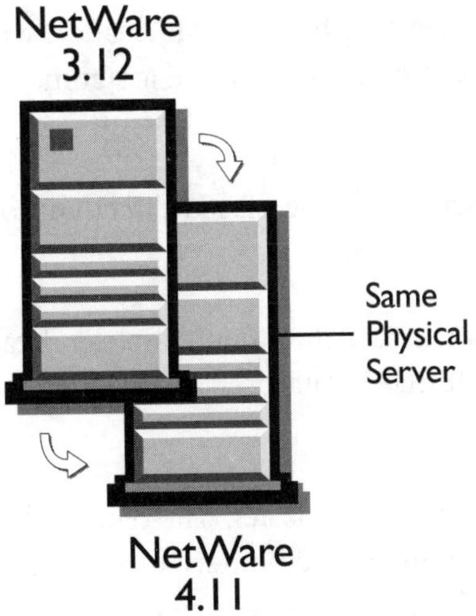

NetWare
3.12

Same Physical Server

NetWare
4.11

Since the file server hardware remains the same, the data volumes remain the same. Only new files are added to the SYS: volume in the system subdirectories. The data files on the other volumes on the server will not be moved or changed.

The In-place migration method is the fastest method for migration because it does not move the data files. The other migration methods are slower because all the data must be migrated across the LAN or WAN. This method is recommended when you are upgrading an existing NetWare 3 server to NetWare 4.11 on the same hardware device. To use this utility to migrate a NetWare 2 server, you'll have to upgrade the server to NetWare 3 first.

The NetWare 4.11 installation program can be started in DOS from the IntranetWare CD-ROM. Then, from the NetWare 4.11 Install main menu, you would select Upgrade a NetWare 3 Server to NetWare 4.11. The In-place migration method is excellent for situations in which you do not have the luxury of migrating from one server hardware to other. The advantages and disadvantages of this method are as follows.

Advantages:

▶ Uses the same physical server hardware. This eliminates the cost of a new server hardware system just to perform the migration.

▶ Passwords are maintained or kept. The user will not change passwords.

▶ Migrates the existing bindery information with full NDS compatibility. All the users, groups, and trustee assignments are migrated or maintained.

▶ User login scripts will be placed directly into the corresponding NDS property for the user.

▶ Preserves all the user print configuration databases. The PRINTCON.DAT and PRINTDEF.DAT databases are written directly into the NDS property for each user.

▶ Migrates all the servers faster. The data in the file system or volumes remain unmodified. The bindery files are the only information that must be converted. They are moved to NDS.

▶ The name spaces are maintained. Since the data files are not changing, the name space (MAC, NFS, and so on) are fully supported.

Disadvantages:

▶ Does not allow the volume block size to be changed. We recommend that each NetWare 4.11 server have 64K volume blocks. But, since the file system remains intact from before the upgrade, you will have the original volume block size set for your server (probably 4K blocks).

▶ Does not allow you to turn on suballocation for the file system. Suballocation can be turned on after the upgrade, but the suballocation will affect only subsequent writes to the disks.

▶ May require a restoration from a tape backup if a failure occurs during the upgrade process. Although the In-place upgrade method is restartable if a failure occurs, there are other windows of vulnerability that may require you to do a tape restore.

 ZEN

Fax hacker — A person who uses a fax machine to send messages that have not been requested by the recipient, usually in large numbers or too many people. Welcome to junk mail in the 21st century.

Across-the-Wire Method

The Across-the-Wire migration utility (AMU) allows you to migrate network servers from a different network operating system including NetWare. This method supports migration from NetWare 2, NetWare 3, LAN Server, LAN Manager, and Banyan VINES.

With this method, the physical server hardware is replaced. The utility migrates the bindery or administrative information and data files from the original server to the NetWare 4.11 server. The Across-the-Wire utility runs on a DOS workstation that should be logged into both the source and destination servers. The workstation will read the administrative information and data files from the source server and write them to the NetWare 4.11 server (see Figure 5.7).

Because this method runs at the workstation and has to move all the data, it is very important that you choose a fast workstation. As a minimum, we recommend a 100-Mhz 486 workstation with at least 480K of free memory. The workstation needs at least a 16- or 32-bit LAN card. Although a slower workstation with an 8-bit LAN card will work, it will increase the time needed to complete the migration. You should find the fastest PC possible and place it on the same network segment as the server being migrated.

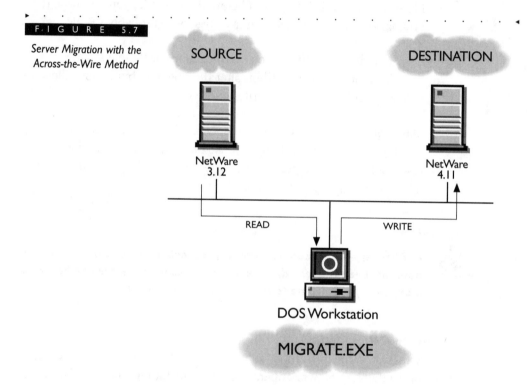

F I G U R E   5.7

Server Migration with the
Across-the-Wire Method

The Across-the-Wire migration utility (MIGRATE.EXE) tracks and logs all the actions of the migration. The log file is written on the hard drive of the workstation. The log file requires approximately 1 MB for every 1 GB of data migrated. The following are the advantages and disadvantages of this method:

Advantages:

▸ Migrates previous NetWare versions as well as other network operating systems (for example, NetWare 2, NetWare 3, LAN Server, LAN Manager, or Banyan VINES). This utility does not support migration from previous versions of NetWare 4 (v4.0x) to NetWare 4.11.

▶ Migrates all the bindery information into NDS (Bindery Services mode). The users, groups, and trustee assignments are maintained.

▶ The server being migrated is read-only and the data files and bindery remain the same. In the event of a network crash, the server being migrated is unmodified.

▶ Allows consolidation of multiple source servers into a single IntranetWare server. The source servers can be from different operating systems.

▶ Gives you the chance to replace or upgrade the server to newer, more powerful hardware. The NetWare 4.11 server must be up and running on the network.

▶ Selectively migrates the data files or bindery information. You can select a volume from the source server to be moved to the new server as a new Volume:Directory combination.

▶ Multiple DOS workstations can migrate the same server, different volumes at the same time. This means that you can have more than one workstation process the information.

▶ Allows you to change the volume block size for the file system. You can select the volume block size during the installation of the NetWare 4.11 server or destination server. You should always select a volume block size of 64K.

▶ Allows you to turn on file suballocation before the migration of the data files.

Disadvantages:

▶ Requires that the DOS workstation be connected concurrently to both the source and destination servers in order to migrate the data files. This could cause a problem if you have to support different network operating systems. You must then load both protocol stacks for each operating system.

▸ Limits the connection to the NetWare 4.11 destination server as Bindery Service access. This will cause a problem when you try to migrate information (for example, login scripts) that must be placed in NDS.

▸ The migration procedure is slow because the DOS workstation is transferring all the data files across the network. The data being copied could be disruptive to the network traffic and may require you to execute the migration process during off-peak hours.

▸ Passwords are not maintained because the workstation doing the migration cannot read the password. You can migrate either with no passwords or with random passwords.

▸ DOS name space or files are the only name space supported. The Mac, NFS, and others are not supported through the DOS workstation. You can do a File Copy using a native desktop machine to move the files.

Same-Server Method

You can also use a modified version of the Across-the-Wire utility to migrate other network operating systems, even if you are not replacing the server hardware. The Same-Server method allows an upgrade without requiring a new server. This option migrates the bindery or bindery-like information from the source server to the DOS workstation.

The Same-Server method does not copy or migrate any data files. To keep your data files, you'll need to back up them before doing the migration. After you have rebuilt the physical hardware device and loaded NetWare 4.11, you can restore the data files. Then you can restore the bindery information from the DOS workstation.

If you want to consolidate hardware, you should also use the Same-Server version of MIGRATE.EXE. It allows you to move the information from several existing servers into one IntranetWare server.

Server Migration Preparation

The server team should also consider performing the following functions in preparation for the migration of each NetWare 4.11 server:

1 • Apply the corporate NDS naming standard while the objects are still in the bindery. NDS does not support different object types having the same name. By contrast, the binderies in previous versions of NetWare do support different object types with the same name. For example, in NetWare 3, a Group object called HP4SI and a print queue called HP4SI have the same name because they are different object types. In NetWare 4.11 you cannot have any leaf object with the same name in the same container. This conflict must be resolved before the migration of the server to NetWare 4.11. If there is a duplicate, the migration utilities will not migrate the second occurrence of a duplicate object name. A Novell utility called DUPBIND (found on NetWire) displays the duplicate object names in the binderies so that they can be changed before a migration begins.

2 • Clean up the binderies and delete users and other objects that are no longer in use. Take this opportunity to remove security and access privileges that are no longer required. The SECURITY.EXE program in NetWare 3 will help you find and expose the detailed security information for each of the objects in the bindery. Users that have left the company or are no longer using that server should be removed.

3 • Make a complete backup of your servers before beginning a migration. Some companies have individuals in an operations group who are responsible for backups. The server team should work with this group to ensure that a recent backup has been performed on any server that is about to be migrated.

4 • Run the BINDFIX utility in NetWare 3 to remove any objects that are corrupted in the bindery.

5 • If you are migrating multiple NetWare 2 or NetWare 3 servers into a single NetWare 4.11 server, the server team should check for users with accounts on the multiple servers. Migrating multiple servers and duplicate users will present you with several challenges during migration to NetWare 4.11. First, the MIGRATE utility prompts you to change the username on the second and subsequent servers. Second, the migrate utility will merge the User objects that have the same name into a single NDS object with cumulative rights. This may not be what you had intended.

6 • If each of the multiple NetWare 2 or NetWare 3 servers are migrated into different containers in the NDS tree (OU's), the duplicate username will be migrated to each individual container with the same name, but a different context. In most cases, you do not want to manage the same user twice in the tree.

7 • Delete old files and applications from the file system. This will free up disk space for other purposes. You may discover many old, unused, and duplicated applications that are wasting disk space.

8 • If you are using Ethernet, ensure that your network uses the IntranetWare default Ethernet frame type of 802.2. Although NetWare 4.11 will support both the 802.3 raw and IEEE 802.2 frame types, 802.2 provides automatic check summing of packets to ensure greater communication reliability and is the preferred standard.

TIP

Always try to use the Ethernet 802.2 frame type and begin phasing out the 802.3 raw frame type if in use at your site. Choosing just one frame type will eliminate additional network traffic considerably.

Refer to Table 5.6 for ACME's server migration schedule. This is the most time-consuming aspect of NDS implementation, because it involves most of the other implementation tasks. At ACME, we will be migrating a total of 52 servers, 3 of which will be part of the earlier pilot program-leaving us with 49 servers. It takes about 1.5 days per server, once you know what you're doing. So, here's the math:

49 servers × 1.5 days = 74 days = 15 weeks

Also, notice that the server migration starts 1.5 months after the client migration. This is because of two factors. First, the NDS implementation must be completed before we can begin (4 weeks after 2/1/97). Second, we have to wait for the procedures from the pilot program (15 days more). That puts us at 3/15/97.

TABLE 5.6

*ACME's Server
Migration Schedule*

TASK	DESCRIPTION	DURATION	START DATE	END DATE	%COMPLETE	PERSON
Main Task: Server Migration		15 weeks	3/15/97			
6.1 Evaluate Inplace Utility						
6.2 Evaluate Across-the-Wire Utility						
6.3 Determine Strategy for Server Migrations						
6.4 Perform Mock Migration in the Lab						
6.5 Test Server Migration Strategy						
6.6 Develop Backup and Restore Strategy						

ZEN

U-turn worker — A professional or skilled worker who returns from unemployment in a big city to work in the nonurban locality from which he or she originally came. Or the propensity of CNEs to return back to the comfortable confines of DOS.

TASK 7 — PRINTING MIGRATION

This printing team is responsible for designing the printing strategies for IntranetWare. All the print software and hardware should be tested for compatibility. This includes connections greater than 250 users. The printing strategies should also encompass printing in a mixed environment — NetWare 3 and IntranetWare. This team should address the following issues for both a pure IntranetWare printing strategy and a mixed NetWare 3 and IntranetWare environment.

Setup for a pure IntranetWare printing strategy:

- ▸ Quick Setup

- ▸ Default print queue for printers

- ▸ Workstations running VLMs

- ▸ Workstations running NETx

Setup for a mixed NetWare 3 and IntranetWare printing strategy:

- ▸ Queues on IntranetWare, with the print servers on NetWare 3

- ▸ Queues on NetWare 3, with the print servers on IntranetWare

- ▸ Queues and print servers on NetWare 3, with client on IntranetWare and VLMs

Refer to Table 5.7 for ACME's printing migration schedule. This process depends entirely on the server migration tasks. Printing implementation takes roughly 2 hours per server:

52 servers × 2 hours per server = 104 hours = 13 days = 2.5 weeks

We will begin implementing printing with the very first pilot server; therefore, this process starts on 3/1/97.

TABLE 5.7

ACME's Printing
Migration Schedule

TASK	DESCRIPTION	DURATION	START DATE	END DATE	%COMPLETE	PERSON
Main Task: Printing Migration		5 weeks	3/1/97			
7.1 Identify Existing Printing Environment						
7.2 Evaluate Proposed Printing Layout						
7.3 Evaluate Direct Print Cards and Printers						
7.4 Determine Printing Migration Strategy						
7.5 Test Printing Migration Strategy						

ZEN

Neoism — An old policy or idea presented in a way that makes it appear new or innovative, such as IntranetWare printing.

TASK 8 — APPLICATION MIGRATION

This application project team is responsible for accomplishing compatibility testing for applications running on both IntranetWare servers and clients. There are several issues to deal with during the compatibility testing, including:

- Bindery-based software programs

- NDS-aware applications

- Connections greater than 250 users

- VLM compatibility

This group is also responsible for the migration and implementation of existing applications into the new IntranetWare production environment. Not all applications need to be tested for compatibility — primarily because NetWare 4 and IntranetWare have been around for a few years and also because mainstream applications are already known to be completely compatible. Applications written by internal staff, however, should be tested.

Novell has introduced two new advancements in the network application arena — the NetWare Application Manager (NAM) and NetWare Application Launcher (NAL).

The NAM utility enables you to represent applications as objects in the Directory tree. As NDS objects, you can manage applications the same way you manage other objects — using NWADMIN. In addition, you can define an application directory, icon, command line parameters, and other attributes in one place, use trustee assignments to manage access to applications, and define startup scripts that establish the appropriate network environment for the application.

The NAL utility (available in both 16-bit and 32-bit versions) enables network users to launch applications represented by application objects. When started, NAL displays a desktop that contains application object icons. When the network user clicks on an icon, NAL sets up the workstation and starts the associated application as defined in the application object's properties. As a CNE, you can control what applications the network user has access to and the user's ability to adjust the NAL desktop. This is just another example of how IntranetWare and NDS are working together to integrate all Enterprise services.

Refer to Table 5.8 for ACME's application migration schedule. Note that the actual migration of the applications occurs during the server migration phase — the duration of which is included in the 15-week estimate for Task 6. In this section, we will estimate the duration of compatibility pretesting. This task also occurs before client and server migration. It takes roughly 1 day to test each application, and

ACME has 24 different applications. Therefore, compatibility pretesting will take approximately five weeks. We'd better start as soon as we can. Note, the client migration may overlap with application pretesting.

TABLE 5.8

ACME's Application Migration Schedule

TASK	DESCRIPTION	DURATION	START DATE	END DATE	%COMPLETE	PERSON
Main Task: Application Migration		**5 weeks**	**2/1/97**			
8.1 Identify all Applications						
8.2 For Internally Written Applications						
8.21 Install						
8.22 Test on a Desktop						
8.23 Test on Server						
8.24 Test Printing						
8.25 Document Compatibility						
8.3 Deliver Applications into Production						

ZEN

Reversible raincoat sentence — A statement that, with a minor change as in word order or word substitution, produces a cleverly expressed idea. Here's a great example: "Ask not what your country can do for you; ask what you can do for your country."

TASK 9 — PILOT PROGRAM

The pilot program is a very important precursor to server migration. It allows you to test the implementation procedures on a few "live" production servers. The goal here is to establish procedures and blueprints for the rest of the server migrations.

It usually takes twice as much time to perform a pilot migration as a regular migration. This is because you're working on your first couple of servers and you're documenting every step. This means that it will take us two weeks to adequately migrate the three Labs pilot servers. Refer to Table 5.9 for ACME's pilot program schedule.

TABLE 5.9

*ACME's Pilot
Program Schedule*

TASK	DESCRIPTION	DURATION	START DATE	END DATE	%COMPLETE	PERSON
Main Task: Pilot Program		**2 weeks**	**3/1/97**			
9.1 Pilot Preparation						
9.11 Clean Up (Objects and Files)						
9.12 Apply Naming Standards on NetWare 3 Servers						
9.13 Run BINDFIX						
9.14 Back Up Servers						
9.2 Pilot Installation or Migration						

T A B L E   5.9

ACME's Pilot
Program Schedule (continued)

TASK	DESCRIPTION	DURATION	START DATE	END DATE	%COMPLETE	PERSON
Main Task: Pilot Program		**2 weeks**	**3/1/97**			
9.21 Upgrade Server to NetWare 4						
9.22 Test Server (Production-like)						
9.23 Document any Problems						
9.24 Modify Procedures Based on Results						
9.3 Acceptance Testing						
9.31 Provide Daily Support to User						

 ZEN

Gridlock — A massive traffic jam in which vehicles are unable to move in a network of intersections. Also can be applied to a variety of nonautomotive situations, including speaking (vocal gridlock), bureaucracy (corporate gridlock), or networking (bindery gridlock).

TASK 10 — ROLLOUT

Well, we finally made it! This is the last leg of a very exhausting race. The rollout schedule is an overview of the entire project. In includes project scope, training, NDS, resource migration, and the pilot program.

As you can see in Table 5.10, we've included a significant cushion in the rollout schedule. Even though the project will theoretically only take 21 weeks, it doesn't factor in scheduling conflicts, traveling, and Murphy's Laws. So, add another 25 percent to the total duration, and we should finish the ACME implementation on September 28, 1997. No sweat, now all we have to do is-just do it! Ready, set, rollout.

T A B L E 5.10
ACME's Final Rollout Schedule

TASK	DESCRIPTION	DURATION	START DATE	END DATE	%COMPLETE	PERSON
Main Task: Rollout		**21 weeks**	**2/1/97**	**9/28/97**		
10.1 Just Do It!						

ZEN

Workquake — An upheaval in the way workers pursue their assignments in the workplace especially as a result of computerization — and IntranetWare is at the epicenter. Now you can better understand the general feeling of WANphobia among users.

Wow, that's a lot of work! I can feel a very large "workquake" approaching. We're going to be very busy over the next eight months. It's a good thing we're attacking this ACME WAN together.

That completes Step 3. As you can see, NDS implementation centers on the implementation schedule. It is truly a road map for ACME success. The remaining ten chapters of this book are dedicated to getting you through the ACME implementation schedule — and beyond.

QUIZ

The plumber left the taps running in the bath with the plug out. The hot water tap would fill the bath in 54 seconds. The cold water tap would fill the bath in 48 seconds. The plug out would release a bath full of water in 30 seconds. Would the water ever fill up?

(Q 5-3)

EXERCISE 5-1: THE SEED

Circle the 20 NDS implementation terms hidden in this word search puzzle using the hints provided.

```
I  L  W  V  F  X  J  M  H  Y  T  X  D  K  W  R  U  P  U  L  G  H
U  A  C  C  E  S  S  I  B  I  L  I  T  Y  P  L  A  N  U  K  P  Q
N  O  V  E  L  L  P  R  E  S  S  B  O  O  K  S  S  G  S  S  M  E
E  I  U  I  C  D  Q  V  T  P  R  L  I  J  P  N  S  J  E  N  D  H
T  C  C  R  X  D  K  N  C  U  A  A  Y  T  L  I  K  B  S  J  F  D
W  F  A  J  S  K  M  R  S  W  F  P  E  H  U  R  Z  P  I  W  P  G
O  H  T  H  T  F  U  S  A  V  E  T  H  E  W  O  R  L  D  V  D  H
R  K  H  A  R  D  W  A  R  E  I  N  S  T  A  L  L  A  T  I  O  N
K  X  S  N  D  S  T  R  E  E  D  E  S  I  G  N  J  L  U  E  U  S
A  M  O  B  I  L  E  U  S  E  R  S  U  U  D  K  M  G  O  R  D  D
P  C  E  G  Q  G  S  Y  B  A  C  K  U  P  R  E  S  T  O  R  E  J
P  R  O  D  U  C  T  I  O  N  E  N  V  I  R  O  N  M  E  N  T  X
L  M  C  O  T  C  I  R  B  M  T  N  W  U  G  O  G  I  Z  P  U  F
I  D  S  S  T  A  N  D  A  R  D  C  C  M  X  M  K  K  W  V  Y  D
C  V  Y  S  O  M  G  H  Q  I  S  O  Q  R  A  M  Z  R  C  W  Z  C
A  V  W  N  H  C  L  U  Z  I  N  U  O  H  Y  Y  R  W  V  D  Y  S
T  E  O  P  G  P  A  Q  M  O  P  I  L  O  T  P  R  O  G  R  A  M
I  E  P  Y  G  U  B  V  X  R  X  P  N  O  X  W  T  Y  Y  Q  F  T
O  F  F  L  I  N  E  T  E  S  T  I  N  G  N  M  P  I  E  U  L  M
N  G  Q  V  Q  W  I  M  P  L  E  M  E  N  T  A  T  I  O  N  N  D
S  H  V  C  F  D  J  W  B  W  M  R  J  Y  F  P  Q  O  O  N  R  K
```

Hints:

1. Task that deals with analyzing and testing login scripts as well as developing and testing mobile user strategies.
2. Important strategy that should be designed and implemented before a disaster occurs rather than after.
3. Off-line modeling tool used to create NDS.
4. Process of setting up network servers, workstations, peripherals, and cabling.
5. Process of executing planned tasks.

6. Type of users that present special implementation and management problems.
7. Critical step that should occur prior to NetWare 4 installation.
8. Third-party software programs that run on the server.
9. Hardware component required for network communication.
10. Valuable source of written information on NetWare 4.
11. Organization that offers NetWare 4 conferences, training, and trade shows.
12. Primary benefit provided by use of a testing lab.
13. Acts as a bridge between the testing lab and a full implementation of NetWare 4 across the entire WAN.
14. This is not the place to do network experimentation if you don't have to.
15. Final task in the implementation schedule.
16. Patented algorithm developed by Rivesi, Shamir, and Adleman for converting text or numerical information to a form that cannot be read by unauthorized personnel.
17. Primary mission of ACME, Inc.
18. Provides a non-production environment for testing hardware installation, NDS implementation, login scripts, network applications, and backup and restore procedures.
19. Critical network-related task that is often given inadequate attention and funding.
20. Type of network which covers larger geographical distances than a LAN.

See Appendix C for answers.

PART II: INTRANETWARE DESIGN

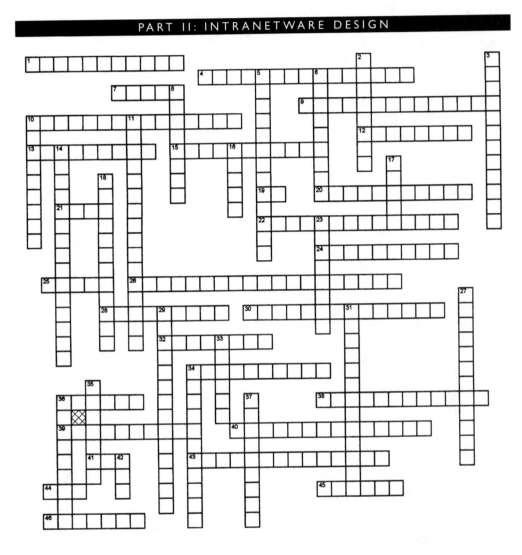

Across

1. One of three reasons to replicate
4. The bad guys
7. Creating more children partitions
9. Step 3 of NDS design
10. A graphical look at ACME's chronicles
12. The heart and soul of NDS implementation

13. Specialist who leads the design team
15. Setting context in NET.CFG
19. NDS Navigation at the command line
20. Step 1 of NDS design
21. The divisional headquarters of ACME's greatest minds
22. Changes context in relative distinguished names
24. "A day in the life of ACME"
25. Building a bigger parent partition
26. Input for *bottom* layers of the NDS tree
28. In charge of the project team
30. One of three reasons to replicate
32. Creating client migration diskettes
34. A great place for NDS experiments
36. Specialist who plans the pilot program
38. Foundation of the *bottom* layers of the NDS tree
39. Focusing in on ACME's WAN layout
40. Customized time communication
41. The center of ACME's New World Order
43. One of three reasons to replicate
44. Server-to-server communication
45. The home of ACME Permaculture
46. Including object class

Down

2. Connection type while accessing MAPped drives and CAPTUREd printers
3. Specialist who gathers WAN layout data
5. Connection type when host server identifies user
6. When
8. The second (and longest) implementation task
10. Design input for *top* layers of NDS tree
11. "Global" design input
14. Very first time server
16. "Young" subordinate partitions
17. Minimum number of replicas per partition
18. Design input for leaf objects

23. An invisible, often-misunderstood NDS object
27. A bridge between NDS design and full-blown implementation
29. Describes and classifies ACME's stuff
31. Establishes distinguished name
33. Step 2 of NDS design
34. Customized time configuration file
35. They "haggle" for time
36. Most popular time server type
37. Foundation for *top* layers of NDS tree
42. The ACME time machine

See Appendix C for answers.

Doctor

IntranetWare Installation

▶ · · · · · · · · · · · · · · · · · ◀

Is your network live?

▶ *It's a carbon-based organic life-form — Silicon is close enough.*

▶ *It consumes food — Your LAN processes valuable information.*

▶ *It propagates — Most IntranetWare WANs include multiple servers.*

▶ *It's self-aware — Many times your network has a mind of its own.*

There you go — your LAN must be alive.
And as a living, breathing life-form, it must be born.
This evolution is both painful and rewarding.
But there's nothing more exciting than being involved from Day One.

That's today!

You are a superhero.

You are a doctor.

You are a gardener.

As an IntranetWare CNE, you are three people in one.

Today, you are a doctor. Not an ordinary human mechanic — no. You are a "Silicon Surgeon." Today, you will deliver an exciting new form of life — an NDS-enhanced newborn. But it won't be an ordinary delivery — no. The birth will involve optical disks (backbone), UTP (circulatory system), a CPU (brain), workstations (limbs), and of course, a birth certificate (license).

Your network will be born today, thanks to IntranetWare installation and migration. But this is only the beginning. Actions you take today will begin the lifespan of a LAN! Later, in Chapters 12 and 13, you'll learn more about LAN childhood and adulthood. But let's not get ahead of ourselves.

Enjoy the moment.

Today, you'll help deliver one of the most exciting forms of life — an NDS-enhanced newborn. And it's only Monday.

IntranetWare/NetWare 4.11 Installation

If you build it, they will come!

There's something terrible about Mondays. First you seem to wake up on the "wrong side" of the bed. Then you burn the toast, pop a shirt button, and hit every red light on the way to work. Well, it can't possibly get any worse. Fortunately, you made it to the office without killing yourself or causing a tsunami to hit Central Park.

You settle into your comfy leather chair and let out a great sigh of relief. All is well. Then it happens! You find that your boss has dumped a menacing white box on your desk labeled "Novell IntranetWare — Intranetwork Software." You need to install it, but where do you begin? You look inside the box, hoping that the installation media consists of a single 3.5-inch diskette and are horrified to find one diskette *and* four CD-ROMs. You're sure this can't be a good sign. You quickly review your options:

- ▶ File a request for an immediate medical leave because of stress.

- ▶ Pawn off the job on some other unsuspecting victim.

- ▶ Give the installation a shot.

Being the weekday warrior that you are, you decide to give the installation a shot. Of course, you keep the other options open in case this proves to be a poor choice.

ZEN

And now for your Monday morning exercises. Ready?
"Up, down — Up, down — Up, down."
That's it. And now, the other eyelid.

Welcome to IntranetWare installation. This is the second of the "three faces of a CNE." Now that you've designed the LAN, it's time to build it. Think of this as IntranetWare Resuscitation" — you're breathing life into an otherwise limp and lifeless LAN. Once the server is "born," you can move into the daily grind of managing it — "childhood" and "adulthood."

WHAT'S NEW

WHAT'S
NEW

I would like to interrupt this book for an emergency broadcast message from Novell. As you know, the latest release of NetWare isn't NetWare at all — it's "IntranetWare." So, what happened to NetWare? Fortunately, it's still here. As a matter of fact, the IntranetWare solution uses "NetWare 4.11" as it's primary operating system. Confusing? Yes.

So, here's the bottom line: IntranetWare is the global WAN connectivity solution and NetWare 4.11 is the server-centric operating system it uses. So, when we talk about installing the server OS, we will use the term "NetWare 4.11." All other references will be to "IntranetWare." After all, that's the product. Now, I will return you to your regularly scheduled programming.

SMART LINK

SMART LINKS

If you want the "real" scoop on IntranetWare and the future of Novell, surf over to their home page at http://www.novell.com

NetWare 4.11 installation is dominated by SERVER.EXE, NLMs, and AUTOEXEC.NCF. It can be a little intimidating at first, especially if you've never installed NetWare before. But have no fear, Dr. David is here. In this chapter, we will traverse every installation obstacle together — all 21 of them. We'll learn about disk partitions, IPX internal network numbers, and NDS context. In addition, there are two extensive installation case studies (walk-throughs) at the end of the chapter. So, sit back, relax, and enjoy the rest of your Monday. After all, it can only get better.

THE BRAIN

This chapter assumes that you will be installing NetWare 4.11 on a DOS server. If you are installing NetWare 4.11 on a Windows 95 server, see the "Prepare to Install on a Windows 95 Machine" section in Chapter 1 of the *Novell NetWare 4.11 Installation* manual. If you'd like to install NetWare 4.11 on an OS/2 server, refer to Chapter 4 of the same manual.

Before You Begin

Installing NetWare 4.11 consists of two main tasks:

- Installation of the NetWare 4.11 operating system and on the server

- Installation of the client software on distributed workstations

You can also install a number of optional products on the server for added functionality. Some of these products are bundled with IntranetWare, including NetWare for Macintosh, MPR (Multiple Protocol Router), DynaText, Novell Internet Access Server, and Novell FTP Services. Others are available at additional cost. We will learn about Intranet installation and management topics later in the "Intranet Management" section of Chapter 13.

The purpose of this chapter is to guide you through the basic steps of the NetWare 4.11 OS server installation process. We will also explore DynaText installation. Wow, we're gonna be busy.

Before you begin, you'll need to install various LAN hardware components, such as:

- Network interface cards

- Cabling and hubs

- Uninterruptible power supplies

An important concern is to make sure that no hardware conflicts exist between your LAN components and server/workstation machines. You'll also need to make sure that your "computer room" meets recommended power and operating environment requirements. You should consult your hardware documentation to determine applicable temperature, humidity, heat-dissipation, and power-consumption requirements. Novell also recommends that you use dedicated electrical lines for all hardware components (such as servers, workstations, printers, and so on). This is a good idea, especially in lightning high-risk zones.

In order to protect your network servers from power surges and voltage spikes, you'll want to connect each server to an appropriate type of uninterruptible power supply (UPS). Novell also recommends that you provide UPS protection for important network workstations and other peripherals. (If this is not feasible, you should at least protect these workstations and peripherals with surge suppressers and ferro-resonant isolation transformers.)

Before purchasing LAN hardware or software applications, you should confirm that they are NetWare-compatible by looking for the following NetWare symbol:

The "Yes" Program provides developers with the opportunity to test their products against Novell's strict quality standards to ensure that their products are compatible with Novell products. Once products have passed the Yes Program's business and certification requirements, they are eligible to use a Yes logo. Novell's customers can then look for these logos to help them identify and purchase Novell-compatible third-party hardware and software products.

Novell releases a Certification Bulletin, also called the bulletin or test summary, on every "Yes" product. The bulletin details what products were used in testing (such as versions of Novell products, network adapters, controller devices, and supported drivers). It also indicates specific product configuration, date of the certification, special network configuration information, or other related information important to the product's interoperability in the network environment.

SMART LINK

You can view Certification Bulletins relating to the "Yes" Program on the Web at http://yes.novell.com. Bulletins are also available under NetWire on CompuServe, the Novell Messenger CD, Novell's Support Connection (formerly NSEPro), and the Yes Smart Solutions CD. You can also have them faxed to you by contacting the Yes Program's FaxBack System at 1-800-414-LABS or 1-801-429-2776.

Really hard-core CNEs have the "YES" icons tattooed on their bodies. (These people really need to get a life.)

MINIMUM HARDWARE REQUIREMENTS

The following checklist can help you prepare for the server installation:

- An IBM-compatible PC with an 80386, 80486 (SX or DX), or Pentium processor.

- 20 MB of RAM for the basic NetWare 4.11 operating system (whether it is being installed from CD-ROM or across the network).

- 115 MB of free disk space on the hard disk: 15 MB for the DOS partition and 100 MB for a NetWare partition (SYS: volume). If you copy all the optional NetWare file groups to the server, you may need a total of 140 MB or more.

- An additional 60 MB of free disk space to install the DynaText viewer and NetWare 4.11 documentation. Additional space will be necessary if you want to install the documentation in more than one language. If you are low on disk space, you can view DynaText directly from the CD-ROM, rather than storing it on the server hard disk.

- One network interface card (NIC).

- The appropriate network cabling (Ethernet, Token Ring, FDDI, ARCnet, baseband, and so on) and related components (hubs, UPS, and so on).

- A CD-ROM drive that can read ISO 9660-formatted CD-ROM disks (if NetWare 4.11 is being installed from CD-ROM).

THE BRAIN

For a more accurate method of calculating the amount of server RAM required, see the article titled "Server Memory — Calculating Memory Requirements for NetWare 3 and 4" in the January 1995 issue of the *Novell Application Notes*, or Appendix A of the *Novell NetWare 4.11 Installation* manual.

REAL WORLD

The hardware requirements listed are minimums, not recommended standards. Realistically, you'll want a fast processor, more RAM, and a larger hard disk.

You'll need to add additional memory, based on the following:

▸ The RAM required for disk caching (1 MB to 4 MB minimum). As a general rule, the more RAM available for disk caching, the better the performance.

▸ RAM that is calculated on the basis of disk size (total disk size in megabytes multiplied by 0.008).

In terms of hard disk size, you'll need a disk that is large enough for all your network needs, including the network operating system, optional network products, applications, documentation, and the file system. Finally, if your server contains more than 20 MB of RAM, you'll need to use 32-bit AT busmastering or DMA boards (unless the driver supports more than 20 MB of RAM). Contact the computer manufacturer for additional information.

TIP

WARNING: If you are installing NetWare 4.11 over the network using Novell Client 32, you should set MAX CACHE SIZE less than or equal to 3 MB. If you don't, Client 32 may allocate up to 8 MB on a computer containing 20 MB of RAM — which could cause you to run out of RAM during the installation process.

There is a method to our madness. As a matter of fact, there are two methods for installing NetWare 4.11:

▸ Local CD-ROM

▸ Server-to-server (called "remote network installation area" by Novell)

The easiest way to install NetWare 4.11 is using the CD-ROM drive installed on the server. The second method, server-to-server, is typically used if your new server doesn't have a CD-ROM drive, or if you will be installing a number of servers at one time. The server-to-server method involves temporarily installing the client software on the new server, then logging into an existing NetWare server that either has a CD-ROM drive mounted as a NetWare device, or a copy of the files from the Novell IntranetWare/NetWare 4.11 Operating System CD-ROM stored on a NetWare (hard disk) volume. In this chapter, we'll cover the CD-ROM method, which is the most common.

THE BRAIN

You'll find a comparison of the two types of installation methods in the "Choose an Installation Method" section in Chapter I of the *Novell NetWare 4.11 Installation* **manual. You can find additional information regarding these two methods in the "Install from a Local CD-ROM" and "Install from a Remote Network Installation Area" sections in the same chapter of the same manual.**

CHOOSING AN INSTALLATION TYPE

Now that you've set up your hardware and chosen your poison (CD-ROM), it's time to get down to business. NetWare 4.11 offers two basic types of server installation:

▸ Simple installation — The faster and easier of the two methods, this type makes a number of assumptions and uses default settings for most configurable parameters.

▸ Custom installation — This type allows you to specify configurable parameters (such as the IPX internal network number, disk mirroring or duplexing), as well as the enabling or disabling of file compression, block suballocation, and data migration features.

Let's take a closer look.

ZEN

"When making your choice in life, do not neglect to live."

Samuel Jackson

Simple Installation

The Simple installation approach should be used if your server meets *all* the following criteria:

▸ A DOS partition of 15+ MB exists on the server.

▸ DOS is installed on the server DOS partition.

▸ The server boots from the DOS partition rather than from boot diskettes.

▸ No disk mirroring, disk duplexing, or disk subsystem is required.

▸ All free disk space not allocated to the DOS partition is available for a NetWare partition.

▸ Each disk will contain only one NetWare volume.

▸ A randomly generated IPX number is acceptable.

▸ AUTOEXEC.BAT and CONFIG.SYS startup files can be used without modification.

▸ IPX is the only communications protocol that will be installed (although TCP/IP and/or AppleTalk can be installed manually at a later date).

▸ Novell Directory Services (NDS) will be installed using a single Organization per tree, which contains all objects.

Custom Installation

The Custom installation method should be used if your server does not meet the requirements for a Simple installation — duh! Some of the configuration options that you can specify in a Custom installation include:

▸ Boot the server from the DOS partition on the server hard disk or from boot diskettes

▸ Assign a nonrandom IPX internal network number

- ▸ Partition hard disks

- ▸ Mirror or duplex hard disks

- ▸ Specify volume names

- ▸ Span volumes across multiple drives

- ▸ Modify time zone parameters for NDS

- ▸ Edit the STARTUP.NCF and AUTOEXEC.NCF startup files

- ▸ Choose nonrouting TCP/IP or AppleTalk protocols in addition to IPX

- ▸ Install NetWare/IP

SMART LINK

For more detailed information about Novell-certified hardware and software, consult the vendor forums on NetWire, testing lab results on Novell Support Connection (formerly NSEPro), or surf to the Novell Lab's Bulletins at http://support.novell.com/sitemap.

Well, there you have it. We've installed the LAN components, inserted the Novell IntranetWare/NetWare 4.11 CD-ROM, and chosen the Simple or Custom installation method — can we finally get started? No! It must be Monday. The last order of business is to walk down the "before you begin" checklist. It looks something like this:

- ▸ The name of the Directory tree. (You'll need to think of one if this is the first server in the tree.)

- ▸ The detailed NDS design. (Remember Chapters 3, 4, and 5.)

- ▸ A password for the Admin user. (If this is the first server in the tree, you'll need to make one up.)

- ▸ A unique server name.

▸ A unique IPX internal network number (applicable to a Custom installation only).

▸ The type and configuration of the disk controller, as well as the appropriate driver(s), if they are not contained on the Novell IntranetWare/NetWare 4.11 Operating System CD-ROM.

▸ The type and configuration of the network board(s), as well as the appropriate driver(s), if they are not contained on the Novell IntranetWare/NetWare 4.11 Operating System CD-ROM.

▸ The IntranetWare/NetWare 4.11 License Diskette.

▸ One of the following IntranetWare CD-ROMs:

 • Novell IntranetWare/NetWare 4.11 Operating System CD-ROM

 • Novell IntranetWare/NetWare 4.11 Online Documentation (optional)

 • Novell IntranetWare Internet Access Server 4 (optional)

 • Novell IntranetWare FTP Services for IntranetWare (optional)

 Or, you can access the NetWare 4.11 installation files on another server. The files can either be located on an Novell IntranetWare/NetWare 4.11 Operating System CD-ROM mounted as an NetWare volume on that server, or the same files copied from the CD-ROM(s) to that server's hard disk.

Now, we're finally ready to roll.

NETWARE 4.11 INSTALLATION PREVIEW

In this chapter, we'll explore the detailed steps of both the Simple and Custom installation types. They both traverse the same 21 steps, but the Simple install automates a few of them — leaving only 16 steps. In either case, the installation process occurs in six stages:

Stage 1 • Prepare the server hard disk

Stage 2 • Run SERVER.EXE

Stage 3 • Load the NetWare 4.11 drivers

Stage 4 • INSTALL.NLM

Stage 5 • Install Novell Directory Services (NDS)

Stage 6 • Create server startup files

The actual process of creating the server occurs during Stages 1 and 2. As you can see in Figure 6.1, control shifts from the primary DOS partition to the NetWare partition. When SERVER.EXE is run, the NetWare 4.11 operating system is loaded into memory and a colon prompt (:) is displayed. It's alive! At this point, the server is alive, but you can't do anything with it. It's sort of like the server being on life support. The remaining four stages add more functionality. Stage 3 adds connectivity by loading LAN and disk drivers. Stage 4 creates a NetWare partition on the hard disk, and then defines one or more volumes. Stage 5 installs NDS. And finally, Stage 6 enables you to create/modify the STARTUP.NCF and AUTOEXEC.NCF server startup files.

F I G U R E   6.1

Understanding NetWare
4.11 Installation

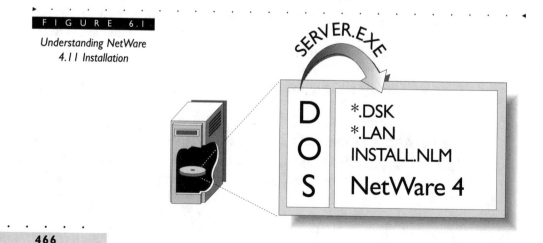

NetWare 4.11 Simple Installation

I know how you feel. It's been a looooong day already, and it's only 9:30 a.m. I feel your pain — because I care. Together we can get through this thing. Together we can conquer the NetWare 4.11 install.

Let's start out slowly (Simple installation), and then work our way into more sophisticated method (Custom installation). Fortunately, the NetWare 4.11 Simple installation is essentially a subset of the Custom installation. It's faster and easier than the Custom method, because it asks a minimum of questions and uses defaults for most configurable parameters. Think of this as a preview to the major steps of the more-detailed Custom Installation.

QUIZ

Just to keep things simple and warm up the old noodle, here's one of my favorites: A train leaves from Boston to New York. An hour later, a train leaves from New York to Boston. The second train is traveling 15 m.p.h. faster than the first, but the first has a 7.5 m.p.h. tail wind. Which train will be nearer to Boston when they meet?

(Q6-1)
(See Appendix C for quiz answers.)

Following is a brief description of what happens during the six phases of a Simple installation. We're just trying to get your feet wet. For detailed information on the 16 steps involved, refer to the appropriate sections of the "Custom Installation" walk-through.

STAGE 1: PREPARE THE SERVER HARD DISK

During Stage 1, the focus is on the DOS operating system. The first step is to boot the server machine with DOS. This is because NetWare 4.11 doesn't have its own "cold boot loader," and, thus, is loaded on the server by executing the SERVER.EXE file from the DOS partition. The Simple install does not give you the option of booting the server from a diskette.

After you boot DOS, the next step is to configure the DOS partition. This consists of making at least two full backups, creating a temporary boot diskette containing C:\DOS\FDISK.EXE and C:\DOS\FORMAT.COM, using the DOS FDISK utility to delete existing server disk partitions and create a new DOS partition of 15+ MB, then using the DOS FORMAT utility to format the new partition as bootable. Wow, that was a mouthful.

Next, you'll need to configure the CD-ROM drive as a DOS device. The reason that you'll need to do this is because IntranetWare is shipped on CD-ROM, and you just blew away the CD-ROM drivers on the server hard disk. Oops. Be sure to follow the CD-ROM manufacturer's instructions for this part. You'll probably find that you must reboot the computer to activate any changes made to the server's AUTOEXEC.BAT and CONFIG.SYS by the CD-ROM installation program.

To begin the automated installation process, insert the Novell IntranetWare/ NetWare 4.11 Operating System CD-ROM disk in the CD-ROM drive and switch to that drive (typically drive D:). Execute the INSTALL.BAT file found in the root directory of the CD-ROM. You will be asked to choose a language to be used during the installation process — your choices are Deutsche, English, Español, Français, Italiano, or Portuguese. After you select a language, you will be asked several questions about the type of installation desired. Make the following menu choices, in order:

1 • NetWare 4.11 Server Installation (see Figure 6.2)

2 • NetWare 4.11

3 • Simple Installation of NetWare 4.11 (see Figure 6.3)

We're cruising now! You will then be prompted for a unique server name. You will *not* be prompted for an IPX internal network number. NetWare will automatically generate a random, eight-digit, hexadecimal IPX internal network number for you — without even asking (how rude). If you were performing a Custom install, you would also be given the option of overriding this default (and so you should).

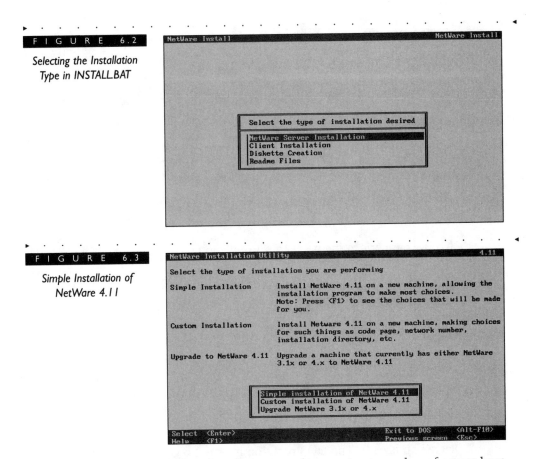

F I G U R E   6.2

*Selecting the Installation
Type in INSTALL.BAT*

F I G U R E   6.3

*Simple Installation of
NetWare 4.11*

As you can see in Figure 6.4, the system then copies a number of server boot files from the CD-ROM to the C:\NWSERVER directory on your DOS partition. This includes such files as SERVER.EXE, disk drivers, LAN drivers, INSTALL.NLM, NWSNUT.NLM, and other NLMs.

During a Simple install, the system automatically selects the locale configuration (country code, character code set, and keyboard mapping server language support parameters) and filename format for you. The defaults assume that you reside in the United States and want to use the DOS filename format. You would need to do a Custom install if you wanted to be able to override these defaults.

FIGURE 6.4

Copying Server Boot Files in INSTALL.BAT

```
NetWare Installation Utility                                    4.11

Copy server boot files to the DOS partition


Copying File: SERVER.EXE
┌─────────────────────────────────────────────────────────────────┐
│███████████████████████████████████████████████████████████████ │
│                              38%                                  │
└─────────────────────────────────────────────────────────────────┘


Source path:   D:\PRODUCTS\NW411\INSTALL\IBM\DOS\XXX\ENGLISH

Destination path:   C:\NWSERVER
```

If you were performing a Custom installation, you would be given the option of customizing startup file SET parameters. Because this is a Simple install, NetWare does it for you. If your server contains a hard disk, CD-ROM, or other device that uses ASPI, the installation program automatically inserts the following line in your STARTUP.NCF file:

```
SET RESERVED BUFFERS BELOW 16 MB = 200
```

If this were a Custom install, you'd also be asked if you wanted the AUTOEXEC.BAT file to automatically execute SERVER.EXE whenever the server is booted. Since this is a Simple install, the SERVER.EXE file will *not* be added to your AUTOEXEC.BAT file.

There you have it. The DOS partition is ready to go. Next stop, SERVER.EXE.

STAGE 2: RUN SERVER.EXE

During Stage 2, the focus shifts from the DOS operating system to NetWare, as shown in Figure 6.5. The installation program automatically executes SERVER.EXE and loads NetWare 4.11 into memory. In other words, this process transfers control of the server from DOS to NetWare. At this point, the server is up and running, but you can't do anything with it. In the next step you'll load the NetWare drivers and establish connectivity between NetWare 4.11 and the hard disk(s) and NIC(s).

FIGURE 6.5

*Automatically Starting the
Server with SERVER.EXE*

```
System Console
SECURE.NCF file will not be executed
Novell NetWare 4.11  August 22, 1996
Processor speed: 16424
(Type SPEED at the command prompt for an explanation of the speed rating)
LCONFIG.SYS file exists, overriding default locale values
Startup file DISTRTUP.NCF will be used
Reserved Buffers Below 16 Meg set to 200
Loading module MAC.NAM
   NetWare Macintosh Name Space Support
   Version 4.11   July 29, 1996
   Copyright 1996 Novell, Inc.  All rights reserved.
Loading module INSTALL.NLM
   NetWare 4.11 Installation Utility
   Version 2.24   August 12, 1996
   Copyright 1996 Novell, Inc.  All rights reserved.
```

REAL WORLD

If your server is an 80386 that was manufactured in 1987, you may find that it doesn't execute certain 32-bit instructions correctly. This could negatively affect the way NetWare 4.11 functions. If a message is displayed indicating that this problem has occurred, you may be able to solve the problem by replacing a ROM chip on the board. Contact the computer manufacturer for further details.

STAGE 3: LOAD THE NETWARE DRIVERS

During Stage 3, we jump-start our barely functioning server. We load and configure various NetWare drivers, including:

▶ Disk drivers for the internal hard disk and CD-ROM drives

▶ LAN drivers for internal NIC(s)

▶ Binding IPX to the LAN driver(s)

The good news is that, unlike earlier versions of NetWare, NetWare 4.11 has two new features called *hardware autodetection* and *automatic selection of drivers* that attempt to automatically detect the type of drivers needed for your particular hard disk(s), CD-ROM(s), and NIC(s). The INSTALL utility will display the drivers that it has selected for each, and will allow you to modify, delete, or accept the defaults, as well as to add additional drivers (see Figure 6.6 and Figure 6.7). Remember, when you load drivers, it's important to make sure that there are no interrupt or address conflicts with other hardware. After you have confirmed the hardware settings, selected disk drivers will be copied to C:\NWSERVER directory, and the appropriate disk and CD-ROM drivers will be loaded. Next, the appropriate LAN driver(s) will be loaded and the IPX communication protocol will be bound to these drivers.

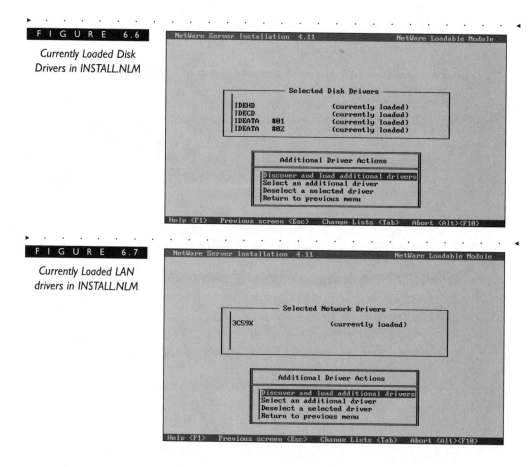

FIGURE 6.6

Currently Loaded Disk Drivers in INSTALL.NLM

FIGURE 6.7

Currently Loaded LAN drivers in INSTALL.NLM

So, what about additional protocols? During the Custom install, you are given the option of installing TCP/IP and/or AppleTalk in addition to IPX. But, in a Simple install, you must add them manually — afterward.

ZEN

"Though we often live unconsciously, 'on automatic pilot,' every one of us can learn to be awake. It just takes vision."

Anonymous

That's more like it. Now that the server is functioning normally, we shift our focus to INSTALL.NLM. This is where the real fun begins.

SMART LINK

Explore the latest IntranetWare drivers on the Web at http://support.novell.com/sitemap

STAGE 4: INSTALL.NLM

Now that you've established connectivity, we're ready to activate the NetWare partition(s). You may be prompted with a warning saying that there is a potential conflict with the DOS CD-ROM driver. If this message is displayed, ignore the warning and select the "Continue Accessing the CD-ROM via DOS" option. No worries.

Next, the installation program automatically creates a NetWare partition on the internal server disk. By default, it occupies the entire disk except for the DOS partition. Then, it creates the SYS: volume using the entire NetWare partition. Finally, NetWare 4.11 mounts the new SYS: volume.

If this were a Custom installation, you would have been given the opportunity of creating additional volumes. You would have also been able to specify a plethora of manual disk options, including specifying the size of NetWare 4.11 partitions, mirroring or duplexing, and specifying the size of the hot fix redirection area. You would also have been given the option of changing the default settings for file compression (default is ON), block suballocation (default is ON), and data migration (default is OFF).

If you were installing NetWare 4.11 from a network volume rather than CD-ROM, you would be given the opportunity to reestablish the server-to-server connection at this point.

Next, the installation utility will automatically begin copying the "preliminary" (pre-installation) files to the SYSTEM and LOGIN directories on the SYS: volume. Later, in Stage 6, you'll copy the remainder of the required SYSTEM and PUBLIC files to the SYS: volume. For now, let's move on to Stage 5.

STAGE 5: INSTALL NOVELL DIRECTORY SERVICES (NDS)

Once the SYSTEM and LOGIN files have been copied to the default SYS: volume, it's time to begin building our tree. Don't forget your protective gloves.

At this point, NetWare searches the WAN for any existing Directory trees. Depending on the number of trees found, the installation utility will display one of three menus. Figure 6.8 shows the menu that will be displayed if no existing Directory trees were found. Depending on your particular configuration, you will need to indicate the appropriate menu choice, then either supply the name of the new tree or select an existing tree.

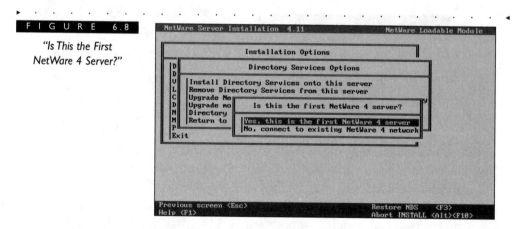

FIGURE 6.8

"Is This the First NetWare 4 Server?"

Once you've selected a tree, NetWare will add this server to the tree indicated and allow you to configure time synchronization for the server, as shown in Figure 6.9. For instance, if you were at ACME's Admin headquarters in Camelot, you would select Great Britain.

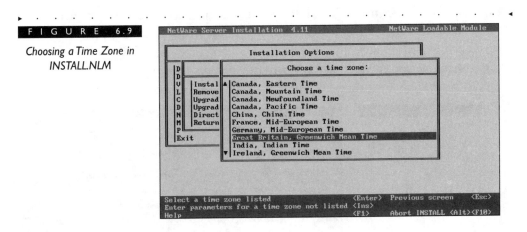

FIGURE 6.9

Choosing a Time Zone in INSTALL.NLM

Next, we move on to NDS context. Remember, we're using the Simple installation method, so the server will be placed in a single Organization container. First, you will be prompted for the name of the Organization. Second, you will be asked to supply a password for the special Admin user. If this is the first server in this tree, you'll have to make this stuff up. If you're adding this server to an existing tree, you'll have to use an established Organization name and Admin password.

After you provide the Admin password, NetWare displays a summary screen with the following information: Directory tree name, Directory context, and Administrator name, an example of which is shown in Figure 6.10. Be sure to write down this information, and keep it in a safe place — maybe next to the License diskette!

FIGURE 6.10

NDS Installation Summary Screen

```
NetWare Server Installation 4.11                    NetWare Loadable Module
┌─────────────────────────────────────────────────────────────────────┐
│                         Installation Options                          │
│ ┌─D─┬──────────────────Directory Services Options────────────────┐   │
│ │ D │                                                             │   │
│ │ U │ Install Directory Services onto this server                 │   │
│ │ L │ Remove Directory Services from this server                  │   │
│ │ C │ Upgra┌──────────────────────────────────────────────────┐  │   │
│ │ D │ Upgra│                                                    │  │   │
│ │ N │ Direc│ For your information (note these for future        │  │   │
│ │ M │ Retur│ reference along with the Administrator password):  │  │   │
│ │ P │      │      Directory tree name:  ACME                    │  │   │
│ │Exit│     │      Directory context:    O=ACME                  │  │   │
│ │    │     │      Administrator name:   CN=Admin.O=ACME         │  │   │
│ │    │     │                                                    │  │   │
│ │    │     │ Press <Enter> to continue.                         │  │   │
│ │    │     └──────────────────────────────────────────────────┘  │   │
│ └───┴─────────────────────────────────────────────────────────────┘   │
│                                                                        │
│ Use the arrow keys to highlight an option, then press <Enter>.         │
└────────────────────────────────────────────────────────────────────────┘
```

You are then prompted to insert the IntranetWare/NetWare 4.11 License diskette, illustrated in Figure 6.11. Make sure that this is a unique server disk not being used on any other server. If you attempt to use the same license on more than one server, you'll get a copyright violation warning.

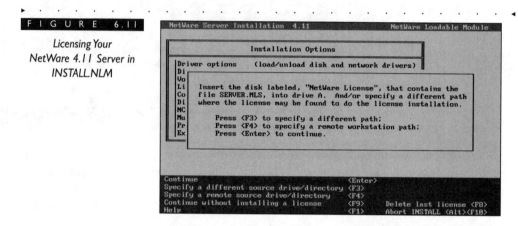

Voilà, we're done. That wasn't so bad. Now you have a living, breathing server. But, in order to automate this process during server startup, you must create the following two configuration files: STARTUP.NCF and AUTOEXEC.NCF. That's Stage 6.

STAGE 6: CREATE SERVER STARTUP FILES

Once Novell Directory Services has been installed, the system automatically creates the STARTUP.NCF and AUTOEXEC.NCF files for you. These files help automate the server startup process. If this were a Custom install, you'd be allowed to modify these files. But since this is a Simple install, you will have to wait until the installation process is complete in order to make any changes to these files by using INSTALL.NLM or SERVMAN.NLM.

The INSTALL utility then copies the main SYSTEM and PUBLIC to the SYS: volume. At this point, you are basically finished with the installation of the NetWare 4.11 operating system itself. Next, you'll be given an opportunity to install other installation items/products. In a Simple Install, the only choice listed is "Make diskettes."

As you can see in Figure 6.12, during a Simple install, you aren't presented with the myriad of optional products to install as you are in the Custom install. Since we don't plan to make any diskettes at this time, choose Continue Installation.

▶ · ◀

FIGURE   6.12

*Installing Optional Products
in INSTALL.NLM*

```
NetWare Server Installation 4.11              NetWare Loadable Module
Other Installation Options

Choose any of the following optional installation items or products.
                    ┌─ Other Installation Items/Products ─┐
                    │Make diskettes                        │
                    │                                      │
                    │                                      │
                    │                                      │
                    │                                      │
                    └──────────────────────────────────────┘
              ┌──────── Other Installation Actions ────────┐
              │Choose an item or product listed above       │
              │Continue installation                        │
              └─────────────────────────────────────────────┘
 Help <F1>    Previous screen <Esc>    Change Lists <Tab>    Abort <Alt><F10>
```

Finally, a screen is displayed advising you that the installation of NetWare 4.11 on the server is complete. Read the screen and press Enter to return to the system console screen. Now, you're *really* done. Congratulations! As a safety measure, you should down the server by typing **DOWN**, and then restart it by typing **RESTART SERVER**. How exciting — your NetWare 4.11 server is alive!

Following is a quick review of the major steps involved in a NetWare 4.11 Simple installation.

SIMPLE INSTALLATION ROAD MAP

Stage 1: Prepare the server hard disk

▶ *Step 1:* Configure the server DOS partition.

▶ *Step 2:* Select the server language and type of installation.

▶ *Step 3:* Assign the server name.

▶ *Step 4:* Copy the server boot files to the DOS partition.

Stage 2: Run SERVER.EXE

▸ *Step 5:* Start the server (happens automatically).

Stage 3: Load the NetWare drivers

▸ *Step 6:* Load and configure the server disk and CD-ROM driver(s).

▸ *Step 7:* Load and configure the server LAN driver(s).

Stage 4: INSTALL.NLM

▸ *Step 8:* Configure the CD-ROM as a DOS or NetWare device.

▸ *Step 9:* Mount the SYS: volume.

▸ *Step 10:* Reestablish the server-to-server connection (conditional).

Stage 5: Install NDS

▸ *Step 11:* Install NDS.

▸ *Step 12:* License the NetWare 4.11 operating system.

Stage 6: Create server startup files

▸ *Step 13:* Copy the SYSTEM and PUBLIC files to the SYS: volume.

▸ *Step 14:* Perform other installation options (optional).

▸ *Step 15:* Complete the installation.

▸ *Step 16:* Boot the server using the STARTUP.NCF and AUTOEXEC.NCF startup files.

SMART LINK

Learn everything there is to know about the NetWare 4.11 Simple Installation process in the *IntranetWare/NetWare 4.11 Installation and Configuration Workshop* at CyberState University (http://www. cyberstateu.com).

Wow, wasn't that fun? Suddenly Mondays aren't so bad anymore. The Simple installation is a breeze. But remember, it makes many assumptions for you. It's not for everyone. If you need more flexibility, or you're feeling a little more daring, you should consider tackling the Custom install. That's the true CNE obstacle course.

Now, let's explore this exciting new thing known as the IntranetWare server.

ZEN

"You'll laugh. You'll cry. You'll hurl!"

Wayne's World

▶ · ◀

NetWare 4.11 Custom Installation

Welcome to the big show. This is where we separate the men from the boys, or the women from the girls. The NetWare 4.11 Custom installation gives you total control over all 21 steps. This is good for you — especially if you're a control freak. But, be forewarned. In order to make it through the Custom install, you must know what you're doing, because there's no one there to hold your hand.

So, in the spirit of goodwill, and to increase your chances of making it through the install in one piece, I offer the following in-depth discussion. Hold onto your hat. And, if this discussion isn't enough for you, there's a detailed, step-by-step walk-through of the ACME Custom installation at the end of the chapter.

STAGE I: PREPARE THE SERVER HARD DISK

The NetWare 4.11 core operating system (OS) consists of a single file called SERVER.EXE. In order to load NetWare 4.11, you must first boot the server using

DOS, and then execute SERVER.EXE. This transfers server control from DOS to the NetWare 4.11 partition. Refer again to Figure 6.1.

Before you can install NetWare 4.11, you must set up the DOS partition. Here's what happens during Stage 1 of the Custom installation process:

- ▶ *Step 1:* Configure the server DOS partition. This consists of booting the server using DOS; making at least two full backups on tape or other media; making a temporary boot diskette; using the DOS FDISK utility to delete existing server disk partitions and to create a new DOS partition of 15 MB to 35 MB (or more); and then using the DOS FORMAT utility to format the new partition. During this step, you will also configure the server CD-ROM drive as a DOS device.

- ▶ *Step 2:* Select the server language and type of installation. In this step, you run the INSTALL.BAT installation program, select the language to be used during the installation process, and select Custom as the installation process to be used.

- ▶ *Step 3:* Assign the server name. This name uniquely identifies your server on the WAN.

- ▶ *Step 4:* Assign the server IPX internal network number. Like the server name, the server IPX internal network must be unique.

- ▶ *Step 5:* Copy server boot files to the DOS partition. In this step, the server boot files are copied to the C:\NWSERVER directory on the DOS partition.

- ▶ *Step 6:* Assign the locale configuration and filename format. Here's where you assign the country code, character code set, and keyboard mapping. (You'll only be asked to assign the filename format if you executed the INSTALL utility with the */file_sys* switch at the beginning of the installation process.) During this step, you also decide whether to customize startup file SET parameters, and whether to modify the server AUTOEXEC.BAT file to automatically execute SERVER.EXE whenever the server is booted.

As you can see, we're pretty busy in Stage 1 — let's get started. Remember, there's a detailed walk-through in the case study titled "Custom Installation for ACME" at the end of the chapter.

Step 1: Configure the Server DOS Partition

Unlike other operating systems (such as NetWare 2.x, OS/2, and UNIX), NetWare 4.11 doesn't have its own cold-boot loader. In order to start the server, you must boot from a DOS partition.

TIP

It is also possible, although not preferable, to boot the server from a pair of diskettes. This added security measure is only necessary if you do not have adequate physical security measures in place. Typically, proper physical security measures, combined with the security features in NetWare 4.11, are adequate for most situations. Instructions for using server boot diskettes can be found in Appendix D of the *Novell NetWare 4.11 Installation* manual.

You should complete the following hard disk preparation tasks prior to installation:

▶ Boot DOS on the server.

▶ Make at least two full system backups (including network security information, if applicable).

▶ Create a temporary boot diskette.

▶ Use FDISK to delete existing partitions and create a new DOS partition of 15 MB to 35 MB (or more).

▶ Use FORMAT to format the DOS partition and make it bootable.

The first task in preparing your hard disk is to boot the server using the version of DOS supplied with your computer.

Next, make at least two full server backups on tape or other storage media. Remember, all the data on the server will be destroyed during the installation process. If the computer is currently being used as a server, be sure to back up network security information as well as the file system.

The third task is to create a temporary boot diskette. Interestingly, this is a task that is often overlooked. Because the FDISK and FORMAT utilities (used later) wipe out existing data, you could find yourself in the unenviable position of trying to make a boot diskette on a computer with no data. If this happens, you'd either need to find an identically configured computer, or restore the data from tape.

To make the diskette bootable, insert a blank diskette in drive A and type

```
FORMAT A: /S
```

This procedure formats the diskette and copies COMMAND.COM and two hidden system files to the root directory. After the diskette is formatted, you'll need to use the DOS COPY command to copy two important utilities to the boot diskette: FDISK.EXE and FORMAT.COM. Also, don't forget CD-ROM and other drivers needed by your computer as well as AUTOEXEC.BAT and CONFIG.SYS. In addition, you may want to copy a few other DOS programs such as EDIT.COM (to edit ASCII files) and MEM.EXE (to display information about available RAM).

The fourth task involves using the DOS FDISK utility to delete existing partitions and to create a DOS partition of 15 MB to 35 MB (or more), depending on your needs. Typically, your server will have a DOS partition occupying the entire internal disk — unless it is currently being used as a server. If it's currently being used as a server, it will probably contain a DOS partition and a NetWare partition.

You're going to need a DOS partition that is large enough to support disk drivers, LAN drivers, name space modules, the SERVER.EXE boot file, and repair utilities. If you plan to store additional utilities on the DOS partition — such as diagnostic software, mouse drivers, SCSI drivers, and antivirus software — you'll need even more space. Although Novell recommends a minimum of 15 MB for the DOS partition, you may want to increase it to 35 MB (or more) to accommodate miscellaneous drivers and utilities. After all, you'll be very unhappy if you run out of disk space on your DOS partition.

To execute the FDISK utility, make sure your temporary boot disk is in drive A:, and then type

```
A:
```

```
FDISK
```

If you look at Figure 6.13, you'll see the main FDISK screen that will be displayed. Follow the appropriate menu options to delete any existing partitions, then create a new DOS partition of 15 to 35 MB (or more) and designate the new partition as "active." Leave the rest of the hard disk as free space, so that it can be converted into an NetWare partition during Stage 4.

F I G U R E   6.13

The Main Menu of FDISK

```
                        MS-DOS Version 6
                     Fixed Disk Setup Program
              (C)Copyright Microsoft Corp. 1983 - 1993

                          FDISK Options

Current fixed disk drive: 1

Choose one of the following:

1. Create DOS partition or Logical DOS Drive
2. Set active partition
3. Delete partition or Logical DOS Drive
4. Display partition information


Enter choice: [1]




Press Esc to exit FDISK
```

REAL WORLD

In some cases, it's easier to troubleshoot server problems if you increase the size of the DOS partition 1 MB for every 1 MB of server RAM. For instance, if your server has 16 MB of RAM, you might want to increase your DOS partition to 31 MB (15 MB + 16 MB), plus additional space for miscellaneous drivers and utilities.

For detailed, step-by-step discussions of how to use FDISK to create and delete DOS partitions, refer to the beginning of the case study titled "Custom Installation for ACME "at the end of the chapter. You can also consult the DOS manual that came with your computer for further information.

When you exit the FDISK program, the computer will reboot. This might be a good time to use the DOS DATE and TIME commands to make sure that your hardware clock is set to the correct time. If this is your only server and the date or time is incorrect, you will probably want to change the "hardware" date and time using the

CMOS setup program built into your computer. (If you have a relatively recent version of DOS, you will probably find that the DATE and TIME commands do this for you.) See the manual that came with your computer for further information.

The fifth task involves formatting the DOS partition and making it bootable. This can be accomplished by typing

```
FORMAT C: /S
```

After you have formatted the DOS partition, remove the temporary boot diskette from drive A and reboot the server. Then, move on to Step 2.

At this point, you might want to use the DOS COPY command to copy the files from the temporary boot diskette to the DOS partition. You won't need to install the full version of DOS unless it tickles your fancy.

After you've copied the files from your temporary boot diskette to the DOS partition, you'll want to clean up your AUTOEXEC.BAT and CONFIG.SYS files so that they contain only those commands that are absolutely necessary. Next, you'll want to update the CONFIG.SYS and AUTOEXEC.BAT files to automatically load any necessary DOS device drivers — such as the ones needed to make your CD-ROM function as a DOS device. (An alternate method would be to use the installation program that came with each device.)

Here's a typical example. The following two lines are required in CONFIG.SYS for the Adaptec 1542 SCSI CD-ROM adapter:

```
DEVICE=A:\ADAPTEC\ASPI4DOS.SYS /D
```

```
DEVICE=A:\ADAPTEC\ASPI CD:SYS /D:ASPICDO
```

In addition, the following line is required in the AUTOEXEC.BAT file:

```
A:\DOS\MSCDEX.EXE /D:ASPICDO /M:12 /S
```

After you have updated AUTOEXEC.BAT and CONFIG.SYS with the appropriate device drivers, make sure there is no diskette in drive A: and reboot the computer — so the changes you made will take effect.

The next step is to determine where to install the NetWare 4.11 operating system from. Your choices are

  ► Local CD-ROM

  ► Server-to-server (called "remote network installation area" by Novell)

TIP

Be sure to copy any and all CD-ROM drivers from the server disk before you run FDISK or FORMAT. Doing so afterward doesn't help you because the drivers are gone. Also, be sure that the logical name of the CD-ROM driver in your AUTOEXEC.BAT file does not conflict with any INSTALL utility filenames. There should be no conflict unless you have changed the name of your CD-ROM driver. In other words, if you have changed the name of your CD-ROM driver to "INSTALL" or to the name of any file that INSTALL copies, the installation procedure will fail.

The easiest way to install NetWare 4.11 is using the CD-ROM drive installed on the server. The second method, server-to-server, is typically used if your new server doesn't have a CD-ROM drive, or if you will be installing a number of servers at one time. The server-to-server method involves temporarily installing the client software on the new server, then logging into an existing NetWare server that either has a CD-ROM drive mounted as an NetWare device, or a copy of the files from the Novell IntranetWare/NetWare 4.11 Operating System CD-ROM stored on a NetWare (hard disk) volume. In this chapter, we'll cover the CD-ROM method, which is the most common.

THE BRAIN

You'll find a comparison of the two types of installation methods in the "Choose an Installation Method" section in Chapter 1 of the *Novell NetWare 4.11 Installation* manual. You can find additional information regarding these two methods in the "Install from a Local CD-ROM" and "Install from a Remote Network Installation Area" sections in the same chapter of the same manual.

At this point, you'll need to switch to the root of the CD-ROM drive by typing

`D: (or the appropriate drive letter)`

`CD \`

TIP

When you purchase a **CD-ROM** drive, be sure that it can also be used as an NetWare device. This is made possible using the **CD-ROM NLM** from Novell. Be sure that the **CD-ROM** is installed on a separate **SCSI** adapter from that being used by the hard drive, because NetWare 4.11 sometimes hangs if the **CD-ROM** drive and hard disk are attached to the same adapter.

Step 2: Select the Server Language and Type of Installation

The INSTALL.BAT program automates most of your early NetWare 4.11 install steps. To begin, access INSTALL.BAT from the root directory of the CD-ROM by typing

```
INSTALL
```

TIP

The NetWare 4.11 installation process automates some of the steps that were involved in installing previous versions of the operating system. For instance, NetWare 4.11 provides hardware autodetection and automatic selection of disk, **CD-ROM**, and **LAN** drivers. It also automatically defaults to the **DOS** filename format. (The filename format controls acceptable naming conventions for all files stored in the **DOS** name space on the server.) You can override these automatic features by using the proper switch when you execute the **INSTALL** command. For instance, you can type **INSTALL** /nad to disable hardware autodetection and automatic selection of drivers, **INSTALL** /file_sys to indicate a different filename format, or **INSTALL** /file_sys /nad to turn off both of these features.

When you execute INSTALL.BAT, a menu is displayed, as shown in Figure 6.14, which allows you to choose the language to be used during the installation process. Choose the Select This Line to Install in English option from the NetWare 4.11 Install menu if you want the installation instructions to be displayed in English. Choose one of the other five options (Deutsche, Español, Français, Italiano, or Portuguese) if you want the installation instructions to be displayed in another language.

QUIZ

To them, "mutual intelligibility" is a necessity. To many of us, it's a mystery. Who are they?

(Q6-2)

F I G U R E   6.14

Selecting a Language in INSTALL.BAT

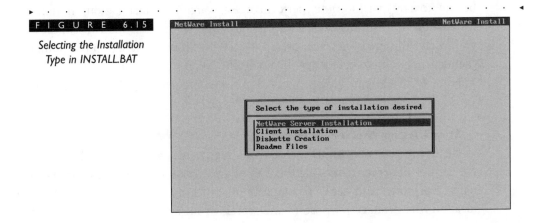

Next, you will be asked several questions about the type of installation you want. When you are asked what type of installation you want to use, choose NetWare Server Installation, as shown in Figure 6.15. When you are asked what product you want to install, select NetWare 4.11. Finally, when you are asked what type of installation you want to perform, select Custom Installation, as shown in Figure 6.16.

F I G U R E   6.15

Selecting the Installation Type in INSTALL.BAT

Custom Installation of
NetWare 4.11

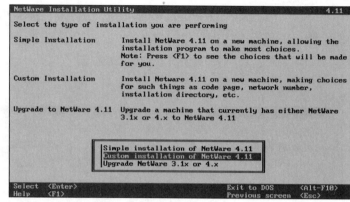

TIP

You can abort the installation process at nearly any point by pressing Alt+F10. You can continue the installation at a later time using a manual process by rebooting the server, executing SERVER.EXE from the DOS prompt, loading INSTALL.NLM, and executing each installation step manually. Alternately, you can restart the automated installation process from the beginning by executing the INSTALL.BAT program found in the root of the Novell IntranetWare/NetWare 4.11 Operating System CD-ROM.

Before proceeding, the installation program checks your server to see if it contains a DOS partition of 15 MB or more and enough free space (that does not belong to any partition) to perform a NetWare 4.11 installation. If not, the installation program displays a warning and asks if you still want to continue. If you receive this error message, press Alt+F10 to exit the installation program, and then fix the problem before you begin again.

Now, we're really making progress. I'm starting to get goose bumps. How about you?

Step 3: Assign the Server Name

Next, you will be prompted for the server name, as shown in Figure 6.17. NetWare 4.11 server names can be 2 to 47 characters long. You should choose a name that's brief and easily recognizable — such as the department name, the location, the primary purpose of the server, or an abbreviated concatenation of such information. Characters that are not allowed include spaces, " * + , \ / : ; = ? [and]. Also, the first character in the server name cannot be a period. Remember, each server on the network must have a unique server name.

FIGURE 6.17

Naming Your Server in INSTALL.BAT

A fairly sophisticated server-naming scheme recommended by Novell includes the use of a set of three three-character codes separated by hyphens (representing the location, division, and server number, respectively). You can use whatever standard you wish for designating these codes, as long as they're consistent. For instance, if your company only has servers in major cities with commercial airports, you could use the three-character airline city code (such as LAX) to designate the location, because all commercial airports in the world have distinct codes. The first server installed in the Small Consumer Electronics Division office in Los Angeles, for instance, could be designated as LAX-SCE-001.

As you saw in Chapter 4, it is wise to plan for future growth when you design a naming scheme. For instance, just because the company only has offices in major cities at the present time doesn't mean this will always be the case.

One disadvantage of this approach is the difficulty in specifying clear standards with only three-character codes. For instance, does the code "IRV" represent Irvine, California, or Irving, Texas? Also, don't forget that you may have network administrators in a number of countries speaking various languages. What might seem like an obvious choice to one person might make no sense whatsoever to someone else. Another disadvantage is that an 11-character server name might prove to be very inconvenient if you're not a good typist. Refer to Chapter 4 for details on ACME's naming standards.

Step 4: Assign the Server IPX Internal Network Number

As you can see in Figure 6.18, when you enter the server name, you will be prompted for a one- to eight-digit IPX *internal network number*. This is an eight-digit hexadecimal number used to uniquely identify this server on the internetwork. You can either accept the randomly generated IPX internal network number displayed on the screen, or enter a new one. You'll probably want to designate a number that is recognizable, because many troubleshooting tools represent servers by their IPX numbers (TRACK ON, for example). The numbers 0 and FFFFFFFF are reserved by NetWare 4.11 and cannot be used. Darn.

F I G U R E   6.18

Choosing an Internal Network Number in INSTALL.BAT

```
NetWare Installation Utility                                      4.11
  Assign an internal IPX number to the server

              A unique IPX internal network number is required. You may accept
              this default or modify it to create a number for your server. For
              guidelines, press <F1>.

              (Example: AEFD2498)

              Press <Enter> to continue.


                 ┌──────────────────────────────────────────┐
                 │ Internal network number:   BADCAFE        │
                 └──────────────────────────────────────────┘




  Continue          <Enter>
  Help              <F1>
  Previous screen   <Esc>
  Exit to DOS       <Alt-F10>
```

TIP

Novell provides a new service called The IPX Registry that keeps track of IPX internal network numbers for you. This ensures that no two servers in your organization share the same number. It also ensures that no two servers *in the world* share the same number. Remember, Novell's goal is to have a private, secure Internet running around the world by the year 2000. What will all the machines be running? IntranetWare 7.21?

As a final check, you'll should make sure that both the server name and IPX internal network number are unique. In other words, if you have a server named SALES at one location, you can't have another server with that same name anywhere else on the WAN.

> **TIP**
>
> **It's a good idea to develop a documented naming convention for server names and IPX internal network numbers. This will help you to quickly identify a server when necessary. When you're asked to supply a server name during the NetWare 4.11 installation process, press F1 to display suggested server naming rules.**

Step 5: Copy the Server Boot Files to the DOS Partition

Next, the system will display the default source and destination paths for copying server boot files, an example of which is shown in Figure 6.19. You'll notice that the default destination path is C:\NWSERVER. The defaults will probably be just fine. Press F2 if you need to change the default source path, or press F4 if you need to change the default destination path. As soon as you make your selection (or press Enter to accept the defaults), the system will automatically copy a number of server boot files from the CD-ROM to the directory indicated (typically, C:\NWSERVER). These include files such as SERVER.EXE, disk drivers, LAN drivers, INSTALL.NLM, NWSNUT.NLM, and other NLMs.

F I G U R E   6.19

Copying Server Boot Files in INSTALL.BAT

```
NetWare Installation Utility                                           4.11
   Copy server boot files to the DOS partition

        The server boot files will be copied from the source directory to
        the destination directory.

        Press <Enter> to continue.




   Source path:   D:\PRODUCTS\NW411\INSTALL\IBM\DOS\XXX\ENGLISH

   Destination path:  C:\NWSERVER

Continue                                 <Enter>
Change current source path               <F2>
Change current destination path          <F4>
Help                                     <F1>
Previous screen                          <Esc>
Exit to DOS                              <Alt-F10>
```

These files enable you to activate the server from the DOS partition and get things started. They include SERVER.EXE, disk drivers, and special LAN drivers. In addition, NetWare 4.11 copies disk and volume utilities to this directory, including VREPAIR.NLM. Once INSTALL is finished copying files, we move on to the final step in Stage 1: entering the server's locale configuration and file information.

Step 6: Assign the Locale Configuration and Filename format

Once the server boot files have been copied to the C:\NWSERVER directory, INSTALL displays the default locale configuration information, as shown in Figure 6.20. Locale information is used to customize server language and keyboard settings. These parameters include:

▶ Country code — A three-character code that designates the country where the server is physically located

▶ Code page — A three-character code that designates the character code set for ASCII

▶ Keyboard mapping — A country-specific keyboard mapping for non-U.S. keyboards (such as Japanese Kanji)

You'll notice that the default values are set up for the United States, so you'll need to change them if your server is located elsewhere. When the locale configuration is correct, select the "Press <Enter> here to continue" field and press Enter.

F I G U R E   6.20

Locale Configuration Screen in INSTALL.BAT

Next, if you executed the INSTALL utility using the */file_sys* switch when you began the installation procedure, you will be asked to select the filename format. Otherwise, NetWare 4.11 will automatically assign the DOS filename format (which is the default).

The DOS filename format enforces DOS naming restrictions as set forth by your country code and code page. The NetWare filename format allows you to use uppercase and lowercase letters, as well as graphics. An obvious advantage of the DOS filename format is that it prevents NETx workstations from creating non-DOS filenames.

TIP

If you choose the DOS filename format, you can still use OS/2 or Macintosh filenames. You'll just have to use NetWare 4.11's name space feature.

Speaking of optional sub-steps — this one fits the bill. INSTALL gives you the option of adding special SET commands to the server startup files. If you select Yes, an edit box will be displayed in which you can specify customized startup commands. For example, if you have disk, CD-ROM, or other devices that use ASPI, add the following line to your STARTUP.NCF file:

```
SET RESERVED BUFFERS BELOW 16MB = 200
```

To determine if a particular device uses ASPI, consult the documentation from the manufacturer. Press F10 when you're finished.

If you don't want to specify any customized SET commands, select No instead.

THE BRAIN

Refer to the "Modify the STARTUP.NCF File" and "Modify the AUTOEXEC.NCF File" sections in Chapter 3 of the *Novell NetWare 4.11 Installation* manual for information on updating NetWare 4.11 startup files. Also, refer to the SET command section in the *Novell NetWare 4.11 Utilities* manual for detailed information about NetWare 4.11 SET commands.

Next, you'll be asked whether you'd like the AUTOEXEC.BAT file to automatically execute SERVER.EXE whenever the server is booted. If you choose Yes, the INSTALL utility will add SERVER to the top of your AUTOEXEC.BAT file. If you choose No, you'll have to switch to the directory containing the server boot files (typically C:\NWSERVER) and type **SERVER** whenever you want to load NetWare 4.11 — too much work.

Well, that does it for the DOS partition. Now, you'll need to transfer server control from DOS to the NetWare 4.11 partition. This is accomplished automatically using SERVER.EXE. This is where the ride gets really thrilling. Hold on to your lunch.

QUIZ

Speaking of thrills, let's take a trip to the "Island of Imperfection." There are three tribes there — the Pukkas, who always tell the truth; the Wotta-Woppas, who never tell the truth; and the Shilli-Shallas, who make statements that are alternatively true and false, or false and true.

An explorer lands on the island and questions three natives — Tom, Dick, and Harry — as follows:

Explorer asks Tom: Which tribe do you belong to?
Tom answers: I'm a Pukka.
He asks Dick: (i) Which tribe do you belong to?
Dick answers: I'm a Wotta-Woppa.
He asks Dick: (ii) Was Tom telling the truth?
Dick answers: Yes.
He asks Harry: (i) Which tribe do you belong to?
Harry answers: I'm a Pukka.
He asks Harry: (ii) Which tribe does Tom belong to?
Harry answers: He's a Shilli-Shalla.

To which tribe does each man belong? Hmmmm.

(Q6-3)

STAGE 2: RUN SERVER.EXE

Your purpose in Stage 1 was to prepare the server hard disk for installation. Most of the first few steps dealt with setting up the DOS partition for booting. During Stage 1, you booted the system to DOS, backed up existing data, deleted existing partitions, configured the CD-ROM as a DOS device, executed INSTALL.BAT, assigned a server name and IPX internal network number, copied server boot files to the DOS partition, and selected the locale configuration and (conditionally) assigned the filename format. You were also given the option of customizing startup file SET parameters and determining whether the AUTOEXEC.BAT file should automatically load SERVER.EXE. No wonder you're already tired.

During Stage 2, the focus shifts from DOS to the NetWare 4.11 operating system. This is accomplished in one easy step:

> *Step 7:* Start the server (happens automatically). The NetWare 4.11 operating system is loaded into memory when SERVER.EXE is executed. This happens automatically.

It's as easy as 1-2-3. Let's take a closer look at the one quick and easy step in Stage 2.

Step 7: Start the Server (Happens Automatically)

SERVER.EXE is the main NetWare 4.11 operating system file — that's what you paid for. When SERVER is automatically executed by INSTALL.BAT, NetWare 4.11 is loaded into server memory and kicks out COMMAND.COM. Now your server is up and running, but you can't do anything with it. It's barely functioning — sort of like being on life support. This is because connectivity has not yet been established between NetWare 4.11 and internal resources, such as hard disk(s) and NIC(s). To jump-start the server, you'll need to load disk and LAN drivers. But not so fast; that's Stage 3. We're not finished with Stage 2 yet. Patience!

TIP

SERVER.EXE runs from the DOS prompt. When you execute it, the server reboots and flushes all DOS programs from memory. This represents a dramatic shift in power from the conservative DOS operating system to liberal NetWare 4.11. You can tell the system is rebooting because the lights on the computer flash. Is this a political statement? Who knows?

Figure 6.21 shows the server console when SERVER.EXE is loaded. Notice the date, SPEED index, and how the server name is displayed with the colon prompt (:). Pretty clever. At this point, the system will automatically load the INSTALL.NLM utility. Now let's breathe life into this otherwise lifeless hunk of silicon — onward to disk and LAN drivers in Stage 3.

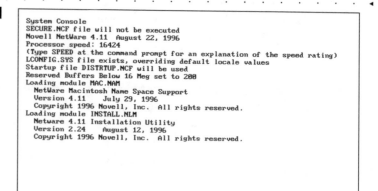

*Automatically Starting the
Server with SERVER.EXE*

```
System Console
SECURE.NCF file will not be executed
Novell NetWare 4.11  August 22, 1996
Processor speed: 16424
(Type SPEED at the command prompt for an explanation of the speed rating)
LCONFIG.SYS file exists, overriding default locale values
Startup file DISTRTUP.NCF will be used
Reserved Buffers Below 16 Meg set to 200
Loading module MAC.NAM
  NetWare Macintosh Name Space Support
  Version 4.11    July 29, 1996
  Copyright 1996 Novell, Inc.  All rights reserved.
Loading module INSTALL.NLM
  Netware 4.11 Installation Utility
  Version 2.24    August 12, 1996
  Copyright 1996 Novell, Inc.  All rights reserved.
```

STAGE 3: LOAD THE NETWARE 4.11 DRIVERS

In Stage 2, INSTALL.BAT loaded the core NetWare 4.11 operating system into
server RAM with SERVER.EXE. Even though our server is alive, as shown by the
colon prompt (:), we can't do anything with it.

Stage 3 jump-starts the server by loading and configuring server disk and LAN
drivers. It also binds the LAN driver(s) to IPX or other communications
protocol(s). Here's how it works:

> ▸ *Step 8:* Load and configure the server disk and CD-ROM driver(s). Disk
> drivers control communication between the server's CPU and the internal
> disk controller. CD-ROM drivers control communication between the
> server's CPU and the internal CD-ROM drive. The NetWare 4.11
> installation program will attempt to automatically detect your hardware
> configuration and select the appropriate hard disk and CD-ROM drivers
> for you.

> ▸ *Step 9:* Load and configure the server LAN driver(s). A LAN driver is
> used as an interface between the file server and the internal NIC. The
> NetWare 4.11 installation program will attempt to automatically detect
> your hardware configuration and select the appropriate LAN driver(s)
> for you. After the server drivers are loaded, you will then be allowed to
> select/accept protocol and frame types for your LAN driver(s). The
> protocol(s) selected will then be bound to the associated LAN driver(s).

With all this in mind, let's continue with "NetWare 4.11 Resuscitation."

THE BRAIN

NetWare 4.11 includes a powerful feature called Symmetric
MultiProcessing (SMP) that allows multiprocessing-enabled NetWare
Loadable Modules (NLMs) to run across multiple processors and
take advantage of the resulting increased processing power. For
information on installing this feature, refer to Chapter 8 of the *Novell
NetWare 4.11 Supervising the Network* manual.

Step 8: Load and configure the Server Disk and CD-ROM Driver(s)

Disk drivers control communication between the server's CPU and internal disk
controllers. CD-ROM drivers control communication between the server's CPU
and internal CD-ROM drives. In many cases, you'll need both a disk driver and a
CD-ROM driver — otherwise they will conflict.

Two of the exciting new features in NetWare 4.11 are hardware autodetection
and automatic selection of drivers. In other words, the INSTALL utility attempts
to automatically detect hardware devices on your machine (such as hard disks,
CD-ROM drives, LAN cards, and so on), then scans for and selects the applicable
drivers. What a great concept! It sure beats trying to figure these things out for
yourself.

If you find that the INSTALL utility is unable to automatically detect your
hardware, you must configure things manually. Some of the reasons might
include:

▸ The server does not have an advanced bus (EISA, PCI, PCMCIA, MCA).

▸ The server hardware is not Plug-and-Play ISA.

▸ The appropriate drivers are not included with this release, or do not
  contain information needed by the autodetection process.

As you can see in Figure 6.22, NetWare 4.11 includes an extensive selection of
hard disk and CD-ROM drivers. With any luck, the INSTALL utility will
automatically detect your server hard disk and CD-ROM hardware and select the
appropriate drivers. You can usually accept the default settings for each unless the

switches on your drives have been changed. If the hardware settings have been changed, refer to the manufacturer's documentation for further information.

▶ • ◀

F I G U R E   6.22

Loading Disk Drivers at the NetWare 4.11 Server

```
NetWare Server Installation 4.11                    NetWare Loadable Module

                              Select a driver:

▲ IDE.DSK       Novell IDE (ATA Compatible) Driver
  IDEATA.HAM    Novell IDE (ATA/ATAPI Compatible) Host Adapter Module (HAM)
  IDECD.CDM     Novell IDE ATAPI CDROM Custom Device Module (CDM)
  IDEHD.CDM     Novell IDE (ATA Compatible) Custom Device Module (CDM)
▼ INI9100.HAM   Initio INI-9100/9100W SCSI Modules

        ┌──────────────────────────────────────────────┐
        │ "IDE.DSK" Help                               ▲│
        │                                              ▓│
        │ Use this driver with IDE or ATA drives that are│
        │ either connected directly to the system board or│
        │ to a paddle board in the system bus. The IDE  ▼│
        │           (To scroll, <F7>-up <F8>-down)       │
        └──────────────────────────────────────────────┘
Select a listed driver <Enter>              Install an unlisted driver <Ins>
Help                    <F1>                Continue without selecting <F10>
```

If your server has more than one hard disk and they're connected to the same controller, you'll only need to load one driver. If the hard disks are connected to different controllers, you'll need to load multiple drivers.

TIP

If you're installing NetWare 4.11 from a CD-ROM that is sharing a SCSI adapter with another internal or external device (such as a hard disk or tape unit), you may find that the system hangs when you are loading drivers or copying files. If this happens, obtain updated drivers from the manufacturer of the SCSI adapter.

Earlier versions of NetWare (such as 3.12) employed an architecture called *monolithic architecture*. It used a single disk driver with a .DSK filename extension as the interface between NetWare and the disk controller. NetWare 4.11 uses a newer architecture, called *NetWare Peripheral Architecture* (NWPA), in which two drivers share this responsibility: a Host Adapter Module (with — what else? — a .HAM filename extension) and a Custom Device Module (with a .CDM filename extension).

The advantage of the monolithic architecture is that it's been around much longer than NWPA, and individual drivers have been more thoroughly tested by

Novell and third parties. A disadvantage of the monolithic architecture is that the driver selected must support all connected devices.

NPA, on the other hand, provides better scalability, because each hardware device uses an individual CDM. Also, NWPA will be the primary disk driver architecture used in future releases of IntranetWare.

SMART LINK

For more information on the new NetWare Peripheral Architecture solution, refer to Appendix H of the *Novell NetWare 4.11 Installation* manual or surf to the Novell Knowledgebase at http://support.novell.com/search/.

Step 9: Load and Configure the Server LAN Driver(s)

The NetWare 4.11 LAN driver serves as an interface between the server and its internal NIC. Activating the appropriate LAN driver enables you to communicate between the internal network board and external cabling system. The appropriate LAN driver to use will depend on your cabling system and network board that you are using.

As we discussed earlier, two of the exciting new features in NetWare 4.11 are hardware autodetection and automatic selection of drivers. In other words, the INSTALL utility attempts to automatically detect hardware devices on your machine (such as hard disks, CD-ROM drives, LAN cards, and so on), then scans for and selects the applicable drivers.

If you find that the INSTALL utility is unable to automatically detect your hardware, you must configure things manually.

If your drivers are automatically selected by the INSTALL utility, a screen will be displayed, showing the selected LAN and disk drivers. You will then be given the opportunity to accept or modify the automatically selected drivers or to select additional drivers, as shown in Figure 6.23.

You should verify that there is at least one LAN driver listed per LAN adapter. Be sure that you take into account adapters that are integrated into the server's motherboard as well as those on the server's expansion cards. With any luck, you will be able to accept the default drivers selected by the INSTALL utility. The INSTALL utility will then load the drivers that were selected.

The next thing that happens is that the INSTALL utility attempts to detect the appropriate protocols for each LAN driver loaded. IPX is the default protocol for NetWare 4.11 and will be chosen automatically.

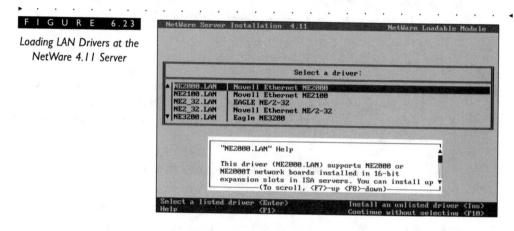

FIGURE 6.23

Loading LAN Drivers at the NetWare 4.11 Server

TIP

The protocols selected at this stage are, by definition, nonrouting protocols. If you require routing protocols, you must configure them after the server is installed by loading the INSTALL.NLM utility and choosing the Configure Network Protocols option.

If you look at the protocol settings for your LAN driver(s), you'll notice one of the parameters that you are allowed to configure is the frame type bound to each protocol (such as IPX). *Binding* is the process of attaching a protocol to a specific server NIC and starting communications.

When you bind IPX to a LAN driver, you must specify the *external network address*. This is a unique hexadecimal number that distinguishes the physical LAN cabling. Unlike the IPX internal network number, the external network address can be the same for two servers as long as they are attached to the same physical cabling trunk. You may find it advantageous to use a strategy that will allow you to differentiate IPX internal network addresses from external addresses just by looking at them — such as by designating that internal address are alphabetic (using the letters A through F) and external address are numeric.

SMART LINK

Explore the latest IntranetWare drivers on the Web at http://support.novell.com/sitemap.

Interestingly, you will find that each NIC can support *multiple* frame types. The *frame type* identifies the packet architecture for LAN communications. It's kind of confusing, but a single cabling trunk can support multiple frame types simultaneously — but they must use different external network addresses. Weird, huh? Anyway, NetWare 4.11 defaults to Ethernet_802.2, whereas NetWare 3.11 defaults to Ethernet_802.3. Be careful. The INSTALL utility, however, selects both of these frame types as default. You will probably want to de-select the Ethernet_802.3 frame type if you don't need it.

THE BRAIN

If you selected the TCP/IP transport protocol when configuring your LAN driver(s), you are given the opportunity to determine whether to install the NetWare/IP product. Refer to the *Novell NetWare 4.11 IP Administrator's Guide* for further information.

STAGE 4: INSTALL.NLM

In Stage 3, we established server connectivity by loading and configuring disk drivers and LAN drivers. In addition, we bound IPX or other communication protocol(s) to the internal NIC and established an external network address for each frame type. Now it's time to get serious about NetWare 4.11 partitions, the SYS: volume, and SYSTEM and PUBLIC files.

ZEN

"History is about to be rewritten by two guys that can't spell."

Bill & Ted's Excellent Adventure

Here's what we have to look forward to in Stage 4:

- *Step 10:* Configure the CD-ROM drive as a DOS or NetWare 4.11 device. A warning may be displayed advising you that there may be a conflict with between the DOS CD-ROM driver and the NetWare 4.11 version of the same driver.

- *Step 11:* Create NetWare 4.11 disk partition(s). By default, NetWare 4.11 creates a single NetWare partition occupying all available server space. Also, you will get the opportunity to configure disk mirroring and change the size of the hot fix redirection area.

- *Step 12:* Create NetWare 4.11 volume(s). By default, NetWare 4.11 creates a single SYS: volume occupying the entire disk partition. You will be given a chance to create additional volumes, as well as to configure other file system options (such as data migration, file compression, and block suballocation).

- *Step 13:* Reestablish a server-to-server connection (conditional). Only applicable with the "server-to-server" installation method (called "remote network installation area" by Novell).

- *Step 14:* Select optional NetWare 4.11 file groups. The "preliminary" SYSTEM and LOGIN files are copied to the SYS: volume during this step.

The server is finally starting to wake up. This is our opportunity to pump some serious muscle. INSTALL.NLM is our friend.

Step 10: Configure the CD-ROM as a DOS or NetWare 4.11 Device

A warning message may be displayed on the screen advising you that the INSTALL utility needs to get a list of drivers from the CD-ROM, but cannot determine if a NetWare 4.11/DOS driver conflict exists. Unless you are sure that such a conflict exists, select the Use the "CD-ROM to Get Drivers" option from the "Select an Action" menu. You will probably be able to continue normally despite the warning. If your keyboard locks up, it probably means there is a conflict. If this happens, reboot the computer and start the installation from scratch — choosing the alternate menu option when you get to this menu.

Step 11: Create NetWare 4.11 Disk Partition(s)

Every NetWare 4.11 server disk requires at least one NetWare 4.11 partition. Only one NetWare 4.11 partition is allowed per hard disk, but each partition can consist of up to eight volume segments.

You'll be given two options for creating NetWare 4.11 partitions: manual or automatic. If you choose to create disk partitions automatically:

▶ *Single hard disk per server*: If the server contains only one hard disk, the INSTALL utility will create a single NetWare 4.11 partition consisting of all free disk space beyond the DOS partition, as seen in Figure 6.24.

▶ *Multiple hard disks per server*: If the server contains more than one hard disk, on the additional hard disks, the INSTALL utility will create one NetWare 4.11 partition per hard disk — where each partition contains all the available space on that disk.

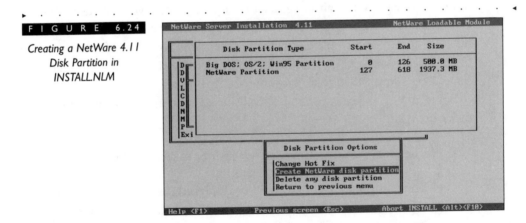

F I G U R E   6.24

Creating a NetWare 4.11 Disk Partition in INSTALL.NLM

You should choose to partition the disk manually if:

▶ You want to selectively delete existing disk partitions.

▶ You want to specify the size of the NetWare 4.11 partition.

▶ You need other operating systems to reside on the same disk.

▶ You need to mirror or duplex disks.

▶ You want to change the size of the hot fix redirection area. (During the NetWare 4.11 installation procedure, the size of the hot fix redirection area is automatically calculated as a percentage of disk capacity.)

TIP

If your disk size seems smaller than anticipated, it may be because NetWare 4.11 lists the true size in megabytes (that is, 1,048,576 rather than 1 million). Also, the disk size listed by NetWare 4.11 does not show the disk space that has been allocated for the hot fix redirection area.

After creating the NetWare 4.11 partitions on each server drive, you can optionally choose to mirror or duplex them — if you have a server with two or more hard disks. With *mirroring*, data is duplicated on two disks using the same controller. With *duplexing*, NetWare 4.11 duplicates the data on two disks using different controllers. Duplexing, which is the more expensive of the two options, offers greater safety because the likelihood of losing two disk controllers at the same time is lower than that of losing two hard drives.

Some things to keep in mind if you are considering mirroring or duplexing disks are:

▶ The same installation process is used for mirroring and duplexing.

▶ The partition sizes of mirrored or duplexed disks should be similar. Otherwise, the remaining space on the larger hard disk will be wasted, because NetWare 4.11 will configure it so that the mirrored partitions are the same size.

▶ Although two mirrored partitions would normally be sufficient, you can mirror up to eight partitions.

▶ Which hard disks are mirrored depends on how you set up the volumes on the server.

You're halfway there. Before you can store files on the new disk partition, you must define at least one volume on it. Look out, that's Step 12.

Step 12: Create NetWare 4.11 Volume(s)

By default, on servers with a single hard disk, NetWare 4.11 allocates all available disk space on the NetWare 4.11 partition to a single NetWare 4.11 volume called SYS:. You can create additional volumes by reducing the size of the SYS: volume and allocating that space to other segments. For servers with multiple hard disks, NetWare 4.11 automatically creates one NetWare 4.11 volume per hard disk.

You can assign whatever name you want to any volume other than SYS:. The SYS: volume is required because it houses all the NetWare 4.11 SYSTEM and PUBLIC files. Chapter 10 takes a closer look at volumes. Also, the SYS: volume is given a "logical" name in the NDS tree: "server_SYS." For example, the first ACME volume is named LABS-SRV1_SYS.

Novell recommends allocating at least 100 MB of disk space to the SYS: volume. You may need to allocate additional space if:

▸ You plan to install several optional products (such as the NetWare 4.11 OS/2 utilities). If insufficient volume space is available when file copying begins, you are prompted to resize the volume before continuing with the file copy.

▸ You plan to print large data or plot files. If so, additional disk space is needed to spool these files.

▸ You plan to install DynaText on the SYS: volume.

Novell recommends that you consider the following guidelines when creating volumes:

▸ Reserve the SYS: volume for NetWare 4.11 files and create one or more additional volumes for applications and data. Also, remember, NDS objects are stored on the SYS: volume. Be sure that you leave adequate room to account for future growth of the NDS database.

▶ If fault tolerance is more important than performance, create one volume per disk.

▶ If performance is more important than fault tolerance, you can span one NetWare 4.11 volume over multiple hard disks, with one segment of the volume on each hard disk. (**Warning**: If any disk on a spanned volume fails, the entire volume is lost. Be sure that you back up spanned volumes on a frequent basis so that you can restore the entire volume from backup once the disk is repaired or replaced.)

▶ If both performance and fault tolerance are important, you can both span and duplex, but Novell recommends that you duplex every hard disk partition of the spanned volume.

▶ For maximum fault tolerant protection, Novell recommend purchasing the NetWare 4.11 SFT III product.

▶ If you will be storing any data files created under an operating system that allows long filenames (such as Macintosh), consider creating one volume for each type of the operating system data files used.

▶ If you are using the NetWare 4.11 auditing feature, and one volume will contain data to be reviewed by two or more auditors, you may want to create a separate volume for each auditor for security reasons.

After you create the server volumes, you are given the chance to modify various volume parameters, as shown in Figure 6.25. They include block size, status, file compression, block suballocation, and data migration. The defaults for these last three parameters are:

▶ File compression: ON

▶ Block suballocation: ON

▶ Data migration: OFF

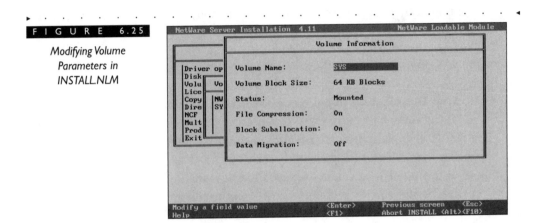

FIGURE 6.25

Modifying Volume Parameters in INSTALL.NLM

Chapter 1 of this book provides additional information on file compression, block suballocation, and data migration. Also, if you plan to use Novell's High Capacity Storage System (HCSS), you'll want to press the Enter key twice on each of these fields to toggle them to the opposite of the default values.

THE BRAIN

Novell's High Capacity Storage System (HCSS) extends the storage capability of an NetWare 4.11 server by moving files between a faster, low-capacity system (the hard disk) and a slower, high-capacity system (rewritable optical disks in a jukebox). This process is transparent to the user. Users (and programs) use the same NetWare 4.11 commands and function calls to access directories and files in both systems. See the High Capacity Storage System section of the *Novell NetWare 4.11 Concepts* **manual for an overview of HCSS. For an in-depth exploration of this topic, refer to the article titled "Inside Novell's High Capacity Storage System (HCSS)" beginning on page 1 of the February 1995 issue of the** *Novell Application Notes* **publication.**

Step 13: Reestablish the Server-to-Server Connection (Conditional)

If you are using the "server-to-server" installation method (called "remote network installation area" by Novell), you'll need to reestablish your remote server connection at this point. This involves identifying the previously used username and password. Here's why. Earlier, when the LAN driver was loaded, we lost our background connection to the other server. IPX can only handle one type of communication at a time, per NIC. Fortunately, INSTALL is smart enough to recognize what has happened. It automatically recalls the source server path from memory, but you must reenter the password.

Now it's time to move on.

Step 14: Select Optional NetWare 4.11 File Groups

In NetWare 4.1, you were asked to select optional file groups to install at this point. In NetWare 4.11, you may find the installation utility skips this step and makes the decisions for you.

At this point, a screen is displayed that lists the default source and destination paths for the so-called "preliminary" (pre-installation) files. If you're installing from the server's CD-ROM, you can probably accept the default — or press F3 to change the defaults. The installation program will then copy only those SYSTEM and LOGIN files that are necessary to continue the installation process. Later, in Step 20, we'll copy the remaining files to the SYS: volume.

We are well on our way to NetWare 4.11 Nirvana. Just a couple more Zen icons, and we'll be there. Also, for those of you out there in NetWare 3 land — this completes the "familiar" part of our show. Please exit to the rear of the cabin. Now, we're going to explore something radically different — installation of "the Cloud."

QUIZ

I've got a great word for ya: **Mukluk.** *But what does it mean?*

(Q6-4)

STAGE 5: INSTALL NOVELL DIRECTORY SERVICES (NDS)

In Stage 4, we set up the NetWare 4.11 partition. This involved five steps: CD-ROM configuration, NetWare 4.11 partition creation, volume definition, reestablishment of the server-to-server connection, and finally, the copying of optional (preliminary) NetWare 4.11 files. Now our server is alive and well.

The most important stage remains. In Stage 5 we finally get to install "the Cloud" — Novell Directory Services (NDS).

▶ *Step 15:* Install NDS. This involves specifying tree names, server context, and time zone information.

▶ *Step 16:* License the NetWare 4.11 operating system. At this point, you will be prompted for a valid, unique License diskette.

Let's take a closer look.

Step 15: Install NDS

Have you ever watched cloud seeding? It helps build bigger clouds to quench the thirst of Mother Earth. Well, in Step 18, we get to do some cloud seeding of our own. At this point, NetWare 4.11 searches the WAN for any existing Directory trees on your network. Depending on the number of trees found, the installation utility will display one of three menus. For example, Figure 6.26 shows the menu that will be displayed if no trees are found. In this example, you are asked to indicate whether or not this is the "first NetWare 4 server."

▶ · ◀

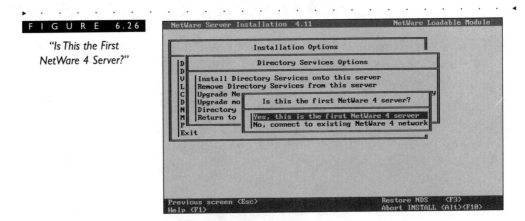

F I G U R E   6.26

"Is This the First NetWare 4 Server?"

If you indicate Yes, you'll be asked to input a unique tree name, as shown in Figure 6.27. Use something creative such as "Elm" or "Redwood." Just kidding. You should use the Organization name followed by "_TREE". For us, that equates to "ACME_TREE". If you select No, you'll be asked to choose from a list of existing trees. This will be the new home of the server. (We'll tell NetWare 4.11 exactly where to put the server in the tree at a later time.)

Next, INSTALL.NLM shifts over to time zone information. Remember, every NetWare 4.11 server must be a time server of some type. As you would guess, most are Secondary time servers. The Time Zone Information screen prompts you to choose among 18 different time zones, as seen in Figure 6.28. (**Note:** This list does not include all time zones.)

*Naming Your NDS Tree in
INSTALL.NLM*

```
NetWare Server Installation  4.11                    NetWare Loadable Module

                            Installation Options
    ┌──────────────────────────────────────────────────────────────────┐
   D│                    Directory Services Options                       │
   D│                                                                     │
   U│  Install Directory Services onto this server                        │
   L│  Remove Directory Services from this server                         │
   C│  Upgrade NetWare 3.x bindery information to the Directory            │
   D│  Upgrade moun┌──────────────────────────────────────────┐           │
   N│  Directory ba│ Enter a name for this Directory tree:     │           │
   M│  Return to th│                                           │           │
   P│              │ >ACME_TREE                                │           │
    │Exit          └──────────────────────────────────────────┘           │
    └──────────────────────────────────────────────────────────────────┘

 Save tree name <Enter>                          Previous screen   <Esc>
 Help            <F1>                             Abort INSTALL <Alt><F10>
```

*Choosing a Time Zone in
INSTALL.NLM*

```
NetWare Server Installation  4.11                    NetWare Loadable Module

                            Installation Options
    ┌──────────────────────────────────────────────────────────────────┐
   D│                      Choose a time zone:                            │
   D│  ┌──────────────────────────────────────────────────────────┐      │
   U│  │▲Spain: Peninsula and Baleares                             │      │
   L│  │ Taiwan, Taiwan Time                                       │      │
   C│  │ United Kingdom, Greenwich Mean Time                       │      │
   D│  │ United States of America, Alaskan Time                    │      │
   N│  │ United States of America, Atlantic Time                   │      │
   M│  │ United States of America, Central Time                    │      │
   P│  │ United States of America, Eastern Time                    │      │
    │  │ United States of America, Hawaiian-Aleutian Time          │      │
    │  │ United States of America, Mountain Time                   │      │
    │  │ United States of America, Pacific Time                    │      │
    │  └──────────────────────────────────────────────────────────┘      │
    └──────────────────────────────────────────────────────────────────┘

 Select a time zone listed                   <Enter>  Previous screen   <Esc>
 Enter parameters for a time zone not listed <Ins>
 Help                                         <F1>    Abort INSTALL <Alt><F10>
```

THE BRAIN

If you are using the INSTALL utility to restore your server after a planned backup or disaster recovery, there are prompts you can follow throughout the process of installing Novell Directory Services. For more information about the circumstances and requirements for backing up and restoring your server, whether the restore is planned or unplanned, see the "Restore Server from Backup" section in Chapter 3 of the *Novell NetWare 4.11 Installation* manual.

This helps automate the input of parameters into the Time Configuration window. As you can see in Figure 6.29, there's a ton of complex time parameters required for every server: "Time server type" (Single Reference, Reference, Primary, or Secondary); "Standard time zone abbreviation"; "Standard time offset from UTC" (Universal Time Coordinated); "Daylight savings time" (DST); "DST offset"; "DST start"; and "DST end." See Chapters 2 and 9.

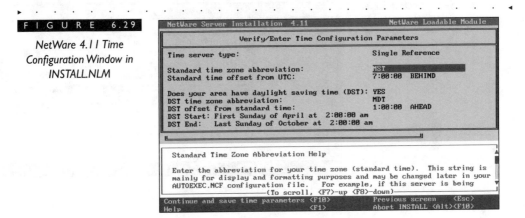

FIGURE 6.29

NetWare 4.11 Time
Configuration Window in
INSTALL.NLM

THE BRAIN

For more information on planning and maintaining a time synchronization strategy, refer to the "Time Synchronization" section in the *Novell NetWare 4.11 Concepts* manual, Chapter 5 of the *Novell NetWare 4.11 Guide to NetWare 4 Networks* manual, and Chapter 7 of the *Novell NetWare 4.11 Supervising the Network* manual.

TIP

Entering incorrect time synchronization information can cause major problems. Don't change the default values unless you know what you're doing.

Next, we get to define the "Cloud." You will be asked for the server's Directory tree context, as shown in Figure 6.30. The context consists of an optional Country code (for example, C=US), an Organization name (for example, O=ACME), and optionally, up to three levels of Organizational Units (for example, OU=NORAD and OU=LABS). In most cases, Novell doesn't recommend the use of Country containers. They are reserved for public service providers. As a matter of fact, the only way to define a Country container is to manually add it to the Server Context field. Notice that there's no option for it.

F I G U R E   6.30

NDS Server Context Screen
in INSTALL.NLM

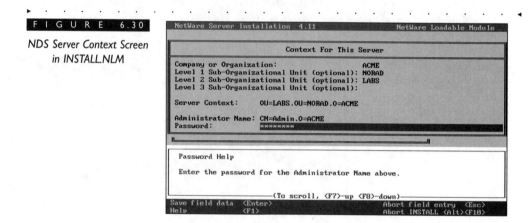

```
NetWare Server Installation 4.11                     NetWare Loadable Module

                              Context For This Server
    Company or Organization:                      ACME
    Level 1 Sub-Organizational Unit (optional): NORAD
    Level 2 Sub-Organizational Unit (optional): LABS
    Level 3 Sub-Organizational Unit (optional):

    Server Context:       OU=LABS.OU=NORAD.O=ACME

    Administrator Name: CN=Admin.O=ACME
    Password:                  ********

    Password Help

    Enter the password for the Administrator Name above.

                        (To scroll, <F7>-up <F8>-down)
Save field data   <Enter>                      Abort field entry   <Esc>
Help              <F1>                          Abort INSTALL <Alt><F10>
```

SMARTLINK

If you need a little more help with your tree design, consult Chapters 3 through 5 of this book, or surf over to CyberState University for the NDS Design course at http://www.cyberstateu.com.

You'll also be asked for an Admin password. If this is the first server in the tree, you get to make one up. Otherwise, you'll need to input the "real" Admin password. This controls who adds servers to *your* tree.

Once you have provided all the requested information, you'll be asked to save the Directory information and continue. Figure 6.31 shows an example of the type of summary window that will be displayed, and lists the Directory tree name, Directory context, and Administrator name. You should write down this information and keep it in a safe place. Whatever you do, don't forget the Admin password.

ZEN

"Everything in moderation, including moderation."

Anonymous

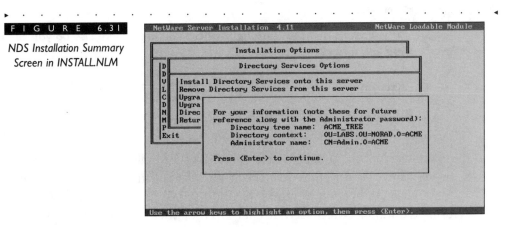

FIGURE   6.31

NDS Installation Summary Screen in INSTALL.NLM

Step 16: License the NetWare 4.11 Operating System

Next, you will be asked to insert the IntranetWare/NetWare 4.11 License diskette into drive A:, as shown in Figure 6.32. Be sure to use a unique License diskette — NetWare 4.11 is kind of picky about such things. If you use the same License diskette on two different servers, NetWare 4.11 will display a license violation warning. And that's not all. It will also cut the user connection number down to 1. This gives you just enough maneuvering room to revalidate the license. Nice try.

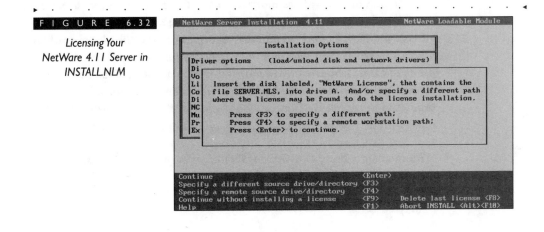

FIGURE   6.32

Licensing Your NetWare 4.11 Server in INSTALL.NLM

ZEN

"If you can't find the truth right where you are, where else do you think you will find it?"

Anonymous

NetWare 4.11 licensing works a bit differently than in previous versions of NetWare. In NetWare 3, licensing was built into SERVER.EXE. This meant Novell had to manufacture 5 million different SERVER.EXE files — too much work. So, in NetWare 4.11, designers developed a way of "validating" a server and "binding" the license information to a generic SERVER.EXE file. This is accomplished by using the IntranetWare/NetWare 4.11 License diskette. Just think of it: $47,995 for a single 3.5-inch floppy diskette. Now that's a serious markup.

Well, there you have it. All done! The server is alive and well, and walking in the clouds. I couldn't be happier for you! Now, we will end the installation process with a little "housekeeping" — creating server startup files, copying SYSTEM and PUBLIC files, and installing optional products. That's Stage 6.

QUIZ

Speaking of "radically different," here's one for the record books: George, John, Arthur, and David are married, but not necessarily respectively, to Christine, Eve, Dana, and Rose. They remember that at a party years ago various predictions had been made. George had said that John would not marry Christine. John had said that Arthur would marry Dana. Arthur predicted that whoever David married, it would not be Eve. David, who at that time was more interested in horses than matrimony, had predicted that Gallant Dancer would win the Kentucky Derby. The only one to predict correctly was the man who later married Dana.

Who married whom? Did Gallant Dancer win the race? Who shot Mr. Burns? (Sorry, that's Chapter 11.)

(Q6-5)

REAL WORLD

Don't tell anybody I told you this, but the NetWare 4.11 Operating System CD actually has two licenses built into it. If you don't have a valid license diskette (for whatever reason), simply press <F9> at this point and the installation will continue. Here's the trick. Even though the server console displays the message, "Maximum connecions has been reduced to one," you actually have two user connections available. Go ahead, try it!

STAGE 6: CREATE SERVER STARTUP FILES

In Stage 5, you installed NDS. As part of this step, you were asked to supply a tree name, the server context, and time zone information. You were also asked for an Admin password — new or used. The final step in Stage 5 was to licensed the NetWare 4.11 operating system

Now, it's time to finish off the Custom installation with some general housekeeping tasks, including:

▶ *Step 17:* Create/modify the STARTUP.NCF and AUTOEXEC.NCF startup files.

▶ *Step 18:* Copy the SYSTEM and PUBLIC files to the SYS: volume.

▶ *Step 19:* Perform other installation options (such as installing NetWare for Macintosh, Creating Registration Diskettes, and DynaText).

▶ *Step 20:* Complete the installation — yeah!

▶ *Step 21:* Boot the server using the STARTUP.NCF and AUTOEXEC.NCF startup files.

These steps are your life in a nutshell. Let's take a look.

Step 17: Create/Modify the STARTUP.NCF and AUTOEXEC.NCF Startup Files

The first housekeeping task involves two server startup files — STARTUP.NCF and AUTOEXEC.NCF. These two files automate the startup process so you don't have to perform these 21 steps every time the server is booted.

It starts with STARTUP.NCF, which contains commands to load disk drivers, name space modules, and special SET parameters. This file can be modified after the installation process is complete by using INSTALL.NLM or the SERVMAN server utility (see Figure 6.33). The STARTUP.NCF file is stored in the C:\NWSERVER directory and is called by SERVER.EXE. When the system displays the proposed STARTUP.NCF file, you'll notice that it includes the disk driver and SET parameter information that you supplied earlier. How kind. Accept the defaults and continue by pressing F10.

FIGURE   6.33

Saving the Server STARTUP.NCF File

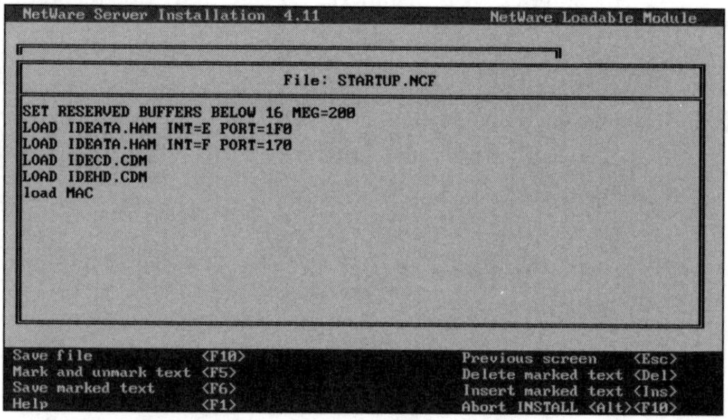

TIP

The SYS: volume is automatically mounted when the corresponding disk driver is loaded by STARTUP.NCF.

Next, it's AUTOEXEC.NCF's turn. This file contains information such as the time zone information, bindery context, server name, IPX internal network number, commands to load and bind the LAN driver(s), and so on. It is stored in the SYS:SYSTEM directory and is called by the STARTUP.NCF file. If necessary, it can be modified after installation is complete by using INSTALL.NLM or the SERVMAN server utility. Once again, you'll notice that the proposed AUTOEXEC.NCF file in

Figure 6.34 includes the values we specified earlier. If this server is installed on an existing network, be sure that each BIND statement includes the correct external network address.

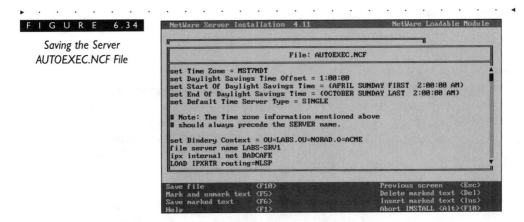

F I G U R E   6.34

Saving the Server AUTOEXEC.NCF File

```
NetWare Server Installation  4.11                    NetWare Loadable Module

                           File: AUTOEXEC.NCF

set Time Zone = MST7MDT
set Daylight Savings Time Offset = 1:00:00
set Start Of Daylight Savings Time = (APRIL SUNDAY FIRST  2:00:00 AM)
set End Of Daylight Savings Time = (OCTOBER SUNDAY LAST  2:00:00 AM)
set Default Time Server Type = SINGLE

# Note: The Time zone information mentioned above
# should always precede the SERVER name.

set Bindery Context = OU=LABS.OU=NORAD.O=ACME
file server name LABS-SRV1
ipx internal net BADCAFE
LOAD IPXRTR routing=NLSP

Save file              <F10>            Previous screen      <Esc>
Mark and unmark text   <F5>             Delete marked text   <Del>
Save marked text       <F6>             Insert marked text   <Ins>
Help                   <F1>             Abort INSTALL <Alt><F10>
```

If you must modify the STARTUP.NCF or AUTOEXEC.NCF files at a later date, you can do so by loading the INSTALL.NLM utility and by choosing NCF files options from the Install Options menu. You can also use the SERVMAN server utility to modify these startup files after-the-fact. If you choose not to create these files, you'll have to load these statements and SET parameters every time the server is booted — major drag!

TIP

You'll notice that the STARTUP.NCF and AUTOEXEC.NCF files are stored in two different locations: The STARTUP.NCF file is stored in the C:\NWSERVER directory on the DOS partition, and the AUTOEXEC.NCF file is stored in the SYS:SYSTEM directory on the NetWare 4.11 partition. This is because the NetWare 4.11 partition isn't available until the disk driver is loaded.

Step 18: Copy the NetWare 4.11 SYSTEM and PUBLIC Files to the SYS: volume

Now you finally get to copy the main SYSTEM and PUBLIC files to the SYS: volume, as shown in Figure 6.35. This is the third time you have copied files to the server disk:

▶ Step 5: Copy the server boot files to the DOS partition —
C:\NWSERVER.

▶ Step 14: Select optional NetWare 4.11 files groups to the SYS: volume.

▶ Step 18: Copy the SYSTEM and PUBLIC files to the SYS: volume.

FIGURE 6.35

Copying the NetWare 4.11 System Files in INSTALL.NLM

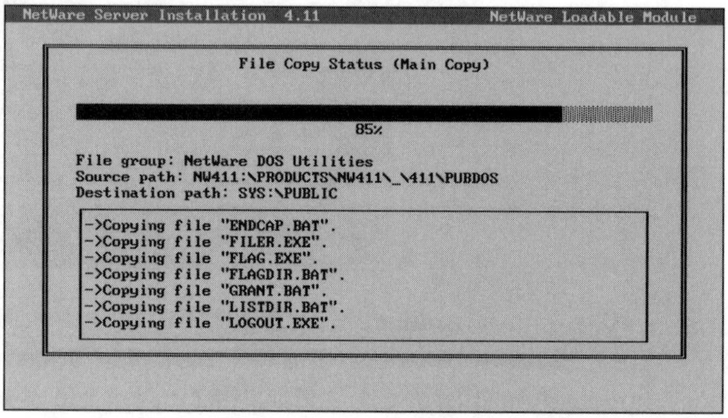

Once it's finished, INSTALL returns with the Other Installation Options screen.
That's Step 19.

Step 19: Perform Other Installation Options (Optional)

Notice in Figure 6.36 that after the main SYSTEM and PUBLIC files have been
copied to the SYS: volume, a list of additional options is displayed, including:

▶ Create Client Installation Directories on Server (see Chapter 13)

▶ Make Diskettes

▶ Install NetWare IP (see Chapter 13)

▶ Install NetWare DHCP

▶ Configure Network Protocols (see Chapter 13)

▶ Install Legacy NWADMIN utility (see Chapter 8)

► Install NetWare Web Server (see Chapter 13)

► Upgrade 3.1x Print Services (see Chapter 7)

► Install an Additional Server Language (see Chapter 13)

► Change Server Language (see Chapter 13)

► Install NetWare for Macintosh (see Chapter 13)

► Install NetWare Client for MAC OS (see Chapter 13)

► Configure Network Licensing Service (NLS)

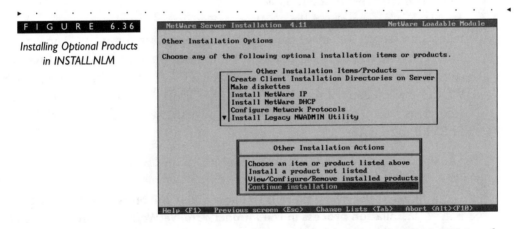

F I G U R E   6.36

Installing Optional Products in INSTALL.NLM

You can access these options at any time by loading INSTALL.NLM and choosing Product Options.

Step 20: Complete the Installation

C O N G R A T U L A T I O N S !

I bet you thought you'd never make it! The last two steps mark the end of a long and rewarding journey. At this point, you should choose Continue Installation from the Other Installation Actions menu. The INSTALL utility then displays the congratulatory message like the one shown in Figure 6.37.

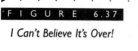

F I G U R E   6.37

I Can't Believe It's Over!

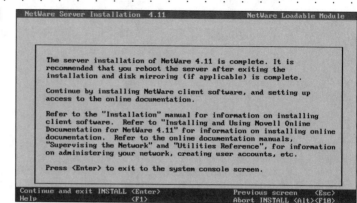

Step 21: Boot the Server Using the STARTUP.NCF and AUTOEXEC. NCF Startup Files

Once you've completed the NetWare 4.11 Custom installation, you'll need to reboot the server to make sure that it is operating properly. Remove the IntranetWare/NetWare 4.11 License diskette from the server's floppy drive and store it in a safe place, such on your refrigerator — just kidding. You may even want to make a copy of the diskette and store it off-site as part of your disaster-recovery strategy. Next, type **DOWN** to down the server, and then **RESTART SERVER** to restart it.

SMART LINK

Learn everything there is to know about the NetWare 4.11 Custom Installation process in the *IntranetWare/NetWare 4.11 Installation and Configuration Workshop* at CyberState University (http://www.cyberstateu.com).

CUSTOM INSTALLATION ROAD MAP

In case you got lost anywhere along the way, here's a road map to get you on the right track. Also, I have added a reference to *"Happens Once"* and *"Happens Every time."* If a step happens once, it only occurs during the initial installation (like creating the DOS partition). However, if a step is marked "Happens Every time," then it occurs each time the server is booted (such as loading disk and LAN drivers). You get the idea. (Also, check out Exercise 6-2 at the end of the chapter.)

Stage 1: Prepare the server hard disk

- ▶ Step 1: Configure the server DOS partition — *"Happens Once."*

- ▶ Step 2: Select the server language and type of installation — *"Happens Once."*

- ▶ Step 3: Assign the server name — *"Happens Every time."*

- ▶ Step 4: Assign the server IPX internal network number — *"Happens Every time."*

- ▶ Step 5: Copy the server boot files to the DOS partition — *"Happens Once."*

- ▶ Step 6: Assign the locale configuration and filename format — *"Happens Once."*

Stage 2: Run SERVER.EXE

- ▶ Step 7: Start the server (happens automatically) — *"Happens Every time."*

Stage 3: Load the NetWare drivers

- ▶ Step 8: Load and configure the server disk and CD-ROM driver(s) — *"Happens Every time."*

- ▶ Step 9: Load and configure the server LAN driver(s) — *"Happens Every time."*

Stage 4: INSTALL.NLM

▸ Step 10: Configure the CD-ROM as a DOS or NetWare device — *"Happens Once."*

▸ Step 11: Create NetWare 4.11 disk partition(s) — *"Happens Once."*

▸ Step 12: Create NetWare 4.11 volume(s) — *"Happens Once."*

▸ Step 13: Reestablish the server-to-server connection (conditional) — "Happens *Once.*"

▸ Step 14: Select optional NetWare file groups — *"Happens Once."*

Stage 5: Install NDS

▸ Step 15: Install NDS — *"Happens Once."*

▸ Step 16: License the NetWare 4.11 operating system — *"Happens Once."*

Stage 6: Create server startup files

▸ Step 17: Create/modify the STARTUP.NCF and AUTOEXEC.NCF startup files — *"Happens Once."*

▸ Step 18: Copy the SYSTEM and PUBLIC files to the SYS: volume — *"Happens Once."*

▸ Step 19: Perform other installation options (optional) — *"Happens Once."*

▸ Step 20: Complete the installation — *"Happens Once."*

▸ Step 21: Boot the server using the STARTUP.NCF and AUTOEXEC.NCF startup files — *"Happens Every time."*

ZEN

"He was 98 lbs of solid nerd until he became ..."

The Toxic Avenger

Okay, put down the champagne. You're not finished yet.

· ◄

DynaText Installation

"What's a Subordinate Reference?"

"List the DSTRACE switches!"

"How many NDS access rights are there?"

These are all great questions, and I know just the place to find the answers — DynaText. The NetWare 4.11 on-line documentation (also called DynaText) enables you to electronically access the information found in NetWare 4.11 manuals. Too bad it's not available *before* you install the server and workstation. Well, actually, it is — you can install DynaText directly from the operating system CD-ROM directly onto your workstation. The case study at the end of this chapter provides instructions for how to do this.

The NetWare 4.11 on-line documentation consists of two main parts:

  ▸ *Document Collection* — Contains the NetWare 4.11 product documentation in the on-line documentation set. Each collection includes a variety of manuals. For example, the "NetWare 4.11 Getting Started" set includes the following five books: *DynaText Installation Guide, Guide to NetWare 4.11 Networks, Installation, New Features*, and *Upgrade*. The collections are also available in several languages.

  ▸ *DynaText Viewer Software* — Enables you to read, search, annotate, and print on-line documentation from the Windows or Macintosh clients.

The on-line documentation can be accessed by using three different methods:

- *From the network* — Once the on-line document collection and viewer have been installed on the server, they can be accessed by any user (with the appropriate rights) from any workstation.

- *From a stand-alone workstation* — If the document collection and DynaText viewer are installed on a workstation, they can only be accessed by a user on that workstation. This method is faster and more convenient, and the documentation is available when the network is down. A disadvantage is the amount of hard disk space required on the workstation — about 60 MB for each language.

- *From the product CD-ROM* — NetWare 4.11 offers the option of accessing the documentation collection directly from the OS CD-ROM. But, you must install the DynaText viewer on a local or network disk. This way you can mount server's CD-ROM as a NetWare 4.11 volume and allow users to run the documentation right off the central server device. This conserves disk space, but negatively impacts performance.

DYNATEXT PREREQUISITES

Following are the prerequisites for installing NetWare 4.11 on-line documentation:

- A minimum of 60 MB of free server hard disk space if you plan to install both the documentation database and the DynaText viewer. Keep in mind that this is for one language only. Each additional language requires approximately 60 MB of additional hard disk space.

- A minimum of 6 MB of free server hard disk space if you plan to install the DynaText viewer only. If you install more than one viewer language, each additional language requires an extra 2 MB of hard disk space. In this configuration, the document collection is read directly from the product CD-ROM.

▸ The server or workstation must have a CD-ROM drive that can read ISO 9660-formatted CD-ROM disks.

▸ A minimum of 4 MB of RAM (although 8 MB is recommended) for any workstation using the Windows DynaText viewer. Plus you need one of the following GUI operating systems: MS Windows 95, Windows 3.11, or OS/2 V.21x. Finally, your workstation display card and monitor must support at least VGA or Super VGA graphics.

DYNATEXT PLANNING

NetWare 4.11 on-line documentation can be accessed from any of the following GUI clients:

▸ Microsoft Windows 95 or 3.1

▸ IBM OS/2 running WIN-OS/2

▸ Apple Macintosh

If you want DynaText to be accessed by all users, you'll need to reference the documentation from the SYS:DOCS.CFG file. This is created during the DynaText installation process. You also must be sure that users have access to the SYS:DOC (documentation) and SYS:DOCU (viewer) directories.

On the other hand, if you want the documentation restricted to only a few people, you should reference the documentation from a platform-specific configuration file and install the software on a local hard disk or secure network directory. Also, you can use SETUPDOC.EXE to configure the viewers on different workstations, and select more than one collection on different servers. This ensures that each user has a specific configuration.

NetWare 4.11 on-line documentation can be installed in the following languages: English, French, German, Italian, and Spanish. Each of these languages is installed into a language-specific directory under SYS:DOC. The command for installing different languages depends on the type of workstation.

As we learned earlier, NetWare 4.11 DynaText can be accessed in one of three different ways — from the network, from a stand-alone workstation, or from the product CD-ROM. Each method has its own advantages and disadvantages:

▸ If you access the documentation directly from the network, you lose access when the network goes down. However, you save disk space on the client and maintain centralized DynaText management control.

▸ If you access the documentation from a stand-alone workstation, the documentation is available if the server is down. However, this costs 60 MB of client disk space for each language and requires local user management.

▸ If you install the DynaText viewer on a local or network hard disk and leave the documentation on the product CD-ROM, you save disk space. However, you will notice a marked decrease in access performance.

Speaking of installation, let's take a closer look at the detailed steps for installing NetWare 4.11 on-line DynaText documentation.

QUIZ

Here's a doozie to finish off what's left of your brain. Andy, Brad, Cole, and Doug all live in different houses on River Road.

By a curious coincidence, the age of each man is either seven greater or seven less than the number of his house. All of them are more than 15 years old and less than 90; all their ages are different.

Andy said that the number of Brad's house was even and Brad remarked that the number of his house was greater than that of Doug's. "My age," he added proudly, "is a perfect cube."

Cole said that the number of his house was greater by three than Andy's, and that Doug's age was an exact multiple of Andy's age.

Doug, who has an unfortunately habit of complicating things, said that Brad's age was either 27 or an even number other than 64. "Furthermore," he commented, "Cole does not live at number 19."

Unfortunately, these remarks were not all true. It was interesting to note that remarks made by those who lived in even-numbered houses were false and remarks made by those who lived in odd-numbered houses were true.

What are their ages and the numbers of their houses? Why do you care?

(Q6-6)

DYNATEXT INSTALLATION STEPS

Now it's time for the "nuts and bolts" of DynaText installation. Before you begin, be sure that your server and workstation meet the minimum hardware requirements listed earlier for DynaText, and that you are logged into the network as the Admin user. Here we go.

Step 1 • Execute the SETUPDOC.EXE file. Insert the Novell IntranetWare/NetWare 4.11 Online Documentation CD-ROM in your workstation's CD-ROM drive. Click on the Windows 95 Start button, then click on the Run button. Type **D:\SETUPDOC** (or the appropriate drive letter for your CD-ROM drive), then click on OK.

Step 2 • Install the NetWare document collections on your server hard drive. Click on the Document Collections Install button. Select D:\DOC (or the appropriate drive letter for your CD-ROM) as the source path for the documentation and click on OK. Select LABS-SRV1\SYS:DOC as the destination directory on your server and click on OK. All the available document collections in English will probably be selected by default. Click on OK to accept the default. A screen will be displayed listing the source directory, destination directory, and document collections you have selected. Click on OK to confirm your selections. The on-line documentation will then be copied to the selected destination directory. When all the documentation files have been copied to the server hard disk, a message will be displayed advising you that the documentation collections have been successfully installed. Click on OK.

Step 3 • Install the DynaText Viewer on your workstation hard drive. Click on the DynaText Viewer Install button. Select D:\DOCVIEW (or the appropriate drive letter for your CD-ROM drive) as the source path and click on OK. Select C:\DOCVIEW (or the appropriate letter for your workstation hard drive) as the destination directory and click on OK. Select the language you want to use for the DynaText Viewer and click on OK. A screen will be displayed listing the source directory, destination directory, and language you selected. Click on OK to confirm your selections. The DynaText viewer files will then be copied to the selected destination directory. When all the view files have been copied to your workstation hard disk, a message will be displayed asking whether to create a Viewer icon. Click on Yes to create the icon. A message will then be displayed indicating that the DynaText viewer has been successfully installed. Click on OK. A message will then be displayed indicating that you have installed at least one documentation collection and at least one viewer. Click on Continue to return to the main setup window.

Step 4 • Configure the viewer to access the documentation collections. Click on Configure Viewer. Select C:\DOCVIEW (or the appropriate drive letter for your hard drive) and click on Configure. Click on Advanced to configure the shared copies of the document collections. Click on <Create>, then click on Select. You will then be asked to select the directory for the new list file. Select LABS-SRV1\SYS:PUBLIC and click on Create, then select the + file and click on Select. The list of available document collections will be listed at the bottom of the screen. Review the list carefully to locate each of the document collections that you just installed on your server, then double-click on each. (If you accidentally select one you don't want, click on it in the upper window to deselect it.) When all the document collections you want are in the upper window, click on Save, then click on Exit. Click Yes to when asked if you really want to quit.

Step 5 • Launch the DynaText Viewer.

a. To launch the DynaText viewer, click on the Windows 95 Start button, next click on Program, then Click on Novell Online Documentation, and, finally, click on DynaText for Windows.

b. Click on the ? button to learn about how to use the DynaText viewer. When you're finished, click on the close button in the upper-right corner of the help screen. (Be sure that you select the correct close button. Otherwise, you will accidentally exit the DynaText viewer itself.)

   c. Use the DynaText viewer to find information about the new features in IntranetWare. (Hint: Double-click on the New Features manual in the title Window, then type **NetWare 4.11** in the Find field, and press Enter. You'll find that all occurrences of "NetWare 4.11" will be highlighted. Click on the forward and backward arrow buttons to locate each occurrence.)

You've done it. The servers and electronic documentation are ready to go. Isn't technology wonderful?

ZEN

"Goodnight stars. Goodnight air."

Margaret Wise Brown

That's it. Mondays aren't so bad! Look, you made it through two server installs and three optional products, and it's not even time to go. It's only 4:59 p.m. I wonder who needs "resuscitation" now — you or the server?

We have been through a lot together today. We created a life — the NetWare 4.11 server. It all started with a review of the NetWare 4.11 Installation prerequisites and some hardware and software requirements. Then we got our feet wet with the easier simple installation method. We strolled through the six stages of server installation with the guidance of INSTALL.BAT and INSTALL.NLM. It was kind of nice letting the server make all the tough decisions.

Unfortunately life isn't always so simple; sometimes it needs to be "customized!" In the second NetWare 4.11 install, we explored all 21 steps in excruciating detail — ouch! You probably learned more about SERVER.EXE, HAM drivers, License diskettes, and time zones than you ever wanted to. But that's the price for knowledge. Besides, who else is going to save the Earth?

That's not all. You also learned about DynaText installation.

Well, that just about does it. It's 5:00 p.m. and time to go home. You should feel proud about what you accomplished today. I wonder what tomorrow has in store for you?

EXERCISE 6-1: CHOOSING THE CORRECT INSTALLATION METHOD

Read each of the scenarios listed here and indicate which NetWare 4.11 installation method (Simple or Custom) you would recommend.

SCENARIO 1

A CAD/CAM software developer wants to install NetWare 4.11 on a 133-MHz Pentium that has 64 MB of RAM and four 1.2 GB hard disks. The network designers use Ethernet thick cabling as a backbone and Ethernet thin cabling between workstations. The development firm has Silicon Graphics and Sun workstations, as well as PCs. Which installation method would you recommend for this company?

SCENARIO 2

A dentist's office has a 486/66 server with 32 MB of RAM and a 510-MB disk. The office is wired for Ethernet 10Base-T and uses 386- and 486-based PCs. Which installation method would you recommend for this office?

SCENARIO 3

A busy medical corporation with multiple hospital and medical clinic locations wants to install a series of NetWare 4.11 servers at its various locations. The corporate office needs to communicate with each of the hospital and clinic locations, as well as with its major suppliers. Because hard disk reliability is important, each of the hard disks will be mirrored. Which installation method would you recommend for this corporation?

See Appendix C for answers.

CASE STUDY: CUSTOM INSTALLATION FOR ACME

Now that you've learned everything there is to know about NetWare 4.11 installation, it's time to tackle ACME. As its resident CNE, it's your responsibility to install all 51 of ACME's servers. Happy, happy, joy, joy!

I know it seems like a daunting task, but just like anything, we'll take it one step at a time. After all, this is why they pay you the big bucks. Let's start with the first server in NORAD at the Labs division. Albert Einstein will be proud.

STAGE 1: PREPARE THE SERVER HARD DISK

a. *Step 1:* Configure the server DOS partition.

(1) Back up existing data. Choose a computer to be used as the server and make at least two verified backup copies of all data. (You never can be too careful. Remember that all existing data on this computer's hard disk will be destroyed during the server installation process!)

(2) Create a boot diskette. Insert a blank diskette in drive A:. Make it bootable by typing **FORMAT A: /S**. After it is formatted, copy the following files to it.

(a) Required files: C:\DOS\FDISK.EXE, C:\DOS\FORMAT.COM, the appropriate CD-ROM drivers, plus any other drivers that your computer needs in order to operate properly. (Be sure that you make a printout of your AUTOEXEC.BAT and CONFIG.SYS so that you can see the proper syntax for executing each driver.)

(b) Optional files: C:\DOS\EDIT.COM and C:\DOS\MEM.EXE.

(3) Use FDISK to delete existing partitions and create a 15 MB DOS partition. (The directions listed below were designed for use with MS-DOS v6.2. The steps required for your version of DOS may differ.)

(a) Display the existing partitions. Be sure the bootable disk you made in the previous step is in drive A:. Type **A:** and press Enter to switch to the floppy drive. Type **FDISK** and press Enter to execute the FDISK command. Type **4** and press Enter to select the Display Partition information option. Note the number and type of partitions that exist on your hard disk. Press Esc to return to the previous menu.

(b) Delete a non-DOS partition. To delete a non-DOS partition, type **3** and press Enter to choose the "Delete Partition or Logical DOS Drive" option. Type **4** and press Enter to choose the Delete Non-DOS Partition option. When you are prompted, key in the number of the non-DOS partitions to be deleted (which will probably be "**2**") and press Enter. Type **Y** and press Enter when you are asked if you wish to continue. Note the number and type of partitions remaining. Press Esc to return to the FDISK Options menu. At this point, the only partition remaining should be your DOS partition. If there are Extended, Logical, or Non-DOS partitions remaining, execute the appropriate menu choices to delete them.

(c) Delete the primary DOS partition. Type **3** and press Enter to select the Delete Partition or Logical DOS Drive option. Type **1** and press Enter to select the Delete Primary DOS Partition option. When you are asked what primary DOS partition to delete, type the number of the Primary DOS partition and press Enter. When you are asked for the volume label of the Primary DOS partition, type the volume label and press Enter. (Press Enter alone if the partition has no volume label.) When you are asked whether you are sure, type **Y** and press Enter. Press Esc to return to the FDISK Options screen.

(d) Create a 15-MB DOS partition. Type **1** and press Enter to select the "Create DOS Partition or Logical DOS Drive" option. Type **1** and press Enter to select the Create Primary DOS Partition option. Type **N** and press Enter when you are asked whether you wish to use the maximum available size for a Primary DOS

Partition. Type **15** and press Enter when you are asked to enter a partition size in megabytes or percentage of disk space. (It will assume that you are entering the number in megabytes if you don't use a percent sign.)

You may notice that the installation program creates a partition that is slightly larger than 15 MB. Press Esc to return to the FDISK options screen. Type **2** and press Enter to select the Set Active Partition option. Type **1** and press Enter when you are prompted for the number of the partition you want to make active. Press Esc to return to the FDISK Options screen. Press Esc again to exit the FDISK utility.

When you are prompted to insert a system diskette into drive A: and strike a key, just press any key. This will cause the computer to reboot. When you are prompted for the correct date, key in the correct date if an incorrect one is displayed and press Enter. (Press Enter alone to accept the default.) When you are prompted for the correct time, key in the correct time if an incorrect one is displayed and press Enter. (Press Enter alone to accept the default.) If this is your only server and the date and/or time listed is incorrect, this would be a good time to change the "hardware" date and time using the CMOS setup program built into your computer. (If you have a relatively recent version of DOS, you may find that the DATE and TIME commands do this for you.) See the manual that came with your computer for the exact procedure.

(4) Format the DOS partition and make it bootable. Type **FORMAT C: /S** and press Enter to format the DOS partition and install system files. Type **Y** and press Enter when you are asked whether to proceed with the format. Type **ACME001** and press Enter when you are asked for a volume label.

(5) Install and configure the CD-ROM drive as a DOS device. Copy the CD-ROM drivers (plus other drivers, if any) from your boot diskette to drive C:, and as well as the AUTOEXEC.BAT and CONFIG.SYS

files. Be sure these configuration files contain only those statements that are absolutely necessary. Also, be sure they are configured to allow the CD-ROM to function as a DOS device. Next, insert the Novell IntranetWare/NetWare 4.11 Operating System CD-ROM in your CD-ROM drive, then type **D:** (or the appropriate drive letter) and press Enter to switch to the CD-ROM drive.

b. *Step 2:* Select the server language and type of installation. Type **INSTALL** and press Enter to execute the INSTALL.BAT file on the CD-ROM. A menu will be displayed allowing you to select the language to be used during the installation process. Choose the "Select This Line to Install in English" option from the NetWare Install menu and press Enter if you want to display the installation instructions in English. Choose one of the other five options (Deutsche, Español, Français, Italiano, or Portuguese) and press Enter if you want the installation instructions to be displayed in another language. A Novell Terms and Conditions screen will appear. Read each screen of this multiscreen agreement carefully, pressing Enter (or any other key) at the bottom of each screen in order to continue to the next screen. Next, choose the NetWare Server Installation option from the Select the Type of Installation Desired menu and press Enter. Then select the NetWare 4.11 option from the Choose the Product You Want to Install menu and press Enter. Finally, select the Custom Installationoption from the Select the Type of Installation You Are Performing menu and press Enter.

c. *Step 3:* Assign the server name. Type **LABS-SRV1** as the server name and press Enter.

d. *Step 4:* Assign the IPX internal network number. A randomly generated internal IPX network number will be displayed. To replace it, type **BADCAFE** and press Enter.

e. *Step 5:* Copy the server boot files to the DOS partition. The default source and destination paths for the server boot files will be displayed. Press Enter to accept the defaults. The system will then begin copying a number of server boot files from the CD-ROM to the C:\NWSERVER directory on the DOS partition.

f. *Step 6:* Assign the locale configuration and filename format. A locale information screen will be displayed on the screen. Defaults include:

▸ Country Code: 001 (United States)

▸ Code Page: 437 (United States English)

▸ Keyboard Mapping: None

If you reside outside of the United States, modify the country code, code page, and keyboard mapping parameters accordingly. Select the "Press <Enter> here to continue" option and press Enter to continue.

If you had executed the INSTALL utility using the */file_sys* switch when you began the installation procedure, you would be asked to select the filename format. Since we didn't, NetWare 4.11 will automatically assign the DOS filename format (which is the default).

Next, you will be given the opportunity to add special startup SET commands. (If you read the screen, you'll notice that the SET Buffers Below 16 Meg=200 statement has been added to your STARTUP.NCF file. Some devices that require an ASPI driver for disk, CD-ROM, or tape drives require additional buffers. You can remove this command if you're sure that the drivers are you loading do not require these buffers. Also, some drivers can't handle more than 16 MB of RAM. Because of this, you may need to add the SET Auto Register Memory Above 16 Megabytes = OFF to your STARTUP.NCF file. In this case study, we are not going to add any startup SET commands. Select No and press Enter when you are asked if you want to include any.

Finally, you will be asked to confirm whether AUTOEXEC.BAT should be modified to execute SERVER.EXE. When the system asks you whether it's okay to have AUTOEXEC.BAT automatically execute SERVER.EXE, choose No and press Enter. (This is the best choice when you're doing practice installations. If you were familiar with the NetWare 4.11 installation procedure and were installing a production server, you would probably want to indicate Yes instead.)

STAGE 2: RUN SERVER.EXE

a. *Step 7:* Start the server. The SERVER.EXE file will be executed automatically. (The system essentially does a warm boot as it flushes the DOS operating system from server RAM and replaces it with the NetWare 4.11 operating system.) The system will load the INSTALL.NLM utility.

STAGE 3: LOAD THE NETWARE 4.11 DRIVERS

a. *Step 8:* Load and configure the server hard disk and CD-ROM driver(s). The INSTALL utility will attempt to detect the hardware in your server and select the appropriate disk, CD-ROM, and LAN drivers. It will then list the ones it has selected for you on the "Choose the Server Drivers — Summary" screen. In Step 8, we are only concerned with hard disk and CD-ROM drivers. (We will worry about LAN drivers in Step 9.) You'll notice that the Driver Names column contains only the first two drivers of each type.

(1) Use the arrow keys on your server keyboard to highlight the disk and CD-ROM driver(s) listed, then press Enter to see a complete list of all disk and CD-ROM drivers selected.

(2) Select the Edit/view parameters for a selected driver option from the Additional Driver Actions menu and press Enter. Select the first disk/CD-ROM driver and press Enter to view its parameters. If the parameters look correct, select the "Save parameters and Continue" option from the "Driver... Parameters Actions" menu and press Enter. (If you don't have a clue, just keep your fingers crossed and assume they are correct for now.) Repeat this procedure for each driver listed.

(3) When you are finished viewing the parameters for the selected driver(s), choose the Continue Installation option from the Additional Drivers Actions menu and press Enter.

b. *Step 9:* Load and configure the appropriate server LAN driver(s).

(1) Use the arrow keys on your server keyboard to highlight the LAN driver(s) listed and press Enter to see a complete list of LAN drivers selected. (There may be only one.)

(2) First, select the Edit/View Parameters for a Selected Driver option from the Additional Driver Actions menu and press Enter. Select the first LAN driver and press Enter to view its parameters. If the parameters look correct, select the Save Parameters and Continue option from the Board... Driver... Actions menu and press Enter. (If you don't have a clue, just keep your fingers crossed and assume they are correct for now.) Repeat this process for any additional drivers that may be listed.

(3) When you are finished viewing the parameters for the selected drivers, choose the Continue Installation option from the Additional Drivers Actions menu and press Enter. Finally, select the Continue Installation option from the Driver Actions menu and press Enter.

(4) The INSTALL utility will then attempt to detect the appropriate protocols for each LAN driver. Select the View/Modify Protocol Settings from the Protocol Options menu and press Enter. Select the IPX protocol and press Enter. You'll notice that if you are using Ethernet, the install program will have selected both the Ethernet 802.2 and 802.3 frame types by default. If you know that you will not have any pre-NetWare 3.12 servers on your network, select the Ethernet 802.3 frame type and press Enter. Then, select Yes and press Enter when asked if you want to deselect the frame type. Press Esc or F10 to return to the previous screen. Finally, select the Continue with Installation option from the Protocol Options menu and press Enter to continue.

THE BRAIN

If you selected the TCP/IP transport protocol when configuring your LAN driver(s), you will be given the opportunity to determine whether to install the optional NetWare/IP product. Refer to the *Novell NetWare 4.11 IP Administrator's Guide* **for further information.**

STAGE 4: INSTALL.NLM

a. *Step 10:* Configure the CD-ROM as a DOS or NetWare device. A warning may be displayed advising you that there may be a conflict with between the DOS CD-ROM driver and the NetWare version of the same driver. Unless you know for certain that there is a conflict, you'll probably just want to keep your fingers crossed and select the "Use the CD-ROM to Get Drivers" option from the "Select an Action" menu and press Enter. You will probably be able to continue normally despite the warning. If your keyboard locks up, it will probably means that there is a conflict. If this happens, reboot the computer and start the installation from scratch — choosing the alternate menu option when you get to this menu.

b. *Step 11:* Create NetWare disk partition(s). Select the Manually option from the Create NetWare Disk Partitions menu and press Enter. Select the "Create, Delete, and Modify Disk Partitions" option from the "Disk Partition and Mirroring Options" menu and press Enter. Select the Device #1 entry from the Available Disk Drives menu and press Enter. Select the Create NetWare Disk Partition option from the Disk Partitions Options menu and press Enter. Press F10 or Esc to accept the default values. When you are asked whether to create the NetWare partition, select Yes and press Enter. If you look at the information on the top of the screen, you'll notice that the NetWare partition now occupies all the remaining space on the disk that is not in use by the DOS partition. Press Esc to return to the previous menu. Select "Continue with Installation" from the "Disk Partition and Mirroring Options" menu and press Enter. Read the information that is displayed on the screen and press Enter.

c. *Step 12:* Create the NetWare 4.11 volume(s):

(1) Create the SYS: volume. Highlight the SYS: volume and press F3 or Ins to be given the opportunity to modify its size. Select the Device 0, Segment 0 entry from the Volume Disk Segment List and press Enter. Key in a number that is approximately equal to half of the disk segment size listed, and press Enter. (Be sure that the number you enter is greater than or equal to 75.) Press F10 or Esc to save the new disk segment size.

(2) Create the VOL1: volume. Select the Device 0, Segment 1 entry from the Volume Disk Segment List and press Enter. When you are asked what you'd like to do with the new segment, select "Make this Segment a New Volume" and press Enter. Type **VOL1** in the disk segment volume name field and press Enter. Press F10 or Esc to save the changes and accept the disk segment size displayed on the screen. (This will assign all remaining free disk space to the VOL1: volume.) Press F10 or Esc to return to the Manage NetWare Volumes screen.

(3) Configure file compression, block suballocation, and data migration. Select the VOL1: volume and press Enter. This case study assumes that you will be using Novell's High Capacity Storage System (HCCS) in the future. If so, Novell recommends that you turn file compression and block suballocation off and data migration on. Select the File Compression field and press Enter twice to toggle the field to OFF. Select the Block Suballocation field and press Enter twice to toggle the field to OFF. You'll get a warning advising you that it's best to have block allocation set to ON. Press Enter to indicate that you have read the warning, then select Yes and press Enter when asked whether to turn off block suballocation. Select the Data Migration field and press Enter twice to toggle the field to ON. Now that you know how to change these parameters, change them back to their original settings, then press Esc to return to the Manage NetWare Volumes screen. Press F10 to save the volume changes and continue. Select Yes and press Enter when you are asked whether to save volume changes.

d. *Step 13:* Reestablish the server-to-server connection (conditional). If you were installing across the network, you'd reestablish your server-to-server connection at this point. Ignore this step, because in this case study you are installing from CD-ROM.

e. *Step 14:* Select optional NetWare file groups. You will find that the NetWare 4.11 installation program skips this step and makes the appropriate decisions for you.

The system will then display a default source path for the "preliminary" (pre-installation) files. Press Enter to accept the default. The system will then automatically copy the appropriate files to the SYSTEM and LOGIN directories on the SYS: volume.

STAGE 5: INSTALL NOVELL DIRECTORY SERVICES (NDS)

a. *Step 15:* Install NDS. When you are asked whether this is the first NetWare server (in this tree), select Yes, this is the First NetWare Server and press Enter. When you are asked to enter the name for this Directory tree, type **ACME_TREE** and press Enter. Next, select the appropriate time zone for the server and press Enter. (For example, this server is located in Colorado, so we'll select United States of America, Mountain Time.) Review the information on the Time Configuration Information screen, then press F10 to save the time parameters and continue.

Next you will be asked to supply an NDS context for this server.

Type **ACME** in the Company or Organization field and press Enter. Type **NORAD** in the Level 1 Sub-Organizational Unit (optional) field and press Enter. Type **LABS** in the Level 2 Sub-Organizational Unit (optional) field and press Enter. Move the cursor down to the Password field and type a password that you are sure you will remember and press Enter. When you are prompted, type the same password a second time and press Enter. Select Yes and press Enter when you are asked whether to save Directory information and continue.

At this point, NDS will automatically be installed on the server. When the Directory tree name, Directory context, and administrator name are displayed on the screen, note them for future reference (along with the Admin password chosen earlier), then press Enter.

b. *Step 16:* License the NetWare 4.11 operating system. When you are prompted, insert the IntranetWare/NetWare 4.11 License disk that contains SERVER.MLS in drive A: and press Enter.

6. CREATE SERVER STARTUP FILES

a. *Step 17:* Create/modify STARTUP.NCF and AUTOEXEC.NCF startup files. The proposed STARTUP.NCF file will be displayed on the screen. Review the file, then press F10 to accept the default values. Select Yes and press Enter when you are asked whether to save the new STARTUP.NCF file. The proposed AUTOEXEC.NCF file will be displayed next. Review the file, then press F10 to accept the default values. Select Yes and press Enter when you are asked whether to save the new AUTOEXEC.NCF file.

b. *Step 18:* Copy the SYSTEM and PUBLIC files to the SYS: volume. At this point, the system will automatically copy the main SYSTEM and PUBLIC files from the CD-ROM to the SYS: volume. (Interestingly, you may find that the time bar says that file copying is 100 percent complete long before it actually is. If so, just wait until the process is complete.

c. *Step 19:* Perform other installation options. Ignore this step. Select the Continue Installation option from the Other Installation Actions menu and press Enter.

d. *Step 20:* Complete the installation. At this point, an information screen will be displayed. Read the information that is displayed on the screen (for future reference) and press Enter to exit to the system console screen.

· · · · ·

e. *Step 21:* Boot the server using the STARTUP.NCF and AUTOEXEC.NCF files. Make sure that you have removed the IntranetWare/NetWare 4.11 license disk from drive A:. Type **DOWN** and press Enter to down the server, then type **EXIT** and press Enter to exit to the DOS prompt. Reboot the server. Finally, type **CD \NWSERVER** and press Enter to switch to the NWSERVER directory, then type **SERVER** and press Enter to reload the NetWare 4.11 operating system.

Congratulations — you have just installed a NetWare 4.11 server using the Custom Installation option. How do you feel?!!

CASE STUDY: CUSTOM INSTALLATION FOR AN EXISTING SERVER

Good work. That's one down and 50 to go. Well, not really. Fortunately, some of the ACME scientists brought their own IntranetWare servers with them. So, instead of installing all of them from scratch, you've got a little bit of a head start.

Of course, it's still Monday, so you can't expect too many miracles. The servers still need to be reinstalled (wrong NDS tree), but you can skip a few early steps. Following is a detailed walk-through for the first "new, yet used" NetWare 4.11 server.

STAGE I: PREPARE THE SERVER HARD DISK

a. *Step 1:* Configure the server DOS partition.

(1) Remove Directory Services from the server. At the server console, type **LOAD INSTALL** and press Enter. Select Directory Options from the Installation Options menu and press Enter. Select the "Remove Directory Services from this Server" option from the Directory Services Option menu and press Enter. Read the warning displayed on the screen, then press Enter to continue. Select Yes and press Enter when asked to remove Directory Services. Key in the Admin password when prompted, then press Enter. Read the warning screen that is displayed, then press Enter to continue. Select Yes and press Enter when asked whether to remove Directory Services anyway. Read the warning screen that is displayed (regarding the fact that this is a Single Reference server), then press Enter to continue. A message should be displayed saying that Directory Services was successfully removed. Press Enter to continue. Press ESC to return to the Installation Options menu. Press Alt+Esc to return to the server console.

(2) Delete the SYS: volume. Type **DISMOUNT SYS:** at the server prompt and press Enter. Press Alt+Esc to toggle back to the Installation Options menu. Select Volume Options from the Installation Options menu and press Enter. Select the SYS: volume

and press Del to delete it. Read the warning and press Enter to continue. Select the Yes option and press Enter when you are asked whether to delete the SYS: volume. Next, select the VOL1: volume and press DEL to delete it. Read the warning and press Enter to continue. Select the YES option when asked whether to delete the VOL1: volume and press Enter. Press ESC to save the volume changes and return to the previous list. Select Yes and press Enter when you are asked whether to save volume changes. Read the warnings that is displayed telling you that the SYS: volume does not exist and installation can be completed without it, then press Enter. Select Yes and press Enter when asked whether to save volume configuration information anyway.

(3) Delete the NetWare 4.11 partition. Select Disk Options from the Installation Options menu and press Enter. Select the "Modify Disk Partitions and Hot Fix" option from the Available Disk Options menu and press Enter. Select the Device #1 entry from the Available Disk Drives menu and press Enter. Select the Delete Any Disk Partition option from the Disk Partition Options menu and press Enter. Select the NetWare Partition option from the Available Disk Partitions menu and press Enter. *Do not delete your DOS partition!* Select Yes and press Enter when you are asked whether to delete the disk partition. Press Esc three times to exit the INSTALL utility. Select Yes and press Enter when asked whether to exit INSTALL.

(4) Bring down the server. Type **DOWN** and press Enter to bring down the server. Type **EXIT** and press Enter to return to the DOS prompt.

(5) Delete the NetWare 4.1 boot files from the DOS partition. Type **CD \NWSERVER** and press Enter to switch to the C:\NWSERVER directory. Type **DEL *.*** and press Enter to delete all files in that directory. Type **CD ** and press Enter to switch to the root directory. Type **RD NWSERVER** and press Enter to remove the NWSERVER directory from the root directory of the DOS partition.

b. Continue with *Step 2* of the case study, "Custom Installation for ACME," discussed earlier.

EXERCISE 6-2: MATCHING SERVER STARTUP STEPS

Before we can go on our IntranetWare exploratorium ride, you must pass a little test. Don't worry, you're tall enough. Segregate and order the following Server Startup steps into two groups — "Happens Once" and "Happens Every time." One set occurs only once during initial IntranetWare installation, and the other set occurs every time you start the server. Good luck.

Happens Once	*Happens Every Time*
1.	1.
2.	2.
3.	3.
4.	4.
5.	5.
6.	6.
7.	7.

Create STARTUP.NCF

Start SERVER.EXE

Define server context

Activate IPX internal network number

Run FDISK

Load AUTOEXEC.NCF

Load LAN driver

Define bindery context

Copy SYSTEM and PUBLIC files

Define volume block size

Create server name

Define locale format

License the server

Activate RMF

EXERCISE 6-3: ONE OF THOSE DAYS

Circle the 20 IntranetWare Installation terms hidden in this word search puzzle using the hints provided.

```
F  D  I  S  K  T  S  V  S  B  F  U  E  F  P  Z  M  R
I  N  S  T  A  L  L  N  L  M  Z  L  M  R  E  S  J  G
L  I  C  E  N  S  E  D  I  S  K  E  T  T  E  G  S  D
E  N  V  B  V  L  L  A  F  H  Q  K  H  M  Y  W  B  F
N  S  A  C  W  E  P  A  R  T  I  T  I  O  N  L  V  L
A  T  D  U  T  J  M  V  L  W  F  W  U  O  Y  K  A  A
M  A  Q  Y  T  V  I  B  Q  J  G  A  I  X  C  K  U  B
E  L  J  C  P  O  S  T  A  R  T  U  P  N  C  F  T  W
F  L  O  C  A  L  E  I  N  F  O  R  M  A  T  I  O  N
O  B  P  I  D  U  R  X  U  U  F  J  U  W  R  W  E  L
R  A  L  W  Z  M  V  R  E  V  R  E  S  W  N  D  X  H
M  T  S  U  O  E  E  F  Y  C  B  I  L  E  Y  D  E  I
A  N  B  R  A  T  R  W  E  H  N  C  Q  N  L  D  C  S
T  A  D  M  I  N  E  H  B  E  P  C  A  G  Y  H  B  S
Y  C  B  X  L  E  X  F  G  O  W  T  F  L  X  Y  A  X
P  Y  U  X  E  I  E  S  L  K  E  T  Z  I  R  S  T  V
R  V  W  E  C  L  F  P  T  X  C  Z  D  S  R  Y  J  T
N  J  U  A  K  C  U  S  T  O  M  D  P  H  T  F  Y  S
```

Hints:

1. Name of User object whose password is required to install a server into an NDS tree.
2. DOS configuration boot file that is typically used to execute SERVER.EXE file.
3. NetWare 4.11 configuration file that contains commands to load and bind LAN driver(s).
4. Default media that IntranetWare installation files are shipped on.
5. Device or application that requests services from a server. A workstation is the most common one.
6. Type of NetWare 4.11 installation method that allows you to specify values for most configurable parameters.

7. Online version of Novell product documentation.

8. Default language for installing NetWare 4.11.

9. DOS utility for deleting partitions on the hard disk.

10. Type of format specified during NetWare 4.11 installation — where choices are DOS or NetWare.

11. Batch file used to automated the NetWare 4.11 installation process.

12. NLM that can be used to install optional NetWare 4.11 products.

13. Name of diskette needed for NetWare 4.11 installation.

14. Category of information which includes country code, character code set, and keyboard mapping.

15. Default directory for server boot files located on the DOS partition.

16. Logical division of the server hard disk. A server's internal hard disk will have a DOS and NetWare 4.11 one.

17. File used to load the NetWare 4.11 operating system into server RAM.

18. Type of installation method that uses defaults for most configurable parameters.

19. NetWare 4.11 configuration file that loads disk driver(s).

20. A default one called SYS: is created during the NetWare 4.11 installation process.

See Appendix C for answers.

IntranetWare/NetWare 4.11 Migration

Ready for Migration!

It's Tuesday morning at 9:00. You carefully unlock your office door, and tiptoe across the ominous gray carpet. An eerie sense of destiny fills the room like low-flying fog over the Golden Gate Bridge. As you settle into the familiar Naugahyde of your office chair, you can't shake the frightening sensation from yesterday. It was at this very desk, yesterday, about this time, that your world turned upside down. Your boss dumped *it* on your desk. You wonder if *it* is still alive. You can't torture yourself for another moment; you have to check. You launch from your Naugahyde and make a beeline for the computer room. Excitement swells as you turn the corner, your legs moving you faster than nerdly possible, then bam! It's there. The worm, a colon prompt (:) — aah, victory. Your NetWare 4.11 server is still alive!

Something magical happened yesterday — a new life was born. But that's only the beginning. Remember, ACME has 51 servers to install. Many of them are already breathing, albeit choking on NetWare 3.12. Now, it's Tuesday, and you approach each new day with a renewed vigor. You thirst for more installation. I think you're ready for *migration!*

ZEN

"Every day is a good day!"

Yun-Men

IntranetWare migration is the ultimate achievement in "nerdiness." It's probably the most popular installation method for NetWare 4.11. After all, there are already 5.7 million NetWare servers out there, and no one wants to start from scratch. With migration, existing CNEs can simply transfer bindery information to the new NDS "Cloud." They don't have to repopulate it. Here's how it works:

Installation methods:

- ▶ Installation (Simple) — Start from scratch and create a new NetWare 4.11 server using the Simple Installation option in INSTALL.NLM — which makes a number of assumptions and uses default settings.

- ▶ Installation (Custom) — Start from scratch and create a new NetWare 4.11 server using the Custom Installation option in INSTALL.NLM — which allows greater flexibility in setting various parameters than the Simple Installation.

Upgrade methods:

▶ In-Place Upgrade (from NetWare 2.1x or NetWare 2.2) — Upgrade the server from NetWare 2.1x or NetWare 2.2 to NetWare 3.12 using the 2XUPGRDE.NLM utility. You can then use the Upgrade option in INSTALL.NLM to upgrade the server from NetWare 3.12 to NetWare 4.11.

▶ Installation Program Upgrade — Upgrade an existing server from NetWare 3.1x or NetWare 4 to NetWare 4.11 using the Upgrade option in INSTALL.NLM.

Migration methods:

▶ Migration (Across-the-Wire) — Migrate bindery information and files from a source NetWare 2.1, NetWare 2.2, or NetWare 3.1x server (or a LAN Manager, LAN Server, VINES, or Windows NT server) to a destination NetWare 4.11 server using the DOS Migration utility (MIGRATE.EXE) *or* DS Migrate (based on DS Standard) and NetWare File Migration.

▶ Migration (Same-Server) — Migrate bindery information and files from a source NetWare 2.1, NetWare 2.2, or NetWare 3.1x server (or a LAN Manager, LAN Server, VINES, or Windows NT server) to a destination NetWare 4.11 server using the DOS Migration utility (MIGRATE.EXE) and the Upgrade option in INSTALL.NLM.

If you're starting from scratch (for example, do not currently have a network operating system on this computer), you'll need to perform a complete installation. As you learned in Chapter 6, there are two types of NetWare 4.11 installation: Simple and Custom. During the Simple install, you rely on NetWare 4.11 to make most of the tough decisions. The Custom method, on the other hand, gives you total control of all 21 installation steps. This may be *too much* control for you — don't let it go to your head.

The NetWare 4.11 installation process assumes that you're starting with a "neoteric" server — no users, no files, no communications. NetWare 4.11 upgrade and migration methods, on the other hand, jump in midstream. Using these methods, you're upgrading or migrating an existing server from NetWare 2 or NetWare 3 all the way to IntranetWare. *This is not an upgrade!* From coach to first class is an upgrade, Windows 95 is an upgrade, better carpeting is an upgrade. NetWare 2 or NetWare 3 to IntranetWare is a "new frontier."

Welcome to Tuesday morning.

REAL WORLD

There is, of course, another option. If you don't care about the server bindery information, you can simply COPY the data files from one server to another. To do so, start with a new server and perform a NetWare 4.11 Custom installation from scratch. Next, copy all of the data files from the old server to the new NetWare 4.11 server. This is a quick-and-easy way of migrating to NetWare 4.11; no fuss, no muss. Be aware that if you use this method, however, that the NetWare 2.x or NetWare 3.1x user, printing system, group, and security information will be lost. Sometimes, though, it just feels good to start over.

So, which one's for you? As you can see in Table 7.1, your choice depends entirely on the operating system you are currently running, available hardware, and which IntranetWare features you plan to use (such as block size, block suballocation, compression, and so on). Here are some examples:

- ▶ If you want to start from scratch, do a Simple or Custom installation.

- ▶ If you're moving from NetWare 2 to NetWare 4.11 on the same hardware, use the In-Place Upgrade method.

- ▶ If you're running NetWare 3 or NetWare 4 and plan to use the same hardware, use the Installation Program Upgrade method.

- ▶ If you have an existing NetWare 2.1, NetWare 2.2, or NetWare 3 server (or LAN Manager, LAN Server, VINES, or Windows NT server), and plan to use new hardware, use the Across-the-Wire method.

- ▶ If you have an existing non-NetWare server (running LAN Manager, LAN Server, VINES, or Windows NT), and plan to use the same hardware, use the Same-Server method.

TABLE 7.1

Comparing Different NetWare 4.11 Migration Methods

	SIMPLE INSTALL	CUSTOM INSTALL	IN-PLACE UPGRADE METHOD	INSTALLATION PROGRAM UPGRADE	ACROSS-THE-WIRE MIGRATION	SAME-SERVER MIGRATION
NetWare 2 to NetWare 4.11			X		X	X
NetWare 3 to NetWare 4.11	X	X		X	X	X
NetWare 4 to NetWare 4.11	X	X		X		
Non-NetWare Operating System to NetWare 4.11					X	X

Before we dive into the detailed steps of the various upgrade and migration methods, let's take a long, hard look at the advantages and disadvantages of each method. Study carefully. The choices you make today can irrevocably alter the path of your destiny — or not!

ZEN

"The clearest way into the universe is through a forest wilderness."

John Muir

▶ · ◀

Advantages and Disadvantages of Each Installation Method

Don't jump the gun. I know you're excited about diving into the ACME migration, but hold on for a second. We need to make a rational decision about which migration method is best for us. After all, it's only 9:23 am, and you have all day to get it done. Let's take a closer look at each of our six options:

- ▸ NetWare 4.11 Simple Installation

- ▸ NetWare 4.11 Custom Installation

- ▸ NetWare 4.11 In-Place Upgrade

- ▸ NetWare 4.11 Installation Program Upgrade

- ▸ NetWare 4.11 Across-the-Wire Migration

- ▸ NetWare 4.11 Same-Server Migration

NETWARE 4.11 INSTALLATION (SIMPLE AND CUSTOM)

If you're starting from scratch, the Simple or Custom installation method is best — assuming that you have sufficient hardware and the know-how to pull it off.

As we discussed in Chapter 6, there are two types of NetWare 4.11 Installation: Simple and Custom. During the Simple Install, you rely on NetWare 4.11 to make most of the tough decisions. The Custom method, on the other hand, gives you total control during all 21 installation steps. This may be *too much* control for you — don't let it go to your head. Refer to Chapter 6 for more details.

As you recall, the NetWare 4.11 installation process consists of six stages:

Stage 1 • Prepare the server hard disk.

Stage 2 • Run SERVER.EXE.

Stage 3 • Load the NetWare 4.11 drivers.

Stage 4 • INSTALL.NLM.

Stage 5 • Install Novell Directory Services (NDS).

Stage 6 • Create server startup files.

The NetWare 4.11 Simple and Custom installation methods require either two or three computers: the new server, a workstation running IntranetWare client software, and the existing server (if applicable).

Following is a list of the key advantages associated with the NetWare 4.11 installation method:

▸ You can design your NDS database and file system structure from scratch, for maximum efficiency.

▸ If you want, you can retain your existing NetWare 3 server while setting up and testing the new NetWare 4.11 server — a pilot system.

But the NetWare 4.11 installation is not all "sugar and cream." It does have disadvantages, including:

▸ It's more time-consuming than other methods because you must create all network objects, security, and configurations from scratch.

▸ It requires additional hardware if you're upgrading from an existing server — namely, the new server. This ensures that you retain your old server while installing NetWare 4.11.

You should be an old pro at NetWare 4.11 installation by now. It's always a good idea to set up a pilot system whenever you migrate to a new frontier. For this reason, you may consider starting out with a few scratch installations. Then, when you have it all figured out, upgrade or migrate the remainder of your production servers using the upgrade and migration methods discussed in this chapter. Let's take a look.

NETWARE 4.11 IN-PLACE UPGRADE

The In-Place Upgrade method allows you to upgrade a NetWare 2.1 or NetWare 2.2 server to NetWare 4.11. In order to do this, you'll need a stepping stone. First, upgrade the NetWare 2 partition to a NetWare 3 partition using 2XUPGRDE.NLM. Be careful — reformatting a NetWare partition is dangerous stuff. Now you're halfway there. Next, use the Upgrade option in INSTALL.NLM to upgrade the server from NetWare 3 to NetWare 4.11. No sweat.

THE BRAIN

The 2XUPGRDE.NLM file is available on NetWire.

The beauty of the In-Place Upgrade is that it's *in-place*. This means you only need one computer — the server. You'll need to perform the following steps to complete this upgrade:

- ▸ Verify that the server meets minimum NetWare 4.11 RAM requirements.

- ▸ Back up your NetWare 2.1 or NetWare 2.2 server (both network security and file system information).

- ▸ Upgrade the NetWare 2 file system to NetWare 3.1x using 2XUPGRDE. NLM. The NLM will ask you to specify the size for the DOS partition it will create. It will then go through four phases to transform the NetWare 2 disk partition to a NetWare 3.1x partition: first, the file system is analyzed; second the disks are analyzed; third, the disks are modified; and fourth, the NetWare 2 bindery is converted to a NetWare 3.1x bindery.

- ▸ Use FDISK to create a primary DOS partition and set it as "active," and then format it with FORMAT.

- ▸ Create a boot directory called C:\NWSERVER and copy the boot files to it.

- ▸ Upgrade the operating system to NetWare 4.11 using the Upgrade option in INSTALL.NLM.

I bet you're wondering how the In-Place Upgrade stacks up (pun intended) against other methods. Very well, here are some of its advantages:

- ▸ You can use your existing hardware if it meets the minimum requirements for NetWare 4.11.

- ▸ This method can be used to upgrade NetWare 2.1 and NetWare 2.2 servers to NetWare 4.11 — welcome to the 1990s.

TIP

If the NetWare 2 server you're upgrading uses the Novell's NetWare 2 IDE disk driver and does not contain a DOS partition, you'll find that you're unable to add a DOS partition once the server has been upgraded to NetWare 3. If you attempt to use the DOS FDISK utility to create a DOS partition on an upgraded IDE disk, it will cause the IDE disk driver to obtain head, sector, and cylinder information from the CMOS tables instead of from the disk drive. The resulting difference in parameters may cause data loss or corruption. This problem arises because the NetWare 2 IDE disk driver does not conform to DOS specifications.

If it looks too good to be true, it probably is. The In-Place Upgrade also has some shortcomings:

▸ If the existing NetWare 2.1 or NetWare 2.2 server uses an IDE disk driver and does not have a DOS partition, you won't unable to add one when you upgrade to NetWare 3. Hmmmm.

▸ You won't be able to take advantage of the IntranetWare disk compression or block suballocation features unless you save off the data, re-create the volume, then restore the data. If you turn on block suballocation after the upgrade without following this procedure, it will affect only files saved after the upgrade. This could be a problem.

▸ This method does not allow you to change the volume size. If you must change the volume size after the upgrade is complete, you'll need to save the information to tape, then delete and re-create the volume. Bummer.

▸ Passwords are not preserved during the upgrade of a NetWare 2 server to NetWare 3. (But they are from NetWare 3 to NetWare 4.11.)

▸ If the upgrade fails for any reason, you'll need to restore the server to its original state before starting over. No way.

The In-Place Upgrade is a great way of quickly moving from NetWare 2 to NetWare 4.11 — on the same server. It also enables you to retain all files in their original, pristine state — without risky transfers. Unfortunately, it provides no

· · · · · ·

"escape pod" in case something goes wrong during upgrade (namely, because you're upgrading *the same server* — also known as "In Place"). Be very leery of upgrade and migration methods that don't include an "escape pod." We're talking unemployment line here.

QUIZ

I'm in a poetic mood. There's a puzzle hidden in the following poem — all you have to do is pick a single letter from each line:

My first is in pansy, but not in rose.
My second in run, but not in goes.
My third is in daze, but not in muddle.
My fourth in haze, but not in puddle.
My fifth is in little, also in small,
My last in tumble, but not in fall.
My whole an amusement, so some guess,
To Others, nothing but a mess.

(Q7-1)
(See Appendix C for all quiz answers.)

INSTALLATION PROGRAM UPGRADE

The Installation Program Upgrade method can be used to upgrade a NetWare 3.1*x* or NetWare 4 server to NetWare 4.11 using the Upgrade option in INSTALL.NLM. Like the In-Place Upgrade, this type of upgrade is done *in-place*. This means you only need one computer — the server. But remember: no "escape pod." The main steps that occur during this type of upgrade are as follows:

Step 1 • NetWare 4.11 boot files are copied to the C:\NWSERVER directory on the DOS partition.

Step 2 • Novell Directory Services (NDS) is installed. If the existing computer is a NetWare 3.1*x* server, its bindery information will be converted to NDS format.

Step 3 • NetWare 4.11 SYSTEM and PUBLIC files are copied to the SYS: volume.

SMART LINK

For more step-by-step detail for the NetWare 2 to NetWare 3 upgrade, consult the on-line NetWare 4.11 documentation at http://www.novell.com/manuals.

Some of the advantages of the Installation Program Upgrade method are as follows:

▶ You can use your existing server hardware if it meets the minimum requirements for NetWare 4.11.

▶ It is probably the most convenient upgrade method.

▶ It allows you to use block suballocation and disk compression on server volumes.

Some of the disadvantages of the Installation Program Upgrade method are as follows:

▶ There is a small risk of data loss. For example, if a power outage occurs during the upgrade and your backup is defective, you could lose data (no "escape pod").

▶ This option can't be used to upgrade NetWare 2 servers or non-NetWare servers to NetWare 4.11

▶ If you're reusing the existing NetWare partition, you can't change block size or activate block suballocation or disk compression on a volume without saving off the data, re-creating the volume, and restoring the data.

For all the reasons I outlined in the previous section, the Installation Program Upgrade is probably a little risky. It is, however, very simple. Now let's leave the upgrade section, and explore some cool *migration* methods.

ACROSS-THE-WIRE MIGRATION

The Across-the-Wire Migration method can be used to upgrade NetWare 2.1, NetWare 2.2, or NetWare 3.1x bindery and data files to IntranetWare. It can also be used to upgrade non-NetWare servers (such as LAN Manager, LAN Server, VINES, or Windows NT) to IntranetWare. You can use either the DOS Migration utility (MIGRATE.EXE) *or* DS Migrate (based on DS Standard) and NetWare File Migration for the migration. This method is considered a *migration* rather than an upgrade because information is copied across the network during the process.

SMART LINK

You can download migration programs for non-NetWare operating systems such as LAN Manager, LAN Server, VINES, and Windows NT from the Programs/Novell Consulting section of the Novell Corporate Home Page on the World Wide Web. Check out http://www.novell.com.

You'll need three computers for the Across-the-Wire migration method:

- ▶ Source (existing) server

- ▶ Destination (NetWare 4.11) server

- ▶ Workstation running Client 32 for Windows

When using this method, you'll want to ensure that you have Supervisor (or equivalent) access to the source and destination server and that both servers have different server names and internal IPX numbers.

You can use either the DOS Migration utility (MIGRATE.EXE) *or* DS Migrate (based on DS Standard) and NetWare File Migration for the migration. If you use the DS Migrate and File Migration utilities to perform an Across-the-Wire migration, the main steps you'll need to perform are as follows:

Step 1 • Discover the bindery information from the source server. It will be displayed in a Directory tree.

Step 2 • Model the bindery information to fit the Directory tree on the destination server. This can involve renaming, deleting, or adding users, containers, servers, or volumes. Check out Chapters 8 and 9 for more information on managing the NDS Directory tree.

Step 3 • Configure the tree to include the new NetWare 4.11 server.

Step 4 • Use the File Migration utility to transfer data files to the new NetWare 4.11 server.

Later in this chapter, we'll explore these steps with DS Migrate and File Migration utilities.

TIP

After you confirm that the migration is successful, you should immediately make at least two full backups of your new NetWare 4.11 server, then destroy the bindery on the source server by deleting the NetWare partition, or by reformatting the hard disk. You can then convert the source server into a NetWare 4.11 workstation or server.

Here's a list of some of the advantages of the Across-the-Wire migration:

▶ It's the safest upgrade method because the source server remains intact. This could prove to be especially useful if a power outage or connection loss occurs during the migration (finally, an "escape pod"). This is probably the single most important advantage in the entire Upgrade/Migration process.

▶ You're given the option of determining whether to migrate all or selected information. We'll talk about this in more detail a little later.

▶ Multiple servers can be migrated to a single destination server. This enables you to consolidate the data from older servers to newer, more powerful computers. Great idea!

▸ Data can be moved from an 80286 server running NetWare 2 to a newer Pentium computer running NetWare 4.11, which is a good idea, given the power of NetWare 4.11.

▸ Data from a non-NetWare network operating system can be moved to a NetWare 4.11 server. Look out, NT.

Don't get too excited — the Across-the-Wire migration does have its downside:

▸ Additional hardware is required — such as an extra server.

▸ The workstation running Client 32 for Windows may require a large hard disk, depending on the number of users on the source server.

What if you don't have any additional servers lying around? Fortunately, there's Same-Server Migration to save the day.

SAME-SERVER MIGRATION

The Same-Server Migration method uses the DOS Migration utility (MIGRATE.EXE) and INSTALL.NLM to upgrade a NetWare 2.1, NetWare 2.2, or NetWare 3.1x bindery to NetWare 4.11. It can also be used to upgrade non-NetWare servers (such as LAN Manager, LAN Server, VINES, and Windows NT) to NetWare 4.11.

SMART LINK

You can download migration programs for non-NetWare operating systems such as LAN Manager, LAN Server, VINES, and Windows NT from the Programs/Novell Consulting section of the Novell Corporate Home Page on the WorldWide Web. Check out http://www.novell.com.

You'll find that the Same-Server and Across-the-Wire Migration methods have a number of things in common. For example, you can use the same DOS utility (MIGRATE.EXE) in each case as well as migrating the same type of source servers. So, what's different? Software — the Across-the-Wire Migration method can also be performed using the DS Migrate and File Migration utilities. And hardware — you only need two machines for the Server-Server Migration method: one server and one workstation (running Client 32 for Windows 95 or DOS/Windows 3.1). Here's how to perform a Server-Server Migration:

Step 1 • Back up the data files on the existing server using a backup device.

Step 2 • Use MIGRATE.EXE to copy the bindery from the existing server to the client workstation (running Client 32 for Windows 95 or DOS/Windows 3.1), then convert the bindery into the IntranetWare format — NDS.

Step 3 • Use INSTALL.NLM to install NetWare 4.11 on the existing server.

Step 4 • Restore the data files from the backup media to the new NetWare 4.11 server.

Step 5 • Use MIGRATE.EXE to move the translated bindery information from the client workstation (running Client 32 for Windows 95 or DOS/Windows 3.1) to the new NetWare 4.11 server.

It sounds pretty tricky to me, but all of this hard work will eventually pay off. Here are some advantages of the Same-Server migration method:

▸ No additional hardware is needed if the existing server meets the minimum requirements for NetWare 4.11.

▸ This method can be used to migrate NetWare 2 servers and non-NetWare servers to NetWare 4.11.

Unfortunately, the Same-Server migration method has more disadvantages than advantages:

▸ Possible risk of bindery data loss during the conversion process because the original bindery is destroyed when NetWare 4.11 is installed on the server — oops (remember, no "escape pod").

▸ File attributes may not migrate because data files are backed up and restored rather than migrated.

▸ The DOS workstation may require a large hard disk, depending on the number of users on the source server — no problem.

▸ Not all tape units will work. Many of the new tape units do not look like a DOS device to the computer, thus they cannot be mapped to a DOS drive letter — blame SMS for this.

Well, there you have it: the advantages and disadvantages of the two installation methods, and the four main NetWare 4.11 upgrade and migration methods. Remember, we're not talking simple upgrade here — this is serious business. In the remainder of this chapter, we'll explore detailed steps of the two most popular upgrade and migration methods: the NetWare 4.11 Installation Program Upgrade method and Across-the-Wire Migration method. But first, let's take a quick look at some important upgrade/migration setup tasks — namely, hardware requirements, prerequisites, and preparation.

ZEN

"Man's main task in life is to give birth to himself."

Erich Fromm

▸ · ◂

Before You Begin

NetWare 4.11 upgrades and migrations are a little tricky, and require some critical preplanning. Before you begin an upgrade or migration, you should verify that your hardware meets the minimum requirements for NetWare 4.11. In addition, you'll need to obtain a few prerequisites, including server information, new drivers, NDS data, and the Admin password.

Let's get prepared.

SMART LINK

For a detailed list of Novell-certified network hardware, consult the Novell Lab's Bulletins at http://support.novell.com/sitemap.

HARDWARE REQUIREMENTS

Before you get too excited about the NetWare 4.11 upgrade/migration methods, ensure that the hardware you plan to use meets the following minimum NetWare 4.11 requirements:

▸ An IBM-compatible PC with an 80386, 80486 (SX or DX), or Pentium processor.

▸ A *minimum* of 20 MB of RAM for the basic NetWare 4.11 Operating System (OS) whether you're upgrading/migrating from CD-ROM or across the network.

▸ A *minimum* of 90 MB of free disk space on the hard disk: 15 MB for the DOS partition and 75 MB (preferably 100+ MB) for the NetWare partition (SYS: volume). If you copy all the optional NetWare file groups available with NetWare 4.11 to the server, you'll need up to 160 MB.

REAL WORLD

It appears that in the real world, you actually need a minimum of 90 MB (or more) for a NetWare disk partition in IntranetWare. Of course, we recommend that you make it 200 MB or larger.

▸ An additional 60 MB of free disk space to install the DynaText viewer and NetWare 4.11 documentation. Additional space will be needed if you want to install the documentation in more than one language. If you are low on disk space, you can view DynaText directly from the CD-ROM, rather than storing it on the server hard disk.

- At least one network interface card (NIC).

- The appropriate network cabling and related components (hubs, UPS, and so on).

- If you're installing NetWare 4.11 from a CD-ROM — a CD-ROM drive that can read ISO 9660-formatted CD-ROM disks.

- The appropriate NetWare 4.11 CD-ROMs and license diskette.

THE BRAIN

For more detailed information on calculating the RAM required for NetWare 4.11, refer to Appendix A of the *Novell NetWare 4.11 Upgrade* manual.

UPGRADE PREREQUISITES

Next, you'll need to gather some important prerequisite information before you begin. For example, following is a list of the stuff you'll need before you begin a NetWare 3.12 to NetWare 4.11 upgrade using the Installation Program Upgrade procedure:

- Server name

- IPX internal network number

- Locale information (country code, code page, and keyboard mapping)

- Filename format — DOS (recommended) or NetWare

- Disk driver information (driver name, hard disk controller I/O port, hard disk controller interrupt setting)

- LAN driver information (driver name, location, frame type, network board I/O port address, network board interrupt, network address)

- Directory tree name

▸ Directory tree context of server

▸ Admin username

▸ Admin user password

UPGRADE PREPARATION

Now we're ready to start. Well, not quite ready. The first step in an "NetWare 4.11 upgrade or migration is preparation!" Before you begin anything, you'll need to ensure that you've properly prepared the source server so that only necessary bindery objects and file system contents are upgraded. For example, here's a detailed list of the things you should do before beginning a NetWare 3.12 to NetWare 4.11 upgrade — "Always Be Prepared."

▸ Make sure that the server meets minimum NetWare 4.11 hardware requirements (see the previous list).

▸ Use the DISABLE LOGIN command to prevent new users from logging into the NetWare 3.1x source server. Broadcast a message to all active users on the source server advising them to log off. Make sure that all the users are logged out of the server and confirm that all files (except bindery files) are closed.

▸ When upgrading multiple servers to the same NDS context, consolidate the usernames of users who exist under different names on different servers. Also, check for other types of objects that may have duplicate names (such as groups and print queues).

▸ Ensure that all bindery objects conform to NDS naming standards — the same ones you created in Chapter 4.

▸ Delete any objects and trustee rights that are no longer needed. If the source server is a NetWare 3 server, you can run SECURITY.EXE to obtain important information on account activity and possible security risks. Make a backup of your server, then run BINDFIX.EXE to delete trustee assignments for users who no longer exist.

▶ Clean up the file system. Delete directories, files, and applications that are no longer needed. Rename any DOS directories and files that have long names. Modify your subdirectory tree so that it is no more than 25 levels deep.

▶ Back up your NetWare 3.1x source server in case you accidentally delete or change something you shouldn't have. Oops.

▶ Load MONITOR.NLM and clear all connections.

▶ Using the NetWare 3.12 version of INSTALL.NLM, edit the NetWare 3.12 AUTOEXEC.NCF file to include the appropriate frame type(s) for each Ethernet LAN driver. The default frame type for NetWare 3.12 and IntranetWare is 802.2; the default frame type for NetWare 3.11 is 802.3.

▶ If you are doing an Across-the-Wire migration, your source and destination servers must have different server names and internal IPX numbers. If you change the server name and/or internal IPX number on one or both servers, don't forget to down the server and bring it up again in order for any changes to take effect.

▶ Write down the security information (such as accounts restrictions, user ID, group information, directory and file assignments, and so on) of sample users so that you can use it after-the-fact to determine if the information was upgraded properly.

▶ Bring down the existing server.

▶ Upgrade the server hardware (CPU, RAM, disk space, and CD-ROM drive) as needed.

THE BRAIN

For more information on updated LAN drivers and disk drivers:

▸ **Contact your Novell Authorized reseller or call 1-800-NETWARE for a list of currently supported drivers.**

▸ **Download a list of currently supported drivers from the NetWire Forum on CompuServe or the Web.**

▸ **Call the Novell Labs FaxBack system at 1-800-414-LABS or 1-801-429-5544 for operator assistance to obtain a list of drivers that have been certified as "Yes, Tested and Approved" with NetWare 4.11.**

Well, there you have it. You've been briefed, required, and prepared. Remember, it's Tuesday morning and we have a whole new attitude. Life is our oyster, and it's time to polish the pearl. So, without any further adieu — ready, set, go!

ZEN

"Life is what happens to you while you're busy making other plans."

John Lennon

NetWare 4.11 Installation Program Upgrade

Here's where we start. Welcome to the Installation Program Upgrade forest. This method enables you to upgrade NetWare 3.1x and NetWare 4 servers to NetWare 4.11 without purchasing additional hardware. The main stages involved in this upgrade are as follows:

Stage 1 • Prepare the server hard disk.

Stage 2 • Run SERVER.EXE.

Stage 3 • Load the NetWare 4.11 drivers.

Stage 4 • INSTALL.NLM.

Stage 5 • Install Novell Directory Services (NDS).

Stage 6 • View/modify the AUTOEXEC.NCF file.

I hope these stages look familiar to you. They follow the same general path as the NetWare 4.11 Custom installation. This section explores each of these stages in detail — and their respective 18 steps.

TIP

To avoid NDS base schema conflicts, always upgrade the server holding the master replica of the [Root] partition first.

STAGE I: PREPARE THE SERVER HARD DISK

During this stage, you will perform two full system backups including both network security information (such as the bindery for NetWare 3 servers or the NDS for NetWare 4 servers) and the file system, configure the CD-ROM as a DOS device, run the INSTALL.BAT utility, copy the server boot files to the DOS partition, and select the server locale and filename format. Let's get started.

Step I: Configure the DOS Partition

The first step in the upgrade process is to boot your NetWare 3 server — nice idea. Next, you should make at least two full server backups on tape or another storage medium — which hopefully, you did during the upgrade preparation process. When you generate your backups, be sure to include network security information (such as the bindery for NetWare 3 servers, or NDS for NetWare 4 servers) as well as the file system. Remember, you *will* want to restore your server back to its original state if something goes wrong.

Next, you should install your CD-ROM as a DOS device — using the directions that came with the drive. Don't forget to reboot the server if you make any changes to AUTOEXEC.BAT or CONFIG.SYS. Next, insert the IntranetWare/NetWare 4.11 Operating System CD-ROM in your CD-ROM drive. At the DOS prompt, type **D:** (or the appropriate drive letter) to switch to the CD-ROM drive, then **CD ** to switch to its root directory.

Step 2: Run INSTALL.BAT and Select the Server Language

The next upgrade step involves INSTALL.BAT. It hangs out in the root directory of the NetWare 4.11 CD-ROM. As you learned in the previous chapter, INSTALL.BAT automates most of the installation and upgrade steps. Start it by typing **INSTALL**.

Choosing a NetWare 4.11 Upgrade Language

INSTALL.BAT then calls a program called SELECT.EXE, which responds with a server language screen like the one in Figure 7.1. If you want the installation instructions displayed in English, choose the Select This Line to Install in English option. Otherwise, choose one of the other five language options (Deutsche, Español, Français, Italiano, or Portuguese). A Novell Terms and Conditions screen will appear. Read each screen of this multi-screen agreement carefully, pressing Enter (or any other key) at the bottom of each screen in order to proceed to the next one. Next, you'll be asked which type of installation you'd like. Select the NetWare Server Installation option. Now we're cooking! Select NetWare 4.11 from the Choose the Product You Want to Install menu. As your last configuration task, choose Upgrade NetWare 3.1x or 4.x from the Select the Type of Installation You Are Performing menu, as seen in Figure 7.2. Now we're ready to start the upgrade for real by copying server boot files.

Step 3: Copy the Server Boot Files to the DOS Partition

The first "real" upgrade step involves copying the server boot files to the existing DOS partition. Because NetWare 3 and NetWare 4 use the same partition type as NetWare 4.11, you won't need to create a new DOS partition. You'll just need to copy the NetWare 4.11 server boot files there. First, the upgrade program asks for destination path. Type **C:\NWSERVER.** You will then be asked whether to create the C:\NWSERVER directory. Select Yes.

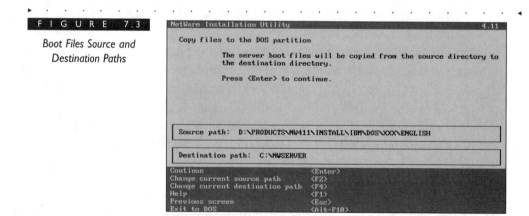

FIGURE 7.2

The NetWare 4.11 Upgrade Screen

```
NetWare Installation Utility                                            4.11

Select the type of installation you are performing

Simple Installation      Install NetWare 4.11 on a new machine, allowing the
                         installation program to make most choices.
                         Note: Press <F1> to see the choices that will be made
                         for you.

Custom Installation      Install Netware 4.11 on a new machine, making choices
                         for such things as code page, network number,
                         installation directory, etc.

Upgrade to NetWare 4.11  Upgrade a machine that currently has either NetWare
                         3.1x or 4.x to NetWare 4.11


                    ┌─────────────────────────────────────┐
                    │ Simple installation of NetWare 4.11  │
                    │ Custom installation of NetWare 4.11  │
                    │ Upgrade NetWare 3.1x or 4.x          │
                    └─────────────────────────────────────┘

Select  <Enter>                              Exit to DOS        <Alt-F10>
Help    <F1>                                 Previous screen    <Esc>
```

At this point, the source and destination paths for the server boot files should be correct. If the source and destination paths listed are correct, press Enter to continue. Otherwise, press F2 to change the source path or F4 to change the destination path. For example, Figure 7.3 shows an example of the source and destination paths for a DOS-based server where the installation language is English and the upgrade is being performed from CD-ROM.

FIGURE 7.3

Boot Files Source and Destination Paths

```
NetWare Installation Utility                                            4.11

Copy files to the DOS partition

           The server boot files will be copied from the source directory to
           the destination directory.

           Press <Enter> to continue.



  ┌─────────────────────────────────────────────────────────────────────┐
  │ Source path:   D:\PRODUCTS\NW411\INSTALL\IBM\DOS\XXX\ENGLISH          │
  └─────────────────────────────────────────────────────────────────────┘

  ┌─────────────────────────────────────────────────────────────────────┐
  │ Destination path:  C:\NWSERVER                                       │
  └─────────────────────────────────────────────────────────────────────┘

Continue                              <Enter>
Change current source path            <F2>
Change current destination path       <F4>
Help                                  <F1>
Previous screen                       <Esc>
Exit to DOS                           <Alt-F10>
```

If the C:\NWSERVER directory doesn't currently exist, you'll be asked whether to create it. Select Yes. If you do, you will then be asked to enter the path for the existing SERVER.EXE file. (If your existing server is a NetWare 3.12 server, this will probably be C:\SERVER.312.) Enter the name of the directory containing the current copy of SERVER.EXE.

INSTALL will then copy a number of server boot files from the CD-ROM to the C:\NWSERVER directory, including SERVER.EXE, disk drivers, LAN drivers, INSTALL.NLM, NWSNUT.NLM, and more. As you can see in Figure 7.4, not all of the existing files are updated. Once the files have been copied, a message pops up listing the drivers that were not updated. Press Enter to continue. (If you need to use any of the drivers listed, be sure that you obtain the latest version of them — then copy them to the C:\NWSERVER directory.)

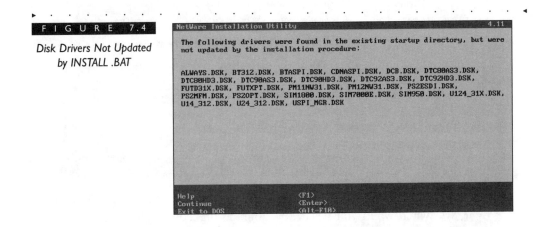

F I G U R E   7.4

Disk Drivers Not Updated
by INSTALL .BAT

REAL WORLD

During the NetWare 4.11 Simple or Custom installation, INSTALL.BAT copies the server boot files to C:\NWSERVER on the DOS partition. During the Installation Program Upgrade, however, you can identify a different destination path, such as C:\SERVER.411. Why, you ask? Because the original NetWare 3 server already has a directory called C:\SERVER.312 that contains the NetWare 3.12 server boot files. By all means, encourage coexistence and stay consistent. If you want, you can indicate C:\SERVER.411 rather than C:\NWSERVER. This way, when NetWare 5 comes along, you can create a similar DOS directory called C:\SERVER.500, or IntranetWare 2 can be placed in the C:\SERVER.IN2. At that point, you'll be the only CNE on the block with all three major NetWare boot file versions on your DOS partition. Very cool!

Step 4: Assign the Locale Configuration and Filename Format

The final disk preparation step focuses on server-specific formatting — namely Locale and Filename Format. It starts with the Locale Configuration screen. As you can see in Figure 7.5, the default values are set up for the United States. If you reside in a different country, here's your chance to modify the Country Code, Code Page, and Keyboard Mapping parameters. When the values listed are correct, select the Press <Enter> Here to Continue field and press Enter to continue

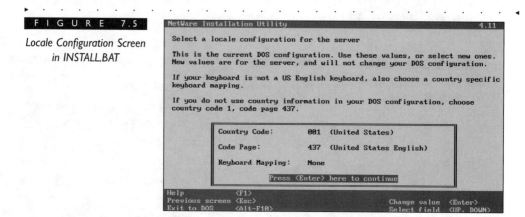

F I G U R E   7.5

Locale Configuration Screen in INSTALL.BAT

Next, is Filename Format. If you had executed the INSTALL utility using the */file_sys* switch when you began the upgrade procedure, you would be asked to select the filename format. Since we didn't, NetWare 4.11 automatically assigns the DOS filename format (which is the default). In case you're curious, there are two types of filename formats from which to choose — DOS and NetWare. The DOS format forces all extended filenames to adhere to strict DOS rules (eight-character names with three-character extensions, all uppercase). The NetWare format, however, gives you move flexibility (lowercase characters). Because most applications and DOS utilities support only DOS filenames, Novell recommends that you use the DOS Filename Format. Remember, we're performing an upgrade, and therefore, the file system already exists. Now you're ready to start SERVER.EXE and switch control to the NetWare partition.

STAGE 2: RUN SERVER.EXE

During Stage 1, we made a minimum of two full server backups (including network security and file system information), configured the CD-ROM as a DOS device, ran the INSTALL.BAT utility, selected the language to be used during the installation process, copied server boot files to the DOS partition, and selected the server locale configuration values. Now it's time for Stage 2.

In Stage 2, INSTALL will automatically execute SERVER.EXE from the C:\NWSERVER directory. This turns control over to the server. Let's take a quick look at the only step in Stage 2.

Step 5: Start the Server

Once the server disk has been prepared, the upgrade program automatically activates SERVER.EXE from the NetWare 4.11 directory — C:\NWSERVER. The server performs a warm boot to flush out DOS and load NetWare 4.11. Once the colon prompt appears, the upgrade program automatically loads INSTALL.NLM. If your server is a symmetrical multiprocessor computer that does not have NetWare SMP installed on it, you will be asked whether to install SMP. If so, select Yes. Otherwise, proceed to Stage 3.

SMART LINK

NetWare 4.11 includes a powerful feature called Symmetric MultiProcessing (SMP) which allows multiprocessing-enabled NetWare Loadable Modules (NLMs) to run across multiple processors and take advantage of the resulting increased processing power. For information on installing this feature, refer to Chapter 8 of the *Novell NetWare 4.11 Supervising the Network* manual or surf the Web to http://www.novell.com/manuals.

STAGE 3: LOAD THE NETWARE 4.11 DRIVERS

In Stage 2, the upgrade program automatically executed SERVER.EXE and shifted control from DOS to NetWare 4.11. In Stage 3, you'll load and configure disk and CD-ROM drivers, possibly reconfigure the internal CD-ROM, and update LAN drivers and name space modules. Let's take a look.

Step 6: Select and Load the Server Disk and CD-ROM Drivers

After executing SERVER.EXE, the upgrade program will list your currently loaded disk and CD-ROM drivers. You will then be allowed to make any changes necessary. With NetWare 4.11, you can either use monolithic disk drivers (.DSK files) or their more-advanced NetWare Peripheral Architecture (NWPA) counterparts. An example of NWPA drivers being selected as disk and CD-ROM drivers is shown in Figure 7.6. In any case, you should make sure you use one driver per controller. When everything's cool, select Continue Installation from the Additional Driver Actions menu.

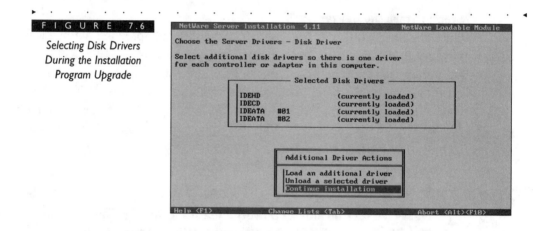

F I G U R E   7 . 6

Selecting Disk Drivers During the Installation Program Upgrade

THE BRAIN

For more information about NetWare Peripheral Architecture (NWPA), see Appendix G of the *NetWare 4.11 Installation* Manual.

Step 7: Configure the CD-ROM as a DOS or NetWare Device (Conditional)

At this point, a warning message may appear indicating a possible conflict with your internal CD-ROM driver, as shown in Figure 7.7. If it happens, calm down — everything is all right. Simply choose Use the CD-ROM to get Drivers option from the Select an Action menu. You should then be able to continue normally, despite the warning. If not, your keyboard will lock up — oops. If this happens, reboot the server and start the Upgrade again — this time choosing Select Only From Previously Copied Driver Files.

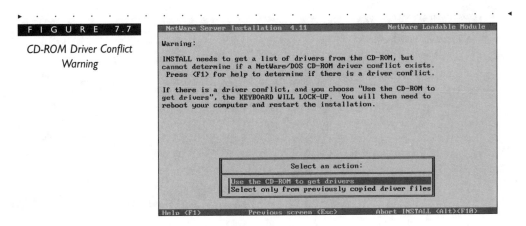

F I G U R E   7.7

CD-ROM Driver Conflict Warning

Step 8: Update LAN Drivers and Name Space Files

Next, another message pops up, indicating that your original AUTOEXEC.NCF file will be scanned for Ethernet frame types. Read the warning shown in Figure 7.8 carefully, then press Enter to continue. Remember, NetWare 3.12 and NetWare 4.11 use a different default frame type (Ethernet_802.2) than NetWare 3.11 (Ethernet_802.3).

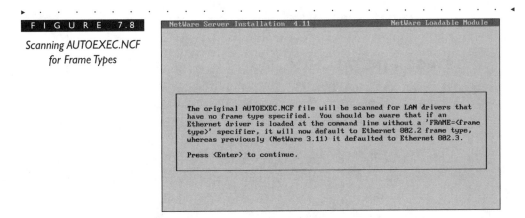

F I G U R E   7.8

Scanning AUTOEXEC.NCF for Frame Types

INSTALL.NLM will then copy a number of LAN drivers and name space modules to your DOS partition. Once the files have been copied, a message will appear that is similar to the one in Figure 7.9, listing the LAN drivers that weren't updated during the upgrade process. Read the message carefully and press Enter to continue. All is well. Are you ready for Stage 4?

FIGURE   7.9

*LAN Drivers Not Updated
by INSTALL.BAT*

```
NetWare Server Installation 4.11                    NetWare Loadable Module




  Note:  An attempt was made to replace drivers in SYS:SYSTEM with more
  current ones.  INSTALL was unable to replace the following driver files:

  NWIPIO.LAN, UBPCETP.LAN, TRXNET.LAN, TOKENDMA.LAN, TOKEN.LAN, TCTOKH.LAN,
  TCNSH.LAN, TCE32MCH.LAN, TCE16MCH.LAN, TCE16ATH.LAN, TCARCH.LAN,
  T30N4X.LAN, T20N4X.LAN, SMCARC.LAN, PCN2L.LAN, NI9210.LAN, NI6510.LAN,
  NI5210.LAN, NE32HUB.LAN, NE1000.LAN, INTEL593.LAN, ILANAT.LAN,
  IBMFDDIO.LAN, IBMETHR.LAN, HP3AT16P.LAN, HP386M16.LAN, HP386E32.LAN,
  HP386A16.LAN, EXP16.LAN, E31N4X.LAN, E21N4X.LAN, DL2000.LAN, DL2.LAN,
  3NW89XR.LAN, 3NW392R.LAN, 3NW391R.LAN, 3CNLAN.LAN, 3C523.LAN, 3C509.LAN,




 Save text to a file <F2>                    Continue        <Enter>
 Help                  <F1>                   Abort INSTALL <Alt><F10>
```

QUIZ

*Before we move on to Stage 4, let's take a little mental break. I'd like you
to meet Guinevere's sister — she's quite an odd bird. She will ride in a
cab, but not a taxi. She will talk to your neighbor, but not to you. She will
eat pasta, but not rice. She will turn left or right, but not around. Will she
like tulips or roses?*

(Q7-3)

STAGE 4: INSTALL.NLM

In Stage 3, we configured the appropriate disk and CD-ROM drivers,
determined whether to continue using the CD-ROM as a DOS device, and updated
the LAN drivers and name space modules. In Stage 4, the upgrade program will
copy the so-called preliminary (pre-installation) files from the CD-ROM to the SYS:
volume, license the NetWare 4.11 operating system, and re-establish a server-to-
server connection (if applicable). This all happens with the help of INSTALL.NLM.
Here's how it works.

Step 9: Copy the Preliminary (Pre-Installation) Files

At this point, the upgrade program will automatically copy the so-called
"preliminary" (pre-installation) files to the server hard disk. These files consist of
those SYSTEM and LOGIN files that are necessary to continue the installation
process. Later, in Step 15, we'll copy the remaining SYSTEM and PUBLIC files to
the SYS: volume.

Step 10: License the NetWare 4.11 Operating System

Now it's time to update the new server license. When you are prompted, insert the IntranetWare/NetWare 4.11 License diskette in Drive A: and press Enter. A greeting pops up stating that the Server Connection License was successfully installed. Press Enter to continue.

TIP

Server connection licenses in NetWare 3 are embedded into the OS file, SERVER.EXE. If you use the same license on two servers, an annoying copyright violation appears on the server console and all workstations — but that's all. NetWare 4.11, on the other hand, relies on a Server License diskette, and its violations are a bit more disruptive. If you share an NetWare 4.11 license on two servers, you'll get copyright violation notices every couple of minutes on both servers and any workstations connected to them. (This will undoubtedly be a real hit with your users.) You'll also get an added little surprise: Your total server licenses will drop to *one!* That's just enough to revalidate the server. Be careful, the server might even put you under citizen's arrest and call in the bounty hunters.

REAL WORLD

Don't tell anybody I told you this, but the NetWare 4.11 Operating System CD actually has two licenses built into it. If you don't have a valid license diskette (for whatever reason), simply press F9 at this point and the Installation Upgrade Program will continue. Here's the trick: Even though the server console displays the message "Maximum connections has been reduced to one," you actually have two user connections available. Go ahead, try it!

Step 11: Load and Bind the LAN Drivers

At this point, a message will be displayed like the one in Figure 7.10, regarding the original AUTOEXEC.NCF file and a temporary version (called AUTOTMP.NCF). Read the message carefully, then press F3 to view the file. Look at the statements that have been disabled (commented out) by the upgrade utility. This includes, for example, those statements that could cause the server to abend (such as Load .NLM). Make any changes necessary, then press F10 to save and execute this file.

F I G U R E   7.10

Information About
AUTOTMP.NCF

Once this happens, INSTALL.NLM will display a screen listing the LAN drivers currently loaded on your server, as seen in Figure 7.11. You will then be given the opportunity to make any changes necessary. You can then select Continue Installation when the LAN driver(s) listed is or are correct. INSTALL.NLM will then load the appropriate LAN driver and bind the communications protocol to it. If multiple LAN drivers have been selected, it will do this for each one. Gee, thanks.

F I G U R E   7.11

Selecting LAN Driver(s)
During Installation Program
Upgrade

Step 12: Re-Establish the Server-to-Server Connection (Conditional)

If you're upgrading over a network, a screen will be displayed listing your username and requesting your password. If so, you'll need to re-establish the server-to-server connection at this point by providing the correct password and pressing Enter twice. Ignore this step if you are running the Installation Program Upgrade from CD-ROM. Now it's the moment you've all been waiting for — NDS installation.

STAGE 5: INSTALL NOVELL DIRECTORY SERVICES (NDS)

In Stage 4, the upgrade program copied the preliminary (pre-installation) files to the server hard disk, licensed the NetWare 4.11 operating system, then re-established a server-to-server connection (if necessary). Now it's time to build the "Cloud." In Stage 5, you get a chance to install Novell Directory Services (NDS) and Time Synchronization. Of course, if you're upgrading an NetWare 4.x server, you can skip most of this step, because NDS is already installed.

Step 13: Install Novell Directory Services (NDS)

This is where the fun begins. If you are upgrading a NetWare 4.x server, you will be informed that you will need to authenticate to the Directory with Supervisory rights in order to continue. The distinguished (complete) name of the Admin user should be listed, as indicated in Figure 7.12. Key in the password for this user to authenticate to the NDS tree. A message will be displayed advising you that Novell Directory Services is already installed on this server and does not need to be re-installed. The message will also say that the Directory schema will be updated, if necessary. Press Enter to continue, then skip to Stage 6.

F I G U R E   7.12

Authenticating to the Directory Tree

```
NetWare Server Installation  4.11                    NetWare Loadable Module

Specify An  Administrator Login Name and Password

You must authenticate to the Directory with
supervisory rights in order to continue.


    Administrator Name: CN=Admin.O=ACME
    Password:           ********


    Password Help

    Enter the password for the Administrator Name above.


                        (To scroll, <F7>-up <F8>-down)

Save field data   <Enter>                      Abort field entry  <Esc>
Help              <F1>                          Abort INSTALL  <Alt><F10>
```

If you're upgrading a NetWare 3.1x server, the upgrade program will display a menu listing any trees it finds. If none is found, it will ask if this is the first NetWare 4 server. Select the ACME_TREE if it exists. Otherwise, select Yes, This is the First NetWare 4.11 Server from the NDS Installation menu — then, type **ACME_TREE** when asked for a tree name.

Next, a list of time zones will appear, somewhat similar to the screen in Figure 7.13. Choose the appropriate one. A Time Configuration window will then be displayed, like the one in Figure 7.14. This screen enables you to customize various Time Synchronization parameters including Time Server type, offset from UTC (Universal Time Coordinated), and Daylight Saving Time options. These are critical NetWare 4.11 configurations. Only make changes if you know what you're doing. When the values listed are correct, press F10 to continue.

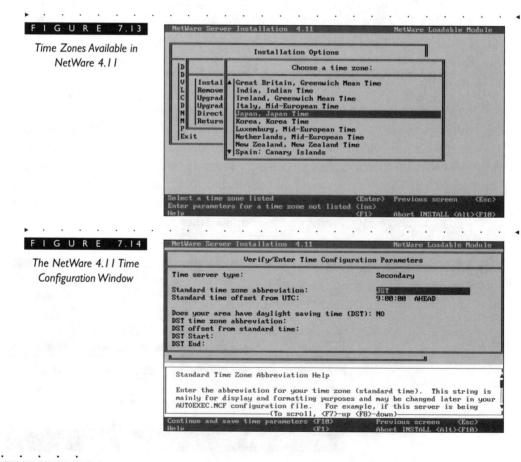

F I G U R E   7.13

Time Zones Available in
NetWare 4.11

F I G U R E   7.14

The NetWare 4.11 Time
Configuration Window

The final NDS configuration is server context, which defines where the server will appear in your NDS tree. Figure 7.15 illustrates the types of information you'd need to provide. For example, if you were upgrading the WHITE-SRV1 server, it would be created with the following context:

```
.OU=WHITE.OU=CRIME.OU=TOKYO.O=ACME
```

F I G U R E   7.15

*Server Context Screen
in the Installation
Program Upgrade*

To create this server context, you would supply the following information:

- ▸ Company or Organization: ACME

- ▸ Level-1 Sub-Organizational Unit: TOKYO

- ▸ Level-2 Sub-Organizational Unit: CRIME

- ▸ Level-3 Sub-Organizational Unit: WHITE

If you want to use more than three levels of Organizational Units (up to 25), you'll need to enter the correct server context manually in the Server Context field. If so, be sure to enter the context using a typeless naming format, with a period (.) between each container. If you want to include a Country object (which is generally *not* recommended), you can enter a country code after the Organization name, separated by a period. For example, if this server is located in the United States, you could add ".C=US" to the end of the server context listed in the Server Context field.

THE BRAIN

Refer to Appendix C of the *NetWare 4.11 Installation* manual for a list of available country codes. See Chapter 4 of this book for a discussion of problems associated with the use of Country objects in NDS trees.

Finally, you'll need to supply the Admin (central administrator) password. This NetWare 4.11 superhero controls access to all branches of the new NDS tree. If this is the first server in the tree, make up a password you're sure you'll remember. When you are prompted, type the password a second time for verification. When you are asked whether to save the Directory information and continue, select Yes.

TIP

By default, **INSTALL.NLM** adds a replica of the partition that contains the server's context if less than three replicas currently exist. If the server is not a NetWare 4 server and contains bindery files (**SYS:SYSTEM\NET$.SYS**), however, a replica will be added regardless of the number of existing replicas. If necessary, you can modify partitions and replicas with **NDS Manager** after the upgrade is complete.

The upgrade program then installs NDS on the server. After the files have been copied, an informational screen appears with the Directory tree name, Directory context, and Administrator name. Note them for future reference, along with the Administrator password that you keyed in earlier.

TIP

IMPORTANT: The Admin password that is assigned during the installation of the first server in an **NDS** tree is also the password used for the bindery **SUPERVISOR** user. If you change the Admin password later (using the NetWare Administrator or **NETADMIN** utilities), the **SUPERVISOR** password will not change until you change it manually using the **SYSCON** or **SETPASS** utility.

Congratulations! The "Cloud" is alive. Now let's finish the remainder of the sky with AUTOEXEC.NCF, NetWare 4.11 SYSTEM and PUBLIC files, Other Installation options, and Rebooting — they're in Stage 6.

STAGE 6: VIEW/MODIFY THE AUTOEXEC.NCF FILE

Welcome to the final stage of NetWare 4.11 Installation Program Upgrade. Now that NDS is in place, it's time to polish off the new server with AUTOEXEC.NCF, the NetWare 4.11 SYSTEM and PUBLIC files, and any optional products you may want. When we're finished, we will down the server, reboot it, and welcome in a new era in computing — the birth of another NetWare 4.11 ACME server. Here are the final five steps.

Step 14: View/Modify the AUTOEXEC.NCF File

Next, a message will be displayed advising you that your AUTOEXEC.NCF file will be scanned to verify Ethernet frame type support, time synchronization parameters, and Directory context information. Read the message, then press Enter to continue. A message will then be displayed explaining changes that may have been made to the AUTOEXEC.NCF file, as shown in Figure 7.16. Read the explanation and press Enter.

FIGURE 7.16

Possible Changes to AUTOEXEC.NCF During Installation Program Upgrade

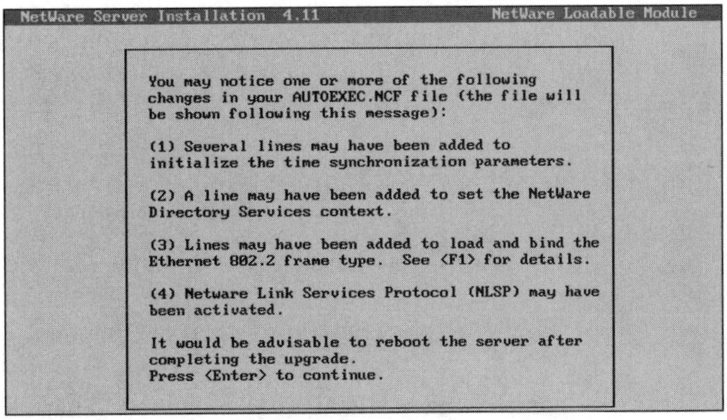

```
NetWare Server Installation  4.11                    NetWare Loadable Module

        You may notice one or more of the following
        changes in your AUTOEXEC.NCF file (the file will
        be shown following this message):

        (1) Several lines may have been added to
        initialize the time synchronization parameters.

        (2) A line may have been added to set the NetWare
        Directory Services context.

        (3) Lines may have been added to load and bind the
        Ethernet 802.2 frame type. See <F1> for details.

        (4) Netware Link Services Protocol (NLSP) may have
        been activated.

        It would be advisable to reboot the server after
        completing the upgrade.
        Press <Enter> to continue.
```

Your AUTOEXEC.NCF file will then be displayed. (If any changes have been made during the installation process, both an old and new version will be displayed.) Make any modifications necessary, then press F10 to save the file, then select Yes to confirm your choice. Remember, AUTOEXEC.NCF is a critical server configuration file that supports LAN drivers, protocol binding, NDS information, and other management NLMs.

> **TIP**
>
> **The upgrade program may insert LOAD commands for both the Ethernet 802.2 and 802.3 frame types in your new AUTOEXEC.NCF file. To reduce network traffic, load only one frame type, preferably 802.2.**

Step 15: Copy the NetWare 4.11 SYSTEM and PUBLIC Files to the SYS: Volume

The upgrade program will then begin copying the main SYSTEM and PUBLIC files to the SYS: volume. This is the follow-up procedure to the preliminary files copied earlier in Step 9.

Step 16: Perform Other Installation Options (Optional)

When all of the required SYSTEM and PUBLIC files have been copied, a list of additional products that can be installed will be displayed, as you can see in Figure 7.17. Select Choose an Item or Product listed above to be allowed to scroll through the list of additional products, such as the following:

- Create Client Installation Directories on Server (see Chapter 13)

- Make Diskettes

- Install NetWare IP (see Chapter 13)

- Install NetWare DHCP

- Configure Network Protocols (see Chapter 13)

- Install Legacy NWADMIN utility (see Chapter 8)

- Install NetWare Web Server (see Chapter 13)

▸ Upgrade 3.1x Print Services (see Chapters 7 and 14)

▸ Install an Additional Server Language (see Chapter 13)

▸ Change Server Language (see Chapter 13)

▸ Install NetWare for Macintosh (see Chapter 13)

▸ Install NetWare Client for MAC OS (see Chapter 13)

▸ Configure Network Licensing Service (NLS)

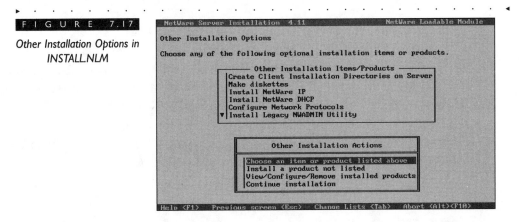

F I G U R E   7.17

Other Installation Options in INSTALL.NLM

Review the various items that can be installed at this point, but don't install any. Instead, select the Continue Installation option from the Other Installation Actions menu. We're almost there. Can't you just feel it?

Step 17: Complete the Upgrade

Wow! You're done. A message that will appear indicating that you've successfully navigated the upgrade forest. It will look like Figure 7.18. Read the message carefully and press Enter to continue — then let out a great big sigh. Now there's only one step standing between you and NetWare 4.11 bliss: Step 18.

F I G U R E   7.18

*Congratulations —
You're Done!*

```
NetWare Server Installation  4.11                   NetWare Loadable Module


    The server upgrade to NetWare 4.11 is complete. It is recommended
    that you reboot the server after exiting the installation.

    Note-1: During the upgrade process, file compression and block
            suballocation on volumes were left unmodified. If you
            upgraded from NetWare 3.x, you may want to load INSTALL.NLM
            after exiting and turn these on.

    Note-2: During the upgrade process, NetWare File Server Auditing
            was disabled.  Please refer to 'Setting up NetWare File
            Server Auditing' to continue to use NetWare Auditing on
            this Server.

    Press <Enter> to exit to the system console screen.


Continue and exit INSTALL <Enter>               Previous screen    <Esc>
Help                      <F1>                   Abort INSTALL <Alt><F10>
```

Step 18: Boot the Server Using the New Startup Files

In order to enjoy the full glory of NetWare 4.11, you must first reboot the server. Remove the IntranetWare/NetWare 4.11 Operating System CD-ROM from the CD-ROM drive and the IntranetWare/NetWare 4.11 license diskette from Drive A: and store them in a safe place. Type **DOWN** to down the server, then **EXIT** to switch back to the DOS partition. Reboot the server.

Switch to the C:\NWSERVER directory by typing **CD\NWSERVER**, then type **SERVER** to start the server. Ensure that all the STARTUP.NCF and AUTOEXEC.NCF commands work properly. Step back and relish your masterpiece. All is well.

ZEN

"There is nothing either good or bad, but thinking makes it so."

Shakespeare

Just in case you missed anything along the way, here's a quick recap of the NetWare 3 to NetWare 4.11 Installation Program Upgrade steps:

Step 1 • Configure the DOS partition.

Step 2 • Run INSTALL.BAT and select the server language.

Step 3 • Copy the server boot files to the DOS partition.

Step 4 • Assign the locale configuration and filename format.

Step 5 • Start the server (happens automatically).

Step 6 • Select and load the server disk and CD-ROM drivers.

Step 7 • Configure the CD-ROM as a DOS or NetWare device (conditional).

Step 8 • Update LAN drivers and name space files.

Step 9 • Copy the Preliminary (Pre-Installation) Files

Step10 • License the NetWare 4.11 operating system.

Step11 • Load and bind the LAN drivers.

Step12 • Re-establish the server-to-server connection (conditional).

Step13 • Install Novell Directory Services (NDS).

Step14 • View/modify the AUTOEXEC.NCF file.

Step15 • Copy the NetWare 4.11 SYSTEM and PUBLIC files to the SYS: volume.

Step16 • Perform other installation options.

Step17 • Complete the migration.

Step18 • Boot the server using the new startup files.

There you are. Your boring NetWare 3.12 server is now a magnificent, sparkling NDS-enhanced IntranetWare roadster. But what happened to your users? They all started in a confining NetWare 3.12 bindery. All of the WHITE02 users were originally defined at the server level. Not anymore. Don't worry — they're all right.

Your NetWare 3.12 users have been magically transformed into IntranetWare NDS objects. During the Installation Program Upgrade, the upgrade program dumps them into the context indicated. Now they can log into the IntranetWare Cloud and have immediate access to all resources in the ACME WAN (provided they have sufficient rights). But before you get too excited about this great new frontier, there's some housekeeping to be done.

AFTER THE UPGRADE

After you complete the upgrade and before you celebrate the birth of your new NetWare 4.11 server, there are a few housekeeping tasks that must be accomplished. These tasks focus on object reorganization, login scripts, security, frame types, utilities, and printing. Here's a quick checklist:

▸ Change user passwords. If you performed an Across-the-Wire migration and assigned random passwords, print out the NEW.PWD file and distribute the password information to each user. Users can then use NetWare Administrator to change their passwords immediately; see Chapter 11.

▸ Install new client software on each workstation. The client files included with IntranetWare are backward-compatible with NetWare 2, NetWare 3, and NetWare 4. Ensure that all users are using the latest version of these files to avoid conflicts. Also, change the Ethernet frame type on each workstation to reflect the new IntranetWare standard (Ethernet_802.2); see Chapter 12.

▸ Assign NDS Object and Property rights to all your upgraded bindery objects; see Chapter 11.

▸ Change the Container and User login scripts to reflect any changes in the server name, directory paths, to add a NO_DEFAULT statement, and so on; see Chapter 12.

▸ Copy the NetWare 4.11 LOGIN.EXE file to the SYS:LOGIN directory on all non-NetWare 4.11 throughout the WAN. This enables NetWare 4.11 login scripts to work with bindery emulation; see Chapter 12.

▸ Use SBACKUP (or other SMS application) to make a copy of all data on the NetWare 4.11 server; see Chapter 13.

▸ Verify that login scripts are operating correctly; see Chapter 12.

▸ Verify that applications are running properly; see Chapter 12.

▸ Modify upgraded object names so they fit your established NDS Naming Standard; see Chapter 4.

▸ Verify that User and Group file system rights are correct; see Chapter 11.

▸ Review the files in merged directories and reorganize them if necessary; see Chapter 10. Also, be sure to update directory and file attributes; see Chapter 11.

▸ Clean up the new printing system. For example, if you performed an Installation Program Upgrade, upgrade your NetWare 3.1x print server and printer objects, print jobs, and PRINTCON and PRINTDEF databases to IntranetWare format using PUPGRADE.NLM. Verify that print queues (which were upgraded with the operating system) are working properly. Assign print queue and print server operators; see Chapter 14.

▸ Take the sample users you choose during the upgrade preparation process and log in as them to check all security and configurations, including passwords, login scripts, NDS security, account restrictions, and drive mappings; see Chapter 11. Also, check to make sure the applications they use still run; see Chapter 12.

▸ Type **ENABLE LOGIN** at the server console to allow IntranetWare users to log in; see Chapter 13.

THE BRAIN

See the "What to Do After the Upgrade" section in Chapter 2 of the *NetWare 4.11 Upgrade* **manual for further hints on what to do after you complete an Installation Program Upgrade.**

· · · · ·

QUIZ

Maid Marion was out on patrol in a strange section of Sherwood Forest and she came across a beautiful princess. The princess was distraught because she lived in the land of the Liars and the Truthtellers. The princess was herself a Truthteller and had no wish to marry a Liar. When a handsome young man from far away asked for her hand in marriage, she devised a simple test to find out whether he was a Liar. She said to him "Do you see that woman walking in the road? I've never seen her before, but I would like to have her as a maid — she looks very nice. Go and ask her if she is a Truthteller or a Liar." The young man returned and said, "She says she is a Truthteller," which solved the problem for the princess very nicely. Was there a happy ending?

(Q7-4)

Well, that just about does it for Installation Program Upgrade method. You've successfully traversed the grand upgrade forest. As you learned earlier, this method enables you to migrate NetWare 3.1x or 4 servers to NetWare 4.11 without purchasing additional hardware. All bindery information (in the case of NetWare 3.12 servers) is transferred to NDS, and the data stays right where it is — on the NetWare partition.

Now, let's take a closer look at the most popular NetWare 4.11 migration method — Across-the-Wire Migration. This approach involves more hardware, more risk, and more heartache. But hey, we get to use a couple of cool new GUI utilities: DS Migrate and File Migration.

Across-the-Wire Migration

The Across-the-Wire migration method transfers bindery information and data from one server to another across the LAN. It requires three machines: two servers and one migration client. The client runs either MIGRATE.EXE or the DS Migrate and File Migration utilities. MIGRATE.EXE is a DOS text-based utility. DS Migrate is a GUI utility that migrates and models bindery information. File Migration is a GUI utility that migrates data files from NetWare 3.1x. Both the DS Migrate and

File Migration utilities operate as snap-ins to NetWare Administrator under Windows 95 and Windows 3.1x.

As you learned earlier, the Across-the-Wire Migration method is the safest upgrade/migration method because the source server remains intact — also known as an "escape pod." You can also use it to migrate all or selected information (which is particularly useful when dealing with a NetWare 3 bindery), or to migrate multiple source servers to a single IntranetWare destination. Let's start our discussion with a look at the IntranetWare information that gets migrated — specifically what is, what isn't, and what should be migrated. Also, you should review the migration prerequisites before you get started. Ready, set, migrate!

MIGRATION PREPARATION

Before you begin your Across-the-Wire Migration, you need to learn a thing or two about what does, doesn't, and should be migrated. In this section, we're going to use the two NEW NetWare 4.11 migration utilities:

- ▶ DS Migrate

- ▶ File Migration Utility

The DS Migrate utility converts bindery information into the new NDS format. NetWare 4.11 migration enables you to choose the categories of information you'd like to migrate. Following is a list of what *is, isn't,* and *should be* migrated.

What *Is* Migrated

- ▶ User login names (merges identical usernames).

- ▶ User print job configurations.

- ▶ User account restrictions (such as account balance restrictions, expiration restrictions, password restrictions, and time restrictions).

- ▶ User login scripts.

- ▶ User bindery login scripts.

▸ Directory- and file-level trustee assignments.

▸ User login names (merges identical usernames).

▸ Group memberships and security equivalences.

▸ NetWare print servers, queues, and printers.

▸ System login script. (The instructions within the system login script become part of the container login script.)

▸ Mail directories and contents for NetWare 3.1x servers.

What *Is Not* Migrated

▸ User passwords. (Passwords can be assigned globally or individually in the modeling process.)

▸ Printer definition database

▸ Mail directories (for NetWare 2.1x or NetWare 2.2 servers only)

What *Should Be* Migrated

▸ All information — This is the default category. It migrates everything except print services, system login scripts, and user passwords.

▸ Data files — Only DOS directories and files that conform to DOS naming conventions are migrated, and their security attributes are preserved. Also, existing directories and files with the same name are not overwritten. Good. Finally, subdirectories greater than 25 levels deep are ignored.

▸ Trustee assignments — User and group trustee rights are migrated (thank goodness). If you select this category, you should also select these other support categories: data files, users, and groups.

▶ Users — Usernames, user login scripts (LOGIN.), and print job configurations (PRINTCON.DAT) are migrated, but passwords are not. You are given the option of assigning randomly generated passwords or allowing users to log into the new system without a password. If you choose to use random passwords, the new passwords are stored in the SYS:SYSTEM directory as the file NEW.PWD. If you choose to have users log in without passwords, you should configure login restrictions so that users are forced to set a password the first time they log in. Existing information on the destination server will not be overwritten, although user rights will be merged.

▶ User restrictions — User login restrictions are migrated. These include account balance restrictions, expiration date, password restrictions, and time restrictions. Unfortunately, user disk restrictions are not migrated. Existing user restrictions on the destination server will not be overwritten. Lucky for us, I was worried about that. How about you?

▶ Groups — Group membership and file system rights are migrated. If a group of the same name exists on the destination server, the source and destination groups are merged.

▶ Default account restrictions — Default account restrictions are migrated and overwrite existing settings on the destination server. That's intense.

▶ Accounting information — NetWare 3 accounting services are migrated and overwrite existing information on the NetWare 4.11 server. This differs from the NetWare 4.11 auditing feature. A few words of advice: Use auditing, it's much more powerful.

▶ Print queues and print servers — NetWare 3 print queues and print servers are migrated. If objects of the same name exist on the destination server, the information is merged. The printing environment itself is not migrated, however. To do so, you must use the MIGPRINT.EXE utility after the migration is completed — and we will.

REAL WORLD

The NetWare 3 system login script is not migrated to the new NetWare 4.11 server. You can move it manually, though, by following any of these strategies:

- Use the NetWare Administrator (or NETADMIN) utility to type in the login script statements manually. They should be placed in appropriate Container login scripts.

- Copy NET$LOG.DAT to the NetWare 4.11 server, then use an MS Windows text editor to copy it to the Clipboard and paste it into the Container login script.

- Copy NET$LOG.DAT to the NetWare 4.11 server, then use an INCLUDE statement in the Container login script to reference it.

Although user login scripts are migrated to the NetWare 4.11 server (that is, SYS:MAIL\USERID#), they're not imported into the NDS database. The migration utility creates two files in the SYS:SYSTEM directory called UIMPORT.CTL and IMPORT.DAT, however, that can be used by UIMPORT to integrate these login scripts into NDS.

MIGRATION PREREQUISITES

In the next section, we'll explore the NetWare 4.11 Across-the-Wire Migration process in great detail using DS Migrate and File Migration. But, first let's start with a quick glimpse of the migration prerequisites. Interestingly, each of the three computers used during this process has its own prerequisites. Check 'em out.

NetWare 2.1x/3.1x Source Server Prerequisites

- Back up both network security information and the file system on the source server.

- Ensure that all users are logged out of the source server.

- Verify that all files (except bindery files) are closed.

- Delete unnecessary files.

- Rename DOS directories and files with long names.

▸ Run BINDFIX on the source server to remove mail subdirectories and trustee rights for users who no longer exist on the source server.

NetWare 4.11 Destination Server Prerequisites

▸ Ensure that the NetWare 4.11 destination server meets the following minimum requirements:

- A 386 or higher processor

- A 15 MB (or larger) DOS partition

- A 75 MB (or larger) NetWare partition (with 100 MB or larger recommended)

- 20 MB of RAM (minimum)

- A unique server name

▸ Create volumes that will contain the migrated data.

▸ Verify the volumes are ready for name spaces (such as DOS, OS/2, and Macintosh).

▸ Log all users out of the NetWare 4.11 server.

Client Workstation Prerequisites

▸ Make sure the client workstation meets the following requirements:

- A 386 or higher processor

- 8 MB (or more) of RAM

- 10 MB of free disk space for MS Migrate executables (17 MB if MS Migrate Assistant is installed)

- 3 MB of additional disk space for each server to be discovered

- Windows 95 or Windows 3.1*x* operating system

- Client 32 for Windows 95 or Windows 3.1*x*

▸ Log into the source server using a bindery connection.

▸ Map a network drive to SYS:PUBLIC on the NetWare 4.11 server.

▸ Verify that the workstation's CONFIG.SYS file includes the FILES=100 command. Reboot the workstation if you add the command.

ZEN

"The creation of a thousand forests is in one acorn."

Ralph Waldo Emerson

DS Migrate and File Migration are GUI utilities that allow you to upgrade your NetWare 2.1*x* or NetWare 3.1*x* server bindery to NetWare 4.11 by migrating modeled bindery information and data files to an existing IntranetWare Directory tree. The following are the four stages involved during this process:

Stage 1 • Discover the Bindery (DS Migrate)

Stage 2 • Model the Directory tree (DS Migrate)

Stage 3 • Configure Objects (DS Migrate)

Stage 4 • Migrate Data (File Migration)

Piece of cake. Wanna learn more? Follow me.

STAGE 1: DISCOVER THE BINDERY (DS MIGRATE)

It all starts with NetWare Bindery discovery. During this stage, DS Migrate searches a NetWare 2.1*x* or 3.1*x* source server and gathers vital data about all its objects and properties. This process is accomplished with the help of four steps. First, you connect to both the source and destination servers. Then, open a new discovery view in DS Migrate. With the view in place, you can choose your discovery parameters and finally initiate the discovery process.

Here's how it works.

Step 1: Connect to the Source and Destination Servers

Log into a NetWare 4.11 destination server as Admin using Client 32 for Windows 95 or Windows 3.1x. Connect to a source NetWare 2.1x or NetWare 3.1x server by mapping a network drive to its SYS: volume.

Step 2: Open a New Discovery View in DS Migrate

Execute the NetWare Administrator utility and click on the Close button if a tip is displayed on the screen. Select DS Migrate from the Tools menu. If this is the first time DS Migrate is run on this server, a working directory will be created. If a message appears advising you of this fact, click on OK.

Click on the Continue button when the initial DS Migrate screen is displayed. To discover the bindery for a NetWare 2.1, NetWare 2.2, or NetWare 3.1x source server, select New View from the File menu, then select Bindery View. Figure 7.19 shows an example of the New View From Bindery screen that will be displayed. Enter a view name in the View Name field, your name in the author field, then click on OK.

F I G U R E   7.19

Creating a New View in DS
Migrate

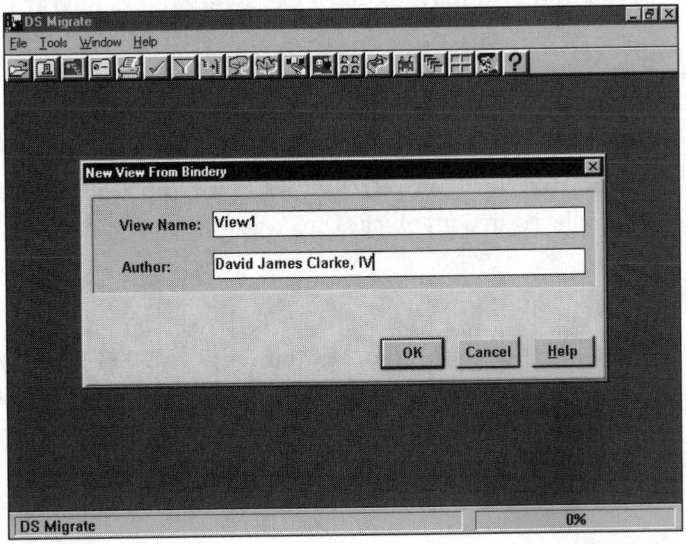

Step 3: Select Discovery Parameters in DS Migrate

A Specify Discover Parameters screen will then appear, as shown in Figure 7.20. Click on the appropriate source server to select the bindery you want to discover, then click on OK to accept the default list of information to be discovered. (The default includes volume, NNS, user, group, and printer information.)

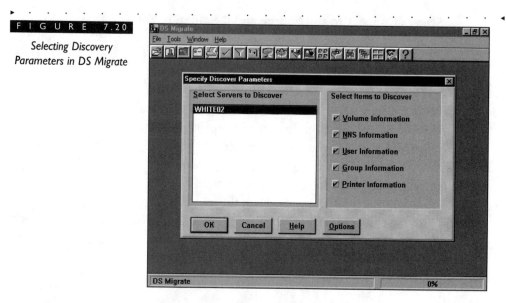

F I G U R E   7.20

Selecting Discovery Parameters in DS Migrate

Step 4: Initiate Bindery Discovery in DS Migrate

As you can see in Figure 7.21, the DS Migrate utility will initiate the discovery procedure, then generate a report in the PSI Viewer that records the results of the discovery process and identifies any bindery problems, as shown in Figure 7.22.

You should review the report to locate any bindery problems, then exit from the PSI Viewer. Figure 7.23 shows an example of how the source server bindery is displayed in a graphical Directory tree structure so that it can be modeled.

SMART LINK

For more information on how DS Migrate works, surf to the Novell Knowledgebase at http://support.novell.com/search/.

▶ . . . . ◀

FIGURE 7.21

Discovery Process in DS Migrate

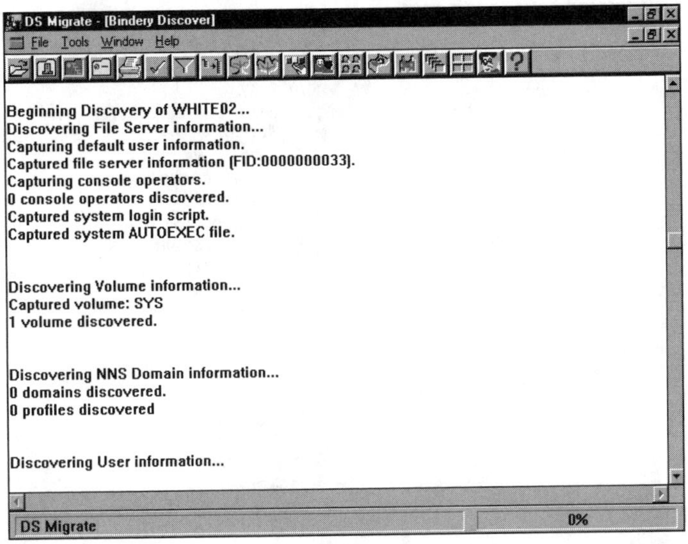

FIGURE 7.22

Discovery Status Log in DS Migrate

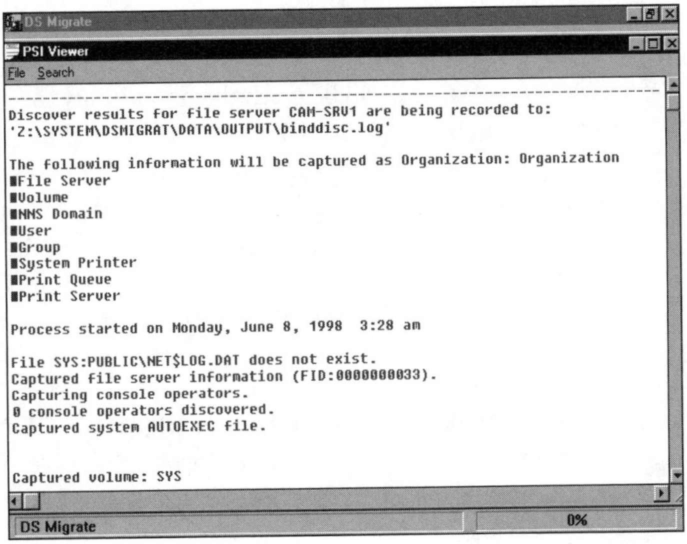

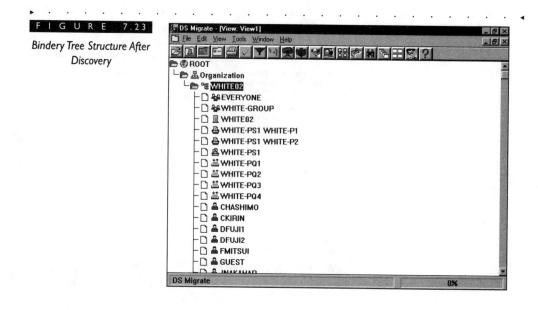

STAGE 2: MODEL THE DIRECTORY TREE (DS MIGRATE)

At this point, you will be given the opportunity to change the bindery's structure to match the IntranetWare Directory tree. Modeling includes adding, deleting, or moving objects; granting or deleting rights and trustee assignments; and merging objects. Modeling is particularly useful when objects that are being migrated already exist in the IntranetWare Directory tree. Once the modeling process is complete, the information displayed in the view can be configured into NDS.

Let's take a closer look at modeling Organization, Organizational Unit, and Leaf objects.

Step 5: Model NDS Organization Objects in DS Migrate

Rename the main Organization object by double-clicking on it, typing a new organization name (such as ACME) in the Name field, then clicking on OK to save the new name.

Step 6: Model NDS Organizational Unit Objects in DS Migrate

Next, rename the existing Organizational Unit (that contains the source server objects) by double-clicking on it, typing the correct name in the Name field, then clicking on OK to save the new name.

Create an Organizational Unit under the Organization object by clicking on the Organization object with the right mouse button, selecting Add Organizational Unit from the pull-down menu, typing the name of the Organizational Unit in the Name field, then clicking on OK to save the new object. Use this method to create additional nested Organizational Units, as needed — by clicking on the parent container and following the procedure listed previously.

If necessary, move the Organizational Unit object containing the source server objects under its parent Organizational Unit by dragging its icon over its parent icon, selecting Add to Container from the dialog box, then clicking on OK.

Step 7: Model NDS Leaf Objects in DS Migrate

Once you've modeled the container objects, it's time to work with the physical resources themselves — also known as leaf objects. Delete the Server and Volume objects in the Organizational Unit containing the source server objects. If desired, delete the SUPERVISOR, GUEST, USER_TEMPLATE, and EVERYONE objects.

Rename all of the User objects in the Organizational Unit object containing the source server objects so that in login names, only the first and last initials of the login name are capitalized (that is, "JSmith" instead of "JSMITH"). Do this by double-clicking on the object, typing in the correct name in the Login Name field, then clicking on OK.

Add any new objects you need by clicking on the parent container icon, selecting Add Object from the Edit menu, selecting the type of object, then clicking on OK.

STAGE 3: CONFIGURE OBJECTS (DS MIGRATE)

Now you're ready to configure the NetWare Bindery and merge it into the Directory tree. This is accomplished with multiple tasks in a single step: Configure and Merge the Bindery in DS Migrate. First, you must configure your new bindery tree, and review the summary report. If all is well, DS Migrate will automatically merge the bindery structure and all its objects into the destination NDS tree. Let's take a closer look.

Step 8: Configure and Merge the Bindery in DS Migrate

We'll begin by configuring the new bindery tree. Select Configure All Objects from the View menu. The names of the objects will be highlighted, as shown in Figure 7.24.

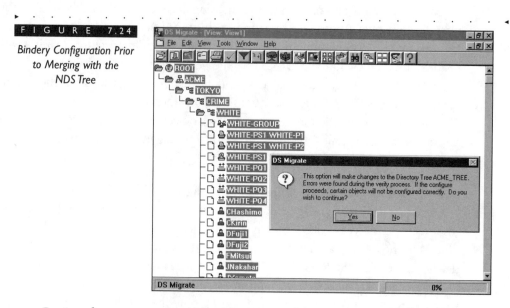

FIGURE   7.24

Bindery Configuration Prior to Merging with the NDS Tree

Review the contents the dialog box to see if any errors were identified by the preconfigure verification. After reviewing the error list, click on OK to indicate acknowledgment of the errors, then click on Yes. If no errors are listed, click on Yes.

When the configuration is complete, a configuration summary report will be displayed in the PSI Viewer, like the one in Figure 7.25. Review the summary report.

Exit the PSI Viewer and DS Migrate. After all replicas have been updated, the new bindery information becomes part of the Directory tree. Take a look at the Directory tree in NetWare Administrator to confirm that the bindery information has been migrated — as shown in Figure 7.26.

ZEN

"Laugh, or I'll blow your lips off...."

From the movie *Dead Men Don't Wear Plaid*

FIGURE 7.25

*Configuration Summary in
DS Migrate*

FIGURE 7.26

*IntranetWare NDS Tree
After Bindery Merge*

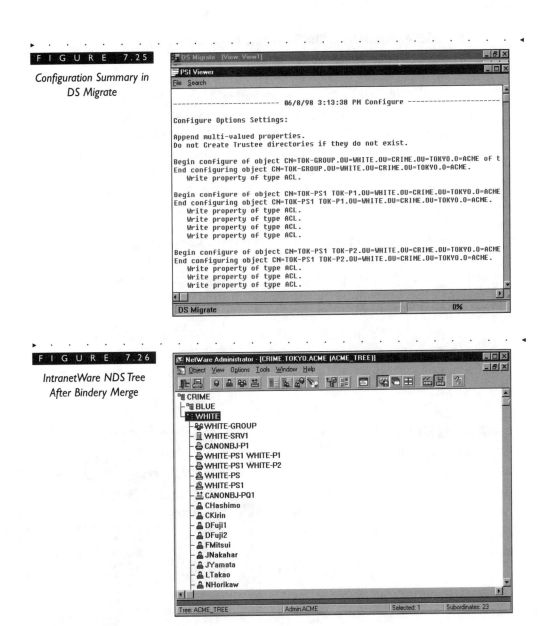

STAGE 4: MIGRATE DATA (FILE MIGRATION)

Now that you've migrated the bindery information using DS Migrate, you're ready to migrate the data files. This is accomplished using the second of the Across-the-Wire GUI tools — File Migration. During this stage, we will migrate old bindery files to IntranetWare in four simple steps. First, you'll start File Migration from within NetWare Administrator. Next, you will need to specify two very important pieces of information — the bindery source server/volume and the IntranetWare destination server/volume. Finally, File Migration will validate the servers and start the migration process. It's as easy as pumpkin pie.

Check it out.

Step 9: Start File Migration from NetWare Administrator

Before you start, you'll need to copy certain NLMs from the IntranetWare/NetWare 4.11 Operating CD-ROM to the source server. See the File Migration documentation for further information. Select File Migration from the Tool menu in NetWare Administrator.

As you can see in Figure 7.27, a NetWare File Migration screen will be displayed indicating the conditions that must be met before beginning the file migration. Verify that the conditions displayed on the screen have been met, then click on Next.

▶ · ◀

F I G U R E   7.27

File Migration Utility Prerequisites

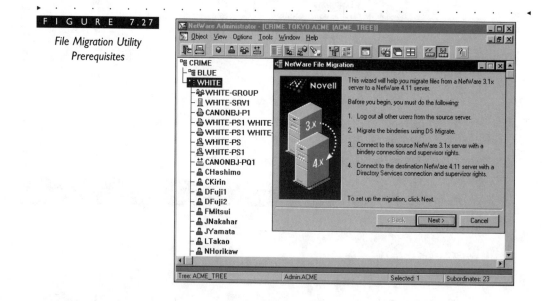

Step 10: Specify the File Migration Source Server

Next, you will be asked to indicate the source server name and volume. Confirm that the correct source server is displayed in the Source server field. and the correct volume is displayed in the Source Volume field. Click on the down arrow next to each of the fields, if necessary, to display the available servers and volumes. A server will only be displayed if your workstation is connected to it. As you can see in Figure 7.28, the screen says that only one volume can be migrated at a time. It also says that all file and directory attributes, name spaces, and trustee rights will be reserved. When the values listed are correct, click on Next.

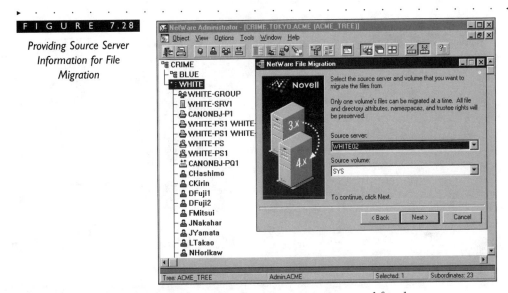

F I G U R E   7.28

Providing Source Server Information for File Migration

You will then be asked to supply the Supervisor password for the source server. Type the source server password in the Password field, then click on Next.

Step 11: Specify the File Migration Destination Server

After you supply the password for the source server, a screen will be displayed requesting the destination server, volume, and directory. Confirm that the correct NetWare 4.11 server has been selected in the Designation Server field, the correct NetWare 4.11 volume in the Destination Volume field, and the correct directory in the Destination Directory field. Click on the down arrow next to each of the fields, if necessary, to displays the available servers, volumes, and directories. A server will only be displayed if your workstation is connected to it. When the values listed are correct, click on Next.

Next, you will be asked to supply the destination server password. Type the NetWare 4.11 destination server password in the Password field, then click on Next.

Step 12: Complete the File Migration

The File Migration utility will confirm that migration conditions have been met and may display a series of error status screens. Review the contents of each error screen and Click on Yes when asked if you want to continue migration.

Finally, a screen like the one in Figure 7.29 will be displayed, advising you that validation is complete. Check to see if any problems were encountered. Click on the Migrate button to begin the actual migration process.

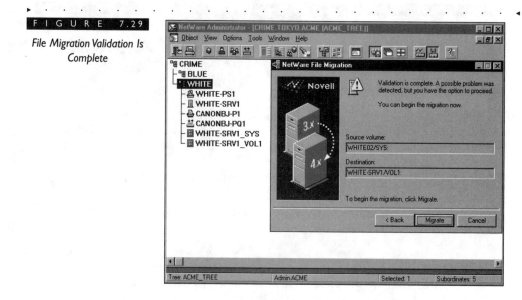

Last, but not least, a screen will appear advising you that the server volume migration is complete. Click on View Log and review the migration log — using it to troubleshoot any migration problems. Click on Close when you are finished. Click on Done to return to the NetWare Administrator screen, then click on Yes when asked to confirm that you want to continue.

THE BRAIN

Refer to Chapter 3 of the *NetWare 4.11 Upgrade* manual for additional information on using DS Migrate and NetWare File Migration.

QUIZ

In another area of Sherwood Forest, fierce winds blow all the time, sometimes in one direction, sometimes in the other. A fast train — or reasonably fast, depending on your ideas — can run under its own steam, if forced — 100 m.p.h. between Never-Never and Sometimes. This particular day it picked up a strong favorable breeze that doubled its speed to 200 m.p.h., at which speed the train completed its 200-mile journey in 1 hour. At the usual time, the train had to make the return journey. Unfortunately, the same wind was still blowing in the same direction at the same speed. How fast would the engineer have to push the train to make the journey home in four hours?

(Q7-5)

You're finished . . . Congratulations! You somehow pulled it off. The Across-the-Wire Migration was a little trickier than the Installation Program Upgrade, but certainly more entertaining. So, your next question is: "Where are my users?" Good question. Once again, they've been transformed from boring NetWare 3 bindery users into magnificent IntranetWare NDS objects. Now, they are free to roam throughout the ACME Cloud.

Here's a quick review of the basic stages involved in a NetWare 4.11 Across-the-Wire Migration if you use the DS Migrate and File Migration utilities:

Stage 1 • Discover the Bindery (DS Migrate)

Stage 2 • Model the Directory Tree (DS Migrate)

Stage 3 • Configure Objects (DS Migrate)

Stage 4 • Migrate Data (File Migration)

Yea, yea, yea! We made it. It's 4:59 p.m. on Tuesday afternoon, and we finished our Installation Program Upgrade and Across-the-Wire Migration. Boy, what a difference a day makes! Remember yesterday about this time, we were feeling a bit overwhelmed. Well, today we have a whole new attitude — we feel great!

Of course, NetWare 4.11 Across-the-Wire Migration is the ultimate achievement in "nerdiness." And now you're an official member of "NLM" — Nerd Liberation Movement. Migration is the most popular NetWare 4.11 installation method, because there are more than 5 million NetWare 2 or NetWare 3 servers out there with already established binderies. As you learned in this chapter, NetWare 4.11 supports two installation methods, two upgrade methods, and two migration methods:

Installation methods:

▸ Installation (Simple) — Start from scratch and create a new NetWare 4.11 server using the Simple Installation option in INSTALL.NLM — which makes a number of assumptions and uses default settings.

▸ Installation (Custom) — Start from scratch and create a new NetWare 4.11 server using the Custom Installation option in INSTALL.NLM — which allows greater flexibility in setting various parameters than the Simple Installation.

Upgrade methods:

▸ In-Place Upgrade (from NetWare 2.1x or NetWare 2.2) — Upgrade the server from NetWare 2.1x or NetWare 2.2 to NetWare 3.12 using the 2XUPGRDE.NLM utility. You can then use the Upgrade option in INSTALL.NLM to upgrade the server from NetWare 3.12 to NetWare 4.11.

▸ Installation Program Upgrade — Upgrade an existing server from NetWare 3.1x or NetWare 4 to NetWare 4.11 using the Upgrade option in INSTALL.NLM.

Migration methods:

▸ Migration (Across-the-Wire) — Migrate bindery information and files from a source NetWare 2.1, NetWare 2.2, or NetWare 3.1x server (or a LAN Manager, LAN Server, VINES, or Windows NT server) to a destination NetWare 4.11 server using the DOS Migration utility (MIGRATE.EXE) *or* DS Migrate (based on DS Standard) and NetWare File Migration.

▶ Migration (Same-Server) — Migrate bindery information and files from a source NetWare 2.1, NetWare 2.2, or NetWare 3.1*x* server (or a LAN Manager, LAN Server, VINES, or Windows NT server) to a destination NetWare 4.11 server using the DOS Migration utility (MIGRATE.EXE) and the Upgrade option in INSTALL.NLM.

ZEN

"How many cares one loses when one decides not to be something but to be someone."

Coco Chanel

So, there you have it. As an official member of "NLM," you can migrate servers anywhere in the world. And this is a good thing, because ACME spans the globe. Now, we're ready to take our new NetWare 4.11 servers to the next level: *IntranetWare Management.*

It's a good thing you have a new attitude. I wonder what Wednesday has in store for us?

SMART LINK

If you need more help with your NetWare 4.11 migration, try the following exercises or get help at http://support.novell.com/sitemap.

Review the scenarios listed here, then answer the questions associated with each scenario.

SCENARIO 1

The Finance department currently has a 486/66 server with 16 MB of RAM that it wants to upgrade from NetWare 3.12 to NetWare 4.11. Because of the nature of the work, the finance manager is concerned that there be no loss of data or corruption during the upgrade. She also mentioned that the department has a new 200 MHz Pentium that just arrived that will take the place of the current server. The original server can then be used for a special project.

The configuration of the old server is as follows:

- A 15 MB DOS partition

- 98 MB of free space on the SYS: volume

- 149 MB of free space in the FINANCE: volume

- A 3C509 NIC

- An IDE disk controller

- A tape unit

- A CD-ROM drive on the workstation (the current server has no CD-ROM drive)

The configuration of the new server is as follows:

- 32 MB of RAM

- 2.1 GB hard disk

- A 3C5X9 NIC

▸ A 1.6/3.2 GB tape unit

▸ A SCSI CD-ROM drive

Your assignment:

1. Indicate which method you would use to upgrade the new server and explain why.

2. Explain which method you would use to upgrade the original server and explain why.

3. Indicate what would be unusual about the method used to upgrade the original server and why it would be necessary.

SCENARIO 2

The Facilities department is currently using NetWare 2.2 on a 386/33 and would like to upgrade to NetWare 4.11. The facilities manager said that the department has no additional server hardware to use during the upgrade. The current configuration for this server is as follows:

▸ 4 MB RAM

▸ 20 MB DOS partition

▸ 25 MB of free space in volume SYS:

▸ 56 MB of free space in volume VOL1:

▸ An NE1000 NIC

▸ An IDE disk controller

Your assignment:

1. Indicate which methods could be used to upgrade this server.

2. Indicate which method you would use to upgrade the server and explain why.

3. Indicate what utility (or utilities) would be used for this method.

4. Determine whether the current hardware configuration is appropriate for running the migration/upgrade method that you chose. If not, describe your recommendations.

5. Specify whether the IDE disk controller would pose a problem in this situation and explain why.

SCENARIO 3

The Pollution department currently has a Pentium 180 MHz computer and is ready to upgrade from NetWare 4.1 to NetWare 4.11. The current configuration for this server is as follows:

▶ 64 MB of RAM

▶ A 3.2 GB hard disk

▶ A 100 MB DOS partition with 62 MB of free space

▶ A CD-ROM drive

Your assignment:

1. Indicate which upgrade or migration methods could be used to upgrade this server.

2. Explain which method you would use if you learned that the department had no additional server hardware to use during the upgrade and explain why.

SCENARIO 4

The Marketing department has a 486/50 and is ready to upgrade from NetWare 3.11 to NetWare 4.11. The marketing manager is quite unhappy with the way the server is currently configured in terms of network security and would just like to start over. The current configuration for this server is as follows:

▸ 16 MB of RAM

▸ A 15 MB DOS partition

▸ 25 MB of free disk space in volume SYS:

▸ 124 MB of free disk space in volume VOL1:

▸ An NE2000 network board

▸ An IDE disk controller and SCSI floppy controller

Your assignment:

1. Indicate what methods could be used to upgrade this server.

2. Indicate which method you would use to upgrade the server and explain why.

3. Determine if the current hardware configuration is appropriate for running NetWare 4.11. If not, describe your recommendations.

4. Explore whether the frame type of the source server would be a concern in this situation.

SCENARIO 5

The Nuclear department currently has a Banyan VINES server and would like to upgrade to NetWare 4.11, but would prefer not to start from scratch. The current configuration for this server is as follows:

- 120 MHz Pentium

- 64 MB of RAM

- A 35 MB DOS partition

- 4 GB hard disk

1. Indicate which upgrade or migration methods could be used to upgrade this server.

2. Indicate which method you would use to upgrade the server and explain why.

3. Explain where you would obtain the upgrade or migration software.

CASE STUDY: MIGRATING A NETWARE 3.12 SERVER TO NETWARE 4.11

In this exercise, you will use the Across-the-Wire Migration method to migrate bindery information from a NetWare 3.12 server called "WHITE02" to the NetWare 4.11 "WHITE-SRV1" server that you upgraded earlier in the chapter. You'll need three computers for this exercise: a NetWare 3.12 source server, a NetWare 4.11 destination server, and a workstation running Client 32 for Windows 95 or Windows 3.1*x*. To perform this migration, you'll need to complete the following steps. Ready, set, migrate!

STAGE 1: DISCOVER THE BINDERY (DS MIGRATE)

▸ *Step 1:* Install a NetWare 3.12 server called WHITE02. Log into your NetWare 4.11 WHITE-SRV1 server as Admin. Map Drive S: to WHITE02\SYS:.

▸ *Step 2:* Execute the NetWare Administrator utility and click on the Close button if a tip is displayed on the screen. Select DS Migrate from the Tools menu. If this is the first time DS Migrate is run on this server, a working directory will be created. If a message appears advising you of this fact, click on OK. Click on the Continue button when the initial DS Migrate screen is displayed. To discover the bindery for the NetWare 3.12 WHITE02 server, select New View from the File menu, then select Bindery View. A New View From Bindery screen will be displayed. Enter View1 as the name of the new view, your name in the author field, then click on OK.

▸ *Step 3:* A Specify Discover Parameters screen will then appear. Click on the WHITE02 server to select the NetWare 3.1*x* bindery you want to discover, then click on OK to accept the default list of information to be discovered. (The default includes volume, NNS, user, group, and printer information.)

▸ *Step 4:* The DS Migrate utility will then generate a report in the PSI Viewer that records the results of the discovery process and identifies any bindery problems. You should review the report to find any bindery problems, then exit from the PSI Viewer. The NetWare 3.12 bindery will be displayed in a graphical Directory tree structure so that it can be modeled.

STAGE 2: MODEL THE DIRECTORY TREE (DS MIGRATE)

▶ *Step 5:* At this point, you will be given the opportunity to change the bindery's tree structure to match the NetWare 4.11 Directory tree structure. Rename the Organization object by double-clicking on it, typing **ACME** in the Name field, then clicking on OK to save the new name.

▶ *Step 6:* Rename the WHITE02 Organization Unit object by double-clicking on it, typing **WHITE** in the Name field, then clicking on OK to save the new name. Create a TOKYO Organizational Unit under the ACME Organization object by clicking on ACME with the right mouse button, selecting Add Organizational Unit from the pull-down menu, typing **TOKYO** in the Name field, then clicking on OK to save the new object. Create a CRIME Organizational Unit under the TOKYO Organization object by clicking on TOKYO with the right mouse button, selecting Add Organizational Unit from the pull-down menu, typing **CRIME** in the Name field, then clicking on OK to save the new object. Move the WHITE Organization Unit object under the CRIME Organizational Unit by dragging the WHITE icon over the CRIME icon, selecting Add to Container from the dialog box, then clicking on OK.

▶ *Step 7:* Delete the Server and Volume objects in the WHITE Organizational Unit. Delete the SUPERVISOR, GUEST, USER_TEMPLATE, and EVERYONE objects in the WHITE Organizational Unit. Rename all of the User objects so that login names only the first and last initials of the login name are capitalized (for example, "FMitsui" instead of "FMITSUI"). Do this by double-clicking on the object, typing in the correct name in the Login Name field, then clicking on OK. Add a User object called NHorikaw (last name Horikawa) to the WHITE container using the following procedure: Click on the WHITE Organizational Unit object. Select Add Object from the Edit menu, then select User and click on OK. Type **NHorikaw** in the Login Name field and **Horikawa** in the Last Name field, then Click on OK to create the object.

STAGE 3: CONFIGURE OBJECTS (DS MIGRATE)

▸ *Step 8:* Now you're ready to configure the NetWare Bindery to the Directory tree. Select Configure All Objects from the View menu. The names of the objects will be highlighted. Review the contents the dialog box to see if any errors were identified by the preconfigure verification. After reviewing the error list, click on OK to indicate acknowledgment of the errors, then click on Yes. If no errors are listed, click on Yes. When the configuration is complete, a configuration summary report will be displayed in the PSI Viewer. Review the summary report. Exit the PSI Viewer and DS Migrate. Take a look at the Directory tree in NetWare Administrator to confirm that the bindery information has been migrated to the Directory tree.

STAGE 4: MIGRATE THE DATA (FILE MIGRATION)

▸ *Step 9:* The File Migration utility requires that you copy certain NLMs from the IntranetWare/NetWare 4.11 Operating CD-ROM to the source server. See the File Migration documentation for further information. Now that you've migrated the bindery information, you're ready to migrate the data files. Select File Migration from the Tool menu in NetWare Administrator. Verify that the conditions displayed on the screen have been met, then click on Next.

▸ *Step 10:* Confirm that the correct NetWare 3.1x server is displayed in the Source server field. and the correct volume is displayed in the Source Volume field. Click on the down arrow next to each of the fields, if necessary, to display the available servers and volumes. A server will only be displayed if your workstation is connected to it. If you read the screen carefully, you'll notice that it says that only one volume can be migrated at a time. It also says that all file and directory attributes, name spaces, and trustee rights will be reserved. When the values listed are correct, click on Next. Type the WHITE 02 (NetWare 3.1x) server password in the Password field, then click on Next.

▸ *Step 11:* Confirm that the correct server has been selected in the Designation Server field, the correct volume in the Destination Volume field, and the correct directory in the Destination Directory field. Click on the down arrow next to each of the fields, if necessary, to displays the available servers, volumes, and directories. A server will only be displayed if your workstation is connected to it. When the values listed are correct, click on Next. Type the WHITE-SRV1 (NetWare 4.11) server password in the Password field, then click on Next.

▸ *Step 12:* The File Migration utility will confirm that migration conditions have been met and may display a series of error status screens. Review the contents of each error screen and Click on Yes when asked if you want to continue migration. A screen will then be displayed advising you that although validation is complete, a possible problem was encountered. Click on the Migrate button to begin the actual migration process. A screen will then be displayed advising you that the server volume migration is complete. Click on View Log and review the migration log. Click on Close when you are finished. Click on Done to return to the NetWare Administrator screen, then click on Yes when asked to confirm that you want to continue.

Congratulations! You've migrated another ACME server to IntranetWare. Three down and only 48 more to go! Ready, set, migrate!

EXERCISE 7-2: TUESDAY MORNING

Circle the 20 NetWare 4.11 Migration terms hidden in this word search puzzle using the hints provided.

```
N E W P W D B I N D E R Y O A M M
C J T L L I S A M E S E R V E R I
O E S Y N S T M C U P H F G T G G
P E F D P E X C I K T E A S H N P
Y K F H S D C M Y G U X D H Q P R
E I I G D I P U B E R P H U C J I
X Z L T S O A J C T M A Q D C O N
V U E T R U P F M X J O T R Q U T
D T M T E J W M I G R A T E E X E
F T I N P L A C E U P G R A D E X
V D G R A C R O S S T H E W I R E
E M R X I N S T A L L N L M N Z Y
B J A W R B W E Y P Y U Q F P Y T
Z Q T C N O I T A R G I M L F L I
R U I S L I B V P D O U G S H I R
F P O R M M L N E D R G P U X F U
I E N I R G T X W U R L N F N B C
X A R E Y N G T W E N T Y F I V E
J X L E R X V K C U E O J R S W S
```

Hints:

1. Migration method that transfers bindery information and data from one server to another across the LAN. It requires three machines: two servers and a workstation.

2. First step in the In-Place Upgrade process. Allows you to return the server to its original state if anything goes wrong.

3. Flat-file database found in earlier versions of NetWare that contains objects such as users, groups, and so on.

4. Workstation command line utility used to detect and correct problems in a NetWare bindery.

5. Graphical utility that can be used during an Across-the-Wire Migration to migrate bindery information to a NetWare 4.11 Directory tree.

6. NLM that is used to detect and correct problems in the Novell Directory Services (NDS) database.

7. Graphical utility that can be used during an Across-the-Wire Migration to migrate bindery-based data files to a NetWare 4.11 server.

8. Type of native disk driver that constitutes a problem when upgrading from a NetWare 2 server that does not contain a DOS partition.

9. Type of upgrade method that requires only one server instead of two.

10. NLM that is used during an Installation Program Upgrade.

11. Utility used to migrate print servers, printers, print queues, and print job configurations from a NetWare 2 or NetWare 3 source server into an NDS tree.

12. Utility used in Across-the-Wire and Same-Server migration methods.

13. Process of converting servers from NetWare 2, NetWare 3, or another network operating system to NetWare 4.11.

14. Workstation command line utility for copying data files only from one server to another.

15. File that contains random passwords generated by the MIGRATE.EXE utility.

16. Migration method that requires only one server instead of two.

17. Workstation command line utility used to detect possible security risks on a NetWare 3 server.

18. Maximum level of subdirectories that will be transferred during a migration or upgrade.

19. Utility that can be used to migrate login scripts from a bindery-based NetWare server into the NDS database.

20. Utility used for doing an In-Place Upgrade of a server from NetWare 2 server to NetWare 3.

See Appendix C for answers.

PART III: INTRANETWARE INSTALLATION

Across

1. The smaller of two server partitions
4. The first phase of DOS preparation
5. MIGRATE.EXE, a workstation, and two servers
8. Old NetWare 3 print job configurations are migrated
10. Printing migration

11. Default VLM directory
12. Default time provider
14. NetWare in Spanish
15. "Off" by default
16. NetWare 4.11 migration insurance
19. NetWare in French
20. Required for Japanese Kanji
21. NetWare 2 or NetWare 3 bindery preparation
22. NetWare in German
25. Automating the server at the NetWare 4.11 partition
26. Server installation with all the bells and whistles
27. Most popular, built-in disk driver
30. Where NetWare 4.11 lives
32. The tool of all great NetWare 4.11 installers
33. Default NetWare 4.11 protocol
35. Minimum server RAM
36. The "brains" of NetWare 4.11
37. Random passwords
38. Not up
39. Approved by Novell Labs and bundled with NetWare 4.11
40. From NetWare 3 with INSTALL.NLM
41. Upgrade name space

Down

1. Communicating with the internal server disk
2. Are not migrated
3. A great on-line source of CNE tidbits
4. ETHERNET_802.2 in the NetWare 4.11 environment
5. First NDS user
6. Automating the server at the DOS partition
7. Loads disk drivers
9. The great server communicator
13. New and improved DSK strategy
15. Built-in disk SFT with enhanced performance
17. User's playground created at installation
18. Communicating with the internal server NIC

19. The second phase of DOS preparation
21. Initializes LAN communications at the server
23. MIGRATE.EXE, a workstation, and a server
24. Activates server NLMs
26. In-Place Upgrade analysis
28. Automating the workstation
29. From NetWare 2
30. Admin's playground created at installation
31. "1234" on the cabling
32. BADCAFE at the server
34. Default NetWare 4.11 media

See Appendix C for answers.

Gardener

PART IV

IntranetWare Management

I wandered lonely as a cloud
That floats on high o'er vales and hills,

When all at once I saw a crowd,
A host of golden daffodils;
Beside the lake, beneath the trees,
Fluttering and dancing in the breeze.

Continuous as the stars that shine
And twinkle on the milky way,
They stretched in never-ending line
Along the margin of the bay:

Ten thousand saw I at a glance,
Tossing their heads in sprightly dance.

William Wordsworth

You are a superhero.

You are a doctor.

You are a gardener.

As an IntranetWare CNE, you are three people in one.

Today, you are a gardener. Welcome to the IntranetWare garden — the last stop on your life-long CNE journey. When you first arrive, the garden is bare. You have a withering sapling (NDS tree), some soil (volumes), a greenhouse (server), and plenty of weeds. Not a promising site. Fortunately, you have plenty of fertilizer (this book) to get you started.

The first step is seeding. Be sure to segment your garden, because certain plants (users) require more attention than others. Once the seeds are in place, it's time for garden management. This is where the magic occurs. It's amazing how quickly your trees will bloom with the right combination of watering, love, sunshine, and weeding. Remember, balance is the key.

Gardening is a very rewarding experience, and your hard work will pay off in the form of productive users, organized resources, and peace on Earth. Good luck, and don't forget your green thumb.

Managing NDS

"There is life in the ground: It goes into the seeds, and it also, when it is stirred up, goes into the person who stirs it."

Charles Dudley Warner

Welcome to the IntranetWare garden!

This is the beginning of an exciting adventure for you — as the IntranetWare gardener. You designed the "Cloud" (as a superhero), installed some servers (as a doctor), and now you get to breathe life into your glorious NDS tree (as a gardener). The next eight chapters will prepare you for the challenge of a lifetime — CNE management. You'll adventure through partitioning, synchronization, the IntranetWare file system, security, configuration, management, printing, and finally, optimization. However, the journey must start somewhere. Welcome to "point A." The challenge begins today — managing NDS.

In the beginning, the garden is bare. You have a withering sapling (NDS tree), some soil (volumes), a greenhouse (server), and plenty of weeds. Not a promising site. Fortunately, you have plenty of fertilizer (this book) to get you started. Once the soil has been prepared, you can start seeding. Be sure to segment your garden because certain plants require more attention than others. Once the seeds are in place, it's time for garden management.

Garden management is the fun part. This is where the magic occurs. It's amazing how quickly your trees will bloom with the right combination of watering, love, sunshine, and weeding. The trick is determining how much is enough. Just as in life, there is such a thing as too much. Too much water, for example, could lead to overhydration, while too much sunshine could cause dehydration. Gardening is a very tricky business — green thumb required.

ZEN

"Water is H_2O, hydrogen two parts, oxygen one, but there is a third thing that makes it water and nobody knows what that is."

D. H. Lawrence

This is your life as an IntranetWare gardener. You start with a sapling NDS tree, some default IntranetWare files, and the Admin user. Now you must turn it into a thriving forest of communication and productivity. Good luck. To make matters worse, ACME's trying to save the world at the same time. Wow, you're going to need plenty of fertilizer!

Before you partition the tree, you must build it. Before you secure the tree, you must build it. Before you configure the tree, you must build it. Before you optimize the tree, you must build it. I see a pattern forming here. And finally, before you build the tree, you must understand the garden.

In this chapter, we'll help you discover your IntranetWare garden and begin planting the seeds of connectivity. We'll learn everything there is to know about NDS objects, their properties, and how to effectively create/manage them. We will build ACME's tree, merge it with another, and even explore some controversial cross-breeding techniques for NetWare 3 and IntranetWare trees — NETSYNCing. Here's a sneak peek at what's ahead:

- ► NDS Gardening — We will get acquainted with the garden, and learn how to browse ACME's NDS tree.

- ► Managing NDS Objects — We will explore the required and most commonly used NDS objects. We'll learn when to use each, and how to segment our garden for maximized productivity.

- ► Building the ACME Tree — We'll finally build ACME's tree and place all our leaf objects in their appropriate containers.

- ► DSMERGing — We will explore the DSMERGE utility and learn how to use it for merging two trees together.

- ► NETSYNCing — Finally, we will discover "crossbreeding" and learn how to make a rose that tastes like corn.

So, that's life in the IntranetWare garden. Let's take a closer look.

NDS Gardening

The first rule of gardening is "know your garden." Know the quality of the soil, know the angle of the sun, and definitely, know the layout of the plants. The IntranetWare garden is a haven for user connectivity. For that reason, you must understand the relationships between objects, and the general layout of the tree. That's where *browsing* comes in.

Browsing is a technical term that means "to walk around the NDS tree looking at stuff." Browsing not only acquaints you with the tree, it also aids in NDS navigation. NDS navigation is required for a myriad of management tasks (such as creating users, adding security, configuring volumes, and partitioning). If you know what your tree looks like and how to navigate it effectively, you'll be well on your way to "green thumb-ship."

In this section, we will learn to browse the NDS tree using a variety of IntranetWare utilities, including

- ▸ NWADMIN — An MS Windows-based utility called NetWare Administrator

- ▸ NETADMIN — A DOS-based version of NWADMIN

- ▸ CX — A command line utility for tree navigation

- ▸ NLIST — A command line utility for searching

- ▸ User Tools — GUI and menu utilities for user navigation

Hold your horses. Before we get too excited about browsing, let's take a quick tour of the NDS garden. Don't pick the flowers.

ZEN

"Anyone who has got any pleasure at all from nature should try to put something back. Life is like a superlative meal and the world is the maitre d'hotel. What I am doing is the equivalent of leaving a reasonable tip."

Gerald Durrell

THE GARDEN

Novell Directory Services (NDS) is the garden. Instead of flowers and tomatoes, this garden organizes network resources (such as users, groups, printers, servers, volumes, and so on). As you can see in Figure 8.1, our garden organizes these resources into a hierarchical Directory tree.

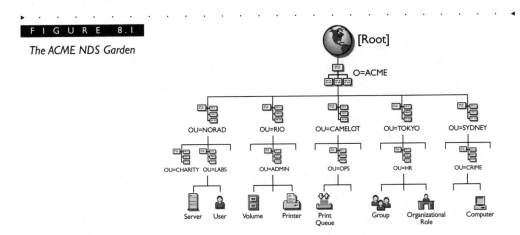

F I G U R E   8.1

The ACME NDS Garden

NDS allows these resources to be managed in a single view. This is significant. It dramatically increases administrative flexibility, allowing you to manage the tree and its objects by using various properties and security capabilities. This contrasts with the earlier NetWare 3 bindery, which was server-centric and inflexible. The Directory is network-centric, that is, it's distributed and replicated on multiple servers throughout the WAN. This increases resource availability and fault tolerance.

All in all, our garden is a pretty amazing place. It seems as though it's been designed for gardening from the very beginning. Management in IntranetWare has never been so accommodating — notice I didn't say "easy." They're not the same thing. NDS accomplishes this with four main principles:

- ▶ NDS provides a single point of login.

- ▶ NDS provides easy administration.

- ▶ NDS is scalable.

- ▶ NDS allows tree walking.

Let's take a stroll through our new NDS garden.

SMART LINK

For a more in-depth discussion of NDS and to download the latest database improvements, surf to "Novell Directory Services" at http://www.netware.com.

NDS Provides a Single Point of Login

IntranetWare users log into the network once — using one username and one password. Once there, they have instantaneous access to all authorized network resources. Very cool. IntranetWare processes the server connections in the background and provides transparent access to resources, regardless of where they are physically located.

In contrast, NetWare 3 bindery users must log into each server individually. This means that they must provide a different username and password for each additional server connection. Too much work.

A single user login also makes your job easier. You create each user account *once* for the entire IntranetWare network. Multiple user accounts on multiple servers are no longer needed in IntranetWare. This feature alone will save you hours of work. As you can see, NDS serves as the central point of management, eliminating tedious duplication and reducing administrative costs.

NDS Provides Easy Administration

IntranetWare consolidates all NDS administrative functions into a single, easy-to-use graphical utility that greatly reduces the time you spend administering the network. NWADMIN is your friend. It is a Windows-based utility that allows you to make changes to the Directory with the simple click of a mouse. It does virtually everything in IntranetWare — get used to it.

With NWADMIN, you can get information about an object simply by clicking on its icon. The icon explodes into a dialog box like the one in Figure 8.2. The main window shows current parameters for each of the 18 page buttons on the right of the screen. In this example, we're looking at the Identification page for George Washington in ADMIN.RIO.ACME.

This object-oriented tool allows you to perform many routine NDS tasks more quickly. Users, directories, and server functions can be accomplished simply by dragging and dropping (don't forget to hold down the Ctrl key), or by clicking on icons. When a user changes departments, for example, you simply drag-and-drop the user to another location. I wish moving my house were so simple.

Adding directory or object rights in previous versions of NetWare involved multilayered menus and tedious processing. Now, all you have to do is drag the user's icon to the specific directory, and IntranetWare takes care of the rest.

Since all the network resources are represented in the NDS tree, managing many IntranetWare servers is no more difficult than managing one IntranetWare server. You don't have to concern yourself with the resources on any one server, but instead you can focus your efforts on managing *all* the network resources as a whole.

We'll explore NWADMIN in great depth later in this chapter. Also, don't miss the great ACME case study at the end of the chapter. It's fun, trust me.

NDS Is Scalable

NDS is a global name service that can be split into pieces and distributed to any number of network servers. In contrast, the NetWare 3 bindery only supports operation from one server at a time. With NDS, the information is not only distributed, but also replicated. As we learned previously, this increases resource availability and fault tolerance. Figure 8.3 shows how NDS could be distributed across the ACME WAN.

F I G U R E   8.3

Scalable NDS

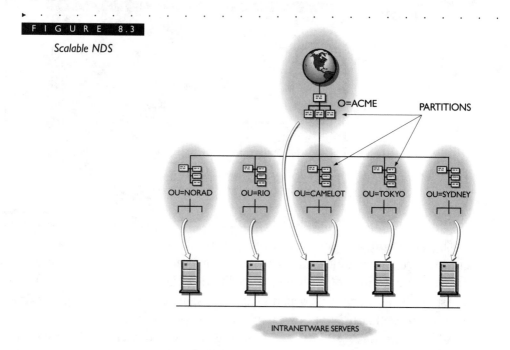

The feature that splits NDS into pieces is called *partitioning* and the process of distributing those pieces is called *replication*. These features makes NDS a powerful tool for storing, accessing, and managing resource information — regardless of where it is physically located.

This means that your NDS tree can easily grow to meet the demands of your environment. In addition, your tree can be quickly transformed to reflect the changes in your company's organization or functionality. We'll discuss NDS partition management and replication in great detail later in Chapter 9 ("Partition Management and Synchronization"). That chapter focuses on "pruning."

Finally, your entire NDS tree doesn't have to be stored on any one server. It can be distributed and replicated on multiple machines. How do the pieces find each other? Good question. NDS provides a mechanism for finding objects in the NDS tree even though they're scattered all over the WAN. This mechanism is called *tree walking*.

NDS Tree Walking

IntranetWare tree walking refers to an automatic background process that locates physically separated resources. Basically, it means that NDS keeps track of objects even if they're scattered from here to eternity. Tree walking allows users to access resources without having to know anything about them. They only need to know the name of the resource, and NDS figures out where it is.

Here's how it works. When a user requests an object and provides its context, NDS searches the user's currently connected server first. If the server doesn't hold the object, NDS contacts all the other servers until it finds the object.

When the object is found, the user's server sends a list of host servers to the user's workstation. This is called a *referral list* and it includes all the servers with the requested object information. Then, the user's workstation determines where to get the information based on a least-cost algorithm. There's one last point. Before the workstation determines a cost for each server, it first checks to see if it's already connected to one of the servers in the referral list. If not, it bases its decision on cost. If the cost is the same, the workstation chooses the first server in the list.

With tree walking, users can always locate specific NDS information without having to worry about where it is. As a matter of fact, NDS uses tree walking to hold your hand while you're browsing. If you try to access resources outside of your server's partition, tree walking takes over immediately. You probably don't even notice what's going on. Very sneaky, and very cool.

Speaking of browsing, I'm ready for a tour of the NDS garden. How about you? As I mentioned, there are five utilities for NDS browsing. Let's start with the most fun one — NWADMIN. And remember, don't pick the flowers — yet.

QUIZ

There were a total of 229 matches played in our local open amateur knockout Tiddlywinks Championships last year. One player scratched out of the preliminary round because of illness and another from the third round because of holidays. Without doing any written calculation can you say how many players entered the competition?

(Q8-1)
(See Appendix C for quiz answers.)

BROWSING THE TREE WITH NWADMIN

NWADMIN (also known as the NetWare Administrator) is a Windows-based tool that allows you to graphically manage objects and properties in the NDS tree. You can also browse the tree by clicking on specific container objects and expanding their contents. Then, detailed resource information is just a double-click away. With this utility, you can view, create, move, delete, and assign rights to any object in the NDS tree. Of course, you can only mess around with the objects for which you have access rights.

> **TIP**
>
> **You may restrict access to NWADMIN by moving it from SYS:PUBLIC into another, more restricted subdirectory (such as SYS:SYSTEM). Everyday users don't need this powerful tree-browsing utility.**

If you want to manage the NDS tree, you must load Client 32 or the NetWare DOS Requester on your workstation (see Chapter 12 and Chapter 13 for details). Once you've done so, you can perform any of the following functions with NWADMIN:

- Create and delete objects (such as users and groups)

- Assign rights to the NDS tree and file system

- Set up IntranetWare print services

- Set up and manage NDS partitions and replicas

- Browse object and property information throughout the tree

- Move and rename NDS objects

- Set up licensing services

NWADMIN runs as a multiple-document interface application. That means you can display up to nine different browsing windows at one time. The primary window is shown in Figure 8.4. It provides a background for viewing one or more secondary windows.

FIGURE 8.4

The Main Browsing Window in NWADMIN

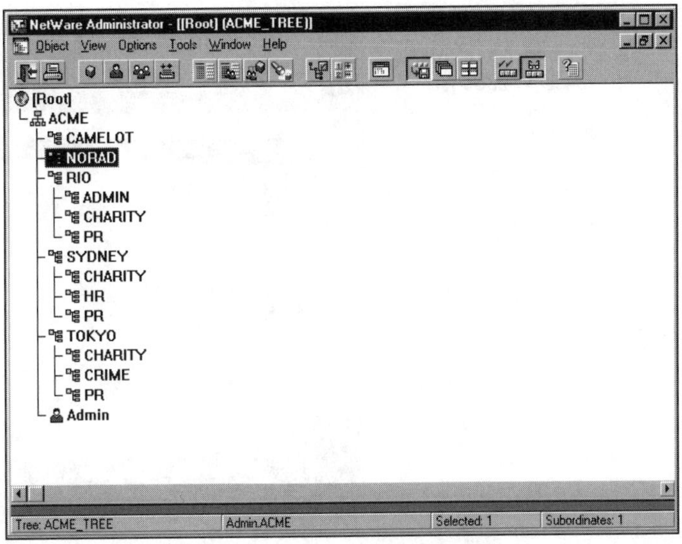

```
NetWare Administrator - [[Root] (ACME_TREE)]
Object  View  Options  Tools  Window  Help

[Root]
  ACME
    CAMELOT
    NORAD
    RIO
      ADMIN
      CHARITY
      PR
    SYDNEY
      CHARITY
      HR
      PR
    TOKYO
      CHARITY
      CRIME
      PR
    Admin

Tree: ACME_TREE          Admin.ACME          Selected: 1    Subordinates: 1
```

REAL WORLD

IntranetWare includes two versions of NWADMIN: Windows 3.1 (SYS:PUBLIC\NWADMN3X) and Windows 95 (SYS:PUBLIC\WIN95\NWADMN95). In this book, we'll focus on the Windows 95 version.

To open a secondary browser window in NWADMIN, select a container object from the primary window, and choose the Browse option from the Tools menu.

The new browser window will display all NDS objects in your new current context. You can now manage any of the objects, directories, and/or files in the window. Figure 8.5 shows a secondary browser window for the CAMELOT container of ACME. Notice all the resources (servers, users, volumes, and so on).

You can open up to nine browser windows at a time. To view multiple windows, select the Tile option from the Windows menu. Figure 8.6 shows three browser windows tiled for [Root], CAMELOT, and NORAD. Once again, notice how easy it is to view multiple ACME resources — regardless of their location.

Finally, the title for each of the browser windows displays its context. This helps you track where all of your resources are — in the logical NDS world.

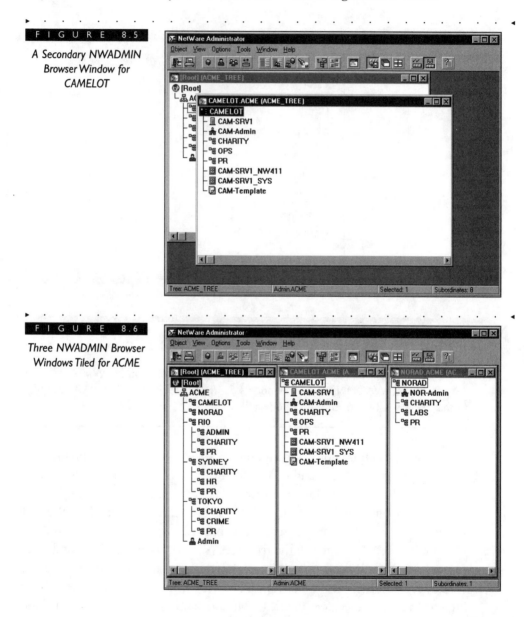

FIGURE   8.5

A Secondary NWADMIN
Browser Window for
CAMELOT

FIGURE   8.6

Three NWADMIN Browser
Windows Tiled for ACME

Now that you have the hang of general NWADMIN browsing, let's try a few special tasks (such as browsing containers, browsing properties, and searching). Ready, set, browse.

Browsing Container Objects

You can also browse the NDS tree by walking through container objects. Since they're glorified Tupperware bowls, containers can be opened and closed. Of the several ways to expand the contents of a container, here are just a few:

1 • Double-click on the container object. When you double-click on a container, it expands its contents. This also shows all subordinate container objects. If the container is expanded, you can collapse it by double-clicking on it again.

2 • Select a container object in the tree and choose the Expand option from the View menu. This will expand the contents of the container. You can collapse the container by using the Collapse option from the same menu.

3 • Select a container object and press the plus (+) key on the numeric keypad of your keyboard. The container object will expand and show its contents (sounds embarrassing). You'll find that the plus (+) key above the equal sign (=), however, doesn't work. You must use the numeric keypad. You can collapse the container by pressing the minus (-) key on the numeric keypad.

4 • Select a container object and press the right mouse button. Select the Browse option from the pull-down menu that appears. This launches a new browser window with the contents of the container object. Figure 8.7 shows the short menu that appears when the right mouse button is pressed. By the way, this is a great shortcut feature. In this case, "right" is right. Draw your own conclusions.

That's good for containers, now let's see what their contents have to offer.

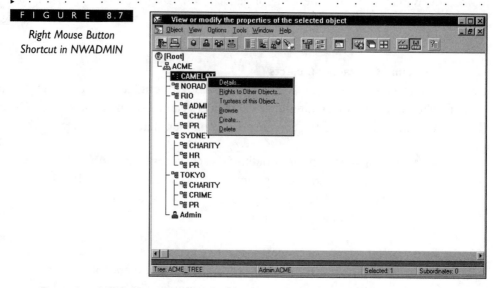

Browsing NDS Properties

You can also browse the properties of any given object by choosing Details from the pull-down menu in Figure 8.7. Or, here are a few other ways to browse NDS properties:

1 • Double-click on a leaf object. Remember, double-clicking on a container object expands and/or contracts it.

2 • Select the object and then choose the Details option from the Object menu. This works for containers as well.

3 • Select the object and press the right mouse button. Choose Details from the pull-down menu that appears. This works for containers as well.

The object dialog box is organized into pages that you can access with the buttons that run down the right side of the dialog. The Identification page always appears first and is shown in Figure 8.2. You can browse specific NDS properties by selecting the corresponding page button. Each object type has a different set of page buttons because each object type has a different set of properties. Earlier, in Figure 8.2, we were browsing the user dialog window. Notice the difference in Figure 8.8 — it shows the page buttons for the O=ACME container object.

*Browsing Properties for
O=ACME*

TIP

The pages in an object dialog box are all part of the same dialog. In other words, when you select a different page, you are still in the same dialog. If you press OK or Cancel on any page, you are affecting the entire dialog box, not just the individual page. For example, OK will save modifications to all of the pages and Cancel will exit the dialog box without saving changes to any page. In order to move between pages of the dialog box, select the desired page.

Searching for NDS Objects and Properties

You can find object and property information in the NDS tree by using the Search feature. You can perform this function without having to expand each of the container objects. It's much easier, trust me. The search operation will browse the entire tree, unless you narrow the search criteria.

For example, in Figure 8.9, the search criteria is configured to find all of the users in the ACME tree who have a Department property equal to Charity. You can further narrow the search by starting at a subcontainer instead of the [Root]. Or, you can expand your searching criteria to include *all* Charity objects, not just users. As you can see, the NWADMIN searching engine is very sophisticated. Maybe you'll find what you're looking for.

F I G U R E   8.9

Searching the ACME Tree
for Charity Users

```
┌──────────────────────────────────────────────────────────────────────┐
│ ┌┐ NetWare Administrator - [[Root] [ACME_TREE]]              _ □ X     │
│ ┌┐ Object  View  Options  Tools  Window  Help               _ ⊟ X     │
│ ─────────────────────────────────────────────────────────────────────│
│  [Root]                                                                │
│   └ ..ACME                                                             │
│      ┌ CAMELOT      ┌───────────────────────────────────────────┐     │
│      ┌ NORAD        │ Search                               X     │     │
│      ┌ RIO          │ Start from:                                │     │
│      ┌ SYDNEY       │ [Root]                              [ ]     │     │
│      ┌ TOKYO        │                                            │     │
│      └ Admin        │ ☑ Search entire subtree                    │     │
│                     │ Search for:                                │     │
│                     │ User                            ▼          │     │
│                     │ Property:                                  │     │
│                     │ Department                      ▼          │     │
│                     │ Equal To        ▼  Charity                 │     │
│                     │   [ OK ] [Cancel] [Save...] [Open...] [Help]│     │
│                     └───────────────────────────────────────────┘     │
│ ─────────────────────────────────────────────────────────────────────│
│ Tree: ACME_TREE        Admin.ACME        Selected: 1   Subordinates: 6 │
└──────────────────────────────────────────────────────────────────────┘
```

ZEN

"What a man needs in gardening is a cast-iron back, with a hinge in it."

Charles Dudley Warner

SMART LINK

If you want to browse an NDS tree of your own, surf over to CyberState University and World Wire at http://www.cyberstateu.com.

This completes our brief tour through NWADMIN. You will quickly come to appreciate this utility — or not. Whatever your feelings are about Windows, you can't argue with NWADMIN's graceful interface and consolidated functionality. It does everything — even things its DOS-based cousin (NETADMIN) can't. Speaking of family, let's check out the other five browsing tools.

BROWSING THE TREE WITH OTHER TOOLS

NWADMIN is great, but it's not the only game in town. IntranetWare provides a myriad of other browsing tools with a variety of different interfaces (GUI, DOS-based menu, and command line). If you're in a bind, or you just hate Windows, these tools are there for you:

- ▸ NETADMIN

- ▸ CX

- ▸ NLIST

- ▸ User Tools (NETUSER and NWUSER)

NETADMIN

NETADMIN is a DOS-based version of NWADMIN. The main difference is the "tunnel-vision" view it provides. Unlike NWADMIN, NETADMIN only displays one container at a time. If you remember from our earlier discussion, NWADMIN allows you to open multiple windows, or view multiple containers in the tree structure. No such luck in NETADMIN. For this reason, it's not a very good browsing tool, especially if you don't know what the garden looks like in the first place. Figure 8.10 shows the main screen of NETADMIN.

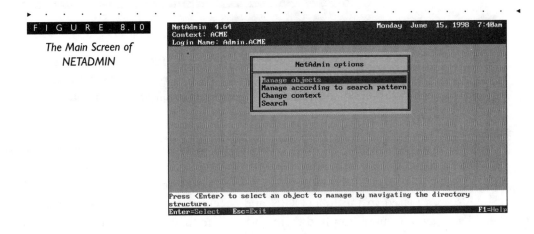

F I G U R E 8.10

The Main Screen of
NETADMIN

In order to browse down the NDS tree with NETADMIN, select a container object from the browse window and press Enter. The container objects are marked with a plus sign (+) in front of the name (see Figure 8.11). Objects without a plus sign are leaf objects and do not contain other objects. In Figure 8.11, the CAMELOT, NORAD, RIO, SYNDEY, and TOKYO objects are containers. The Admin user is a leaf object.

To browse up the NDS tree to the parent container, select the double-dot (..) or parent marker. To view or edit the properties of the current container object, select the dot (.) or current container marker. Pretty fancy, huh? I guess it depends on your definition of "fancy."

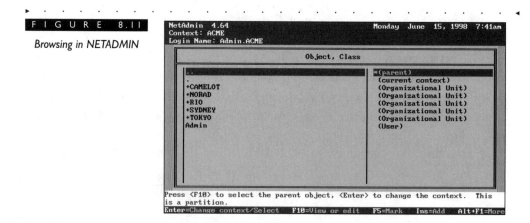

F I G U R E   8.11

Browsing in NETADMIN

THE BRAIN

For more information on using the NETADMIN utility, see the AppNote entitled "Using NETADMIN to Create and Administer NDS Objects" in the July 1993 issue of *Novell Application Notes*.

CX

Change Context (CX) is a DOS-based command line utility that allows you to navigate the tree by changing your current context. You can only use CX to view container and leaf objects in the tree. It doesn't provide any property information. Also, it's placed in the SYS:LOGIN and SYS:PUBLIC subdirectories, by default. This way, your users can find themselves before they log in. Figure 8.12 displays the help screen for CX.

FIGURE 8.12

The CX Help Screen

```
┌─────────────────────────────────────────────────────────────────────┐
│ CX                          Options Help                        4.20  │
│ Syntax:  CX [new context ¦ /VER] [/R] [/[T ¦ CONT] [/A]] [/C] [/?]    │
│                                                                        │
│ To:                                                     Use:          │
│   View all container objects below the                  /T            │
│     current or specified context.                                      │
│   View container objects at the current                 /CONT         │
│     or specified level.                                                │
│   Modify /T or /CONT to view All objects                /A            │
│     at or below the context                                            │
│   Change context or view objects relative to root       /R            │
│   Display version information                           /VER          │
│   Scroll continuously                                   /C            │
│                                                                        │
│   For example, to:                                      Type:         │
│   View directory tree below the current context         CX /T         │
│   View containers within a specific context             CX .O=Novell /CONT│
│                                                                        │
│ >>> Enter = More    C = Continuous    Esc = Cancel                    │
│                                                                        │
└─────────────────────────────────────────────────────────────────────┘
```

Following is a brief description of the CX browsing options. If you want to learn more about using CX to change your current context, refer to Chapter 2 ("Understanding NDS").

▸ /CONT — List just the container objects in the current context.

▸ /R — List all the container objects starting at the [Root] object. This option also changes your current context to the top of the tree — also known as the [Root].

▸ /T — List all the container objects below the current context.

▸ /A — List all the objects when used in conjunction with /T. This includes all the leaf objects.

SMART LINK

For a complete list of "CX" options, consult the *NetWare 4.11 Utilities Reference* at http://www.novell.com/manuals.

Figure 8.13 displays the output of the CX /T command for the ACME tree when the current context is set to [Root]. Check out all of the interesting information. I sure hope it doesn't fall into the wrong hands — like the Alpha Centurions. Stay tuned for more information concerning security loopholes and CX — check out Chapter 11 ("IntranetWare Security").

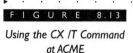

```
*** Directory Services Mapping ***

ACME
  ├CAMELOT
  │   ├CHARITY
  │   ├OPS
  │   │  ├FIN
  │   │  └DIST
  │   └PR
  ├NORAD
  │   ├CHARITY
  │   ├LABS
  │   │  ├R&D
  │   │  │  ├POLL
  │   │  │  ├NUC
  │   │  │  └UR
  │   │  └WHI
  │   └PR
  └RIO
      ├ADMIN
      │  ├FAC
      │  ├AUDIT
      │  └MRKT
      ├CHARITY
>>> Enter = More    C = Continuous    Esc = Cancel
```

NLIST

NLIST allows you to browse objects *and* properties in IntranetWare. It replaces
a number of NetWare 3 utilities, including USERLIST, SLIST, SECURITY, and so
on. NLIST works on most NDS objects (including Aliases, Computers, Directory
Maps, Groups, Organizational Units, Printers, Profiles, Servers, Users, and
Volumes). NLIST includes a multitude of options, most of which are shown in
Figure 8.14.

```
NLIST                    Basic Options Help Screen                    4.20

Purpose: Specify basic options for viewing objects.
Syntax: NLIST class type [= object name] [basic option]

To display:                                             Use:
  Active users or servers                                 /A
  Objects throughout all subordinate contexts             /S
  Objects in a specified context                          /CO <context>
  Objects at [ROOT] context                               /R
  Continuously without pausing                            /C
  Bindery information                                     /B
  Version information                                     /VER
  Available Directory Services trees                      /TREE

For example, to:                                        Type:
  See servers in all subordinate contexts                 NLIST Server /S
  See logged in users (active)                            NLIST User /A
  See volumes in the context O=My Org                     NLIST Volume /CO "O=My Org"
  See servers in bindery mode                             NLIST Server /B
  See Directory trees in bindery mode                     NLIST /Tree = *

J:\PUBLIC>
```

Please be sure to use the proper syntax for NLIST. It's kind of picky that way.
Here's how it works:

```
NLIST [object type] [=object name] [/options]
```

Here are some examples:

▸ NLIST user /R /S — Searches for all User objects in the tree starting at [Root]

▸ NLIST server /B — Displays all the servers (even bindery ones)

You can also use NLIST to view property information. In this case, you must use WHERE and SHOW, as follows:

```
NLIST [object type][=object name] [WHERE [property] [value]]

        [SHOW [property]]
```

Here are some great property examples:

▸ NLIST user=AEinstein /D — Shows all property details about a user named AEinstein in the current context

▸ NLIST user WHERE "Security Equal To" = CAM-Admin — Shows all the users in the current context that are security equivalent to the CAM-Admin Organizational Role

NLIST is a very powerful tool from the command line. The syntax is a little tricky, but once you get the hang of it, you'll love it.

User Tools

What about users? They like gardens, too. Well, my best advice to you is — watch them like a hawk. You never know what mischief they'll get themselves into.

Fortunately, IntranetWare provides two gardening tools just for users — NWUSER and NETUSER. They provide the same functionality, except that NWUSER is Windows-based and NETUSER is DOS-based. With these utilities, users can change their own context, manage server connections, manage the drive and search mappings, change their passwords, modify login scripts, capture printers/print queues, and send messages.

REAL WORLD

NWUSER is a Windows 3.1 tool. You can access the same functionality in Windows 95 by using the Microsoft "Network Neighborhood."

In the case of NWUSER, it even does Windows (sorry). Refer to Figure 8.15 for a snapshot of the NWUSER browsing tool. In this case, we're mapping drives to the LABS-SRV1 server. Cool.

FIGURE 8.15

The Mapping Window in NWUSER

NetWare Drive Connections

Path:
\\\CN=LABS-SRV1_SYS.OU=LABS.OU=NORAD... \PUBLIC

Drives:
A:
B:
C:
D:
E:
F: \\\CN=LABS-SRV1_SYS.OU=LABS.OU=NORA
G:
H:
I:
J:
K:
L:
M:
N:
O:

Resources:
..ACME
OU=CAMELOT
OU=NORAD
OU=RIO
OU=SYDNEY
OU=TOKYO

Drive Connections (Alt+D)   Drive Info...   Permanent   Map Delete   Map

This completes our tour of the IntranetWare garden. That was a rather nice, quiet stroll through NDS. We really should do this more often — stop to smell the roses. I especially enjoyed the browsing part, how about you?

Now that you're familiar with the garden, it's time to get down to business. To succeed in the NDS garden, you must be down-to-Earth (literally), and focus on the NDS objects. Now it's time to put on your canvas gloves and dig in. Ready, set, garden.

ZEN

"Bees are not as busy as we think they are. They just can't buzz any slower."

Kin Hubbard

Managing NDS Objects

What does it mean to have a green thumb? Does it mean you're a Martian? No. Does it mean you should bathe more often? Probably not. Does it mean you get along well with plants? Bingo. The term green thumb implies that you understand the delicate balance of life in the garden. It means that you appreciate your chlorophyll-based friends and constantly nurture them. It means that you love the smell of fresh-cut flowers, dirt between your toes, and the hot sun beating down the back of your neck. To have a green thumb is to be blessed — and dirty.

As a CNE, you need a red thumb. You must appreciate the delicate balance of life on the WAN. To have a red thumb means that you appreciate your users and their resources. It means that you like the smell of LaserJet toner, NDS objects between your toes, and disgruntled users breathing down the back of your neck. It means that you need to get a life.

So, what is garden management all about? It involves a combination of tools, knowledge, luck, and experience. You must know when to fertilize, when to water, and when not to spray pesticide. Similarly, NDS management is a combination of CNE tools (NWADMIN), knowledge of NDS objects, luck, and WAN experience. In this section, we will explore all the most important NDS objects and learn how to manage them effectively. This is the most important aspect of IntranetWare gardening because after all — objects *are* NDS. Let's start by getting acquainted with NDS objects and learning what makes them tick.

GETTING TO KNOW NDS OBJECTS

Objects *are* NDS. In order to manage NDS, you must learn the intricacies of NDS objects. But you can't stop there. You must understand the relationships *between* objects as well. Sometimes it doesn't make sense to place a sunflower next to a rose. They're just not compatible.

In Chapter 2, we gained a fundamental understanding of NDS objects and their purposes. We learned about object classifications, and settled on two types: container objects and non-container (leaf) objects. The critical issue here is *containment* — that is, who contains whom. From a management perspective, it's important to understand how containment works. You must make sure that objects are correctly placed in the tree. Figure 8.16 shows how containers and non-containers interact with each other.

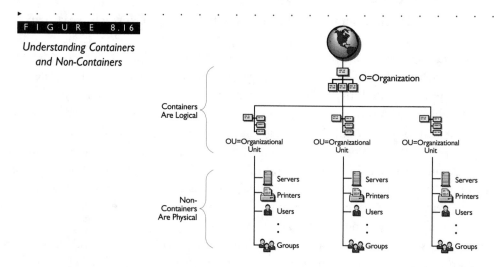

In general, containers are logical and non-containers are physical. This is another important distinction. It means the sole purpose of containers is to organize and store physical network resources — non-containers. So, if you think about it, the non-containers are doing all the work. They add productivity to the WAN. They are the sole reason you and I have a job. Wow, it sure puts things in perspective. Once you understand the relationships of these object types, it helps you better manage them. After all, roses are pretty, but tomatoes feed us — and, therefore, keep us alive.

The containment of an object specifies where it can appear in the Directory and which objects can be created underneath it. Table 8.1 provides a list of the NDS container objects and their containment rules. Notice the Locality container. It's there, but unavailable to the IntranetWare utilities. That means you can't play with it. Also, refer to Figure 8.17 for a graphical representation of the NDS containment rules. This figure also includes non-container (that is, leaf) objects.

T A B L E 8.1	OBJECT TYPE	CONTAINMENT
Containers and Their Containment	[Root]	Locality, Country, Organization
	Country	Locality, Organization
	Locality	Locality, Organization, Organizational Unit
	Organization	Locality, Organizational Unit, Leaf Objects
	Organizational Unit	Locality, Organizational Unit, Leaf Objects

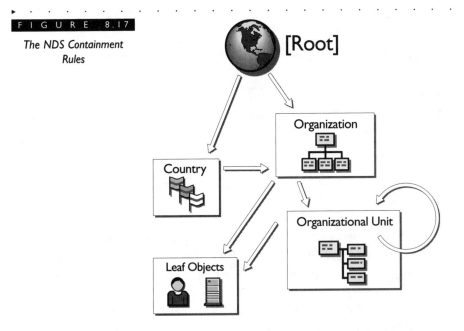

F I G U R E   8.17

The NDS Containment Rules

You will quickly discover (if you haven't already) that some objects are more popular than others. The User object, for example, is the most commonly used leaf object because it defines everybody in your tree. On the other hand, you might never use an external entity or bindery queue. That's OK, your tree is unique, and it's nice to know that they're there for you if you ever need them.

Inside each object is a predefined subset of properties that describes characteristics about it. The User object, for example, has 55 different properties defining everything from First Name to Network Address. As a CNE, it's your job to manage these properties and to make sure that the right people have access to the right information. Approximately 142 available properties are defined in the base NDS object definitions. Various combinations of these properties apply to all objects. You can easily view this information through any of the NWADMIN, NETADMIN, or NLIST tools. Take your pick.

ZEN

"Man is a complex being who makes deserts bloom and lakes die."

Gil Stern

For now, I'd like to take you on a magic carpet ride through some required and commonly used NDS objects. The more you learn about them, the better off you'll be.

Following is a list of the five required NDS objects. These containers and leaves are created automatically during the installation of the first server in the tree:

▸ [Root] — The top (or the bottom) of the tree — it depends on your point of view. [Root] is created during installation of the very first IntranetWare server in the tree.

▸ Organization — Usually located directly under the [Root] (unless a Country or Locality is used). Think of it as the "trunk." The first server must exist somewhere, and it can't exist under the [Root], so here it is.

▸ User — You, me, them — leaves. The first, and only, default user is Admin and he or she is placed inside the first Organization container.

▸ Server — IntranetWare must run somewhere. Regardless of what you might think, the logical NDS garden still exists inside the server greenhouse.

▸ Volume — The soil.

Next, we must shift our focus from required to commonly used NDS objects. The following 11 object classes provide additional functionality to your tree. As a matter of fact, you'll probably use all or most of them. Remember, don't force the issue. Only use the object types that make sense for your unique situation. This is not a popularity contest.

▸ Bindery Object — Created by NDS for backward compatibility. It represents a bindery-based resource (such as an upgraded NetWare 3 print queue).

▸ Organizational Unit — The real branches of our tree. True geographic and organizational structure is provided through multiple OU layers.

▸ Organizational Role — Defines a role or position within the company. A useful tool for managing "turnstile" User objects.

▸ Group — A collection of unrelated users. Very useful management object.

▸ Directory Map — An independent pointer for automating application search drive mappings.

▸ Alias — Beware, they're not what they appear to be.

▸ Print Server — Serves printing.

▸ Printer — It prints.

▸ Print Queue — It queues.

▸ Profile — A special management group for sharing global, location, or special-function login scripts.

▸ Unknown — If all else fails . . . .

Now, let's explore each of these objects in more detail. In each case, we will learn three important pieces of information: Purpose, Use, and Recommendations.

Purpose describes what the objects do. *Use* provides some examples of how you might use the objects. *Recommendations* are provided to help you manage these objects in your own NDS tree. So, without any further adieu, allow me to introduce IntranetWare's 16 most exciting NDS objects — starting, of course, with the [Root].

SMART LINK

For more information on NDS objects or the architecture of the Directory, surf to the Novell Knowledgebase at http://support .novell.com/search/.

[ROOT]

Purpose

The [Root] object is at the top of our inverted tree structure. The [Root], from a visual standpoint, is the starting point of your tree and branches downward, as shown in Figure 8.18. The name of the [Root] object is the same as the name of your tree. When you install the very first IntranetWare server, you are prompted for a tree name. At this point you are actually naming the [Root] object. Each tree can have only one [Root] object. In our case, it's called ACME_TREE, but NWADMIN shows it as [Root].

The [Root] object's name is broadcast on the WAN using the Service Advertising Protocol (SAP). If you have multiple trees running on the same network infrastructure, you must ensure that the names are unique.

Use

Choose a name for [Root] that will clearly identify your organization or company. Keep in mind that renaming the [Root] can only be done with the DSMERGE utility (discussed later in this chapter) and becomes more difficult the larger your tree becomes. This is because your entire NDS naming structure relies on the [Root].

Recommendations

Most companies simply use the same name as their Organization object and add the extension _TREE. For example, our tree name is ACME_TREE, because the organization name is O=ACME. Ensure that you choose a name you will be able to recognize when you're monitoring server-to-server communications.

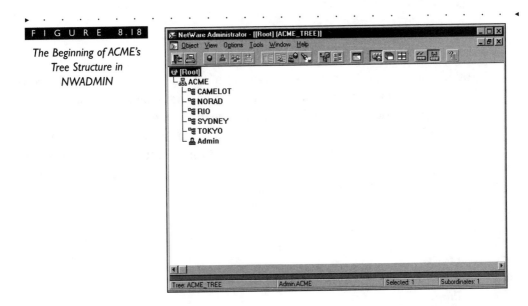

F I G U R E   8.18

The Beginning of ACME's Tree Structure in NWADMIN

ZEN

"Spring has come when you can put your foot on three daisies."

Folk Wisdoms

ORGANIZATION

Purpose

This object class is used to define your company. An Organization object will be located directly under the [Root] object unless, of course, you are using one or more Country objects. You are required to define at least one Organization in your NDS tree. Multiple Organization objects may be used directly below the [Root], if needed.

Use

As you learned previously, ACME's tree contains only one Organization object, namely O=ACME (see Figure 8.18). The Organization represents the name of your company and should be an overall descriptor of your business. If you are a nonprofit group or university, it can be the name of your campus (O=UCB, for example).

Recommendations

Most companies define only one Organization object in their tree. The rule of thumb for determining whether to use multiple Organization objects is based on your network infrastructure. For example, if you are a large conglomerate with separate network infrastructures, you can use a separate Organization object for each entity. This type strategy may be used, for instance, if each company is separately managed with a separate network infrastructure. If all business are connected with the same network, then a single Organization may more accurately represent your WAN. In the latter case, you would use an Organizational Unit to represent each business unit.

 ## USER

Purpose

The most common object in your tree will probably be the User object. The NDS User object is similar to the bindery user in NetWare 3, but ours contains many more configurable attributes.

Use

During installation of the first IntranetWare server in your tree, you are prompted to create the first user in the tree. This user, usually named Admin, initially has Supervisor rights to the entire NDS structure (see Figure 8.19). At this point, Admin is the only object with such complete and extensive access to your tree. The importance of maintaining Admin is well-documented — see Chapter 11 ("IntranetWare Security"). If you delete Admin without making any backup contingencies, you will lose all administrative control of the tree. Your options under such circumstances would be to reinstall NDS or to call Novell Technical Support to provide you with re-entrance to your tree. Be very careful with the Delete key.

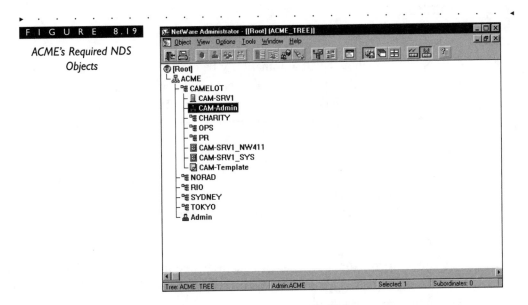

ACME's Required NDS
Objects

Recommendations

After you install the first couple of IntranetWare servers, ensure that the Admin password is protected. Follow these simple steps:

1 • Your first IntranetWare server installation will prompt you for the Admin password. Remember, this password is also assigned to the bindery [Supervisor] object. If you change the Admin password at a later date, the bindery [Supervisor] password does *not* change. Choose a secure password and don't forget it. Change your passwords periodically for greater security.

2 • Create an Organizational Role at the Organization level and grant it all object rights [BCDRS] to the [Root] object (see CAM-Admin in Figure 8.19). In addition, create a user called Backup and put him or her into the Organizational Role. Whatever you do, don't make the Organizational Role object security equivalent to the original Admin user. This creates a loophole. If the Admin is deleted, the Organizational Role becomes useful — effectively, the security equivalent to dirt! Refer to Chapter 11 for more in-depth security analyses.

SERVER

Purpose

An NDS Server object will automatically be created for any server installed or upgraded to IntranetWare. The Server object holds key WAN information (such as the network address, NetWare version, and serial number). Refer to Figure 8.19 for an illustration of CAMELOT's first server (CAM-SRV1).

Use

The Server object is managed primarily by NDS and requires little or no attention from you. You may want to assign yourself Supervisor [S] rights to the server for administrative purposes. Once again, see Chapter 11.

Recommendations

Be sure to follow the naming standards presented in Chapter 4 ("NDS Design") when creating Server objects. Consistent and appropriate naming will help the tree walking process considerably.

VOLUME

Purpose

At least one server volume (SYS:) is created when you install an IntranetWare server (see Figure 8.19). This is a logical representation of your physical server file system. It is possible to create multiple logical Volume objects, but each must point to a physical NetWare volume (such as CAM-SRV1_SYS).

Use

This object exists primarily to give you greater flexibility in volume management, if needed. It also increases file access by spreading the logical file system throughout the tree. It's important to note that the actual files always stay on the server — they are *not* distributed throughout the tree with the Volume object. That's IntranetWare 3.

Recommendations

IntranetWare gives you the flexibility of placing print queues on any IntranetWare volume. We recommend that you always create at least one other volume in addition to the SYS: volume so that your print queues will not fill up the SYS: volume. This can cause the server to shut down. In addition, use volume restrictions to limit the size of your volumes before they fill up completely. You can also limit the disk space occupied by user files with NWADMIN.

QUIZ

A Greek was born on the 260th day of 20 BC, and died on the 260th day of AD 60. How many years did he live?

(Q8-2)

This completes our discussion of the five required NDS objects. Refer to Figure 8.19 for a review of the CAMELOT subtree. Now, let's take a closer look at some commonly used NDS objects.

BINDERY OBJECT

Purpose
This leaf object represents any object created by Bindery Services and designated as such by the Directory. The Bindery object has the format of "Bindery Identifier + Object ID" and is used to provide backward compatibility for bindery-oriented applications or utilities.

Use
Bindery objects typically appear after an upgrade or migration from NetWare 2 or 3 to IntranetWare. They only occur if NDS can't identify them. For applications that require the bindery, a Bindery object will be created. Although these objects appear in utilities such as NWADMIN, they are nonmanageable and are present for informational purposes only.

Recommendations
Do not delete a Bindery object until you verify its purpose. Some installation utilities create a Bindery object for specific purposes. If removed, they will cause problems for your applications. Also, some Bindery objects can't be removed at all, and may require the use of DSLOAD — a special "repo-man" for IntranetWare.

ORGANIZATIONAL UNIT

Purpose

Nearly all NDS trees contain Organizational Units. They are, however, optional. Organizational Units serve the purpose of subdividing the tree into functional units. As we learned in Chapter 4, this subdivision can be based on either location or organization — it's up to you.

Use

As shown in Figure 8.19, the ACME tree uses containers to make logical divisions in the tree. Notice that the first level of OU's represent geographic sites based on the network infrastructure. Subsequent levels are organized according to departments. Many trees will be designed in this fashion, with several levels of nested Organizational Units. For more information on designing an IntranetWare tree, see Chapter 4 ("NDS Design").

Recommendations

Most companies use Organizational Units to represent geographic locations, divisions, and workgroups. You generally use an Organizational Unit to group common users and resources in the same container. Organizational Units should not be created to represent a single person or a single resource. They are used to provide access to a group of resources in a particular part of the tree.

ORGANIZATIONAL ROLE

Purpose

An Organizational Role is typically used to define a functional position within the company. It is extremely useful as an administrative tool because it acts as a holding cell for NDS and file system security. Once you make a user an occupant of an Organizational Role, that user immediately inherits the rights of the position.

Use

Organizational Roles can be used to create subadministrators. Users can be moved in and out of the role quickly to facilitate short-term assignments. For example, if the regular administrator is absent for any length of time, another user can be moved into the Organizational Role temporarily. While there, he or she can manage the network.

As shown in Figure 8.19, we have created an Organizational Role for each ACME location. Each Organizational Role will have complete administrator privileges to all resources within that location. This includes all containers and subcontainers.

Recommendations

Organizational Roles allow you to distribute access rights to various container administrators. It also allows you to switch occupants at a moment's notice (for instance, if an administrator goes on vacation, gets sick, or goes crazy). This system also allows you to easily track security by centralizing it all in one object. It sure beats assigning administrator rights to each user independently. Refer to Chapter 11 ("IntranetWare Security"), for more information on NDS security.

GROUP

Purpose

Groups allow you to organize users from any part of the NDS tree. Groups function exactly the same way as they did in NetWare 3 — they are primarily used for assigning rights. There is very little difference between Group objects and Organizational Units (OUs). As a matter of fact, containers are called natural groups because they naturally group all the users within their context. Both have the same function — placing common users close together.

It is true that users as members of both objects receive rights by security equivalence, but there are some differences. Because of security equivalency, any member of an OU will receive whatever rights the OU possesses, provided that there is not an intervening Inherited Rights Filter (IRF) placed on that user. Users who are members of Group objects also receive whatever rights the Group possesses, but there is no IRF provision.

OK, I can't hold out any longer. There is one major difference between OUs and groups — groups can contain users from separate parts of the tree. So, here's the bottom line: If all the users are in the same container, and they have similar resource needs, use the OU for assigning rights. Otherwise, use a Group object.

Also, use a Group object if you want to assign rights to a small subset of users *within* a container.

Use

In order to provide rights to a small subset of users in the CHARITY.SYDNEY. ACME OU, for example, you can use a Group object. Figure 8.20 shows an Organizational Unit called OU=CHARITY and its populated users and resources. Within this OU are two sets of users — HP4SI and WP. Each group needs to access different software on the server and requires different rights assignments. Within the Container login script, the "IF MEMBER OF GROUP" statements are used to determine which group a user belongs for assigning rights. When each user logs into the network, the login script determines if a user is a member of a group, and sets the appropriate environmental variables. Very cool.

Understanding Groups in the OU=CHARITY Container of ACME

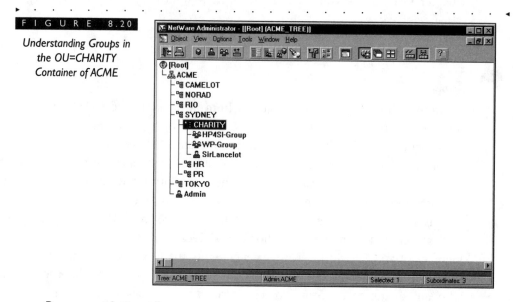

Recommendations

Groups are great for associating users in the same or different containers. They define rights for a subset of users. Typically, you'll want to create groups within a container instead of creating more functional containers. If it's a geographically separated site, it's a different story. Limit your number of groups to less than 15 in a Container login script, if possible. The more groups, the longer the Container login script will be and the slower login will be. Also, if you have that many groups, you should most likely create additional containers.

ZEN

"A plant is like a self-willed man, out of whom we can obtain all which we desire, if we will only treat him his own way."

Goethe

DIRECTORY MAP

Purpose
The Directory Map object is a centralized pointer that refers to a directory on a NetWare volume. They're used in login scripts to point to applications. We'll explore them in much greater depth in Chapter 10 ("IntranetWare File System").

Use
Let's assume that you have WordPerfect installed in a directory called WP60. Then, let's assume you upgrade your software to WordPerfect 6.1 — and rename the subdirectory WP61. Normally, you would have to change every login script to reflect this change. Too much work. The Directory Map object allows you to centralize applications by pointing to the Directory Map object instead of the directory itself. Then, when you upgrade, all the login scripts remain the same and you only make one change — to the Directory Map object itself.

Recommendations
Directory Maps are useful for providing a standard Container login script on multiple servers. We recommend that you have standard file structures for all your IntranetWare volumes. There are also some security considerations when using Directory Maps, which we'll talk about in Chapter 11 ("IntranetWare Security").

ALIAS

Purpose

An Alias object points to another object in the tree. It's IntranetWare incognito — the object of a million disguises. An Alias object can point to either a container or leaf object.

Use

An Alias object is a name containing at least one *relative distinguished name* (RDN). As a CNE, you may want to use aliases to give users access to specific resources in other parts of the tree. You could create an alias to reference a printer in another container, for example. The Alias object can be considered a relay to another object in a different part of the tree.

You can also alias an Organizational Unit to another OU. This basically gives all the objects in one container access to the resources in another.

The object being aliased is known as the *primary object*. When you create an Alias object, you may or may not want to name it with an Alias flag. For example, the name might include the word "alias," as in "AEinstein-Alias". You should use the Alias flag to distinguish between the primary and Alias object. Otherwise, they both use the same icon and act the same. How do you tell who is who? I'm glad you asked. In Windows 95, NWADMIN will display the Alias object with two icons: the primary object icon and the alias mask shown in the left margin. Pretty cool, huh?

Recommendations

The Alias can be useful for some companies that create mobile users who do not want to have to remember their user contexts. The Alias can be created at the top of the tree below the Organization object to shorten the user's context. If a user named Dr. Watson in CRIME.TOKYO.ACME wants to log into the network, he only has to remember that his context is Dr Watson.ACME because the alias points to his actual context in the tree. This example is shown in Figure 8.21.

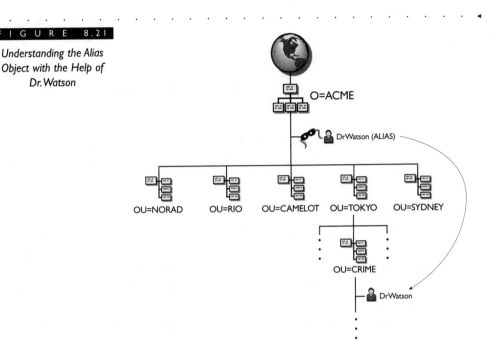

F I G U R E   8.21

*Understanding the Alias
Object with the Help of
Dr. Watson*

PRINT SERVER

Purpose

The Print Server leaf object represents a server that takes print jobs out of a print queue and sends them to a network printer. This object is used in conjunction with the Printer and Print Queue objects. A Print Server object must be created for every actual print server that exists on the IntranetWare network.

Use

All IntranetWare networks offering printing services will have at least one Print Server object. You can also define print server operators using this object.

PRINTER

Purpose

Used in conjunction with the Print Server object, you use this object to manage a printer. The assignment for a print queue can be made within the object.

Use

You can attach to the network printers in several different ways (for example, directly to the network cable, to a printer port of a NetWare server, or to a printer port of a PC).

Recommendations

Place the Printer object along with the Print Queue object as high as possible in your NDS tree. This provides support for as many users as possible. If your printer will be accessed by users in this container only, then place the printer in this container. If more containers need access to the printer, place the object in the next higher level in the tree. We also recommend that you configure printers as network-direct printers in queue server mode. Intrigued? Check out Chapter 14.

PRINT QUEUE

Purpose

This object represents a print queue defined on an IntranetWare server volume. The queue actually represents the physical directory in an IntranetWare volume where the print jobs reside while they're waiting to be printed.

Use

Place Print Queue objects along with Printer objects at the highest level possible in your tree. This way, they can service the most users.

Recommendations

All IntranetWare print queues should be placed on a volume other than the SYS: volume. This provides greater fault tolerance for the server. At least one Print Queue object must be created for IntranetWare printing. Also, don't forget to assign each Print Queue object to the appropriate Printer object.

PROFILE

Purpose

The Profile object is used as a special-purpose scripting object that executes a shared login script after the execution of a user's Container login script. The Profile script can contain special drive mappings or environment settings for a select group of people.

One of the properties of a User object is the Profile. When a user is first created, you can specify that the user participate in a Profile. You can also add a user to a Profile after the fact, through the user's Login Script property.

Use

The three notable uses for a profile script are

- ▶ Global login scripts

- ▶ Location login scripts

- ▶ Special Function login scripts.

Global Login Scripts

IntranetWare does not use a global System login script. Instead, each container can have its own login script. The order of execution of login scripts is

1 • Container login script (if used)

2 • Profile login script (if used)

3 • User login script (if used)

4 • Default login script (if no other script is available)

Therefore, if you want to create a more global login script and include users from multiple Organizational Units, you could employ the Profile object for group-specific settings.

Location Login Scripts

A Profile can also be used for determining resource allocation based on location. For example, each department of a company may have three printers and three print queues. With a Profile, you have the ability to assign a particular group of users to a specific print queue. You can use a Profile login script to capture to a particular print queue and then automatically print to the right printer.

Special Function Login Scripts

A Profile can also be used as a special-function script to assign access for applications. For example, you can create a Profile script that will be used by administrators only. This script could be used to give these users a specific drive assignment to a help desk utility. In this scenario, you would move the help desk utility out of the SYS:PUBLIC directory and into a new subdirectory you create called SYS:APPS\HELPDESK. When a user logs into the network, the Admin Profile executes and assigns the user a drive mapping to the HELPDESK directory. Only the users executing the Profile script will be assigned appropriate rights.

Recommendations

Typically, the Profile is used as a global login script for an entire organization. Keep in mind that the Profile object will execute from one container, although users may be participating from other containers and may see some performance issues if the script is executing over a wide area connection.

 ## UNKNOWN

Purpose

This class represents any restored object whose base class is currently undefined in the schema. Objects of this class are only created by the IntranetWare server. They usually occur when a mandatory property of an object has been lost.

Use

This object is automatically created by NDS. If you have an Unknown object appear in your tree, check to see if some other object has been deleted. In the case of a deleted Server object, the server's Volume objects will appear as Unknown objects and must be deleted by an administrator. In other circumstances, an Unknown object may appear temporarily as the NDS background processes work through a synchronization procedure.

Recommendations

Check before deleting an Unknown object, as the object may resolve itself. If you have verified that the object is not needed, then remove it from your tree. There is no point in maintaining unknown and unusable objects.

QUIZ

Very few of us now have dial (rotary) telephones, but the letter and number system is the same as it was when telephone dials were used for codes. Here is a coded message based on a telephone numbering system. For example, 2 would equal A, B, or C. All you have to do is select the correct letter from each group of three to solve the puzzle.

8447 47 4273 2322873 84373 273 84733 2464237 367 3224 686237

(Q8-3)

There you have it! Those are your NDS objects. Hopefully, you have a better appreciation for the complexity of NDS gardening. There's a lot of diversity in life, and it seems there's an NDS object for every occasion. As a matter of fact, it's possible to customize the IntranetWare schema and create additional object types and properties. Once again, genetic engineering is put to good use.

However, before you get too excited about merging and crossbreeding, let's learn how to create these NDS objects. In the next two sections, we will explore IntranetWare's two main object creation tools:

▸ NWADMIN

▸ UIMPORT

Ready, set, create.

THE BRAIN

Check out these AppNotes for more information on creating and naming NDS objects: "Implementing Naming Standards for NetWare Directory Services" (February 1994) and "Understanding and Using NDS Objects" (January 1995).

CREATING NDS OBJECTS WITH NWADMIN

As we learned previously, NWADMIN is your friend. It allows you to create and manage NDS objects quickly and easily. We already discovered NWADMIN's browsing capabilities; now we're going to learn about its object-creation capabilities. Keep in mind that you can also use the DOS-based NETADMIN utility to accomplish these tasks.

After enabling NWADMIN from your Windows 3.1x or Windows 95 workstation, the main browsing screen appears. First, select a container in which to create your User objects. In our case, we're starting with OU=CAMELOT (see Figure 8.22).

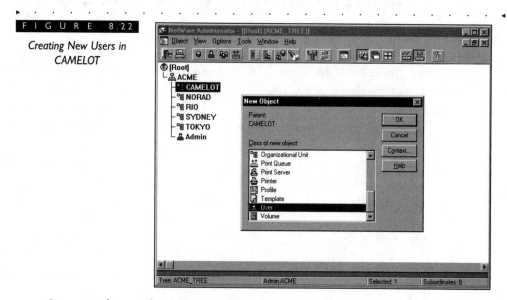

F I G U R E   8.22

Creating New Users in CAMELOT

Once you have selected a container, you can choose the Create option from the Object menu (or from the shortcut menu that can be displayed by pressing the right mouse button). Next, you are presented with a list of objects (as shown in Figure 8.22). Select the User object and press Enter or double-click on it with the mouse.

If you want to create multiple users at once, the intermediate dialog window has a dialog box for this. Also, you can specify a home directory for the user at this point. Finally, if you're going to create many similar users, consider the special User Template object. You'll find it in the Object menu of the main browsing screen. Figure 8.23 shows the default User Template input window. Once you create a User Template object, future objects that you create by using it can inherit its properties (such as Group Membership, Trustee Assignments, or Time Restrictions).

F I G U R E   8.23

The User Template
Identification Page in
NWADMIN

REAL WORLD

To change properties common to multiple users, you can use the new "Details on Multiple Users" option in the Object menu of NWADMIN. This also works for all users associated with an OU, Group, and/or Template object.

You can also create Group objects with NWADMIN. Instead of selecting the User object in the New Object window, simply choose Group. Next, the dialog window in Figure 8.24 appears. Follow this same process for any or all IntranetWare NDS objects. As you can see, NWADMIN takes the pain out of user creation.

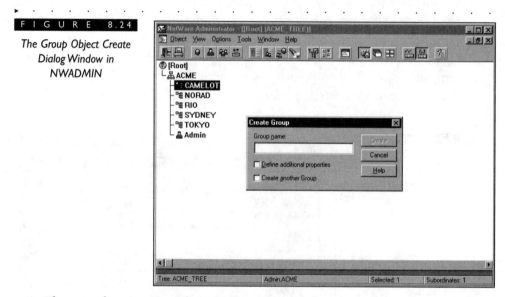

F I G U R E   8.24

The Group Object Create
Dialog Window in
NWADMIN

There is, however, another option. You can use UIMPORT to create large numbers of users from database records. Let's see how it works.

CREATING NDS USERS WITH UIMPORT

UIMPORT allows you to import users from a database application to Novell Directory Services. This utility can also be used to create, delete, and update User objects and their existing properties. If you are using a database that has the ability to convert records to a comma-separated ASCII file, you can use UIMPORT to migrate this data to the NDS. Here's how it works:

1 • Create a data file based on your existing database.

2 • Create a control file to interpret and act on the data file.

3 • Just do it!

The UIMPORT utility consists of two files: the data file and the import control file. The creation of your data file involves generating an ASCII comma-separated file from an existing database. The control file consists of some control parameters and field definitions. It defines where the information should be placed in NDS. Let's check them out.

THE BRAIN

To read more about UIMPORT, see the AppNote entitled "Importing User Information into NetWare Directory Services Using UIMPORT" in the April 1995 *Novell Application Notes*.

ZEN

"There is no season when such pleasant and sunny spots may be lighted on, and produce so pleasant an effect on the feelings, as now in October."

Nathaniel Hawthorne

The Data File

This is the easy part. The data file is created by your database application when you save the information in a comma-separated ASCII file (sometimes referred to as a *comma-delimited* file). A comma in the data file indicates a separation of fields in the NDS database. When a record is read through UIMPORT, a comma indicates the transfer of a new property. An example of the structure of your database might be as follows:

```
Last Name:
First Name:
Local Address:
Street:
City:
State or Country:
Zip Code:
Description:
Job Title:
```

After you have created a data file in delimited ASCII format, it should look something like this:

```
Madison,James,"111 Calle de Carnival","Rio de Janeiro",
Brazil,57775,Facilities,Administrator
```

We named our file ACMEDATA as we exited from the ASCII editor. Next, we must define a control file so that UIMPORT can match field values with properties in the NDS database. Here's how it works.

The Control File

Next, you must create the import control file. This file actually controls how the data information is written to NDS. The control file can be created using any ASCII text editor. You will enter a set of control parameters first, followed by a list of field definitions. Control parameters define how the information is separated in the data file. The field parameters define how the information is to be written to NDS. Table 8.2 displays a list of the control parameters, along with a brief definition of each.

TABLE 8.2	CONTROL PARAMETER	EXPLANATION
UIMPORT Control Parameters	Separator	Defines the type of separator used in the data file (such as a comma or a semicolon).
	Quote	Defines the character used for string data in the data file.
	Name Context	Defines the NDS context where the users will be created.
	Replace Value	Enables you to overwrite or add data to multivalue fields (such as overwrite an existing telephone number in a User object).
	User Template	Specifies the use of a user template in the creation of your users.
	Import Mode	Defines how User objects will be created. C = Create, B = Create and Update, and U = Update data for existing objects.
	Delete Property	Enables you to delete a property from a User object in NDS.

TABLE 8.2	CONTROL PARAMETER	EXPLANATION
UIMPORT Control Parameters (continued)	Create Home Directory	Allows the creation of a home directory for user objects.
	Home Directory Path	Required if you create a home directory for users. The volume name is not necessary in the inclusion.
	Home Directory Volume	Required if you create a home directory for users.

Next, the field definitions define which properties correlate with established user properties. These fields are listed below and can be selected based on your particular needs:

Name	Telephone	Location
Last Name	Fax Number	Group Membership
Other Name	Job Title	See Also
Postal Address	Description	Skip
E-Mail Address	Department	Login Script

Using our previous data file as an example, this is what our import control file would look like:

```
Import Control
Name Context="OU=FAC.OU=ADMIN.OU=RIO.O=ACME"
User Template=Y
Fields
Last Name
Other Name
Postal Address
Postal Address
Postal Address
Postal Address
Department
Job Title
```

That's our ACME control file and we've named it ACMECTRL. Notice the NAME CONTEXT line. This ensures that the users are imported into the correct container. If you don't specify one in the control file, UIMPORT places them into your current context — all users in the same container.

Now, there's only one step left — just do it!

Just Do It!

Once you've created your data and control files, you're ready to run UIMPORT. Type the following at your workstation command line:

```
UIMPORT <control file> <data file>
```

In our example, we would type

```
UIMPORT ACMECTRL ACMEDATA
```

Off it goes. Keep in mind, you must have Supervisor access rights to the UIMPORT container in order to import users. This prevents random users from overpopulating your NDS database. Also, if an error should occur during the process, it will be displayed at the workstation command line. Consider using the redirect symbol to create an error log file:

```
UIMPORT ACMECTRL ACMEDATA > UIMPORT.LOG
```

That does it for NDS objects. I bet you didn't think gardening could be so much fun. It really pays off if you get to *know* your plants intimately. Put yourself in their roots, try to understand what makes them tick. Understand their dreams, their goals. Plants have feelings, too, you know.

SMART LINK

For more experience with "UIMPORT", consult the *NetWare 4.11 Utilities Reference* at http://www.novell.com/manuals.

In this section, we have done that with IntranetWare's NDS objects. We explored the 16 most interesting objects, and learned some valuable management lessons about each one. In addition, we explored object creation with NWADMIN and UIMPORT. Now I think you're ready for Prime Time. Now I'm gonna let you loose on ACME's tree. Now you get to pick the flowers!

Building the ACME Tree

Welcome to ACME's garden. Don't step on the daffodils. Now that you understand the fundamentals of NDS gardening, it's time to put your knowledge to the test. Did somebody say "test"?

Anyway, today's the *big* day. We finally get to build ACME's tree. Here's where we've been:

- In Chapter 2, we learned about NDS objects and their purposes.

- In Chapter 3, we learned all about ACME and the design process. We also discovered some key ACME design inputs, including the critical resource list.

- In Chapter 4, we designed ACME's tree with locations at the top and departments down below. In addition, we created a naming standards document and updated the ACME resource list to match.

- In Chapter 5, we started the ACME rollout with a testing lab and pilot program. We also created a detailed NDS implementation schedule.

- In Chapters 6 and 7, we installed and migrated most, if not all, of ACME's NetWare 4.11 servers. The "Real Thing"!

With experience, NWADMIN, design inputs, and a little luck, you're ready to build ACME's tree. This consists of two stages. First, build the container structure as outlined in the ACME design in Chapter 4 ("NDS Design"). Then, place the leaf objects according to the resource list and managerial experience you gained earlier in this chapter. Are you ready? Go!!

THE NORAD SITE

At the NORAD site (as well as all other sites), we have placed a central server in the top OU=NORAD container (see Figure 8.25). This server will hold the Master replica of the NORAD partition and can also function as an e-mail server for internal and external communications. The same process is repeated at all five sites.

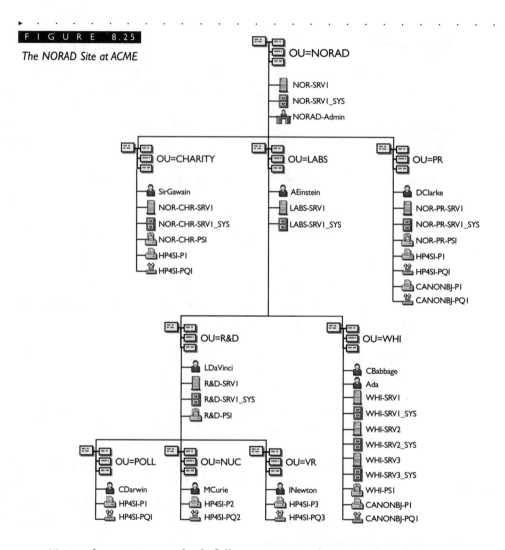

Notice the naming standards follow a very simple pattern based on our naming standards document. Servers are always defined by unique names across the entire tree because of the SAP requirement. Printers and print queues, however, can have the same name as long as they reside in different containers.

THE RIO SITE

Figure 8.26 shows the placement of resources in each of the Rio site's departments. It's not necessary to place all the users in your tree at this point. We have included a user in each location as an Administrative example. At the very least, you should include the container administrators, as we've done here.

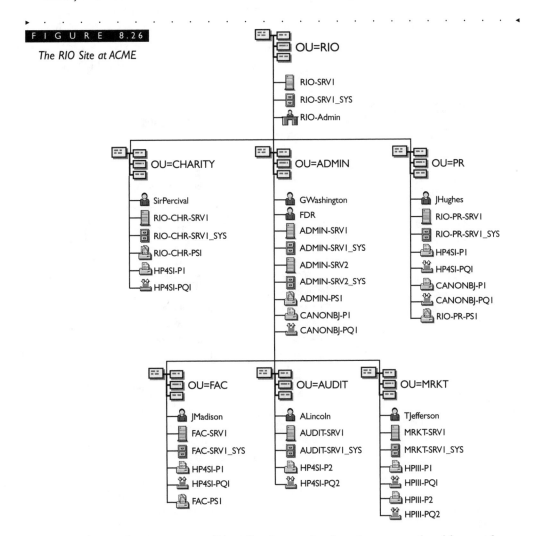

F I G U R E   8.26

The RIO Site at ACME

OU=RIO
- RIO-SRV1
- RIO-SRV1_SYS
- RIO-Admin

OU=CHARITY
- SirPercival
- RIO-CHR-SRV1
- RIO-CHR-SRV1_SYS
- RIO-CHR-PS1
- HP4SI-P1
- HP4SI-PQ1

OU=ADMIN
- GWashington
- FDR
- ADMIN-SRV1
- ADMIN-SRV1_SYS
- ADMIN-SRV2
- ADMIN-SRV2_SYS
- ADMIN-PS1
- CANONBJ-P1
- CANONBJ-PQ1

OU=PR
- JHughes
- RIO-PR-SRV1
- RIO-PR-SRV1_SYS
- HP4SI-P1
- HP4SI-PQ1
- CANONBJ-P1
- CANONBJ-PQ1
- RIO-PR-PS1

OU=FAC
- JMadison
- FAC-SRV1
- FAC-SRV1_SYS
- HP4SI-P1
- HP4SI-PQ1
- FAC-PS1

OU=AUDIT
- ALincoln
- AUDIT-SRV1
- AUDIT-SRV1_SYS
- HP4SI-P2
- HP4SI-PQ2

OU=MRKT
- TJefferson
- MRKT-SRV1
- MRKT-SRV1_SYS
- HPIII-P1
- HPIII-PQ1
- HPIII-P2
- HPIII-PQ2

For the Rio location, as well as all other major locations, you should consider creating an Organizational Role object as the site administrator with Supervisor rights. In our example (Figure 8.26), notice the RIO-Admin object at the top of the subtree. Finally, you should assign key administrators as occupants of the Role (in Rio that includes George Washington, Sir Percival, and Jeff Hughes).

THE CAMELOT SITE

Since Camelot is the center of ACME activity, you may want to maintain control over Admin from this location. Change the password frequently and limit the number of users who know it. Also, make Admin a member of the site Organization Role, CAM-Admin. See Figure 8.27 for an illustration of the CAMELOT subtree.

The CAMELOT Site at ACME

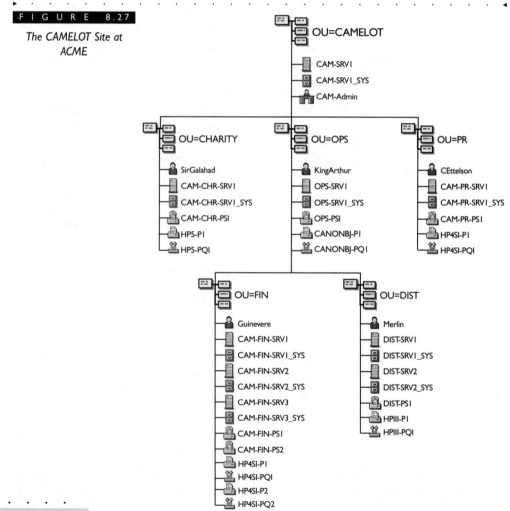

THE SYDNEY SITE

Use Directory Map objects to simplify administration of your users. For example, the Sydney office uses Directory Maps in all its Container login scripts. As versions of its specialized software change, the Sydney site administrator only changes the pointer of the Directory Map object to the new version of the software. This automatically enables all users in Sydney to see the new version of software, because all Container login scripts use the same Directory Map.

As you can see in Figure 8.28, we've placed the Directory Maps higher in the tree. This provides access to all users underneath. The Human Rights application, for example, is accessed from a Directory Map object in the OU=HR container (HR-APP). This way, all the HR employees can have access to the application. Follow this same conventions for all the other Sydney divisions.

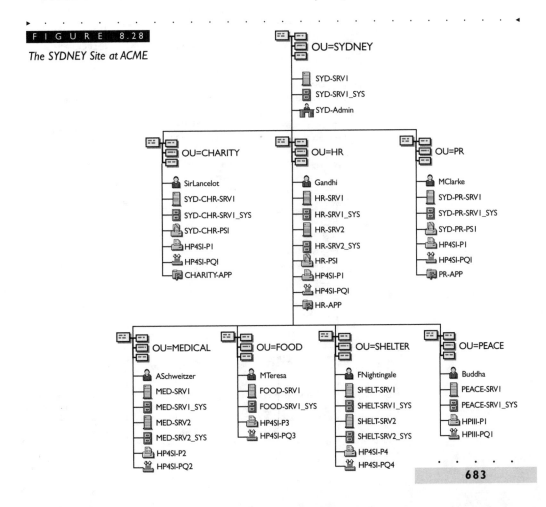

F I G U R E   8.28

The SYDNEY Site at ACME

THE TOKYO SITE

The Tokyo office has traveling users (see Figure 8.29). We will create an alias for these users at the top of the ACME tree (at O=ACME). With the alias in place, a traveling user such as DHoliday in OU=THEFT can log in with the following simple context — DHoliday.ACME. This makes the login process much easier for users who travel, but do not carry their own laptop computers. For more information on these Nomads, refer to Chapter 4 ("NDS Design").

FIGURE 8.29

The TOKYO Site at ACME

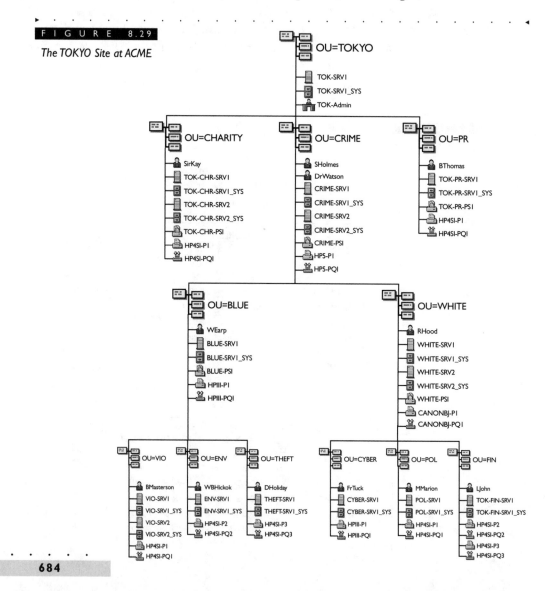

Congratulations! You've taken a very big step today toward saving the world. ACME's garden is in place. Now all you have to do is water, fertilize, weed, and manage it. Be sure the users get enough sun, and whatever you do, don't let the snails get them.

This is the beginning of a wonderful friendship. This tree will follow you everywhere you go. In subsequent chapters, you will learn how to partition, secure, configure, and optimize it. You should be very proud of yourself. Also, if you want some hands-on practice building the tree, check out the case study at the end of this chapter. It explores three important creation utilities — NWADMIN, NETADMIN, and UIMPORT. Otherwise, you can practice off-line with DS Standard.

SMART LINK

If you want to hang out at ACME and meet all its great heroes in cyberperson, surf the Web to http://www.cyberstateu.com/clarke/ acme.htm.

So, what's next? In the remainder of this chapter, we will discuss two auxiliary NDS management responsibilities — DSMERGing and NETSYNCing. You never know when you're going to need a little genetic engineering to help your plants.

▶ · ◀

DSMERGing

Now, your gardening experience takes a strange scientific turn. In the next two sections, we will explore some "bizarre" ways of improving your NDS tree — through genetic engineering:

▶ Merging — DSMERGE allows you to combine two unrelated NDS trees. This functionality adds greater flexibility to diverse and distributed organizations. It also doubles the size of your oak tree.

▶ Crossbreeding — NETSYNC allows you to cross-pollinate between NetWare 3 binderies and IntranetWare NDS trees. It's a strange operation, but the result is mind-blowing — a rose that tastes like corn.

In this section, we will explore the details of DSMERGE. This utility allows you to combine multiple trees (two at a time) into a single, cohesive NDS WAN. Imagine what life was like before DSMERGE. Earlier versions of NetWare 4 forced CNEs to agree on a master plan before installing the very first server. Distributed organizations had to design and build the tree from a central location, or *rebuild* the tree later.

DSMERGE has added an important level of flexibility by allowing CNEs to merge existing trees once the organization agrees on a single NDS design. This way, distributed departments can implement NDS early, and merge into the parent tree at a later date.

DSMERGE occurs in the following four steps:

- ▶ Step 1 — Check status of IntranetWare servers.

- ▶ Step 2 — Check time synchronization status.

- ▶ Step 3 — Rename a directory tree (if necessary).

- ▶ Step 4 — Perform the DSMERGE.

Let's explore each of these exciting steps. Refer to Figure 8.30 as you go. It shows the main screen of DSMERGE. Ready, set, merge.

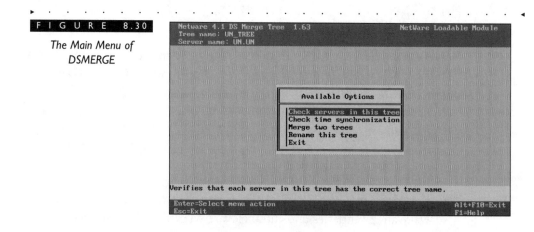

FIGURE 8.30

The Main Menu of DSMERGE

STEP 1: CHECK STATUS OF INTRANETWARE SERVERS

Before and after you merge two trees, it is important to check the status of your IntranetWare servers. Before the merge, you want to check the version of each IntranetWare server and its current status. Table 8.3 shows the possible server status values and a brief description of each.

T A B L E 8.3 *Understanding Server Status in IntranetWare*	SERVER STATUS	DESCRIPTION
	!DS Locked	The server responds with an error condition indicating that the NDS database is locked and inaccessible.
	!Inaccessible/Down	The server does not respond and is considered to be inaccessible.
	!Error <-N>	N is the Directory Services error code number. This status indicates that the server is not responding because of the error condition listed in the value N.
	!Wrong Tree	The server is responding with a tree name that does not match the tree name of the local server containing the Master replica of [Root].
	UP	The server is up and functioning.

The check phase of DSMERGE also ensures that the host DSMERGE server holds a replica of the [Root] partition. If it cannot find a replica of [Root], the operation will abort.

Next, the utility will attempt to find all IntranetWare servers in the tree. DSMERGE will search an array of server IDs that are contained in the Master replica of the [Root] partition to collect the server name, version of NDS, and tree name. If a server in the list cannot be found, or has an incorrect tree name, the utility will issue an error code.

Once all the servers have been contacted, DSMERGE will display a list of servers and their respective statuses. Now, you're ready for Step 2 — time synchronization check.

ZEN

"However much you knock at nature's door, she will never answer you in comprehensible words."

Ivan Turgenev

STEP 2: CHECK TIME SYNCHRONIZATION STATUS

The next important DSMERGE check involves time synchronization. Both trees must be synchronized and they must refer to the same time source. Once DSMERGE is loaded on a server containing a replica of the [Root] partition, you can initiate time synchronization as shown in Figure 8.31.

▶ · ◀

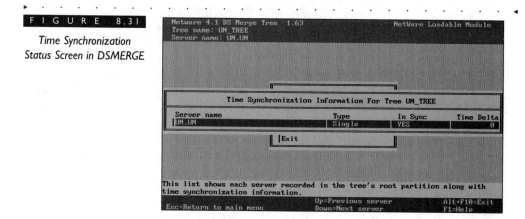

F I G U R E   8.31

Time Synchronization Status Screen in DSMERGE

DSMERGE will check the time status of all servers for the server name, NDS version, and the time synchronization status. If there is a *Time Delta* between an IntranetWare server and the local server running DSMERGE, the difference is shown on the screen in hours, minutes, and seconds (see Figure 8.31).

Your merged directory tree must only have one Reference or Single-Reference time source. If more than one server is a Reference or a Single-Reference server, you must assign all but one of them as Secondary time servers prior to initiating the merge.

STEP 3: RENAME A DIRECTORY TREE (IF NECESSARY)

Next, you should rename one of the trees — but only if you are merging two trees that have the same name. Keep in mind that this is the only IntranetWare utility that currently allows you to change the name of your NDS tree.

First, load DSMERGE.NLM on the server that contains the Master replica of the [Root] partition and follow the previous checking steps.

Next, DSMERGE begins by changing the name of the local tree's [Root] object to the new tree name. If an error occurs during this process, the operation is aborted. After the local server has changed the name of the [Root] object, a command is issued to change all servers in the local tree to the new tree name. Keep in mind that once this process has been completed, we're not finished. There are many more synchronization activities occurring in the background — you just can't see them. Once initiated, this process is irrevocable. After completion of the operation, you should check the status of the servers once again to verify that all servers have received the new name.

STEP 4: PERFORM THE DSMERGE

It's time! Once you have checked and verified the status of your IntranetWare servers, along with time synchronization, you are ready to perform the merge. Get out your protective gloves. At the completion of DSMERGE, you will have a single tree with a common [Root]. Very cool.

Here's how it works:

▸ Phase 1: Merge Check

▸ Phase 2: Merge Preparation

▸ Phase 3: Merge Trees

▸ Phase 4: Merge Completion

THE BRAIN

A good reference on DSMERGE is "Using the DSMERGE Utility in NetWare 4.1" in the March 1995 *Novell Application Notes*.

Phase I: Merge Check

The Merge Check ensures that your source server running DSMERGE.NLM contains the Master replica of the [Root] partition. If this check is successful, you will see a screen similar to the one shown in Figure 8.32. This screen asks for the tree name of both the source and target trees, along with their Admin names and passwords.

FIGURE   8.32

The Merge Tree Information
Screen of DSMERGE

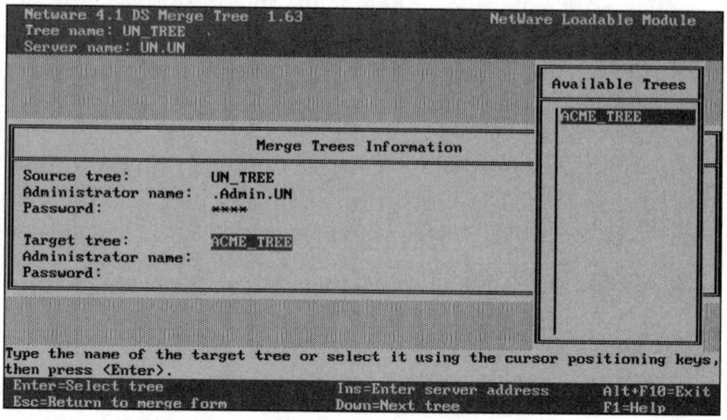

```
Netware 4.1 DS Merge Tree  1.63                    NetWare Loadable Module
Tree name: UN_TREE
Server name: UN.UN
                                                            Available Trees
                                                         ┌──────────────────┐
                                                         │ ACME_TREE        │
        ┌─────────────────────────────────────────────┐ │                  │
        │           Merge Trees Information             │ │                  │
        │                                               │ │                  │
        │ Source tree:          UN_TREE                 │ │                  │
        │ Administrator name:   .Admin.UN               │ │                  │
        │ Password:             ****                    │ │                  │
        │                                               │ │                  │
        │ Target tree:          ACME_TREE               │ │                  │
        │ Administrator name:                           │ │                  │
        │ Password:                                     │ │                  │
        └─────────────────────────────────────────────┘ └──────────────────┘

  Type the name of the target tree or select it using the cursor positioning keys,
  then press <Enter>.
  Enter=Select tree              Ins=Enter server address      Alt+F10=Exit
  Esc=Return to merge form       Down=Next tree                F1=Help
```

Phase 2: Merge Preparation

This phase modifies the source tree partitions. The utility will remove all [Root] replicas from any non-IntranetWare servers. It will also split the [Root] partition from all other objects in the tree, making a partition that contains only the [Root] object. Any other Read/Write or Read-Only replicas of [Root] also will be removed from any servers in the tree.

Once this operation is completed, DSMERGE can actually merge the two trees. Keep in mind that the partitioning operations mentioned here also could be performed beforehand with NWADMIN or PARTMGR. But why perform extra work if DSMERGE is willing to do it for you? The first two phases are displayed (see Figure 8.33) before you continue to Phase 3.

Phase 3: Merge Trees

Once the first two phases are completed, the merge operation begins. Once again, DSMERGE will gather the server IDs from the source server's replica list and check their statuses. Each server in the source tree will be contacted to obtain its server address and distinguished name in preparation for merging the source servers to the target tree.

The merge operation actually changes the name of the source tree [Root] object to match the [Root] object of the target tree. Once this process occurs, the source server receives a new name and issues a command to change the tree name of all servers in the source tree.

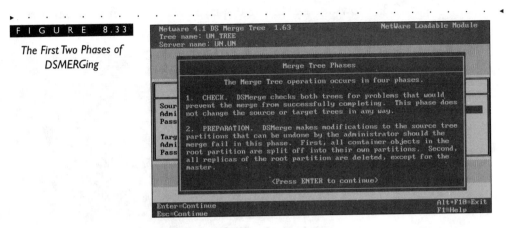

FIGURE 8.33

The First Two Phases of
DSMERGing

Phase 4: Merge Completion

The merge completion phase continues renaming source tree servers until all are done. A copy of the target tree's [Root] replica is then copied to each source server. This operation may take some time, depending on the size of the target's [Root] replica and the bandwidth of WAN links. Any objects that are no longer needed will be removed by the background synchronization process.

As with most gardening tasks, DSMERGing makes a mess. Some manual tasks may have to be completed after the two trees are merged:

1 • Place copies of the [Root] replica on strategic servers throughout the new tree.

2 • You may have to restore any objects that were deleted before the DSMERGE process.

3 • Because the source tree has had significant changes to its partitions below [Root], you will have to replace most of its child partitions. Refer to Chapter 9 ("Partition Management and Synchronization") for more information.

4 • Finally, you may have to check workstations that have the PREFERRED TREE statement in their NET.CFG configuration file. Each workstation with the source tree name will have to be changed to reflect the target tree name. This can be accomplished through the use of batch files or a WSUPDATE program in each user's Container login script.

Figure 8.34 shows the DSMERGE display screen for the final two phases.

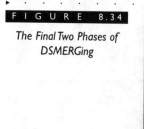

F I G U R E   8.34

The Final Two Phases of DSMERGing

Netware 4.1 DS Merge Tree 1.63   NetWare Loadable Module
Tree name: UN_TREE
Server name: UN.UN

```
                          Merge Tree Phases

     3.  MERGE.  DSMerge modifies the target tree and then the source
     tree so that the source tree's root replica appears as a new
     replica of the target tree's root.  If an error occurs before
Sour both trees are modified, DS will eventually clean up both trees
Admi so that they are separate and operating.
Pass
     4.  COMPLETION.  At this point the trees are irrevocably merged.
Targ DSMerge waits for synchronization to begin and for the new
Admi replica on the source tree to be turned on.  If this does not
Pass happen in a reasonable amount of time, it probably indicates
     that there is a synchronization problem in the tree.  When this
     is fixed, the tree will be functional.

                       <Press ENTER to continue>
```

Enter=Continue   Alt+F10=Exit
Esc=Continue   F1=Help

QUIZ

Some things are enough to scare anyone. You might be able to go from warm to cold quite easily, but how about from cold to warm? Can you change one letter at a time and make a proper English word with each step? You should be able to do it in four steps.

C   O   L   D

—   —   —   —

—   —   —   —

—   —   —   —

W   A   R   M

(Q8-4)

Voila! You're finished with DSMERGing. That wasn't so bad. How does it feel to be a full-fledged genetic engineer? Well, not quite yet. There's one more scientific experiment left — NETSYNCing. This is where it gets really weird.

SMART LINK

If you really feel the urge to DSMERGE, consult the *NetWare 4.11 Utilities Reference* at http://www.novell.com/manuals or try it out for yourself at http://www.cyberstateu.com.

NetSyncing

As promised, we now get to cross-pollinate NetWare 3 binderies and IntranetWare trees. Don't forget your protective clothing. This is genetic engineering at its finest.

All of this scientific wizardry is accomplished by using NetSync — a special part of IntranetWare. It is a management utility designed to expand the benefits of Novell Directory Services to NetWare 3 file servers. With NetSync, you can synchronize NetWare 3 users and groups with objects that are contained in an IntranetWare Directory. Therefore, when you create or modify a user in the bindery context of an IntranetWare server, the changes are synchronized with all NetWare 3 servers in the NetSync cluster.

An IntranetWare server can have up to 12 NetWare 3 servers in its NetSync cluster. A *cluster* is simply a collection of NetWare 3 servers that are synchronized with a single IntranetWare server — inside its bindery context. Because all servers in the cluster are synchronized, you only need to create a user once. That information is then automatically distributed to all NetWare 3 binderies in the cluster. This is amazing stuff! See Figure 8.35 for an example of a five-server NetSync cluster.

You can also use IntranetWare utilities (such as NWADMIN, NWADMIN95, or NETADMIN) to create and manage the NetWare 3 users and groups in a NetSync cluster. Printing is also manageable with the IntranetWare versions of PCONSOLE and NWADMIN. Wow! So, how does it work? Smoke and mirrors — watch.

*Creating a Five-server
NetSync Cluster*

NETSYNC3.NLM

NETSYNC4.NLM

3.1 3.1 3.1 3.1 3.1

4.1

N E T W O R K   S E R V E R S

NetSync Cluster

REAL WORLD

So, when should you use NetSync? The answer is when you want to synchronize NetWare 3 servers using NetWare Name Services (NNS); when you need an interim solution for a mixed bindery/NDS environment before a full migration to IntranetWare; or when you want to make NetWare 3 users, groups, and print queues part of the NDS directory without upgrading all your servers. Whatever the reason, be sure to download the latest NetSync drivers (NLMs) from NetWire before you start.

UNDERSTANDING NETSYNC

All great magic involves smoke and mirrors. NetSync is no exception. It is intended as a temporary solution for central administration of a mixed NetWare 3 and IntranetWare environment. For those servers running versions of NetWare 3 that cannot immediately be moved to IntranetWare, NetSync provides a good (albeit, temporary) solution. Don't get too attached to this concept. Life would be much easier if you just upgraded your NetWare 3 servers to IntranetWare. But if you can't (or don't want to), NetSync is an option.

NetSync uses two NLMs. NETSYNC4 is loaded on a single IntranetWare server, while NETSYNC3 operates on up to 12 NetWare 3 servers (once again, check out Figure 8.35). The NetSync NLM loaded on each server provides communication between the NetWare 3 binderies and the emulated bindery context of IntranetWare. From the IntranetWare point of view, NetSync performs the following functions:

1 • Holds bindery objects that are copied to its bindery context. When NETSYNC4.NLM is first enabled on the IntranetWare server, it copies all users and groups from the NetWare 3 server's binderies into the first bindery context of the IntranetWare server.

2 • Downloads all objects in the IntranetWare bindery context to the connected NetWare 3 servers. A combined bindery of NDS users and groups (along with the NetWare 3 binderies) is downloaded to each NetWare 3 server in the NetSync cluster. This process gives all servers (NetWare 3 and IntranetWare) a common, synchronized bindery, called a *Super Bindery*.

3 • Monitors any changes to the bindery context of the IntranetWare server. The NetSync utility will monitor any user or group changes made on the IntranetWare server, and synchronize these changes with all NetWare 3 servers in its cluster.

4 • Synchronizes bindery information of any NetWare 3 server that has been temporarily removed from the cluster. Any changes that may have occurred to the bindery during its absence will be sent down by the IntranetWare server and redistributed automatically. By the way, password synchronization through the NetWare 3 cluster is handled by REMAPID NLM. It is autoloaded by NETWYNC3.NLM.

Genetic engineering is an amazing science. How do they do it? Now, let's find out how to install NetSync for ourselves. Ready, set, sync.

INSTALLING NETSYNC

Installing NetSync is not difficult. All of the components are already stored on your IntranetWare file server. The SYS:SYSTEM directory contains the necessary IntranetWare files and the SYS:SYSTEM\NETSYNC directory contains the NetWare 3 files. At least one IntranetWare server is required, but you can have up to 12 NetWare 3 servers in the cluster. For authentication purposes, each NetWare 3 server will also need an available licensed connection to the IntranetWare server.

As we learned previously, NetSync consists of two server modules:

▸ NETSYNC4 — on the IntranetWare server

▸ NETSYNC3 — on each NetWare 3 server in the NetSync cluster

Let's take a closer look.

Loading NETSYNC4

To load NetSync on the host IntranetWare server, simply type **LOAD NETSYNC4** at the server console. Always load NETSYNC4 first and authorize the NetWare 3 servers before loading NETSYNC3 on the NetWare 3 servers in the NetSync cluster.. If you don't, the NetWare 3 servers won't become part of the NetSync cluster. NETSYNC4 automatically creates the SYS:SYSTEM\NETSYNC directory — it contains log files and the other critical NetSync information.

Before activating NETSYNC3, you must authorize each NetWare 3 server on the IntranetWare server. When you load NETSYNC4, you will see the screen shown in Figure 8.36. Select Edit Server List and press Enter to add NetWare 3 servers by name. This begins the authorization process. You can enter up to 12 NetWare 3 servers on the list.

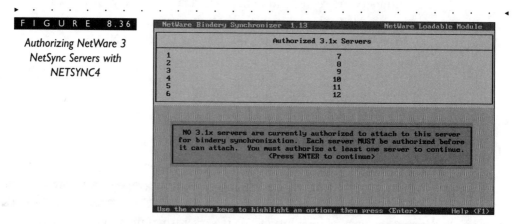

FIGURE 8.36

Authorizing NetWare 3 NetSync Servers with NETSYNC4

As an added measure of security you will also need to enter a NetSync password. This password will then be required as each NetWare 3 server requests entry into the NetSync cluster. The password is used only once.

TIP

You can use a different password for each NetWare 3 server. However, since this password is used only once, for simplicity we recommend the same password for all NetWare 3 servers in the cluster. Additionally, do *not* use your ADMIN or Supervisor password as your NetSync password — as it may pose a security risk.

Next, you will be asked if you want to copy the NetSync files to the NetWare 3 server. This option appears when you first authorize a NetWare 3 server during installation. It sounds like a grand idea to me.

Loading NETSYNC3

Every NetWare 3 server that participates in the cluster must load the NETSYNC3 NLM. Again, be sure that you have completed the NetSync installation steps on the IntranetWare server before starting this phase. The next step is to reboot the NetWare 3 servers because they will need to execute some new files that were downloaded by the NETSYNC4 process. Once your NetWare 3 server is back up and running, you can now type LOAD NETSYNC3 at the server's console.

Once loaded, you will be asked a couple of questions regarding NetWare Name Services (NNS). If you are not running NNS, select No to these questions and proceed. If you are running NNS, refer to Novell's NetSync documentation for more information.

The utility will ask you to enter the name of the IntranetWare host server and the correct NetSync password. After successful entry, NETSYNC3 will upload the NetWare 3 bindery information to the IntranetWare server's bindery context. The users and groups in the IntranetWare server's bindery context, in turn, are loaded onto the NetWare 3 server.

For further NetSync configurations, you can use the NetSync Options menus within NETSYNC3.NLM and NETSYNC4.NLM. These include viewing or editing the log file, editing a server list, and other activities.

Now that NetSync is installed, it's time to explore NetSync management. You're off and running. Isn't this exciting?

ZEN

"Earth laughs in Flowers."

Ralph Waldo Emerson

MANAGING NETSYNC

Once you've successfully installed NetSync, you can manage your NetWare 3 bindery objects with the IntranetWare NWADMIN or NETADMIN utilities. *Do not go back and use SYSCON* to modify user and group information on these NetWare 3 servers. The use of SYSCON will not synchronize changes on NDS and should be avoided with this configuration.

NetSync will also provide printing support. After you have completed your installation of NETSYNC3 and NETSYNC4, all workstation print utilities are copied to the NetWare 3 servers. Also, PRINTCON and PRINTDEF databases are updated to the IntranetWare formats. You can also choose to move your NetWare 3 print servers into a single print server on the IntranetWare server. Your printers are moved into Directory Services where they can be managed from a single IntranetWare print server.

In addition, IntranetWare print utilities are immediately available for use in your NetWare 3 printing environment. For more information on using print utilities with NetSync, refer to your Novell documentation.

Since NetSync synchronizes NetWare 3 users and groups with objects in the IntranetWare bindery context, you must enable Bindery Services on the host IntranetWare server. The IntranetWare server will periodically download its bindery context changes to all the participating NetWare 3 servers in the cluster. If more than one IntranetWare server is using the same bindery context, you will have all servers with the same context synchronizing with the NetWare 3 servers in the cluster. Although there is no theoretical limit to how many servers can be using the same bindery context, the NetSync operation is CPU-intensive. Thus, the more objects to synchronize, the more overhead placed on the server.

Finally, if you want to set multiple bindery contexts for a server, the process is also governed by the number of objects and the speed of your links during synchronization. Have a nice day!

ZEN

"When the oak is felled, the whole forest echoes with its fall, but a hundred acorns are sown by an unnoticed breeze."

Thomas Carlyle

Congratulations! You're tree is alive and well. It's been grown, browsed, accessed, fertilized, merged, and finally, cloned. Now there's only one thing left to do — chop, chop. T-I-M-B-E-R!

Just kidding. I wouldn't do that to you. It's a beautiful tree, and besides, this is only the beginning. Speaking of beginnings, let's review where we've been.

It all started with a brief tour of the garden. Then, we discovered a variety of tree browsing tools (including NWADMIN, NETADMIN, CX, NLIST, and various user tools). In the next section, we explored the purposes and uses of many required and commonly used NDS objects. As a matter of fact, most of these objects found their way into the ACME tree — it's a good thing we were paying attention.

Then, the chapter took a scientific turn into the realm of merging and crossbreeding. In the DSMERGing section, we learned the four steps for merging two unrelated NDS trees. Then, in the NETSYNCing section, we learned how to cross-pollinate NetWare 3 and IntranetWare LANs. Scary.

Now what? Well, like I said before, this is only the beginning. In the next chapter, we will continue the gardening stint and learn about pruning (partitioning), grafting (replication), and pollination (time synchronization). And that's not all. In subsequent chapters, we'll file, secure, configure, manage, print, and optimize your new NDS tree. You have so much more gardening to look forward to. I bet you can't wait. Go wash the dirt from under your fingernails. You're about to inherit a pair of green, uh, I mean Novell red, thumbs.

ZEN

"To own a bit of ground, to scratch it with a hoe, to plant seeds, and watch their renewal of life — this is the commonest delight of the race, the most satisfactory thing a man can do."

Charles Dudley Warner

Congratulations! You're ready to start building the ACME tree. The world is in very good hands with you on the job. In this exercise, we are going to build the ACME tree using three different utilities: NWADMIN (a Windows-based utility), NETADMIN (a menu utility) and UIMPORT (a batch utility). This exercise assumes that you have completed the case study entitled "Custom Installation for ACME" in Chapter 6.

In this exercise, you will create Organizational Unit, User, Printer, and Print Server objects in the CAMELOT, RIO, and SYDNEY branches of the tree. (You can't create Server objects because they are created automatically when you install or migrate to IntranetWare. You also can't create Print Queue objects because they require volume names for servers that haven't been installed.)

You will need the following additional information when building the tree:

> ▸ The Location property for each container or leaf object should always contain the city or Location (such as Camelot, Rio, or Sydney). The Department should always be the full name of the container (such as Administration, Financial, Marketing, and so on).

> ▸ The address, phone, and fax information for the CAMELOT Organizational Unit and its subcontainers is as follows:

> London Road
> Bracknell, Berkshire RG12 2UY
> United Kingdom
> Phone: (44 344) 724000
> Fax: (44 344) 724001

> ▸ The address, phone, and fax information for the RIO Organizational Unit and its subcontainers is as follows:

> Alameda Ribeirao Preto 130-12 Andar
> Sao Paulo 01331-000
> Brazil
> Phone: (55 11) 253 4866
> Fax: (55 11) 285 4847

▸ The address, phone, and fax information for the SYDNEY Organizational Unit and its subcontainers is as follows:

18 Level
201 Miller St.
North Sydney NSW 2060
Australia
Phone: (61 2) 925 3000
Fax: (61 2) 922 2113

▸ Each Organizational Unit will have the following Intruder Detection/Lockout limits:

Incorrect Login Attempts: 5
Intruder Attempt Reset Interval: 10 days
Intruder Lockout Reset Interval: 20 minutes

▸ User Templates and each User object should contain the following account restrictions, unless otherwise specified:

• Each user will be limited to logging in on one workstation at a time (that is, one concurrent login).

• Each user will be required to have a unique password consisting of 8 characters or more, and will be required to change their password every 60 days. Each user will be allowed six grace logins.

• Each user will be restricted from logging in each day between 3:00 a.m. and 4:00 a.m. (when backups and system maintenance are finished).

Now that you know the plan, let's go ahead and implement it! Ready, set, build!!

PART I: NWADMIN

1. Execute the NetWare Administrator utility.

a. Make sure that you are logged into the network as .ADMIN.ACME.

b. Execute the NetWare Administrator utility under Windows 3.1x or Windows 95. (If you haven't created an icon yet, you can find the NetWare Administrator utility under SYS:PUBLIC\NWADMN3X if you're using Windows 3.1x, or SYS:PUBLIC\WIN95\NWADMN95 if you're using Windows 95.)

2. Set the current context for the NetWare Administrator utility.

a. A portion of the NDS tree should be displayed. If not, select the NDS Browser option from the Tools menu to open a browser window. Next, be sure that your current context for this utility is set to the [Root]. If the [Root] icon is displayed at the top of the screen, proceed to Step 3.

b. If the [Root] icon is not displayed at the top of the screen, set the context to the [Root] by clicking on the Set Context option in the View menu, typing [Root] in the Context field, then clicking on the OK button.

3. Create the CAMELOT Organizational Unit.

a. At this point, the [Root] icon and the ACME Organization icon should be displayed. If no icons are listed under the ACME Organization, you will need to expand it to display its contents using one of the following three methods: double-clicking on its icon; clicking on its icon and selecting the Expand option from the View menu; or clicking on its icon and pressing the plus sign (+) on the numeric keypad of your keyboard. The Admin User object icon should then be displayed under the ACME Organization container.

b. To create a CAMELOT Organizational Unit under the ACME Organization, be sure the ACME Organization is highlighted, then press the Insert key. (Alternately, you could select the Create option from the Object menu, or click on the ACME Organization with the right mouse button, and choose Create from the pop-up menu that appears.) A New Object dialog box appears. Choose the Organizational Unit object type by using the scroll bar on the right side of the dialog box to bring it into view, then double-clicking on it. (An alternate method would be to type the letter **O**, which happens to be the first letter in the term Organizational Unit. This would highlight the Organizational Role object class, since Organizational Role is the first object in the list that begins with the letter "O." You could then press the down-arrow key once to highlight the Organizational Unit object class, then double-click on it or click on OK.) A Create Organizational Unit dialog box will be displayed. Type **CAMELOT** in the Organizational Unit Name field, then click the Define Additional Properties check box to select it. Finally, click on the Create button to create the new Organizational Unit called CAMELOT.

c. Because you selected the Define Additional Properties check box in Step 3b, a dialog box will appear. You'll notice that, by default, the Identification page button has been selected, allowing you to type in property information for that category. Click on each Identification field in turn, typing in the following values:

Other Name: **CAMELOT**

Location: **CAMELOT**

Telephone: **44 344 724000**

Fax Number: **44 344 724001**

d. Next, Click on the Postal Address page button and click on each field. Fill in the following fields:

Street: **London Road**

City: **Bracknell**

State or Province: **Berkshire, United Kingdom**

Postal (Zip) Code: **RG12 2UY**

TIP

If you suddenly find yourself on the Login Script page instead of the Postal Address page, it means that you forgot to click on the first field of the Postal Address screen before you began typing. If this happens, click on the Postal Address page button, then click on the Street field before you begin typing. This is a strange idiosyncrasy of NWADMIN.

   e. Next, click on the Intruder Detection/Lockout page button and fill in the following information:

      Detect Intruders: (click on check box)

      Incorrect Login Attempts: **5**

      Intruder Attempt Reset Interval: **10 days, 0 hours, 0 minutes**

      Lock Account after Detection: (click on check box)

      Intruder Lockout Reset Interval: **0 days, 0 hours, 20 minutes**

   f. Finally, click the OK button to return to the main browser window in the NetWare Administrator utility.

  4. Create a User Template in the CAMELOT container. To create a User Template object in the CAMELOT Organizational Unit container, be sure that the CAMELOT Organizational Unit is highlighted, then press the Insert key. (Alternately, you could select the Create option from the Object menu, or click on the CAMELOT Organizational Unit with the right mouse button and choose Create from the pop-up menu that appears.) A New Object dialog box appears. Choose the Template object type by using the scroll bar on the right side of the dialog box to bring it into view, then double-clicking on it. (An alternate method

would be to type the letter **T**, which happens to be the first letter in the word Template. You could then double-click on it, or click on OK.) A Create Template dialog box will be displayed. Type **CAM-UT** in the Template Name field, then click the Define Additional Properties box to select it. Finally, click on the Create button to create the new User Template called CAM-UT.

a. Fill in the same location, telephone, fax, and address information as you did for the CAMELOT Organizational Unit in Step 3c. (You won't be able to set any Intruder Detection parameters for this User Template, as Intruder Detection parameters are set per container, not per leaf object.) If you can't find the property page button that you're looking for, don't forget to use the scroll bar to the right of the page buttons to locate it.

b. Next, click on the Login Restrictions page button, then click on the box in front of the Limit Concurrent Connections property. The Limit Concurrent Connections property should then list a maximum connection value of "1."

c. To set password restrictions for this User Template, click on the Password Restrictions Page button, then do the following:

(1) Make sure there is a checkmark in the Allow User to Change Password check box.

(2) Click on the Require a Password check box and type in a password length of **8**.

(3) Click on the Force Periodic Password Changes check box and type in a Days Between Forced Changes value of **60**.

(4) Click on the Require Unique Passwords check box.

(5) Click on the Grace Logins check box and make sure that Grace Logins Allowed field shows a value of "6."

(6) Click on the Set Password after Create check box so that you'll be prompted to indicate a password each time you create a new user using this user template.

d. Next, go ahead and restrict login privileges between 3:00 a.m. and 4:00 a.m. every day. Click on the Login Time Restrictions page button. A grid will be displayed on the screen showing days of the week along the left edge, and time of day across the top. Each cell in the grid represents a half-hour period during the week. You'll notice that when you place the mouse cursor in a cell, the day and time represented by that cell is displayed. White (blank) cells represent times during which the user is allowed to log in. Gray cells indicate times that the user is prevented from logging in. Click on the 3:00 and 3:30 cells for each day of the week. (Alternately, you can drag the cursor to select multiple cells.) When you are finished updating the User Template, click on OK to accept the changes you made.

e. Finally, click on the OK button to return to the main NetWare Administrator browser window.

5. Create the CHARITY Organizational Unit under the CAMELOT container.

a. Use the same method listed in Step 3b to create a CHARITY Organizational Unit under the CAMELOT Organizational Unit, except that you'll highlight the CAMELOT Organizational Unit instead of the ACME Organization. Next, use the method described in Steps 3c, 3d, and 3e to fill in the appropriate location, phone, fax, address, and Intruder Detection information.

b. Create a User Template for the CHARITY Organizational Unit using the method described in Step 4. This time, however, we'll save time by copying the properties from the User Template you created in the CHARITY Organizational Unit earlier, rather than having to key them in again. To do this, click on the Use Template or User

check box instead of the Define Additional Properties check box
when you create the User Template. Next, click on the Browse
button to the right of the Use Template or User field and either
walk the tree or change the context so that the CAM-UT User
Template object appears in the Available objects window on the left
of the screen. To walk the tree, double-click on the double dot (..)
entry in the Browse Context window on the right of the screen to
move up the tree one level, since the CAM-UT object is located in
the CAMELOT Organizational Unit, which is one level above the
current context. Alternately, you could set the context by clicking
on the Change Context button, typing in CAMELOT.ACME as the
context, then clicking on OK. At this point, the CAM-UT User
Template should be displayed in the Available Objects window on
the left side of the screen. Click on it, then click on OK. Finally,
Click on the Create button to create the new User Template.

c. Create the SirGalahad User object by clicking on the CHARITY
Organizational Unit and pressing Insert. A New Object dialog box
will appear. Select the User object type by typing **U** and pressing
Enter. (Alternately, you could have clicked on OK instead of
pressing Enter.) The Login Name and Last Name fields are required
properties for a User object. Type in a login name of **SirGalahad**
and a Last Name of **Galahad**, then click on the Use Template
check box. Next, click on the Browse button to the right of the Use
Template field. The CAM-UT User Template object should be
displayed in the Available Objects window on the left side of the
screen. If so, click on OK to select this User Template. (Normally,
you would also create a home directory for this user, but you can't
at this time because the CAM-CHR-SRV1 server has not been
installed yet.) Finally, click on the Create button to create this user
by using the defaults in the CHAR-UT User Template.

d. Create the HP5-P1 Printer object by making sure the CHARITY
Organizational Unit is highlighted and pressing Insert. A New
Object dialog box appears. Choose the Printer object type by using
the scroll bar on the right side of the dialog box to bring it into

view, then double-clicking on it. A Create Printer dialog box will be displayed. Type in a Printer object name of **HP5-P1** and click on the Define Additional Properties check box, then click on the Create button. A Printer dialog box will appear. Type in **HP5-P1** in the Other Name field, **CAMELOT** in the location field, **CHARITY** in the Department field, and **ACME** in the Organization field. Then click on OK to return to the main NetWare Administrator browser screen.

e. Create the CAM-CHR-PS1 Print Server object by clicking on the CHARITY Organizational Unit and pressing Insert. A New Object dialog box appears. Choose the Print Server object type by using the scroll bar on the right side of the dialog box to bring it into view, then double-clicking on it. A Create Print Server dialog box will be displayed. Type in a print server name of **CAM-CHR-PS1**, click on the Define Additional Properties check box, then click on the Create button. A Print Server dialog box will appear. Click on the Assignments page button, then click on the Add button. A Select Object dialog box will appear. The HP5-P1 printer you created in the previous step should appear in the Available Objects list box on the left side of the screen. Double-click on the HP5-P1 printer object, then click on the OK button to return to the main NetWare Administrator browser window.

6. Create the .OPS.CAMELOT.ACME Organizational Unit using the method listed in Step 5a, then create a User Template called OPS-UT using the method described in Step 5b. Next, create the KingArthur User Object, the CANONBJ-P1 Printer object, and the OPS-PS1 Print Server object under it by using the methods covered in Steps 5c through 5e.

7. Create the .FIN.OPS.CAMELOT.ACME Organizational Unit, then create the following objects under it: the FIN-UT User Template object, the Guinevere User object, the HP4SI-P1 and HP4SI-P2 Printer objects, and the CAM-FIN-PS1 and CAM-FIN-PS2 Print Server objects.

8. Create the .DIST.OPS.CAMELOT.ACME Organizational Unit, then create the following objects under it: the DIST-UT User Template, the Merlin User object, the HPIII-P1 Printer object, and the DIST-PS1 Print Server object.

9. Create the .PR.CAMELOT.ACME Organizational Unit, then create the following objects under it: the PR-UT User Template, the CEttelson User object, the HP4SI-P1 Printer object, and the CAM-PR-PS1 Print Server object.

10. To exit the NetWare Administrator utility, chose the Exit menu option from the File menu.

PART II: NETADMIN

1. Execute the SYS:PUBLIC\NETADMIN utility.

2. Create the RIO Organizational Unit under the ACME Organization.

   a. Select the Manage Objects menu option from the NetAdmin Options menu. Walk the tree until you locate the ACME Organization. Highlight the ACME Organization using the up-arrow key and down-arrow key, press Enter to change context, then press the Insert key.

   b. A Select an Object menu will appear. Highlight the Organizational Unit object class and press Enter. A Create Object Organizational Unit dialog box appears. Type in **RIO** in the New Name field, **Y** in the Create User Template field, press Enter, then press F10 to continue. You will be informed that an Organizational Unit has been created. When asked whether to create another, select No and press Enter. The RIO Organizational Unit will be displayed in the appropriate position in the NDS tree.

   c. Highlight the RIO Organizational Unit and press Enter to change context. Highlight the User Template and press F10 to select it. An

Actions for Users: User Template menu will be displayed. Select the "View or edit properties of this object" option and press Enter. You'll see a list of property categories. Select the Identification option and press Enter. Type in the information listed below in the fields specified. (To update a field, highlight the field and press Enter to select it, then press Insert to add information. After you've finished adding information to a field, press Enter then F10 to save the information that you've added.)

Other Name: **Rio de Janeiro**

Telephone: **(55 11) 253 4866**

Fax Number: **(55 11) 285 4847**

Location: **Rio**

d. When you are finished, press F10 to save the information on the Identification screen. Next, select the Postal address option from the View or edit user menu and press Enter. Type in the following information in the fields indicated:

Street: **Alameda Ribeirao Preto 130-12 Andar**

City: **Sao Paulo**

State or Province: **Brazil**

Postal (Zip) Code: **01331-000**

When you are finished, press F10 to save. Press Esc twice to return to the Object, Class window.

e. Highlight the period (.) representing the current context, then press F10 to select it. Select the View or edit properties of this object option from the Actions for Organizational Unit: Rio menu and press Enter. Select the Intruder Detection option from the

Viewer, or edit Organizational Unit menu and press Enter. Fill in the following information:

Detect Intruders: **Yes**

Incorrect Login Attempts: **5**

Intruder Attempt Reset Interval: **10 days**

Lock Account After Detection: **Yes**

Intruder Lockout Reset Interval: **20 minutes**

Press F10 to save when you are finished. Press Esc three times to return to the Object, Class menu.

3. Create the ADMIN, CHARITY, and PR Organizational Units under the RIO Organizational Unit, then create the AUDIT, FAC, and MRKT Organizational Units under the .ADMIN Organizational Unit. When asked whether you want to create another Organizational Unit after creating the PR Organizational Unit, type **N** instead of Y. When creating each Organizational Unit, make sure that you create a User Template under it. You'll notice there are some disadvantages to creating a User Template using the NETADMIN utility rather than the NetWare Administrator utility. One problem is that NETADMIN creates a User object named "USER_TEMPLATE" rather than a User Template object with the name of your choice. Another problem is that NETADMIN does not allow you to copy the properties of an existing User Template when creating a new one — which means you have to type in the properties for each User Template manually. After you've done so, you can continue to create objects in this portion of the tree using the instructions listed below.

4. Create the GWashington User object under the ADMIN.RIO.ACME Organizational Unit object.

a. Highlight the ADMIN Organizational Unit and press Enter, then Insert. The Select an Object Class menu appears. Type **U** to select the User Object class, then press Enter. A Create Object User dialog box will appear. Type **GWashington** in the Login Name field and **Washington** in the Last Name field. (Normally, you would create a home directory for this user, but you can't at this time, because neither the ADMIN-SRV1 nor ADMIN-SRV2 servers have been installed.) Be sure that the Copy the User Template Object field has a value of Yes, then press F10 to continue. You will then be notified that the User has been created. When asked if you'd like to create another user, select No and press Enter.

b. Try to create a Printer object and Print Server object in the same container. If you press Insert, the Select an Object Class menu appears. You'll notice that the Print Server, Printer, and Print Queue object classes are not listed. This is because you cannot create or manage the printing environment using the NETADMIN utility. These objects can, however, be created with the NetWare Administrator and PCONSOLE utilities.

5. Create the SirPercival User object under the CHARITY.RIO.ACME Organizational Unit.

6. Create the JHughes User object under the PR.RIO.ACME Organizational Unit.

7. Create the ALincoln User object under the AUDIT.ADMIN.RIO.ACME Organizational Unit.

8. Create the JMadison User object under the FAC.ADMIN.RIO.ACME Organizational Unit.

9. Create the TJefferson User object under the MRKT.ADMIN.RIO.ACME Organizational Unit.

10. To exit the NETADMIN utility, press the Esc key repeatedly until the "Exit?" question is displayed, then select Yes and press Enter.

PART III: UIMPORT

1. Before you can run the UIMPORT utility, you must have created two files: an ASCII control file and a comma-delimited ASCII data file. The data file is typically created by exporting user information from a database file. The control file consists of some control parameters and field definitions that define where information should be placed in the NDS. The UIMPORT utility can only be used to add users. It cannot be used to create other objects in the NDS tree. Because of this, before you run UIMPORT, you must create any Organization or Organizational Unit objects that you will need.

    a. Since you don't have a database containing the information for the users in the SYDNEY subtree, you'll need to create a data file from scratch using an ASCII text editor. Let's try a very simple test case. Let's try importing the User objects for the network administrators for HR Organizational Unit and each of its four subcontainers into the HR container. To create the data file, type in the following lines into an ASCII file you create called ACMEDATA:

        Ghandi,Ghandi,"Human Resources"

        MTeresa,Teresa,Food

        ASchweitzer,Schweitzer,Medical

        FNightingale,Nightingale,Shelter

        Buddha,Buddha,Peace

        You'll notice that Human Resources is enclosed in quotation marks. This is because it contains a space.

b. Next, create an import control file by typing in the following lines in an ASCII file you create called ACMECTRL:

Import Control
   Name Context=.OU=HR.OU=SYDNEY.O=ACME
   User Template=Y
Fields
   Name
   Last Name
   Department

2. Before you can import this data, you must create the NDS subtree structure using the NWADMIN or NETADMIN utilities. Use the utility of your choice (hint: NetWare Administrator is the best choice) to create the initial SYDNEY subtree structure, including:

   • A SYDNEY Organizational Unit under the ACME Organization

   • CHARITY, HR, and PR Organizational Units under the SYDNEY Organizational Unit.

   • FOOD, MEDICAL, PEACE, and SHELTER Organizational Units under the HR Organizational Unit.

   When you create each of these containers, be sure to create a User Template object for each. Don't forget to update both the containers and the User Templates with the property values listed at the beginning of this chapter.

3. After you've set up the NDS subtree structure for the SYDNEY portion of the tree, you can execute the UIMPORT utility by typing UIMPORT ACMECTRL ACMEDATA at the DOS prompt and pressing Enter. To see the result of using this utility, type CX .HR.SYDNEY.ACME /A / T.

PART IV: SPECIAL CASES

Now that you've had an opportunity to build the basic ACME tree, let's explore some of their special conditions. Following is a list of some of ACME's more challenging NDS management requirements. Please help them out.

1. ACME needs a site administrator in each location. This will be a revolving position among each of the division heads. For example, the NORAD administrator (named NORAD-Admin), will have administrative access to all divisions of NORAD and the position will alternate among AEinstein, DClarke, and SirGawain.

2. In addition, all of the site administrators will share a common login script. It will be a mechanism for global security, drive mappings, and special messaging.

3. The Human Rights Tracking application is constantly being updated. Can you think of an easier way to manage its search drive mappings?

4. Also, each of the Human Rights department administrators needs access to the Human Rights Tracking program. Security could be a problem.

5. All of the employees in the Auditing department need easy access to all the resources in the Financial container — for auditing purposes. Also, the auditors don't want to have to navigate the tree to see them.

6. In addition, the Auditing application is constantly being updated. Searching drive mapping is becoming a problem.

7. As a matter of fact, the Financial database is due for some major changes as well. I see a pattern forming here. Please help us out.

8. The following traveling users need a simpler context for accessing ACME from distributed locations: AEinstein, DHoliday, and MCurie.

9. Everyone in the Crime Fighting division needs to share a common login script.

10. Finally, Leonardo DaVinci believes in empowering his scientists. After all, he's a "labrat," not a bureaucrat. To distribute the administrative load evenly, he and his scientists take turns managing the R&D department — each scientist takes the helm for three months out of the year.

EXERCISE 8-1: THE NDS GARDENER

Circle the 20 NDS management terms hidden in this word search puzzle using the hints provided.

```
U  S  E  R  T  E  M  P  L  A  T  E  X  Y  X  D  W
S  X  O  T  V  S  G  D  L  F  F  J  Q  Z  A  U  Y
E  E  G  B  U  M  I  G  I  H  G  U  P  T  D  E  M
R  E  F  E  R  R  A  L  L  I  S  T  J  C  U  E  V
E  R  C  R  N  N  S  I  N  G  L  E  L  O  G  I  N
P  N  E  T  A  D  M  I  N  E  T  U  S  E  R  F  A
L  A  L  W  Q  A  O  N  C  P  S  E  R  V  E  R  U
I  M  P  O  R  T  C  O  N  T  R  O  L  F  I  L  E
C  N  X  I  F  A  D  Q  E  G  E  D  G  C  J  P  M
A  E  F  K  L  F  G  R  K  U  S  M  Q  K  G  F  D
P  T  K  E  B  I  N  D  E  R  Y  O  B  J  E  C  T
O  S  C  S  R  L  C  B  W  J  H  Y  O  D  V  B  E
I  Y  B  J  O  E  D  M  O  E  Q  M  G  Q  Z  I  I
N  N  E  T  W  O  R  K  R  E  S  O  U  R  C  E  T
T  C  U  J  S  C  A  L  A  B  I  L  I  T  Y  Y  W
E  D  S  M  E  R  G  E  N  L  M  U  U  O  N  Q  Y
R  I  A  F  R  N  B  R  Y  K  H  S  T  J  O  J  R
```

Hints:

1. Leaf object which represents an object created by bindery services and designated as such by the Directory.

2. Type of window in NWADMIN which allows you to view a portion of the Directory tree.

3. NetSync term which refers to an IntranetWare server and up to 12 associated NetWare 3 servers.

4. Comma-delimited ASCII text file exported from a database for use with UIMPORT.

5. NetWare Loadable Module that can be used to rename an NDS tree.

6. ASCII file used by UIMPORT containing a set of control parameters, followed by a list of field definitions.

7. Leaf object that is created when you install IntranetWare on a server.

8. Menu utility used by network administrators to manage NDS objects and properties.

9. Utility that allows you to link the bindery security of up to 12 NetWare 3 servers to a context in the Directory tree.

10. Menu utility that allows users to manage network tasks.

11. Physical or logical entity represented by an NDS object (such as a user, group, printer, server, or volume).

12. Command line utility used to view NDS object and property information.

13. A NetWare naming service product that was a predecessor of NDS.

14. List of servers containing information on an NDS object that is returned to a client requesting information about the object.

15. Property of a partition root object that contains a list of all of the replicas in the partition and their locations.

16. Term used to describe Novell Directory Services as a global database that can be split into sections and distributed to any number of network servers.

17. Feature of NDS where users log into the network once, using one ID and password, to access all authorized network resources.

18. The most common leaf object in an NDS tree.

19. File containing default property values that can be applied to new User objects created in a container.

20. OSI standard used by Novell in the initial design of many NDS objects.

See Appendix C for answers.

Partition Management and Synchronization

Pruning is an interesting phenomenon. You cut away branches in order to make them grow. You kill something so it may live. You break up the tree into little pieces so it can become whole again. Gardening is a strange science!

You are an IntranetWare gardener now. It's time to take control of your horticulture — green thumb required. In the previous chapter you created the tree. Now you will get a chance to prune it as we take the bull-weed by the horns and implement ACME's partition design. Think of this as "tough love" for the chlorophyll set.

IntranetWare pruning focuses on three important sciences:

1 • NDS Partition Management (pruning)

2 • NDS Replication (grafting)

3 • Time Synchronization (pollination)

In Chapter 2 we learned about partition boundaries and their purpose. Then, in Chapter 4, we discovered various guidelines for NDS partition design. Our first step here is partition management.

The next step is NDS replication — grafting. Once you have set the partition boundaries, you must scatter them around. This serves two purposes — fault tolerance and resource accessibility. In Chapter 2 and Chapter 4, we also learned about replica design. Now we get a chance to create ACME's replicas (using NWADMIN) and distribute them to servers throughout their global WAN.

The final step is time synchronization — pollination. Time is as important to NDS as seeds and sunlight are to daffodils. As an IntranetWare gardener, it's your job to ensure accurate time throughout the WAN. In ACME's case, that's 5 time providers and 47 time consumers (see Chapter 4). In this chapter we'll learn how to implement and manage ACME's custom time synchronization design. Cool.

So, there you have it — your agricultural future. NDS pruning is important business, and today we're going to learn all about it. Ready, set, prune.

ZEN

"Pressure is playing for ten dollars when you don't have a dime in your pocket."

Lee Trevino

SMART LINK

For more experience with NDS pruning, consider *Novell Course 532: NDS Design and Implementation* at CyberState University: http://www.cyberstateu.com, or surf to Novell Education at http://education.novell.com.

NDS Partition Management

The beauty of NDS is its scalability and flexibility. NDS is *scalable* because it allows you to make the database as small, medium, or large as you want. NDS is *flexible* because it allows you to store the database (or pieces of it) anywhere you want. This beauty has a price, though — work. And guess who gets to do the work — *you*, the CNE gardener.

NDS Partition Management deals with the daily tasks involved in scaling the database. In the next section, "NDS Replication," you'll explore flexibility by distributing the database (or pieces of it) to distributed servers throughout the WAN. These scaling chores are your responsibility alone. Fortunately, they don't impact the user. As you can see in Figure 9.1, NDS partitioning provides two main benefits:

1 • NDS allows you to break the database into smaller pieces and distribute those pieces to multiple servers — NDS partition management.

2 • Regardless of how it's partitioned, NDS appears to users as a single, unified cloud — user transparency.

F I G U R E   9.1

Benefits of NDS and
Partitioning

Although portions of NDS can be distributed to multiple IntranetWare servers, users see a single view of its resources. With NDS, the information is not only distributed, but also replicated multiple times to increase fault tolerance. In Figure 9.1, three of ACME's containers are distributed to location-specific servers. This is the best NDS partitioning approach for large, multisite corporations such as ACME.

Smaller companies, on the other hand, can get away with centralizing the NDS database. In this case, all the network information can reside on a few central file servers. The benefit of centralized control is easier administration. Also, synchronization operations are minimized. This will work as long as the total number of users and network resources remains small.

The bottom line is: *You* get to choose how NDS is partitioned and replicated. You are in control. Later in this section we'll discuss some key partition management strategies, including managing the [Root] partition, creating partition boundaries, and merging partitions. But first, let's spend a few moments reviewing NDS scalability and user transparency — also known as *partitioning*.

TIP

Small companies can greatly simplify partition management by placing all their objects in a single O=Organization NDS container.

UNDERSTANDING NDS PARTITIONS

NDS uses a hierarchical tree structure to organize network resources. As we've learned throughout the book, this tree consists of logical branches (container objects) and leaves (leaf objects).

NDS partitions are logical sections of the tree. Partitioning allows you to split a very large tree into smaller subtrees. These subtrees are easier to manage, and they provide users with better NDS accessibility and performance (see Figure 9.2). You can even distribute copies (replicas) of the subtrees to improve NDS fault tolerance. If all of this sounds too good to be true — it is! NDS partition management is hard work, and *you* get to do it.

NDS Partitioning at ACME

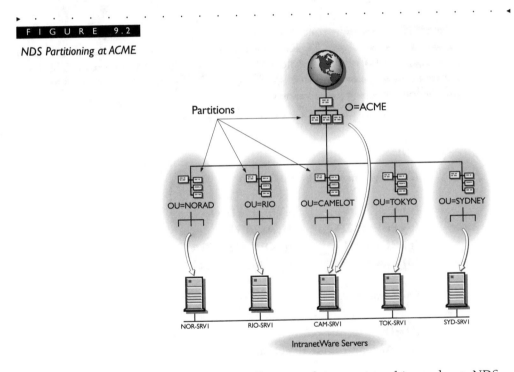

In earlier chapters, we learned all sorts of interesting things about NDS partitions. In Chapter 2 we discovered how they work, and in Chapter 4, we built a partition design for ACME. Now it's time to create them. Before we start, however, I want to point out three concepts that have an important impact on partition management:

1 • The Parent/Child Relationship

2 • Partition Transparency

3 • Partitioning Rules

Let's take a quick look.

· ◄

REAL WORLD

Partition management is accomplished by using one of two different tools: NDS Manager (Windows) or PARTMGR (MS-DOS). NDS Manager is a stand-alone utility for Windows 3.1 (SYS:PUBLIC\NDSMGR16) or Windows 95 (SYS:PUBLIC\WIN95\NDSMGR32). It can also be "snapped" into NWADMIN. In this chapter, we'll focus on the Windows 95 stand-alone version.

QUIZ

All anagrams of animals:

(a) **CORONA**   (e) **SOMEDAY**
(b) **PAROLED**   (f) **ALPINES**
(c) **RETIRER**   (g) **ORCHESTRA**
(d) **LESIONS**   (h) **CALIFORNIA***

two words

(Q9-1)
(See Appendix C for all quiz answers.)

The Parent/Child Relationship

Partition boundaries follow the same logical, hierarchical flow as the NDS tree. If your tree looks like a pyramid, so does your partition map. This is called *natural partitioning*. As you can see in Figure 9.3, ACME's partition map includes five PARENT partitions and many CHILDREN.

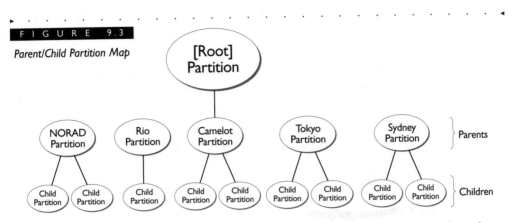

FIGURE 9.3

Parent/Child Partition Map

This relationship is known as the *parent/child partition relationship*. When the boundaries between two partitions meet, the partition closest to the [Root] is considered the parent, and the one further away is the child. In Figure 9.3, the OU=<*location*> containers are parents to lower organizational containers. In fact, the OU=<*location*> partitions are also children of the [Root] partition. That's an interesting "double whammy."

As in life, partition parents must manage their subordinate children. This is ensured in NDS through a concept known as *Subordinate References*. When new partitions are created under an existing container, their parent must maintain pointers to the new partitions. Therefore, any server holding a partition can end up with a large number of Subordinate Reference pointers to children of that container.

As a matter of fact, the [Root] is a very sensitive partition. Let me emphasize that NDS creates a Subordinate Reference pointer automatically when a server holding a parent partition creates a link to its child partitions. This is a big problem for the [Root], because it is a parent to all second-tier containers. For this reason I recommend that you make the [Root] partition very small, with only the [Root] and an Organization container inside. Later in the chapter we'll explore some special management strategies for the [Root] partition.

Partition Transparency

Partitioning is hard work. Fortunately, it's completely transparent to the user. In a nutshell, users can access the entire NDS tree, regardless of which server they are connected to. Furthermore, it doesn't matter how the tree has been partitioned and replicated. It appears as a single, unified "cloud" to the user.

How does this work? Well, NDS maintains a background connection between all parent and child partitions. Although a specific server may not contain the complete NDS database, users still have the ability to get the information from a variety of scattered sources. NDS pieces it together for them in the background. As an IntranetWare gardener, you must tell NDS where to put all the copies — that's work.

NDS partitioning is not foolproof, however. If there aren't enough distributed replicas, and a number of servers or WAN links crash, it is possible to temporarily (or permanently) lose access to NDS information. That's why I recommend at least three replicas of every partition. It's better to be safe than sorry.

NDS Partitioning Rules

Now let's review some of the more important NDS partitioning rules. It's as easy as 1-2-3-4.

1 • Each partition must be named and requires a single container object as the top (or root) of the partition (not to be confused with the [Root] partition). The container object used as the start of the partition is called the *partition root object*. Only one partition root object exists for each partition, and it is the topmost container object. In Figure 9.2, for example, OU=NORAD is the root object for the NORAD partition.

2 • Two containers at the same level cannot share a partition without a parent watching over them. Play nicely, children.

3 • Partitions cannot overlap with any other part of the NDS tree. This means that one object will never reside in two partitions.

4 • Each partition contains all the information for the connected subtree, unless another subordinate partition is created underneath. For example, each location partition in Figure 9.2 includes all the NDS information for all resources in that ACME location.

Now that we know the rules, it's time to move on to NDS partition management. In the next two sections we'll explore some interesting partitioning tasks, including creating, merging, moving, and aborting NDS partitions. But first, let's learn a little more about the [Root] partition and discover why it's so special. Don't forget to bring your green thumb along.

MANAGING THE [ROOT] PARTITION

You know what they say about the first child — or, in this case, the first parent. In either case, it's a very special partition. The [Root] partition is created during the installation of the very first IntranetWare server in your Directory tree. And this server gets a Master copy of it.

In IntranetWare, the [Root] partition is the only default partition. For this reason, it is often called the *default partition*. All other partitioning is your responsibility. Since this [Root] partition is the only partition created during installation, Figure 9.4 shows how INSTALL.NLM creates the [Root] partition. It happens when you provide the first server's context.

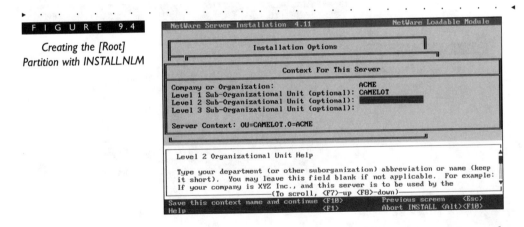

F I G U R E   9.4

Creating the [Root]
Partition with INSTALL.NLM

Once the first server has been installed, you can start adding your container and leaf objects. This process was outlined in the previous chapter. As you can see in Figure 9.5, ACME is starting to take shape. This is accomplished by using any of the three NDS construction tools: NWADMIN, NETADMIN, or UIMPORT.

All the second-tier container objects in Figure 9.5 are held within the [Root] partition. Remember, it's the only partition that exists until *you* create some new ones. This is shown in Figure 9.6.

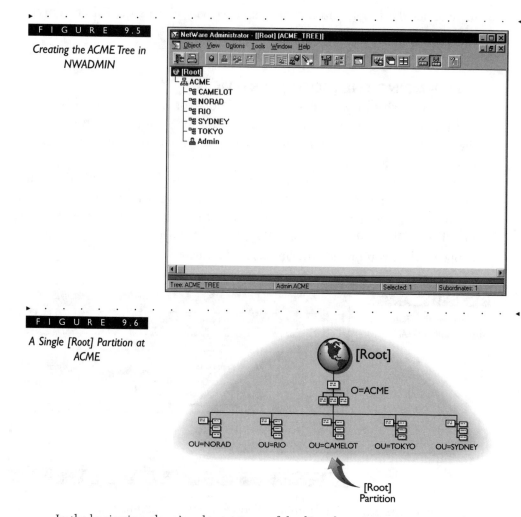

Creating the ACME Tree in
NWADMIN

A Single [Root] Partition at
ACME

In the beginning, there's only one copy of the [Root] partition. It exists on the very first server (CAM-SRV1) as a Master replica. When you install a new IntranetWare server, it will immediately create a Read/Write replica of the [Root] partition and place it on the new server (NOR-SRV1). This can also be accomplished using NDS Manager or PARTMGR (see Figure 9.7). In this figure, two copies of the [Root] partition have been placed on ACME's first two servers — CAM-SRV1 and NOR-SRV1. Incidentally, you should follow this rule for the first ten servers only. We don't want 200 copies of the [Root] partition floating around!

F I G U R E   9 . 7

Distributing ACME's [Root]
Partition

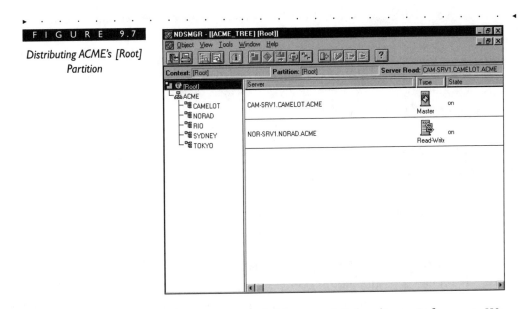

Earlier we learned about parents, children, and Subordinate References. We also learned about the downfalls of a large [Root] partition. So, to keep things working efficiently, we need to "split" the [Root] partition so only two objects remain — [Root] and O=ACME. In order to accomplish this, we need to create five new partitions — one for each location (see Figure 9.8).

F I G U R E   9 . 8

"Splitting" ACME's [Root]
Partition

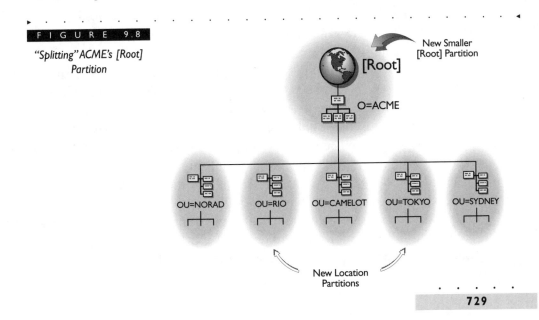

Now that ACME's [Root] partition is more manageable, we can concentrate on creating other child boundaries. But first, IntranetWare must distribute one more copy (replica) of the [Root] partition — this time to the third ACME server (TOK-SRV1). For an illustration of this process, refer to Figure 9.9 in the next section. OK, finished. Now we're ready to create, merge, move, and abort ACME's partitions. Ready, set, prune.

ZEN

"I have too much money invested in sweaters."

Bob Hope, on why he will never give up golf

MANAGING NDS PARTITIONS

With the [Root] partition in place, you can get on with the rest of ACME's pruning. This is hard work, but rewarding. And if you think the tree is screaming while you prune, it's just your imagination. It's not that painful. Besides, we're doing it for their own good — the trees know that.

NDS pruning requires special gardening tools; namely, NDS Manager (Windows-based) and PARTMGR (DOS-based). NDS Manager is a Windows-based GUI tool that allows you to manage all NDS partitions in the tree. As we learned earlier (in a "Real World" icon), IntranetWare supports two different versions of NDS Manager. We'll be using the 32-bit version for Windows 95. Check out Figure 9.9.

As you can see in the figure, NDS Manager splits the screen between partitions (left side) and servers (right side). It uses a "Replica Table" concept similar to the one introduced in Exercise 9-1 at the end of the chapter. Also, each replica is shown as a server icon. We'll discuss replicas a little later in the chapter.

PARTMGR is the other IntranetWare partition management tool. It's a DOS-based program that provides functionality similar to NDS Manager. As you can see in Figure 9.10, PARTMGR lacks a little grace in the user-interface realm. It is, however, a very effective partition tool for those of you who don't do Windows.

In order to perform any partition management operation, you must have access to the Master replica for that partition. It locks the partition before you start working. This ensures NDS database consistency and limits management to one partition at a time. In addition, all the replicas of a specific partition must be available in order to complete the entire operation. If one replica is missing, NDS Manager will wait until it is available.

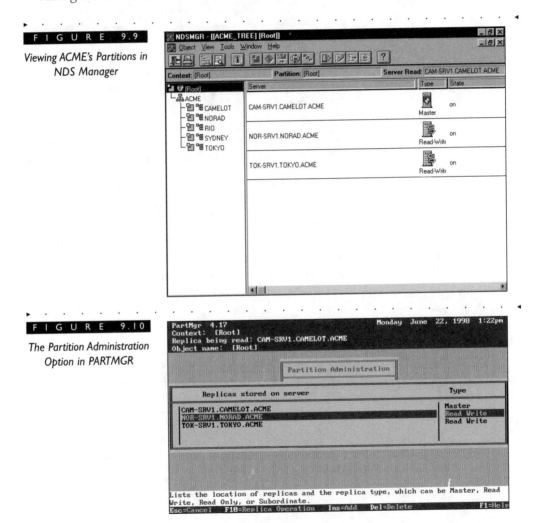

F I G U R E   9.9

Viewing ACME's Partitions in NDS Manager

F I G U R E   9.10

The Partition Administration Option in PARTMGR

Preparation is a virtue — especially in NDS pruning. Before you start a partition operation, you should check the status of its replicas. DSREPAIR is your friend. It provides valuable status reports on replicas and their synchronization process. Figure 9.11 shows a sample status check for the [Root] partition. Notice the default/replica status Edit Log File — SYS:SYSTEM\DSREPAIR.LOG.

F I G U R E   9.11

The Replica Status Edit Log
in DSREPAIR

```
NetWare 4.1 DS Repair  4.40                             NetWare Loadable Module
DS.NLM 5.73   Tree name: ACME_TREE
Server name: NOR-SRV1.NORAD.ACME                              Total errors: 0

         View Log File (Last Entry): "SYS:SYSTEM\DSREPAIR.LOG"  (83069)


/***********************************************************************************/
Netware 4.1 Directory Services Repair 4.40 , DS 5.73
Log file for server "NOR-SRV1.NORAD.ACME" in tree "ACME_TREE"
Start:  Thursday, June 18, 1998   4:51:03 pm Local Time

Synchronizing Replica: [Root]
Performed on server: NOR-SRV1.NORAD.ACME

Servers that contain a replica                     Replica Type   Status
──────────────────────────────────────────────────────────────────────
NOR-SRV1.NORAD.ACME                                Read/Write     Host
TOK-SRV1.TOKYO.ACME                                Read/Write     OK
CAM-SRV1.CAMELOT.ACME                              Master         OK

Synchronizing Replica: [Root]
Performed on server: TOK-SRV1.TOKYO.ACME

Esc=Exit the editor                 F1=Help                    Alt+F10=Exit
```

Another pruning virtue is patience. Once you have started an NDS partition operation, you should wait for all the synchronization activities to complete. NDS is a "loosely consistent" database, and it takes time for partition changes to be reflected across the network. A partition with many objects and replicas will naturally take longer than one with just a few objects. In this case, DSTRACE is your friend. Among other things, it notifies you when replica synchronization is finished (see Figure 9.12). We will explore DSTRACE in great depth later in the chapter.

F I G U R E   9.12

Monitoring Replica
Synchronization with
DSTRACE

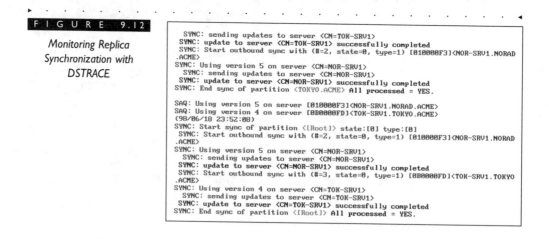

```
   SYNC: sending updates to server <CN=TOK-SRV1>
   SYNC: update to server <CN=TOK-SRV1> successfully completed
   SYNC: Start outbound sync with (#=2, state=0, type=1) [010000F3]<NOR-SRV1.NORAD
   .ACME>
SYNC: Using version 5 on server <CN=NOR-SRV1>
   SYNC: sending updates to server <CN=NOR-SRV1>
   SYNC: update to server <CN=NOR-SRV1> successfully completed
SYNC: End sync of partition <TOKYO.ACME> All processed = YES.

SAQ: Using version 5 on server [010000F3]<NOR-SRV1.NORAD.ACME>
SAQ: Using version 4 on server [0B0000FD]<TOK-SRV1.TOKYO.ACME>
(98/06/18 23:52:08)
SYNC: Start sync of partition <[Root]> state:[0] type:[0]
   SYNC: Start outbound sync with (#=2, state=0, type=1) [010000F3]<NOR-SRV1.NORAD
   .ACME>
SYNC: Using version 5 on server <CN=NOR-SRV1>
   SYNC: sending updates to server <CN=NOR-SRV1>
   SYNC: update to server <CN=NOR-SRV1> successfully completed
   SYNC: Start outbound sync with (#=3, state=0, type=1) [0B0000FD]<TOK-SRV1.TOKYO
   .ACME>
   SYNC: Using version 4 on server <CN=TOK-SRV1>
   SYNC: sending updates to server <CN=TOK-SRV1>
   SYNC: update to server <CN=TOK-SRV1> successfully completed
SYNC: End sync of partition <[Root]> All processed = YES.
```

SMART LINK

**For a more in-depth look at DSREPAIR and DSTRACE, consult the
NetWare 4.11 Utilities Reference at http://www.novell.com/manuals.**

If possible, you should centralize your partition management operations. Only one person or a small group of people should be responsible for all of the partitioning and replication operations within your company. Typically, the central IS staff has control over initiating partition operations. This central management approach minimizes the chance that two network administrators are working on the same partition simultaneously. If this does occur, it can have unpredictable results — a bad thing.

In the following section, we will explore four key partition management operations:

1 • Creating Partitions

2 • Merging Partitions

3 • Moving Partitions

4 • Aborting Partition Operations

Creating Partitions

Creating a new partition is actually "splitting" a child partition from its parent. This sounds sad, but it really isn't. At some point all children must leave the nest and go out into the cruel world to find themselves. It just happens sooner for NDS partitions, that's all. We refer to partition creation as a *partition split*.

Normally, partition splits occur on a single server, because the parent partition already resides there. Therefore, it doesn't generate any traffic and happens very quickly. The bottom line? A partition split divides one NDS database into two, with all the information staying on the same server. In addition, this split operation will create a new child partition on all the servers that contain a replica of the parent partition. This is an important point.

For example, in Figure 9.13, you can see that partitions have already been created for OU=CAMELOT and OU=NORAD. We are currently in the process of creating a partition for OU=TOKYO.

When we create the OU=TOKYO partition, copies of it (replicas) are automatically placed on all servers that already have a copy of TOKYO's parent ([Root] partition). As you can see in Figure 9.14, both CAM-SRV1 and NOR-SRV1 get Read/Write replicas of the new OU=TOKYO partition. This ensures database reliability and NDS connectivity — mostly for tree walking.

When the partition is created, it takes its name from the topmost container object (partition root object). All NDS objects in the new subtree become part of the new partition. This is always true, unless there's a previously defined partition lower in the tree. In that case, the old partition is unaffected. By partitioning the NDS tree, you can keep the location information in each location and still find and use the resources throughout ACME. Therefore, you should partition locally and replicate locally. As we add servers in TOKYO, we will place our recommended three replicas on servers in TOKYO. As you'll see in just a minute, it's not a good idea to partition or replicate over WAN links.

In order to perform the Create Partition operation, you need Supervisor object rights to the partition root objects — the highest container in the partition. You can also get away with the Write property right to the container's Access Control List (ACL) property. Both of these rights assignments will work. Figure 9.15 illustrates the NDS security necessary for AEinstein to create a partition at

NORAD. In this case, OU=NORAD is the partition root object at the top of the new subtree.

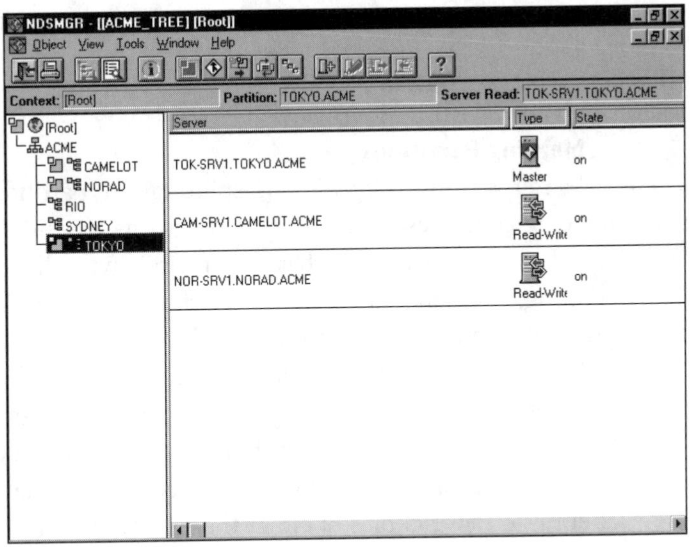

FIGURE 9.14

Distributing OU=TOKYO's Replicas in NDS Manager

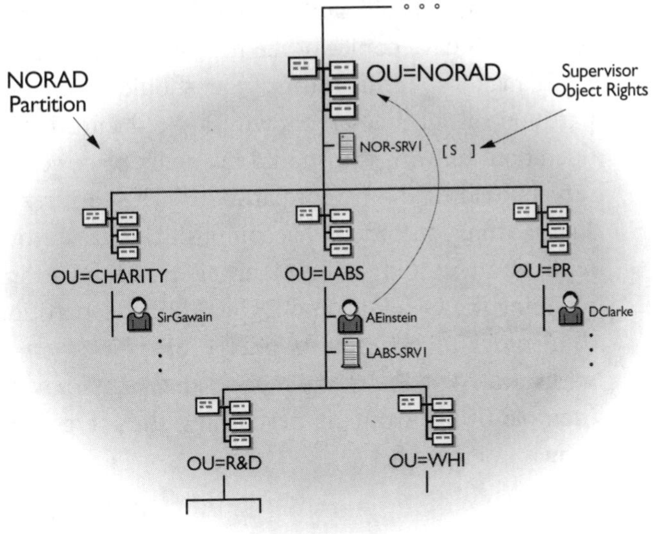

FIGURE 9.15

AEinstein Creates the OU=NORAD Partition

ZEN

"It's nice to look down the fairway and see your Mother on the left and your Father on the right. You know that no matter whether you hook it or slice it, somebody is going to be there to kick it back in the fairway."

Larry Nelson

Merging Partitions

Merging is the opposite of splitting. In partition management vernacular, merging combines a child partition with its parent. This operation is sometimes called *partition join* — what a surprise! Typically, merging takes longer than splitting, and generates a great deal of WAN traffic, depending, of course, on the physical location of all servers in both partitions' Replica Rings.

In order to merge partitions, each server holding a replica of the parent partition must receive a copy of the child partition — before the merge can happen. In return, each server holding a copy of the child partition must receive a copy of the parent — before the merge can complete. The merge operation will attempt to move copies of either the parent or child partitions to the appropriate servers as needed. After the copies have been successfully moved, the merge operation will begin and ultimately join the two partitions together. Then, all servers will have copies of the new, larger partition.

To make your life easier, you should manually place copies of the parent partition on all the servers with a child partition before you initiate the merge operation. In turn, you should manually place copies of the child partition on the servers holding the parent partitions. This ensures a smooth merger — if there is such a thing. In order to accomplish this task, you must know where all of the replicas are stored. NDS Manager. Here's an example. In Figure 9.16, we are rejoining the OU=OPS and OU=CAMELOT partitions.

In order to perform the Merge operation, you must have Supervisor object rights (or Write property rights) to *both* parent and child containers. In this example, King Arthur is performing the merger, and his NDS access rights are shown in Figure 9.17.

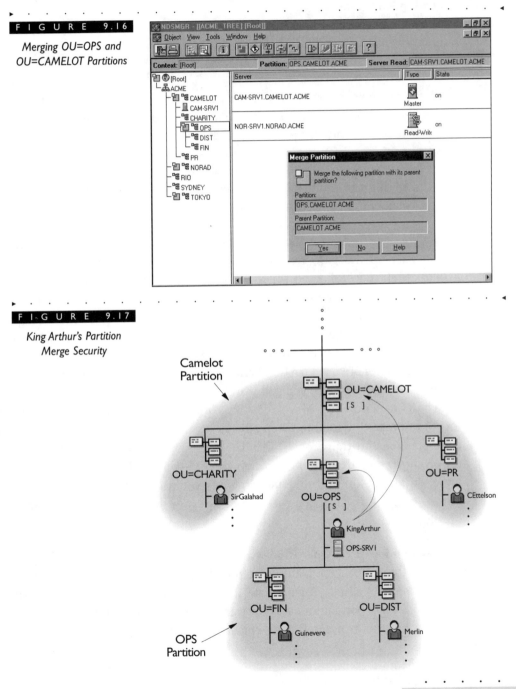

FIGURE 9.16

Merging OU=OPS and
OU=CAMELOT Partitions

FIGURE 9.17

King Arthur's Partition
Merge Security

Moving Partitions

Moving partitions is a tricky business. NDS allows you to move entire subtrees from one location to another. In order to perform this maneuver, you must satisfy two important conditions:

1 • The moving container must be a partition root. This means that the source container must be at the *top* of an existing partition. You may need to create this partition if it doesn't exist.

2 • The partition (or subtree) you want to move cannot have any child partitions. You may be forced to merge child partitions with the above parent if they're currently split.

Moving containers (and their contents) is essentially moving a partition from one location in the NDS tree to another. This operation can generate *mucho* network traffic depending on where the source partition's replicas are.

Here's an example. In Figure 9.18, we're going to move the OU=OPS subtree to the OU=NORAD location. I don't know why, we just are. Also, NDS Manager gives you the option of leaving an Alias of OU=OPS behind. This recommendation is a temporary action that helps ensure continuity during the move. It's like leaving cardboard copies of your furniture behind when you move to a new house. For a while, the neighbors think you still live there. Notice the check box.

In order to perform the Move operation, you must have Supervisor object rights (or Write property rights) to all containers involved. In this case, that's OU=OPS (the source partition root), OU=CAMELOT (its parent partition), and OU=NORAD (the destination partition root). I see a pattern forming here. The more serious the work gets, the more security you need. Makes sense. Speaking of serious work, what happens if something goes wrong during the partition operation? Let's see.

Aborting Partition Operations

If something goes wrong during the pruning process, you can always try to stop and return the tree to its original state. This feature would really help the medical profession. It's important to note, however, that this is not an undo feature. It's just a way to back out of a partitioning operation that didn't complete.

FIGURE 9.18

Moving the OU=OPS
Subtree to OU=NORAD

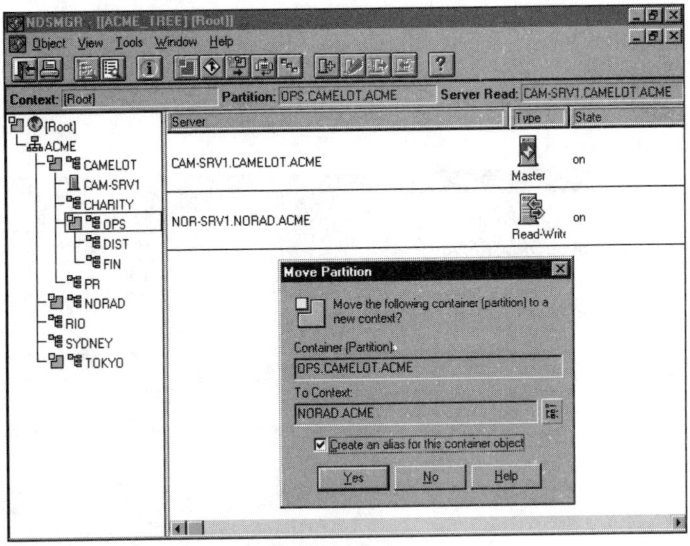

For example, only one partition operation can take place at a time. So, if you start an operation and it stalls, everyone else is stuck. No other operations can take place on that partition. You're probably wondering why a partition operation would stall. Typically, it's because one of the partition's replicas becomes unavailable — because of a server crash, WAN link going down, corrupted NDS database; take your pick.

If your partition operation stalls, you have two choices:

1 • Wait until the server comes back up or the WAN link is restored.

2 • Abort the partition operation and try again later.

To abort a partition operation, you can use NDS Manager or PARTMGR. Select the partition and right-click the mouse. Choose Abort Partition and OK to confirm the action. It's that simple.

Once the partition operation has been aborted, the replicas will be turned back ON. This means all is well in the kingdom, and you can try again later.

All of this excitement can also be accomplished in DSREPAIR — there's something comforting in the term *repair*. From the DSREPAIR main menu, select Advanced Options. Next, select Replica and Partition Operations, and a list of all replicas stored on this server will appear. Choose your troublesome replica and press Enter (CAMELOT.ACME, in this case). The Replica Options menu will appear, as shown in Figure 9.19. Finally, choose Cancel Partition Operation and press Enter.

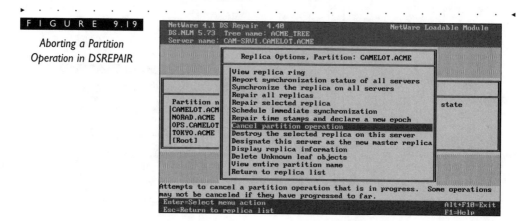

F I G U R E   9.19

Aborting a Partition Operation in DSREPAIR

Since you're running DSREPAIR from the server, you'll need to provide a valid username and password at this point. In addition, this user must have Supervisor object rights (or Write property rights) to all of the affected partitions. When you do, DSREPAIR takes care of the rest, and all is well again.

You're finished. That's all there is to NDS pruning — a piece of cake. In this section, we learned about [Root] pruning; creating, merging, and moving partitions; and how to back out when something goes wrong. This has been an invaluable lesson to all you aspiring NDS gardeners out there. But it's just the beginning. The *real* fun is in grafting. "Spread the partitions," that's what I always say. Let's see how.

ZEN

"Golf is a good walk spoiled!"

Mark Twain

NDS Replication

NDS grafting is almost as intriguing as pruning. As if cutting up the tree weren't enough, now we have to piece it back together somewhere else. They say it's good for the tree. They say it adds years to the tree's life. Do you buy it? I don't know.

NDS grafting is a similar prospect. They say it's good for the NDS tree. They say it adds years to the life of your network. Do you buy it? Well, you have to. The good news is that NDS replication makes more sense than grafting. Replication is the process of "spreading the partitions" around the WAN. This serves three purposes:

1 • *Fault tolerance* — Replication increases the availability of partitions — it spreads them around. This also increases reliability. For example, if a server holding a replica of your partition goes down, you can simply use another copy for authentication and updates.

2 • *Performance* — Distributed replicas increase NDS performance. Replication enables you to distribute partition copies to local servers throughout the WAN. Having a local replica decreases the time needed for certain NDS tasks, including authentication, NDS changes, searches, and data gathering. This does not imply that replicas should be used for mobile users. Having a replica locally means on the server where the majority of the users need the information.

3 • *Name Resolution* — Replication enhances name resolution because users requesting NDS information first have to locate a server with the data's information on it. Replication spreads the data around. If the requested information is not found on the server that the user is already authenticated to, then NDS will automatically connect the user to the proper server through the process of name resolution. This connection process is simplified when there are more replicas to choose from. It also happens faster and more reliably.

The main difference between NDS partitioning and NDS replication is the difference between "logical" and "physical." NDS partitions are logical boundaries that split the hierarchical database into subtrees. A partition doesn't actually "exist" until you place a copy (replica) of it on a server — replication. NDS replicas are physical pieces of the NDS database. They have mass. In Figure 9.20, for example, physical copies of the logical [Root] partition have been placed on three physical servers — CAM-SRV1, NOR-SRV1, and TOK-SRV1.

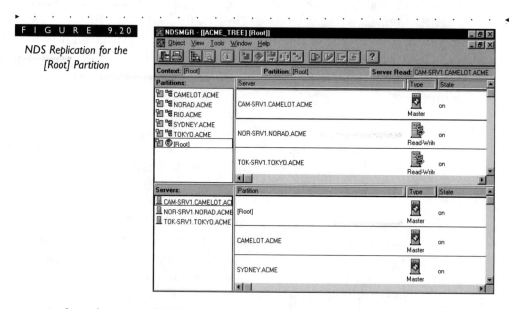

F I G U R E   9.20

NDS Replication for the [Root] Partition

So, how does it work? The IntranetWare installation program gets things started for you by creating three replicas for each partition. When you install a new server, NDS places a Read/Write replica of the server's home partition on it by default. It does this three times, then stops. If you want more than three replicas of any given partition, you must create them yourself using NDS Manager or PARTMGR.

SMART LINK

For a more in-depth discussion of NDS and the benefits of replication, surf to "Novell Directory Services" at http://www.netware.com.

Novell has a great way of demonstrating the relationship between NDS replicas and IntranetWare server. They use a replica replacement matrix called a *Replica Table*. Here's how it works. Let's say that you are part of a simple manufacturing company called "ABC." Your simple tree is shown in Figure 9.21. Notice the positioning of the six servers (S1 through S6).

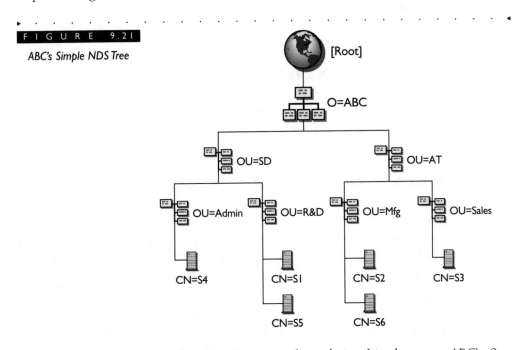

ABC's Simple NDS Tree

A Replica Table graphically illustrates the relationship between ABC's 8 partitions, 6 servers, and 18 replicas (see Figure 9.22). For practice using these tables, check out Exercise 9-1 at the end of this chapter.

ABC's Replica Table

Partitions

	[Root]	ABC	SD	AT	Admin	R&D	Mfg	Sales
S1	M	M	M	M	M	M	M	M
S2	R/W	R/W		R/W			R/W	
S3								R/W
S4			R/W		R/W			
S5	R/W					R/W		
S6							R/W	

(Columns represent partitions, rows represent servers;
M=Master replica, R/W=Read/Write replica, and R-O=Read-Only replica.)

In this section, we will explore three important aspects of Replica Management:

▸ Managing NDS Replica Types

▸ Managing NDS Replica Operations

▸ Managing NDS Replica Synchronization

Let's take a closer look at NDS Replication. This is a very important part of NDS gardening, so try to stay awake. Ready, set, replicate.

MANAGING NDS REPLICA TYPES

Replication is important business. It dramatically affects the speed and reliability of your NDS tree. The IntranetWare server is the focal point. A server can contain any number of replicas, as long as they're from different partitions. On the other hand, a server doesn't have to contain any replicas at all. It's up to you.

In order to understand where and when to place NDS replicas, you must understand the different types of replicas and their characteristics. Certain replica types react differently in certain circumstances. It's your job to know when to hold them and when to fold them. Here's a list of the replica types:

▸ Master — King of the hill. There's only one Master replica per partition.

▸ Read/Write — Second in command. Allows users to make changes to the NDS database.

▸ Read-Only — For browsing the tree only.

▸ Subordinate Reference — A special replica created by NDS when the parent partition exists but the child does not.

As I said, each of these replica types has its own strengths and weaknesses. In the next section we will explore all four types and provide some management insight for each. Let's begin at the top with the Master replica.

Managing Master Replicas

The Master replica is king of the hill. It's the first replica created during initial partition creation. Although the first replica is always designated as the Master, it can be changed as other replicas are added. There can be only one Master replica for each partition. In short, the Master replica is in charge — it controls all partitioning operations. The Master essentially locks the partition for the duration of any partition operation. This ensures that only one operation happens at a time.

For example, if you want to create or merge a partition, you must have access to its Master replica. The Master then works with the other replicas to complete the operation. As we learned earlier, you must also have Supervisor object rights or Write property rights to the partition root container.

It's important to note that the Master replica is equal to all other replicas during replica synchronization. This is a peer-to-peer mechanism, not a master-to-slave. In addition, the Master replica provides complete access to the object and property information within the partition. This means users can log in through this replica and make changes to the database — such as adding, deleting, renaming, and modifying NDS objects. Of course, they'll need sufficient NDS rights to do so.

The Master replica for the [Root] partition is stored on the CAM-SRV1 server. There is only one Master replica, but multiple Read/Write replicas. Makes sense. As a matter of fact, the Read/Write replica is probably the most popular type. Let's see why.

Managing Read/Write Replicas

The Read/Write replica is the most popular because there can be any number of them for a given partition. Although in theory there is no limit to the number of Read/Write replicas, you shouldn't go hog wild. Keep the number manageable for the sake of synchronization traffic and managerial overload. Remember, replicas are distributed to increase fault tolerance and accessibility — not for the fun of it.

Like Master replicas, Read/Write replicas provide complete access to NDS object and property information. Users can log into the "Cloud" and manage objects with this replica type. Refer to Figure 9.20 for an illustration of ACME's replica strategy for the [Root] partition. Notice the single Master and multiple Read/Write replicas. I told you they were popular. As a matter of fact, the Master and Read/Write replicas are the only ones that can support authentication and Bindery Services. Read-Only and Subordinate References don't provide much management help. They do, however, provide a purpose. Let's discover what it is...together.

ZEN

"We have 51 golf courses in Palm Springs. He never decides which course he will play until after his first tee shot."

Bob Hope, on Gerald Ford

Managing Read-Only Replicas

The Read-Only replica, as its name implies, will not accept changes from users. The only way it discovers changes in the database is through synchronization with other replicas; namely, Masters and Read/Writes. Since the Read-Only replica can't be updated, it can't support login authentication or Bindery Services. All you can do is browse the tree. Boring.

TIP

When a user logs into NDS, three of his/her properties are updated — Network Address, Last Login Date, and Last Login Time. In order for users to change or update these three properties, they must log into a Master or Read/Write replica. The Read-Only replica cannot accept user logins because these properties cannot be updated.

Here's an idea. Suppose you want to provide read access to the NDS database, but not allow updates. Then the Read-Only replica is for you. For example, you want to build an off-site disaster-recovery center for your servers. You could place a Read-Only replica there. This way, the server would be updated through replica synchronization, but users couldn't bother it; that is, there would be no login activity. I know I'm stretching it, but it's a good example. Actually, now is a good time to move on to Subordinate References.

Managing Subordinate References

A Subordinate Reference pointer contains only one object, the partition root object. This container stores partition information linking it to other containers in the tree. The bottom line? Subordinate Reference replicas provide tree connectivity by acting as a link between the parent partition and child partitions.

Subordinate Reference replicas are completely managed by NDS and IntranetWare servers. You do not need to manage them. You should understand them, though. NDS will place a Subordinate Reference on any server that contains a replica of its parent partition, but not the child. In summary, where the parent is but the child is *not*. Refer to Figure 9.23 for a graphical summary.

▶ · ◀

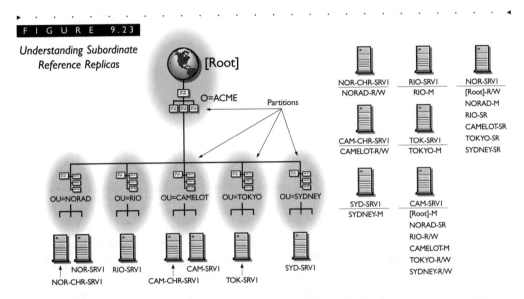

F I G U R E 9.23

Understanding Subordinate Reference Replicas

A lot of interesting replication is going on in Figure 9.23. As you can see, some servers have Subordinate References because they have a copy of the parent partition ([Root] partition in this case), but not the child. For example, NOR-SVR1 holds a copy of the [Root] Partition and itself, but no other partitions. Since all the location partitions are children of the [Root], NOR-SRV1 gets a Subordinate Reference of them all (except itself and the [Root]).

In a similar example, CAM-SRV1 also has a copy of the [Root] and itself. But it additionally holds a Read/Write replica of RIO, TOKYO, and SYDNEY. Therefore, the only child (of the [Root]) it doesn't have a replica of is NORAD, so NDS gives it a Subordinate Reference. How kind.

Subordinate References are visible in NDS Manager and DSREPAIR. They are not visible in NETADMIN or PARTMGR. Check out the CAM-SRV1 replicas in Figure 9.24. Since Subordinate References are just pointers, they don't actually contain any object information. Therefore, users can't log in, manage, or view NDS objects with this replica type. It's basically a tree-walking nuisance.

F I G U R E   9.24

The Different Replica Types for CAM-SRV1

NDSMGR - [[ACME_TREE] [Root]]

Object   View   Tools   Window   Help

Context: [Root]   Partition: Server Read: CAM-SRV1.CAMELOT.ACME

Servers:	Partition	Type	State
CAM-SRV1.CAMELOT.AC	[Root]	Master	on
NOR-SRV1.NORAD.ACME			
TOK-SRV1.TOKYO.ACME			
	CAMELOT.ACME	Master	on
	SYDNEY.ACME	Read-Write	on
	RIO.ACME	Read-Write	on
	TOKYO.ACME	Read-Write	on
	NORAD.ACME	Subordinate	on

TIP

Subordinate References may be a "nuisance," but they're a very important part of becoming a CNE. Learn them, know them, test them. Check out the challenging activities in Exercise 9-1 at the end of the chapter. Also, don't add R/W replicas to avoid Subordinate References. It will actually increase synchronization traffic.

SMART LINK

If you need more help with Subordinate References, check out the exercise at the end of this chapter or find a friend at http:// support.novell.com/sitemap.

This completes our first phase of Replica Management. How do you like it so far? Aren't replicas fun? Now that you have a new understanding of the four different replica types, let's spend some time learning what to do with them; namely, Add, Remove, Change, and Rebuild. Funny, it looks a lot like Add, Subtract, Multiply, and Divide. Maybe I learned this stuff somewhere else. Maybe in a previous life. You never know . . .

QUIZ

Without changing the order of the digits, insert four plus signs, one division sign and three minus signs between them to make the calculation correct:

9 8 7 6 5 4 3 2 1 = 0

(Q9-2)

MANAGING NDS REPLICA OPERATIONS

There are a lot of interesting things you can do to NDS replicas. First, you can create them — that's a good place to start. And, of course, anything you can create you can delete. But that's not all — you can also change and rebuild replicas. Wow, all this and so much more. Let's review the four options:

1 • *Add Replicas* — To distribute partitions throughout the WAN.

2 • *Remove Replicas* — If you change your mind, or the synchronization traffic is too much to bear.

3 • *Change Replicas* — To upgrade or downgrade existing replica types. This is also a great troubleshooting aid if the Master gets corrupted.

4 • *Rebuild Replicas* — Just in case.

Adding Replicas

Adding replicas is how we distribute partitions throughout the WAN. All you need is an existing partition and a host server; NDS Manager takes care of the rest. When you add replicas to other servers, all the NDS data is copied to the new server over the WAN. This operation causes significant network traffic. It depends, though, on the size of the replicated partition and the speed of the WAN links. It's a good idea to schedule replication operations when the network isn't very busy.

Figure 9.25 shows the NDS Manager screen for adding NDS replicas. First, choose a partition (CAMELOT.ACME in this case), then select Add Replica, and, finally, choose a server, NOR-SRV1.

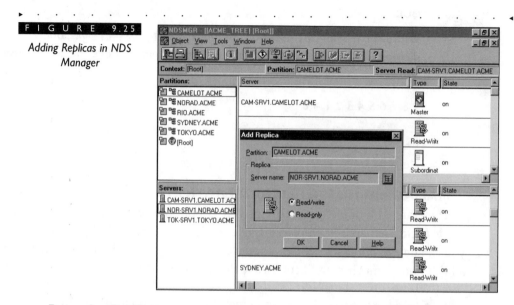

Removing Replicas

Whatever you create you can also destroy. Such power. NDS Manager also allows you to remove NDS replicas from specific servers. This operation is not as simple as it looks. When you remove a replica from an IntranetWare server, NDS creates an external reference pointer to every object in the original partition. The external reference points to another reference. The creation of all these external references may take some time, depending on the size of the partition. Be careful.

ZEN

"I figure practice puts your brains in your muscles."

Sam Snead

Changing NDS Replica Types

NDS also allows you to change a replica's type. This is particularly important when you want to manage NDS partitions or log into the "Cloud." Here's a quick summary:

▶ Partition Management — As we learned earlier, NDS requires access to the Master replica of a partition for any partition management operation. If the Master is unavailable, you can temporarily change an existing Read/Write or Read-Only replica into the Master.

▶ Login Authentication — We also learned that you need access to a Read/Write replica of your home partition in order to log in. If no Master or Read/Write replicas are available, you can upgrade an existing Read-Only replica. Cool.

Figure 9.26 shows how to change replica types in NDS Manager. It's pretty simple. First you select a partition, then a server, and finally, a new replica type. In this case, we're upgrading the [Root] partition on NOR-SRV1 from Read/Write to Master.

FIGURE 9.26

Changing Replica Types in NDS Manager

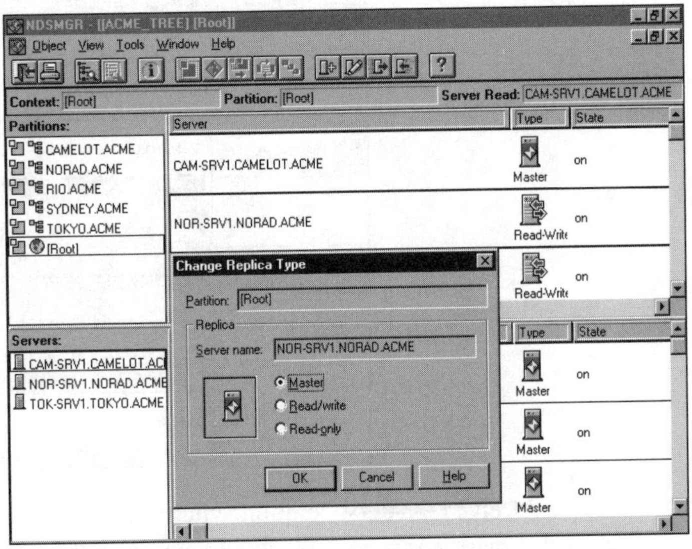

Rebuilding Replicas

Stuff happens. Some good, some bad. If your replicas lose their accuracy or become corrupted, you can always rebuild them. NDS Manager provides two methods for rebuilding replicas:

1 • Send Updates

2 • Receive Updates

The Send Updates option synchronizes all other replicas with the one you have selected. You would perform this operation when the partition information on some of the other servers is inaccurate or has become corrupted. This way you can control the source replica. Just make sure you select the best one — the one with the most recent, most accurate information. Figure 9.27 shows an example of the Send Update operation. In this example, NOR-SRV1 has a Master replica of the [Root] partition. It has been chosen as the source replica server. With the click of a button, we will update all other replicas in this Replica Ring.

F I G U R E   9.27

Sending Replica Updates in
NDS Manager

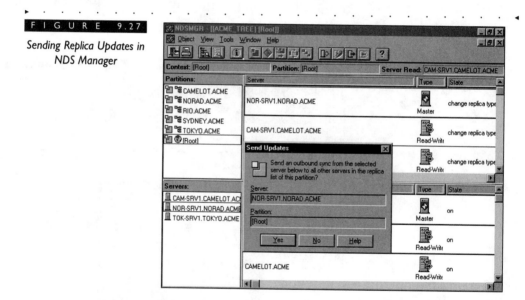

The Receive Updates operation synchronizes selected replicas with information from the Master replica. You would perform this operation when the partition information on one of your servers is not as complete as the Master. You can perform this task in either NDS Manager or DSREPAIR. Figure 9.28 shows an example of the Receive Updates operation in DSREPAIR. In this example, the CAM-SRV1 server is receiving replica updates from the Master [Root] replica. For more help troubleshooting NDS replicas, check out the "NDS Maintenance" section of Chapter 13.

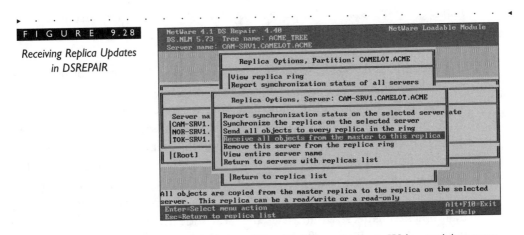

FIGURE 9.28

Receiving Replica Updates in DSREPAIR

This completes the second phase of Replica Management. We're cruising now. The final topic deals with a very important replica operation — synchronization. Replica synchronization affects NDS management more than any other partitioning task. Your goal is to maximize replica efficiency and minimize replica synchronization. It's a tough balancing act, and I'm here to help. So, without further adieu, let's synchronize.

SMART LINK

For more help fixing your broken replicas, check out the "NDS Maintenance" section of Chapter 13 or surf the Novell Knowledgebase at http://support.novell.com/search/.

MANAGING REPLICA SYNCHRONIZATION

Life is full of synchronization. We synchronize our watches; everyone wants synchronicity; the world even tolerates synchronized swimming. So, it's no surprise that NDS synchronizes, too.

Why? Because the database is distributed, and all pieces must be updated. Synchronization takes place within a special group of replicas called a *Replica Ring*. The Replica Ring is a list of all servers with replicas of a given partition. For example, Figure 9.29 illustrates the Replica Ring for the [Root] partition — CAM-SRV1 (Master), NOR-SRV1 (Read/Write), and TOK-SRV1 (Read/Write). Replica Rings are important because they dictate the speed and efficiency of synchronization. If a

Replica Ring spans slow WAN links, updates are going to be cumbersome and slow. On the other hand, if you keep a Replica Ring local, synchronization will be no sweat.

In addition, NDS replica synchronization is said to be loosely consistent. This means that changes within a Replica Ring are not always instantaneous and consistent. One server may get updated while the others hang out in the dark for a few more minutes. This loose consistency is caused because NDS receives updates from a variety of places, including itself, users, and CNE gardeners. As we'll see in just a moment, a variety of events activate synchronization updates. However, to ensure the integrity of the database, NDS will, over time, automatically synchronize all the replicas within the ring. Some just take longer than others. Figure 9.29 illustrates the "real" ACME Replica Ring for the [Root] partition. Notice all the traffic generated when the servers try to synchronize.

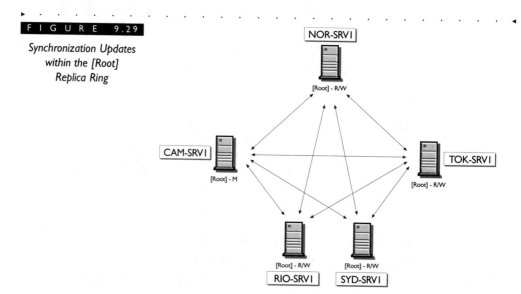

F I G U R E   9.29

Synchronization Updates within the [Root] Replica Ring

This synchronization process introduces a new level of complexity to WAN traffic efficiency. Fortunately, the information passed between replicas is limited to only updates, so this reduces the total amount of network traffic created by synchronization. But, as you can see in Figure 9.29, it's still quite significant. So, as the IntranetWare gardener, it's your job to minimize replica synchronization traffic. How do you do this? Well, here are three issues to consider:

1 • The total number of replicas per partition — Replica Ring

2 • The total number of replicas per server

3 • Subordinate Reference replicas

In general, you should avoid both having too many replicas in the ring and having too many total replicas per server. These two factors go hand-in-hand in minimizing the workload of replica servers and the background network traffic generated by synchronization. Also, Subordinate Reference replicas have a big impact because they are automatically created, generating more background traffic. Finally, consider controlling the types of replicas you create. Master and Read/Write replicas initiate synchronization, while Read-Only replicas don't.

Now, let's dive a little bit deeper into the scary world of replica synchronization management. Boo.

Total Number of Replicas per Partition — Replica Ring

The amount of replica synchronization for any given partition depends on the size of the partition (the number of objects), the number of updates or changes to the object information, the number of replicas or servers participating (Replica Ring), and the speed of the network (LAN and WAN links).

I encourage you to keep the size of the partitions small — no more than 5,000 objects per partition. This way the synchronization process can efficiently update all the replicas as needed. If a partition grows too large, consider splitting it to minimize large periodic updates.

Next, the level of partition activity impacts synchronization traffic. A lot of changes means a lot of traffic. Makes sense. Also, if the object information changes in one replica, it must change in all the replicas of the ring. Finally, remember that the NDS database is loosely consistent. This means that not all of the replicas are instantaneously updated. For example, each user login initiates synchronization because changes are made to three of the user's properties: Network Address, Last Login Date, and Last Login Time. When the user logs in, these changes are automatically written to the replica on the server that authenticated the user. Of course, updates of these changes must be synchronized to all other replicas in the ring. You can see that if a particular partition is active with logins and changes it will generate an inordinate amount of background traffic. In addition, you can increase replica synchronization traffic by simply having more objects in the partition and more replicas in the ring.

 ZEN

"This suit is so stiff. I can't do this with two hands, but I'm going to try a little sand trap shot here."

Alan Shepard, on the first golf shot on the moon

Total Number of Replicas per Server

Another synchronization consideration is the total number of replicas per server. A server cannot hold two replicas of the same partition. A server *can*, however, hold multiple replicas of different partitions. Many multiples, in some cases.

You should always place NDS replicas on high-end servers, so they can keep up with the other servers in the WAN. The synchronization process between all replicas in a ring is only as fast as the weakest link. The bottom line is: Don't place active replicas on a low-end server because it negatively affects all servers in the Replica Ring.

The total number of replicas per server varies according to the server's purpose. For example, an application/data server shouldn't hold more than 10 to 15 replicas. An e-mail server, on the other hand, can hold up to 20 to 25 replicas because it's not as disk-intensive. Finally, a dedicated NDS replica server can hold up to 100 to 150 replicas.

There is also an extreme case. Suppose, for example, you brought in a Super Server as a centralized NDS replica server. It could possibly maintain up to 200 replicas, but I wouldn't want to go much higher than that. Of course, this assumes an incredibly large NDS tree with at least 200 distributed partitions.

Subordinate Reference Replicas

There is a special consideration when it comes to the distribution of Subordinate Reference replicas. They are created like crazy all over the system, and do participate in daily synchronization activity. In some cases, this one event can impact a WAN so severely that it effectively shuts everything down. So, what can you do about it? Well, Subordinate References are the end product of poor partitioning. If you design natural partitions according to a pyramid design, the number of Subordinate References will automatically be reduced.

Don't be too hard on Subordinate References. Remember, they're good in that they provide tree connectivity by linking parent partitions with their children. Using this mechanism, NDS operates more efficiently because it does not have to place a full replica (Master, Read/Write, and Read-Only) to provide tree connectivity. As we learned earlier, NDS will place a Subordinate Reference replica on a server that contains a replica of the parent but does not contain a replica of the child. In summary, where the parent is, but the child is not.

Since NDS manages Subordinate Reference replicas automatically, you can only sit on the sidelines and watch. But, if you're perceptive and diligent, you can discover ways to change your partition design and minimize the number of Subordinate Reference pointers. The only way to reduce Subordinate References is to reduce the number of replicas of the parent partition. This can be done by reducing the number of servers that contain a copy of the parent partition. Let's see how it works.

QUIZ

One candle was guaranteed to burn for six hours, the other for four hours. They were both lit at the same time. After some time one was twice as long as the other. For how long had they been burning?

(Q9-3)

Let's return to ACME — but this time we've "phased" into a parallel universe (accidentally, of course). This new, weird ACME has 200 locations, all placed directly below the [Root] partition (see Figure 9.30). Assume that this new ACME follows the same partitioning strategy as our original ACME — that is, a partition in each of its locations. So, as you can see in Figure 9.30, there's one [Root] partition and 200 location partitions directly below it.

Consider what would happen each time you place a replica of the [Root] partition on a server. NDS would be forced to create 200 Subordinate References on that server, one for each of the [Root]'s child partitions. From the server perspective, it now must participate in each of the 200 partitions' synchronization processes. This amount of work will probably overload the servers entirely, unless they have special super-fast servers in the parallel universe. So, how would you solve this problem?

ACME's Partition Strategy in a Parallel Universe

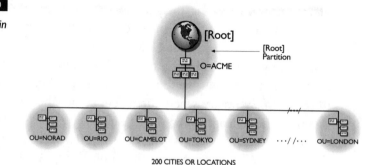

The simplest way to minimize Subordinate References is to create a more pyramid-like partition design. In ACME's case, you could simply add another layer of regional partitions directly under the [Root] partition. This would help distribute Subordinate Reference replicas across more IntranetWare servers. Figure 9.31 illustrates this simple solution.

F I G U R E   9 . 3 1

Adding Regional Containers to Spread-Out Subordinate References at ACME

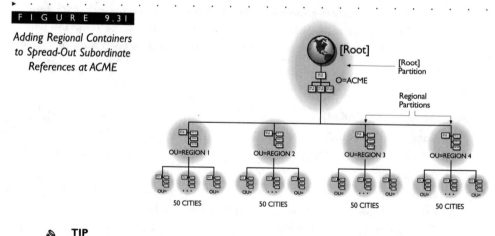

TIP

Be sure to place Regional OU replicas on separate servers from the location replicas. This will distribute the load of Subordinate References across the ACME WAN.

Partitioning also affects the placement of Subordinate Reference replicas. By the way, welcome back to the correct ACME universe. During any partitioning operation, all of the replicas in the ring must be available. This includes the Subordinate Reference replicas. If for any reason one of them isn't available, the partition operation will not complete. The total number of Subordinate Reference replicas could affect the efficiency of partitioning operations because each Subordinate Reference is part of the Replica Ring. This increases the chances of a failure. In this case, more is *not* merrier.

REAL WORLD

You may wonder why a Subordinate Reference replica is contacted during a partition operation. Even though Subordinate References do not contain any NDS partition information, they do contain information on the partition root container. This container changes during the partition operations. Bummer.

THE BRAIN

For more guidelines on working with **NDS partitions and replicas,** see "Management Procedures for Directory Services in NetWare 4" in the March 1994 *Novell Application Notes.*

OK, that's enough synchronization. I am fully synchronized at this moment. Synchronicity has been achieved. Now I'd like to introduce you to a pal of mine. He's a swinging NDS utility from downtown. His name is DSTRACE.

ZEN

"I don't answer the phone. I get the feeling whenever I do that there will be someone on the other end."

Fred Couples

USING DSTRACE

DSTRACE is your friend.

This is IntranetWare's version of TRACK ON — an old NetWare 3 SAP and RIP tool. DSTRACE allows you to track NDS activity between IntranetWare servers. DSTRACE will provide you with information on how NDS is functioning and whether or not the NDS synchronization processes are complete. DSTRACE will also assist you in diagnosing NDS errors.

The DSTRACE screen can be enabled at the IntranetWare server console by typing

```
SET DSTRACE = ON
```

or

```
SET NDS TRACE TO SCREEN = ON
```

Once DSTRACE is on, you can switch back and forth between console screens using the Alt-Esc keys. At some point, settle on the Directory Services console — this is DSTRACE. IntranetWare displays the major synchronization activities in color to help you identify the most important information. If a problem pops up, NDS errors will be displayed as well. In a few moments I'll provide you with a detailed NDS Error Code listing. This will be a big help when something unexpected happens to the NDS database.

There are plenty of DSTRACE commands that can assist you in capturing trace information for further review. This feature is handy because on a very busy server your information may scroll across the screen too fast. The default report file name is SYS:SYSTEM\DSTRACE.DBG. To save screen output to this disk file, type

```
SET TTF = ON
```

To stop screen output to disk file, type

```
SET TTF = OFF
```

SMART LINK

For a more in-depth look at DSTRACE Error Codes, consult the *NetWare 4.11 Utilities Reference* **at http://www.novell.com/manuals.**

To change the name of the report file, type

`SET NDS TRACE FILENAME = <filename>`

DSTRACE filter settings allow you to view specific NDS activity. They are activated by typing

`SET DSTRACE = <name>`

Notice that some of the filters must be preceded by a plus sign (+). To disable the filters, type

`SET DSTRACE -<name>`

Other commands are preceded by an asterisk (*) and will be noted where necessary. For your reading pleasure, I have listed the most useful DSTRACE filters in Table 9.1. And if that's not enough fun, check out the NetWare 4.11 documentation for a list of the most popular DSTRACE Error Codes. They may seem superfluous now, but believe me, these codes will save your hide some day.

TABLE 9.1	COMMAND	DESCRIPTION
DSTRACE Filter Commands	ALL	View all DSTRACE activity.
	+AUDIT	View audit messages that may be created while using the AUDITCON utility.
	+AUTHEN	View authentication time stamp information as users are logging into the network.
	+BACKLINK	View backlink information processing from server to server (BLINK also works).
	+COLLISION	View NDS timestamp collisions (COLL also works).
	+JANITOR	View the janitor process which cleans up deleted entries (J also works).
	+LIMBER	View a server's verification of name, network address, and replica placement for that server.
	OFF	Disable the DSTRACE screen.
	ON	Enable DSTRACE minimal tracking.

(continued)

TABLE 9.1	COMMAND	DESCRIPTION
DSTRACE Filter Commands (continued)	PART	View NDS partition information as an operation occurs.
	+SYNC	View the synchronization process for replicas stored on this server.
	SCHEMA	View the schema synchronization process.
	+VC	View virtual client (server to server) activity as replicas synchronize.
	*H	Begin the synchronization process immediately.
	*L	Begin the limber process immediately.
	*R	Reset the DSTRACE.DBG file to 0 length.
	*U	Reset all servers in the replica list to "Up."

You can use DSTRACE to track replica management and synchronization activity as well. When you do so, it lists the replica type according to the following codes:

▸ Master is replica type 0

▸ Read/Write or Secondary is replica type 1

▸ Read-Only is replica type 2

▸ Subordinate Reference is replica type 3

REAL WORLD

DSTRACE can also be activated at the IntranetWare server by typing **SET NDS TO SCREEN = ON**. For more troubleshooting tips with DSTRACE and other tools, check out the "NDS Maintenance" section of Chapter 13.

This completes our discussion of NDS grafting. Good work. In this section, we explored the three main aspects of replica management: replica types, replica operations, and replica synchronization. There's much more to replication than meets the eye. The good news is, we've made it through two of the three main NDS gardening tasks: pruning and grafting. That leaves pollination. I wonder if we have enough time to finish?

ZEN

"If you think it's hard to meet new people, try picking up the wrong golf ball."

Jack Lemmon

Time Synchronization

No matter how you look at it, time controls everything. This is especially true in NDS. Time impacts every aspect of your IntranetWare life — NDS partitioning operations, replica synchronization, and resource access, to name just a few. For this reason, time synchronization becomes a priority.

In Chapter 2 and Chapter 4 we learned all about what makes NDS time synchronization "tick." We learned that it coordinates and maintains consistent time for all the servers in your NDS tree. We also learned that IntranetWare provides two different time configuration options: default (small trees) and custom (large trees).

The *default* time synchronization option works best for small networks with few servers in a single location. This configuration is commonly referred to as the *single reference* configuration because it uses a Single Reference time provider. The *custom* time synchronization option provides more flexibility for larger networks with multiple servers in distributed locations. It uses a special time provider group. The time provider group is designed to provide greater fault tolerance and efficiency for communicating time across multiple servers and wide area networks.

In this section, we will explore the realm of time management. This deals primarily with the custom time configuration method. We will re-introduce

ACME's time provider group and learn everything there is to know about TIMESYNC.CFG. But first, let's take a quick stroll down memory lane and review some key time concepts.

UNDERSTANDING TIME SYNCHRONIZATION

Time synchronization provides IntranetWare servers with a mechanism for coordinating NDS time stamps. IntranetWare uses the TIMESYNC NLM to coordinate time stamps between all servers on the WAN. TIMESYNC.NLM maintains each server's Universal Time Coordinate (UTC) — a fancy name for Greenwich Mean Time (GMT).

All IntranetWare servers are time servers of some type, either providers or consumers. Time providers provide time to time consumers. Makes sense. IntranetWare supports three different time providers: Primary server, Reference server, and Single Reference server. On the other hand, there's only one type of time consumer: Secondary server. The majority of your IntranetWare servers will be time consumers.

All IntranetWare time servers perform three functions in relation to time synchronization:

1 • They provide UTC time to any NLM or requesting client workstation.

2 • They provide status information regarding the synchronization of UTC time.

3 • They adjust their clock rates to correct for time discrepancies and maintain UTC synchronization.

Time management operates on two important principles: time configuration and time communication.

Time configuration defines how your time servers are distributed. In addition, it outlines which servers are providers and which servers are consumers. As we learned earlier, IntranetWare supports two basic time configuration designs:

1 • Default: Single Reference

2 • Custom: Time Provider Group

Whatever you do, be sure to choose the correct configuration method for your WAN. If your network is distributed over multiple sites and there are WAN links to consider, definitely use the custom method. A time provider group gives your network greater fault tolerance by distributing the time servers to multiple locations. If your network has less than 30 servers and they are all at a single location, you can probably use the default configuration method.

THE BRAIN

For more information on NDS time synchronization, see the following *Novell Application Notes:* "An Introduction to NetWare Directory Services" (April 1993) and "Time Synchronization in NetWare 4" (November 1993).

REAL WORLD

Occasionally it may be necessary to change the time on an IntranetWare server. Never change time at a server by typing **TIME** at the server's console and entering a new value. You can change a server's time by following these steps:

1. After hours, bring the IntranetWare server down.

2. At the DOS prompt, type **TIME** and enter the new time value.

3. Restart IntranetWare by typing **SERVER.EXE**.

NDS will get the new time value from DOS and the server's CMOS. This is the sole source of time for this server, unless it's getting time from an outside source. Also, remember to change the time zone information in SERVMAN, if necessary.

In Chapter 4 we learned that ACME will be using the custom time configuration approach. They will place a Reference time server in CAMELOT and Primary time servers in the other four hubs: NORAD, TOKYO, SYDNEY, and RIO. The next question is, How will these time servers communicate with one another?

Time communication occurs in two instances. First, when time providers "vote" with one another to determine the network's correct time. And second, when Secondary time servers "poll" time providers for the correct time. This occurs at regular polling intervals. Since ACME is using the custom time communication design, we'll need to create Configured Lists for server-to-server communications.

That's enough review for now. Let's dive into time management with a comprehensive exploration of TIMESYNC.CFG and ACME's time synchronization strategy.

MANAGING TIME SYNCHRONIZATION WITH TIMESYNC.CFG

IntranetWare time synchronization is activated by default. It uses a Single Reference server configuration and SAP (Service Advertising Protocol) communications. You can start with this design if you'd like — just to test out the waters. But pretty soon, you'll probably need greater flexibility and synchronization control. That's where time management comes in. Time management is the process of customizing two important time synchronization principles:

▸ Time Provider Group — Determines which servers are providers. Also determines who gets to be the Reference time server and who are Primaries.

▸ Configured Lists — Determines who gets time from whom. For providers, this list determines the voting patterns, and for consumers, this list determines where Secondary servers go for the correct network time.

Most time management tasks are accomplished using the Time Parameters option in SERVMAN. You can load this tool by typing **LOAD SERVMAN** at the file server console. Figures 9.32 and 9.33 show the two main Time Parameters window. This window, and subsequent screens, list 24 different time management options. These options help us define time provider groups and build Configured Lists for every server. Let's check them out.

ZEN

"They call it golf because all the other four-letter words were taken."

Raymond Floyd

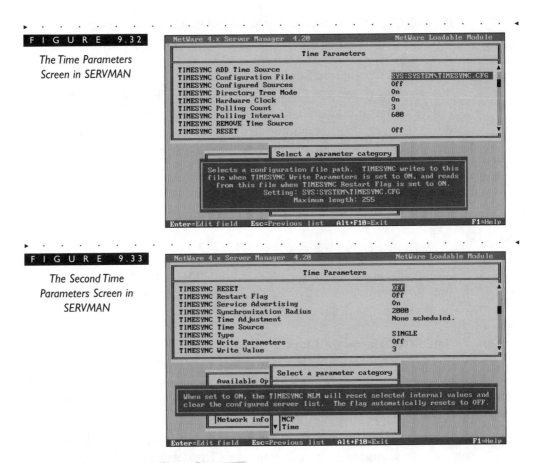

FIGURE 9.32

The Time Parameters Screen in SERVMAN

FIGURE 9.33

The Second Time Parameters Screen in SERVMAN

TIMESYNC Add Time Source

This option allows you to add the name of a server to your Configured List. The server name that you enter here will eventually find its way to the TIMESYNC.CFG configuration file. TIMESYNC.CFG is updated if you choose the Update TIMESYNC.CFG option after exiting the Time Parameters screen. In most cases, you will only use this option if you are adding a new source time server to the Configured List. Again, the default is Empty.

TIMESYNC Configuration File

The TIMESYNCE.CFG configuration file is the default name given to the file that stores all the settings for time management. There is little (if any) need to change the name of this file, and I recommend you accept the default,

TIMESYNC.CFG. This file can easily be copied to multiple IntranetWare servers if needed. Again, the default value is SYS:SYSTEM\TIMESYNC.CFG.

TIMESYNC Configured Sources

This option activates the Configured List strategy. It is also shown in Figure 9.32. This option must be set to ON if you are using Configured Lists. When activated, this server only communicates with servers in its configured list — SAP broadcasts are ignored. The default is OFF.

If you need to view your server's Configured List, you can type the following command at the server console:

```
SET TIMESYNC TIME SOURCE =
```

TIMESYNC Directory Tree Mode

This option specifies that SAP packets from other Directory trees can influence the time synchronization on this server. Do not change this parameter if this server is a time source. The default is ON.

TIMESYNC Hardware Clock

This option controls the hardware clock synchronization and instructs the server to read its hardware clock at the beginning of each polling loop (see Figure 9.32). A Single Reference server or Reference server will read its hardware clock at the start of each polling loop. A Primary server or Secondary server will not read its hardware clock during each polling loop. Instead, they will adjust their software clocks during each polling interval. The default is ON.

TIMESYNC Polling Count

This option sets the number of times the polling packets should be exchanged. Typically, the default of three works adequately. In cases where you may have a long delay of communications between two time servers, you may want to increase this option by a few.

TIMESYNC Polling Interval

Every 10 minutes (600 seconds), a server will poll for time. After initial installation of your IntranetWare servers, you may want to increase this value to 20 minutes or even one hour. The time polling process does not generate an inordinate amount of traffic on your network, so the default setting does not create large problems. The default is 600 seconds.

TIMESYNC REMOVE Time Source

This option allows you to remove a server from your list of configured time sources. The server name entered in this field will be removed from the TIMESYNC.CFG configuration file if you exit and choose Yes to update TIMESYNC.CFG. You can also use EDIT to change an entry in the TIMESYNC.CFG file.

TIMESYNC RESET

This option will return all values in your TIMESYNC.CFG configuration to the default values. If you issue a reset and write the configuration file after exiting, any changes previously made to the TIMESYNC file will be lost. Be careful with this paramter. The default is, kindly, OFF.

TIMESYNC Restart Flag

This option will cause the time synchronization process to restart using the parameters found in the TIMESYNC.CFG configuration file. These parameters will cause TIMESYNC.NLM to reload without bringing down the server. The default is OFF.

TIMESYNC Service Advertising

This parameter enables the Service Advertising Protocol (SAP) as the communication mechanism. If you are using Configured Lists, turn this parameter OFF. The default, as you can see in Figure 9.33, is ON.

TIMESYNC Synchronization Radius

The synchronization radius is the amount of time that a server's clock can vary and still be considered synchronized. The default of 2,000 milliseconds works well for most installations. This time parameter can be increased if more time is required for travel across satellite links or congested WAN links. The default polling interval is shown in Figure 9.33.

TIMESYNC Time Adjustment

This parameter is used to schedule adjustments to the server's network time. Use caution when executing this command because changing time can disrupt network operations. For example, entering the command

```
+00:00:01 at 11/17/99 08:59:00 PM
```

will adjust the time ahead three hours and one minute before midnight on November 17, 1999. Use this field only when a significant one-time correction must be made to the network time. The default is None Scheduled.

TIMESYNC Time Source

This parameter is used to add time sources to your TIMESYNC.CFG file. The same functionality is provided through the field ADD Timesync Time Source at the top of the screen. To reduce confusion, leave this field alone.

TIMESYNC Type

This field allows you to specify a type of time server to be configured. You will only need to modify this parameter when creating a Time Provider Group (as in ACME's case). You specify which type it is by typing Reference, Single, Primary, or Secondary.

TIMESYNC Write Parameters

This parameter is used to write changes to the TIMESYNC.CFG file. Use EDIT rather than this parameter. The default is OFF.

TIMESYNC Write Value

This is used to modify the TIMESYNC.CFG file. Use EDIT rather than this parameter for making modifications.

If you are using the SERVMAN utility to make edits to TIMESYNC.CFG, you can save those edits when you exit the Time Parameters screen. The main SERVMAN screen will prompt you to save the changes, as shown in Figure 9.34.

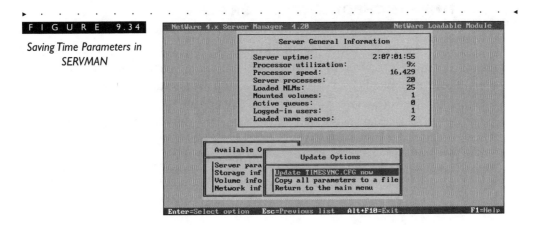

FIGURE 9.34

Saving Time Parameters in SERVMAN

You can easily view the status of TIMESYNC.CFG by typing **SET** at the file server console. You can then select list option 9 to give the settings for all Time Parameters as discussed earlier. Finally, TIMESYNC.NLM supports a debug mode for time troubleshooting. This is helpful for determining if the servers are contacting one another during the expected intervals. Here's how it works:

```
SET TIMESYNC DEBUG = 7     (enables debug)
SET TIMESYNC DEBUG = 0     (disables debug)
```

That's everything you need to know about managing TIMESYNC.CFG. Now you're ready to attack ACME's time synchronization design. Ready, set, time.

QUIZ

Without changing the order of the digits, form a calculation equal to 100. Only four plus and/or minus signs can be inserted between the digits:

9 8 7 6 5 4 3 2 1 = 100

(Q9-4)

SMART LINK

If you want to know what time it REALLY is, check out the U.S. Government's atomic clock in Boulder, Colorado at http://www.bldrdoc.gov/doc-tour/atomic_clock.html.

TIME SYNCHRONIZATION FOR ACME

Now it's "time" (pun intended) to implement ACME's time synchronization design. As you may remember from earlier discussions, their corporate headquarters are in CAMELOT. Furthermore, they have a Reference time server there that is linked to an external time source. This source provides time for both the IntranetWare server clock and the PC hardware.

Primary servers are located in each of the other WAN hubs; namely, RIO, NORAD, SYDNEY, and TOKYO. These time sources will work together to determine the actual network time during each polling interval. The ACME tree uses customized Configured Lists for time communication. The following information shows what it takes to make time work at ACME.

Reference Server in CAMELOT

TIMESYNC.CFG (CAMELOT)

- ▶ Configured Sources = ON
- ▶ Directory Tree Mode = ON
- ▶ Hardware Clock = ON
- ▶ Polling Count = 3
- ▶ Polling Interval = 10
- ▶ Service Advertising = OFF
- ▶ Synchronization Radius = 2000
- ▶ Type = REFERENCE

Configured List (CAMELOT)

- ▶ Time Source = RIO
- ▶ Time Source = TOKYO
- ▶ Time Source = SYDNEY
- ▶ Time Source = NORAD
- ▶ Time Source = CAMELOT

Primary Servers in RIO, TOKYO, NORAD, and SYDNEY

TIMESYNC.CFG (TOKYO as example)

- Configured Sources = ON
- Directory Tree Mode = ON
- Hardware Clock = ON
- Polling Count = 3
- Polling Interval = 10
- Service Advertising = OFF
- Synchronization Radius = 2000
- Type = PRIMARY

Configured List (TOKYO as example)

- Time Source = CAMELOT
- Time Source = RIO
- Time Source = TOKYO
- Time Source = NORAD
- Time Source = SYDNEY

Secondary Servers

TIMESYNC.CFG (Secondary Servers)

- Configured Sources = ON
- Directory Tree Mode = ON
- Hardware Clock = ON
- Polling Count = 3
- Polling Interval = 10

- Service Advertising = OFF

- Synchronization Radius = 2000

- Type = SECONDARY

Configured List (depends on location NORAD as example)

- Time Source = NORAD

- Time Source = RIO

- Time Source = SYDNEY

- Time Source = CAMELOT

- Time Source = TOKYO

Congratulations! Your green thumb is shining brightly. You're going to be a great IntranetWare gardener. Today, we added an in-depth knowledge of pruning to our agronomic repertoire. We learned about NDS partition management (pruning), NDS replication (grafting), and time synchronization (pollination). Doesn't it feel wonderful to be in the great outdoors?

This is not only the end of a chapter, this represents the end of an era. An era in NDS gardening that started seven chapters ago — way back in Chapter 2. In the beginning . . . We learned all about the "Cloud" and what it meant to live there. We learned about objects, naming, partitions, replicas, and time synchronization. Our innocence and naivete was only eclipsed by our insatiable curiosity.

Then, we took this rudimentary knowledge and used it to save the world. In Chapter 3 we discovered ACME and promptly designed their tree in Chapter 4. NDS design consisted of naming standards, tree design, partition design, replica placement, and time synchronization design. There are those topics again. But this time, we expanded our understanding of NDS into the realm of design and implementation. Tricky stuff.

We took a well-deserved rest from NDS until Chapter 8. Then bang! It hit us — NDS management. We brought our design to life with tools such as NWADMIN, CX, NetSync, and so on. We learned about special NDS objects, naming rules, Bindery Services, and management tricks. I never knew NDS had such a complex personality. Then things got even weirder in this chapter. We expanded our gardening skills into the realm of pruning — you know, kill a tree so it can live. Strange stuff.

So, here we are. We've learned all there is to know about NDS. Of course, we're not done learning. There's a plethora of IntranetWare Management tasks left; namely, the file system, security, configuration, management, printing, and optimization. And the good news is, NDS permeates them all.

I wonder if there's life after gardening. Something tells me that NDS will always be there — like a guardian "cloud" floating above our heads. Of course, it's especially beautiful at sunrise. Tomorrow is a new dawn.

Welcome to the real fun part of NDS pruning. Subordinate Reference replicas are one of the most challenging management topics of IntranetWare CNEship. As such, you'll be expected to master them during several Novell Education exams, including *NDS Design*, *Advanced Administration*, *Update*, and the *Installation and Configuration Workshop*.

In this exercise, I have devised three detailed and challenging Subordinate Reference exam questions. If you can figure these out, then you're a few steps closer to being a CNE. Good luck, and let the games begin.

SR CHALLENGE #1

Refer to Figure 9.35 for an illustration of the "O=ABC" company tree. Then, check out the NDS replica placement table in Figure 9.36. It shows the distribution of eight different partitions on six different servers.

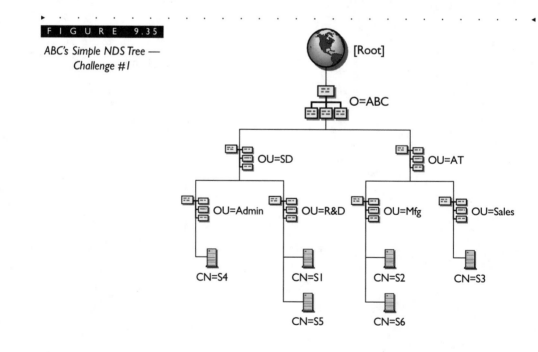

F I G U R E   9.35

ABC's Simple NDS Tree —
Challenge #1

FIGURE 9.36

ABC's Replica Table — Challenge #2

Partitions

Servers	[Root]	ABC	SD	AT	Admin	R&D	Mfg	Sales
S1	M	M	M	M	M	M	M	M
S2	R/W	R/W		R/W			R/W	
S3								R/W
S4			R/W		R/W			
S5	R/W					R/W		
S6								R/W

(Columns represent partitions, rows represent servers;
M=Master replica, R/W=Read/Write replica, and R-O=Read-Only replica.)

Now, which of the following statements is true concerning the placement of SR replicas on ABC's servers:

A. Server 2 would have a Subordinate Reference replica for the SD and Sales partitions.

B. Server 3 would have a Subordinate Reference replica for the Mfg partition.

C. Server 4 would have a Subordinate Reference replica for the R&D partition.

D. Server 5 would have a Subordinate Reference replica for the ABC partition.

E. Server 6 would have a Subordinate Reference replica for the Sales partition.

Bonus: for extra credit (and to prove you're true CNE material), finish the matrix in Figure 9.36 by placing an "SR" wherever Subordinate Reference replicas would appear.

SR CHALLENGE #2

Refer to Figure 9.37 for another version of the "O=ABC" NDS tree. Then, check out the NDS replica placement table in Figure 9.38. It shows the distribution of nine different partitions on seven different servers.

FIGURE 9.37

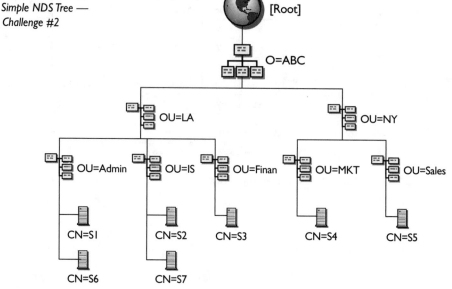

ABC's Simple NDS Tree — Challenge #2

FIGURE 9.38

ABC's Replica Table — Challenge #2

Partitions

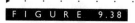

Servers	[Root]	ABC	LA	NY	Admin	IS	Finan	Mkt	Sales
S1		M			M	M	R/O	M	
S2	M					M			
S3				R/W			R/W		
S4	R/W			M				M	R/W
S5		R/W	R/W					R/W	M
S6			M		R/W				
S7	M					R/W	R/W		

(Columns represent partitions, rows represent servers;
M=Master replica, R/W=Read/Write replica, and R-O=Read-Only replica.)

Now, which of the following statements is true concerning the placement of SR replicas on ABC's servers:

A. The Finan partition is missing a Master replica.

B. Server 5 would have a Subordinate Reference replica for the [Root] partition.

C. Server 3 would have a Subordinate Reference replica for the Mkt and Sales partitions.

D. Servers 2 and 7 can't both have Master replicas for the [Root] partition.

E. Server 2 would have a Subordinate Reference replica for the LA and NY partitions.

Bonus: for extra credit (and to prove you're true CNE material), finish the matrix in Figure 9.38 by placing an "SR" wherever Subordinate Reference replicas would appear.

SR CHALLENGE #3

Refer to Figure 9.39 for another version of the "O=ABC" NDS tree. Then, check out the NDS replica placement table in Figure 9.40. It shows the distribution of ten different partitions on eight different servers.

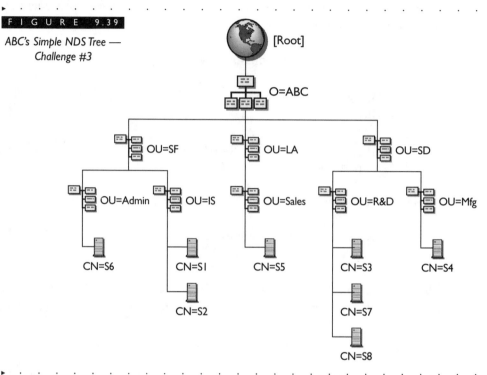

FIGURE 9.39

ABC's Simple NDS Tree —
Challenge #3

FIGURE 9.40

ABC's Replica Table —
Challenge #3

Partitions

Servers	[Root]	ABC	SF	LA	SD	Admin	IS	Sales	R&D	Mfg
S1	M	M	M				M			
S2						R/W	R/W			
S3	R/W			M					M	
S4		R/W			R/W					M
S5	R/O	R/O		M				M		
S6			R/W			M				
S7									R/W	
S8									R/W	R/W

(Columns represent partitions, rows represent servers;
M=Master replica, R/W=Read/Write replica, and R-O=Read-Only replica.)

Now, which of the following statements is true concerning the placement of SR replicas on ABC's servers:

A. Server 1 would have a Subordinate Reference replica for the Sales, R&D, and Mfg partitions.

B. Server 4 would have a Subordinate Reference replica for the SF, LA, and R&D partitions.

C. Server 1 would have a Subordinate Reference replica for the LA, SD, and Admin partitions.

D. Server 3 would have a Subordinate Reference replica for the ABC and Mfg partitions.

E. Server 6 would have a Subordinate Reference replica for the LA and SD partitions.

Bonus: for extra credit (and to prove you're true CNE material), finish the matrix in Figure 9.40 by placing an "SR" wherever Subordinate Reference replicas would appear.

See Appendix C for answers.

EXERCISE 9-2: INTRANETWARE PRUNING

Circle the 20 partition management and synchronization terms hidden in this word search puzzle using the hints provided.

```
V  H  U  V  K  D  E  V  N  O  I  T  I  T  R  A  P  T  O  O  R
F  L  O  O  S  E  C  O  N  S  I  S  T  E  N  C  Y  Y  A  S  E
K  J  A  L  Y  F  A  W  M  A  S  T  E  R  R  E  P  L  I  C  A
Q  V  F  S  N  H  R  E  W  X  W  U  D  H  X  M  O  N  S  V  D
P  P  A  R  T  I  T  I  O  N  R  O  O  T  O  B  J  E  C  T  O
J  A  A  R  H  V  S  Y  N  C  H  R  O  N  I  Z  A  T  I  O  N
J  R  F  R  E  A  D  W  R  I  T  E  R  E  P  L  I  C  A  D  L
S  E  B  F  T  H  H  P  J  L  Y  K  K  H  W  L  D  V  K  Q  Y
Q  N  G  P  I  I  K  I  S  Y  S  F  B  J  Q  I  F  H  W  O  R
P  T  C  A  C  V  T  P  A  R  T  I  T  I  O  N  M  E  R  G  E
Y  P  A  R  T  I  T  I  O  N  O  P  E  R  A  T  I  O  N  S  P
T  A  T  T  I  S  U  U  O  K  O  K  H  B  O  V  D  E  M  L
I  R  T  I  M  D  X  L  E  N  H  L  D  M  I  L  X  Y  X  Q  I
M  T  P  T  E  H  M  N  W  Y  M  C  Z  Y  N  L  Y  Z  E  X  C
E  I  Y  I  L  S  P  S  E  Q  N  A  Y  N  P  V  S  M  R  M  A
S  T  K  O  R  X  H  U  K  J  J  N  N  P  S  W  O  V  G  G  L
Y  I  T  N  V  M  B  M  M  R  Q  L  R  A  X  P  O  L  M  P  I
N  O  X  S  E  N  D  U  P  D  A  T  E  S  G  W  D  X  T  B  S
C  N  Q  P  N  X  S  Q  V  E  O  Q  K  B  K  E  D  G  R  V  T
C  H  I  L  D  P  A  R  T  I  T  I  O  N  J  K  R  A  A  V  Q
F  V  T  I  M  E  P  R  O  V  I  D  E  R  G  R  O  U  P  G  U
G  E  J  T  U  L  U  C  N  J  R  R  J  J  Q  H  H  O  G  F  A
```

Hints:

1. A subordinate partition.
2. Utility that can be used to determine how NDS is functioning, whether NDS synchronization is complete, and to assist in diagnosing NDS errors.
3. Concept that replicas are not instantaneously changed as updates are made to NDS.

4. The name of the first replica created for a partition.
5. When partition boundaries meet, the partition that is closer to the [Root].
6. NWADMIN utility option that can be used to manage NDS partitions.
7. Also known as a "partition join."
8. Tasks include creating new partitions, merging partitions, moving partitions or subtrees, adding replicas, removing replicas, changing replica types, rebuilding replicas, and aborting partition operations.
9. The topmost object in a partition.
10. The process of dividing the NDS tree into subtrees.
11. Workstation utility used to manage partitions and their replicas.
12. Type of replica that cannot support login or authentication requests from users.
13. Most common type of replica.
14. Indicates all of the replicas for a given partition.
15. The only partition created by the installation program.
16. An NWADMIN menu option can be used to force all of the other replicas of a partition to synchronize with the one you have selected.
17. Process used to ensure that changes made to one replica of a partition are automatically made to all replicas of that partition.
18. An indication that time may have been set back on a server.
19. Most commonly used configuration for installations with 30 or more servers connected through a WAN link.
20. Server configuration file used to store time synchronization settings.

See Appendix C for answers.

IntranetWare File System

Just when you think you have IntranetWare and NDS figured out, a little voice inside your head whispers, "There is another . . . ."

Another what? Listen more closely, ". . . directory structure."

Another directory structure? How could that be? You may think that there's only one NetWare directory structure and it's the foundation of NDS. Well, that's where you're wrong. If you look closely at Figure 10.1, you'll see *two* directory trees — one above the server and one below it.

▶ · ◀

F I G U R E   10.1

The Two IntranetWare Directory Trees

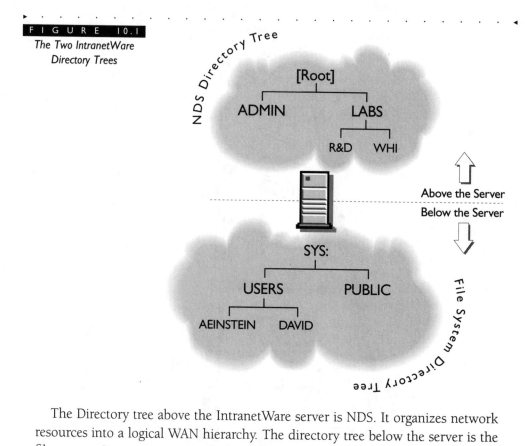

The Directory tree above the IntranetWare server is NDS. It organizes network resources into a logical WAN hierarchy. The directory tree below the server is the file system. It organizes network data files into a functional application hierarchy. Pretty simple, huh? The important thing is to separate the two in your mind. NDS handles resource data and the file system handles application data. Think of it as the "File Cabinet of Life."

ZEN

"To me, if life boils down to one significant thing — it's movement. To live is to keep moving. Unfortunately, this means that for the rest of our lives we're going to be looking for boxes!"

Jerry Seinfeld

In the past, cave — LANs relied on "sneakernet" for file sharing. First, they copied files to a diskette, then ran them down the hall to a coworker's machine. Finally, the coworker transferred the files from diskette to his or her own directory structure. Voilá!

With the advent of NetWare (and coaxial cabling), society experienced the dawning of a new age — the file server. The file server became the central repository of shared data and applications. Life was good.

Then, IntranetWare came along. Once again, society experienced the dawning of a new age — NDS. The file server suddenly became a small fish in a very large, global pond. Volumes took on a life of their own. People started treating them as independent objects; free from the servers that house them. Is this progress? I'm not so sure. It underemphasizes the importance of the file server. Let's be honest. It's still the most important resource in the WAN. And what do file servers do? They serve files. How? Through the IntranetWare file system.

Let's check it out.

SMART LINK

Go meet Jerry Seinfeld on the Web at http://www.nbc.com/entertainment/shows/seinfeld.

Understanding the IntranetWare File System

Every IntranetWare file server contains a hierarchical directory structure for storing shared data files and applications. It is called the *file system*. The file system organizes internal disks into one or more volumes. Volumes are then divided into directories that contain subdirectories or files. On the surface it looks a lot like DOS. But don't be fooled; it's a whole new world. Check out Figure 10.2!

TIP

In earlier versions of NetWare, the "file system" was referred to as the "directory structure." In IntranetWare, it is referred to as the "file system" to distinguish it from the NDS directory structure.

F I G U R E   10.2

The IntranetWare File System

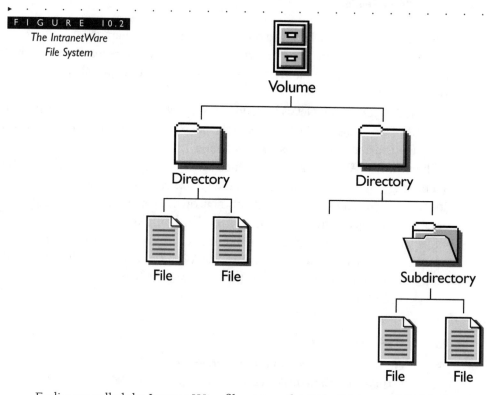

Earlier we called the IntranetWare file system the "File Cabinet of Life." It fits. See Figure 10.3. In such an analogy, the file server is the filing cabinet and the volumes are the drawers. Also, the directories are hanging folders, the subdirectories are file folders, and the files become individual sheets of paper. Pretty nifty, huh?

With this analogy in mind, let's explore the key components of IntranetWare's exciting new file system: volumes and directories. In the first section, we will re-discover the volume, and learn about its dual personality as a logical NDS object and physical disk resource. Then, we'll focus our journey even further into the IntranetWare directory structure — starting with system-created directories, which are defined automatically on the SYS: volume during IntranetWare/NetWare 4.11 server installation (see Chapter 6). Next, we'll expand our horizons beyond default directories and into the realm of DOS, application, configuration, home, and shared directories. Finally, you'll get a taste of two different directory designs — shallow and deep.

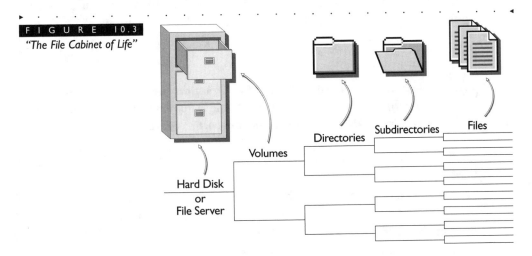

F I G U R E 10.3
"The File Cabinet of Life"

And that's only the first section. Later in the chapter, we'll explore file system management and the land of drive mapping. Wow! So much to learn and so little time. So, without any further interruptions, let's get on with the show.

UNDERSTANDING INTRANETWARE VOLUMES

Volumes are cool — mostly because they're so unique. They can span multiple disks, or they can be subdivisions of a single disk. They are physical storage units within the file server, but also independent logical objects that stand alone. They are neither here nor there — they are everywhere!

The volume represents the highest level in the IntranetWare file system. It is the root of the server directory structure. Volumes are also leaf objects in the NDS Directory tree. Because of this unique position, they act as a bridge between NDS and the file system. The first volume on each IntranetWare server is named SYS:. It is created automatically during NetWare 4.11 installation. In addition, an NDS volume leaf object is created in the server's home container. In our example, it is called WHITE-SRV1_SYS — a logical representation of the physical SYS: volume on server WHITE-SRV1.

None of this is set in stone, of course. You can change the context of a Volume object using NetWare Administrator (NWADMIN) or NETADMIN. You can also rename volumes. To rename a physical volume, you'll need to change its server definition with INSTALL.NLM. To rename a logical volume, on the other hand, you can use either NWADMIN or NETADMIN. Finally, you can create a special pointer to a different physical volume using the Alias object type.

ZEN

Infobit — An individual item of information, such as a recipe or a description of a place, that meets the requirements for inclusion in a databank. Also used to describe properties of NDS objects.

So, what are they? IntranetWare *volumes* are fixed units of hard disk storage that are created during server installation. They can be formed from any hard disk that contains a NetWare partition. Think of it as NetWare formatting. You can place 64 volumes on a IntranetWare server, and each one can span up to 32 hard disks. Do the math. That means a IntranetWare server can support 2,048 disks — wow! Also, a volume can support 32 terabytes of disk space and as many as 16 million directory entries (with only the DOS name space).

How does it work? Volumes are divided into physical volume segments. Different segments can be stored on one or more hard disks. Each volume can support up to 32 segments, and/or each hard disk can support up to 8 volume segments from one or more volumes. Because of this, a volume can

▸ Contain a portion of a hard disk

▸ Occupy an entire hard disk

▸ Span multiple hard disks

The simplest configuration is, of course, one hard disk per volume. The advantage of spreading a volume across multiple hard disks is performance. It allows the server to read from or write to different parts of the same volume simultaneously — thus speeding up disk input/output. The disadvantage of such a technique, however, is fault tolerance. If you span volumes across multiple disks, it increases the chances that something will go wrong. If any disk fails, the entire volume fails, and you lose all your data. Consider protecting your volumes with mirroring, duplexing, or RAID (Redundant Array of Inexpensive Disks).

TIP

RAID provides numerous performance and SFT (System Fault Tolerance) advantages. From a performance standpoint, it uses data striping, which means that files are stored across multiple disks. Read and write performance is enhanced dramatically because blocks can be accessed simultaneously. In addition, RAID employs a parity algorithm that protects volumes even when a disk crashes. Cool.

SMART LINK

For more information on RAID, surf to the Novell Knowledgebase at http://support.novell.com/search/.

IntranetWare volumes are further organized into *directories* and *files*. Directories are logical volume subdivisions that provide an administrative hierarchy to network applications and data files. They allow you to further organize your data into content-specific file folders. Directories can contain other directories (called *subdirectories*) or files.

Files are individual items of data. They represent the bottom level of the file-server food chain. Files can contain valuable user data or network applications. It doesn't matter. What does matter is their location. Files should be stored in logical subdirectories according to their purpose and security level. That's the ultimate goal of the IntranetWare file system — organize the user's data so that it's secure and easy to find.

To accomplish this goal, you must follow specific file syntax and naming rules. As with NDS object naming, filenames define the data's name and location:

```
Server/Volume:Directory\(Subdirectory)\Filename
```

Standard directory names and filenames support eight characters and an optional three-character extension. Special non-DOS filenames can extend as far as 32 characters (Macintosh) or even 255 characters (OS/2 and Windows 95).

These special files require an additional volume feature called *name space* (see Chapter 13). Also, make sure to support the path conventions of standard or special filenames. NetWare allows 255 characters in a directory path (counting the drive letter and delimiters), whereas DOS only allows a maximum of 127 characters. Refer to Table 10.1 for more IntranetWare file system naming rules.

T A B L E 10.1 *IntranetWare File System Naming Rules*	PATH COMPONENT	RULES
	File Server	Name is limited to 2 to 47 characters.
		First character in name cannot be a period.
		Name cannot contain spaces or special characters such as * + , \ / | : ; = < > [ ].
	Volume	Name length is limited to 2 to 15 characters.
		Physical name must end with a colon (:), which is added automatically.
		First volume on server must be SYS:.
		Two physical volumes on the same server cannot have the same name.
		Name cannot contain spaces or special characters such as * + , \ / | : ; = < > [ ].
	Directory	Name length is limited to a maximum of 11 characters (a directory name consisting of one to eight characters plus an optional directory name extension of up to three characters).
		A period (.) is used to separate the directory name from the (optional) extension.
		Directories should be limited to functional groups.
		Name cannot contain spaces or special characters such as * + , \ / | : ; = < > [ ].
	Subdirectory	Name length is limited to a maximum of 11 characters (a directory name consisting of one to eight characters plus an optional directory name extension of up to three characters).
		A period (.) is used to separate the directory name from the (optional) extension.
		Subdirectories share common functionality.

TABLE 10.1	PATH COMPONENT	RULES
IntranetWare File System Naming Rules (continued)	Subdirectory	The size of subdirectories is limited by disk size. Name cannot contain spaces or special characters such as * + , \ / | : ; = < > [ ].
	Files	Name length is limited to a maximum of 11 characters (a filename consisting of 1 to 8 characters plus an optional filename extension of up to 3 characters). A period (.) is used to separate the directory name from the (optional) extension. Name cannot contain spaces or special characters such as * + , \ / | : ; = < > [ ].

Before you get too carried away with IntranetWare configuration and management, you should design the basic structure of the file system. This is just as important as designing the NDS tree. In both cases, you need to consider a number of important WAN factors, including security, administration, and accessibility. Except, this time, we're working below the server, not above it.

ZEN

Nonchaotic attractor — A pattern of movement in a system with motion that settles down to an easily describable and predictable pattern, such as a pendulum or IntranetWare volume. This can also be thought of as a normal attractor in that it is the opposite of a "strange" attractor.

Because volumes are at the top of the file system tree, they should be planned first. Here are a few things to think about:

▸ The simplest strategy is one-to-one. That is, one volume for each internal disk. In this scenario, stick with the default SYS: volume and let it occupy your entire internal disk. Then rely on directories and subdirectories for file organization and security.

▸ If the one-to-one strategy isn't for you, be sure to reserve the SYS: volume for files needed by the IntranetWare operating system. Additional volumes can be created for applications, data files, and print queues.

. . . . .

▸ Create a separate volume for each client operating system that allows long filenames. For instance, if you have OS/2, Windows 95, or Macintosh users in addition to DOS users, you might want to create a separate volume for the OS/2, Windows 95, or Macintosh files. This is particularly important because it enhances administration, backup procedures, and disk space usage. Also, name space adds performance overhead to ALL files on the host volume. So, minimize the files on that volume.

▸ If fault tolerance is more important than performance, create one volume per disk. If performance is more important than fault tolerance, span one NetWare volume over multiple hard disks (with one segment of the volume on each hard disk). If fault tolerance and performance are equally important, you can still spread volumes across multiple hard disks, but you should make sure that they are duplexed or RAIDed.

SMART LINK

For a little more input on IntranetWare volume structures, consult the on-line IntranetWare documentation at http://www.novell.com/manuals.

Once the volumes are in place, it's time to shift your focus to directories. This is when it gets interesting. Fortunately, IntranetWare gives you a big head start with system-created directories and files. Let's check them out.

SYSTEM-CREATED DIRECTORIES

With the IntranetWare server installation, you get a default user (Admin) and two directory trees:

▸ The default NDS tree (server context)

▸ The default file system on SYS:

In our discussion of the IntranetWare file system, we will explore the default tree and go a few steps beyond:

▸ System-created directories

▸ DOS directories

▸ Application directories

▸ Configuration directories

▸ Home directories

▸ Shared data directories

System-created directories contain IntranetWare operating system files, NLMs, and utilities. They are divided into two main categories: Admin directories and User directories. This is a security issue. The Admin directories (SYSTEM, for example) are reserved for administrators only — they require Supervisor access rights. User directories, on the other hand, contain public utilities and are open to all users throughout the WAN (PUBLIC, for example). Next, with the system-created directories as a platform, you will spring forward into the world of file-system creativity.

DOS directories are optional. They are required only if you want users to access DOS from the server instead of from their local drives. Application directories contain third-party application programs such as word processing, spreadsheet, or database programs. Configuration directories hold user- or group-specific configuration files. These files help you manage network applications. Home directories hold user-specific files and create a cozy, productive network environment. Finally, shared data directories contain global files for groups of users throughout the WAN.

Let's start our discussion with a detailed look at the nine system-created directories. Refer to Figure 10.4. Here they are:

LOGIN	ETC
SYSTEM	QUEUES
PUBLIC	DELETED.SAV
MAIL	DOC
NLS	

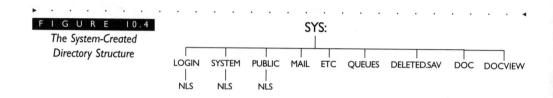

The System-Created Directory Structure

LOGIN

LOGIN is your doormat to the WAN. From there you can knock on NetWare's door and provide the secret password for entrance. This is all accomplished with the help of LOGIN.EXE. In addition to logging in, there are other administrative tasks you (and users) can perform from the LOGIN directory — such as changing context (CX), viewing the NDS tree structure (NLIST), and mapping drives (MAP).

LOGIN is the only directory available to users prior to login. Be careful which programs you place there, because they are available to users without any security. Finally, there's an additional subdirectory under LOGIN, called OS2, which contains login programs for OS/2 clients.

Once you log in and pass through the magic NDS gates, the rest of the world opens up to you — namely the other eight system-created directories.

WHAT'S NEW

To access the LOGIN directory and log in, users must first change their network drive to D: or F:. Then they must access LOGIN.EXE and provide a valid username. This entire process is automated in the GUI environment with Client 32.

SYSTEM

SYSTEM is Admin's workroom. This directory contains special administrative tools and utilities, including OS files, NLMs, and dangerous NDS programs. For this reason, SYSTEM should be kept out of the reach of users and small children. Fortunately, it contains a "child-proof cap" in the form of Supervisor access rights. Only Admin can gain access by default.

PUBLIC

PUBLIC, on the other hand, is the user's playground. This directory contains general user commands and utilities, such as NWADMIN, NETADMIN, NWUSER, and MAP. By default, all users in the server's home container have access to PUBLIC — but only after they've logged in. In addition, a subdirectory under PUBLIC, called OS2, contains NetWare programs and utilities for OS/2 users.

MAIL

The MAIL directory may or may not contain subdirectories and files. It is left over from the old days when NetWare shipped with an e-mail application. Well, guess what, it does again (see Chapter 12), but it doesn't use the MAIL directory. Go figure. Instead, the MAIL subdirectory is a repository for old user-specific system configuration files, like bindery login scripts (LOGIN.) and print job configurations (PRINTCON.DAT). Of course, these files are now properties of each User object. Ah, NDS.

Oh yeah. MAIL is sometimes used by third-party e-mail applications, but not very often. It is also used by IntranetWare for bindery emulation.

NLS

NLS is IntranetWare's translator. It stands for NetWare Language Support (or something like that). Each of the main system-created directories has its own NLS subdirectory. These NLS directories contain message and help files for multilingual IntranetWare utilities. If multiple languages have been installed, each language has its own subdirectory under NLS.

Later in Chapter 13, we'll learn how multiple languages are supported in IntranetWare. But here's a quick preview. Each utility and message file has a general language pointer. The workstation determines which language the user wants and tells the pointer where to go for language-specific modules (that is, which NLS directory). Then, NLS displays the utility or message in the appropriate language. It is very cool.

SMART LINK

If you're interested in more information on IntranetWare's support for multiple languages, consult the "Product and Programs Quick Reference Guide" at http://www.novell.com/manuals.

ETC

ETC is aptly named. It contains a bunch of other stuff, like sample TCP/IP configuration files and, you know, other stuff.

QUEUES

QUEUES is one of the great advancements in IntranetWare. Earlier versions stored print queues on the SYS: volume only. This caused serious problems if the print job was large and SYS: ran out of space — namely, the server crashed. Now, CNEs can offload print queue storage to any volume they want. When you do, IntranetWare automatically creates a QUEUES directory off the root of the host volume.

DELETED.SAV

DELETED.SAV is file heaven. This is where files go when they die. You see, files can be brought back to life in IntranetWare — it's called *salvaging*. Normally, the files must be salvaged from their parent directory. If, in some horrible plane crash, their parent directory was also deleted, the children files can be salvaged from DELETED.SAV. This directory is only created when it's needed. Keep in mind, you can only salvage files as long as the user hasn't *purged* them.

DOC

Welcome to IntranetWare's electronic documentation — DynaText. The interesting thing about DynaText is that it becomes available *after* you need it. For example, the IntranetWare installation instructions are available once you install DynaText — *after* the server's been installed! Life has a funny way of surprising you. Remember, Murphy's law number 142: "I'm an optimist."

Anyway, IntranetWare DynaText is installed in the DOC directory using INSTALL.NLM. Refer to Chapter 6 for specific details.

DOCVIEW

The DOCVIEW directory contains the viewer files required by the DynaText utility. The DOC and DOCVIEW directories can be installed on the volume of your choice.

ZEN

"Pioneers took years to cross the country. Now people will move thousands of miles just for the summer. I don't think any pioneers did that, 'Yeah, it took us a decade to get there, and we stayed for the summer. It was nice, they had a pool, the kids loved it. And then, we left about ten years ago and we just got back. We had a great summer, it took us twenty years, and now our lives are over!'"

Jerry Seinfeld

This completes our brief pilgrimage through the IntranetWare system-created directory structure. Be sure that you do not accidentally delete, move, or rename any of these system-created directories — especially LOGIN, SYSTEM, PUBLIC, MAIL, and NLS. These directories are critical to the server and bad things will happen if they're removed.

O.K. We're cruising now. Next, let's expand our horizons beyond the default directory structure and explore the land of additional directories. You'll be amazed at what you can find there.

EXPANDING BEYOND THE DEFAULT DIRECTORY STRUCTURE

IntranetWare provides you with a big head start by building the default directory tree (see Figure 10.4). The next step is to add some productive DOS, user, application, and data directories. Think of it as a transition from Figure 10.4 to Figure 10.5. It boils down to five suggested directory components:

- ▸ DOS directories

- ▸ Application directories

- ▸ Configuration directories

- ▸ Home directories

- ▸ Shared data directories

Let's take a closer look.

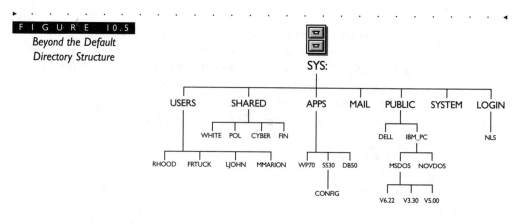

FIGURE 10.5

*Beyond the Default
Directory Structure*

DOS Directories

DOS directories are vital because they provide support for various workstation operating systems (namely DOS and OS/2). They are, however, optional. You can choose to have users execute DOS commands and utilities from their local workstation drives or from a shared DOS directory on the server — it's up to you.

If you choose to have users run DOS from the server, you'll need to make a separate subdirectory for each version of DOS. It is preferable, of course, to have all users run the same version of DOS, but dream on — it'll never happen. Here's the trick: You'll need to somehow interrogate each workstation and point the user to the correct version of DOS. Fortunately, IntranetWare supports login script identifier variables for this very purpose. We'll explore them in more depth in Chapter 12 ("IntranetWare Configuration").

For now, you'll need to create a DOS directory structure that supports all the different types of machines and DOS versions on your WAN. As you can see in Figure 10.5, the DOS structure starts under SYS:PUBLIC because users already have access there. Next, you'll need to create a subdirectory structure for each of the following three components:

▸ MACHINE — IBM_PC, DELL, or other

▸ OS — MSDOS, NOVDOS, OS2, and so on

▸ OS VERSION — V7.01, V6.22, or whatever version you're using

So why should you bother? Many users simply access DOS utilities from their local drives. Well, if you're using a diskless workstation, you'll need to get DOS somewhere else — such as the server. Also, some users get better performance from the server because of file caching and a slow local disk channel. Finally, a centralized DOS structure allows you to update DOS once (on the server), instead of hundreds of times on each distributed workstation. The bottom line is that it's your choice, central DOS or local DOS — whatever you do, just DOS it!

Application Directories

A subdirectory structure should be created under SYS:APPS for each network application. For security's sake, restrict this structure to application files only — no data. Users can store their data in home directories, group areas, or SYS:SHARED — a global data directory (see the "Shared Data Directories" section).

Configuration File Directories

What about application configuration files, such as templates, interface files, and style sheets? It depends on the type of configuration file it is. Application-specific configuration files, like style sheets, should be placed in a CONFIG directory under the application. User-specific configurations, on the other hand, such as interface files, should be placed in user home directories. Let's take a closer look.

Home Directories

Each user needs a place he or she can call home. Typically, a special subdirectory is created under SYS:USERS for each user, which gives each of them a private, secure retreat for his or her own stuff. User directories serve two functions: security and organization. From a security viewpoint, they provide a secure place for private user files — a place away from coworkers' prying eyes (of course, you can look at their files because you are a CNE!). From an organizational viewpoint, user directories become the parent of a complex user-specific directory structure — a place for personal games and applications.

Each user's home directory name should exactly match their login name — or at least be very close. This simplifies administration and makes them easy to find. Also, be sure to give users sufficient access rights to move around in there (see Chapter 11).

Shared Data Directories

The proper organization of network data strongly impacts user productivity. Let's be honest — the sole purpose of the IntranetWare file system is to organize data efficiently. This is accomplished in three ways:

- ▸ Personal data — should be stored in user home directories

- ▸ Group-specific data — should be stored in special group data directories under SYS:SHARED

- ▸ Globally shared data — should be stored in the SYS:SHARED directory off the root of SYS:

There you go. That's the IntranetWare file system. So, the only question that remains is, "What should it look like?" You have two choices: shallow or deep. Check it out.

QUIZ

I'm on this numbers kick. Numbers have an unavoidable fascination. Try this one on for size:

What is the five-digit number, no zeros, in which the first number is one-fourth of the second, the second is twice the third, the third is two-thirds of the fourth, and the fifth is half of the fourth, with the sum of all the digits being 23?

(Q10-1)
(See Appendix C for quiz answers.)

DESIGNING YOUR DIRECTORY STRUCTURE

Now that you know what the file system is made of, you need to decide what it's going to look like. You can either create a flat tree with many directories stored off the root of the volume, or you can have a deep directory structure with many levels of subdirectories (see Figure 10.6). Novell recommends that, for ease of administration, you design a directory structure that is no more than five levels deep.

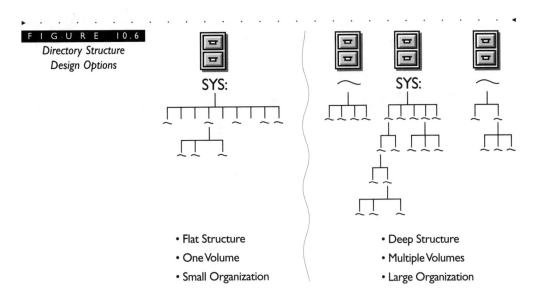

SYS:

SYS:

• Flat Structure
• One Volume
• Small Organization

• Deep Structure
• Multiple Volumes
• Large Organization

A flat directory structure, such as the one in Figure 10.7, could be used for a very small company with few users. In this example, all home directories are stored in the root of the volume — not recommended, but easy to use. On the up side, this design limits file storage to a single volume, and the path names are very short. Also, the application programs are separated from data files.

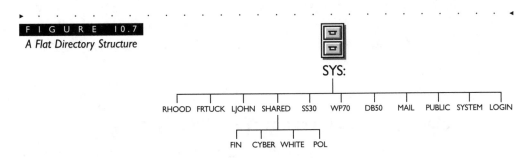

SYS:

RHOOD FRTUCK LJOHN SHARED SS30 WP70 DB50 MAIL PUBLIC SYSTEM LOGIN

FIN CYBER WHITE POL

On the down side, the SYS: volume shares its space with everyone else. Sometimes it just needs to be alone. Also, home directories are located in the root of the volume, and there is no shared data area.

A deeper directory structure is shown in Figure 10.8. In this design, system-created directories and applications share SYS:, while all other components have their own volumes. On the up side, the SYS: volume is more stable, because files are not added or deleted very often. Also, applications are more secure because they hang out with SYS:. Finally, you can consider using a different file system administrator for each volume.

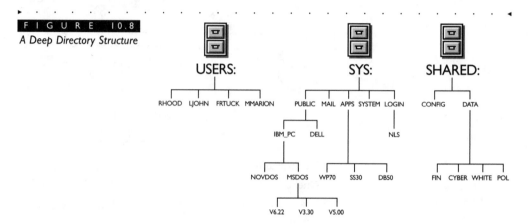

F I G U R E   10.8
A Deep Directory Structure

On the down side, this design places users on different volumes, which makes security much more difficult to administer. Also, you may run out of room on a given volume, even though you have sufficient disk space on the server.

So, there you are. The "other" IntranetWare directory structure. It's not so bad. It's a lot easier than those crazy leaf objects and distinguished names. As you can see, the IntranetWare file system provides a simple, straightforward structure for sharing valuable WAN files. But what about management? How do you keep it running on a daily basis? I'm so glad you asked. That's the next topic.

Managing the IntranetWare File System

Once you've designed your file system, you'll need to develop a plan to maintain it — every day! You'll need to ask yourself the following questions:

- How much disk space is left on each volume?

- How much disk space is still available to users with volume space restrictions?

▶ How much room is being taken up by files that have been deleted but not yet purged?

▶ Which files have not been accessed in a long time?

▶ Are there any directories or files with no owner?

For the most part, the IntranetWare file system looks like DOS. For this reason, you can perform a lot of DOS file management tasks in IntranetWare as well. In addition, DOS tools such as DIR, COPY, and the MS Windows File Manager work just fine in the NetWare environment.

This is not nearly enough, however. Networking, in general, puts a great strain on file management. Fortunately, IntranetWare includes a number of file management utilities that are specifically designed to work in a network environment, such as:

▶ *FILER* — A text-based utility that is used to manage directories and files, display volume information, and salvage and purge deleted files.

▶ *FLAG* — Allows you to view or modify directory and file attributes. It can also be used to modify the owner of a directory or file and to view or modify the search mode of executable files.

▶ *NCOPY* — Allows you to copy network files from one location to another.

▶ *NDIR* — Lets you view the files once they've been copied. In addition, this utility allows you to view a plethora of information about volumes and directories — but you can't modify anything with it.

▶ *NLIST* — A new IntranetWare NDS utility that displays information about NDS objects and/or properties. It can be used to display information about volumes, as long as they're represented as Volume objects in NDS.

▶ *NWADMIN* (runs under MS Windows) and *NETADMIN* (runs under DOS) — NDS-based tools that can be used to perform a variety of file management tasks such as creating, deleting, renaming, copying, or moving directories and/or files. You can also use them to assign trustee rights, determine effective rights, and modify Inherited Rights Filters. In addition, they display Volume object information and, finally, allow you to purge and salvage deleted files. Wow!

> **TIP**
>
> **Many of thse file system utilities are DOS-based command line utilities (such as FLAG, NDIR, and NLIST). If you ever need help at the command line, type the utility name followed by "/?".**

It's a good thing you have so many friends to help you out. In this section, we will explore these and other IntranetWare file management tools. But we're going to approach them in a slightly unique way. Instead of talking about each utility alone, we are going to explore how they combine to help you manage three key file-system components:

- ▶ Volumes

- ▶ Directories

- ▶ Files

In each area, we will explore all the file management tools that apply to that component. Also, we'll provide some examples of how they can be used to simplify your life. This makes sense, because we're managing volumes, directories, and files — not utilities. So, without further adieu, let's start out with IntranetWare volumes.

> **ZEN**
>
> *"My parents live in Florida now. They moved there last year. They didn't want to move to Florida, but they're in their seventies now and that's the law!"*
>
> **Jerry Seinfeld**

MANAGING INTRANETWARE VOLUMES

Volumes are at the top of the file-system food chain. They also represent a bridge between physical files on server disks and logical leaf objects in the NDS tree. For your managing pleasure, IntranetWare includes five key tools for managing volumes:

- ▶ FILER

- ▶ NWADMIN

- ▶ NETADMIN

- ▶ NLIST

- ▶ NDIR

Let's check them out.

SMART LINK

If you want to get some real "hands-on" practice managing IntranetWare volumes, surf on over to CyberState University and World Wire: http://www.cyberstateu.com.

FILER

The DOS-based FILER menu utility can be used to display a variety of volume information, including:

- ▶ Volume statistics relating to space usage, directory entries, and compression

- ▶ Volume features such as volume type, block size, name space, and installed features (such as compression, migration, suballocation, or auditing)

- ▶ Date and time information, including creation date/time, owner, last modified date/time, last archived date/time, and archiver

To view information relating to the current volume, choose the "View volume information" option from the "Available options" menu, as shown in Figure 10.9. A Volume menu will appear that gives you the option of viewing volume statistics, features, or dates and times.

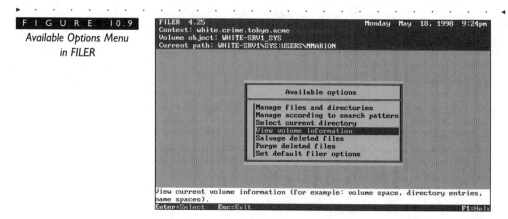

F I G U R E   10.9
Available Options Menu in FILER

If you select the "Volume statistics" option, a screen will appear that is similar to the one in Figure 10.10. This screen lists statistics relating to volume space usage, maximum and available directory entries, and file-compression space usage.

F I G U R E   10.10
Volume Statistics in FILER

```
FILER 4.25                                    Monday  May  18, 1998  9:29pm
Context: white.crime.tokyo.acme
Volume object: WHITE-SRV1_SYS
Current path: WHITE-SRV1\SYS:USERS\MMARION


                        ┌─────────────────────────────────────┐
                        │           Volume statistics           │
                        ├─────────────────────────────────────┤
                        │ Total space in KB(1024 bytes):   1,024,000  100.00% │
                        │ Active space used:                 297,728   29.08% │
                        │ Deleted space not yet purgeable:         0    0.00% │
                        │ Space remaining on volume:         726,272   70.92% │
                        │                                                     │
                        │ Maximum directory entries:          11,264          │
                        │ Directory entries available:         2,835   25.17% │
                        │                                                     │
                        │ Space used if not compressed:      132,608          │
                        │ Total space compressed:             55,808          │
                        │ Space saved by compressing data:    76,800   57.92% │
                        │ Uncompressed space used:           260,096          │
                        └─────────────────────────────────────┘


Esc=Escape                                                          F1=Help
```

If you select the "Volume features" option, a screen will appear that is similar to the one in Figure 10.11. This screen includes information about the volume type (that is, non-removable), the block size, the name space(s) installed, and installed features (such as compression, migration, suballocation, or auditing).

· ◄

FIGURE 10.11
Volume Features in FILER

```
FILER  4.25                          Wednesday  May  20, 1998  7:58pm
Context: white.crime.tokyo.acme
Volume object: WHITE-SRV1_SYS
Current path: WHITE-SRV1\SYS:USERS\MMARION


                         ┌──────────────────────────┐
                         │      Volume features     │
                         │                          │
                         │ Volume type:   Non-removable│
                         │ Block size:    65,536 bytes │
                         │                          │
                         │ Name spaces:   DOS       │
                         │                          │
                         │ Installed features: Compression│
                         │                     Suballocation│
                         └──────────────────────────┘




Esc=Escape                                              F1=Help
```

THE BRAIN

Some of the most exciting IntranetWare volume features are file compression, data migration, and block suballocation. Learn them, use them, live them. Refer to Chapter 1 for an introduction to these features and Chapter 15 for details on how to optimize volumes using them, or surf the Web at http://www.novell.com/manuals.

Finally, if you choose the "Dates and times" option, a Volume dates and times window will be displayed. This window displays information such as the volume creation date/time, owner, the last modified date/time, the last archived date/time, and the archiver.

FILER is the most useful non-NDS file management tool. It focuses on volumes, directories, and files as physical storage units within the IntranetWare server — no NDS nonsense to confuse you. This is appealing to many CNEs. If you want fancy NDS footwork, refer to NWADMIN.

Hey, good idea!

NWADMIN

The NetWare Administrator (NWADMIN) tool treats volumes as NDS objects. It displays roughly the same information as FILER, but from a slightly different point of view:

- ▸ Identification

- ▸ Dates and Times

- ▸ User Space Limits

- ▸ Trustee Security

- ▸ Attributes

To display volume information using NWADMIN, walk the tree until you find your desired volume — in our case it's .CN=WHITE-SRV1_SYS.OU=WHITE. OU=CRIME.OU=TOKYO.O=ACME. When you select a volume, the Identification page button activates by default. Because of this, a screen similar to the one in Figure 10.12 magically appears. It's marginally interesting, containing information on volume name, host server, NetWare version, host volume, and location.

FIGURE 10.12

Identification Page for
Volumes in NWADMIN

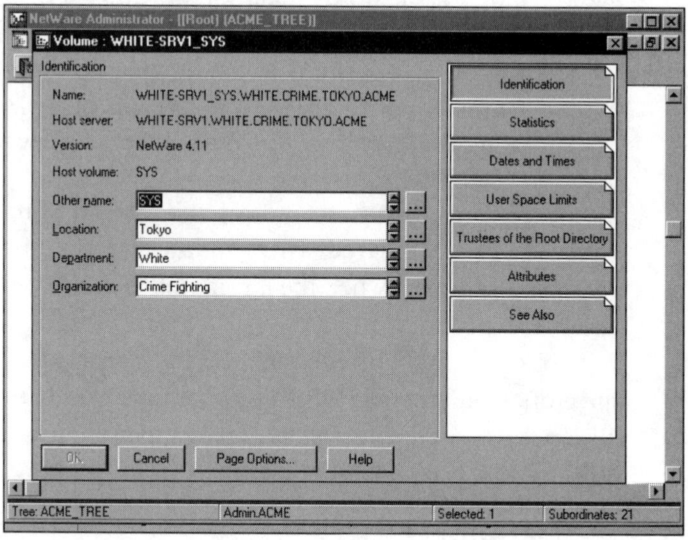

The Statistics page is the really interesting NWADMIN volume page (see Figure 10.13). It displays statistical information relating to the volume type (non-removable), deleted files, compressed files, block size, name spaces, and installed features (such as suballocation, data compression, and data migration). Colorful pie charts are also displayed, showing the percentage of disk space and directory entries used. Very cool.

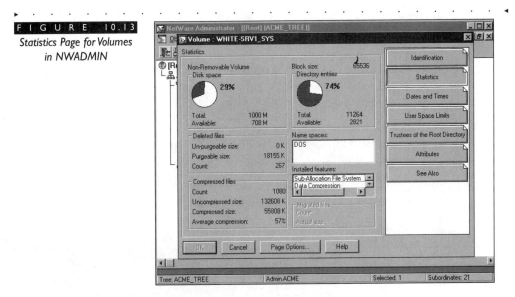

In addition to Identification and Statistics, NWADMIN provides numerous other volume-related page buttons:

- *Dates and Times* — Displays values for the volume creation date and time, owner, last modified date, last archived date, and "user last archived by." The latter option offers valuable information for managing data backup (see Chapter 13).

- *User Space Limits* — Displays information regarding user space limits imposed on particular users (if any). This is an effective way of controlling "disk hogs."

- *Trustees of the Root Directory* — Displays security information concerning the trustees of the root directory, their effective rights, and the directory's Inherited Rights Filter. You should be careful about who gets access rights to the root directory of *any* volume — especially SYS:.

- *Attributes* — Displays directory attributes for the root directory of the given volume. This is another security option (see Chapter 11).

► *See Also* — Displays who and what is related to the Volume object. This is basically a manual information record for tracking special volume details.

NETADMIN

NETADMIN is the DOS-based version of NWADMIN for those of you who break out into hives every time you touch a mouse. It provides the same type of information as NWADMIN, but in a slightly (or greatly) less user-friendly way. This means it's very hard to use.

To view volume information with NETADMIN, you have to find the volume first. This involves a labyrinth of tree-walking through three menu choices: Manage objects, Object class, and View or edit properties of this object. Once you arrive at your destination, it looks something like Figure 10.14.

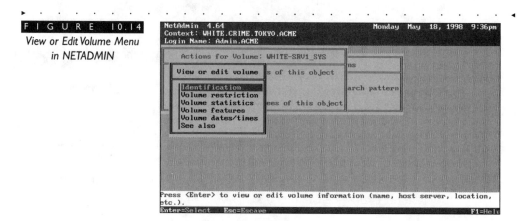

FIGURE 10.14

View or Edit Volume Menu in NETADMIN

If you select the Identification option from this menu, a screen appears showing the same type of NDS information as the NWADMIN Identification page, including volume name, host server, NetWare version, host volume, and location. Once again, the really interesting data is in the "Volume statistics" screen (see Figure 10.15). This screen lists numerous statistics related to volume space, maximum and available directory entries, and file-compression space. As a matter of fact, it looks a little familiar — like the Statistics screen in FILER. It's exactly the same data, just using a different DOS-based menu tool. Hmmm.

F I G U R E   10.15

Volume Statistics in
NETADMIN

```
NetAdmin  4.64                              Monday  May  18, 1998  9:36pm
Context: WHITE.CRIME.TOKYO.ACME
Login Name: Admin.ACME
┌──────────────────────────────────────────────────────────────────────┐
│                           Volume statistics                            │
│  Total volume space in KB (1024 bytes):        1,024,000    100.00%    │
│  Active space used:                              276,096     26.96%    │
│  Deleted space not yet purgeable:                      0      0.00%    │
│  Space remaining on volume:                      747,904     73.04%    │
│                                                                        │
│  Maximum directory entries:                       10,240               │
│  Available directory entries:                      2,181     21.30%    │
│                                                                        │
│  Space used if not compressed:                   132,600               │
│  Total space compressed:                          55,800               │
│  Space saved by compressing data:                 76,800     57.92%    │
│  Uncompressed space used:                        220,800               │
│                                                                        │
└──────────────────────────────────────────────────────────────────────┘
This is information pertaining to the physical volume.  These fields can't be
changed.  Press <Esc> when done.
Esc=Escape                                                       F1=Help
```

In addition to Identification and Statistics, NETADMIN provides a combination of options from both NWADMIN and FILER, including:

▶ Volume restrictions

▶ Volume features

▶ Volume dates/times

▶ See also

NLIST

As we learned earlier, NLIST is a special IntranetWare NDS command line utility. It displays all related property information for any NDS object — including volumes. For our purposes, NLIST gives us access to:

▶ Object class

▶ Current context

▶ Volume name

▶ Host server name

▶ Physical volume name

▸ The number of Volume objects in the NDS tree

▸ Property values for Volume objects

NLIST can only be used to display information about NDS objects — it cannot be used to modify NDS information. Some of the most common commands used to display NDS volume information are included in Table 10.2. Check it out.

T A B L E 10.2	COMMAND	RESULT
Partial List of NLIST Options	NLIST VOLUME	Lists information for all volumes in the current context
	NLIST VOLUME /D	Lists detailed information about a specific volume in the current context
	NLIST VOLUME /N	Lists the names of the volumes in your current context

Output from the "NLIST VOLUME /D" command is shown in Figure 10.16. Notice the detailed volume-based information you can view from the command line.

F I G U R E 10.16
Results of the NLIST VOLUME /D Command

```
Object Class: Volume
Current context: white.crime.tokyo.acme
Volume: WHITE-SRV1_SYS
        Name: WHITE-SRV1_SYS
        Object Trustees (ACL):
                Subject: [Root]
                Property: Host Resource Name
                Property Rights: [ R    ]
        Object Trustees (ACL):
                Subject: [Root]
                Property: Host Server
                Property Rights: [ R    ]
        Host Resource Name: SYS
        Host Server: WHITE-SRV1
        Object Class: Volume
        Object Class: Resource
        Object Class: Top
        Revision: 1
---------------------------------------------------------------------------
Volume: WHITE-SRV1_VOL1
        Name: WHITE-SRV1_VOL1
        Object Trustees (ACL):
                Subject: [Root]
>>> Enter = More    C = Continuous    Esc = Cancel
```

Now let's explore the final volume management tool — NDIR. Just imagine "the forest moon of NDIR."

NDIR

NDIR, as its name implies, is mostly a directory and file utility. It does, however, offer a few statistics for IntranetWare volumes, namely:

▶ Volume space statistics

▶ Directory entry statistics

▶ Compression space statistics

Figure 10.17 shows an example of the type of information that can be displayed by typing:

```
NDIR /VOL
```

You'll notice that it lists a variety of volume information, including space used, space remaining, deleted space not yet purged, space available for use by you, maximum and available directory entries, as well as compression statistics, such as space used by compressed files, space saved by compressed files, and uncompressed space used. It's amazing that all this information can be viewed from such a small utility!

```
U:\USERS\MMARION>NDIR /VOL

Statistics for fixed volume WHITE-SRV1/SYS:
Space statistics are in KB (1024 bytes).

Total volume space:                          1,024,000   100.00%
Space used by 8,059 entries:                   276,096    26.96%
Deleted space not yet purgeable:                     0     0.00%
                                             ------------
Space remaining on volume:                     747,904    73.04%
Space available to Admin.ACME:                 747,904    73.04%

Maximum directory entries:                      10,240
Available directory entries:                     2,181    21.30%

Space used if files were not compressed:       132,608
Space used by compressed files:                 55,808
                                             ------------
Space saved by compressing files:               76,800    57.92%

Uncompressed space used:                       220,800

U:\USERS\MMARION>
```

SMART LINK

For more information on these great IntranetWare volume management tools, check out the "IntranetWare Utilities Reference" at http://www.novell.com/manuals.

There you go. That's everything you wanted to know about volume management but were afraid to ask! Now that you've gotten cozy with some of IntranetWare's finest file system tools, let's see what they can do with directories and files. Who knows, you might even meet some new tools along the way.

ZEN

"If professional wrestling didn't exist, could you come up with this idea? Could you envision the popularity of huge men in tiny bathing suits pretending to fight?"

Jerry Seinfeld

MANAGING INTRANETWARE DIRECTORIES

Volumes are important, but directories win the prize. These are the true organizational containers of the IntranetWare file system. As we learned earlier, a logical directory design can save hours of security and file management. In this section, we will explore many of the same utilities as we just discussed, but from a totally different point of view:

- FILER

- NWADMIN

- NDIR

- NCOPY

- RENDIR

So, let's get started.

SMART LINK

If you want to get some real "hands-on" practice managing IntranetWare directories, surf on over to CyberState University and World Wire: http://www.cyberstateu.com.

FILER

FILER is IntranetWare's most comprehensive directory and file management tool. Earlier we learned about its volume savvy, but you ain't seen nothing yet. In its natural element, FILER can

- ▸ Create, delete, and rename directories

- ▸ Copy and move entire subdirectory structures

- ▸ View or change directory information such as owner, directory creation date/time, directory attributes, trustees, Inherited Rights Filter, and space limitations

- ▸ View your effective rights for directories

- ▸ Set up search and view filters (include and exclude options)

The first step is to select the default directory. If you look at the top of the screen, you'll notice that it lists the current path. To choose a different directory, choose the "Select current directory" option from the "Available options" menu, as shown in Figure 10.18. You can either modify the path manually or walk the tree by pressing Insert. If you walk the tree, don't forget to press Esc when you're finished selecting directories. When the correct directory is selected, press Enter to return to the "Available options" menu.

The next step is to determine if you want to use any search or view filters to limit the directories that are displayed. If so, select the "Manage according to search pattern" option from the "Available options" menu. As you can see in Figure 10.19, a screen appears with the directory include and exclude patterns. You can also specify Hidden and/or System directories. After you've made your selections, press F10 to return to the "Available options" menu.

F I G U R E   10.18

Available Options Menu
in FILER

```
FILER  4.25                                Monday   May   18, 1998   9:44pm
Context: white.crime.tokyo.acme
Volume object: WHITE-SRV1_SYS
Current path: WHITE-SRV1\SYS:USERS\MMARION

                        ┌─────────────────────────────────────┐
                        │          Available options          │
                        ├─────────────────────────────────────┤
                        │ Manage files and directories        │
                        │ Manage according to search pattern   │
                        │ Select current directory            │
                        │ View volume information             │
                        │ Salvage deleted files               │
                        │ Purge deleted files                 │
                        │ Set default filer options           │
                        └─────────────────────────────────────┘


Select a volume object to view that volume's information or to change your
position in the tree structure.
Enter=Select    Esc=Exit                                           F1=Help
```

F I G U R E   10.19

Set the Search Pattern and
Filter Menu in FILER

```
FILER  4.25                                Monday   May   18, 1998   9:45pm
Context: white.crime.tokyo.acme
Volume object: WHITE-SRV1_SYS
Current path: WHITE-SRV1\SYS:USERS\MMARION

        ┌──────────────────────────────────────────────────────┐
        │         Set the search pattern and filter            │
        ├──────────────────────────────────────────────────────┤
        │  Pattern: *.*                                        │
        │                                                      │
        │  Exclude directory patterns: ↓  <empty>              │
        │  Include directory patterns: ↓  *                    │
        │                                                      │
        │  Exclude file patterns: ↓  <empty>                   │
        │  Include file patterns: ↓  *                         │
        │                                                      │
        │  File search attributes: ↓  <empty>                  │
        │  Directory search attributes: ↓  <empty>             │
        └──────────────────────────────────────────────────────┘

Type a pattern (for example: *.EXE) to search by, or press <Enter> to edit the
pattern.
Enter=Select    Esc=Escape    F10=Continue                         F1=Help
```

Now you're ready to go exploring — inside the selected directory. Select the "Manage files and directories" choice from the "Available options" menu. You'll notice that the subdirectories and files in the current directory appear as well as a double-dot (..), representing the parent directory, and a dot (.), representing the current directory.

You can do a number of different things with this screen. For instance,

▶ If you want to make another directory the current directory, you can walk the tree again.

▶ If you want to create a new subdirectory, press Insert and type in the name.

▶ If you want to delete a subdirectory, press Del. If you want to delete multiple directories at once, mark them all using F5 before pressing Del.

▶ If you want to rename a subdirectory, highlight it and press F3, then enter the new name.

To display information about this directory, highlight the period (.) and press F10. The "Subdirectory options" menu will be displayed. Press Enter to select the "View/Set directory information" option. A directory information screen will pop up, similar to the one in Figure 10.20. This screen lists information about the directory, such as the owner, the creation date/time, the directory attributes, the inherited rights filter, the trustees of the directory, the directory space limitations, and your effective rights for this directory.

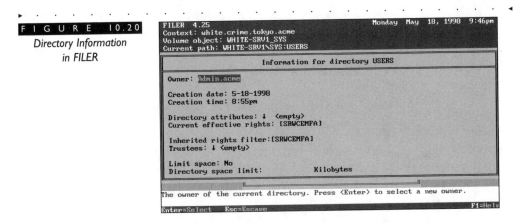

FIGURE 10.20

Directory Information in FILER

If you have the appropriate rights, you can change any parameter listed, except for effective rights, which are calculated by IntranetWare (as you'll see in painstaking detail in Chapter 11). Go ahead and press Esc twice to return to the "Directory contents" screen.

If you highlight a subdirectory and press F10, a "Subdirectory options" screen will be displayed, as shown in Figure 10.21. Two of the most interesting options allow you to move or copy an entire branch of the tree at one time. Cool.

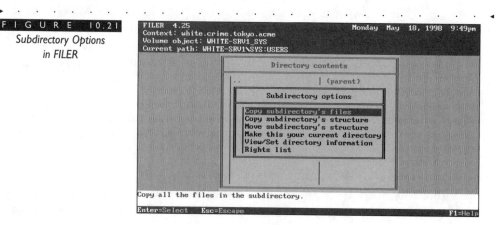

Subdirectory Options
in FILER

That does it for FILER. Now, let's see what NWADMIN can do for IntranetWare directories.

QUIZ

Here's another numbers game:

Find the product of (x-a)(x-b)(x-c) ... (x-z), where x is any number between 22 and 42.

(Q10-2)

NWADMIN

NWADMIN is primarily an NDS-management tool; however, it offers a few directory-related functions, such as:

- ► Create, move, delete, and rename directories

- ► Copy, move, and delete entire subdirectory structures

- ► View or change directory information, such as owner, attributes, trustees, Inherited Rights Filter, or space limitations

- ► Set up search and view filters (include and exclude options)

First of all, walk the tree until the directory with which you want to work is in view. Click on the directory, then click on the Object menu. If you look at the options in the Object menu, you'll notice that you can perform the following file management tasks: create a directory; delete a directory; rename, copy, and/or move a directory. You can also select the Details option to view information about your directory.

If you select Details, the Identification page button is activated by default. As you can see in Figure 10.22, this page includes two important pieces of information: the directory name and the name spaces available on the volume.

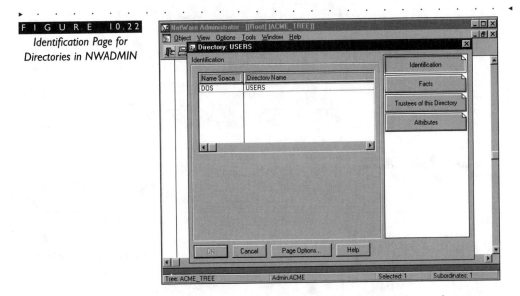

FIGURE 10.22

Identification Page for Directories in NWADMIN

If you select the Facts page button, as shown in Figure 10.23, another screen appears with more detailed directory information, including the owner, the directory creation date/time, the last modified date/time, the last archived date/time, and the archiver. It also lists the volume space available on this directory and the space limitations (if any).

Figure 10.24 illustrates the first of two directory-specific security options in NWADMIN — the Trustees of this Directory page. This page allows you to list trustees and their effective rights as well as the inherited rights filter for this directory.

The second NWADMIN file system security option deals with Attributes (see Figure 10.25). Don't worry, you'll get plenty of chances to work with security in Chapter 11.

FIGURE 10.25

*Attributes Page in
NWADMIN*

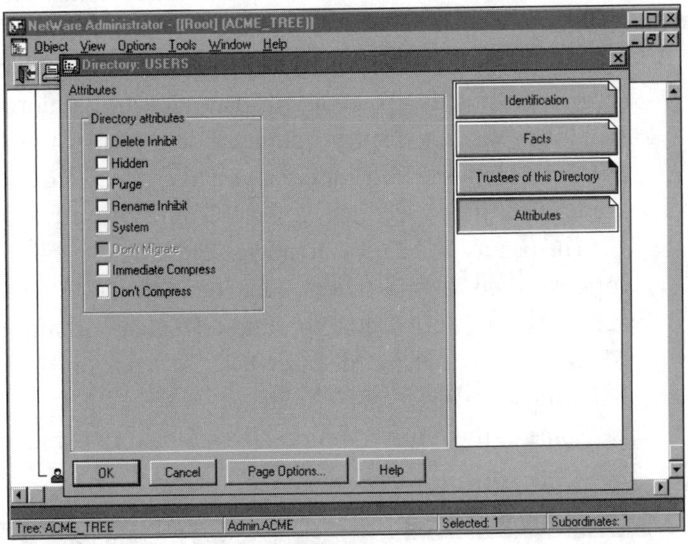

That's enough of NWADMIN for now. As you can see, it augments the FILER functions in a prettier Windows-based user interface. Now, for something completely different. Let's go back to the command line — starting with the forest moon of NDIR.

NDIR

NDIR gives us limited functionality at the volume level — because it's not a volume utility; it's a directory/file utility. NDIR opens a new world of directory information to you, including:

▶ Owner, creation date, attributes, and archive information

▶ Subdirectories/files

▶ Inherited Rights Filter

▶ Effective rights

In addition, directory information can be sorted according to almost any criteria (owner, creation date, attributes, and so on). If you don't specify any formatting options, NDIR lists the following information about each directory: the directory name, Inherited Rights Filter, your effective rights, the creation date/time, and the owner.

By default, NDIR lists all subdirectories and files in the specified directory (unless otherwise noted). You can display directory information selectively by using wildcards, and/or display options. For example, use /C to scroll continuously or /SUB to include subdirectories and their files. You can also list directories that contain (or do not contain) a specific directory attribute.

The beauty of NDIR is its logic searching capabilities. NDIR also supports date options such as AFT (after), BEF (before), and EQ (equals); size options such as LE (less than), EQ (equal to), and GR (greater than); and sorting options such as /REV SORT (reverse order), /SORT CR (creation date), /SORT OW (owner), and /UN (unsorted).

Some of the more common NDIR directory commands are listed in Table 10.3.

TABLE 10.3

Common NDIR Directory Commands

COMMAND	RESULT
NDIR	Displays subdirectories and files in the current directory
NDIR /DO	Displays directories only
NDIR /DO /SUB	Displays directories and subdirectories only
NDIR /SPA	Displays space limitations for this directory
NDIR /DO /C	Displays directories only — scrolls continuously when displaying information
NDIR /DO CR	Displays directories only — those created AFT 10/01/99 after 10/01/99
NDIR /DO /REV	Displays directories only — sorts by SORT CR directory creation date, with newest listed first

Figure 10.26 shows an example of output from the NDIR /DO command. Use it or lose it.

FIGURE   10.26

The NDIR /DO Command

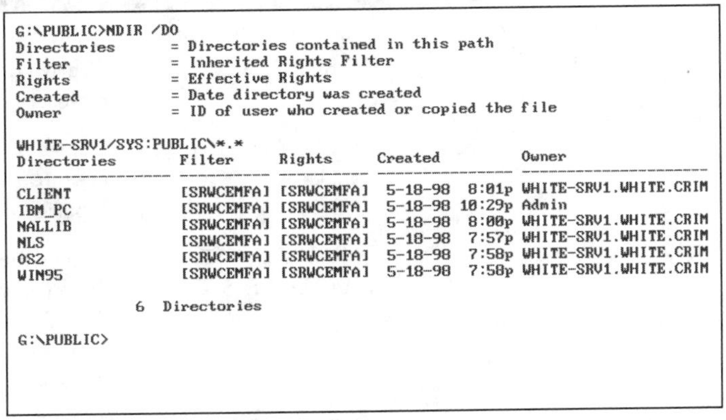

```
G:\PUBLIC>NDIR /DO
Directories      = Directories contained in this path
Filter           = Inherited Rights Filter
Rights           = Effective Rights
Created          = Date directory was created
Owner            = ID of user who created or copied the file

WHITE-SRV1/SYS:PUBLIC\*.*
Directories         Filter        Rights       Created          Owner
----------------    ----------    ----------   --------------   --------------------------
CLIENT              [SRWCEMFA]    [SRWCEMFA]    5-18-98  8:01p   WHITE-SRV1.WHITE.CRIM
IBM_PC              [SRWCEMFA]    [SRWCEMFA]    5-18-98 10:29p   Admin
NALLIB              [SRWCEMFA]    [SRWCEMFA]    5-18-98  8:00p   WHITE-SRV1.WHITE.CRIM
NLS                 [SRWCEMFA]    [SRWCEMFA]    5-18-98  7:57p   WHITE-SRV1.WHITE.CRIM
OS2                 [SRWCEMFA]    [SRWCEMFA]    5-18-98  7:58p   WHITE-SRV1.WHITE.CRIM
WIN95               [SRWCEMFA]    [SRWCEMFA]    5-18-98  7:58p   WHITE-SRV1.WHITE.CRIM

            6  Directories

G:\PUBLIC>
```

NCOPY

NCOPY is the NetWare version of COPY. Can you guess what it does? Very good — it copies stuff. NCOPY is similar in function to the DOS XCOPY command and allows the use of the same wildcards. Benefits of using NCOPY include:

▸ Directory/file attributes and name space information are automatically preserved.

▸ Read-after-write verification feature is ON by default. (You must use the /V switch to use verification if you're copying files on local drives.)

▸ NetWare physical or object volume names can be specified in a path.

TIP

Because NCOPY is a NetWare utility, it accesses the NetWare file allocation table (FAT) and directory entry table (DET) more efficiently than the DOS COPY or XCOPY commands. It is faster than COPY and XCOPY if the files are being copied from one directory to another on the server, because it works within server RAM rather than copying the directories and/or files to and from workstation RAM. It is also a safer method because it uses the IntranetWare read-after-write verification fault tolerance feature by default.

Some of the more common NCOPY commands are listed in Table 10.4.

COMMAND	RESULT
NCOPY G:REPORTS C:REPORTS	Copies the REPORTS directory from the G: drive on the server to the default directory on your workstation C: drive
NCOPY F:DATA C:DATA /S	Copies the DATA directory from the F: drive to the C: drive, including subdirectories
NCOPY G:1995 ..\ARCHIVE /S /E	Copies the 1995 directory on the G: drive (as well as its subdirectories and their files, including empty subdirectories) to an ARCHIVE directory under the current directory's parent directory
NCOPY . TEMP /V	Copies the current directory to the TEMP directory and verifies that the procedure was accurate (only needed if copying files on a local drive)

RENDIR

RENDIR allows you to rename directories — what a surprise. Wildcards can be used, as well as a period (.) to represent the current directory or a colon followed by a forward slash (:/) to represent the default drive and volume. Check out Table 10.5 for some examples of the more common RENDIR commands in IntranetWare.

COMMAND	RESULT
RENDIR REPORT REPORTS	Renames the directory called REPORT under the current directory to REPORTS
RENDIR U:USER USERS	Renames the directory on Drive U: called USER to USERS
RENDIR S: SAMPLES	Renames the directory to which drive S: is mapped as SAMPLES
RENDIR . DATA	Renames the current directory to DATA
RENDIR :/QTR1 95QTR1	Renames the directory called QTR1 on the current drive and volume to 95QTR1
RENDIR /?	Displays on-line help for the RENDIR command

TIP

If you rename a directory, don't forget to modify any configuration files that reference it — like login scripts.

SMART LINK

For more information on these great IntranetWare directory management tools, check out the **NetWare 4.11** *Utilities Reference* at http://www.novell.com/manuals.

That completes our discussion of directory management. Wasn't that fun? There's only one more file system component left — and we've saved the best for last. Hold on to your hats; we're entering the file management zone.

ZEN

Sick-building syndrome — A condition found in humans, caused by a substance that pollutes the environment becoming trapped in a building, especially as a result of poor design or hazardous materials being used in construction. How are you feeling? Need some fresh air?

MANAGING INTRANETWARE FILES

Earlier, I said that directories win the prize — I lied. Files are really the most important components. After all, what's the ultimate goal of the IntranetWare file system? File sharing. What do users ask for when they log into the "Cloud"? Files. Why are we here?

Anyway, file management looks a little like directory management, and it uses most of the same tools. But that's where the similarities end. Directories are for organization; files are for productivity. And what's more important? Here's a list of the tools we'll explore in this section:

▶ FILER

▶ NWADMIN

▶ MS Windows

▸ NDIR

▸ NCOPY

Don't just sit there; get moving. There are only a few utilities left. Ready, set, go.

SMART LINK

If you want to get some real "hands-on" practice managing IntranetWare files, surf on over to CyberState University and World Wire: http://www.cyberstateu.com.

FILER

Let's visit our old friend FILER just one last time. Now we're focusing on real file management, including:

▸ Creating, deleting, renaming, copying, and moving files

▸ Managing files attributes

▸ Setting up search and view filters (include and exclude options)

▸ Salvaging and purging deleted files

As before, the first FILER step is to select the default directory. Refer to the directory management section for more details. Once you're there, you can alter the include and exclude filters for specific files or even check out Hidden and/or System documents. After you've made your selections, you can press F10 to return to the "Available options" menu.

In addition to the search/view filters, FILER presents Copy and Delete options when working with files. First, select the "Set default filer options" choice from the "Available options" menu. A "Filer settings" screen will appear, as shown in Figure 10.27. You can set a number of defaults for copying and deleting files, including confirmations and messaging help. When all of file management settings are correct, press Esc to return to the "Available options" menu.

FIGURE 10.27
FILER Settings Screen

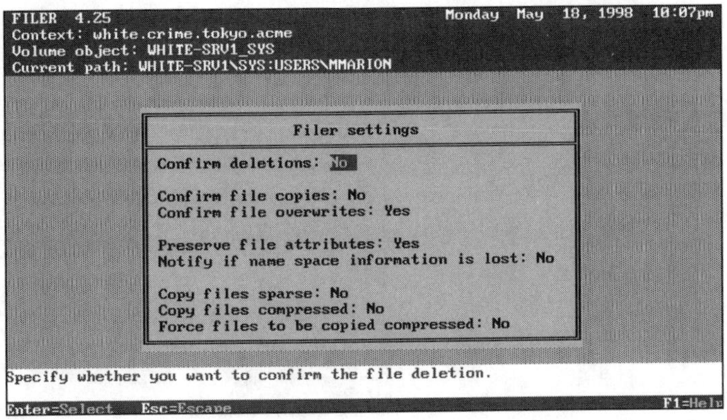

```
FILER  4.25                              Monday  May  18, 1998  10:07pm
Context: white.crime.tokyo.acme
Volume object: WHITE-SRV1_SYS
Current path: WHITE-SRV1\SYS:USERS\MMARION

                          ┌─────────────────────────────┐
                          │       Filer settings        │
                          │                             │
                          │ Confirm deletions: No        │
                          │                             │
                          │ Confirm file copies: No      │
                          │ Confirm file overwrites: Yes │
                          │                             │
                          │ Preserve file attributes: Yes│
                          │ Notify if name space information is lost: No │
                          │                             │
                          │ Copy files sparse: No        │
                          │ Copy files compressed: No    │
                          │ Force files to be copied compressed: No │
                          └─────────────────────────────┘

Specify whether you want to confirm the file deletion.

Enter=Select    Esc=Escape                              F1=Help
```

Now you're ready to display your files. Select the "Manage files and directories" option from the "Available options" menu. You'll notice a plethora of subdirectories and files in the current directory, as well as a double-dot (..) for the parent directory and a dot (.) for the current directory. Now, you're ready to get busy:

▶ Walk the tree to select another directory as the current directory.

▶ Delete a file by highlighting it and pressing Del. If you want to delete multiple files at once, mark them all with the F5 key before pressing Del.

▶ Rename a file by highlighting it and pressing F3.

Next, select a particular file to work with (SAMPLE.SRC) by highlighting it and pressing F10. The "File options" menu appears. This menu gives you the option of copying, viewing, or moving the file; displaying trustees of the file; or viewing/modifying file information. If you select the "View/Set file information" option from the "File options" menu, a file information screen pops up, similar to the one in Figure 10.28. This screen lists information about the file such as the owner; access, archive, creation, and modification dates; file attributes; the Inherited Rights Filter; the trustees of the file; the owning name space; the file size and EA size; as well as your effective rights.

If you have appropriate rights, you can change most of the parameters listed, except for effective rights, owning name space, file size, and EA size. Press Esc three times to return to the "Available options" menu.

F I G U R E   10.28
File Information Screen in
FILER

There are two more choices in the "Available options" menu that relate to files, namely "Salvage deleted files" and "Purge deleted files." Salvage allows you to recover deleted files that have not yet been purged. Purge is the process of permanently removing deleted files from the system.

If you choose "Salvage deleted files," you will be given three options:

▶ Salvage files from an existing directory

▶ Salvage files from DELETED.SAV (because the parent directory has been deleted)

▶ Set salvage options (that is, indicate whether to sort the list by filename, file size, deletion date, or deletor)

If you choose "Purge deleted files" from the "Available options" menu, you can specify the filename pattern to be used when selecting purged files. It will also allow you to choose whether to purge files in the current subdirectory only, or to purge the files in the entire subdirectory tree structure. Be very careful when purging files: You can never recover these files.

This completes our discussion of FILER all together. It's been a wonderous journey, and I hope you have learned to appreciate how helpful it can be for volume, directory, and file management. Now, let's visit NWADMIN one last time.

QUIZ

I like these number brainiacs so much, I thought I'd try another one:

What is the five-digit number in which the first digit is two-thirds of the second, the third is one-third of the second, the fourth is four times the last, and the last is one-third of the first. The digits total 28.

(Q10-3)

NWADMIN

NWADMIN is another important file management tool. It allows us to perform any of the following functions from a friendly Windows-based interface:

▸ Create, delete, and rename files

▸ Copy and move files

▸ View or change file information such as owner, attributes, trustees, and nherited Rights Filter

▸ Set up search and view filters (include and exclude options)

▸ Salvage and purge deleted files

First of all, walk the tree until the desired file is in view. Click on the file, then click on the Object menu. If you look at the options in the Object menu, you'll notice file management options that allow you to delete the file, rename it, copy it or move it. The same options can be accessed from the Details menu as well.

If you select the Facts page button, a screen appears with the file's owner, size, file creation date/time, last modified date/time, last archived date/time, and archiver. If you have the appropriate rights, you can modify all of these parameters except for the size and creation date.

If you select the Trustees of this File page button, you will be allowed to view, add, or modify trustees and display their effective rights, as well as view or change the Inherited Rights Filter for the file. Similarly, if you select the Attributes page button, you can view the attributes that have been set for this file, and you can change them if you have the appropriate access rights (see Chapter 11).

In addition to the usual file management stuff, NWADMIN allows you to salvage or purge deleted files. Interestingly, both of these functions are handled by the same menu option: Choose Salvage from the Tools menu (see Figure 10.29).

FIGURE 10.29

Salvage Menu in NWADMIN

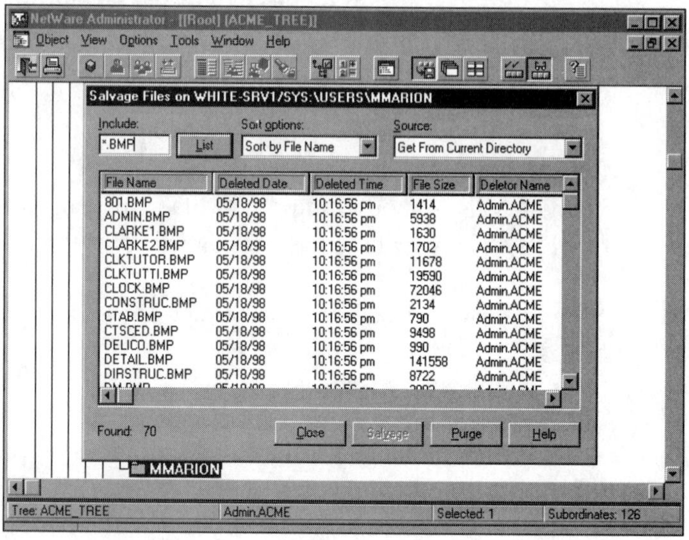

You can select three sets of options from the Salvage menu:

- ▶ Include pattern using wildcards or filenames

- ▶ Sort options (deletion date, deletor, filename, file size, or file type)

- ▶ Source (current directory or deleted directories)

When all of the options are set correctly, click on the List button to list the files indicated. As with other MS Windows or Windows 95 utilities, to select the desired files, you can

- ▶ Select a single file by clicking on it

- ▶ Select sequentially listed files by clicking on the first file, holding down the Shift key, then clicking on the last file in the range

▶ Select nonsequentially listed files by holding down the Ctrl key while selecting files

When you have selected all of the desired files, you can click on either the Salvage or Purge button at the bottom of the screen to salvage or purge the selected file(s). If salvaged, the NetWare files will be restored with their original trustee rights and extended attributes intact. Finally, when you're finished, click on the OK button to return to the NWADMIN browse screen.

MS Windows

Both the 16-bit and 32-bit versions of MS Windows provide built-in file management functions. Client 16 and Client 32 allow you to use their native Windows for managing NetWare volumes, directories, and files. This gives you the ability to manage the network file system just like you would your local drives.

MS Windows supports NetWare file management from three different platforms:

▶ Windows 95 Network Neighborhood

▶ Windows 3.1 File Manager

▶ NetWare User Tools for Windows

Client 32 allows you to manage the NetWare file system from within the Windows 95 Network Neighborhood. As you can see in Figure 10.30, it provides much of the same functions as NWADMIN. Windows 95 supports the following file management tasks:

▶ Name

▶ Owner

▶ Creation date

▶ Available space

▶ Directory entries

- ▸ File attributes

- ▸ Archive dates

- ▸ Size

- ▸ Effective rights

- ▸ Trustees

NetWare File Management in Windows 95 Network Neighborhood

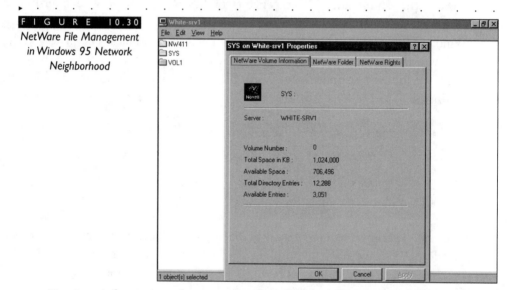

To view information about a specific NetWare file object in Windows 95, simply highlight a volume, directory, or file, and click the right mouse button. Then choose "Properties" from the abbreviated menu. You should get a screen similar to the one in Figure 10.30.

Windows 3.1 also allows limited access to directory and file information through File Manager (see Figure 10.31). This screen provides the following information:

- ▸ Name

- ▸ Owner

- Size
- Creation date
- Access date
- Last update
- Last Archive
- Attributes

FIGURE 10.31
NetWare File Management in Windows 3.1 File Manager

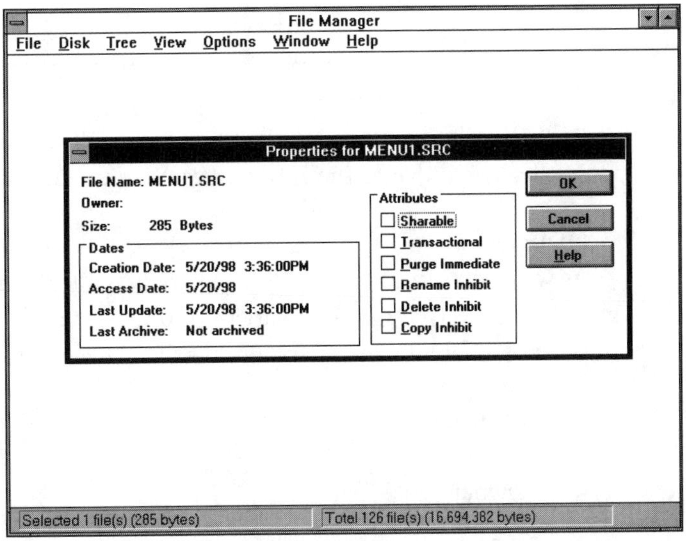

To access this property page, select a file and choose Properties from the File menu. Then click the NetWare button to view these NetWare-specific properties.

You can also use the NetWare User Tools for Windows graphical utility to view effective rights for volumes and directories. This utility can be launched from within the Windows 3.1 File Manager by selecting Network Connection from the Disk menu. As you can see in Figure 10.32, this property screen provides valuable information about your NDS tree name, server, path, username, and effective rights in a given directory.

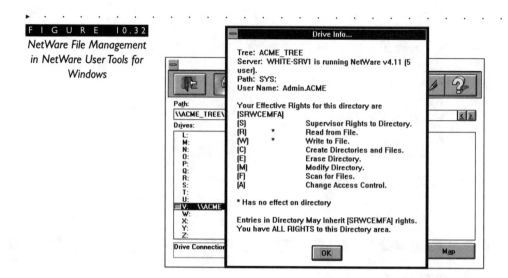

F I G U R E   I 0 . 3 2
NetWare File Management
in NetWare User Tools for
Windows

Well, that does it for Windows. You can bid the GUI environment a fond farewell as we move to the IntranetWare command line. NDIR awaits!

NDIR

As we discussed earlier, NDIR is a very versatile command line utility that allows you to selectively list a large variety of directory and file information, sorted by a number of different parameters. From a file management standpoint, NDIR displays:

- ▶ Filename

- ▶ Owner

- ▶ Creation date and time

- ▶ Last modified date and time

- ▶ Size

- ▶ File attributes

▶ Access rights

▶ Macintosh files

▶ Version information for application files

▶ Extended details

If you don't specify any formatting options, NDIR lists the following information about each file: the filename, size, last update (modified) date, and owner. You can customize the output by specifying one of the following formatting options: /COMP (compression statistics), /DA (Dates), /D (detail), /L (long names), /M (Macintosh), and /R (rights).

By default, NDIR lists all subdirectories and files in the current directory, unless otherwise noted. You can selectively list the information by specifying a particular file, using wildcards, or by indicating a display option such as /C (scroll continuously), /FI (list every occurrence within your current directory and path), /FO (list files only), /SUB (include subdirectories and their files). You can also list files that contain (or do not contain) a specific file attribute.

NDIR also lets you restrict files by specifying date options such as AFT (after), BEF (before), and EQ (equals); size options such as LE (less than), EQ (equal to), and GR (greater than); and NOT (all except).

NDIR lists files in alphabetical order by default. You can change the order files are sorted in by specifying one of the following options: /REV SORT (reverse order), /SORT AC (access date), /SORT AR (archive date), /SORT CR (creation date), /SORT UP (update date), /SORT OW (owner), /SORT SI (size), or /SORT UN (unsorted).

THE BRAIN

For further information on the options available with the NDIR command, refer to the NDIR section of the *Novell NetWare 4.11 Utilities* manual, or surf the Web at http://www.novell.com/manuals.

Get to really know the NDIR command by checking out Table 10.6.

Common NDIR Commands

COMMAND	RESULT
NDIR /FO	Displays files only — those in the current directory
NDIR /FO /C	Displays files only — scrolls continuously
NDIR /FO /SUB	Displays files only — those in the current directory and its subdirectories
NDIR /FO /REV SORT SI	Displays files only — sorts by size, starting with the largest file
NDIR /FO /SORT UP	Displays files only — sorts by last modified date
NDIR /FO /SORT OW	Displays files only — sorts by owner
NDIR /FO OW EQ DAVID	Displays files only — where the owner is David
NDIR R*.* /SIZE GR 500000	Displays files and directories that exceed 500K in size
NDIR *.BAT /FO	Displays files only — those in the current directory with an extension of .BAT
NDIR /FO /AC BEF 06-01-99	Displays files only — those not accessed since 06/01/99
NDIR \WHOAMI.EXE /SUB /FO	Displays files only — lists all occurrences of the WHOAMI.EXE file, starting the search at the root of the volume
NDIR Z:*.EXE /VER	Displays the version number for those files on the Z: drive with an .EXE extension
NDIR *.* /R /FO	Displays files only — lists your effective rights for each file
NDIR Z:NWADMIN.EXE /D	Displays detailed file information for the Z:NWADMIN file
NDIR SYS:SHARED*.* /RO	Displays those files in the SYS:SHARED directory that have the Read Only attribute set
NDIR *.* /FO /NOT RO	Displays files only — those that do not have the Read Only attribute set
NDIR F:*.* /FO /REV SORT AC	Displays files only — sorts by access date, listing the file with the most recent access date first
NDIR /FO DA	Displays files only — lists access, archive, creation, and update dates

Output from the NDIR /FO command is shown in Figure 10.33. And that does it for NDIR. Now, let's explore the final NetWare file management tool — NCOPY.

FIGURE 10.33

The NDIR /FO Command

```
G:\ETC>NDIR /FO
Files            = Files contained in this path
Size             = Number of bytes in the file
Last Update      = Date file was last updated
Owner            = ID of user who created or copied the file

WHITE-SRV1/SYS:ETC\*.*
Files                   Size Last Update      Owner
---------------------  ----- -------------   ------------
ATTYPES.CFG               237  9-23-93  6:56p WHITE-SRV1
BUILTINS.CFG           18,825  3-13-96  3:09p WHITE-SRV1
GATEWAYS                  500  5-24-93  4:59p WHITE-SRV1
HOSTS                     441  9-11-92  2:31p WHITE-SRV1
NETWORKS                  288  9-11-92  2:31p WHITE-SRV1
PROTOCOL                  370  9-11-92  2:31p WHITE-SRV1
SERVICES                1,570  9-11-92  2:31p WHITE-SRV1
TRAPTARG.CFG            1,697  3-17-93  8:50a WHITE-SRV1


      15,928  bytes (17,920  bytes of disk space used)
          8  Files

G:\ETC>
```

NCOPY

NCOPY can be used to copy files as well as directories. What a surprise. As we discussed earlier, NCOPY is similar in function to the DOS XCOPY command, except that directory attributes and name space information are automatically preserved. Refer to Table 10.7 for an exploration of NCOPY from a file management point of view.

THE BRAIN

For further information on the options available with the NCOPY command, refer to the NCOPY section of the *Novell NetWare 4.11 Utilities* manual, or surf the Web at http://www.novell.com/manuals.

TABLE 10.7

Common NCOPY
Commands

COMMAND	RESULT
NCOPY JULY.RPT F:	Copies a file in the default directory called JULY.RPT to the F: drive.
NCOPY F:PHONE.NUM C:	Copies the PHONE.NUM file from the F: drive to the C: drive.
NCOPY F:*.RPT A: /A	Copies files with a *.RPT extension that have the archive bit set (and thus, need to be backed up) from F: to A:.

(continued)

TABLE 10.7

*Common NCOPY
Commands (continued)*

COMMAND	RESULT
NCOPY DOC1.WP TEMP1.* /C	Copies the DOC1.WP file and renames the new version TEMP1.WP without preserving extended attributes and name space information.
NCOPY F:R*. G: /F	Copies files beginning with the letter "R" from the F: drive to the G: drive, forcing the copying of sparse files.
NCOPY *.DOC A: /I	Copies files with a .DOC extension from the current directory to the A: drive and notifies you when extended attributes or name space information cannot be copied because the target volume doesn't support these features.
NCOPY F:*.DOC A: /M	Copies files with the *.DOC extension that have the archive bit set (and thus need to be backed up) from F: to A:, then turns off the archive bit of the source files. (This allows NCOPY to be used for backup purposes.)
NCOPY C:FRED.LST C:TOM.LST /V	Copies FRED.LST to TOM.LST on the C: drive using the verify option.
NCOPY /?	Displays on-line help for the NCOPY utility.

Well, there you have it — the wonderful world of IntranetWare file system management. Aren't you a lucky camper? Now you are an expert in gardening NDS and non-NDS trees. In this section, we focused on the three main components of the IntranetWare file system — volumes, directories, and files. We discovered a variety of tools and learned how they help us manage each of these components. See Table 10.8 for a complete summary. The important thing is to focus on the file system, not the tool — a unique, but effective approach.

*IntranetWare File
Management Utilities
Summary*

MANAGEMENT OBJECT	MANAGEMENT TASK	MANAGEMENT UTILITY
Managing volumes	Displaying volume space usage	NetWare Administrator, NETADMIN, MS Windows, Filer, and NDIR
	Modify user space limits	NetWare Administrator and NETADMIN
	Manage file compression	NetWare Administrator, NETADMIN, Filer, and NDIR
	Manage data-migration attributes	NetWare Administrator, NETADMIN, and FLAG
Managing Directories	View directory information such as creation date, last access date, owner, and attributes	NetWare Administrator, MS Windows, Filer, NDIR
	Modify directory information such as last access date, owner, and attributes	NetWare Administrator, MS Windows, Filer
	Create a directory	NetWare Administrator, MS Windows, Filer
	Rename a directory	NetWare Administrator, MS Windows, Filer, RENDIR
	Delete the contents of a directory	NetWare Administrator, MS Windows, Filer
	Remove a directory and its contents, including subdirectories	NetWare Administrator, MS Windows, Filer
	Remove multiple directories simultaneously	NetWare Administrator, MS Windows, Filer
	Copy a directory structure (while maintaining all NetWare information)	NetWare Administrator, MS Windows, Filer, NCOPY
	Move a directory structure	NetWare Administrator, MS Windows, Filer

(continued)

T A B L E   10.8

*IntranetWare File
Management Utilities
Summary (continued)*

MANAGEMENT OBJECT	MANAGEMENT TASK	MANAGEMENT UTILITY
Managing files	View file information such as creation date, last access date, owner, and attributes	NetWare Administrator, MS Windows, Filer, NDIR
	Modify file information such as creation date, last access date, owner, and attributes	NetWare Administrator, MS Windows, Filer
	Copy files	NetWare Administrator, MS Windows, Filer, NCOPY
	Copy files while preserving NetWare attributes	NetWare Administrator, Filer, NCOPY
	Salvage deleted files	NetWare Administrator, Filer
	Purge deleted files	NetWare Administrator, Filer
	Set a file or directory to purge upon deletion	NetWare Administrator, Filer, FLAG

I guess we're done then, huh? Wrong! We haven't journeyed into the mysterious land of drive mapping yet. I'm sure you'd rather not go there, but buck up soldier, you're a CNE — you can handle it. But can your users?

ZEN

"Fear of success is one of the newest fears that I've heard about lately. I think it's definitely a sign that we're running out of fears. A person suffering from fear of success is scraping the bottom of the fear barrel."

Jerry Seinfeld

Drive Mapping

Drive mapping is one of the great mysteries of life. Forget about the pyramids, alien cornfields, or quarks — drive mapping has them all beat.

It doesn't have to be this way. As a matter of fact, drive mapping is really pretty simple. The problem is that it requires you to unlearn the fundamentals of DOS. Let me explain. In the DOS world, drive letters point to *physical* devices. In Figure 10.34, the A: and B: letters point to floppy drives, C: and D: point to hard drives, and the E: drive is a CD-ROM. Pretty simple, huh? Well, it works fine on workstations, because they typically use multiple storage devices.

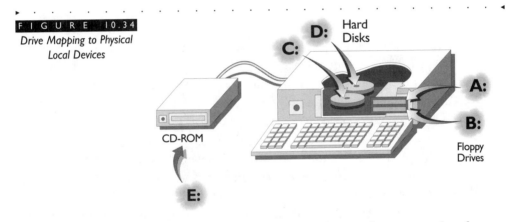

FIGURE 10.34

Drive Mapping to Physical Local Devices

So, how does this theory apply to IntranetWare drives? If we extrapolate from the local theory, we would use 21 different drive letters (F-Z) to point to 21 physical devices — not very likely. So, Novell returned to the proverbial drawing board and came up with a slightly different approach — just different enough to confuse you, me, CNEs, and especially users. Here's how it works:

IntranetWare drive letters point to logical directories instead of physical drives.

This is also pretty simple; a little too simple (see Figure 10.35). As a matter of fact, users treat the NetWare drives just like local drives — *mistake.* The first time they use the CD command, all heck breaks loose. Let me tell you a little story — ironically, about Little John.

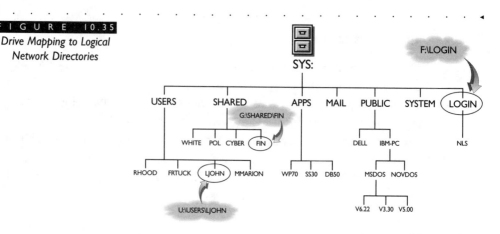

FIGURE 10.35

Drive Mapping to Logical Network Directories

One seemingly innocent summer day in August, Little John was working on his financial files in the SYS:SHARED\FIN directory. For his convenience, you have mapped this directory to drive letter G: (see Figure 10.35). He suddenly realizes that his report templates are at home, that is, SYS:USERS\LJOHN (drive map U:). Any other time he would simply type U: and press Enter to get home, but not today. Today he confuses his network and local drives. Today is a bad day for Little John.

Instead of using the existing U: drive mapping, Little John types CD\USERS\LJOHN from the G: drive. This would work fine in the DOS world, but it's unforgivable in the IntranetWare world. What has he done? Correct. Little John has inadvertently re-mapped his G: drive to SYS:USERS\LJOHN. Remember, IntranetWare drive letters are logical pointers to IntranetWare directories, not physical devices. As you can see in Figure 10.36, Little John now has two letters mapped to his home directory. Of course, he doesn't realize this. Let's return to the story.

Oblivious to the changes in his world, Little John searches the G:\USERS\LJOHN directory for his report templates. He can't find them. "Ah," he thinks. "They're in my home directory. That's drive U:." He quickly switches over to U:\USERS\LJOHN, unaware that this is the same directory. Remember, he thinks the G: and U: drives are different hard disks. He searches in vain and doesn't find the report templates on the U: drive either — he wouldn't. This is where it gets interesting.

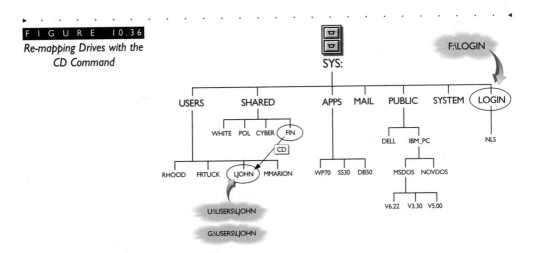

FIGURE 10.36

Re-mapping Drives with the
CD Command

Disgruntled, Little John decides to return to his financial directory and continue work without the missing templates. Naturally, he types G: and presses Enter to return to the G:\SHARED\FIN directory — it doesn't work. "That's odd," he thinks. "It's always worked before." Much to his dismay, all of the financial files seem to have been removed from the G: drive and replaced by a duplicate copy of his home files. At least that's how it appears to Little John. Remember, he thinks the G: and U: drives are different hard disks. In actuality, Little John has re-mapped the G: drive to G:\USERS\LJOHN with the CD command. Oops.

In a panic, Little John deletes the duplicate copy of his home files — hoping it will clear enough space for his financial files to return. Of course, he has inadvertently deleted *all* his home files, because they are *not* duplicates. It's simply a duplicate drive mapping. He comes rumbling down the hall to your office, screaming at the top of his lungs, "Somebody has deleted my financial files!" Incidentally, Little John is not a little man. After picking yourself off the floor, you proceed to explain to him that the IntranetWare CD command doesn't change directories as it does in DOS. Instead, it *cancels data*. Of course this is a lie, but it stops him from using the CD command in the future. Fortunately, you're a CNE and you can save the day! Use SALVAGE to undelete his files and MAP to return G: back to G:\SHARED\FIN where it belongs. Just another day in the life of an IntranetWare CNE.

ZEN

"I once had a leather jacket that got ruined in the rain. Now why does moisture ruin leather? Aren't cows outside a lot of the time?"

Jerry Seinfeld

This story has been brought to you by IntranetWare and your local neighborhood DMV (Drive Mapping Vehicle). It's a great example of what can happen when users get local and network drive mappings confused. For this reason, you have a choice to make: Do you perpetuate the myth or tell your users the truth? If you perpetuate the myth that IntranetWare drives point to physical disks, you'll need to use the MAP ROOT command to make them appear as such. This will also nullify the effects of CD. If you decide to tell your users the truth, consider that knowledge is power. Also consider that they may not want to know the truth. Either way, IntranetWare provides you with three different approaches to drive mapping:

▸ Network Drive Mapping

▸ Search Drive Mapping

▸ Directory Map Objects

Network drives use a single letter to point to logical directory paths. The previous example uses network drives. *Search* drives, on the other hand, provide additional functionality by building a search list for network applications. Finally, *Directory Map objects* are centralized NDS resources that point to logical directory paths. They help ease the transition from one application version to another. Let's take a closer look.

NETWORK DRIVE MAPPINGS

Network drive mappings have a singular purpose — convenience. They provide simple directory navigation for accessing data files. As we learned earlier, IntranetWare supports 21 network drives by default: F-Z. In Figure 10.35, the F: drive points to SYS:LOGIN and the U: drive points to SYS:USERS\LJOHN. These mappings make it easy for users to find their stuff — as long as they don't use the dreaded CD command. Little John simply types U: followed by Enter to get home to U:\USERS\LJOHN. Without drive mappings, movement throughout the directory tree would be cumbersome and time consuming. It would involve long path names and confusing directory searches. Yuck!

TIP

On DOS and MS Windows clients, the availability of network drives is dictated by the NetWare DOS Requester configuration at the workstation. By default, the VLMs specify F: as the first network drive. You can change this by removing the FIRST NETWORK DRIVE = F statement from NET.CFG. As a matter of fact, you can use 26 network drive letters by overwriting all existing local drives. Cool!

Network drive mappings are user-specific, temporary environment variables. Each user has a different set of drive mappings within his or her workstation RAM. These mappings are created each time the user logs in. When the user logs out or turns off the machine, these mappings are lost. For this reason, you'll want to automate the creation of drive mappings in Container and Profile login scripts (see Chapter 12). Also, you can place your mappings in the Windows 95 Registry and make them permanent. This way, they'll always be available when you access the network.

Network drive mappings are created using the MAP command. We'll explore this command in depth later in this chapter. For now, consider creating any or all of the following drive mappings for your users:

▸ U: — each user's home directory (for example, SYS:USERS\LJOHN)

▸ F: — SYS:LOGIN

▸ G: — group-specific data directories (for example, SYS:SHARED\FINAN)

▸ H: — global shared directory (for example, SYS:SHARED)

Now, let's expand our understanding of IntranetWare drive mapping with search drives. They help us build an internal search list for network applications.

SEARCH DRIVE MAPPINGS

Search drive mappings extend one step beyond network mappings by helping users search for network applications. When a user executes an application, IntranetWare searches two places for the program file:

1 • The current directory.

2 • The internal IntranetWare search list. Search drive mappings build the internal search list. They are the IntranetWare equivalent of local PATH statements.

TIP

Most DOS applications cannot access IntranetWare volumes by their volume name. Instead, they typically rely on network and search drive mappings.

The beauty of the IntranetWare search list is that it allows you to prioritize application directories. IntranetWare searches for programs in the order in which they are listed. The list can be a combination of local and network directories. For example, the following search list would find Windows on the local drive first; otherwise, it would use the network version in SYS:APPS\WINDOWS:

```
S1:=SYS:PUBLIC
S2:=SYS:PUBLIC\IBM_PC\MSDOS\V6.22
S3:=C:\WINDOWS
S4:=SYS:APPS\WINDOWS
S5:=SYS:APPS\SS30
```

Because search drive mappings are primarily used to build search lists, you should be more concerned with the order of the list than with the letter assigned to each directory. As you can see from this list, IntranetWare assigns search drive mappings in search order — and each is preceded by the letter S. As a matter of convenience, IntranetWare also automatically assigns a drive letter to each search directory — in reverse order (to avoid using network drive letters). For example, the first search drive (S1:) inherits the letter Z:, the second mapping (S2:) gets the letter Y:, and so on (see Figure 10.37). This allows you to navigate through search directories if necessary, although I don't recommend it. You are limited to a total of 16 search drives that inherit network drive letters. That is, you can have more than 16 search drives, but the extra ones will have to point to already-existing drive letters — such as C:.

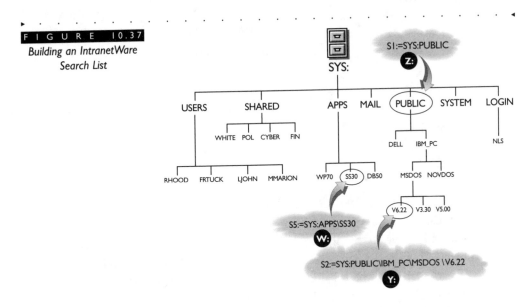

Building an IntranetWare
Search List

> **TIP**
>
> If a search drive encounters an existing network drive letter, the drive skips the letter and inherits the next one. For this reason, you should always assign network drive mappings first.

Because the IntranetWare search list and DOS PATH statements accomplish the same thing, there's a little conflict of interest. As a matter of fact, the IntranetWare search list systematically eliminates directories in the DOS path. To avoid this problem, consider incorporating your DOS path into the IntranetWare search list. This is accomplished using the MAP INSERT command (see the "Drive Mapping" section).

This completes our discussion of network and search drive mappings. Refer to Table 10.9 for a summary of how they work.

TABLE 10.9

Comparing Network and
Search Drive Mappings

FUNCTION	NETWORK DRIVE MAPPING	SEARCH DRIVE MAPPING
Purpose	Movement	Searching
Assignment Method	As the letter	In search order
Letter Assignment	By you	By NetWare
First Letter	F:	Z:
Directory Types	Data	Applications

Now, let's take a moment to explore Directory Map objects before we dive into the MAP command.

DIRECTORY MAP OBJECTS

In earlier chapters, we learned about a special NDS leaf object that helped us deal with drive mapping in the IntranetWare file system — the Directory Map object. This special-purpose object allows us to map to a central logical resource instead of to the physical directory itself, mainly because physical directories change and logical objects don't have to.

This level of independence is very useful. Let's say, for example, that you have a central application server in the TOKYO container that everybody points to. On the server is an older copy of WordPerfect (WP5). You have two options for adding this application to your internal search lists:

1 • Search Drive Mapping — Use a traditional search drive mapping in each container's login script (five of them). This mapping would point to the physical directory itself — TOKYO-SRV1\SYS:APPS\WP5.

2 • Directory Map Object — Create a central Directory Map object in TOKYO called WPAPP. Then, each of the five search drive MAP commands can point to the logical object instead of the physical APPS\WP directory. Finally, here the WPAPP object points to the physical directory as TOKYO-SRV1\SYS:APPS\WP5.

Both of these scenarios accomplish the same thing: They create a search drive mapping to WordPerfect 5 for all users in the Tokyo location. But, once you upgrade WordPerfect, you'll find the second option is much more attractive. In the first scenario, you'll need to change five different search drive statements in five distributed login scripts on five different servers. This is a lot of work!

In the second scenario, however, you'll only need to change the one Directory Map object reference, and all the other MAP statements will automatically point to the right place. Amazing! In the next section, we'll explore the MAP command and learn how it can be used to reference Directory Map objects.

ZEN

"The movie ad I don't get is this one: 'If you see only one movie this year ....'
Why go at all? You're not going to enjoy it — there's too much pressure.
You're sitting there, 'Alright, this is it for 51 more weekends, this better be
good!'"

Jerry Seinfeld

MAPPING DRIVES WITH MAP

So, now that you know everything there is to know about network, search, and NDS drive mappings, the next logical question is, "How?" It's simple — the MAP command. The IntranetWare MAP command allows you to

▸ View drive mappings

▸ Create or modify network or search drive mappings

▸ Point to Directory Map objects

▸ Map drives to a fake root — to fool users or install special applications

▸ Change mappings from one type to another

▸ Integrate the network and local search lists

▸ All sorts of other stuff

TIP

The DOS CD command will change the MAP assignment in the DOS window, but not in the current Windows applications. Also, the MAP command is faster than CD because it has drive letters. Finally, the IntranetWare MAP command is most like the DOS SUBST command.

As I'm sure you've probably guessed, the MAP command is the heart and soul of IntranetWare drive mapping. Now, let's take a closer look at some fun and exciting MAP commands — starting with plain, old MAP. Also, there's a MAP summary table at the end of this section for your review. Ready, set, MAP!

MAP

You can use the MAP command without any options to display a list of your current drive mappings. As you can see in Figure 10.38, the local drives (A: through E:) are listed first, followed by the network drives, and finally, the search drives. Also, note the cool dashes in the middle. They separate the network drives from the search drives.

FIGURE 10.38

The Plain Old MAP
Command

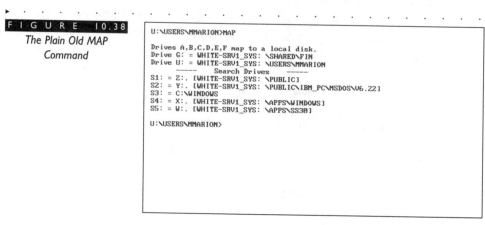

```
U:\USERS\MMARION>MAP

Drives A,B,C,D,E,F map to a local disk.
Drive G: = WHITE-SRV1_SYS: \SHARED\FIN
Drive U: = WHITE-SRV1_SYS: \USERS\MMARION
          ------  Search Drives  ------
S1: = Z:. [WHITE-SRV1_SYS: \PUBLIC]
S2: = Y:. [WHITE-SRV1_SYS: \PUBLIC\IBM_PC\MSDOS\V6.22]
S3: = C:\WINDOWS
S4: = X:. [WHITE-SRV1_SYS: \APPS\WINDOWS]
S5: = W:. [WHITE-SRV1_SYS: \APPS\SS30]

U:\USERS\MMARION>
```

TIP

IntranetWare does not track information on local drive assignments. Even though a map list will show that drives A: through E: are assigned to local drives, that doesn't necessarily mean they point to real devices. If you really want to mess with your users, map network drives to local devices. Or, even better, map local drives to network directories.

MAP G:=WHITE-SRVI\SYS:SHARED\FINAN

You can use the MAP command followed by a drive letter (A: through Z:) to create network drive mappings. In this case, the G: drive is assigned to the SYS:SHARED\FIN directory on the WHITE-SRV1 file server.

TIP

We also could have used the relative distinguished name or distinguished name for the volume instead of using the physical volume name. For instance, we could have typed

```
MAP G:=WHITE-SRV1_SYS:SHARED\FIN
```

or

```
MAP G:=.WHITE-SRV1_SYS.WHITE.CRIME.TOKYO.ACME:SHARED\FIN
```

If the G: drive already exists, it will replace the existing assignment without displaying a warning. However, if you attempt to re-map a local drive (that is, Drive A: through Drive E:), you will receive a warning that the drive is currently assigned to a local device. IntranetWare is polite and asks you if you want to assign it to a network drive anyway.

MAP NP E:=SYSMAIL

Using the NP parameter allows you to overwrite local or search drives without being prompted. It must be listed first or second. In this example, the E: drive would be re-mapped without the usual warning:

```
Warning: You are attempting to re-map a local drive.
```

MAP S3:=SYS:APPS\WP70

You can use the MAP SEARCH command followed by a search drive number (S1: through S16:) to map a directory to a specific search drive. The number in the search drive defines the pointer's place in the search list (that is, its priority).

TIP

Search drive mappings share the same environment space as the DOS path. As a result, if you assign a IntranetWare search drive number using the MAP SEARCH command, it will overwrite the corresponding pointer in the DOS path. (For instance, if you use the MAP S1: command, it will overwrite the first pointer in the DOS path.) The only way to retain existing pointers in the DOS path is to use the MAP INS or MAP S16: commands (listed later in this section), which insert new search drives into the DOS path rather than replacing existing ones.

In this example, the SYS:APPS\WP70 directory will be assigned as search drive S3:, which is the third item in the search list. It will also map the directory to the next available drive letter, starting with Z: and moving backward. Review the "Search Drive Mappings" section.

TIP

There is a way to specify which network drive letter is assigned when creating a search drive. In the previous example, if you want to assign network drive letter W: to the S3: search drive, you can use the following command:

```
MAP S3:=W:=APPS\WP70
```

MAP INS S1:=SYS:PUBLIC

The MAP INSERT command can be used to insert a new search drive into the search list, at the number specified, without overwriting an existing drive mapping. All existing search drives below the new pointer are then bumped up one level in the list and renumbered accordingly.

In this example, we are inserting a new drive as S1:. Therefore, IntranetWare bumps up and renumbers all other search drives in the list. Then, it inserts the new drive at the top of the list as search drive S1:.

The interesting thing about this scenario is that it has no effect on existing network drives. All previous drives retain their original drive letters, even though they change positions in the search list.

REAL WORLD

A very interesting thing happens if you re-map an existing search drive number. IntranetWare assigns the new directory, as specified, without warning you that an existing search drive with the same number already exists. It does not, however, overwrite the network drive letter that was originally associated with the search drive number. Instead, it assigns a new network drive letter to the new directory and converts the old network drive letter into a full-fledged network drive mapping — thus stripping away its searching ability. Conversely, if you attempt to re-map the network drive associated with a search drive, you will receive a warning that the drive is already in use as a search drive and will be asked if you want to overwrite it. If you say "Yes," both the network drive and its associated search drive will be mapped to the new directory. Weird, huh?

Earlier, we learned that both the MAP INSERT and MAP S16: commands could be used to preserve the DOS path. This way, when you log off the network, your NetWare search drives will be deleted, but your local PATH statements will remain intact. Remember, DOS PATH drives don't count toward your limit of 16 network search drives.

TIP

So, what happens when you mix the **MAP INSERT** and **MAP S16:** statements? You create a strange "genetic" breed. The resulting command, **MAP INSERT S16:** places your search drives in the IntranetWare search list but after the **DOS PATH** directories. Weird.

QUIZ

One final numbers game: This is one of my personal favorites (see if you can figure out why). Change the position of only one number to make this a palindromic sequence:

1, 4, 2, 9, 6, 1, 5, 10, 4

Hint: When in Rome . . .

(Q10-4)

MAP DEL G:

The MAP DEL command deletes an existing drive mapping. This command can be used with both network and search drive pointers. The MAP REM command performs the same function. Remember, network drive mappings and search drive mappings are deleted automatically if you log off the network or turn off your workstation.

MAP ROOT H:=SYS:ACCT\REPORTS

You can use the MAP ROOT command to create a false root. This command solves user problems like the one we had with Little John. The user sees this drive as if it were the root directory; therefore, he can't wander off too far with the dreaded CD command.

MAP ROOT can also be used for application programs that need to be installed in the root directory. For security reasons and administrative purposes, you should never install applications in the actual root, so here's a great compromise. The Install program thinks it's installing WordPerfect, for example, in the root directory, when it's actually a false root pointing to SYS:APPS.

To determine if a drive mapping is actually a false root, use the MAP command alone. As you can see in Figure 10.39, the H: drive is shown differently than are the other network drives. Instead of showing a blank space between the volume name and the directory name, it shows a blank space followed by a backslash following the directory name. This clues you in that we're dealing with a different breed — a false root.

▶ · ◀

F I G U R E   10.39
The MAP ROOT Command

```
U:\USERS\MMARION>MAP

Drives A,B,C,D,E,F map to a local disk.
Drive G: = WHITE-SRV1_SYS: \SHARED\FIN
Drive H: = WHITE-SRV1_SYS:ACCT\REPORTS \
Drive U: = WHITE-SRV1_SYS: \USERS\MMARION
             Search Drives
S1: = Z:. [WHITE-SRV1_SYS: \PUBLIC]
S2: = Y:. [WHITE-SRV1_SYS: \PUBLIC\IBM_PC\MSDOS\V6.22]
S3: = C:\WINDOWS
S4: = X:. [WHITE-SRV1_SYS: \APPS\WINDOWS]
S5: = W:. [WHITE-SRV1_SYS: \APPS\SS30]

U:\USERS\MMARION>
```

MAP N SYS:DATA

You can use the MAP NEXT (N) command to assign the next available drive letter as a network drive mapping. It doesn't work, however, with search drive pointers.

TIP

Although the MAP NEXT command doesn't work with search drives, there is another technique that you can use to achieve the same effect, namely the MAP S16: command. The MAP S16: command assigns the next available search drive number to the specified directory. Because search drives update the DOS Path, IntranetWare does not allow you to assign search drive numbers that would cause holes to exist in the DOS path. For instance, if only search drives S1: through S4: exist, IntranetWare would not let you create search drive S7:. Instead, it would just assign the next search drive number in the list (S5:, in this example).

MAP C I:

The MAP CHANGE (C) command can be used to change a regular IntranetWare drive to a search drive, or vice versa. In this example, Drive I: will still point to the same directory to which it was originally assigned, but it would also be added to the end of the IntranetWare search list. Conversely, if you use the MAP CHANGE command with a search drive, the search drive number is deleted from the search list, but the network drive letter originally associated with it is retained as a network drive mapping.

MAP S5:=.WPAPP.TOKYO.ACME

You can also map a drive to a Directory Map object (WPAPP) instead of to the directory itself. This is especially useful if the directory name changes from time to time — such as every time you upgrade WordPerfect or Microsoft Word — and you don't want to change every MAP statement in every login script.

In this case, you only need to change the reference in the central Directory Map object. All other drive mapping commands will reflect that change instantly. It's fun at parties. But whatever you do, don't place a colon (:) at the end of the Directory Map object.

TIP

Directory Map objects appear as folders in the Windows 95 Network Neighborhood. You can activate them with the Map Network Drive option from the File menu. Also, you can access Directory Map objects on the Resource side of the NetWare User Tools for Windows.

MAP /?

The MAP /? command displays on-line help for all variations of the MAP command.

MAP /VER

The MAP /VER command lists the version of the MAP utility that you are using as well as the files the utility needs to execute. If you use the /VER option, all other parameters will be ignored.

Table 10.10 provides a quick summary of all the really amazing MAP commands you've learned today.

T A B L E   10.10

Getting to Know the MAP
Commands

COMMAND	RESULT
MAP	Displays a list of current drive mappings.
MAP G:=WHITE-SRV1\SYS: SHARED\FINAN	Maps the G: drive as a network drive that points to the SHARED\FINAN directory on the SYS volume of the WHITE-SRV1 server (using the physical volume name).
MAP G:=.WHITE-SRV1_SYS.WHITE. CRIME.TOKYO.ACME:SHARED\FINAN	Maps the G: drive as a network drive that points to the SHARED\FINAN directory on the SYS volume of the WHITE-SRV1 server (using the Volume object name).
MAP NP E:=SYS:HR\EVAL	Maps the E: drive to the HR\EVAL directory, suppressing the warning that you are about to re-map a local drive.
MAP S3:=SYS:APPS\WP70	Maps the S3: search drive to the SYS:APSS\WP70 directory and assigns the next available drive letter in reverse alphabetical order as a network drive.

T A B L E   10.10

Getting to Know the MAP
Commands (continued)

COMMAND	RESULT
MAP S3:=W:=SYS:APPS\WP70	Maps the S3: search drive to the SYS:APPS\WP70 directory and assigns W: as the associated network drive.
MAP INS S1:=SYS:PUBLIC	Inserts a new S1: search drive at the beginning of the search list, renumbering all existing search drives accordingly. Also assigns the next available drive letter in reverse alphabetical order as a network drive.
MAP DEL G:	Deletes the G: network drive (see MAP REM command).
MAP REM G:	Deletes the G: network drive (see MAP DEL command).
MAP ROOT H:=SYS:ACCT\REPORTS	Maps the H: drive as a false root pointing to the ACCT\REPORTS directory.
MAP N SYS:DATA	Maps the next available network drive letter to the SYS:DATA directory.
MAP C I:	Changes the I: network drive to the next available search drive number.
MAP C S4:	Changes the S4: search drive to a network drive.
MAP S5:=WPAPP	Maps the S5: search drive to a Directory Map object called WPAPP in the current container.
MAP /?	Displays on-line help information for the MAP command.
MAP /VER	Displays version information about the MAP utility, including the files it needs to execute.

MAPPING DRIVES WITH MS WINDOWS

In addition to the MAP command, IntranetWare allows you to create network and search drive mappings using MS Windows. Specifically, you can use the following two Windows environments:

▶ Windows 95

▶ NetWare User Tools for Windows

Let's take a closer look.

Windows 95 Drive Mappings

In Windows 95, you can use the Network Neighborhood to map network drives to volumes and directories. This facility does *not* allow you to create search drive mappings. To map a network drive in the Windows 95 Network Neighborhood, consult Figure 10.40 and follow these steps:

1 • Select the volume or directory you want to map.

2 • From the File menu, choose "Map Network Drive." The Map Network Drive window appears, showing the path you have selected.

3 • Choose a drive letter.

4 • Select the "Reconnect at Logon" option so that this drive will be available the next time you log in. Incidentally, these permanent settings are stored in the WIN.INI file.

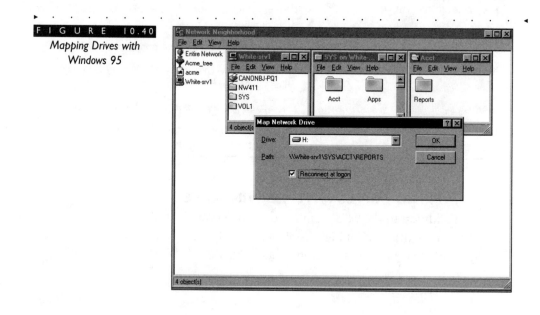

F I G U R E   10.40

Mapping Drives with
Windows 95

It's important to note that all drive mappings are viewed globally by Client 32. Therefore, any time a drive is mapped within Windows (Windows 95 Network Neighborhood, File Manager, or at the MS-DOS prompt), the drive's accessible and visible everywhere else in Windows. In addition, whenever a drive is changed to a different directory, the directory change affects only that specific instance of the drive. For example, if the drive is changed to the SHARED directory at the MS-DOS prompt, no other MS-DOS prompt or Windows application will display this change. For this reason, you want to be sure to use the Network Neighborhood or NetWare User Tools for Windows utilities.

NetWare User Tools for Windows Drive Mappings

In Windows 3.1, you can change mappings or create new mappings with the NetWare User Tools for Windows interface. Figure 10.41 shows the split screen graphical interface. On the left side is a list of all available drives and on the right side is a list of available resources (volumes and directories).

To map a drive, drag the directory or volume object from the right size of the screen and drop it on top of the drive letter on the left side. (See Figure 10.41)

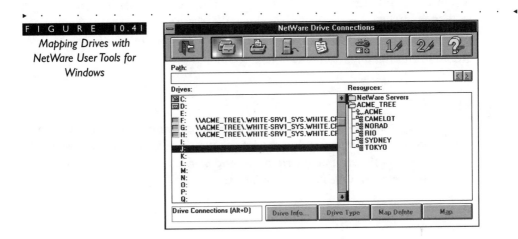

FIGURE 10.41

Mapping Drives with NetWare User Tools for Windows

Unlike Windows 95, the NetWare User Tools for Windows utility allows you to create search drives. Follow these simple steps:

1 • Select the drive from the left side of the drive mapping window.

2 • Click the Drive Type button on the bottom of the screen.

3 • In the dialog box that appears, select Search Drive.

4 • Click OK.

This converts an already existing network drive into a IntranetWare search drive.

In addition, NetWare User Tools for Windows allows you to create permanent network or search drive mappings. Like Windows 95, these permanent settings are stored in the WIN.INI file.

In the beginning . . . there was the NDS directory tree. We discovered the [Root], leaf objects, proper naming, and Read/Write replicas. We learned how to name it, partition it, design it, install it, manage it, and groom it. Just when we thought we understood the true meaning of IntranetWare life, another tree appeared — the non-NDS directory tree.

This strange new tree is very different. Instead of a [Root], it has a root; instead of leaves, it has files; and instead of replicas, it has duplexing. But once you get past its rough exterior, you'll see that the non-NDS tree shares the same look and feel as the NDS one. And they approach life together with a similar purpose — to logically organize user resources, except this time the resources are files, not printers.

In this chapter we learned everything there is to know about our non-NDS friend. We learned how to name it, partition it, design it, install it, manage it, and groom it. All in a day's work.

ZEN

Megatrend — A far-reaching or widespread change in society such as the advent of computers and the information revolution, aerobics and physical fitness, microwave ovens and convenience food, or, most importantly, CNEs becoming florists.

So, what does the future hold? Well, now that we've learned everything about NDS and non-NDS trees, we can expand our minds to the rest of IntranetWare management. We will combine our "treeologist" skills and forge ahead into the great CNE abyss:

- ▸ Security

- ▸ Configuration

- ▸ Management

- ▸ Printing

- ▸ Optimization

During your journey through the rest of this book, look back to the fun times you had in gardening class. Count on your NDS and non-NDS gardening skills — because you will need them. Oh yes, you will.

Good luck, and by the way . . . thanks for saving the world.

CASE STUDY: CREATING A DIRECTORY STRUCTURE FOR ACME

You're ready to create the basic file system directory structure for the WHITE-SRV1 server. Using the scenario listed below, design the directory structure on paper first, then use the DOS MD command or the IntranetWare FILER utility to create the directory structure on the system.

As you know, initially, the Crime Fighting division, the White-Collar Crime department, and the three White-Collar Crime units (Cyber Crime, Financial Crime, and Political Crime) will all be sharing the same server (WHITE-SRV1.WHITE.CRIME.TOKYO.ACME). Although there will be some sharing of programs and data, each group will essentially function as an independent workgroup with a separate network administrator.

Because the WHITE-SRV1 server has already been installed, the system-created LOGIN, SYSTEM, PUBLIC, MAIL, and ETC directories already exist.

The USERS directory should be created in the root of the volume. It will serve as the parent directory for the home directories for each user. (The home directories will be created when you actually create the users at a later time). Each of the workgroups will have access to the SHARED directory, which will be located in the root of the volume. This directory will be used for the sharing of files between workgroups. In addition, each workgroup will have exclusive access to its own group directory under the SHARED directory (called WHITE, CYBER, FIN, and POL, respectively).

The users in the various workgroups will be running different versions of DOS. Although each user will normally run DOS off his/her local workstation, there will also be a copy of each DOS version stored on the server in case anything happens to the copy on a particular workstation. Because the DOS versions differ in manufacturer, type, and version, you will want to use the standard DOS directory structure recommended by Novell (that is, a three-level directory structure under the SYS:PUBLIC directory: the machine type on the first level, the DOS type on the second level, and the DOS version on the third). So far, you know that there will be:

- Two types of machines (DELL and IBM_PC)

- Two types of DOS (MSDOS and NOVDOS)

- Three versions of MSDOS (v3.30, v5.00, and v6.22).

The first three applications that will be installed on the server include:

- A word processing application (in the WP70 directory)

- A spreadsheet application (in the SS30 directory)

- A database application (in the DB50 directory)

Each of these subdirectories will be stored under the APPS directory, which will be located in the root of the volume.

EXERCISE 10-1: MAPPING DRIVES WITH MAP

Follow the steps listed below to create sample drive mappings for the directory structure that was created in the case study titled "Creating a Directory Structure for ACME."

1. Display on-line help information for the MAP command.

2. Display your current drive mappings.

3. Map drive F: to the USERS directory. (Normally, it would point to each user's individual home directory, but they have not been created yet.)

4. Map drive G: to the POL subdirectory under the SHARED directory, using the physical name of the volume.

5. Map the J: drive to the same directory as the F: drive.

6. Map drive S: to the SHARED directory, using the Volume object name.

7. Map the S1: search drive to the SYS:PUBLIC directory without overwriting the existing pointers in the DOS path.

8. Map the S2: search drive to the V6.22 directory without overwriting the existing pointers in the DOS path.

9. Map the S3: search drive to the SS30 subdirectory.

10. Map the S4: search drive as a false root to the DB50 subdirectory.

11. Display your current drive mappings again. How does the system indicate a false root?

12. Map the S5: search drive to the WP70 subdirectory, specifying that W: be assigned as the associated network drive. Did it work?

13. To view the effect of the CD command on search drive mappings, switch to the Z: drive. Type CD .. and press Enter to switch to the root directory. Type the MAP command to list your current drive mappings. What happened? What should be done to fix the problem? Fix the problem.

14. Delete the J: drive.

15. Delete the S3: search drive using a different command than you did in Step 14. What happened to your other search drive mappings? What happened to the network drive associated with those search drives?

16. Change the S4: drive from a search drive to a network drive. What happened to the search drive itself? What happened to the network drive associated with it?

See Appendix C for answers.

EXERCISE 10-2: MAPPING DRIVES WITH MS WINDOWS

In addition to the MAP command, IntranetWare allows you to create network and search drive mappings using MS Windows. Specifically, you can use the following two Windows environments:

▸ Windows 95

▸ NetWare User Tools for Windows

Let's run these utilities for a test drive (*pun intended*).

Mapping Network Drives with Windows 95

In Windows 95, you can use the Network Neighborhood to map network drives to volumes and directories. To map a network drive in Network Neighborhood, perform the following steps:

1. Double-click on the Network Neighborhood icon on your Windows 95 desktop. Double-click on the server icon. Double-click on the SYS: volume icon. Click on the folder corresponding to the PUBLIC directory.

2. Choose "Map Network Drive..." from the File menu. The Map Network Drive window appears, showing the path you have selected.

3. The next available network drive letter will be displayed. If you wish to choose a different drive letter, key it in, or click on one from the list (see Figure 10.40).

4. Click on the "Reconnect at logon" option so that this drive will be available the next time you log in. Click on OK to map the drive. Back out of this utility by clicking on the Close button in the upper-right corner of each of the open windows relating to this utility.

Mapping Drives with NetWare User Tools for Windows

In Windows 3.1, you can change mappings or create new mappings with the NetWare User Tools for Windows. Figure 10.41 shows the mappings with the graphical interface. To map a drive to a directory or volume listed on the right side of the window, you can drag the directory or volume over to the drive letter on the left side.

It's as simple as that!

In this exercise, we will use the MS Windows-based graphical NetWare Administrator utility to manage IntranetWare directories and files. First, we will create an ADMIN subdirectory under the USERS subdirectory, then we'll create subdirectories and files under the ADMIN directory. Finally, we will manipulate the files and directories we have created under the ADMIN directory using NetWare Administrator.

Follow these simple steps very carefully:

1. Run NetWare Administrator. Execute the NetWare Administrator utility. The contents of your Directory tree should be displayed.

2. Open an independent browse window for the SYS: volume. Click on the SYS volume icon. Select NDS Browser from the Tools menu and click on OK. This will set the current context for this browse window to that of the SYS: volume.

3. Create an ADMIN directory under the SYS: volume. Click on the SYS volume to see its contents. Click on the USERS directory using the right mouse button. Click on Create from the pull-down menu. Type ADMIN in the Directory name field, then click on Create to create the directory. Finally, double-click on the USERS directory to open it and see its contents.

4. Create the following three directories under the ADMIN directory: PROJECT1, PROJECT2, and PROJECT3.

   a. Create the PROJECT1 directory. Click on the ADMIN directory to select it. Press the Ins key or select Create from the Object menu. Type **PROJECT1** in the Directory name field. Click on the "Create another Directory" box, then click on Create to create the PROJECT1 directory.

b. Create the PROJECT2 directory. Enter **PROJECT2** in the Directory name field, then click on Create to create the PROJECT2 directory.

c. Create the PROJECT3 directory. Enter **PROJECT3** in the Directory name field, then click on the "Create another Directory" to turn off the feature. Finally, click on Create to create the PROJECT3 directory.

d. Double-click on the ADMIN directory to view the directories you have just created.

5. Open a second browse window for the SYS: volume. Click on the SYS volume icon. Select NDS Browser from the Tools menu and click on OK. This will set the current context for this browse window to that of the SYS: volume. Select the Tile option under the Window menu to reshape the browse windows and view the contents of all three windows at the same time.

6. Display the contents of the ETC directory in the second browse window. Double-click on the ETC directory to open the directory and see its contents.

7. Copy each of the following files in the ETC directory to the corresponding directory you created in Step 4:

    ► ATTYPES.CFG to the PROJECT1 directory

    ► BUILTINS.CFG to the PROJECT2 directory

    ► TRAPTARG.CFG to the PROJECT3 directory

a. Copy the files. Drag the ATTYPES.CFG file from the source browser window to the PROJECT1 directory in the target browser window. You'll notice that the Copy button is selected by default. Click on OK to copy the file. Repeat this same procedure for the remaining two files — making sure to drop each one in the appropriate directory.

b. Confirm the files were copied. Double-click on each destination directory to confirm that the files were copied successfully.

c. Close the source browser window. Click on the Close button in the upper-right of the browser window that shows the contents of the ETC directory.

8. Move the BUILTINS.CFG and TRAPTARG.CFG files from the PROJECT2 and PROJECT3 directories to the PROJECT1 directory. Click on the BUILTINS.CFG file. Hold down the Ctrl key and click the TRAPTARG.CFG file. Continue to hold down the Ctrl key and drag the files on top of the PROJECT1 directory. You'll notice that the move button is automatically activated. Click on OK to move the files to the PROJECT1 directory.

9. Rename the PROJECT1 directory to DONE1. Click on the PROJECT1 directory. Select Rename from the Object menu. Type DONE1 in the New name field, then click on OK to rename the directory.

10. Copy the DONE1 directory and its contents to the PROJECT2 directory. Drag the DONE1 directory onto the PROJECT2 directory, then click on OK to confirm the copy.

11. Move the new DONE1 directory and its contents from the PROJECT2 directory to the PROJECT3 directory. Double-click on the PROJECT2 directory to open the directory and see its contents. Click on the DONE1 directory under the PROJECT2 directory and hold down the mouse button. While holding down the Ctrl key, drag the DONE1 directory from the PROJECT2 directory to the PROJECT3 directory, then click on OK to confirm the move.

12. Set the Purge attribute for the TRAPTARG file under the PROJECT3\DONE1 directory. Double-click on the PROJECT3 and DONE1 directories to open them and see their contents. Double-click on the TRAPTARG.TXT file under the PROJECT3/DONE1 directory. Click on the Attributes page button. Click on the Purge Immediately attribute, then click on OK.

13. Simultaneously delete the three files in the PROJECT3/DONE1 directory. Click on the first filename listed. While holding down the Shift key, click on the last filename listed. Press the Del key, then select Yes when prompted to confirm the deletion.

14. Salvage the files you deleted in Step 13.

    a. Salvage the files. Click on the DONE1 directory under the PROJECT3 directory. Select Salvage from the Tools menu. Click on the List button at the top left of the window. You'll notice that TRAPTARG.CFG is unavailable for salvaging because you set it to "immediate purge" before deleting it. Click on the *first filename*. While holding down the Shift key, click the *second name*, then click the Salvage button. Click on the Close button to close the salvage window.

    b. Confirm the deletion. Double-click on the DONE1 directory to confirm that the two files have been salvaged.

Circle the 20 IntranetWare File System terms hidden in this word search puzzle using the hints provided.

```
S   Y   S   T   E   M   C   T   E   R   R   B
Y   E   U   U   J   N   E   Q   E   K   B   U
S   N   E   A   K   E   R   N   E   T   S   R
I   W   L   L   S   J   Q   X   Y   F   Q   Z
X   A   U   C   P   P   T   V   Q   L   V   G
T   D   E   L   E   T   E   D   S   A   V   C
E   M   Z   O   V   X   V   M   W   G   P   Q
E   I   F   N   C   O   P   Y   P   L   U   N
N   N   I   G   O   L   P   R   I   B   G
R   I   D   N   L   S   D   U   A   A   L   Q
V   Q   U   E   U   E   S   I   M   M   I   K
T   A   N   B   H   K   R   W   M   E   C   D
```

Hints:

1. Directory that contains deleted files from directories that no longer exist.
2. Directory that contains NetWare on-line documentation files.
3. Directory that contains sample programs for use in configuring the network for TCP/IP.
4. IntranetWare file management menu utility that can be used to salvage and purge files.
5. Command line utility that can be used for assigning directory or file attributes.
6. The only directory available to users prior to login.
7. This directory may or may not contain User ID subdirectories.
8. Comand line utility used for assigning network or search drive mappings.

9. Command line utility that be used for copying files from one location to another.
10. Command line utility that can be used to selectively list volume, directory, and file information.
11. Directory that contains subdirectories for different languages.
12. MS Windows-based file management utility.
13. Directory that contains NetWare utilities available to network users.
14. Directory that contains print queue subdirectories.
15. Another name for Redundant Array of Inexpensive Disks.
16. Maximum number of network search drives available.
17. Process used for filesharing before the advent of LANs.
18. First volume on every IntranetWare server.
19. A directory that contains operating system files, NLMs, and administrator utilities.
20. The highest level in the IntranetWare file system.

See Appendix C for answers.

IntranetWare Security

"You won't find a more secure system anywhere"

Security is an interesting thing. Everyone wants it but how much are you willing to pay? On the one extreme, you could live in a titanium vault — secure, but very uncomfortable. On the other extreme, you could live in a 1960s Woodstock fantasy — fun, but way too risky. No, I believe you live somewhere in between. Whether you know it or not, your security requirements fall in a spectrum between a titanium vault and the 1960s. The key to security is gauging the range of your boundaries.

Goal: *Let the good guys in and keep the bad guys out!*

Security in the Information Age poses an even more interesting challenge. Computers and communications have made it possible to collect volumes of data about you and me — from our last purchase at the five-and-dime to our detailed medical records. Privacy has become a commodity to be exchanged on the open market. Information is no longer the fodder of afternoon talk shows. It has become *the* unit of exchange for the 21st Century, more valuable than money.

A recent study has shown that 92 percent of the Fortune 500 companies think security is important enough to do something about. Even the government is getting involved with the "clipper chip" and other anti-theft policies. I bet you thought you left cops and robbers behind in childhood. Well, this is a variation on the game and the stakes are very high. As a CNE, it is your responsibility to design, install, and manage the IntranetWare network. But, most importantly, you must protect it. You need a brain filled with sophisticated security strategies and a utility belt full of advanced protection tools. Think of this chapter as your impenetrable network armor.

IntranetWare security is, in general, fairly good. But for many of today's WANs, it's not good enough. As a matter of fact, most of IntranetWare's security features need to be "turned on." It's not secure right out of the box. A truly *secure* network protects more than just user data — it protects everything! So, what is "everything"? The definition of "everything" has changed in IntranetWare. Now the world exists in a nebulous cloud full of Tupperware containers and User objects. As the IntranetWare universe becomes more open and interconnected, security becomes more and more important.

So, what is "security"? Simply stated, security is freedom from risk. Therefore, network security can be considered as any effort you take to protect your network from risk. Of course, it's difficult to protect your network from things you cannot see or understand. So, the first thing you need to do in developing a security model is to learn about risks.

So, what is "risk"? Risk is a combination of value and threat. The value you determine is the cost of your network resources should you lose them. Value extends well beyond monetary value — it encompasses data integrity, confidentiality, and the value of data to competitors. Threats are more difficult to define. They come from a variety of different sources, including people, technology, and the environment. The very nature of computer networks puts them at continual risk. In summary, sharing data makes it harder to protect data. Of course, you don't have a choice. The first step toward true network security is *risk analysis*.

The goal of risk analysis is to define your network security principles and identify the threats against them. A "threat" is a person, place, or thing that poses some danger to a network asset. Threats can be physical (file servers and workstations), topology (wire tapping), network-related (back/trapdoors, impersonation, and piggybacking), data (logic bombs and Trojan horses), and people (intentional sabotage or unintentional bumbling).

The goal of your threat-based security model is to determine how likely your network is to experience any of these threats. What are the chances, for example, that your system has a back/trapdoor in place? Is wiretapping a possibility? How about impersonation or, even worse, logic bombs? The best approach is to make a realistic judgment of each threat's probability on your WAN. This becomes the foundation of your network's risk index. You can then use this index to develop a successful system of security countermeasures.

Countermeasures are actions that create a protective barrier against network threats. In many cases, countermeasures can reduce the probability of serious threats. In addition, vulnerability decreases as countermeasures increase. There is, however, never a vulnerability level of zero because countermeasures themselves have vulnerabilities built in. The bad news is that countermeasures cost money. As a matter of fact, the more serious the threat, the higher the cost of the countermeasure. Because it's difficult to quantify the decrease in threat probability due to countermeasures, cost justification becomes a challenge. But all in all, countermeasures are necessary to keep your network running, and, therefore, money must be spent on them. After all, money makes the world go 'round.

SMART LINK

Download and Read "The Orange Book" of security from http://www.sevenlocks.com/evaluati.htm.

As a CNE, it's your job to identify network threats and implement appropriate countermeasures to eliminate them. This isn't easy. You have many factors working against you — including money, office politics, and user productivity. But there are some quick and easy countermeasures that can dramatically improve your network security:

- Restrict physical access to file servers. In Chapter 13, we'll learn a few strategies for physical file server protection.

- One of your network's most insecure entry points is through virtual links.

- Consider using dial-back systems with multilayered password protection. Remember, anyone with a modem and phone line can gain access to your network.

- Background authentication and NCP packet signing protect data packets as they travel over topology lines. In addition, data is encrypted for further protection.

- Many advanced routers allow you to filter SAPs, RIPs, and specific frame types. Consider filtering non-essential packets to increase performance and keep out the bad guys.

- Don't use the Supervisor or Admin accounts — use an equivalent instead. Also, don't delete the original Admin account once you have made yourself equivalent. There's some existentialist ramifications in there somewhere.

- Always create a backdoor. Consider using Alt+255 as a null character. It's hard to track. The beauty of null characters is they appear as spaces. Intruders will see a username or password with a space and never assume it's a null character. Also, many times you can't tell how many null characters are involved — especially when they're sequentially added to the end of a username.

- IntranetWare includes an extensive auditing system that allows you to audit login events as well as file/directory events. Use it!

▸ Consider restricting the following file server access rights: Supervisor, Access Control, and Modify [SAM].

▸ Track rights carefully and make sure you know what you're doing before you get started. Calculating effective rights can be very tricky, especially if you use an Inherited Rights Filter (IRF). Many times users end up with rights they shouldn't have.

▸ Classify people into security levels and identify the highest security risks, then implement countermeasures against these people, including training sessions, tracking, or extensive auditing.

▸ Be careful when assigning distributed administrative responsibility. Remember, power corrupts and absolute power corrupts absolutely.

Well, there you go. Risk analysis and countermeasures. These are key factors in protecting your IntranetWare WAN. Sometimes, however, IntranetWare security isn't good enough. You need to develop appropriate countermeasures for *all* network threats, not just a few. After all, the '60s was a great decade but welcome to the '90s. This is the Information Age and your data is a valuable commodity.

Fortunately, IntranetWare has a dramatically improved security model for creating and maintaining your impenetrable network armor. This model allows us to perform risk analysis at five different levels. It also includes numerous countermeasures for dealing with "bad guys." Whatever you do, don't let this information fall into the wrong hands. Let's take a closer look.

ZEN

As you progress through this chapter, you'll find that "true security" is a mystery. What is it? How do you get it? Many times, it's not what it seems. You'll find it in the least likely places. As an example, let's rewind a few years to one of the greatest mysteries of our time — "Who shot Mr. Burns?" It all started with a simple question, from a key witness: "Who shot who in the what, now?"

Old Man

SMART LINK

Surf the Web with Homer, Marge, Bart, Lisa, and Maggie at http://www.foxinteractive.com.

IntranetWare Security Model

IntranetWare improves on earlier NetWare security models by adding supplemental front-end barriers for filtering unauthorized users. Once again, the same security goal applies:

Let the good guys in and keep the bad guys out!

As you can see in Figure 11.1, the IntranetWare security model consists of five different barriers. They are:

1 • Login/Password Authentication

2 • Login Restrictions

3 • NDS Security

4 • File System Access Rights

5 • Directory/File Attributes

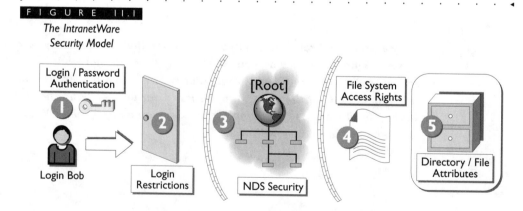

F I G U R E   II.I
The IntranetWare Security Model

As you can see, each layer creates an increasingly strong barrier against user access. Each time you pass through a door, you are greeted with an even stronger barrier. This works much the same way as the opening to the TV show *Get Smart*. Maxwell would have to travel through numerous barriers until he finally reached the telephone booth. After entering the correct code, he was allowed access to Control headquarters. Users pass through similar barriers on their way to the ultimate prize — data.

Let's take a quick look.

LAYER ONE — LOGIN/PASSWORD AUTHENTICATION

As you can see from Figure 11.1, it all starts with login/password authentication. Remember, users don't log into NetWare servers anymore — they log into the "Cloud." First, the user requests access by typing **LOGIN** followed by a valid username. Once this occurs, authentication begins. There are two phases:

▶ Initialization — The server and workstation authenticate the session with an encrypted key. You are required to enter a valid password to decrypt the key.

▶ Background — IntranetWare continues to attach the key to all messages to ensure data integrity. This process is known as *background authentication*. In addition, you can enhance background security with a related feature called *NCP packet signing*. We'll explore both features later in this chapter. In addition to authentication, IntranetWare accepts passwords up to 127 characters. This is a substantial improvement over earlier versions. The limit is decreased significantly, though, for Macintosh clients. Once you have been authenticated, IntranetWare matches you against a list of global and personal login restrictions. These restrictions allow for conditional access according to a variety of criteria. That's Layer One.

WHAT'S NEW

WHAT'S
NEW

This process occurs the same way for Client 32, except that it's a little more hidden behind GUI "windows."

LAYER TWO — LOGIN RESTRICTIONS

Once you provide a valid login name and password, you are authenticated. Congratulations! IntranetWare responds with conditional access and NDS rights take over. At this point, I stress the word *conditional* access. Permanent access is made possible by a variety of login restrictions. These login restrictions include:

▸ Account Restrictions — includes anything from "Account locked" to "Force periodic password changes"

▸ Password Restrictions — includes "Minimum password length" and "Force unique passwords"

▸ Station Restrictions — limits users to specific workstation node IDs

▸ Time Restrictions — determines when users can and cannot use the system

▸ Intruder Detection/Lockout — a global feature that detects incorrect password attempts and locks bad guys out

Each of these restrictions are configured by *you* using a variety of IntranetWare tools, including NWADMIN and NETADMIN. We'll learn all the details of how and why later in this chapter.

LAYER THREE — NDS SECURITY

Once you enter the "Cloud," your ability to access leaf and container objects is determined by a sophisticated NDS security structure. At the heart of NDS security is the Access Control List (ACL). The ACL is a property of every NDS object. It defines who can access the object (trustees) and what each trustee can do (rights). The ACL is divided into two types of rights:

▸ Object Rights — Defines an object's trustees and controls what the trustees can do with the object.

▸ Property Rights — Limits the trustees' access to only specific properties of the object.

Here's a great example (see Figure 11.2). Let's say the Group object Admin-Group has rights to the User object LEIA. Admin-Group has the Browse object right, which means that any member of the group can see LEIA and view information about her. But LEIA is shy. She wants to limit what the group can see (reasonable enough). She only wants them to see her last name, postal address, and telephone number. So, LEIA limits the group's rights by assigning the Read property right to only these three properties: Last Name, Postal Address, and Telephone Number. No sweat.

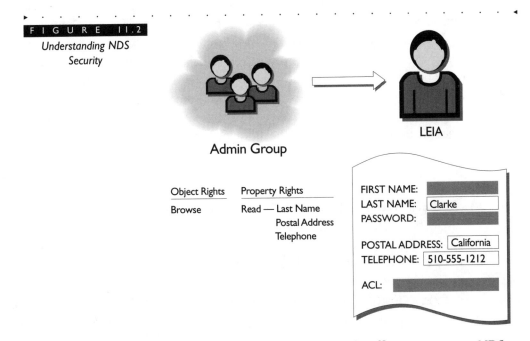

F I G U R E   11.2

Understanding NDS Security

Object and property rights are designed to provide efficient access to NDS objects without making it an administrative nightmare. You be the judge. Users can acquire object rights in a variety of ways, including trustee assignment, inheritance, and security equivalence. Property rights, on the other hand, are a bit trickier. Global property rights can be inherited, but rights to specific properties must be granted through a trustee assignment.

Trustee assignments occur when an object is given explicit access to any other object or its properties. These trustee assignments are administered by adding the user to a host object's ACL property. This is accomplished using the NWADMIN or NETADMIN utilities.

Inheritance is a little simpler. If rights are granted at the container level, they are inherited by all container and leaf objects within. This means that rights assigned to the [Root] object, for example, are inherited by every object in the NDS tree. Be very careful. Fortunately, IntranetWare includes an Inherited Rights Filter (IRF), which can be used to block inherited rights.

Finally, there's *security equivalence*. This means objects can absorb rights by being associated with other objects. Sometimes the associations are obvious, but most of the time, they're not. For this reason, you should only use security equivalences for temporary assignments, or not at all. In reality, users can inherit rights ancestrally from containers, groups, organizational roles, and [Public].

Regardless of how you acquire object and property rights, the concept of *effective rights* still applies. This means the actual rights you can exercise with a given object are the combination of explicit trustee assignments, inheritance, and the IRF. The mathematical product of this mess is known as *effective NDS rights* — "modern math." And that effectively ends our discussion of NDS security and moves us on to Layer Four of the IntranetWare security model — file system access rights.

LAYER FOUR — FILE SYSTEM ACCESS RIGHTS

Well, here we are. Congratulations! You've finally made it to IntranetWare Nirvana. You've passed through three very difficult barriers of network armor and the search is over — your files await you. Ah, but not so fast! Before you can access any files on the IntranetWare server, you must have the appropriate file system access rights. Once again, another barrier pops up to bite you. Following is a list of the eight rights that control access to IntranetWare files (they almost spell a word):

- ▶ W — Write: Grants the right to open and change the contents of files.

- ▶ (O) — Doesn't exist but is needed to spell a word.

- ▶ R — Read: Grants the right to open files in the directory and read their contents (or run applications).

- ▶ M — Modify: Grants the right to change the attributes or name of a file or directory.

▸ F — File Scan: Grants the right to see files and directories.

▸ A — Access Control: Grants the right to change trustee assignments and IRFs.

▸ C — Create: Grants the right to create new files and subdirectories.

▸ E — Erase: Grants the right to delete a directory, its files, and subdirectories.

▸ S — Supervisor: Grants all rights to a directory and the files and subdirectories below. This right cannot be blocked by the IRF.

Holy anatomical nematodes, Batman! That spells "WoRMFACES." It's not a pretty sight but certainly a name you will not forget. IntranetWare file system access rights are administered in much the same way as NDS object rights. They are granted with the help of trustee assignments, inheritance, and ancestral inheritance. In addition, file system rights are subject to the same rules as NDS effective rights. All in all, NDS and file server security parallel one another — one operating in the clouds (NDS) and one with its feet firmly planted on the ground (file system).

Well, that completes the majority of the IntranetWare security model. There's only one layer left, and it is seldom used — directory/file attributes. Let's take a closer look.

LAYER FIVE — DIRECTORY/FILE ATTRIBUTES

Directory and file attributes provide the final and most sophisticated layer of the IntranetWare security model. These attributes are rarely used, but provide a powerful tool for specific security solutions. If all else fails, you can always turn to attribute security to save the day.

IntranetWare supports three different types of attributes:

▸ Security Attributes — The main attribute category. Some attributes apply to both directories and files.

▸ Feature Attributes — Applies to three key features: backup, purging, and the Transactional Tracking System (TTS).

▸ Disk Management Attributes — For file compression, data migration, and block suballocation.

QUIZ

There's a hidden message in everything. The following coiled sentence contains a profound truth. Start at the correct letter, move to any touching letter, and you will find a mystery unfold.

V	E	O	E	T
E	U	Y	L	P
R	Y	S	L	A
H	T	R	O	M
I	N	A	A	D
G	E	X	R	T
E	C	O	E	I
P	O	T	F	D
T	H	W	O	L

(Q11-1)
(See Appendix C for all quiz answers.)

SMART LINK

You can learn even more about "IntranetWare Security" on the Web. Check it out in "NetWare 4 Product Information" at http://www.netware.com.

Well, there you have it. That's a brief snapshot of IntranetWare's five-layered security model. Now we'll take a much closer look at each of these layers and learn how they can be used to create your impenetrable network armor. Of course, if somebody should get lucky enough and break through your network armor, it would be nice to know what they're doing there. That's where IntranetWare auditing comes in. And, yes, we'll discuss it, too. But not yet. Now it's time to attack the first layer of IntranetWare security — login/password authentication.

REAL WORLD

In October 1967, a task force was assembled by the Department of Defense (DOD) to address computer security safeguards that would protect classified information and computer networks. The task force was formed primarily because networks were just beginning to make an impact on all the world's computers. Of course, they had no idea what they were in for the next 30 years. The DOD now explores security alternatives through the National Computer Security Center (NCSC). In December 1985, the DOD published a document affectionately known as "the Orange Book." Yes, I've seen it — it is orange. The document was entitled *The Department of Defense Trusted Computer System Evaluation Criteria* (TCSEC). The Orange Book was designed to provide security guidelines for both developers and administrators. The major goal of the document is "to encourage the computer industry to develop trusted computer systems and products making them widely available in the commercial marketplace." The book basically consists of a spectrum of evaluation criteria for differing levels of security. It lists basic requirements for very low and very high levels of security.

In order to be truly secure, your system must satisfy six fundamental requirements:

1 • It must have a clear and well-defined security policy enforced.

2 • All system elements must be associated with access control labels.

3 • All individuals accessing the system must be identified.

4 • Audit information must be selectively kept and protected so that all security actions can be traced.

5 • The computer system must contain hardware/software mechanisms that can be independently evaluated.

6 • The countermeasures that enforce these basic requirements must be continuously protected against tampering and/or unauthorized changes.

So, there you have it. Is your system truly secure? Well, in addition to these six requirements, the Orange Book includes evaluation criteria for four different divisions

(continued)

> **REAL WORLD** *(continued)*
>
> of security — A through D. Just like in school, *A* is good and *D* is bad. Working your way from the bottom, Division D is simply the bottom of the totem pole. This classification is reserved for those systems that have been evaluated, but have failed to meet the requirements for a higher evaluation class.
>
> Division C, on the other hand, provides security on a "need to know" basis. Division C security includes auditing and accountability. The Orange Book further classifies Division C into two classes — C-1 and C-2. Most of today's network operating systems, including IntranetWare and NT, vow to meet C-2 requirements at the very minimum (the Government requires it). Class C-2 is entitled "Controlled Access Protection." Systems in this class enforce a more finely grained discretionary control than C-1 systems. C-2 users are individually accountable for their actions through login procedures, auditing of security-related events, and resource isolation. The idea here is to permit or refuse access to any single file.
>
> The bottom line is that IntranetWare satisfies Class C-2 security through an integrated trust suite called NetWare Enhanced Security (NES). NetWare Enhanced Security is a distributed network operating system made up of three types of network components: servers, workstations, and network media.
>
> The server component of NES contains a Network Trusted Computing Base (NTCB) partition, which is used to enforce the security policies and protect data stored on the server. The Trusted Network Interpretation (TNI) describes a Network Trusted Computing Base (NTCB) as, "the totality of protection mechanisms within a network system — including hardware, firmware, and software — the combination of which is responsible for enforcing a security policy."
>
> For NetWare Enhanced Security, the NTCB is distributed among multiple heterogeneous server and workstation NTCB partitions. The server NTCB partition contains the trusted hardware, firmware, and software that implement the security policies enforced by the server component. Because untrusted software is not permitted on the server, the entire server is included in the server NTCB partition.
>
> Now that you understand the importance of NTCB, let's review the requirements for each of the three NES components:
>
> ▸ Servers — The server is evaluated as a Class C-2 IAD component, which means that it provides Identification and Authentication (I), Audit (A) and

Discretionary Access Control (D) functions within the enhanced security architecture. The architecture allows you to connect an arbitrary number of servers within your network. These servers must be evaluated as Class C-2 or higher security with respect to architecture, and may provide one or more of the IAD security functions. The architecture does not permit use of unevaluated servers such as NetWare 3.11 or NetWare 4.01.

▶ Workstations — The architecture permits an arbitrary number of single-user client workstations, potentially from different vendors. These products must be evaluated as Class C-2 or higher security with respect to architecture, and may provide none, some, or all of the IAD security functions. In particular, a diskless workstation might be evaluated as a Class C-2 "nil" component. This means that the workstation does not provide local enforcement of Identification and Authentication, Direct Access Control, or Auditing, but is capable of being securely used within the enhanced security network.

▶ NetWork media — Network media components are usually "nil" components, such as passive cabling.

You can compose a trusted Class C-2 network system by interconnecting an arbitrary number of IntranetWare servers, other servers, client workstations, and passive network cabling. To determine the ratings of server and client workstation components, ask the vendor for the Evaluated Products List (EPL) entry for the product.

SMART LINK

To learn more about IntranetWare security and Class C-2, check out the *NetWare Enhanced Security Administration* manual at http://www.novell.com/manuals.

Layer One — Login/Password Authentication

When you log into an IntranetWare server, the world changes. Suddenly you have access to a plethora of resources that weren't available before — printers, files, users, and e-mail. Whatever you do, don't take the login process for granted. It's a complex series of sophisticated communication steps between your client and the server.

As you'll see in the next two chapters, logging in involves ODI drivers, VLMs, context, and STARTNET.BAT. But the real goal of logging in is security. After all, it's the only way to differentiate between real users and "bad guys." Now let's take a closer look at how hard it is to get into a IntranetWare server.

GETTING IN

The first two layers of the IntranetWare security model are concerned with gaining access to the network — that is, "getting in." Once you're in, the bottom three layers take over. They control what you can do once you get there — access to NDS resources and the file system. As you can see in Figure 11.3, there's a lot going on during the login process. Also notice that there are three ways to be denied, and only two ways to be granted access to, the IntranetWare Cloud. This is because of authentication. Let's take a closer look at the flowchart in Figure 11.3.

FIGURE 11.3

Login Process Flowchart

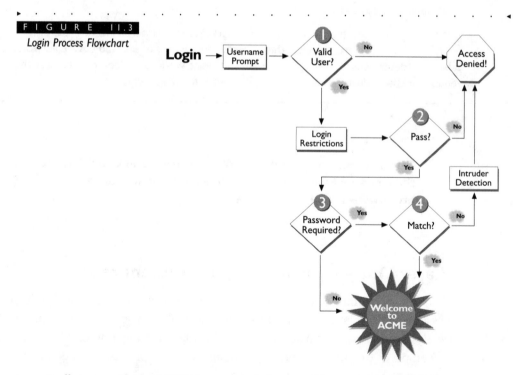

It all starts with the LOGIN command. IntranetWare responds with a username prompt. You'll need to provide your login name with complete NDS context. This is so that IntranetWare can match you against specific user properties in the NDS database. Once you enter a username, IntranetWare goes to the nearest Read/Write replica of your parent partition to verify that you exist. If you don't exist in the context specified, you'll be denied access and the following two error messages will be displayed:

```
LOGIN  -  4.12  -  895: The user does not exist in the
specified context.
```

```
LOGIN  -  4.12  -  130: Access has been denied and you have
been logged out.
```

If you do provide a valid username and context, the system continues to decision two — login restrictions. Using the information provided by the Read/Write replica, IntranetWare checks all your major login restrictions including time restrictions, station restrictions, and account lockout. If you try to log in from an unauthorized workstation or during the wrong time of day, access will be denied and the following error message appears:

```
LOGIN  -  4.12  - 860: You have tried to log in during an
unauthorized time period.
```

If you pass login restrictions, IntranetWare moves on to the final two decisions — passwords. First, it uses your NDS information to determine whether a password is required. If a password is not required, you are authenticated automatically and access is granted. Bad idea. If a password is required, you are prompted for it. Good idea. That brings us to the final login decision: Does the password you provided match the one in the NDS database? If not, access is denied, Intruder Detection is incremented, and the following brief error message appears:

```
LOGIN  -  4.12  -  100: Access has been denied.
```

SMART LINK

For more detail on IntranetWare login error codes, consult the on-line documentation at http://www.novell.com/manuals.

If you provide the correct password, IntranetWare uses it to decrypt the private authentication key. This completes the initialization phase of login authentication and access is granted. We'll discuss the two phases of authentication in just a moment.

In summary, the IntranetWare login process consists of four decisions:

1 • Are you using a valid username?

2 • Do you pass login restrictions?

3 • Is a password required?

4 • Does your password match?

If all of these conditions are met, access is granted. As you can see in Figure 11.3, there are three ways to be denied access — you type an invalid username, you don't pass login restrictions, or you provide the incorrect password. Now you should have a new appreciation for all the work that's involved when you type that one magic word: **LOGIN**.

WHAT'S NEW

WHAT'S NEW

This process is identical for Client 32, but the details are hidden behind GUI "windows."

ZEN

"Nancy Drew says that all you need to solve a mystery is an inquisitive temperment and two good friends."

Lisa Simpson

INITIAL AUTHENTICATION

From a security standpoint, the entire login process points to one goal — authentication. This is the only way you can gain access to a IntranetWare network. Authentication involves the username, the password, the client, NDS, and the IntranetWare server. There sure are a lot of cooks in the kitchen. Once you've been initially authenticated, IntranetWare activates a secondary authentication scheme — background authentication. Background authentication keeps the user validated throughout the current session. An additional feature, called *NCP packet signing*, validates *every* user packet as it's sent from the workstation to the server. This also applies to the active session only. We'll take a look at background authentication and NCP packet signing in just a moment.

In both cases, IntranetWare authentication guarantees the following:

▶ Only the purported sender built the message.

▶ The message came from the workstation where the authentication data was created.

▶ The message pertains to the current session.

▶ The message contains no information counterfeited from another session.

▶ The message has not been tampered with or corrupted.

▶ You are who you say you are.

▶ You're doing what you say you're doing.

IntranetWare authentication is based on the RSA (Rivest Shamir and Adleman) scheme. This is a public key encryption algorithm that is extremely difficult to break. In addition to RSA, authentication uses a independent private key algorithm as well. One key is public (which means that all users on the network can have access to it) while the other is kept private (which means only a designated user knows about it). If a message is encrypted with a private key, it can be decrypted with a public key and vice versa. As you can see in Figure 11.4, initial authentication consists of four sophisticated steps. Let's take a closer look.

Step One: Client Requests Authentication

IntranetWare authentication requires Client 32 or the NetWare DOS Requester. It uses a special file to control the encryption and decryption of public and private keys. In Step One, Admin logs in by providing his or her full NDS context. The client requests authentication from the IntranetWare server. The request is then handled by a special program within the core OS — Authentication Services.

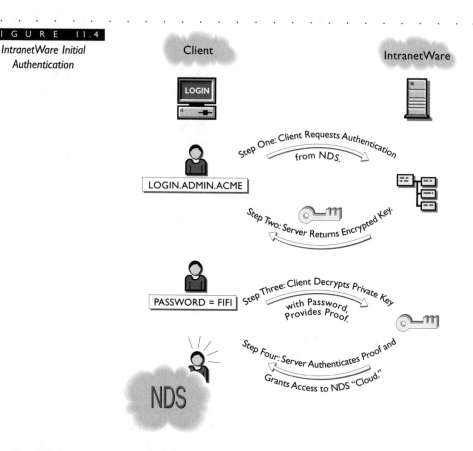

Step Two: Server Returns Encrypted Key

Once the authentication request has been accepted, IntranetWare matches the user information with an encrypted private key. This private key can only be decrypted by the user password. That's Step Three.

Step Three: Client Decrypts Private Key

In Step Three, the user provides a valid password to decrypt the private key. The password is then erased from memory to prevent a hacker from obtaining it illegally. This is where the fun begins. With the private key, the client creates an *authenticator*. This credential contains information identifying the user's complete name, the workstation's address, and a validity period (the duration of time the authenticator is valid). In addition, there are other undocumented values that make up the authenticator.

The client then creates an encryption called a *signature* using the authenticator and private key. The private key is then removed from memory while the authenticator and signature remain in workstation RAM throughout the login session. The signature is used for background authentication and validates all packets sent during this session.

Finally, the client requests authentication using a *proof*. The proof is constructed from the signature, the request for authentication, and a random-generated number. It is further encrypted by the user's private key. The proof is sent across the WAN instead of the signature to prevent anyone from illegally obtaining the valuable signature. An internal client random number generator ensures that each message sent from this workstation includes a different proof. The proof also assures IntranetWare that the message has not been modified. This is the goal of background authentication and NCP packet signing.

Step Four: Server Authenticates Proof and Grants Access

During the final step, authentication services validates the proof as an authentic construct of the authenticator, the private key, and the message (request for authentication). Once the proof has been validated, the user is granted conditional access to the NDS Cloud. Permanent access is granted once you successfully pass Layer Two of the NetWare security model — login restrictions.

Table 11.1 summarizes the key concepts in initial authentication. Here's a madcap recap: Admin logs in by providing his or her complete name. The client (RSA.VLM) requests authentication from the server (authentication services). The server returns an encrypted private key. Admin enters a valid password and the private key is decrypted. The client then creates an authenticator with the private key, which includes Admin's complete name, the workstation address, a validity period, and other undocumented values. Next, the client creates a signature by encrypting the authenticator with the private key. Finally, a proof is constructed from the signature, private key, and a random number for traveling over the WAN. The proof is sent to authentication services which validate it and grant Admin access to the NDS Cloud. All of this magic occurs in less than a second. Wow!

	AUTHENTICATION ELEMENT	DESCRIPTION
TABLE 11.1 *Understanding IntranetWare Authentication*	Client	Participates in initial authentication on behalf of the user. Controlled by special RSA VLM.
	Authentication Services	Participates in initial authentication on behalf of the server. Consists of features built into the core IntranetWare OS.
	Username	Initiates initial authentication through login request. Also is used by the server in combination with the user password to create an encrypted private key.
	Encrypted Private Key	A specific key for each user, which can be decrypted only with the valid password.
	RSA Public Key	Used by authentication services to validate user information.
	Password	Entered by the user to decrypt the private key. Once this occurs, the password is removed from workstation RAM for security purposes.
	Authenticator	A special credential created by the client with user- and session-specific information including the user's complete name, the workstation address, a validity period, and other undocumented values.
	Signature	A background authentication credential created by a combination of the authenticator and encrypted private key. The signature is used to validate all packets sent during this session. It is also the foundation of the proof.
	Proof	A temporary encryption created for traveling over the WAN. It is constructed from the signature, a message, the user's private key, and a randomly generated number. The random number generator ensures that each message contains a unique proof.

THE BRAIN

If you feel inspired to delve more deeply into the mysteries of NDS authentication, check out the AppNote entitled "Understanding the Role of Identification and Authentication in NetWare 4" in the October 1994 issue of Novell Application Notes, or surf to http://www.novell.com/manuals.

Once you have been initially authenticated, the second phase begins — background authentication. In this phase, the signature and proof are used to continually authenticate all packets during the current session. Let's take a closer look.

BACKGROUND AUTHENTICATION

Welcome to the second phase of IntranetWare incognito. Background authentication and NCP packet signing are designed to protect the WAN from experienced hackers who forge data packets or pose as unauthenticated clients. In earlier versions of NetWare, hackers could use protocol analyzers to capture server requests and forge their own instructions. For example, I could request something simple like login as Guest, then capture the packet and add something harmful like, "While you're at it, please make me Supervisor Equivalent." This is a bad thing. NCP packet signing solved this problem by requiring a unique signature on all messages. The signature is represented as a *unique proof*, which is the combination of the workstation signature and a random number. If a message doesn't have the correct proof attached, it is discarded. When this occurs, an error message is sent to the error log, the affected workstation, and the server console. The alert message contains the login name and the station address of the invalid client.

NCP packet signing occurs at both the workstation and the server. IntranetWare contains a default level of packet signing — the client signs only if the server requests it and the server signs only if the client requests it. Therefore, signing doesn't occur. You can customize NCP packet signing by using the SET server console command and NET.CFG client configuration file. Here's how it works:

▶ At the server — Use the following SET command:

SET NCP PACKET SIGNATURE OPTION=*n*

- ► At the workstation — Add the following statement to the NETWARE DOS REQUESTER section of NET.CFG:

SIGNATURE LEVEL=n

In both cases, n represents a signature level from zero to three: 0 deactivates NCP packet signing and 3 creates the highest level of protection available. Table 11.2 shows some common client-server combinations (this is not an exhaustive list). Notice what happens when either the client or server uses packet signing levels of 0 and 3. This can cause havoc on the WAN. Consider activating minimal packet signing — client (1) and server (2).

Finally, packet signing does have a cost. This background protection scheme causes a slight decrease in server performance because of the overhead involved. Not only is the header of each packet marginally larger, but the workstations perform additional processing for each packet transmitted. The server must also perform processing to validate each signed packet. That's okay; your security is worth it.

You've been authenticated. How does it feel? Isn't it nice to know that your life has a purpose? We all need a little validation. But we're not finished yet. Remember, we just have *conditional* access to the WAN. In order to become a permanent resident of the NDS Cloud, we must successfully pass through the second layer of the IntranetWare security model — login restrictions. Login restrictions offer much more administrative flexibility because you can limit users according to a large number of criteria including time of day, workstation, intruder detection, and so on. Let's get restricted.

REAL WORLD

NCP packet signing and background authentication recently became necessary because of the overzealous activities of a group of students at Lieden University in the Netherlands. These mischievous students are considered "the Netherlands hackers." This means they expose security loopholes as a means of plugging them. A few years ago, they discovered a simple piggyback intrusion mechanism for NetWare 2.2 and 3.11 servers. The NCP packet signing feature was implemented in NetWare 3.12 and all future versions as a way of slamming this backdoor. Way to go team.

TABLE 11.2 *Understanding NCP Packet Signing Options*	CLIENT LEVEL	SERVER LEVEL	DESCRIPTION
	0	3	The client does not sign packets and the server requires it; therefore, the workstation cannot log into this server.
	3	0	Packet signing is required by the workstation, but the server does not support it. Workstations with this level will not communicate with unsigning servers because they consider them to be unsecure.
	1	1	This is the default. The client signs only if the server requests it, and the server signs if the client requests it. Therefore, signing doesn't occur.
	1	2	Client signs only if the server requests it and the server does request packet signing. This is the minimal setting for activating background authentication.
	3	3	Client always signs and requires server to sign. Server always signs and requires clients to sign. Therefore, everyone signs and all is well. This is the maximum level of packet signature protection.

Layer Two — Login Restrictions

Login restrictions further scrutinize WAN access by matching the login name with a variety of NDS qualifications:

- ▸ Is this user authorized to log in during this time period?

- ▸ Is this user authorized to log in from this particular workstation?

- ▸ Is this user authorized to log in on this date?

- ▸ Will this user ever get the password right?

- ▸ Will this user ever change the password?

▸ Who shot Mr. Burns?

▸ What is the meaning of life?

The first layer of IntranetWare security (login authentication) restricts *invalid* users. Login restrictions, on the other hand, restrict *valid* users. At this point, IntranetWare assumes a valid username has been provided and authentication can probably be guaranteed.

As you can see in Figure 11.5, NDS supports a variety of login restriction properties. A quick scan of the right side of Figure 11.5 shows four obvious user restrictions — Login, Password, Login Time, and Network Address. In addition, IntranetWare supports a password tracking feature called Intruder Detection/Lockout. This security feature tracks unauthorized login attempts and automatically locks accounts when the attempts exceed a given bad login threshold count. The user account can only be unlocked by an administrator.

F I G U R E   11.5

Login Restrictions for Maid Marion

In summary, IntranetWare login restrictions fall into five different categories:

▸ Account Restrictions

▸ Password Restrictions

► Time Restrictions

► Station Restrictions

► Intruder Detection/Lockout

Account Restrictions only apply to specific users. Maid Marion, for example, can have her account expired, concurrent connections limited, or access disabled altogether. *Password Restrictions* impact login authentication. In this screen, we can define a variety of Maid Marion's password settings, including allowing her to change her password, requiring a minimum password length, forcing periodic password changes, requiring unique passwords, and limiting grace logins. Remember, the password is used by the client to decrypt the authentication private key.

The next option is *Time Restrictions*. These limitations simply apply to when users can be connected to NDS. Time restrictions are not login restrictions per se; they are "connection restrictions." This means users cannot log in or be connected to the tree during inactive time periods.

Similarly, *Station Restrictions* do not allow users to log in or attach from unauthorized stations. NWADMIN calls this "Network Address Restrictions" because it allows you to limit user access to a specific protocol, LAN address, or node ID.

Finally, *Intruder Detection/Lockout* is a global feature that is activated at the container level. All objects within the container are tracked according to a variety of parameters including Incorrect Login Attempts, Intruder Attempt Reset Interval, and Account Lockout. If, for example, Maid Marion logs in with her correct context and an incorrect password seven times within an hour, intruder lockout activates. Once her account has been locked, she has two options — wait the Intruder Lockout Reset Interval or have an administrator unlock her account. This feature allows you to sleep better at night knowing that IntranetWare is doing all it can to keep intruders out of your WAN.

SMART LINK

For more detail on IntranetWare Login Restriction parameters, consult the on-line documentation at http://www.novell.com/manuals.

All of these restrictions (except Intruder Detection/Lockout) are activated at the user level. This means you have to set them for each individual user — too much work. Fortunately, IntranetWare includes a User Template object for global configurations. If, for example, you'd like to set a minimum password length for all users in the WHITE container, you could create a User Template object with the correct settings. Then all users will dynamically inherit the properties of the User Template. This applies to all properties, not just login restrictions. Figure 11.6 shows a sample User Template configuration screen for the WHITE container. Notice all the page buttons listed on the right-hand side. I'm a big believer in the theory "Less work and more play makes life worth living." And the User Template object is right up my alley. Use it or lose it.

User Template Saves the Day!

![NetWare Administrator screen showing Template: WHITE-UT identification page with fields for Name, Other name, Title, Description, Location, Department, Telephone, Fax number, and page buttons on the right: Identification, Environment, Login Restrictions, Password Restrictions, Login Time Restrictions, Network Address Restriction, Login Script, Group Membership, Security Equal To, Trustees Of New Object.]

REAL WORLD

The User Template object maintains a link with the User object created with it. This is a dynamic link — much different from previous versions of NetWare. Also, this new wonder includes a global change button called "Details on Multiple Users." Very cool!

ZEN

"And when he tried to steal our sunlight, he crossed over that line between everyday villainy and cartoonish super-villainy."

Mr. Wayland Smithers

Now let's take a much closer look at each of the five IntranetWare login restrictions, starting with account restrictions.

ACCOUNT RESTRICTIONS

IntranetWare account restrictions provide a method for controlling and restricting user access to the NDS tree. Account restrictions can be found in the Login Restrictions screen of NWADMIN (see Figure 11.7). As you can see, there are four main options:

- ▶ Account Disabled

- ▶ Account Has Expiration Date

- ▶ Limit Concurrent Connections

- ▶ Last Login

Account Disabled

This option is pretty self explanatory. The account is either disabled or not. This option is not related to Intruder Detection/Lockout. It is possible for an account to be locked but not disabled. In both cases, the effect is the same — the user can't log in. In order to disable a IntranetWare account, you have two choices — manually check this box or use an expiration date.

F I G U R E   II.7
Account Restrictions in
NWADMIN

NetWare Administrator - [[Root] [ACME_TREE]]

User : MMarion

Login Restrictions

☐ Account disabled
☑ Account has expiration date
Expiration date and time:
01 /01 /00   12 :01 :00 AM

☑ Limit concurrent connections
Maximum connections: 3

Last login: 05/18/98 10:39:36 am

Identification
Environment
Login Restrictions
Password Restrictions
Login Time Restrictions
Network Address Restriction
Print Job Configuration
Login Script
Intruder Lockout
Rights to Files and Directories

OK   Cancel   Page Options...   Help

Tree: ACME_TREE   Admin.ACME   Selected: 1   Subordinates: 0

REAL WORLD

Disabling an account will cause any connections in use by that account to be terminated within 30 minutes and will prevent future tree logins from that account. However, it does not prevent anyone who is already logged in from authenticating to another server. Therefore, the only way to force a user off the network immediately is to delete the user's NDS object. Once this change has propogated throughout the tree, the user is blocked from authenticating to *any* server!

Account Has Expiration Date

This option is a useful tool for temporary employees or students in an academic environment. It allows you to lock an account after a specific date. As you can see in Figure 11.7, the default is inactive. If you check the Account Disabled box, NOW appears as the default date and time. This means as soon as you exit NWADMIN, Maid Marion's account will be disabled. Be sure to increase the value before you leave. In Figure 11.7, Maid Marion's expiration parameters have been set to just before midnight on January 1, 2000. At this point, she will either be gone or celebrating the success of ACME.

Limit Concurrent Connections

Let's face it, users are nomadic. They like to migrate throughout the WAN and log in from multiple workstations. You can limit a user's concurrent connections by changing the inactive parameters in Figure 11.7 to something greater than zero. As you can see, an ideal setting is three concurrent connections. This means that Maid Marion can only log in from three workstations simultaneously. That's plenty. This account restriction works in conjunction with station restrictions. You can enhance a user's concurrent connection limitation by combining it with a specific physical workstation address. In this case, Maid Marion can only log in from three specific machines simultaneously.

Last Login

The Last Login parameter allows users to track activity on their login account. You should train users to periodically check this parameter for intruder logins. If, for example, Maid Marion was gone for a week, but saw that the last login was three days ago, she would have reason to believe an intruder had used her account.

That does it for login restrictions. Now let's take a closer look at password restrictions.

PASSWORD RESTRICTIONS

The next set of login restrictions properties deal with passwords. As you can see in Figure 11.8, there are five main options:

- Allow User to Change Password

- Require a Password

- Force Periodic Password Changes

- Require Unique Passwords

- Limit Grace Logins

Password restrictions directly impact login authentication. As we learned earlier in Figure 11.3, IntranetWare access can be granted in one of two ways — by providing the correct password (if one is needed) or automatically (if no password is required). Requiring a password is absolutely mandatory. Otherwise, authentication is crippled. Once you require a password, the question remains, "Who manages it?" If you place the burden of password management on the user, the other four password restriction parameters become important. Let's take a closer look

Allow User to Change Password

If you allow users to change their passwords, you're opening a can of worms. On the one hand, it shifts the burden of password management from you to them — this is a good thing. On the other hand, it allows them to mess around with an important authentication parameter — this is a bad thing. Most annoying user complaints deal with password management and printing. Well, one out of two ain't bad. If you don't allow users to change their passwords, all the work falls on you. It's your call — a balance between security and practicality.

Require a Password

By default, IntranetWare does not require a password — this is bad. This should be the very first parameter that you change when creating user accounts.

If you activate Require a Password and Force Periodic Password Changes, the system will ask for a password the very first time users log in. Once you activate the Required Password parameter, it's a good idea to set a minimum password length of more than five characters (the default). There are many password hacking routines that can guess a five-character password in less than 20 minutes. On the other hand, you want a password length that doesn't intimidate fragile users. Consider that most users can't easily remember strings in excess of seven to ten characters. The last thing you want to do is force large passwords so that users have to write them down on a piece of paper and tape them to the front of their monitors. IntranetWare supports passwords up to 127 characters in length. It also supports any alphanumeric and ASCII characters. Consider creating passwords that join two unrelated words with a punctuation mark such as:

▸ DOOR!GROUND

▸ SHOE;QUARK

▸ LATCH PURPLE

Note the last example did not use a space — it used a null character (Alt+255). Funny, it looks like a space — that's the whole point. Intruders will assume it's a space. Also, it's even trickier when used in succession at the end of a password or username. I bet you can't tell there are seven successive null characters at the end of the second example. Once you've required a password, all the other restrictions light up.

Force Periodic Password Changes

Once a password has been required and a minimum password length of seven characters has been set, you should explore using the Force Periodic Password Changes restriction. This parameter forces users to change their passwords at periodic intervals. If you activate the option, NetWare asks you to input the days between forced changes. The default is 40 days. This is a little short and can become a nuisance very quickly. Remember, users love to complain about password problems. A periodic password interval of 90 days seems to be optimal.

Password expiration seems to be a touchy topic for users and administrators alike. We want the interval to be short for better security, and they want the interval to be long for less interference. Either way, someone has to track it. You can train your users to check NWADMIN periodically and view the Date Password

Expires property within Password Restrictions. This will tell them exactly on what date and at what time their password will expire. Once the password interval has expired, the user is required to change his or her password. This is where grace logins come in. We'll talk about them in just a second.

REAL WORLD

Many times password expiration and grace logins cause unneeded friction between CNEs and users, especially when users abuse the privilege and CNEs ultimately have to change the passwords anyway. Consider making password expiration a big "event." Use the PASSWORD_EXPIRES login script identifier variable to count down the number of days until password expiration (see Chapter 12). Then when the day arrives, throw a party, bring in balloons and cake, and have everyone change their passwords at once. Turning this event into a party makes password transition every 90 days fun and unobtrusive. It's also a great excuse to have four parties a year.

Require Unique Passwords

The Require Unique Passwords restriction works in conjunction with forcing periodic password changes. When the periodic password interval expires and the user must change his or her password, unique passwords forces him or her to enter a new *different* value. If you're going to endure the effort of forcing periodic password changes, do yourself a favor and make them unique. It doesn't make sense to have users change their passwords every 90 days if they're going to use the same one. IntranetWare only tracks the last 20 passwords. Don't let your users learn this. They will create numerical intervals such as FIFI1, FIFI2, FIFI3, and so on. Also, I've seen users change their passwords 20 times in succession so they can reuse the original ones. To solve this problem, IntranetWare requires at least 24 hours between password changes. Perpetuate the myth that IntranetWare keeps track of all passwords forever.

Limit Grace Logins

When the periodic password interval has expired, IntranetWare responds with the following statement during login:

```
Your password has expired. Would you like to change it now?
```

This provides users with an opportunity to change their passwords right away. If they do not, the system will lock their accounts. The problem with this message is the words "Would you like." It should say something like, "You better change your password now or your computer will explode." Unfortunately, this message is not configurable. So, many users see it as a choice and decide to move on using their existing passwords. This is where *grace logins* come in. Grace logins allow the users to log in without changing their passwords. This is a temporary situation because even grace logins expire. As you can see in Figure 11.8, we're giving Maid Marion six grace logins. This means she can log in six times without changing her password. But then her account will be locked. Once again, encourage your users not to rely on grace logins. There's a convenient Change Password button on the Password Restrictions screen for user access. Otherwise, they can use the SETPASS command at the NetWare prompt.

QUIZ

Even numbers have a certain mystery. Try to find the five-digit number, no zeros, in which the first digit is the sum of the last two digits, the second digit is twice the first digit and three times the fourth digit, and the total of all five digits is 16.

Hmmm.

(Q11-2)

SMART LINK

For more information on IntranetWare passwords, surf to the Novell Knowledgebase at http://support.novell.com/search/.

This completes our discussion of password restrictions. Aren't they fun? As you can see, there's much more to IntranetWare passwords than meets the eye. Remember, this is the foundation of our login authentication strategy. Don't underestimate the importance of passwords. Use them or suffer the consequences.

TIME RESTRICTIONS

The next two login restrictions deal with *when* and *where* you get to log in. Time restrictions determine *when*. How many of you have suffered from the Curious Custodial Syndrome (CCS)? Let's see a show of hands. Ah, just as I thought — almost all of you. CCS is a problem that afflicts most of today's modern businesses. It's caused by the simple fact that the network stays up 24 hours a day and you don't. Since nighttime janitors have access to your equipment, they can easily hack your networks. One simple solution is time restrictions. Deactivate the network after 9:00 at night and before 6:00 in the morning. This way, no matter how curious the custodial staff is, they can't access the network after hours.

Each square in Figure 11.9 represents a 30-minute interval. The shaded area represents inactive time periods. The white area shows that users can log in any time between 6:00 a.m. and 9:00 p.m. Time restrictions go beyond login restrictions and become connection restrictions. Not only can they not log in, but they can't be connected. If Maid Marion is using the network at 8:55 p.m., she will receive a message:

```
Time expires in five minutes. Please logout.
```

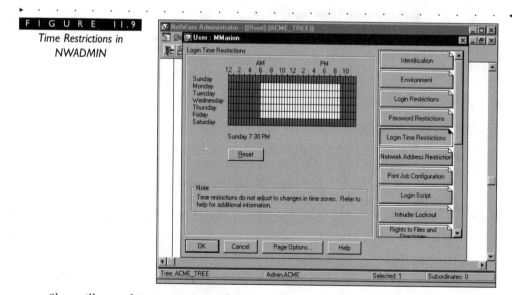

She will get this message at five- and one-minute intervals. When a time restriction is encountered and the user connection is cleared, the system does not perform a proper logout. The system simply *clears* the connections without saving the file. This is a very serious problem. Clearing Maid Marion's connection could result in bindery corruption, hardware failure, or even worse, data loss. When you see a five-minute or one-minute message, be sure to pay attention and log out.

Here are some common time restriction strategies:

▶ Restrict After Hours — ACME doesn't expect employees to work between the hours of 9:00 p.m. and 6:00 a.m. They want to avoid burnout. Setting a time restriction during this period protects them from curious custodians.

▶ Restrict Weekends — Also to avoid burnout, ACME restricts anybody from accessing the network during the weekend. Remember, all work and no play . . . .

▶ Activate Backup Periods — One down side of time restrictions is that it doesn't allow a window for backup. If you're backing up the system late at night, you'll have to activate a backup time window. Test your backup to determine how long it takes and give the system a large enough window — let's say from 11:00 p.m. till 1:00 a.m.

▶ Restrict Specific Users — Remember, time restrictions are a user configuration. You can restrict everybody in a container using the User Template object or specific users individually. If temporary users, for example, only work on Tuesdays and Thursdays, consider deactivating their accounts on other days.

Don't go crazy with time restrictions. Intelligent time restrictions increase network security, but careless time restrictions can significantly hinder user productivity. You want to give users time to work but not leave the network susceptible to CCS.

STATION RESTRICTIONS

Station Restrictions are the other half of the when/where dynamic duo. They deal with *where*. Now that we've solved our CCS problem, another one will arise — Nomadic User Syndrome (NUS). NUS hinders network security for a variety of reasons. First, nomadic users take up multiple network connections and block access to other users. Secondly, NUS implies that users are logging in from workstations other than their own. And, finally, NUS impairs your ability to limit intruders from accessing physical workstations.

Station restrictions solve NUS. They allow you to virtually chain users to specific machines. Instead of restricting them with passwords, disk restrictions, or time slots, you're physically restricting the workstation from which they can log in. As you can see in Figure 11.10, IntranetWare station restrictions go a few steps farther:

▸ Protocol Restrictions

▸ Network Address Restrictions

▸ Node Restrictions

FIGURE 11.10

Getting to Know Station Restrictions

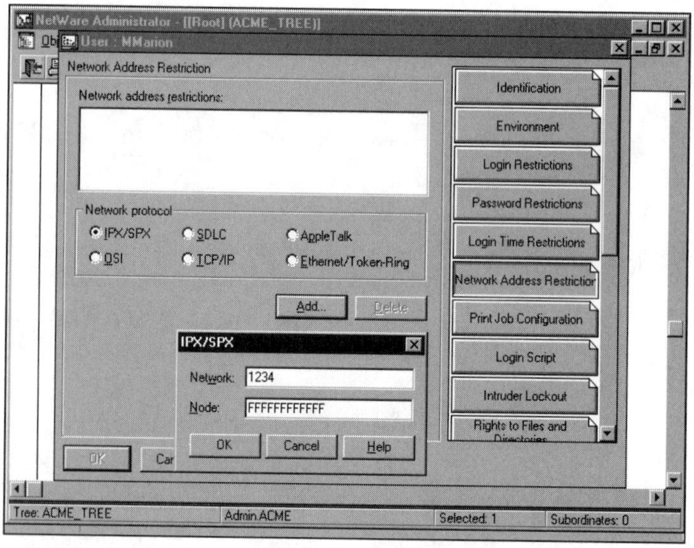

First you pick a protocol. IntranetWare defaults to the IPX/SPX protocol. Other options include OSI, SDLC, TCP/IP, AppleTalk, and Ethernet/Token Ring. Each protocol treats network address restrictions differently. The IPX/SPX address format consists of an 8-digit external network address and 12-digit hexadecimal node ID. The network address identifies an external LAN segment, while the node ID identifies a specific workstation. Maid Marion, for example, is restricted to any workstation (FFFFFFFFFFFF) on the 1234 LAN. We could further refine her restriction by listing one or more physical node IDs on the 1234 LAN.

The TCP/IP address format expresses logical and physical IDs in the dotted-dash decimal notation. In this case, you can also restrict to all workstations on a logical network or a specific physical machine. Finally, the Ethernet/Token Ring address format uses a SAP (Service Access Point) address, block ID, and PU ID (physical unit). Once again, these values specify all stations on a LAN segment or a specific workstation.

Unfortunately, NWADMIN doesn't dynamically interrogate the LAN to determine addresses for you. You must use other IntranetWare or third-party utilities to gain network and node ID information. As a word of warning, don't go hogwild with station restrictions. Use it only if you suffer from NUS. Like other login restrictions, if it's abused or mishandled, station restrictions can significantly impede user productivity. What happens, for example, when Maid Marion travels to another location? Or, what if we restrict her to one workstation and the machine goes down? These are all important considerations. Although station restrictions are a useful security tool, they can also be detrimental to user relationships.

This completes our discussion of what, when, and where. Now only one question remains: "Who?"

ZEN

"If you've ever handled a penny, the government's got your DNA. Why do you think they keep them in circulation?"

Scientist Smith

INTRUDER DETECTION/LOCKOUT

Welcome to Whoville. This is not so much a restriction as it is a security tracking feature. Intruder Detection/Lockout tracks invalid login attempts by monitoring users who try to log in without correct passwords. As you recall from Figure 11.3, this feature increments every time a valid user provides an incorrect password. It also leads directly to Access Denied! Once Intruder Detection has reached a threshold number of attempts, the account is locked completely.

There's one very important thing you need to know about this final login restriction — it's a container-based configuration. All the previous restrictions have been user-based. As you can see in Figure 11.11, intruder detection is activated at the Organization or Organizational Unit level. Once an account has been locked, it must be reactivated at the user level. There are two main configuration elements:

▸ Intruder Detection Limits

▸ Lock Account after Detection

Once Intruder Detection/Lockout has been activated at the container level, all users in that container are tracked. Let's take a closer look.

Intruder Detection Limits

Intruder Detection is turned off by default. In order to activate it, you simply click on the Detect Intruders box. Once you activate Intruder Detection, it begins tracking incorrect login attempts. This parameter is set to seven by default. As soon as the incrementing number exceeds the threshold, account lockout occurs. Finally, the Intruder Attempt Reset Interval is a window of opportunity, so to speak. The system uses it to increment the incorrect login attempts. It is set to 30 minutes by default.

Here's how it works. Assume the Incorrect Login Attempts parameter is set to 7 and Intruder Attempt Reset Interval is set to 1 day, 12 hours (see Figure 11.11). The system will track all incorrect login activity and lock the user account if the number of incorrect login attempts exceeds 7 in the 36-hour window. Pretty simple, huh? Now let's take a look at what happens once Intruder Detection is activated.

Lock Account After Detection

This is the second half of Intruder Detection/Lockout. After all, the feature wouldn't be much good if you didn't punish the intruder for entering the wrong password. When you activate the Lock Account After Detection parameter, NetWare asks for an Intruder Lockout Reset Interval. By default, this value is set to 15 minutes. Doesn't make much sense, does it? This invites the hacker to come back 15 minutes later and try all over again. Typically, a value equal to or exceeding the Intruder Attempt Reset Interval is adequate. As you can see in Figure 11.11, we're locking the account for two days, giving you enough time to track down the intruder.

So, what happens to the user when the account is locked? As you can see in Figure 11.12, IntranetWare tracks account lockout at the user level. The Intruder Lockout screen provides three important pieces of information:

- ▶ *Incorrect Login Count* — A dynamic parameter that tells the user how many incorrect login attempts have been detected during this reset interval. If the account is locked, the incorrect login count should equal the lockout threshold.

- ▶ *Account Reset Time* — Informs the user how much time is remaining before the account is unlocked automatically.

- ▶ *Last Intruder Address* — Shows the network and node address of the workstation that attempted the last incorrect login. This parameter provides you with valuable information regardless of whether the account is locked. This is pretty undeniable evidence that someone tried to hack this account from a specific workstation. You don't have to worry about disputed evidence or planted gloves.

So, who's going to unlock Maid Marion's account? You! Only Admin or distributed administrators can unlock accounts that have been locked by the Intruder
Detection feature. But what about Admin? After all, Admin is the most commonly hacked account — with good reason. If you don't have an Admin-equivalent
user to unlock the Admin account, consider using ENABLE LOGIN at the file
server console. It's always nice to have a back door.

There you have it. This completes our discussion of Intruder Detection/Lockout
and login restrictions in general.

Congratulations, you are in! You've successfully navigated the first two layers of the
IntranetWare security model — login/password authentication and login restrictions.

In login/password authentication, we discussed the first two phases of WAN access —
initial authentication and background authentication. Initial authentication is a sophisticated four-step process that develops a user-specific, session-specific signature and proof.
This signature is then used by background authentication to validate incoming workstation packets. Once you've been authenticated, IntranetWare grants you conditional access
to the WAN. Permanent access relies on login restrictions.

Login restrictions are the second layer of the IntranetWare security model. They
define what, when, where, and who gets access to the system. "What" is account
and password restrictions, "when" is time restrictions, "where" is station restrictions, and "who" is Intruder Detection/Lockout.

IntranetWare has never been more secure. And we haven't even accessed any resources yet. The first two layers get us in, but what we do inside the "Cloud" relies on NDS and file system security. How secure do you feel now?

Layer Three — NDS Security

Welcome to the "Cloud"!

The NDS park is a great place to hang out. It has trees, swings for the kiddies, a bike trail, and external entities. Feel free to look around. Browse all day if you'd like. But don't touch anything. You haven't been secured yet.

Access to the tree is one thing; being able to do anything there is another. Until you've been granted sufficient NDS access rights, all the pretty objects are useless to you. No trees, no swings, no bike paths. Once you enter the NDS park, your ability to access leaf and container objects is determined by a sophisticated NDS security structure. At the heart of NDS security is the Access Control List (ACL). The ACL is a property of every NDS object. It defines who can access the object (trustees) and what each trustee can do with it (access rights).

This strategy poses two important questions:

- ▸ What rights do I need to do stuff?

- ▸ How do I get these rights?

These are good questions. Fortunately, I have some simple answers. First, NDS supports two types of access rights — object and property. *Object rights* define an object's trustees and control what they can do with the object. *Property rights*, on the other hand, further refine NDS security by limiting access to only specific properties of the object. Fortunately, these rights are fairly self-explanatory. Browse, for instance, allows you to see an object. Hmmmm, no "brain drain" there.

So, that leaves us with an answer to the second question: "How do I get these rights?" It's a simple three-step process:

- ▸ *Step One:* Assigning Trustee Rights — Someone gives you specific rights to specific objects through trustee assignments, inheritance, and/or security equivalence.

▸ *Step Two:* Filtering IRF Rights — Someone else can filter certain rights if they want to.

▸ *Step Three:* Calculating Effective Rights — The result is effective rights, which define what you can actually do to the object.

As easy as A-B-C. And you thought NDS security was going to be hard — nope. It can get weird, though. As I'm sure you can imagine, the potential combination of object/property rights can be staggering — almost infinite. So, you're going to want to try to keep it under control. In this section, we'll talk about default NDS rights and how you can use the simple three-step method for limiting potential loopholes. Finally, we'll talk about NDS administration and explore Admin, distributed administrators, and "special" cases. So, without any further ado, let's get on with the show — starting with NDS access rights.

QUIZ

While establishing the credibility of Mr. Smithers' testimony, we learned a few interesting things about him. He prefers pneumonia to a cold. He likes sequoias, but not pine trees. He is facetious, but not amusing. So, the question remains, is he abstemious or sober?

(Q11-3)

UNDERSTANDING NDS ACCESS RIGHTS

Access to NDS objects is controlled by ten different NDS access rights — sounds reasonable. These ten rights are organized into two functional groups:

▸ Object rights

▸ Property rights

Let's use the famous "box analogy" to understand the difference between these two different sets of NDS access rights. Think of an NDS object as a box. Like any other three-dimensional rectangloid, the box has external characteristics. You can look at the box and describe its color, size, and shape. By describing the outside of the box, you have a good idea of the type of box it is. But you don't know anything else about it, especially what's inside the box. With object rights, you can look at the box, destroy the box, relabel the box, or create a new one. But you can't get specific information about what's inside the box — that requires property rights.

The contents of the box are similar to what's inside an NDS object — properties. In most cases, the contents of different boxes will vary. One box may contain caviar while another contains video games. In order to see what's inside the box, you need permission to open it and look inside. With the proper rights, you can compare properties in this box with properties in other boxes, you can read the packing list, or you can change the contents of the box altogether. It all depends on which property rights you have.

If you're feeling a little boxed in, that's okay. We'll try and take it slow. But before we can move on to the three-step NDS security model, we must explore each of these ten rights in depth. You'll need to have a firm understanding of default NDS rights before you start changing things around. The default rights in IntranetWare are very sophisticated. In many cases, they're good enough. Let's start with a closer look at object and property rights.

Object Rights

Object rights control what a trustee can do with any object. As you can see in Figure 11.13, the five object rights spell a word — BCDRS. So, what do NDS object rights have to do with dinosaurs? Absolutely nothing, but it's an easy way to remember the five rights. Just visualize *Jurassic Park* and all the sick dinosaurs. What would they do without dinosaur doctors?

Following is a description of the five object rights and their functions:

▶ *Browse* — Grants the right to see objects in the Directory tree. With this right, you can see the outside of the box.

▶ *Create* — Grants the right to create a new object within this container. Obviously, the Create right is only available for container objects. With this right, you can create a new box.

▸ *Delete* — Grants the right to delete the object from NDS. With this right, you can throw away the box.

▸ *Rename* — Grants the right to change the name of the object, in effect changing the naming property. This is the only object right that has any impact on properties, except Supervisor. With this right, you can relabel the box.

▸ *Supervisor* — Grants all access privileges. Anyone with Supervisor rights to an object has access to all its properties. The Supervisor right *can* be blocked with the Inherited Rights Filter (IRF). In effect, anyone with Supervisor rights owns the box.

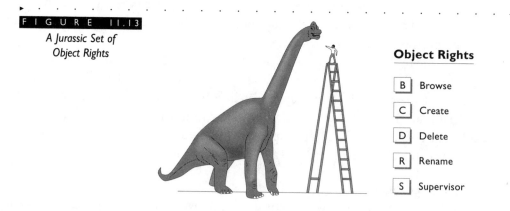

▸ · ◂

FIGURE 11.13

A Jurassic Set of
Object Rights

Object Rights

B   Browse

C   Create

D   Delete

R   Rename

S   Supervisor

Except for a few minor exceptions, object rights have no impact on properties. Remember, we're dealing with the outside of the box at this point. If you want to have control over the contents of the box, you'll need to be granted property rights.

TIP

One of the most notable object/property exceptions involves the Supervisor [S] object right. Be careful. It gives the user Supervisor [S] property rights to all properties.

Property Rights

Property rights control access to the information stored within an NDS object. They allow users to see, search for, and change the contents of the box. At the very minimal level, you must be a trustee of an object in order to be granted rights to its properties. As you can see in Figure 11.14, the property rights almost spell a word — SCRAW(L). In order to cure the dinosaur, you'll have to write a pretty big prescription. This involves that unique medical skill known as SCRAWling — wait 'til you see my signature at the end of Chapter 15!

▶ . . . . ◀

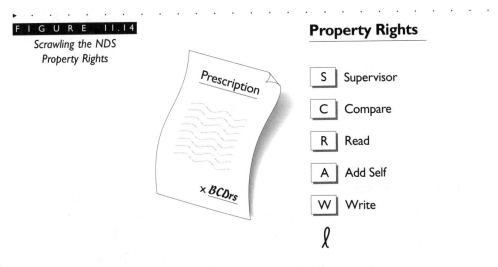

FIGURE 11.14

Scrawling the NDS Property Rights

Property Rights

Here's a description of the five IntranetWare property rights:

▶ *Supervisor* — Grants all rights to the property. The Supervisor right *can* be blocked by an object's Inherited Rights Filter (IRF).

▶ *Compare* — Allows you to compare any given value to the value within the property. This is analogous to saying, "I'm not going to tell you what my phone number is, but I'll let you guess it." With the Compare right, an operation can return True or False but will not give the value of the property. Compare is automatically granted when users have the Read property right.

▶ *Read* — Grants the right to read values of the property. This is better than Compare because it actually allows you to view the value.

▸ *Add Self* — Allows you to add or remove yourself as a value of a property. This right is only meaningful for properties that contain object names as values, such as group membership lists and mailing lists. This right is automatically granted with the Write right.

▸ *Write* — Grants the right to add, change, or remove any values of the property. This is better than Add Self because it allows you to change any value, not just yourself.

▸ (L) — This is not a property right but is needed to spell a word.

Property rights can be assigned in one of two ways — All Properties and/or Selected Properties. As you can see in Figure 11.15, NWADMIN provides two choices. The All Properties option assigns the rights you indicate to *all* properties of the object. A list of these properties is displayed in the Selected Properties window. The Read right to All Properties, for example, would allow you to view the value of all the properties for a given object.

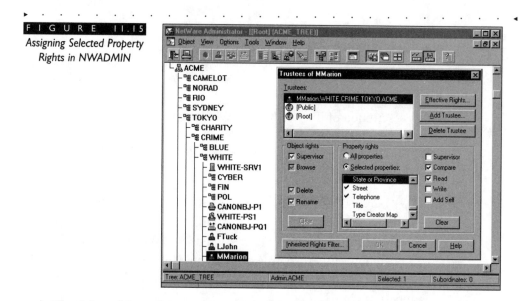

FIGURE 11.15

Assigning Selected Property Rights in NWADMIN

The Selected Properties option, on the other hand, allows you to fine-tune NDS security for specific properties. Simply choose the right you want to assign and highlight one or more properties from the Selected Properties window. It's important to note that the list will change for each object type. Users, for example, have 55 properties, whereas groups have only 23. Finally, granting rights to selected properties overwrites anything granted through the All Properties option. This is very powerful because it allows you to get very specific with certain properties even though a general assignment already exists.

SMART LINK

For more information concerning NDS Object and Property rights, consult the on-line NetWare 4.11 documentation at http://www.novell.com/manuals.

TIP

Later, in Step One of the NDS security model, we're going to learn about a concept called *inheritance*. Inheritance is based on the concept that object and property rights flow down the NDS tree from container to container to leaf objects. It's a fairly simple concept, but there's one exception you need to be aware of. Object rights and All Properties rights are inherited, but Selected Properties rights are not. This means rights you assign to selected properties apply to the specific object only — they do not flow down the tree. Keep this in the back of your mind when we get to inheritance later.

Now that you understand the ten different NDS access rights, it's time to start our three-step model. Before we do, however, let's take a detailed look at default NDS security. This discussion will help you determine when, where, and if you need to assign additional object and property rights.

Default NDS Rights

You have to start somewhere, and default NDS rights are a great place. As I said earlier, default IntranetWare security is extremely sophisticated. In many cases, it's enough. Every time a Server and/or User object is created, IntranetWare assigns a variety of object and property rights to them. Before you move on to the three-step model, you'll want to learn what these defaults are in case you can use them. There's no sense in re-inventing the wheel. Use IntranetWare's default NDS rights as a foundation and build from there.

IntranetWare assigns default NDS rights during four major events:

▸ Initial NDS installation

▸ File server installation

▸ User creation

▸ Container creation

Let's take a closer look.

Initial NDS Installation   When NDS is installed on the very first server on a network, two key objects are created — [Root] and Admin. [Root] represents the very top of the NDS tree (the Earth) and Admin has Supervisor control over the entire network. Incidentally, Admin is placed in the Organization level of the first server's context. The following default rights are granted when NDS is first installed:

▸ Admin — Granted Supervisor [S] object rights to [Root]. This allows the first User object to administer the entire NDS tree. Distributed administrators can be created using supplemental rights. We'll take a look at this later in the chapter.

▸ [Public] — A special system-owned trustee object also created at initial installation. Every object in the NDS tree inherits the rights of [Public]. This is analogous to the EVERYONE group in NetWare 3. By default, [Public] is granted the Browse [B] object right to [Root]. This allows every object in the NDS tree to see every other object.

File Server Installation   When a new file server is installed in NDS, default rights are given to the creator of the Server object, the server itself, and [Public]. Remember, in order to create a Server object, you must have the Supervisor object right to that portion of the tree. By default, INSTALL.NLM asks for the Admin password. If Admin doesn't exist or has been locked out of this portion of tree, a container administrator's username and password is sufficient. In either case, this person is known as the *Creator*. Let's take a look at the default rights assigned during server installation.

▸ Creator — Either Admin or a container administrator. By default, this user is granted Supervisor [S] object rights to the server. This allows Admin or the container administrator to manage the Server object.

▸ Server — The server itself is granted Supervisor [S] object rights to itself. This allows the server to modify the parameters of its own object. Of course, in order for this to occur, the server would have to sprout arms.

▸ [Public] — Granted the Read [R] property right to a specific server property — Messaging Server. This allows any network client to identify the messaging server assigned to this file server. As you'll see in Chapter 12, this is required for MHS Services for IntranetWare. Also, [Public] gets the Read [R] property right to the Network Address property. This allows any client to identify the server.

REAL WORLD

A special trustee called [Public] is created during initial NDS installation and granted the Browse [B] object right to the [Root]. This trustee establishes a global assignment for all objects. Think of it as a minimum trustee assignment. There's one problem, though — users do not have to be logged in to inherit the rights of [Public]. They simply need to be *attached*!

Therefore, any hacker with a notebook and VLMs can attach to your network and download the entire NDS tree. Consider removing [Public] as a trustee of the [Root] object and assign each Organization or Organizational Unit container Browse [B] rights to itself. This will allow users to see their portion of the NDS tree and not the entire tree. But, more importantly, users must be logged in (not just attached) to inherit these rights.

> **TIP**
>
> Layers Three and Four of the IntranetWare security model are completely independent. This means rights assigned at the NDS level do *not* apply to the file system. These rights only apply to network resources like printers, users, and servers. There is, of course, one exception. If you grant anybody Supervisor [S] object rights to a Server object, they also inherit Supervisor file system rights to the [Root] of all volumes on that server. Therefore, by default, the creator of a server gets all rights to its NDS properties and file system. If you're lucky, this could be you.

User Creation   When you create a new User object in NDS, certain necessary rights are granted automatically. These rights are granted to provide the user with some degree of access to WAN resources. Remember, default NDS rights provide a very good beginning. In many cases, these rights are enough for users to be productive. In general, the User object receives enough rights to modify its own login script and print job configurations. If you don't like this idea, consider revoking these rights. Let's take a closer look:

▶ User — Each user is granted three sets of property rights by default. First, he or she is granted the Read [R] right to All Properties. This allows users to view information about themselves. Next, the user is granted the Read and Write [RW] property rights to two selected properties — Login Script and Print Job Configuration. This allows users to execute and change their own User script and/or print job configurations. As you will learn in Chapter 12, this is a moot point since User login scripts are avoided at all costs. Finally, an obvious object right assignment is missing — Browse [B] rights to yourself. While this is not explicitly granted at user creation, the right is inherited from initial NDS installation. Remember, [Public] is granted the Browse [B] right to the [Root], and, therefore, all users can see all objects, including themselves.

▶ [Root] — Granted the Read [R] property right to two specific user properties — Network Address and Group Membership. This allows anyone in the tree to identify the user's network address, location, and any groups the user belongs to.

▶ [Public] — Granted the Read [R] property right to a selected user property — Default Server. This allows anyone to determine the default server for this user. The difference between the [Public] and [Root] assignment is that [Public] rights are granted upon attaching, where [Root] rights imply a valid login authentication.

Container Creation   Any Container you create in NDS receives default rights to itself. This is to ensure that all objects in the container receive the rights they need to access their own family members (that is, resources that share a home container). Remember, the goal of NDS administration is to organize network resources (servers, printers, volumes, users, and directory maps) near the users that need them. If you accomplish this successfully, the default container rights will create an implied security equivalence for all users in the container. Very cool!

Whenever an NDS container is created it gets certain critical NDS rights to itself. First, it gets Read and Write [RW] property rights to its own Login Script property. This allows users in the container to modify the container login script. As you'll see in Chapter 12, this is not always such a good idea. Next, the container receives Read and Write [RW] property rights to its own Print Job Configuration property. This allows users in the container to modify the container's print job configurations. Also not a great idea. See Chapter 14 for more information.

This completes our discussion of the default NDS rights. Refer to Table 11.3 for a summary. Hopefully, you've gained an appreciation for the sophistication of IntranetWare default security. As you can see, users and servers are well taken care of. The only additional security you'll need to add are for special container administrators, traveling users, or groups. We'll discuss these special NDS circumstances later in the chapter.

But for now, let's put our understanding of object, property, and default rights to the test. Let's learn the simple three-step model for assigning NDS security:

▶ Step One: Assigning trustee rights

▶ Step Two: Filtering IRF Rights

▶ Step Three: Calculating effective rights

ZEN

*"When I took your father's name, I took everything that came with it —
including his DNA!"*

Marge Simpson

	NDS EVENT	TRUSTEE	DEFAULT RIGHTS
TABLE 11.3 *Default NDS Security Summary*	Initial NDS installation	Admin	[S] — Supervisor object rights to [Root]
		[Public]	[B] — Browse object rights to [Root]
	File server installation	Creator	[S] — Supervisor object rights to server
		Server	[S] — Supervisor object rights to self
		[Public]	[R] — Read right to selected server property (Messaging Server)
	User creation	User	[R] — Read right to All Properties
			[RW] — Read and Write rights to selected user property (Login Script)
			[RW] — Read and Write rights to selected user property (Print Job Configuration)
		[Root]	[R] — Read right to two selected user properties (Network Address and Group Membership)
		[Public]	[R] — Read right to a selected user property (Default Server)
	Container creation	Container	[RW] — Read and Write rights to Login Script property
			[RW] — Read and Write rights to Print Job Configuration property

STEP ONE: ASSIGNING TRUSTEE RIGHTS

I keep talking about how simple the NDS security model is — easy as 1-2-3. Well, now I get a chance to prove it. A lot has been written about NDS security and most of it is intimidating. Granted, there are a lot of complexities involved, but if you approach it with an open mind, everything falls into place. So far, we've talked about object and property rights. Understanding these rights is a prerequisite to building an NDS security model. But it's certainly not enough. Now you have to learn how to implement these rights in the ACME NDS tree.

Step One deals with assigning these rights. In many cases, this is enough. You only need Steps Two and Three under special circumstances. NDS rights can be assigned in one of three ways:

- ► Trustee assignments

- ► Inheritance

- ► Security equivalence

Trustee assignments involve work — this is bad, of course, since our goal is to minimize the amount of work we do. But you have to start somewhere. Trustee assignments are granted using NWADMIN, NETADMIN, and/or RIGHTS. Inheritance, on the other hand, doesn't involve work — this is good. Inheritance happens automatically when you assign trustee rights at the container level. Just like water flowing down a mountain, trustee rights flow down the NDS tree — from top to bottom. The beauty of this feature is that you can assign sweeping rights for large groups of users with a single trustee assignment.

Finally, security equivalence gives us the added flexibility we need in today's modern world. There are a variety of security equivalence strategies including ancestral inheritance (AI), Organizational Roles, Groups, and Directory Map objects. You'll learn that security equivalence is a way of augmenting the other two trustee assignment strategies. Let's take a closer look at Step One, starting with trustee assignments.

Trustee Assignments

You have to start somewhere and Step One starts with work. A trustee is any NDS object with rights to any other object. Trustees are tracked through the ACL (Access Control List) property. Every object has an ACL property, and the ACL lists the trustees of that object and the rights they have. IntranetWare supports a variety of trustees, including:

▶ User — A leaf object in the NDS tree. It represents a person with access to network resources. Individual users can be assigned specific NDS rights through the User trustee type.

▶ Group — A leaf object with a membership list. The membership list includes users from anywhere in the NDS tree. When NDS rights need to be assigned to unrelated users (in different containers), the Group object is a great option. Rights granted to a Group object are passed to all members of the group.

▶ Container — All container objects are considered "natural groups" and can be used to assign NDS rights to multiple trustees. If you make any container object a trustee of any other object, all users and subcontainers inherit those same rights. The ultimate rights to all objects in the tree are granted using the [Root] object.

▶ Organizational Role — A leaf object, much like groups, except that users are identified as occupants. This object is used to specify a particular role in the organization and not a group of unrelated users. Container administrators, for example, inherit the rights from the Organizational Role they occupy.

▶ [Public] — A special system-owned trustee. Rights granted to [Public] are passed to every object connected to the network. This means users do not have to be logged in in order to inherit [Public] rights. Be very careful when using the [Public] trustee.

Once you identify *who* is going to get the rights, you have to determine *what* rights you're going to give them and *where* the rights will be assigned. *What* consists of any of the ten object and property rights — simple. *Where* can be any object in the NDS tree — also simple. Take Figure 11.16, for example. As you can see, Sherlock Holmes is granted all object rights to the .OU=TOKYO.O=ACME container. In the figure, we have satisfied all three of the trustee assignment elements — who, what, and where.

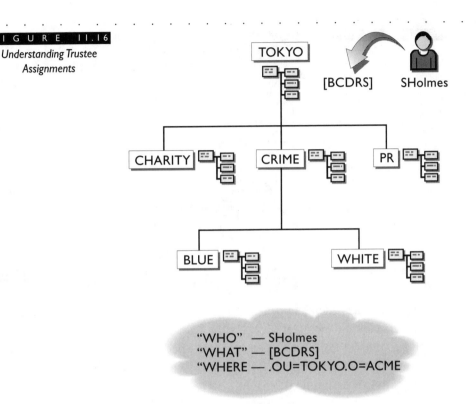

F I G U R E   11.16

Understanding Trustee
Assignments

So, how is this accomplished in NWADMIN? It depends on your point of view. You have two choices:

▸ Rights to Other Objects — This is from Sherlock Holmes's point of view.

▸ Trustees of this Object — This is from OU=TOKYO's point of view.

It really doesn't matter which option you choose. You can either assign rights from the user's point of view or the object's point of view. In the first example, we assign security from Sherlock Holmes' point of view. In NWADMIN, highlight SHolmes and click on the right mouse button. An abbreviated dialogue box appears. As you can see in Figure 11.17, there are two security options. In this case, we're interested in Rights to Other Objects.

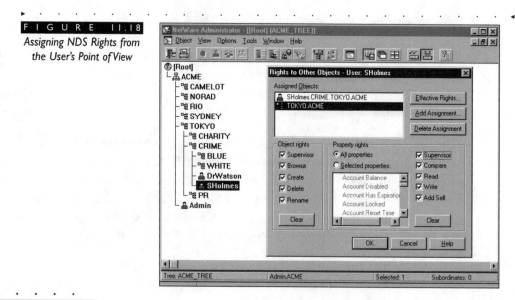

NWADMIN Security
Window for SHolmes

The SHolmes menu appears. Figure 11.18 shows the security window from Sherlock Holmes' point of view. As you can see, he has been granted all object rights to the TOKYO Organizational Unit. Specifically, the Supervisor object right implies the Supervisor property rights to All Properties. This was accomplished using the Add Assignment button.

Assigning NDS Rights from
the User's Point of View

The second option allows you to assign NDS rights from TOKYO's point of view. In this case, you would select OU=TOKYO.O=ACME from the Browse window and click using the right mouse button. The same window will appear (as shown in Figure 11.17). This time, though, choose Trustees of this Object. Figure 11.19 shows the NDS security window from TOKYO's point of view. Notice the default trustees. In addition, SHolmes has been added with all object and property rights. This was accomplished using the Add Trustee button.

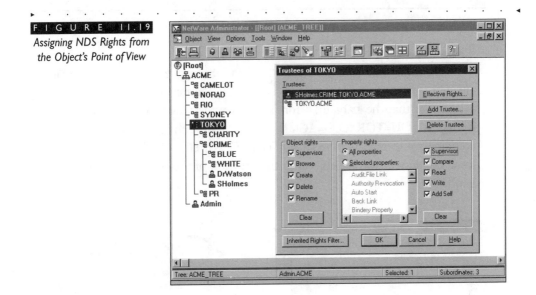

FIGURE 11.19

Assigning NDS Rights from the Object's Point of View

SMART LINK

Get some real "hands-on" experience assigning NDS trustee rights in IntranetWare Administration at CyberState University: http://www.cyberstateu.com.

There you have it. As you can see, it doesn't matter how we assign trustee rights. Both methods accomplish the same thing — Sherlock Holmes (who) is granted [BCDRS] object rights (what) to .OU=TOKYO.O=ACME (where). I told you trustee assignments would be simple. Now that we've explored the "work" part, let's take a closer look at inheritance — the "no work" part.

REAL WORLD

All of this fancy trustee assignment footwork is accomplished using a special NDS property called the Access Control List (ACL). It controls who can access objects and what they can do with them. Some important ACL objects include Applications, printers, and users.

Inheritance

NDS rights can also be assigned through inheritance. This is an automatic side effect of trustee assignments. As you can see in Figure 11.20, Sherlock Holmes got a lot more than he bargained for. When you assigned him the [BCDRS] object rights to .OU=TOKYO.O=ACME, he actually inherited these rights for all containers and objects underneath TOKYO as well. Now he has all object rights to all containers and all objects in that portion of the tree — this might not be a good thing.

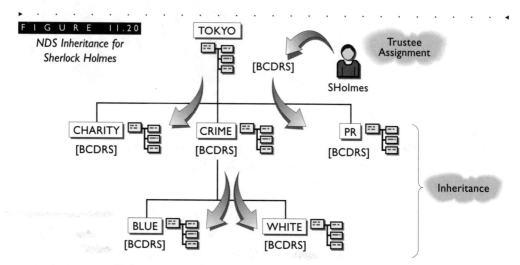

FIGURE 11.20

NDS Inheritance for
Sherlock Holmes

As you recall from our ACME overview in Chapter 3, Sherlock Holmes heads up the Crime Fighting division. He probably shouldn't have Supervisor object rights to Charity and PR. Fortunately, we can rectify the situation. IntranetWare provides two methods for overriding inheritance:

▸ **New trustee assignment** — Trustee assignments override inherited rights. If we assigned SHolmes Browse [B] rights to Charity and PR, he would lose his inheritance in these containers. The new trustee assignment would become his effective rights and inheritance within these containers would reflect the changes.

▸ **Inherited Rights Filter (IRF)** — The IRF is much more serious. It overrides inherited rights for *all* objects in the tree. A [B] filter on Charity and PR wouldn't allow anybody to inherit [CDRS], including SHolmes. So, who manages these containers? What about SirKay and BThomas? Stay tuned for the answer.

Inheritance is a great thing. It allows you to assign sweeping NDS object rights with minimal effort. Remember, as a CNE, "work" is a bad word. As far as property rights go, only one type is inherited. Remember, there are two ways of assigning property rights — All Properties or Selected Properties. The rights assigned using the All Properties option are inherited. Rights assigned to Selected Properties are not. Combine this with what we learned about trustee assignments and we could have an effective strategy for property customization.

Here's an example. Remember, Maid Marion is shy. She's a user in the .OU=WHITE.OU=CRIME.OU=TOKYO.O=ACME container. She doesn't want Sherlock Holmes to see any of her properties except Telephone and Postal Address. This can be a problem since he inherits all rights from his [BCDRS] assignment to the TOKYO container. Fortunately, as a CNE, you have a solution. You simply assign SHolmes the Read [R] property right to Maid Marion's Selected Properties — Telephone and Postal Address. This trustee assignment overrides his inheritance through All Properties. Voilà, Maid Marion is safe. (See Figure 11.21.)

Trustee assignments and inheritance are the two main strategies of Step One. But special situations may arise when you need something more. This is where security equivalence comes in. Let's take a closer look.

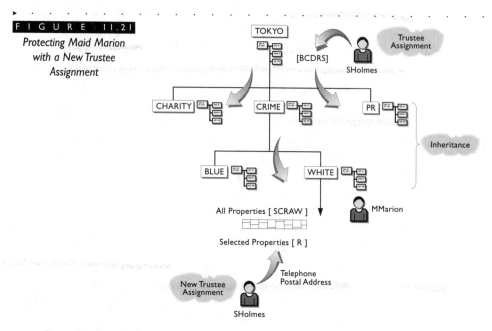

FIGURE 11.21
Protecting Maid Marion
with a New Trustee
Assignment

Security Equivalence

If trustee assignments or inheritance aren't quite getting the job done, security equivalence may be the answer. Security equivalence simply states "one object is equivalent to another with respect to NDS rights." Users, for example, are security equivalent to their parent container. Security equivalence is different from inheritance in that it operates at the trustee assignment level. Please do not confuse the two. Security equivalence applies when an object is made equivalent to another object's explicit trustee assignments. Therefore, security equivalence overrides the IRF.

IntranetWare provides four strategies for security equivalences:

- Ancestral inheritance (AI)

- Organizational Role

- Groups

- Directory Map objects

Ancestral Inheritance (AI) Ancestral inheritance (AI) is a very cool term. But, before you get too caught up in it, you should know a little secret — it doesn't really mean anything. AI simply implies that an object is security equivalent to its ancestor (parent container). This means any rights you assign to an NDS container are absorbed by all the objects in the container. This is not inheritance; this is security equivalence. Therefore, AI can get very strange. Earlier we learned that containers can be trustees and they're thought of as "natural groups." This is true. But, remember, any rights that you assign to a container are implicitly assigned to all objects within the container. For example, suppose we assigned OU=CRIME [BCDRS] rights to TOKYO instead of SHolmes (see Figure 11.16). Now, both users in OU=CRIME — Sherlock Holmes and Dr. Watson — gain the same trustee assignments and inheritance shown in Figure 11.20. Pretty simple.

Well, that's not all. Not only do the objects in OU=CRIME absorb its trustee assignments, but all objects underneath CRIME as well! This means Maid Marion, Robin Hood, and all their friends would get the same trustee assignments as Sherlock Holmes and Dr. Watson. Wow. This concept is also called implied security equivalence. However tempting it is, avoid AI unless you know what you're doing.

Organizational Role (OR) Organizational Roles are another type of security equivalence. These special NDS objects are designed as task identifiers. Jobs that require multiple temporary users are excellent candidates for Organizational Roles. Postmaster, for example, is a job that can be assigned to multiple users on a rotating basis. When a user is performing the Postmaster duties, he or she will need special NDS and file system rights. Let's say the White Collar Crime Division has a Postmaster OR that changes occupants every three months. This person needs special NDS security to e-mail objects and the file system. Instead of continually moving trustee assignments around, you can define security once for the Organizational Role, then switch occupants. Let's say it's Little John's turn, for example. When you remove Maid Marion from the Postmaster OR and replace her with LJohn, he immediately absorbs the NDS security of that object. Suddenly, Little John has all the security he needs to perform Postmaster duties. An elegant solution. Later we'll explore the Organizational Role as one solution for creating distributed administrators. For now, let's move on to the next security equivalence option — Groups.

▶ · ◀

REAL WORLD

AI allows you to make broad trustee assignments at high levels in the tree. For example, you could place a mail server at O=ACME and grant the container rights to it. Because of AI, all objects in the ACME organization will have immediate access to the mail server. This also applies to file system rights. You could place all the CRIME files on a single server in the OU=CRIME container, then assign appropriate file system rights to OU=CRIME. Because of AI, all users in the CRIME division would have immediate access to the central server.

Groups   As we learned earlier, groups are another trustee type for assigning NDS rights. This allows us to distribute similar rights to unrelated users. That is, users not within the same area of the NDS tree. First, create a group, then assign it rights, and finally, add members. This is similar to the Organizational Role object in that it works on the security equivalence concept. Members of any group absorb (not inherit) rights assigned to the host group object. Groups also differ from AI containers in that they don't involve "implied inheritance." Rights assigned to groups only apply to specific members of the group. And, as we all know, users can be easily removed from groups.

Directory Map Objects   In very special circumstances, security equivalence can be used to facilitate Directory Map objects. As we learned in Chapter 10, these objects allow us to map directory paths to a centralized object instead of to a physical location. To accomplish this, you must first create a Directory Map object that points to a physical location in the file system, then create a logical drive pointer to the Directory Map object using the MAP command. There's one problem with this scenario: The drive mapping doesn't work until the user is assigned explicit or inherited file system rights to the physical directory. This involves a lot of planning, a lot of work, and some careful tracking. An easier solution would involve assigning the file system rights to the Directory Map object itself, then making each user a security equivalent of the NDS object. This makes security assignments much clearer.

In summary, when you create a Directory Map object, be sure to assign adequate file system rights to its physical directory. Then when you use the MAP command to create logical pointers, be sure to assign the host user security equivalence to the Directory Map object. Believe me, this will make drive mapping and security much easier to manage. Really!

REAL WORLD

Don't forget about NDS rights when dealing with Directory Map objects. If the Directory Map is outside your container, you'll need at lease Read [R] property rights to the object's PATH property.

There you have it — Step One. Don't get discouraged — this is the tricky part. Once you assign NDS rights, the rest takes care of itself. In Step One, we learned there are three different ways of assigning rights to NDS trustees — trustee assignments, inheritance, and security equivalence. We also learned there are a variety of different trustee types and to be aware of ancestral inheritance (implied security equivalence). The good news is, most of your work stops here. Only in special cases do you need to go on to Steps Two and Three. Of course, you remember Murphy's Law Number 342 — special cases will appear just when you least expect them. So, in honor of Murphy and to decrease your stress level, let's take a quick look at Steps Two and Three.

ZEN

"DNA .... Positive ID .... Those won't hold up in any court. Run Dad!"

Bart Simpson

STEP TWO: FILTERING IRF RIGHTS

Earlier we learned there are two ways of blocking unwanted inherited rights:

▸ New trustee assignments

▸ Inherited Rights Filter (IRF)

Let's propose a problem with Sherlock Holmes's inheritance. Since he's been assigned [BCDRS] object rights to .OU=TOKYO.O=ACME, he becomes distributed administrator of that entire section of the tree — this is bad. Sherlock Holmes is responsible for the Crime Fighting division. He has no authority over Charity or PR. However, his inheritance model shows [BCDRS] object rights to both OU=CHARITY and OU=PR (see Figure 11.20 earlier). We're going to have to do something about this right away.

Welcome to planet IRF. IntranetWare includes an Inherited Rights Filter that blocks inherited rights at any point in the tree. Right off the bat, you'll need to understand two very important points about how the IRF works:

▸ It's an inclusive filter, which means the rights that are in the filter are the ones that are allowed to pass through.

▸ The IRF applies to everyone in the NDS tree. Once you've assigned an IRF to a container, everyone is blocked, including Admin.

TIP

The Supervisor object right can be blocked by an NDS IRF. It cannot be blocked, however, by an IRF in the file system. If you attempt to block the Supervisor [S] right with an IRF, NWADMIN will first require you to make an explicit Supervisor [S] trustee assignment to someone else (assuming, of course, that one does not already exist). This is so that access to that portion of the tree is not permanently removed. Imagine how much fun it would be if the Supervisor object right was filtered for everybody. Does the term *reinstall* mean anything to you?

The IRF can be used to block inheritance of either object rights or property rights assigned through the All Properties option. Remember, Selected Properties aren't inherited. Figure 11.22 shows how the IRF can be used to solve our Sherlock Holmes problem. We create an inclusive IRF of [B] to block everything but the Browse right. His inheritance in OU=CRIME, however, remains unaffected.

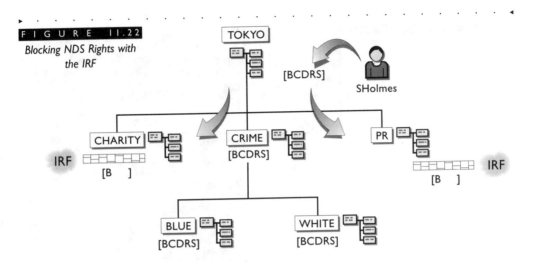

FIGURE 11.22
Blocking NDS Rights with
the IRF

So, how do we assign an IRF? Once again, NWADMIN is our friend. Earlier we learned that trustee assignments can be assigned in one of two ways — "Rights to other objects" and "Trustees of this object." IRFs are accomplished using only one of these two choices. Can you figure out which one? Correct — it's "Trustees of this object." Remember, IRFs are host-object specific. They work from the host's point of view and apply to every object in the NDS tree. Figure 11.23 shows the IRF input screen for OU=CHARITY. Notice the downward arrows that appear next to each option box. These differentiate IRF rights from trustee assignments. Anywhere you see a downward arrow, you can assume it's an IRF filter.

REAL WORLD

Even though the IRF input window in Figure 11.23 gives you the option of choosing Selected Properties, it's not a feasible configuration. Why? Because Selected Properties are *not* inherited. Therefore, the IRF is useless. Please don't let the utility confuse you. That's my job.

F I G U R E   11.23
Filtering NDS Rights in
NWADMIN

NetWare Administrator - [[Root] [ACME_TREE]]

Object View Options Tools Window Help

- [Root]
  - ACME
    - CAMELOT
    - NORAD
    - RIO
    - SYDNEY
    - TOKYO
      - CHARITY
      - CRIME
      - PR
    - Admin

Trustees of CHARITY

Trustees:
- CHARITY.TOKYO.ACME
- SirKay.CHARITY.TOKYO.ACME

Effective Rights...

Add Trustee...

Delete Trustee

Inherited Rights Filter

Object rights
- Supervisor
- Browse
- Create
- Delete
- Rename

Property rights
- All properties
- Selected properties:
  - Audit:File Link
  - Authority Revocation
  - Auto Start
  - Back Link
  - Bindery Property

- Supervisor
- Compare
- Read
- Write
- Add Self

OK   Cancel   Help

Tree: ACME_TREE   Admin.ACME   Selected: 1   Subordinates: 1

If the IRF applies to all objects in the tree, who is going to administer the OU=CHARITY and OU=PR containers? As you can see in Figure 11.22, no one can have the [CDRS] object rights. Fortunately, trustee assignments override the IRF. Remember, the "I" in IRF stands for "inherited." It only works on inherited rights. Figure 11.24 introduces two new players — SirKay (the administrator of OU=CHARITY) and BThomas (the administrator of OU=PR). We will simply assign SirKay the [BCDRS] object rights to OU=CHARITY. Now he is the container administrator for this section of the tree and everyone else, including Sherlock Holmes and Admin, has been locked out. The same holds true for BThomas and OU=PR.

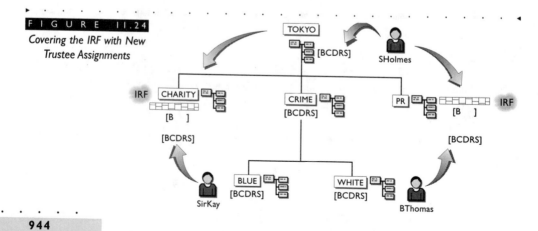

F I G U R E   11.24
Covering the IRF with New
Trustee Assignments

So, let me ask you — which activity occurs first? The IRF or the new trustee assignment? Correct, the new trustee assignment. Remember, NWADMIN will *not* allow us to set an IRF for OU=CHARITY until someone else has explicitly been granted Supervisor privileges. So, first we assign SirKay [BCDRS] privileges, then we set the IRF to [B].

Good work.

So, what's the bottom line? What can Sherlock Holmes *really* do in the TOKYO portion of the tree? "It's elementary, my dear Watson, elementary." More accurately, it's Step Three: calculating effective rights.

STEP THREE: CALCULATING EFFECTIVE RIGHTS

Effective rights are the bottom line. This is the culmination of our three-step process. In Step One, we assign the rights. In Step Two, we filter the rights. In Step Three, we calculate exactly what the rights are.

Calculating effective rights is about as simple as modern math. Any object's effective rights are the combination of NDS privileges received through any of the following:

▸ Trustee assignments made to the user

▸ Inheritance minus rights blocked by the IRF

▸ Rights granted to the special [Public] trustee

▸ Security equivalences to parent containers, groups, or Organizational Roles

I don't know if you've ever done modern math, but it's ugly. It would be easy if any of the assignments shown above canceled out the others. But, unfortunately, life isn't easy. These assignments work in combination with each other. Consider it modern math in the 7th Dimension.

Let's start with a simple example. Refer to Figure 11.25. In this first example, Sherlock Holmes is assigned [BCDRS] object rights to OU=CRIME. On the right side of the figure, we've created an effective rights calculation worksheet. This is an *effective* (pun intended) tool for helping you get through modern math. You can create one at home with paper, a pencil, and a ruler.

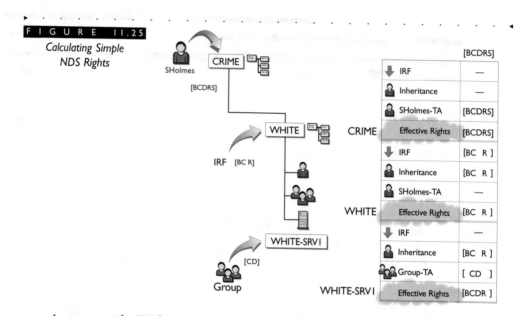

FIGURE 11.25

Calculating Simple NDS Rights

It starts with SHolmes' trustee assignment to OU=CRIME. Since there's no inheritance or IRF involved, his effective rights in this container are the same. Those effective rights become inherited rights in all subcontainers — one of which is OU=WHITE. To further complicate things, there's an IRF of [BCR] on the WHITE container. Since the IRF blocks [DS], Sherlock Holmes's inherited rights become [BCR]. With no other trustee assignments, his effective rights in OU=WHITE are the same — [BCR].

Finally, we arrive at the WHITE-SRV1 server object. It has no IRF, so SHolmes' inherited rights are equal to the effective rights of the WHITE container — [BCR]. In addition, one of Sherlock Holmes's groups is assigned the [CD] object rights to the WHITE-SRV1 server. These rights combine with his inherited rights to create ultimate effective rights of [BCDR] for the server object. You see, that wasn't so hard. In this simple example, we had a limited number of different elements — one user trustee assignment, one group trustee assignment, and one IRF. Of course, the world is not always this simple. Now let's take a look at a more complex example.

TIP

One of the trickiest aspects of NDS effective rights is deciding when trustee assignment rights override inherited rights, and when they're combined. It's simple: If the trustee is the same, then TA overrides I; if trustees are different, then TA combines with I. In summary, Same = override; Different = combine!

Just when you think you understand it, they throw something like this at you. In this example (see Figure 11.26), there's one user assignment, one group trustee, an Organizational Role equivalent, AI, and three IRFs. Hold on to your hat!

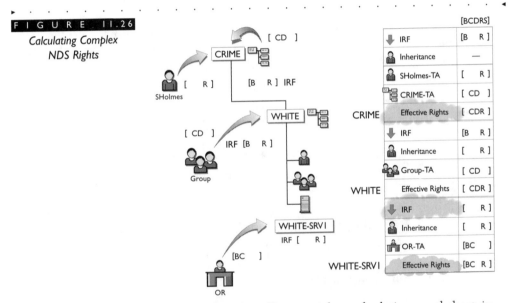

FIGURE II.26

Calculating Complex NDS Rights

Once again, we're going to use the effective rights calculation worksheet in Figure 11.26. As before, it begins with Sherlock Holmes at the OU=CRIME container — trustee assignment of [R]. In addition, the container is granted [CD] rights to itself. Since Sherlock Holmes lives in this context, he gains an ancestral inheritance of [CD]. This, combined with his user assignment, gives the effective rights [CDR]. In this case, the IRF is useless — simple window dressing. Remember, trustee assignments override the IRF.

Sherlock Holmes's effective rights in OU=CRIME become his inherited rights in OU=WHITE. The IRF, however, blocks [CDS] so his inheritance becomes [R]. This combines with a group trustee assignment of [CD] to give the effective rights [CDR].

These effective rights pass through the [R] filter at WHITE-SRV1. These inherited rights combined with his OR equivalence give effective rights of [BCR] at the WHITE-SRV1 server object. Piece of cake.

SMART LINK

Get some more experience calculating NDS effective rights at CyberState University: http://www.cyberstateu.com.

As you can see, effective rights get very hairy very quickly — just like modern math in the 7th Dimension. This is probably because there're so many forces at work. Remember, effective rights are the combination of trustee assignments, inheritance, [Public], and security equivalence. The default NDS rights are looking better and better all the time.

There you have it. The simple three-step NDS security model:

- *Step One:* Assigning NDS Rights — through trustee assignments, inheritance, and/or security equivalence.

- *Step Two:* Filtering IRF Rights — The inclusive filter allows you to block inherited rights. Remember to avoid isolating sections of the tree by using new trustee assignments with IRFs.

- *Step Three:* Calculating Effective Rights — just like modern math in the 7th Dimension.

Now I bet you're glad you made it through the simple steps of NDS security. Fortunately, there's a sophisticated foundation of NDS default rights to start from. And Steps Two and Three are optional. Your security system doesn't need to be this complex, but in case it is, you have *Novell's CNE Study Guide for IntranetWare/NetWare 4.11* to fall back on.

THE BRAIN

For more expert tips on NDS rights, see "Designing NetWare 4.x Security" in the November 1993 *Novell Application Notes* or surf the Web to http://www.novell.com/manuals.

Before we move on to the Fourth Layer of the NetWare security model (file system access rights), let's spend a few moments exploring NDS administration. These are some supplemental strategies to help you deal with the daily grind of NDS security management.

QUIZ

OK, Bart. To prove your innocence, tell me: What is the English word most often pronounced wrong?

(Q11-4)

NDS ADMINISTRATION

NDS security is a daunting task. Don't feel like you have to accomplish it all alone. The advantages of NDS are that it enables you to section off certain areas of the network and delegate network administration tasks. You can, for example, delegate portions of the tree to distributed container administrators. On the other hand, what if it's a very highly secured government installation? You may only be involved in setting up the network. The daily administration tasks may be accomplished by a high-security work group.

NDS allows you to approach administration in one of two ways:

▶ Central administration

▶ Distributed administration

Central administration means you have only one user (Admin) with Supervisor rights to the entire tree. This is the IntranetWare default. *Distributed administration*, on the other hand, allows you to designate users with Supervisor rights for branches of the Directory tree. This container administrator can either work in conjunction with Admin or replace him or her for that portion of the tree. Let's take a closer look.

Admin

The Admin user is created during installation of the first server and initially has all rights to manage NDS. As you saw in our earlier discussion, Admin is granted the [S] object right to [Root] by default. He or she consequently inherits all rights to the rest of the tree unless an IRF is applied. These rights also extend into IntranetWare file systems unless blocked by an IRF in the NDS tree.

Centralized administration is appropriate for small organizations or large implementations with a central MIS department. Some tasks that could easily be centrally administered include:

▸ Naming the Directory tree

▸ Installing the first server

▸ Creating the top layers of the NDS tree

▸ Partition management and synchronization

▸ Assigning container administrators

It may be difficult for one person to administer the entire tree. A central Admin may not be able to meet the daily requests of user creation, file system rights, login scripts, and so on. Therefore, you may consider assigning container administrators for busy portions of the tree.

TIP

The Admin user has few special properties beyond [S] rights to the [Root]. This user can be deleted, replaced, or generally abused. This is unlike the special Supervisor account from previous versions of NetWare, which was a "Super User" and couldn't be deleted. The moral of the story is, "Don't get delusions of grandeur if you log in as Admin." Remember, anyone can be Admin as long as he or she has Supervisor [S] rights to the [Root].

Distributed Administrators

Distributed administration means that designated users are given enough NDS rights to manage distributed branches of the NDS tree. This special type of user is often referred to as a *container administrator*. Distributed administration tends to allow you to respond to users' needs more quickly, especially in a large implementation. The following tasks can be distributed:

- ▶ Creating user accounts

- ▶ Creating and configuring print services

- ▶ Backing up and restoring data

- ▶ Assigning file system trustees

- ▶ Installing additional servers

- ▶ Creating workgroup managers

Of course, the optimum administrative strategy combines a central Admin with a few distributed administrators. As we saw in our earlier discussion, there are two ways of creating distributed administrators — IRF/new trustee assignments and Organizational Role. If only one person will administer a container, consider using the first option. Otherwise, Organizational Roles can act as a host to rotating administrators. Remember our Postmaster example.

· ▶ · ◀ ·

REAL WORLD

There is a third way of creating distributed administrations — security equivalence. You can create a single container administrator and then make other users security equivalent to that object. This is not recommended, however. If you happen to delete the host administrator, all security equivalent users lose their rights. If the host was an exclusive container administrator, you've just lost all administrative control over a section of the tree. Does the term *reinstall* mean anything to you?

As we saw in an earlier example, it's possible to create an exclusive container administrator. Refer back to Figure 11.24. When the IRF was used to block all rights in the CHARITY container, all administrators, including Admin, were locked out. But before we could block [S], we needed to make Sir Kay an exclusive administrator by granting him [BCDRS] object rights. Remember, NWADMIN requires you to make the trustee assignments first, then the IRF.

There are two other types of distributed administrators in addition to Admin and the container administrator:

▸ Print server operator — Responsible for managing print services. This role is often incorporated into the role of the container administrator.

▸ Print queue operator — Can assist the print server operator or container administrator in managing print jobs.

Table 11.4 summarizes the actions and requirements of central and distributed administrators. For now, suffice it to say — you don't have to do it alone. No matter who you are, there will always be some special circumstances to deal with. Let's take a look at some clever solutions for Profile login scripts, Directory Map objects, mailing list administrators, and traveling users.

T A B L E I I . 4

Summary of Distributed Administrators

ROLE	ACCOUNT INFORMATION	FUNCTIONS
Admin	Default Admin User object [S] object rights to [Root] (by default).	Name the Directory tree; install the first server; create the top levels of the NDS tree; handle partition management and synchronization; assign distributed administrators; issue initial auditor password(s); and upgrade servers, clients, and applications.
Distributed Administrator	Exclusive container administrator or Organizational Role. Requires [BCDRS] object rights to appropriate container.	Install supplemental servers; perform data backup and restoration; create and configure print services; write and maintain login scripts; monitor file server performance; track errors; monitor disk space usage, assign file system security; and upgrade respective servers, clients, and applications.

	T A B L E 11.4

Summary of Distributed
Administrators (continued)

ROLE	ACCOUNT INFORMATION	FUNCTIONS
Print Server Operator	Print Server Operator object or Organizational Role. Must be added to "Print Server Operator" property of the respective Print Server object.	Load and shut down the print server, manage and maintain print server configurations.
Print Queue	Print Queue Operator object or Organizational Role. Must be added to the "Print Queue Operator" property of the respective print queue.	Delete print jobs, change the order of print jobs, change queue status.

Special NDS Security

If you only learn one thing in this crazy chapter, I hope it's this:
Expect the unexpected.

ZEN

"Doh!"

Homer Simpson

There are many special circumstances that require a unique approach toward NDS security. Certain objects in the tree, for example, require additional NDS rights beyond the defaults. This usually occurs when a user is defined in a different container than the resource he or she is trying to access. Also, there are special considerations for traveling users and mailing list administrators. Here are some proven solutions for dealing with special security circumstances:

▶ *Profile Login Scripts* — As you'll learn in Chapter 12, IntranetWare provides a facility for group login scripts — the Profile object. In order for a user to access a Profile script, he or she requires special rights. If the User and Profile objects are in the same container, no additional rights are required because he or she gets them by default. If, however, the User is in a different container, the Read [R] right to the Profile login script property is required.

▸ *Directory Map* — In Chapter 10, we discovered the Directory Map object as a way of reducing redundant network administration. It allows you to map logical pointers to NDS objects instead of physical volume locations. In order to access Directory Map objects, users need two sets of rights. First, NDS rights (Read [R] to the "Path" selected property of the Directory Map object) and, second, file system rights to the volume in question. If the user resides in the same container as the Directory Map object, no additional NDS rights are required. Otherwise, you'll need to make the above NDS assignment.

▸ *Mailing list administrator* — postal workers are special people, too. Mailing list administrators need special NDS rights to manage certain user properties. Specifically grant him or her Read and Write [RW] properties rights to the following Selected Properties of each user in the mailing list — Telephone, Street, City, State or Province, Postal (Zip) Code and other postal office box properties. Whatever you do, don't use the All Properties option. This would give the mailing list administrator unintended power. Remember, if you grant anyone the Write [W] property right to a user's ACL property, he or she can change the user's security. This is a bad thing.

▸ *Traveling user between two offices* — As we learned in Chapter 4, traveling users can cause havoc on NDS administration. These users typically bounce from location to location demanding access to distributed and centralized resources. Several of the NDS security issues you should consider when working with traveling users include access to applications, file storage in a central volume, access to distributed files, access to local and distributed printers and e-mail, login authentication, and the type of computer they're using (notebook or desktop). The user who divides his or her time between two offices needs similar resources in two different locations. The easiest way to approach this problem is create two User objects, one in each location. Give appropriate rights to any resources needed in the local location. Then give him or her the Read [R] property rights to Profile login script and Directory Map Objects (as shown above).

► *Traveling users between various locations* — Users who travel to various locations on a regular basis require a slightly different type of NDS security. In this case, you may want to create an Alias object in each location. You can also use groups or Organizational Roles, then assign the appropriate rights to the Alias for access to directories and network resources. Finally, don't forget the Profile and Directory Map objects. This strategy can also be used for traveling users who find themselves stuck in a remote location for a temporary period of time.

This completes all the "special" and not-so-special aspects of IntranetWare NDS Administration. As you can see, it's a tricky, critical piece of your life as a CNE. To help, Table 11.5 outlines all the rights necessary to create and manage daily NDS resources. Just think of it as a blueprint for NDS success. Hey that rhymes.

TABLE II.5

*Summary of NDS Resource
Access Rights*

NDS RESOURCE	ADMINISTRATIVE ACTION	NECESSARY RIGHTS
Alias	Grant users appropriate NDS rights to the Alias Host object	Authority to grant NDS rights to objects in other containers (i.e. Write [W] privileges to the object's ACL property)
Application	1) Grant users appropriate file system rights to the application referred to by the Application object.	To perform Step 1, you must have Supervisory or Access Control file system rights to the directory or file.
	2) Associate users with Application objects.	To perform Step 2, you must have the Write [W] property right to ACL property of the Application and User objects.
Directory Map	1) Grant users appropriate file system rights to the directory referred to by the Directory Map object.	To perform Step 1, you must have Supervisory or Access Control file system rights to the directory or file.

(continued)

*Summary of NDS Resource
Access Rights (continued)*

NDS RESOURCE	ADMINISTRATIVE ACTION	NECESSARY RIGHTS
Directory Map	2) Grant users the Read [R] property right to the Path property of the Directory Map object.	To perform Step 2, you must have the Write [W] property right to ACL property of the Directory Map object.
Group	Add users to the Group Membership list of the Group object.	Write [W] property right to the ACL property (that is, Member and Object Trustees) of the Group object.
Organizational Role	Add users to the Occupant list of the Organizational Role object.	Write [W] property right to the ACL property (that is, Occupant and Object Trustees) of the Organizational Role object.
Print Queue	Add users to the Print Queue Users list of the Print Queue object.	Print Queue Operator status.
Printer	Add users to the Print Queue Users list of the Print Queue object that services this printer.	Print Queue Operator status.
Profile	1) Add the Profile object to each User object's Profile property. 2) Grant users the Read [R] property right to the Login Script property of the Profile object.	To perform both Steps 1 and 2, you must have the Write [W] property right to the ACL (that is, Object Trustees) property of the Profile object.
Volume/directory	Grant users the appropriate file system rights to the directory or file you want to target in the Volume object. (By default: Read and File Scan rights to SYS:PUBLIC)	Supervisory or Access Control file system rights to the directory or file you want to target in the Volume object.

SMART LINK

For more information on **NDS Administration and security,** surf to
the **Novell Knowledgebase at http://support.novell.com/search/.**

Wow. That's NDS security! In this section, we've explored the simple three-step model for configuring NDS access rights. We've learned about trustee assignments, inheritance, and security equivalence. The IRF came along to help us lock inherited rights and quickly became the foundation of "modern math" in the 7th Dimension — calculating effective rights. That's all there is to it. Finally, we learned you don't have to do it alone. You can share all this fun with distributed administrators.

At the beginning of the chapter, we learned that security is "freedom from risk." At this point, you're probably thinking NDS security is freedom from sanity. Don't worry — it's not as crazy as you think. We've provided a detailed exploratorium at the end of the chapter for your enjoyment. And in the next section — file system access rights — you'll get a chance to review the three-step approach. Here's the good news. File system security is very similar to NDS security. Let's check it out.

QUIZ

So, you wanna be the next Sherlock Holmes? Let's see if you've got what it takes. Each of the following six words is the odd one out for a different reason.

ABORT

ACT

AGT

ALP

OPT

APT

Can you find all six answers? If so, you are well on your way to answering the question, "Who shot Mr. Burns?"

(Q11-5)

Layer Four — File System Access Rights

IntranetWare security exists on two functional planes:

▸ Above the server

▸ Within the server

In order to understand the two functional planes of IntranetWare security, use the server as a midpoint (see Figure 11.27). NDS security occurs above the server — the "Cloud." In this plane, the server is at the bottom of the tree. It is treated as any other leaf object, just like users, printers, and groups. NDS security applied above the server ends when it gets to a leaf object. There's no transition into the file system.

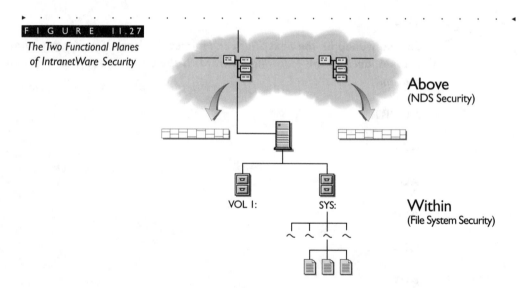

FIGURE 11.27

The Two Functional Planes of IntranetWare Security

Above
(NDS Security)

VOL 1:   SYS:

Within
(File System Security)

File system security, on the other hand, occurs within the server. In this case, the server is the top of the tree. The server contains the volumes that contain the directories that house the files. Again, file system security ends once it gets to the server. There's no transition into the NDS security structure. Understanding the server's point of view will help you understand NDS and file system security.

The good news is NDS and file system security have a lot in common. You don't have to learn a whole new model. The same simple three-step approach applies. There're trustee assignments, inheritance, and security equivalence. The file system uses an IRF and calculating effective rights is still ugly. There are, however, a few minor differences between NDS and file system security:

▸ NDS has ten access rights broken into two groups — object and property. The file system uses eight access rights.

▸ Rights do not flow from NDS into the file system except in one special instance — Supervisor [S] object right to the Server object, which grants the trustee Supervisor file rights to the [Root] of all the server's volumes.

▸ The Supervisor NDS right can be blocked by the IRF. The Supervisor file system right, on the other hand, *cannot* be blocked by the IRF.

That does it. As you can see, the file system and NDS have much more in common than you think. Let's start our discussion of security *within* the server by describing the eight file system access rights.

UNDERSTANDING FILE SYSTEM ACCESS RIGHTS

Welcome inside the server. It's kind of dark and cold in here, but very secure. Before you can access any files, though, you must have appropriate file system access rights. As you can see in Figure 11.28, they also spell a word — WoRMFACES (the "O" is implied). Holy anatomical nematodes, Batman! It's not a pretty sight, but certainly a name you will not forget. Let's check them out.

▸ W — *Write:* Grants the right to open and change the contents of files and directories.

▸ (O) — Doesn't exist but is needed to spell a word.

▸ R — *Read:* Grants the right to open files in the directory and read their contents or run applications.

▸ M — *Modify:* Grants the right to change the attributes or name of a file or directory. As we'll learn in just a second, the Modify right has a dual personality.

▸ F — *File Scan:* Grants the right to see files and directories.

▸ A — *Access Control:* Grants the right to change trustee assignments and the IRF.

▸ C — *Create:* Grants the right to create new files and subdirectories.

▸ E — *Erase:* Grants the right to delete a directory, its files, and subdirectories.

▸ S — *Supervisor:* Grants all rights to a directory and its files and subdirectories. This right *cannot* be blocked by the IRF (unlike NDS security).

FIGURE 11.28

WoRMFACES

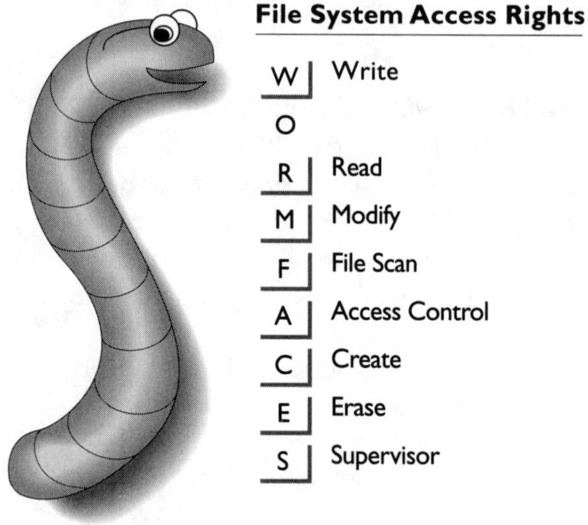

File System Access Rights

W	Write
O	
R	Read
M	Modify
F	File Scan
A	Access Control
C	Create
E	Erase
S	Supervisor

In this list, there are three rights you may want to steer clear of — [SAM] (and they also spell a word). The Supervisor right grants all privileges to files and directories and it cannot be filtered. Users with the Supervisor right can make trustee assignments and grant all rights to other users as well. Access Control also allows users to make trustee assignments, but they can only grant the rights they possess. In addition, these users can modify the IRF. Finally, the Modify right has a split personality — Dr. Jekyll and Mr. Hyde. As Dr. Jekyll, Modify allows users to rename files and directories. Many applications require this. As Mr. Hyde, Modify allows users to change file and directory attributes. As we'll see a little later, attributes constitute the fifth layer of the IntranetWare security model. I don't think you want users messing around with it.

REAL WORLD

The Supervisor access right is just as dangerous in the file system as it is in NDS. The tricky part is that it can leak its way into the file system without you knowing it. Any user with the Write [W] property right to a server's ACL will implicitly receive Supervisor file rights to the Root of all volumes on the server. And to make things worse, the user will not appear on any file or directory trustee list. There's a variety of ways to get the Write [W] property right to a server's ACL, including Supervisor object rights, Supervisor All Properties rights, and security equivalence. You may consider blocking these rights with a server IRF.

Recognizing the eight file system access rights is only the beginning. In order to effectively configure and manage file system security, you must understand what they do. Individually, the rights are useless. But in combination, they become valuable security tools. Table 11.6 summarizes the file system rights requirements for common network tasks. Believe me, this will be an invaluable aid when it comes time to configure application and data security. Use it or lose it.

SMART LINK

For more information on IntranetWare file system access rights and appropriate configurations, surf to the Novell Knowledgebase at http://support.novell.com/search/.

TABLE 11.6	FILE SYSTEM TASK	RIGHTS REQUIREMENTS
Rights Requirements for Common File System Tasks	Open and read a file	Read
	See a filename	File Scan
	Search a directory for files	File Scan
	Open and write to an existing file	Write, Create, Erase, and Modify
	Execute an .EXE file	Read and File Scan
	Create and write to a file	Create
	Copy files *from* a directory	Read and File Scan
	Copy files *to* a directory	Write, Create, and File Scan
	Make a new directory	Create
	Delete a file	Erase
	Salvage deleted files	Read and File Scan for the file and Create for the directory
	Change directory or file attributes	Modify (Mr. Hyde)
	Rename a file or directory	Modify (Dr. Jekyll)
	Change the IRF	Access Control
	Change trustee assignments	Access Control
	Modify a directory's disk space restrictions	Access Control

So, where do you begin? As with NDS, file system security starts with the defaults. IntranetWare provides a sophisticated set of default file system access rights. These rights should become the foundation of your application and data security strategies. They aren't, however, as comprehensive as NDS defaults. You'll need to assign security whenever you create new application and data directories. Let's take a quick look at the IntranetWare defaults:

▶ *User* — A unique user directory is created under SYS:USERS during User object conception. By default, the user gets all file system rights except Supervisor to the directory — [RWCEMF]. This directory will exactly match the User object name unless otherwise specified. Its location is also configurable.

▶ *[Supervisor]* — The Bindery Services Supervisor object is granted Supervisor [S] file rights to the [Root] of all volumes. This user performs special bindery functions using the Admin password.

▶ *Creator* — Whoever creates the File Server object (usually Admin) automatically gets Supervisor [S] file system rights to all volumes. This can be blocked by filtering the Supervisor [S] object right with a server IRF.

▶ *Container* — The server's parent container is granted Read and File Scan [RF] access rights to SYS:PUBLIC. This way all users and objects in the server's home container can access IntranetWare public utilities.

This completes our discussion of file system access rights. As you can see, there's a lot more than meets the eye. Be sure to use Table 11.6 when assigning rights to new application and data directories. Also, test these rights before you let the users loose. Many times, applications have strange unobvious requirements. Now that you know what to do, let's learn how to do it. Remember, the IntranetWare file system behaves exactly the same as NDS:

▶ Step One: Assigning Trustee Rights

▶ Step Two: Filtering IRF Rights

▶ Step Three: Calculating Effective Rights

Ready. Set. Go!

ZEN

"I am Melvin Van Horn, and this is my associate Hershel Krustovsky. Officers, you have arrested an innocent man!"

Krusty's Sidekick

FILE SYSTEM THREE-STEP SHUFFLE

This gives us an opportunity to review the three-step NDS security model. Fortunately, file system security imitates it to the letter. Remember, IntranetWare security starts with two simple questions:

▸ What rights do I need to do stuff?

▸ How do I get these rights?

Well, so far we've learned about the eight file system access rights and what rights are needed for common network tasks. Now we get to answer the question, "How do I get these rights?" As with NDS, file system security is as easy as 1-2-3:

▸ *Step One:* Assigning Trustee Rights — You assign the access rights through trustee assignments, inheritance, and/or security equivalence.

▸ *Step Two:* Filtering IRF Rights — In special circumstances, you can filter inherited rights at the directory or file level.

▸ *Step Three:* Calculating Effective Rights — The result is effective rights (that is, what users can actually do to directories and files).

Once again, it's as easy as A-B-C. Except in this case, we're assigning access rights to files and directories, not NDS objects. Let's take a closer look at this simple three-step model from the file system's point of view.

Step One: Assigning Trustee Rights

You have to start somewhere, and Step One starts with work. A trustee is any NDS object with rights to directories or files. Trustees are tracked through the DET (directory table). The file system supports the same trustee types as NDS — users, groups, containers, Organizational Roles, and [Public]. Once you identify who is going to get the rights, you have to determine what rights you're going to give them and where the rights will be assigned. This is shown in Figure 11.29. MMarion is granted all rights except [SAM] to the SYS:SHARED directory. These rights are then inherited for all subdirectories underneath. As you can see, the *who* is MMarion, the *what* is [RWCEF], and the *where* is SYS:SHARED. This is an explicit trustee assignment.

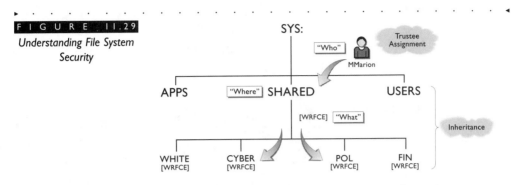

FIGURE 11.29

Understanding File System
Security

So, how is this accomplished in NWADMIN? Once again, it depends on your point of view, and you have two choices:

▸ Rights to Files and Directories — This is from Maid Marion's point of view.

▸ Trustees of this Directory — This is from SYS:SHARED's point of view.

It really doesn't matter which option you choose. You can either assign rights from the user's point of view or the directory's point of view. In the first example, we assign security from Maid Marion's point of view. In NWADMIN, double-click on Maid Marion and her User Information window appears. Choose Rights to Files and Directories from the right-hand list and voilà — Figure 11.30 appears.

REAL WORLD

The Security Information window shown in Figure 11.30 only displays trustee assignments for a single volume at a time. By its very nature, NDS allows you to view information about multiple volumes throughout the WAN. In order to bring up the trustee assignments for a different volume, use the Show . . . button. You can also explore for other volumes by using the Find . . . button. In Figure 11.30, we're only looking at Maid Marion's trustee assignments for WHITE-SRV1_SYS.

Figure 11.30 shows the security window from Maid Marion's point of view. As you can see, she has been granted [RWCEF] access rights to SYS:SHARED. In addition, she's also a trustee of SYS:\USERS\POLIT\MMARION — by default. You can create trustee assignments by using the Add . . . button.

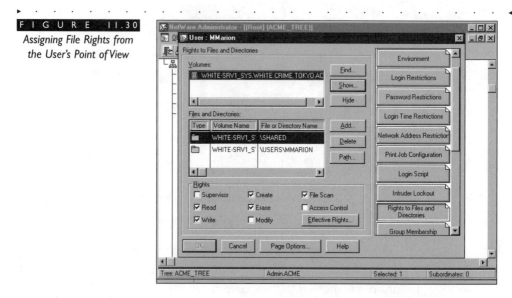

FIGURE 11.30

Assigning File Rights from the User's Point of View

The second option allows you to assign access rights from SYS:SHARED's point of view. In this case, you would double-click on WHITE-SRV1_SYS from the Browse window of NWADMIN. All of its directories should appear. Then, highlight SHARED and click the right mouse button. A pull-down menu will appear — choose Details. Once the SYS:SHARED Details window appears, choose Trustees of this Directory from the righthand list (see Figure 11.31). In this screen, NWADMIN gives you the choice of adding trustees or setting the IRF (Inherited Rights Filter). Notice that MMarion has been added with the [RWCEF] access rights. You can create other trustee assignments for SYS:SHARED using the Add Trustee . . . button. Also, notice the IRF allows all rights to flow through — this is the default.

There you have it. As you can see, it doesn't matter how we assign access rights. Both methods accomplish the same thing — Maid Marion (who) is granted [RWCEF] trustee rights (what) to SYS:SHARED (where).

FIGURE II.31
*Assigning File Rights from
the Directory's Point of View*

NetWare Administrator - [[Root] [ACME_TREE]]

Directory: SHARED

Trustees of this Directory

Trustees:
MMarion.WHITE.CRIME.TOKYO.ACM

Effective Rights...
Add Trustee...
Delete Trustee

Identification
Facts
Trustees of this Directory
Attributes

Access rights
☐ Supervisor
☑ Read
☑ Write
☑ Create
☑ Erase
☐ Modify
☑ File Scan
☐ Access Control

Inheritance filter
☑ Supervisor
☑ Read
☑ Write
☑ Create
☑ Erase
☑ Modify
☑ File Scan
☑ Access Control

OK   Cancel   Page Options...   Help

Tree: ACME_TREE   Admin.ACME   Selected: 1   Subordinates: 1

REAL WORLD

In addition to NWADMIN, you can use FILER and RIGHTS (command line utility) to assign file system access rights.

Now that we've explored the "work part," let's take a closer look at inheritance — "no work."

As we learned earlier, access rights are also assigned through inheritance. This is an automatic side effect of trustee assignments. As you can see in Figure 11.29 earlier, Maid Marion inherits [RWCEF] access rights in all subdirectories of SYS:SHARED. Inheritance is a great thing. It allows you to assign sweeping file system access rights with minimal effort. Remember, as a CNE, work is bad.

But many times, inheritance gets out of hand. Fortunately, IntranetWare allows you to override inheritance using a new trustee assignment or an IRF. We'll explore these topics in just a moment.

If trustee assignments or inheritance aren't quite getting the job done, security equivalence may be the answer. Security equivalence simply states "one object is equivalent to another with respect to file system access rights." As we learned earlier, users, for example, are security equivalent to their parent container. We also learned that security equivalence operates at the trustee assignment level — this is *not* inheritance. Therefore, security equivalence overrides the IRF.

SMART LINK

Get some real "hands-on" experience assigning file system access rights in the CNE program at CyberState University: http://www.cyberstateu.com.

IntranetWare provides four strategies for security equivalence:

▸ *Ancestral Inheritance (AI)* — Any object is security equivalent to its ancestors (parent containers). This means any rights you assign to an NDS container are absorbed by all the objects in the container. This is not inheritance — this is security equivalence.

▸ *Organizational Role* — Our special NDS objects designed as task identifiers. Jobs that require multiple temporary users are excellent candidates for Organizational Roles. Simply assign file system access rights to the Role and they are absorbed by all occupants of the Role. Once again, this is not inheritance.

▸ *Groups* — Allows you to distribute similar rights to unrelated users. That is, users not within the same area of the NDS tree. Members of any group absorb (not inherit) rights assigned to the host Group object.

▸ *Directory Map* — In very special circumstances, security equivalence can be used to facilitate Directory Map objects. When you create a Directory Map object, be sure to assign adequate file system rights to its physical location. Then when you use the MAP command to create logical pointers, be sure to assign the host user security equivalence to the Directory Map object.

This completes Step One of the file system security model. Remember, this is the hard part. Step Two and Step Three are optional. Step Two allows us to filter inherited rights, and Step Three combines all rights assignments into a single mathematical formula — math in the 7th Dimension. Let's keep rolling!

Step Two: Filtering IRF Rights

Earlier we learned there are two ways of blocking unwanted inherited rights: new trustee assignments and the Inherited Rights Filter (IRF). The IRF blocks inherited rights at any point in the tree. There are, however, two very important points you must understand about how the IRF works:

- It's an inclusive filter, which means the rights that are in the filter are the ones that are allowed to pass through.

- The IRF applies to everyone in the NDS tree. Once you've assigned an IRF to a directory, everyone is blocked *except* Admin (or anyone else with the [S] file system right).

This is the only place where file system and NDS security differs. The NDS IRF blocks the Supervisor right. The file system IRF, on the other hand, *cannot* block the Supervisor right. As you saw earlier in Figure 11.31, the IRF is assigned using the Trustees of this Directory option. Also notice that the Supervisor right has been grayed out. This means it cannot be removed. Also notice the downward arrows that appear next to each option box. These differentiate IRF rights from trustee assignments. Anywhere you see a downward arrow, you can assume it's an IRF filter.

When you assign an IRF, all sorts of crazy things happen. My word of advice is, "Avoid them at all cost." But if you can't, you'll need to deal with Step Three — calculating effective rights.

Step Three: Calculating Effective Rights

As we learned earlier, effective rights are the bottom line. This is the culmination of our three-step process. In Step One, we assign the rights. In Step Two, we filter the rights. In Step Three, we calculate exactly what the rights are. We also learned that calculating effective rights is as simple as modern math — in the 7th Dimension! Any object's effective rights are the combination of file system privileges received through any of the following:

▸ Trustee assignments made to the user

▸ Inheritance minus rights blocked by the IRF

▸ Rights granted to the special [Public] trustee

▸ Security equivalences to parent containers, groups, or Organizational Roles

As we learned earlier, calculating effective rights for NDS can be mind-boggling and fun. The file system is no different. Let's use Maid Marion as an example. Suppose we're concerned about users making changes to our political database. To protect it, we assign an [RF] filter to SYS:SHARED\POL. This will block MMarion's inherited rights of [RWCEF]. Therefore, her effective rights should be Read and File Scan [RF]. But as you can see in Figure 11.32, her effective rights in SYS:SHARED\POL are, in fact, [RWF]. How did this happen? She must be getting the [W] right from somewhere else. Ah, I remember. She's a member of the POL-Group and they've been granted Write privileges to SYS:SHARED\POL. Therefore, her effective rights become inherited rights minus the IRF *plus* group trustee assignments.

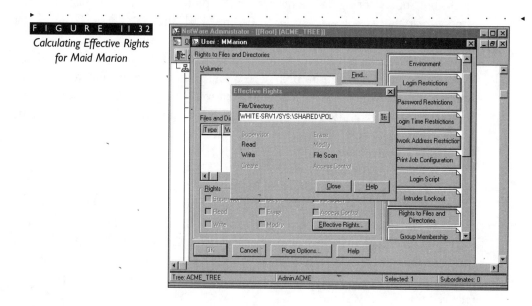

F I G U R E   11.32

Calculating Effective Rights for Maid Marion

NWADMIN provides an excellent tool for viewing effective rights — check out Figure 11.32. All you have to do is identify the user (MMarion) and the directory (SYS:SHARED\POL) — NWADMIN does all the rest.

There you have it. The simple three-step file system security model:

- *Step One:* Assigning NDS Rights — Through trustee assignments, inheritance, and/or security equivalence.

- *Step Two:* Filtering IRF Rights — The inclusive filter allows you to block inherited rights.

- *Step Three:* Calculating Effective Rights — Just like modern math in the 7th Dimension.

That was a fun review. It's fortunate for us that IntranetWare uses the same model for both NDS and file system security. Even though these two layers apply to dramatically different network elements, they approach security in a similar way. Hopefully, now you have a firm handle on access rights, default assignments, trustees, inheritance, the IRF, and effective rights. They all work together as a synergistic solution for risk management. Of course, there's always that isolated exception when four layers of security aren't quite enough. You never know when a hacker will show up with armor-piercing bullets. Fortunately, IntranetWare has one more layer for just these emergencies — file/directory attributes. Let's check it out.

ZEN

"Shot . . . by you? I'm afraid not, my primitive friend. Your kind has neither the cranial capacity nor the opposable digits to operate a firearm."

Mr. Montgomery Burns

Layer Five — Directory/File Attributes

Welcome to the final layer. I bet you never thought you'd get here. Directory and file attributes provide the final and most sophisticated layer of the IntranetWare security model. These attributes are rarely used, but provide a powerful tool for specific security solutions. If all fails, you can always turn to attribute security to save the day.

Attributes are special assignments or properties that are assigned to individual directories or files. Attribute security overrides all previous trustee assignments and effective rights. Attributes can be used to prevent deleting a file, copying a file, viewing a file, and so on. Attributes also control whether files can be shared, mark files for backup purposes, or protect them from data corruption using the Transactional Tracking System (TTS).

Attributes allow you to manage what users can do with files once they have access to them. Attributes are global security elements that affect all users, regardless of their rights, and they override all previous levels of security. Let's say, for example, Maid Marion has all rights except [SAM] to the SYS:APPS\WP directory — [RWCEF]. You can still restrict her from deleting a specific file by assigning it the Read-Only attribute. Therefore, the true effective rights for Maid Marion in this directory are the combination of her effective file system rights *and* file attributes.

IntranetWare supports two types of attributes: directory and file. Directory attributes apply to directories only, whereas file attributes can be assigned to files. In both of these cases, attributes fall into one of three categories:

- ▶ Security attributes

- ▶ Feature attributes

- ▶ Disk management attributes

Security attributes affect users' security access — what they can do with files. Feature attributes, on the other hand, affect how the system interacts with files. That is, whether the files can be archived, purged, or transactionally tracked. Finally, disk management attributes apply to file compression, data migration, and block suballocation.

Let's take a closer look at IntranetWare attribute security, starting with security attributes.

SECURITY ATTRIBUTES

Security attributes protect information at the file and directory level by controlling two kinds of file access — file sharing and file alteration. File access security controls not so much *who* can access the files but *what kind of access* they have. Once users have been given the proper trustee assignments to a given directory, they're in the door. Security attributes tell users they what he or she can do with the files once they're there. Here's a list of IntranetWare's security attributes and a brief description. An asterisk (*) indicates any attribute that affects both directories and files.

- ▶ *Copy Inhibit* (Ci) — Only valid on Macintosh workstations. Prevents users from copying the file. Even if users have been granted the Read and File Scan [RF] rights, they still can't copy this specific file. Macintosh users can, however, remove the Ci attribute if they have been granted the Modify [M] access right.

- ▶ *Delete Inhibit* (Di)* — Prevents users from erasing the directory or file.

- ▶ *Execute Only* (X) — This is an extremely sensitive attribute and provides a very high level of IntranetWare security. Only the Supervisor, Admin, or anyone with the Supervisor [S] right can set this file attribute — and it *cannot* be cleared. The only way to remove X is to delete the file. The Execute Only attribute can only be assigned to .EXE and .COM files. These files cannot be copied or backed up — just executed or deleted. You should note that many applications don't work on files with the Execute Only attribute attached.

- ▶ *Hidden* (H)* — Valid on both DOS and OS/2 machines. Hidden is reserved for special files or directories that should not be seen, used, deleted, or copied over. However, the NDIR command will display the directory if the user has File Scan [F] access rights.

- ▶ *Normal* (N)* — No directory or file attributes have been set. This is the default. Normal files are typically flagged non-sharable, Read/Write automatically.

▸ *Read-Only* (Ro) — No one can write to the file. When Read Only is set or cleared, IntranetWare also sets or clears the Delete Inhibit and Rename Inhibit attributes. Consequently, a user can't write to, erase, or rename a file when Read Only is set. A user with the Modify access right can remove the Di and Ri attributes without removing Ro. In this case, the file can be deleted or renamed, but not written to.

▸ *Read/Write* (Rw) — Allows users to change the contents of the file. This attribute is assigned automatically using the Normal (N) attribute.

▸ *Rename Inhibit* (Ri)* — Prevents a user from renaming the file or directory.

▸ *Sharable* (Sh) — Allows the file to be accessed by more than one user at a time. This attribute is usually used in combination with Ro for application files. The default "Normal" setting is non-sharable.

▸ *System* (Sy)* — Applies to DOS and OS/2 workstations. The IntranetWare OS assigns this attribute to system-owned files and directories. System files are hidden and cannot be deleted, renamed, or copied. However, the IntranetWare NDIR command will display the file if the user has File Scan access rights.

That does it for security attributes. Now let's take a closer look at feature attributes.

FEATURE ATTRIBUTES

Feature attributes provide access to special IntranetWare functions or features. These features include backup, purging, and transactional tracking. As a matter of fact, there are only three feature attributes in IntranetWare, and one of them applies to both directories and files (P). Here's how they work:

▸ *Archive Needed* (A) — A status flag set by IntranetWare, which indicates that the file has been changed since the last time it was backed up. IntranetWare sets this attribute when a file is modified and clears it during SBACKUP full and incremental sessions. We'll learn more about this in Chapter 13.

▸ *Purge* (P)* — Tells IntranetWare to purge the file when it is deleted. The file then cannot be salvaged with FILER. Purge at the directory level clears all files and directories from the salvage table once they're deleted. This attribute is best used on sensitive data.

▸ *Transactional* (T) — Indicates that the file is protected by IntranetWare's internal Transactional Tracking System (TTS). TTS prevents data corruption by ensuring that either all changes are made or no changes are made when a file is being modified. The Transactional attribute should be assigned to TTS-tracked database and accounting files.

That does it for IntranetWare feature attributes. Now let's take a quick look at disk management.

DISK MANAGEMENT ATTRIBUTES

The remaining seven file and directory attributes apply to IntranetWare disk management — file compression, data migration, and block suballocation. File compression allows more data to be stored on a volume by compressing files that are not being used. Once you enable this disk management feature, volume capacity increases up to 63 percent. Data migration is the transfer of inactive data from a NetWare volume to an external optical disk storage device — called a *jukebox*. The process is transparent to the user because files appear to be stored on the volume. Data migration is made possible because of IntranetWare's internal High Capacity Storage System (HCSS). Finally, block suballocation increases disk storage efficiency by segmenting disk allocation blocks. Suballocation is also automatic, and you can turn it off using one of the following seven attributes. Here's a quick look at IntranetWare's disk management attributes:

▸ *Can't Compress* (Cc) — A status flag set by IntranetWare. Indicates that the file can't be compressed because of insignificant space savings. To avoid the overhead of uncompressing files that do not compress well, the system calculates the compressed size of a file before actually compressing it. If no disk space will be saved by compression, or if the size difference does not meet the value specified by the "Minimum Percentage Compression Gain" parameter, the file is not compressed. This attribute is shown on attribute lists, but cannot be set by users or CNEs.

▸ *Compressed* (Co) — A status flag set by IntranetWare. Indicates that the file has been compressed by the system. Once again, this attribute is shown on attribute lists but cannot be set by the user or CNEs.

▸ *Don't Compress* (Dc)* — Marks a file or directory so that it is never compressed. It is a way of managing file compression. This attribute is used in combination with Ic (immediate compression). We'll check this out in just a moment.

▸ *Don't Migrate* (Dm)* — Marks a file or directory so that it is never migrated to a secondary storage device. This is the only way you can directly manage data migration. Otherwise, all files are automatically migrated once they exceed the timeout threshold.

▸ *Don't Suballocate* (Ds) — Prevents an individual file from being suballocated even if suballocation is enabled on the volume. This is typically used for files that are huge or appended to frequently, such as databases. This attribute is your only tool for managing suballocation once it's been activated.

▸ *Immediate Compress* (Ic)* — Marks a file or directory for immediate compression. IntranetWare will compress the file as soon as it can without waiting for a specific event to initiate compression — such as a time delay. As a CNE, you can use Ic to turn on compression and Dc to turn it off. Both attributes operate at the file and directory level.

▸ *Migrated* (M) — A status flag set by IntranetWare. Indicates that the file has been migrated. This attribute is shown on an attribute list, but can't be set by the user or CNE.

TIP

Any of these attributes can be modified using the FLAG command line utility or NETADMIN menu utility and/or NWADMIN graphical utility. In addition to these tools, attributes can be viewed using NDIR.

These file and directory attributes, when used in combination, can create effective security tools to control who has access to do what with specialized IntranetWare files. The default attribute combination for all files is Normal — nonsharable Read/Write. There are special instances, however, when you can justify customizing these attributes, such as

▶ Stand-alone applications that are not to be shared should be flagged nonsharable Read-Only.

▶ Data files that are shared but not written to simultaneously should be flagged nonsharable Read/Write.

▶ Data files that are part of larger multiuser applications can be flagged Sharable Read/Write only if the application supports internal record locking.

▶ Application files that are accessed by simultaneous users should be flagged Sharable Read-Only.

▶ Large important database files should always be flagged with the Transactional (T) attribute, but be sure the application supports TTS.

▶ Sensitive archive files should be flagged with the attribute Hidden. These include records that are only accessed once a month.

▶ All System files owned by IntranetWare should be flagged System. This is an attribute assigned by IntranetWare, not you.

▶ Sensitive application files that cost a significant amount of money should be flagged Execute Only by the network administrator. However, be careful, because not all applications will run when flagged "X."

Congratulations! You've completed the IntranetWare's five-layered security model. Wow, what a wild ride. It all started with risk analysis and countermeasures. We learned the absolute goal of IntranetWare security:

Let the good guys in and keep the bad guys out.

We also learned that IntranetWare's five-layered security model is an increasingly more secure series of barriers against network threats — users. In Layer One, they log into the "Cloud" with initial and background authentication. Then login restrictions take over. This barrier controls the user's conditional access through five different types of restrictions — account, password, station, time, and Intruder Detection/Lockout. Once the user passes through the first two barriers, their ability to access leaf and container objects is determined by a sophisticated NDS security structure. At the heart of NDS security is a simple three-step process — trustee assignments, IRF, and effective rights.

But what about security *within* the server? NDS security isn't enough. Now we must protect the file system. File system security operates in much the same way as NDS object rights. They're granted with the help of trustee assignments, inheritance, and security equivalence. We learned how the eight different access rights can be used to protect IntranetWare files and directories. But sometimes this isn't enough. That's where attributes come in. The final barrier allows you to override previous security with three different attribute types — security, feature, and disk management.

SMART LINK

For an in-depth review of IntranetWare's file system attributes, consult the on-line documentation at http://www.novell.com/manuals.

Well, there you have it. The IntranetWare five-layered security model. Of course, we're not quite finished. Should someone get lucky enough to break through your network armor, it would be nice to know what he or she is doing there. That's where IntranetWare auditing comes in. Fortunately, IntranetWare includes a sophisticated suite of event tracking services called auditing. Check out the following Real World icon for more details.

REAL WORLD

Have you ever had the feeling you're being watched? Paranoia is a good thing. Especially when it comes to IntranetWare security. Fortunately, IntranetWare includes an Auditing feature (using the AUDITCON utility) that allows an independent auditor to track a variety of NDS, file system, and user events. NDS auditing allows you to track a variety of interesting events, including changes to the ACL, security equivalence, enable/disabling user accounts, intruder lockout, partition management, replication, and time stamp repairs. File system auditing allows you to track numerous events according to three key elements — files, print queues, and servers. Finally, user auditing allows you to track logins, logouts, trustee assignments, connection termination, and disk space restrictions.

The beauty of IntranetWare auditing is that auditors can audit — and nothing else. In addition, auditors can track Admin without his or her interference. Too bad we didn't have this facility around during the S&L days of the late 1980s. Here's how it works:

Step One: Activate AUDITCON — The Admin user gets things rolling by activating the AUDITCON utility from SYS:PUBLIC.

Step Two: Enable auditing — Next, Admin enables auditing for a specific NDS container or volume. Only Admin or a distributed administrator can enable auditing. Once auditing is enabled, only the auditor can disable it.

Step Three: Assign auditor password — When Admin chooses "Enable Volume Auditing" from the Available Audit Options menu, a password prompt appears. This is Step Three. **Note:** You can only enable auditing at the volume or container level. Auditing does not extend to subcontainers. This way, distributed auditors can track different areas of the tree simultaneously. When you assign an auditor password at this point, you're only assigning the password to a specific volume or container. Once you assign a password, it's time to transfer control over to the independent auditor.

Step Four: Auditor login — Now control shifts from Admin to the new auditor. Once auditing has been enabled, he or she can log in to AUDITCON using the new password. This activates volume or container auditing and expands the Available Audit Options menu to include Audit files maintenance, Auditing configuration, and Auditing reports. The auditor is in! The next step is to protect the auditor's independence by assigning a new password.

(continued)

REAL WORLD *(continued)*

Step Five: Change auditor password — In order to maintain independence from Admin, the auditor should first change the auditing password. This is accomplished using the Auditing configuration option from the main menu. Remember, any changes made to this password take effect for the current volume or container only. Once the password has been changed, the setup phase of auditing has been completed and it's time to get to work — Steps Six and Seven.

Step Six: Auditing configuration — This is where the auditor earns his or her pay. The Auditing Configuration window provides the "meat-and-potatoes" of auditing setup. From here, the auditor can activate tracked events, change configuration options, or disable auditing. Nothing happens until the auditor switches on Tracked Events — they're all off by default.

Step Seven: Auditing reports — This is the pinnacle of IntranetWare auditing. It doesn't do us any good to track volume and NDS events unless we generate reports on them. After you've configured tracked events, you'll have to determine which ones you want to include in the report. Then you'll have to decide what the reports are going to look like, and finally how often the reports should be printed. Auditing reports are based on a filtering concept. AUDITCON generates so much information it would be impossible to wade through all the tracked entries. Report filters allow you to print out only the information you're interested in. This includes date and time, specific container and volume events, include and exclude users, files or directories.

That's it — IntranetWare auditing. And if you want to be *super secure*, you can activate some additional auditing functions as part of IntranetWare's NES (NetWare Enhanced Security) feature. This allows you to achieve full Class C-2 security for NDS, the file system, and user access. Now, that's what I call SECURITY!

QUIZ

This mystery doesn't seem to have any "rhyme or reason." Speaking of which, each of the following six "rhymes" provides clues to a word. When you've uncovered the mysterious list, use the first and last letters of each word to discover the "reason" for our journey. Ready, set, go.

A tiny note, it's in quick time,
All you need to solve this rhyme?

Cry to Mark, it's so abrupt,
Delight or horror will erupt.

Set a course to steer the ship,
Plot the route when off you trip.

Just a drop to come apart,
Joy perhaps, or sad at heart?

Describe a lad who now is striving,
One day his hopes may be arriving.

Sculpture of freedom and all is well,
Here's independence and the marching bell.

Good luck. You're going to need a lot of mental energy to solve this mystery.

(Q11-6)

Let me ask you a simple question:
So, how secure do you feel?
Now that you know everything about IntranetWare security, how much are you willing to pay? Are you going to place your server in a titanium vault or live in a 1960s Woodstock fantasy? Remember, the key to security is gauging the range of your boundaries:
Let the good guys in and keep the bad guys out!

THE BRAIN

If you just can't get enough of NetWare security and auditing, Novell has devoted an entire special edition of Application Notes to the subject. It's the April 1994 issue, entitled "Building and Auditing a Trusted Network Environment with NetWare 4" or surf the Web to http://www.novell.com/manuals. Check it out!

As a CNE, it is your responsibility to design, install, and manage the IntranetWare network. But most importantly, you must protect it. Hopefully now you've gained a new appreciation for the value of an impenetrable network armor. We've filled your brain with sophisticated security strategies and given you a utility belt full of advanced protection tools — like NWADMIN and AUDITCON.

So, where do you go from here? The world is your oyster. It's amazing what a little security can do for your fragile psyche. Once all your risks are in check, there's no limit to what you can do. So far, you can manage NDS, synchronize time, map drives, and secure the WAN. I'd say you're becoming a full-fledged "IntranetWare gardener"! But what about the big picture? Now I think you're ready to journey through the life span of a LAN — starting with childhood (IntranetWare configuration) and continuing through adulthood (IntranetWare management). It all starts with a single seed.

REAL WORLD

Now you're a IntranetWare security expert — a real Sherlock Holmes of the WAN. But before you can move on to IntranetWare Configuration and Management, you should take a moment to explore a few final tips concerning NetWare Enhanced Security. Remember, information is valuable and many of today's advanced networks require Class C-2 security configurations. Here's a few "Dos" and "Don'ts".

<u>Do List</u>

Do read the on-line manuals before installing the server software.

Do physically restrict the console to prevent access by nonadministrative users.

REAL WORLD *(continued)*

Do make and securely store frequent backups of TCB configuration files. Your computer system can be replaced, but it may not be possible to replace the data stored on your system.

Do set the console parameter to disable use of audit passwords (as required for the NetWare Enhanced Security configuration).

Do configure your audit trails properly: only trusted users as Audit Administrators and Audit Viewers; only workstation TCBs as Audit Sources.

Do provide sufficient space for audit data collection.

Do archive audit files on a regular basis.

Do keep a manual record of per-user and per-file audit configuration flags, since they are not backed up by SBACKUP.

Do file reports (User Comment Forms) with Novell if you find any problems with the server programs or documentation.

Do create a separate account (for example, BBAILEY-ADM) for administrative work.

Do set up a separate administrative account for each administrator. (Don't share administrator accounts.)Do use a strong password for your administrative accounts.

Do change the password frequently for your administrative accounts.

Do set up a separate administrative account for each dministrator (that is, do not share the ADMIN account).

Do configure the server to remove DOS (either UNLOAD DOS or SECURE CONSOLE) after IntranetWare has booted.

Do configure the IPX restriction on all printer objects so that print servers will accept connections only from valid printer drivers.

Do protect SYS:PUBLIC, SYS:SYSTEM, and SYS:MAIL by defining the appropriate file system rights settings.

(continued)

REAL WORLD *(continued)*

Do set up print queues, print servers, and printers such that only trusted users are on the list of operators, only evaluated print servers are on the list of servers, and all users are on the list of users.

Do modify the "User Template" settings before creating any users: set minimum password length to at least eight characters, password required to "yes," and account disabled to "true."

Do use the user template when creating new users.

Do develop a site policy for password changes, and enforce it.

Do configure the "User Template" and all NDS User objects so that each user can change his or her own password.

Do enable password expiration.

Do configure audit trails to shut off operations when audit trails fill, to avoid audit loss.

Do physically protect the licensing diskette.

Do protect printed output and instruct users to do likewise.

Do protect removable media (such as tapes and floppy disks) and instruct users to do likewise.

Don't List

Don't allow general (nonadministrative) users to have access to the server console.

Don't type your administrative password at any time other than (a) when running INSTALL to set up the server, (b) at the server console SBACKUP prompt, or (c) to the TCB of an evaluated client component.

Don't specify the optional parameters (—s, —na, —ns) when you boot the server for normal operation. This is because the STARTUP.NCF, AUTOEXEC.NCF, and INITSYS.NCF files help initialize the server's secure state.

Don't install arbitrary untrusted NLM executables.

REAL WORLD *(continued)*

Don't give the [Public] object any additional rights beyond those available in the standard distribution (that is, "out of the box"). Rights given to the [Public] object are available to all users on the network.

Don't give sensitive names to what is public information (such as usernames, container names, server names, email addresses, or people's names).

Don't add unevaluated peripherals to the server hardware configuration.

Don't use workstations as queue servers or queue operators, unless the queue server is an evaluated part of a workstation component.

Don't install name space NLM programs that are not part of the NetWare Enhanced Security configuration. Consequently, only the DOS name space is supported on the server.

Don't use undocumented console operations, as they may place the server into an unevaluated configuration.

Don't load NLM programs associated with the AppleTalk Filing Protocol (AFP) or TCP/IP protocol suite.

Don't use undocumented console operations, as they violate the servicer's NetWare Enhanced Security configuration

Don't believe all telephone calls or e-mail messages you receive. For example, the Computer Emergency Response Team (CERT) has documented cases of messages telling users to temporarily change their passwords to a certain value "for debugging purposes."

QUIZ

Here's another doozy:

"Who shot Mr. Burns?"

Now that you have all the clues, let's see if you have what it takes to be a "Silicon Sleuth."

(Q11-7)

In this exercise, we are going to explore the exciting world of IntranetWare NDS and file system security. In order to complete this exercise, you will need to install a server called WHITE-SRV1 in the WHITE.CRIME.TOKYO.ACME container.

Initially, the Crime division, the White-Collar Crime department, and the three White-Collar Crime units (Cyber Crime, Financial Crime, and Political Crime) will be sharing the same server (.WHITE-SRV1.WHITE.CRIME.TOKYO.ACME)—but not the same data. The Users in the Crime division office will be located in a container called CRIME.TOKYO.ACME. The White-Collar Crime department and its three Crime units will be located in a subcontainer called WHITE.CRIME.TOKYO.ACME.

You will need to create Group objects for each of these workgroups (namely, CRIME-Group, WHITE-Group, CYBER-Group, FIN-Group, and POL-Group).

Temporarily, the managers of each workgroup will act as network administrators for their respective workgroups. Because these administrator assignments are temporary, you will need to create an Organizational Role for each (called CRIME-Admin, WHITE-Admin, CYBER-Admin, FIN-Admin, and POL-Admin, respectively).

Each workgroup will be given rights to the SYS:SHARED directory as well as to its own subdirectory under the SYS:SHARED directory (namely, SYS:SHARED\CRIME, SYS:SHARED\WHITE, SYS:SHARED\CYBER, SYS:SHARED\FIN, and SYS:SHARED\POL). The SHARED directory will contain those files that are shared by the entire division, whereas the individual subdirectories will contain those files that are shared by each workgroup. An Inherited Rights Filter (IRF) will be placed on each of the subdirectories under SHARED, so that users from one department cannot see the files from another.

Everyone in these five workgroups will have access to the word processing program (stored in SYS:APPS\WP70). In addition, the Financial Crime unit will have access to the spreadsheet program (stored in SYS:APPS\SS30) and the Cyber Crime unit will have access to the database program (stored in SYS:APPS\DB50). Each workgroup is currently generating a list of other applications that they'd like on the server.

User Template objects will be used for consistency in creating User objects and will contain the following account restrictions:

> ▸ Each User will be limited to one concurrent login.

▸ Each User will be required to have a *unique* password consisting of 7 characters or more and will be required to change their password every 90 days. Each User will be allowed six grace logins.

▸ Because employees in this division work long hours, there will be no time restrictions on anyone's account except between 3:00 a.m. to 4:00 a.m. daily (when system backups and network maintenance are performed).

▸ Intruder detection will be set to lock for 24 hours after 6 incorrect attempts in 24 hours. Intruder detection statistics will be kept for 30 days.

Now that you know the plan, let's go ahead and implement it!

1. Execute the NetWare Administrator utility.

   a. Make sure that you are logged into the network as .Admin.ACME.

   b. Execute the NetWare Administrator utility under Windows 3.1x or Windows 95. (If you haven't created an icon yet, you can find the NetWare Administrator utility under SYS:PUBLIC\NWADMN3X if you're using Windows 3.1x or SYS:PUBLIC\WIN95\NWADMN95 if you're using Windows 95.)

2. Set the current context for the NetWare Administrator utility.

   a. Click on the maximize button in the upper-right corner of the browser window to maximize the browser screen. A portion of the NDS tree should be displayed. If so, move on to Step 2b. If not, select the NDS Browser option from the Tools menu to open a browser window. A Set Context dialog box will be displayed. Make sure that ACME_TREE is listed in the Tree field. Type **[Root]** in the Context field, then click on OK to set the context to the [Root]. Now that you've set the context, proceed to Step 2c below.

b. Next, be sure that your current context for this utility is set to the [Root]. If the [Root] icon is displayed at the top of the screen, proceed to Step 2c. Otherwise, set the context to the [Root] by clicking on the Set Context option in the View menu. A Set Context dialog box will be displayed. Make sure that ACME_TREE is listed in the Tree field. Type **[Root]** in the Context field, then click on OK.

c. Finally, you'll want to get a visual perspective of where these containers are located in the NDS tree. If the contents of the WHITE Organizational Unit are displayed, proceed to Step 3. Otherwise, double-click on the following containers, in order: ACME , TOKYO, CRIME, and WHITE.

3. Create the basic file system directory structure. Double-click on the WHITE-SRV1_SYS Volume object in order to display the directories under it. (Use the scroll bar on the right side of the screen, if necessary, to bring it into view.)

a. Press the Insert button to display the Create Directory dialog box. To create the USERS directory, type **USERS** in the Directory Name field, then click on the Create Another Directory box, then click on the Create button.

b. Another Create Directory dialog box will be displayed. To create the SHARED directory, type **SHARED** in the Directory name field, then click on the Create Another Directory box to de-select it, then click on the Create button.

c. To create the CRIME subdirectory under the SHARED directory, click on the SHARED folder icon, then press the Insert button to display the Create Directory dialog box. Type **CRIME** in the Directory Name field, then click on the Create Another Directory box, then click on the Create button. Follow the same procedure to create the WHITE, CYBER, FIN, and POL directories under the SHARED directory.

     d. Finally, use the same procedure to create a SYS:APPS directory, then create the following directories under it: DB50, SS30, and WP70.

4. Set Intruder Detection/Lockout defaults for the CRIME and WHITE containers. Click on the CRIME container with the right mouse button, then click on the Details menu option with the left mouse button. Next, click on the Intruder Detection page button. Click on the Detect Intruders box, then key in the following Intruder Detection limits:

        Incorrect Login Attempts: **6**

        Intruder Attempt Reset Interval: **1 days, 0 hours, 0 minutes**

  Next, click on the Lock Account After Detection box and type in the following information:

        Intruder Lockout Reset Interval: **30days, 0 hours, 0 minutes**

  Finally, click on the OK button to save these changes, then use the same procedure to set the Intruder Detection/Lockout parameters for the WHITE container.

5. Create a User Template object for TOKYO container. As you know, changes to a User Template object affect only those users created after the changes are made. Since no users have been created yet, this will not be a problem. Make sure that the TOKYO container is highlighted, and press Insert. The New Object window will be displayed. Type **T** and press Enter to select the Template object. Type **TOKYO-UT** in the Name field, then click on the Define Additional Properties box. Finally, click on the Create button to create the User Template. You'll notice a set of page buttons along the right side of the screen. Select the page buttons listed below and make the changes indicated.

     a. Identification page button. The Identification object dialog will be displayed by default. Type the following information on this screen:

Location: **Tokyo, Japan**

Telephone: **813-5481-1141**

Fax Number: **813-5481-855**

b. Environment page button. Click on the Environment page button. Walk the tree to select the following Home Directory information:

Volume: **WHITE-SRV1_SYS.WHITE.CRIME.TOKYO.ACME**

Path: **USERS**

c. Login Restrictions page button. Click on the Login Restrictions page button.

Click on the Limit Concurrent Connections box. A value of 1 will be displayed in the Maximum Connections field.

d. Password Restrictions. Click on the Password Restrictions page button, then perform the following tasks:

Make sure the Allow User to Change Password box is checked.

Click on the Require a Password box.

Indicate a Minimum Password Length of **7**.

Click on the Force Periodic Password Changes box.

e. Indicate a value of 90 for Days Between Forced Changes.

Click on the Require Unique Passwords box.

Click on the Limit Grace Logins box.

Accept the default of six Grace Logins Allowed.

Click on the Set Password after Create box so that you will be prompted to supply a login password whenever you create a User object using this User Template object.

f. Login Time Restrictions page button. Next, go ahead and restrict login privileges between 3:00 a.m. and 4:00 a.m. every day. Click on the Login Time Restrictions page button. A grid will be displayed on the screen showing days of the week along the left edge and time of day across the top. Each cell in the grid represents a half-hour period during the week. You'll notice that when you place the mouse cursor in a cell, the day and time the cell represents is displayed. White cells represent times during which the user is allowed to log in; gray cells indicate times that the user is prevented from logging in. Click on the 3:00 and 3:30 cells for each day of the week. (Alternately, you can click on the cell corresponding to 3:00 a.m. Sunday, and while holding down the mouse button, drag the mouse cursor to the rectangle representing 3:30 a.m. Saturday before releasing the mouse button.)

g. Postal Address page button. Click on the Postal Address button and fill in the following information:

Street: **Toei Mishuku Building; 1-13-1, Mishuku**

City: **Setagaya-ku, Tokyo 154**

State or Province: **Japan**

When you have finished updating the User Template, click on the OK button at the bottom of the screen to save the changes that you have made.

6. Copy the TOKYO User Template to the CRIME and WHITE containers. Click on the CRIME container and press Insert. Type **T** and press Enter to select the Template object. Type **CRIME-UT** in the Name field, then click on the Use Template or User box to copy the properties of the TOKYO-UT User template located in the TOKYO.ACME container. Follow the same procedure for copying the User Template to the WHITE container.

7. Create Group objects. Before you can create users, you will need to create the Group objects that they will be members of. Click on the CRIME container and press Insert. The New Object window will appear. Type **G** and press Enter to select the Group object. Type **CRIME-Group** in the Group Name field, then click on the Define Additional Properties box, then click on the Create button. The Group Object Identification screen will be displayed. Fill in the following information:

   Location: **Tokyo, Japan**

   Department: **Crime-Fighting**

   Organization: **ACME**

   Click on the OK button when you are finished. Follow the same procedure for creating the WHITE, CYBER, FIN, and POL groups (called WHITE-Group, CYBER-Group, FIN-Group, and POL-Group respectively) in the WHITE container.

8. Create User objects. Next, you'll need to create the SHolmes and DrWatson User objects in the CRIME container and the RHood, LJohn, MMarion, and FrTuck User objects in the WHITE container.

a. Click on the CRIME container and press Insert. Type **U** and press
    Enter to select the User object. Type **SHolmes** in the Login Name
    field and **Holmes** in the Last Name field. Click on the Use
    Template, Create Home Directory, and Define Additional Properties
    boxes. Type **CRIME-UT.CRIME.TOKYO.ACME** in the Use
    Template field. Finally, click on the Create button. You will be
    asked to supply a password. Choose a password you will
    remember in the Password field, the same password in the Retype
    Password field, then click on OK.

b. The Identification screen for the SHolmes User object will be
    displayed. Click on the Group Membership page button to select it.
    (You may have to use the scrollbar along the right side of the screen
    to bring it into view.) Click on the Add... button to display the
    Select Object dialog box. Double-click on the CRIME-Group object
    in the Available Objects box on the left side of the screen, then click
    on OK to add this user as a member of the CRIME-Group.

c. Follow the procedure listed above for adding the DrWatson User
    Object to the CRIME container and the RHood, LJohn, MMarion,
    and FrTuck User objects to the WHITE container (indicating the
    CRIME, WHITE, FIN, POL, and CYBER groups, respectively).

9. Create Organizational Role objects. Your next task will be to create an
    Organizational Role object for each workgroup manager. Create an
    Organizational Role object for SHolmes by clicking on the CRIME
    container, then pressing Insert. Type **O** and press Enter to select the
    Organizational Role object. Type **CRIME-Admin** in the Organizational
    Role Name field, click on the Define Additional Properties box, then
    click on the Create button. The CRIME-Admin Organizational Role
    Identification screen will be displayed. Click the browser button to the
    right of the Occupant field, then click on the Add ... button. Double-
    click on the SHolmes icon in the Available Objects list box on the left
    side of the screen, then click on the OK button in the Occupant
    Window. Finally, click on the OK button at the bottom of the screen to
    accept the changes you've made to this Organizational Role object.

Using this same technique, create Organizational Roles for the following users in the WHITE container: RHood (WHITE-Admin), FrTuck (CYBER-Admin), LJohn (FIN-Admin), and MMarion (POL-Admin).

10. Now that you've created the Organizational Roles for container administration, let's give them the rights they need. In this section, we will create an exclusive container administrator for CRIME (SHolmes) and WHITE (RHood). As you know, an exclusive administrator has all NDS rights to a container and blocks most rights (especially S) from everyone else.

   a. To start, assign SHolmes as the administrator for .CRIME.TOKYO.ACME. Click on the CRIME container, then press the right mouse button. Choose Trustees of this Object … from the pull-down menu. Click on the Add Trustee … button. Walk the tree until the SHolmes User object is listed in the Available Objects list box, then double-click on SHolmes to select it.

   b. Next, we'll need to assign SHolmes' object rights. Click on the Supervisor, Create, Delete, and Rename object rights, because the Browse box is already selected. Next, select the Supervisor, Add Self and Write property rights, because the Read and Compare property rights are already selected. With all rights in place, he's well on his way.

   c. Finally, click on the OK button at the bottom of the screen. Good work.

11. You have successfully made SHolmes an administrator of the .CRIME.TOKYO.ACME container. He currently shares this role with Admin. Now comes the "exclusive" part. We need to create an IRF of [B] for the CRIME container. This will block Admin, but not SHolmes.

a. The CRIME container should still be highlighted in the NWADMIN Browser. Press the right mouse button, and choose Trustees of this Object.... Click on the Inherited Rights Filter.... button. Currently, the defaults are selected—that is, all five object rights [BCDRS] and all five property rights [SCRWA].

b. To make SHolmes an exclusive administrator, click on "all rights except Browse". This will leave only the [B] object right selected. Next, click on "all five property rights" to de-select them. Finally, click on OK twice to return to the main NetWare Administrator browser window.

c. Very good work. Now, repeat these steps (10 and 11) to make RHood the exclusive container administrator of .WHITE.CRIME.TOKYO.ACME.

12. Assign file system rights to the file system. You are now ready to start assigning rights to the file system.

a. Assign rights to the SHARED directory. Because all five workgroups will have the same level of access to the SHARED directory, you can grant these rights at the container level rather than at the Group level. Click on the SHARED folder (which is located under the WHITE-SRV1_SYS volume object), then select the Details option from the Object menu. Click on the Trustees of this Directory page button, then click on the Add Trustee ... button. Walk the tree until the CRIME container is displayed in the Available Objects list box on the left side of the screen, then double-click on it. You'll notice that the container is automatically granted the Read and File Scan rights. Click on the Write, Create, and Erase rights, then click on the OK button to accept this trustee assignment. You will need to make the same trustee assignment to the WHITE container, because the Inherited Rights Filter (IRF) on the WHITE container will prevent these rights from flowing down from the CRIME container.

b. Assign rights to the CRIME directory under the SHARED directory. Double-click on the SHARED directory to display its contents, then click on the CRIME directory under it. Select Details from the Object menu, then click on the Trustees of this Directory page button. Next, click on the Add Trustee ... button, then walk the tree until the CRIME-Group is displayed in the Available Objects list box. Double-click on the CRIME-Group to select it.

c. As you can see, Read and File Scan rights are assigned by default when you create a trustee. Click on the Write, Create, and Erase rights to assign these rights to the CRIME-Group. Next, you'll want to change the Inherited Rights Filter for this directory so that most rights are not inherited from above. Click on each of the rights, except for the Supervisor right, in order to de-select them. The net effect will be to assign an IRF of [S]. Finally, click on OK to save your changes.

13. Assign trustee rights for the APPS subdirectories. Now that you know how to grant trustee rights for directories to containers and Group objects, use the same techniques to make the trustee assignments. If you'd really like a challenge, see if you can make these assignments from the trustee's perspective (that is, container or group) rather than the directory's perspective. (**Hint:** You can use the Rights to Other Objects ... option in the Object menu.)

a. Grant the CRIME container [RF] rights to the SYS:APPS\WP70 directory (since all five workgroups will have access to the word processing application).

b. Grant the FIN-Group [RF] rights to the SYS:APP\SS30 directory.

c. Grant the CYBER-Group [RF] rights to the SYS:APPS\DB50 subdirectory.

14. Assign trustee rights to Organizational Role objects. Grant the trustee rights listed below to the Organizational Roles indicated:

   a. All five Organizational Roles should be granted all rights to the SHARED directory.

   b. Each Organizational Role should be granted all rights to their corresponding workgroup's subdirectory under the SHARED directory.

   c. Each Organizational Role should be granted all rights to the home directories of each user in their workgroup.

15. Verify effective rights. You can verify an object's effective rights to a directory from the object's perspective or the directory's perpective.

   a. To verify an object's effective rights from the directory's perspective, you can click on the object with the right mouse button, then select the Details option from the pulldown menu that is displayed. Next, click on the Trustees of this Directory page button, then click on the Effective rights ... button. An Effective rights window will be displayed. Click on the Browser button to the right of the Trustee field. Walk the tree until the desired object is displayed in the Available Object list box on the left side of the screen. Double-click on the object to select it. The Effective rights screen will again be displayed. This time, the effective rights for this object will be displayed in black. (The rights they do not have will be displayed in gray.)

   b. Practice verifying the effective rights of different objects for various directories that we worked with in this exercise from the directory's point of view.

   c. Practice verifying the effective rights of different objects for various directories that we have worked with in this exercise from the object's point of view. (**Hint:** Use the Rights to Other Objects menu option.)

EXERCISE 11-1: CALCULATING NDS EFFECTIVE RIGHTS

OK, now that you're a pro with IntranetWare security, let's experiment with "modern math." Earlier in the chapter, we explored IntranetWare's version of calculus — calculating effective rights. We learned that both NDS and the file system have their own versions of effective rights — and they work exactly the same way:

Effective Rights = trustee assignments + inheritance - IRF (Inherited Rights Filter)

In this exercise, we'll begin Calculus 101 with NDS access rights. Then, in Exercise 11-2, you'll get an opportunity to explore file system access rights. Also, we've included some beautiful graphic worksheets to help you follow along. You can create your own at home with a pencil, some paper, and a ruler.

So, without any further adieu, let's get on with CASE #1.

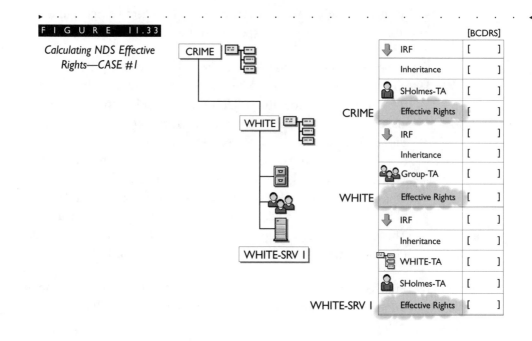

FIGURE 11.33

Calculating NDS Effective Rights—CASE #1

CASE #1

In this case, we are helping Sherlock Holmes gain administrative rights to the Crime Fighting division. Refer to Figure 11.33. It all starts at .CRIME.TOKYO.ACME, where he is granted [CD] NDS privileges. There is no IRF or inheritance in CRIME.

In the next container, WHITE, SHolmes gets [S] from his "CRIME-Group" group. Also, there's an IRF of [D]. Finally, these privileges flow down to the WHITE-SRV1 Server object and become inherited rights. But the server's IRF is set to [BR], so some of them are blocked. Also, SHolmes has an explicit trustee assignment of [D] to the WHITE-SRV1 server. Finally, Sherlock's home container, WHITE, is granted [C] privileges to the Server object.

CASE #2

After careful consideration, you decide that the above rights are inappropriate. So, let's try it one more time. But, in this case, we're going to use the WHITE-Admin Organizational Role instead of the "WHITE-Group" group. This gives us more administrative flexibility and narrows the scope of rights assignments. For this case, refer to Figure 11.34.

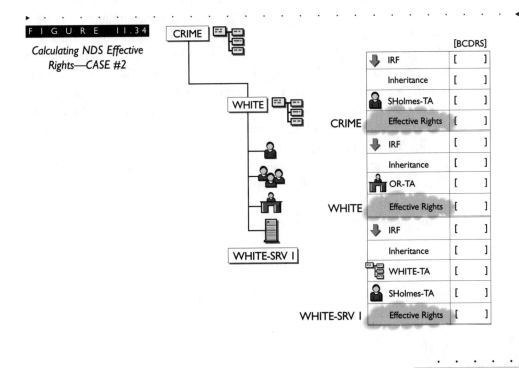

FIGURE 11.34

Calculating NDS Effective Rights—CASE #2

As before, it starts in the .CRIME.TOKYO.ACME container. Sherlock Holmes is granted the [BR] rights to the container. Also, there is no inheritance in CRIME, but the IRF has been set to [CD] anyway.

In the next container, WHITE, SHolmes gets [BCD] through his CRIME-Admin Organizational Role. Also, there's an IRF of [CDRS]. Finally, the container's effective rights flow down to the WHITE-SRV1 Server object and become inherited rights. But the server's IRF is set to [BR], so some of them are blocked. In addition, SHolmes has an explicit trustee assignment of [CD] to the WHITE-SRV1 server. Finally, Sherlock's home container, WHITE, is granted [B] privileges to the Server object. Now, let's see what he ends up with.

CASE #3

In this final case, let's bounce over to the .BLUE.CRIME.TOKYO.ACME container and help out Wyatt Earp—their administrator. Refer to Figure 11.35. As with most NDS trees, it actually starts much higher up—above TOKYO. Wyatt Earp inherits [BCDR] to .TOKYO.ACME through his User object. The IRF is identical, so all rights are allowed to flow through. In addition, he's granted Rename privileges as a user and Browse privileges through his home container—BLUE.

In the next container, CRIME, WEarp gets all object rights through his BLUE-Admin Organization Role. This overshadows the Browse privileges he ancestrally inherits from BLUE. Also, don't forget the CRIME IRF of [BCD]. Finally, all rights flow down to the BLUE container and become inherited. But the Organizational Unit's IRF is set to [DR], so most of them are blocked. In addition, WEarp has an explicit trustee assignment of [C] to BLUE. This assignment is enhanced by the Browse privilege he inherits from BLUE. Good luck.

Well, there you have it. Great work. Now that you're a security guru, let's dive into file system access rights. Rustle on over to Exercise 11-2.

Good luck, and by the way, thanks for saving the world!

See Appendix C for the answers.

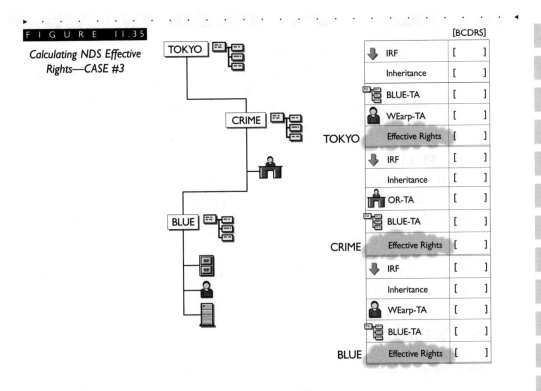

FIGURE   11.35

Calculating NDS Effective Rights—CASE #3

EXERCISE 11-2: CALCULATING FILE SYSTEM EFFECTIVE RIGHTS

Here you are. In case you're lost, here is modern math, part II. In this exercise, we're going to explore the wonderful world of file system effective rights. Now that you've helped "administrate" Sherlock Holmes and Wyatt Earp, it's time to "liberate" the rest of the crime-fighting team, namely Robin Hood, Maid Marion, Dr. Watson, Little John, and Friar Tuck. Ah, a CNE's job is never done.

CASE #1

FrTuck has been made a trustee of the SYS:SHARED directory and granted Read, Write, Create, and File Scan rights. The IRF for the SYS:SHARED directory contains all rights; the IRF for the SYS:SHARED\CYBER directory contains Supervisor, Read, and File Scan; and the IRF for the CYBER.DOC file contains Read, Write, Create, and File Scan. Calculate FrTuck's effective rights in the SYS:SHARED directory, the SYS:SHARED\CYBER directory, and the CYBER.DOC file, using the worksheet in Figure 11.36.

FIGURE 11.36

Calculating File System Effective Rights—CASE #1

SYS:SHARED	S	R	C	W	E	M	F	A
Inherited Rights Filter								
Inherited Rights-User								
Inherited Rights-Group								
Trustee Assignment-User								
Trustee Assignment-Group								
Effective Rights								

SYS:SHARED\CYBER	S	R	C	W	E	M	F	A
Inherited Rights Filter								
Inherited Rights-User								
Inherited Rights-Group								
Trustee Assignment-User								
Trustee Assignment-Group								
Effective Rights								

CYBER.DOC	S	R	C	W	E	M	F	A
Inherited Rights Filter								
Inherited Rights-User								
Inherited Rights-Group								
Trustee Assignment-User								
Trustee Assignment-Group								
Effective Rights								

CASE #2

DrWatson was granted the Read, Write, Create, and File Scan rights to the SYS:SHARED directory. The CRIME Group, of which he is a member, was granted Read, Write, Create, Erase, Modify, and File Scan rights to the SYS:CRIME directory. The CRIME Group was also granted Read and File Scan rights to the CRIME.DB file. The IRF for the SYS:SHARED directory is all rights; the IRF for the SYS:SHARED\CRIME directory is Supervisor and Access Control; and the IRF for the CRIME.DB file is Supervisor, Read, Write, Create, and File Scan. Calculate DrWatson's effective rights in the SYS:SHARED directory, the SYS:SHARED\CRIME directory, and the CRIME.DB file, using the worksheet in Figure 11.37.

FIGURE 11.37

Calculating File System Effective Rights—CASE #2

SYS:SHARED	S	R	C	W	E	M	F	A
Inherited Rights Filter								
Inherited Rights-User								
Inherited Rights-Group								
Trustee Assignment-User								
Trustee Assignment-Group								
Effective Rights								

SYS:SHARED\CRIME	S	R	C	W	E	M	F	A
Inherited Rights Filter								
Inherited Rights-User								
Inherited Rights-Group								
Trustee Assignment-User								
Trustee Assignment-Group								
Effective Rights								

CRIME.DB	S	R	C	W	E	M	F	A
Inherited Rights Filter								
Inherited Rights-User								
Inherited Rights-Group								
Trustee Assignment-User								
Trustee Assignment-Group								
Effective Rights								

CASE #3

MMarion was granted the Modify and Access Control rights to the SYS:SHARED\POL directory. In addition, the POL Group was granted the Read, Write, Create, Erase, and File Scan rights to both the SYS:SHARED and SYS:SHARED\POL directories. The IRF for the SYS:SHARED directory contains all rights; the IRF for the SYS:SHARED\POL directory contains the Supervisor right; and the IRF for the CRIME.RPT file contains all rights. Calculate MMarion's effective rights to the SYS:SHARED directory, the SYS:SHARED\POL directory, and the CRIMEP.RPT file, using the worksheet in Figure 11.38.

SYS:SHARED	S	R	C	W	E	M	F	A
Inherited Rights Filter								
Inherited Rights-User								
Inherited Rights-Group								
Trustee Assignment-User								
Trustee Assignment-Group								
Effective Rights								

SYS:SHARED\POL	S	R	C	W	E	M	F	A
Inherited Rights Filter								
Inherited Rights-User								
Inherited Rights-Group								
Trustee Assignment-User								
Trustee Assignment-Group								
Effective Rights								

CRIME.RPT	S	R	C	W	E	M	F	A
Inherited Rights Filter								
Inherited Rights-User								
Inherited Rights-Group								
Trustee Assignment-User								
Trustee Assignment-Group								
Effective Rights								

CASE #4

SHolmes was granted all rights to the SYS:SHARED directory. The CRIME Group, of which he is a member, was granted Read, Write, Create, and File Scan rights to the SYS:SHARED\CRIME directory. The CRIME Group was also granted Read and File Scan rights to the CRIME.DB file. The IRF for the SYS:SHARED directory contains all rights; the IRF for the SYS:SHARED\CRIME directory contains the Supervisor right; and the IRF for the CRIME.DB file contains Supervisor, Read, and File Scan rights. Calculate SHolmes' effective rights to the SYS:SHARED directory, the SYS:SHARED\CRIME directory, and the CRIME.DB file, using the worksheet in Figure 11.39.

Calculating File System Effective Rights—CASE #4

SYS:SHARED	S	R	C	W	E	M	F	A
Inherited Rights Filter								
Inherited Rights-User								
Inherited Rights-Group								
Trustee Assignment-User								
Trustee Assignment-Group								
Effective Rights								

SYS:SHARED\CRIME	S	R	C	W	E	M	F	A
Inherited Rights Filter								
Inherited Rights-User								
Inherited Rights-Group								
Trustee Assignment-User								
Trustee Assignment-Group								
Effective Rights								

CRIME.DB	S	R	C	W	E	M	F	A
Inherited Rights Filter								
Inherited Rights-User								
Inherited Rights-Group								
Trustee Assignment-User								
Trustee Assignment-Group								
Effective Rights								

The answers to all of these cases are in Appendix C.

Circle the 20 IntranetWare Security terms hidden in this word search puzzle using the hints provided.

```
T  S  M  W  O  D  N  Z  S  R  Y  L  L  O  R  U  G  X  K  D  W
R  T  I  M  E  R  E  S  T  R  I  C  T  I  O  N  S  K  E  T  L
U  A  S  E  F  F  E  C  T  I  V  E  R  I  G  H  T  S  L  X  D
S  T  S  Q  N  U  N  I  Q  U  E  P  A  S  S  W  O  R  D  S  Y
T  I  Q  F  V  Y  O  L  I  T  U  N  W  P  X  S  B  E  I  G  M
E  O  F  R  O  X  T  B  S  Y  W  M  Y  N  P  J  H  S  W  F  K
E  N  V  I  N  T  R  U  D  E  R  D  E  T  E  C  T  I  O  N  F
R  R  H  F  O  O  R  P  R  O  P  E  R  T  Y  R  I  G  H  T  S
I  E  C  I  P  T  R  N  J  X  I  O  F  O  E  U  Q  F  T  X  S
G  S  E  C  U  R  I  T  Y  E  Q  U  I  V  A  L  E  N  C  E  S
H  T  Z  Y  V  C  Z  Z  W  Q  L  O  R  C  C  Y  Z  M  M  M  E
T  R  D  Q  C  I  W  N  R  K  O  B  U  N  A  E  M  L  A  Q  O
S  I  N  U  F  I  F  O  M  M  S  K  V  S  L  K  F  P  G  T  Y
M  C  M  P  G  R  A  C  E  L  O  G  I  N  S  C  Y  J  H  X  G
A  T  O  B  J  E  C  T  R  I  G  H  T  S  D  I  L  R  O  Y  P
J  I  S  H  K  P  R  I  V  A  T  E  K  E  Y  L  Y  B  C  D  W
I  O  K  U  B  M  E  D  D  L  M  Y  P  N  R  B  I  B  E  H  D
Y  N  R  E  J  R  F  U  V  D  L  D  R  R  Q  U  E  Q  Y  T  F
R  S  J  X  U  E  D  A  T  A  E  N  C  R  Y  P  T  I  O  N  Q
G  O  U  N  C  P  P  A  C  K  E  T  S  I  G  N  A  T  U  R  E
C  F  G  J  X  G  O  J  G  L  Q  S  D  Q  S  V  Y  S  D  X  T
```

Hints:
1. Property of an object that lists trustees of the object.
2. Workstation command line utility used to audit network transactions.
3. Method of encoding data for security purposes.
4. The rights that an object can actually exercise for an object, directory, or file.
5. The number of times a user can log in with an expired password.
6. Feature that tracks invalid login attempts.

7. Controls the rights that can be inherited from a parent container or directory.

8. Security feature that protects servers and workstations by preventing packet forgery.

9. Privileges that are assigned to an object that control its access to other objects, directories, or files.

10. An encryption scheme element that is user-specific and which can only be decrypted with a valid password.

11. A temporary encryption that is constructed from the signature, a message, the user's private key, and a randomly-generated number.

12. Privileges required to view or modify the property of an object.

13. Special trustee which is similar to the EVERYONE Group found in earlier versions of NetWare.

14. Encryption element that is available to all users on the network that is used by authentication services to validate user information.

15. Method of granting a User object the same rights as another object.

16. Login restriction which limits a user to specific workstation node IDs.

17. Login restriction which limits the hours during which a user can log in.

18. Privileges granted to an object which determine its access to another object, directory, or file.

19. System Fault Tolerance feature that protects database applications from corruption by backing out incomplete transactions.

20. Login restriction that requires a User to supply a new password that is different from previous passwords.

See Appendix C for answers.

CHAPTER 12

IntranetWare Configuration

5. E-Mail

4. Network Applications

3. Menu System

2. Login Scripts

1. Workstation Connectivity

The birth of a LAN.

There are many different definitions of "life." The one that you choose depends entirely on your point of view. Regardless of your choice, the fundamental question remains — is your LAN alive? Judging from the following guidelines, I think so:

▸ Carbon-based organic life form — Silicon is close enough.

▸ Consumes food — Your LAN processes valuable information.

▸ Propagates — Most IntranetWare WANs include multiple servers.

▸ Self-awareness — Many times your network has a mind of its own.

There you go — your LAN must be alive. And, as a living, breathing life form, it must pass through the three phases of "life span" — birth, childhood, and adulthood. This evolution (that we all experience) can be both painful and rewarding. But there's nothing more exciting than watching it happen and being involved from Day One.

During birth, the IntranetWare server is installed. In the grand scheme of things, this event is theoretically quick and painless (although I don't know about the latter part). In Chapter 6, you learned about the six stages of NetWare 4.11 installation and how they can be automated using the STARTUP.NCF and AUTOEXEC.NCF files. Decisions you make during installation may have an irrevocable impact on the server, LAN, and WAN. Birth is especially important in IntranetWare because of the importance of the NDS infrastructure.

Once the server has been installed, you are left with a simple directory structure, some workstations, and a few users — a LAN version of a cute little baby girl. Over time, this adorable little monster will learn to walk, talk, and start getting along with others. She will go to school and learn some valuable skills — ranging from how to climb the social ladder to how to deal with integral calculus. Finally, at some point, she will make an abrupt transition to adulthood — buy her first car, get her first job, and move into her first apartment.

SMART LINK

Explore your own IntranetWare Childhood at http://www.kids.com.

In IntranetWare, childhood is dominated by *IntranetWare Configuration*. During configuration, your server undergoes five important steps:

Step 1 • *Workstation connectivity* — Leia takes her first steps. In IntranetWare, workstation configuration files provide an initial attachment to the server and NDS. This is accomplished using Client 32 and Windows 95, or the 16-bit DOS solution.

Step 2 • *Login scripts* — Leia finally begins to talk (and doesn't stop for 85 years). In IntranetWare, login scripts enable you to customize user connections and establish important login settings.

Step 3 • *Menu system* — She learns how to share and begins getting along with others. In IntranetWare, the menu system provides a vital interface between users and the network. Just as Leia learns to get along with others, your users learn to get along with IntranetWare.

Step 4 • *Network applications* — Leia goes to school and learns important (and not so important) skills. In IntranetWare, applications are productivity tools that give the network value. These tools are undeniably bound to the aforementioned menu system — just like Leia is likely to make most of her friends in school.

Step 5 • *E-mail* — Leia makes a quick transition into adulthood by getting her first car, first job, and first apartment — all in the same week. In IntranetWare, e-mail provides a vital link between applications, interface, and management. Think of it as "the force that binds the network together."

ZEN

"Life is like a ten-speed bike. Most of us have gears we never use."

George Schultz

The third and final phase of "life span" is adulthood. At this point, your LAN is secure in its new purpose and the goal shifts from conception to "keeping it going."

These are the golden years. During adulthood, your LAN will get married, have children of its own, plan for the future, and finally retire. Where do I sign up? This phase is controlled by *IntranetWare Management*. It goes something like this:

▸ *Server management* — Your LAN gets married and becomes part of a team. Remember LAN synergy — the whole is greater than the sum of its users. In IntranetWare, marriage takes the form of console commands, NetWare Loadable Modules (NLMs), and server protection.

▸ *Intranet Management* — You get a career and become part of a collective community. You and your married friends join softball teams, bowling leagues, and sewing circles. The server expands to become part of a "collective whole" — the *intranet*.

▸ *Workstation management* — The family grows larger with the addition of three little "rug rats" — aka, children. Life suddenly takes on a whole new meaning. Your thoughts switch from "me" to "them" — cute little people who rely on you. In IntranetWare, these cute little people are represented by users and workstations. You'll never truly understand the frustration and joy of running a network until you have children of your own.

▸ *Storage Management Services* (SMS) — With the family firmly in place and your children advancing through childhood, focus shifts to the future. You need to develop disaster recovery plans and begin saving for retirement. This is life's little backup (insurance) policy. In IntranetWare, backup management ensures job security.

▸ *Remote Management Facility* (RMF) — Your children leave home and are off to a LAN of their own. Now it's time for you to take it easy. Through remote management, you can retire to Happy Acres and enjoy the good life. In IntranetWare, RMF enables you to manage the central server from the comfort of your own office, or even from the luxury of your own sofa.

SMART LINK

For a more in-depth discussion of these IntranetWare management topics, refer to Chapter 13 or surf the Web to http://www.novell.com/manuals.

Wow, I bet you didn't think becoming a CNE would be such a life-changing experience! So far, the LAN has been relatively quiet — this will change. Remember, babies are cute until they learn to walk and talk and eat furniture. The daily bustle of humming workstations and crazed users will quickly take its toll on an unorganized IntranetWare LAN. That's why it's important to carefully configure it now — while things are still under control. It's imperative for you to establish workstation connections, write login scripts, and develop menu systems before the network goes into hyperactivity — configuring an active network is like tuning a moving car.

Consider this scenario: Guinevere walks into her office every morning, eager to begin a new day. She hangs up her coat, turns on the radio, and shifts her focus to the center of worklife — the computer. She gracefully reaches for the on/off switch and gives it a gentle nudge. Voilà! The day begins! During the booting process, Guinevere takes an opportunity to slip out for a quick cappuccino. When she returns, the machine displays a friendly network menu and her e-mail for the morning.

Magic! Although Guinevere doesn't pay much attention to what occurs while she's sipping her cappuccino, the LAN has undergone an entire childhood in only an instant. As a CNE, it's your responsibility to configure the system so that Guinevere doesn't have to worry about connectivity software, login scripts, VLMs, NMENU.BAT, or MHS. As a parent, it is your responsibility to make childhood as painless as possible.

Let's start our journey through the life span of a LAN with the first step — workstation connectivity.

SMART LINK

You can download the new Client 32 connectivity files for free at http://www.novell.com.

Step 1: Establishing Workstation Connectivity

Leia begins to walk.

The first step is always the most exciting. I hope you have your camcorder. While Leia's taking her first step, the network begins life anew as well. During this step, the client computer boots and activates a variety of configuration files. These configuration files establish the client environment and attach Guinevere to the network. All this magic can occur in a 32-bit or 16-bit world:

- ▶ *Client 32* — Provides 32-bit graphical access to NetWare 2.2, 3.12, and 4.11 servers. It is the new and preferred way of networking from Windows 95, Windows 3.1, and/or DOS workstations.

- ▶ *Client 16* — Provides simple 16-bit DOS access to NetWare 2.2, 3.12, and 4.11 servers. This is the older, stable method of accessing servers with ODI drivers, VLMs, and NET.CFG.

ZEN

In walking, just walk. In sitting, just sit. Above all, don't wobble.

Yun-Men

Once the first step of the configuration has been taken, Leia is well on her way toward childhood and Guinevere is well on her way toward LAN productivity. Let's take a closer look at these respective first steps, starting with Client 32.

WORKSTATION CONNECTIVITY WITH CLIENT 32

Client 32 is the newest and most powerful workstation connectivity software for IntranetWare. It is a 32-bit protected mode IntranetWare client that allows Windows 95, Windows 3.1, and DOS workstations to connect to NetWare 2.2, 3.12, and 4.11 servers. In addition, it provides a graphical login utility for logging in from MS Windows. Finally, if you are running Windows 95, you can access network files and printers using the Network Neighborhood, the Windows Explorer, and various application dialog boxes.

All in all, this is a pretty powerful client system. Here's a quick checklist that will help you prepare your workstations for Client 32:

▸ An 80386 processor or better

▸ At least 6 MB of RAM for Windows 95, and at least 5 MB for Windows 3.1 and DOS

▸ 6K of conventional memory (with remaining memory allocated to extended space)

▸ A memory manager (such as HIMEM.SYS, EMM386.EXE, QEMM, or 386 MAX)

▸ Network board with the appropriate 32-bit LAN driver

▸ Physical connection to a IntranetWare WAN

▸ A supported local operating system

Before we explore the detailed steps of workstation connectivity with Client 32, let's take a moment to review the basic components of our network connection.

Understanding the Network Connection

Throughout this book, we have focused on the "network" as a distributed synergistic collection of computers. So far, we've learned everything there is to know about how to design, install, manage, and secure the network. However, we haven't explored the basics of the workstation-to-server connection. This is the most fundamental platform of local and wide area networking.

In Chapter 1, we learned that the network workstation is made up of three fundamental components (see Figure 12.1):

▸ Network interface card (NIC)

▸ Workstation connectivity software

▸ Local operating system

FIGURE 12.1

Understanding the Network Connection

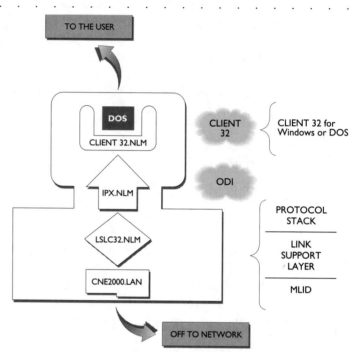

It all starts with the NIC, which is the hardware component that provides electronic communication between the LAN cabling scheme and local operating system.

The local operating system provides a point of access for the LAN user. Without a local OS (like Windows 95 or DOS), there would be no way to tell the LAN what you need.

The vital connection between the NIC and local OS is provided by a collection of files called the "Workstation Connectivity Software." As you can see in Figure 12.1, this software consists of the following four main components:

▸ *NIC driver* — A driver that ontrols communications with the internal NIC. This is a hardware-specific LAN driver such as CNE2000.LAN. It's also known as the Multiple Link Interface Driver (MLID).

▸ *Link Support Layer* — Acts as a switchboard to route network protocol packets between the LAN driver and appropriate communications protocol. LSL is implemented at the workstation as LSLC32.NLM.

▶ *Communications Protocol* — A set of rules that determines the *language* used to move data across the network. The protocol guarantees that two devices using the same protocol can communicate because they speak the same language. This is accomplished at the Client 32 workstation using IPX.NLM.

▶ *Client 32* — A platform-independent NLM that provides 32-bit workstation access for Windows 95, Windows 3.1, and DOS operating systems. This facility is accomplished using the CLIENT32.NLM file.

Client 32 is the only client software for Windows 95 or Windows 3.1 that enables full support of NDS. Using Client 32, you can browse through network services, across multiple trees, and print from Network Neighborhood and Windows Explorer.

THE BRAIN

For more information on Client 32 architecture, refer to the "Workstation Management" section of Chapter 13.

Now that we understand the basics of workstation connectivity, let's check out Client 32 in action starting with Windows 95.

Connectivity with Windows 95

Workstation connectivity for Windows 95 and Windows 3.1 differ in one critical respect — Windows 95 is a true 32-bit native operating system environment. Windows 3.1, on the other hand, is an application that runs on top of 16-bit DOS. Because of this fact, Windows 95 benefits from all the 32-bit advantages of Client 32, including

▶ NIOS, the core Client 32 component, runs as a virtual device driver (VXD) rather than as an executable file.

▶ Client 32 does not require a STARTNET.BAT file. Windows 95 loads Client 32 at startup automatically.

- Client 32 does not need a NET.CFG file. Configuration settings are saved in the Windows 95 Registry allowing Client 32 parameters to be managed using the Windows 95 System Policy Editor (SPE).

- Client 32 for Windows 95 supports long filenames.

- Client 32 for Windows 95 is fully integrated into the Explorer and Network Neighborhood utilities. In addition, you can log into IntranetWare networks and run login scripts from the Windows 95 desktop environment.

- You're able to upgrade Windows 3.1 workstations to Windows 95 and Client 32 for Windows 95 in one installation process called the "Batch Install."

- Client 32 for Windows 95 supports the Windows 95 implementations of TCP/IP, WinSock, Named Pipes, and NetBIOS industry-standard protocols.

- Client 32 IPX protocol stack supports the Windows 95 WSOCK32.DLL.

- Simple Network Management Protocol (SNMP).

In addition, Windows 95 provides its own client for IntranetWare and Microsoft networks. The good news is Client 32 can coexist with the Microsoft client for Microsoft or IntranetWare networks.

Client 32 can be installed in a variety of ways using the Windows 95 Network Device Installer (NDI) and .INF script files to ensure full integration with the Windows 95 environment. Check out Chapter 13 ahead for more details.

During the Client 32 installation, a directory named C:\NOVELL\CLIENT32 is created on the local hard drive. All the required files for Client 32 connectivity are placed in this directory and changes are made to the Windows 95 Registry. Refer to Table 12.1 for a list of these files and their specific load order.

It all starts when Guinevere turns on her computer. This activates an internal 32-bit DOS system, which immediately loads the Windows 95 Registry. Once Windows 95 starts, the NIOS.VXD file activates and Table 12.1 takes over. It's as simple as 1-2-3-4-5-6-7.

	STEP	FILE	DESCRIPTION
T A B L E 12.1 *Client 32 Connectivity for* *Windows 95*	1	NIOS.VXD	The core Client 32 component. In Windows 95 it runs as a virtual device driver (VXD).
	2	LSLC32.NLM	Link Support Layer for protocol switchboarding.
	3	CNE2000.LAN	NIC driver. Remember this file is hardware-specific. Be sure to obtain the latest driver from your NIC manufacturer.
	4	CMSM.NLM	A C-based version of the Media Support Module in the ODI architecture.
	5	ETHERTSM.NLM	Client 32 uses Topology Support Modules (TSMs), which are components of the IntranetWare OS LAN Driver Architecture. ETHERTSM.NLM provides Ethernet topology support for the NIC driver.
	6	IPX.NLM	Communications protocol for the native IntranetWare IPX language.
	7	CLIENT32.NLM	The platform-independent module for all Client 32 services.

Connectivity With Windows 3.1

Client 32 workstation connectivity for Windows 3.1 follows the same basic guidelines as Windows 95. The main difference is Windows 3.1 relies on a non-native, 16-bit version of DOS. For this reason, it uses the same client connectivity files as Client 16:

▸ CONFIG.SYS

▸ AUTOEXEC.BAT

▸ STARTNET.BAT

▸ NET.CFG

It all starts when Guinevere turns on her computer. At this point, DOS executes and calls CONFIG.SYS. Next AUTOEXEC.BAT activates the network-specific STARTNET.BAT batch file. Each command in STARTNET.BAT performs a specific function in creating the network connection. Check out Table 12.2.

TABLE 12.2	STEP	FILE	DESCRIPTION
Client 32 Connectivity for Windows 3.1	1	NIOS.EXE	The core Client 32 component, NIOS, runs as an executable file (.EXE) in Windows 3.1.
	2	LSLC32.NLM	Link Support Layer for protocol switchboarding.
	3	CNE2000.LAN	NIC driver. Remember this file is hardware-specific. Be sure to obtain the latest driver from your NIC manufacturer. At this point, the CMSM.NLM and ETHERTSM.NLM modules also must be loaded.
	4	IPX.NLM	Communications protocol for the native IntranetWare IPX language.
	5	CLIENT32.NLM	The platform-independent module for all Client 32 services.

Once STARTNET.BAT is completed, it returns control to AUTOEXEC.BAT. Keep in mind, it's best to eliminate STARTNET.BAT and place the specific connectivity steps from Table 12.2 directly into AUTOEXEC.BAT.

Refer to the "Workstation Connectivity with Client 16" section of this chapter for more information on client connectivity in a 16-bit environment.

Once you have connected using Client 32, you'll find that there are a few tricks for customizing its environment. The good news is Client 32 is designed to minimize the need for configuration. Most settings have default values that work well in most environments. As a matter of fact, Client 32 uses some settings as a guide, and then dynamically adjusts them for optimum performance. Therefore, you should not have to spend a lot of time configuring Client 32. However, if you have unique needs or preferences, a number of customizable configurations are available.

After you have installed Client 32, you can choose to customize the client for your workstation. To customize Client 32, select "Novell NetWare Client 32" in the Installed Components window and click Properties.

Figure 12.2 shows the Client 32 Properties page. As you can see, it allows you to change Client 32 settings at any given workstation. These properties include Preferred Server, Preferred Tree, Name Context, and First Network Drive. Incidentally, all these configurations and more can be customized in Client 16 using NET.CFG.

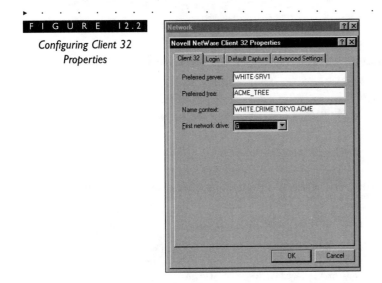

F I G U R E   12.2

Configuring Client 32 Properties

Logging In

Once you've connected to the network using Client 32, there's only one task left — *logging in*. As a CNE, you've already accomplished the hard part — automating the workstation connection. Now it's the user's turn. The good news is Client 32 provides a friendly GUI login utility for Windows 95 and Windows 3.1 users (see Figure 12.3).

As you can see in Figure 12.3, the GUI login utility provides simple Name and Password input boxes within the native MS Windows environment. In addition, the "Connection" page allows you to specify an NDS tree, server, and/or login context. Similarly the "Script" page allows users to override container and profile scripts with local text files. And finally, the "Variables" page provides customizable login script variables. We'll discuss these last two pages later in this chapter.

▶ · ◀

FIGURE 12.3

*GUI Login Utility for
Windows 95*

Novell NetWare Login ⊠

NetWare

Login	Connection	Script	Variables

OK

Cancel

Help

Logging into NetWare using:

▯ WHITE-SRV1

Name: |Admin|

Password: |********|

TIP

**Both bindery and NDS connections are supported by the Client 32
GUI login utility.**

As you can see in Figure 12.3, the GUI login page asks for two pieces of
information:

▶ *Name* — This piece of information represents the user's login name,
which is the same as the User object name. A user cannot log in until
the network administrator has created a User object for that user. Once
the User object has been created, the user can log in using this name.

▶ *Password* — After the user has entered a login name, the user should
specify a password. Passwords are optional but *highly* recommended. As
you can see in Figure 12.3, they do not appear on the screen when they
are typed in. The letters of the password are replaced by asterisks. Refer
to Chapter 11 for more information on login authentication and
password restrictions.

Before a user can log into an IntranetWare server, the user must create a network
connection. This is accomplished by using the connectivity files described earlier.
But that's not all. The user must also change to a valid network drive. For example,
drive F: is usually the default letter used for the first network drive. However, Client
32 can use the D: drive as well. Once the user has switched to the first default drive,
the system will place the user in the SYS: login directory. By default, each user has

the Read and File Scan rights to the directory, and, therefore, can run the appropriate login utility.

Speaking of the login utility, IntranetWare provides three different varieties for Windows and DOS users:

▸ LOGINW95.EXE — The GUI login utility for Windows 95 users. It is found in the C:\NOVELL\CLIENT32 subdirectory on the workstation.

▸ LOGINW31.EXE — The GUI login utility for Windows 3.1 users. It is found in the C:\NOVELL\CLIENT32 subdirectory on the workstation.

▸ LOGIN.EXE — The non-GUI login utility for DOS users. It is found in the SYS:LOGIN directory on the IntranetWare server.

Congratulations . . . you're in! That's all there is to it for workstation connectivity with Client 32. Not so bad, huh? Now let's shift gears a little bit and return to a simpler time — a time when bicycles had three wheels, a movie cost a dime, and clients connected to the network using 16-bit software.

WORKSTATION CONNECTIVITY WITH CLIENT 16

In the previous section, we learned about Leia's first step from the 32-bit point of view. Now let's explore the configuration files required for Guinevere's 16-bit DOS workstation. It all happens with the help of four simple files:

▸ CONFIG.SYS — This is the first configuration file loaded during the boot process. Because DOS and the NetWare DOS Requester share drive table information, CONFIG.SYS must include the LASTDRIVE statement.

▸ AUTOEXEC.BAT — This autoexecuting batch file is modified to activate STARTNET.BAT from the default C:\NWCLIENT subdirectory.

▸ STARTNET.BAT — This file automates the workstation connection. By default, it resides in the C:\NWCLIENT subdirectory and initializes the workstation-specific ODI and VLM drivers.

▶ NET.CFG — This is the final workstation configuration file that is used to customize ODI and VLM settings.

Once the first step of configuration has been taken, Leia is well on her way toward childhood and Guinevere is progressing toward LAN productivity. Let's take a closer look at these respective first steps, starting with CONFIG.SYS.

CONFIG.SYS

CONFIG.SYS is the first configuration file loaded when Guinevere turns on her computer. It is used by DOS for registering devices, managing memory, and establishing local drives. In addition, the NetWare DOS Requester uses CONFIG.SYS to identify a range of letters available for network drives. Here's how it works.

Because the NetWare DOS Requester and DOS share drive table information, we need a convention to determine where the local drives end and the network drives begin. Fortunately, the IntranetWare VLMs do this for us. They read the workstation hardware configuration and determine where the local drives end. From that point forward, they make all remaining drive letters available to the network. The key is determining exactly which drive letters are available. This is accomplished using the LASTDRIVE command.

If you place the following statement in each workstation CONFIG.SYS file, all drive letters from A through Z will be available for local and network drives:

```
LASTDRIVE=Z
```

Remember, you don't have to determine where the network drives begin because VLMs do it for you. For example, most standard workstations have a single floppy drive (A:), an internal hard disk (C:), and a CD-ROM (D:). This means that the first available network drive is E:. Similarly, if you have only a local floppy drive (A: — a more simple configuration), your first network drive will be B:. Undoubtedly, this sounds strange because you're used to pointing to F: as the first network drive. Fortunately, IntranetWare includes a statement in NET.CFG (by default) that ignores drives A: through E: and treats F: as the first network drive regardless of what your workstation thinks.

Once CONFIG.SYS is loaded and the LASTDRIVE statement has been activated, control shifts over to AUTOEXEC.BAT.

TIP

The LASTDRIVE statement works a little bit differently when used with NETx. In the NETx universe, the LASTDRIVE statement identifies local drives only — which means that the LASTDRIVE=Z command has an entirely different effect. In such a case, users are left with no network drives at all.

This is not entirely true because IntranetWare reserves certain ASCII characters for emergencies. If you use the LASTDRIVE=Z statement with NETx, the first available network is [: (a smiley-face). It really works. Try it — it's fun at parties.

AUTOEXEC.BAT

AUTOEXEC.BAT is a DOS configuration file used for activating a variety of workstation parameters, including PATH statements, the PROMPT command, SET parameters, and internal TSRs (terminate-and-stay-resident programs). By default, the IntranetWare client installation creates a file called STARTNET.BAT and places it in the C:\NWCLIENT subdirectory. It then adds the following line to the top of AUTOEXEC.BAT:

```
@CALL C:\NWCLIENT\STARTNET.BAT
```

This is a great way to automatically load workstation connectivity files while separating them from normal DOS operations. There is, however, one problem with this strategy. By placing this line at the top of AUTOEXEC.BAT, none of the other DOS statements load until STARTNET.BAT is finished — which is never. Remember, the goal of workstation connectivity is to load the drivers, automatically execute login scripts, and leave Guinevere in a menu system. This means IntranetWare will never execute the remaining statements in AUTOEXEC.BAT. A better solution is to move the @CALL C:\NWCLIENT\STARTNET statement to the end of AUTOEXEC.BAT.

Speaking of STARTNET.BAT, let's take a closer look.

STARTNET.BAT

As you recall from Chapter 1, IntranetWare workstation connectivity consists of two main components:

- ▶ Communications — ODI drivers

▸ NetWare DOS Requester — VLM files

STARTNET.BAT automates the loading of these files — isn't that special. By default, it consists of the following commands:

```
C:
cd \NWCLIENT
LSL.COM — the first ODI file
NE2000 — or other MLID driver
IPXODI.COM — or other communications protocol file
VLM.EXE — loads the NetWare DOS Requester
F: — switches to the first default network drive
LOGIN Guinevere — or other username
```

By default, this file is stored in the C:\NWCLIENT subdirectory. This is also where the older NetWare 4 client installation process stores ODI drivers and VLMs. The beauty of this scenario is that it enables you to separate workstation connectivity files from other DOS programs. Also, it gives you a central point of workstation management. Once STARTNET.BAT has loaded and the workstation connectivity files are initialized, control shifts from the workstation to server login scripts.

QUIZ

Here's an easy one to warm up your gray matter. Twenty-four red socks and 24 blue socks are lying in a drawer in a dark room. What is the minimum number of socks I must take out of the drawer that will guarantee that I have at least two socks of the same color?

(Q12-1)
(See Appendix C for quiz answers.)

But not so fast. Before we move on to Step 2, you need to learn a little bit more about how these workstation connectivity files are configured. That is, you need to learn more about NET.CFG.

REAL WORLD

As a CNE, you'll decide how transparent the login process should be. Do you want Guinevere to input her login name and password, or have the system do it for her? While the latter is not the most secure alternative, it certainly removes the burden from Guinevere. The following line inputs Guinevere username and password automatically:

```
LOGIN GUINEVERE < C:\NWCLIENT\PASSWORD.TXT
```

This statement logs Guinevere into the network and redirects her password from a text file on the C: drive. In order for this to work, make sure to place only her password (followed by a carriage return) in the text file. Although this isn't great security, you can deter would-be hackers by placing the text file in a hidden directory or on a secure boot disk. Remember, there's always a compromise between user transparent and security.

NET.CFG

The final workstation connectivity file is NET.CFG. This file is not executed, it's simply used as a support file for customizing ODI and VLM settings for STARTNET.BAT. By default, NET.CFG must be stored in the same subdirectory as the other workstation connectivity programs. You only need to create a NET.CFG file if you plan to deviate from the established ODI/VLM defaults. You can create NET.CFG with any ASCII text editor, and it must follow these general conventions:

- ► Left-justify section headings

- ► Place options under each section heading and indent them with a tab or at least one space

- ► Use upper- or lowercase for section headings and options

- ► Precede comments with a semicolon (;) or pound sign (#) for documentation purposes

- ► End each line with a hard return

▸ Write all numbers in decimal notation except where noted

NET.CFG is your friend. Use it to customize ODI and VLM parameters as well as to automate the login process.

For a complete list of NET.CFG parameters, consult the NetWare 4.11 documentation.

QUIZ

What is Bullwinkle Moose's middle initial? You have a 1 in 26 chance!

(Q12-2)

This completes our discussion of NET.CFG and workstation connectivity files in general. Now the first step of configuration has been completed. Leia is well on her way to toddlership and Guinevere is well on her way to LAN productivity. At this point, the workstation computer has booted, the connectivity software has been activated, and Guinevere has been logged in. The next step is to customize Guinevere's network connection via login scripts. Let's dive in.

▸ · ◂

Step 2: Login Scripts

Chatterbox.

The next step in Leia's development is learning to talk. One day, your LAN's mindless babbling will begin to form words. Of course, we all know her first word will be "Daddy." Embrace these early days because soon she'll begin to form sentences and "Daddy" will become "Daddy, where're the car keys?" or "Daddy, I'm getting married" or, even worse, "Daddy, I want to be a CNE." Aah, the innocence of youth!

ZEN

"But the Emperor has nothing on at all!," cried the little child.

Hans Christian Andersen

Login scripts are an expression of your LAN's vocal cords. Once Guinevere has been authenticated with a valid username and password, IntranetWare greets her with login scripts. In short, login scripts are batch files for the network. They provide a simple configuration tool for user customization — drive mappings, text messages, printer redirection, and so on.

Login scripts are one of your most important configuration responsibilities. From one central location, they enable you to customize *all* users or just specific groups of users. Many of the configurations we've talked about are session-specific and disappear when users log out. Login scripts give you the ability to reestablish these settings every time Guinevere logs in. Don't underestimate the power of IntranetWare login scripts.

IntranetWare supports four types of login scripts, which are executed in systematic progression. As you can see in Figure 12.4, there's a flowchart logic to how login scripts are executed. Here's a quick look:

▶ *Container login scripts* are properties of Organization and Organizational Unit containers. They enable you to customize settings for all users within a container.

▶ *Profile login scripts* are properties of the Profile object. These scripts customize environmental parameters for groups of users. This way, users who are not directly related in the NDS tree can share a common login script.

▶ *User login scripts* are properties of each User object. They are executed after the Container and Profile scripts and provide customization to the user level.

▶ *Default login script* is executed for any user who does not have an individual User script. This script contains some basic mappings for the system and a COMSPEC command that points to the appropriate network DOS directory.

Login scripts consist of commands and identifiers just like any other program or batch file. In addition, login script syntax must follow specific rules and conventions. Let's start our discussion with a more detailed look at the four login script types and then explore the commands that make them productive.

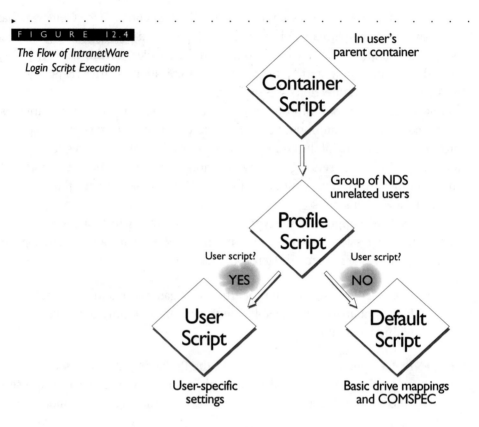

FIGURE   12.4

*The Flow of IntranetWare
Login Script Execution*

In user's
parent container

Container
Script

Group of NDS
unrelated users

Profile
Script

User script?   User script?

YES   NO

User
Script

Default
Script

User-specific
settings

Basic drive mappings
and COMSPEC

LOGIN SCRIPT TYPES

We just saw that there are four types of IntranetWare login scripts — Container, Profile, User, and Default. All four work in concert to provide LAN customization for containers, groups, and users. As you'll quickly learn, login scripts are an integral part of your daily CNE grind. Let's start with a description of the four different login script types.

Container Login Script

Container login scripts are properties of Organization and Organizational Unit containers. In previous versions of NetWare, there was one System login script that was executed for all users. In IntranetWare, it is possible for every container to have its own login script. As you can see in Figure 12.4, the container is the first login script executed — Profile and User scripts follow.

There is one important difference between the IntranetWare Container login script and earlier System login scripts. A container script only executes for users *within* the container. As you can see in Figure 12.5, the Admin user executes the ACME Container login script. SHolmes, on the other hand, doesn't execute any Container login script because the CRIME Organizational Unit doesn't have a script. Similarly, RHood executes the WHITE Container login script, whereas AEinstein executes none.

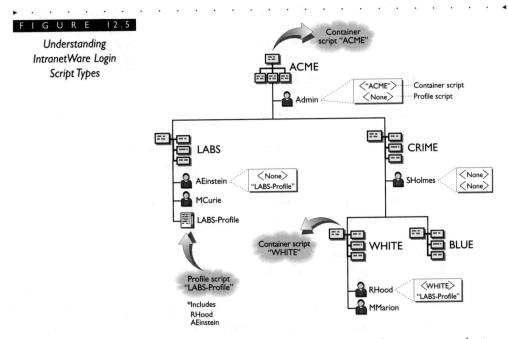

F I G U R E   1 2 . 5

Understanding IntranetWare Login Script Types

This is an important point because many CNEs assume that Container login scripts can be inherited by lower containers. This is *not* the case. If you wish to have one login script for all users to share, you have three options: (1) You can create a Profile login script and have all users point to it; (2) you can use the cut-and-paste feature within NWADMIN to copy one script to all containers; or (3) you can use an INCLUDE statement in each Container login script, which executes a text file containing these commands. Regardless, the moral of the story is IntranetWare no longer provides a single script for all users.

As you plan login scripts for your network, keep in mind that at some point you'll need to maintain them. Use Container login scripts to provide access to network resources, Profile scripts for a specific group's needs, and User login scripts only in special circumstances. Following are the types of things you might do within a Container login script:

▶ Send messages to users within a container

▶ Establish the first search drive mapping to SYS:PUBLIC

▶ Establish the second search drive mapping to DOS directories

▶ Create other search drive mappings for application directories

▶ Establish a network drive mapping U: to each user's home directory

▶ Connect users within a container to appropriate network printers

▶ Use IF . . .THEN statements for access to specific resources based on times, group memberships, and other variables

▶ Transfer users to an appropriate container-based menu system and/or application

Profile Login Script

The Profile login script is a property of the Profile object. This script customizes environmental parameters for groups of users. Each User object can be assigned a single Profile script — that's all. This way, users who are not directly related in the NDS tree can share a common login script. For example, Figure 12.5 shows how the AEinstein and RHood can share the LABS-Profile login script even though they live in different parts of the tree. Also note how the Profile login script executes after the Container script, and in Mr. Einstein's case, the Profile login script is the only script that executes.

Figure 12.6 shows an example of how the Profile login script is created in NWADMIN. Once the script has been defined, two things must happen so you can use it. One, each user must have the Browse right to the object and the Read property right to the Profile object's Login Script Property (assuming the user and Profile are defined in different containers). Two, the complete name of the Profile object must be defined in the user's Profile Login Script Property. See the case study at the end of this chapter.

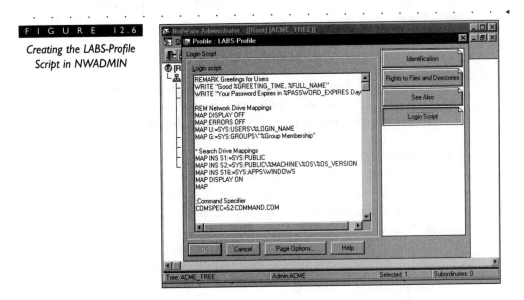

F I G U R E   12.6

Creating the LABS-Profile
Script in NWADMIN

TIP

Remember, users can be assigned to only one Profile object, but other Profile login scripts can be specified at the command line. For example, the following line would allow RHood to execute the "WHITE-Profile" script in addition to his default "LABS-Profile" script:

```
LOGIN RHOOD /P.CN=WHITE-Profile.OU=WHITE.OU=CRIME.OU=
TOKYO.O=ACME
```

Wasn't that fun?

Profile login scripts should be used to customize specific group configurations. Some tasks you can accomplish with Profile login scripts include

▶ Send messages to users within a group

▶ Establish network drive mappings to special data directories, report files, or other servers that contain critical group information

▸ Establish search drive mappings to group application directories

▸ Connect to group-specific printers such as high-resolution LaserJets, plotters, or faxes

SMART LINK

For more information about ACME's login scripts and a chance to try out NetWare Administrator on your own, surf on over to CyberState University and World Wire: http://www.cyberstateu.com.

User Login Script

The User login script is a property of each User object. The User script is executed after the Container and Profile scripts, and provides customization all the way down to the user level. Although User scripts are a nice feature, they can quickly become a maintenance nightmare — imagine hundreds and hundreds of User login scripts constantly screaming for attention. Nope, one baby is enough. A better strategy is to use Container and Profile scripts as much as possible and eliminate the User scripts altogether.

The primary purpose of the User login script is user-specific customization. This level of customization can be accomplished in the Container and Profile scripts by using IF . . .THEN logic commands. But, if you absolutely have to create a user-specific script, it's nice to know that it's there.

User login scripts should be created only in special circumstances. Remember, you have to *maintain* any scripts you create. Some instances when a User script might be justified include:

▸ Establish network drive mappings to specific user directories, provided that these directories do not correspond with the drive mappings made in the Container script

▸ Connect to commonly used printers, in addition to the ones selected in the Container and Profile scripts

▸ Send weekly messages to remind the user about time-sensitive tasks

▸ Activate a special user-specific menu system and/or application

Default Login Script

The Default login script is executed for any user who does not have an individual User script. This poses an interesting dilemma. Earlier we said it's a good idea not to have a User script. This means the Default script will automatically execute. Oops. This is a problem because the default script typically overrides already-established drive mappings and COMSPEC settings. Fortunately, Novell has recognized this problem and provides you with the means to disable the Default login script using the following statement:

```
NO_DEFAULT
```

This command must be placed in a Container or Profile login script.

TIP

The Default login script cannot be edited because it is included in the SYS:LOGIN\LOGIN.EXE command code. It can, however, be disabled by including the NO_DEFAULT command in a Container or Profile script.

QUIZ

So, you think you're so smart? Let's see if you can think in three dimensions. A man is 100 yards due south of a bear. He walks 100 yards due east, then faces due north, fires his gun due north, and hits the bear.

What color was the bear?

Don't underestimate this one. The answer is much more involved than you think.

(Q12-3)

This completes our discussion of the different login script types. In leaving this little discussion, consider the factors that determine how you use login scripts and which types you'll need. These factors include the needs of users, their knowledge level, the size of your network, the complexity of the WAN, the type of groups, and access requirements for different containers. Remember, login script design can go a long way toward increasing your CNE quality of life and decreasing your daily workload. This is your first shot at parenthood (system customization); don't underestimate it.

LOGIN SCRIPT COMMANDS

Login scripts consist of commands and identifiers just as any other program or batch file. In addition, login script syntax must follow specific rules and conventions. The syntax for login script programming is quite simple, but you must be sure to organize identifier variables and commands with appropriate grammar — much like learning to talk. For example, consider the following line:

```
MAP U:=SYS:USERS\%LOGIN_NAME
```

This line uses proper login script syntax — it starts with the login script command MAP and uses appropriate identifier variable grammar — %LOGIN_NAME. The cool thing about this line is that it changes for each user. For example, when Dr. Watson logs in, the system creates a U: drive for him, and it points to SYS:USERS\ DRWATSON. On the other hand, when SHolmes logs in, his U: drive points to SYS:USERS\SHOLMES. Cool!

Another good example of login script vernacular is the WRITE command. Consider the following statement:

```
WRITE "Good %GREETING_TIME, %FULL_NAME!"
```

Depending on the time of day and user who logs in, this single statement will provide a custom message. For example, Guinevere gets the following message when she turns on her machine in the morning:

```
"Good Morning, Guinevere Wannamaker!"
```

This can go a long way in making users feel warm and fuzzy about the LAN. As a matter of fact, some users get the perception that IntranetWare actually *cares* about them and is personally wishing them a nice day. Regardless of the LAN's motivation, the point is that users feel good about using the network!

All this configuration magic is made possible because of two login script elements — identifier variables and commands. Let's take a closer look at how they work.

Identifier Variables

Identifier variables enable you to enter a variable (such as LAST_NAME) rather than a specific name (Wannamaker). When the login script executes, it substitutes real values for the identifier variables. This means that you can make your login scripts more efficient and more flexible. In addition, it makes the concept of a single Container script feasible. As we saw in earlier examples, identifier variables are preceded by a percent sign (%) and written in all uppercase. This is the ideal syntax for identifier variables because it allows you to use them anywhere in the script, including inside quotation marks (" "). Table 12.3 lists identifier variables available in IntranetWare. Learn them. These cute little guys can go a long way in customizing Container and Profile scripts.

T A B L E 12.3

Login Script Identifier
Variables for
IntranetWare

CATEGORY	IDENTIFIER VARIABLE	DESCRIPTION
Date	DAY	Day number 01 through 31
	DAY_OF_WEEK	Day of week (Monday, Tuesday, and so on)
	MONTH	Month number (01 through 12)
	MONTH_NAME	Month Name (January, February, and so on)
	NDAY_OF_WEEK	Weekday number (1 through 7, where 1 equals Sunday)
	SHORT_YEAR	Last two digits of year
	YEAR	All four digits of year
Time	AM_PM	a.m. or p.m.
	GREETING_TIME	Time of day (morning, afternoon, or evening)
	HOUR	Hour of day on a 12-hour scale
	HOUR24	Hour of day on a 24-hour scale
	MINUTE	Minutes (00 through 59)
	SECOND	Seconds (00 through 59)

(continued)

TABLE 12.3

Login Script Identifier
Variables for
IntranetWare (continued)

CATEGORY	IDENTIFIER VARIABLE	DESCRIPTION
User	CN	User's full common name as it exists in NDS
	ALIAS_CONTEXT	Y if REQUESTER_CONTEXT is an Alias
	FULL_NAME	User's unique full name as it appears in both NDS and the bindery
	LAST_NAME	User's last name in NDS or full name in bindery-based IntranetWare
	LOGIN_CONTEXT	Context where user exists
	LOGIN_NAME	User's unique login name truncated to eight characters
	MEMBER OF "GROUP"	Group object that user is assigned to
	NOT MEMBER OF "GROUP"	Group object that the user is not assigned to
	PASSWORD_EXPIRES	Number of days before password expires
	REQUESTER_CONTEXT	Context when login started
	USER_ID	Unique hexadecimal ID assigned to each user.
Workstation	MACHINE	Type of computer (either IBM_PC or other name specified in NET.CFG)
	NETWARE_REQUESTER	Version of Requester being used (NetWare Requester for DOS or OS/2)
	OS	Type of operating system on the workstation (MSDOS, OS/2, and so on)
	OS_VERSION	Operating system version loaded on the workstation
	P_STATION	Workstation's 12-digit hexadecimal node ID
	SHELL_TYPE	Version of the workstation's DOS shell for NetWare 2 and 3 users
	S_MACHINE	Short machine name (IBM, and so on)
	STATION	Workstation's connection number

CATEGORY	IDENTIFIER VARIABLE	DESCRIPTION
Miscellaneous	FILE_SERVER	IntranetWare server name that workstation first attaches to
	NETWORK_ADDRESS	IPX external network number for the cabling system (8-digit hexadecimal number)
	ACCESS_SERVER	Shows whether the access server is functional (true or false)
	ERROR_LEVEL	An error number (0 equals no errors)
	%n	Replaced by parameters entered after the LOGIN command (starting with %0)

In addition to these identifier variables, you can use any NDS property name within an IntranetWare login script. Just be sure to use the same syntax — that is, uppercase and preceded by a percent sign.

These identifier variables have to be used with valid login script commands. As you can see in Figure 12.7, IntranetWare includes a plethora of commands that can be used in various configurations. In this discussion, we'll present the commands as part of a productive IntranetWare Container login script. In each case, refer to Figure 12.7 for appropriate syntax.

A: WRITE and REMARK

Login scripts should always start with documentation. This is accomplished using the REMARK command. Any line beginning with REMARK is ignored by IntranetWare. It does, however, provide a useful tool for documenting the many different sections of your Container and Profile scripts. Besides the word REMARK, IntranetWare supports three other variations — REM, an asterisk (*), and a semicolon (;). As you can see in Figure 12.7, all possibilities have been used. Another use of documentation is edit tracking. When multiple supervisors are maintaining the same container login script, it's a good idea to document who does what when. Finally, documentation is necessary for CNEs who follow you. After all, you do plan on winning the lottery, don't you?

A
```
REMARK Greetings for users
WRITE "Good %GREETING_TIME, %FULL_NAME!"
WRITE "Your Password Expires in %PASSWORD_EXPIRES Days"
```

B
```
REM Network Drive Mappings
MAP DISPLAY OFF
MAP ERRORS OFF
MAP U:=SYS:USERS\%LOGIN_NAME
MAP G:=SYS:GROUPS\"%Group Membership"
```

C
```
*Search Drive Mappings
MAP INS S1:=SYS: PUBLIC
MAP INS S2:=SYS: PUBLIC \%MACHINE\%OS\%OS_VERSION
MAP INS S16:=SYS:APPS\WINDOWS
MAP DISPLAY ON
MAP
```

D
```
; Command Specifier
COMSPEC= S2:COMMAND.COM
```

E
```
SET PROMPT= "$P$G"
SET TEMP= "U:\USERS\%LOGIN_NAME\TEMP"
```

F
```
IF DAY_OF_WEEK= "Friday" THEN BEGIN
   MAP R:=.REPORTS.LABS.NORAD.ACME
   DISPLAY R:FRIDAY.TXT
   PAUSE
END
```

G
```
IF MEMBER OF "OPS-Group" THEN #CAPTURE P=HP4S1-P1 NT T1=10
IF MEMBER OF "ADMIN-Group" THEN #CAPTURE P=HP5-P1 NFF NT
IF MEMBER OF "LABS-Group" THEN #CAPTURE P=CANONBJ-P1 NB
```

H
```
NO_DEFAULT
```

I
```
PCCOMPATIBLE
DRIVE U:
EXIT "Start"
```

ZEN

"Miami Beach is where neon goes to die."

Lenny Bruce

One of the most popular login script commands is WRITE. With it, you can display a variety of friendly messages during login script execution. One of the friendliest is shown in Figure 12.7. Other identifier variables you can use with the WRITE command include

```
Your password expires in %PASSWORD_EXPIRES days.
Today is %MONTH_NAME %DAY.
```

```
At the tone, the time is %HOUR:%MINUTE %AM_PM.
You're connected as workstation %STATION.
You're attached to %FILE_SERVER.
```

Don't underestimate the power of communication. Goodwill flourishes with a quick note to your users now and again.

REAL WORLD

Here's a list of things to think about when creating IntranetWare login scripts. It's always a good idea to have a few guidelines in mind before you begin exploring all the possibilities:

▶ Minimum — One. All four login script types are optional. Of course, if no User script exists, the default will run. So, at the absolute minimum, you must have one User script with one command — EXIT.

▶ Case — Not case-sensitive, except for identifier variables in quotation marks. They must be uppercase and preceded by a percent sign (%). See the "WRITE" example.

▶ Characters per line — 150 maximum, although 78 is recommended for readability.

▶ Commands per line — One. Also press Enter to mark the end of each line. Lines that automatically wrap are considered one command.

▶ Blank lines — Have no effect. Use them to visually separate groups of commands.

▶ Documentation — Use any variation of the REMARK command to thoroughly document what's going on.

B: Network Drive Mappings

The next section in Figure 12.7 establishes user-specific and group-specific drive mappings. Drive mapping is the single, most important purpose of login scripts. Mappings are essential to IntranetWare navigation and provide a facility for representing large directory paths as drive letters. The problem with mapping is that it's both session-specific (meaning drive pointers disappear when users log out) and user-specific (meaning they're unique for each user). The temporary nature of drive mappings makes them particularly annoying — because complex MAP commands must be entered each time a user logs in. Fortunately, this process can be automated using IntranetWare login scripts.

> **TIP**
>
> In addition to standard **MAP** statements, IntranetWare login scripts support **MAP NEXT** and **MAP %1** commands. The latter will map the first network drive to a specific directory or volume. Also, the "1" can be replaced by any number from 1 to 26.

Before you get too excited about network and search drive mappings, it's a good idea to turn off the display of drive mapping and drive mapping errors. MAP DISPLAY OFF stops complex mappings from displaying during execution, and MAP ERRORS OFF avoids confusing users with mappings to directories they don't have rights to. Don't worry, we'll turn them back on later.

The MAP command is most useful when combined with identifier variables. This way, you can accomplish user-specific and group-specific mappings with only one command. Notice the second network drive mapping in Figure 12.7. Here we're using the Group Membership property from NDS. The trick is getting the quotes in the right place.

C: Search Drive Mappings

Once the network drive mappings have been established, it's time to shift your attention to search drive mappings. By default, the first two should always be SYS:PUBLIC and the network DOS directory structure. Notice our creative use of identifier variables in search mapping 2. This single statement intelligently maps every workstation to the appropriate version of DOS. Of course, these statements must be combined with the exact DOS structure outlined in Chapter 10. The three key identifier variables are

▶ %MACHINE — Identifies the machine such as IBM_PC, Dell, NEC, and so on. These values are established using the LONG MACHINE TYPE parameter in NET.CFG.

▶ %OS — Identifies the operating system as MSDOS, OS/2, PCDOS, DRDOS, and so on.

▶ %OS_VERSION — Identifies the specific version of DOS running on the workstation (for example, v5.00, v7.01, v6.22). This value is determined by the IntranetWare client.

Next, you should create a search drive mapping for every application that users are likely to access. In these cases, you can use MAP INS S16 to systematically create mappings in order. In each case, S16 will drop to the next available search number. Finally, turn MAP DISPLAY back on and issue one final MAP command to show the user what he or she has available.

TIP

Remember from Chapter 10 that IntranetWare search mappings systematically replace the DOS path statement. Also, remember that using MAP INSERT eliminates this problem by adding the DOS path to the end of the IntranetWare search list. In addition, an interesting thing happens when you use "MAP INS S16." The IntranetWare search drives are added _after_ the DOS path. This means users will execute local applications before network ones. Sometimes, this is a good thing!

QUIZ

What is the name for the upper portion of the brain? You know, the part that really hurts right now.

(Q12-4)

D: COMSPEC

The next step is to create a COMSPEC for the new DOS directory mapping. COMSPEC stands for "Command Specifier," and it helps IntranetWare find COMMAND.COM when it's lost. This happens all the time when TSRs and Windows applications need extra space. If COMMAND.COM cannot be found, your users will get one of these messages:

```
Invalid COMMAND.COM
COMMAND.COM cannot be found
Insert Boot Disk in Drive A
```

Interestingly, this causes the hair to stand up on the back of your neck — especially if it happens all day. It must be a kinetic reaction.

COMSPEC solves the "lost DOS" problem by telling the system where to search for appropriate COMMAND.COM file. Keep in mind that each version of DOS on each of your workstations supports a different type of COMMAND.COM. You must make sure to point to the correct file. This is accomplished by using the S2: drive mapping we created earlier. Remember, it points to the correct DOS directory structure for each workstation.

SMART LINK

For more information on the IntranetWare COMSPEC strategy, surf to the Novell Knowledgebase at http://support.novell.com/search/.

TIP

Setting COMSPEC to a network directory for COMMAND.COM has its advantages. However, many CNEs still insist on pointing to a local drive such as C:\DOS. It's your choice. Here are some reasons to use the IntranetWare DOS directory structure:

- ▸ **Speed (with file caching)**
- ▸ **Central management (all workstations point to the file server)**
- ▸ **Diskless workstations (it's required)**

E: SET

The SET command enables you to configure DOS environment variables within the login script. You can use the SET command exactly the same as you would in DOS (except that you'll need to surround the values with quotation marks). Otherwise, most SET variables are configured in the user's AUTOEXEC.BAT file. In Figure 12.7, we've included two important SET variables:

```
SET PROMPT="$P$G"
```

This configures the local and network prompt to display the current directory path. We want users to feel like they're at home.

```
SET TEMP="U:\USERS\%LOGIN_NAME\TEMP"
```

This points the Windows TEMP directory to an IntranetWare drive under the user's area.

Whatever you do, don't use the SET PATH command in a Container login script; it overwrites local and network search drives.

F: IF . . .THEN . . . ELSE

The IF . . .THEN command enables you to use script programming logic. It checks a given condition and executes your command only if the condition is met. In addition, you can add the ELSE statement to selectively execute another command only when the condition is *not* met. For example, you can have the system display a fancy message and fire phasers whenever it is the user's birthday (using MONTH and DAY identifier variables). Otherwise, display a message pointing out that it's not his/her birthday the other 364 days of the year.

The IF . . .THEN command is the most versatile login script tool. Learn it, use it, be it. IF . . .THEN effectively enables you to execute any command based on condition, including login name, context, day of the week, or group membership. As you can see in Figure 12.7, we are executing these three commands only on Friday:

▶ MAP — Maps the R: drive to a Directory Map object.

▶ DISPLAY — Displays a text file that is stored on the R: drive.

▶ PAUSE — Temporarily stops execution of the login script to allow the user time to read the display. Just as with the DOS PAUSE command, execution resumes when the user presses any key.

Also notice the use of BEGIN and END. If you plan on including multiple commands within a nested IF . . .THEN statement, you must use BEGIN to start and END to mark the bottom of the nest. As a side note, IF . . .THEN statements can be nested up to ten levels.

You can do anything with an IF...THEN statement. Don't be shy. Before you resign yourself to creating Profile and User login scripts, explore the use of IF . . .THEN statements in Container scripts.

G: # (DOS Executable)

The DOS executable (#) command has been included by Novell to support external programs. Because IntranetWare has a limited number of login script commands, you might run across a case where you need to run a non-login script program. The most obvious oversight that comes to mind is CAPTURE, which is an IntranetWare printing command that redirects local ports to shared network printers. This command should be included in Container and Profile scripts for user and group automation. You can do so with the following command:

```
#CAPTURE P=HP4SI-P1 NT TI=10
```

There is one problem with this scenario. While CAPTURE is running, the entire login script and LOGIN.EXE is swapped to workstation RAM. Once the # command is finished, IntranetWare reloads the login script from memory. But what if the external program is a TSR or never returns stolen RAM to the workstation? In both of these cases, you run the risk of wasting 70K to 100K of workstation RAM. This is a bad thing. By default, IntranetWare swaps login scripts and LOGIN.EXE into extended or expanded memory.

Fortunately, CAPTURE is not one of those misbehaving # commands. As you can see in Figure 12.7, we've combined the #CAPTURE program with IF . . .THEN statements to customize group-specific printing captures within a single Container login script. Once again, the goal is to satisfy all of your users' needs from within a single, centrally managed login script.

H: NO_DEFAULT

Here's another command that helps you avoid conflicts between a central Container script and the Default login script. As you remember from our earlier discussion, the Default login script is contained in LOGIN.EXE and cannot be edited. In addition, it conflicts with drive mappings and the COMSPEC command from Container and Profile scripts. Finally, the Default login script executes only if there is no User script, which conflicts with our goal of having one centrally managed Container login script. Fortunately, by using the IntranetWare NO_DEFAULT statement, you can skip the Default login script even without a User script. Simply place it toward the end of your Container or Profile script and everything will be fine. Sometimes life can be so easy.

I: EXIT

Congratulations, you've made it to the end of our mammoth Container login script. Don't forget Guinevere. She's counting on finding a menu system and e-mail somewhere in her future. As a CNE, it is your job to orchestrate a smooth transition from Guinevere's login script to her menu system. Fortunately, you have the EXIT command.

EXIT terminates any login script and executes a specific network program. The program can be an .EXE, .COM, or .BAT file and must reside in the default directory. When combined with the DRIVE command (as shown in Figure 12.7), EXIT can facilitate a smooth transition from a login script to a menu system. In the case of Figure 12.7, we're exiting to a START batch file residing in either SYS:PUBLIC or the user's home area. Here's what START looks like:

```
ECHO OFF
CLS
CAPTURE P=HP4SI-P1 NFF NT
TSA_SMS /SE=CAM-FIN-SRV1 /P=RUMPELSTILTSKIN /D=C /B=30
NMENU GUINEVER.DAT
```

In this scenario, the DRIVE command dumps Guinevere into her own home directory, where the menu system resides. Otherwise, she would be placed in the first available network drive (by default). In addition, the PCCOMPATIBLE line ensures that her clone workstation returns a %MACHINE value of IBM_PC.

It's important to note that the EXIT command skips all other login scripts. For this reason, you'll want to be careful where you place it. Only use EXIT in a Container login script if you're convinced there are no Profile or User scripts, or if you'd rather not execute those scripts because they've been created by nonauthorized managers. All in all, this is a great strategy for skipping unnecessary login scripts and making a smooth transition to Guinevere's menu system.

ZEN

"When love and skill work together, expect a masterpiece."

John Ruskin

Before we move on to Step 3: Menu System, let's take a quick look at some other powerful login script commands.

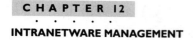
Other Login Script Commands

In addition to the commands shown in Figure 12.7, IntranetWare includes a potpourri of other login script commands. For a complete listing, refer to "THE BRAIN" after this discussion.

▸ BREAK — If "BREAK ON" is included in a login script, you can press Ctrl+C or Ctrl+Break to abort the normal execution of a login script. This is not a good thing, especially in the hands of users. The default is BREAK OFF.

▸ CLS — Use CLS to clear the user's screen during login script execution.

▸ CONTEXT — This command changes the workstation's current NDS context during login script execution. It works similarly to the workstation CX utility.

▸ FDISPLAY — Works the same as DISPLAY, except that it filters out formatting codes before showing the file on the screen. In other words, it can be used to display the text of an ASCII file without showing all the ASCII formatting codes.

▸ FIRE PHASERS — Beam me up, Scotty. FIRE PHASERS can also be combined with identifier variables to indicate the number of times the phaser sound should blare. For example, FIRE PHASERS %NDAY_OF_WEEK will fire five phasers on Thursday.

▸ GOTO — This command enables you to execute a portion of the login script out of regular sequence. GOTO jumps to login script labels — text followed by a colon (TOP:, for example). Do not use GOTO to enter or exit a nested IF . . .THEN statement. This will cause the keyboard to explode. You can go through a lot of users that way.

▸ INCLUDE — As if one login script isn't enough. The INCLUDE command branches to subscripts from anywhere in the main Container script. These subscripts can be text files with valid login script syntax, or entire login scripts that belong to different objects in the NDS tree. Once the subscript has been completed, control shifts to the next line in the original script. Now we're really getting crazy. Consider using INCLUDE subscripts with IF . . .THEN statements to ultimately customize Container login scripts. Now there's no excuse for using Profile, User, or Default scripts. As a matter of fact, everyone in the WAN can share the same Container script by distributing INCLUDE statements to all Organizational Units. Think of the synergy.

▶ LASTLOGINTIME — As you've probably guessed, displays the last time the user logged in. This can be combined with WRITE statements to ensure that nobody is logging in as *you* while you're on vacation. When the cat's away, the mice will play.

▶ SWAP — As you recall from our earlier discussion, the # command swaps 100K of stuff into workstation RAM and doesn't always give it back. The SWAP command can be used to force the 100K out of workstation RAM onto the local or network disk. Simply identify a path with the SWAP command and LOGIN.EXE will bother you no more. When the # command is completed, LOGIN.EXE continues on its merry way. If this bothers you, NOSWAP will force LOGIN.EXE into conventional workstation RAM.

GUI LOGIN SCRIPT MANAGEMENT

The IntranetWare GUI login utility and Client 32 provide two important pages for login script management. They are:

▶ Script page

▶ Variables page

Let's take a closer look.

GUI Script Page

The *Script* page of the IntranetWare GUI login utility is shown in Figure 12.8. It allows users to bypass default scripts by running specified login scripts, or choosing not to run any scripts at all. As you can see in Figure 12.8, this is accomplished by entering the path and name of a text file in the login script box.

This will run the file as a login script and bypass all other scripts assigned to you. Also, if you know the name of a Profile object that contains a login script you would like to run, you can enter the name in the Profile Script box.

F I G U R E   12.8

GUI Login Script Page

To avoid running any login scripts, deselect the Run Scripts option. By doing so, no login scripts (even those entered above) will run.

As a CNE, the GUI login utility gives you much better control over specific user login script execution. Keep in mind, however, it also places such control in the hands of the user. This power can easily be abused. Consider this fact when giving your users access to the GUI login utility.

GUI Variables Page

The *Variables* page of the IntranetWare GUI login utility can be seen in Figure 12.9. It allows you to enter different values for variables that are referenced in any login script associated with the user. As you can see in Figure 12.9, each variable is assigned to an environmental designator — %2, %3, %4, and %5.

F I G U R E   12.9

GUI Login Variables Page

To use the variables, type the desired value in the corresponding field in Figure 12.9. Then reference the variables in all login scripts associated with this user.

For example, users can customize home directories by using the following MAP ROOT command and the GUI login script Variables page:

```
MAP ROOT U:=LABS-SRV1_SYS:%2
```

With this combination, users can map drive U: to different directories each time they log in. All they have to do is simply enter the desired path in the "%2" variable box in Figure 12.9.

Once again, be careful when granting this login power to users. It can be used to override your login script automation strategy.

THE BRAIN

For a complete list of IntranetWare login script commands and identifier variables, refer to page 187 of the *NetWare 4.11 Supervising the Network I* manual. Another good reference is "Using NDS User Object Properties in NetWare 4.1 Login Script" in the May 1995 *Novell Application Notes*. Or, surf the Web at http://support.novell.com/sitemap.

QUIZ

Now that you're warmed up, let's try something a little more interesting. Besides, Guinevere could solve it — how about you?

Alice, Brett, Catherine, and Deirdre went to school together. They became, but not necessarily respectively, an author, a biologist, a cartoonist, and a doctor. Years before, they belonged to A, B, C, and D sororities, and they came from Australia, Brazil, Canada, and Denmark. The letters of each woman's house, the initial letters of her profession, her home, and her name are all different from each other. The doctor had never been to Brazil, and the biologist had never been to Canada. Back at school, Catherine, the girl from Australia, and the biologist used to spend all their spare time together.

What was the profession, the home, and the house of each of them?

Good luck.

(Q12-5)

This completes our discussion of IntranetWare login scripts. I hope you've gained an appreciation for how these cute little tools help you customize user and group connections. Once the Container and Profile scripts have been executed, IntranetWare automatically loads Guinevere's menu. As we saw, this is accomplished by using the EXIT login script command.

She can walk, she can talk; your LAN is an unstoppable bundle of joy. Now that all of the fundamentals have been accomplished, it's time to put her to the test — preschool. It's time for your LAN to learn how to get along with others.

Step 3: Creating the Menu System

Leia goes to preschool.

One of the most rewarding aspects of a child's development is watching how she gets along with others. You can't beat the thrill of discovery and the sight of two toddlers bonding. Of course, this peaceful picture hinges on the ability of children to "share" — a lesson the world hasn't quite caught onto yet. Although with Barney the dinosaur as our ambassador of sharing, I can understand why some people have resorted to violence. Not my baby! Leia's going to learn how to share without resorting to Barney-isms.

Social interaction is a valuable skill on any level. It's how the world works. Learning to get along with others is as practical a skill as tying your shoes or signing your name. As a matter of fact, you'll run into questions on your CNE job application that deal with this very topic.

SMART LINK

Preschool is a self-defining moment in LAN Childhood. Check it out at http://www.kids.com.

Social interaction is also important to our IntranetWare LAN. In order for Guinevere to get anything done, she needs a friendly menu interface for all her network applications and e-mail. A turnkey custom menu environment provides transparent access from "point A" (turning on the computer) to "point Z" (accessing her e-mail with cappuccino in hand). Fortunately, IntranetWare has a built-in menu system that provides custom NetWare-looking menus. This system uses a simple script format and is versatile enough to support large groups of users with a single menu file.

Menus are a good thing. They provide a comfortable, friendly interface for Guinevere and eliminate the need to learn IntranetWare command line utilities. They present information in multiple layers instead of all in one place. But let's be honest. You're probably using MS Windows. On the most fundamental level, MS Windows is a simple graphical menu. It controls what kind of information is presented and enables users to launch applications from a single place. If you're using MS Windows, you don't need this menu system. However, it does have merits as a simple network-oriented interface for small IntranetWare LANs. So, with that in mind, you're prepared to learn about it.

TIP

The IntranetWare menu system is a subset of the Saber Menu System. This software acquisition falls into the Novell category of "if you can't build it, buy it." As a partial version, IntranetWare menus have limitations. For example, you can't specify the location of menus on the screen nor avoid the default color palette — blue and gold. In addition, IntranetWare's internal menu system is limited to 11 cascading screens — 1 main menu and 10 submenus. Finally, there's limited security and many missing features. So, if you're intrigued by what you learn here, consider contacting Saber and buying the full-blown version.

IntranetWare menus are built using two simple command types:

▸ Organizational commands — providing the menu's look and feel

▸ Control commands — doing the work

In addition, IntranetWare has specific rules about how menus are executed and what rights are necessary to get at them. These are the topics we're going to discuss in this section — starting with organizational commands.

ORGANIZATIONAL COMMANDS

It all starts with organizational commands. They provide the menu's look and feel. IntranetWare supports two organizational commands:

▸ MENU — identifies the beginning of each menu screen and provides a title

▸ ITEM — defines the options that appear within the menu and includes a variety of built-in "squiggly" options

REAL WORLD

The first menu defined in the source file is always the first menu displayed — no matter what number it uses. Subsequent submenus are referenced by their numbers. In Figure 12.10, the first menu has the number 01. This will be the first menu displayed for Guinevere — not because it's menu 01 but because it's the first menu shown in the source file. Branching to other submenus is accomplished with the SHOW command, not their numeric order. Bottom line: Menu numbers are for reference only; they don't have any systematical significance (there's a mouthful).

As you can see in Figure 12.10, the MENU command is left-justified and followed by a number. The menu number is then followed by a comma and the title of the menu. Next, options are listed under the MENU command using the organizational tool — ITEM. Items can be specific applications or other submenus — it doesn't matter. Using Figure 12.10 as a guide, let's explore these two organizational commands.

MENU

MENU identifies the beginning of each menu screen. It is left-justified and followed by a number. A single IntranetWare menu file can support 255 different menus — 1 through 255. The menu number is then followed by a comma and the title of the menu. As you can see in Figure 12.10, the first menu displays the title "Guinevere's Main Menu." Subsequent menus have systematically higher numbers (10, 15, and 20). Each menu number identifies the beginning of a new submenu for branching purposes (using the SHOW control command). Menu titles are limited to 40 characters.

FIGURE 12.10

Guinevere's Menu System

```
MENU 01, Guinevere's Main Menu
    ITEM  ^AApplications
          SHOW 10
    ITEM  ^EE-Mail {BATCH}
          EXEC WIN WMAIL
    ITEM  ^FFun Stuff
          SHOW 15
    ITEM  ^MAdmin Menu
          LOAD G:\GROUPS\ADMIN\ADMIN.DAT
    ITEM  ^LLogout
          EXEC LOGOUT

MENU 10, Guinevere's Applications
    ITEM  ^1Windows '95 {BATCH}
          EXEC WIN
    ITEM  ^2Network Utilities
          SHOW 20
    ITEM  ^3Word Perfect {CHDIR}
          EXEC WIN WPWIN

MENU 15, Guinevere's Fun Stuff
    ITEM  Pick your Doom
          GETO ENTER THE VERSION OF DOOM (1-3):{DOOM}1,1,{}
          EXEC
    ITEM  Solitaire {BATCH}
          EXEC WIN SOL

MENU 20, Network Utilities
    ITEM  NetWare User Tools {BATCH}
          EXEC WIN NWUSER
    ITEM  Network Copy {PAUSE} {SHOW}
          GETP ENTER SOURCE FILE(S):{ }80,,{}
          GETP ENTER DESTINATION FILE(S):{ }80,,{}
          EXEC NCOPY %1 %2
```

ITEM

Options are listed under each menu title using the ITEM command. Each item is automatically preceded by a letter (from A through Z) and appears in the exact order in which it is written. If you'd like to force a different letter or number for any option, simply precede the text with a caret (^) and the desired letter or number. For example, refer to menu 01 in Figure 12.10. Notice how the five items are each preceded by a caret and a letter. This forces the letter E, for example, to appear in front of "E-mail." Otherwise, it would get the letter B. Numbers can also be used as shown in Menu 10 of Figure 12.10. **Note:** If you force the letter assignment of one item, you should force the letter assignment of every item —

but you don't have to. The menu program does not track forced assignments and might duplicate letters — this is a bad thing.

ITEM options can be customized using one of four built-in parameters. These are called "squiggly options" because they live inside cute "squiggly" brackets. Let's take a look:

- ▸ {BATCH} — shells the menu to disk and saves 32K of workstation RAM (see Figure 12.10)

- ▸ {CHDIR} — returns the user to the default directory upon completion of the item

- ▸ {PAUSE} — temporarily stops menu execution and displays the message

    ```
    Press any key to continue.
    ```

ZEN

"Where's the Any key?"

Guinevere

- ▸ {SHOW} — displays DOS commands in the upper left-hand corner of the screen when they're executed

Once you've created the "look and feel" of your menus, it's time to move on to the real workhorses of IntranetWare menuing — control commands.

CONTROL COMMANDS

The second IntranetWare command type is control commands. These little wonders are the workhorses of the menu system. They execute menu instructions and enable branching to internal and external submenus. The IntranetWare control commands are

- ▸ EXEC — Executes any internal or external program.

▶ SHOW — Branches to another menu within this menu file. This is used for submenuing.

▶ LOAD — Branches to a completely different external menu file (with the .DAT extension).

▶ GETO — Supports optional user input.

▶ GETR — Supports required user input.

▶ GETP — Assigns user input to a programmable variable.

As you can see in Figure 12.10, the EXEC and SHOW control commands are the most popular. In Guinevere's main menu, for example, she has the option of branching to one of two submenus. This submenuing strategy continues throughout her complex menu file. Let's take a closer look at how these little dynamos work.

EXEC

EXEC is the most popular IntranetWare control command. It executes internal or external commands. These commands can be either an .EXE file, a .COM file, a DOS internal command, or one of four special EXEC options:

▶ EXEC CALL — Runs a batch file and returns to NMENU.

▶ EXEC DOS — Temporarily returns the user to the IntranetWare command line. Users must type **EXIT** to return to the custom menu.

▶ EXEC EXIT — The only way to exit a IntranetWare menu. Don't lock yourself in — use this command.

▶ EXEC LOGOUT — Exits NMENU and logs the user out. Guinevere is left at the DOS prompt without access to the network.

Be sure to include at least one of these EXEC commands toward the bottom of your main menu. As you can see in Figure 12.10, we're giving Guinevere the option of logging out. If you don't include one of these special EXEC options, the user will be trapped in the menu forever. This might not be a bad thing.

SHOW

SHOW is the second most popular IntranetWare control command. Because you can create 255 submenus within a single script file, you need a way of getting to them. SHOW branches to another menu number from within any item. This is a way of submenuing from WITHIN the same script file. Notice in Figure 12.10 how the SHOW command is used with the Applications and Fun Stuff submenus. Also, notice how Network Utilities is called as a submenu from within the Applications submenu.

TIP

Try not to confuse the SHOW control command with the SHOW squiggly option. It's unfortunate that they share the same name. The SHOW control command is used for submenuing, whereas the SHOW squiggly option displays executed DOS commands in the upper left-hand corner of your screen.

LOAD

LOAD performs exactly the same function as SHOW, but in a slightly different way. Instead of executing submenus within the same script file, LOAD branches to submenus in completely different files. Refer to Figure 12.10 for an example of how the LOAD command is used. The Admin Menu item includes a branch to ADMIN.DAT. This external menu file must be in the default directory or specified with an exact path.

There is no limit to the number of menus that you can LOAD at any one time. But remember, you can only display 11 cascading menus simultaneously.

GETO

The final three control commands allow for user input. This feature was previously not available in NetWare menus and is hard to find in MS Windows. GETO, GETR, and GETP are powerful tools, but their syntax is a little tricky:

```
GETx prompt{PREPEND}length,prefill,{APPEND}
```

▸ x is replaced with the type of GET command you wish to use — O for optional, R for required, and P for programmable user input.

▸ *prompt* is replaced by the message you want to send to the user. For example, in Figure 12.10, the last item asks Guinevere to "Enter source file(s):". This is the prompt.

▸ {PREPEND} data is attached *before* the user input. This works oppositely from {APPEND}. For example, in Figure 12.10, refer to the Pick your Doom item. The user is asked to enter the version of Doom he or she wish to play. The number they choose is prepended by the DOOM command, and it executes a batch file to load the appropriate game. This is a {PREPEND}. If no {PREPEND} is necessary, use the braces without any characters between them. Refer to the last item in Figure 12.10.

▸ *length* is the maximum number of characters the user can enter. Again, a length is required and the maximum is 80 characters. In the DOOM example, users can only enter a one-character answer.

▸ *prefill* displays a default response if none is given. It is separated from *length* by a comma and no spaces. Again, in the DOOM example of Figure 12.10, you're forcing a 1 to appear if no input is given. This will run the original game.

▸ {APPEND} defines a value that will always be appended to the user input. Once again, these braces are required, and if no data are needed, type the brackets without any characters. Refer to the last item in Figure 12.10.

TIP

Wow, what a mind-boggling collection of IntranetWare control commands. Don't GET too excited about using GETx. But if you have to, here are a few things to think about:

▸ **The GETO, GETR, and GETP commands must be entered between the ITEM line and the EXEC command associated with them.**

▸ **You can have a maximum of 100 GET commands per ITEM, although you want to limit each prompt to 1 line.**

▸ **Commands can be entered in either upper- or lowercase.**

▸ **You can enter up to 10 prompts in each dialog box. If you want a prompt to appear in its own dialog box, type a caret (^) at the beginning of the prompt text.**

▸ **During execution, the Enter key accepts input, but does not cause the command to execute. To activate the appropriate EXEC command, you must press F10.**

Now it's time to GET on with the show.

GETO allows for optional user input. As you can see in Figure 12.10, the Pick your Doom item uses an optional GET control command. If the user does not enter any input and simply presses Enter, IntranetWare executes the {PREPEND} and {prefill}, which is "DOOM1."

ZEN

"The computer is a great invention. There are just as many mistakes as ever. But now they are nobody's fault."

Anonymous

GETR

GETR requires user input. The menu will not continue until some valid information has been entered. However, the user can press Esc to return to the main menu.

GETP

GETP assigns user input to a programmable variable. If you need a variety of inputs from the user, assign each to a GETP prompt. The corresponding EXEC command can then use these prompts in combination with some valid external commands. As you can see in the final item of Figure 12.10, two GETP prompts are shown. The first input is assigned to %1 and the second to %2. The EXEC NCOPY command then uses these variables to satisfy the user's request. In addition, the {PAUSE} squiggly option enables the user to view the results as long as necessary.

Well, wasn't that fun? If you're feeling a little dizzy, now's a good time to put down the book and grab a soda . . . welcome back. Now that we've conquered the IntranetWare menu syntax, let's take a look at how these babies execute.

SMART LINK

The new and exciting Saber menu system has been integrated in a full line of network management tools. Surf over to McAfee and check them out: http://www.mcafee.com/prod/netmgt/saber.html.

MENU EXECUTION

So, how are IntranetWare menu files executed? Good question. It all starts with the source file. Menu source files are created by using any text editor, and they must have the .SRC extension. As you can see in Figure 12.11, these source files are then compiled into .DAT files using MENUMAKE.EXE. The compiled files are smaller, more flexible, and easily swapped to and from the local disk. You cannot, however, edit .DAT files. You must edit the source file and recompile it for testing.

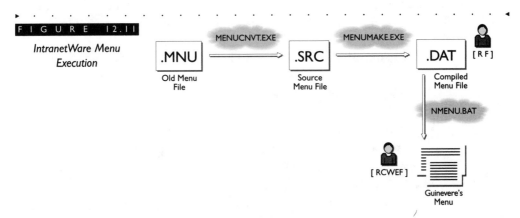

FIGURE 12.11

IntranetWare Menu Execution

The smaller, more flexible .DAT file is finally executed using NMENU.BAT. This step finally brings Guinevere's menu to life. (See Figure 12.12.)

That's not all — IntranetWare also supports older menus. NetWare 3.11 menu files (with the extension .MNU) can be converted into IntranetWare source files using MENUCNVT.EXE. These .SRC files are then compiled and displayed using MENUMAKE.EXE and NMENU.BAT. However, this is not the end of menu conversion. You must also edit some of the .SRC syntax changes, including invalid commands (such as SYSCON), preceding letters or numbers from the old menu system, and the conversion of "@1" variables into newer GETP statements.

▶ · ◀

FIGURE 12.12

Looking at Guinevere's Menu

```
Novell Menu System  4.11                      Wednesday  May  20, 1998  3:36pm




                    ┌─ Guinevere's Main Menu ─┐
                    │ A. Applications          │
                    │ E. E-Mail                │
                    │ F. Fun Stuff             │
                    │ M. Admin Menu            │
                    │ L. Logout                │
                    └──────────────────────────┘






F2=Session Information                                              F1=Help
```

So, what about security? The NMENU.BAT program is stored in SYS:PUBLIC so it can be accessed from anywhere by any IntranetWare user. In addition, there are access right issues concerning the location of .DAT files. Here's a summary:

▸ Users must have the Read and File Scan (RF) access rights to directories that hold the .DAT files. This is typically their home directory or a shared area such as SYS:PUBLIC.

▸ The IntranetWare menu system creates many temporary files. For this reason, users need special rights in the current default directory when executing NMENU.BAT. These rights are Read, Create, Write, Erase, and File Scan (RWCEF). Typically, this is the user's home or a temporary directory. Recall that in the previous discussion, you used EXIT to bail out of the Container login script and automatically accessed NMENU.BAT. You did this from Guinevere's home directory (with the DRIVE command) for security purposes. I knew there was a reason.

▸ If the menu file is going to be used by multiple users, it should be flagged as Sharable.

Once again, refer to Figure 12.11 earlier for a summary of the access rights required at different points of menu execution.

So, what does Guinevere's menu look like? Check out Figure 12.12. As it shows, the IntranetWare menu program creates an extremely NetWare-looking interface. As a matter of fact, it's difficult to tell the difference between Guinevere's main menu and NETADMIN. I just hope Guinevere can tell the difference. Let's review. IntranetWare menu source files are created using any text editor. Their filenames contain the .SRC extension. These files are then compiled using MENUMAKE.EXE into a .DAT file. The smaller, more flexible .DAT file is then executed using NMENU.BAT. Piece of cake.

ZEN

"Never eat more than you can lift."

Miss Piggy

Remember, "wherever you go, there you are." With that in mind, let's take a moment to reflect on our LAN's brief, but exciting, life so far. First, she was born (installation), and then she took her first step (workstation connectivity). Once she learned to talk (login scripts), we sent her off to preschool to learn how to get along with others (menu system).

Now, it's time for our talented toddler to scurry off to kindergarten. There she'll start her long and winding journey down the road known as "SCHOOL"! During this journey, Leia will expand her body and mind to new levels — gaining valuable skills in the process. She'll make friends, buy clothes, ignore you, go to the prom, and, finally, graduate. This all leads to one inevitable climax — adulthood. Where did all the time go?

Step 4: Installing Network Applications

Leia goes to school.
Aah, school:
  "The chalice of wisdom, to drink once more from thee."

I don't know what's more memorable, school or all the extracurricular activities that surround it. Regardless, this is the fire in which we forge our personalities. So many memories — my fourth grade music teacher, recess, stomach-churning school lunches, mind-boggling math homework, field trips, sports, and the junior prom. As we help Leia through this phase of her childhood, we get an opportunity to live our own school days all over again. This is probably one of the most rewarding and excruciating experiences for any parent.

In addition to life lessons, school teaches you a few academic things. With knowledge comes productivity and wisdom. Suddenly, Leia's eyes open to the wonders and possibilities of calculus, art, and prepositional phrases. And sometimes the lessons aren't so obvious. I'm sure you'll never use algebra again in your life, but consider the problem-solving skills it taught you — skills that you'll put to good use as a CNE.

SMART LINK

Speaking of school, check out Novell Education at http://education.novell.com or CyberState University at http://www.cyberstateu.com.

As your LAN learns more and more from school, your users' productivity will increase as well. After all, a network is only as useful as the users who use it (that's a triple-word score). In Step 4 of IntranetWare Configuration, you will give Guinevere all the productivity tools she needs to get her job done. That includes network applications, utilities, and a consistent user environment. Don't underestimate the value of the latter. This means if Guinevere wants to use MS Windows, her application should be in Windows. However, if she breaks out in hives every time she touches the mouse, consider giving her DOS-based applications. Please try not to mix interfaces — it gets ugly fast.

A SIMPLE SEVEN-STEP MODEL

Network applications are the productivity tools of your LAN — and IntranetWare has great support for them. This is accomplished with the help of a simple seven-step model. For the most part, these seven steps help you foster synergy between user productivity and shared application software — I learned those big words in school.

Step 1 • Make sure your applications are IntranetWare-compatible *before* you buy them.

Step 2 • Ensure that the software is truly multiuser.

Step 3 • Create an appropriate directory structure for the applications and all their support components.

Step 4 • Install them.

Step 5 • Establish file attributes for Sharable and Nonsharable network applications.

Step 6 • In addition to file attributes, assign user access rights to network application subdirectories.

Step 7 • Customize the workstation for specific application needs.

This is just a general discussion. Most network applications include specific instructions for making them work on a LAN. However, the previous guidelines are a great place to start.

INTRANETWARE APPLICATION MANAGEMENT

In addition to the simple seven-step model for generic network applications, IntranetWare provides a complete GUI application management system. The NetWare Application Manager (NAM) allows users to run network applications that have been configured and centralized on the server. NAM consists of application objects and a special launcher called the NetWare Application Launcher (NAL). The application's setup information is stored as an Application object in the NDS tree. This eliminates the need for users to have a drive mapping or path to an application's directory. They simply double-click on the NAL icon within Windows and the system takes care of the rest.

To configure NDS and the file system for NAM, you must complete the following three tasks:

▶ Task 1 — Create Application objects

▶ Task 2 — Configure Application objects

▸ Task 3 — Configure workstations

Task 1 — Create Application Objects

NAM supplies three new objects in the NDS tree, one each for Windows 95, Windows 3.1, and DOS applications.

You can create these Application objects in the same way you create any other NDS leaf. Simply select the container where the Application object will reside and choose Create from the Object menu. When creating the Application object, you must provide a name for it and a path to the application's directory. This information can be seen in Figure 12.13.

▸ . . . . ◂

FIGURE   12.13

*Configuring NAM
Application Objects*

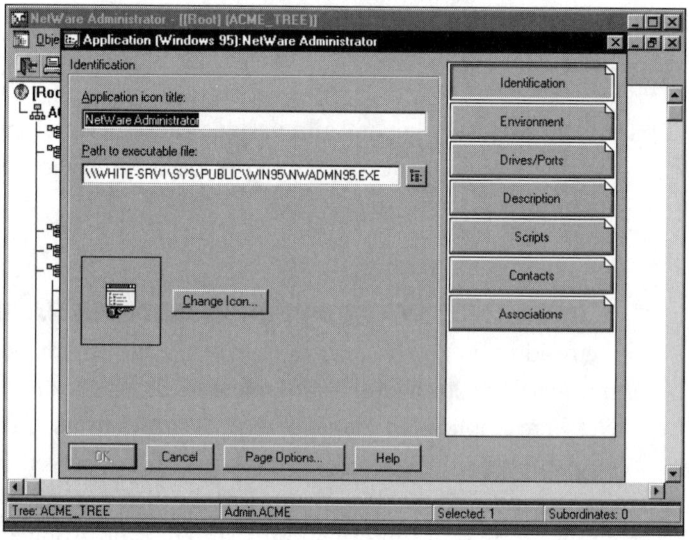

Task 2 — Configure Application Objects

Application objects contain many pages of information. However, the only data necessary is the path to the application and a list of User objects that are allowed to access it.

Figure 12.13 shows the NetWare Application object configuration screen. In the identification page, you can define an application icon title, path, and icon type. In other pages, you can associate users with the object, provide any special commands for startup, and create special scripts that define custom drive mappings when the application is launched.

As previously mentioned, Application objects can map network drives and capture printer ports when they're launched from the workstation. These drives and ports are only active as long as the application is running. When the user exits the application, the mappings and captures are deleted. This is accomplished using the Drives/Ports page.

In addition, scripts can be added to the Application object, which perform login script functions during application launching. This is accomplished using the Scripts page in Figure 12.13. Finally, you can also enter description and names of contacts for the application that is viewed by users.

One tip from the security front: Ensure that users have the appropriate NDS and file system rights to Application objects and corresponding directories before activating NAL. Speaking of NAL, that's the final task in our Application Management model.

TIP

If two or more Application objects create a drive map to the same drive letter, the first application launched from NAL will take precedence. The same is true when using Application objects to capture the same port. Be very careful when using the Drives/Ports option in NAM.

Task 3 — Configure Workstations

No special configuration is needed to run NAL from a workstation. Users can run NAL from the SYS:PUBLIC directory or from a copy of NAL that is stored on the workstation's hard disk.

However, if you want to get fancy and increase network application security, you can configure NAL to replace the normal Windows interface — EXPLORER.EXE in Windows 95 or PROGMAN.EXE in Windows 3.1. This feature automates network application access and only displays the applications to which users have rights.

To replace the Windows interface with NAL, complete the following steps:

▶ Step 1A — If you are using Windows 95 copy the following files to a directory on the local hard drive: NALW95.EXE, NALRES32.DLL,NALBMP32.DLL, and NAL.HLP.

▸ Step 1B — If you are using Windows 3.1 copy the following files to a directory on the local hard drive: NALW31.EXE, NALRES.DLL, NALBMP.DLL, and NAL.HLP.

▸ Step 2 — Edit the SYS.INI file to set NAL as the SHELL. Find the line in the [boot] section that starts with "SHELL=". Here's an example of the syntax for Windows 95:

```
SHELL=EXPLORER.EXE
```

This would be replaced with the location of the NAL files on the local hard drive:

```
SHELL=C:\NALW95.EXE
```

▸ Step 3 — Save the changes and restart Windows.

Once the workstation has been customized with NAL, users can launch applications by simply double-clicking the icon within Windows. When the application is launched, NAL runs any scripts associated with the Application object, checks for the path to the application, and then launches the application. Similarly, when the user exits the application, any mappings or other special commands that were set within an Application object script are reset to their original configurations.

This is a great way of further automating network applications. In addition, NAM gives you better application security and centralized control. These are all important parts of growing up in the IntranetWare universe.

SMART LINK

For more information on NetWare Application Management, surf to the Novell Knowledgebase at http://support.novell.com/search/.

Once the application software has been installed, your LAN is well on its way to enlightenment: "sipping from the chalice of knowledge." In addition, the menu interface can provide a friendly, centrally managed arena for application launching. I know this is a lot of work, but "warm and fuzzy" is a good thing. Customization increases productivity by giving users the tools they need and decreasing their LAN-phobia — not to be confused with parent-phobia!

ZEN

"Actually I'm 18. I've just lived hard."

Clint Eastwood

Speaking of phobia, Guinevere is growing up way too fast. In the blink of an eye, the prom is over and she's ready for the fifth and final step of IntranetWare childhood — moving out.

Step 5: E-mail

The time has come. Your LAN becomes a woMAN (metropolitan area network).

It's inevitable. At some point, your child grows up and becomes an adult. The transition to adulthood is a scary time for everybody. She gets her first car, her first job, and her first apartment. Suddenly, the chalice of knowledge takes on a whole new importance. Her ability to survive depends on how many business classes she slept through. Suddenly, all those nights you spent helping her with math homework equate to food on the table. Suddenly, Mom and Dad aren't so wrong anymore. It's weird how that happens — and it always does.

With adulthood comes new challenges and a new level of communication. To succeed, it's vital that you develop a high level of LAN synergy. All your users, configurations, workstations, and applications must work together as one cohesive unit. This is made possible through e-mail. The final step in IntranetWare configuration focuses on tying all of these components together.

E-mail has become one of the most critical LAN services, next to filing and printing. That's because it performs the following functions:

- ▶ *Improves communication* — E-mail enables employees to communicate even when business meetings, travel schedules, and distributed locations prevent them from seeing each other.

- ▶ *Increases productivity* — E-mail improves the success rate for communications because unlike other forms of communication, messaging does not require conversing participants to be available at the same time. No more "telephone tag."

▸ *Maximizes the use of existing resources* — E-mail leverages file, printing and connectivity services by providing a way of tying them altogether, much the same way as time ties together the fabric of our universe. (Is that *esoteric* enough for you?)

QUIZ

Speaking of esoteric, here's a doozy for you. There are five men —
A, B, C, D, and E — each wearing a disc on his forehead selected from a
total of five white, two red, and two black. Each man can see the colors
of the discs worn by the other four, but he is unable to see his own.

They are all intelligent people, and they are asked to try to deduce the
color of their own disc from the colors of the other four whom they can
see. In fact, they are all wearing white discs. After a pause for reflection,
C, who is even more intelligent than the others, says,
"I reckon I must be wearing a white disc."

Huh? How did he do that?

(Q12-6)

E-mail in IntranetWare relies on an integrated messaging platform called MHS Services for IntranetWare. MHS (Message Handling Service) stores, forwards, and routes user messages. These messages can be text, binary, graphics, digitized video, or audio data. MHS Services is integrated with NDS and uses many NDS objects to accomplish these magic messaging tasks.

Let's take a closer look.

REAL WORLD

MHS Services for IntranetWare is *not* included in IntranetWare. It is, however, available for free from NetWire (Web or CompuServe). Incidentally, Novell would prefer that you used GroupWise as your e-mail engine. They have a good point!

SMART LINK

If you really want to use Novell's "MHS Service for IntranetWare," you can download it for free from http://support.novell.com/sitemap.

UNDERSTANDING MHS SERVICES

MHS Services for IntranetWare is an "engine" that provides messaging capabilities. Various messaging programs can now take full advantage of this technology. In the simplest terms, this "engine" takes input from various e-mail applications and routes it to any user on the internetwork running any other type of e-mail interface. This is much like the way IntranetWare file services stores a variety of different types of files from various network applications. However, unlike file services, MHS actively deals with the communication interactions between computer users. Instead of simply storing data files, MHS moves the data from point to point and notifies the user of waiting messages.

All of this magic is accomplished with three key components:

▶ Messaging server

▶ User mailboxes

▶ MHS applications

Messaging Server

The *messaging server* is IntranetWare's implementation of the MHS "engine." The server accepts data from a variety of user e-mail packages and delivers it to any type of mailbox (as Figure 12.14 shows). The server can deliver messages to local user mailboxes or route them through the internetwork to other messaging engines for eventual delivery. The main point is — MHS Services supports a variety of e-mail applications and can deliver to a variety of other engine types. Also, messages can be composed of text, graphics, video, or audio data.

All of this fancy footwork occurs within the messaging server. Each network server that has MHS Services installed is called a *messaging server.* A *message routing group* is a group of messaging servers that communicate with each other directly — to transfer messages. In a large WAN such as that in Figure 12.14, for example, this would be all the IntranetWare servers that share a common backbone. Each message routing group has one or more *Postmaster Generals*. This special user is automatically granted the privilege of modifying message routing groups and configuring all of the messaging servers. In addition, each of these servers has one or more *Postmasters* that configure and manage user mailboxes.

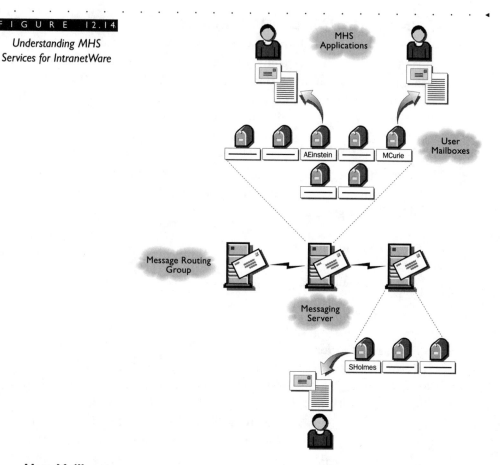

FIGURE 12.14

Understanding MHS Services for IntranetWare

User Mailboxes

A *user mailbox* is a physical location on the messaging server where messages are delivered. You can use any MHS application to send messages to any NDS object that can be assigned a mailbox. This includes Users, Groups, Organizational Roles, and Organizational Units. Also, you can send mail to special *Distribution List* objects, which in turn copy the mail to multiple mailboxes. This reduces network traffic throughout the message routing group by creating and routing only one copy of the message and then replicating it for every mailbox on the list. Finally, user mailboxes can be configured and managed using either NWADMIN (MS Windows) or NETADMIN (DOS). Once again, refer to Figure 12.14 for an illustration of the relationship between messaging servers and user mailboxes.

MHS Applications

All this IntranetWare messaging magic is made possible through a front-end e-mail application. Without these applications, there's no way to create or read MHS messages. Just your luck, IntranetWare includes two rudimentary MHS applications — FirstMail for DOS and FirstMail for Windows. Both starter MHS applications are automatically installed in the SYS:PUBLIC subdirectory on each messaging server. The good news is, FirstMail automatically imports all user and group information from NDS. You don't need to lift a finger. This means that as soon as you install MHS Services, users can begin sending messages via FirstMail.

The bad news is, you get what you pay for. Although FirstMail for Windows has a nice interface (as shown later in Figure 12.15), it doesn't include any advanced messaging features. FirstMail is a simple starter application that can tide you over until you buy a real MHS front-end. Think of it as Guinevere's first broken-down VW or her one-room apartment under the train tracks. Even though it's not the Taj Mahal, it does represent her first shot at freedom. For this reason, you'll probably never forget FirstMail or that adorable VW Bug.

There you have it. MHS Services in a nutshell. Even though I'm sure you absorbed it all the first time, let's take a quick review — just for the heck of it. Table 12.4 is your friend.

TABLE 12.4	MHS COMPONENT	DESCRIPTION
Getting to Know MHS Services for IntranetWare	MHS Services for IntranetWare	"The Product."
	MHS engine	Implementation of "The Product."
	Messaging server	Each IntranetWare server running "The Product." Also the central communications point and storage location of user mailboxes.

(continued)

T A B L E 12.4	MHS COMPONENT	DESCRIPTION
Getting to Know MHS Services for IntranetWare (continued)	Message routing group	A collection of interconnected messaging servers.
	Postmaster general	Manages the message routing group.
	Postmaster	Manages the messaging server.
	User mailboxes	Physical storage location for MHS messages. They hang out on messaging servers.
	MHS applications	E-mail front-ends that send and receive MHS messages.
	Distribution list	A special NDS object that forwards messages to numerous user mailboxes.

Now that you're a pro with MHS Services, let's explore the details of managing it. Don't have any illusions; nobody said moving out would be easy.

MANAGING MHS SERVICES

So, you've learned about Novell's MHS. Now, what do you do with it? Moving out can be such a traumatic experience. One morning you wake up and bam! It hits you that you're on your own. A thousand questions pop into your head: Who's going to make breakfast? What am I going to do with my life? Where's the laundry machine? In order to survive in this cruel and exciting world, you must have a plan and, above all, you must have friends.

Managing MHS Services is not so different. One day you'll come into work and bam! It hits you that you're using e-mail. Then a thousand questions pop into your head: Who's the Postmaster? Where's my mailbox? What's a Distribution List? Fortunately, IntranetWare provides numerous NDS objects especially for MHS Services — your friends. They are

- ▶ Message Routing Group

- ▶ Messaging Server

- ▶ Distribution List

- ▶ External Entity

In addition to these MHS-only objects, you'll need to create and manage various mailbox owners — Users, Groups, Organizational Roles, and Organizational Units.

Now let's take a closer look at how these MHS "friends" can help you get along in the cruel and exciting world of IntranetWare messaging.

Message Routing Group

As you remember from our earlier discussions, the MHS Message Routing Group is a collection of interconnected messaging servers. As an NDS object, it represents a cluster of messaging servers that communicate directly with each other for transferring messages. A default Message Routing Group object is created during the installation of MHS Services and placed in the same container as the host IntranetWare server. Subsequent messaging servers are defaulted to this group.

Also recall that the Postmaster General manages the Message Routing Group. This is usually the Admin user but can be assigned a unique name during initial MHS Services installation.

Messaging Server

In earlier discussions, you learned that the messaging server is the central communications point and storage location of MHS Services for IntranetWare. As an NDS object, it identifies the host IntranetWare server and the location of the MHS directory structure (SYS:MHS). The SYS:MHS directory houses all user mailboxes assigned to this messaging server. During a standard MHS Services installation, the Messaging Server object is created automatically and placed in the same container as the Host IntranetWare server object.

In order for numerous messaging servers to communicate with one another, they must be part of the same message routing group. Once these first two MHS objects have been created, you're well on your way to e-mail paradise. With the groundwork in place, it's time to turn our attention toward the people who will be sending and receiving MHS messages. Look out, Guinevere.

Distribution List

As you recall, the Distribution List is a special NDS object that forwards messages to numerous user mailboxes. It accomplishes this in an interesting way. Only one copy of the message is delivered to the Distribution List mailbox. The message is then replicated for every mailbox in the Distribution List. This decreases network traffic between messaging servers because multiple messages are routed with only a single packet.

Group objects can also be used for messaging, but they *do* increase network traffic. Unlike Distribution List, Group objects generate a packet for every message routed between Messaging Servers. Distribution Lists also differ from Groups in that membership can be nested. In other words, a Distribution List can contain other distribution lists. This is not true for NDS group objects.

That completes our discussion of the three main MHS management objects — Message Routing Group, Messaging Server, and Distribution List. For a more practical hands-on approach toward MHS management, consult the case study at the end of this chapter. Now, let's take a quick look at the final two management objects: External Entity and Mailbox objects.

ZEN

"The only Zen you can find on the tops of mountains is the Zen you bring up there."

Robert M. Pirsig

External Entity

The *External Entity* object represents non-native NDS MHS objects. It's basically an NDS placeholder that enables you to send messages to users who are not part of the NDS tree. External Entity objects are not created during MHS Services installation; they are normally imported from special gateway software. This gateway software allows MHS to interface with other non-NDS systems.

Mailbox Objects

The discussion so far has focused on the key MHS management objects you need to deal with in order to make MHS Services work. But all of this lexicon doesn't mean a hill of beans if you don't have anyone to send the messages to. MHS Services for IntranetWare supports four types of Mailbox objects:

- ▶ User

- ▶ Group

- ▶ Organizational Role

- ▶ Organizational Unit

Each of them can send and receive MHS mail with varying degrees of sophistication. In the exercise at the end of the chapter, we will explore how to assign mailboxes to each of these objects and use them in the grand MHS scheme of things. For now, suffice it to say that you probably fall into one of these four categories — maybe more.

QUIZ

Which "Star Trek" character waited until the second season to beam aboard the Starship Enterprise?

(Q12-7)

USING FIRSTMAIL

As you learned earlier, MHS Services for IntranetWare includes a rudimentary e-mail application called FirstMail, available by default in two versions (DOS and Windows), that are copied to the SYS:PUBLIC directory on each Messaging Server.

FirstMail for Windows is an intuitive messaging application with simple icons for sending, receiving, and reading e-mail. As seen in Figure 12.15, FirstMail lists all of your new messages and enables you to open, reply, forward, move, copy, or delete them. In addition, the Button Panel provides five management tasks:

- ▸ Send mail

- ▸ Read new mail

- ▸ Mail folders

- ▸ Address books

- ▸ Distribution Lists

The greatest thing about FirstMail (other than it being free) is the fact that it's NDS-aware. This means you don't have to bother with user configurations; FirstMail gets everything it needs from the NDS database. Otherwise, if you're using an MHS-compatible application that's not NDS-aware, you have to register it with Directory Services and add the e-mail name to each user's list of applications. Too much work.

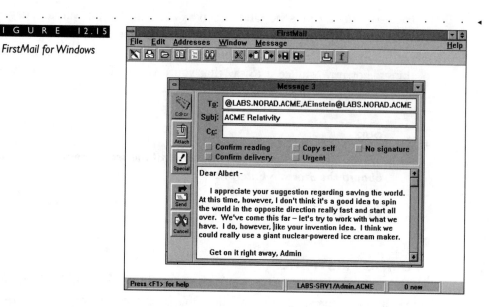

FirstMail for Windows

ZEN

"Ring the bells that still can ring.
Forget your perfect offering.
There is a crack in everything.
That's how the light gets in."

Leonard Cohen

THE BRAIN

For more information on using MHS Services in IntranetWare, see the AppNote entitled "Integrating MHS Services with Other Novell Products" in the October 1995 issue of *Novell Application Notes*, or surf the Web at http://support.novell.com/sitemap.

Well, there you have it. That completes the final step of IntranetWare configuration. Childhood isn't so bad. Let's quickly review where we've been.

It all started with Leia's first step (workstation connectivity). Once she became connected to the network, Step 2 took over — Leia learned to talk. This involved Container, Profile, and User login scripts.

Leia went to preschool. The next stage in your network's development was dominated by a friendly IntranetWare menu system. The menu system acted as a central repository for user interface, network applications, and e-mail. In Step 4, you installed and configured the network applications as Leia went to "real" school. This was the most important phase of the child's development. After all, without school (or network applications), there would be no productivity and purpose to life.

Finally, in Step 5, Leia moved out. She got her first car, her first apartment, and her first job. Although it seemed like a difficult time for everyone, moving out represented an important stage in Leia's life. She made a smooth transition from childhood to adulthood. In much the same way, your network needs a smooth transition from IntranetWare configuration to management.

In a side story, we were tracking Guinevere as she started her day with a computer and cappuccino. As a CNE, it's your responsibility to establish the configuration so that Guinevere never knows what's happening while she's sipping her cappuccino. In an ideal world, Guinevere never suspects that when she turns on her computer, it initializes workstation connectivity files, runs login scripts, establishes a menu system, and provides transparent access to network applications and e-mail — just like a child never understands what her parents go through while she's growing up. Of course, life doesn't end there; it is only the beginning. Now that you've made it through childhood in one piece, it's time to move on to the third and final phase of life — adulthood.

Get out of the way, we're coming through!

SMART LINK

Learn to find yourself in IntranetWare Adulthood at http://www.aronson.com/ppp/birth.html.

In this exercise, we will walk through some very important Client 32 workstation connectivity steps: namely *Connection* and *Login*. Follow very carefully, and try this at home — if you dare!

1. On a Windows 95 workstation, click on the Start button, then select the following, in order:

    ▸ Programs

    ▸ Novell

    ▸ NetWare Login

2. Make sure the Login tab is selected.

    A. You'll notice that this dialog box lists the network or server to which you are currently attached. You will probably find it lists ACME_TREE.

    B. Type **Admin** in the Name field. (If you wanted to log in as a different user, you could specify the common or distinguished name of that user.)

    C. Type the password for the Admin user in the Password field. You'll notice that asterisks, rather than the actual password, are displayed for security reasons.

3. Click on the Connection tab.

    A. Make sure that the radio button in front of the Tree field is selected and that ACME_TREE is displayed in this field. If not, you can either type it in, or select it from a list by clicking on the tree icon to the right of this field.

    B. Type **"ACME"** (including the quotation marks) in the Context field to indicate the location of your User object in the NDS tree.

(If you had keyed in a distinguished name in Step 2b, it would override the context listed in this field.)

C. Don't type anything in the Server field. In this exercise, we are going to log into the network itself, rather than logging into a specific server. (If you wanted to specify a server, you could click on the radio button in front of the Server field, then key in the server name, or select it from a list by clicking on the server icon to the right of this field. You'll notice that it's asking for the common name of the server — not its distinguished name.) Ensure that the Bindery connections box is not checked, as we want to log in as an NDS connection, not a Bindery Services connection.

D. Ensure that there is an "X" in the Clear current connections box to clear any existing connections. You should always check this box if you are switching trees or servers, or logging in under a new username. If you didn't check this box, it would indicate that you wanted to make an additional tree or server connection. If you did so, you'd find that the login scripts for the new connection would overwrite any existing mappings that use the same drive letters, port numbers, and so on.

4. Click on the Login Script tab. Sit back and relax while you read this paragraph. We are not going to make any changes to this dialog box. It is for informational purposes only. This tab allows you to control the processing of login scripts. It allows you to override existing User and Profile login scripts assigned to this user, as well as to bypass all login scripts. For example, if you indicated a login script name in the Login Script field, it would override your existing User login script (if you had one). If you entered a login script name in the Profile Script field, it would override your existing Profile login script (if one existed). If you were to click on the Run scripts box, it would run any login scripts that had been set up for you, including any listed in this dialog box. Because the Close script results automatically box is not checked, it will keep the Login Results window open so that you can examine

the results of login script processing when you have completed the login process.

5. Click on the Variables tab. If you wanted to pass on any variables to the login script processor, you would indicate them here. (We don't want to do so, so don't make any changes to this dialog box.)

6. Click on OK to initiate the login process. A Login Results window should be displayed on the screen. You will notice that it lists information such as your current context, your User object's current context, your current tree, and the server to which you are currently attached. Review the contents of the window, then click on OK. Congratulations! You have successfully logged into the network.

CASE STUDY: CONFIGURING ACME'S LOGIN SCRIPTS

Just as the day was winding down swimmingly at ACME (at 4:50 p.m.), FDR came cruising into your office. "I'm sorry it's so late," he said, "but something's up with the Net. Can you take a quick look?" Grudgingly (because that's how you do things at 4:59 p.m.), you agree to check it out. "Oh, right," he adds, "I want all the public relations managers to share some applications and report files — any ideas?"

Of course you have ideas; after all, you are a CNE! Quickly you discover that the PR Container script has been destroyed — fortunately, you have notes from the old one in your IntranetWare Log book.

1. Here's the PR Container login script notes:

   A. Insert a comment at the top of the login script indicating the purpose of the login script, the author (who is you), and the date the file was created.

   B. Set the DOS prompt to display the drive and directory name.

   C. Display a greeting that is displayed each time a user in this container logs in, including the username, day, and date.

   D. Turn off the display of drive mappings and assign the following regular drive mappings:

      1) Drive U: should point to the User's home directory.

      2) Drive G: should point to the user's shared group directory.

   E. Assign the following search drive mappings, making sure not to overwrite existing drive mappings in the DOS path:

      1) S1: pointing to SYS:PUBLIC

      2) S2: pointing to the DOS directory on the network

      3) S3: pointing to the SYS:APPS\WINDOWS directory

F.   Insert a COMSPEC command that points to the DOS directory on the network.

G.   Prevent the Default login script from executing when a user logs in that has no User login script.

H.   Set up a printer capture of the HP4SI-P1 printer, specifying no tabs, no banners, and a timeout of 20 seconds.

I.   On Wednesdays, fire phasers and display a reminder to members of the PR-Group that the weekly Manager meeting is at 9:00 a.m. in Conference Room 3-D.

J.   Every time a user logs into the network, display a file called G:PR.NEW containing the important news of the day for the public relations department.

K.   Set the default drive to U:.

L.   Execute a custom menu called G:PRMAIN.DAT (which you will create in the next exercise).

M.   General notes:

   1)   Whenever you display a message, don't forget to insert a PAUSE statement so that the message doesn't scroll off the screen before the user has a chance to read it.

   2)   Insert appropriate remarks through the login script so that someone else that looks at it can easily understand what you have done.

2.   Next, you decide to create a PRMGRS-Profile login script for the public relations managers. Then you discover, astonishingly enough, that one already exists in the ACME container! Hmmmm. Must be those crazy ACME fairies again. Anyway, you might as well make FDR a member of the PRMGRS-Profile login script while you're there. (See Appendix C for hints on the basic steps involved.)

3. Log in as FDR to check things out:

   ```
   LOGIN .FDR.ADMIN.RIO.ACME
   ```

   Watch the screen as the Container and Profile login scripts are
   automatically executed. Fix any errors that occur.

Well, the fun never stops. It seems as though FDR has opened Pandora's box. Now, for some unexplainable reason, the ACME gremlins have hit — the PR menu system has disappeared. If you don't get home soon, you're gonna miss "Friends." You'd better hurry.

Once again, the IntranetWare Log book has saved the day. Using the criteria outlined here, create a custom menu for the Public Relations department.

A. PR Main Menu

   1) Applications (which displays an Applications submenu)

   2) E-mail (which runs the Windows version of First Mail)

   3) IntranetWare Commands (which displays a IntranetWare Commands submenu)

   4) Log off network (which exits the user from the menu and logs him or her off the network)

B. Applications Menu (submenu called by option in the Main Menu)

   1) Database (where executable file is DB)

   2) Spreadsheet (where executable file is SS)

   3) Word Processing (where executable file is WP)

C. IntranetWare Utilities Menu (submenu called by an option in the Main Menu)

   1) File Management

   2) NCOPY

   3) NETUSER

4) User Tools

5) WHOAMI

Next, you'll need to quickly compile and debug the new menu. Once you're finished, you can place it in the default SYS:PUBLIC subdirectory and test it. Ensure that the new login script can automatically find and execute the menu system. After all, you don't want another visit from FDR tonight.

Sweet dreams.

EXERCISE 12-2: INTRANETWARE CHILDHOOD

Circle the 20 IntranetWare Configuration terms hidden in this word search puzzle using the hints provided.

```
R D R B E U T A B T E N T R A T S U J
F I L E A T T R I B U T E N E Q H E K
I S B U S P R O F I L E G F C T E N R
R T L L S O J Q X Y Q Z U C P P L T V
S R Q V G S E X E C C Z O O X V L M W
T I Q P N T G Q V O I K T A T N C B H
M B K S H M E N U M A K E E X E F W M
A U P R I A N I N S T A L L C F G R J
I T F R B S O U P U H X N H L O L H
L I D E N T I F I E R V A R I A B L E
F O C X S E H N W C L I E N T S C P W
N N J W B R L Q K R Y B K M P T X E K
L L T U I K G Q E C T D O B U D S P Q
B I Y L O G I N S C R I P T Z R C D A
N S V C W C B Z P I M C K B O I G Z J
N T T N P L E C V W E R N X L V C C D
B Q O S N A M E C O N T E X T E P K G
X G T O X S R F R K V H O B W Z W X N
```

Hints:

1. Login script command used to indicate the location of the command specifier to be used (typically COMMAND.COM).
2. Leaf object that represents a list of E-mail recipients.
3. Menu system control command used to execute a DOS or IntranetWare command.
4. Set when installing network applications through the use of the FLAG or FILER utility.
5. E-mail application that is included with IntranetWare.
6. Menu system command that requests (optional) information from the user before a menu item is executed.

7. Used in a login script instead of using literal values.
8. File that is used to create customized NET.CFG file during client installation.
9. Statement required in CONFIG.SYS for VLMs.
10. Section heading in NET.CFG.
11. File that is similar to a batch file and is executed when a user logs in.
12. Used to compile menu system source files.
13. Integrated messaging (e-mail) engine included in IntranetWare.
14. NET.CFG statement used to set workstation context prior to login.
15. Workstation boot file containing network-related information used by IntranetWare.
16. Workstation directory that contains IntranetWare client files.
17. Name of the supervisor for an MHS Server object.
18. Type of login script that can contain members that reside in different containers.
19. Workstation configuration that was used in earlier versions of NetWare.
20. Batch file that is used to automate the loading of client connection files on the workstation.

See Appendix C for answers.

IntranetWare Management

"As an IntranetWare CNE, I consider them part of the family."

Welcome to adulthood.

An interesting thing happens on the way to adulthood — we grow up. All through childhood we look forward to the days when we can drive our own car, eat junk food, and play loud music 24 hours a day — freedom!

Then it happens! What a shock. Once we grow up and become adults, we yearn for the days when life was simple. We dream of the simplicity and innocence of childhood. Wow, we need therapy. Well, you're an adult now, so deal with it. But being an adult doesn't mean you have to lose the child within. It just means the toys get bigger.

So, you have a new car, a new job, and a new apartment. Now your focus shifts from starting the "life span" (configuration) to keeping it going (management). As a CNE, you move into LAN adulthood with a new focus on IntranetWare management. Once the network is up and running, you can step back and shift your attention to the long term. Suddenly, your mind is filled with thoughts of a family (servers and workstations), a pension (SMS), and retirement (RMF). Aah, adulthood is a many-splendored thing.

IntranetWare management is the most time-consuming aspect of being a CNE. Think about it: *IntranetWare configuration occurs only once, but management dominates your life forever.* In IntranetWare, network management occurs through five strategies:

- ▸ Server management

- ▸ Intranet management

- ▸ Workstation management

- ▸ Storage Management Services (SMS)

- ▸ Remote Management Facility (RMF)

Server management is marriage. It involves daily tasks for creating, protecting and maintaining your relationship with the IntranetWare server. This includes console management, NetWare Loadable Modules (NLMs), and server protection. At this point, monitoring the server involves more than just walking by it once a day and making sure the green light is on. You must nurture your new-found relationship.

Intranet management explores the limbo world between marriage and children. At this point, your focus is career and community. You, your spouse, and your married friends join softball teams, bowling leagues, and sewing circles. The server expands to become part of a "collective whole" — the intranet! This involves NDS maintenance, internationalization, NetWare MPR, the NetWare Web server, and more. It feels good to be part of a group.

Workstation management is like having children. It can be even more challenging than the other three strategies because you're dealing with the IntranetWare users (your children). And we all know that the user's primary purpose in life is to make CNEs miserable. In addition to battling users, our workstation management duties involve Client 32 installations, Client 16 connectivity strategies, and support for diverse client environments — DOS, Windows 95, OS/2, and Macintosh.

As the adage goes, "You never miss anything until it's gone." This holds especially true for IntranetWare data. Welcome to your pension plan. One of the most important things you can do as an IntranetWare CNE is to plan for the future by using backups. *Storage Management Services (SMS)* is an IntranetWare backup engine that provides data storage and retrieval from various front-end applications to numerous back-end storage devices. In this chapter, you'll learn about the fundamental architecture of SMS and explore the many features of SBACKUP.NLM.

Finally, *RMF (Remote Management Facility)* enables you to manage the server console from anywhere in the world — including Happy Acres. You've worked hard, and now it's time for retirement. RMF will become the cornerstone of your server maintenance schedule. Of course, it's hard to maintain the server when it's chained up and locked away in a hidden closet. Fortunately, by using RMF, you can access the server console from any distributed workstation.

ZEN

"Every wakeful step, every mindful act is the direct path to awakening. Wherever you go, there you are."

Anonymous

Like adulthood, IntranetWare management doesn't always come naturally. You must work at it. Children have their parents to rely on, but now (as an adult) you're on your own. So, to help guide you through the mine field of CNE adulthood, I suggest these few management strategies.

First, build an IntranetWare Log book. Although few CNEs have one, it should become the foundation of your daily management life. The IntranetWare Log book is a detailed, step-by-step log of all activity from LAN conception to the present. It includes worksheets, floor plans, security restrictions, file management, pictures of LAN hardware, pictures of your mother, cabling layouts, application information, and weekly management tasks. It's vital that you take the Log book seriously, because you never know when you might need it.

Next, use the worksheets provided with IntranetWare documentation. The *Installation* manual includes various worksheets that can help you document LAN details including file server hardware, workstation hardware, configuration files, IntranetWare directories, users and group information, default login restrictions, trustee assignments, and login scripts. Then, put these worksheets in your IntranetWare Log book for future reference. I see a pattern forming here.

Reference material is the fodder of creative minds. I don't know what that means, but it sounds good. The bottom line is, you can't know everything. Create an extensive library of reference material so that you don't have to know everything. Some of the best sources include Novell Press books, *Novell Application Notes*, the latest Novell Support Connection CD-ROM, Web pages, documentation, and, of course, this book. Don't forget your library card.

Finally, your mindset has an important impact on IntranetWare management. Psychologically, you must be committed to the network and recognize management as an important aspect of your daily life. Take time to embrace these management tasks and make sure that everyone in the organization recognizes that you need time to do them. Many times, users and management don't understand why the network must be down for VREPAIR or SMS backup. Educate them gracefully.

With these strategies in mind, let's now dive into the wild and wacky world of IntranetWare management. Remember, this is the foundation of your daily life as a CNE. NDS design happens once, installation happens once, and IntranetWare configuration happens once. On the other hand, management happens every day until you win the lottery. So, without any further adieu, let's start our jaunt through LAN adulthood, beginning with marriage.

ZEN

*"I know it is wet
And the sun is not sunny.
But we can have
Lots of good fun that is funny!"*

Dr. Seuss

Server Management

Eventually you will find Mr. or Ms. Right. Your eyes will meet across a crowded dance floor, you will feel that wonderful flutter in the pit of your stomach. Your knees will buckle and then bang — you're married! Marriage changes everything. Suddenly, your focus shifts from "me, me, me" to "the family." Your spouse becomes the center of your life. It's like sharing a lifeboat with that "special someone" while careening down the whitewater rapids of love. Yuck.

Similarly, the IntranetWare server is at the center of your LAN. At some point, your focus shifts from "users, users, users" to "the server." After all, the entire WAN will crumble if your servers aren't running correctly.

IntranetWare server management consists of three components:

▶ Console commands — keep the server running at peak performance

▶ NetWare Loadable Modules — everything else

▶ Server protection — keep users away from the server console

It all begins at the colon prompt. The colon (:) prompt is the server console. This is where you'll spend most of your server management time. It's a comforting feeling seeing the server running smoothly — seeing the familiar "WORM" prance around the screen (assuming that MONITOR.NLM is loaded), hearing the constant hum of IntranetWare workstations, and following the IntranetWare packets as they bounce merrily along the cabling segment.

The colon prompt accepts two kinds of commands — console commands and NLMs. IntranetWare includes numerous console commands for various server management and maintenance tasks (including NDS management, time synchronization, Bindery Services, sending messages, activating NLMs, server protection, and network optimization). This chapter explores most of the IntranetWare console commands and provides some hints on how to use them.

All remaining server activity is accomplished by using NLMs. NLMs are modular Legos that provide supplemental functionality to the IntranetWare server. There are four kinds of NLMs: disk drivers, LAN drivers, name space modules, and management utilities. In this chapter, we'll explore each of these and some key server management tools — INSTALL.NLM, MONITOR.NLM, SERVMAN.NLM, and DSREPAIR.NLM. You can think of NLMs as network management applications at the server.

Finally, we'll learn how to protect our precious IntranetWare server. This includes locking up the physical server machine, preventing access to the keyboard with MONITOR.NLM, using the SECURE CONSOLE command, and adding a password for RMF. Also, don't forget to use The Club. Server protection is a serious management task because of the vulnerability of the console — users can cause a lot of damage there. Many times, this security feature is overlooked and CNEs discover their inadequate security measures when it's too late — in the unemployment line.

ZEN

"What is the sound of one hand clapping?"

Zen Koan

As you can see, marriage takes a great deal of work. Fortunately, the rewards greatly outweigh the pain. As a CNE, you must work hard at your network marriage to keep the server running and in peak condition (and, with luck, the rewards will also outweigh the pain). In both marriage and server management, communication is the key.

Well, there you have it. Our CNE life in a nutshell. Let's get started with console commands — also known as marriage tools.

QUIZ

Just to keep things simple and warm up the old noodle, here's one of my favorites: A train leaves from Boston to New York. An hour later, a train leaves from New York to Boston. The second train is traveling 15 MPH faster than the first, but the first has a 7.5 MPH tailwind. Which train will be nearer to Boston when they meet?

(Q13-1)
(See Appendix C for quiz answers.)

CONSOLE COMMANDS

To be successful in anything, you need the right tools. Marriage is no exception. In order to make any marriage work, both both partners must bring the right tools — love, compassion, understanding, respect, flexibility, truth, and a spirit of compromise. But more important than anything is communication. You need to work together as a team and develop synergy. This strategy revolves around the single most important tool — "honey-do's." Honey-do's make the world go around. "Honey, do this," "honey, do that." As long as you pay attention to honey-do's, you'll never have to miss another Sunday football game or "mushy" movie like *On Golden Pond*. Don't forget those compromises.

IntranetWare marriage is not any different. In order to develop server management synergy, you must bring along the right tools — console commands and NLMs. *Console commands* are internal management tools that enable you to perform various server management maintenance tasks, including NDS management, time synchronization, bindery services, sending messages, activating NLMs, server protection, and network optimization. They are built into the NetWare 4.11 core OS. *NLMs*, on the other hand, are modular Legos that provide supplemental functionality to the core OS. IntranetWare includes four kinds of NLMs — disk drivers, LAN drivers, name space modules, and management utilities. Let's start our discussion of IntranetWare honey-do's with a look at some important console commands.

Console commands enable CNEs to interact directly with the IntranetWare OS core. These commands are internal to SERVER.EXE and do not require any other support commands. One of the most powerful IntranetWare console commands is SET. This utility enables you to customize the OS core with more than 100 advanced parameters. These parameters are organized into 13 categories ranging from communications to file system to time synchronization. Warning: Don't mess around with SET unless you've been adequately trained and you're wearing protective gloves.

The syntax of console commands is relatively straightforward. The command itself is entered at the colon prompt and is followed by an Enter. Also, IntranetWare supports various command switches that customize their execution. Anybody can execute a console command as long as he/she has physical access to the file server console. This is a good reason to severely limit access to the machine and implement many of the protection schemes we discussed earlier. Also, console tools can be hazardous to the server if not handled correctly. You should ensure that they are kept out of the reach of small children and IntranetWare users. Fortunately, they have their own childproof cap (by being placed in the SYS:SYSTEM subdirectory by default).

Let's take a closer look at IntranetWare's top 15 console commands (provided here in alphabetical order). For a complete list of the console commands, refer to the *Novell NetWare 4.11 Utilities Reference Manual*.

SMART LINK

For a complete list of IntranetWare console commands, surf the Web to NetWare 4.11 documentation at http://www.novell.com/ manuals.

TIP

Console commands are internal operating system tools that are similar to DOS's internal commands. They are built into SERVER.EXE just like CD or CLS is built into COMMAND.COM. You don't need to have any searching or IntranetWare directories available to access console commands.

BIND

BIND is an installation console command. As we saw earlier, it links LAN drivers to a communications protocol. Once the LAN driver is loaded, BIND must be issued to activate LAN communications. The default IntranetWare communication protocol is IPX. Here's the syntax for activating communications on the 3C5X9 NIC:

```
BIND IPX to 3C5X9
```

When you issue the BIND statement at the server console, you'll be asked for the external network number. Refer to Chapter 6 for more information.

BROADCAST

BROADCAST is an administrative console command that enables CNEs to send brief alert messages to all attached workstations. Another related command (SEND) enables you to broadcast messages to specific users or groups of users. In both cases, the message appears at the bottom of the workstation monitor and prompts the user to press Ctrl+Enter to clear it from the screen. Only users who are currently logged in will receive these messages. BROADCAST messages can be up to 40 characters, whereas SEND supports larger messages (55 characters maximum). Here's the syntax:

```
BROADCAST message
```

The downside of BROADCAST and SEND is that they lock up the destination computer until Ctrl+Enter is pressed. This lockup can create harmful effects if the computer is being used for unattended backups. To avoid having messages lock up unattended machines, consider issuing SEND with the following parameters:

/A=C — Accept messages only from the server console

/A=N — Accept no messages (dangerous)

/A=P — Store the last message sent until you poll to receive it

/P — Polls the server for the last stored message

/A=A — Accept all messages

CLEAR STATION

CLEAR STATION is an administrative console command that enables you to abruptly clear a workstation's connection. Be forewarned — this command removes all file server resources from the workstation and can cause file corruption or data loss if it is executed while the workstation is processing transactions. This command is only useful if workstations have crashed or users have turned off their machines without logging out. Here's the syntax:

```
CLEAR STATION n
```

The *n* specifies the connection number of the workstation you want to clear. These connection numbers can be viewed from MONITOR.NLM or with the help of NLIST. Connection numbers are incrementally allocated as workstations attach to the server and are not the same from one session to another.

CONFIG

CONFIG is a maintenance console command. It displays hardware information for all internal communication components. Figure 13.1 shows the CONFIG information for ACME's first LABS-SRV1 server, and Table 13.1 describes CONFIG parameters.

F I G U R E   13.1

The CONFIG Console Command

```
LABS-SRV1:CONFIG
File server name: LABS-SRV1
IPX internal network number: 0BADCAFE
     Node address: 000000000001
     Frame type: VIRTUAL_LAN
     LAN protocol: IPX network 0BADCAFE
Server Up Time:  1 Minute 38 Seconds

3Com EtherLink III 3C5X9 Family
     Version 4.01b   October 19, 1994
     Hardware setting: I/O ports 320h to 32Fh, Interrupt Ah
     Node address: 0020AFE28F2D
     Frame type: ETHERNET_802.2
     Board name: 3C5X9_1_E82
     LAN protocol: IPX network 00001234

Tree Name: ACME_TREE
Bindery Context(s):
     LABS.NORAD.ACME

LABS-SRV1:
```

T A B L E   13.1

Understanding CONFIG Parameters

PARAMETER	VALUE	DESCRIPTION
File server name	LABS-SRV1	The name of the server.
IPX internal network number	BADCAFE	The eight-digit hexadecimal network number used to uniquely identify this server.

TABLE 13.1	PARAMETER	VALUE	DESCRIPTION
Understanding CONFIG Parameters (continued)	Node address	000000000001 0020AFE28F2D	The internal server node and unique factory address for internal 3C5X9 NIC.
	Frame type	VIRTUAL_LAN ETHERNET_802.2	Modular communications within the server and external communications for this NIC.
	LAN protocol	IPX 1234	Identifies the internal IPX address as BADCAFE and external cable segment as 1234.
	Board name	3C5X9_1_E82	The unique board name given to this NIC's frame type and external address.
	Tree name	ACME_TREE	The name of the NDS tree in which this server participates.
	Server Up Time	1 minute 38 seconds	The amount of time the server has been active.

DOWN

DOWN is a dangerous administrative console command. It completely shuts down file server activity and closes all open files. This is probably one of the most dramatic and potentially harmful IntranetWare console commands, so treat it with kid gloves. Before DOWN deactivates the server, it performs various tasks including clearing all cache buffers and writing them to disk, closing all open files, updating appropriate directory and file allocation tables, dismounting all volumes, clearing all connections, and closing the operating system. Once DOWN has been entered at the file server console, you have various options:

▸ Type **EXIT** to return to the DOS partition.

▸ Type **RESTART SERVER** to bring things back up again.

▶ Type **UP** to reactivate the server console (take a look at the following Real World section).

. . . . ◀

REAL WORLD

In many of my trials and tribulations in the NetWare world, I've seen frustrated users trying to reactivate the server by typing "UP." I've come to the conclusion that Novell missed the boat in creating a cure for the DOWN command. Because turnabout is fair play, I offer this simple solution: Create a server batch file named "UP.NCF." In it, place a single command: "RESTART SERVER." Then add the following line to the end of your AUTOEXEC.NCF file:

```
SEARCH ADD C:\NWSERVER
```

Finally, copy UP.NCF to the C:\NWSERVER directory. Now, whenever the server is brought DOWN, you can simply type UP to reactivate it. I just love it when a plan comes together.

ZEN

"Unformed people delight in the gaudy and in novelty. Cooked people delight in the ordinary."

Mao Pau Zen

DSTRACE

DSTRACE is a maintenance console command. It enables CNEs to monitor NDS replica-related activities, including advertising, synchronization, and replica-to-replica communications. As you can see in Figure 13.2, DSTRACE provides various statistics concerning ACME partitions and replicas. Here's a snapshot of some of the more interesting messages:

▶ Date and time — The date and exact second of replica synchronization is shown in parentheses.

▸ SYNC: Start sync of partition [Root] — This indicates the start of a synchronization interval. A state of [0] indicates a normal synchronization check. A value greater than [0] (such as [30]) shows replica activity like a partition being created or a partition being merged back into its parent.

▸ SYNC: End sync of partition [Root] — This line indicates the end of the synchronization interval. The message "All processed=YES" indicates that all updates were successfully incorporated into the master replica of this partition.

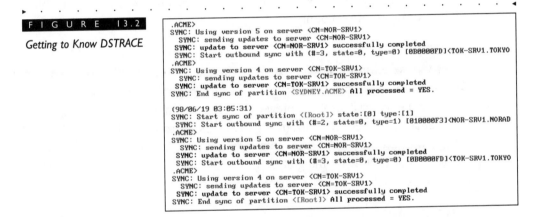

F I G U R E   13.2

Getting to Know DSTRACE

DSTRACE can be activated at the IntranetWare server console by issuing one of the following two commands at the file server console:

```
SET DSTRACE=ON
```

```
SET NDS TRACE TO SCREEN=ON
```

THE BRAIN

For more information on using DSTRACE and its parameters, consult the SET discussion in the *Novell NetWare 4.11 Utilities Reference Manual*, or Chapter 5 of the *Novell NetWare 4.11 Manual Supervising the Network I*, or the "Using DSTRACE" section of Chapter 9 earlier in this book.

ENABLE/DISABLE LOGIN

ENABLE LOGIN and its counterpart are both maintenance console commands. DISABLE LOGIN enables you to prevent access to the server for troubleshooting or maintenance activities. DISABLE LOGIN is particularly useful when you are working on the NDS database, backing up files, loading software, or dismounting/repairing volumes. Keep in mind that DISABLE LOGIN does not affect users who are currently logged in. You may consider combining this command with the CLEAR STATION statement.

As I'm sure you've probably guessed, ENABLE LOGIN enables file server logins if they've been disabled. It also provides one other facility — Supervisor unlocking. If the bindery Supervisor account has been locked because of intruder detection, ENABLE LOGIN will unlock it. This only works on the bindery Supervisor or Admin accounts.

EXIT

EXIT is an administrative console command. It enables you to return to the DOS partition once the file server has been brought DOWN. You may want to EXIT the file server console to prevent any other commands from being activated or to reissue SERVER.EXE with new parameters. In addition, EXIT can be used in conjunction with REMOVE DOS to remotely reboot the file server. Of course, this facility has already been integrated into RESTART SERVER or our new UP.NCF utility. Who needs EXIT when you've got UP?

HELP

HELP is definitely an administrative console command. Many times when you feel the CNEship is weighing you down, simply type HELP at the server console and IntranetWare will come to your rescue. You can view help about a specific console command by identifying it with the HELP command, or view a short description of all console commands by typing

HELP ALL

Press Enter after each description to view the next command. Then press Esc to exit altogether.

LOAD/UNLOAD

LOAD is an installation console command. It is used to activate NLMs and attach them to the core OS. As you recall, the IntranetWare architecture consists of two pieces — core OS and NLMs. The LOAD console command is used to activate these NLMs and bring them to life. You can also UNLOAD NLMs when you're finished with them and free up valuable server RAM.

MODULES

MODULES is a maintenance console command. It displays a list of currently loaded NLMs and some brief information about each, including the module short name, a descriptive string for each module, and the version number if it's a disk driver, LAN driver, or management utility. MODULES can be an important part of your IntranetWare optimization strategy in that it enables you to identify which modules are occupying valuable server RAM. Also, it displays support NLMs you might not have known you're using.

MOUNT

MOUNT is an installation console command. It activates internal IntranetWare volumes. The MOUNT command makes volumes available to users and can be used on specific volumes or all of them:

```
MOUNT ALL
```

MOUNTing and DISMOUNTing volumes can be used as a security measure for volumes that are rarely accessed. You can MOUNT them during access hours and DISMOUNT them when they are not in use. No matter how clever the hacker is, no one can access a dismounted volume. Murphy's Law Number 142 — never say "no one."

REMOVE DOS

REMOVE DOS is an administrative console command. As you learned earlier, REMOVE DOS eliminates COMMAND.COM from background file server RAM. This memory is then returned to IntranetWare for file caching. REMOVE DOS can also be used to increase file server security. When DOS is removed, NLMs cannot be loaded from the DOS partition — it doesn't exist any more. Also, users cannot EXIT to the DOS partition. If they try, the file server is automatically rebooted back to the NetWare partition. Recall that the SECURE CONSOLE command automatically removes DOS from file server RAM.

RESTART SERVER

RESTART SERVER is an administrative console command. It can be used to reactivate the server after it has been DOWNed. This is most useful when your troubleshooting duties require that you frequently DOWN the server. RESTART SERVER is not one of your normal daily activities. This command also has a couple of interesting parameters that improve its troubleshooting value:

▸ -NS — Restarts the server without invoking STARTUP.NCF

▸ -NA — Restarts the server without invoking AUTOEXEC.NCF

Remember, this console command is the foundation of our earlier server UP scheme.

TRACK ON

TRACK ON is a maintenance console command. It activates the router information protocol (RIP) tracking screen. This screen displays RIP traffic on your IntranetWare server. Keep in mind that IntranetWare NDS activities do not rely on RIP. Instead, they broadcast their own information over separate channels. In addition, it's possible to filter RIP activity using additional products such as Novell's MultiProtocol Router. As you can see in Figure 13.3, TRACK ON fills up the server console very quickly. You can bounce between this and other screens by pressing the Alt+Esc keys simultaneously, or by using Ctrl+Esc to view a list of all active console screens.

▸ · ◂

Getting to Know TRACK ON

```
Router Tracking Screen
OUT  [0BADCAFE:FFFFFFFFFFFF]  3:13:49 pm   0000DAD  2/3      00001234  1/2
OUT  [00001234:FFFFFFFFFFFF]  3:13:49 pm   0BADCAFE  1/2
IN   [0BADCAFE:000000000001]  3:13:56 pm   LABS-SRV1      1
IN   [00001234:0020AFE8B0B5]  3:13:56 pm   ACME_TREE____  1      ACME_TREE____  1
         WHITE-SRV1    1    WHITE-SRV1    1    WHITE-SRV1    1
IN   [00001234:0020AFC855F3]  3:14:07 pm   Get Nearest Server
OUT  [00001234:0020AFC855F3]  3:14:07 pm   Give Nearest Server LABS-SRV1
IN   [00001234:0020AFC855F3]  3:14:07 pm   Route Request
IN   [00001234:0020AFC855F3]  3:14:07 pm   Route Request
OUT  [00001234:0020AFC855F3]  3:14:07 pm   0BADCAFE  1/2
IN   [0BADCAFE:000000000001]  3:14:16 pm   ACME_TREE____  1
OUT  [0BADCAFE:FFFFFFFFFFFF]  3:14:19 pm   ACME_TREE____  2      ACME_TREE____  2
         WHITE-SRV1    2    WHITE-SRV1    2    WHITE-SRV1    2
         LABS-SRV1     1                       ACME_TREE____  1
OUT  [00001234:FFFFFFFFFFFF]  3:14:19 pm   ACME_TREE____  1      LABS-SRV1      1
         LABS-SRV1     1
OUT  [0BADCAFE:FFFFFFFFFFFF]  3:14:19 pm   LABS-SRV1      1
IN   [0BADCAFE:000000000001]  3:14:23 pm   LABS-SRV1      1
IN   [0BADCAFE:000000000001]  3:14:25 pm   LABS-SRV1      1
IN   [00001234:0020AFE8B0B5]  3:14:26 pm   0000DAD   1/2
<Use ALT-ESC or CTRL-ESC to switch screens, or any other key to pause>
```

TRACK ON information is formatted according to whether the file server is receiving the information (IN) or broadcasting the information (OUT). Figure 13.3 shows the format of TRACK ON for the ACME LAB server and provides information about the many components it tracks, including sending file server's network address, node address, name, hops from that file server to this one, network addresses known by the sending file server, and the number of ticks it takes to traverse the WAN. Refer to Table 13.2 for a more detailed discussion of these TRACK ON components. Finally, you can activate the RIP tracking screen by issuing the following command at the server colon prompt (:):

    TRACK ON

T A B L E   13.2

*Understanding TRACK ON
Parameters*

PARAMETER	VALUE	DESCRIPTION
IN	IN [network address] 3:14:07 PM	Indicates inbound information originating outside this server and the time at which it was accepted.
OUT	OUT [network address] 3:14:19 PM	Indicates outbound information originating from this server and going across the WAN.
[network address]	[0BADCAFE:000000000001]	Identifies the IPX internal network address and node address of the internal virtual LAN. This is the server's unique internal network address.
	[00001234:FFFFFFFFFFFF]	The outbound network and node address for packets being sent from this server. The odd node address indicates this packet is meant to be broadcast to all workstations and servers on the 1234 external cabling segment.
	[00001234:0020AFC055F3]	Indicates a packet arriving from a specific machine — in this case, a workstation.

(continued)

TABLE 13.2

Understanding TRACK ON
Parameters
(continued)

PARAMETER	VALUE	DESCRIPTION
SAP Information	LABS-SRV1 1	Service advertising protocol (SAP) information. This includes server names and a number. The number 1 represents how many hops the server is from this server. Each router counts as a hop. Servers displaying SAP information include file servers, print servers, and mail servers, and so on.
	WHITE-SRV1 2	SAP information showing the WHITE-SRV1 server as "2" hops from LABS-SRV1. Internal IPX routing does count as a hop.
RIP Information	00001234 1/2	Routing information protocol data. The number 00001234 indicates the destination network address for this packet. The values "1/2" indicate the number of hops and ticks it will take to reach the network. A tick is 1/18th of a second and typically one more than the number of hops. If you're sending packets over a large WAN, the ticks could take much longer.
GET NEAREST SERVER	Get Nearest Server	This is a broadcast from a client seeking a connection from any server. If you do not get this message, it indicates that the workstation is having trouble communicating with the server.
GIVE NEAREST SERVER	Give Nearest Server LABS-SRV1	This server's response to the "GET NEAREST SERVER" request.

THE BRAIN

For more information on using **TRACK ON** and other server console commands, see the AppNote entitled "Using TRACK and Other Console Utilities in a Mixed NetWare Environment" in the October 1995 issue of *Novell Application Notes*.

If you haven't figured it out yet, almost every ON switch in the world has an OFF. TRACK ON is no exception. To deactivate the RIP tracking screen, simply issue the command

    TRACK OFF

This completes our discussion of IntranetWare marriage tools. With this knowledge, comes responsibility. Remember, wield these tools wisely. Power corrupts and absolute power corrupts absolutely. Now let's complete our journey through the world of IntranetWare server management with a final discussion of "honey-do's."

ZEN

"The story of a girl who gets mad, gets big, and gets even."

From the movie *Attack of the 50 Foot Woman*

ZEN

"I know it is wet
And the sun is not sunny.
But we can have
Lots of good fun that is funny!"

Dr. Seuss

NETWARE LOADABLE MODULES

NLMs are IntranetWare honey-do's. If you ever need any help, it's nice to know NLMs are there for you. These cute little server dynamos attach to the core OS and provide additional IntranetWare functionality. As you can see in Figure 13.4, IntranetWare doesn't have much to offer without NLMs. The core operating system provides these basic network services:

▸ Novell Directory Services (NDS)

▸ File system

▸ Security

▸ Authentication

▸ Routing

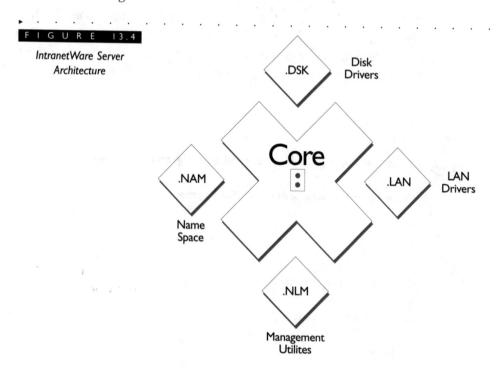

*IntranetWare Server
Architecture*

Of course, this is only the beginning. Without NLMs, the IntranetWare server would be limited to communications and file storing. Here's a list of the additional services provided by IntranetWare NLMs:

▸ Network Printing — PSERVER

▸ Storage Management Services (SMS) — SBACKUP and drivers

▸ Remote Server Console — REMOTE and RSPX/RS232

▸ Server Monitoring — MONITOR

▸ Server Customization — SERVMAN

▸ Communications — NetWare Connect (purchased separately)

▸ Network Management — Managewise (purchased separately)

▸ Messaging — Groupwise (purchased separately)

WHAT'S NEW

It's important to note that server NLMs are very different from Client 32 workstation NLMs. Unfortunately, they have the same name (that is, NLMs). Server NLMs are modular utilities and drivers that interface between IntranetWare and server components. On the other hand, Client 32 workstation NLMs are connectivity programs that interface between the server and local resources (such as Windows 95 and the internal NIC). Got it? Good.

None of these facilities is available until NLMs activate internal communications and mount the file system volumes. In addition to saving the day, IntranetWare NLMs have the following advantages:

▸ NLMs free up RAM by enabling CNEs to remove inactive modules.

▸ NLMs can be loaded and unloaded without bringing down the server — hence the Lego analogy.

▸ NLMs provide an easy method for outside developers to write their own modules for IntranetWare.

From Figure 13.4, you can see that IntranetWare supports four NLM types: disk drivers, LAN drivers, name space, and management NLMs. Disk drivers are primarily responsible for the interface between IntranetWare and the internal hard disks. LAN drivers initiate communications with the internal NIC, and name space modules provide support for non-DOS naming schemes. Management NLMs are the real stars of the show. They're used for monitoring, maintenance, and configuration of the IntranetWare server environment. Let's take a closer look at each of these NLM types and explore how they can improve your quality of life — or at least your marriage.

QUIZ

Here's a nice easy one to warm up with. Two U.S. coins add up to 30 cents, yet one of them is not a nickel. What coins are they? Don't spend it all in one place.

(Q13-2)

Disk Drivers

As I just mentioned, disk drivers control communications between IntranetWare and the internal shared disk (and/or CD-ROM devices). You can load and unload disk drivers as needed. You learned earlier in this chapter that disk drivers activate the NetWare partition. They have the .DSK extension and are stored in the C:\NWSERVER directory. During the installation or startup process, your first task (after running SERVER.EXE) is to activate disk driver NLMs. This mounts the IntranetWare file system and makes all other utilities available from the SYS:SYSTEM directory. Some common .DSK drivers include ISADISK.DSK, IDE.DSK, and DCB.DSK for disk coprocessor boards. Newer disk modules written to the Novell Peripheral Architecture (NWPA) standard come in pairs and have the .CDM and .HAM extensions. In summary, .HAM (Host Adapter Modules) drivers control the host bus adapter, while .CDM (Custom Device Module) drivers control the hardware devices that are attached to the host bus adapter. For more details, refer to Chapter 6.

SMART LINK

For more information on the new Novell Peripheral Architecture solution, surf to the Novell Knowledgebase at http://support.novell. com/search/.

LAN Drivers

LAN drivers, on the other hand, control communication between IntranetWare and internal network interface cards (NICs). You can load and unload these drivers as needed to make communications available to all LAN users. Bear in mind that when you load the LAN driver, you must specify hardware configuration options such as interrupt, port address, memory address, and frame type.

Although disk drivers are automatically activated from STARTUP.NCF, LAN drivers are loaded from AUTOEXEC.NCF. This is because they are available from the SYS:SYSTEM directory once the NetWare partition has been activated. LAN drivers have the .LAN extension and include NE2000.LAN, TOKEN.LAN, 3C5X9.LAN, and TRXNET.LAN for ARCNet.

WHAT'S NEW

IntranetWare introduces an exciting new NLM loading feature: automated hardware detection. When the server is first installed, IntranetWare will automatically detect any hardware devices attached — such as disk controllers, Network Interface Cards, CD-ROMS, and so on. It will then automatically load the correct NLM drivers for each device. Wow! Things are getting easier. Imagine that.

Name Space

Name space modules enable files using non-DOS naming conventions to be stored in the IntranetWare file system. Also, native naming conventions are maintained for diverse workstations throughout the WAN. Name space is important because it allows Windows 95, Windows NT, Macintosh, Unix, and OS/2 names to be supported along with the default DOS environment. Name space modules have the .NAM extension and are stored in the SYS:SYSTEM directory with other NLMs. Some common name space modules include MAC.NAM for Macintosh users, LONG.NAM for Windows and OS/2 users, and NFS.NAM for Unix workstations. In addition to LOADing name space NLMS, you must use a console command to activate the new file system — ADD NAME SPACE.

INSTALL.NLM

This is where the fun begins. INSTALL.NLM is the first of a slew of management NLMs that help you install, manage, maintain, troubleshoot, and optimize the IntranetWare server. As you can see in Figure 13.5, INSTALL consists of ten options.

FIGURE 13.5

*Checking Out
INSTALL.NLM*

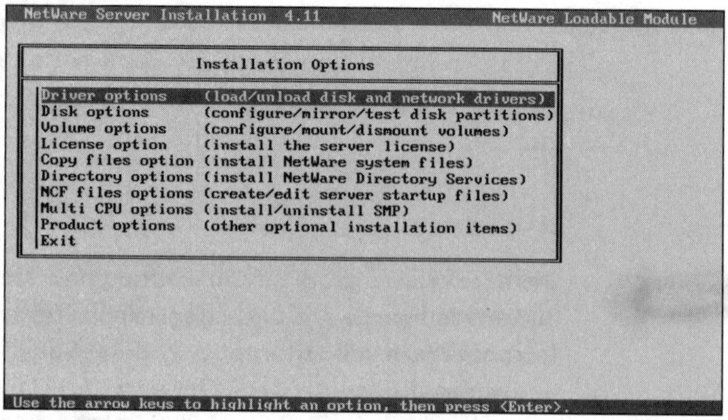

```
NetWare Server Installation  4.11                    NetWare Loadable Module
┌────────────────────────────────────────────────────────────────────────┐
│                          Installation Options                            │
│  ┌────────────────────────────────────────────────────────────────┐     │
│  │ Driver options     (load/unload disk and network drivers)        │    │
│  │ Disk options       (configure/mirror/test disk partitions)        │    │
│  │ Volume options     (configure/mount/dismount volumes)             │    │
│  │ License option     (install the server license)                   │    │
│  │ Copy files option  (install NetWare system files)                 │    │
│  │ Directory options  (install NetWare Directory Services)           │    │
│  │ NCF files options  (create/edit server startup files)             │    │
│  │ Multi CPU options  (install/uninstall SMP)                        │    │
│  │ Product options    (other optional installation items)            │    │
│  │ Exit                                                              │    │
│  └────────────────────────────────────────────────────────────────┘     │
│                                                                          │
│                                                                          │
└────────────────────────────────────────────────────────────────────────┘
Use the arrow keys to highlight an option, then press <Enter>.
```

These ten INSTALL steps systematically walk you through the server install process beginning with SERVER.EXE. Once the core OS has been activated, you load the disk driver(s) and create the NetWare partition. Next, you create the default SYS: volume. Once you copy SYSTEM and PUBLIC files to the new volume, it's time to install NDS, and activate the server license. Installing NDS is the trickiest of the ten installation options. Once time synchronization and server context have been established, you can automate the whole kit and caboodle with AUTOEXEC.NCF and STARTUP.NCF files. Finally, Product Options provides support for installing other products, and Server Options gives you the choice of starting all over again. Of course, like any management NLM, if things get too hairy, you can always EXIT.

This INSTALL.NLM utility is a dramatic improvement over earlier versions. In the past, the installation process wasn't nearly as systematic or organized. Also, you can jump to any point in the journey from the main menu. Some of the tasks you might want to perform after the IntranetWare installation include:

- Disk duplexing

- Adding drives and volumes

- Adding incremental server licenses

- Redefining the hot fix redirection area

▶ Editing server configuration files

▶ Loading an upgraded IntranetWare license

▶ Installing and configuring additional products, including Web Server, NetWare/IP, additional languages, Macintosh connectivity, and Unix support

For a more detailed walkthrough of the server installation process, refer to Chapter 6.

MONITOR.NLM

MONITOR.NLM has always been the "mother of all server utilities." It provides a plethora of information about key memory and communication processes. The types of resources that can be tracked using MONITOR.NLM include file connections, memory, disk information, users, file lock activity, and processor usage. Of course, with the advent of SERVMAN, there's some competition at the top of the mountain.

ZEN

"My grandfather once told me that there are two kinds of people: those who do the work and those who take the credit. He then told me to try to be in the first group, there was much less competition there."

Indira Gandhi

As you can see in Figure 13.6, MONITOR.NLM consists of two main menu screens — General Information and Available Options. Like most MONITOR windows, General Information contains dynamic statistics that change every second or so. Some of the most interesting General Information statistics include:

▶ *Utilization* — Reflects CPU utilization. This number is roughly the amount of time the processor is busy. For a more accurate reading of CPU utilization, use the histogram displayed from the Processor Utilization option from the main menu.

▸ *Total cache buffers* — The number of blocks available for file caching. This number decreases as NLMs and other server resources are loaded. Because file caching has the most dramatic impact on server file performance, you want this number to remain high. For a more accurate measure of available cache buffers, use the Resource Utilization option from the main menu.

▸ *Dirty cache buffers* — The number of file blocks in memory waiting to be written to disk. If this number grows large, you may have a bottleneck problem with the internal hard disk. A server crash at this point would corrupt saved data.

▸ *Current service processes* — Indicates the number of task handlers IntranetWare allocates to service incoming requests. This can dramatically impact server performance, because requests have to wait in line when service processes are busy. Consider what happens at the grocery store around 5:00 p.m. each evening. The default maximum number of service processes is 50, with a possible range of 5 to 1,000.

▸ *Current licensed connections* — The number of active licensed connections the server currently recognizes. This number will always be less than the maximum number of licensed connections your server supports. If this number approaches the maximum, consider upgrading your license using INSTALL.NLM.

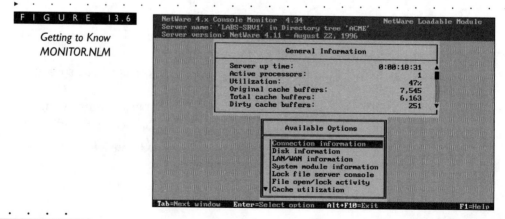

F I G U R E   13.6

*Getting to Know
MONITOR.NLM*

In addition to these general information statistics, MONITOR.NLM includes a plethora of Available Option submenus. Each submenu focuses on a specific subcomponent of the IntranetWare server architecture. Here's a quick look:

▸ Connection information — Lists all active connections and tracks their current activity. CNEs can use this option to clear specific user workstation connections.

▸ Disk information — Lists all available internal disks and valuable hot fix redirection statistics. CNEs can use this option to activate, deactivate, or modify internal disks.

▸ LAN/WAN information — Lists LAN driver configurations and statistics as well as node and network addressing.

▸ System module information — Lists all loaded modules by name, size, and version. In addition, you can track resource "tags" and memory usage for each module.

▸ Lock file server console — As you learned earlier, enables you to protect the console by specifying a password.

▸ File open/lock activity — Monitors files, lock activity, and status. It also enables you to view which stations have open files and general information about mounted volumes and directory structures.

▸ Cache utilization — View detailed caching statistics, including total cache block requests, the number of times a block request had to wait because there were no available cache blocks, long- and short-term cache hits, and dirty cache hits. This option enables you to assess the efficiency of server RAM and take corrective actions.

▸ Processor utilization — Provides a detailed histogram of all selected processes and their CPU usage.

▸ Resource utilization — View memory usage statistics for cache buffer pool, allocated memory, and movable and nonmovable memory pools, and code/data memory. You can also view resource tags and determine which NLMs are "hogging" valuable server RAM.

▸ Memory utilization — View detailed memory statistics such as percent of allocated memory in use, memory blocks and bytes in use, and free blocks. This option also enables you to activate garbage collection routines. You never know when you might need it.

▸ Scheduling information — View and change the priority of a process by delaying CPU execution until a later time. This options also provides a management window to IntranetWare's new SMP (Symmetric MultiProcessing) feature.

▸ EXIT — Sounds like a good time for this.

You could spend a lifetime exploring MONITOR.NLM, and we probably will in Chapter 15. Stay tuned. But for now, settle for the MONITOR.NLM exploritorium at the end of this chapter.

SERVMAN.NLM

Look out, there's a new superhero in Gotham. He is faster than a speedy microprocessor, has more storage than a CD-ROM, and is able to search huge databases in a single second. He's SERVMAN!

SERVMAN, the new SERVer MANager, is at the core of IntranetWare's new server utility strategy. It is the most exciting and versatile new server utility. SERVMAN provides a menu interface for SET parameters and displays valuable IntranetWare configurations. As you can see in Figure 13.7, SERVMAN includes two windows — Server General Information and Available Options. Each of the statistics in the Server General Information window is updated every second. Here's a quick look:

▸ *Server uptime* — Length of time the server has been running since it was last booted.

▸ *Processor utilization* — Percentage of time the server CPU is busy.

▸ *Processor speed* — Speed at which the processor is running based on CPU clock speed, CPU type, and the number of memory wait states. For example, the LABS-SRV1 server has a rating of 16,429. This is an average setting for a Pentium 200 MHz machine.

▸ *Server processes* — The number of tasks handlers currently available to handle incoming user requests.

▸ *Loaded NLMs* — The number of modules currently loaded on the server.

▸ *Mounted volumes* — The number of volumes currently active on the server.

▸ *Active queues* — The number of active print queues currently servicing user print jobs.

▸ *Logged-in users* — The number of users logged into the server.

▸ *Loaded name spaces* — The number of name spaces loaded on the server, and yes, DOS counts as one.

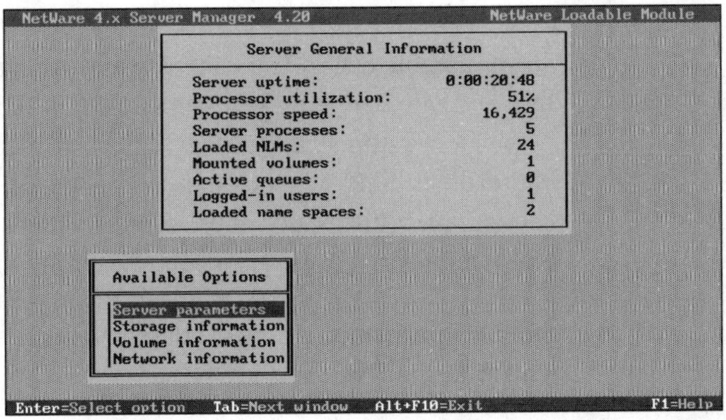

FIGURE 13.7

SERVMAN — The New IntranetWare Superhero

```
NetWare 4.x Server Manager  4.20              NetWare Loadable Module

                     ┌─────── Server General Information ───────┐
                     │  Server uptime:             0:00:20:48    │
                     │  Processor utilization:            51%    │
                     │  Processor speed:               16,429    │
                     │  Server processes:                   5    │
                     │  Loaded NLMs:                       24    │
                     │  Mounted volumes:                    1    │
                     │  Active queues:                      0    │
                     │  Logged-in users:                    1    │
                     │  Loaded name spaces:                 2    │
                     └──────────────────────────────────────────┘


          ┌─ Available Options ─┐
          │ Server parameters   │
          │ Storage information │
          │ Volume information  │
          │ Network information │
          └─────────────────────┘

  Enter=Select option   Tab=Next window   Alt+F10=Exit            F1=Help
```

REAL WORLD

The processor speed rating is a measurement of the server's processing capabilities as determined by the CPU clock speed (such as 120 MHz), the CPU type (such as Pentium), and the number of memory wait states (for example, 0). For instance, a 386/33 machine should get a rating of about 320, a 486/50 should get a rating of around 1,370, a Pentium/120 should get a rating of approximately 6,576, and a Pentium/200 should get a rating around 16,429.

As you can see, there's a little overlap between MONITOR.NLM and SERVMAN.NLM. This is not where the similarities end. Throughout SERVMAN, you'll see references back to statistics displayed in INSTALL.NLM and MONITOR.NLM. And, of course, you'll see some new configurations not available anywhere else. The idea is this: With SERVMAN, you get a single management utility for all server maintenance and customization tasks. Although it doesn't provide a facility for *all* server management tasks, SERVMAN does help you accomplish many of them. Murphy's Law Number 342 — never say "all."

The Available Options menu within SERVMAN offers some valuable management capabilities, including:

▸ Server parameters — You can view and configure "almost all" IntranetWare operating system parameters. This includes SET parameters automated by AUTOEXEC.NCF and STARTUP.NCF. Changes you make in SERVMAN can optionally be reflected in the server configuration files. Cool! Plus, you can view a quick description of each SET parameter and its default settings from within a menu interface.

▸ Storage information — View adapter, device, and partition information similar to INSTALL and MONITOR.

▸ Volume information — View information about volumes mounted on the file server (similar to INSTALL).

▸ Network information — View network information such as number of packets received and transmitted. This is a summary screen of the detailed LAN statistics provided by MONITOR.NLM.

All in all, SERVMAN is a great superhero. Remember, never tug on Superman's cape.

SMART LINK

For more information about IntranetWare optimization using MONITOR/SERVMAN and a chance to try out these server utilities on your own, surf over to CyberState University and World Wire: http://www.cyberstateu.com.

DSREPAIR

It's nice to know that if SERVMAN can't save the day, you can rely on DSREPAIR.NLM. This replaces the BINDFIX utility used in previous bindery-based versions of NetWare. DSREPAIR makes repairs and adjustments to the NDS database and solves inconsistencies with time and replica synchronization. Figure 13.8 shows the main menu of DSREPAIR and both synchronization options. In addition, the Advanced Options menu enables you to set advanced repair configurations such as "Log file management," "Repair local DS database," "Servers known to this database," "View remote server ID list," "Replica and Partition operations," "Check volume objects and trustees," "Check external references," "Security equivalence synchronization," "Global schema operations," and "Create a database file." If you're not sure you have a corrupted NDS database, consider the following symptoms:

▸ You cannot create, delete, or modify objects even though you have sufficient rights.

▸ You have unknown objects appearing in the tree that do not disappear after all servers are synchronized.

▸ You cannot create, merge, or modify partitions.

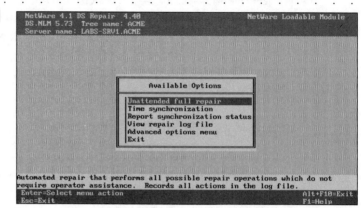

FIGURE 13.8

*If Only I Knew
DSREPAIR.NLM*

Once DSREPAIR is completed, you can read through the DSREPAIR log as the file DSREPAIR.LOG in the SYS:SYSTEM subdirectory (see Chapter 9). Remember, DSREPAIR is your friend, but should only be used in emergency situations.

ZEN

"Computers come in two varieties: the 'prototype' and the 'obsolete.'"

Anonymous

IntranetWare is a great operating system for our global electronic village. Now that we've installed, configured, activated, and maintained our server, it's time to "protect" it. In the next section, you'll learn how to create a maximum security server. If we do it right, our server will be more impenetrable than Alcatraz. Interestingly, we're trying to keep the users from breaking *in*, not *out*.

QUIZ

Speaking of Security, at the next minute, it will be exactly twice as many seconds after the half-hour as it was minutes before the same half-hour last time the two hands were at right angles this afternoon. Hmmmm, help me out here — what time is it?

(Q13-3)

SERVER PROTECTION

If the server is at the heart of your IntranetWare WAN, it makes sense to take all measures you can to protect it. As we saw in Chapter 11, IntranetWare has an elaborate security system that protects NDS and data files from would-be hackers. This system does nothing, however, to protect the server console itself. Any user with mischievous intent and a little bit of knowledge can cause a lot of harm at the IntranetWare server console. For this reason, you should take extra measure to install an impenetrable network armor at the file server console. Following are four scenarios that can go a long way in protecting your server:

▸ Physical — Lock up the physical server

▸ MONITOR.NLM locking — Use the password feature

▸ SECURE CONSOLE — Restrict access to the DOS partition

▸ REMOTE.NLM — Add a password to the built-in RMF facility

Now, let's take a closer look at how to create a "maximum security server."

Physical

No matter what security locks you put in place, someone's going to break them if they have physical access to the server. It's amazing how much information can be stolen from the physical server console, including SERVER.EXE, NLMs, optimization data, and company secrets. The first step in creating a maximum security server is locking up the physical machine itself. This involves three steps:

1 • Lock the server into a wiring closet or other restricted room.

2 • Remove the keyboard to discourage physical access to the console.

3 • Remove the server monitor and leave the hacker "in the dark."

Although this is a great plan, you're probably wondering, "How am I supposed to manage server operations from within a locked closet and with no keyboard or monitor?" That is a good question. Fortunately, IntranetWare includes a built-in

Remote Management Facility (RMF) that provides virtual access to the file server console — from a direct workstation or asynchronously remote machine. Later in this chapter, we'll explore RMF and show you how it can be used to supplement the server protection plan. For now, let's move on to the next protection scenario — MONITOR.NLM.

MONITOR.NLM Locking

If locking up the server is not an option, or if you want to increase your level of server protection, consider "locking" the console with MONITOR.NLM. This way, even if someone does get physical access to the machine, he or she can't access the console unless he or she has the MONITOR.NLM password. First, load the MONITOR.NLM utility by typing:

```
LOAD MONITOR
```

at the file server console. Next, choose the Lock Server Console option from the main menu. IntranetWare will ask for a password. Enter a unique password and press Enter. All done. Now anyone accessing the server console must first enter the MONITOR.NLM password.

> **TIP**
>
> If intruder detection/lockout disables either the bindery supervisor or Admin account, the password won't unlock **MONITOR. This is a bad thing. The only way to reactivate the accounts is to issue the **ENABLE LOGIN** console command at the server — but we can't get there! So, as a backup measure, consider issuing a different **MONITOR** locking password.

By default, IntranetWare accepts the bindery supervisor's password for unlocking the server console. As you learned earlier, this is the first password assigned to the Admin user when you installed the first server in this NDS tree. Even if you delete Admin or change his or her password, the supervisor bindery password remains the same. You should specify a different password when you lock the monitor — just in case. You can also automate monitor locking by placing the following command in the server's AUTOEXEC.NCF configuration file:

```
LOAD MONITOR L
```

In this example, only the supervisor bindery password can be used to unlock the server console. Next, let's expand our server protection scheme to include the SECURE CONSOLE command.

SECURE CONSOLE

To further enhance server protection, you can use the SECURE CONSOLE command at the colon prompt (:) or, even better, place it in the AUTOEXEC.NCF file so it executes automatically when the server is booted. This command accomplishes four things:

▶ Path specifiers are disabled. Only the SYS:SYSTEM search path remains in effect. This means NLMs can only be loaded from the SYS:SYSTEM directory. SECURE CONSOLE provides protection against Trojan horse modules that are loaded from the DOS partition or diskette drives. These modules enter the core OS and access or alter valuable server information. Remember, anyone can load an NLM at the server from diskette unless he or she is physically restricted from accessing it, or the SECURE CONSOLE command has been used.

▶ Keyboard entry into the NetWare 4.11 OS debugger is disabled. This stops super-nerdy hackers from altering the OS itself.

▶ This command prevents the server date and time from being changed by an intruder. This closes a loophole in the intruder detection/lockout feature. Without SECURE CONSOLE, users whose accounts have been disabled can simply access the server colon prompt and manually expire their lockout period. Bad user.

▶ COMMAND.COM is removed from server memory. This protects files on the DOS partition by preventing access to it. Remember, one of your most important IntranetWare files (SERVER.EXE) resides on the DOS partition.

I'm feeling more secure already. With the server locked up tight as a drum, there's only one more back door to close — RMF access.

REMOTE.NLM

The final server protection strategy involves restricting access to RMF — IntranetWare's built-in remote management facility. As you recall from our first protection strategy, we've already locked the server in a closet and removed the keyboard and monitor. Now, the only way to perform daily monitoring tasks is RMF. We'll talk more about the details of RMF later in this chapter, but here's the "Cliff Notes" version.

RMF enables you to access the server console from a local or remote workstation. In either case, it relies on two key components — REMOTE.NLM at the server and RCONSOLE.EXE at the workstation. It's reasonable to assume that if *you* can access the server console from a remote workstation, so can any malevolent hacker. So, let's take measures to protect REMOTE.NLM.

When you activate REMOTE at the server console, you can specify a password using the following syntax:

```
LOAD REMOTE password
```

Replace *password* with any alphanumeric name you can remember. With the password in place, RCONSOLE prompts you for it before enabling access to the server console. Here's the catch — you'll probably want to automate this step by placing REMOTE in the AUTOEXEC.NCF file. Because AUTOEXEC.NCF is a text file in the SYS:SYSTEM subdirectory, it's reasonable to assume that any hacker worth his or her salt would be able to view the REMOTE password. Oops. But we have a solution. You can use null characters in the password or, better yet, encrypt it. Null characters appear as spaces but are actual, valid, alphanumeric characters. You can issue a null character by pressing the Alt+255 keys simultaneously. When hackers view AUTOEXEC.NCF, they'll never know the difference between a null character and a space. Or, better yet, you can encrypt the REMOTE password using LDREMOTE. For more details, see the Real World that follows.

Don't you feel much better now, knowing that you have a maximum security server? Just like Alcatraz, it should be almost impossible for IntranetWare criminals to "break in."

REAL WORLD

In pre-NetWare 4.1 versions of NetWare, REMOTE.NLM accepted the supervisor's bindery password in addition to its own. This meant you could issue the LOAD REMOTE command in AUTOEXEC.NCF without having to disclose the password. In IntranetWare, the REMOTE password is required and the Supervisor bindery password no longer works. Fortunately, Novell has included an encryption scheme that enables you to encrypt what appears in AUTOEXEC.NCF. Here's how it works:

1. Load REMOTE.NLM at the server console by typing **LOAD REMOTE** and pressing Enter. IntranetWare will prompt you for an RMF password. Enter it now (for example, **Cathy**).

2. RMF is now active, but your password is not protected. Next, you can encrypt the password by typing **REMOTE ENCRYPT** at the server console and pressing Enter. Once again, IntranetWare will ask you for a password. Enter the same one from Step 1 (**Cathy**).

3. IntranetWare then responds with an encrypted LOAD statement, such as:

    ```
    LOAD REMOTE -e 14572BFD3AFEAE4E4759
    ```

This is the encrypted representation of the password "Cathy."

Next, REMOTE will ask you a simple question:

```
Would you like this command written to SYS:SYSTEM\LDREMOTE.NCF?
```

You should probably answer Yes.

4. Now you're ready to add the REMOTE statement to AUTOEXEC.NCF without any concerns about giving away the password. Simply enter these two commands toward the end of AUTOEXEC.NCF:

    ```
    LDREMOTE
    ```

    ```
    LOAD RSPX
    ```

There you have it! We've increased server protection by requiring an RMF password and closed a loophole by encrypting it. In summary, use LOAD REMOTE with the password, then issue the REMOTE ENCRYPT command to encrypt the password. Provide the same password again and have IntranetWare create the LDREMOTE configuration file. Finally, automate RMF by placing LDREMOTE in the AUTOEXEC.NCF file.

ZEN

"We could tell you what it's about. But then, of course, we'd have to kill you."

From the movie *Sneakers*

Well, there you have it — the tools of a good marriage. No matter what you do, remember: Communication is the key. If you work hard at it and develop a synergistic team, I guarantee the rewards will greatly outweigh the pain.

Now it's time to expand your marriage and embrace the community. Become part of the "collective whole" — as long as their name isn't *The Borg*. Beam me up!

Intranet Management

Just when you were beginning to get comfortable with marriage, the *intranet* came along. From a technical standpoint, the intranet is simply a Web server that is confined to a private internal network and publishes files to a private audience (such as the employees of a corporation). A true WWW server is connected to the Internet and publishes files to the world. From a less technical standpoint, the intranet is nosy neighbors, bowling leagues, and poker on Saturday night.

IntranetWare is Novell's comprehensive platform for a modern, full-service intranetwork. It starts with NetWare 4.11, then adds the following intranet and Internet features:

▸ *IPX/IP Gateway* — This gateway enables administrators to allow IPX-based workstations to access TCP/IP-based resources (such as FTP and the World Wide Web) without having to install or configure TCP/IP on those workstations. The gateway also lets you implement access control — you can limit users by TCP port number, IP address or the target host, and the time of day.

▸ *NetWare MPR* (MultiProtocol Router 3.1) — This feature provides WAN (wide area network) connectivity, routing multiple protocols over leased lines, frame relay, or ISDN lines. This capability allows you to connect network users to an Internet Service Provider (ISP).

▸ *The NetWare Web Server* — A full-feature Web server that allows you to publish HTML pages over the intranet and Internet. It also includes the Netscape Navigator browser that lets you locate and read information stored on the Web.

▸ *FTP Services for IntranetWare* — FTP services let you configure FTP access for your intranetwork.

REAL WORLD

As we learned in Chapter 6, IntranetWare includes the following CD-ROMs:

▸ *NetWare 4.11 Operating System* CD-ROM, which contains the regular NetWare 4.11 product software and the NetWare Web Server. The NetWare Web Server also contains the Netscape Navigator Web browser (and a single-user license for the browser).

▸ *NetWare 4.11 Online Documentation* CD-ROM, which contains the DynaText documentation for NetWare 4.11.

▸ *Novell Internet Access Server 4* CD-ROM, which contains most of the IntranetWare features: the IPX/IP gateway, MultiProtocol Router 3.1 for WAN connectivity, and the Netscape Navigator Web browser (multiuser license). This CD-ROM also contains HTML-formatted documentation for the IPX/IP gateway.

▸ *FTP Services for IntranetWare* CD-ROM, which contains the FTP services and configuration utilities.

In this section, we will expand our understanding of the IntranetWare server to the "collective whole" — *intranet*. We will explore each of the previously mentioned four solutions in excruciating detail. But first, let's take a moment to explore two other important Enterprise topics:

- ▸ *NDS Maintenance* — Novell Directory Services is the heart of IntranetWare's enterprise solution. Keeping it running smoothly should be your #1 priority. The next section explores some time-proven techniques for NDS maintenance and troubleshooting. Also, review Chapters 4, 8, and 9 earlier in the book.

- ▸ *Internationalization* — IntranetWare allows diverse users to "speak different languages" and transport messages across different communication protocols. This is accomplished with the help of built-in IntranetWare internationalization. Language enabling and special keyboard support ensure that international users can access resources in their native languages.

There's only one guarantee in marriage — anything goes! I have a feeling there's a lot of fun ahead for us, so let's get started.

NDS MAINTENANCE

NDS is a "sticky wicket." (I don't know what that means, but doesn't it sound great?) As a sticky wicket, NDS requires special precautions to make sure everything runs smoothly. If anything bad happens to NDS, it's only a matter of time before it starts to happen to you. That's karma.

As you learned in Chapters 8 and 9, many different bad things can happen to NDS. The network begins to wig out when replicas are unsynchronized. The NDS database gets corrupted, servers crash, or containers get moved around too much. You also learned some strategies for dealing with these unwanted realities. Now, let's take a look at a few additional NDS maintenance strategies that can help us deal with, or even prevent, NDS crises:

- ▸ Preventative Maintenance

- ▸ Identifying NDS Database Inconsistencies

> ▸ Repairing NDS with NDS Manager

> ▸ Removing a Server from the Network

> ▸ Recovering from a Crash

Because NDS is a distributed, replicated database, the NetWare 4.11 server must continually share information and synchronize changes in the database. In addition, the database is *loosely* consistent and requires time to replicate and synchronize major changes. For these reasons, it's critical that you take numerous preventative measures to maintain the health of your NDS database.

If these measures don't work, then you'll need a sure-fire plan for identifying and dealing with database inconsistencies. That's what this section is all about. Think of it as a disaster-recovery plan for database synchronicity (and a great way to keep your job!).

REAL WORLD

NDS synchronization occurs differently for *simple* and *complex* changes. Simple changes (such as changing a user's phone number) occur almost instantaneously. More complex changes take more time. For example, joining two partitions that exist on two different servers will take a few minutes to synchronize throughout the network. In the meantime, Unknown objects may appear. This doesn't mean the database is corrupted; it just means it's temporarily "out-of-sync".

Preventative Maintenance

There are a number of measures you can take to prevent NDS database disasters. Following is a quick summary of some of the most useful:

> ▸ *Plan replica placement* — As we learned in Chapter 4, you should have at least three replicas of every partition. At the same time, don't get carried away. Too many replicas can cause serious synchronization problems. Also, distribute replicas intelligently. Most should be local, and a few should be at distributed locations.

▸ *Regulate partition management rights* — Partition operations (such as splitting and joining) have a dramatic impact on NDS synchronization. For this reason, you'll want to regulate who gets to perform these operations. One method of regulating is by only giving one or two people Supervisor NDS rights to the partition root object. Also, limit partition operations to one workstation at a time. Remember: Partitions lock as they are split and joined, so you can only perform one operation at a time.

▸ *Backup the Directory* — Backing up the file system doesn't backup the Directory. Be very careful about NDS backups, and be sure to test them with proper restores. Also, consider backing up the Directory at least every week — maybe everyday. Finally, you should restore an NDS backup only when all other options have been exhausted.

▸ *Maintain a standard NDS version* — Each update of NDS fixes problems and increases functionality. When a new version of NDS is released, the new features are not available until all servers in the Replica Ring are updated. So, how do you update NDS? Simple — change the server's "DS.NLM" module. You can use NDS Manager to view your NDS version by selecting "View from NDS Version" (see Figure 13.9) in the Objects menu. Similarly, you can update a server's DS.NLM version by choosing "Update from NDS Version." The server with the newest version is the *source* server and the one being updated is the *target* — makes sense.

TIP

The Version Update feature of NDS Manager can be used to upgrade DS.NLM within Operating System versions, but not across them. This means you can upgrade any NetWare 4.1 version to another NetWare 4.1 version (Versions 463 through 499) and any NetWare 4.11 version to another NetWare 4.11 version (Version 500 and above). But you can't upgrade version 477 to version 522, for example. Sorry.

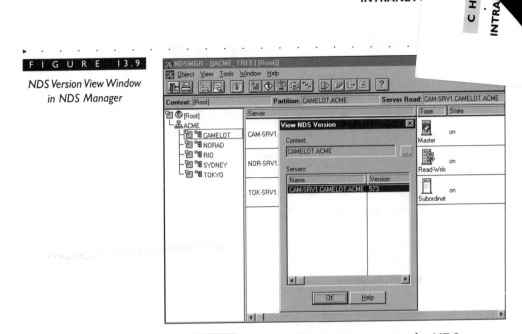

FIGURE 13.9

*NDS Version View Window
in NDS Manager*

Important *Monitor SYS: volume space* — The SYS: volume contains the NDS database in a hidden directory on every server. Furthermore, NDS is protected by the Transactional Tracking System (TTS). If the SYS: volume fills up, TTS shuts down and the NDS database is closed to future changes. This is bad. To avoid running out of disk space on SYS:, try some of these sure-fire tips: set minimum space requirements to receive a warning before SYS: runs out of space; store print queues and user files on other volumes; don't add replicas to full servers; control-audit data files; don't disable TTS; and consider removing CD-ROM drives, because they create huge index files on the SYS: volume.

▶ *Prepare a server for downtime* — Don't just turn off your server! If you must shut down a server for more than a few hours, use NDS Manager to move replicas to other servers. If you want to shut down the server or WAN link for an extended period of time (more than a few days), remove NDS from the server by using INSTALL.NLM. Fortunately, the Directory is designed to withstand these problems, and all replicas are resynchronized when the servers come back on-line. But it's always a good idea to use prevention rather than troubleshooting.

That's it for NDS prevention. Remember: *An ounce of prevention is worth more than a ton of cure.* Unfortunately, life doesn't always fit so nicely into nursery rhymes. Sometimes prevention doesn't work. In those cases, you'll need a ton-and-a-half of cure. Let's start with identification.

Identifying NDS Database Inconsistencies

The first sign of NDS trouble is an "inconsistent database." This occurs when replicas of a partition cannot be synchronized, and the shared information becomes dissimilar and/or corrupted. Sometimes, inconsistency is temporary — as when splitting or joining multiple partitions. But most of the time it's a tell-tale sign of something wrong.

Here are three things to look for when identifying database inconsistencies:

- Client symptoms

- Unknown objects

- NDS error codes

Let's take a closer look.

Client Symptoms The following client problems may indicate that the database is out of sync:

- The client prompts for a password when none exists.

- Client logins take much longer than they should.

- Modifications to the Directory disappear.

- Previously assigned NDS rights disappear.

- Client problems are inconsistent and cannot be duplicated.

Unknown Objects The presence of *Unknown* objects in the tree can indicate problems with synchronization. However, Unknown objects don't always point to a problem. For example, sometimes objects become Unknown during partition Create and Merge operations. This is normal, because the partition root is changing.

Volume objects also become Unknown when their host server is deleted. Finally, Alias objects become Unknown when their host objects are deleted.

So, as you can see, being Unknown isn't always a problem — just most of the time!

NDS Error Codes The NetWare 4.11 server console produces NDS error messages whenever the server is unable to complete a synchronization process. These messages can be seen in the File Server Error Log, on the DS TRACE console, or in NDS Manager. Refer to NetWare 4.11 documentation for a complete listing of important NDS error codes in DS TRACE.

Repairing NDS with NDS Manager

Once you have identified an NDS database inconsistency, you must use NDS Manager to do something about it. Following are some of the most valuable repair tasks available in NDS Manager:

> ▸ *Check partition synchronization* — To view partition synchronization information in NDS Manager, first highlight the appropriate partition. Then, choose Check Synchronization from the Object menu (see Figure 13.10). A synchronization problem appears when the "All Processed = No" line has a value greater than 0. One word of warning: Check Synchronization may provide incomplete information because it only checks for synchronization errors on the first server in the Replica Ring. If you want to check all servers in the ring, use Partition Continuity.

TIP

Check Synchronization in NDS Manager doesn't work on NDS versions earlier than Version 489.

> ▸ *Check partition continuity* — To check for synchronization errors on all servers in a Replica Ring, choose Partition Continuity from the Object menu in NDS Manager (see Figure 13.11). The Continuity window is a matrix showing each server in a partition's Replica Ring (row) and the different type of replicas it supports (column). A replica icon with an exclamation point

indicates a server with synchronization errors (see CAM - SRV1 in the figure). Also, you can track Replica Ring inconsistencies in this window by matching row and column icons (they should match).

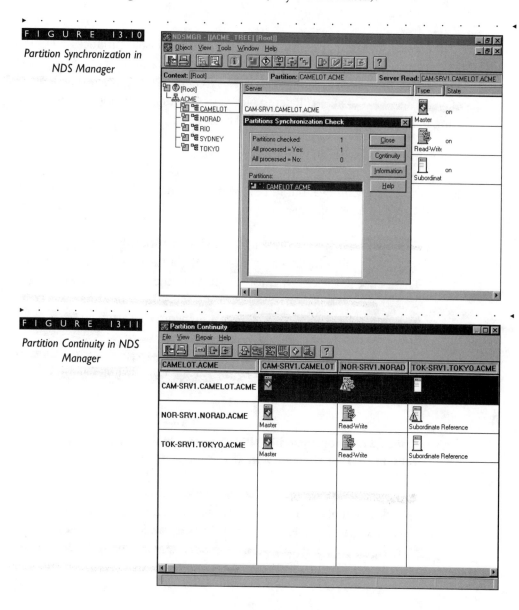

F I G U R E 13.10

Partition Synchronization in NDS Manager

F I G U R E 13.11

Partition Continuity in NDS Manager

▶ *Help* — Once you identify a database inconsistency, you can use the NDS Manager Help system for a list of possible solutions. First, double-click on the suffering icon and an error code is displayed. To view more information and a list of solutions, click on the ? (Help) button. You can also find Help information by selecting List of Codes from NDS and Server Codes in the Contents window of Help (see Figure 13.12).

SMART LINK

You can get a complete list of NDS error codes in the NetWare 4.11 System Messages manual, or surf the Web to http://www.novell.com/ manuals.

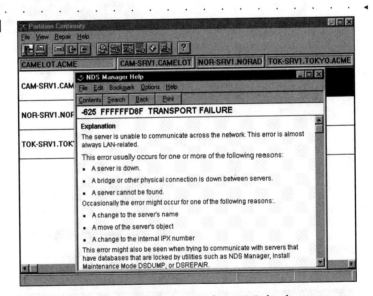

F I G U R E   13.12

*NDS Error Codes Help
Screen in NDS Manager*

▶ *General Guidelines* — the action you take to resolve NDS database inconsistencies depends entirely on the specific error begin reported. This is where the Help information can be very valuable. There are, however, a few general guidelines which sometimes work. First, let the system run for a few hours. You might get lucky and synchronization will take care of itself. Whatever you do, don't shut down the server. This will prevent self-healing. Also, follow error-code repair guidelines very carefully. You can cause more harm if you don't follow the directions precisely. Finally, don't attempt any partition operations on a partition that is already experiencing problems. They'll spread like a virus.

Most NDS repair procedures can be found in the Repair menu of Partition Continuity within NDS Manager (see Figure 13.13). Refer to Table 13.3 for a detailed explanation of each of these great NDS Manager repair tasks. Use them, or lose them!

F I G U R E   1 3 . 1 3

NDS Repair Menu in NDS
Manager

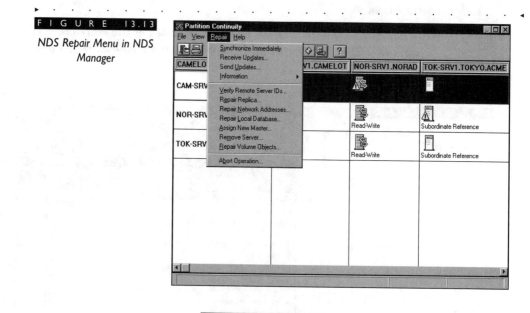

T A B L E   1 3 . 3

Exploring the NDS Repair
Menu in NDS Manager

MENU CHOICE	ACTION
Synchronize Immediately	Forces all servers in the Replica Ring to sychronize immediately.
Receive Update	Deletes a replica on a server, and replaces it with a copy from the Master replica. This is performed on a target server when its replicas are known to be corrupted. Note: This operation can cause excessive traffic on the WAN, because the entire replica is sent.
Send Update	Selected server. Forces the server to synchronize immediately with all servers in its Replica Ring.

*Exploring the NDS Repair
Menu in NDS Manager
(continued)*

MENU CHOICE	ACTION
Verify Remote Server IDs	Selected server. Confirms and corrects the Replica Ring and server IDs for all replicas held on this server. This ensures that the server can communicate with all servers holding the same replicas.
Repair Replica	Selected replica. Confirms and corrects the Replica Ring and server IDs for the replica. This ensures that the server can communicate with all servers holding this replica (also known as a Replica Ring).
Repair Network Addresses	Corrects inconsistencies in network address information between servers in a Replica Ring. Incorrect network address information can result in communication failure between servers (NDS Error code -625)
Repair Local Database	Selected server. Corrects specific inconsistencies within all replicas on this server. This action is similar to the repairing performed by VREPAIR on local volumes.
Assign New Master	Selected replica. Changes a Read/Write or Read-Only replica into the Master replica. Performed when the Master replica becomes corrupted or unavailable.
Remove Server	Selected server. Removes a server from a chosen Replica Ring. Performed when a server becomes corrupted or unavailable. Note: This operation is performed in the Partition Continuity window of NDS Manager, and differs from "Delete Server."
Repair Volume Objects	Selected server. Confirms that NDS Volume objects exist for all physical volumes on this server. In addition, this operation will create Volume objects if they are missing. Finally, this operation can also confirm that all Trustees are, in fact, NDS object in the Directory.
Delete Server	Selected server. Deletes a server object from the NDS Directory tree. You should only perform this operation when the server has been permanently removed from the network. Note: This operation is performed from the Object menu of NDS Manager, and differs from "Remove Server."

Removing a Server from the Network

If any of the above repair tasks don't solve your problem, you may need to remove your server from the Directory tree. Removing a server requires special consideration, because it might contain replicas and other essential references to NDS. These references must be deleted so that the rest of the servers in the Replica Ring can synchronize properly.

Removing NDS is the recommended way of removing a server object from NDS because it accomplishes several auxiliary tasks you may not have thought of (such as deleting Volume objects relating to this server, solving replica placement problems, informing other servers in the Replica Ring, and removing all essential NDS references).

Follow these simple steps for removing a server from the NDS Directory:

1 • Load INSTALL at the server console

2 • Select Directory Options

3 • Select Remove Directory Services from this server. A warning message will appear. Press Enter to close the window and continue.

4 • Select Yes to confirm.

5 • Log into the server as Admin (or any user with Supervisor rights to all replicas). You will receive a message that Master replicas exist on this server. Press Enter to close the window.

6 • If this is the only server in the NDS tree, then you're finished. You will receive a message confirming that "NDS has been removed."

7 • If this is not the only server in the NDS tree, you will need to send the Master replica to another server. Choose "Do it automatically" if you want INSTALL to find an appropriate Read/Write replica and upgrade it. Otherwise, choose "Designate which servers yourself" and choose the Read/Write replica manually. Either way, you're finished!

Recovering from a Crash

As we learned earlier, NDS is stored in hidden files on the SYS: volume. If the hard disk crashes or the SYS: volume becomes unavailable, it's the equivalent of losing NDS *and* the entire Operating System.

REAL WORLD

INSTALL.NLM might not be able to remove NDS if certain preconditions aren't met. You can still "force" INSTALL to remove NDS by using the following option:

```
LOAD INSTALL -DSREMOVE
```

This is a very traumatic event and it can cause unusual side effects. Only use it as a last resort.

Recovering from a crash this serious is very tricky. You must first resolve any NDS problems that were caused by the crash, then back out the Server and Volume objects, Install the hard disk and NetWare 4.11, and finally, restore the replicas and file system.

Navigate the following steps very carefully when recovering from a SYS: crash:

1 • *Determine replica status* — Use NDS Manager to document the replicas that were stored on this server. Highlight the Server object from another server and document the replica list. This is a lot easier if the server is still up. If any of the replicas were Masters, you'll need to upgrade another Read/Write to Master status (also in NDS Manager).

2 • *Delete the server object* — Use NDS Manager to delete the Server object from NDS.

3 • *Delete volume objects* — Use NetWare Administrator to delete any Volume objects associated with this server.

4 • *Resolve NDS problems* — Use NDS Manager to resolve any outstanding NDS problems caused by the crash. Highlight the server's home partition and activate Partition Continuity. If you receive a "-625" NDS error, use the Remove Server task as outlined in Table 13.3.

5 • *Install NetWare 4.11* — Install the new hard disk and NetWare 4.11 Operating System (as outlined in Chapter 6). When the NDS Server Context screen appears, install the server in its original context.

6 • *Restore the replicas* — Use NDS Manager and your replica list from Step 1 to replace all replicas (including Masters) on the new server. This step may take a long time because of extensive updates across WAN links. Take a nap.

7 • *Restore the file system* — use Storage Management Services (SMS) to restore the file system from tape (or optical) backup. Refer to the "Storage Management Services" section later in this chapter.

8 • *Confirm the correct bindery context* — use SERVMAN to restore the server's bindery context.

Congratulations! Your NDS server has been restored. See? There isn't any disaster you can't recover from. All you need is a quick wit and really heavy book (preferably *Novell's CNE Study Guide for IntranetWare/NetWare 4.11*).

SMART LINK

For an on-line glimpse of *Novell's CNE Study Guide for IntranetWare/ NetWare 4.11*, surf to http://corp.novell.com/programs/press/hot.htm.

This completes our discussion of NDS Maintenance. These strategies should help you sleep better at night by decreasing the chances that something horrible will happen to your NDS database. Now that your LAN is more stable, you can consider expanding its boundaries with Internationalization.

REAL WORLD

So, where do the NDS files really live? Like I said, off the root of the SYS: volume. NDS lives in a hidden system-owned directory called _NETWARE. You can view the files and their size through RCONSOLE. Simply choose Directory Scan from the Available Options menu and use the following path: SYS:_NETWARE. It's amazing what you can learn in a book these days.

INTERNATIONALIZATION

If will be extending the boundaries of your WAN to "span the globe," you're going to need to speak everyone's language. And we're not just talking protocol languages — we're talking humans' written and spoken languages. This falls under the category of "knowing what your spouse means" when he or she says something crazy. For example, "You should've known I meant 'yes' when I said 'no.'" Once again, we find ourselves in a sticky wicket. Understanding spouses and IntranetWare internationalization can be the difference between sweet dreams and a night on the sofa. Imagine waking up to Figure 13.14. Language support in IntranetWare includes:

▶ Text displayed in non-English languages for utilities and system messages.

▶ Alternate display formats for numbers, dates, times, and other parameters that differ around the world.

▶ Double-byte character support for Asian languages as part of the UniCode specification. (I'm sorry, did someone say unicorn?)

▶ Non-English filename characters and path separators.

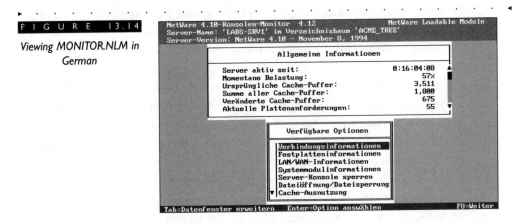

FIGURE 13.14

Viewing MONITOR.NLM in German

Here's the deal. Language support will enable you to use IntranetWare in your native language, but it won't translate messages for you. Sorry, we're not quite there yet — that's IntranetWare 7.2. So, how does it work? Language enabling in IntranetWare is possible because message strings have been separated from the source code and placed in separate files called "language modules." If message strings were in the source code, for example, you'd have to recompile and relink the code every time you wanted to change the language. Having the language modules separate enables us to switch languages on-the-fly. Pretty cool, huh?

Language modules use the same file-naming as utilities, but have an .MSG extension. For example, the language module for MONITOR.NLM is MONITOR.MSG. Here's the kicker: Language modules for different languages all have the same name (MONITOR.MSG, for example). Therefore, they must be kept in separate directories. If you mix language modules, you'll end up with something like Figure 13.14. This is fine if you happen to live in Germany. But it's a little confusing any other place in the world.

In order to keep language modules separated, IntranetWare creates a numbered subdirectory under the SYS:SYSTEM\NLS directory structure. Each subdirectory corresponds with the "languages designator" — there are 22 of them (German is number 7). Fortunately, you don't have to worry too much about this because INSTALL automatically puts each language module in an appropriate NLS subdirectory each time a new international version is installed. IntranetWare currently ships with six different languages by default — English, French, German, Italian, Spanish, and Portuguese. IntranetWare will create an NLM search hierarchy based on the default language designator. For example, you can have all utilities appear in English, but if that's not available, the system will default to Canadian French. And if that's not there, maybe Chinese would be nice. You get the idea.

Earlier I said language support is enabled using INSTALL.NLM. Here's how it works. First, load INSTALL at the server console. Then choose Product Options from the Installation Options main menu. Next, select Choose an Item or Product Listed Above and INSTALL will bounce over to the Other Installation Items/Products menu. In there, you'll see a detailed list of all available additional products. Refer to Chapter 6 for a complete list. In this case, we're interested in the following option — Install an Additional Server Language. From there, you'll get a list of available languages and their corresponding size. In order to create Figure 13.14, we had to choose NetWare 4.11 German Language-specific Files (5 MB). There you go, that's all there is to it.

REAL WORLD

Keep in mind, all of this international activity only allows us to view utilities, system messages, and display formats in alternative languages. It doesn't do much for the core operating system. If you want NetWare 4.11 itself to operate in a different language, replace SERVER.EXE in C:\NWSERVER with the appropriate SERVER.MSG language module.

Once you've installed the languages you need, changing the server language is a snap. This is accomplished by using the LANGUAGE console command and an appropriate language designator. Remember, the language designator directs the utility to the correct NLS subdirectory for the .MSG language module. To change to German, for example, issue the following command at the server colon prompt:

LANGUAGE 7

Table 13.4 lists the 22 default language designators included with IntranetWare.

TABLE 13.4

IntranetWare Language Designators

NUMBER	LANGUAGE	NUMBER	LANGUAGE
0	French (Canadian)	9	Japanese
1	Chinese (Simplified)	10	Korean
2	Danish	11	Norwegian
3	Dutch	12	Portuguese (Brazil)
4	English	13	Russian
5	Finnish	14	Spanish (Latin America)
6	French (France)	15	Swedish
7	German	16	Chinese (Traditional)
8	Italian	17	Polish

(continued)

T A B L E   1 3 . 4

*IntranetWare Language
Designators (continued)*

NUMBER	LANGUAGE	NUMBER	LANGUAGE
18	Portuguese (Portugal)	20	Hungarian
19	Spanish (Spain)	21	Czech

Now that all of your server utilities are appearing in German, there are two other parameters you might want to configure — keyboard type and locale format. International server keyboard types are activated using KEYB.NLM. To define a German keyboard, for example, you would type the following at the server colon prompt:

```
LOAD KEYB GERMANY
```

Here's a more complete list of the IntranetWare international keyboard types:

United States	Denmark
Germany	Norway
France	Sweden
Italy	Latin America
Japan	Netherlands
Spain	Swiss German
United Kingdom	Swiss French
Portugal	Russia
Belgium	Brazil
Canadian French	US International

Also note that keyboard types are dependent on the code page set by DOS. Code pages are available to IntranetWare only if you have the correct UniCode files that match your code page number and country code. These settings are defined during Stage 1 of the NetWare 4.11 installation process. For more information, refer to Chapter 6.

You may also want to define the Locale Format for international languages. Locale determines how time, dates, and numbers are formatted. This information is stored in C:\NWSERVER\LCONFIG.SYS. Once again, locale formatting is defined during Stage 1 of the NetWare 4.11 installation process.

So, that's what happens at the server. But what about the workstation? After all, you have international users to think about as well. Fortunately, IntranetWare clients can access the same NLS language modules as the server. You just need to designate the name of the language. This is accomplished by using the following SET parameter at the workstation DOS prompt:

```
SET NWLANGUAGE=Deutsch
```

This line would set up the workstation for German utilities. IntranetWare also includes support for English, Español, Français, Italiano, and Portuguese. This SET parameter tells the client to look for specific messaging files in specific NLS subdirectories. If no message files exist, the default English message files are used instead.

QUIZ

My first is in day, but not in night.
My second, in flame, but not in light.
My third is in milk, but not in tea.
My fourth in slip, but not in plea.
My last in yellow, not in whale.
My whole for love will tell a tale.
What am I?

(Q13-4)

Well, there you have it. NDS has been maintained and the server has been internationalized. Now it's time to enter a whole new frontier:

IntranetWare's Global Electronic Village

IntranetWare is Novell's enterprise solution for intranet and Internet WANs. It's based on the NetWare 4.11 operating system, but that's not enough. The real exciting stuff is in the Novell Internet Access Server. Let's activate it!

INTRANETWARE'S GLOBAL ELECTRONIC VILLAGE

As we learned earlier, IntranetWare is made up of five main components:

▶ NetWare 4.11 Operating System

- ▸ IPX/IP Gateway

- ▸ NetWare MPR

- ▸ The NetWare Web Server

- ▸ FTP Services for IntranetWare

In Chapter 6, we learned how to install the NetWare 4.11 Operating System. Now, let's take a closer look at each of the other IntranetWare components. Here are the step-by-step installation instructions for Novell's Internet Access Server:

1 • Insert the Novell Internet Access Server 4 CD-ROM in a drive on the server and mount the CD-ROM as a NetWare volume.

2 • At the server console, load INSTALL.NLM.

3 • From the Installation Options menu, choose Product Options, then choose Install a Product Not Listed.

4 • To specify a path to the installation software, press F3 and type

NIAS4:\NIAS\INSTALL

5 • Choose Install Product. The Install To Servers list displays the local server name. The value in the title reflects the number of servers to be installed. If you want to install Novell Internet Access Server software on a remote server, press Insert to add the server to the list. If an expected server is not displayed, ensure that the latest version of RSPAWN.NLM is loaded on that server. To remove a server from the Install To Servers list, select the server, press Delete, and select Yes at the prompt.

6 • From the Install To Servers menu, press Enter and select Yes to begin the installation. Servers are installed in alphabetical order. If you are installing to a remote server, you will be prompted to log in as an administrator. Enter the administrator's full login name and password.

7 • When the prompt "Install previously created configuration files?" appears, select No.

8 • When prompted for the Novell Internet Access Server license diskette, insert the IntranetWare/NetWare 4.11 license diskette in the specified drive and press Enter. Once the login, license, and configuration file information for each server are provided, the installation begins copying files to the destinations.

9 • When the installation is completed, you can read the installation log file if you desire. Choose Display Log File. When you're finished reviewing the log, press Esc to return to the Installation Options menu.

10 • To verify that the Novell Internet Access Server software installed correctly, choose Product Options from the Installation Options menu, then select Configure/View/Remove Installed Products. The Currently Installed Products list appears, showing entries for the NetWare MultiProtocol Router 3.1 software, WAN Extensions 3.1, and Novell Internet Access Server 4. Press Esc to return to the Installation Options menu.

11 • From the Installation Options menu, select NCF Files Options, then choose the Edit STARTUP.NCF file. Modify the STARTUP.NCF file for each installed server to include the following line at the end of the file if you are using the IntranetWare server to make a WAN connection:

```
SET MINIMUM PACKET RECEIVE BUFFERS=400

SET MAXIMUM PACKET RECEIVE BUFFERS=1000
```

The value of the second parameter can be increased as needed.

12 • To exit the installation screen, press Esc and then select Yes to save the changes.

13 • Bring down and restart the server to make sure all the correct NLMs are loaded. At the server's console, type

```
DOWN
RESTART SERVER
```

In addition to updating server NLM files stored in SYS:\SYSTEM, the installation process installs the client files in the SYS:\PUBLIC\CLIENT\WIN95 and SYS:\PUBLIC\CLIENT\WIN31 directories. The Netscape Navigator files are installed in the SYS:\NETSCAPE\32 and SYS:\NETSCAPE\16 directories.

SMART LINK

For a more in-depth discussion of Novell's Internet Access Server and installation instructions, surf the Web to http://www.novell.com/ manuals.

Once you've installed the Internet Access Server, you're ready to configure and explore it's many wonderous solutions. Let's start with the IPX/IP Gateway.

IPX/IP GATEWAY

The IPX/IP gateway is a very important part of IntranetWare. With this gateway, IPX-based clients can access the Internet and other IP-based resources without having to install TCP/IP on the workstations themselves. The IPX/IP gateway gets installed on the server as part of the Novell Internet Access Server installation. To take advantage of the gateway, you must install IPX/IP Gateway support on each workstation. Client gateway support is included as an option in the NetWare Client 32 installation (see the "Workstation Management" section later).

Not having to use TCP/IP on each workstation is a benefit in many cases because there are significant management tasks associated with maintaining TCP/IP workstations. With TCP/IP, you must manually keep track of and configure many items for each individual workstation (such as the unique IP address, subnet mask, IP addresses of the default router and the domain name servers, as well as the domain name).

An IPX/IP gateway removes much of the individual management hassles that occur with maintaining TCP/IP workstations by letting you retain IPX on those workstations.

When the IPX/IP gateway is installed on the IntranetWare server, the server runs IPX to communicate with the IPX workstations on the network and TCP/IP so that it can communicate with the Internet. From the viewpoint of a remote host on the Internet, all traffic through the gateway seems to originate from the IP address assigned to the gateway server. Because the IPX/IP gateway uses only a single IP address, regardless of the number of users it supports, the private network is safe from outside interference. Using the Novell IPX/IP Gateway alleviates the difficulties of administering a TCP/IP environment by providing ease of management and centralized control over Internet access.

By using Novell's IPX/IP gateway, you can run only IPX on the network workstations. Compared to IP, IPX is simple to manage. It assigns user connections dynamically, eliminating the need for a registered address to be configured at each desktop. Since IPX addresses are assigned dynamically, workstation IPX address conflicts do not occur. Users can move transparently between IPX networks, and traveling IPX users can roam between multiple networks within an enterprise.

The Novell IPX/IP Gateway allows you to limit access to Internet services by the type of traffic (for example, Web browsing or FTP) and by remote host. Either type of restriction can be limited to specific times during the day to reduce "rush hour" traffic on an Internet connection.

Configuring the IPX/IP Gateway

After you've installed Novell's Internet Access Server on the server, you can configure the IPX/IP gateway. To do this, complete the following steps:

1 • At the server console, load INETCFG.NLM. If you are asked if you want to transfer your LAN driver, protocol, and remote access commands, choose Yes. What this really means is that you will move the LOAD and BIND commands from the AUTOEXEC.NCF file to INETCFG's startup files.

2 • From the main menu, select Protocols, then choose TCP/IP, then choose IPX/IP Gateway Configuration.

3 • Specify "enabled" in the Enabled for the IPX/IP Gateway field so that the gateway will become operational.

4 • If you want to record when clients access a service over the gateway, enable the Client Logging field. The log is stored in a filed called GW_AUDIT.LOG in the SYS: volume.

5 • In the Console Messages field, specify the type of messages you want to display on the gateway logging screen and the gateway status log file (GW_INFO.LOG in the SYS: volume). You can choose "Informational, warning, and errors" (the default), "Warnings and errors only," or "Errors only."

6 • To enforce access restrictions (which you set using the NetWare Administrator utility), enable the Access Control field.

7 • In the Domain Name field, specify the name of the domain in which the gateway is installed. Your Internet Service Provider may provide you with this name.

8 • In the Name Server fields, specify the IP addresses of any active domain name servers. Your Internet Service Provider may provide these addresses.

9 • Press Esc twice, then log in as user Admin when prompted.

10 • If you want to configure the gateway to use leased lines, frame relay, or ISDN lines, complete the following steps (see the documentation that came with Novell's Internet Access Server for more specific details about parameters):

a. Choose Boards from the INETCFG.NLM main menu. Then specify the appropriate WAN driver and configure any necessary parameters.

b. Choose Network Interfaces from the INETCFG.NLM main menu. Then configure the appropriate WAN interfaces.

c. Choose WAN Call Directory from INETCFG's main menu and press Insert to configure a new WAN call destination, then configure any necessary parameters.

d. Choose Bindings from INETCFG's main menu, press Ins, and bind TCP/IP to the appropriate board or driver.

11 • Exit INETCFG.NLM and save the changes you made.

12 • Reboot the server to make the changes take effect.

After you've enabled and configured the gateway, a gateway server NDS object appears in the NDS tree in the same context as the server on which it is installed. The gateway object's name is the same as the server's name, with "-GW" added to the end of the name. This gateway object assists gateway clients in locating active IPX/IP gateway servers.

Adding IPX/IP Gateway Tools to NWADMIN

To work with the IPX/IP gateway object, you'll need to add the gateway's snap-in utility to the NetWare Administrator utility. This will allow NWADMIN to recognize the new gateway object and the new access control property that was added to certain objects.

The IPX/IP gateway snap-in utility works only with the 16-bit version of NetWare Administrator (which runs on Windows 3.1*x*). To add the IPX/IP gateway support to the NetWare Administrator utility on a Windows 3.1 workstation, complete the following steps.

1 • If you haven't yet opened the NetWare Administrator utility, open it and close it.

2 • From the Windows File Manager on your workstation, double-click on the NWADMN3X.INI file (located in the WINDOWS directory) to open it for editing.

3 • Under the heading [Snapin Object DLLs WIN3X], add the following line:

```
IPXGW3X=IPXGW3X.DLL
```

4 • Save and close the file. Now the NetWare Administrator utility will recognize the IPX/IP gateway object.

Controlling Access to the IPX/IP Gateway

After the IPX/IP Gateway server is fully installed and configured, you can use the NetWare Administrator utility to give the IPX/IP gateway server access control information for the various objects in the NDS tree. Then you can use NWADMIN to set restrictions for users, groups, or containers.

To give the gateway server access control information, use the NetWare Administrator utility to make the following changes to the NDS tree:

- ▶ Make the [Public] object a trustee of the Gateway object, with browse object rights and read and compare property rights (for all properties).

- ▶ Make the [Public] object a trustee of the File Server Object that is running the IPX/IP Gateway, with browse object rights and read and compare property rights for the Network Address property only (under selected properties).

- ▶ Make the Gateway object a trustee in the Root object, with browse object rights and read and compare property rights (for all properties).

You control user access through the IPX/IP Gateway by using the NetWare Administrator utility. As the point of connection between a NetWare network and a TCP/IP network, an IPX/IP gateway is in an ideal position to enforce restrictions on traffic between the two networks.

These access restrictions can be stored in two properties that are added to the User, Group, Organization, or Organizational Unit objects when the gateway is enabled:

- ▶ The first property, service restrictions, tells the gateway object which applications may be used by the object and which are restricted. These restrictions are based on the port number.

▸ The second property, host restrictions, tells the gateway which remote hosts are restricted from the object. These restrictions are based on the IP address.

Storing access restrictions in the NDS objects provides a single database of restrictions that all gateway servers share. You do not need to configure access control separately on each gateway. Restrictions are active on all gateways regardless of whether they are applied to an entire organization or created individually for each user.

To place access restrictions on a User, Group, Organization, or Organizational Unit object, use the NetWare Administrator utility and select the object in question. Then choose Details under the Object menu and open the IPX/IP Gateway Service Restrictions page. On this page, you can enter restrictions for this object.

To restrict access to a specific Internet site, place a host restriction on the IP address of that site. To prevent certain types of traffic from being forwarded by the server, create a service restriction for the appropriate port number. For example, you might restrict Web browser access to certain hours during the day, but allow FTP or TELNET access during those same hours. You could also place the remote host "www.games.com" off limits. To prevent news readers from operating across the gateway, you might place a restriction on traffic to port number 119 (News) at any site.

Installing the IPX/IP Gateway Client for Windows 3.1

The IPX/IP gateway support is installed as an option in the NetWare Client 32 workstation software. The following instructions explain how to install this support on Windows 3.1x workstations and Windows 95 workstations.

To configure the IPX/IP gateway support on a Windows 3.1x workstation, you install NetWare Client 32 as explained later in the "Workstation Management" section. During the installation process when the Additional Options screen appears, complete the following steps:

1 • Select the NetWare IPX/IP Gateway check box, then select Next to continue.

2 • When the Configuration menu for these options appears, enter the appropriate information and select Next to continue.

3 • When you've finished, choose OK to restart your computer. When the workstation comes back up, the Novell IPX/IP Gateway Switcher icon appears in the NetWare Tools program group. The gateway switcher program switches the client from gateway operation to native TCP/IP operation (if TCP/IP is available on the client).

4 • Double-click the Gateway Switcher icon, then click Enable Gateway to enable the gateway. You can also enter the name of a preferred gateway server if you have more than one gateway installed in the network. If a preferred gateway server is configured, the gateway task will attempt to locate that gateway server through NDS and connect to it. If the preferred gateway server is not available, the gateway client will search for other gateway servers, first in the user's NDS context, then in the bindery of the attached server, then finally it will query for a SAP broadcast of any gateway server.

Note: There is no linkage between the preferred file server and the preferred gateway server. A user may be attached to file server A while using a gateway server that resides on file server B.

Installing the IPX/IP Gateway Client for Windows 95

To configure the IPX/IP gateway support on a Windows 95 workstation, first install NetWare Client 32 as explained later in the "Workstation Management" section. When the installation is finished, complete the following steps:

1 • Click on Customize to customize the client.

2 • Choose Add.

3 • In the Type of Network Component You Want to Install box, double-click on Protocol.

4 • In the Manufacturers box, choose Novell, then double-click on Novell NetWare IPX/IP Gateway.

5 • Choose OK to exit the Network configuration screen.

6 • If you receive a prompt to select a preferred gateway server, click Yes, enter the name of your preferred IPX/IP Gateway server, and select OK. If a preferred gateway server is configured, the gateway task will attempt to locate that gateway server through NDS and connect to it. If the preferred gateway server is not available, the gateway client will search for other gateway servers, first in the user's NDS context, then in the bindery of the attached server, then finally it will query for a SAP broadcast of any gateway server.

> **Note:** There is no linkage between the preferred file server and the preferred gateway server. A user may be attached to file server A while using a gateway server that resides on file server B.

7 • If you asked for additional files, type the location of those files in the Copy Files From box. If you are asked for Client 32 files, type in the path to the directory from which you ran SETUP.EXE.

8 • Click Yes to restart the computer. The IPX/IP Gateway Switcher program runs automatically during the first restart after installation. This switcher program switches the client from gateway operation to native TCP/IP operation (if TCP/IP is available on the client).

To enable the gateway, click the Enable IPX/IP Gateway button, then click OK. Well, that was fun. Now our IntranetWare LAN is becoming a fully-functional IPX/IP IntranetWare WAN. Not yet. True the protocol gateway is in place, but we have to activate the MultiProtocol Router (MPR) before the new WAN packets can find their way around.

ZEN

Luis Ponce de Leon, returning to his university after five years imprisonment by the leaders of the Inquisition, resumed his lectures with the words: "As we were saying yesterday . . ."

NETWARE MPR

IntranetWare includes a suite of programs that provide internetworking among dissimilar workstations and servers. This is the third of the five IntranetWare solutions, and it's called "NetWare MPR." This suite runs on standard PC hardware and enables you to integrate various LANs regardless of the communication protocols being used. In short, IntranetWare includes a full version of the NetWare MultiProtocol Router (MPR). Check out Figure 13.15.

FIGURE 13.15

Internetworking with MPR

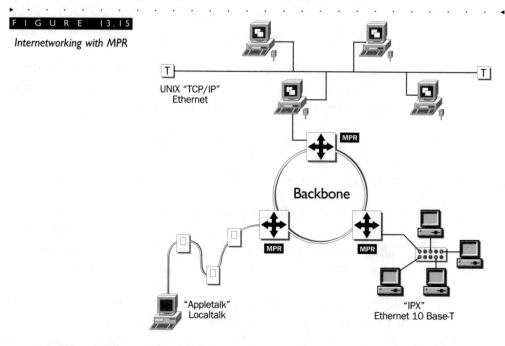

NetWare MPR provides the following services:

▸ It connects dissimilar media, frame types, and transports at all levels in the ODI model using an advanced type of routing called NetWare Link Services Protocol (NLSP).

▸ It offloads routing tasks from busy servers to dedicated machines.

▸ It provides security by isolating traffic on LAN segments.

NetWare MPR 3.1 includes routing capabilities for several communications protocols, including — IntranetWare IPX/SPX (default), Unix TCP/IP, Macintosh AppleTalk, and NetWare Link Services Protocol (NLSP). It also allows you to connect LANs over leased lines, frame relay, or ISDN. It even allows you to connect network users to Internet Service Providers (ISP). Wow, all that in just one box!

Like most other additional products, MPR is installed using INSTALL.NLM. Once it's installed, you can manage and configure MPR by using a server application called INETCFG.NLM. INETCFG is a menu-driven utility that simplifies routing and bridging configuration. It also provides an extensive list of configurable parameters for IPX, TCP/IP, and AppleTalk (see Figure 13.16). When you load INETCFG for the first time, it performs two important initialization tasks:

▶ AUTOEXEC.NCF — INETCFG saves your old AUTOEXEC.NCF file as SYS:SYSTEM\AUTOEXEC.BAK. Then it prompts you to transfer five important commands from the old AUTOEXEC.NCF to the new file — LOAD, BIND, LAN driver, protocol, and route access commands. Answering YES to the prompts will enable INETCFG to automatically initialize AUTOEXEC.NCF for the new internetworking suite.

▶ CONLOG — Next, INETCFG inserts three commands into the new AUTOEXEC.NCF file in this order. First, LOAD CONLOG enables the server to begin a log file of all messages that appear during the initialization. These messages are stored in SYS:ETC\CONSOLE.LOG. Second, it loads INITSYS.NCF to configure server communications using the INETCFG database. Finally, the utility unloads CONLOG and startup is complete.

Once INETCFG has been initialized, you're ready to configure and manage your new multiple protocols. Figure 13.16 shows the INETCFG main menu. In general, these choices are selected systematically from top to bottom during protocol configuration. It all starts with the Boards option. Here, you configure LAN and WAN boards so INETCFG can place the correct LOAD commands in AUTOEXEC.NCF. You can also customize hardware parameters for internal NICs. The next two INETCFG menu choices are somewhat optional. That is, they're required if needed. The Network Interfaces option enables you to configure ports on multiport boards. Each port can be configured for a different WAN protocol such as PPP, frame relay, or X.25. Also, the WAN Call Directory option provides further customization for PPP WAN protocols.

```
 Internetworking Configuration  3.10a                NetWare Loadable Module


     ┌─────────────────────────────────────┐
     │  Internetworking Configuration       │
     │ ┌───────────────────────────────────┐│
     │ │ Boards                            ││
     │ │ Network Interfaces                ││
     │ │ WAN Call Directory                ││
     │ │ Protocols                         ││
     │ │ Bindings                          ││
     │ │ Manage Configuration              ││
     │ │ View Configuration                ││
     │ └───────────────────────────────────┘│
     └─────────────────────────────────────┘




 Add, delete, and configure interface boards.
 ENTER=Select ESC=Exit Menu                                          F1=Help
```

The next step in INETCFG customization is accomplished by using the Protocols menu choice. This option enables you to configure routing protocol operation such as IPX, RIP, and NLSP. Once again, INETCFG.NLM will build the correct LOAD commands for AUTOEXEC.NCF. On to Step 3.

The Bindings menu choice enables you to initialize MPR by binding protocols to each NIC as needed. For example, one interface could bind IPX RIP and another could initialize NLSP. Configuring the bindings in INETCFG builds the correct BIND statements for AUTOEXEC.NCF. Once you have configured network boards, protocols, and bindings, MPR is ready to go. The final two INETCFG options deal with managing SNMP, remote access, and viewing LOAD and BIND statements. This falls under the category of daily multiprotocol management.

THE BRAIN

Here are some good AppNotes on MultiProtocol Router, NLSP, and other IntranetWare internetworking topics: "Optimizing NetWare Wide Area Networks" (May 1994), "Wide Area Networking with Frame Relay and IntranetWare MultiProtocol Router" (February 1995), and "Configuring Asynchronous Connections with the IntranetWare MultiProtocol Router 3.0 Software" (July 1995).

Now that we've extended the boundaries of our WAN, let's explore IntranetWare's built-in Web Server. We're really surfin' now!

SMART LINK

For more information on NetWare MPR consider attending Novell Education Course 740: *Internetworking with NetWare MultiProtocol Router.* **Surf the Web to http://education.novell.com.**

THE NETWARE WEB SERVER

The NetWare Web Server 2.5 is an easy-to-install, high-performance World Wide Web (WWW) server that comes with IntranetWare. Installation and configuration is so easy that, if you already have TCP/IP configured on your server, you can view the sample NetWare Web Server home page in approximately 15 minutes. If you know how to create your own *HyperText Markup Language* (HTML) files, you can be viewing your own home page just a few minutes later.

This section introduces you to the basics of the NetWare Web Server and teaches you how to install it, explore it, and configure it. So, without any further adieu, let's surf the Web.

TIP

Creating Web pages (usually called "authoring") and administering a NetWare Web Server require different skills and are often performed by different people. This section focuses on NetWare Web Server administration, but it is undeniable that you can be a much better administrator if you also learn at least some of the basics of Web page authoring. Your first indication of this will come when Web page authors start linking pages to files all over the server and requesting write permissions. To learn more about Web page authoring, consider taking Novell Education Course 654, Web Authoring and Publishing.

SMARTLINK

SMARTLINK

If you want first-hand experience surfing a NetWare Web Server, check out World Wire at http://www.world-wire.com. It's running on a NetWare Web Server.

What Is the NetWare Web Server?

A WWW server, such as the NetWare Web Server, is a file server that serves or *publishes* files in HTML format. You read these HTML files from workstations by using client applications called *browsers*. HTML files are text files with special tags (usually enclosed in less-than and greater-than symbols, < >) that tell the browser how to format the file on screen. The main differences between HTML files and standard word processing files are

- HTML files do not contain proprietary custom symbols or formatting characters. All formatting is specified with special combinations of ASCII text characters. For example, to indicate that text should be printed in bold, you might use the following command:

  ```
  <B>This will appear as bold text.</B>
  ```

- HTML files can include text or graphic *links*, which users can click on to move to another location in the same file or to another file on any Web server in the world.

Many people get confused by the terms HTML and HTTP, and they are overwhelmed when WWW and Internet are also thrown into the same sentence. A WWW Web server publishes files in HTML format. A Web server communicates with browsers using the HyperText Transfer Protocol (HTTP), which runs over TCP/IP. The Internet is a global network of computers that provide many services, one of which is the WWW.

The NetWare Web Server provides the following features:

- Easy installation and configuration

- A Windows-based administration utility

- NDS Access control for Internet/intranet users and systems

▸ File security through NDS

▸ Internet/intranet access logging

▸ Browser access to NDS trees

▸ Support for dynamic Web pages

▸ NetBasic for creating Internet scripts

▸ Netscape Navigator (multiuser license — up to your allowed IntranetWare user limit)

Dynamic Web page support allows Web page authors to add commands to HTML files that enhance the pages in ways that are not possible with HTML tags. For example, Web page authors can add commands that automatically insert variables (such as the date or time) into a page as it is sent to a browser. Other commands allow Web page authors to display animations or perform calculations on data entered by a browser user. The NetWare Web Server supports dynamic Web pages with the following features:

▸ Server Side Include (SSI) commands

▸ Local Common Gateway Interface (L-CGI)

▸ Remote Common Gateway Interface (R-CGI)

▸ BASIC script interpreters

▸ PERL script interpreters

▸ Support for Java applets

▸ Support for JavaScript

Installing the NetWare Web Server
Installing the Web Server consists of configuring the network to support TCP/IP and then running INSTALL.NLM to install the Web Server product.

To set up a NetWare Web Server site, you need the following hardware and software:

- A NetWare 4.11 server with a CD-ROM drive.

- At least 2.5 MB of hard disk space for the NetWare Web Server software, plus additional disk space for your new HTML files.

- A client workstation running Windows 3.1*x*, Windows 95, or Windows NT. The workstation must have an 80386 processor, 4 MB of RAM, and 2.5 MB of hard disk space available for the Netscape Navigator browser installation. (You can use a different browser if you prefer.)

- Although you can use Windows word processing tools to create and edit HTML documents, you may want to add HTML authoring software, which would require additional disk space and memory. An HTML authoring tool is not included with the NetWare Web Server.

The Web Server documentation is in HTML format on the IntranetWare/ NetWare 4.11 Operating System CD-ROM. To read or print this documentation, you must use a Web browser such as Netscape Navigator (included with the NetWare Web Server) on a workstation.

If you don't have a browser installed yet, complete the following steps to install the Netscape Navigator browser on a Windows 3.1*x* workstation:

1 • Insert the NetWare 4.11 Operating System CD-ROM into a Windows 3.1*x* workstation's CD-ROM drive.

2 • From the workstation's Program Manager, choose Run from the File menu. Click Browse, and locate the SETUP.EXE file for the Web Server in the following directory: PRODUCTS\WEBSERV\BROWSER\ N16E201. Select OK to begin the setup process.

To install the Netscape Navigator on a Windows 95 workstation, complete the following steps:

1 • Insert the NetWare 4.11 Operating System CD-ROM into a Windows 3.1x workstation's CD-ROM drive.

2 • From Windows 95, click Start. Then choose Run and locate the SETUP.EXE file for the Web Server in the following directory: PRODUCTS\WEBSERV\BROWSER\N32E201. Select OK to begin the setup process.

After you've installed the viewer, launch it. From the Navigator's File menu, select Open File and select the drive and directory that contains the Web Server documentation (such as the CD-ROM drive or a directory if you've copied the documentation files to the server or the client). Then double-click on the file you want to open.

To prepare for NetWare Web Server installation, install NetWare 4.11 on the server and establish IPX and TCP/IP communications between the two. (TCP/IP software is provided with IntranetWare) Use INETCFG.NLM to specify an IP address for the server and to bind TCP/IP to the network board (see the "NetWare MPR" section earlier in this chapter). Then load the PING NLM on the server and use it to verify TCP/IP communications with the client.

ZEN

"If you watch a game, that's fun. If you play it, that's recreation. But if you work at it, that's golf."

Bob Hope

NetWare Web Server installation is easier than most NetWare installations because the critical configuration is completed when you configure TCP/IP. Simply load INSTALL.NLM on the server, choose Product Options, and then choose Install NetWare Web Server. Follow the instructions that appear on the screen.

When the NetWare Web Server installation is complete, press Alt-Esc at the server console to switch between the following active services:

▸ Novell HTTP Server 2.5, which is the NetWare Web Server NLM

▸ Novell Basic language interpreter, for dynamic Web page support

▸ Novell Perl language interpreter, for dynamic Web page support

You have now created a Web site. Any network browser can now view the default home page if the user knows the TCP/IP address of your server.

To view the Web site you have just created, start the browser on your client workstation, select Open Location from the file menu, and enter the following *Universal Resource Locator* (URL):

```
http://server_ip_address
```

After you enter this command with your server IP address, you should see a sample Web page. The default Web site contains a number of sample pages and links. Browse through these pages to get an idea of what can be published on a NetWare Web Server. To see the HTML commands used to create any page, display the page and then select Document Source from the View menu.

SMART LINK

To view the default NetWare Web Site and explore sample pages and links, surf to http://www.world-wire.com. It's running on a NetWare Web Server.

Exploring Your Web Site

You are now a Web site manager (or maybe even a "Web Master") and, depending on your TCP/IP network connections, your site is available to your organization and possibly the world. Let's take a closer look at what you have.

When you look at the default directory structure of the NetWare Web Server, you'll notice the INDEX.HTM file. This is the default HTML file that Web browsers see when they access your site using your IP address. We'll talk about changing the defaults and using names instead of IP addresses later. For now, what you need to know is that this is the entry point for your Web site. To create your own home page, start by editing this file or by replacing it with your own INDEX.HTM file.

By default, the INDEX.HTM file is in the SYS:\WEB\DOCS directory, which is the document root directory of your Web site. At least three root directories are on your NetWare Web Server. The one you are most familiar with is the SYS: root directory, which is the NetWare volume root directory.

The NetWare Web Server has two root directories of its own: the server root directory and the document root directory. The *server root directory* contains all the configuration and control files associated with your Web site. These are the files that you don't want your Web site visitors to see. The server root directory on any NetWare Web Server is SYS:\WEB and cannot be changed.

The *document root directory* is the default path to all the files you want to publish. To protect your server configuration files from undesired access, the document root directory should be a subdirectory of the server root directory, or it should be placed on another volume.

TIP

When browsers access your site, they are restricted to files and directories that are contained in the document root directory — with one exception. You can configure the NetWare Web Server to allow browsers to access user home pages in the users' home directories.

The document root directory can be changed to another directory or another volume, but it should be changed only after careful planning. Many links in the Web pages will use relative references that define the path from the document root directory to another file. Carelessly moving the document root can make all your internal Web site links invalid, rendering your Web site useless.

TIP

A NetWare Web Server is a live Web site. Users can connect to it at any time. To avoid user access errors, always edit published Web pages off-line in your home directory or on another computer. Otherwise your word processor or Web authoring tool may lock the file and prevent other users from accessing it. Also, test all links that you create in your Web pages. It's less embarrassing to find the mistakes yourself.

Configuring Name Services

Your Web server is up, but your customers (both internal and external) must remember your server's IP address to access it. Simplify your customers' access by creating a *name service*.

Name services use a table of IP addresses and names to establish names that can be used in place of IP addresses. Each IP address can be associated with one or more names or aliases.

There are two common ways to add a name service to your network. The easiest is to create a hosts file on your server. The second is to configure your server as a Domain Name Service (DNS) server or as a client of a DNS server. The hosts file approach provides name services only on your network or subnet. DNS provides name services over an entire network or the Internet.

To create a table of IP addresses and host names for your network or subnet, use a text editor to create a file named HOSTS.TXT in the SYS:ETC directory. Create a name table similar to Table 13.5.

TABLE 13.5	#IP ADDRESS	ALIASES	COMMENTS
Sample Name Table for The NetWare Web Server	ip_address	alias1 alias2	#NetWare Web Server
	ip_address	alias3	#jim's pc
	ip_address	alias4	#carol's pc

The "#" character indicates that all text to the right of it is a comment and is to be ignored. Each line starts with the IP address of a host, followed by one or more spaces. The second item on each line is the name you want to assign to the host. You can add several names, but be sure to separate each name with one or more spaces.

Domain name service (DNS) is an Internet protocol that allows administrators to associate Internet addresses with names that people can remember. A DNS server stores the names and their corresponding IP addresses, and responds to clients that need names services. DNS is provided with NetWare IP and FTP Services for IntranetWare. You can use these products to add DNS to your network, or you can use an existing DNS server.

To configure your NetWare Web Server to use the name services of a DNS server, use a text editor to create a file named RESOLV.CFG in the directory SYS:ETC. Enter the following text in this file:

```
domain domain_name
nameserver IP_address
```

The *domain_name* variable is the name of the domain in which your server is installed. The *IP_address* variable is the IP address of the DNS server. You should be able to get this information from the administrator of the DNS server.

TIP

To use the services of a DNS server, you must create the RESOLV.TXT file. Installing the DNS server on the same server as your NetWare Web Server does not remove this requirement.

All finished! Congratulations, you lived through a lesson in Web surfing. Now all you have to do is move to California, dye your hair blonde, and pick up a virtual boogie board. Hang ten! Now, let's finish our journey through Intranet Management with a brief glimpse of FTP Services for IntranetWare.

THE BRAIN

If all this surfing talk wasn't enough, check out the NetWare 4.11 documentation for more details.

FTP SERVICES FOR INTRANETWARE

The final component in the IntranetWare electronic global village is a bridge to the sometimes understandable, always bizarre world of Unix. FTP Services for IntranetWare is a subset of the NetWare UNIX Print Services 2.11 product that allows NetWare clients to use FTP to work with files on the Internet or intranet.

Here's how it works.

Installing FTP Services

To install FTP Services for IntranetWare on your server, complete the following steps:

1 • Mount the FTP Services CD-ROM as a volume on the NetWare 4.11 server.

2 • Load INSTALL.NLM on the server.

3 • Choose Product Options, then choose Install a Product Not Listed.

4 • Press F3, then type in the following path to the FTP Services files on the CD-ROM:

NWUXPS:\NWUXPS

5 • If you are asked to specify a host name, either press Enter to accept the default name displayed or enter the correct host name.

6 • Accept the default boot drive (or specify the correct drive from which the server boots).

7 • To install the online documentation for FTP Services, choose Yes. This documentation is separate from the regular NetWare online documentation and describes how to install and use FTP Services.

8 • If you have already installed the NetWare 4.11 DynaText viewer, choose No when asked if you want to install a new one.

   Note: If you receive the message "hosts.db does not exist," ignore it.

9 • When prompted for a user name, enter the ADMIN name and password.

10 • Choose the name service option you want to use on this server and answer any prompts necessary for the name service you choose. If you choose to use a local name service, the database that holds the name service information will be stored on this server and will be the master database. You can use the UNICON.NLM utility to work with the master database on a local server. If you choose to use a remote name service, that database will reside on another server. You can use UNICON.NLM only to view the database information but not modify it. You can choose one of the following options:

▶ Local DNS and Local NIS. This option stores both master databases on this server.

▶ Remote DNS and Remote NIS. This option uses the master databases stored on another server.

▶ Remote DNS and Local NIS. This option stores the master NIS database on this server and the DNS database on another server.

▶ No DNS and Remote NIS. This option stores the master NIS database on another server and does not provide DNS service at all.

11 • Follow any prompts necessary to initialize the name service and the product.

12 • To start FTP Services, press Ins and choose FTP Server. FTP Services will start running and will appear in the Running Services menu.

13 • To exit the installation program, press Esc as many times as necessary.

14 • Restart the server to make the new settings take effect, by typing:

```
DOWN
RESTART SERVER
```

Configuring FTP Services

With FTP Services, users can use FTP to access and transfer files from the intranet or Internet. If you desire, you can create an Anonymous FTP account for users to use. With an Anonymous account, any user can access the FTP service by typing in any password. (Any password will work; the FTP service doesn't actually authenticate the password.)

To configure an Anonymous FTP account, complete the following steps:

1 • At the server console, load UNICON.NLM.

2 • When prompted, enter the ADMIN user name and password.

3 • Choose Manage Services, then choose FTP Server, then choose Set Parameters.

4 • Choose Default Name Space and enter NFS. This will install the NFS name space on the server, which will allow the server to store UNIX files.

5 • Change the Anonymous User Access field to Yes so that the Anonymous account will be enabled.

6 • Choose Anonymous User's Home Directory and change the path from the volume SYS (displayed as /sys) to a directory you prefer to use as the login directory for Anonymous FTP users.

7 • When finished, press Esc to exit the installation program and save the changes you've made.

8 • Return to the main menu by pressing Esc twice, then choose Perform File Operations, then choose View/Set File Permissions.

9 • Enter the path to the Anonymous user's home directory (specified in Step 6) and press F9 to see the permissions (the UNIX equivalent of trustee rights) that have been set for this directory. If the permissions are not correct, modify them on this screen. The permissions should be

```
[U = rwx] [G =  -- -] [o =  -- -]
```

10 • Press Esc multiple times to exit UNICON and save the changes you've made.

11 • Even though you specified the NFS name space in Step 4, you still need to add it to the volume. (You only need to add the name space to the volume once. To see if you've already added NFS name space to a volume, type **VOLUMES** at the server console — the display will show which name spaces are supported on each volume.) If you need to add the name space, type the following command, replacing *volume* with the name of the volume:

```
ADD NAME SPACE NFS TO volume
```

QUIZ

I was out house-hunting the other day, and this one really bothered me. There was this odd house, on which the two halves of the roof were unequally pitched. One half sloped downward at an angle of 60° (left) and the other half at an angle of 70° (right). I wondered, if a rooster layed an egg on the exact peak, where would the egg roll — left or right? Help.

(Q13-5)

Wow, that was fun! I had no idea community activities could be so time-consuming, and rewarding. It sure puts your own marriage in perspective when you see how well (or not) the "Jones'" are getting along. Suddenly, server-centric NetWare is looking so easy. Regardless, we now live in an electronic global village and you better get used to it, or you'll get run over by an IP packet.

Now let's shift our attention to the *citizens* of the village — rugrats!

Workstation Management

So, you're cruising along through life, minding your own business, and wham — it hits you. Suddenly, your family is twice as big as it was a few years ago. It's an abrupt wake-up call when you finally realize *you're* not the child anymore. A strange thing happens when children have children. Even though Leia is 27 years old — firmly planted in adulthood — she's still our little baby. We were there through the rough years — login scripts, menu system, and e-mail. Now Leia's having children of her own. Suddenly her focus shifts from marriage to her baby.

Now is a good time for your focus to shift as well — from the server to your IntranetWare children (workstations). As a CNE, you will spend just as much time managing the workstations as you will managing the server — probably more. In addition, managing workstations can be even more challenging because it encompasses a much more diverse collection of users, applications, and operating systems. And we all know users can act like babies sometimes. In order to fully optimize the client connection and keep things running smoothly, you'll have to employ a stern, yet caring, workstation management strategy.

ZEN

"If my heart can become pure and simple like that of a child, I think there probably can be no greater happiness than this."

Kitaro Nishida

Of all the places you'll go in your life, few will be as interesting as the IntranetWare client. There you'll find fun, adventure, and NetWare (or Virtual) Loadable Modules (NLMs). The client is one of the most important aspects of an IntranetWare system because it's where the users meet the network. Someday, I guarantee you'll get the question, "Where's the ANY key?" In order to help you sleep at night, the interface should be as transparent as possible — avoid confusion and unnecessary support calls. In order to achieve client transparency, IntranetWare breaks the workstation into two key components (see Figure 13.17):

▶ *NIC* — The internal network interface card that provides communications between the local workstation operating system (WOS) and the IntranetWare server. This hardware device is managed by a series of workstation connectivity files called ODI (Open Datalink Interface). We use LAN drivers and NLMs in the Client 32 world, and simple COM files on 16-bit workstations.

▶ *Workstation operating system (WOS)* — The WOS manages all local workstation services. It coordinates among local applications (word processing, spreadsheets, and databases) and local devices (file storage, screens, and printers). All of these local activities must be somehow orchestrated with network services. In the Client 32 universe, this is accomplished using CLIENT32.NLM. On the other hand, Client 16 uses relies on complex suite of workstation Legos called VLMs (Virtual Loadable Modules).

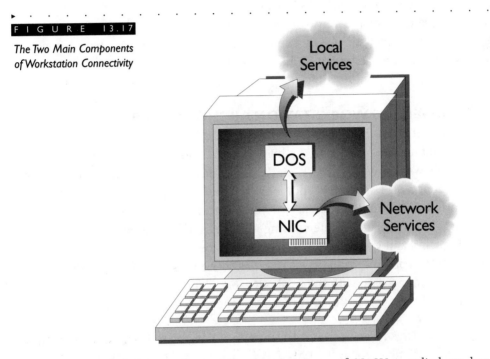

F I G U R E   13.17

The Two Main Components
of Workstation Connectivity

Here's a quick history lesson. Previous versions of NetWare relied on less-integrated client connectivity files. NetWare 3.11 and before used programs such as WSGEN or SHGEN to generate an IPX.COM file that implemented the IPX/SPX stack and provided the link between the workstation and internal NIC. In addition, most of the DOS Requester functionality was accomplished using one rigid file — NETX.EXE.

More recent versions of NetWare (NetWare 3.12 through 4.1) relied on Client 16 connectivity files. They introduced ODI (Open Datalink Interface) drivers that provided a more flexible way of binding the IPX/SPX protocol stack. In addition, the DOS Requester functionality was expanded to include a suite of 16-bit Virtual Loadable Modules (VLMs). These VLMs together form the "NetWare DOS Requester," which provides support for DOS and MS Windows client workstations in the 16-bit environment.

Now, in IntranetWare, Novell has introduced a more integrated 32-bit client. It uses an enhanced version of ODI and 32-bit NetWare Loadable Modules at the workstation. The 32-bit solution provides graphical access to NetWare 2.2, 3.12, and 4.11 servers. It is the new and preferred way of networking from Windows 95, Windows 3.1, and/or DOS workstations.

Regardless of the way you go, you must be intimately familiar with BOTH platforms. After all, CNEs should always be prepared. So here we go . . . . workstation management in the 32-bit and 16-bit sandboxes.

CLIENT 32 WORKSTATION ARCHITECTURE

Client 32 is the newest and most powerful workstation connectivity software for IntranetWare. It is a 32-bit protected mode NetWare client that allows Windows 95, Windows 3.1, and DOS workstations to connect to NetWare 2.2, 3.12, and 4.11 servers. In addition, it provides a graphical login utility for logging in from MS Windows. Finally, if you are running Windows 95, you can access network files and printers using the Network Neighborhood, the Windows Explorer, and various application dialog boxes.

In Chapter 12, we learned that Client 32 uses a variety of LAN drivers and NLMs to interface with the local NIC and WOS. As you can see in Figure 13.18, this software consists of four main components:

▸ *NIC driver* — Controls communications with the internal NIC. This is a hardware-specific LAN driver such as CNE2000.LAN. It's also known as the Multiple Link Interface Driver (MLID).

▸ *Link Support Layer* — Acts as a switchboard to route network protocol packets between the LAN driver and appropriate communications protocol. LSL is implemented at the workstation as LSLC32.NLM.

▸ *Communications Protocol* — A set of rules that determines the *language* used to move data across the network. The protocol guarantees that two devices using the same protocol can communicate because they speak the same language. This is accomplished at the Client 32 workstation using IPX.NLM.

► *Client 32* — A platform-independent NLM that provides 32-bit workstation access for Windows 95, Windows 3.1, and DOS operating systems. This facility is accomplished using the CLIENT32.NLM file.

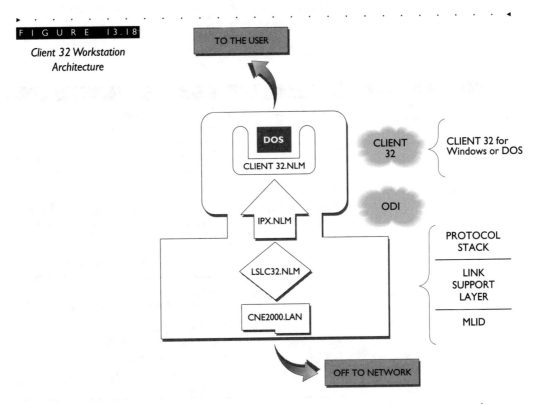

FIGURE 13.18

Client 32 Workstation Architecture

Client 32 is the only client software for Windows 95 or Windows 3.1 that enables full support of NDS. Using Client 32, you can browse through network services, across multiple trees, and print from Network Neighborhood and Windows Explorer.

Probably the most important workstation management topic for CNEs is Client 32 installation. This is a very complex and troublesome task because the workstation is such a diverse battleground. It's where the users plot their assaults against *your* network. Also, in IntranetWare, the Client 32 installation is much more integrated with the workstation's native GUI environment than previous versions. For this reason, you must be intimately familiar with both Client 32 and MS Windows (95 and 3.1).

And that's not all. You also must understand the installation and management procedures for diverse network hardware — such as NIC boards, cabling, and related components. Also, you must make sure there are no hardware conflicts. Refer to Table 13.6 for some client install-related action items.

TABLE 13.6 Network Board Configuration	TYPE OF BOARD	ACTION REQUIRED
	ISA Network Boards	Look at the network board to determine the settings. The documentation that came with the board should describe where each setting is located. Configurations are typically accomplished using jumpers or DIP switches.
	EISA or MCA Network Board	Run the workstation's reference or setup program. The program will list the settings for your network board.
	PCI Local Bus Network Boards	Run the workstation's reference or setup program. The program will list the settings for your network board. Configurations are stored in firmware chips on the NIC.
		NOTE: If you already have a network connection established, switch to the SYS:\PUBLIC directory and type NVER and then press Enter. This will verify your configuration.

Once you're an expert in workstation hardware, it's time to move onto some even more puzzling topics: Client 32 and MS Windows (egad!). Let's start with Windows 95.

SMART LINK

You can check out and download the new Client 32 connectivity files for free at http://www.novell.com.

CLIENT 32 INSTALLATION FOR WINDOWS 95

Client 32 can be installed in four different ways using the Windows 95 Network Device Installer (NDI) and .INF script files. In addition, Novell's Client 32 installation incorporates Windows 95 property pages that were created specifically to set Client 32 configuration parameters contained in the Windows 95 registry. These pages use a graphic user interface to replace NET.CFG and other configuration files.

Here's a list of the four different Client 32 installation options for Windows 95:

▸ *MSBATCH SETUP* — This installation method allows you to install Client 32 files at the same time as Windows 95. It prepares the Windows 95 and Client 32 files on the server so they can be copied to the workstation simultaneously. To accomplish this, simply place the Windows 95 install image on the server and then update it to default to Client 32 instead of Microsoft's Client for NetWare Networks. Then when you run the MSBATCH SETUP, it will take care of the rest for you.

▸ *NetWare 4.11 SETUP* — If Windows 95 is already installed on the workstation or you're upgrading from Client 16, you can use the SETUP program on the NetWare 4.11 operating system CD-ROM. This is the typical single-user install.

▸ *Custom Windows 95 Setup* — The custom installation option removes the Microsoft NetWare Client and any other NetWare network component. Then it sets up files that the Microsoft NDI uses to install Client 32. A knowledgeable network user can configure network parameters, including the client parameters, manually. This is accomplished using the Windows 95 Network Control Panel and other property page features. Refer to the "Step 1: Establishing Workstation Connectivity" section of Chapter 12 for more information.

▸ *Automatic Client Upgrade (ACU)* — Executes an instruction placed by the CNE in a login script and then seamlessly upgrades clients during login. This method can be used to automatically upgrade NetWare Client 32 for Windows 95 or the Microsoft Client for NetWare Networks. It doesn't, however, upgrade NETx or VLM clients.

Client 32 Installation Steps for Windows 95

Once you've determined which installation method to use, it's time to get on with the show. Following are the general steps for Client 32 installation in Windows 95:

▸ *Step 1:* Run SETUP.EXE from within Windows 95. On the server, it will be in the SYS:PUBLIC\CLIENT\WIN95\IBM_ENU directory. On the NetWare 4.11 operating system CD-ROM, it can be found in the D:\PRODUCTS\WIN95\IBM_ENU directory.

▸ *Step 2:* The NetWare Client 32 Installation window appears once you bypass the Software License Agreement. Select Start to begin the installation.

TIP

Microsoft Networks use NDIS drivers for protocol connectivity. The NetWare Client 32 prefers ODI drivers. To upgrade NDIS drivers to ODI automatically, click the appropriate box in the Client 32 installation screen.

▸ *Step 3:* SETUP will automatically install and configure Client 32 with default properties. During this process, you may be asked to insert your Windows 95 CD-ROM and supply a source location for the CAB files. They can be found in the D:\WIN95 subdirectory.

▸ *Step 4:* When SETUP is complete, click on Customize, Novell NetWare Client 32, and finally, Properties. This allows us to personalize many Client 32 properties such as

• Preferred Server

• Preferred Tree

• Name Context

- Login Scripts

- NIC Settings

Once you're finished inputting custom configurations, Windows 95 will build a driver information database. When it's completed, restart your computer and the Network Login Dialog Box appears. Congratulations, installation complete!

Now that wasn't so bad. As you can see, the Client 32 Installation for Windows 95 is simple, graphical, and straightforward. Unfortunately, however, it is not *Automated*. Have no fear — ACU is here!

Automatic Client Upgrade for Windows 95

You can also use the Automatic Client Upgrade (ACU) program to upgrade older Client 32 files to the newest 32-bit connectivity drivers. It also upgrades the Microsoft Client for NetWare Networks. This version doesn't, however, upgrade NETx or VLM drivers. That functionality is provided by the Client 32 for Windows 3.1 ACU program (see the section, "Client 32 Installation for Windows 3.1" later in this chapter). ACU uses fancy login scripts to automate the upgrade process. Here's how it works in the Windows 95 world:

▶ *Step 1:* To use ACU, you must first place the Client 32 installation files and Windows 95 .CAB files in a directory where they can be read during client login. We recommend the SYS:LOGIN subdirectory. Remember, the user must have Read and File Scan [RF] access rights to this directory.

▶ *Step 2:* Next, you must place the following statement in a Container or Profile login script:

```
#SYS:PUBLIC\CLIENT\WIN95\IBM_ENU\SETUP.EXE /ACU
```

This instruction will automatically upgrade old workstations to Client 32 during the next login. When the workstation logs in, ACU checks the client's file to see if the System files are newer. If they are, the user gets a dialog with the following message:

"A newer version of the Novell Client Software is available. Click Continue to install the newer version or Cancel to retain your existing client software."

▸ *Step 3:* If the user chooses Continue, the upgrade starts automatically and the files are copied to the workstation.

▸ *Step 4:* If the user chooses Cancel, the workstation continues to use the older client software. However, each time the user logs in with the older client, ACU will again attempt to upgrade the workstation's software.

▸ *Step 5:* Finally, once the client has been upgraded, the user is prompted to reboot the workstation in order to utilize the new Client 32 software.

Well, that does it for Windows 95. Simple, huh? But, that's not the end. We can't ignore all our older 16-bit GUI users. That wouldn't be polite. Now let's take a moment to explore Client 32 installation for Windows 3.1.

CLIENT 32 INSTALLATION FOR WINDOWS 3.1

DOS and Windows 3.1 workstations need a different set of Client 32 files to connect to an IntranetWare WAN. During the Client 32 installation process, several drivers and configuration files are copied to C:\WINDOWS and C:\WINDOWS\SYSTEM.

In addition, the following workstation configuration files are modified:

▸ CONFIG.SYS — Automates drive mapping settings

▸ AUTOEXEC.BAT — Automates workstation connectivity at startup

▸ NET.CFG — Establishes driver settings

Client 32 Installation Steps for Windows 3.1

Here's a brief overview of the Client 32 installation process for DOS/Windows 3.1 workstations:

▶ *Step 1:* To start the Client 32 installation, run INSTALL.EXE from DOS or SETUP.EXE from Windows 3.1. Both of these applications are located on the IntranetWare Client 32 Installation diskettes. You can create these diskettes using the "Other Products" option of INSTALL.NLM (see the "Custom Installation" section of Chapter 6 earlier in this book).

▶ *Step 2:* Once the installation program begins, you will be greeted with a language selection screen, welcome message, and Software License Agreement. Click **OK**, Continue, and Yes, in order.

▶ *Step 3:* Next, you will be presented with the Directory Locations dialog box. You can accept the default (C:\NOVELL\CLIENT32), or choose a directory of your own. Click Next to move onto the LAN driver selection screen. Choose the correct ODI-compliant driver that matches your workstation's NIC card. Click Next to continue.

▶ *Step 4:* At this point, SETUP.EXE will copy necessary drivers to your workstation and make adjustments to local configuration files. Finally, click Next to bypass the Additional Options screen and choose Restart Computer to complete the installation. Piece of cake.

▶ *Step 5:* Not so fast. Now you must customize the Client 32 installation properties to automate workstation connectivity. This can be accomplished using two utilities — NET.CFG and NetWare User Tools for Windows. First, use a DOS text editor to customize NET.CFG in the C:\NOVELL\CLIENT32 directory (check out the "NET.CFG" section of Chapter 12 for more information). Second, activate NetWare User Tools for Windows and click the NetWare Settings option. Next, click Startup and Login. Make sure the following options are selected: "Display Connection Page," "Display Script Page," Display Variables Page," and "Restore Permanent Connections." Now you're really finished. Congratulations!

Automatic Client Upgrade for Windows 3.1

You can also use the Windows 3.1 Automatic Client Upgrade (ACU) program to upgrade NETx, VLMs, or older Client 32 files to the newest 32-bit connectivity drivers. As we learned earlier in the "Client 32 Installation for Windows 95" section, ACU uses fancy login scripts to automated the upgrade process. Here's how it works in the Windows 3.1 world:

▸ *Step 1:* Choose a login script — container, profile, or user. The type of script you use depends on the type of workstation you want to upgrade. Refer to Chapter 12 for more information on IntranetWare login scripts.

▸ *Step 2:* Install the Client 32 for Windows 3.1 files on a shared network server. Make sure users have Read and File Scan [RF] access rights to the SYS:PUBLIC\CLIENT\DOSWIN32 directory.

▸ *Step 3:* Copy the ACU utilities and files to the Client 32 directory. These files are located in the SYS:PUBLIC\CLIENT\DOSWIN32\ADMIN\DOS_ACU directory. Note: Be sure to use the "NCOPY /S" command for comprehensive copying. When your finished, create a "LOG" subdirectory under SYS:PUBLIC\CLIENT\DOSWIN32 to store status information about each client upgrade process.

▸ *Step 4:* Edit INSTALL.CFG. This ACU configuration file is located in the Client 32 parent directory (that is, SYS:PUBLIC\CLIENT\DOSWIN32). Make sure the "InstallType" setting is configured as "AUTO" so ACU workstations can be upgrade without user intervention:

```
[Setup]

    InstallType=AUTO
```

▸ *Step 5:* Finally, it's time to configure the ACU login script. Add the following statements to the container, profile, or user script you chose in Step 1:

```
MAP I:=ACME-SRV1/SYS:PUBLIC\CLIENT\DOSWIN32
#I:NWDETECT Novell_Client32 4.1.0
```

```
IF ERROR_LEVEL = "1" THEN
    #I:INSTALL
    IF ERROR_LEVEL = "0" THEN
        #I:NWSTAMP Novell_Client32 4.1.0
        #I:NWLOG /F I:.\LOG\UPDATE.LOG
        #I:REBOOT
    END
END
MAP DEL I:
```

So, what's going on here? Here's a detailed description of this mysterious and magical ACU login script statement:

- *Line 1:* First, the "I:" drive is temporarily mapped to the Client 32/ACU parent directory. In this case, it's SYS:PUBLIC\CLIENT\ DOSWIN32. The drive is removed at the end of the statement (Line 11).

- *Line 2:* NWDETECT is executed from the ACU parent directory using the "#" login script command. NWDETECT looks in the workstation's NET.CFG file for an Install Stamp. If no Install Stamp exists or if the stamp doesn't match "Novell_Client32 4.1.0," then NWDETECT returns an error code of "1".

- *Line 3:* If NWDETECT returns an error code of "1", the IF/THEN statement executes.

- *Line 4:* The Client 32 for Windows 3.1 installation program (INSTALL.EXE) runs from the Client 32 parent directory.

- *Line 5:* If the INSTALL.EXE program doesn't run successfully, it returns an error code of "1" and the nested IF/THEN statement doesn't run.

- *Line 6:* This is the first of three nested programs, once the Client 32 for Windows 3.1 installation program upgrades the workstation. NWSTAMP updates the client's NET.CFG file with the correct Install Stamp.

- *Line 7:* NWLOG writes a log file called "UPDATE.LOG" to the Client 32 LOG directory. It contains the date, time, username, IPX number, node address, and optionally, any message defined by you.

- *Line 8:* Finally, REBOOT automatically reboots the workstation so it can benefit from the new upgrade client software.

 ZEN

"If I have the belief that I can do it, I shall surely acquire the capacity to do it, even if I may not have had it at the beginning."

Mahatma Gandhi

Children aren't so bad. Once you get the hang of it, I think you might even enjoy adulthood. Having servers and workstations enables you to relive a little bit of your own childhood and adds years to your life (yeah, right). Of course, all the while, you must be thinking about the future and what happens when your children get children of their own. What a disaster. But let's not get ahead of ourselves. Now let's take a moment to return to a simpler time and play in the 16-bit sandbox.

CLIENT 16 WORKSTATION ARCHITECTURE

Welcome to 16-bit land.

Earlier we learned that 16-bit workstations attack the local NIC and WOS in a slightly less-GUI way. As with most family matters, it all starts with communications. Figure 13.19 illustrates the bottom three layers of the 16-bit workstation architecture. Together, these files are part of a solution called ODI (Open Datalink Interface). Then, further workstation management is handled by a group of VLMs called the NetWare DOS Requester. They lie between the WOS and ODI to make transparent network communications possible. This is Leia making sure her sister Sophie doesn't get into any trouble.

Let's take a closer look at these two important pieces of the 16-bit workstation puzzle.

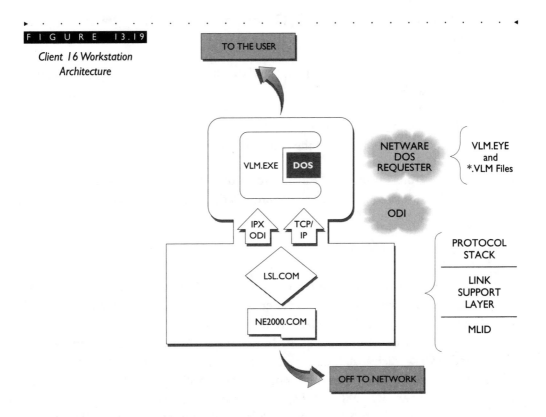

F I G U R E   13.19

Client 16 Workstation
Architecture

Open Datalink Interface

Interestingly, Open Datalink Interface (or ODI) is also the name of an old TV character and a cartoon dog. What does this mean? Using ODI, your network can run multiple protocols on the same cabling system. This enables devices that use different communication protocols to coexist on one WAN, thus increasing your network's functionality and flexibility. For example, both IPX and TCP/IP can run on the same workstation using the same NIC. This means that a user may concurrently access services from an IntranetWare server using IPX and a Unix host using TCP/IP. Very cool.

As you can see in Figure 13.19, the workstation ODI architecture consists of three main components:

▸ MLID (the Multiple Link Interface Driver) — This component interfaces with the internal NIC.

▸ LSL (the Link Support Layer) — Acts as a switchboard to route packets between MLID and the protocol stack.

▸ Protocol stack — One of three protocol-specific files used to translate and negotiate network communications. This is the real star of the ODI show.

Let's take a closer look.

MLID   It all starts at the bottom of the ODI picture — MLID. Each physical NIC has its own specific MLID driver. MLIDs accept any type of packet and either send them up to LSL or down to the NIC. In either case, MLIDs handle workstation communications. In IntranetWare, MLIDs come in various shapes and sizes — each matching the specific NIC. The MLID driver NE2000.COM, for example, handles communications for the Novell NE2000 NIC. Similarly, the MLID driver 3C5X9.COM handles communications for the popular 3COM 3C5X9 NIC. The beauty of the modular ODI approach is that MLID drivers can be loaded and unloaded as needed. Also, their configuration settings are handled by a single text file — NET.CFG.

Link Support Layer   The Link Support Layer (LSL) is the next point in the ODI picture. It acts as a switchboard to route packets between the MLID driver and appropriate protocol stack. LSL identifies the packet and then passes it to either IPX/SPX, TCP/IP, or AppleTalk. At the DOS workstation, LSL is implemented as LSL.COM. An IntranetWare client can use any of the three protocols because LSL directs information to the appropriate one. Think of it as your client traffic cop.

Protocol Stack   The final ODI layer contains protocol stacks such as IPX/SPX, TCP/IP, and AppleTalk. Once a packet arrives at the specific protocol stack, it either passes through and communicates with the NetWare DOS Requester, or is sent back down to another network. One of the main features of ODI is that it supports multiple protocols on the same cabling segment. This enables devices that allow different communication protocols to coexist on one network, thus increasing your WAN's functionality and flexibility. This is particularly important in IntranetWare because it is the foundation of a multiprotocol, multinational, and multilingual operating system. Protocol implementation for the default IPX/SPX LAN is handled by IPXODI.COM, whereas TCP/IP implementation works through TCPIP.EXE.

ODI loading at the workstation works a little bit differently. Although the MLID layer is the bottom and is the first point of contact for incoming packets, it is not the first ODI driver loaded — go figure. Here's how it works:

- ▶ LSL.COM

- ▶ 3C5X9.COM (or other *MLID*)

- ▶ IPXODI.COM (or other *protocol stack*)

As you learned in Chapter 12, customization and configuration of the ODI files is implemented using NET.CFG. So, how do you unload them? It's easy. Simply type the name followed by a /U. Make sure, however, that you unload the drivers in reverse order, because they build on top of each other. And always unload the NetWare DOS Requester before unloading ODI drivers.

ZEN

"Dishes. Relationships. Wind. This guy breaks everything!"

From the movie *Drop Dead Fred*

Once the packet finds its way up through the correct protocol stack, it's time for the WOS to take over. WOS connectivity at the IntranetWare client is handled by VLMs — the NetWare DOS Requester.

REAL WORLD

The ODI drivers have some interesting command line switches. Although these are not widely known, they can help you in special circumstances:

▸ IPXODI /C — Indicates an alternate filename for configuration information. This way, you can specify a different NET.CFG for ODI settings. The /c parameter also works with LSL and VLM.

▸ IPXODI /A — Eliminates the diagnostic responder and SPX communications. Although this reduces the memory size by 9 KB, it does eliminate support for RCONSOLE and dedicated print servers. Be careful when you use this option.

▸ IPXODI /D — Eliminates the diagnostic responder only reducing memory size by 3 KB.

▸ IPXODI /F — Forcibly unloads IPXODI from memory, even if other modules are loaded above it. Use this only in extreme circumstances, because it might cause the system to hang.

▸ IPXODI /? — All the ODI and VLM drivers have detailed help screens.

NetWare DOS Requester

The NetWare DOS Requester is a connection point between your WOS and network services. A DOS workstation, for example, is typically a stand-alone computer. It uses a local operating system to provide basic local services. These services include file storage to local disks, screen display access, printer access, and communications. DOS itself and most WOSs are not capable of communicating with the network. Therefore, they need a little help.

VLMs to the rescue! As you can see in Figure 13.19, the NetWare DOS Requester is a marshmallow-looking thing that surrounds DOS and provides transparent connectivity between user applications and the network. It shares drive table information with DOS, therefore reducing memory usage. The Requester performs such tasks as file and print redirection, connection maintenance, and packet handling. This is all made possible through various modular files, VLMs. Each VLM performs a specific function including

PRINT.VLM for printer redirection, CONN.VLM for connectivity, FIO.VLM for file services, and NETX.VLM for backward compatibility to NETx. Of course, none of this could be possible without the conductor of our orchestra — VLM.EXE.

VLM.EXE manages 16-bit VLMs in an interesting load-order architecture. This model consists of three layers:

▸ Transport protocol — Maintains server connections and provides transmission and other transport-related services.

▸ Service protocol — Handles requests for specific services such as broadcast messages, file reads and writes, and print redirection. Service protocol VLMs are the heart and soul of IntranetWare client connectivity.

▸ DOS redirection — REDIR.VLM is responsible for DOS redirection services. The Requester makes an IntranetWare server look like a DOS driver to the user by having REDIR.VLM make decisions about client requests. This is analogous to the major functionality of NETX.EXE.

So, who's in charge here? The VLM manager — VLM.EXE. When you run it, it oversees the loading and sequencing of VLM files. Because VLMs are load-order dependent, you have to make sure VLM.EXE activates them in the correct order. In addition, the NetWare DOS Requester supports two types of VLMs — core and optional. Core VLMs are activated automatically in a specific order when you execute VLM.EXE. There are 13 of them shown in Table 13.7 — and they're listed in respective load order. Optional VLMs, on the other hand, can be activated by issuing the following commands under the NetWare DOS Requester section heading of NET.CFG:

```
NetWare DOS Requester
    VLM=C:\NWCLIENT\AUTO.VLM
    VLM=C:\NWCLIENT\RSA.VLM
    VLM=C:\NWCLIENT\NMR.VLM
```

T A B L E   1 3 . 7

Load Order for Core VLMs

LOAD ORDER	VLM	DESCRIPTION
1	BIND.VLM	NetWare protocol implementation using bindery services. This is an optional core VLM for IntranetWare NDS. (Child)
2	CONN.VLM	Connection table manager. Communicates between the three layers of VLM architecture. (Parent)
3	FIO.VLM	File input and output services. (Parent)
4	GENERAL.VLM	Miscellaneous functions for NETX.VLM and REDIR.VLM. (Child)
5	IPXNCP.VLM	Transport protocol using IPX/SPX. (Child)
6	NDS.VLM	NWP implementation using NDS support. This VLM is required for IntranetWare NDS. (Child)
7	NETX.VLM	NetWare shell compatibility for previous versions of NetWare. (Parent)
8	NWP.VLM	NetWare protocol multiplexer. This parent VLM oversees key IntranetWare client services. (Parent)
9	PNW.VLM	NWP implementation for Personal NetWare. (Child)
10	PRINT.VLM	Printer redirector that provides CAPTURE capabilities for the DOS workstation. (Parent)
11	REDIR.VLM	DOS redirector. This VLM performs most of the tasks of earlier NETx. (Parent)
12	SECURITY.VLM	NetWare-enhanced security. (Parent)
13	TRAN.VLM	The transport protocol multiplexer that oversees IPX and TCP/IP communications. (Parent)

As you can see in Table 13.7, these are the three most popular optional VLMs. In addition, you can exclude core VLMs from loading, but only if you follow these two steps: First, add the following statement to the NetWare DOS Requester section of NET.CFG

```
USE DEFAULTS=OFF
```

Then, second, specify every VLM you do want to load in correct order. The bottom line is, you either load all 13 core VLMs, or specify the ones you want in correct order.

The Requester supports DOS 3.1 and above, and works with extended, expanded, and conventional memory. VLM.EXE, by default, tries to load all VLMs in extended memory first. Expanded memory is the second choice, and, if extended or expanded memory is unavailable, conventional memory is used. VLM.EXE itself can be loaded in high memory, but this is not the default state. In addition to memory support, VLM has various switches that customize its activities.

- /? — Displays the help screen.

- /M*x* — Loads VLM.EXE and associated files in conventional (C), expanded (E), or extended (X) memory.

- /V*x* — Displays the detailed level of messaging where *x* runs from 0 to 4. Verbosity can display copyright messages and critical errors (0), warning messages (1), program load information (2), configuration information (3), or everything, including diagnostics (4).

- /PS — Specifies the preferred server during connection.

- /PT — Specifies the preferred tree during connection.

- /D — Displays file diagnostics such as status information, memory type, current ID, and VLM manager functioning.

Well, that just about does it for the NetWare DOS Requester and ODI. Both of these workstation connectivity strategies rely on workstation-specific configuration files for implementation and customization. As you learned in Chapter 12, NET.CFG enables CNEs to increase user transparency and pinpoint communication problems. In summary, here's what it does for ODI and VLMs:

- ODI — NET.CFG provides vital information for NIC configuration. It includes a section heading called LINK DRIVER for ODI support. CNEs can use this section to name the MLID file and specify hardware and software settings, including interrupt, I/O port, memory address, and frame type. Fortunately, you only need to use NET.CFG if you plan on deviating from the established ODI defaults.

▶ VLMs — NET.CFG can also be used to customize default VLM settings. As we saw earlier, it includes a NetWare DOS Requester section heading for defining workstation connections, the first network drive, and activating specific core and optional VLMs.

QUIZ

The "Puzzler" strikes again:

What will you break even if you name it?
What fastens two people yet touches only one?
What grows larger the more you take away?
What grows larger the more you contract it?

(Q13-6)

Well, there you have it. Life in the 32-bit and 16-bit sandboxes. Aren't children grand. Don't they just take you back to a simpler life — no work and all play. Speaking of play, let's take a second to explore workstation management in the twilight zone — that is, OS/2, Macintosh, and Unix. I know you want to.

DIVERSE CLIENTS

IntranetWare prides itself on the ability to transparently support a multitude of workstation environments. After all, IntranetWare was designed to provide centralized connectivity for diverse WANs spanning the globe. In other words, IntranetWare lets lots of different people talk to each other. So, how does it do it? As you can see in Figure 13.20, IntranetWare supports five workstation environments: three on the client side and two on the server side. If you access the network from a DOS, OS/2, or Windows 95 client, the connectivity software resides on the workstation. On the other hand, if you access the network from a Macintosh or Unix client, the connectivity software resides on the IntranetWare server. I wonder if Novell is making a subtle statement here.

Either way, the goal is to allow all of these five diverse clients to coexist on the same WAN. In addition, file and print services appear to each client using their native interface. Cool! This means DOS users operate with the C:\, and GUI users (Windows 95, Macintosh, and OS/2) hang out in folders. This may seem magic to the user, but it requires a great deal of work for you, the CNE.

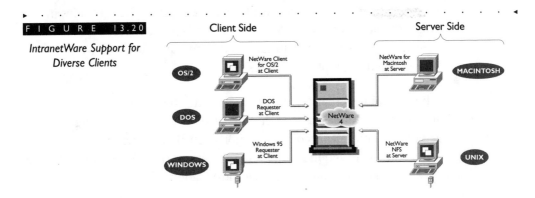

FIGURE 13.20

IntranetWare Support for Diverse Clients

Let's take a quick look at life beyond DOS, including OS/2, Macintosh, and Unix.

ZEN

"If I have the belief that I can do it, I shall surely acquire the capacity to do it even if I may not have had it at the beginning."

Mahatma Gandhi

OS/2

IntranetWare client support for OS/2 is provided through a new system called NetWare Client for OS/2. Makes sense. The client software runs on the OS/2 workstation and is included with the IntranetWare operating system. File service support for OS/2 is provided through NetWare's own IPX protocol stack. So, what do OS/2 clients gain from IntranetWare services? Here are some benefits:

▸ Long names — OS/2 supports much longer names than those used by DOS. DOS restricts a filename to eight characters plus a three-character extension, whereas OS/2 can use names up to 255 bytes.

▸ Extended attributes — In addition, OS/2 attaches extended attributes to files that describe them and provide better management capabilities.

▸ GUI utilities — NetWare Client for OS/2 supports NDS utilities in OS/2's native, graphical Presentation Manager interface. This is a critical feature because most of IntranetWare's administrative tasks are performed in graphical utilities.

The bottom line is that OS/2 clients running the IntranetWare connectivity software have equal access to IntranetWare services (including NDS, file management, printing, and communications). In this discussion, we're going to explore the two main requirements for providing IntranetWare support to OS/2 clients: OS/2 name space and OS/2 client installation.

OS/2 Name Space   OS/2 workstations use High Performance File System (HPFS) to store data with long names and extended attributes. IntranetWare support for HPFS is provided through the OS/2 name space. As you learned earlier, name space NLMs have the .NAM extension and provide non-DOS support to the IntranetWare file server. Once you've loaded the OS/2-specific name space, you must use the ADD NAME SPACE command to configure the volume. The following example would prepare the default SYS: volume for OS/2 files:

```
LOAD OS2
ADD NAME SPACE OS2 TO SYS:
```

You only need to execute the ADD NAME SPACE command once during initial configuration. After a volume has been configured for a new name space, you only need to load the appropriate NLM. This can be automated by placing the LOAD OS2 statement in STARTUP.NCF. Incidentally, Macintosh name space can also be configured on IntranetWare volumes using a similar approach.

OS/2 Client Installation   Once the IntranetWare file system has been prepared to accept OS/2 filenames, it's time to install the client software. The NetWare Client for OS/2 software provides access to the IntranetWare file system and print services. The OS/2 client installation software can be found on the IntranetWare/NetWare 4.11 Operating System CD-ROM, or in the SYS:PUBLIC\CLIENT\OS2 directory. In addition, you can create installation diskettes with the "MAKEDISK" utility — also found on the CD-ROM or in the OS2 subdirectory.

Well, there you go. OS/2 has been configured and installed. Now we have three client platforms accessing the same IntranetWare files — DOS, Windows 95, and OS/2. Anyone for a foursome?

> **TIP**
>
> To remove a non-DOS name space, you must load **VREPAIR.NLM.** This repairs the volume and strips away any unused name space. But what if you want to run **VREPAIR** without removing name space — to repair volumes maybe? Fortunately, IntranetWare includes protective shields that prevent name space stripping when **VREPAIR** is loaded. For OS/2, it's **V_LONG.NLM,** and for Macintosh it's **V_MAC.NLM.**

Macintosh

Macintosh connectivity is provided through one of two solutions:

▸ NetWare Client for Mac OS — the *new* way.

▸ NetWare for Macintosh — the *old* way.

In the old days (pre-IntranetWare), Macintosh clients relied on a special suite of NLMs at the server called "NetWare for Macintosh" (see Figure 13.20). With this suite in place, Macintosh users could access NetWare files and printers in their native AppleTalk (AFP) and Chooser environments. It was slow, inconvenient, and messy.

In the new IntranetWare global village, Macintosh users are treated as equal citizens. Their voice has been heard, and now they can access the IntranetWare server using the native IPX protocol. This magic is made possible by a new solution called "NetWare Client for Mac OS." With this new client-based strategy, Macintosh users move from the right side of Figure 13.20 to the left (with the rest of us).

Here's some of the great benefits of the new NetWare Client for Mac OS solution:

▸ It provides a NetWare Directory Browser that runs at the Macintosh workstation. The Browser provides full-feature access to NDS from within the native Chooser interface.

▸ It provides context-sensitive help within the NetWare Directory Browser. In addition, users with System 7.5 or greater get integrated Apple Guide Help as well.

▸ It gives network administrators and Macintosh users the ability to create icons for NDS objects on the desktop.

▸ It supports drag-and-drop interfacing between NDS objects and the Macintosh Desktop. This allows users to integrate NDS Application and Printer objects into their daily GUI routine.

In order to activate NetWare Client for Mac OS, you must first install the software onto the Macintosh workstation. Then, you must prepare the IntranetWare server for Macintosh connectivity and files. This is accomplished by loading the appropriate server components and Macintosh Name Space NLMs.

SMART LINK

For more information on the new Macintosh solution for IntranetWare, consult the on-line IntranetWare documentation at http://www.novell.com/manuals.

Now let's move on to the final non-DOS client: Unix.

Unix

In much the same way as Macintosh clients, Unix workstations have built-in, native networking functionality for attaching to IntranetWare servers: NFS. NFS is the Unix network file system. It coordinates file storage and communications between Unix clients and hosts. Using a special server component called NetWare NFS, Unix clients can attach to IntranetWare servers and use its file, printing, and connectivity services.

NetWare NFS can be used with NetWare's native IPX protocol or the Unix TCP/IP. However, if you want your IntranetWare server to hang out on a TCP/IP-only network, you'll need another product — NetWare IP (also included with IntranetWare).

NetWare IP is a suite of server and client software that allows you to switch the default network protocol from IPX to TCP/IP. It provides the following features:

► It transparently extends NetWare and IntranetWare services and applications to nodes on an existing TCP/IP network.

► It migrates the entire WAN from IPX to TCP/IP

► It interconnects IPX and TCP/IP networks, thus enabling users on both LANs to access IntranetWare resources.

In order to activate NetWare/IP, you must first prepare the IntranetWare server by loading appropriate NLMs. Then, you can configure the TCP/IP workstations for NetWare connectivity. It's as easy as 1-2.

As you can tell, it's not easy to incorporate various workstations into one cohesive, happy WAN. Although IntranetWare provides a facility for transparent connectivity, some serious massaging is required in order for it to work smoothly. Once again, it may appear as magic to the user, but it's no mystery to you (the CNE) — just hours and hours of hard work. Don't get discouraged, though. It's ultimately rewarding when all the diverse users come together into one big happy family.

ZEN

"In dwelling, live close to the ground.
In thinking, keep to the simple.
In conflict, be fair and generous.
In governing, don't try to control.
In work, do what you enjoy.
In family life, be completely present."

Tao Te Ching

Speaking of family, ours is growing quickly. We watched Leia go through a childhood of her own and now she's experiencing the growing pains of parenthood. Of course, one of our most important parent responsibilities is the family. And we can learn an important lesson from the Girl Scouts of America — be prepared! Let's continue our journey through adulthood with a detailed look at the "second half" of life — pension and retirement.

Storage Management Services

Call it a pension, a "nest egg," or whatever you like, planning for the future is important business. With a family comes serious financial concerns — college education, emergency fund, and retirement. And these financial decisions aren't as simple as they used to be. You must choose among IRAs, annuities, mutual funds, pension plans, and (my old favorite) the "sock in the bedpost." Regardless of what you do, it's critical that you plan for the future.

One of the most exciting things about life is that you never know what's around the corner. To be prepared, you must have a backup plan. Also, as your network grows in complexity, the value of its services grows as well. And we all know nothing becomes more valuable until it is lost. That's Murphy's Law Number 193.

Welcome to IntranetWare backup. Backup provides both a prevention and maintenance strategy:

▸ Prevention — Backup is a proactive strategy toward disaster recovery. You don't want to be wondering what to do *after* the data is lost.

▸ Maintenance — Backup doesn't always prevent a disaster from occurring; it simply expedites recovery.

As soon as your network data is lost, file backup should be the first thing that pops into your mind. In many cases, having current backups can spell the difference between a successful and prosperous CNE career and the unemployment line. *Never* neglect your IntranetWare backup duties. Fortunately, IntranetWare includes a versatile new backup feature called Storage Management Services (SMS).

SMS is a combination of related services that enable data to be stored and retrieved. The SMS backup process involves a *host* server and a *target*. The host server is the IntranetWare machine on which the backup program resides. The target is the IntranetWare server or client that contains the data needing to be backed up. In addition, SMS uses an application on the host server to communicate with modules on target devices — SBACKUP.NLM is included for free. This discussion first explores the fundamental architecture of SMS. Then we'll take a closer look at backing up and restoring data using the default SMS application — SBACKUP.NLM. What are we waiting for? Let's go.

SMS ARCHITECTURE

As you learned earlier, SMS is a combination of related services that enable you to store and retrieve data from various targets — Target Service Agents (TSAs). SMS operates as a backup engine that is independent from the front-end application and back-end device. As you can see in Figure 13.21, SMS supports various TSA front-ends, including IntranetWare file systems, NDS, DOS and OS/2 file systems, and BTRIEVE databases. Any or all of these resources can be backed up to various back-end devices including DOS read/write disks, tape, and optical drives.

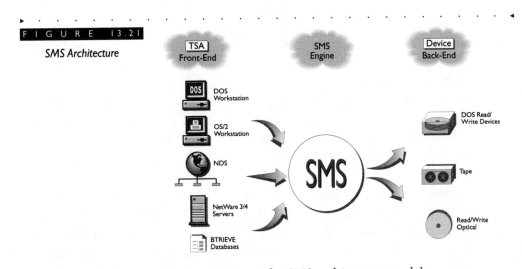

F I G U R E   13.21

SMS Architecture

There are three main components to the SMS architecture model:

- ▸ Device drivers

- ▸ SBACKUP.NLM

- ▸ Target Service Agents

You can see the interaction among these components in Figure 13.22. The device drivers interface between SBACKUP.NLM and the internal host device. Then, SBACKUP uses Target Service Agents to activate source file systems. Let's take a closer look.

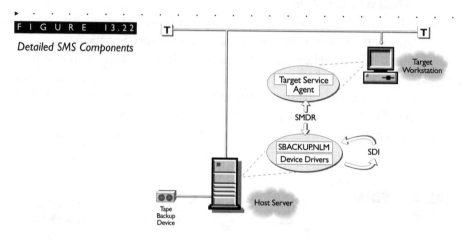

FIGURE 13.22

Detailed SMS Components

Device Drivers

Device drivers lie at the bottom of the SMS model. They control the mechanical operation of the host storage device. In addition, they must be specifically configured for each backup device and interface with the SBACKUP.NLM application. When device drivers are loaded, SBACKUP recognizes the storage device.

Device drivers are loaded at the host server and therefore must be NLMs. The following files are included with IntranetWare: TAPEDAI.DSK (Novell's generic tape driver for most ASPI-compatible SCSI controllers); MNS*.DSK (Mountain Backup devices); PS2SCSI.DSK (for IBM PS2 SCSI controllers); and AHA*.DSK (Adaptec SCSI devices). Before SBACKUP.NLM recognizes the host device, you must register it with IntranetWare using the following command:

```
SCAN FOR NEW DEVICES
```

SBACKUP.NLM

The backup application (SBACKUP, in this case) communicates with device drivers through SDI — the Storage Device Interface. It is loaded as an NLM on the host server. Once the backup device is activated, you can enter the SMS application — SBACKUP.NLM. This utility works within the SMS architecture to route data requests from the source and to the device through SDI. Interestingly, we are now backing up clients from the server — isn't this backward? Later in this section, we'll explore the ins and outs of using SBACKUP.NLM.

Target Service Agents

The final component in the SMS architecture model is TSAs — Target Service Agents. TSAs must be loaded on target servers or workstations. SBACKUP.NLM recognizes TSAs through the Storage Management Data Requester (SMDR), which is an NLM running on the host server. IntranetWare supports various TSAs, including:

▶ IntranetWare server — TSA411

▶ NetWare 4 server — TSA410 or TSA400

▶ NetWare 3 server — TSA312 or TSA311

▶ DOS workstation — TSADOS and TSASMS

▶ OS/2 workstation — TSAPROXY and TSAOS2

▶ Macintosh workstation — TSAMAC and TSASMS

▶ NDS database — TSANDS

▶ Btrieve SQL Databases — TSASQL

Remember, if you're backing up data on the host server, you still have to load TSA410 and TSANDS. Finally, SBACKUP.NLM only recognizes targets that have loaded the appropriate TSA module.

Now that you understand the fundamental SMS architecture, let's explore SBACKUP.NLM in more depth. Keep in mind, any third-party backup application can be used with SMS, as long as it follows this fundamental design.

ZEN

"Don't hurry, don't worry. You're only here for a short visit. So be sure to stop and smell the flowers."

Walter Hagen

USING SBACKUP

At the heart of the SMS model is the backup application. IntranetWare includes a starter program called SBACKUP.NLM. You can use any server application, as long as it's SMS-compliant. SBACKUP, for example, is an NLM that operates at the IntranetWare server and communicates directly with the host backup device. Running SBACKUP at the server has its advantages. First, it supports multiple file server connections at one time. Also, it operates faster because it doesn't cause an additional communications load on the network. Because the tape unit is connected directly to the file server, SBACKUP doesn't route packets over the LAN. Finally, SBACKUP supports a wide variety of backup devices because of their independent *.DSK device drivers.

Just like any application, you'll have to learn the SBACKUP "lingo" to use it efficiently. Following are a few terms you should be aware of:

- ▸ Host — The IntranetWare server running SBACKUP.NLM. Also, the backup device is attached to it.

- ▸ Target — Any IntranetWare server, workstation, or NDS database that has a TSA loaded. This is where the backup source material resides.

- ▸ Parent — A data set that may have subordinate data sets. In IntranetWare, a parent would be a directory, a subdirectory, or a container.

- ▸ Child — A data set that has no subordinates. In IntranetWare, for example, a child would be a file or leaf object.

Let's explore SBACKUP.NLM by first learning about its four main backup strategies. Then we'll discuss some guidelines before diving into the detailed steps of SMS backup and restore.

SMART LINK

SMART LINK

For a more in-depth discussion of SBACKUP and backup/restore procedures, surf the Web to http://www.novell.com/manuals.

Backup Strategies

So, how does it work? SBACKUP provides four strategies that can be used for backing up and restoring data. Each strategy provides a different balance of performance and efficiency. In Figure 13.23, you can see the three main strategies — full, incremental, and differential. Here's how they work.

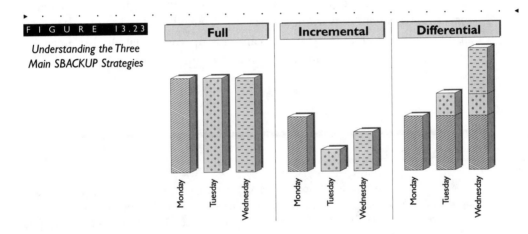

FIGURE 13.23

Understanding the Three Main SBACKUP Strategies

As you can see in Figure 13.23, the full backup option is the most thorough. It is, however, not practical. During a full backup, all data is copied, regardless of when or if it has been previously backed up. While this option is the most time-consuming, it does allow for very fast and easy restores — you only have to restore the latest full backup. During a full backup, the "Modify" bit of each file is cleared — we'll discuss why a little later. (Incidentally, the "Modify" bit is a file attribute that changes each time a file is modified. It is the same as the "Archive Needed" attribute from Chapter 11.)

The second option (incremental) backs up only the files that have changed since the last backup. Although this option offers a quick backup, restoring can be quite a nightmare. In order to restore all the data, you must restore the last full backup and every incremental backup since then, *in order.* If one is missing or doesn't work, you're up a creek. During an incremental backup, the "Modify" bit of each file is cleared, so SBACKUP skips them the next time.

The differential backup is a new and interesting strategy. It backs up all the data that has been modified since the last full backup. Differential backup is the best balance of efficiency and performance because it minimizes the number of restore sessions. You only need to restore the last full and the latest differential. Also, the backup session is optimized because only the files that have changed are being copied.

The main improvement with the differential strategy is the state of the "Modify" bit — it is *not* cleared. This way, all the files that have changed since the last full backup are copied each time. This is why the full backup strategy clears the modify bit. Notice in Figure 13.23 how the volume of data systematically increases. One word of warning, however — since the "Modify" bit is also cleared during an incremental backup, this can mess up your differential strategy. Make sure you never perform an incremental backup between differential and full backups.

REAL WORLD

As you can see, the incremental and differential backup strategies provide many options when backing up and restoring IntranetWare data. They don't, however, allow you to back up NDS. Only the full backup strategy can backup the NDS database. This is a very important point to keep in mind when planning your backup schedule.

The fourth and final SBACKUP strategy is "custom." The custom method enables you to specify which files are backed up, and whether the "Modify" bit is cleared. This provides the ultimate level of flexibility.

Table 13.8 shows a comparison of the four SBACKUP strategies. The best combination is

- ▶ Every day — Differential

- ▶ Once a week on Friday — Full

- ▶ Once a month — Custom

	SBACKUP STRATEGY	BACKUP	RESTORE	MODIFY BIT
	Full	Slow	Easy	Cleared
	Incremental	Quick	Hard	Cleared
	Differential	Quick	Easy	Not cleared
	Custom	Whatever	Your choice	Doesn't matter

T A B L E   13.8

Understanding the Four Main SBACKUP Strategies

Once you've chosen your backup strategy, you must follow some simple SBACKUP guidelines during backup and restore sessions. Let's take a look.

Guidelines

You gotta have rules. Without rules, the world would be a very wacky place. Let me rephrase that — the world would be an even wackier place. SBACKUP is no exception. Here are a few guidelines you must follow when using this SMS application:

▸ Make sure you have enough disk space on the host server's SYS: volume for temporary files and log files (1 MB should be sufficient). Run SBACKUP.NLM from an IntranetWare server and attach the backup device to the same host server. Also, be sure to run updated support NLMs (such as STREAMS, SPXS, TLI, CLIB, and NWSNUT).

▸ Limit access to SBACKUP to maintain the security of your IntranetWare server and to ensure data integrity. Also, be aware that security can be compromised if a delayed backup session does not fit on inserted media. If you are prompted to insert another tape, the program pauses at that point and does not exit. To reduce this risk, set APPEND to NO.

▸ When you are entering a filename that has a non-DOS format, use the DOS equivalent naming scheme. SBACKUP does support OS/2 and Macintosh naming schemes, but the application interface doesn't. So, even though you're backing up long filenames (September99, for example), they appear in their DOS equivalent (September, for example). You can track this by using the SBACKUP error and backup log files. They display both the DOS equivalent and the name space version of each directory or file.

▸ Monitor the size of SBACKUP temporary files. SBACKUP creates temporary files on the target server as well as the host machine. These temporary files may become quite large if you have extended attributes or linked Unix files.

▸ Do not mount or dismount volumes or unload drivers during a backup session. You may corrupt data or abend the host server — duh!

▸ Know the passwords assigned to target servers and workstations.

ZEN

"Don't wait for your ship to come in; swim out to it!"

Anonymous

Backup Steps

Once you understand these guidelines, you're ready to perform your first SMS backup using SBACKUP.NLM. I can hardly contain my excitement. Follow the bouncing ball as we outline the seven steps of an SMS backup. For a more detailed walkthrough, try it yourself. C'mon in, the water's fine.

1 • Load the backup device driver on the host server.

2 • Load appropriate TSA drivers on all target devices. This includes the host server, if you plan on backing it up. When you load the TSAs, all support modules are activated automatically.

3 • Load SBACKUP.NLM at the host server. Once you've activated SBACKUP, certain support modules are automatically loaded, including SMDR. The SBACKUP main menu is then displayed, as shown in Figure 13.24.

4 • Select a target to be backed up from the TSA list. **Note:** Targets will only appear if the appropriate TSAs have been loaded properly. You can get to the TSA list by choosing "Change Target to Back Up From or Restore To" from the main menu of SBACKUP.NLM. If you choose a remote server, you'll be asked for a valid username and password for authentication. Recall you can only back up files matching that user's access rights.

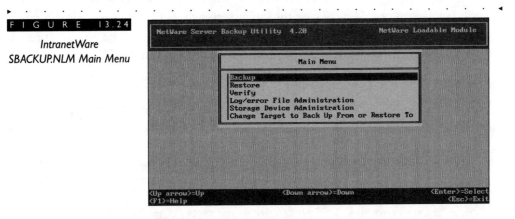

FIGURE 13.24

IntranetWare
SBACKUP.NLM Main Menu

```
NetWare Server Backup Utility  4.20            NetWare Loadable Module

                          Main Menu

                  Backup
                  Restore
                  Verify
                  Log/error File Administration
                  Storage Device Administration
                  Change Target to Back Up From or Restore To

<Up arrow>=Up              <Down arrow>=Down          <Enter>=Select
<F1>=Help                                              <Esc>=Exit
```

5 • Select the backup device from an Available Options list. The list should reflect all devices that are attached to the host server and have appropriate drivers loaded. If only one backup device driver is loaded, SBACKUP automatically selects this device. The list appears when you choose Storage Device Administration from the main menu of SBACKUP.NLM.

6 • Perform appropriate SBACKUP administration, including selecting a location for the log and error file, selecting the type of backup, and providing a session description. All of these tasks are accomplished using the Log/Error File Administration option within the main menu.

7 • Finally, you're ready to back up. You can either proceed "now" or "later." If you choose "later," you'll be prompted for a date and time. If you choose "now," you'll be asked to insert the backup media and enter a unique label for it.

You're finished. That wasn't so hard. Whatever you do, don't *trust* your backup. Always test SBACKUP tapes by selectively restoring them at regular intervals. This might involve restoring random files to a secondary volume or the entire SBACKUP session. Whatever you do, don't discover SBACKUP doesn't work after you've lost your disk.

Restore Steps

This is where "Murphy" comes in. If you must restore, something bad happened. Let's hope you never have to implement the following seven steps. But, before you begin, make sure the target server or workstation has enough free disk space. It must have approximately 20 percent *more* than the amount needed to restore. The overhead space stores temporary files and additional name space information. Here's a brief outline of the SBACKUP restore steps:

1 • Load the backup device driver on the host server (same as Backup Step 1).

2 • Load the appropriate TSA software on all targets you wish to restore to. This includes the host server if you plan on restoring to it.

3 • Load SBACKUP.NLM at the host server (same as Backup Step 3).

4 • Select a target to restore to. The Available Options within SBACKUP should reflect all devices that have loaded the appropriate TSA. Once again, this is accomplished using the "Change Target to Backup From or Restore To" option from the main menu of SBACKUP. Once you choose a TSA, a list of recognized restore sessions will appear. Select one.

5 • Perform SBACKUP administration, including selecting a location for the log and error file and inserting the backup media.

6 • Select a restore device from the Available Options list. This list should match all attached devices and loaded drivers. If only one backup device driver is loaded, SBACKUP automatically selects this device.

7 • Now, we finally get to restore. First select the type of restore from the following list of three — "One File or Directory," "Entire Session," or "Custom Restore." Second, choose the files and objects you wish to restore. Finally, select one of the following restore options — "Proceed now" or "Later."

There you have it. Let's hope you never have to perform a "real" SBACKUP restore. You should practice, though — every week.

ZEN

"Learn not to sweat the small stuff."

Dr. Kenneth Greenspan

THE BRAIN

When backing up NDS with SBACKUP, there are a number of issues to be aware of. These are covered in detail in an AppNote entitled "Backing Up and Restoring Netware Directory Services in NetWare 4" in the August 1995 *Novell Application Notes*.

Well, that wasn't so hard, was it? That's SBACKUP.NLM in a nutshell. After you've completed the SBACKUP steps each day, you'll find a certain peace of mind knowing that you have these hot little tapes in your hands. It matches the peace of mind knowing that your children can go to college and someday you'll finally get to retire to the beaches of Tahiti. But, that time is not now, so stop daydreaming and move on to the final section of IntranetWare SMS — other SMS considerations.

OTHER SMS CONSIDERATIONS

We're not quite finished yet. In order to take full advantage of IntranetWare's SMS feature, you'll need to explore a few other considerations. They are

- ▸ Who does it?

- ▸ Workstation backup

- ▸ SMS management

So, who's the lucky person? Probably you. Count your blessings because you're the lucky person chosen to be the SBACKUP administrator. Remember, you wanted to be a CNE. In addition to understanding the rights needed for SMS duties, you must understand the special drivers that load at the SMS workstation. Finally, there are a few SMS management issues that can help you troubleshoot and optimize SBACKUP duties. Any questions? Good, time to move on.

Who Does It?

Being assigned SBACKUP responsibilities is a dubious distinction. Although it has its status in the IntranetWare management realm, it also has a price. You don't want to mess up here. The person you assign to back up your network must have certain qualifications and access privileges, including:

- ▸ The backup administrator needs Read and File Scan (RF) access rights to the files he or she plans to back up. The administrator will also need additional rights for restoring (RWCEMF).

- ▸ The backup administrator will need the Browse Object right and Read Property right for backing up NDS information.

- ▸ The backup administrator must know the password on all servers and workstations that act as hosts and targets. A standard naming scheme would be a great idea at this point.

If you're the lucky soul chosen as SBACKUP administrator, continue with the next two considerations. If not, go grab a soda.

Workstation Backup

As if by some inspiration, Novell finally allows workstation backup from the server. This long-awaited feature has been implemented in the new SMS. SMS uses SBACKUP.NLM to back up and restore information from local DOS or OS/2 workstations. You can back up certain directories or the entire workstation including floppy and hard drives.

The DOS workstation TSA is a TSR (terminate-and-stay-resident) program that you can run on any target workstation. Some DOS TSA options include /P for password, /T for no password, and /D for drive designation. Here's how the TSA works:

1 • Load TSADOS.NLM at the server for DOS workstations and TSAPROXY.NLM for OS/2.

2 • Load TSASMS.COM at the DOS workstation and TSAOS2.COM at the OS/2 workstation. This is where you specify the TSA parameters we just discussed. One additional parameter you may want to employ is

/N to give the workstation a unique name. This name will appear in the TSA list of SBACKUP.NLM.

3 • Select the appropriate DOS TSA from the SBACKUP target list. The name that appears should match the name given in Step 2.

Workstation backup is a cool feature, but make sure that you use the correct parameters with the DOS TSA and that you remember to load the appropriate NLMs at the host server. And, if those are not enough to worry about, check out the next discussion.

SMS Management

A few SMS management issues can help you journey through the SBACKUP jungle. Let's start with performance. The speed of SBACKUP varies depending on the configuration and location of the data being backed up. If a file server backs up its own data, for example, it runs about four times faster than if it backs up data from a remote server. The difference is because of the communications required between the host server and the target servers. The speed of communications also depends on the availability of packet receive buffers at the host server; see Chapter 15.

Next, let's talk about SBACKUP session files. Session files are "backup logs" that contain information to help you effectively manage SMS backups. The information also facilitates the restore process and helps you to troubleshoot anything that goes wrong. The two most important session files are the backup log and error log. The backup log consists of a list of all data backed up during the session and the media ID, session date and time, session description, and location of data on the storage media.

The error file, on the other hand, is generated on the host server when a particular group of data is initially backed up. It contains the same header data as the backup log but also provides error information (such as the names of files that were not backed up, files that were not restored, who accessed the NDS database, and error codes). As you recall from our earlier discussion, we identified the location of these session files during Step 6 of the backup process.

Now we're really finished. Congratulations! You've been made SBACKUP administrator. I hope you understand the responsibility that accompanies this honor. But, if you perform your duties admirably, everyone will treat you like a hero.

Pension planning works much the same way. Although it's a dubious honor to be responsible for the family's financial future, many times the rewards greatly outweigh the pain. I see a trend here. All I know is, retirement in Tahiti is sounding better and better all the time.

QUIZ

Here's a quick brain-stretching exercise before you tackle IntranetWare retirement:

A common English word can be made from the letters on the top row of a standard typewriter. For those of you who do not have a typewriter keyboard handy, the letters are Q, W, E, R, T, Y, U, I, O, P. Not all letters must be used and some letters may be used more than once.

(Q13-7)

Remote Management Facility

The final step in our life journey is retirement — RMF. Our life's been an exciting adventure and now it's time to kick back and put it in cruise control. Welcome to Happy Acres!

Now, no one is saying that retirement has to be boring. Quite the contrary: It provides us with an opportunity to enjoy all the adventures we never had time for in the past. You can learn to scuba dive, hang-glide, golf, and even bungee jump. And the best part is, you get to do it on your own terms. It sure sounds appealing — where do I sign up?

RMF is the final step in IntranetWare configuration and management. It enables you to manage all your IntranetWare file servers from one central location. This is particularly useful because file server security states that the machine should be locked away in a cabinet with no monitor or keyboard. Also, IntranetWare prides itself on managing multiple servers spanning wide geographic boundaries. In both cases, you'll spend more time trying to access the servers than doing the important stuff — maintaining and managing them.

Now let's take a moment to explore the details of RMF and learn how it can help you enjoy your new IntranetWare retirement.

RMF ARCHITECTURE

So, how does it work? As you can see in Figure 13.25, RMF supports access from both the workstation and a modem. In either case, it consists of two main components: server NLMs and RCONSOLE.EXE.

▶ . . . . ◀

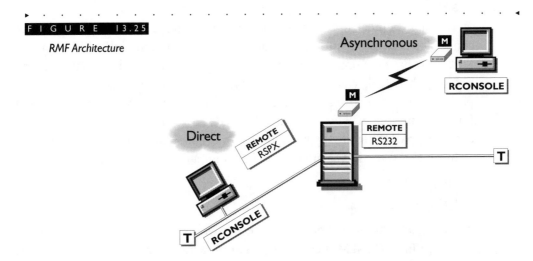

F I G U R E   13.25

RMF Architecture

The RMF server NLMs are broken into two functions — REMOTE and connection services. The REMOTE.NLM module manages information exchange to and from the workstation and the server. In addition, REMOTE.NLM enables you to specify an RMF password.

Connection services are a little bit trickier. As you remember from our earlier discussion, RMF supports access from both a direct workstation or from a modem. In either case, the connection NLM is different. When you access RMF from a direct workstation, connection services are provided by RSPX.NLM. This module provides communication support and advertises the server's availability for remote access. On the other hand, when you access RMF from an asynchronous modem, connection services are provided by RS232.NLM. This module initializes the server modem port and transfers screen and keystroke information to REMOTE.NLM.

Let's take a closer look.

ZEN

"Millions long for immortality who do not know what to do with themselves on a rainy Sunday afternoon."

Susan Ertz

SPX

The most popular RMF connection approach is direct — through SPX. Direct connection services are provided through the RSPX.NLM module. When you load RSPX, you have the option of requiring packet signatures — this ensures security. The default is ON, which means that packet signatures are required. However, packets with signatures are not compatible with NetWare 3.11. If your IntranetWare server coexists with NetWare 3.11 machines, you'll need to deactivate packet signing by using the SIGNATURES OFF switch with RSPX.

In summary, the server modules required for a direct RMF connection are

```
LOAD REMOTE
LOAD RSPX
```

Finally, a quick note about REMOTE passwords. As you learned earlier in the chapter, REMOTE.NLM includes a password facility that enables you to restrict access to the server console. As a matter of fact, in IntranetWare, a REMOTE password is required. This creates a security loophole when the command is placed in AUTOEXEC.NCF. To work around this weakness, consider using LDREMOTE and encrypted passwords. See the earlier "Server Protection" discussion for more details.

TIP

If you use the IPXODI /A parameter to deactivate SPX and gain conventional workstation RAM, RCONSOLE won't work. I wouldn't want you to be surprised at a bad time.

Asynchronous

In addition to a direct connection, RMF supports asynchronous connectivity. As you can see in Figure 13.25, the remote workstation can be attached to the server via a modem. This means you really can manage the IntranetWare server from Tahiti. In this case, connection services are provided by the RS232.NLM module. When you load RS232.NLM, IntranetWare will ask you for some simple modem configurations, including the communications port number, baud rate, and an option for callback.

A callback list enables you to create a list of authorized modem numbers that can be used to access the server. When a connection attempt is made, the server notes the number of the modem that is calling and then terminates the connection. The server then compares the number to the numbers in the call-back list. If the number is in the list, the server calls the modem at that number and re-establishes the connection. If it is not, the server ignores the call. This is another security feature that limits "hacker" access to your server console.

In summary, the following NLM command entries must be given at the IntranetWare server to activate asynchronous RMF:

```
LOAD REMOTE
LOAD RS232 1 9600 C
```

In this example, "1" is the com port, "9600" is the modem speed, and "C" activates the call-back option. The authorized list is defined as CALLBACK.LST in the SYS:SYSTEM directory.

Table 13.9 summarizes these two RMF options.

TABLE 13.9	DIRECT SPX	ASYNCHRONOUS MODEM
Understanding RMF	REMOTE.NLM	REMOTE.NLM
	RSPX.NLM	RS232.NLM

Whether you're accessing RMF from a direct workstation or asynchronous modem, you're going to need RCONSOLE.EXE.

REAL WORLD

The SPX and Asynchronous connections differ dramatically in how they affect network traffic and server utilization. The SPX method increases network traffic, but doesn't have a noticeable effect on server utilization. Conversely, the Asynchronous method generates little network traffic, but causes considerable overhead at the server. For this reason, the Asynchronous connection method shouldn't be used during peak hours.

USING RCONSOLE

RCONSOLE is the front-end for IntranetWare RMF. It provides direct access to the IntranetWare server console screen from a workstation and enables you to perform any task as if you were standing right in front of it. In addition, RCONSOLE provides an Available Options menu with supplemental tasks, including changing screens, scanning server directories, and performing a remote install. All in all, RCONSOLE is your friend because it enables you to enjoy the good life without having to run around like a chicken with your head cut off.

Like most IntranetWare utilities, RCONSOLE has both DOS and Windows versions. The DOS version is executed as RCONSOLE.EXE at any workstation DOS prompt. RCONSOLE.EXE resides in the SYS:PUBLIC subdirectory, but you may want to move it to SYS:SYSTEM to ensure that it doesn't fall into the wrong hands.

Whether you access RCONSOLE from DOS or Windows, you'll get the same main screen asking the same simple question: "What connection type do you want?" The available choices are SPX (for a direct connection) or Asynchronous (for a modem connection). The SPX option brings up a list of available servers as shown in Figure 13.26. Once you choose a server, the password prompt appears. Upon entering the correct password, you'll find yourself staring at the all-too-familiar colon prompt (:). Figure 13.27 below shows the Remote Server console screen from the "Tools" option in NWADMIN.

On the other hand, if you choose the asynchronous connection type, a different menu appears. The Asynchronous Options menu provides two choices: Connect to Remote Location and Configuration. From here, you can either dial a remote server or configure your local modem. Once your connection is established, a callback list will be activated and/or the password prompt will appear. Once again, after you enter the correct password, you'll find yourself staring down the barrel of the IntranetWare console (as in Figure 13.27).

FIGURE 13.26

Available Servers Option in RCONSOLE.EXE

FIGURE 13.27

Accessing the Remote Server Console from NWADMIN

ZEN

"Go ahead: Make my day!"

Clint Eastwood

Once the RCONSOLE session is established, you can perform any available server task as if you were standing in the wiring closet yourself — closed quarters. In addition to standard console activities, you can perform various special RCONSOLE tasks, including:

▶ Change screens

▶ Scan server directories

▶ Transfer files to the server

▶ Shell to DOS

▶ End remote session

▶ Resume remote session

▶ View your local workstation address

▶ Configure keystroke buffering

SMART LINK

Access a "real" IntranetWare server using RCONSOLE. It's as easy as http://www.cyberstateu.com

All of these fun-filled activities are accomplished using the RMF Available Options menu. This menu is activated by pressing the Alt+F1 keys simultaneously and can be seen in Figure 13.28. Also, a list of RCONSOLE function keys can be found in Table 13.10.

Whenever a remote session is granted to RCONSOLE, the file server broadcasts a message to the error log and console prompt indicating that a remote session was attempted at a particular node address and whether or not it was granted. This is useful information if you like to track who's accessing the file server colon prompt using RMF — good idea!

Well, that does it. Your life in a nutshell!

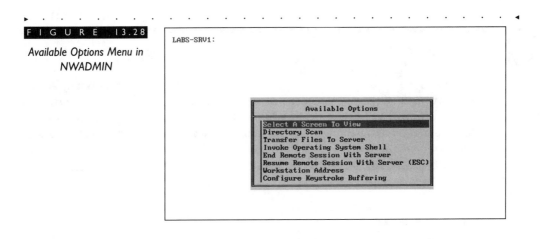

LABS-SRU1:

Available Options

Select A Screen To View
Directory Scan
Transfer Files To Server
Invoke Operating System Shell
End Remote Session With Server
Resume Remote Session With Server (ESC)
Workstation Address
Configure Keystroke Buffering

	KEYS	TASK
TABLE 13.10	Alt+F1	View the RMF Available Options menu.
IntranetWare RCONSOLE Function Keys	Alt+F2	Exit RCONSOLE.
	Alt+F3	Move forward through the server console screens. Similar to Alt+Esc at the physical server console itself.
	Alt+F4	Move backward through the server console screens.
	Alt+F5	Show your workstation address.
	F1	Display remote console help from within the Available Options menu.
	Esc	Resume remote session with server.

We've brought our LAN from birth through childhood and the rewards of adulthood. Through IntranetWare configuration and management, we've transformed a relatively limp and lifeless LAN into a powerful and productive business tool. How did we do it?

In IntranetWare configuration, we walked Leia through the five steps of childhood. She learned to walk (workstation connectivity), talk (login scripts), and get along with others in preschool (menu system). Then she enjoyed the many splendors of school (network applications) and finally moved out (e-mail).

In IntranetWare management, Leia continued her "life span" through marriage (server management) and children of her own (workstation management). Now, in her later years, Leia planned her pension (SMS) and finally retired to Tahiti (RMF).

REAL WORLD

RMF is cool. RMF is so cool, in fact, that it enables you to remotely install IntranetWare. Talk about extended vacations! This means you can actually install an IntranetWare server in Camelot from Tahiti. Think of it. Sand between your toes and SERVER.EXE bouncing through your head. Just be sure to copy the PUBLIC files locally, or you're in for an unhappy phone bill!

SMART LINK

Explore your own IntranetWare Childhood at http://www.kids.com or Adulthood at http://www.aronson.com/ppp/birth.html.

QUIZ

This pretty much sums up IntranetWare childhood and adulthood:

"Individuals who are completely devoid of sapience in all respects indicate a propensity to cast themselves without hesitation onto those areas where beings of a heavenly nature would reflect seriously and be timorous about proceeding."

(Q13-8)

It was a long and winding road but certainly an adventure for all of us. No matter how much you might want to, you can't just set up the server and walk away. You're a CNE, and, as one, your life is irrevocably bound to the childhood and adulthood of IntranetWare.

Have a Nice Day!

CASE STUDY: WINDOWS 95 CLIENT 32 INSTALLATION FOR ACME

Very good. Now that Albert and his gang have their servers up and running, it's time to activate the workstations. Your next mission, should you choose to accept it, is to install the ACME Labs clients. We're going to use the CD-ROM method, because we like it. Besides, it's the most common.

All right, here we go. Don't fall asleep at the wheel — remember, the fate of the whole world is in your hands. "No, not that key!" Just kidding.

Complete the following steps:

1. Execute the Client 32 for Windows 95 installation program. Insert the Novell IntranetWare/NetWare 4.11 Operating System CD-ROM in your CD-ROM drive. Click on the Windows 95 Start button, then click on the Run ... button. Type **D:\PRODUCTS\WIN95\IBM_ENU\SETUP** (or the appropriate drive letter for your CD-ROM drive), then click on OK. The NetWare Client 32 License Agreement screen will be displayed. Read the agreement, then click Yes to accept the terms of the agreement. (You won't be allowed to install the client software otherwise.) The Client 32 Installation screen will then be displayed.

2. Click on the Start button in the NetWare Client 32 Installation window to begin the installation. The program will then automatically install and configure Client 32 with default properties. You may be asked to insert your Windows 95 CD-ROM and supply a source location for the CAB files. If so, insert your Windows 95 CD-ROM, then key in D:\WIN95 (or the appropriate drive letter for your CD-ROM) as the location of the files.

3. When setup is complete, click on Customize. Click on Novell NetWare Client 32, then click on Properties.

    a. The Client 32 tab should be active.

        *   Leave the Preferred Server field blank. (This field is used for Bindery Services connections.)

        *   Type **ACME_TREE** in the Preferred Tree field.

- Type **ACME** in the Name context field.

- The first network drive is drive F: by default. If drive F: is unavailable because you are already using it for a local device, indicate the first available drive letter in the "First network drive" field.

b. Click on the login tab. Make sure that "Display connection page," "Display script page," "Display variables page," and "Save settings when exiting Login" boxes are all checked, then click on OK.

c. Click on OK again.

4. If prompted to configure the resources for your board, add the values for the interrupt, I/O address range, and the memory address.

5. Wait while Windows builds a driver information database.

6. Click on Yes to restart your computer.

7. After your workstation reboots, the Network login dialog box will be displayed. Key in the Admin password in the password field and click on OK. The Login Results screen will be displayed next. Review the contents of the screen, then click on Close.

CASE STUDY: SERVER MANAGEMENT AT ACME

Now you're ready. Let's go on an "incredible journey" through one of ACME's most exciting servers — ACME-SRV1. Don't blink; you might miss something. This IntranetWare exploratorium is packed with console commands, NLMs, NDS, and pixie dust. Hold on tight!

Let's start at the beginning. As you know, before you can log into the network, you must load the 16-bit client connection files. This is accomplished using the "Client-16 Connectivity" guidelines from Chapter 12. During this process, the 16-bit connection files are automatically loaded each time you boot your workstation. Let's investigate how this is accomplished.

First, take a look at your AUTOEXEC.BAT file. You'll notice that the Client Installation program added two lines: one to call the STARTNET.BAT batch file and the other to add C:\NWCLIENT to the path. Next, review the STARTNET.BAT file. You'll see that it designates the language to be used and loads the connection files and the NetWare DOS Requester. Finally, examine the CONFIG.SYS file. You'll find that the client installation program added a LASTDRIVE statement that is used by the DOS Requester to determine what drives are available to be used as IntranetWare drives.

Now that you understand how these files are loaded, try to accomplish the following tasks:

1. First, check to see if the files are currently loaded in workstation RAM by typing

   MEM /C /P

2. Next, unload the connection files in the reverse order from which they were originally loaded, using the /U (that is, unload) switch with each command. (Look at the C:\NWCLIENT\STARTNET.BAT file if you want to see how they were originally loaded.)

   Question 1: What commands did you use to unload the connection files from workstation RAM?

3. Finally, load all four of the connection files manually, specifying "maximum verbosity" for VLM.EXE. (If you don't remember which switch to use, use the command line help method for viewing options that can be used with VLM.EXE.)

> **Question 2**: What command did you use to list the options available for use with VLM.EXE?

> **Question 3**: What command did you use to load VLM.EXE with maximum verbosity?

As soon as you execute VLM.EXE with the appropriate switch, various information will be displayed on the screen. Use the information displayed to answer the following questions:

> **Question 4**: Which version of VLM.EXE are you running?

> **Question 5**: What type of RAM is being used to load the VLMs?

> **Question 6**: Which is the first VLM loaded by VLM.EXE? Which is the last?

4. Once you have successfully loaded the connection files, log into the network by typing

```
F:
```

```
LOGIN .ADMIN.ACME
```

5. The next thing you want to do is to explore the Remote Management Facility (RMF). As you know, RMF is a wonderful feature you can use to access the file server console screen from your workstation. Because security is a concern, we will load this utility using an encrypted password.

The first thing you must do is to activate the RMF on the server by performing the following tasks at the server console, ending each entry by pressing Enter:

a. Load the REMOTE.NLM utility by typing

   LOAD REMOTE

   IntranetWare will prompt you for an RMF password. Enter it now:

   CATHY

b. RMF is now active, but your password is not protected. You can encrypt the password by typing

   REMOTE ENCRYPT

   Once again, IntranetWare will ask you for a password. Enter the same one:

   CATHY

c. IntranetWare then responds with an encrypted LOAD statement such as: LOAD REMOTE -e 14572BFD3AFEAE4E4759. (The number will be different every time you try this.) This is the encrypted representation of the password CATHY. Next, when you are asked whether you'd like for this command to be written to SYS:SYSTEM\LDREMOTE.NCF, type

   Y

d. Load RSPX.NLM by typing

   LOAD RSPX

e. Now that you've activated the RMF on the server, you need to run the RCONSOLE utility on the workstation by typing:

   RCONSOLE

   Read the message that is displayed regarding the fact that MS Windows may cause RCONSOLE to behave erratically, then press Enter. Because our workstation is connected to the server via cable rather than via modem, select SPX when you are asked to choose the connection type. Next, choose the IntranetWare file server from the Available Servers menu by selecting ACME-SRV1.

Finally, when you are asked to provide the password, type:

CATHY

At this point, the same information that is displayed on the file server console screen should be displayed on your workstation screen.

Question 7: How can you tell that you are viewing the file server console screen?

Question 8: What type of warning is displayed at the bottom of the screen? Why is this important?

Because you are running the RCONSOLE utility, you can now execute console commands at your workstation rather than having to type them at the file server console.

6. Next, let's take a look at the INSTALL.NLM utility. This utility is used for various functions such as installing the NetWare operating system and additional products, creating NetWare partitions and volumes, mirroring the hard disk, copying SYSTEM and PUBLIC files to the SYS: volume, and creating/editing the AUTOEXEC.NCF and STARTUP.NCF configuration files. To load the INSTALL.NLM utility, type

LOAD INSTALL

The first thing you want to do in this utility is to add the RMF commands to the AUTOEXEC.NCF file so that it will be activated with the encrypted password every time you boot the server. Select the NCF Files options choice from the Installation Options menu and press Enter, then select the Edit AUTOEXEC.NCF file option from the Available NCF Files Options menu and press Enter. The AUTO-

EXEC .NCF file will then be displayed on the screen. Add the following two lines to the end of the file:

```
LDREMOTE
```

```
LOAD RSPX
```

Save the file and return to the Available NCF Files Options menu. Next, choose the appropriate options to view (edit) the AUTO EXEC.NCF and STARTUP.NCF configuration files so that you can answer the questions listed here:

> **Question 9:** Which configuration file loads the LAN driver? Which one loads the disk driver?

> **Question 10:** What time server type is designated for this server?

> **Question 11:** If you have an Ethernet network board, what frame type is being used?

Next, press Esc once to return to the Installation options menu. Choose the appropriate options from this menu to answer the following questions:

> **Question 12:** What percentage of the NetWare partition is reserved for the hot fix area?

> **Question 13**: Is this disk mirrored?

> **Question 14:** What volume block size is being used for SYS:, and why? On the SYS: volume are file compression, block suballocation, and data migration turned on or off?

> **Question 15:** For how many connections is this server currently licensed?

> **Question 16**: Which menu choice would you select to install DOS/Windows Client files?

7. Let's leave INSTALL.NLM and move onto the MONITOR.NLM utility. To load the MONITOR.NLM utility, type

    `LOAD MONITOR`

    Press the Tab key to expand the General Information window.

    Question 17: How long has your server been up and what do the four sets of numbers separated by colons represent? At what level is your CPU processor utilization? What is the total number of cache buffers currently being used? What is the number of current service processes in use? How many licensed connections are available at the moment? Press Esc to contract the General Information window.

    Question 18: What is the server's hot fix status? Have any blocks been redirected to the hot fix area?

    Question 19: What protocol(s) is/are currently supported on your server?

    Question 20: What is the load filename of the IntranetWare Directory Services Module? What is the size of this file?

    Question 21: Finally, cruise over to Processor Utilization. Which IntranetWare process occupies the most server CPU time?

8. Now let's exit MONITOR and warp ahead to SERVMAN. To load SERVMAN, type

    `LOAD SERVMAN`

    Question 22: Which general statistics overlap MONITOR functionality?

    Question 23: Explore some SET parameters. What console command could be used instead of SERVMAN to change SET parameters?

Question 24: Next, switch to the server console without exiting SERVMAN. What method did you use? Next, check out the RMF Available Options menu. What method did you use to activate it?

Question 25: Which option is similar to one found in INSTALL.NLM? How is this one different?

Question 26: Press Esc to switch back to the server console. Use the appropriate console command to activate the RIP tracking screen. What command did you use? What is ACME's tree name? How about the IPX internal network number of other servers? Where else can you get this information?

Question 27: Switch to the server console and send yourself a message. What command did you use? Acknowledge receipt of the message. How did you do so? Aren't such messages annoying? How can you set your workstation so that it does not receive messages from other users?

Question 28: What name spaces are loaded on the SYS: volume?

9.   Turn off the RIP tracking screen and exit the SERVMAN utility.

Question 29: What method could you use to review a quick list of IntranetWare console commands that are available?

Question 30: Use a console command to see what NLMs are currently loaded. Which console command did you use? What NLM would give you a count of the NLMs that are currently loaded?

10. Exit RCONSOLE, log off the network, and call it a day! Very good, you lived through the exploratorium without a scratch. Now, wasn't that fun?

See Appendix C for answers.

Circle the 20 IntranetWare Management terms hidden in this word search puzzle using the hints provided.

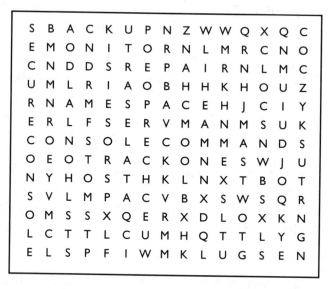

```
S  B  A  C  K  U  P  N  Z  W  W  Q  X  Q  C
E  M  O  N  I  T  O  R  N  L  M  R  C  N  O
C  N  D  D  S  R  E  P  A  I  R  N  L  M  C
U  M  L  R  I  A  O  B  H  H  K  H  O  U  Z
R  N  A  M  E  S  P  A  C  E  H  J  C  I  Y
E  R  L  F  S  E  R  V  M  A  N  M  S  U  K
C  O  N  S  O  L  E  C  O  M  M  A  N  D  S
O  E  O  T  R  A  C  K  O  N  E  S  W  J  U
N  Y  H  O  S  T  H  K  L  N  X  T  B  O  T
S  V  L  M  P  A  C  V  B  X  S  W  S  Q  R
O  M  S  S  X  Q  E  R  X  D  L  O  X  K  N
L  C  T  T  L  C  U  M  H  Q  T  T  L  Y  G
E  L  S  P  F  I  W  M  K  L  U  G  S  E  N
```

Hints:

1. Executed at the colon prompt.
2. NLM used to detect and correct problems in the NDS database.
3. Term used to refer to the server to which a tape backup unit is attached.
4. ODI layer that acts as a switchboard to route packets between MLID and the protocol stack.
5. NLM used to view server RAM activity for troubleshooting and optimization purposes.
6. Module that is used to allow the storage of non-DOS files on a NetWare 4.11 server.
7. Modular server programs.
8. Architecture that allows multiple LAN drivers and protocols to coexist on network systems.
9. Workstation command line utility used to remotely access the server console.

10. IntranetWare feature that allows remote access of the file server console.
11. NLM used to allow RCONSOLE to access a server over a direct connection.
12. Protocol used by servers to advertise their services on an IntranetWare internetwork.
13. NLM used to back up and restore data for a server, workstation, or service.
14. Console command used to increase security at the server console.
15. NLM used to view and configure system parameters. Can be used in place of the SET command.
16. Used to pass commands and information between SBACKUP and Target Service Agents.
17. IntranetWare backup/restore engine used by the SBACKUP utility.
18. Console command used to display the RIP tracking screen.
19. Program used to process data moving between a target and an SMS-compliant backup engine such as SBACKUP.
20. Modular executable program that runs on a DOS workstation and enables communication with an IntranetWare server.

See Appendix C for answers.

IntranetWare Printing

Adding users to IntranetWare printing is like putting Godzilla in a mosh pit.

Now that you've lived through the life span of a LAN, I think you're ready to discover one of the greatest mysteries of life — printing. The meaning of life? — Nah. The Great Pyramids? — Nah. The Sphinx? — No chance. Printing has them all beat. More brain cells have been lost pondering IntranetWare printing than any other philosophical question.

Why? It's not that printing itself is so puzzling. As a matter of fact, the concept of printing is fairly easy to comprehend — you click a button on the workstation, and a piece of paper comes out of the printer down the hall. No rocket science here. It's true. The fundamental architecture of IntranetWare printing is solid — rock solid. So, why is it such a mystery? One word — users! It's the users' fault. They introduce so much complexity to printing, it's a wonder the paper finds its way anywhere, let alone to the correct printer. And to make matters worse, users expect too much:

▸ They want the page to be formatted correctly every time.

▸ They want their print jobs to arrive at the "correct" printer (when they don't even know what that means).

▸ They always want their jobs to come out first.

So, how do you possibly satisfy the lofty expectations of your users while maintaining a rock-solid IntranetWare printing architecture? That's the greatest mystery of them all. Fortunately, Novell is on your side, and they've come up with some answers. The IntranetWare printing system has been improved dramatically in several ways — easier setup, better management, more flexibility. They certainly haven't solved your mystery entirely, but they've given you some great tools to help you crack the case — and we're gonna learn all about them.

In this chapter, we're going to explore this great printing mystery and discover some startling answers. You're going to learn about the four steps of printing setup, all the great tools available for printing management, and some tips for printing troubleshooting. But first, we need to spend a few moments meditating on the true essence of printing. You must become one with the printer. It works. Trust me.

The Essence of Printing

Now, repeat after me — I *am* a printer, I *am* a printer. The best way to handle IntranetWare printing is to *be* IntranetWare printing. This is the essence of printing.

Actually, the essence of printing is a little more technical than that. It is a wondrous journey from the user's workstation to the network printer down the hall. Here's how it works:

- ▶ *Capturing* — The job moves from the local workstation to the IntranetWare server.

- ▶ *Moving to the queue* — It waits in line (first come; first served).

- ▶ *The print server* — The brains behind the process.

- ▶ *At the printer* — Finally, the print job arrives at the printer and prints correctly (fingers crossed).

This is the Printing Journey. But before we take a closer look at the Journey, let's take a history lesson in network printing. Get out your notebooks.

ZEN

"School, thank God for school. I need those seven hours of personal time. I mean, how can I continue to be the bright, vivacious Nanny everyone knows and loves if I have to spend all day with the kids?"

Nanny Fine

GETTING STARTED

We already know what a great job IntranetWare does with its file services, but printing is just as important to users. Initially, all users need access to file storage and shared print services to get the most out of IntranetWare.

Setting up and using printing services under IntranetWare can be a challenging part of setting up the network. But printing isn't as difficult as it seems — especially if you understand the system's essence. This chapter provides some insight into the overall architecture of network printing, and, in the process, should make print services setup a whole lot easier.

Printing By Yourself

Most people are familiar with printing from a local workstation. In this scenario, a PC or other station has a stand-alone printer (a LaserJet, dot matrix, or other type of printer) that is dedicated to that station. With a dedicated printer, you have much less to worry about when it comes to printing documents. Issues such as *print drivers* or notification when the print job is complete do not apply. You can see the printer on your desk (or nearby, at least), and hopefully the correct print driver (with the proper version) has already been set up. When the document is printed, you need only reach over and grab it from the printer.

To better understand network printing, it helps to have a solid foundation of how local printing works. Starting from the beginning, the workstation has one or more local ports. Most PCs have at least one *parallel* port, labeled LPT1, LPT2, and so on. Many PCs also have a *serial* port as well. Serial ports typically are used as communication ports (that is, for modems), because they work faster than do parallel ports.

When you begin printing (if a printer is attached), the default output for printing is LPT1. LPT1 outputs to parallel port one, LPT2 outputs to parallel port two, and so on. Serial output is not enabled by default. If you print something, the software program you are using will usually default to LPT1. Otherwise, it may ask you which port you prefer (LPT1-LPT*n*).

Once you have hit the magic button to print something, the machine takes over. If you are running strictly DOS (no Windows in sight), then the machine may halt while printing. This is because DOS is set up to do only one thing at a time. But there are ways to trick DOS into not halting your machine, such as by using the PRINT command. This command will take the print data and store it locally on the hard disk while it feeds the data to the printer in the background. This will allow you to do other things while the system is printing (for more information on the PRINT command, see your DOS reference manual). If you don't trick the computer, you'll have to wait for the document (or other print job) to finish printing before the machine will return control back to you (just like the old *Outer Limits* program, huh!).

If you are printing to a serial port under DOS, you'll need to do a bit of preparation. First, you must *redirect* the LPT output from the parallel port to a serial port. This is done by using another DOS command called MODE. The MODE command works similarly to how network printing works in general. MODE simply takes LPT1 output and redirects it to the serial port. The program *thinks* it's sending to the LPT port. DOS takes the output, however, and streams it to the serial device (see Figure 14.1).

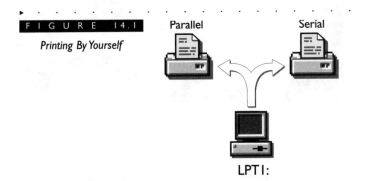

FIGURE 14.1

Printing By Yourself

Parallel   Serial

LPT1:

If you are using Windows (3.*x* or Windows 95), a neat little program called Print Manager can be used to manage local printing from Windows. Print Manager also provides the same capabilities as the DOS PRINT program — such as the ability to spool the print data locally and feed it to the printer. Print Manager has a few more features than PRINT. For example, it will allow you to view the current printing job, delete it, or postpone it.

Typically, when you are printing to the network, those features are already provided by IntranetWare utilities, thereby making Print Manager functions unnecessary. Many users will disable Print Manager when using IntranetWare for this reason. Print Manager can actually slow network printing because the print job will be spooled once locally, and then again to the network queue.

Instead of disabling Print Manager, you can select the Print Net Jobs Direct option (select Options and then Network Settings from the Print Manager). This will enable any network print jobs to spool directly to a IntranetWare queue and bypass local hard disk spooling. Check out the screen in Figure 14.2.

FIGURE 14.2

Network Printing in
Microsoft Windows

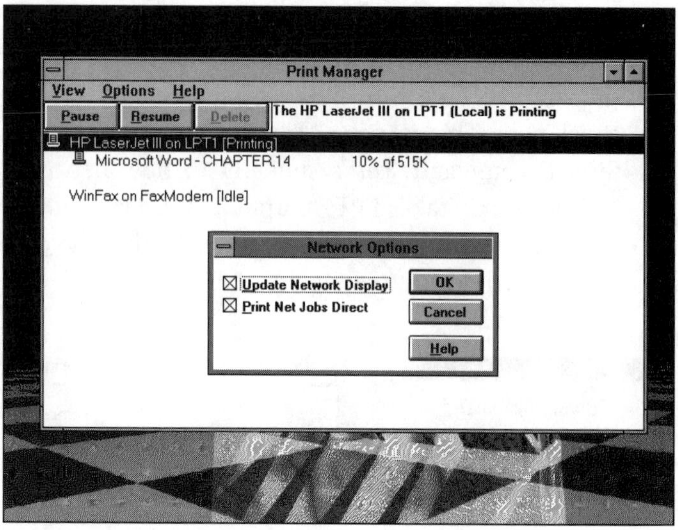

Once you attach a workstation to a network, the rules change a little. Some considerations are

1 • Does the workstation have the proper driver for the network printer?

2 • How will you know when the document has completed printing?

3 • How does the server know when you have stopped sending print data?

4 • What if the printer runs out of paper? How will you or the administrator be notified?

Printing on a Network

The flow for network printing works something like this. The user has enabled printing to a network device from the workstation, or the administrator has automatically enabled it via a batch file (AUTOEXEC.BAT) or a login script (Container, System, Personal, and so on). This is similar to using the MODE command under DOS, except that when an application prints, the output gets redirected to a queue on a server somewhere. The workstation command line utility to enable printing is called CAPTURE.

When CAPTURE is executed, the local LPT port that is being redirected to the network is specified. By default, this is usually LPT1. With this approach, the application may send output via LPT2 and the IntranetWare shell knows to capture data coming from the LPT2 port and redirect it to the appropriate queue. As a default, the CAPTURE command automatically assumes that data will be sent via LPT1. Most applications also assume that this is the default port on which to send data. Remember, the LPT port is merely a channel, port, or stream as far as the application knows. It may *point* at a parallel port, a serial port, a file, or the network queue. This concept is shown in Figure 14.3.

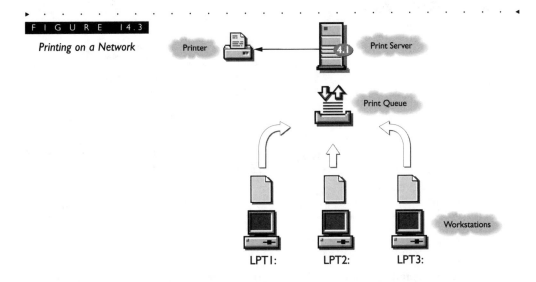

F I G U R E   14.3

Printing on a Network

Printer

Print Server

Print Queue

Workstations

LPT1:   LPT2:   LPT3:

Understanding Print Queues   Now that capturing is on, the user starts to print via the application, DOS, or Windows. The output can be an existing file (such as DATA.TXT) or raw data from a word processing program (such as WordPerfect). The data being printed will be sent to an area on a specified server called a *queue*. Queues are nothing more than a subdirectory with a *.QDR extension. The data will be spooled into an automatically created file. When the user signals that he or she is finished sending data, the file is closed and prepared for printing.

Understanding Print Servers   Now that the data file is closed and ready, it can be serviced from the QUEUE directory. A *print server* is a device that is assigned to watch a particular queue or queues. When it sees a job waiting to be serviced, it opens the job (file) and starts to read from it. The print server then prints the data in the file to a printer attached to the print server. *Which* printer it sends the file to depends on the setup of the print server (see the "IntranetWare Printing Setup" section). See Figure 14.4 for a quick preview. Incidentally, the IntranetWare native print server must by loaded on the server as PSERVER.NLM.

▶ . . . . ◀

F I G U R E   14.4

Understanding Print Servers

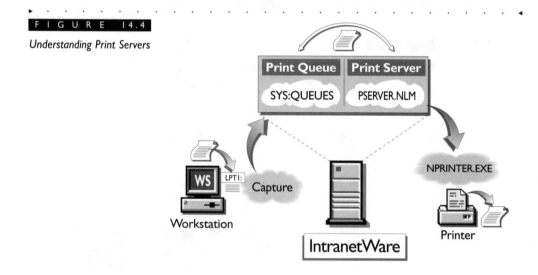

Understanding Printers   As the print server services the request, it attempts to print the data to a locally attached printer (physically attached to the print server) or a remotely attached printer (perhaps a printer attached to a workstation, but remotely attached via software to the print server). If the printer is a remote printer, the print server *thinks* it is attached locally, when, in fact, the data is being sent across the network to where the remote printer physically resides.

Once the contents of the data file have been printed, the data file residing in the queue will be deleted to recover the disk space. In addition, if it has been set up to do so, a notification will be sent to the user (and possibly others) that the job has been successfully printed and is ready to be picked up.

QUIZ

*Let's begin our IntranetWare "sleuthing" with a simple one. Here goes . . . .
At a college reunion, a group of men and women were discussing their
lives after they had received their undergraduate degrees. It turned out
that everyone in the group had gone on to receive an advanced degree, so
each of them had two degrees. Each degree holder had both a B.A. and
an M.S., an M.A., an M.B.A., or an M.F.A. Half of them had an M.S., one-
quarter had an M.A., one-sixth had an M.B.A., and just one had an M.F.A.
How many were there in total?*

(Q14-1)
(See Appendix C for all quiz answers.)

THE BEGINNING: CAPTURING

This is the beginning of your printing journey. Hold on to your hat. As we
learned earlier, IntranetWare printing is a wondrous journey from the user's
workstation to the network printer down the hall. Here's how it works:

▸ *The Beginning: Capturing* — The job moves from the local workstation to
the IntranetWare server.

▸ *Moving to the queue* — It waits in line (first come; first served).

▸ *The print server* — The brains behind the process.

▸ *The Destination: At the printer* — Finally, the print job arrives at the
printer and prints correctly (fingers crossed).

In this first stop, we will explore the details of IntranetWare printing from the
PC workstation's perspective. Two areas will be covered: printing from DOS and
printing from Windows. This discussion assumes that you have some knowledge
of DOS and Windows in order to understand the elements of network printing.

This section also assumes that a printing system has already been set up (print
server, print queue, and remote/local printer) and that the user has been granted
access. If not, you can jump ahead to the section "IntranetWare Printing Setup"
and then return to this section.

Capturing with DOS

To enable network printing, you must first tell the network client (for example, Client 32, VLM, or NETx) that you want to print to the network. You can do this by using the IntranetWare command-line utility CAPTURE, or the IntranetWare menu utility NETUSER (see Figure 14.5).

▶ · ◀

F I G U R E   14.5

Capturing a Local Port

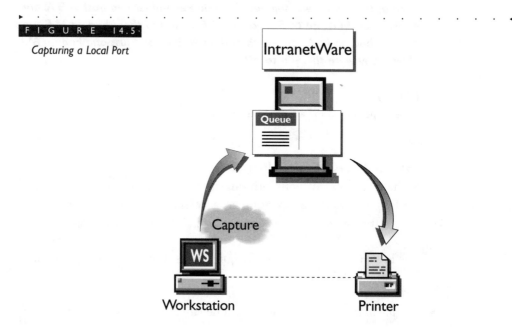

WHAT'S NEW

WHAT'S NEW

The printer redirection information stored in Client 32 is temporary and is lost when you log out or disconnect from the network. For this reason, you should automate Capturing with the help of login scripts or batch files.

The CAPTURE command is included with IntranetWare, and allows you to start and end network printing. It can be used in a DOS-only environment, or it can be executed *before* starting Windows 3.*x* to allow capturing under Windows. In Windows 95 environments, you can use the Win95 Print Manager or NWUSER (a Windows 3.1 IntranetWare tool). We'll explore these options in a little while.

CAPTURE has several command line options that allow you to customize how the network capture will work. These options include:

- ► /? — This option will show help for the CAPTURE command if you need it. You can also use CAPTURE /? ALL to show every possible option and explanation for CAPTURE.

- ► /SH (Show) — This is a very useful command to see how you are currently captured to the network. CAPTURE /SH will show all LPT ports currently enabled for network printing, as well as other flags (such as banners, copies, and so on). The Show parameter will *not* initiate a print capture. It is for informational purposes only.

- ► /S (Server) — This option allows you to specify the server to which you want to print. In IntranetWare environments, this is usually unnecessary because the user is oblivious to servers per se. When capturing, the user can just specify the printer name using a distinguished name (for example, HP5-P1.CRIME.TOKYO.ACME), and the server will automatically be found and attached. In a NetWare 3 environment, however, /S can be used to point to a server with a particular printer/queue that you want to use. If you are not logged in/attached to that particular server, then the CAPTURE command will attempt to log in as GUEST. If the GUEST account does not exist, printing on that server will be denied to the user. This is a good reason (in an open environment) to keep the GUEST account around on a public NetWare 3 server.

- ► /Q (Queue) — This command line option allows the user to specify the queue to which data should be sent. In a NetWare 3 environment, it can be combined with the /S option to specify a server name and queue name that the user desires. In a IntranetWare network, the queue name can be a relative distinguished name (for example, HP5-PQ1) or a distinguished name (for example, HP5-PQ1.CRIME.TOKYO.ACME). If a distinguished name is used, there is much less of a chance of ambiguity between printer and queue names. For example, if the user is in context CYBER.WHITE.CRIME.TOKYO.ACME, and he or she wants to print to a queue in BLUE.CRIME.TOKYO.ACME, there is a chance that the relative distinguished name HPIII-PQ1 may exist in both locations (and it does). In such a case, if a user types in the command **CAPTURE /Q=HPIII-PQ1**, the printer captured will be the one in CYBER.WHITE.CRIME.TOKYO.ACME.

▸ /AU (AutoEndCap) — This option allows the application to decide if the user is finished sending capture data. For example, when a user sends data, how does the network shell know when the application/user is finished sending data? There are three ways:

  1. The user stops sending capture data (via the CAPTURE command — discussed later).

  2. The application sends a NetWare-specific command to signal the end of capture data (this is the case with network-aware applications such as WordPerfect).

  3. The shell assumes you are finished via AutoEndCap or timeouts. When AutoEndCap is enabled, the shell assumes you are finished sending data if you leave the application that began sending capture data. Consider a user who enables capture (via the CAPTURE command), sends a print job via the application (such as WordPerfect), and then exits the application. The shell can safely assume that since the user exited, he or she was finished sending data. If AutoEndCap were *not* enabled, the user would still have to terminate CAPTURE to signal the end of capture data.

▸ /TI (TimeOut) — This option is similar to the AutoEndCap command, except that the user does not need to exit the application. Instead, a timeout is specified when capture was started (such as CAPTURE TI=8). This means the network shell will assume that once capture data has been sent, if no more data has been sent after 8 seconds, the job will automatically be completed and scheduled for printing. The only problem with this command is what happens when an application pauses between spurts of data. For example, if a database program were sending data and then paused 10 seconds before sending page totals, the first data would be sent as one print job and the page totals would be sent as a second, thereby violating the integrity of the job.

▶ /K (Keep/No Keep) — This option tells the shell what to do if something interrupts the flow of data from the workstation to the queue on the server. For example, if a print job were started and then interrupted when the workstation lost power, all data sent to the queue up to that point would be lost if Keep were not enabled. If Keep is enabled, any data sent up to that point will be printed.

▶ /T (Tabs) — The Tabs option was included from the earlier versions of IntranetWare when printing documents was not always done through the application. As a result, when a document was printed, the proper spaces were not inserted for a tab character. Therefore, the IntranetWare shell was enabled to observe a tab character during the print process, remove it, and send the proper amount of spaces to the printer. This option was enabled in versions of NetWare 3.11 and below. The default amount of spaces per tab character was eight. Current versions no longer support this as a default. This is because most applications now format their own printing and convert tabs to the proper spaces. This option, if enabled, can cause printing problems, since some graphics programs or other raw text may have characters that signify a tab. If T is enabled, the shell will strip the tab, send the spaces, and you'll end up with garbled print output. NT (No Tabs) is the default.

▶ /C (Copies) — This option specifies the number of copies you want of the printout. The default is 1.

▶ /B (Banner) — This option (enabled by default) will send a print banner at the beginning of the print job. You can specify the name of the person who submitted the document, as well as the name of the job itself (B=user name and N=job name). If nothing is specified, then the document will either be the name of the file being printed (if an existing file is being printed) or PRN: if the print job is output from an application. The name will be the username of the person who submitted it.

▸ /NB (No Banner) — This option disables the Banner option. It is usually used when a small office is involved or with a local workgroup.

▸ /NFF (NoFormFeed) — This option prevents an additional page from being sent at the end of the print job. This may be necessary with some applications that do not send a form feed after a print job has been submitted.

▸ /FF (FormFeed) — This option sends a form feed after the job has been completed (default). This is necessary when the application doesn't do this automatically, since the last page of the document may not be ejected by the printer (especially when using a LaserJet printer). NFF (No Form Feed) turns off form feed.

▸ /L=n (Local Port Number) — DOS provides several channels for print output. The first and primary channel is LPT1. There can be more than one, however. Many applications today can output print data on LPT2-LPT*n*. Most default to LPT1. If your application is outputting on LPT2, you must use this command to tell IntranetWare which LPT port is being used. For example, you might have a local printer attached to LPT1 and you want network printing to go out via LPT2. The CAPTURE command would look like this: **CAPTURE /L=2**. That way, through the application, you can print to LPT1 and the output will go to the local printer. If you print out to LPT2, however, the output will go to the network. Keep in mind, you can print to "logical" parallel ports even if a physical one doesn't exist.

▸ /F (Form) — Forms allow network users to share the same printer for a variety of functions. When (and if) forms are defined, a user can submit a job of a particular form type and the print server will ensure that the printer being used is ready to accept a print job of that form type. For example, this option would allow one user to submit a purchase requisition (that requires a preprinted form), while another user could submit an invoice (also requiring a preprinted form). When the job is submitted, a form name or number is used to specify which form is to be used when printing the job. Form names and numbers are defined using the PRINTDEF utility.

▸ /CR (Create) — This option allows the user to send output to a file instead of to a print queue. When this option is specified, the user must also specify the filename to which output should be directed. If the file does not exist, it will be created automatically. After the first print job output has completed, subsequent print jobs will be sent to a normal queue. For example, if we typed **CAPTURE /CR=SYS:TEST.TXT /Q=.HP5-PQ1.CRIME.TOKYO.ACME,** the data will be captured to the printer HP5-P1, but the initial output will go to file TEST.TXT. We then submit data for print (through the application or an existing file). The data will go into the file TEST.TXT instead of being printed! If we print again, the data will be spooled to HP5-P1 and printed on the physical printer. This parameter is useful when you need to encapsulate an entire print job (printer escape codes and all) into a file. Another user could merely submit the entire file for printing (without the source application being available), and the data will print successfully.

▸ /NOTI (Notify) — With this option, provided the print server has been created to support it, a message will be sent to the user *after* the job has been printed successfully. In addition, the print server can be created to notify the user or other responsible parties (such as Admin or the print server administrator) if any problems arose (for example, if the printer ran out of paper or if it went off-line). NNOTI disables notification.

▸ /EC (EndCapture) — This option is used to return LPT output to the local port (usually the local parallel port). Since the CAPTURE command could have been started for LPT2, LPT3, and so on, ENDCAP can be used with the L=n switch to turn off CAPTURE on a specific port.

A sample CAPTURE command might look like this:

```
CAPTURE /NB /L=2 /K /Q=HP5-PQ1.CRIME.TOKYO.ACME /TI=10
```

For this print job:

▸ No banner will be prefixed to the print job.

▸ Output will be via LPT2.

▸ Data will be kept and printed *if* the capture is not formally closed.

▸ The queue to be used is HP5-PQ1.CRIME.TOKYO.ACME.

▸ A timeout of 10 seconds will be used.

SMART LINK

For a complete list of the IntranetWare CAPTURE parameters, consult the on-line IntranetWare documentation at http://www.novell.com/manuals.

In the menu world, NETUSER provides a simpler capturing interface for users. The NETUSER (also known as NetWare User Tools for DOS) main menu is shown in Figure 14.6. As you can see, it's a full-service user utility. From a printing point of view, it allows users to capture local ports and manage their current print jobs.

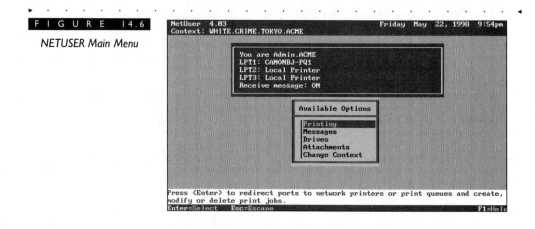

FIGURE 14.6

NETUSER Main Menu

Just like with the other DOS utilities, it's important to note the context at the very top of the NETUSER screen. Anything done in NETUSER from this point will be from the .WHITE.CRIME.TOKYO.ADMIN context.

You should also notice the box above the "Available options" menu, indicating current user and capturing information. In Figure 14.6, we are currently logged in as Admin and LPT1 is captured to the queue servicing the Canon Bubble Jet. To capture a printer port with NETUSER, under the Printers option, select the port you want to capture and choose Change Printers. You are then presented with a list of printers and print queues in your current context. Use the arrow keys to highlight the printer you want (or the print queue assigned to it) and press Enter. Any capturing done through NETUSER will remain active during the current login session only. One disadvantage this utility has in comparison with its Windows (NWADMIN) counterpart is that there is no way to make the capturing permanent.

In addition to capturing, NETUSER allows users to manage their current print jobs. When you select Printing from the "Available options" menu, you are shown a list of the available LPT ports. If you select an LPT port, you are given two options: Print Jobs and Change Printers. Since we have already captured LPT1 to the CANONBJ-PQ1 queue, we can select the queue by pressing Enter and view a list of print jobs currently in the queue. If you select a print job, you are presented with the Printing Management menu. This is the same screen we'll use later to manage printing in PCONSOLE. Be patient.

Now let's explore the GUI world, and see what capturing is like with Windows.

Capturing with Windows

There are three ways to CAPTURE a local port under Windows:

▶ Use the CAPTURE command, and then start Windows.

▶ Use the Windows 95 Print Manager.

▶ Use the Windows 3.1 NWUSER utility.

Since we have already covered CAPTURE, let's start our GUI journey with a closer look at the Windows 95 Print Manager.

You can redirect print jobs in Windows 95 using the Printer Properties screen shown in Figure 14.7. Here's how you get there. Click Start, Settings, and then Control Panel. Finally, click Printers and you'll get a list of available printers.

Highlight your printer, click the right mouse button, and choose Properties. You will be greeted with the input screen shown in Figure 14.7.

F I G U R E   14.7

Windows 95 Print Manager

As you can see, there's a plethora of great printing functionality available in this screen. You can

► Redirect print jobs to a printer or queue.

► Configure print job redirection using options such as Enable Banner. This is the equivalent to the switch settings in CAPTURE

► Make redirection permanent (unlike CAPTURE or NETUSER).

► Select the correct parallel port and print driver.

Windows 95 provides a native configuration screen for printer redirection (as seen in Figure 14.7). Windows 3.1, however, relies on a special IntranetWare utility for capturing. It's called NetWare User Tools for Windows (or NWUSER). To start NWUSER, find the icon under the NetWare Tools Program Group. This is installed as part of the NetWare DOS Requester or Client 32 connectivity software. NWUSER is simply a launcher for the Novell Driver for Windows. Another option is to launch File Manager and choose Disk/Network Connections. This will also launch the NetWare Tools utility.

TIP

If you have a sound card, choose the NetWare Settings option from the button bar (the one that has a key) and click once over the Novell icon in the upper left-hand corner — surprise!

Once the tool is running, choose the printer icon (third icon from the left on the button bar). This will display all the printers available to you in the browser window to the right. You can also walk the tree to find other printers and queues in your network. You will also see any queues available for any NetWare 3.12 or 2.2 servers that you are logged into.

To capture to a printer, select the printer/queue you want and then choose Capture (or merely drag and drop the chosen printer from the right window to the desired LPT port on the left). Once completed, you can double-click on the newly captured printer and select Printing Options. These options correspond to the flags used under CAPTURE at the DOS prompt (see Figure 14.8).

· ·

FIGURE 14.8

Capture Settings in NetWare User Tools for Windows

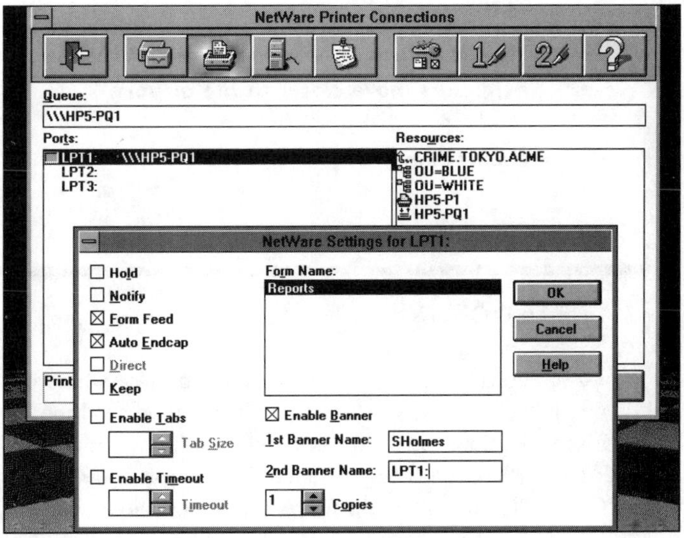

Like Windows 95, NWUSER allows you to select the Permanent option after capturing a printer. This will automatically recapture the printer every time you start Windows. If it is a NetWare 3.12 or 2.2 printer/queue, you may be required to log into the server again before capturing is complete.

To end CAPTURE under Windows, drag the printer mapping from the left window to the right. You can also select the desired printer/queue and choose End Capture from the lower button bar.

REAL WORLD

Printers and queues are referred to in the same way, since they are so closely related. More will be explained later, but for clarification's sake, a print job always must be submitted to a queue before it can be serviced by a printer via a print server. To minimize complexity, Novell allows you to choose a printer by name, and you will be captured automatically to the queue that services that printer. This way, you don't need to know which queue services which printer.

ZEN

"Don't underestimate the power of these adenoids. I had next-door neighbors move closer to the airport."

Nanny Fine

REAL WORLD

If you don't want to capture your local ports for whatever reason, you still have another option. You can print your job to a file and then send the file to an IntranetWare queue. Most applications can send a print job to a file on disk. Simply provide a filename (such as C:\TEMP\PRINT) instead of a local port name (like LTP1). Next, use NRPRINT or PCONSOLE to redirect the file to an IntranetWare queue. It's pretty easy and very flexible.

MOVING TO THE QUEUE

Once capturing has begun, the print data is sent to the print queue from an application via the local port. Before the data is sent, however, some very interesting things occur. If you analyze the anatomy of a print stream (see Figure 14.9), you'll see there are three parts: the print header, the print body (data sent), and the print tail. The purpose of these other components becomes important when drivers are involved.

▶ • ◀

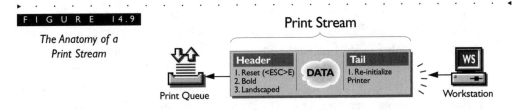

FIGURE 14.9

The Anatomy of a
Print Stream

IntranetWare allows the user to specify escape codes that can be sent before the print data reaches the printer (a *print header*). And, at the end of the print data, a *print tail* sends the proper escape codes to reset the printer to a default state. This leaves the printer ready for the next user. To use this feature, two things must have been created:

▶ PRINTDEF database — includes escape code information for printers and modes of operation (collections of escape codes)

▶ Print Job Definition — specifies details about how the capture should be handled

Remember the options for CAPTURE? Well, these can be incorporated into a file stored in NDS that is read and utilized when the user begins a CAPTURE session. Any command line options used when executing the CAPTURE command will override the Print Job Definition options.

The print server's job is to control the flow of the print job from its beginning until it is finally printed on a printer *somewhere*. That somewhere is dictated by the queue typically.

Several server elements are involved in printing: the queue (which always resides on a server volume somewhere), the print server (which may reside on a file server, IntranetWare router, any other NLM platform, or even inside the printer itself), and finally, the printer (which prints the data and notifies the print server of completion and any problems that may arise).

IntranetWare queue services are designed to provide more than just support for printing. Other applications can take advantage of the queue API under IntranetWare to service jobs based on a queuing mechanism. As a result, not all queue characteristics look related to printing.

A queue is basically comprised of a subdirectory stored on a volume of a server somewhere. Since the queue is there to hold files waiting to be printed, it must be on a storage area (volume) on a file server. Where the subdirectory exists is up to the person who created it. In NetWare 3 and below, the directories always existed under the SYS:SYSTEM subdirectory. IntranetWare, on the other hand, allows you to create them anywhere — under the subdirectory QUEUES on any volume.

Once a print job has begun from the client, the queue servicing the request (selected by the user via CAPTURE, Print Job Settings, or NWUSER) will create a temporary file inside the queue's subdirectory. This file is used to keep track of the job as it flows through the system. One of the data items kept in the file is the *Job Entry Record,* which contains information such as

- ▸ When the job was submitted

- ▸ Who submitted the job

- ▸ Size of the data

- ▸ Whether the job can be printed immediately

- ▸ How many copies to print

And more. This information can be called up via NWADMIN or PCONSOLE. See Figure 14.10 for an example of the Print Job Detail screen in NWADMIN.

The queue also has security assigned to it. During setup, we can designate users, groups, or containers that may submit jobs to the queue. We can also restrict which print servers may service jobs from our queue. Finally, there is a security designation called Queue Manager. This entity, when designated, may delete jobs submitted by other users. In this manner, print queue administration may be delegated to other users.

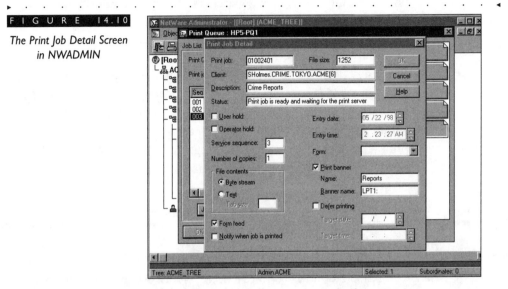

The Print Job Detail Screen
in NWADMIN

There are some utilities available that allow users and administrators to manage and view the flow of printing, including PCONSOLE (under DOS) and NWADMIN (under Windows). We'll explore printing management later in the chapter.

THE PRINT SERVER

Once the print server is loaded and functioning, it must then log into the servers it is servicing. This allows it to poll the queues it has been assigned. It is a very good idea to password-protect all the print servers in the network to minimize security problems.

Once the server is fully initialized, it will begin polling the queues it has been assigned and service print jobs within those queues. Some factors may affect which queues get serviced first. They include:

  ▶ *Queue priorities* — When a queue is assigned to a print server, a priority can be assigned. This priority tells the print server that if any jobs are waiting in the highest priority queue, it must service them once the currently serviced job has completed. This can be set up as part of security, allowing certain users to have better access to a printer than others. This would be the case if two queues were servicing the same physical printer. Users having access to the higher priority queue will have their jobs completed before the users that submitted jobs to a lesser priority queue.

▸ *Forms servicing* — This topic will be covered later in the chapter, but the Print Server Manager can designate how forms are serviced. As such, a print server may be required to service all forms of a particular type within a queue before it can move to the next queue. Or, it may have to print all jobs that have a certain designated Form Type across all queues to which it is assigned, before servicing jobs with a different form type.

REAL WORLD

Here's an example of how "Forms Servicing" works. Suppose print server Alpha were supporting Q1 and Q2. And further assume that it must service all jobs using a particular form before moving to the next form. If User1 submits a job of form type 0 into Q1, and User2 submits a job with form type 5 thereafter, User2 will have to wait if User3 submits a job of form type 0 into Q2, even if User3 submitted it *after* User2. Once User3's job is complete, the print server can begin to service jobs using form type 5.

Much like a print queue, print servers have security:

▸ *Print server users* — These are users, groups, and containers that can view current jobs being serviced. Print server users can also abort their jobs if they wish.

▸ *Print server operators* — These are users, groups, and containers that can abort anyone's job currently being serviced. They can also view the status of any currently printing job.

Other things that can be controlled on print servers include how often the print server polls the assigned queues looking for jobs. As mentioned earlier, you can modify the queue priority and how forms get serviced using Admin utilities described later in this chapter. When setting up print services, you should know the options available. The relationship of queues and print servers to printers can be

- One to many

- One to one

- Many to many

- Many to one

Print servers usually reside at the file server, although they may reside as NLMs elsewhere, such as in a special third-party printer or IntranetWare router. Print servers, when created, are assigned the queues they are to service and which printers they will support. Unlike queues, print servers do not require disk storage; therefore, they can reside just about anywhere.

THE DESTINATION: AT THE PRINTER

Once a print server has been initialized, it will first attempt to find any printers it is supposed to support. Print servers support two types of printers: local and remote. The print server software, in NLM form, is called PSERVER.NLM, which, by itself, does not know how to talk to a printer. Therefore, a separate printer support module must be provided. Let's take a closer look.

Local Printers

If the printer is local (as defined during print server creation), then the PSERVER.NLM automatically loads a local NLM called NPRINTER.NLM. NPRINTER.NLM has a bidirectional communication with the print server, as well as a communication to the local port it is servicing. The local port is usually either a parallel or serial port. These printers are known as "Auto-Load" because NPRINTER is automatically loaded at the server.

This design has several advantages, including:

- PSERVER can theoretically talk to devices other than serial and parallel ports.

▸ By design, IntranetWare SFTIII has two parts: one that talks to hardware (IOEngine) and one that is common to both servers. Using this method, the PSERVER resides in the shared engine and NPRINTER resides in the IOEngine.

Remote Printers

If the designated printer is a remote printer, PSERVER.NLM attempts to contact it using SPX as the communications method. This necessitates loading the NPRINTER.EXE module on a workstation that has the desired remote printer attached to it. Once NPRINTER.EXE has been loaded, a communication will be established and remote printing can be supported. This printer is known as "Manual Load" because NPRINTER is loaded manually at the workstation.

REAL WORLD

You can automate the loading of NPRINTER.EXE by placing it in the workstation's AUTOEXEC.BAT file. It is not necessary to log in, but you must load IPX/SPX with IPXODI.COM (or IPX.NLM with Client 32). Also, make sure the following three files are available on the local disk: NPRINTER.EXE, NPRINTER.HLP, and NPRINTER.MSG. You can find them on the Install CD-ROM or in the SYS:PUBLIC directory. Finally, use the "/U" switch to unload NPRINTER.

ZEN

"Some people say Yoga is a great way to keep your energy up. For me, it's a Snickers and a Diet Coke."

Nanny Fine

That finishes our discussion of IntranetWare printing fundamentals. But, hold on, we're not done yet. Just when you think you're at the end of your journey, the tour guide throws in a few side stops. Don't you just hate that? In our case, it's time to explore a few third-party printing solutions, before we move on to setup and management.

THIRD-PARTY PRINTING SOLUTIONS

Several good add-ons are available for the IntranetWare printing system. These usually can augment the services already provided within the printing infrastructure.

For example, in a generic IntranetWare environment using remote printers, the job must go from the user to the queue, to the print server, and finally to the remote printer. Using a device that encapsulates these functions into one subsystem can greatly reduce the network traffic required to print. Two of these devices are the HP JetDirect Card and Intel's NetPort.

HP JetDirect Card

This device resides in a printer (such as an HP LaserJet4M or 4SI) and acts as a peer device on the network. It can be configured either as a print server or as a remote printer.

Ideally, the JetDirect card should be configured as a print server. This reduces the flow of network printing since the print job only has to go from the user to the queue, and then to the JetDirect card in the printer. The challenge is when you are running a system that the JetDirect card can't log into (for example, with an older JetDirect card and IntranetWare).

The other option is to set up the JetDirect as a remote printer. In this scenario, the JetDirect will have a name assigned to it when configured. This name must correspond to the name given to the remote printer when it was defined under IntranetWare. This way, the print server knows how to communicate with the JetDirect card. The down side is that you still have the same traffic, but you do not need a machine dedicated to support the remote printer. Finally, HP has developed a wonderful Windows-based printing management system called JetAdmin. It helps you set up and manage HP JetDirect cards.

SMART LINK

Explore Hewlett Packard's home page for more information on the HP JetDirect printing solution: http://www.hp.com.

Intel NetPort

Intel's solution is similar to HP's, except an Intel NetPort can only be configured as a peer device on the network. It plugs into an Ethernet cable just like another node on the network. It can then have a standard parallel cable attached to it, enabling it to communicate with a standard printer (unlike the HP JetDirect card, which only plugs into HP printers). The other options typically apply to the NetPort. Both modes can be supported, either as a remote printer or a print server.

Now, we're really at the end of our journey. They say, "A well-traveled person is an enlightened person." Do you feel well traveled? Do you feel enlightened? You should feel *something* right about now.

So, that's the essence of printing. It's not so bad. I think IntranetWare printing gets a bad rap. It's not very mysterious — you click a button on the workstation and your document comes out of the printer down the hall, assuming, of course, that you set it up correctly. Now would be a good time to explore that aspect of IntranetWare printing.

SMART LINK

Explore Intel's home page for more information on the Intel NetPort printing solution at http://www.intel.com.

IntranetWare Printing Setup

Welcome to IntranetWare printing setup. Now that you understand the essence of printing, it's time to do something about it. This is where the mystery begins to unfold. This is where the clues appear. This is "Sherlock Holmes 101."

SMART LINK

Visit Sherlock Holmes at http://www.citsoft.com/holmes.html.

Creating print services for a IntranetWare network requires a little bit of planning. In a simple environment, IntranetWare allows you to create a basic printing system by using the DOS utility PCONSOLE.

Under Windows, you must create the items separately and associate them. This is a relatively simple process — once you understand how printing works under IntranetWare. If you have read the previous section, this should appear relatively obvious.

As you recall, there are three elements to the printing system that must be present in order to print. They are

▸ *The Queue* — used to store the print jobs on the way to the printer

▸ *The Print Server* — polls the queue for jobs and prints them on assigned printers

▸ *The Printer* — defines whether the printer is local to the file server or remotely attached

You can use NWADMIN to create the IntranetWare printing system. NWADMIN is a Windows-based graphical utility that integrates several aspects of managing IntranetWare (including rights assignments and user creation) into one easy-to-use application.

The order in which you create the print system items (queue, print server, and printer) really makes no difference. The most efficient way is to start with the queue, since it is central to the printing system. Here's how I like to do it:

▸ Step 1: Create the print queue

▸ Step 2: Create the printer

▸ Step 3: Create the print server

▸ Step 4: Activate the printing system

There you have it. Four simple steps. No mystery here. Let's take a closer look, and don't forget your IntranetWare magnifying glass.

ZEN

"I've often wondered how the British know what everyone's feeling. They all must wear mood rings."

Nanny Fine

STEP 1: CREATE THE PRINT QUEUE

It is important to remember that when you create a queue, it should be central to the users who are going to use it. When using NDS, you usually want to keep the queues and print servers proximal to each other.

TIP

IntranetWare Printing Setup is closely related to NDS and partitioning. It is more efficient to have the area where the jobs get stored (Queue Volume) as close to the users as possible. If you reside in Camelot, it makes no sense to print something to a queue in Tokyo (unless you *want* the print job to print in Tokyo). See Chapter 9 for more information on replica distribution.

The first step is to choose the context where you create the queue. This is usually in the container where the users reside who will be using the queue the most.

To create the queue under NWADMIN, select Object/Create or select the container and press Insert. You'll be presented with a dialog box asking for the type of object you wish to create. Choose Print Queue and press Enter (see Figure 14.11). The items you need to define next are shown in Table 14.1 and Figure 14.11.

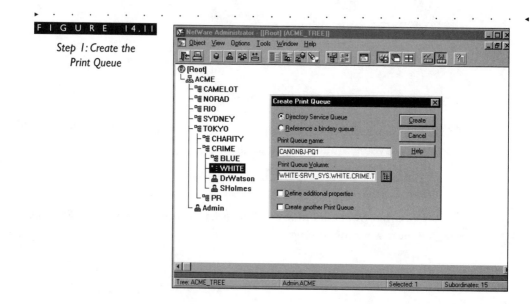

F I G U R E   14.11

Step 1: Create the
Print Queue

T A B L E   14.1

Important Print Queue Properties

PROPERTY	DESCRIPTION
Directory Queue vs. Bindery Queue	If you are creating a regular queue (and we are), choose Directory Services Queue. A Bindery Reference Queue can service jobs out of a queue that resides on a 2.x or 3.x server. This can be useful if you have a mixed environment and must support queues from a single location. In addition, you can submit a job to Bindery Reference Queue and it will be sent automatically to the reference queue on the 3.x server.
Print Queue Name	Usually you want to name a queue descriptively. It is easier to find a queue named CANONBJ-PQ1 than just Bubble Printer.
Print Queue Volume	This is the physical space where the job will be stored as it is spooled and when it is serviced. Therefore, this property must reference a volume somewhere in the IntranetWare tree. In addition, the container in which the queue is created must have rights to that volume in order to create print jobs there.

▶ · ◀

REAL WORLD

In previous versions of NetWare, the queue was *always* stored under SYS:SYSTEM in the volume SYS:. In IntranetWare, the NWADMIN utility will create a subdirectory off of the root of the volume chosen (which can be other than SYS: now!) and call it QUEUES. This is where the data will be stored for the queue.

At this point, you can choose to define other queue properties (which will be brought up in a dialog box), or let IntranetWare create the queue and allow you to create another. For our example, let's click the Define Additional Properties check box, then click on Create.

Data added to the Print Queue Identification page (such as Other Name and Location) can be useful when searching for queues under NWADMIN. This allows the user to find a queue based on unique information entered here, but the additional data is purely optional (see Figure 14.12 and Table 14.2).

FIGURE 14.12

The Print Queue
Identification Page in
NWADMIN

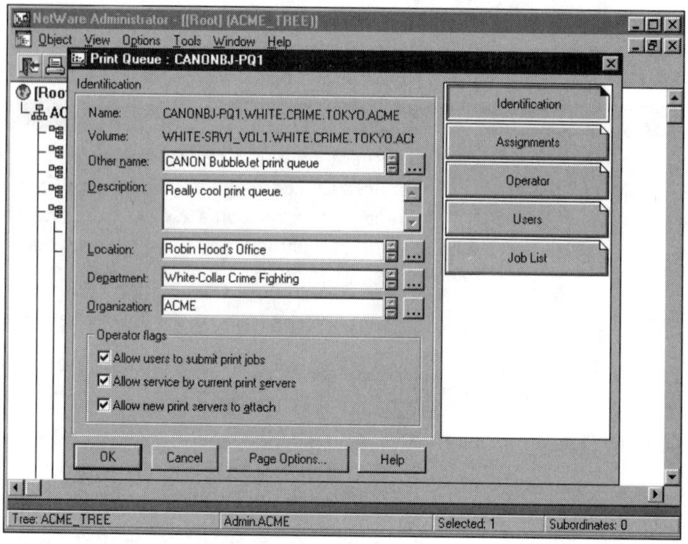

TABLE 14.2

Additional Print Queue
Pages

PRINT QUEUE PAGE	DESCRIPTION
Assignments	The Assignments page is a view-only screen used to show which printer(s) the queue is servicing and which print server is servicing this queue.
Operator	The Operator page contains some of the most important information for the queue. Print queue operators can do several valuable management items, such as: Create new jobs in the queue Delete jobs submitted by other users Affect the availability of the queue Place holds on their own submitted jobs Place holds on jobs submitted by other users Grant access to other users to use the queue By default, the user that created the queue is the queue operator. You can add other users, if necessary.

TABLE 14.2

*Additional Print Queue
Pages (continued)*

PRINT QUEUE PAGE	DESCRIPTION
Users	The Print Queue Users page is the most important item for the queue because it is where you designate who may use the queue (that is, who may submit jobs via CAPTURE or through Windows). By default, anyone in the container where the queue was created as well as any containers below this container may submit print jobs to this queue. To limit this, you can assign other objects such as Groups, Organizational Roles, or specific users the ability to submit print jobs to the queue.
Job List	Job List is a management function available to users and operators alike. It allows a user to view the current jobs in the queue as well as change details about the job. If you are a print queue operator, you can change aspects of jobs submitted by other users in addition to your own. To do this, highlight the job you want to change and click on Job Details. If the job is not actively being serviced, you can change aspects of the job such as number of copies, form feed after print, and so on.
	A print queue operator can change the priority of a job by changing its sequence number. For example, changing a job from sequence 3 to sequence 1 bumps the first job to sequence 2, 3 to 4, and so on. More of this function will be covered in the section "IntranetWare Printing Management."

STEP 2: CREATE THE PRINTER

The next step is to create a printer that will be serviced by the queue. Creating the printer is similar to creating the queue. Choose the container where the printer will be stored by selecting it with your mouse and pressing Insert (or choosing Create from the Object option on the toolbar). Choose Printer and give it a descriptive name. Click on Define Additional Properties and choose Create.

TIP

You don't have to create the printer, print server, and queue in the same container. You can locate them in three different areas and then associate them. For our example, it is easier to create them all in the same container.

You can use the Printer Identification page to provide information that NDS can use for searches, as well as to provide more descriptive information for users and other administrators. Check out Figure 14.13 and Table 14.3.

F I G U R E   14.13

The Printer Identification Page in NWADMIN

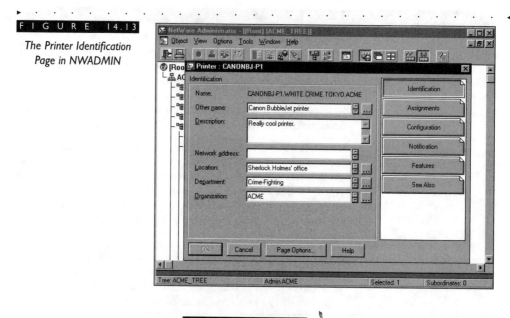

T A B L E   14.3

Additional Printer Pages

PRINTER PAGE	DESCRIPTION
Assignments	This page is where you tell the printer which queue(s) it will be servicing. You may have one printer that services multiple queues, or multiple printers servicing one queue. If you have more than one queue per printer, you can assign a *priority,* the highest being 1. Any jobs submitted to a higher-priority queue will get serviced before any waiting jobs in a lower-priority queue (see Figure 14.14).
	The default queue is used when a user chooses to capture to the network by using a printer name instead of a queue name. When you choose a printer name, the job will be sent to the default queue.
	For this option, choose the queue that you just created.

Additional Printer Pages
(continued)

PRINTER PAGE	DESCRIPTION
Configuration	This option determines whether the printer is physically attached to the print server or remotely attached to a workstation.
	The first option, Printer Type, determines what kind of printer this is.
	Typically, it is either serial or parallel. The other options (such as AppleTalk and XNP) are configured and used with additional software.
	The Communication option specifies the local port that will be used. If the printer is polled, it will be sent printer output in a polled fashion instead of using interrupts to control print flow. Manual Load indicates that the remote printer software (NPRINTER.EXE) will be loaded instead of the local NPRINTER.NLM. If you choose Auto Load, the print server will know to load the NPRINTER.NLM at the server to service a locally attached printer.
	Another security feature of remote printers is the ability to limit the network address that the remote printer can use. This way, only the allowed address can load NPRINTER.EXE and support the print server as a remotely defined printer.
Notification	The Notification page is where you determine who will be notified in the event the printer has a problem. This is different than notifying the user when the print job submitted is complete.
	The default user is whoever submitted the print job. In a small office, this setting works just fine, but in a larger network, this setting is usually deleted and an IS group or person is added instead. This makes servicing the printer (for example, when it is out of paper) the job of such a person.
	You can also specify how often (in minutes) the person gets notified. First indicates how long before the first message is sent, and Next is the interval at which subsequent messages will be sent.
Features	This page allows more descriptive data to be placed in NDS, which allows for better searching. For example, a user/administrator could search for printers supporting PCL with 4 MB memory and a fax card. This search could occur network-wide, or could be limited to a subarea of the directory tree.

F I G U R E   14.14

The Printer Assignments
Page in NWADMIN

NetWare Administrator - [[Root] [ACME_TREE]]

Object View Options Tools Window Help

Printer : CANONBJ-P1

Assignments

Print server:
WHITE-PS1.WHITE.CRIME.TOKYO.ACME

Print queues:

Queue	Priority
CANONBJ-PQ1.WHITE.CRIME.TOKYO.ACME	1

Add...   Delete   Priority: 1

Default print queue:
CANONBJ-PQ1.WHITE.CRIME.TOKYO.ACME

OK   Cancel   Page Options...   Help

Identification

Assignments

Configuration

Notification

Features

See Also

Tree: ACME_TREE   Admin.ACME   Selected: 1   Subordinates: 0

REAL WORLD

The Printer Configuration page in NWADMIN is where you configure options for third-party printer support such as HP JetDirect cards or Intel's Netport. These devices can act either as a remote printer or as a print server to an IntranetWare server. Older versions of these products may only be used as remote printers and not as print servers in an IntranetWare environment.

STEP 3: CREATE THE PRINT SERVER

To create a print server, use the NWADMIN utility. Select the container that will store the print server and press Insert while the container is highlighted. Choose Print Server off of the list, and then choose OK.

First, you need to give the print server a name. Once again, descriptive names work best (such as WHITE-PS1). This will help you search for print servers later.

After entering the name, click on the Define Additional Properties check box and choose Create. The Print Server Identification page will appear (see Figure 14.15). Table 14.4 lists the basic information you will need to provide to complete print server creation.

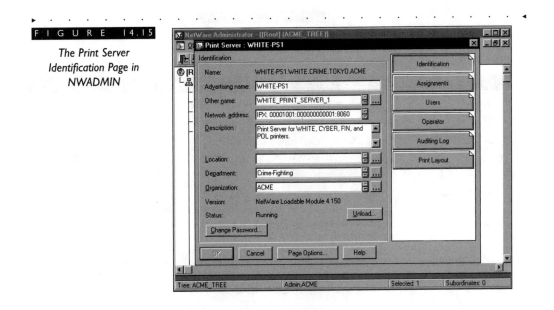

FIGURE 14.15

The Print Server
Identification Page in
NWADMIN

T A B L E   14.4

Additional Print Server
Pages

PRINT SERVER PAGE	DESCRIPTION
Assignments	This page allows you to tell the print server which printers it will be servicing. Note that it may support several (up to 256) for one print server. Naturally, not all the printers can be attached physically to the print server (only 5). The rest would be attached remotely.
	Select the printer you just created by choosing Add (see Figure 14.16). The printer will be added with a *Printer Number*. Usually this number will not be referenced on a day-to-day basis. One or two IntranetWare utilities still require it, such as Print Server Control (PSC), which is covered in the "IntranetWare Printing Management" section.
Users	Users information is not necessary for a user to print, even if this print server is servicing jobs in queues where the user has submitted a print job. This page is provided so that users can check the status of a print server using the management utilities (such as PSC or NWADMIN). If the user never needs to do this (for example, if printer management is handled by IS), then the user doesn't need the print server user status.

(continued)

T A B L E   1 4 . 4

*Additional Print Server
Pages (continued)*

PRINT SERVER PAGE	DESCRIPTION
Users (continued)	By default, all users in the container where the print server was created are given the print server user status.
Operator	Print server operators are similar to queue operators in that they can manage the print server. For example, print server operators may take printers off-line remotely, shut down the print server, and abort jobs in process.
Auditing Log	This page allows you to enable an auditing function for the print server. You can limit the size of the audit file, as well as how many jobs it will keep in its auditing log. The file can be printed or it can be viewed under NWADMIN.
Print Layout	This is a very handy function in that you can graphically see the printing layout in one screen. This function works for all printers and queues associated with this print server.
Print Layout	An additional function called Status allows the print server operator to view the status of all elements in the printing hierarchy. Simply select one of the printing components and click on Status. Figure 14.17 shows an example of the Print Server Status screen.

F I G U R E   1 4 . 1 6

*The Print Server
Assignments Page in
NWADMIN*

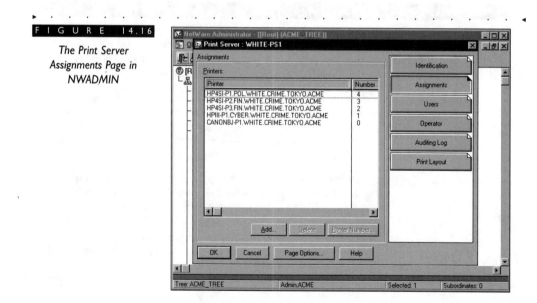

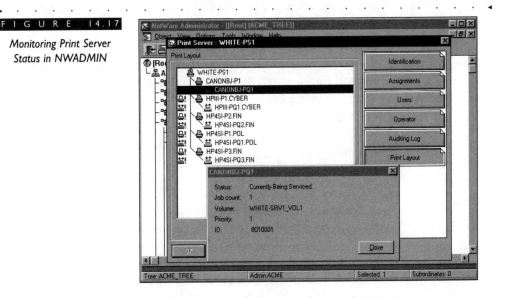

FIGURE 14.17

Monitoring Print Server
Status in NWADMIN

When you create a print server, you should set a password for the print server for security reasons. You can set a password under the Print Server Creation screen by pressing the Change Password button. You will be asked for the password at server load time.

ZEN

"Danny bought me some lingerie for my birthday. It was so inappropriate. It's a good thing my mother's birthday was two days later or I'd still be stuck with the thing."

Nanny Fine

STEP 4: ACTIVATE THE PRINTING SYSTEM

Now that the configuration is set, the last step is to start the print server. This is done either at the server, or remotely by using RCONSOLE.

To start the print server, load PSERVER.NLM at the console by typing

```
LOAD PSERVER
```

This will bring up the menu for PSERVER. It will show the context that the server is in within the directory tree. If you need to change where the print server is, you can either type in the new context or browse by pressing Enter. Selecting ".." moves up in the tree or you can select another container by choosing a container name and hitting enter. Once you have found the print server, load it by highlighting it and pressing Enter.

Three things will happen:

1 • The print server will load. Any printers that are locally defined for this print server will be supported by NPRINTER.NLM, which is loaded automatically if it is needed by local printers. The local printers will have a status of "Waiting for Jobs" once this is complete.

2 • Remote printers defined for this server will attempt to find a remote printer. If they cannot, they will wait for remote printer software to contact them (either IntranetWare's NPRINTER.EXE, or a third-party solution such as HP's JetDirect card or Intel's Netport).

3 • The print server will ask for a password before loading. Passwords are desirable especially in larger networks. If you need to add or change a print server password, use NWADMIN and select the print server. PCONSOLE also allows you to change passwords as well.

TIP

When the IntranetWare print server loads, it looks to the corresponding NDS Print Server object for three vital pieces of information: password for access to printing console, available printers serviced by this print server, and the user/operator list. If you change any of these values in NDS, they will not take effect until the print server is brought down and back up again.

The print server Main Menu provides you with two options: Printer Status and Print Server Information.

Printer Status

This option allows you to view status of all printers defined for this print server (see Figure 14.18). You can also execute some printer management functions, such as:

▶ Abort currently printing jobs

▶ Stop printer output

▶ Start printer output

▶ Eject a page (form feed)

The Print Server Status Window

```
NetWare Print Server  4.15                    NetWare Loadable Module
Print server: WHITE-PS1.WHITE.CRIME.TOKYO.ACME
                        Status: Running

Printer:   CANONBJ-P1.WHITE.CRIME.TOKYO.ACME
Type:      Manual Load (Remote), LPT1
Address:   00001234:00A024563DEE:403B                Printer control

Current status:   Waiting for job

Queues serviced:  (See list)                        Abort print job
Service mode:     Minimize form changes within print qu  Form feed
Mounted form:     0                                 Mark top of form
                                                    Pause printer
NetWare server:                                     Private / Shared
Print queue:                                        Start printer
Print job ID:                                       Stop printer
Description:
Print job form:

Copies requested:                    Finished:
Size of 1 copy:                      Finished:
Percent complete:
```

In addition, you can change how forms (discussed later) get serviced on the selected printer. All of these functions can also be done via NWADMIN and PSC (a DOS utility).

Print Server Information

The Print Server Information screen has two functions:

▶ Allows you to view print server information such as version and name

▶ Allows the print server to be shut down gracefully

Ideally, the print server should be shut down either remotely (via NWADMIN or PCONSOLE), or at the server using this option.

To shut down the print server, choose Current Status and press Enter. You can then shut down the print server in one of two ways:

1 •   Immediately — With this option, any currently running jobs are suspended. They will continue when the print server is restarted.

2 •   Unload after active print jobs — This allows any printing jobs to complete before the print server terminates.

In either case, the print server will advertise that it is no longer available and then terminate. Let's take a look at how changes to print servers take effect.

When you make the following changes, the print server must be unloaded and reloaded at the file server/router where the print server is running. This way, IntranetWare can read the new information and effect the changes.

Changes made directly to a print server:

▸ Assigned printers

▸ Passwords

Changes made to printers and queues assigned to a print server:

▸ Queue assignments

▸ Printer definition (parallel, serial, remote, or local)

▸ Forms servicing

▸ Notification of service alerts

Changes to the following take place immediately:

▸ Queue users

▸ Print server users

▸ Queue operators

▸ Print server operators

Understanding that some changes take place immediately and others take place after loading/reloading will help you avoid frustration when the print server appears to accept changes, but does not effect them immediately.

SMART LINK

If IntranetWare printing setup is still a great mystery to you, join us in the CNE program at CyberState University at http://www.cyberstateu.com

This completes our discussion of the fundamentals of IntranetWare printing setup. But before we dive into the depths of printing management, let's take a moment to explore some extracurricular setup options — namely, setup customization with forms and devices.

CUSTOMIZING INTRANETWARE PRINTING

Forms and devices add another dimension to the IntranetWare printing system. You should be able to determine now if forms or device definitions are needed in your network.

The first step is to determine where in the tree the devices need to exist. If forms or devices do not exist in a particular context, the printing system will look into the next higher context until it finds a definition. This would allow an administrator to create forms and devices at the Organization level of the tree, and all users in the entire organization would benefit.

Users will always use the forms and devices in their own contexts if they exist. If they do exist within the context, then the users cannot see any others above their own context.

Creating forms and definitions can be done either under NWADMIN (graphically under Windows) or using the DOS menu command PRINTDEF. Once they have been created, you can assign forms or devices to users with either NWADMIN (under Windows) or PRINTCON (under DOS). This is accomplished by creating a print job configuration for the user or container.

Building Forms

1 • Choose the context where you wish the form or forms to exists. This could be at the root or deep within the directory.

2 • Select the Organizational Unit (container) and click the right mouse button.

3 • Choose Details.

4 • Choose Printer Forms.

5 • Choose Create.

6 • Give the new form a descriptive name. Typically form 0 is the first form. Therefore, it should be the most commonly used form. This might be labeled BLANK or WORDPROC.

7 • The form number is used from the command line under CAPTURE, although CAPTURE can now use form names as well. Usually the form is referenced by name not by number.

8 • Choose OK.

This will create the form desired within the selected context. The next step is to assign it to a user. This can be done two ways:

▸ Set up a *print job configuration*. This is a collection of printing attributes that the user can select by a given name. One of the attributes can be the form name used when submitting jobs.

▸ Select a form name when capturing a printer under NWUSER (Windows 3.1). This is usually chosen by the user before printing, as opposed to using a preset configuration such as print job configurations.

Creating print job configurations will be covered later (see the section "Tying It All Together").

Building Devices

Creating devices requires two steps:

▶ *Step 1: Creating functions* — These are printing-specific. They would include codes for things such as Reset, Landscape, Portrait, Letter-size, Graphics mode, and so on. To get these codes, you must refer to the manual that came with your printer.

▶ *Step 2: Creating modes* — These are made of up one or more functions. They allow you to send a series of functions to the printer before your job prints. For example, you can

▶ Reset the printer

▶ Change to landscape

▶ Change to A4 format

Together, functions and modes constitute a *device* definition. The idea is that when you start to print to the network printer, IntranetWare will send these codes to the desired printer and properly initialize it for you.

TIP

As stated before, it is much more desirable to allow the application (such as WordPerfect) to send its own codes. If that is not possible, then IntranetWare can send them for you via this interface.

To create functions and modes, you must decide where you want them to be available. As with forms, you can create them once at the root of the tree and make them globally available, or deeper in the directory tree. Also as with forms, when looking for devices, IntranetWare looks in the current container, and, if none is found, it continues to looks into superior containers until one is found. If none is found, no devices will be available.

REAL WORLD

NWUSER allows you to choose a form when capturing under Windows. However, NWUSER doesn't look into superior containers for other forms if none exists in the current context. Therefore, you may need to create a form in the users' context anyway, or change contexts.

To create a device, first choose the container where the device will be stored. As noted previously this will have an impact on who will be able to see and use the device. Then create the device as follows:

1 • Click the right mouse button on the desired container.

2 • Choose Details.

3 • Choose Print Devices.

4 • Choose Create.

5 • Next, we must create a device name (such as HP4SI). To do this, put in a name under Name and press Enter.

6 • Next, we must create functions, since modes are created from one or more functions. As a sample, we'll create a reset function. Choose Modify.

7 • Choose Create Function (see Figure 14.19).

8 • First you must give the function a name. This should be descriptive of the function. As described previously, you can obtain the function codes from your printer manual. There are some codes that you cannot type in (such as ESCAPE). These codes are typed in within delimiters to tell IntranetWare that a special character is needed. For example, you can indicate ESCAPE in other ways, such as <ESC> or <ESCAPE>. To represent reset string of Escape E, you would represent it as <ESCAPE>E.

9 • Once you have created one or more functions, you can now create a mode. To create a mode, choose Create Mode. There is a default mode called *reinitialize* that is automatically created. This mode can be populated with the reset function (created earlier) for the print device you are defining. To add the reset function we just created, choose Add Above or Add Below.

TIP

Above and **Below** will make a difference in how the mode works. Naturally, you would want to send a reset function before you send the function for Landscape. It the functions were reversed, it wouldn't do you any good (setting Landscape, then reset!). Adding **Above** and **Add Below** allows you to place functions where they need to be in the mode list.

10 • Be sure to give the mode a name. This should be descriptive of what the mode needs to do. In our case, the mode name Reset is perfect. You may also want to add the reset function to the predefined mode reinitialize.

F I G U R E   14.19

Creating a New Function in NWADMIN

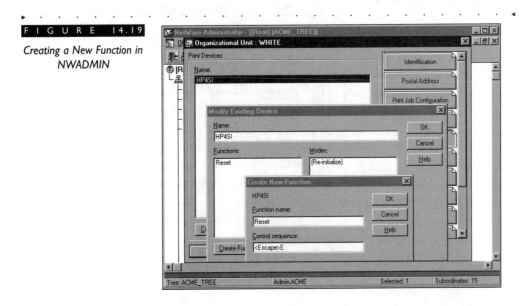

Importing Devices   A nice capability is importing into the system predefined devices defined by someone else. This does not include device drivers from application manufacturers. Only NetWare-defined devices can be imported (and exported).

An example might be where another administrator already went through the pain of creating a print driver for a new device. They can export that device (see the "Exporting Devices" section) into a file that can then be imported into your system.

To do this, follow these steps:

1 •   Choose the container where you wish to import the device.

2 •   Click the right mouse button and choose Details.

3 •   Choose Print Devices.

4 •   Choose Import.

5 •   Under filename, type **Z:\PUBLIC** and press Enter (this step is shown in Figure 14.20).

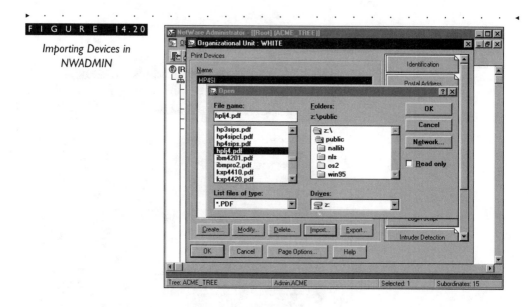

TIP

Novell includes many predefined devices as examples for real applications. They are stored in SYS:PUBLIC during install.

6 • Choose a device name, such as HPLJ4.PDF. (PDF stands for Printer Definition File.) Then choose OK.

7 • The file will now be imported into NDS as a new device. To verify, check the modes and functions defined for this device.

Remember that to utilize these forms and devices, you must create a print job configuration for a user and either make it a default for the user or allow the user to activate the configuration via a batch file or command line.

Exporting Devices   This option is similar to import. The steps are as follows:

1 • Choose the container where the device exists.

2 • Open Details on the container.

3 • Choose Print Devices.

4 • Choose Export.

5 • Choose a filename and directory where you want to store the exported device in the form of a file.

6 • Choose OK.

NWADMIN will then export all functions and modes for the device and store them in a file. At that point, you may copy it to a diskette, e-mail it, or otherwise make it available for other administrators.

QUIZ

Let's test your mystery-solving abilities. What English word can have four of its five letters removed and still retain the same pronunciation?

(Q14-2)

Tying It All Together

You now know how to create forms and devices, but how do you assign them to users? That is the next step. IntranetWare has a method for integrating together a series of printing options into a named grouping of items. This is called a *print job configuration*. Print job configurations can be used in several ways:

▶ They can be created for a particular user

▶ They can be created for a container. Then all users/objects in the container can use it.

▶ You can use a print job configuration defined for another user and assign it to another user in lieu of creating a duplicate configuration.

▶ You can make a print job configuration *default*. This means that if the user issues a CAPTURE command (under a Login Script or command line), then the items defined in the job will take effect.

To create a print job (either for a user or a container):

1 • Choose the item in NWADMIN and select Details.

2 • Choose Print Job Configuration.

3 • Choose New.

4 • Give the job a name.

5 • You must choose a print queue for this job. Other options (for example, banners, copies, and form feed) are at the discretion of the creator. You can also assign a device, mode, and form (if they are created and within the scope of the configuration being created (see Figure 14.21).

6 • Choose OK.

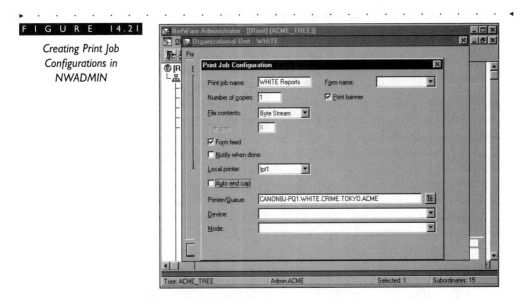

*Creating Print Job
Configurations in
NWADMIN*

After creating the print job configuration, you can now optionally make it a default. For obvious reasons, there can be only one default. You can make other configurations the default if you wish. To select the default, highlight the desired configuration and click on Default. You should see a small printer icon next to the chosen configuration.

To use a configuration other than the default, use the /J option with the CAPTURE command on the command line (or when using CAPTURE in a Login Script).

Congratulations! You've passed the first test. You successfully set up IntranetWare printing. Now comes the fun part — keeping it running. This is the *real* mystery of life.

IntranetWare Printing Management

IntranetWare printing setup was a breeze. And now the system is working flawlessly. You've tested a few documents, and they printed fine. You're probably getting a little overconfident right about now. Be careful, it happens to the best of us.

Now for the real test — letting the users loose on your new, clean, "working" printing system. You know it can print in a vacuum, but what about in a war zone?

Welcome to IntranetWare printing management. In this section, we will explore five key management responsibilities, and learn about five key printing management tools. They are

- ▸ Managing printing with PCONSOLE

- ▸ Managing printing with NWADMIN

- ▸ Managing print servers with PSC

- ▸ Configuring print jobs with PRINTCON

- ▸ Customizing printing with PRINTDEF

With the release of IntranetWare, many of the DOS-based administration utilities that have been around since the beginning of NetWare were replaced by new utilities that support NDS. Even though the new NDS utilities have the same C-worthy look and feel, most of them have changed entirely — much to the dismay of some of us old NetWare junkies! Fortunately, for those who prefer to work under DOS, the DOS-based printing utilities under IntranetWare survived the cut with a few minor changes.

This section describes how IntranetWare print services can be managed in a distributed environment. We'll also cover some common printing issues and how to resolve them.

SMART LINK

For a comprehensive discussion of NetWare's numerous printing utilities, check out "NetWare Printing and Utilities" at http://support.novell.com/sitemap.

The main areas that can be managed are shown in Table 14.5. Take a look.

Some of the same general-purpose utilities that you use to create print services are the same ones that you use for management. Some special-purpose utilities (such as PSC) are only used for management. Table 14.6 summarizes these utilities.

T A B L E   14.5

IntranetWare Printing
Management Components

COMPONENT	HOW YOU CAN MANAGE THIS COMPONENT
Print Servers	If you are a print server operator, you can: Unload the print server View auditing records
Queues	For queue operators and users, the queue allows for great flexibility in what can be seen and changed remotely (under NWADMIN and PCONSOLE). For example, you can: Delete a job (NWADMIN and PCONSOLE) Create a job (PCONSOLE) Suspend a queue from receiving new jobs (NWADMIN and PCONSOLE) Suspend servicing of jobs (NWADMIN and PCONSOLE) Place an operator hold on a job (NWADMIN and PCONSOLE) Place a user hold on a job (NWADMIN and PCONSOLE)
Printers	For printers, you can: View how much of a job has been completed (NWADMIN and PCONSOLE) Mount a new form (NWADMIN and PCONSOLE) Pause and restart a printer (NWADMIN and PCONSOLE) Abort a currently printing job

T A B L E   14.6

IntranetWare Printing
Management Tools

TOOL	FUNCTION
NWADMIN	Used to do most print system component management. This includes: Deleting jobs Changing mounted forms Stopping and starting printers Checking the status of jobs in the queue Placing holds on jobs Aborting currently printing jobs

(continued)

TOOL	FUNCTION
PCONSOLE	This is a DOS/MENU utility and encompasses most of the queue and print server creation and management functions. These include: Deleting jobs from a queue Submitting a new job (not possible under NWADMIN) Placing holds on a job Stopping and starting printers Aborting currently printing jobs
PSC	This is a command line utility that can be used to manage print servers from a command line. This includes: Mounting new forms Stopping and starting printers Aborting currently printing jobs

For the most part, users are more interested in getting information about print jobs than they are in completing particular tasks. Most of the time, users need to know when a job will complete, or if the printer is available. They might need to delete a submitted job, but otherwise, they probably don't need to be able to do too many things to a printer or print job. The double-X's in Table 14.7 show the minimum rights needed to complete certain tasks.

Now that you've got your battle plan, let's arm you with some powerful printing management weapons, starting with the strongest of them all — PCONSOLE.

ZEN

"Men can't be rushed. They're like children. You cook them too fast, they get tough. Whereas, you take your time, let them simmer for a while, they fall apart in your hands."

Nanny Fine

T A B L E   14.7

*IntranetWare Printing
Management Administrators*

FUNCTION	QUEUE OPERATOR	QUEUE USER	PRINT SERVER OPERATOR	PRINT SERVER USER
View any submitted job		XX		
Delete a submitted job (personal)		XX		
Delete another user's jobs	XX			
Create a new job		XX		
Prevent users from submitting jobs to a queue	XX			
Suspend servicing of print jobs	XX			
Abort a printing job on a printer			XX	
Stop a printer			XX	
Restart a printer			XX	
Mount a new form for a printer			XX	
Check printer status			XX	
Place a user hold on a job (personal)		XX		
Place an operator hold on a job	XX			
Check printer status				XX
Check percentage of the job printed				XX

MANAGING PRINTING WITH PCONSOLE

PCONSOLE is the general of printing utilities. IntranetWare's print console allows for the configuration and administration of NDS printing objects. Let's take a look at the PCONSOLE main menu (see Figure 14.22).

Before we begin exploring the PCONSOLE menu options, you should be aware of a few important things about PCONSOLE. First, notice the top of the screen. In addition to the version of PCONSOLE that is running and the date and time, you will see your current context. This is very important, because any menu option we choose at this point will affect this context only. For example, if we were to choose

. . . . .

Print Queues, we would see the print queues configured in the current context only. A common mistake when using PCONSOLE is to be in the wrong context, select one of the menu items, and then find yourself wondering, "What happened to all of my printing objects?" So, before beginning your printing administration, be sure that you are in the proper context.

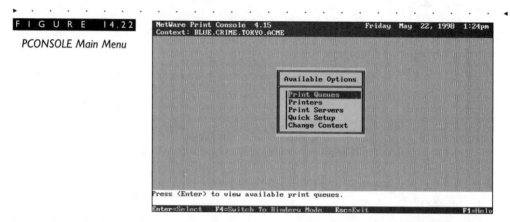

FIGURE 14.22

PCONSOLE Main Menu

The default PCONSOLE context will be whatever context you were in when you ran PCONSOLE.EXE. Generally, this will be the context you were placed in at login. If your current context isn't correct, you can use the Change Context option to move to the proper context. Let's do that now. When you select Change Context, you are prompted to either type the context you desire, or to use the Insert key to browse for the desired context. Using the Insert key is the easiest, most foolproof method since it eliminates any guessing. When you press Insert, you will be presented with the Container object below your current context.

By selecting the Organizational Unit, you can move deeper in the tree. Just like in a DOS file system directory structure, the two dots indicate "parent," so, if you press Enter at the two dots, you'll move up the tree to the parent container. When you have finished browsing for the desired context, press F10 or Esc to save the new context.

The second important item to notice on the PCONSOLE main menu is the menu bar at the bottom of the screen. Most of the options are self-explanatory: Enter to select, F10 or Esc to exit, F1 for help, but the one you should pay close attention to is F4=Switch To Bindery Mode. This option is a toggle switch. By pressing F4, PCONSOLE will change the display from NDS objects to Bindery objects. This option is normally used when you are logged into a bindery-based

IntranetWare server (that is, NetWare 3 or NetWare 2). It can also be used if you are logged in as a user who is in the bindery context of the server to which you are authenticated. If you are not, when you press F4, you will receive a bindery context error message.

This option is useful in a mixed NetWare 3 and IntranetWare environment because it allows you to toggle back and forth between NDS and bindery, and easily manage network printing in both environments.

Using Quick Setup

Before we get into the details of PCONSOLE, let's take a look at the best part of the utility — Quick Setup. One of the most frustrating parts of configuring network printing is trying to remember the next step in the process. Administrators frequently create all of the necessary printing objects correctly, but miss one step in the process of linking print queues to printers and printers to print servers. The result: hours of trying to figure out why jobs go to the print queue but never print.

Quick Setup allows you to set up a print server, printer, and print queue very quickly (hence the name), making all of the necessary assignments for you. This option is great for the administrator who doesn't like to hop back and forth between menus, trying to remember the next step in the print setup process.

If you choose Quick Setup from a context that does not have print services configured, the system will present you with default print object names, as shown in Figure 14.23.

FIGURE 14.23

The Print Services Quick Setup Screen in PCONSOLE

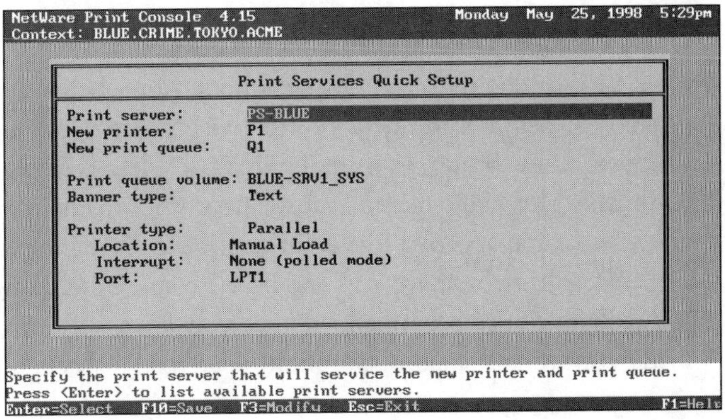

```
NetWare Print Console  4.15                    Monday  May  25, 1998  5:29pm
Context: BLUE.CRIME.TOKYO.ACME

                          Print Services Quick Setup

        Print server:         PS-BLUE
        New printer:          P1
        New print queue:      Q1

        Print queue volume:   BLUE-SRV1_SYS
        Banner type:          Text

        Printer type:         Parallel
          Location:           Manual Load
          Interrupt:          None (polled mode)
          Port:               LPT1


Specify the print server that will service the new printer and print queue.
Press <Enter> to list available print servers.
Enter=Select   F10=Save   F3=Modify   Esc=Exit                     F1=Help
```

Print servers will be named PS-<*Container_Name*>, the first printer will be named P1, and the first print queue will be named Q1. These defaults can be changed as necessary to match the naming standards of your organization.

Default assumptions will also be made about the print queue volume, banner type, and printer configuration. These defaults can also be changed as necessary.

To change the printer configuration, arrow down to Printer type and press Enter. Select the appropriate printer type — Parallel, Serial, or other printer type — and press Enter. You will also need to specify whether this printer is an Auto Load printer (directly attached to the print server) or a Manual Load (workstation or network attached).

Generally, the Interrupt field can be left at the default of None (polled mode). If you choose to use an interrupt method, this field can be configured to indicate the interrupt of the port hardware. This field must match the port hardware if an interrupt is used. The Port field must match the port to which this printer is physically attached — LPT1, LPT2, and so on.

Quick Setup is the foolproof method for configuring IntranetWare printing. Unfortunately, this option is only available in PCONSOLE, not NWADMIN. So, for those of you who are die-hard GUI administrators, if you find yourself caught in a DOS utility, this is the easiest way to set up IntranetWare printing.

Quick Setup is not the only way to create printing objects in PCONSOLE — it's just the easiest! The objects can also be created using the individual Print Queues, Printers, and Print Servers options from the PCONSOLE main menu as described in the following sections.

Managing Print Queues

By selecting the Print Queues option from the PCONSOLE main menu, you are shown a list of print queues currently configured in the current context. By pressing Insert, a new print queue can be created. When creating a new print queue, you will be asked for two pieces of information: print queue name and print queue volume.

The name assigned to a print queue can be any hexadecimal name from 1 to 64 characters, including spaces and underscores. Even though this provides tremendous flexibility, it is recommended that you keep your print queue names short and descriptive. For example, a print queue that is serviced by an HPIII LaserJet printer might be named HPIII-PQ1.

The second piece of information that will be required when creating a new print queue is the print queue volume. This is the volume where the print jobs sent to this queue will be spooled. Since the volume name entered here must be the full NDS name of the volume, use the Insert key to browse the tree to find the appropriate volume. When you have found the volume on which you want to create this queue, press Enter or F10 to accept your selection.

Remember, before any new print queue created can be used, all of the proper printing assignments must be made, including assigning a print server to service this queue and attaching a printer. This process is described in the following discussion.

By selecting Print Queues from the PCONSOLE Available Options menu you can also manage existing NDS print queues. The left side of Figure 14.24 shows the print queues configured in the context .BLUE.CRIME.TOKYO.ACME.

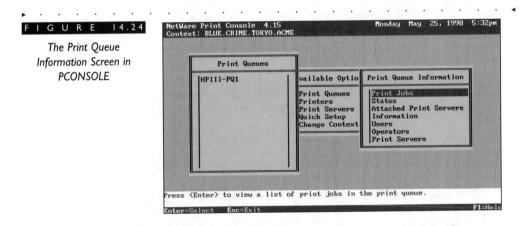

F I G U R E   14.24

The Print Queue Information Screen in PCONSOLE

When you select an available print queue, you will see the available information about this print queue displayed on the right side of the screen (see Figure 14.24). Table 14.8 summarizes the information found in each menu option listed.

Viewing Jobs in a Print Queue   By selecting Print Jobs from the Print Queue Information menu, you can see all of the print jobs in this queue that are waiting to be serviced. Print queue operators will be shown all jobs in the queue. Regular users, or non-operators of the queue, will only be shown the jobs that they submitted. By selecting a specific print job, you will see information about that job, as shown in Figure 14.25.

TABLE 14.8

*Print Queue Information
Parameters*

MENU OPTION	PURPOSE
Print Jobs	Allows you to view the current print jobs in this queue. Also allows a print queue operator to delete jobs from the queue, reorder jobs in the queue, and put an operator hold on the jobs in the queue. Regular users (non-operators) can only modify jobs that they have submitted.
Status	Allows you to view the status of this print queue, including number of jobs, number of print servers servicing this queue and operator flags.
Attached Print Servers	Shows a list of active print servers servicing this print queue. The print server must be loaded in order to be active.
Information	Allows you to view the print queue identification number, and the server and volume in which this queue is created on. The print queue ID number is the subdirectory name of this print queue plus a .QDR extension. This subdirectory will be in the QUEUES directory of the indicated volume.
Users	Shows a list of users and groups who are authorized to submit jobs to this queue. Also allows you to add new users.
Operators	Shows a list of users and groups who are authorized to manage this queue. Also allows you to add new operators.
Print Servers	Allows you to view the print servers authorized to service this queue. Also allows you to authorize additional print servers to service this queue.

FIGURE 14.25

*The Print Job Information
Screen in PCONSOLE*

```
NetWare Print Console 4.15                    Monday  May  25, 1998  5:54pm
Context: BLUE.CRIME.TOKYO.ACME

                          Print Job Information

  Print job:          0193E001             File size:         5522
  Client:             WEarp[7]
  Description:        J:USERS\WEARP\BLUCRIME.RPT
  Status:             Print job is ready and waiting for the print server.

  User hold:          No                   Entry date:        5-25-1998
  Operator hold:      No                   Entry time:        5:52:39 pm
  Service sequence:   1
                                           Form:              Reports
  Number of copies:   1                    Print banner:      Yes
                                           Name:              WEarp
  File contents:      Byte stream          Banner name:       LPT1
  Tab size:
                                           Defer printing:    No
  Form feed:          Yes                  Target date:
  Notify when done:   No                   Target time:

Enter up to 49 characters to describe the print job.

Esc=Exit                                                            F1=Help
```

This screen shows the print job ID number, who submitted the job, the filename, and the status of the job. This screen also allow a user or operator hold to be placed on the job. If the job is placed on hold, it will stay in the queue until the hold is removed.

The "Service sequence" field allows you to reorder jobs in the queue. In our example, there is only one job currently in the queue, so the service sequence is 1 — indicating that this job is next in line to be serviced by the print server. If there were jobs in the queue ahead of this one, we could change the service sequence number, thereby moving it up in the queue. Only print queue operators can place one user's job ahead of another's. Users can only reorder their own jobs.

If you look closely at the remaining options, you'll notice that these are all of the parameters used with CAPTURE. So, if you send a print job with CAPTURE parameters and would like to change the parameters after the job is sent, you can do that here.

The last option on this screen is "Defer printing." If this option is set to Yes, you will be able to specify the date and time for which you would like this job to print. This option is useful if you are printing large jobs that you would like to defer until a later, less busy, time.

Putting Print Queues on Hold   Using the Status option of the Print Queue Information menu, a print queue operator can put the select print queue on hold. There are three hold options in this menu:

▸ Allow users to submit print jobs — When set to No, this option prevents users from placing additional jobs in the queue. Any jobs already in the queue will continue to be serviced by the print server. This is useful when you are planning to do maintenance on a printer, or if you are planning to change print queue definitions.

▸ Allow service by current print servers — This option, when set to No, will allow users to continue to place jobs in the queue, but those jobs will not be printed until this flag is removed. Again, this option is useful when doing printer or print server maintenance.

▸ Allow new print servers to attach — This option prevents new print servers from attaching to this queue.

Assigning Print Queue Users and Operators The Users option of the PCONSOLE Print Queue Information menu allows you to authorize users and groups to place jobs in this queue. When you select this option, you are presented with a list of current print queue users. Use the Insert key to browse the tree and then authorize new users, groups, or containers as users of this print queue by highlighting an object and pressing F10. Multiple objects can be selected by using the F5 key to mark them and F10 to select. To remove print queue users, highlight the object in the user list and press Delete.

Assigning print queue operators is done is a similar fashion. Select the Operators menu option and use the Insert key to browse and F10 to select.

Attaching Print Servers to a Queue To assign a print server to service a queue, select the Print Servers option from the Print Queue Information menu. You will be shown a list of the print servers currently assigned to service this queue. Use the Insert key to browse the NDS tree to find the print server you would like to service this queue. To add a print server to the list, highlight the server name and press F10 or Esc. Before the print server will actively service this queue, it must be loaded at a file server.

ZEN

"Big hair makes your hips look smaller."

Nanny Fine

Managing Printers

When you select the Printer option from the PCONSOLE main menu, you will be shown a list of print queues configured in the current context. Use the Insert key to create a new printer. When you create a printer in PCONSOLE, the only information you are asked for at this point is the printer name. This can be a little deceiving because additional steps are required to complete the printer setup.

Once the printer is created, you will need to select the printer by pressing Enter and configure it from the resulting Printer Configuration screen (shown in the background of the screen in Figure 14.26).

FIGURE 14.26

The Printer Configuration Screen in PCONSOLE

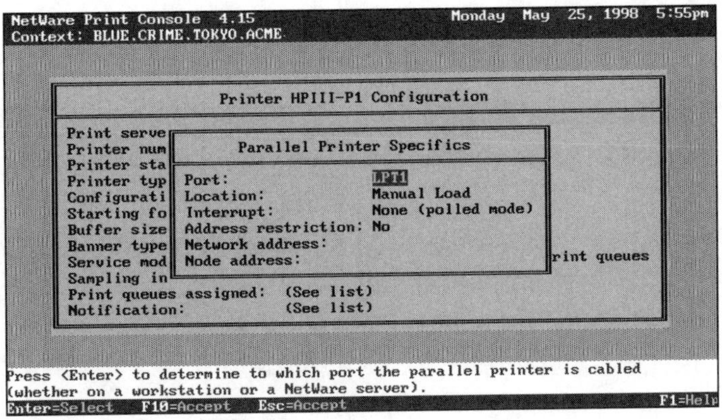

This default configuration assumes that you are configuring a parallel printer attached to LPT1 of a remote workstation. So, in order to complete the configuration, you must provide the following information if the default configuration is not correct:

▸ *Printer type* — Whether this printer is a parallel, serial, or other type of printer.

▸ *Configuration* — To which port this printer is attached (LPT1, LPT2, and so on), and the location of this printer; that is, locally (directly) attached or remotely (workstation) attached.

▸ *Interrupt* — IntranetWare defaults to a polled mode when checking a print queue for new print jobs. If you choose to use an interrupt mode instead, this field can be configured to indicate the interrupt of the port hardware. This field must match the port hardware if an interrupt is used.

▸ *Address restriction* — This optional field allows you to restrict this printer to being loaded on the specified workstation or network.

To complete the printer configuration, you must assign a print queue for this printer to service and link a print server.

To manage NDS printing objects with PCONSOLE, select the Printers option from the PCONSOLE main menu. This allows you to manage NDS printer objects in the current context. By selecting an available printer, you can see the current configuration of this printer (see Figure 14.27).

FIGURE 14.27

Printer Configuration Screen for an HPIII LaserJet Printer

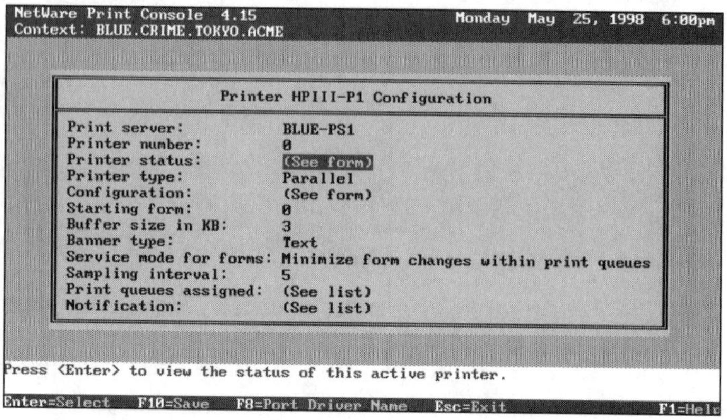

Table 14.9 summarizes the information found in Figure 14.27.

TABLE 14.9

Printer Configuration Parameters

PARAMETER	FUNCTION
Print server	Specifies the active print server currently servicing this printer.
Printer number	Displays the logical printer number assigned to this printer.
Printer status	Displays the status of this printer and the active print job. Also allows a print server operator to change the queue service mode, change the currently mounted form, and issue printer control commands.
Printer type	Displays the configured printer type. Available printer types include parallel, serial, UNIX printer, AppleTalk printer, Other/Unknown, XNP, and AIO.
Configuration	Displays the configuration information about this printer, including port, location, and interrupt. For serial printers this field also includes COM port configuration information, such as baud rate, stop bits, data bits, and parity.
Starting form	Indicates the PRINTDEF form that the print server will assume is mounted on the printer when the print server starts.

TABLE 14.9

Printer Configuration
Parameters (continued)

PARAMETER	FUNCTION
Buffer size in KB	Indicates the size of the print server's internal buffer for this printer. Increasing this number may improve printer performance if the printer stops and restarts in the middle of a print job.
Banner type	Specifies the default banner type for this printer. Options are Text or Postscript.
Service mode for forms	Specifies how the print server will service jobs in the queue when forms are used.
Sampling interval	When the printer is idle, this number specifies how often (in seconds) that the print server will poll the queue assigned to this printer for new print jobs. When the printer is active, the print server will automatically service the next job in the queue.
Print queues assigned	Allows you to view the print queues this printer is assigned to service. Also allows you to add new print queues to be serviced.
Notification	Displays the users and groups assigned to be notified if there is a problem with this printer. Also allows you to add users or groups to the notification list.

Assigning a Print Queue   Assigning a print queue to a printer can be done through the Printer Configuration screen as well. To do so, select the Print queues assigned option and press Enter. You can then use the Insert key to browse the directory tree for the print queue to which you would like to assign this printer. Once you have located the desired print queue, press Enter or F10 to select it.

When you assign a print queue to a printer, you can also set the priority level and default status of the queue. After you select the print queue, a Priority Configuration screen appears. The priority of this queue can be set to any number between 1 and 10. Priority 1 is the highest; 10 is the lowest.

If this printer is servicing multiple queues, you can use the "Make this the default queue" option to define the default queue for this printer. When network users capture to this printer instead of a queue assigned to it, print jobs will be spooled to the default queue assigned here.

In the background, you will see to what priority this queue is set and the state. As shown at the bottom of this screen, a printer's state can be one of the following:

▸ [A]: Active

▸ [C]: Configured

▸ [AC]: Active and configured

▸ [D]: Default

Using Forms   If you have defined print forms using NWADMIN or PRINTDEF, the Printers option under PCONSOLE will also allow you to configure how those forms are used. Referring back to the Printer Configuration screen (Figure 14.27), there are a number of areas that affect forms.

Under the "Printer status" option, there are two forms options. The first is "Service mode." This option determines how the printer will service the print queue when forms are being used. The next option is "Mounted form." This is the form that is currently mounted at this printer. You would use this option to change the currently mounted form through PCONSOLE. The currently mounted form can also be change through NWADMIN, PSC, and at the print server console.

The next option that affects forms from the Printer Configuration menu is "Starting form." This option defines the default starting form to be used when the printer starts up. This form number should represent the most commonly used form on this printer.

Finally, there is the "Service mode for forms" option. When you select this option, you are presented with the screen in Figure 14.28. Take a quick peek.

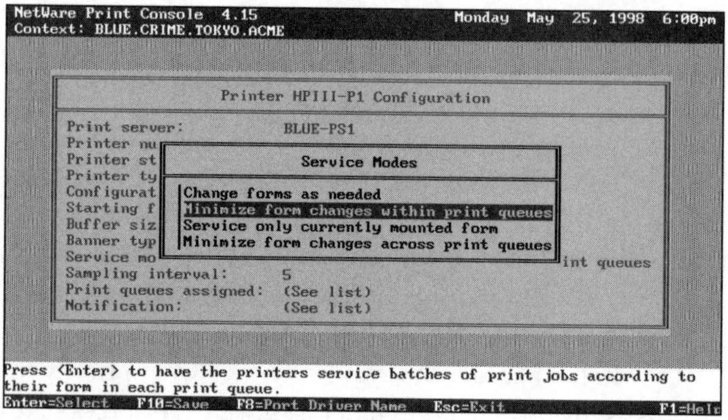

FIGURE 14.28

Service Modes for Custom Forms in PCONSOLE

```
NetWare Print Console  4.15                    Monday  May  25, 1998  6:00pm
Context: BLUE.CRIME.TOKYO.ACME

                        Printer HPIII-P1 Configuration

    Print server:          BLUE-PS1
    Printer nu ┌──────────────────────────────────────────────────────┐
    Printer st │               Service Modes                          │
    Printer ty │                                                      │
    Configurat │Change forms as needed                                │
    Starting f │Minimize form changes within print queues             │
    Buffer siz │Service only currently mounted form                   │
    Banner typ │Minimize form changes across print queues             │
    Service mo └──────────────────────────────────────────────────────┘int queues
    Sampling interval:     5
    Print queues assigned: (See list)
    Notification:          (See list)


Press <Enter> to have the printers service batches of print jobs according to
their form in each print queue.
Enter=Select   F10=Save   F8=Port Driver Name   Esc=Exit              F1=Help
```

The first option, "Change forms as needed," requires you to mount a new form at this printer each time a print job with a different form number is submitted to the queue. The print jobs in the queue will be serviced based on priority (on a first-in, first-out basis). So, if many different form types are used, this option may require you to change forms often.

To minimize the number of times form changes occur, you may consider leaving the default ("Minimize form changes within print queues") enabled. With this option enabled, all of the print jobs with the same priority submitted to the queue with the currently mounted form requested will be serviced first. Lower-priority jobs with a different form requested will require a form change before being serviced.

The next option, "Service currently mounted form," will only service jobs submitted with the mounted form type. If this option is enabled, the print server will not prompt for a form change if a job with a different form type is submitted to the queue. These jobs will never be printed unless this option is changed to one of the other options.

The final option on this menu, "Minimize form changes across print queues," is similar to the default option, except, in this case, all jobs with the currently mounted form will be serviced first, regardless of priority.

ZEN

"If it ain't half off, it ain't on sale."

Nanny Fine

Managing Print Servers

When you select the Print Servers option from the PCONSOLE main menu, you are shown a list of print servers configured in the current context. When you press Insert, a prompt appears, at which you enter the print server name.

The print server can be any hexadecimal name from 1 to 64 characters, including spaces and underscores. Even though this gives you tremendous flexibility, you should keep your print server names short and descriptive. For example, the second print server created to service printers in the BLUE division might be named BLUE-PS2. When you press Enter to create the print server, a message appears on the screen indicating that it may take up to 60 seconds for the print server to be created. Though it rarely takes 60 seconds to create a new print server, this message is just to reassure you that the system is still working.

Once the print server is created, to complete the configuration you will need to assign this print server to service printers and print queues.

To manage NDS print servers with PCONSOLE, select the Print Servers option from the PCONSOLE main menu. By selecting Print Servers you can create new NDS print server objects or view existing print servers in the current context. The left side of Figure 14.29 shows the print servers configured in the current context.

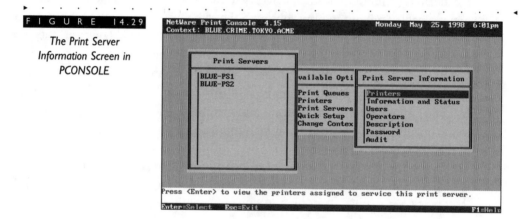

F I G U R E   14.29

The Print Server
Information Screen in
PCONSOLE

After you select an available print server, all of the available information about that server will be displayed on the right side of the screen, as seen in Figure 14.29. Table 14.10 summarizes the information found in each menu option.

T A B L E   14.10

Print Server Information
Parameters

MENU OPTION	PURPOSE
Printers	Displays the printers assigned to be serviced by this print server and their state. Also allows printers to be assigned or removed from this print server.
Information and status	Displays print server type, status, version, number of printers serviced, and advertising name. If the print server is running, this option also allows it to be taken down.
Users	Displays users and groups who are authorized to view the print server's status and active configuration. Allows print server users to be added or removed.

TABLE 14.10

*Print Server Information
Parameters (continued)*

MENU OPTION	PURPOSE
Operators	Displays users and groups who are authorized to manage the print server's status and active configuration. Allows print server operators to be added or removed.
Description	Allows an optional text description to be entered for this print server.
Password	Allows a print server password to be entered. This prevents unauthorized users from loading the print server.
Audit	Allows you to view or modify this print server's auditing information.

Assigning Printers to Be Serviced To assign printers to this print server, select Printers from the Print Server Information menu. A list of the printers currently being serviced by this print server will be displayed. Pressing Insert will allow you to browse the directory tree for the desired printer.

The Printers option will also show you the state of the attached printers. A printer's state can be one of the following:

- ▶ [A]: Active

- ▶ [C]: Configured

- ▶ [AC]: Active and configured

Selecting a configured printer from this screen will take you to the same Printer Configuration screen we saw when we were creating and configuring printers (see Figure 14.27). This is a nice shortcut when you are setting up printing services with this utility.

Assigning Print Server Users and Operators Print server users are network users who have the ability to view the information and status of a print server. Print server operators have the ability to actually change that information. Selecting the Users option from the PCONSOLE Print Server Information menu allows you to authorize users and groups as print server users. You do not have to be a print server user to have print jobs routed by a particular print server, but you do to view its configuration and status. When you select the Users option, you will be presented with a list of current print server users. Use the Insert key to browse the tree for users, groups, or containers to be authorized as print server users. To select an object, highlight the object and press F10. Multiple objects can be selected by using the F5 key to mark them, and then using F10 to select. To remove print server users, highlight the object in the user list and press Delete.

Assigning print server operators is done in a similar fashion. Select the Operators menu option and use the Insert key to browse and F10 to select. To remove a print server operator, use the Delete key.

Using the Auditing Feature

To keep track of printing transactions, print server auditing can be enabled. When auditing is enabled, information about each completed print job will be logged in an audit file called PSERVER.LOG. This log file can be viewed using PCONSOLE or NWADMIN. Also, because PSERVER.LOG is a text file, it can be viewed with any text editor.

To enable auditing, or to view or delete the audit file for a particular print server, choose Audit from the Print Server Information menu. Figure 14.30 shows the resulting screen.

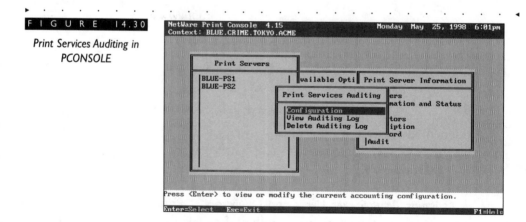

F I G U R E   14.30

Print Services Auditing in PCONSOLE

To enable auditing, choose Configuration and set the "Enable auditing field" to Yes. When you enable auditing, you are given the option of limiting the size of the audit file. If you do not limit this file's size, it could grow to the maximum of the available disk space. To prevent the file from getting out of hand, you may want to limit its size. When the file size is limited, the print server will log entries until the maximum size is reached, and then it will stop until the file is deleted or this field is changed.

Any time a change is made in the Auditing Information screen, the print server must be shut down and restarted before the changes will take place.

QUIZ

To be a crack sleuth, you have to know your codes. Decode the following:

$C_{18}V_2C_{99}$ $C_3V_4C_{11}V_2!$ $C_{10}V_2C_{1515}V_1C_5V_2$ $C_{15}V_2C_{22}V_5C_{15154}V_5C_{9920}$ $C_3V_2C_2V_4C_3V_2C_3.$

(Q14-3)

That completes our in-depth exploration of PCONSOLE. As you can see, it provides a lot of printing management punch. But for those of you who still prefer a GUI world, NWADMIN provides some printing management capabilities as well, albeit, not as many as PCONSOLE. Let's check it out.

SMART LINK

For more detail on the PCONSOLE printing utility, surf to the *NetWare 4.11 Utilities Reference* **at http://www.novell.com/manuals.**

MANAGING PRINTING WITH NWADMIN

Management under Windows is one of the easiest ways to track jobs and the status of print servers. NWADMIN and NWUSER are the main tools for doing this. Even though NWADMIN is primarily an administrator's tool, users can benefit from it as well.

Printing management under NWADMIN is broken into two sets of tasks:

▶ CNE tasks

▶ User tasks

Let's take a closer look.

CNE Tasks

As a manager of printers and queues, you will need to do several things:

- ▶ Mount new printer forms

- ▶ Stop/start printers

- ▶ Unload the print server

- ▶ Place a hold on a job

- ▶ Delete a job

Remember, you must be an operator (printer or queue) to carry out these management functions. Table 14.11 shows the steps required to accomplish these functions. This assumes you are already in NWADMIN and at the context where the objects resides.

T A B L E 14.11
CNE Printing Tasks in NWADMIN

TASK	STEPS INVOLVED
Mount new printer forms	1 • Choose the printer (highlight and double-click).
	2 • Select Printer Status.
	3 • Select Mount Form.
	4 • Choose the form name (or number).
Stop/start printers (see Figure 14.31)	1 • Choose the printer.
	2 • Select Printer Status.
	3 • Select Pause to stop or Start to resume printer output.
Unload the print server	1 • Choose the print server.
	2 • At the lower middle of the screen, choose Unload.
	3 • Choose Immediately or After Jobs based on whether you wish current jobs to complete before the print server terminates.

CNE Printing Tasks in
NWADMIN (continued)

TASK	STEPS INVOLVED
Place a hold on a job (see Figure 14.32)	1 • Select the queue that is servicing the job. 2 • Select Job List. 3 • Select Hold Job.
Release a job hold	1 • Select the queue that is servicing the job. 2 • Select Job List. 3 • Select Resume.
Delete a job	1 • Select the queue that is servicing the job. 2 • Select Job List. 3 • Highlight the specific job. 4 • Select Delete.

The Printer Status Screen in
NWADMIN

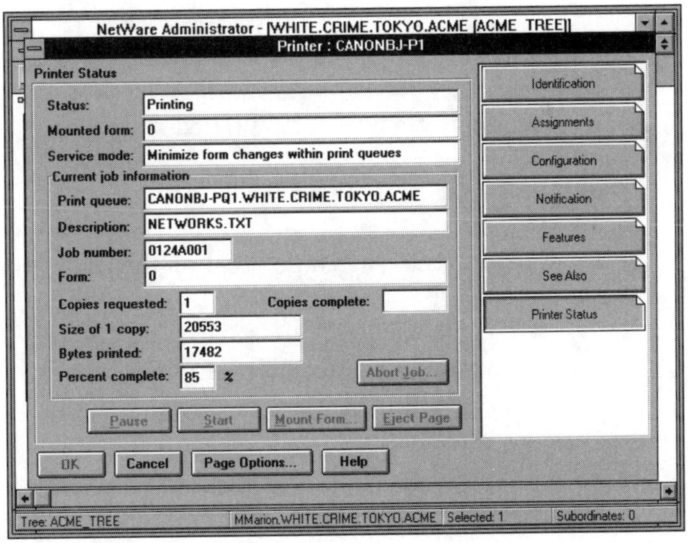

NetWare Administrator - [WHITE.CRIME.TOKYO.ACME [ACME TREE]]
Printer : CANONBJ-P1

Printer Status

Status: Printing
Mounted form: 0
Service mode: Minimize form changes within print queues

Current job information
Print queue: CANONBJ-PQ1.WHITE.CRIME.TOKYO.ACME
Description: NETWORKS.TXT
Job number: 0124A001
Form: 0
Copies requested: 1   Copies complete:
Size of 1 copy: 20553
Bytes printed: 17482
Percent complete: 85 %   Abort Job...

Pause   Start   Mount Form...   Eject Page

OK   Cancel   Page Options...   Help

Identification
Assignments
Configuration
Notification
Features
See Also
Printer Status

Tree: ACME_TREE   MMarion.WHITE.CRIME.TOKYO.ACME   Selected: 1   Subordinates: 0

The Print Queue Job List
Screen in NWADMIN

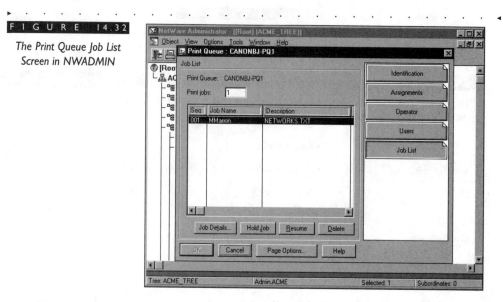

User Tasks

Some user management functions are similar to operator functions. Typically, they are basic view functions to check on the status of a job. These functions include:

- ▸ Viewing status of a job in a queue

- ▸ Viewing amount of job printed on a printer

- ▸ Deleting a job submitted

- ▸ Placing/releasing a user hold on the job

These functions require that you have at least user access on the print server or queue in question. Refer to Table 14.12 for a quick review.

ZEN

"Ma has plastic on the furniture. I think she's preserving it for the afterlife!"

Nanny Fine

TABLE 14.12	TASK	STEPS INVOLVED
User Printing Tasks in NWADMIN	View job status	1 • Select the queue that is servicing the job.
		2 • Select Job List.
		3 • Locate the job in question.
		4 • Scroll right to view status (Active, Held, Ready).
	View percent completed	1 • Select printer that is printing the job.
		2 • Select Printer Status.
	Delete a job	1 • Select the queue that is servicing the job.
		2 • Select Job List.
		3 • Highlight the chosen job.
		4 • Select Delete.
	Place/release a user (see 14.33)	1 • Select the queue that is servicing the hold Figure job.
		2 • Select Job List.
		3 • Select the job to hold/release.
		4 • Select Hold Job to hold and Resume to release.

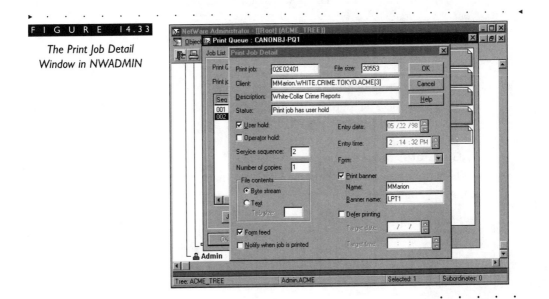

FIGURE 14.33

The Print Job Detail Window in NWADMIN

This completes our discussion of general printing management with PCONSOLE and NWADMIN. These two tools are the cornerstone of your arsenal. But you never know when you might need a special utility. So, the next four topics deal with less common printing management components — such as print servers, print job configurations, and print forms customization. Ready, set, explore.

SMART LINK

For more detail on NWADMIN as a printing utility, surf to the "IntranetWare Utilities Reference" at http://www.novell.com/manuals.

MANAGING PRINT SERVERS WITH PSC

Print Server Control (PSC) is the first of the printing-specialty tools. To use PSC, you need the following information:

1 • The print server name — This could be either the name of the print server on a Bindery (3.x, 2.x server) or an NDS name (such as WHITE-PS1. WHITE.CRIME.TOKYO.ACME).

2 • The name of the printer to manage — This could be P1, HP4SI-P1, and so on. The names were defined under PCONSOLE or NWADMIN.

3 • The command desired (for example, STATUS, MOUNT, or DISMOUNT)

One of the more helpful options is the /? option, which will show all the options available for the PSC command. The next section covers some of the fun things that you can do with PSC.

Get Status of All Printers

This option shows all printers for the print server and their status (see Figure 14.34). Following is the syntax:

```
PSC PS=WHITE-PS1.WHITE.CRIME.TOKYO.ACME P=ALL STAT
```

FIGURE 14.34

*Getting Printer Status
with PSC*

```
Z:\PUBLIC>PSC PS=.WHITE-PS1.WHITE.CRIME.TOKYO.ACME P=ALL STAT
Printer CANONBJ-P1 (printer number 0)
        Status:Not connected

Printer HPIII-P1 (printer number 1)
        Status:Not connected

Printer HP4SI-P3 (printer number 2)
        Status:Not connected

Printer HP4SI-P2 (printer number 3)
        Status:Not connected

Printer HP4SI-P1 (printer number 4)
        Status:Printing job
        Off-line
        Print job name: LPT1
        Print job ID: 212001
        Complete: 93%


Z:\PUBLIC>
```

Mount a New Form in a Printer

This option will make the desired form number the currently mounted form. Here's the syntax:

```
PSC  PS=WHITE-PS1.WHITE.CRIME.TOKYO.ACME  P=CANONBJ-P1  Mount
Form=Reports
```

You may also indicate the printer and/or form by number:

```
PSC PS=WHITE-PS1.WHITE.CRIME.TOKYO.ACME P=0 Mount Form=1
```

Stop/Start a Printer from Servicing Jobs

This option will tell the printer to stop printing once its local buffer is empty. This would be useful if it's necessary to change paper or fix a problem without deleting jobs in the queue.

In this example, we'll assume that we're already in the context WHITE.CRIME. TOKYO.ACME. Therefore, we only need to specify the name of the print server.

```
PSC PS=WHITE-PS1 P=CANONBJ-P1 STOP
```

To restart the printer, type

```
PSC PS=WHITE-PS1 P=CANONBJ-P1 START
```

Show Print Server Configuration

This option will show you the printer layout for the specified print server. This includes all printers and queues assigned to the print server. The syntax for this option is

```
PSC PS=WHITE-PS1 LIST
```

This option helps you to find the name of the printers attached to the print server so that you can use the other options to get more specific details (see Figure 14.35).

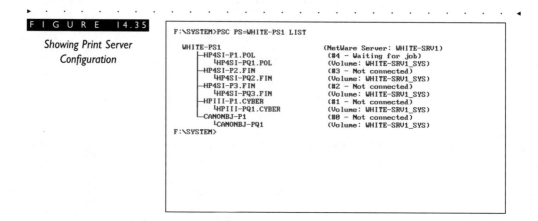

```
F:\SYSTEM>PSC PS=WHITE-PS1 LIST

WHITE-PS1                               (NetWare Server: WHITE-SRV1)
        ├─HP4SI-P1.POL                  (#4 - Waiting for job)
        │   └HP4SI-PQ1.POL              (Volume: WHITE-SRV1_SYS)
        ├─HP4SI-P2.FIN                  (#3 - Not connected)
        │   └HP4SI-PQ2.FIN              (Volume: WHITE-SRV1_SYS)
        ├─HP4SI-P3.FIN                  (#2 - Not connected)
        │   └HP4SI-PQ3.FIN              (Volume: WHITE-SRV1_SYS)
        ├─HPIII-P1.CYBER                (#1 - Not connected)
        │   └HPIII-PQ1.CYBER            (Volume: WHITE-SRV1_SYS)
        └─CANONBJ-P1                    (#0 - Not connected)
            └CANONBJ-PQ1                (Volume: WHITE-SRV1_SYS)
F:\SYSTEM>
```

That's it for PSC. The next specialty printing tool is PRINTCON.

SMART LINK

For more detail on the PSC printing utility, surf to the *NetWare 4.11 Utilities Reference* at http://www.novell.com/manuals.

CONFIGURING PRINT JOBS WITH PRINTCON

Back in the days before NetWare supported Windows, the only way to capture printers was with the CAPTURE command, either through a login script or a batch file. To make this process easier, PRINTCON was used to create print job configurations that consisted of common user CAPTURE statements. Then, rather than having to enter long and cryptic CAPTURE statements, the CAPTURE command was simply

```
CAPTURE J=<job_configuration>
```

Today, with the NWUSER Windows utility, we have an easier option: Just drag and drop to capture a printer once and select the Permanent option. But, even with this easier option, PRINTCON is still around for those who would like to use it. Figure 14.36 shows the PRINTCON main menu.

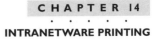

FIGURE 14.36

PRINTCON Main Menu

```
Configure Print Jobs  4.15                    Friday  May  22, 1998  2:46pm
Object: Admin.acme




                        ┌──────────────────────────────────┐
                        │          Available Options         │
                        ├──────────────────────────────────┤
                        │ Edit Print Job Configurations      │
                        │ Select Default Print Job Configuration │
                        │ Change Current Object              │
                        └──────────────────────────────────┘




Press <Enter> to add, change or delete print job configurations.
Enter=Select    F4=Switch to Bindery Mode    Esc=Exit                F1=Help
```

The first thing to notice in the PRINTCON main menu is the object at the top of the screen. Any print jobs configured during this session will be for the .Admin.ACME object. If we would like to set up print job configurations for another user, we can use the Change Current Object option. When we select that option, we are prompted to enter the object name. This can be done by either typing the full NDS name, or by using the Insert key and browsing.

Print job configurations can be created for users or Container objects. If a print job configuration is created for a Container object, all the users in that container can use it. This is an improvement over the PRINTCON of yesterday. In previous versions of NetWare, there was no way to assign print job configurations to groups of users — each user had an individual PRINTCON database. The database itself was a file called PRINTCON.DAT, which was located in each user's individual SYS:MAIL directory. In IntranetWare, the PRINTCON job configurations are not separate databases, but rather are part of the NDS database and are properties of each user or container object.

To create a print job configuration, select Edit Print Job Configurations from the "Available options" menu. A list of the current job configurations will be displayed. To create a new job configuration, press the Insert key and enter the job configuration name. The name can be just about anything you wish, but it should be descriptive of the configuration type. For example, if you are creating a job configuration to be used when you are printing letters on company letterhead, you may want to name the job configuration "letters."

After you name the job configuration, select it by pressing Enter. The Job Configuration screen will appear. If you look closely at the job configuration's options, you'll notice that they are essentially all of the CAPTURE parameters. Since CAPTURE was covered previously, we won't cover each of these options in depth.

The only options listed that aren't regular CAPTURE options are Device and Mode. These options represent print devices and modes defined in the PRINTDEF utility. Print devices and modes generally are used when the application you are using doesn't support the print mode you want. However, most of today's applications support print modes for common printers. When selecting print devices and modes, be sure that you have selected a print queue first. Otherwise, the devices and modes defined in the user's context will not appear.

If you have more than one print job configuration defined, you can choose one of them as the default. The benefit of having a default job configuration is that you can use the CAPTURE command without other parameters and the default job configuration will be used. To change the default job configuration, choose Select Default Print Job Configuration, highlight the desired job configuration, and press Enter. To remove the default job configuration, press Delete.

SMART LINK

For more detail on the PRINTCON printing utility, surf to the NetWare 4.11 Utilities Reference at http://www.novell.com/manuals.

CUSTOMIZING PRINT DEVICES AND FORMS WITH PRINTDEF

Now that everything is set up and running smoothly, we must shift our printing focus to customization. These are the advanced tasks that separate CNEs from pretenders. PRINTDEF is our friend. This DOS-based printing utility allows us to customize two important printing components:

- ▶ Print forms

- ▶ Print devices

Multiple print forms can be supported by attaching special instructions to specific print jobs. In addition, customized formatting is allowed with special print devices. All of this is accomplished using PRINTDEF.

The PRINTDEF utility is used to define and store printer definitions or command strings and printer form definitions. It's probably the least frequently used of all of the IntranetWare printing utilities, but it comes in handy when you have multiple paper types used on a single printer, or when you want to exploit printer functionality that your application doesn't support. Let's take a look at the PRINTDEF main menu (see Figure 14.37).

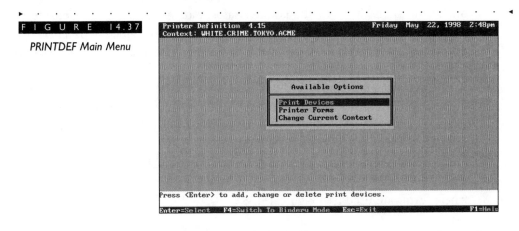

F I G U R E   1 4.37

PRINTDEF Main Menu

As with the other DOS-based print utilities, it's important to notice the context at the top of the screen before creating or modifying devices or forms. When creating or modifying devices or forms, the context shown at the top of the screen is where they will be created. Any user under the context where the forms or devices are defined will have access to them.

Devices and forms will flow down through the NDS tree until another definition is defined at a lower level. For example, if a print form is defined in ACME, all users in all Organizational Units below ACME will have access to that form. If forms are then defined in the .WHITE.CRIME.TOKYO.ACME container, users in that container will get only those forms and not the ones defined in ACME.

ZEN

"My Aunt Miriam always says, 'The more the merrier, unless you're talking about chins.'"

Nanny Fine

Using Custom Forms

In certain cases, a printing environment may require the use of preprinted forms for print jobs such as invoices, paychecks, return forms, and purchase orders. If this is the case, the administrator and the network must ensure that submitted print jobs get printed on the proper forms. Imagine if a paycheck were printed on an invoice form. The person on the receiving end of the paycheck wouldn't be too happy.

One way around this is to have a dedicated printer for every type of possible print job that requires the form. In fact, in companies that require high-volume print services, this is usually the case. This means the printers seldom have to be reset, except to add new forms when they run out.

In environments where the volume is lower, preprinted forms may be required, but multiple form types may need to be consolidated to a single printer. This is where forms are used (see Figure 14.38).

TIP

In the situation where you have dedicated forms printers, you can ignore forms altogether. Configuring forms where not needed just adds another layer of complexity.

A good example would be where the company ACME needs to print invoices and purchase requisitions on the same printer. ACME needs to have two forms defined, plus a potential third if normal draft printing is also done on the same printer. In our example, we have defined three forms:

- INVOICE (0)

- PURCHASE (1)

- DRAFT (2)

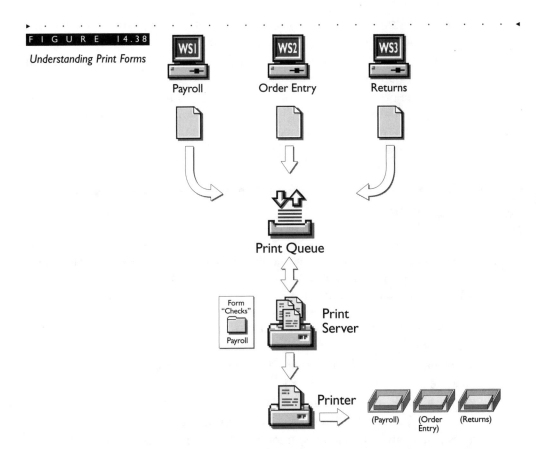

Understanding Print Forms

Notice that each form also has a number. When referencing forms, you can use either a form name or a reference number — IntranetWare doesn't care which.

To specify the form to use, when the workstation is initially captured, you can use the /F option under the CAPTURE command, or a form may be specified under a user's print job configuration. The administrator may also have more than one print job configuration per user specifically for that reason. That way, the workstation will default to the standard print configuration for the user (perhaps using a draft form — standard blank paper, for instance), but the user can still choose a print job that specifies a particular form.

Ideally, form selection could be set via a batch file, login script, or Windows PIF file. This would eliminate the burden on the user of choosing the right print job configuration.

Servicing Print Forms Once a user has submitted a print job with a specific form, the form number (and the name) will be kept as part of the Job Entry Record. If you recall, a Job Entry Record is kept for every print job submitted to the IntranetWare print system.

When the print server first comes up, it defaults to form type 0, even though form 0 may be undefined. Typically, most administrators make form 0 the most used form in a multiple-forms environment.

REAL WORLD

IntranetWare needs only the form number and not necessarily the form name. Therefore, when any print server initializes, it will default to form 0 for all printers serviced by that print server.

Once the print server has found a job in the queue to service, it will look to see what form type the job requires. It then decides whether to service the job immediately or to hold it temporarily for efficiency reasons. We'll assume for now that the print server will service jobs on a first-come, first-served basis.

The print server then opens the data file associated with the print job and checks the form type currently being used for the printer. Remember that the print server usually initializes the printer with form 0 (the default can be set when the printer is defined with IntranetWare). If the print server notes that the job submitted requires a different form than the currently mounted type, then the server halts the printer and sends a message to the designated persons that a new form must be mounted.

The printing administrator (or whoever is designated to manage the print server) can then take several steps to continue printing:

▸ Remove the current paper type in the printer

▸ Feed in the required form type

▸ Use a server set command to indicate that the proper form is now in the printer

▶ Restart the printer

If the next print job requires a different form type, the process must be repeated.

Changing Print Forms   As you can see, changing forms can become quite tiresome if many different types of jobs are passing through, all with different form types. To minimize the number of form changes, IntranetWare allows you to optimize how forms get serviced.

By default, a print server services form types on a first-come, first-served basis. But, if you're in a multiform environment, you may want to change this default. When the print server is configured, you can specify how to handle forms when the print server encounters them. Options include:

▶ *Minimize form changes within queues* — This option will ask you to change form types only when all of the currently mounted forms have been serviced within the queue. If there were one form 0, three form 3, and five form 4 print jobs, here's what would happen. Assume that form 0 is currently mounted. First, the form 0 job would be printed, then the three form 3 jobs, followed by the five form 4 jobs, regardless of their submission order. When all jobs were completed, if there were another queue being serviced by the printer, the print server would rotate to the next queue and do the same.

▶ *Minimize form changes across queues* — This option is similar to the previous, except that the print server will do all the form 0 print jobs across all queues being serviced by the one printer, then move on to the next form and so on, until all print jobs had been serviced. This is used only when more than one queue services a single printer.

▶ *Service only the currently mounted form* — This option allows the print server operator to control when jobs with forms get printed. The currently mounted form type will be the only type serviced until the operator changes the printer's mounted form. Then the print server will only service that form. This is useful in an environment where the main form (invoices, for example) are being printed all day long, and the other form(s) only must be batch-printed at intervals (such as at the end of the day).

Remember, in an ideal situation, each preprinted form should have its own dedicated printer, in which case, no forms definition is necessary. If forms are necessary (more than one form printed per printer), then there are two ways to configure forms: CAPTURE and NWADMIN.

Under NWADMIN, you may define forms under a container to service the objects (users, for example) of that container. To do this:

1 · Start NWADMIN and locate the container where the desired print server resides.

2 · Place the pointer over the container icon and click the right mouse button once.

3 · Choose Details.

4 · Choose Forms.

In most cases, applications send all the formatting information needed by a plotter or a printer via their own native print drivers. In addition, Windows has support for every major printer available today.

In certain cases, IntranetWare may need to send printer formatting functions along with the actual print data. This is accomplished through the printer definition database (PRINTDEF), which can be defined by the administrator.

To review, every print job has three parts in the actual data stream: the print header, the print data, and the print tail. When you are using the PRINTDEF database, you are telling IntranetWare what to put in the *print header*. The header information reaches the printer first and will format it properly before the *data* starts to print. The *print tail* is used normally to reset the printer to its initial state so that it's ready for the next print job.

Once you have assigned a user either a form or a device (or both) using PRINTCON or NWADMIN, when the user prints, the device information will be appended to the print job data. For example, if you have chosen HPLaserJet4 and Landscape as a function, the proper escape codes will be part of the print header. In addition, if the function for printer reset (under the reinitialize mode) has been set, IntranetWare will automatically send the reset string after the job data has been sent. This way, IntranetWare can ensure that the printer is left in a reset state after a function has been used.

Using Print Devices

To define a new print device, select Print Devices from the PRINTDEF main menu. Print devices can be created manually by using the Insert key and entering each escape sequence that represents your printer's command strings. The easiest way to define a new printer definition is to take advantage of the 57 predefined print devices that come with IntranetWare. Those print devices are stored in the SYS:PUBLIC directory of each IntranetWare file server. These print devices can be imported into your current context by selecting Import Print Devices from the Print Device Options menu.

If the printer you are using is not on the list, check your printer manual because your printer may emulate a printer that is on the list.

PRINTDEF print devices consist of two parts: print devices and print modes. *Print devices* are the various printer command strings that you often find in the back of printer manuals. *Print modes* are made up of one or more print functions and represent the various modes a printer supports. For example, the reinitialize mode will reset the printer after each print job. Another example of a common printer mode is landscape mode.

That pretty much finishes our journey through printing management LANd — otherwise know as the IntranetWare "war zone."

SMART LINK

For more detail on the PRINTDEF printing utility, surf to the *NetWare 4.11 Utilities Reference* at http://www.novell.com/manuals.

QUIZ

Try this one on for size. A man is walking his dog on a leash toward home at a steady 3 m.p.h. When they are 7 miles from home, the man lets his dog off the leash. The dog immediately runs off toward home at 8 m.p.h. When the dog reaches the house, it turns around and runs back to the man at the same speed. When it reaches the man, it turns back for the house. This is repeated until the man gets home and lets in the dog. How many miles does the dog cover from the time it is let off the leash to the time it is let into the house?

(Q14-4)

This completes our discussion of IntranetWare's printing management tools. Wow, there's a lot to work with. We learned about PCONSOLE, NWADMIN, PSC, PRINTCON, and PRINTDEF. With all of these tools, it should be easy to keep IntranetWare printing running smoothly. It is . . . until somebody tries to print something! That's when it gets a little out of hand.

Congratulations! Mystery solved. I enjoy a good mystery, how about you? IntranetWare printing is a great place to start. We discovered a lot of interesting things about it today, and I think you're definitely ready to attack it on your own. But if you're still feeling a little skittish, here's a quick review.

It all started with the essence of printing. In the old days, we used to print by ourselves. Now, we get to share this honor with hundreds of strangers. Network printing has probably had a major impact on the social fabric of humanity — we just don't notice it. We went on a little journey through the life of a print job — starting with CAPTURE, then to the queue, print server, and ultimately the printer. Wasn't that fun?

Then, we learned all the steps involved in printing setup. It's not so bad. There are only four steps and they're not very hard. First, you create the print queue, then the printer, and finally the print server. Then, to top it all off, you activate the print server. No sweat. We also discovered a few secrets about customizing IntranetWare printing with print forms and devices.

Once it's up an running, the fun part starts — keeping it running. IntranetWare printing management focused on five CNE and user tools, namely PCONSOLE, NWADMIN, PSC, PRINTCON, and PRINTDEF. We learned how to configure, manage, and customize the IntranetWare printing system. I bet you didn't realize how much help there is out there! Don't worry — you're not alone.

ZEN

"I was thinking about the Pilgrims. How'd they know what to pack? I mean, you're going to a new world. Is it hot, . . . cold, . . . rainy? There are no brochures! So, they all wear the same thing and what a mistake. Very few people look good in a big hat, a big collar, and a big buckle. What were they thinking?"

Nanny Fine

So, how do you feel now? A little better? Did all that wisdom from Nanny Fine soothe your brain? Well, if you're still a little worried about going out on your own, I have a surprise for you — exercises! You want practice, I've got practice. A bunch of hands-on exercises are just the cure for printing cold feet. Once you've cruised through the following seven exercises, you'll be a printing pro. You'll be ready for anything . . . except a shopping spree with Nanny Fine — ouch! Go get them, and I'll see you in the final frontier.

SMART LINK

Visit Nanny Fine at http://www.cbs.com/primetime/nanny.html.

QUIZ

Here's the ultimate numbers mystery. Let's see if you're up to the task. Fill the grid below with the numbers 1 to 16 to form a magic square so that each vertical and horizontal line, each corner to corner diagonal line, the four corner numbers, each block of four corner squares and the middle four block of numbers each add up to 34. The number 7 has been filled in for good luck. Ready, set, calculate.

7			

(Q14-5)

████ CASE STUDY: BUILDING ACME'S PRINTING SYSTEM ████

This exercise will walk you though the creation and loading of a basic print system using the NWADMIN (Windows) graphical interface. This assumes you have already created ACME's NDS tree. We'll be working in the Crime Fighting department today. Seems appropriate, since we're trying to solve a mystery. Where's Sherlock Holmes when you need him?

For the exercise, we will assume the following names:

▶ *Print server:* WHITE-PS1

▶ *Print queue:* CANONBJ-PQ1

▶ *Printer:* CANONBJ-P1

First we will create the queue.

QUEUE CREATION

1. Log into the network as .Admin.ACME, then execute the NetWare Administrator utility under Windows 3.1 or Windows 95.

2. Click on the WHITE.CRIME.TOKYO.ACME container, then press Insert or choose Object/Create from the menu bar. A New Object dialog box will be displayed. Select Print Queue as the type of object to be created, then click on OK.

3. A Create Print Queue dialog box will be displayed. Type **CANONBJ-PQ1** in the Print Queue Name field, then click on the browser button to the right of the Print Queue Volume field. Walk the tree until WHITE-SRV1_SYS volume is shown in the Available Objects list box. Click on WHITE-SRV1_SYS volume, then click on OK to select it. The Create Print Queue dialog box will be displayed again at this point. Click on the Define Additional Properties box, then click on the Create button.

4. The CANONBJ-PQ1 Print Queue Identification page will be displayed by default. Type **MainQ** in the Other Name field and **Downtown** in the Location field.

5. Click on the Users page button. Who is/are assigned as queue users? Why?

6. Temporarily switch to a DOS prompt. Type **F:** (or the appropriate network drive letter) and press Enter. Type **DIR \Q*.*** and notice what you see.

7. Use the DOS CD command to switch to the directory found. Count how many subdirectories exist with a .QDR extension.

8. Return to the NWADMIN utility. Click on OK to save your changes to the CANONBJ-PQ1 print queue.

Next, we need to create the printer.

PRINTER CREATION

1. Select the WHITE.CRIME.TOKYO.ACME container again. Press Insert (or Object/Create), and choose a printer as the type of object to be created.

2. Name the printer **CANONBJ-P1**. Click on Define Additional Properties and then click on Create.

3. Type **Booking Printer** in the Other Name field.

4. Click on the Assignments page button and add the print queue just created.

5. Click on the Configuration button, then the Communication button, then click on Auto Load (local to Print Server), then click on OK.

6. Click on the Notification page button. Click on Notify Print Job Owner to deselect the option. Note what happens.

7. Click on Notify Print Job Owner again to re-select, and note what happens.

8. Click on Features. Type **Fingerprint** in the Supported Cartridges field, then click on OK.

Finally, it's time to build the print server.

CREATING THE PRINT SERVER

1. Select the WHITE.CRIME.TOKYO.ACME container again.

2. Press Insert (or Object/Create), and select "print server" as the type of object to create.

3. Name the print server **WHITE-PS1**, then click on the Define Additional Properties box and click on CREATE.

4. Click on Change Password Enter the password **Secret** and reconfirm, then click on OK.

5. Click on the Assignments page button. Add the CANONBJ-P1 printer click on OK.

6. Click on the Users page button. Who is the current print server user? Why?

7. Delete the current print server user and add yourself.

8. Click on the Operator page button. Who is the operator and why?

9. Click on the Auditing Log page button, then click on the Enable Auditing button. Finally, click on OK to save your changes to this print server.

10. Double-click on the WHITE-PS1 print server, then click on the Print Layout page button. Note the exclamation point next to the print server. What do you think this means?

11. Click on the print server to select it, then click on Status. Note what you see.

12. Click on Close, then click on Cancel to return to the main NetWare Administrator browser screen.

Congratulations! You've built ACME's printing system. Now all you have to do is find the right printer and load the print server. Ready, set, print.

FINDING THE PRINTER

1. Click on the [Root] of the tree. Choose Object/Search from the menu bar. A Search dialog box will be displayed.

2. You'll notice that [Root] is listed in the Search From field.

3. Click on the Search Entire Subtree box.

4. Type **Printer** in the Search For field, then type **Cartridge** in the Property field.

5. Type **Fingerprint** in the blank entry box to the right of Equal To field, then click on OK to start the search.

6. A message will be displayed advising you that searching the entire tree could take a long time and asking if you want to continue. Click on Yes.

7. Note the results from the search.

8. Double-click on the printer to verify that it's correct.

LOADING THE PRINT SERVER

1. At the server console, ensure that you are at the colon prompt.

2. Type **LOAD PSERVER** and press Enter.

3. Enter **WHITE-PS1.WHITE.CRIME.TOKYO.ACME** as the name of the print server and press Enter.

4. What happens next?

5. Take steps to allow loading to continue.

6. Select Printer Status from the Available Options menu and press Enter. The CANONBJ-P1.WHITE.CRIME.TOKYO.ACME printer should be highlighted. Press Enter to select it.

7. Note the status of the printer.

8. Press Escape twice to return to the Available Options screen.

9. Choose Print Server Information from the Available Options screen.

10. Choose Current Status.

11. Select Running and press Enter, then select Unload and press Enter. What happens?

12. Reload the print server again.

See Appendix C for answers.

CASE STUDY: USING ACME'S PRINTING SYSTEM

This section assumes that you have two users set up in the WHITE.CRIME.TOKYO.ACME container. This will allow us to test capturing data and enabling print job configurations. You should have already completed the previous exercise.

You will log in as two different users in this exercise:

▸ Robin Hood (RHood)

▸ Maid Marion (MMarion)

1. Make sure you are logged into the network as .Admin.ACME.

2. Go to a DOS box under Windows.

3. Type **CAPTURE SH** and note the results.

4. Type **CAPTURE** and note what happens.

5. Change to the context where the CANONBJ-PQ1 exists. How do you do this?

6. CAPTURE to the CANONBJ-PQ1 using the Q option. What does the command look like?

7. End the capture using CAPTURE. How do you do this?

8. Return to Windows.

9. Run the NWUSER utility. (This utility is only available under Windows 3.1x. If you are running Windows 95, skip to Step 15.)

10. Click on the printer icon.

11. Walk the tree in the Resources list box on the right side of the screen to locate the WHITE.CRIME.TOKYO.ACME context.

12. Drag either the CANONBJ-P1 printer or the CANONBJ-PQ1 print queue onto LPT1: in the Ports list box.

13. Double-click on the new printer mapping. Note the default settings for the capture.

14. Leave the NWUSER utility.

15. Log out as the .Admin.ACME user, then log in as RHood. Before you do this, ensure that he has at least Read and File Scan rights, and a search drive mapping to the SYS:PUBLIC directory.

16. From a DOS box, change to the WHITE.CRIME.TOKYO.ACME container using the CX command.

17. Attempt to CAPTURE to the CANONBJ-PQ1 queue. What happens and why?

18. Re-login as yourself again. How would you grant access to the user RHood?

19. Change to the context WHITE.CRIME.TOKYO.ACME and re-enable CAPTURE to the network queue CANONBJ-PQ1. How can you do this?

20. Start the NetWare Administrator utility.

21. Choose Object/Print from the NWADMIN menu bar and print the current NetWare Administrator screen.

22. Ensure that the capture is working. Where can you look in NWADMIN to verify this?

23. Return to a DOS box and ensure that the capture is working. What is the command to do this?

24. Print a DOS text file to the network. How can you do this while CAPTURE is activated?

25. End the capture and return to Windows.

26. Create a print job configuration for the container WHITE.CRIME.TOKYO.ACME and call it **Main**. Where would this be done?

27. Grant the container WHITE.CRIME.TOKYO.ACME access to the print queue CANONBJ-PQ1. How would you do this?

28. Log in as RHood.

29. Under DOS, type **CAPTURE** and note what happens.

30. Log in as .Admin.ACME to modify the queue.

31. Return to the NetWare Administrator utility. Right mouse-click on the WHITE.CRIME.TOKYO.ACME container and select Details from the pull-down menu that is displayed. Click on the Print Job Configuration page button and ensure that the Main print job configuration is highlighted. Click on the Default button to make this the default print job configuration for this container. Note the printer icon that now appears next to the configuration. Also note the options for the configuration (copies, queue, notification). Finally, click on OK to save this change.

32. Log in as RHood again.

33. Return to a DOS box and execute CAPTURE. What happens now?

34. Type **CAPTURE SH.** What do you note about the settings?

See Appendix C for answers.

CASE STUDY: MANAGING ACME'S PRINTING SYSTEM

This case study assumes the following: that the WHITE-PS1 print server is running on the .WHITE.CRIME.TOKYO.ACME server; that a printer is attached to the server and is ready to print (that is, on-line, with paper); and that you are using a Windows 3.1x workstation. (This case study will not work with a Windows 95 workstation.)

1. Log in as .Admin.ACME on a Windows 3.1x workstation and execute the NetWare Administrator utility.

2. Select the CANONBJ-P1 printer by double-clicking on it.

3. Click on the Printer Status page button, then click on the Pause button. What changes with the printer?

4. Send two jobs to the queue CANONBJ-PQ1.

5. Double-click on CANONBJ-PQ1, then click on the Job List page button. What do you see?

6. Select the first print job and click on the Details button.

7. Click on the User Hold box. What status is displayed?

8. Return to the main NetWare Administrator browser screen. Click on the CANONBJ-P1, then click on Printer Status.

9. Click on the Resume button to re-enable the printer. What happens?

10. Place the printer off-line after the job has completed printing. (Use the printer's on-line/off-line button for this.)

11. View the CANONBJ-P1's status under NetWare Administrator. Note the status of the printer.

12. With the printer status up (viewing percentage and such), place the printer back on-line and watch what happens.

13. Once the job has completed printing, click on the CANCEL button, then double-click on WHITE-PS1.

14. Click on the Print Layout page button. Select each item, one at a time, then click on the Status button to check its status. What do you see?

15. Click on the Identification page button, then click on the UNLOAD button. Select Unload Print Server Immediately, then click on OK. Monitor the file server console screen, if possible. What happens?

16. Click on the Cancel button to leave the Print Server Identification screen. Double-click on WHITE-PS1, then click on the Print Layout page button. What do you notice that's different? What do you think it means?

17. Click on WHITE-PS1, then click on the Status button. Does this verify your assumption?

18. Submit another job to CANONBJ-PQ1.

19. Double-click on CANONBJ-PQ1, then select Job List. Select any job other than the first (Seq 1) and click on Job Details. Locate the Service Sequence field on the middle left-hand side. Change the Service Sequence to **1**, then click on OK.

20. What looks different?

See Appendix C for answers.

The following exercise will walk you through the process of creating IntranetWare printing objects using the Quick Setup option of PCONSOLE. Before beginning this exercise, be sure that you are in the context that you want to create new printing objects in, and logged in as a user with sufficient rights to create objects.

1. From the DOS command line, run the PCONSOLE utility by typing **PCONSOLE** and pressing Enter.

2. Use the arrow keys to select Quick Setup and press Enter.

3. From the Print Services Configuration menu, modify the print server, printer, and print queue name to match the naming standards of your organization.

4. Verify the volume you want this print queue to be created on. If necessary, select the existing volume and press Enter, then press the Insert key to browse the tree and select the appropriate volume.

5. Specify the banner type. This should be based on the type of printer you are using. PCL printers use text banners.

6. Specify the printer type (parallel, serial, and so on), location (manual load —workstation or network attached; or auto load — locally attached to the print server).

7. Specify the interrupt or polled mode (recommended). If interrupt is chosen, it must match the configuration of the physical printer port.

8. Specify the port to which this printer is attached.

9. When configuration is complete, press Esc and Yes to save, then Esc and Yes to exit the PCONSOLE utility.

EXERCISE 14-2: MANUAL PRINTING SETUP IN PCONSOLE

The following exercise will walk you through the process of creating IntranetWare printing objects using the individual print queues, printers, and print server options of PCONSOLE. Before beginning this exercise, be sure that you are in the context that you want to create new printing objects in, and logged in as a user with sufficient rights to create objects.

1. From the DOS command line, run the PCONSOLE utility by typing **PCONSOLE** and then pressing Enter.

2. Choose the Print Queues option from the Available Options menu.

3. Use the Insert key to create a new print queue.

4. Enter a print queue name that matches the naming standards of your organization and press Enter.

5. Enter the print queue's volume. Press the Insert key and browse the NDS tree to choose the appropriate volume and press Enter to select.

6. Press Esc to return to the Available Options menu.

7. Choose the Printers option from the Available Options menu.

8. Press the Insert key to create a new printer.

9. Enter a printer name that matches the naming standards of your organization and press Enter.

10. Select the printer by pressing Enter.

11. Highlight the Configuration field and press Enter. Specify the port to which this printer is attached, the printer type (parallel, serial, and so on), the location (manual load — workstation or network attached; or auto load — locally attached), the interrupt or polled mode (recommended). If interrupt is chosen it must match the configuration of the physical printer port. Specify an address restriction, if desired. When configuration is complete, press Esc.

12. If forms are being used, specify the starting form number.

13. Specify the banner type. This should be based on the type of printer you are using. PCL printers use text banners.

14. If multiple form types are being used, specify the forms service mode you desire.

15. Press Enter at *Print queues assigned* and use the Insert key to add a print queue to service this queue. Use the arrow keys to select the queue you created above and press Enter to select. When you have finished, press Esc.

16. **Optional:** Press Enter at Notification to add users or groups to be notified of printer problems. Use the Insert key to browse the NDS tree. Use the arrow keys to select the person to be notified, and press Enter to select. When you have finished, press Esc, then select Yes, then press Esc.

17. When you have completed the printer configuration, press Esc to save the changes, then press Esc to return to the Available options menu.

18. Select the Print Servers option from the Available options menu.

19. Use the Insert key to add a new print server. Enter a print server name that matches the naming conventions of your organization and press Enter.

20. Press Enter to select the print server you have just created.

21. Select Print Servers from the Print Server Information menu and press Enter.

22. Press the Insert key. Select the printer you created above, then press Enter.

23. Press Esc three times to return to the Available Options menu.

24. Press Esc, then select Yes and press Enter to exit the PCONSOLE utility.

This exercise will walk you through the process of creating a print job configuration for the user you are currently logged in as.

1. From the DOS command line, run the PRINTCON utility by typing **PRINTCON** and then pressing Enter.

2. Select Edit Print Job Configurations from the Available Options menu and press Enter.

3. Press the Insert key to create a new print job configuration.

4. Enter a name for this new print job configuration and press Enter.

5. Press Enter to select the job configuration you just created.

6. Use the arrow keys to select Local printer.

7. Enter the printer port you wish to capture (1=LPT1, 2=LPT2, and so on).

8. Use the arrow keys to select print queue and press Enter. Press Insert and browse the NDS tree to find the desired print queue, then press Enter to select it.

9. Specify other desired options such as form feed, banner, and form number.

10. When you have finished, press Esc, select Yes, and press Enter to save changes.

11. Press Esc twice, select Yes, and press Enter to exit.

Circle the 20 printing terms hidden in this word search puzzle using the hints provided.

P	R	I	N	T	Q	U	E	U	E	O	P	E	R	A	T	O	R	I
A	R	P	R	E	V	I	R	D	T	N	I	R	P	V	G	G	P	R
R	I	I	Q	D	R	T	H	G	C	E	Z	R	R	L	S	P	S	L
A	M	A	N	U	A	L	L	O	A	D	I	Q	I	L	Q	Q	H	A
L	C	G	D	T	I	Z	N	P	O	N	O	K	N	W	U	S	E	R
L	K	B	P	O	S	C	A	P	T	U	R	E	T	O	B	G	B	F
E	D	F	S	S	T	E	K	E	S	Y	F	D	Q	L	N	K	B	K
L	U	K	V	V	Z	K	R	S	K	N	D	C	U	K	T	Y	P	A
P	R	I	N	T	S	E	R	V	E	R	O	P	E	R	A	T	O	R
O	P	M	A	P	L	T	V	W	E	T	L	K	U	K	V	W	L	F
R	P	Q	J	S	H	I	S	N	A	R	U	D	E	W	H	P	L	K
T	V	B	P	E	C	O	P	S	K	F	A	P	R	I	C	G	E	D
D	W	D	X	R	F	C	R	I	F	O	I	J	X	O	L	M	D	E
S	O	D	X	V	I	X	I	U	L	Z	S	L	N	Q	P	T	M	D
M	O	P	O	E	R	N	N	O	O	Y	V	S	B	D	R	T	O	F
B	X	G	P	R	I	N	T	C	O	N	O	P	W	O	V	L	D	T
Z	T	E	F	N	Z	U	J	D	A	L	X	Q	X	S	K	S	E	I
T	Y	H	J	L	A	T	O	W	E	E	B	B	B	O	H	H	S	O
J	X	O	Y	M	P	E	B	C	C	F	M	B	D	G	Q	Y	Q	E

Hints:

1. Designation that indicates that a printer is directly connected to the print server.
2. Command line utility used to redirect DOS and OS/2 print jobs from applications designed to print to parallel ports.
3. Designation that indicates that a printer is connected to a workstation, the network cable, or a server other than the print server.
4. New printing architecture developed by a partnership between HP, Novell, and Xerox.

5. Graphical utility running under MS Windows that can be used for printer redirection.

6. Type of port that typically provides better performance than a serial port.

7. Menu utility that can be used to set up the IntranetWare printing environment.

8. Default IntranetWare printer configuration option (where alternate choice is Interrupt mode).

9. Software that can be used to convert a print job into a format that can be used by a particular printer.

10. File stored in a print queue while waiting to be printed.

11. User or Group member who can edit the print jobs of other users, delete print jobs from the print queue, or modify the queue status.

12. Network directory used for storing print jobs.

13. User or Group member who has the rights needed to manage a print server.

14. Server used to direct print jobs from a print queue to a network printer.

15. Command line utility that can be used to create print job configurations for use with the CAPTURE, NETUSER, NPRINT, or PCONSOLE utilities.

16. Command line utility used to view, modify, import, or export print device definitions and create or modify printer forms.

17. A leaf object that represents a physical printing device on the network.

18. NLM used for loading print server software on a server.

19. Directory name extension used to indicate that a subdirectory is a IntranetWare print queue.

20. PCONSOLE option that provides a fast method for creating the initial printing environment.

See Appendix C for answers.

IntranetWare Optimization

Optimization . . . the final frontier. This is the voyage of the Starship IntranetWare. Its continuing mission is to explore strange, new NDS trees. To seek out new users and new wide area networks. To boldly go where no CNE has gone before!

Congratulations! You made it. Welcome to the next generation of IntranetWare. And more importantly, welcome to the end of this book. It's been a long and winding road, but we struggled through it together. We designed the "Cloud," built the tree, secured the users, configured the WAN, and managed the printers. It's all in a day's work for a CNE superhero/doctor/gardener.

Now, we've reached the final frontier of IntranetWare — optimization! This is the last great journey. A journey of self-realization; learning to be the best you can be; reaching for the stars; expanding your horizons; and so on. But don't stop there; IntranetWare optimization is more than just a collection of trite phrases, it is "warp" speed!

Before you can cruise the intergalactic information highway, you must make a few last-minute adjustments to your server's warp drive. It will need to operate at peak performance in order to handle the demands of strange aliens and IntranetWare users. Fortunately, you're Captain CNE, and you know how to optimize the warp drive. You know that it consists of two important tasks:

- ▸ Monitoring

- ▸ Optimization

Monitoring involves periodic interrogation of key performance components, such as file cache buffers, packet receive buffers (PRBs), and disk allocation blocks. IntranetWare CNEs use MONITOR.NLM for daily performance monitoring. Optimization is the next step. Now you must proactively fine-tune each of these components so the server operates at peak performance. CNEs use SERVMAN.NLM and SET parameters for optimization tasks.

Balance is the key. Balance among server performance, reliability, and security. They all live in cohesive harmony. If you exaggerate any component over the others, it could throw the server out of balance — this is not a good thing. The bottom line is this: Don't optimize the server in a vacuum. Consider the impact of your actions on the server as a whole. Believe it or not, that extra nanosecond of performance isn't always worth it overall — consider the big picture.

Speaking of the big picture, let's start our journey with a discussion of optimization components. They are the "di-lithium crystals" that make up your IntranetWare server. We must understand them before we start fiddling around. Warp speed ahead.

ZEN

"Victory belongs to the most persevering!"

Napoleon

Optimization Components

There are many factors that affect your network's overall performance. Most of them center around the file server. It is a source of great misunderstanding and confusion. Administrators from the mainframe world tend to overemphasize the importance of file server processing. The bottom line is: This is a distributed computing system, not a centralized one. The file server handles only 5 percent of the network's overall processing. The majority of the work is handled by the workstation — it says so right there in the name.

If the file server CPU isn't the most important optimization component, then what is? Well, that depends on your bottlenecks. *Bottlenecks* are optimization hot spots that slow down file server performance. They can exist anywhere — server NIC, disk channel, memory, workstation, cabling, and so on. The best place to start is the server network interface card (NIC).

The file server NIC sees the most network traffic. It should be fast — at least 16-bit, but hopefully 32-bit. Also, consider bus-mastering NICs and disk controllers to alleviate chatter from the CPU. Finally, some LANs benefit from splitting the network segment and placing two NICs in the file server. This is called *Internal Routing*.

The next bottleneck is created by the disk channel. It relies on controller and hard drive speed. If the hard drive channel is slow, it won't matter how much memory or processor power you put in the server. You can make an 80386 server (with a fast hard drive) run just as fast as an 80486 server (with a slow hard drive).

Remember, the IntranetWare server is simply serving files. You also must be aware of what sorts of tasks you're asking the server to perform. If most users access a customer database for reading information, then you must optimize the file system for fast "reads." If the same users spend all day changing the database, you'll want to optimize for fast "writes."

Third, take a long hard look at your client workstations. Because IntranetWare distributes processing to clients, the quality of your workstations makes a big difference. You could have a super-fast file server, but if your clients are running on 80286 workstation with 1 MB RAM, they're going to complain that the network is slow. Remember, distributed applications are running at the speed of the client station. While you're upgrading the clients, upgrade their NICs as well. There's no sense leaving an 8-bit card in a PC when you can essentially double the network throughput with a 16-bit card.

Fourth, explore the bottlenecks created by local operating systems. If your users are using Windows, consider adding local bus video to their workstations. Windows bottlenecks are frequently screen redraws. Speeding up that process sometimes compensates for other slow components. As new versions of Windows are released, you'll also want to increase the amount of memory and hard disk space at the desktop.

ZEN

"We are here and it is now. Further than that, all knowledge is moonshine."

H. L. Mencken

There are a few good bottlenecks to explore before you get too wrapped up in IntranetWare optimization. Many times these simple fixes make the world of difference. But, no matter how you slice it, optimization focuses on three main components:

- ▸ Blocks and buffers

- ▸ Tables

- ▸ Memory management

A *block* is an allocation unit on the server disk. They store files permanently. *Buffers* are allocation units in server memory. They store files temporarily. Block and buffer sizes dramatically affect memory utilization, and, therefore, network performance.

Tables, on the other hand, transcend blocks and buffers. Some tables are stored on disk, then copied into memory as needed. Some are only memory constructs, and are created and discarded as needed, but never saved. We care about server tables because they use up file server memory and impact read/write performance.

Finally, *memory management* impacts every facet of IntranetWare optimization. In earlier versions of NetWare, the server relied on a fragmented memory pool architecture that was inefficient and slow. IntranetWare uses the same architecture, but memory utilization has improved — now it's more efficient and not as slow (faster). In addition, IntranetWare memory management relies on a new memory protection scheme for fault tolerance and reliability. After all, performance is *really* bad when the server crashes.

Let's take a closer look at these three main optimization components and prep ourselves for the onslaught of MONITOR.NLM (monitoring) and SERVMAN.NLM (optimization).

BLOCKS AND BUFFERS

As we learned earlier, blocks are storage allocation units on disk and buffers are storage allocation units in server memory. Since the file server is primarily involved in serving files, performance optimization relies on the efficient management of blocks and buffers. Also, you'll find that many of the monitoring tasks in MONITOR.NLM and optimization tasks in SERVMAN.NLM focus on special blocks and buffers — such as file allocation blocks, file cache buffers, packet receive buffers, and directory cache buffers. Refer to Figure 15.1 for an illustration of IntranetWare blocks and buffers.

When a volume is created (initial installation or when a new disk is added), the file allocation blocks are created as well. One of your most important installation decisions is block size. Valid answers are 4K, 8K, 16K, 32K, and 64K. There will be a default, and it will vary with the size of the volume itself. For example, a 100 MB volume will default to 4K blocks, while a 10,000 MB volume defaults to 64K.

The trade-off between a small and large block size is speed and space. Each file takes up at least one block — suballocation works only on excess data; the first file segment always reserves an entire block. This fact argues for a small block size. At the other extreme, a large file can be read far more efficiently if its blocks of data are contiguous. So, a 64K file in one block provides much better performance than the same file stored in sixteen 4K blocks scattered around the disk (see Figure 15.2).

F I G U R E   15.1

Blocks and Buffers in IntranetWare

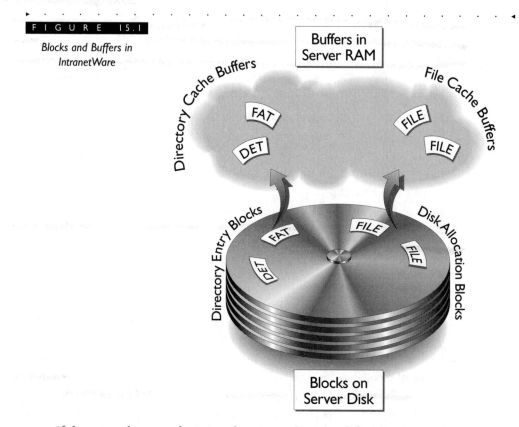

If there is only one volume on the server, then the default is almost always fine especially if you've activated the block suballocation feature. On the other hand, if the server supports multiple volumes, it is often worth the effort to find the optimal block size and standardize it across all volumes. This makes file cache memory utilization far more efficient. Let me explain.

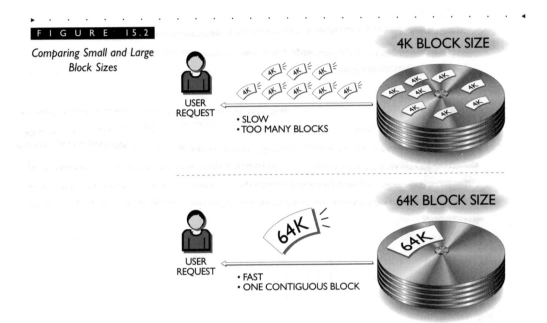

Comparing Small and Large
Block Sizes

4K BLOCK SIZE

USER
REQUEST
• SLOW
• TOO MANY BLOCKS

64K BLOCK SIZE

USER
REQUEST
• FAST
• ONE CONTIGUOUS BLOCK

File cache buffer sizing doesn't have as dramatic an effect on performance as file allocation block sizing. But there is one hard and fast rule: File cache buffer sizing must be consistent across all volumes on a server. (IntranetWare does this for you.) And, the size must match the smallest file allocation block size on any volume. IntranetWare will not mount a volume whose file allocation block size is smaller than the file cache buffer size.

This means that a server with several large volumes and a single small one will be forced to use smaller buffers — this is less efficient. The defaults will set a small block size for the small volume, and then force the file cache buffers to match that small allocation size. This will have a negative impact on the performance of the larger disks with their larger blocks. To tune dissimilar hardware properly, you should increase the size of the smaller volume's allocation units to match the size of the large disk's blocks. Easy as pie.

That completes our discussion of blocks and buffers. Don't worry; we'll explore them in more depth throughout the chapter. Now let's take a look at IntranetWare tables.

TABLES

Tables are involved in every facet of file reads and writes. IntranetWare relies on two file system tables to store location and configuration information about internal files and directories. To understand them, let's review the steps the server goes through in accessing a user's data file.

First, IntranetWare checks the directory entry table (DET) to make sure that the user has sufficient rights to access the file. Then it looks at the DET entry to find the first File Allocation Table (FAT) entry for that file. The FAT has an entry for every physical sector on the disk. Every time a file is created, the FAT entry for that cylinder, head, and sector address is updated. If the file is big enough to take up more than one sector, the first FAT entry also points to the next FAT entry for that file, and so on.

When a user requests a block of data toward the end of a big file, IntranetWare reads all of the intervening FAT entries until it has found the correct file, then it actually retrieves the file and sends it to the user.

In order to speed up data access, IntranetWare does several things:

- ▶ First, IntranetWare keeps files in RAM as long as it can. This way files are retrieved from file cache buffers, thus avoiding disk access. This can increase server read performance up to 100 times!

- ▶ Second, IntranetWare keeps part of the DET in RAM, so that frequently accessed directories can be checked without first having to go to disk.

- ▶ Third, IntranetWare keeps the entire FAT in server memory to speed up the FAT scanning time.

- ▶ Fourth, and finally, IntranetWare creates an index of the FAT entries (for large files only). This index is called the "Turbo Fat." It is created when the file is first accessed, then maintained as long as any client has the file open. It is discarded a short time after the last user closes it — five and a half minutes is the default; it can be changed with a SET command.

Table 15.1 summarizes IntranetWare file and directory hashing (indexing) and caching. As you can see, the FAT is held in memory (cached), as are the most recently accessed files. Furthermore, parts of the FAT are indexed (hashed). Files themselves are not indexed. It would be rather useless to have the system alphabetize all the words in your memos, for example.

TABLE 15.1		CACHING	HASHING
A Summary of File/Directory Hashing and Caching options	FAT	Yes	Yes
	File	Yes	No

MEMORY MANAGEMENT

Memory management has the most dramatic impact on IntranetWare server optimization. After all, everything happens there. Of course, disk and NIC optimization run a very close second. Memory management operates in two important spheres:

▸ Memory Utilization

▸ Memory Protection

Let's take a closer look.

Memory Utilization

IntranetWare includes a substantially improved memory utilization strategy. In order to best understand it, let's take a moment to explore our roots — NetWare 3.

When NetWare 3 arrived, everyone applauded its new memory utilization scheme. That was appropriate because it was a vast improvement over the strategy used in NetWare 2. As experience with NetWare 3 accumulated, certain minor problems became apparent. The most troublesome of them was memory pool inefficiencies. It turned out that memory pools grew as needed, but never contracted. They never returned unused RAM. In some cases, this could result in the loss of a significant portion of file server memory.

The designers of IntranetWare decided to fix this, and reengineered the memory pool concept. It still uses the memory pool architecture, but unused RAM is returned. The biggest change is that memory pools can both request and free memory. In NetWare 3, there were some pools, most notably Permanent Memory and Alloc Short-Term Memory, that would take memory as needed, but never return it when finished. The only cure for this problem was to periodically shut down and restart the server. This reset all the memory pools to their default (smaller) sizes. In IntranetWare, memory is still assigned to pools, but they return RAM to the file cache pool when they're done.

So, why do we need the memory pools at all? To off-load memory resource tracking from SERVER.EXE. You see, when a particular resource requests a buffer of RAM (for an NLM, LAN driver, or console screen image), IntranetWare takes it from file caching. Therefore, SERVER.EXE can ignore the pooled chunk of memory. If it wasn't "pooled," SERVER.EXE would have to track all its memory-related parameters — too much work for one little file.

SERVER.EXE does, however, track other memory-related events — such as dirty. If the contents of a memory buffer change, the file cache buffers marks the buffer as "dirty" — who washes them? You can track dirty cache buffers in MONITOR.NLM.

ZEN

"Look, I really don't want to wax philosophic, but I will say that if you're alive, you got to flap your arms and legs, you got to jump around a lot, you got to make some noise, because life is the very opposite of death."

Mel Brooks

The process of recovering available memory is called *garbage collection*. NLM programmers can tell the operating system that they no longer need a particular block of memory via the FREE command. Once freed, those blocks are ready for collection. **Note:** Can't you just see the little garbage trucks running about inside file server memory looking for discarded bits and collecting them together to make new pools? I can see you're going to have strange dreams tonight.

The garbage collection process is a low-priority process that runs in the background when the file server is experiencing periods of low activity. Nevertheless, there are three SET parameters that control the process. Table 15.2 lists the commands, their defaults, minimum and maximum settings, and their meanings. In use, they provide three different triggers for garbage collection. In other words, if either 15 minutes have elapsed, or 5,000 FREEs have been issued, or 8,000 alloc memory bytes are available, then garbage collection will begin.

T A B L E 15.2	COMMAND	DEFAULT	MIN.	MAX.	MEANING
SET Parameters for Garbage Collection	Garbage Collection Interval	15 min.	1 min.	60 min.	The interval between times that the collection process is initiated
	Number of FREEs for Garbage Collection	5000	100	100,000	Number of FREEs that will trigger the collection process
	Minimum Free Memory For Garbage Collection	8K	1000	1 MB	The minimum number of bytes that must be available in Alloc memory for successful collection

We'll explore SET commands and SERVMAN later in the chapter. But here's a quick preview. SET is an IntranetWare console command. The great news about SET is that once you select a category, the current values for each parameter are displayed on the screen. In addition, the range of parameters is also displayed so you know how high or low you can go. Beats looking it up in a manual.

SMART LINK

Explore *all* the garbage collection SET parameters in the "Utilities Reference" book at http://www.novell.com/manuals.

In addition to SET, MONITOR.NLM provides numerous memory utilization statistics. Most of them are found under the Resource Utilization option. Figure 15.3 illustrates the IntranetWare memory pools and their current utilization statistics. Later in the chapter, we'll use this screen to determine how our server resources utilize available RAM. For now, let's move on to memory protection.

FIGURE 15.3

Memory Utilization in
MONITOR.NLM

```
NetWare 4.x Console Monitor  4.34                    NetWare Loadable Module
Server name: 'LABS-SRV1' in Directory tree 'ACME_TREE'
Server version: NetWare 4.11 - August 22, 1996
                        Server Memory Statistics

        Allocated memory pool (bytes):        2,543,616    8%
        Cache buffers (bytes):               23,330,816   71%
        Cache movable memory (bytes):         1,249,280    4%
        Cache non-movable memory (bytes):        81,920    8%
        Code and data memory (bytes):         5,607,424   17%
        Total server work memory (bytes):    32,813,056  100%


                        Tracked Resources

    AES Process Call-Backs
    Alloc Memory (Bytes)
    Alternate Debugger Handlers
    Alternate Key Handler
    Audit Services
    Cache Memory Below 16 Meg (Bytes)
  ▼ Cache Movable Memory (Bytes)

Tab=Next window    Enter=Select option    Alt+F10=Exit              F1=Help
```

Memory Protection

Ever since Intel released the 80286 chip in 1986, PC-based processors have had the capability to protect various areas of memory. *Protected* means that if a program wants to use a chunk of RAM, it asks the operating system for an allocation, then it can do whatever it wants to do within that allocated space. If, however, it tries to access or manipulate storage areas outside of its allocated range, the CPU gets mad (and even).

As you might imagine, asking the CPU to watch every memory access command for every task running on the server would seriously impact performance. On the other hand, there are times when some tasks or resources need to be watched very closely. Well, good news: You have the best of both worlds with IntranetWare. It has the capability to monitor tasks — NLMs — if and only if necessary.

Here's how it works. Intel designed its 80286 chip with four logical *rings*. Ring 0 is where the operating system lives. Nothing can interrupt the operating system without its permission. Ring 1 surrounds Ring 0 and can be interrupted by the operating system running in Ring 0. Ring 2 surrounds Ring 1 and can be interrupted by both Rings 0 and 1. Finally, Ring 3 surrounds Ring 2 and can be interrupted by any of the other three rings. Refer to Figure 15.4 for more details.

A well-behaved, polite program in a multitasking environment will, from time to time, stop to see if any higher-priority program is waiting for execution. If so, it will suspend itself and defer to the other task. A program that does not give up the processor can cause the server to appear dead — aka SERVER CRASH! This rudeness cannot be allowed. When the operating system, running in Ring 0, detects that some other program is hogging the processor, it can intervene and kick that program out. Similarly, when a program running in Ring 3 accesses memory that has not been allocated to it, the Ring 0 program can detect it and deal with it harshly; for example, unload the NLM from memory altogether.

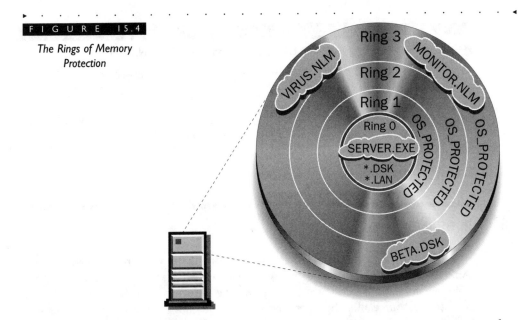

F I G U R E   15.4

*The Rings of Memory
Protection*

IntranetWare allows developers to create programs that can run in Ring 3 and gives administrators the ability to load them there. If you get a new NLM and you want to run it on a mission-critical server, you're taking a risk that the NLM will be well-behaved and not interrupt the core operating system — SERVER.EXE. To prevent this, use DOMAIN.NLM to run new NLMs in Ring 3 for a while. This Ring 3 domain is referred to by Novell as the Operating System Protected Domain (OS_PROTECTED in Figure 15.4). If the NLM proves safe, you can move it to Ring 0 with the rest of the operating system and get a little better performance.

DOMAIN monitors NLMs running in Ring 3 for time or data violations and will abort those processes when a violation occurs. To enable this Miss Manners of the operating system, DOMAIN must be loaded before the operating system loads any other NLMs. Therefore, it must be loaded via STARTUP.NCF. Next, you're ready to place specific NLMs in Ring 3. To do so, type the command **DOMAIN 3** before loading the new NLM. This switches console control to the OS_PROTECTED Ring 3. Then load the NLM. Finally, when you're finished, return console control to the OS domain (Ring 0) by typing **DOMAIN 0**. Table 15.3 summarizes the DOMAIN command.

T A B L E 15.3	COMMAND	DESCRIPTION
Protecting Server Memory with DOMAIN.NLM	LOAD DOMAIN	Loads the DOMAIN. NLM
	DOMAIN	Provides a list of the available domains
	DOMAIN HELP	Provides a list of the DOMAIN help screens
	DOMAIN = *<domain name>*	Switches console control to a specific domain for loading new NLMs

REAL WORLD

In previous versions of NetWare, NLMs sometimes were responsible for fatal ABEND errors. ABEND stands for Abnormal End — every CNE's nightmare. If the software developer made a mistake when writing the program, the NLM might allocate a system resource that the operating system does not have available, and thus the server comes crashing to its knees, only capable of one last ABEND message.

By loading the DOMAIN.NLM and using the DOMAIN=OS_PROTECTED command, NLMs can be loaded into an area of memory that will protect the server from ABENDing. If the NLM fails, the memory that the NLM had allocated is locked up, but the rest of the server's resources are still available. The idea is to test out new NLMs in protected memory and later let them run in unprotected memory.

Unfortunately, not just any NLM will successfully load into protected memory. In fact most NLMs will not. The EDIT NLM is one NLM that will load into protected memory. Use the DOMAIN command to confirm which NLMs are in protected and unprotected memory.

That's it. Everything you need to know about optimization components. Now I think you're ready for prime time. The rest of this chapter is dedicated to the two main stages of IntranetWare optimization:

▶ Monitoring with MONITOR.NLM

▶ Optimization with SERVMAN.NLM

In addition, we'll explore some other optimization strategies, including file compression, block suballocation, packet burst protocol, and large internet packets (LIPs). Wow, I had no idea IntranetWare has so much to offer. But wait, that's not all. We'll throw in a lengthy discussion of optimization and troubleshooting. Now how much would you pay?

I'll see you on the other side.

QUIZ

Five men had a race at the annual picnic of the Associated Widget and Dingbat factory. They were, not in order, Tom, John, Bill, Pat, and Kevin. Pat was neither first nor last. Kevin was four behind the winner. Bill beat Pat, John came in after Tom, but ahead of Pat. Bill was neither first nor second. Tom was not second or third. Give the rankings.

(Q15-1)
(See Appendix C for all quiz answers.)

▶ - ◄

Monitoring with **MONITOR.NLM**

It all starts with MONITOR.NLM. I know you're good, but not even a CNE Superhero can fix problems he or she doesn't know about. Monitoring is important because it allows you to create an Optimization Plan. Your plan should include weekly server statistics and threshold values. You check the numbers every week, and if they eclipse a certain value, you perform an optimization task (usually in SERVMAN.NLM).

Having said that, it's interesting that many people claim IntranetWare is "self-tuning." While there is some truth to this statement, it still takes hands-on work and good optimization techniques to get a finely tuned server.

In this section, we'll take a closer look at IntranetWare monitoring with MONITOR.NLM — the grandfather of IntranetWare server tools. We will start with a quick view of the main screen, and then dive into its most useful options:

▸ Memory Utilization

▸ Cache Utilization

▸ LAN/WAN Information

▸ Processor Utilization

You'll spend most of your monitoring time in these four areas. But MONITOR doesn't stop there. To get a jump on IntranetWare optimization, you'll need to explore *all* aspects of this great utility. That's what the ACME Exploratorium is for at the end of the chapter. Don't miss it. So, without any further adieu, let's get on with the show!

SMART LINK

Explore MONITOR.NLM in detail with the *NetWare 4.11 Utilities Reference* **at http://www.novell.com/manuals.**

THE MAIN SCREEN

It all starts with the main screen of MONITOR.NLM. From there, the IntranetWare server can be watched, prodded, tweaked, and cooed at. Yes, it's the last of the great IntranetWare utilities.

To get to the main screen, type **LOAD MONITOR** at the file server console prompt. You're greeted with a screen similar to the one in Figure 15.5. You can spend days going through all the detailed information provided in this handy dandy tool. There is one serious limitation, though. There is no convenient way to print out all the information available — no reporting function. For that, you must look at some third-party products. Bummer.

F I G U R E   15.5

*The Main Screen of
MONITOR.NLM*

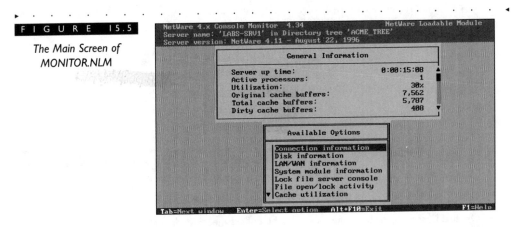

If you're familiar with NetWare 3, MONITOR will look and feel familiar. It has undergone some major and some minor changes, though. Among the minor changes is a small tweak to the main screen. When you first start the program, or while you're changing from one subscreen to another, the box at the top shows six important items. If you hit the Tab key, or wait 10 seconds, the box will expand to show seven more items. In its expanded state, it nearly covers the Available Options menu. Refer to Table 15.4 for a description of all 14 server parameters.

MEMORY UTILIZATION

IntranetWare introduced several new subscreens to MONITOR. One of them is the Memory Utilization screen. From this screen, you can choose any of the NLMs loaded on your system and see that it is using server memory. If you add a new NLM, perhaps as a result of purchasing a new server-based program (SMS Backup, for example), you might want to track its supporting resources through Memory Utilization.

A well-behaved NLM will take the memory it needs and then free it after use. Let's explore our new SMS backup NLM. When you activate the backup program, the application NLM will begin to swell in size. Once it finishes, the NLM should release nearly all the memory it had allocated, leaving just enough for it to be accessed and started again at the appropriate time.

RCONSOLE is another good example. Figure 15.6 shows the Memory Utilization screen for RCONSOLE when it's being used. At this moment, it is using ten blocks of 4K each, with about two-thirds in use and the remainder freed. These freed blocks will be picked up by garbage collection the next time it is activated.

TABLE 15.4 *important*

Monitoring Parameters on the Main Screen of MONITOR.NLM

ITEM	MEANING
Server Up Time	Days:hours:minutes:seconds since server last started.
Utilization	Percentage of time the CPU is working (versus idle).
Original Cache Buffers	Number of cache buffers measured just after the OS Kernel (SERVER.NLM) is loaded.
Total Cache Buffers	Number of currently available buffers. This number is reduced as other memory pools convert cache buffers for their use; it increases when they return it.
Dirty Cache Buffers	Number of buffers that have updated data not yet written to disk.
Current Disk Requests	Number of disk I/O requests currently pending.
Packet Receive Buffers	Pool of buffers set aside for incoming network packets
Directory Cache Buffers	Pool of buffers set aside for volume directory tables.
Maximum Service Processes	Ceiling on the number of service processes that will be allocated.
Current Service	Number of service processes currently Processes allocated.
Maximum License Connections	Total of all licenses applied to this server. Up to ten licenses can be "stacked" on top of each other.
Current License	Number of license connections currently Connections in use.
Open Files	Number of files currently being accessed by both the server itself and any connected workstations.

TIP

Several third-party programs are in circulation that provide cache utilization statistics for NetWare 3 servers.

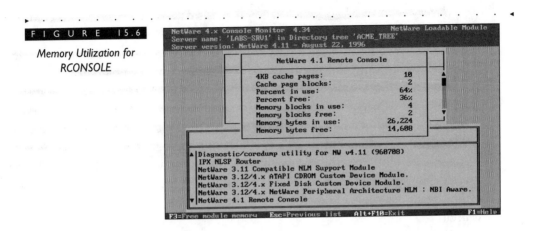

F I G U R E   15.6

Memory Utilization for
RCONSOLE

CACHE UTILIZATION

IntranetWare has also reintroduced an old friend to the MONITOR family — cache utilization. These terrific statistics were available in NetWare 2, but were removed from view in NetWare 3. Now they're back. Check out Figure 15.7.

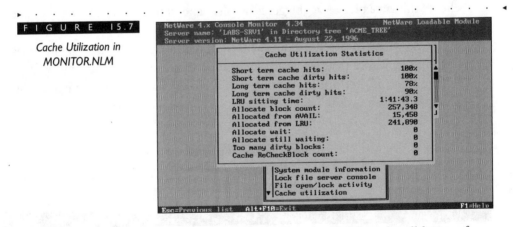

F I G U R E   15.7

Cache Utilization in
MONITOR.NLM

Having enough cache memory is essential to the health and well-being of any IntranetWare file server — especially IntranetWare. The good news is that you can easily increase available cache by installing more memory in your server. However, as a frugal CNE, you don't want to add memory needlessly. This screen gives you all the information you need to make the right decision. Here's how it works.

Cache hits occur when a workstation requests data, and the server gets the data from RAM instead of from disk. IntranetWare uses an LRU (Least Recently Used) algorithm to determine which data stays in memory and which data goes. Cache hits are broken down into two parts: short-term hits and long-term hits.

Short-term hits are those that have occurred within the last second. *Long-term hits* include all cache requests since the server was last booted. The short-term numbers should be more than 98 percent and the long-term numbers more than 90 percent. If not, add more memory. If the numbers are lower than that, Novell suggests performing some short-term fixes, such as unloading unneeded NLMs or removing DOS from memory. These actions won't hurt, but please remember that they treat a symptom of a problem (not enough memory) rather than the problem itself.

In addition, cache utilization can be optimized during volume creation. How? Well, performance is best when cache size equals buffer size. If you have volumes with different sizes, it is impossible to optimize. If you remember from our earlier discussion, IntranetWare requires that you select a buffer size equal to the smallest block size mounted. If you are installing multiple volumes, you would do well to choose the same block size (bigger is usually better if they're close) for all volumes, and then set cache buffer size to match. No sweat.

OK, so what can you do about cache utilization? Well, IntranetWare includes a few important SET parameters that allow you to manage file reads and writes. If your server is performing many small writes, consider optimizing these parameters as shown in Table 15.5.

T A B L E 15.5

SET Parameters for
Write-Intensive Servers

COMMAND	SETTING	MIN.	MAX.	MEANING
Dirty Disk Cache Delay Time	7 sec.	0.1	10 sec.	Minimum amount of time the system waits before writing a not-completely-dirty disk cache buffer. Default: 3.3 sec.
Maximum Concurrent Disk Cache Writes	50	10	4,000	Maximum number of disk cache writes that will be scheduled on one pass of the read/write head. Default: 50.

COMMAND	SETTING	MIN.	MAX.	MEANING
Dirty Directory Cache Delay Time	2 sec.	0	10 sec.	Minimum amount of time the system waits before writing a not-completely-dirty directory cache buffer. Default: 0.5 isec.
Maximum Concurrent Directory Cache Writes	25	5	50	Maximum number of directory cache writes that will be scheduled on one pass of the read/write head. Default: 10.

On the other hand, if your server performs a lot of read operations, consider optimizing cache utilization parameters according to Table 15.6.

TABLE 15.6

SET Parameter for
Read-Intensive Servers

COMMAND	SETTING	MIN.	MAX.	MEANING
Maximum Concurrent Disk Cache Writes	10	10	4,000	Maximum number of disk cache writes that will be scheduled on one pass of the read/write head. Default: 50.
Maximum Concurrent Directory Cache Writes	5	5	50	Maximum number of directory cache writes that will be scheduled on one pass of the read/write head. Default: 10.
Directory Cache Buffer Non-Referenced Delay	1 min.	1 sec.	5 min.	Minimum time to hold a directory block in cache after it was last accessed. Default: 5.5 sec.

SMART LINK

Explore *all* the cache utilization SET parameters in the *NetWare 4.11* *Utilities Reference* book at http://www.novell.com/manuals.

LAN/WAN INFORMATION

All network interface cards (NICs) maintain a set of statistics about themselves. Items such as Packets Received and Packets Sent are common to every protocol, and are reported for every board. Others such as Collisions or Beacons are particular to one protocol or another (Ethernet and Token Ring, respectively, in this example). Those statistics are stored in counters called *registers*, and are accessible via special commands to the NIC itself. The manufacturer of the board writes the LAN driver, which MONITOR uses to access and interpret the statistics. There are whole shelves of third-party programs that access these registers on every station on the LAN, and produce pretty reports that help identify dead or dying NICs. Check them out; they're fun at parties.

ZEN

"To change one's life: Start Immediately! Do it flamboyantly. No exceptions."

William James

Welcome to the WAN. MONITOR has an internal mechanism that allows it to access NIC registers. You can view these statistics on the LAN/WAN Statistics screen (see Figure 15.8). When you first select this item, you will be presented with a list of all your LANs. If you happen to have two protocols loaded for a single LAN card (the default for Ethernet), that card will be listed twice, since it represents two logical LANs. Don't worry; the data will be identical — you can pick either one.

Figure 15.8 shows the registers for ACME's Ethernet card — a 3COM 3C5X9. As you can see, there are several pages of statistics you can look at, and they're all explained in the NIC's reference manual. Remember, different manufacturers write different LAN drivers and capture different statistics. You might find a register called Enqueued Sends Count for an NE2000, but not find it for our 3C5X9 — even though they're both Ethernet cards. By the way, the NE2000 Enqueued Sends Count field represents the number of times the server wanted to send something, but the NIC was still busy dealing with the previous packet. The solution is to get a faster NIC.

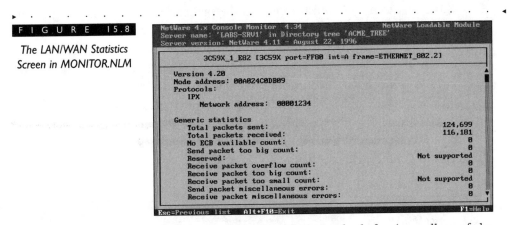

FIGURE 15.8

The LAN/WAN Statistics
Screen in MONITOR.NLM

There is one particular statistic you should always look for (regardless of the card) — the No ECB Available statistic. This register gets updated whenever an incoming packet must be rejected because there is no available packet receive buffer (PRB). We'll discuss PRBs in just a second. If this figure is above zero and climbing, then the number of buffers allocated has reached the maximum and many more are needed.

Another important set of statistics deals with collisions. Ethernet packets are subject to collisions, and when they occur, packets must be retransmitted. If there is a high number of collisions, it is usually because of a very busy segment (too busy). And the retransmissions only make it worse. On the second page of statistics (not shown here), MONITOR lists collision count registers. On one of our test servers, with 1.3 million packets sent since it was brought up, there were 26 collisions. Any number less than 2 percent is acceptable. When it climbs above that, the proper remedy is to split or segment the LAN.

PROCESSOR UTILIZATION

Under most conditions, the server CPU is not taxed. In fact, most servers have far more CPU power than they really need. MONITOR's Utilization percentage is often well under 30 percent, and on many machines it is in the single-digit range. On the off chance that you have a server with a significant CPU load, there are a few things you can do about it.

The first thing you must do is find the process or task that is using the most CPU power. It would be a waste of your time, for example, to move the print server NLM to another machine if, in fact, the print server was taking only 5 percent of the CPU's time. However, if it were taking 35 percent of the computer power in your server, then moving it might be a great idea.

Refer to Figure 15.9 for a snapshot of the Processor Utilization screen in MONITOR.NLM. To get to this screen, choose Processor Utilization from the menu, then press F3 to see utilization statistics for all tasks. If there are just a few tasks to monitor, choose them with the F5 key.

FIGURE 15.9

Processor Utilization in MONITOR.NLM

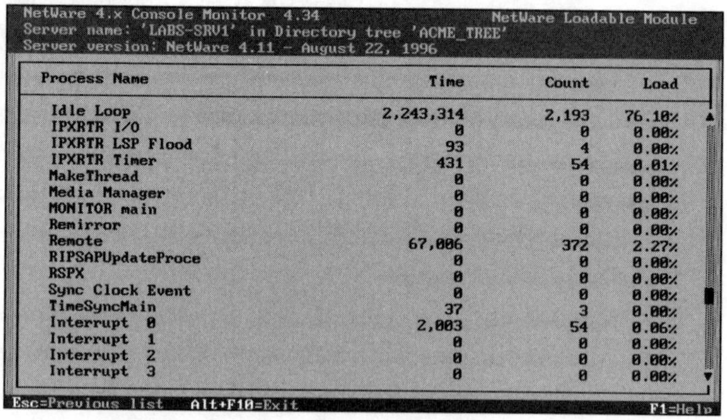

The four columns in the Processor Utilization screen are

- ▸ *Name* — The name of the process. Some processes spawn other subtasks (the PSERVER process on this screen is an example) and so they get numbered sequentially in order to distinguish them.

- ▸ *Time* — The amount of time the CPU spent executing this process since the last sample was taken.

- ▸ *Count* — The number of times this process was executed at all during the sample period.

▶ *Load* — The percent of CPU load attributable to this task. The total of this column equals 100 percent, so if you have a CPU Utilization (from the opening screen) of 75 percent and a load of 33 percent for Task-A, then Task-A is using 25 percent of the CPU's capacity (a third of 75 percent = 25 percent).

One of the tasks always listed is the Idle Loop. When the CPU has nothing to do, it simply hangs out for one tick — there are 18.2 ticks per second on every Intel-based CPU. Then it checks again for something to do. This checking, idling, and checking again is called the Idle Loop Process. Its load will vary inversely with CPU utilization.

Bus mastering can also help. These special SCSI and LAN cards have 80188 CPUs on them. So, they can handle some of the workload that usually must be passed to the main processor. If your processor utilization statistics point to a system that has a lot of disk activity taking the CPU's time, then get a bus mastering SCSI card. Similarly, if your CPU is busy handling LAN traffic, then a bus mastering NIC will offer significant help.

Finally, here are a few tips to consider for lowering your server's processor utilization:

▶ Compile baseline data to determine your server's typical utilization, then take action when it gets high.

▶ Place some services (printing, database, application, gateway, and communications) on other dedicated servers. Also, consider upgrading the hardware in this server.

▶ Set low-priority threads to remain low priority.

▶ Manage compression and backup activity during off-hours.

Well, that does it for monitoring. Are you getting the feeling someone is watching you? Is it paranoia, or does MONITOR.NLM extend to your living room? Regardless, we can all agree it's a great server monitoring tool.

Now that you're comfortable with the first phase of IntranetWare optimization, let's move on to the second phase — SERVMAN.NLM. In the next section, we'll explore the details of proactive optimization with SERVMAN.NLM. Move over Batman; there's a new Superhero in town.

QUIZ

Let's test your monitoring capabilities. Three men are standing in front of you. Each is either a Truthteller or a Liar. You ask if any of them is a Truthteller. The first one says, "There are three Truthtellers here." The second says, "No, only one of us is a Truthteller," and the third one answers, "The second man is telling the truth." Well, what are they: Liars, Truthtellers, or a mixture, and how many of each? Note: You can't use MONITOR.NLM to help you.

(Q15-2)

Optimization with SERVMAN.NLM

Novell has performed countless market analysis studies and found that most LANs still have fewer than 20 workstations per server — very surprising. They've also found that LANs with more than 50 workstations per server also have at least a part-time LAN administrator (CNE). Taking these two factors into account, Novell designed a server that would have default tuning parameters covering the 20 to 50 workstation range.

For example, we'll discuss something called packet receive buffers later in this section. Without even defining them, let's look at their defaults. IntranetWare sets an initial size of 50 packet receive buffers, and allows the operating system to allocate up to 50 more (a ceiling value of 100). They even tell you that a good rule of thumb is two per workstation plus ten for the server. This default calculation is perfect for that 20 to 50 workstation range. After that, Novell expects the LAN administrator to make adjustments.

You can make similar adjustments with respect to IntranetWare's three most popular optimization components:

- ▸ Memory

- ▸ LAN

- ▸ Disk

To check the current status of these three areas, use MONITOR. If you must make changes to the items reported in MONITOR, you'll use the SET parameters listed in SERVMAN. It's that easy — a one-two punch. First, check it out in MONITOR, then fix it in SERVMAN.

SMART LINK

Explore SERVMAN.NLM in detail with the "Utilities Reference" at http://www.novell.com/manuals.

In this chapter, we've already explored a few different SET parameters. As you've seen, IntranetWare provides several scores of tuning parameters that can be changed in environments that demand it. Some (such as the minimum and maximum packet receive buffer parameters) are essential in all but the smallest LANs. Others (such as the ones that adjust the volume log file size) are almost never changed. In this section, we'll look at the SERVMAN screens that pertain to memory, LAN, and disk optimization.

MEMORY OPTIMIZATION

Three separate SERVMAN screens deal with memory. The first is called Directory Caching and is shown in Figure 15.10. The second is simply called Memory and is shown in Figure 15.11. And finally, the File Caching parameters are shown in Figure 15.12.

Let's check them out.

Optimizing Directory Caching in SERVMAN

IntranetWare file servers keep a part of the directory entry table (DET) in memory at all times. The DET contains information such as ownership, attributes, dates, and times about the files and directories on each volume. As files and directories are added, updated, deleted, and even accessed, the respective DET entry must be updated. These SET parameters adjust how much file server RAM should be allocated to the DET, how often to make new buffers (up to the limit), and how long to keep old ones around after they're no longer being referenced. The only parameter most CNEs are likely to modify is the one that is highlighted in Figure 15.10:

```
SET Maximum Concurrent Directory Cache Writes
```

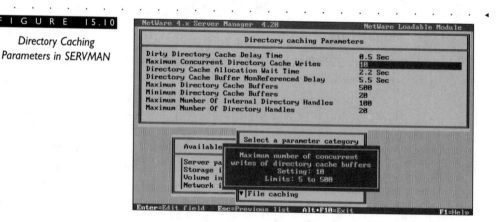

FIGURE 15.10

Directory Caching
Parameters in SERVMAN

SMART LINK

Explore *all* the directory caching SET parameters in the *NetWare 4.11 Utilities Reference* book at http://www.novell.com/manuals.

In Figure 15.12 (later), there is a related SET parameter called Maximum Concurrent Disk Cache Writes. This is similar to the SET command for directory cache writes, in that it tells IntranetWare how many updated file cache buffers can be written to disk at once.

When requests to write to the disk are made, they are placed in a queue. Each time the read/write head on the disk swings in or out, a list of clusters to read or write is given to the controller. The size of the list is different for each controller. For some, it is as low as 100 entries; for others there's room for a thousand.

By default, up to 20 of them can be DET buffer writes, and 50 can be file cache buffers. As a CNE, you can increase this number, but it will be at the expense of potential read requests. For controllers that can only handle a few at a time, these numbers are too high. For those that are capable of handling a thousand at a time, feel free to increase these values. You'll know if they need to be increased by looking at the Cache Utilization Monitor screen and examining the too many dirty cache buffers count. If it is non-zero, you need to take action.

ZEN

"The most incomprehensible thing about the world is that we think it's comprehensible."

Albert Einstein

Optimizing Memory in SERVMAN

Figure 15.11 focuses on the general Memory window in SERVMAN. In this case, we've highlighted AUTO REGISTER MEMORY ABOVE 16 MB. On EISA-, MCA-, and PCI-based machines, IntranetWare will be told the exact amount of available RAM. You can set this to ON, so that the server knows about and uses all of the memory you have installed. While it seems obvious that everyone would always want to use all the available memory, this isn't the case.

FIGURE 15.11

The Memory Screen in SERVMAN

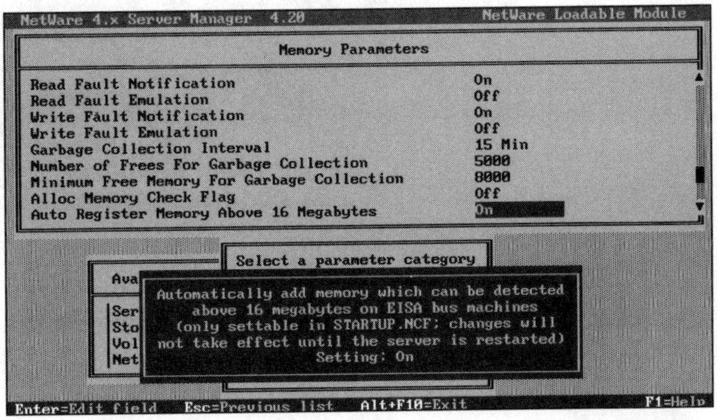

There are many drivers that are written in such a way that they have to be loaded in the first 16MB of RAM. If they are located at a higher address, they won't be able to function properly. IntranetWare defaults to loading drivers (both LAN and disk) at the highest available memory address, while it loads other NLMs just above the operating system itself. (It does this because drivers are very seldom unloaded, so loading them together at the top of memory reduces RAM fragmentation.) If this parameter is set to ON, and you use these low-memory-only drivers, your network will bog down. The solution is to set the parameter to OFF, then load the drivers, then tell IntranetWare about the additional memory after the drivers are loaded. (Use the REGISTER MEMORY console command.)

Optimizing File Caching in SERVMAN

SERVMAN also allows you to optimize file caching. Check out Figure 15.12. In this case, we've highlighted Read Ahead LRU Sitting Time Threshold. When buffers are in such high demand that they are reused after being idle only 10 seconds, the server is seriously short on memory. Leaving data in RAM for extended periods reduces demands for disk activity. If the buffers have to be used again in such a short time, it is likely that additional read requests will be made for data that was just recently overwritten.

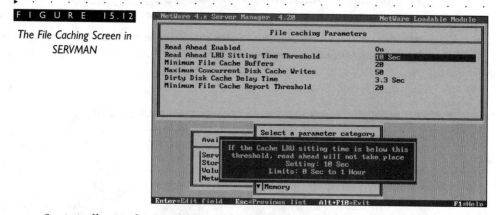

FIGURE 15.12

The File Caching Screen in SERVMAN

Statistically speaking, when a block is read, the most likely next read request will be for the adjacent block. IntranetWare takes advantage of this possibility by reading the next block right away, thus saving the time it takes for the controller to position the head over the right cylinder and track. When memory is tight, IntranetWare forgoes this potential time-saver.

As a CNE, you probably understand your server much better than the IntranetWare designers. If most access is random, then increase this parameter, because it will be better to retain already read data than to read adjacent blocks. On the other hand, if the data is often searched in a sequential manner, then a decrease is in order. Read-ahead is far more important than retention. Note, though, that either choice merely treats a symptom of too little file server RAM. The only real solution is to install more memory.

That completes our discussion of memory optimization. Now let's take a look at the LAN itself.

LAN OPTIMIZATION

Data is transferred across the LAN in small chunks known as packets. As you might imagine, the server sends and receives far more of these packets than do normal workstations. When a packet arrives, it is likely that the server will be busy servicing a previously sent packet. When this is the case the newly arrived packet has to wait in an area known as the *packet receive buffer pool* (sometimes called the *PRB pool*).

If a packet arrives when there is no more room in the PRB pool, it gets dropped. Packets are normally received in the memory area of a LAN card, then transferred to the PRB pool, then erased from the card's memory so that the card is ready for the next incoming packet. If the PRB pool is full, then it is erased immediately after it is received, without the transfer. LAN architectures are able to recognize missing packets and so the sender will just send another one, but this wastes LAN capacity, or bandwidth.

On the other hand, if the pool is much larger than ever needed, then precious server RAM is wasted. Why reserve a big chunk of memory for the PRB pool if it just sits idly by in case a flurry of incoming packets should arrive? Better to have that memory available for file caching or an NLM task.

Novell's surveys of its customers show that the average LAN still has fewer than 20 workstations, so the default number of PRBs is just 50, with permission to grow to a maximum of 100. A good starting rule of thumb is two buffers per workstation, plus ten for the server. Look at Figure 15.5, the MONITOR main screen. Around the middle of the list you'll see the number of currently allocated PRBs. For this server, the number allocated is the minimum. No more than 50 have been needed so far. If the number was 100, it might mean that this was the high-water mark, or it might mean that more were needed, but couldn't be allocated because the server did not have permission to do so.

If your server is consistently using all the allocated PRBs then you should raise the ceiling by typing the following SET command:

```
SET Maximum Packet Receive Buffers=200.
```

Wait to see if the number climbs to the new maximum. Repeat this command until the ceiling is high enough that you don't hit it. Then type a similar line:

```
SET Minimum Packet Receive Buffers=nnn
```

Place this line in the STARTUP.NCF file so that the server will start out with the proper number. Incidentally, *nnn* is the observed high-water mark, the maximum should be a hundred or two higher.

Ah, but there is another solution. You can cure overloaded PRB pools by processing the packets faster once they arrive. This feature is controlled by two SET parameters: Minimum and Maximum Service Processes. As we learned earlier, Service Processes handle incoming user requests at the server. If you increase the number of processes available, then the server can move the PRBs out of the PRB pool more quickly. This eliminates the need for fiddling around with Minimum and Maximum PRBs. Refer to Table 15.7 for more details.

Finally, you can solve the problems of too many packets and high bandwidth utilization by increasing the size of the packets themselves. This feature is controlled by the Maximum Physical Receive Packet Size parameter. Ideally, you want to use the largest packet size available. This is because the IntranetWare server negotiates to the smallest packet size being used by the workstations. The allowable range for a workstation is 512 to 24,682 bytes, depending on the LAN driver. Check out Table 15.7 for a closer look at available server packet sizes.

SMART LINK

Explore *all* the LAN optimization SET parameters in the "Utilities Reference" book at http://www.novell.com/manuals.

Packet-Related SET Parameters

COMMAND	DEFAULT	MIN.	MAX.	MEANING
Maximum Packet Receive Buffers	100	50	25,000	Maximum number of PRBs supported at the server for incoming packets.
Minimum Packet Receive Buffers	50	10	20,000	Minimum number of PRBs allocated at server startup.
Maximum Physical Receive Packet Size	4,202 (Token Ring); 1,514 (Ethernet); 512 (Arcnet)	512	24,682	Largest client packet size supported at this server. This statistic is determined by the LAN driver.
Maximum Service Processes	40	5	1,000	Maximum number of service processes available for handling incoming user requests.
Minimum Service Processes	10	10	500	Number of service processes automatically available when the server boots. Allocated processes are dynamically added until the reach the maximum.

We'll discuss packet sizing in a little more detail later in the chapter. As a matter of fact, IntranetWare includes an optional optimization strategy known as Large Internet Packets, or LIP.

Don't give me any lip; it's time to move on to the final optimization component — the disk.

DISK OPTIMIZATION

Now we get to optimize the Disk. SERVMAN provides two screens for this task:

▶ File System Parameters (see Figure 15.13)

▶ Disk Parameters (see Figure 15.14)

Let's check them out.

Optimizing the File System in SERVMAN

Figure 15.13 shows the SERVMAN parameters for optimizing the IntranetWare File System. We've highlighted a key parameter, Immediate Purge Of Deleted Files. Normally, this parameter is set to OFF, so that files can be salvaged or recovered long after they've been deleted. There is one time, however, when you might consider setting the parameter to ON.

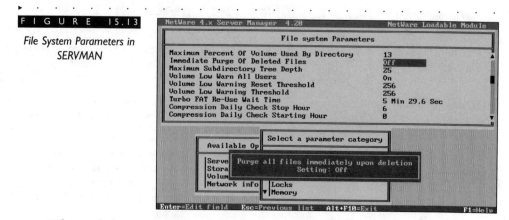

F I G U R E   15.13

File System Parameters in SERVMAN

When a disk is new, all files written to it are placed on the disk in never-before-used blocks. Files and directories that are deleted are simply marked as deleted and otherwise left alone. When the system runs out of this never-used space, it begins reusing it, taking first the space that has been deleted the longest. The only exception is that space from files that have been purged (either manually or because of the purge attribute) will be reused before space from the file deleted for the longest time. Normally, this scheme works to keep recently deleted files available for recovery as long as possible. However, there is one case in which it doesn't work as planned.

When a disk is more than half full, and a full restore from the backup tape is being done, you'll want to turn this parameter to ON temporarily. Otherwise, the files will be restored from the backup tape and as they are created, they will automatically delete the version already on disk. By the time the restore is finished, nearly all of the files that were on the disk before the restore will have been deleted. Those files that happened to have been deleted before the restore will no longer be salvageable (and remember, as deleted files they weren't backed up). By setting the parameter to ON, IntranetWare will immediately reuse the space taken by files deleted during the restore process. When finished, the old deleted files will still be salvageable.

Optimizing the Disk in SERVMAN

Figure 15.14 shows the SERVMAN parameters for optimizing the IntranetWare Disk. We've highlighted a key parameter Enable Disk Read After Write Verify.

• ▸ • ◂

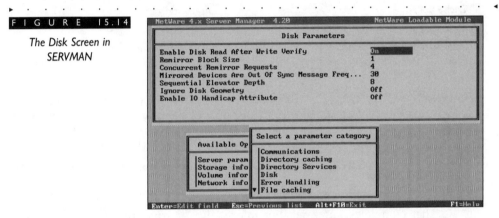

| FIGURE 15.14 |

The Disk Screen in SERVMAN

```
NetWare 4.x Server Manager  4.20              NetWare Loadable Module
┌──────────────────────────────────────────────────────────────────┐
│                         Disk Parameters                            │
│  Enable Disk Read After Write Verify          On                   │
│  Remirror Block Size                          1                    │
│  Concurrent Remirror Requests                 4                    │
│  Mirrored Devices Are Out Of Sync Message Freq... 30               │
│  Sequential Elevator Depth                    8                    │
│  Ignore Disk Geometry                         Off                  │
│  Enable IO Handicap Attribute                 Off                  │
│                                                                    │
│                                                                    │
│                                                                    │
│                    ┌────────────┐ Select a parameter category ┐   │
│                    │ Available Op│                             │   │
│                    │             │ Communications              │   │
│                    │ Server param│ Directory caching           │   │
│                    │ Storage info│ Directory Services          │   │
│                    │ Volume infor│ Disk                        │   │
│                    │ Network info│ Error Handling              │   │
│                    │           ▾ │ File caching                │   │
│ Enter=Edit field   Esc=Previous list    Alt+F10=Exit        F1=Help│
└──────────────────────────────────────────────────────────────────┘
```

One of InternetWare's fault-tolerance features is its habit of rereading every block of data just after writing it, just to make sure that it was written correctly and that it can be read from disk. This is a holdover from days when disks were not nearly as reliable as they are today. In fact, many of today's disks (all IDEs and some SCSIs) are automatically reread by their controller before the operating system is told that the write is complete. If you have one of these disks in your server, then leaving this parameter ON wastes resources for no valid reason.

Finally, there are a variety of additional SET parameters which help manage disk optimization. Refer to Table 15.8 for a complete list.

QUIZ

What is the five-digit number in which the last number is the product of the first and second, the last number is twice the second, the fourth is the sum of the third and the last, and the sum of all the digits is 24?

(Q15-3)

COMMAND	DEFAULT	MIN.	MAX.	MEANING
Maximum Directory Cache Buffers	500	20	4,000	Maximum number of cache buffers the server has allocated for Directory tree.
Minimum Directory Cache Buffers	20	10	2,000	Minimum number of cache buffers the server automatically allocates for DET/FAT searches at startup.
Immediate Purge Files	OFF	OFF	ON	Automatically purge files once of Deleted they are deleted. This parameter disables "SALVAGING."
Fast Volume Mounts	ON	OFF	ON	When ON, this parameter increases the speed of volume mounts by only checking the most important volume fields. Turn OFF if volumes dismount abnormally.
Auto Restart ABEND	OFF	OFF	ON	Automatically restarts the server once it After ABENDs (also known as ABnormal END).

That completes our brief, but informative, journey through SERVMAN. You should really explore this wonderful optimization tool whenever you get a chance. We've given you a big headstart here, but there's so much more to learn. As a matter of fact, there are a few miscellaneous parameters I'd like to leave you with. Check them out.

MISCELLANEOUS OPTIMIZATION

SERVMAN and SET parameters are primarily used for memory, LAN, and disk optimization. But there are a few other cases where they can be very helpful, namely:

- ▸ WatchDog

- ▸ Bells and Whistles

- ▸ Saving Your Work in SERVMAN

Let's explore these miscellaneous optimization strategies before we leave SERVMAN and enter the realm of packet bursting — sounds painful.

WatchDog

As much as we tell them otherwise, users often fail to log out. Sometimes they just turn off their machines and then leave; sometimes they wind up having to reboot. In either case, the server has no way of knowing that the workstation is no longer actively using its connection.

IntranetWare has a series of SET parameters, shown in Table 15.9, that are collectively known as WatchDog. You can tell IntranetWare to contact workstations that it has not heard from in a while, and if they don't respond after several such contacts, to assume that they're no longer around and to clear their connection. As an administrator, you must balance the need to avoid wasting connections with the possible data loss from an improperly cleared connection. The SET parameters control how long to wait before checking to see if a workstation is still there, how many times to check, and how long to wait between tries. With these defaults, it takes 15 minutes for the WatchDog to clear a connection. The minimum would be 65 seconds; the maximum is almost 15 days.

SMART LINK

Explore _all_ the WatchDog SET parameters in the "Utilities Reference" book at http://www.novell.com/manuals.

TABLE 15.9

WatchDog SET Parameters

COMMAND	DEFAULT	MIN.	MAX.	MEANING
Delay Before First WatchDog Packet	5 min.	15 sec.	14 days	The length of time that has to elapse before the server will send the first WatchDog packet
Number Of WatchDog Packets	10	5	100	The number of packets to send without a response from the workstation before clearing the connection
Delay Between WatchDog Packets	1 min.	10 sec.	10 min.	The amount of time to wait before sending the next WatchDog packet

Bells and Whistles

Of all the things you can do for the system, there is one parameter that's primarily useful to you — the IntranetWare CNE. When the server issues an alert, it displays a message on the screen and rings the "bell" (sounds a tone on the server's speaker). If you are dealing with a problem in the computer room, the last thing you need is a beep going off every few seconds. At those times, the SET parameter shown in Figure 15.15 will be especially useful.

Saving Your Work in SERVMAN

Whenever a change is made via SERVMAN, it is in effect immediately (except those changes that have to be issued from STARTUP.NCF). To save you the trouble of entering them over and over again, SERVMAN offers to write them to the STARTUP.NCF and AUTOEXEC.NCF files for you when you exit the SET Parameters section. Figure 15.16 shows how changes are written to the STARTUP.NCF and AUTOEXEC.NCF files.

Now it's time to explore a few additional optimization strategies, including file compression, block suballocation, packet bursting, and Large Internet Packets. These are the "other" topics people keep talking about. They are primarily unique to IntranetWare, and are very cool. So, let's not waste any time. Ready, set, optimize!

F I G U R E   15.15

Miscellaneous Parameters in SERVMAN

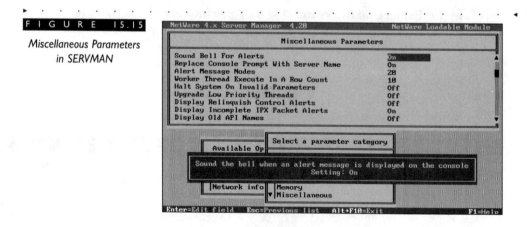

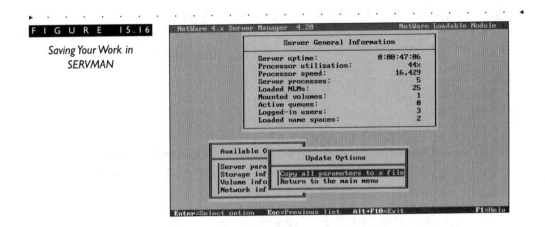

Saving Your Work in
SERVMAN

Other Optimization Strategies

So, what's left? After MONITOR and SERVMAN, it's hard to believe that there are more ways to optimize IntranetWare. Well, prepare yourself — there's a lot more! As a matter of fact, IntranetWare includes four more optimization strategies beyond what you've already seen. They are

- ► File Compression

- ► Block Suballocation

- ► Packet Burst protocol

- ► Large Internet Packets

There are two keys to optimizing disk space: file compression and block suballocation. For users of DOS, compression is old news. Programs such as Stacker and DoubleSpace have been around for a few years. Adding it to the IntranetWare operating system was a bold step forward. Suballocation is an entirely new concept. We'll take a closer look at both.

In addition, IntranetWare offers two ways of optimizing LAN/WAN communications: packet bursting and Large Internet Packets (LIPs). Packet bursting sends more packets per session, while LIPs send bigger packets each time. We'll also take a closer look at these.

What are you waiting for, Ensign — let's optimize.

SMART LINK

For more information on File System and WAN optimization, surf to the Novell Knowledgebase at http://support.novell.com/search/.

OPTIMIZING FILE COMPRESSION

Some files are read and reread every day, or even every few minutes (LOGIN.EXE, WP.EXE, and so on). These files are always stored in their fully expanded form. Other files, however, are only read a few times, and then sometimes left untouched for months or years. Think of the last memo or letter you wrote. While composing and editing it, you probably saved and retrieved it several times, but after printing and mailing, you saved for the last time. That memo will live on the disk forever. Other examples of files that stay idle for extended periods are on-line documentation for many applications, IntranetWare's own Electrotext or Dynatext files, prior years' accounting data, and so on.

With IntranetWare, you can enable compression. After a file is left idle for several days (the default is seven, but you can change it), it will be compressed. Reading it once in any day won't change that, but if it's accessed more than that, it will be stored back in expanded form. Even when it's compressed, if it's accessed, it will be expanded in file server memory before being delivered to the requester. Except for a small delay for decompression, this whole process is invisible to the user.

If there are files that you want to compress right away and leave compressed or, alternatively, if there are files that you never want compressed, IntranetWare has a solution. IntranetWare contains some new attributes. Use FLAG or FILER or NWADMIN to set the Ic (Immediate Compress) or Dc (Don't Compress) attributes on any file or directory, and IntranetWare will comply.

Figure 15.17 shows a screen from the INSTALL program, indicating that both compression and suballocation are turned on. It is important to note that once on, they cannot be turned off; but if they are off, they can be turned on (once). Maximum disk savings are realized with compression and suballocation are enabled, and disk allocation blocks are large (16K, 32K, or 64K).

F I G U R E   15.17

Activating File Compression in INSTALL.NLM

ZEN

"An atom (and thus all matter) is mostly empty space. Therefore, things are not what they appear."

Encyclopedia Britannica

Figure 15.18 shows the File Compression statistics in NWADMIN. These statistics are also available via the NDIR program (NDIR /VOL) and through FILER. The volume has 1,933 MB of space, of which 1,582 MB are free, yet there are more than 450 MB of data already stored on it. Fortunately, 143 MB is compressed. Apparently, you can get six pounds of sand into a two-pound bag, if you have a good compression program. IntranetWare has an average compression ratio of 63 percent.

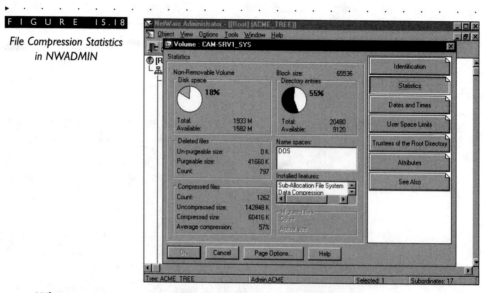

When compression is enabled, IntranetWare will scan the volumes each night looking for files that have been idle for seven days. Those files will be compressed. If they are accessed once in any day, they will remain compressed, but if they are accessed a second time, IntranetWare will write them back to disk in expanded form. If the disk is nearly full, however, IntranetWare will leave them compressed to avoid running out of disk space. If IntranetWare tries to compress a file and it doesn't save at least 2 percent of the file's space, it will leave it in its fully expanded form, and will set the Can't Compress (Cc) attribute to remind itself not to bother trying again. All of these defaults can be changed using SET commands described later.

You have some control over this situation. You can set the attribute of a file or directory to Immediate Compress (Ic), which will cause IntranetWare to compress the file as soon as possible and to always leave it on disk in compressed form, no matter how many times it is accessed. On the other hand, you can set a Don't Compress (Dc) attribute, which tells IntranetWare to always maintain a file or directory in fully expanded form. You might choose Ic for large, infrequently accessed files (such as documentation), while choosing Dc for infrequently accessed databases (where retrieving a record from a large database would take quite a bit of time). Finally, you can also disable compression by using the following SET parameter:

```
SET Enable File Compression=OFF
```

> ## REAL WORLD
>
> During file compression, IntranetWare builds a temporary file describing the contents of the original. It compresses the temporary file and eventually replaces the original. If the server should fail during compression, the original (uncompressed) file is left intact.

Figure 15.19 from the SERVMAN.NLM shows the compression-related SET commands. Table 15.10, which follows, explains these commands in detail. Check out Chapter 1 for a more detailed discussion of file compression.

SMART LINK

Explore *all* the file compression SET parameters in the *NetWare 4.11 Utilities Reference* book at http://www.novell.com/manuals.

F I G U R E   15.19

*File Compression
Parameters in SERVMAN*

```
NetWare 4.x Server Manager  4.20                    NetWare Loadable Module
                            File system Parameters
 Compression Daily Check Stop Hour                   5
 Compression Daily Check Starting Hour               0
 Minimum Compression Percentage Gain                 20
 Enable File Compression                             On
 Maximum Concurrent Compressions                     2
 Convert Compressed To Uncompressed Option           1
 Decompress Percent Disk Space Free To Allow C...    10
 Decompress Free Space Warning Interval              31 Min 18.5 Sec
 Deleted Files Compression Option                    1

 The hour (0 = midnight, 23 = 11pm) when the file compressor ends scanning
 each enabled volume for files that need to be compressed (if Compression
 Daily Check Stop Hour is equal to Compression Daily Starting Hour then
 start checking every day at Compression Daily Starting Hour and run as
 long as necessary to finish all files meeting the compressible criteria.)
                     (also settable in STARTUP.NCF)
                             Setting: 6
                             Limits: 0 to 23
 Enter=Edit field   Esc=Previous list   Alt+F10=Exit              F1=Help
```

T A B L E   15.10

*Understanding File
Compression SET
Commands*

COMMAND	DEFAULT	MIN.	MAX.	MEANING
Compression Daily Check Stop Hour	6:00 a.m.	0	23	When system should stop scanning for compression candidates. If equal to start hour, then run until done.
Compression Daily Start Hour	0	0	23	Time when system should start scanning for candidates to compress.
Minimum Compression Percentage Gain	2%	0	50 percent	If a file compresses less than this percent (or expanded), then leave it expanded.
Enable File Compression	ON	OFF		If OFF, then don't scan for compression and queue all IC flag requests.
Maximum Concurrent Compressions	2	1	8	Number of volumes that can be scanned for compression at once. IntranetWare still only compresses one file per volume. Novell does not recommend increasing the default.
Convert Compressed to Uncompressed	1	0	2	0 = leave it compressed; 1 = store uncompressed after second access in "untouched" period; 2 = store uncompressed after a single touch.
Uncompress Percent Disk Space Free to Allow Commit	10%	0	75 percent	Minimum percentage of free space that must exist before a compressed file will be rewritten uncompressed. An updated file is always written uncompressed.
Uncompress Free Interval	31 min., 18.5 sec.	0	29 days	Frequency of Space Warning warning alerts when volume has too little space to write decompressed files. Setting of 0 disables messages.

T A B L E   15.10

Understanding File
Compression SET
Commands (continued)

COMMAND	DEFAULT	MIN.	MAX.	MEANING
Deleted File Compression Option	1	0	2	0 = Don't; 1 = Compress next day; 2 = Compress immediately.
Days Untouched Before Compression	7	0	100,000	Number of days to wait before an unmodified file becomes a candidate for compression.

OPTIMIZING BLOCK SUBALLOCATION

In most operating systems, including prior versions of IntranetWare, a small file takes an entire allocation block. In the typical NetWare 3.12 file system, that block size is 4K, so a 1-byte file takes 4096 bytes of disk space. As it grows, the next 4095 bytes are "free." Byte 4097 gets a second allocation block, and so on.

For most of today's hard disks, the minimum size chunk of data that can be read or written is 512 bytes, meaning that eight separate files might fit into that same 4K block.

To further complicate things, if a volume has large files, an even bigger block size is more efficient when reading and writing them, but the few small files on that volume can waste a tremendous amount of space.

IntranetWare solves these problems through a technique called *block suballocation*. When a new file is created, it always gets assigned to a new block. As it grows into a second block, the suballocation process begins. IntranetWare takes a block and breaks it into 512-byte segments. When the 4097th byte is written (on a volume with 4K blocks), the file takes a full block, plus one suballocation chunk. If it grows by another 512 bytes, then it gets a second suballocation chunk. Since multiple files are being managed this way by the operating system, it's possible that these two suballocation chunks might, for a moment, be in separate blocks. In its spare time, IntranetWare rearranges the suballocation units so that the pieces are moved to contiguous spaces. In that way, by the time the file grows to 8192 bytes (8K) it will occupy two full 4K blocks. If the file continues to grow, the process is repeated.

Since this saves so much space that would otherwise be wasted, IntranetWare now defaults to assigning larger block sizes when creating volumes. Depending on the size of the volume, IntranetWare will assign block sizes ranging from a low of 4K (volumes under 64 MB) to a high of 64K (volumes over 1 GB). During the volume-creation portion of the installation, this number can be changed if the installer so desires. Also, block suballocation is enabled by default during installation. If you want to disable it, you must do it when the volume is created. Otherwise, you would have to re-create the volume with INSTALL.NLM (and lose all your data!). See Figure 15.17 (earlier).

Check out Chapter 1 for a more detailed discussion of block suballocation.

OPTIMIZING PACKET BURST PROTOCOL

There is yet another way to improve packet transmittal performance, and that is to use the Packet Burst protocol. Normal IntranetWare procedure is for the receiver to acknowledge ("ack") the receipt of each packet. When the sender hears the ack, it sends the next packet. If it does not hear an ack for an extended period of time (this occurs when a packet is dropped), it resends the same packet. This back-and-forth process is extraordinarily time-consuming and wastes a tremendous amount of bandwidth. A much better alternative is to send a bunch of packets and then wait for an ack from the group. If one part of the group is received OK and another part is bad, the ack can simply indicate which part needs to be retransmitted. This is called Packet Burst. In the NetWare 3.12 environment, it has to be added to both the workstations and the servers by the administrator. In IntranetWare it is automatically turned on for both.

The largest packet size is 64K, but on a busy day it would be unfair to other waiting stations if the LAN permitted some stations to send that much. The server can decide how big the burst size should be, and that size is called the *Window Size*. Also, it is possible for a really fast sender to overwhelm a slower receiver. To prevent this, the receiver (usually a workstation) can dictate the *burst gap time*, which is a delay time between bursts that gives the slower station time to process the last burst. As the server dictates smaller window sizes, the workstation can reduce the burst gap time.

Using Packet Burst protocol can increase LAN performance by 10 to 300 percent, depending on such factors as bandwidth, memory, and file sizes. You might choose to eliminate the use of Packet Burst for a station or group of stations.

(For example, the administrator might know that the packets have to cross a router or bridge that does not know how to handle burst traffic.) To do that, all you have to do is alter (or add) a line to the NET.CFG file on the workstation that says

```
PB BUFFERS = 0
```

To reverse that decision, changing the value to any non-zero number will turn it on. It doesn't matter which non-zero number is used. For now, Novell recommends using 2, so that future enhancements might be implemented more easily.

So, let's see what it takes to enable packet bursting in Windows 95:

1. Access Start and Settings. Choose Control Panel and double-click on Network. This provides access to the Windows 95 network settings.

2. At the Configuration tab, select Novell IntranetWare Client 32 and click Properties.

3. Select the Advanced Settings tab. Scroll down the choices until you find three packet bursting parameters: Packet Burst, Packet Burst Read Window Size, and Packet Burst Write Window Size. Remember: Packet bursting is automatically activated at the IntranetWare server.

OPTIMIZING LARGE INTERNET PACKETS (LIPS)

When NetWare was first introduced, CPUs were slow (8 MHz was a fast machine), memory was expensive, and there was plenty of extra bandwidth. The engineers at Novell quite properly decided to make IPX smaller and faster by eliminating the code that could break a large packet into smaller parts for retransmission (a process known as *fragmentation*). This meant that whenever a LAN had two segments of different sizes, packets from the larger capacity segment could not be retransmitted to the smaller unless, somehow, the larger packet size LAN was forced to issue smaller packets to begin with. To make matters worse, the servers couldn't be sure what size might be in use on any segment. The solution was to force all packets to the smallest packet size of any commonly available protocol whenever a server detected that there was more than one segment on that LAN.

The ARCnet protocol was one of the available protocols, and it uses 576-byte packets. Therefore, IntranetWare forces all packets to that size whenever it detects multiple segments. Since ARCnet's popularity has dwindled to almost nothing, this is a major waste of resources for most networks. The solution was to tell the server to use larger packets. It still could not fragment, but at least it could be told to operate at the smallest size in use on that LAN. Ethernet packets top out at 1514 bytes, and both Token Ring and FDDI use 4202-byte packets. A mixed Ethernet/Token-Ring LAN would need to use 1514 as the maximum packet size; a Token Ring only or mixed Token-Ring/FDDI LAN could set its packet size at 4202. The SET command that tells the server what packet size to use is

```
SET Maximum Physical Receive Packet Size=nnnn.
```

One of the new features of IntranetWare is a routing process called NetWare Link State Protocol (NLSP). Among its features is the capability to fragment and reassemble packets so that mixed LANs can exist. Very cool.

QUIZ

I love a good math problem — how about you? Aren't they wonderfully relaxing? Anyway, here's a doozy for your calculating pleasure: Using the figure "5" eight times together with any mathematical symbols, with the exception of the plus sign, write out a calculation to give the answer 110. Ready, set, calculate (hey, that rhymes).

(Q15-4)

"That's not all. It slices, it dices. . . ." Oops, sorry. I was working on my latest infomercial. Check it out at 2 a.m. on any local access channel near you. What I was trying to say was "Optimization is not just for optimizing." It can also be used for troubleshooting. As a matter of fact, optimization and troubleshooting are forever tied together. Are you confused? Watch (I mean "Read") . . . .

Optimization and Troubleshooting

Optimization and troubleshooting are forever tied together. Here's how it works. Optimization is a proactive strategy to increase server performance. True. Troubleshooting is a reactive strategy to fix a broken server. True. How optimized is your server when it's broken? Not very. So, it stands to reason that fixing your server increases its performance, and in some strange way, is a form of optimization. Hmmmm.

Let's begin our discussion of optimization and troubleshooting with a review of how the server works and how data flows.

SMART LINK

For more help troubleshooting and optimizing your network and server, surf over to http://support.novell.com/sitemap.

HOW THE SERVER WORKS

By now it should be clear that memory plays a huge part in how well your file server responds to your users' requests. Every process that takes place on your file server requires memory. These processes are loaded into file server memory because you have loaded an NLM. While you may think the solution is to not load any NLMs, you would quickly find that you could do very little, including logging in. You can't log in unless your network card driver, which is an NLM, is loaded and bound to the right protocol stack.

This is the most basic of NLMs, but there are other essential NLMs you'll want to leave in file server memory. Many backup and virus protection programs are implemented as NLMs. You certainly don't want to do without these. You may want to leave the MONITOR.NLM loaded so you can view statistics on an ongoing basis. Many management utilities (such as inventory and metering programs) require NLMs. All these processes may be essential to maintaining your file server. So, after all the administrative trivia, how much memory do you have left for your users? Specifically how many file cache buffers do you have left?

Your job is to make sure there is enough memory left over for those pesky users. You can control how much memory will be allocated to various processes by using the SET command and the SERVMAN utility. SET commands can be issued directly at the file server console prompt, except for those that can be issued only in STARTUP.NCF. The good news is that SET will tell you which ones must be in STARTUP.NCF. You can't hurt the file server by accidentally issuing this subset of SET commands at the prompt. You'll just get a message that says you can only set the particular parameter in STARTUP.NCF. There are a couple of SET commands that can also be issued in STARTUP.NCF. You can use the INSTALL.NLM or SERVMAN to edit STARTUP.NCF to include the appropriate commands.

Note: If you change your STARTUP.NCF, the changes won't take effect until the next time you shut down and restart your file server. Some are parameters settable only in STARTUP.NCF, including:

▸ *Minimum Packet Receive Buffers* — This makes sense if you think about it. You want to make sure enough memory is set aside for incoming packets before all the other memory gets allocated.

▸ *Maximum Physical Receive Packet Size* — This works with the previous parameter. Not only do you want to set aside memory buffers for incoming packets, but you must know how big each of those buffers needs to be.

Other parameters can be set in STARTUP.NCF, but don't have to be, including:

▸ Maximum Packet Receive Buffers

▸ Fast Volume Mounts

▸ Auto Restart After ABEND

▸ Garbage Collection Interval

▸ Number of Frees for Garbage Collection

▸ Minimum Free Memory for Garbage Collection

ZEN

"Life consists not in holding good cards but in playing those you hold well."

Josh Billings

Before you start tuning your file server, you should figure out if it needs tuning. You do this by monitoring how well your file server is performing without tuning it. Obviously, if you start your file server and watch what's going on, it will look like you don't need to do anything. The trick is to watch how your file server is doing when all your users are pounding on it. So, wait until most everyone has logged in, say around 10:30 in the morning, or after they come back from lunch, but before they leave early to pick up their kids — say around 2:30 in the afternoon. These are generally considered peak times in most environments. Your environment may be different.

The process of tracking how your file server is doing on a regular basis is called *baselining*. You're establishing the baseline or most normal levels at which your file server operates. By baselining, you can spot when the file server isn't behaving at its most normal level. It makes it much easier to figure out if something is wrong (or different) if you have some information to compare it to.

You know how to move around MONITOR, so you know how to find out the baseline parameters of your file server. Because MONITOR doesn't contain a print option, you'll want to write down the parameters you're tracking. (The IntranetWare Log book would be a good place.) If you decide to use a third-party management utility that prints reports, make sure they make it to the log book instead of the trash can.

Despite the fact that we seem to be focusing exclusively on memory, you'll remember that we discussed how important the disk system is to optimal performance of an IntranetWare file server. The two are intimately related because everything you read or write from or to the disk goes through memory. So, how well do you understand the path data takes through file server memory on its way to and from the file server disk? Time to learn.

HOW DATA FLOWS

When a workstation wants a data file from the file server, it first has to ask permission to open it. This is different from actually reading the contents of the file, which depends on your trustee rights. So, there you are at your workstation and you issue a command to open a file. What happens? First the DOS Requester wraps your request into a NetWare Core Protocol (NCP) request. NCP is the language the server speaks. The packet then travels across the cable to the file server, where it sits in a packet receive buffer. Packet receive buffers are also referred to as event control blocks (ECBs).

If no ECB is available, the packet is dropped into the euphemistic bit bucket. The more packets that get trashed into the bit bucket, the higher the No Available ECB Count number gets. If there is an available buffer, the request gets parked in one. From the packet receive buffer, the request moves up to the appropriate protocol stack. If the request is for this server, the server looks around to see if a File Server Process (FSP) is available to handle the request. Remember that FSPs are task handlers. They do the work. If the requesting packet is for another file server, it will get routed appropriately. If no FSPs are available, the packet will just twiddle its thumbs in the packet receive buffer until one becomes available.

Once an FSP starts to handle the request, it will look in the FAT for the location on the hard disk where the requested file blocks are located. If the requested file block is in file cache, the server sends a reply to the workstation that the file is available. If the file blocks are not in cache already, the server will read the file from disk into cache memory. Then the file server asks the workstation if it needs anything else.

If you want to write a file to the file server's hard disk, the first part of the process is the same — up until the FAT search. If no hard disk blocks have been allocated before (for example, this is a new file you want to save), then hard disk space and cache buffers are allocated for use. If the file is associated with previously allocated hard disk blocks, the server checks to see if the relevant blocks are currently in cache memory. If they are cached, then the data is written to the buffer. The buffer is then marked as "dirty." At this point the workstation ceases to worry about the data.

It's now up to the file server to keep track of the dirty buffers and to get the data permanently stored on the file server's hard disk. Now we start the data countdown. If the data has been in the dirty buffer for more than 3.3 seconds, the file server sends it to the hard disk waiting line — the write queue — and frees up the buffer for other caching needs.

Now that you know the details of the read and write paths that data takes through file server memory, it will be easier to understand why you may want to tune certain parameters such as packet receive buffers. Let's look at some common performance symptoms, their possible causes, and what you might want to do to alleviate them. Now we're flying through the Troubleshooting Nebula at warp factor 12.

SMART LINK

If all this optimization and troubleshooting material is still a little greek to you, try the IntranetWare Installation and Configuration Workshop in the CNE program at CyberState University: http://www.cyberstateu.com.

SYMPTOM: SLOW SERVER RESPONSE

The server seems really slow in responding to requests. A request might be running an NDIR *.* /SUB or just logging in and asking for a file. There are several possible solutions. Let's take them one by one.

Solution #1 — High LAN traffic

It may be that you have truly outgrown how much traffic your network cable can handle. Your user population may have grown faster than you (or management) anticipated. You may have moved to more traffic-intensive applications such as multimedia, or graphic design applications.

Redesign your network cable layout. You can do this by just segmenting what you have. Put another network card in your server and put some of your users on the cable segment attached to this new card. Or, you can upgrade your cable plant by moving to something faster.

Note: Sometimes the only problem is a bad network card. Amazingly, network cards can be deaf, dumb, or dead. Deaf cards can't hear, and so they keep requesting stuff that drives the network traffic up. Dumb cards hear but don't speak — they send. Dead cards — well, they're just dead.

What parameters might you want to watch for trouble indicators?

- *Utilization* — If it's high, you should probably add another server instead of just more cable.

▶ *Dirty Cache Buffers* — If they're consistently high, you may consider favoring Disk Cache Writes over reads. Refer to Table 15.5.

▶ *Current Disk requests* — This may indicate the problem is really with a slow disk system.

▶ *Packet Receive Buffers* — If they're maxing out, there could be a communications bottleneck between the server NIC and processor. Consider increasing the Maximum Packet Receive Buffers parameter as a short-term fix.

▶ *Service Processes* — If these are maxing out, you can either adjust them with SERVMAN or SET, as long as there is enough memory left over for file caching. If not, consider adding more memory.

Solution #2 — Packet Receive Buffers have maxed out

This one is easy. Check your baseline statistics for packet receive buffers. Next, shut down the server (your users won't notice, right?) and watch how quickly the buffers max out again. If it's just a matter of minutes, you probably have a bad network board or network board driver somewhere. If it takes days or months to max out, then if you have enough memory left over for caching. Just increase the number of PRBs using SERVMAN or SET.

Solution #3 — Not enough cache buffers

Do you have any NLMs loaded that you aren't using? Do you have the INSTALL.NLM loaded? If your server is up and running, you don't need to leave INSTALL in memory. You also might be loading NLMs from products you aren't using, or aren't using anymore. Unload them. You can use the MEMORY console command to see if the server knows about all the memory you actually installed. You may need to use the REGISTER MEMORY command to make sure it realizes that there is more memory installed than it recognizes. Occasionally, RAM chips go bad. A bad RAM chip may lower the amount of memory the server can access. Unfortunately, bad RAM chips more likely will just crash your server.

Solution #4 — Slow disk

We've talked about this in detail already. As a good CNE, you'll check to see if there is a hardware problem, and if the disk driver is the correct one for your hardware. You may have to upgrade your disk driver by calling your disk manufacturer. Most vendors have bulletin boards or libraries on services such as CompuServe where you can download the latest driver instead of waiting for a disk to arrive in the mail. Diagnostic software for your disk system should be provided by the vendor. They know their hardware the best.

If you have only one disk or disk channel in your file server, you should consider expanding. You can increase disk throughput by adding another disk controller and drive, as well as a Host Bus Adapter (HBA). If one disk channel is busy performing a read or write, the next disk request in the queue (remember the disk request queue from above?) can use the other disk channel.

You could also just speed up the entire process by upgrading all the disk channel components to faster, newer components. If you have CD-ROM drives hanging off your file server disk channel, move them. There is no reason shared CD-ROMs need to be physically on the file server. They only need to be shareable somehow. Microtest in Arizona makes a whole range of sharable CD-ROM solutions that take advantage of IntranetWare performance features and off-load the CD-ROM processing from your file server.

Solution #5 — The file server CPU is overburdened

In other words, the CPU utilization is consistently high and you've already added more memory and off-loaded or unloaded everything you can think of.

Buy a faster CPU. That's pretty obvious. Not so obvious is buying another CPU. Split the server tasks among multiple servers. This is called *load balancing*. To do this efficiently you need to know which processes are the most computer-intensive. But you already know how to find that out, right? Use MONITOR to track which tasks are using most of the CPU's time. Also check for new NLMs that may not have read Miss Manners. Misbehaving NLMs frequently hog the CPU. Usually you can reconfigure the errant NLM. If not, you may have to get rid of it.

Solution #6 — The Directory Tables aren't all cached

Remember that IntranetWare likes to cache the Directory Tables so that file lookups are faster. You'll especially notice this problem when running NDIRs of whole volumes or large parts of the directory structure.

Check if the directory cache buffers have reached their maximum. You know what to do. Increase the amount of memory that can be used for directory caching. You also know the impact this will have on file caching. There will be less memory for caching files. Feels sort of like robbing Peter to pay Paul.

Solution #7 — File Service Processes (FSPs) are maxed out

Running out of task handlers is not a pretty picture, and is usually caused by a misbehaving NLM. If that's not the problem, you may have too many users accessing the file server. Again, load balancing is the answer here. It is pretty common to see networks in which the user population outgrows the original design of the network. While every company likes to imagine itself growing, very few enjoy paying for hardware for the future. CNEs are responsible for recognizing when the future has arrived.

QUIZ

What is unique about the number 854,917,632? (Be careful, this is a tricky one!)

(Q15-5)

As you can see, there are lots of reasons users may be legitimately complaining about slow network response. Whichever solution works for your environment, be sure to document it in your network log book. Time for a new symptom.

SYMPTOM: ABEND (ABNORMAL END)

The IntranetWare server can crash for a variety of reasons. But many times it ends up as an ABEND. This is a special kind a crash that can be caused by a variety of server problems, including NMI I/O and System Board parity errors. Let's check them out.

Solution #1 — ABEND Due to NMI parity error (I/O)

The server console says ABEND and refers to an NMI parity error generated by I/O.

ABEND is short for Abnormal End of Operation. It's a bad thing. You'll know right away because your users will tell you the network is down. The NMI part refers to bad memory. Really. A memory chip someplace gave up the ghost. The I/O part points you toward an input output device instead of the memory on your motherboard.

The tough part about this is that locating exactly the bad memory chip is tricky and takes time, which your users won't be happy about. The fastest solution is to replace the offending board containing the bad memory. It could be memory on any board in your system, including your network card, HBA, or video card.

Sometimes memory chips go bad because of bad power. If you have had brownouts or blackouts, you'll probably notice because the lights will go out or dim perceptively. Spikes and surges are tougher to notice unless you disobey your mother and put your finger in a wall socket. The solution is a line-conditioning UPS.

It is also conceivable that the power supply in the file server, or disk subsystem, has decided to go on the fritz. You can check the power supply voltages, but again, the fastest solution is to replace the power supply. This is also a good reason to maintain a parts inventory.

Solution #2 — ABEND Due to NMI parity error (System Board)

You get an ABEND error with an NMI parity error generated by the system board.

You guessed it! Bad memory on the system board. It is also conceivable that the system board has some other problem, but the NMI part almost always refers to memory-related problems.

Change your system board. Frequently you can get away with swapping memory chips until you find the faulty set. At least that way you don't have to order a new motherboard.

SYMPTOM: SERVER CRASH

If you server doesn't ABEND, it will probably just plain, old CRASH. This is a bad thing. Following are a few follow-up procedures for dealing with IntranetWare server crashes.

Solution #1 — Error message on server console

The server crashes. Any old crash. Now what? There may be an error message displayed to point you in the right direction.

If there is an error, try to figure out what process caused it. It is likely to be NLM-related. If you can pinpoint the NLM, start up the server without the suspect NLM. If it's a newly installed NLM, unload the program, contact the vendor, and review any compatibility issues or installation configuration options that might cause problems, and start again. If the error persists, get rid of the NLM. It could also be that the NLM doesn't get along with the other NLMs in the sandbox. You may have to re-evaluate your older NLMs. You might have to upgrade them so they get along with the new kid (NLM). You may simply have to download a patch and install it. Now would be a good time to check your NSEPro or NetWire to find out about new patches for the operating system or other vendor's NLMs.

Solution #2 — GPPE error

The server crashes (a technical term) with a GPPE error.

All the same problems occur with NLMs as described previously, *plus* you may have a corrupt SERVER.EXE.

Get a new copy of SERVER.EXE from your original disks or CD-ROM, and copy it to your file server.

SYMPTOM: NLM WON'T LOAD

NLMs are usually pretty well-behaved. But, in some cases, they like to cause a fuss. Most of the time, they're missing a supporting NLM or the server is out of memory. Let's take a closer look.

Solution #1 — Supporting NLMs didn't load

A pesky NLM just will not load. This happens more often than you would think, especially with third-party NLMs.

The good news is that this is a pretty easy problem to solve. Check for messages claiming that supporting NLMs (such as CLIB.NLM or STREAMS.NLM) are not loaded. You might also see a message claiming a ". . . public symbol could not be found." You could also just flat be out of available memory for the NLM to load.

Check the NLM's documentation to find out what other NLMs must be loaded first. If you got the "public symbol could not be found" message, you need to load CLIB. If you have CLIB loaded and you're still getting this message, check the version. You may need to download a newer CLIB from NetWire and load it. Third-party NLMs can be very picky about which version of CLIB they run with.

You'll need to pay special attention to the letter associated with the CLIB version (for example, CLIB version 3.12g, d, or e).

If there isn't enough memory available to load the NLM, you know what to do — add more memory. But be sure. There are several NLMs for third-party developers who claim they don't have enough memory to load, and when you check with MONITOR you see megs and megs worth. Contact the NLM vendor and have a long heart-to-heart talk with them about what else could be going on.

Solution #2 — Out of server memory

An NLM won't load because there really isn't enough memory available.

You may have installed plenty of memory, but SERVER.EXE may not know about it. This can happen frequently with ISA machines and occasionally on EISA machines.

Time to dig out the REGISTER MEMORY command. It is possible that you manually issued this command at the console prompt. Then the server was restarted and the command was forgotten about. Of course, you made a note of the need for this command in your log book, but, to make your life even simpler, you should put it in the STARTUP.NCF file so that it runs automatically each time the server comes up. If this isn't the solution, fall back on the old standby — add more memory.

SYMPTOM: CACHE ALLOCATOR IS OUT OF AVAILABLE MEMORY

The console displays an error message saying that the cache allocator is out of available memory.

One of the boards in the file server, most likely the HBA(s), may be trying to use memory above 16 MB, but the driver for the board freaks out because it doesn't know how to work above the magic 16 MB line. To top it off, there probably isn't space available below the 16 MB line. Now, how is the server supposed to give memory for this board?

Well, double-check with MONITOR to make sure there really isn't enough memory, and double-check with your startup files to see if you're trying to load items "high" or "low." Then double-check with the vendor to see if they have a newer driver that can use any memory the cache allocator wants to give it. If none of that works, you can reserve memory below 16 MB.

SYMPTOM: SERVERS ARE LOST IN RCONSOLE

You can't see any of your IntranetWare servers when you try to access them via RCONSOLE.

Guess what? You probably have an old version of RCONSOLE. Earlier versions of RCONSOLE did not support packet signing. It's a relatively new feature of IntranetWare. It's also possible that you neglected to load RSPX and REMOTE on the file server. Without them, you won't be able to get to the file server console via any version of RCONSOLE.

Check to make sure RSPX and REMOTE are loaded. Then check the version of RCONSOLE that you are running. Look at the very top of the screen when you bring it up. You can install the IntranetWare RCONSOLE.EXE on your NetWare 3.x servers by simply copying it to the SYS:SYSTEM directory on the 3.x servers. If you find this odious and packet signature level security is of no consequence in your environment you can issue the following command:

```
LOAD RSPX SIGNATURE OFF
```

SYMPTOM: DRIVE DEACTIVATION ERROR

The users lose their connection to the file server. You race to the console and see a drive deactivation error message.

You definitely have a hardware problem with the disk channel. There may just be loose connections on the drive channel. Remember that a hardware problem may mean that the driver doesn't match the hardware setup.

Check all the connections. Unplug and replug all the drive channel cables. Then check the configuration, especially if you have SCSI drives. The addressing may be off or the final device in the chain may not be terminated. If you have recently upgraded the drivers, try to un-upgrade them. Check for compatibility issues with your existing firmware by calling the vendor.

Well, that should keep you busy managing your file server. It's amazing how simple things like slow network access can get so detailed when you start troubleshooting them. Understanding how the file server allocates memory and manages the disk processes helps a lot in determining where to start. If in doubt, start with the simple stuff like checking all the cable connections, power connections, and error messages. Sometimes the error message is right. Sometimes a pencil is just a pencil.

This completes our discussion of IntranetWare optimization. As you can see, it's definitely the new frontier of IntranetWare networking. Optimization is more important now than ever before, mostly because NDS taxes the server so much. In this chapter, we've learned everything there is to know about optimization components, monitoring with MONITOR, and optimization with SERVMAN.

 ZEN

"Any sufficiently advanced technology is indistinguishable from magic!"

Arthur C. Clarke

Oh, my goodness! Would you look at the time — where has it all gone? I've just been rambling away here . . . sorry, if you missed your train or something. I guess I'm done. There's not much more that can be said about IntranetWare. Are you interested in golf? We could talk about that for a while. Nah, I better save that for another book.

Before you leave, let's take a quick moment to review your journey. It's been quite a wild ride, and you should be very proud of yourself for surviving it in one piece — or so it seems. Do you still want to be a CNE? An IntranetWare superhero, doctor, and gardener? Good. Because the world needs a few good CNEs, and you're a great place to start. Speaking of starting . . .

The journey began with a brief introduction into the next generation of IntranetWare. Chapter 1 was a preview of IntranetWare and the entire book. Then, we focused on the fundamentals of NDS in Chapter 2. It's a whole new ball game. With all of that knowledge under our collective belt, we began the great journey of life — quest for IntranetWare CNEship and saving the world.

Throughout this book, we learned that CNEs have three main tasks: design, installation, and management. First, you design the NDS tree — as a superhero. Second, you install the servers using an established design — as a doctor. And third, you get to configure and manage it — as an NDS gardener. Talk about split personalities! CNEs must excel in all three jobs, although each is very different. Fortunately, this book helped us every step of the way. First stop — IntranetWare design.

In Chapter 3, we discovered ACME — A Cure for Mother Earth. We learned about its plight and helped develop the ACME project team. We gathered a large list of design inputs, including WAN layouts, an organization chart, and workflow diagram. Then, in Chapter 4, we explored the nuts and bolts of NDS design — a very important CNE task. We learned about tree design, partitioning, time sychronization, and most important, accessibility design. Things really started hopping right about now. Finally, with the design in place, we started NDS implementation — that's Chapter 5. With water, sunlight, and a little love, our seedling quickly grew into a fruitful, majestic tree. Next stop — IntranetWare installation.

SMART LINK

Visit ACME in cyberperson, surf the Web to http://www.cyberstateu.com/clarke/acme.htm.

In Chapter 6, the network was born. During NetWare 4.11 installation, we followed 6 stages and 23 steps toward IntranetWare Nirvana. It was a great place to start. Next, in Chapter 7, we discovered the miracle of NetWare 4.11 migration. IntranetWare is so different from earlier versions, upgrading really is "migrating." It's a whole new frontier of networking. In Chapter 7, we outlined the steps of migrating from NetWare 2 or 3 all the way to IntranetWare. It seemed like a breeze next to installation. Final stop — IntranetWare management.

Once the tree had been designed and installed, we entered the wonderful world of NDS gardening. We covered object naming, NWADMIN, object types, and Bindery Services — all the time trying to keep the dirt out from under our fingernails. As we learned in Chapter 9, the tree also needs to be pruned periodically. This provides better health and efficiency (distributed databases) as well as tree stability and longevity (fault tolerance). Also, we learned how to use time synchronization for better access to sunlight. That completed our journey above the server; next, we dove inside.

In Chapter 10, we learned that the file system represents IntranetWare life within the server. All of our focus shifted to IntranetWare's big, electronic filing cabinet. Chapter 11 continued this journey with a look at security. Information is now the new commodity — more valuable than money. We need to take new measures to protect our information. We discovered IntranetWare's five-layered security model — login/password authentication, login restrictions, NDS rights, file system access rights, and attributes. Think of it as your impenetrable network armor.

SMART LINK

It was a pleasure saving the world with you. Come say "Hi!" at http://www.cyberstateu.com/clarke.htm.

Once the LAN has been installed (born), it enters the second and third phases of its lifespan — configuration (childhood) and management (adulthood). In Chapter 12, the first of two related chapters, we walked through the five steps of configuration using Leia as an example. Then in Chapter 13, we discovered the final phase of LAN life span — adulthood. Here your network got married, had children, planned for retirement, and finally retired. How about you?

In the final two chapters, we ended the journey with IntranetWare printing and optimization. Printing (Chapter 14) was the greatest challenge. IntranetWare printing is simple, and works great until . . . you add users. In Chapter 14, we explored some time-proven methods for successful IntranetWare printing (installation, management, and troubleshooting). Then, we completed the journey with Chapter 15 — the final frontier. Once you'd lived through the LAN lifespan and set up IntranetWare printing, only one task was left — optimization.

ZEN

"All good things must come to an end!"

Q

Well, that does it! The End . . . Finito . . . Kaput. Everything you wanted to know about IntranetWare, but were afraid to ask. I hope you've had as much fun reading this book as I've had writing it. It's been a long and winding road — a life-changer. Thanks for spending the last 1,600 pages with me, and I bid you a fond farewell in the only way I know how:

"See ya' later, alligator!"

"After a while, crocodile!"

"Hasta la vista, baby!"

"Live long and prosper!"

"So long and thanks for all the fish!"

"May the force be with you . . ."

GOOD LUCK, AND BY THE WAY....
THANKS FOR SAVING THE WORLD!!

:)

BEST WISHES,

David James Yorke IV

EXERCISE 15-1: THE FINAL FRONTIER

Circle the 20 optimization terms hidden in this word search puzzle using the hints provided.

```
G  A  R  B  A  G  E  C  O  L  L  E  C  T  I  O  N  F
F  I  L  E  C  A  C  H  I  N  G  M  K  U  Y  G  G  Y
I  A  J  N  I  N  O  P  T  I  M  I  Z  A  T  I  O  N
L  U  T  U  R  B  O  F  A  T  L  B  V  K  W  E  S  Q
E  U  P  V  X  J  E  Y  O  C  T  W  S  D  X  L  G  E
S  B  I  W  O  G  B  P  A  C  K  E  T  B  U  R  S  T
E  G  H  B  L  O  C  K  S  I  Z  E  S  Y  K  X  G  E
R  W  G  N  I  H  S  A  H  Y  R  O  T  C  E  R  I  D
V  D  I  R  T  Y  C  A  C  H  E  B  U  F  F  E  R  S
E  V  E  N  T  C  O  N  T  R  O  L  B  L  O  C  K  N
R  R  Q  T  J  L  Y  V  Y  M  Q  Q  D  G  R  U  E  B
P  L  O  O  P  Y  R  O  M  E  M  Y  E  R  Y  C  N  R
R  D  J  M  N  K  C  T  N  E  B  O  I  H  H  I  B  P
O  D  S  K  C  E  N  E  L  T  T  O  B  O  G  L  L  G
C  A  C  H  E  U  T  I  L  I  Z  A  T  I  O  N  K  L
E  F  E  O  P  D  S  T  I  H  E  H  C  A  C  O  E  Q
S  U  G  E  Q  X  Q  P  S  W  J  Y  H  J  U  J  F  M
S  R  E  F  F  U  B  E  H  C  A  C  L  A  T  O  T  E
```

Hints:

1. Set automatically set during server installation, based hard disk size.
2. Something to be avoided if performance is important.
3. Occur when a workstation requests data and the server is able to satisfy the request from file server RAM without having to issue a disk read request.
4. Statistic that will show best performance when cache size equals buffer size.
5. An acronym for the table that contains information about files, directories, directory trustees, and so on.

6. Process that uses algorithms to calculate a file's address in cache memory and on the hard disk.
7. Portions of server RAM that contain data that has not yet been written to disk.
8. Another name for packet receive buffer.
9. Index that keeps track of where files are located.
10. Process of storing files in server RAM to improve access time.
11. Task handler.
12. Process of recovering available memory.
13. Acronym for feature that allows a workstation to determine packet size based on the maximum size supported by a router.
14. IntranetWare temporarily allocates portions of this area of server RAM to various processes, instructions, and data.
15. Fine-tuning your server so that it operates at peak performance.
16. Unit of information used in network communications.
17. Protocol used to increase the transfer speed of multiple-packet NCP file reads and writes.
18. Command line utility used to view and configure operating system parameters.
19. Number of currently available Cache buffers.
20. Special index used to group together all entries for a file that exceeds 64 blocks (and the corresponding number of FAT entries).

See Appendix C for answers.

PART IV: INTRANETWARE MANAGEMENT

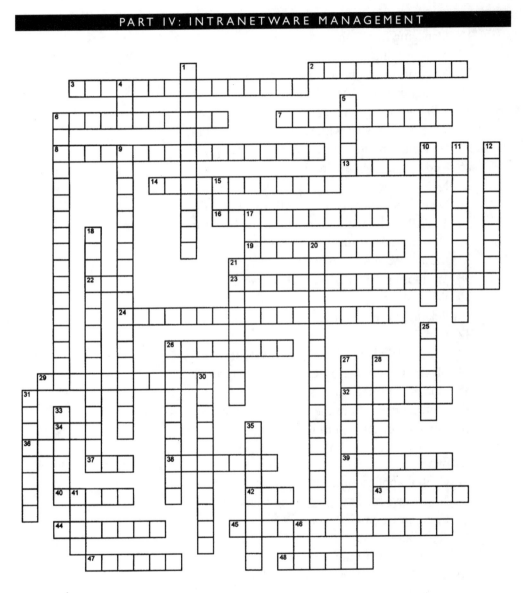

Across

2. Your password has expired, but c'mon in anyway
3. Timing is the key
6. Weapons in the new frontier
7. All your replication buddies

8. The second layer of IntranetWare security
13. Managing from Tahiti
14. NDS pruning
16. #1 performance benefit in IntranetWare
19. Configuring ODI MLID in NET.CFG
22. Filing phone book
23. Who can do what with whom
24. Programming in IntranetWare login scripts
26. Auditing in the new frontier
29. NLM test-bed
32. Where, oh where is my COMMAND.COM?
34. TCP/IP configuration files in the IntranetWare file system
36. Optimization at the server console
37. IntranetWare backup engine
38. Monitoring server SAP and RIP traffic
39. Where I live
40. Relating unrelated users
42. DynaText
43. The Dr. Jekyll and Mr. Hyde of WORMFACES
44. Maximum number of search drive mappings
45. One of the three reasons to replicate
47. A graceful exit from the IntranetWare WAN
48. The king of the replica hill

Down
1. Central application control
4. "Don't give me any_____" (big packets)
5. Filing in a non-GUI world
6. Task handler
9. Don't mess with my packets
10. The Albert Einstein of server utilities
11. NDS cloning
12. Skipping the Default login script
15. Filtering effective NDS rights
17. The ODI "traffic cop"
18. A two-dimensional view of the 3-D NDS world

20. Group mail
21. A non-DOS client included with IntranetWare
25. Printing on a different volume
26. The final layer of IntranetWare security
27. Better security at the file server
28. Protecting memory at the IntranetWare server
30. Fixing a broken tree
31. Login script messaging without all the mess
33. Workstation configuration file
35. Speaking to the whole "Cloud"
41. High-capacity from a bunch of cheap stuff
46. IntranetWare encryption

See Appendix C for answers.

PART V

Appendixes

Overview of Novell Education and the CNE Program

"I wanna be a CNE!"

In a world where people and businesses and organizations and governments and nations are being connected and sharing information at a dizzying rate, Novell's primary goal is to be the infrastructure that connects people and services together all over the world.

To help fulfill this goal, Novell Education is providing quality education programs and products to help create a strong support base of trained networking professionals. By itself, the Novell Education department isn't nearly large enough to provide high-quality training to the vast number of people who will require it. Therefore, Novell Education has developed authorized training partnerships throughout the world to provide authorized training. In addition, Novell Education created certification programs to help ensure that the standard for networking skills is maintained at a high level.

Today, Novell has more than 1,500 authorized education partners worldwide, including colleges, universities, professional training centers, and the like.

This appendix describes Novell Education and the CNE program. It also provides some practical tips, such as alternatives to formal classes, finding out how to take the test, and so on.

Certification Partners

Two types of education partners work with Novell worldwide: Novell Authorized Education Centers (NAECs) and Novell Education Academic Partners (NEAPs). These education partners provide top-quality training on Novell products. In fact, Novell guarantees complete customer satisfaction for all Novell courses when they are taught at Novell-authorized training partners.

NAECs are private, independent training organizations that meet Novell's strict quality standards. Some NAECs are also Novell product resellers, but many operate independent of Novell's reseller channels.

The advantage of attending an NAEC is that these organizations typically have a great deal of experience in technology training, and since their livelihood depends on enticing students to take their courses, they are driven to provide quality education.

ZEN

"Don't waste time learning the 'tricks of the trade.' Instead, learn the trade."

H. Jackson Brown, Jr., *Life's Little Instruction Book*

To become an NAEC, the training organization must meet the following strict education guidelines:

▶ The facility must use Novell-developed course materials.

▶ The course must be taught within a recommended time frame.

▶ The facility itself must be Novell-authorized. Authorization is based on a strict set of standards for equipment, instructional soundness, and student comfort.

▶ The course must be taught by a Certified Novell Instructor (CNI), who is certified to teach the specific course.

In addition, the prospective NAEC must submit an extensive application to Novell Education. The training center also pays an initiation fee and annual licensing fees. NAECs are required to offer various courses in a consistent, timely manner.

NEAPs are colleges or universities that provide Novell-authorized courses in a semester- or quarter-length curriculum. There are more than 100 such colleges and universities in the United States, as well as some in Canada, and the list is growing.

NEAPs must follow the same strict guidelines as NAECs and provide Novell courses as part of their standard curriculum.

Both NAECs and NEAPs offer the same courses, based on the same education materials, objectives, and information. They also offer a wide variety of classes (more than 40) on various Novell products and technologies. If you want to pursue Novell-authorized training in a classroom setting, with hands-on labs and knowledgeable instructors, either type of education partner will be beneficial.

Novell-authorized courses (through either NAECs or NEAPs) often offer the best way to get direct, hands-on training, using approved techniques, technologies, and training materials.

Certification Levels

Because Novell has so many different products, and because networking professionals have different reasons for getting trained on those products, Novell offers four different certification levels.

Depending on the level of certification you want to achieve, you take different exams (and, if you desire, the associated courses to prepare for the exams). While one or more certain core exams are required for all levels, you may also take exams for additional "electives" to achieve the certification and specialization you want.

 ZEN

"Argue for your limitations, and sure enough, they're yours."

Richard Bach, *Illusions*

The following certification levels are available for Novell products:

- ▸ CNA (Certified Novell Administrator)

- ▸ CNE (Certified Novell "E")

- ▸ Master CNE

- ▸ CNI (Certified Novell Instructor)

Within each of these levels, there are areas of specialization. Let's look at these four programs in more detail.

CNA (CERTIFIED NOVELL ADMINISTRATOR)

The CNA certification is the entry-level certification for network administrators. It prepares you to manage your own IntranetWare network on a day-to-day basis.

The CNA level does not delve into the more complex and technical aspects of IntranetWare network design, troubleshooting, and implementation. Instead, it is designed for people who perform day-to-day general network administration tasks (such as adding and deleting users, setting up desktop environments, backing up network data, and maintaining network security).

 TIP

As a prerequisite to taking the IntranetWare CNA exam, be sure you have a thorough knowledge of DOS, Windows, and general microcomputer concepts.

To prepare for the IntranetWare CNA exam, you can take the Novell-authorized course entitled IntranetWare Administration (course number 520). In addition to being the preparatory course for the CNA exam, this course is also a required course for the IntranetWare track of the CNE certification level (described in the next section). So, if you have plans to continue past the CNA level to get your CNE certification, too, you're killing two birds with one stone.

For a list of the course objectives for the *IntranetWare Administration* course, see Appendix B. That appendix cross-references all the course objectives with locations in this book that will help prepare you to meet those objectives.

 TIP

CNAs qualify for associate membership in the Network Professional Association (NPA), which is explained in Appendix D.

You can pursue five different CNA specialization tracks. Each CNA track involves a single exam that proves you have mastered the tasks associated with being a system administrator on that type of Novell product. You can achieve your CNA status in multiple tracks simply by passing the appropriate exam for each track.

Table A.1 shows the CNA tracks that are currently available.

CNE

The CNE certification ensures that you can adequately install and manage IntranetWare networks on a more advanced level than the CNA. The CNE starts with the basic CNA skills, then adds high-end skills that will allow you to support IntranetWare networks more fully.

TABLE A.1	CNA TRACK	DESCRIPTION
Current CNA Tracks	IntranetWare	This track certifies that you understand and can administer LAN features of the WAN-based IntranetWare platform.
	NetWare 4	This track certifies that you understand and can administer features of your NetWare 4.1 network.
	NetWare 3	This track certifies that you understand and can administer features of your NetWare 3.12 network.
	GroupWise 4	This track certifies that you understand and can administer the GroupWise GroupWare product, including creating post offices and users, creating links between domains, installing GroupWise clients, and performing basic troubleshooting tasks.
	SoftSolutions 4	This track certifies that you understand and can administer the SoftSolutions product, including adding users, setting up basic applications, operating full-text indexers, and designing screens, reports, and workstation IDs.
	InForms 4	This track certifies that you understand and can administer the InForms product and its features, including creating forms, queries and reports; linking forms to the database; and creating simple macros.

While pursuing your CNE certification, you "declare a major," meaning that you choose to specialize in any of the following three particular Novell product families:

- ▸ IntranetWare

- ▸ NetWare 4

- ▸ NetWare 3

- ▸ GroupWare

Some skills you are expected to master as a CNE include managing multiple networks, performing network upgrades, improving network printing performance, and managing network databases.

CNEs are expected to provide support at the network operating system and network applications level.

TIP

CNEs qualify for full membership in the Network Professional Association (NPA), which is explained in Appendix D.

MASTER CNE

The Master CNE certification level allows you to go beyond basic CNE certification. To get a Master CNE, you declare a "graduate major." These areas of specialization delve deeper into the integration- and solution-oriented aspects of running a network than the CNE level.

While CNEs provide support at the operating system and application level, Master CNEs are expected to manage advanced access, management, and workgroup integration for multiple environments. Master CNEs can support complex networks that span several different platforms, and can perform upgrades, migration, and integration for various systems.

There are three areas in which Master CNEs can specialize:

▶ Network management

▶ Infrastructure and advanced access

▶ GroupWare integration

TIP

Master CNEs qualify for membership in the Network Professional Association (NPA), which is explained in Appendix D.

The ECNE level is being phased out. The ECNE level's series of tests emphasized aspects of networking encountered in larger, enterprise-wide networks (such as routing, gateways, Novell Directory Services, and so on).

The Master CNE program is replacing the ECNE level because it adds more flexibility to the type of specialization the candidate can pursue. If you've already achieved ECNE status, you will retain the title, and Novell will still recognize it. However, Novell stopped certifying new ECNEs on September 30, 1995.

CNI (CERTIFIED NOVELL INSTRUCTOR)

The CNI certification level qualifies instructors to teach authorized IntranetWare courses through NAECs. The tests and classes specific to this level ensure that the individual taking them will be able to adequately teach others how to install and manage IntranetWare.

This CNI program is designed for people who want to make a career of teaching others how to install, configure, and use Novell networking products.

CNI candidates must attend the Novell courses they wish to be certified to teach, and they must pass proficiency tests at a higher level than other certification candidates. (The course they attend must be taught by an official NAEC or NEAP, and must be taught in the standard Novell format.)

In addition, CNIs must successfully complete a rigorous Instructor Performance Evaluation, as well as meet continuing certification requirements (which include additional training and testing as Novell updates courses and releases new products).

ZEN

"You are never given a wish without also being given the power to make it true. You may have to work for it, however."

Richard Bach, *Illusions*

Testing Your Mettle

Okay. You've finished the course, you've studied this book, you've spent hours in the lab or on your own network using the NetWare Administrator and other utilities to add users, change passwords, back up files, and the like. You're ready to show your stuff, and prove that you have the baseline of knowledge required to take on network administrator duties in the real world.

You're ready to take the test and become a CNE.

So, how do you sign up for the exam?

The IntranetWare Administrator exam is offered at NAECs and NEAPs all over the world. The first thing you must do is find one of these centers to administer the exam.

HOW DO YOU SIGN UP FOR AN EXAM?

All Novell exams are administered by a professional testing organization: Sylvan Prometric.

If you take the Novell-authorized course, you may be able to sign up to the take the test at the same location, because some (but not all) NAECs are also affiliated with Sylvan Prometric. In fact, the instructor most likely can give you information about where to take the exam locally.

Otherwise, to find a location that administers this exam, simply call one of the following numbers:

▸ The Novell Education phone number at 1-800-233-EDUC (toll-free in Canada and the USA) or 1-801-222-7800

▸ Sylvan Prometric, at 1-800-RED-TEST (toll-free), 1-800-RED-EXAM (toll-free), or 1-410-880-8700

Outside of the USA and Canada, contact your local Novell office, or a local Sylvan Prometric office.

REAL WORLD

In the past, there were two testing organizations that Novell used to administer its tests: Sylvan Learning Systems and Drake Prometric. However, Drake Prometric was recently bought by Sylvan Learning Systems. The merged organization changed its name to Sylvan Prometric, so now it's all just one big, happy family.

WHAT IS THE EXAM LIKE?

The IntranetWare Administrator exam, like all Novell exams, is computer-based. You take the exam by answering questions on the computer. However, unlike more traditional tests, the IntranetWare Administrator exam is performance-based. This means that instead of just asking you to regurgitate facts, the exam actually requires you to apply your knowledge to solve problems. For example, the exam may include simulations of network problems or tasks, such as adding a user. You must actually use IntranetWare utilities to complete the task or solve the problem.

The exam is also adaptive. This means that the exam offers easier or more difficult questions to you based on your last answer, in an effort to determine just how much you know. In other words, the exam starts off asking you a fairly easy question. If you answer it correctly, the next question will be slightly harder. If you answer that one correctly, too, it will offer you a slightly harder one again, and so on. If you answer a question incorrectly, on the other hand, the next question will be slightly easier. If you miss that one, too, the next will be easier yet, until you get one right. Then the questions will get more difficult again.

The number of questions you'll be asked will vary, depending on your level of knowledge. If you answer all of the questions correctly, you will continue to be offered questions until you have been tested on the full range of knowledge. If you answer incorrectly, you'll only answer questions until your level of knowledge is determined. Obviously, the higher the level of knowledge the computer determines you have, the better score you receive.

It will probably take you from 20 to 40 minutes to take this exam.

ZEN

"Be brave. Even if you're not, pretend to be. No one can tell the difference."

H. Jackson Brown, Jr.

The exam is closed-book and is graded on a pass/fail basis. The standard fee for the exam is $85. When you go to take the exam, remember to take two forms of identification with you (one must be a picture ID). You will not be allowed to take any notes into or out of the exam room.

If you fail the test, take heart. You can take it again. In fact, you can take it again as many times as you want — there are no limits to repeating it. You can repeat it as soon as you like, and as many times as it takes to pass (or until your checkbook runs dry, whichever comes first). Because of the way the exam is designed, questions are randomly pulled from a giant database. Therefore, chances are slim that you will ever get the same test questions twice, no matter how often you take the exam.

TIP

If you want to know what you're in for before signing up for a CNE exam, check out *The Clarke Tests v3.0*. We've included a special edition of this best-selling software on the CD-ROM bound in this book. It will give you a great taste of the Novell exams *before* you have to spend $85. Try it . . . believe me, they'll save you time and money!

After the Test — Now What?

Congratulations! You passed the exam with flying colors, just like we knew you would! Now comes the easiest part — getting your official certification.

To receive your official certification status, you must sign a Novell Education Certification Agreement.

The certification agreement contains the usual legal jargon you might expect with such certification. Among other things, it grants you permission to use the trademarked name "CNE" on your resume or other advertising, as long as you use the name in connection with providing network administration services on a IntranetWare network. It also reminds you that if the network administration services you offer don't live up to Novell's high standards of quality, Novell can require you to meet those standards within "a commercially reasonable time."

After you've passed the exam, you can read the agreement, sign the "Signature Form," and mail it back to Novell. (Because Novell needs your legal signature on the form, they can't accept faxed copies of the form.) For your convenience, we've included a copy of the agreement, along with the signature form, at the end of this chapter. You can also receive additional copies of the form by calling your local NAEC, or by calling Novell's FaxBack phone line at 1-801-222-7800 or 1-800-233-EDUC and requesting a copy to be faxed to you. Novell Education, of course, reserves the right to change this form without notice.

For More Information . . .

You can get more information about Novell Education courses, exams, training supplements, programs, and so on, by using one of the following avenues:

- ▶ Call Novell Education at 1-801-222-7800 or 1-800-233-EDUC (toll free in the USA and Canada)

- ▶ Use Novell's FaxBack system to receive information by fax. The FaxBack system is available through the same numbers listed here. Select Option 3 for the FaxBack system, and follow the instructions to order the FaxBack master catalog of available documents. After you've received the FaxBack catalog of documents, you can call back and request the specific documents you want. You can order up to four documents per call.

- ▶ Call your local NAEC, NEAP, or Sylvan Prometric testing center.

- ▶ Go on-line to Novell Education's Internet site. You can get to the Novell Education information either through Novell's Internet site (GO NETWIRE on CompuServe, or *http://www.novell.com*), or by going directly to *http://education.novell.com*.

- ▶ Visit my personal education site for CNE updates: *http://www.cyberstateu. com/clarke.htm*.

Novell Education Certification Agreement

1 **PURPOSE.** NOVELL is in the business of, among other things, manufacturing, distributing, selling, offering for sale, and promoting network computing products. Many of NOVELL's products are technically complex and require competent pre- and post-sales support. In order to provide adequate support, NOVELL has devised several programs under which individuals become certified to competently provide appropriate support. These are the Certified Novell Administrator (or "CNA"), the CNE, the Enterprise CNE (or "ECNE"), the Master CNE, and the Certified Novell Instructor (or "CNI") certification programs. Successful participants in these programs, through education, training, and/or testing become authorized to provide services and to use the NOVELL Marks pertaining to the particular certification program or programs that the participant has completed. Individuals may participate in one or more of these certification programs. Completion of one certification program does not entitle a participant to use the Marks or provide the services pertaining to any other certification program.

2 **DEFINITIONS.**

2.1 **Program** means one of the programs of certification that is offered by NOVELL, is available to participants, and may lead to certification under this Novell Education Certification Agreement ("Agreement"). The Programs include the CNA, CNE, Enterprise CNE, Master CNE, and CNI certification programs. As further provided in this Agreement, participants cannot administer Licensed Services under or otherwise use the Marks of a particular Program, claim any Program certification or status, or exercise any rights granted under this Agreement, except through the successful completion of NOVELL's requirements for that Program.

2.2 **MARKS** means, as the case may be, the Certified Novell Administrator and CNA marks and logos, the CNE marks and logos, Enterprise CNE and ECNE marks and logos, Master CNE marks and logos, and the Certified Novell Instructor and CNI marks and logos.

2.3 **LICENSED SERVICES** means the particular administration or pre- and post-sales service and support of NOVELL's network computing products that correspond with the Program or Programs successfully completed by the participant. The LICENSED SERVICES for each particular Program are described below. LICENSED SERVICES does not mean (i) any services provided with respect to non-NOVELL products or (ii) the teaching of courses relating to NOVELL products other than those courses permitted to be taught according to the CNI LICENSED SERVICES and described below.

2.3.1 **If YOU have successfully completed the CNA Program requirements, LICENSED SERVICES** means handling the day-to-day administration of the installed NOVELL networking product or products for which YOU have successfully completed a CNA Program. Successful completion of a particular CNA Program will allow YOU to administer the above services for one of several particular products, including (but not limited to) NetWare, GroupWare (GroupWise, InForms and SoftSolutions) and UnixWare.

2.3.2 **If YOU have successfully completed the CNE, Enterprise CNE and/or Master CNE Program requirements, LICENSED SERVICES** means the pre- and post-sales service and support of the NOVELL network computing product or products for which YOU have successfully completed a CNE, Enterprise CNE and/or Master CNE Program. Successful completion of a particular CNE Program will allow YOU to administer the above services in one of several particular products, including (but not limited to) NetWare, GroupWare (GroupWise, InForms and SoftSolutions) and UnixWare. Successful completion of a particular Master CNE Program will allow YOU to administer the above services in one of several particular service areas, including (but not limited to) Network Management, Infrastructure and Advanced Access, and GroupWare Integration.

2.3.3 **If YOU have successfully completed the CNI Program requirements, LICENSED SERVICES** means the teaching of NOVELL authorized courses under the auspices of a Novell Authorized Education Center. CNI Licensed Services does not mean the teaching of a course not authorized by NOVELL.

2.4 **NOVELL AUTHORIZED EDUCATION CENTER or NAEC** means any organization that has been approved by NOVELL as an authorized training facility and includes Novell Authorized Internal Training Organizations and Novell Education Academic Partners.

2.5 **NOVELL** means Novell Ireland Software Ltd. If YOU provide LICENSED SERVICES in Europe, the Middle East, or Africa (EMEA). If YOU do not provide LICENSED SERVICES in EMEA, Novell means Novell, Inc.

3 **CERTIFICATION.** YOUR Program certification is based on completing the required testing and complying with the requirements set forth in the brochure corresponding with the Program YOU have successfully completed. YOU acknowledge that NOVELL has the right to change the requirements for receiving Program certification, or

Novell

maintaining a Program certification, at any time. Once certification is granted, it will automatically renew if all continuing certification requirements are met. YOU are responsible for maintaining YOUR certification. To maintain certification, YOU must complete all Program continuing certification requirements, if any, corresponding with YOUR particular Program certification within the time frame specified by NOVELL. If YOU do not complete the continuing certification requirements within the time frame specified by NOVELL, YOUR certified Program status for that particular Program may expire, resulting in de-certification. NOTWITHSTANDING ANYTHING IN THIS AGREEMENT TO THE CONTRARY, NOVELL HAS THE RIGHT NOT TO GRANT OR RENEW YOUR CERTIFICATION IF NOVELL REASONABLY DETERMINES THAT YOUR CERTIFICATION OR USE OF THE MARKS WILL ADVERSELY AFFECT NOVELL. THIS AGREEMENT APPLIES TO ANY AND ALL PROGRAMS COMPLETED BY YOU.

4 **WHAT HAPPENS WHEN YOU LEAVE AN ORGANIZATION?** YOU retain YOUR Program certification if YOU move to a new organization.

5 **GRANT AND CONSIDERATION.** NOVELL grants to YOU a non-exclusive and non-transferable license to use the MARKS solely in connection with providing the LICENSED SERVICES corresponding to the Program certification YOU have achieved. YOU or YOUR agents may use the MARKS on such promotional display and advertising materials as may, in YOUR judgment, promote the LICENSED SERVICES corresponding to YOUR Program certification. YOU may not use the MARKS for any purposes that are not directly related to the provision of the LICENSED SERVICES corresponding to YOUR particular Program certification. YOU may not use the MARKS of any Program unless YOU have completed the Program certification requirements and have been notified by NOVELL in writing that YOU have achieved certification status for that particular Program. YOUR CNI certification, if applicable, is subject to the restrictions of Section 5.1 of this Agreement.

5.1 **AFFILIATION WITH NAECS/CNI LICENSE GRANT**

5.1.1 **Affiliation with NAECs.** YOU are authorized, if YOU achieve the status of CNI, to teach authorized Novell courses only at NAECs. YOU may be employed by one NAEC or YOU may work independently, contracting with one or more NAECs on a case-by-case basis. If YOU are employed by an NAEC and move to another NAEC or obtain independent status, YOU retain the CNI certification status. It is YOUR responsibility to notify NOVELL of any address or NAEC change.

6 **TERM AND TERMINATION.**

6.1 **Term.** This Novell Education Certification Agreement will commence on the date YOU receive written notice from NOVELL that YOU have met all the requirements necessary to attain YOUR particular Program certification and will terminate in accordance with the terms and provisions of this Agreement. YOU understand that, for convenience of processing, YOU will indicate assent to this Agreement via the use of a computer as indicated electronically prior to YOUR completion of the Program requirements, or, in certain circumstances and when authorized by NOVELL, YOU will indicate assent by signing this Agreement. YOU acknowledge that this Agreement will not take effect until NOVELL has notified YOU in writing that all Program requirements have been met. YOU further acknowledge that this Agreement will remain in effect in the event YOU upgrade YOUR status to include any other Program certifications, and that those subparagraphs specific to those certification(s) will also apply to YOU.

6.2 **Termination by Either Party.** Either party may terminate this Agreement without cause by giving thirty (30) days or more prior written notice to the other party.

6.3 **Termination by NOVELL.** Without prejudice to any rights it may have under this Agreement or in law equity or otherwise, NOVELL may terminate this Agreement upon the occurrence of any one or more of the following events (called "Default"):

6.3.1 If YOU fail to perform any of YOUR obligations under this Agreement;

6.3.2 If YOU render the LICENSED SERVICES without complying with the testing required under this Agreement, or if YOU discontinue offering the LICENSED SERVICES;

6.3.3 If any government agency or court finds that LICENSED SERVICES as provided by YOU are defective in any way, manner or form; or

6.3.4 If actual or potential adverse publicity or other information, emanating from a third party or parties, about YOU, the LICENSED SERVICES, or the use of the MARKS by YOU causes NOVELL, in its sole judgment, to believe that NOVELL's reputation will be adversely affected.

Novell.

In the event any Default occurs, NOVELL will give YOU written notice of termination of this Agreement. In the event of a Default under Section 6.3.3 or 6.3.4, NOVELL may terminate this Agreement with no period for correction, and it will terminate automatically without further notice. In the event of a Default under Section 6.3.1 or 6.3.2, or at NOVELL's option under Section 6.3.3 or 6.3.4, YOU will be given thirty (30) days from receipt of notice in which to correct any Default. If YOU fail to correct the Default within the notice period, this Agreement will automatically terminate on the last day of the notice period.

6.4 Return of Materials. Upon termination of this Agreement, YOU agree to immediately cease to render the LICENSED SERVICES and to return all badges or other trademark collateral to NOVELL. Upon termination, all rights granted under this Novell Education Certification Agreement will immediately and automatically revert to NOVELL.

7 CONDUCT OF BUSINESS. YOU agree to (i) conduct business in a manner which reflects favorably at all times on the products, goodwill and reputation of NOVELL; (ii) avoid deceptive, misleading or unethical practices which are or might be detrimental to NOVELL or its products; and (iii) refrain from making any representations, warranties, or guarantees to customers that are inconsistent with the policies established by NOVELL. YOU further agree that YOU will not represent YOURSELF to possess the certification of any Program category until such time as YOU have completed all requirements for that Program and have been notified by NOVELL in writing that YOU have achieved the certification of that Program, including but not limited to the Program certifications of CNA, CNE, Enterprise CNE, Master CNE, and CNI.

8 OWNERSHIP. No title to or ownership of the MARKS or of any software or proprietary technology in hardware licensed to YOU pursuant to this Agreement is transferred to YOU. NOVELL, or the licensors through which NOVELL obtained the rights to distribute the products, owns and retains all title and ownership of all intellectual property rights in the products, including all software, firmware, software master diskettes, copies of software, documentation and related materials and, all modifications to and derivative works from software acquired as a Program certification holder which are made by YOU, NOVELL or any third party. NOVELL does not transfer any portion of such title and ownership, or any of the associated goodwill to YOU, and this Agreement should not be construed to grant YOU any right or license, whether by implication, estoppel or otherwise, except as expressly provided. YOU agree to be bound by and observe the proprietary nature of the products acquired as a CNA, CNE, Enterprise CNE, Master CNE, and/or CNI.

9 QUALITY OF LICENSED SERVICES. YOU agree that it is of fundamental importance to NOVELL that the LICENSED SERVICES be of the highest quality and integrity. Accordingly, YOU agree that NOVELL will have the right to determine in its absolute discretion whether the LICENSED SERVICES meet NOVELL's high standards of merchantability. In the event that NOVELL determines that YOU are no longer meeting accepted levels of quality and/or integrity, NOVELL agrees to so advise YOU and, except as otherwise provided in Section 6.3 of this Agreement, to provide YOU with a commercially reasonable time of no less than one (1) month to meet the above-referenced standards of quality and integrity.

10 RESERVATION OF RIGHTS AND GOOD WILL IN NOVELL. NOVELL retains all rights not expressly conveyed to YOU by this Agreement. YOU recognize the value of the publicity and goodwill associated with the MARKS and acknowledge that the goodwill will exclusively inure to the benefit of, and belong to, NOVELL. YOU have no rights of any kind whatsoever with respect to the MARKS licensed under this Agreement except to the extent of the license granted in this Agreement.

11 NO REGISTRATION BY YOU. YOU agree not to file any new trademark, collective mark, service mark, certification mark, and/or trade name application(s), in any class and in any country, for any trademark, collective mark, service mark, certification mark, and/or trade name that, in Novell's opinion, is the same as, similar to, or that contains, in whole or in part, any or all of Novell's trade names, trademarks, collective marks, service marks, and/or certification marks, including, without limitation, the MARKS licensed under this Agreement. This section will survive the expiration or other termination of this Agreement.

12 PROTECTION OF RIGHTS. YOU agree to assist NOVELL, to the extent reasonably necessary (and at NOVELL's expense), to protect or to obtain protection for any of NOVELL's rights to the MARKS. In addition, if at any time NOVELL requests that YOU discontinue using the MARKS and/or substitute using a new or different mark, YOU will immediately cease use of the MARKS and cooperate fully with NOVELL to ensure all legal obligations have been met with regards to use of the MARKS.

13 INDEMNIFICATION BY YOU. YOU agree to indemnify and hold NOVELL harmless against any loss, liability, damage, cost or expense (including reasonable legal fees) arising out of any claims or suits, whatever their nature and however arising, which may be brought or made against NOVELL (i) by reason of YOUR performance or non-performance of this Agreement; (ii) arising out of the use by YOU of the MARKS in any manner whatsoever except in the form expressly licensed under this Agreement; and/or (iii) for any personal injury, product liability, or other claim arising from the promotion

Novell.

and/or provision of the LICENSED SERVICES. In the event NOVELL seeks indemnification under this Section, NOVELL will immediately notify YOU, in writing, of any claim or proceeding brought against it for which it seeks indemnification under this Agreement. In no event may YOU enter into any third party agreements which would in any manner whatsoever affect the rights of, or bind, NOVELL in any manner, without the prior written consent of NOVELL.

14 **REVISION OF TERMS.** NOVELL reserves the right to revise the terms of this Agreement from time to time. In the event of a revision, signing a new agreement may be a condition of continued certification.

15 **GENERAL PROVISIONS.**

15.1 **Governing Law and Venue.** This Agreement will in all respects be governed by the law of the country of Your residence, and venue of any actions will be proper either in the courts of the State of Utah of the United States of America or in those of the country of Your residence.

15.2 **Non-Waiver.** No waiver of any right or remedy on one occasion by either party will be deemed a waiver of such right or remedy on any other occasion.

15.3 **Course of Dealing.** This Agreement will not be supplemented or modified by any course of dealing or usage of trade.

15.4 **Assignment.** Neither this Agreement nor any of Your rights or obligations arising under this Agreement may be assigned without Novell's prior written consent. This Agreement is freely assignable by Novell, and will be for the benefit of Novell's successors and assigns.

15.5 **Independent Contractors.** YOU acknowledge that both parties are independent contractors and that YOU will not, except in accordance with this Agreement, represent YOURSELF as an agent or legal representative of NOVELL.

15.6 **Compliance with Laws.** YOU agree to comply, at YOUR own expense, with all statutes, regulations, rules, ordinances, and orders of any governmental body, department or agency which apply to or result from YOUR obligations under this Agreement. All holders of the CNE designation must not represent themselves as "engineers" or otherwise misrepresent the meaning of the CNE designation, which is an inventive and symbolic phrase only and not an acronym. Such holders must use only the "CNE" marks and logos, the "ECNE" or "Enterprise CNE" marks and logos, and/or the "Master CNE" marks and logos, as applicable and corresponding to your certification(s).

15.7 **Modifications.** Any modifications to the typewritten face of this Agreement will render it null and void. All modifications must be in writing and signed by both parties.

1428

Novell.

Signature Form

This Signature Form relates to and incorporates the terms and conditions of the Novell Education Certification Agreement ("Agreement") to which it is attached. YOU must either indicate assent electronically or sign this Agreement Signature Form and return it to the applicable address below:

Novell Education
c/o Agreements
5001 W 80th St, Suite 401
Bloomington, MN 55437
USA

Novell Education
c/o Agreements
Level 6, Suite 602
25 Bligh Street
Sydney, NSW 2000
Australia

Novell Education
c/o Agreements
Pelmolenlaan 12-14
3447 G W Woerden
The Netherlands

Please note: If YOU are a minor under the laws of the state or country (whichever applies) where you sign this Signature Form, it needs to be countersigned below by YOUR parent, court-appointed curator, or legal guardian. The Agreement will automatically terminate when YOU reach the age of majority *unless* you affirm the Agreement by completing and signing the Novell Education Certification Agreement being used generally by Novell at that time and returning it to Novell. If YOU allow the Agreement to lapse, YOU will be decertified.

Certification Candidate:

[ ] Parent / [ ] Curator / [ ] Legal Guardian:
(Check appropriate box)

By signing this form, YOU confirm that YOU have read and agree to be bound by the terms and conditions of the Novell Education Certification Agreement, including, but not limited to, the terms relating to YOUR limited right to use Novell's Marks (as that term is defined in the Agreement).

By signing this form, the candidate's parent / curator / legal guardian confirms that he / she has read the Novell Education Certification Agreement and accepts full responsibility for the candidate's compliance with its terms and conditions and will be liable for any breach of the candidate's obligations thereunder.

Signature _____

Print Name _____

Date _____

Test ID# _____

Daytime Phone # _____

Signature _____

Print Name _____

Date _____

To receive a copy of the complete agreement from Certification Administration or by fax, call 1-800-233-EDUC or 1-801-222-7800.

Due to legal restrictions we cannot accept faxed copies of the signed form.

1429

CNE Cross-Reference to Novell Course Objectives

Following is a list of the Novell-authorized course objectives for the entire CNE curriculum. These objectives are the foundation of the "new" IntranetWare/ NetWare 4.11 CNE program. Novell Education uses these objectives to write authorized courseware and to develop certification exams. In order to become an IntranetWare CNE, you must be intimately familiar with every objective in the following courses:

- ▸ Novell Education Course 520 — *IntranetWare/NetWare 4.11 Administration*

- ▸ Novell Education Course 525 — *IntranetWare/NetWare 4.11 Advanced Administration*

- ▸ Novell Education Course 526 — *NetWare 3 to IntranetWare Update*

- ▸ Novell Education Course 532 — *IntranetWare/NDS Design and Implementation*

- ▸ Novell Education Course 804 — *IntranetWare/NetWare 4.11 Installation and Configuration Workshop*

Novell's CNE Study Guide for IntranetWare/NetWare 4.11 enables you to learn these objectives (see page numbers cross-reference) in conjunction with Novell-authorized courseware. This appendix clarifies that relationship by pointing you in the right direction. Have fun and good luck!

Novell Education Course 520 — *IntranetWare/NetWare 4.11 Administration*

This is the foundation of the IntranetWare curriculum. In the *IntranetWare/ NetWare 4.11 Administration* course, you are introduced to the fundamental technologies of IntranetWare, namely Novell Directory Services, the File System, Security, Backup, Login Scripts, and, of course, Printing. It's a 5-day course covering almost 100 objectives.

It's time to learn, and this is a great place to start.

SECTION 1: INTRODUCTION TO INTRANETWARE

1 • Describe a network, including its basic function and physical components. . . **(18-26)**

2 • List several responsibilities of a network administrator. . . **(1-5, 206-217)**

3 • List the IntranetWare network services you will learn to administer in this course. . . **(18-90, 205)**

4 • Describe Novell Directory Services (NDS) and explain its role on the network. . . **(37-49)**

5 • Describe the Directory, including its function and basic components. . . **(99-107)**

6 • Describe the Directory tree, including leaf and container objects. . . **(97-126)**

7 • Browse the Directory tree. . . **(172-178, 638-650)**

8 • Demonstrate correct object-naming techniques. . . **(127-144, 179-180)**

SECTION 2: CONNECTING TO THE NETWORK AND LOGGING IN

1 • Describe how a workstation communicates with the network, and list the files required to connect a workstation to the network. . . **(1014-1028)**

2 • Describe the function of the software and hardware, including local operating systems, Client 32, communications protocols, and network boards necessary to connect a workstation to the network. . . **(1173-1178)**

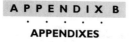

3 • Connect a workstation to the network by executing the appropriate workstation files. . . **(1080-1082)**

4 • Explain and perform the login procedure. . . **(1021-1023)**

SECTION 3: ACCESSING DATA FILES AND APPLICATIONS ON THE NETWORK

1 • Explain the basic components of network file storage, including volumes, directory structures, network drives, and search drives. . . **(786-794, 843-850)**

2 • Display volume, directory, and file information. . . **(813-815, 823-824, 836-839)**

3 • Define IntranetWare command line utilities, describe how they are used, and activate Help information for them. . . **(59, 804-842)**

4 • Using a Volume object and a Directory Map object, map a network drive to a volume and navigate between the volumes. . . **(850-862)**

5 • Using a Volume object and a Directory Map object, map a network drive to a directory and navigate the directories of a volume. . . **(850-862, 866-869)**

6 • Using a Volume object and a Directory Map object, map a search drive to a directory containing an application. . . **(848-862)**

SECTION 4: PRINTING TO A NETWORK PRINTER

1 • Describe the basic components of network printing and how they interrelate in processing a print job. . . **(1236-1262)**

2 • View network printing information in Windows 95 and Windows 3.1. . . **(1251-1254)**

3 • Set up print job redirection, and print from Windows 95 and Windows 3.1. . . **(1251-1254, 1329-1331)**

4 • Set up print job redirection with CAPTURE and print a document from an application. . . **(1243-1250, 1329-1331)**

SECTION 5: SETTING UP USER ACCOUNTS AND LOGIN SECURITY

1 • Describe the function of a User object and its property values. . . **(116-117, 658-659)**

2 • Create a User object and enter user identification property values. . . **(700-716)**

3 • Create and modify User objects with the same property values using the Template object. . . **(704-707, 986-997)**

4 • Create a user home directory automatically while creating a User object. Create user home directories. . . **(988-990, 707)**

5 • Modify parameters for multiple users. . . **(673)**

6 • Manage NDS objects by creating, deleting, and renaming objects, and by entering and modifying property values. . . **(632-650, 700-716)**

7 • Create users with UIMPORT. . . **(674-678, 713-714)**

8 • Identify the levels and functions of network security. . . **(878-889)**

9 • Describe and establish login security, including user account restrictions, time restrictions, station restrictions, and intruder detection. . . **(891-919)**

SECTION 6: SETTING UP THE NETWORK FILE SYSTEM

I • Explain guidelines for planning and creating custom volumes and directories in the network file system. . . **(786-794)**

2 • List the system-created volumes and directories. Describe their contents and function. . . **(794-799)**

3 • List suggested directories for organizing the file system. . . **(799-802)**

4 • Identify the strengths and weaknesses of sample directory structures. . . **(802-804)**

5 • Design and create a directory structure based on a given scenario. . . **(864-865)**

SECTION 7: MANAGING THE FILE SYSTEM

I • Manage the file system directory structure by creating, deleting, renaming, and moving directories. . . **(816-827, 870-873)**

2 • Manage files in the file system by copying, moving, deleting, salvaging, and purging files. . . **(827-842, 870-873)**

3 • Manage the use of volume space by viewing volume usage statistics; restricting space usage by user and directory; changing file ownership; locating files based on usage, owner, and size; setting compression attributes; and setting data migration attributes. . . **(807-816, 870-873)**

SECTION 8: SETTING UP FILE SYSTEM SECURITY

I • Describe IntranetWare file system security, including the concepts of directory and file rights, trustee assignments, inheritance, rights reassignment, Inherited Rights Filters (IRFs), security equivalence, and effective rights. . . **(958-971)**

2 • Determine a user's effective rights. . . **(1002-1005)**

3 • Perform basic security implementation tasks, such as assigning a trustee and granting rights, setting a directory IRF, creating a Group object and assigning members, and making a user security equivalent to another user. . . **(986-977)**

4 • Describe guidelines for planning a directory structure based on security considerations. . . **(786-804)**

5 • Given a directory structure and the function of its directories, recommend the rights that should be granted and the trustee object that will make security implementation and management easiest. . . **(986-997, 962)**

6 • Describe and set the directory and file attributes that can be used to regulate access to files. . . **(972-977)**

7 • Use NetWare Administrator to navigate NDS and the IntranetWare file system. Use NetWare Administrator Help. . . **(987-989, 995-997)**

8 • Based on a scenario, create and implement a file system security plan that appropriately grants directory and file rights to container, Group, and User objects, and sets directory IRFs. . . **(986-997)**

SECTION 9: ACCESSING AND PROTECTING THE NETWARE SERVER CONSOLE

1 • Describe the function of a NetWare 4.11 server and its interface. . . **(1095-1098, 1109-1111, 1225-1231)**

2 • Define *console command* and *NetWare Loadable Module (NLM)*. . . **(1097-1122)**

3 • Describe the function of the LOAD command. . . **(1105)**

4 • Describe remote console management. List the steps necessary to set up a server for both SPX and asynchronous remote connections. . . **(1214-1218)**

5 • Use RCONSOLE to remotely access the server console, switch between console screens, and activate the RCONSOLE Available Options menu. . . **(1218-1222)**

6 • Describe security strategies for a NetWare 4.11 server, such as setting a password on the monitor, setting a password for Remote Console, and placing the server in a secure location. . . **(1123-1127)**

SECTION 10: SETTING UP NETWORK PRINTING

1 • Set up a network printing environment by creating and configuring related Print Queue, Printer, and Print Server objects. . . **(1262-1273, 1324-1327)**

2 • Set up network printing hardware by bringing up a print server on a NetWare 4.11 server and connecting a printer to the network through a NetWare server or DOS workstation. . . **(1273-1277, 1328)**

3 • Regulate who can do any of the following: print to a print queue, manage print jobs in the print queue, be notified by a printer when a problem occurs, view the status of the print server, or manage the print server. . . **(1288-1289)**

4 • Manage the flow of print jobs into and out of a print queue by managing the status of the print queue. . . **(1287-1310, 1332-1333)**

5 • Manage print jobs in a print queue by pausing, rushing, delaying, and deleting print jobs in the print queue. . . **(1287-1310)**

6 • Describe how to customize print jobs using print job configurations, printer definitions, and printer forms. . . **(1277-1285, 1312-1322, 1337)**

SECTION 11: INSTALLING AND CONFIGURING CLIENT 32 ON WORKSTATIONS

1 • Use the NetWare Client software to install Client 32 for Windows 95. . . **(1179-1181, 1223-1224)**

2 • Use the Network Configuration Page to modify the network connection for Windows 95. . . **(1020-1021)**

3 • Use the NetWare Client software to install Client 32 for Windows 3.1. . . **(1182-1183)**

4 • Modify the network connection for Windows 3.1 by modifying the NET.CFG file. . . **(1027-1028)**

5 • Upgrade the client automatically to the most current version of Client 32. . . **(1181-1182, 1183-1186)**

SECTION 12: CREATING LOGIN SCRIPTS

1 • Describe the types of login scripts and explain how they coordinate at login. . . **(1028-1035)**

2 • Recommend procedures that should be executed during login. . . **(1040)**

3 • Plan login scripts with correct login script command syntax. . . **(1036-1051)**

4 • Create, execute, and debug a login script. . . **(1083-1085)**

SECTION 13: CONFIGURING NETWORK APPLICATIONS FOR USERS

1 • Describe how to manage and launch network applications using Application objects and the NetWare Application Launcher (NAL). . . **(1065)**

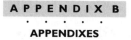

2 • Configure NDS and the file system to access network applications with NAL. . . **(1065-1068)**

3 • Use NAL to launch a network application from Windows. . . **(1068)**

SECTION 14: MANAGING NDS SECURITY

1 • Explain how access to the Directory is controlled by object trustees, object rights, and property rights. . . **(919-930)**

2 • Given a Directory tree, determine effective rights for objects and properties and troubleshoot an NDS security scenario. . . **(945-948, 998-1001)**

3 • Explain guidelines and considerations for managing NDS security. . . **(931-948, 953-957)**

4 • Implement NDS security by making trustee assignments; modifying Object, All Property, and Selected Property rights; and setting Inherited Rights Filters (IRFs). . . **(931-948, 986-997)**

SECTION 15: MANAGING RESOURCES IN A MULTICONTEXT ENVIRONMENT

1 • Describe how the Directory tree structure affects network use and management skills. . . **(632-637)**

2 • Describe sample Directory structures and discuss basic guidelines for organizing resources. . . **(679-685)**

3 • Demonstrate correct object-naming techniques. . . **(127-144, 179-180)**

4 • Change the current context and navigate the Directory tree. . . **(129-134, 172-178)**

5 • Log in, map network drives, and redirect print jobs to resources in other contexts. . . **(129-134, 141, 1245-1246)**

6 • Grant rights to file system and network printing resources in other contexts. . . **(931-937)**

7 • Create shortcuts to objects in other contexts using Directory Map and Alias objects. . . **(665-667)**

8 • Establish an initial context at login for a DOS workstation. . . **(131, 388-392)**

9 • Edit login scripts to access resources in other containers. . . **(1048, 392-394)**

SECTION 16: BACKING UP SERVERS AND WORKSTATIONS

1 • Compare and contrast backup strategies. . . **(1205-1207)**

2 • Describe the process of backing up a NetWare 4.11 server and workstation's file systems with SBACKUP. . . **(1200-1209)**

3 • Describe the process of restoring file system information with SBACKUP. . . **(1210-1214)**

SECTION 17: PERFORMING A SIMPLE NETWARE 4.11 INSTALLATION

1 • Compare the requirements of the NetWare 4.11 Simple and Custom Installation options. . . **(458-465, 530)**

2 • Identify the major steps for installing NetWare 4.11. . . **(477-478)**

3 • Install a NetWare 4.11 server using the Simple Installation option. . . **(467-477)**

Novell Education Course 525 —
IntranetWare/NetWare 4.11 Advanced Administration

Your CNE education continues with *IntranetWare/NetWare 4.11 Advanced Administration*. In this course, you explore the advanced topics that separate CNEs from pretenders. You learn all about Server Management, advanced NDS Design and Maintenance, Partitioning and Time Synchronization, better Security, Diverse Clients, and Optimization.

Pay attention to these objectives, because they can be a little tricky.

SECTION 1: SERVER STARTUP PROCEDURES AND CONFIGURATION FILES

1 • Identify and describe the server components. . . (457-462, 1095-1098)

2 • Perform a server startup procedure. . . (519-522, 545)

3 • Identify and describe server configuration files. . . (515-517)

4 • Identify commands and options used to customize the appropriate server configuration file. . . (515-517, 541)

5 • Select the appropriate utility and edit the server configuration files. . . (517)

6 • Create server batch files that perform specific tasks, such as remotely rebooting the server. . . (1102, 1104, 1127)

SECTION 2: DESIGNING THE DIRECTORY TREE

1 • Identify the process for designing the Directory tree, which includes determining naming standards and planning the Directory structure. . . (190-205)

2 • Create a structural design of NDS based on company information. . . (300-327)

SECTION 3: SECURING THE DIRECTORY TREE

I • Explain guidelines and considerations for managing NDS security in a multicontext environment. . . **(931-948, 953-957)**

2 • Describe the differences between centralized and distributed NDS management. . . **(949-952)**

3 • Create NDS administrators by granting the appropriate rights based on scenarios of centralized and distributed NDS management. . . **(952-953)**

SECTION 4: MANAGING PARTITIONS AND REPLICAS

I • Describe NDS partitioning and replication. . . **(144-159)**

2 • Describe the process of partitioning and replicating the NDS database. . . **(721-727, 741-748)**

3 • Identify which partitions and replicas are created by default when a server is installed in a Directory tree. . . **(342-353)**

4 • List and explain the guidelines for planning partition boundaries and replica placement. . . **(149, 157-159, 344-345, 360, 726, 741)**

5 • Manage NDS partitions and replicas in NDS Manager by viewing partition and server information, creating and merging partitions, adding and removing replicas, and moving containers. . . **(727-740, 749-759, 776-781)**

SECTION 5: IMPLEMENTING AND MANAGING TIME SYNCHRONIZATION

1 • Configure servers to synchronize time in an IntranetWare network. . . **(159-170)**

2 • Given a scenario that includes a WAN topology, choose an appropriate time provider and communication method. . . **(360-373)**

3 • Manage time synchronization by viewing time synchronization status, changing time, and bringing new servers on-line appropriately. . . **(763-774)**

SECTION 6: COMPLETING YOUR NDS DESIGN

1 • Given a company scenario including the Directory tree design, plan NDS security for the Directory tree and determine any Directory design changes. . . **(327-329)**

2 • Given a company scenario including the Directory tree design, plan partitions and replica placement, and determine any Directory design changes. . . **(330-332, 344-349, 352-360)**

3 • Given a company scenario, plan time synchronization for the network and determine any Directory design changes. . . **(367-373)**

SECTION 7: MAINTAINING NOVELL DIRECTORY SERVICES

1 • Explain preventive maintenance procedures for the NDS database. . . **(1131-1134)**

2 • In NDS Manager, identify NDS database inconsistencies and find Help information about resolving the error. . . **(1134-1135, 1137)**

3 • Explain NDS database repair procedures that can be accomplished in NDS Manager. These include creating a new master replica, repairing a local database, sending and receiving updates, repairing network addresses, and repairing server IDs. . . **(1135-1139)**

4 • Explain the procedure for recovering NDS from a failed server or volume. . . **(1139-1142)**

SECTION 8: INTEGRATING AND MANAGING NETWARE 3

1 • Use Bindery Services to integrate NetWare 3.1x with IntranetWare. . . **(46-49, 334-336, 356-358)**

2 • Use NetSync to manage NetWare 3.1x resources from NetWare Administrator. . . **(693-699)**

SECTION 9: OPTIMIZING THE NETWORK AND SERVER (important)

1 • Describe IntranetWare memory allocation and configure the server for memory deallocation and garbage collection. . . **(1342-1355)**

2 • Interpret the MONITOR Statistics screen. . . **(1355-1359)**

3 • Monitor and modify file and directory cache performance. . . **(1359-1361, 1367-1371)**

4 • View and modify server buffer and packet parameters. . . **(1362-1365, 1371-1377)**

5 • Define and enable block suballocation. . . **(1385-1386, 50-52)**

6 • List the steps to enable file compression. . . **(1380-1385, 52-53)**

7 • Enable and manage the Packet Burst protocol. . . **(1386-1387)**

8 • Enable and manage Large Internet Packets (LIPs). . . **(1387-1388)**

SECTION 10: CONFIGURING INTRANETWARE FOR DIVERSE CLIENTS

1 • Configure the server to support diverse clients such as Macintosh and OS/2. . . **(1194-1199)**

2 • Install and configure NetWare/IP. . . **(1150-1157, 1169-1173)**

3 • Define the purpose of the NetWare MultiProtocol Router (MPR) 3.1 and give an example of its function within a network. . . **(1158-1161)**

4 • Enable internationalization. . . **(1143-1147)**

Novell Education Course 526 — *NetWare 3 to IntranetWare Update*

This course is the Administration alternative for advanced NetWare 3 CNEs. Everything you learn in the *NetWare 3 to IntranetWare Update* course is carefully hand-picked from the previous two Administration courses. Novell Education removed the NetWare 3 material with the assumption that CNE-3 students should already know it. The result is a fun-packed three days of insanity and NDS wizardry.

Don't forget your magic wand.

SECTION 1: PERFORMING NETWARE 3 TASKS WITH INTRANETWARE

1 • View the NetWare 4.11 server startup components and compare them with NetWare 3. These components include server configuration files, the server startup process, server utilities (such as MONITOR and INSTALL), and commands (such as DISPLAY SERVERS and CONFIG). . . **(567-568, 1095-1122)**

2 • Use Novell Directory Services (NDS) to organize network resources in IntranetWare. . . **(96-126, 630-685, 700-716)**

3 • Demonstrate correct object-naming techniques. . . **(127-144, 179-180)**

4 • Connect with Client 32 and log into an IntranetWare server from DOS, Windows 3.1, and Windows 95 workstations. . . **(1014-1023)**

5 • Manage objects in Novell Directory Services (NDS) that have been migrated from the NetWare 3 bindery. Such objects include users, groups, servers, and volumes. . . **(590-592, 651-671)**

6 • Use the Volume object in the NetWare Administrator utility to manage the file system. . . **(807-816, 870-873)**

7 • Use NetWare Administrator to control file system security, view effective rights, assign rights to users and groups, and modify the Inherited Rights Filter (IRF). . . **(964-971, 986-997)**

8 • Set up and manage printing using NetWare Administrator and the IntranetWare DOS text print utilities. . . **(1262-1337)**

SECTION 2: MANAGING THE USER ENVIRONMENT

1 • Create and modify user, profile, and container login scripts. . . **(1028-1051, 1083-1085)**

2 • Use UIMPORT to create users. . . **(674-678, 713-714)**

3 • Describe how to manage and launch network applications using Application objects and the NetWare Application Launcher (NAL). . . **(1065)**

4 • Configure NDS and the file system to access network applications with NAL. . . **(1065-1068)**

5 • Use NAL to launch a network application from Windows. . . **(1068)**

SECTION 3: INTEGRATING AND MANAGING NETWARE 3

I • Use Bindery Services to integrate NetWare 3.1*x* with IntranetWare. . . **(46-49, 334-336, 356-358)**

2 • Use NetSync to manage NetWare 3.1*x* resources from NetWare Administrator. . . **(693-699)**

SECTION 4: DESIGNING THE DIRECTORY TREE

I • Identify the process for designing the Directory tree, which includes determining naming standards and planning the Directory structure. . . **(190-205)**

2 • Create a structural design of NDS based on company information. . . **(300-327)**

SECTION 5: SECURING THE DIRECTORY TREE

I • Identify differences and similarities between NDS security and file system security in IntranetWare. . . **(958-959)**

2 • Identify how access to the Directory is controlled by object trustees, object rights, and property rights. . . **(919-930)**

3 • Given a Directory tree, determine effective rights for objects and properties and troubleshoot an NDS security scenario. . . **(945-948, 998-1001)**

4 • Explain guidelines and considerations for managing NDS security in a multicontext environment. . . **(931-948, 953-957)**

5 • Implement NDS security by making trustee assignments; modifying Object, All Property, and Selected Property rights; and setting Inherited Rights Filters (IRFs). . . **(931-948, 986-997)**

6 • Describe the differences between centralized and distributed NDS management. . . **(949-952)**

7 • Create NDS administrators by granting the appropriate rights based on scenarios of centralized and distributed NDS management. . . **(952-953)**

SECTION 6: MANAGING PARTITIONS AND REPLICAS

I • Describe NDS partitioning and replication. . . **(144-159)**

2 • Describe the process of partitioning and replicating the NDS database. . . **(721-727, 741-748)**

3 • Identify which partitions and replicas are created by default when a server is installed in a Directory tree. . . **(342, 353)**

4 • List and explain the guidelines for planning partition boundaries and replica placement. . . **(149, 157-159, 726, 741, 344-345, 360)**

5 • Manage NDS partitions and replicas in NDS Manager by viewing partition and server information, creating and merging partitions, adding and removing replicas, and moving containers. . . **(727-740, 749-759, 776-781)**

SECTION 7: IMPLEMENTING AND MANAGING TIME SYNCHRONIZATION

I • Configure servers to synchronize time in an IntranetWare network. . . **(X159-170)**

2 • Given a scenario that includes a WAN topology, choose an appropriate time provider and communication method. . . **(360-373)**

3 • Manage time synchronization by viewing time synchronization status, changing time, and bringing new servers on-line appropriately. . . **(763-774)**

SECTION 8: COMPLETING YOUR NDS DESIGN

1 • Given a company scenario including the Directory tree design, plan NDS security for the Directory tree and determine any Directory design changes. . . **(327-329)**

2 • Given a company scenario including the Directory tree design, plan partitions and replica placement and determine any Directory design changes. . . **(330-332, 344-349, 352-360)**

3 • Given a company scenario, plan time synchronization for the network and determine any Directory design changes. . . **(367-373)**

SECTION 9: MAINTAINING NOVELL DIRECTORY SERVICES

1 • Explain preventive maintenance procedures for the NDS database. . . **(1131-1134)**

2 • In NDS Manager, identify NDS database inconsistencies and find Help information about resolving the error. . . **(1134-1135, 1137)**

3 • Explain NDS database repair procedures that can be accomplished in NDS Manager. These include creating a new master replica, repairing a local database, sending and receiving updates, repairing network addresses, and repairing server IDs. . . **(1135-1139)**

4 • Explain the procedure for recovering NDS from a failed server or volume. . . **(1139-1142)**

SECTION 10: MANAGING A MULTICONTEXT ENVIRONMENT

1 • Access network resources in other contexts by changing the current context and navigating the Directory tree. . . **(129-134, 172-178, 388-392)**

2 • Log in, map network drives, and redirect print jobs to resources in other contexts. . . **(129-134, 141, 1245-1246)**

3 • Grant users in one context access to file system and network printing resources in other contexts. . . **(931-937)**

4 • Create shortcuts to objects in other contexts using Application, Directory Map, Alias, and global Group objects. . . **(665-667)**

5 • Edit login scripts to access resources in other containers. . . **(392-394, 1048)**

SECTION 11: OPTIMIZING THE NETWORK AND SERVER

1 • Describe IntranetWare memory allocation and configure the server for memory deallocation and garbage collection. . . **(1342-1355)**

2 • Interpret the MONITOR Statistics screen. . . **(1355-1359)**

3 • Monitor and modify file and directory cache performance. . . **(1359-1361, 1367-1371)**

4 • View and modify server buffer and packet parameters. . . **(1362-1365, 1371-1377)**

5 • Define and enable block suballocation. . . **(50-52, 1385-1386)**

6 • List the steps to enable file compression. . . **(52-53, 1380-1385)**

7 • Enable and manage the Packet Burst protocol. . . **(1386-1387)**

8 • Enable and manage Large Internet Packets (LIPs). . . **(1387-1388)**

SECTION 12: CONFIGURING INTRANETWARE FOR DIVERSE CLIENTS

1 • Use the NetWare Client software to install Client 32 for Windows 95. . . **(1179-1181, 1223-1224)**

2 • Use the Network Configuration Page to modify the network connection for Windows 95. . . **(1020-1021)**

3 • Use the NetWare Client software to install Client 32 for Windows 3.1. . . **(1182-1183)**

4 • Modify the network connection for Windows 3.1 by modifying the NET.CFG file. . . **(1027-1028)**

5 • Describe the appropriate options needed in the CONFIG.SYS, AUTOEXEC.BAT, and NET.CFG files to automate the network connection and login processes. . . **(1023-1027)**

6 • Upgrade the client automatically to the current version of Client 32. . . **(1181-1182, 1183-1186)**

Novell Education Course 532 — *IntranetWare/NDS Design and Implementation*

With NDS comes great responsibility. Gone are the days when you could yank NetWare 3.12 out of the box and slam it into a server over lunch. Now you must fully understand the "purpose" of your WAN before installing the very first server. The good news is Novell Education has developed a special "new" course just for you — *IntranetWare/NDS Design and Implementation*. In this thorough three-day journey, you'll grasp the fundamentals of Project Team creation, NDS Tree Design, Partitioning and Replica Design, Time Synchronization, and IntranetWare Implementation.

This is the trickiest test of them all. Study hard.

SECTION 1: DETERMINING THE PROJECT APPROACH

1 • Identify the sequence of the tasks in the IntranetWare design and implementation process and determine the dependencies for each task. . . **(190-205)**

2 • Given a project team, identify roles and assign project tasks and responsibilities for each role. . . **(205-218)**

3 • Given a case company that will implement an IntranetWare network, identify the types of information required to create a design and implementation strategy. . . **(218-251)**

4 • Given a company scenario, define the scope of the IntranetWare implementation and design project, assess the company situation for factors that affect design, and use the information to set project expectations. . . **(251-253)**

SECTION 2: DESIGNING THE DIRECTORY TREE

1 • Given a case company, revise a naming standards document that specifies a unique Directory tree name and ensures consistent object names, property values, and other network names (such as IPX addresses). . . **(260-295)**

2 • Given a case company's WAN topology and geographic location, draw the structure for the upper layers of the Directory tree. . . **(295-324)**

3 • From an analysis of corporate documents that include the organization chart, resource chart, and workflow chart, draw a first draft of the lower layers in the Directory tree. . . **(325-327)**

4 • Modify the Directory tree for a centralized or decentralized administration approach and login script maintenance strategy. . . **(327-329, 333-334)**

5 • Given a draft Directory tree, verify that all containers are appropriately placed for efficient partitioning. . . **(330-332)**

6 • Given a draft Directory tree, place leaf objects in the Directory tree to facilitate efficient user access. . . **(334-337)**

SECTION 3: DETERMINING A PARTITION AND REPLICATION STRATEGY

1 • Assess a company scenario (including WAN topology, a map of physical locations, numbers of servers, and server location) to determine where to draw partition boundaries in the Directory tree structure. . . **(337-350)**

2 • Given a scenario with new servers, upgraded servers, and merged Directory trees, determine how the default replica placement should be modified. . . **(350-360)**

3 • Given a company scenario, adapt the replica placement plan to accommodate additional considerations. . . **(350-360)**

4 • Given a Directory tree structure with partition boundaries, create a table showing appropriate replica placement on servers for each partition. . . **(742-744, 776-781)**

SECTION 4: PLANNING A TIME SYNCHRONIZATION STRATEGY

1 • Given a company scenario with a resource map, a location map, LAN topology, and WAN topology, use guidelines to determine the configuration of the time server types. . . **(360-371)**

2 • Given a company scenario with a resource map, a location map, and WAN topology, use guidelines to determine the method of communicating time across the network. . . **(371-374)**

SECTION 5: CREATING AN ACCESSIBILITY PLAN

1 • Given an evaluation of users' accessibility needs, analyze the needs and complete an accessibility guidelines document. . . **(375)**

2 • Design administrative strategies for using container login scripts, Profile login scripts, Directory Map objects, Alias objects, Organizational Role objects, and Group objects. . . **(381-386)**

3 • Given a company scenario and suggested guidelines, create a security strategy and guidelines that can be used by network administrators. . . **(385-386, 949-957)**

4 • Given a company scenario with mobile users and a draft Directory tree, develop a strategy for mobile users to access resources from two or more geographical locations. . . **(386-394)**

SECTION 6: DEVELOPING A MIGRATION STRATEGY

1 • Given a company scenario, create a client migration strategy that includes configuration parameters and plans for automating the migration process. . . **(421-426)**

2 • Given a company scenario with an existing network, create a migration strategy for existing servers to become IntranetWare servers. . . **(427-439)**

SECTION 7: CREATING AN IMPLEMENTATION SCHEDULE

1 • Given a company scenario, identify the proper sequence of tasks to implement an IntranetWare network. . . **(398-410)**

2 • Set timelines and milestones for the implementation of an IntranetWare network by matching available people with the required tasks. . . **(411-446)**

SECTION 8: DESIGNING ADDITIONAL SCENARIOS

1 • Given a company scenario, design a Directory tree structure with associated partition, replica, time synchronization, and accessibility plans. . . **(295-394)**

2 • Given a company scenario, develop a migration strategy and implementation schedule for IntranetWare. . . **(398-446)**

Novell Education Course 804 — *IntranetWare/ NetWare 4.11 Installation and Configuration Workshop*

The final IntranetWare course is the most interesting. You get to spend two fun-filled days of "hands-on" bliss. The entire *IntranetWare/NetWare 4.11 Installation and Configuration Workshop* course consists of exercise after exercise, including Installing NetWare 4.11 (seven times), Migrating from NetWare 3, Building NDS, Troubleshooting NDS, Maintaining NDS, Partitioning NDS, Time Synchronization, Securing Everything, and finally, Optimizing the File System and Server. As if that's not all, they even throw in a "DynaText" installation for good measure.

Your fingers sure are going to be sore after this one.

SECTION 1: UPGRADING NETWARE 3.1X TO NETWARE 4.11

1 • Describe, compare, and choose the upgrade or migration method that best fits your needs. . . **(550-564)**

2 • Identify the software and hardware required for a NetWare 4.11 server. . . **(564-567)**

3 • Describe the critical components and software for the NetWare 4.11 server as compared to NetWare 3 servers. . . **(567-568)**

4 • Identify the high-level steps for upgrading NetWare 3.12 servers to NetWare 4.11. . . **(569-570, 588-589)**

5 • Upgrade a NetWare 3.12 server to NetWare 4.11. . . **(570-590)**

6 • Confirm the NetWare 4.11 upgrade. . . **(590-592)**

SECTION 2: PERFORMING A SIMPLE NETWARE 4.11 INSTALLATION

1 • Compare the requirements of the NetWare 4.11 Simple Installation and Custom Installation options. . . **(462-465, 530)**

2 • Identify the major steps for installing NetWare 4.11. . . **(466, 477-478)**

3 • Install a NetWare 4.11 server using the Simple Installation option. . . **(467-477)**

SECTION 3: MIGRATING FROM NETWARE 3.1X TO NETWARE 4.11

1 • Identify the two types of upgrades available using the Migration utilities. . . **(592-593, 610-611, 612-616)**

2 • Discuss which elements of the NetWare 3.12 environment will migrate and which will not when using DS Migrate. . . **(593-595)**

3 • Discuss the prerequisites of an Across-the-Wire Migration. . . **(596-598)**

4 • Identify the major steps to upgrading a NetWare 3.1x server using the Across-the-Wire Migration method. . . **(598)**

5 • Upgrade a NetWare 3.1x server using the Across-the-Wire Migration method with DS Migrate and File Migration. . . **(598-609, 617-620)**

SECTION 4: PERFORMING A CUSTOM NETWARE 4.11 INSTALLATION

1 • Identify the major steps for installing NetWare 4.11 using the Custom Installation option. . . **(520-522)**

2 • Install NetWare 4.11 using the Custom Installation option. . . **(479-520, 531-544)**

3 • Discuss the two methods used to install TCP/IP and AppleTalk protocols. . . **(499-501, 1147-1157, 1197)**

SECTION 5: INSTALLING NOVELL ONLINE DOCUMENTATION

1 • Identify the steps for preparing to install the online documentation on your server from a Windows client. . . **(523-526)**

2 • Install the DynaText viewer and install the document collections. . . **(527-529)**

3 • Set up and configure clients to view the on-line documentation. . . **(528-529)**

SECTION 6: CONFIGURING THE INTRANETWARE ENVIRONMENT

1 • Set up network user accounts and configure property information. . . **(700-716)**

2 • Create the file system structure and provide appropriate security for users. . . **(986-997)**

3 • Set up a network printing environment by creating and configuring a print queue, printer, and print server. . . **(1262-1273, 1324-1327)**

SECTION 7: MERGING, CONFIGURING, AND TROUBLESHOOTING NDS

1 • Merge small Directory trees in a departmental-to-organizational implementation. . . **(685-692)**

2 • Given a Directory tree, create and merge partitions using NDS Manager. . . **(733-737)**

3 • Move an NDS container from one context to another. . . **(738)**

4 • Execute the procedures to recover from a failed Master replica. . . **(750-753, 1139)**

5 • Set the bindery context for multiple servers in multiple contexts. . . **(47)**

SECTION 8: MANAGING THE INTRANETWARE SERVER

1 • Describe IntranetWare memory components, memory requirements, and memory allocation. . . **(1349-1354)**

2 • View critical components to verify memory status and use commands to optimize memory allocation. . . **(1349-1354, 1355-1359)**

3 • Describe the components that affect server and network performance. . . **(1343-1349)**

4 • Implement appropriate SET parameters to increase performance. . . **(1366-1377)**

5 • Describe the maintenance utilities and use them to verify the integrity of the server data and hardware. . . **(1389-1401)**

SECTION 9: NETWORK ADMINISTRATION TIPS

1 • Identify tips for designing, installing, and maintaining IntranetWare. . . **(295-299, 1092-1094, 1123-1127, 1214-1220)**

2 • Given scenarios, apply the tips for designing, installing, and maintaining IntranetWare. . . **(295-299, 1092-1094, 1123-1127, 1214-1220)**

SECTION 10: INSTALLING AND CONFIGURING THE NETWARE WEB SERVER

1 • Install and configure the NetWare Web Server. . . **(1161-1164)**

2 • Install the Netscape browser and view your home page. . . **(1165-1169)**

Solutions to Quizzes, Puzzles, Exercises, and Case Studies

"Scanner indicates no life forms Captain . . . only the answers to CNE exercises."

IntranetWare CNE — A New Frontier

▶ · ◀

Chapter 1: Introduction to IntranetWare

ANSWERS TO QUIZZES

Q1-1
The only available matching color for the large present is red. Next, the only contrasting color available for the small wrapping is silver. Finally, that leaves green wrapping and a gold bow for the medium-sized gift. Happy birthday.

Q1-2
15

Q1-3
Decimal point.

Q1-4
$(7777 \times 7)/(\bar{\ } (7 \times 7)$ Told ya so.

Q1-5
It doesn't. It takes place "A long time ago . . . in a galaxy far, far away."

Q1-6
Assume that the total number of birds is 240 — that is, 6 trees with 40 birds, or 40 trees with 6 birds, or 3 trees with 80 birds, or 80 trees with 3 birds. Remember, I said, "If you know the number of birds, you can figure out the number of trees." Therefore, it can't be 240, or any number that factorizes.

Now try prime numbers. A *prime number* is any number that can only be divided by 1 and itself. If 229 were the number, there would only be 1 tree with 229 birds in it, or 229 trees with only 1 bird each. Nope — there's more than one tree, and you have to have more than one bird per tree.

That leaves only the square of a prime number. Voilà, there's only one answer between 200 and 300 — 289. Therefore, there are 17 trees, each with 17 birds. Now, wasn't that fun!

Q1-7

The average is calculated as the total distance (240 miles) divided by the total time (2 hrs. + 3 hrs. = 5 hrs.). Therefore, it's not 50 m.p.h., but 48 m.p.h.

EXERCISE 1-1: GETTING TO KNOW INTRANETWARE

1.	D	11.	A
2.	J	12.	K
3.	O	13.	H
4.	F	14.	Q
5.	R	15.	E
6.	B	16.	P
7.	I	17.	N
8.	L	18.	M
9.	G	19.	T
10.	S	20.	C

EXERCISE 1-2: GETTING TO KNOW NDS — PART I

1.	L	6.	L
2.	C	7.	L
3.	L	8.	L
4.	L	9.	L
5.	C	10.	C

EXERCISE 1-2: GETTING TO KNOW NDS — PART II

1. Container (Organizational Unit)
2. Leaf
3. Leaf
4. Leaf
5. Container (Organization)
6. Leaf
7. Container (Country or Organizational Unit)
8. Leaf
9. Organizational Unit
10. Leaf

EXERCISE 1-3: THE CLOUD

```
N  B  X  E  T  X  E  T  N  O  C  Y  R  E  D  N  I  B  E  S  L
G  D  I  R  E  C  T  O  R  Y  G  Y  R  W  N  N  R  I  X  L  O
Y  I  S  I  N  G  L  E  R  E  F  E  R  E  N  C  E  N  E  B  L
N  S  D  X  V  J  R  B  F  P  K  S  T  E  C  X  Y  D  J  T  C
T  T  G  S  B  Q  P  X  V  E  L  E  A  F  O  B  J  E  C  T  F
B  I  D  U  X  M  L  D  L  T  E  E  N  U  B  Q  C  R  O  K  I
H  N  U  U  E  E  I  X  U  E  S  R  Z  E  T  T  E  Y  N  Z  L
G  G  A  U  T  H  E  N  T  I  C  A  T  I  O  N  U  Z  T  V  H
I  U  O  W  T  I  M  E  S  E  R  V  E  R  F  R  M  N  A  F  B
S  I  H  Y  D  C  O  L  M  U  F  X  E  Q  G  B  C  F  I  W  R
S  S  U  B  O  R  D  I  N  A  T  E  R  E  F  E  R  E  N  C  E
Y  H  Y  R  N  F  J  M  I  L  X  B  J  T  C  O  N  T  E  X  T
T  E  F  V  Z  S  U  O  O  Y  T  R  E  P  O  R  P  G  R  T  J
K  D  D  F  C  F  C  L  F  O  D  C  H  V  M  O  A  B  K  P  G
Z  N  G  C  D  V  U  J  M  D  X  H  B  S  M  N  R  L  B  Q  H
C  A  T  W  P  H  Z  W  U  J  X  W  P  L  O  E  T  W  W  L  E
J  M  K  C  Q  V  I  K  P  G  K  K  G  S  N  V  I  T  L  P  E
F  E  E  R  M  S  J  V  X  I  F  O  G  W  N  D  T  H  Y  H  O
T  I  M  E  S  Y  N  C  H  R  O  N  I  Z  A  T  I  O  N  K  L
S  W  V  I  N  E  X  J  Y  W  H  E  G  E  M  D  O  P  E  W  V
E  O  N  Q  S  G  R  S  I  G  M  J  Q  Z  E  N  N  O  E  E  Y
```

1. AUTHENTICATION	11. OBJECT
2. BINDERY	12. PARTITION
3. BINDERY CONTEXT	13. PROPERTY
4. COMMON NAME	14. [ROOT] (with no brackets)
5. CONTAINER	15. SINGLE REFERENCE
6. CONTEXT	16. SUBORDINATE REFERENCE
7. DIRECTORY	17. TIME SERVER
8. DISTINGUISHED NAME	18. TIME SYNCHRONIZATION
9. LEAF OBJECT	19. TREE
10. NDS	20. UTC

► · ◄

Chapter 2: Understanding NDS

ANSWERS TO QUIZZES

Q2-1

The only days the Lion can say "I lied yesterday" are Mondays and Thursdays. The only days the Unicorn can say "I lied yesterday" are Thursdays and Sundays. Therefore, the only day they can both say it is Thursday.

Q2-2

On no day of the week is this possible! Only on Mondays and Thursdays could he make the first statement; only on Wednesdays and Sundays could he make the second. So, there is no day he could say both. Poor Alice is stuck in the Land of Forgetfulness forever.

Q2-3

This is a very different situation! It illustrates well the difference between making two statements separately and making one statement that is the conjunction of the two. Indeed, given any two statements X and Y, if the single statement "X and Y" is true, then it follows that X and Y are true separately; but if the conjunction "X and Y" is false, then at least one of them is false.

Now, the only day of the week it could be true that the Lion lied yesterday and will lie again tomorrow is Tuesday (this is the only day that occurs between two of the Lion's lying days). So, the day the Lion said that couldn't be Tuesday, for on Tuesdays that statement is true, but the Lion doesn't make true statements on Tuesdays. Therefore, it is not Tuesday; hence, the Lion's statement is false, so the Lion is lying. Therefore, the day must be either Monday or Wednesday. Tricky little Lion.

Q2-4

A-4
B-5,8
C-1
D-2, 6
E-3

Q2-5

The Hint (Synergy) means the whole is greater than the sum of its parts. This means we must be dealing with a whole number. Therefore, half of "What I'd be" must be a whole number. "What I'd be" must be an even number. "What I am" cannot end in 1. There are four possible arrangements of the three digits:

	(a)	(b)	(c)	(d)
What I am	1?3	13?	31?	?13
What I'd be	3?4	34?	43?	?34

"What I am" is "Nine less than half what I'd be." So, ("What I am" + 9) • 2 = "What I'd be." Examination shows that only "A" fits the bill and "What I am" must be 183. No sweat.

EXERCISE 2-1: "TREE WALKING" FOR TODDLERS

1a. Answers will vary in terms of what objects are displayed when you activate the NetWare Administrator utility. Your current context is the topmost icon displayed on the screen. (You may need to use the scroll bar on the right side of the screen to get to the top of the screen.) When you first activate the NetWare Administrator utility, your *current context* is the one that was in effect the last time you used the utility on this workstation. This is because your current context in NetWare Administrator is utility-specific. In other words, it is independent of your current context as displayed at the command line.

1b. Answers will vary for all questions in this section.

EXERCISE 2-2: UNDERSTANDING NDS NAMING

1. .BMasterson.BLUE.CRIME.TOKYO.ACME

2. .CN=RHood.OU=WHITE.OU=CRIME.OU=TOKYO.O=ACME

3. CRIME.TOKYO.ACME

4. CN=BLUE-SRV1.OU=BLUE.OU=CRIME.OU=TOKYO.O=ACME (since the default current context is the [Root])

5. SHolmes

6. LJohn.WHITE.CRIME

7. CN=SirKay.OU=CHARITY.

8. Admin...

9. CN=BThomas.OU=PR..

10. CN=BLUE-SRV1_SYS.OU=BLUE.OU=CRIME.OU=TOKYO.O=ACME....

11. BLUE.CRIME.TOKYO.ACME (since it's the context of the server)

    LOGIN .DHolliday.BLUE.CRIME.TOKYO.ACME

    LOGIN DHolliday (since NetWare 4 searches the server's context by default)

12. CX CHARITY..

13. Add the following statement to his NET.CFG file (if he has an MS Windows workstation):

    ```
    NAME CONTEXT="OU=CHARITY.OU=TOKYO.O=ACME"
    ```

    Add the following to the Name Context field on the Client 32 page of the Novell NetWare Client 32 Properties dialog box:

    ```
    OU=CHARITY.OU=TOKYO.O=ACME
    ```

14. LOGIN .CN=SHolmes.OU=CRIME.OU=TOKYO.O=ACME

    LOGIN .SHolmes.CRIME.TOKYO.ACME

    LOGIN SHolmes.

    LOGIN CN=SHolmes.

    LOGIN SHolmes.CRIME..

    LOGIN CN=SHolmes.OU=CRIME..

    LOGIN SHolmes.CRIME.TOKYO...

    LOGIN CN=SHolmes.OU=CRIME.OU=TOKYO...

LOGIN SHolmes.CRIME.TOKYO.ACME....

LOGIN CN=SHolmes.OU=CRIME.OU=TOKYO.O=ACME....

15. CX /R

EXERCISE 2-3: PLANT A TREE IN A CLOUD

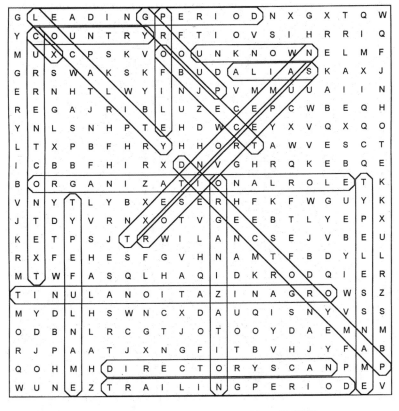

1. ALIAS
2. COUNTRY
3. CURRENT CONTEXT
4. CX
5. DIRECTORY MAP
6. DIRECTORY SCAN
7. GROUP
8. LEADING PERIOD
9. LOCALITY
10. NAME CONTEXT
11. OBJECT
12. ORGANIZATION
13. ORGANIZATIONAL ROLE
14. ORGANIZATIONAL UNIT
15. PROFILE
16. SUPERVISOR
17. TRAILING PERIOD
18. TYPEFUL NAME
19. TYPELESS NAME
20. UNKNOWN

Part I: IntranetWare CNE Basics

▶ · ◀

Chapter 3: Step 1 — NDS Preparation

ANSWERS TO QUIZZES

Q3-1
* = asterisk (ass to risk)

Q3-2
William Shakespeare

Q3-3
It was raining.
". . . country at the top of the Himalayas" = Nepal = PLANE
". . . man from the Far East" = China = CHAIN
". . . man from the Middle East" = Iran = RAIN

Q3-4
NECKLACE

EXERCISE 3-1: ACME — A CURE FOR MOTHER EARTH

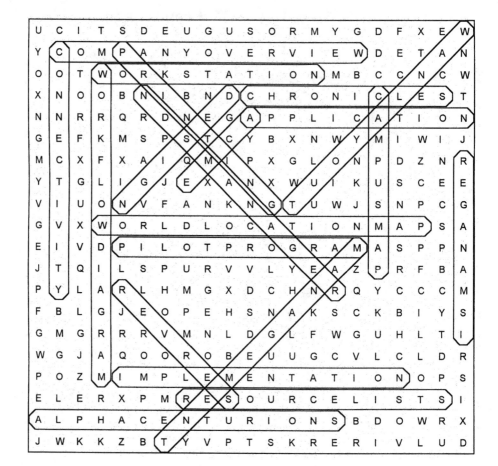

1. ACME
2. ALPHA CENTURIONS
3. APPLICATION
4. CAMPUS MAP
5. CHRONICLES
6. COMPANY OVERVIEW
7. CONNECTIVITY
8. DESIGN
9. IMPLEMENTATION
10. IS MANAGER

11. MANAGEMENT
12. NDS MANAGER
13. PILOT PROGRAM
14. PRINTING
15. RESOURCE LISTS
16. SERVER
17. WAN LAYOUT
18. WORKFLOW DIAGRAM
19. WORKSTATION
20. WORLD LOCATION MAP

Chapter 4: Step 2 — NDS Design

ANSWERS TO QUIZZES

Q4-1

Certainty. The sum of the digits 1 to 8 is 36. Any number divides by 9 exactly when the sum of its digits are also divided by 9 exactly. It does not matter in which order the balls are drawn out as the sum will always be 36.

Q4-2

17 (seventeen). All numbers containing only "E" vowels.

Q4-3

The names are all anagrams:
Zena le Vue = Venezuela (the Americas)
Dr. A. Glebe = Belgrade (Europe)
Rob E. Lumen = Melbourne (Australia)
Ann Ziata = Tanzania (Africa)
That tricky Sherlock Holmes — got me again!

Q4-4

You = 4/7
Me = 2/7
Albert = 1/7
(Because you go first, you have twice the chance as I do. And since I go second, I have twice the chance that Albert does — therefore, the chances are 4 to 2 to 1.)

Q4-5

[(1.5 + 0.25) • 60/50] = 2 minutes 6 seconds

Q4-6

It helped me remember pi to 8 decimal places. The number of letters in each word represents the digits of pi: 3.141559265. I really had a "warped" childhood.

Q4-7

In a pack of 52 cards there are 32 cards of nine or below. The chance that the first card dealt is one of the 32 is 32/52, for the second card the chance is 31/51, and so on. The chance of all 13 being favorable is 32/52 × 31/51 ×...× 20/40 = 1/1828. The odds were strongly in Lord Yarborough's favor.

EXERCISE 4-1: THE RIDE OF YOUR LIFE

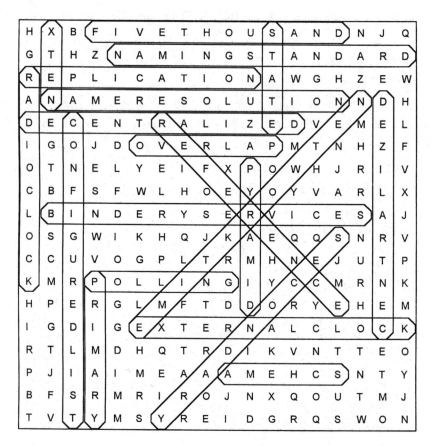

1. BINDERY SERVICES
2. CENTRALIZED
3. CONFIGURED LIST
4. DECENTRALIZED
5. EXTERNAL CLOCK
6. FIVE THOUSAND
7. NAME RESOLUTION
8. NAMING STANDARD
9. NETWORK TIME
10. NETX

11. OVERLAP
12. POLLING
13. PRIMARY
14. PYRAMID
15. RADIO CLOCK
16. REFERENCE
17. REPLICATION
18. SCHEMA
19. SECONDARY
20. STATE

Chapter 5: Step 3 — NDS Implementation

ANSWERS TO QUIZZES

Q5-1
You win $59.00. You will always win the same number of units that heads comes down in the sequence, as long as the final toss is heads.

Q5-2
12365

Q5-3
Yes, in 2.777 minutes.
54 seconds = 0.9 minutes, reciprocal(*) = 1.11
48 seconds = 0.8 minutes, reciprocal   = 1.25
     Add   2.36
30 seconds 0.5 minutes, reciprocal   = 2.00
     Deduct   0.36
     Reciprocal = 2.777 minutes

(*) *A reciprocal is a number or quantity that, when multiplied by a given number or quantity, gives the product of 1, that is, $0.8 \times 1.25 = 1$. To find the reciprocal of 0.8, it is necessary to divide 1 by 0.8, which gives the reciprocal 1.25.*

EXERCISE 5-1: THE SEED

I	L	W	V	F	X	J	M	H	Y	T	X	D	K	W	R	U	P	U	L	G	H
U	A	C	C	E	S	S	I	B	I	L	I	T	Y	P	L	A	N	U	K	P	Q
N	O	V	E	L	L	P	R	E	S	S	B	O	O	K	S	S	G	S	S	M	E
E	I	U	I	C	D	Q	V	T	P	R	L	I	J	P	N	S	J	E	N	D	H
T	C	C	R	X	D	K	N	C	U	A	A	Y	T	L	I	K	B	S	J	F	D
W	F	A	J	S	K	M	R	S	W	F	P	E	H	U	R	Z	P	I	W	P	G
O	H	T	H	T	F	U	S	A	V	E	T	H	E	W	O	R	L	D	V	D	H
R	K	H	A	R	D	W	A	R	E	I	N	S	T	A	L	L	A	T	I	O	N
K	X	S	N	D	S	T	R	E	E	D	E	S	I	G	N	J	L	U	E	U	S
A	M	O	B	I	L	E	U	S	E	R	S	U	U	D	K	M	G	O	R	D	D
P	C	E	G	Q	G	S	Y	B	A	C	K	U	P	R	E	S	T	O	R	E	J
P	R	O	D	U	C	T	I	O	N	E	N	V	I	R	O	N	M	E	N	T	X
L	M	C	O	T	C	I	R	B	M	T	N	W	U	G	O	G	I	Z	P	U	F
I	D	S	S	T	A	N	D	A	R	D	C	C	M	X	M	K	K	W	V	Y	D
C	V	Y	S	O	M	G	H	Q	I	S	O	Q	R	A	M	Z	R	C	W	Z	C
A	V	W	N	H	C	L	U	Z	I	N	U	O	H	Y	Y	R	W	V	D	Y	S
T	E	O	P	G	P	A	Q	M	O	P	I	L	O	T	P	R	O	G	R	A	M
I	E	P	Y	G	U	B	V	X	R	X	P	N	O	X	W	T	Y	Y	Q	F	T
O	F	F	L	I	N	E	T	E	S	T	I	N	G	N	M	P	I	E	U	L	M
N	G	Q	V	Q	W	I	M	P	L	E	M	E	N	T	A	T	I	O	N	N	D
S	H	V	C	F	D	J	W	B	W	M	R	J	Y	F	P	Q	O	O	N	R	K

1. ACCESSIBILITY PLAN
2. BACKUP/RESTORE
3. DS STANDARD
4. HARDWARE INSTALLATION
5. IMPLEMENTATION
6. MOBILE USERS
7. NDS TREE DESIGN
8. NETWORK APPLICATIONS
9. NIC
10. NOVELL PRESS BOOKS
11. NUI
12. OFF-LINE TESTING
13. PILOT PROGRAM
14. PRODUCTION ENVIRONMENT
15. ROLLOUT
16. RSA ENCRYPTION
17. SAVE THE WORLD
18. TESTING LAB
19. TRAINING
20. WAN

Part II : IntranetWare Design

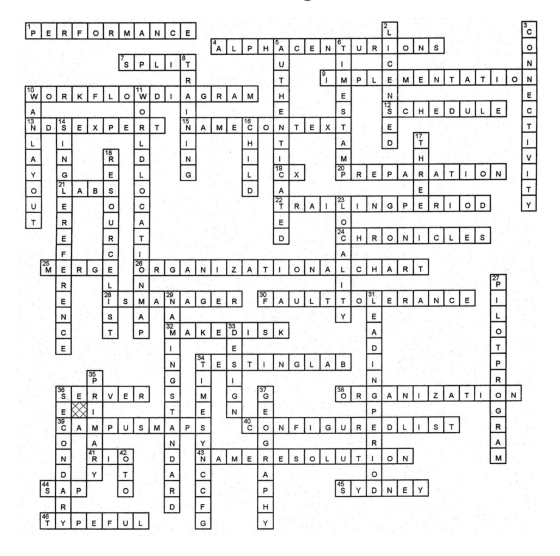

▶ . . . . ◀

Chapter 6: IntranetWare/NetWare 4.11 Installation

ANSWERS TO QUIZZES

Q6-1
Actually, the two trains will be at the *same* distance from Boston when they meet.

Q6-2
Linguists. *Mutual intelligibility* is when two people can understand each other without instruction.

Q6-3
The first answer from Dick cannot be true (if true, it is false). Therefore, Dick is not a Wotta-Wooppa. Because he has made a false statement, Dick can't be a Pukka either. Therefore, Dick is a Shilla-Shalla, and his second answer is true.

Because Dick's second answer is true, Tom is a Pukka. Therefore, Harry's second answer is false as is his first answer, which makes Harry a Wotta-Woppa.

So, Tom is a Pukka, Dick is a Shilli-Shalla, and Harry is a Wotta-Woppa. No sweat.

Q6-4
Mukluks are Eskimo boots made from seal or reindeer hide.

Q6-5

1. Since the only one to predict correctly was the man who married Dana, John did not predict correctly (that Arthur would marry Dana). Therefore, Arthur did not marry Dana, and John did not marry Dana.

2. Therefore, Arthur did not predict correctly. Therefore, David married Eve.

3. Therefore, by elimination, Dana married George. Therefore, George (and only George) predicted correctly.

4. Therefore, John did not marry Christine. Therefore, by elimination, Arthur married Christine and John married Rose.

Complete result: George married Dana; John married Rose; Arthur married Christine; David married Eve; Gallant Dancer did not win the race.

Q6-6

Let's start with a quick summary of their comments.

Andy: The number of Brad's house is even.

Brad: (1) The number of my house is greater than the number of Doug's, and (2) My age is a perfect cube.

Cole: (1) The number of my house is greater than the number of Andy's, and (2) Doug's age is a multiple of Andy's age.

Doug: (1) Brad's age is either 27 or an even number other than 64, and (2) Cole does not live at number 19.

Now, here's my reasoning. The difference between age and house number is always 7. Therefore, if the house number is even, age is odd; and if the house number is odd, age is even. Therefore, false remarks are made by those with odd ages and even houses; true remarks are made by those with even ages and odd houses.

If Brad (2) is true, Brad's age is 27 or 64, but if his age is 27, the remark is false. Therefore, either Brad's age is 64 (and the remark true), or Brad's age is an odd number other than 27 (and the remark is false). Doug (1) contradicts this; therefore, Doug (1) is false.

Therefore, Doug's age is odd and his house number is even, and Doug (2) is false.

Therefore, Cole lives at number 19, and Cole's age is 26 (it cannot be 19 - 7 = 12).

Therefore, Cole's remarks are true, and from Cole (1), Andy's house is number 16.

Therefore, Andy's age is 23 (it cannot be 16 - 7 = 9).

Therefore, Andy's remark is false.

Therefore, Brad's house number is odd and Brad's age is even.

But we know that Brad's age is either 64 or an odd number other than 27. Therefore, Brad's age is 64.

Therefore, Brad's remarks are true.

Since Cole (2) is true, Doug's age is a multiple of 23.

But Doug's age is odd (see above). Therefore, Doug's age is 69.

Brad (1) is true. Therefore, the number of Brad's house is greater than the number of Doug's.

But Brad's age is greater than Doug's. Brad's house must be 64 + 7 (71), and Doug's house must be 69 - 7 (62).

Complete results: Andy is 23 and lives at number 16; Brad is 64 an lives at number 71; Cole is 26 and lives at number 19; Doug is 69 and lives at number 62.

Wasn't that fun — Jell-O brain!

EXERCISE 6-1: CHOOSING THE CORRECT INSTALLATION METHOD

1. Simple Installation

2. Simple Installation

3. Custom Installation

EXERCISE 6-2: MATCHING SERVER STARTUP STEPS

HAPPENS ONCE	*HAPPENS EVERY TIME*
1. Run FDISK	1. Start SERVER.EXE
2. Define locale format	2. Load AUTOEXEC.NCF
3. Define volume block size	3. Create server name
4. Define server context	4. Activate IPX internal network number
5. Copy SYSTEM and PUBLIC files	5. Load LAN driver
6. License the server	6. Define bindery context
7. Create STARTUP.NCF	7. Activate RMF

EXERCISE 6-3: ONE OF THOSE DAYS

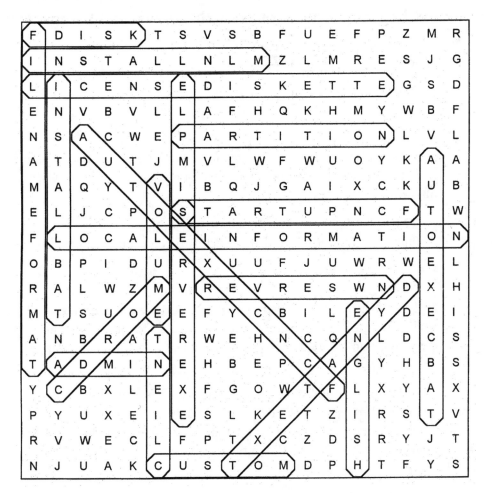

1. ADMIN
2. AUTOEXEC.BAT
3. AUTOEXEC.NCF
4. CD-ROM
5. CLIENT
6. CUSTOM
7. DYNATEXT
8. ENGLISH
9. FDISK
10. FILENAME FORMAT

11. INSTALL.BAT
12. INSTALL.NLM
13. LICENSE DISKETTE
14. LOCALE INFORMATION
15. NWSERVER
16. PARTITION
17. SERVER.EXE
18. SIMPLE
19. STARTUP.NCF
20. VOLUME

Chapter 7: IntranetWare/NetWare 4.11 Migration

ANSWERS TO QUIZZES

Q7-1
Puzzle!

Q7-2
Podunk is an unincorporated area in Massachusetts about six square miles in size. It houses about 100 families within East Brookfield town about 15 miles west of Worcester.

Q7-3
Tulips. She only likes words in which two consecutive letters of the alphabet appear.

Q7-4
If the woman were a Liar, she would have said she was a Truthteller. If she were really a Truthteller, she certainly would have said she was a Truthteller. Therefore, the young man reported truthfully, proving he was a Truthteller. Happy ending.

Q7-5
If his top speed is 100 m.p.h., he'll never get there. He'll be going 100 m.p.h. and be pushed backward at 100 m.p.h. He'll just have to wait until the wind dies down. Of course, if he could get the train up to 150 m.p.h., he could do it in four hours, but we've just said 100 m.p.h. is the top speed. Sorry.

EXERCISE 7-1: CHOOSING THE CORRECT MIGRATION METHOD

Scenario 1 — Finance Department

1. Across-the-Wire Migration. The original server would still be intact if anything went wrong during the upgrade.

2. Custom Installation. Because the original server is going to be used for a special project, it is not necessary to retain any of the current information. Thus, when the new server is fully up and operational,

you can delete the NetWare partition on the original server and do a Custom Installation of NetWare 4.11. Doing a Custom Install rather than a Simple Install would provide you with greater control of configurable parameters (such as specifying the container in which the server would be installed and creating multiple volumes).

3. Because the current server does not have a CD-ROM drive, you'd need to use the remote network installation area (that is, server-to-server) method for doing the installation. Using this method, you could mount the CD-ROM drive as a network drive on the new server, then log into the new server from the original server to do the installation. Also, you'd need to purchase additional RAM so that the server had a minimum of 20 MB total.

Scenario 2 — Facilities Department

1. Across-the-Wire, In-Place Upgrade or Same-Server.

2. In-Place Upgrade because it would allow you to upgrade a NetWare 2.2 server without purchasing additional hardware. (You might want to upgrade the hardware anyway, however, to take full advantage of NetWare 4.11 capabilities.)

3. You would need to perform the upgrade in two steps: First, you'd have to use the 2XUPGRD.NLM utility to upgrade from NetWare 2.2 to NetWare 3.1x and then would use the Upgrade option in the INSTALL.NLM utility to upgrade from NetWare 3.1x to NetWare 4.11.

4. There is too little RAM available. The Facilities department would need to purchase enough additional RAM so that the server had a total of 20 MB or more.

5. The IDE.DSK driver would not be a concern because the DOS partition is already of sufficient size (that is, at least 15 MB) and, thus, would not have to be re-created.

Scenario 3 — Pollution Department

1. Installation Program Upgrade

2. Installation Program Upgrade. This is the preferred method for upgrading from NetWare 4.1 to NetWare 4.11 and would not require a second server.

Scenario 4 — Marketing Department

1. Simple Installation method or Custom Installation method

2. Custom Installation. The Custom Installation method makes sense because the Marketing Manager wants to set up network security from scratch. Another reason for choosing the Custom Installation method is that you'd like to have more control over configurable parameters during the installation process than the Simple Installation method would allow — such as setting up multiple volumes.

3. There is insufficient hard disk space available on the SYS: volume. You'd either need to delete files to free up an appropriate amount of free space or move files to the VOL1: volume. There is also insufficient RAM — you'd need a minimum of 20 MB total.

4. The frame type of the source server would be a concern (since the default frame type for NetWare 3.11 is Ethernet 802.3 and the default frame type for NetWare 4.11 is 802.2).

Scenario 5 — Nuclear Department

1. Server-Server or Across-the-Wire

2. Same-Server because the Nuclear Department Manager does not want to start from scratch and there are no other NetWare 4.11 upgrade or migration methods available that are compatible with Banyan VINES which do not require additional hardware.

3. You can download migration programs for non-NetWare operating systems such as LAN Manager, LAN Server, VINES, and Windows NT from the Programs/Novell Consulting section of the Novell Corporate Home Page on the WorldWide Web (www.novell.com).

EXERCISE 7-2: TUESDAY MORNING

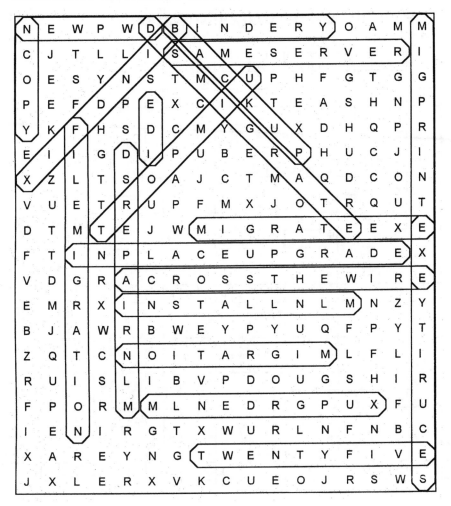

1. ACROSS-THE-WIRE
2. BACKUP
3. BINDERY
4. BINDFIX
5. DS MIGRATE
6. DSREPAIR.NLM
7. FILE MIGRATION
8. IDE
9. INPLACE UPGRADE
10. INSTALL.NLM

11. MIGPRINT.EXE
12. MIGRATE.EXE
13. MIGRATION
14. NCOPY
15. NEW.PWD
16. SAME SERVER
17. SECURITY.EXE
18. TWENTY-FIVE
19. UIMPORT
20. 2XUPGRDE.NLM

Part III: IntranetWare Installation

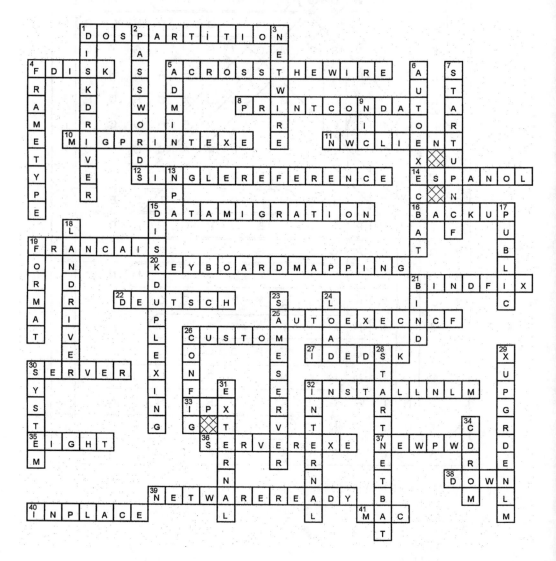

Chapter 8: Managing NDS

ANSWERS TO QUIZZES

Q8-1

232 entries — 229 matches were played; therefore, there must have been 229 losers. Add the two who scratched out without playing and then add the winner of the championship and you arrive at the total number of entries — 232.

Q8-2

79 years (there was not a year 0)

Q8-3

"This is hard because there are three choices for each number."

Q8-4

COLD, CORD, WORD, WARD, WARM

CASE STUDY: BUILDING ACME'S NDS TREE

We need a little help building ACME's NDS tree. In addition to the normal network resources, they have some special needs. Here's a quick list.

1. Each site needs a revolving administrator. This sounds like a job for Organizational Roles. Create an Organizational Role under each location OU. Use the following naming standard:

    NORAD-Admin in OU=NORAD.O=ACME

    RIO-Admin in OU=RIO.O=ACME

    CAM-Admin in OU=CAMELOT.O=ACME

    SYD-Admin in OU=SYDNEY.O=ACME

    TOK-Admin in OU=TOKYO.O=ACME

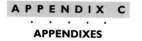

Then, assign the divisional administrator as the first occupant in each location O — AEinstein, GWashington, KingArthur, Gandhi, and SHolmes, respectively.

2. Next, create a common Profile Login Script object for all the administrators to share. It should be called ADMIN-Profile and placed in the O=ACME container. Remember, shared objects are placed higher in the tree. Finally, attach each Organizational Role to the shared login script by referencing the Profile object within each Organizational Role's Login Script property.

3. The Directory Map object saves the day. If the Human Rights (HR) tracking program is constantly changing, consider creating a Directory Map object as a point of central control. Then, all the HR login scripts can point to the central object, not the physical application directory. In this case, create an HR Directory Map object called HR-App, and place it in the .OU=HR.OU=SYDNEY.O=ACME container. Then, place the following directory in the Directory Map object's Path property:

    ```
    HR-SRV1/SYS:APPS\HRT
    ```

4. In addition, each of the HR administrators need access to the Human Rights tracking application in HR-SRV1/SYS:APPS\HRT. Security could be a problem. The Group object is your friend. Create a Group leaf object called HR-Group, and place it in the .OU=HR.OU=SYDNEY.O=ACME container. Then, create a Group Membership list with each of the HR administrators — Gandhi, ASchweitzer, MTeresa, FNightingale, and Buddha.

5. The people in the Auditing department need easy access to the Financial resources. There's a simple solution, and it allows the auditors to access these resources from within their home .OU=AUDIT container. Simply create an Alias object for .OU=FIN.OU=OPS.OU=CAMELOT.O=ACME, and place it in the .OU=AUDIT container. The Alias will point to the original objects from within the auditor's home context. Clever, huh?

6. In addition, the auditors and financial accountants need access to the ever-changing financial database program. Once again, the Directory Map object saves the day. In this case, create a Directory Map object called FIN-App and place it in the .OU=AUDIT.OU=ADMIN.OU=RIO.O=ACME and .OU=FIN.OU=OPS.OU=CAMELOT.O=ACME containers. Then, place the following directory in the Directory Map object's Path property:

    `CAM-FIN-SRV1/SYS:APPS\FIN`

7. The same holds true for the auditing application, except this time only the auditors need access to the Directory Map object. In this case, create a Directory Map object called AUD-App, and place it in the .OU=AUDIT.OU=ADMIN.OU=RIO.O=ACME container. Then, place the following directory in the Directory Map object's Path property:

    `AUDIT-SRV1/SYS:APPS\AUDIT`

8. To accommodate traveling users, we will create corresponding Alias objects for them in the very top of the ACME tree. This way, they can log in from anywhere with a very simple name context. For example, MCurie's alias becomes .MCurie.ACME. That's a big improvement over MCurie.NUC.R&D.LABS.NORAD.ACME. To accomplish this, create three user Alias objects (MCurie, AEinstein, and DHoliday), and place them in the O=ACME container. All done.

9. Everyone in the Crime Fighting division needs access to a common login script. Simply create a global Profile Login Script property called CRIME-profile, and place it in the .OU=CRIME.OU=TOKYO.O=ACME container. Don't forget to add CRIME-profile to each user's Login Script property.

10. To empower Leonardo's scientists, you'll need to create an Organizational Role called R&D-Admin. Place it in the OU=R&D.OU=LABS.OU=NORAD.O=ACME container, and give the Organizational Role Administrative rights over all R&D resources. Then, you can rotate the scientists through the Organizational Role, starting with LDaVinci. Make him the first occupant. It's as easy as 1-2-3.

Thanks for helping out. The world's in good hands with a CNE like you on the job!

EXERCISE 8-1: THE NDS GARDENER

U	S	E	R	T	E	M	P	L	A	T	E	X	Y	X	D	W
S	X	O	T	V	S	G	D	L	F	F	J	Q	Z	A	U	Y
E	E	G	B	U	M	I	G	I	H	G	U	P	T	D	E	M
R	E	F	E	R	R	A	L	L	I	S	T	J	C	U	E	V
E	R	C	R	N	N	S	I	N	G	L	E	L	O	G	I	N
P	N	E	T	A	D	M	I	N	E	T	U	S	E	R	F	A
L	A	L	W	Q	A	O	N	C	P	S	E	R	V	E	R	U
I	M	P	O	R	T	C	O	N	T	R	O	L	F	I	L	E
C	N	X	I	F	A	D	Q	E	G	E	D	G	C	J	P	M
A	E	F	K	L	F	G	R	K	U	S	M	Q	K	G	F	D
P	T	K	E	B	I	N	D	E	R	Y	O	B	J	E	C	T
O	S	C	S	R	L	C	B	W	J	H	Y	O	D	V	B	E
I	Y	B	J	O	E	D	M	O	E	Q	M	G	Q	Z	I	I
N	N	E	T	W	O	R	K	R	E	S	O	U	R	C	E	T
T	C	U	J	S	C	A	L	A	B	I	L	I	T	Y	Y	W
E	D	S	M	E	R	G	E	N	L	M	U	U	O	N	Q	Y
R	I	A	F	R	N	B	R	Y	K	H	S	T	J	O	J	R

1. BINDERY OBJECT
2. BROWSER
3. CLUSTER
4. DATA FILE
5. DSMERGE.NLM
6. IMPORT CONTROL FILE
7. NCP SERVER
8. NETADMIN
9. NETSYNC
10. NETUSER
11. NETWORK RESOURCE
12. NLIST
13. NNS
14. REFERRAL LIST
15. REPLICA POINTER
16. SCALABILITY
17. SINGLE LOGIN
18. USER
19. USER TEMPLATE
20. X.500

Chapter 9: Partition Management and Synchronization

ANSWERS TO QUIZZES

Q9-1

(a) Raccoon   (e) Samoyed

(b) Leopard   (f) Spaniel

(c) Terrier   (g) Carthorse

(d) Lioness   (h) African lion

Q9-2
$9 + 8 + 7 + 6 \div 5 - 4 - 3 + 2 - 1 = 0$

Q9-3
Three hours. After x hours,
A had burned $x/6$ leaving $6-x/6$.
B had burned $x/4$ leaving $4-x/4$.
But after x hours, A was twice as long as B. Therefore, $6-x/6 = 2(4-x)/4$. Therefore, $x = 3$.

Q9-4
$98 - 76 + 54 + 3 + 21 = 100$

EXERCISE 9-1: MASTERING SUBORDINATE REFERENCES

Challenge #1

A (Server S2 would have a Subordinate Reference for the SD and Sales partitions)

C (Server S4 would have a Subordinate Reference for the R&D partition)

D (Server S5 would have a Subordinate Reference for the ABC partition)

	[Root]	ABC	SD	AT	Admin	R&D	Mfg	Sales
S1	M	M	M	M	M	M	M	M
S2	R/W	R/W	SR				R/W	SR
S3								R/W
S4			R/W		R/W	SR		
S5	R/W	SR				R/W		
S6							R/W	

Challenge #2

B (Server S5 would have a Subordinate Reference for the [Root] partition)

E (Server S2 would have a Subordinate Reference for the LA and NY partitions)

	[Root]	ABC	LA	NY	Admin	IS	Finan	Mkt	Sales
S1		M	SR	SR	M		R/O		
S2	M	SR				M			
S3				R/W			R/W	SR	SR
S4	R/W	SR		M				M	R/W
S5		R/W	R/W					R/W	M
S6			M		R/W	SR	SR		
S7	M	SR					R/W	R/W	

Challenge #3

B (Server S4 would have a Subordinate Reference for the SF, LA, and R&D partitions)

C (Server S1 would have a Subordinate Reference for the LA, SD, and Admin partitions)

D (Server S3 would have a Subordinate Reference for the ABC and Mfg partitions)

	[Root]	ABC	SF	LA	SD	Admin	IS	Sales	R&D	Mfg
S1	M	M	M	SR	SR	SR	M			
S2						R/W	R/W			
S3	R/W	SR			M				M	SR
S4		R/W	SR	SR	R/W				SR	M
S5	R/O	R/O	SR	M	SR			M		
S6			R/W			M	SR			
S7									R/W	
S8									R/W	R/W

EXERCISE 9-2: INTRANETWARE PRUNING

```
V H U V K D E V N O I T I T R A P T O O R
F L O O S E C O N S I S T E N C Y Y A S E
K J A L Y F A G M A S T E R R E P L I C A
Q V F S N H R E W X W U D H X M O N S V D
P P A R T I T I O N R O O T O B J E C T O
J A A R H V S Y N C H R O N I Z A T I O N
J R F R E A D W R I T E R E P L I C A D L
S E B F T H H P J L Y K K H W L D V K Q Y
Q N G P I K I S Y S F B J Q I F H W O R
P T C A C V T P A R T I T I O N M E R G E
Y P A R T I T I O N O P E R A T I O N S P
T A T T I S U U O U K O K H B O V D E M L
I R T I M D X L E N H L D M I L X Y X Q I
M T P T E H M N W Y M C Z Y N L Y Z E X C
E I Y I L S P S E Q N A Y N P V S M R M A
S T K O R X H U K J J N N P S W O V G G L
Y I T N V M B M M R Q L R A X P O L M P I
N O X S E N D U P D A T E S G W D X T B S
C N Q P N X S Q V E O Q K B K D G R V T
C H I L D P A R T I T I O N J K R A A V Q
F V T I M E P R O V I D E R G R O U P G U
G E J T U L U C N J R R J J Q H H O G F A
```

1. CHILD PARTITION	11.	PARTMGR.EXE
2. DSTRACE	12.	READ-ONLY REPLICA
3. LOOSE CONSISTENCY	13.	READ/WRITE REPLICA
4. MASTER REPLICA	14.	REPLICA LIST
5. PARENT PARTITION	15.	[ROOT] PARTITION (with no brackets)
6. PARTITION MANAGER	16.	SEND UPDATES
7. PARTITION MERGE	17.	SYNCHRONIZATION
8. PARTITION OPERATIONS	18.	SYNTHETIC TIME
9. PARTITION ROOT OBJECT	19.	TIME PROVIDER GROUP
10. PARTITION SPLIT	20.	TIMESYNC.CFG

Chapter 10: IntranetWare File System

ANSWERS TO QUIZZES

Q10-1

28463

Q10-2

It doesn't matter what x is, because at some time during the calculation you will be multiplying by $(x-x)$, which equals 0; therefore, the product will be 0. Tricky!

Q10-3

69382

Q10-4

1, 4, 9, 6, 1, 5, 10, 4, 2

Now change to Roman numerals:

I, IV, IX, VI, I, V, X, IV, II

Very tricky, and I like it for that reason and because the Roman numeral IV appears in my name. Touché.

EXERCISE 10-1: MAPPING DRIVES WITH MAP

1. MAP /?

2. MAP

3. MAP F:=SYS:USERS

4. MAP G:=SYS:\SHARED\POL

5. MAP J:=F:

6. MAP S:=.WHITE.SRV1_SYS.WHITE.CRIME.TOKYO.ACME:SHARED

7. MAP INS S1:=SYS:\PUBLIC

8. MAP INS S2:=SYS:\PUBLIC\IBM_PC\MSDOS\V6.22

9. MAP S3:=APPS\SS30

10. MAP ROOT S4:=SYS:\APPS\DB50

11. MAP

    In the map list, the false root has no space after the volume name but does have a space followed by a backslash after the name of the directory it points to.

12. MAP S5:=W:=SYS:\APPS\WP70

    Yes.

13. The MAP command didn't work. To fix the problem, type **CD \PUBLIC.**

14. MAP DEL J:

15. MAP REM S3:

    The search drives with higher search drive numbers were renumbered accordingly.

    The network drive associated with the search drive was deleted.

16. MAP C S4:

    The search drive was deleted.

    The network drive associated with the search drive was moved to the top portion of the map list.

EXERCISE 10-4: NETWARE 4 FILE CABINET

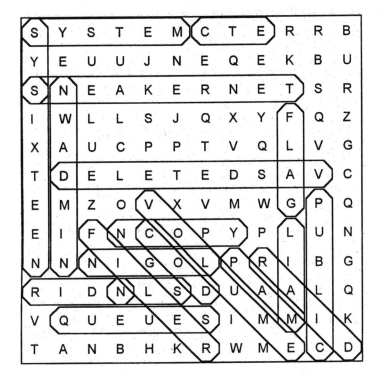

1. DELETED.SAV
2. DOC
3. ETC
4. FILER
5. FLAG
6. LOGIN
7. MAIL
8. MAP
9. NCOPY
10. NDIR
11. NLS
12. NWADMIN
13. PUBLIC
14. QUEUES
15. RAID
16. SIXTEEN
17. SNEAKERNET
18. SYS:
19. SYSTEM
20. VOLUME

Chapter 11: IntranetWare Security

ANSWERS TO QUIZZES

Q11-1

"A road map tells you everything except how to refold it." (Start at *A* in center.)

Q11-2

36421

Q11-3

He is abstemious. We discovered that he only likes words with all five vowels in them — an odd bird.

Q11-4

That's easy, man. It's "wrong."

Q11-5

ABORT: It is five letters long.
ACT: Last letter cannot be placed first to form another word.
AGT: Not an actual word. ALP: Does not end with a "T."
OPT: Does not start with "A."
APT: Not in alphabetical order with rest.

Q11-6

Here's the mysterious list:
MinutE
ExclamatioN
NavigatE
TeaR
AspirinG
LibertY
And, of course, the purpose of our journey is to generate as much "MENTAL ENERGY" as possible. Did we succeed?

QII-7

Maggie Simpson. That's what he gets for trying to steal candy from a baby. Mr. Burns certainly learned his lesson the hard way. Kudos to you, for figuring it out.

EXERCISE 11–1: CALCULATING NDS EFFECTIVE RIGHTS

CASE #1

See Figure C11.1 for answer to this case.

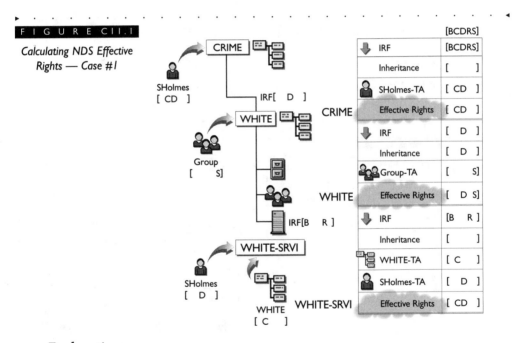

FIGURE C11.1

Calculating NDS Effective Rights — Case #1

Explanation:

Sherlock Holmes is granted CD rights to the CRIME Organizational Unit. Since he has no rights from any other source, and explicit trustee assignments override the Inherited Rights Filter (IRF) for this container, his effective rights for the CRIME Organizational Unit are [CD].

These rights then flow down to the WHITE Organizational Unit as inherited rights, where they are partially blocked by an IRF of [D] — leaving inherited rights of [D]. Sherlock Holmes also gets the [S] right to the WHITE Organizational

Unit as a member of the CRIME Group. If you add his inherited right of [D] to the [S] right granted to the CRIME-Group, you'll find that his effective rights for the WHITE container are [D S]. (Note: The fact that he has the [S] object right means that he implicitly has all object rights and all property rights for this object.)

Finally, his effective rights of [D S] in the WHITE container flow down and become inherited rights at the WHITE-SRV1 server, where they are blocked by an IRF of [B R]. (Even though he implicitly had all rights to the WHITE container, implied rights do not flow down — only explicit rights. Also, remember, that the [S] right CAN be blocked by an IRF in the NDS tree.) Sherlock Holmes does, however, receive an explicit trustee assignment of [D] to the WHITE-SRV1 server. His home container, the WHITE Organizational Unit, also receives a trustee assignment of [C] — meaning that his effective rights for the WHITE-SRV1 server are [CD].

CASE #2

See Figure C11.2 for answer to this case.

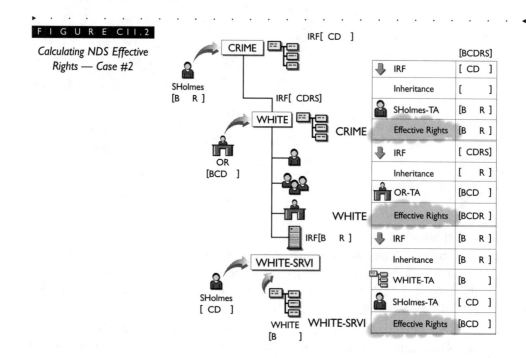

FIGURE C11.2

Calculating NDS Effective Rights — Case #2

Explanation:

In Case #2, Sherlock Holmes receives an explicit trustee assignment of [B R] to the CRIME Organizational Unit. Because he has no rights from other sources, and an explicit assignment overrides the IRF, his effective rights in the CRIME Organizational Unit are [B   R].

These rights then flow down and become inherited rights at the WHITE Organizational Unit, where they are partially blocked by an IRF of [CDRS] — leaving an inherited right of [R]. Sherlock Holmes also gets [BCD] rights through the CRIME-Admin Organizational Role, of which he is an occupant. If you add his inherited right of [R] to the [BCD] rights granted to the CRIME-Admin Organizational Role, you'll find that his effective rights for the WHITE container are [BCDR].

Finally, these rights flow down and become inherited rights at the WHITE-SRV1 server. These rights are partially blocked by the IRF of [B R] — leaving inherited rights of [B R]. The [R] inherited right is also blocked by a new trustee assignment made to the SHolmes User object (since explicit trustee assignments granted to the same object lower in the tree block inheritance to that same object from higher in the NDS tree.) In other words, the [CD] rights granted to the SHolmes User object for the WHITE-SRV1 server block the [R] inherited right that he originally received at the CRIME container. Sherlock Holmes also receives the [B   ] right that is granted to WHITE Organizational Unit, which is his home container. This means that Sherlock Holmes effective rights for the WHITE-SRV1 server are [BCD], which is a combination of his inherited right of [B   ], the [B   ] right he receives from the WHITE container, and the [CD] rights he receives from his User object.

CASE #3

See Figure C11.3 for answer to this case.

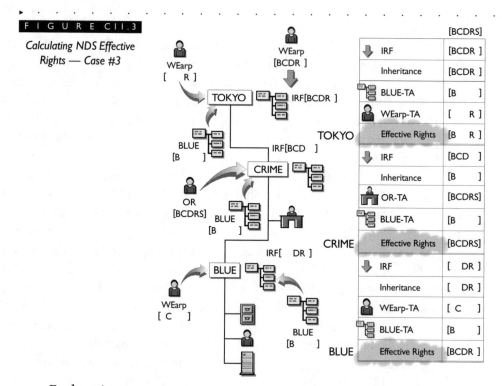

FIGURE C11.3

Calculating NDS Effective Rights — Case #3

Explanation:

In Case #3, Wyatt Earp inherits [BCDR] rights to the TOKYO Organizational Unit through a trustee assignment to his User object somewhere higher in the tree. These rights are then filtered by the Tokyo Organizational Unit's IRF of [BCDR] — which allows all four rights to flow through. He doesn't get to keep these rights, however, because his User object receives a new trustee assignment to the Tokyo Organizational Unit at this level — and such an assignment blocks inheritance from his User object from higher in the tree. Wyatt Earp does, however, receive the [B] trustee right for the TOKYO Organizational Unit from the Blue Organizational Unit, which is his home container, and the [R] right from his User object. This means that his inherited rights for the TOKYO container are [B] plus [R] or [B R].

These rights then flow down and become inherited rights at the CRIME Organizational Unit, where they are partially blocked by an IRF of [BCD] — leaving an inherited right of [B   ]. This right is also blocked, however, because the BLUE Organizational Unit receives a new trustee assignment to the CRIME Organizational Unit at this level — and such an assignment blocks inheritance for the BLUE Organizational Unit object from higher in the tree. Wyatt Earp does, however, receive [BCDRS] rights through the BLUE-Admin Organizational Role, of which he is an occupant and the [B   ] from the BLUE Organizational Unit, which is his home container. If you add the [BCDRS] rights that he receives from the BLUE-Admin Organizational Role to the [B   ] right he receives from the BLUE Organizational Unit, you'll find that his effective rights for the CRIME Organizational Unit are [BCDRS].

Finally, these rights flow down and become inherited rights at the BLUE Organizational Unit and are partially blocked by an IRF of [DR] — leaving inherited rights of [DR]. (Remember, the [S] right CAN be blocked by an IRF in the NDS tree.) Wyatt Earp also receives the [C   ] right to the BLUE Organizational Unit from his User object and the [B   ] right from the BLUE Organizational Unit, which is his home container. This means that his effective rights to the BLUE Organizational Unit are the [DR] rights, which he received through inheritance, plus the [C   ] right which he received from his User object, plus the [B   ] right which he received from the BLUE Organizational Unit — or [BCDR].

EXERCISE 11-2: CALCULATING FILE SYSTEM EFFECTIVE RIGHTS

CASE #1
See Figure C11.4 for the answer to this case.

FIGURE C11.4

Calculating File System Effective Rights — CASE #1

SYS:SHARED	S	R	C	W	E	M	F	A
Inherited Rights Filter	S	R	C	W	E	M	F	A
Inherited Rights-User								
Inherited Rights-Group								
Trustee Assignment-User		R	C	W			F	
Trustee Assignment-Group								
Effective Rights		R	C	W			F	

SYS:SHARED\CYBER	S	R	C	W	E	M	F	A
Inherited Rights Filter	S	R					F	
Inherited Rights-User		R					F	
Inherited Rights-Group								
Trustee Assignment-User								
Trustee Assignment-Group								
Effective Rights		R					F	

CYBER.DOC	S	R	C	W	E	M	F	A
Inherited Rights Filter		R	C	W			F	
Inherited Rights-User		R					F	
Inherited Rights-Group								
Trustee Assignment-User								
Trustee Assignment-Group								
Effective Rights		R					F	

CASE #2

See Figure C11.5 for the answer to this case.

► . . . . ◄

FIGURE C11.5

Calculating File System
Effective Rights —
CASE #2

SYS:SHARED	S	R	C	W	E	M	F	A
Inherited Rights Filter	S	R	C	W	E	M	F	A
Inherited Rights-User								
Inherited Rights-Group								
Trustee Assignment-User		R	C	W			F	
Trustee Assignment-Group								
Effective Rights		R	C	W			F	

SYS:SHARED\CRIME	S	R	C	W	E	M	F	A
Inherited Rights Filter	S							A
Inherited Rights-User								
Inherited Rights-Group								
Trustee Assignment-User								
Trustee Assignment-Group		R	C	W	E	M	F	
Effective Rights		R	C	W	E	M	F	

CRIME.DB	S	R	C	W	E	M	F	A
Inherited Rights Filter	S	R	C	W			F	
Inherited Rights-User								
Inherited Rights-Group		R	C	W			F	
Trustee Assignment-User								
Trustee Assignment-Group		R					F	
Effective Rights		R					F	

CASE #3

See Figure C11.6 for the answer to this case.

*Calculating File System
Effective Rights —
CASE #3*

SYS:SHARED	S	R	C	W	E	M	F	A
Inherited Rights Filter	S	R	C	W	E	M	F	A
Inherited Rights-User								
Inherited Rights-Group								
Trustee Assignment-User								
Trustee Assignment-Group		R	C	W	E		F	
Effective Rights		R	C	W	E		F	

SYS:SHARED\POL	S	R	C	W	E	M	F	A
Inherited Rights Filter	S							
Inherited Rights-User								
Inherited Rights-Group								
Trustee Assignment-User						M		A
Trustee Assignment-Group		R	C	W	E		F	
Effective Rights		R	C	W	E	M	F	A

CRIME.RPT	S	R	C	W	E	M	F	A
Inherited Rights Filter	S	R	C	W	E	M	F	A
Inherited Rights-User						M		A
Inherited Rights-Group		R	C	W	E		F	
Trustee Assignment-User								
Trustee Assignment-Group								
Effective Rights		R	C	W	E	M	F	A

CASE #4

See Figure C11.7 for the answer to this case.

*Calculating File System
Effective Rights —
CASE #4*

SYS:SHARED	S	R	C	W	E	M	F	A
Inherited Rights Filter	S	R	C	W	E	M	F	A
Inherited Rights-User								
Inherited Rights-Group								
Trustee Assignment-User	S	R	C	W	E	M	F	A
Trustee Assignment-Group								
Effective Rights	S	R	C	W	E	M	F	A

SYS:SHARED\CRIME	S	R	C	W	E	M	F	A
Inherited Rights Filter	S							
Inherited Rights-User	S							
Inherited Rights-Group								
Trustee Assignment-User								
Trustee Assignment-Group		R	C	W			F	
Effective Rights	S	R	C	W			F	

CRIME.DB	S	R	C	W	E	M	F	A
Inherited Rights Filter	S	R					F	
Inherited Rights-User	S							
Inherited Rights-Group								
Trustee Assignment-User								
Trustee Assignment-Group		R					F	
Effective Rights	S	R					F	

EXERCISE 11-3: HOW SECURE DO YOU FEEL?

T	S	M	W	O	D	N	Z	S	R	Y	L	L	O	R	U	G	X	K	D	W
R	T	I	M	E	R	E	S	T	R	I	C	T	I	O	N	S	K	E	T	L
U	A	S	E	F	F	E	C	T	I	V	E	R	I	G	H	T	S	L	X	D
S	T	S	Q	N	U	N	I	Q	U	E	P	A	S	S	W	O	R	D	S	Y
T	I	Q	F	V	Y	O	L	I	T	U	N	W	P	X	S	B	E	I	G	M
E	O	F	R	O	X	T	B	S	Y	W	M	Y	N	P	J	H	S	W	F	K
E	N	V	I	N	T	R	U	D	E	R	D	E	T	E	C	T	I	O	N	F
R	R	H	F	O	O	R	P	R	O	P	E	R	T	Y	R	I	G	H	T	S
I	E	C	I	P	T	R	N	J	X	I	O	F	O	E	U	Q	F	T	X	S
G	S	E	C	U	R	I	T	Y	E	Q	U	I	V	A	L	E	N	C	E	S
H	T	Z	Y	V	C	Z	Z	W	Q	L	O	R	C	C	Y	Z	M	M	M	E
T	R	D	Q	C	I	W	N	R	K	O	B	U	N	A	E	M	L	A	Q	O
S	I	N	U	F	I	F	O	M	M	S	K	V	S	L	K	F	P	G	T	Y
M	C	M	P	G	R	A	C	E	L	O	G	I	N	S	C	Y	J	H	X	G
A	T	O	B	J	E	C	T	R	I	G	H	T	S	D	I	L	R	O	Y	P
J	I	S	H	K	P	R	I	V	A	T	E	K	E	Y	L	Y	B	C	D	W
I	O	K	U	B	M	E	D	D	L	M	Y	P	N	R	B	I	B	E	H	D
Y	N	R	E	J	R	F	U	V	D	L	D	R	R	Q	U	E	Q	Y	T	F
R	S	J	X	U	E	D	A	T	A	E	N	C	R	Y	P	T	I	O	N	Q
G	O	U	N	C	P	P	A	C	K	E	T	S	I	G	N	A	T	U	R	E
C	F	G	J	X	G	O	J	G	L	Q	S	D	Q	S	V	Y	S	D	X	T

1. ACL
2. AUDITCON
3. DATA ENCRYPTION
4. EFFECTIVE RIGHTS
5. GRACE LOGINS
6. INTRUDER DETECTION
7. IRF
8. NCP PACKET SIGNATURE
9. OBJECT RIGHTS
10. PRIVATE KEY
11. PROOF
12. PROPERTY RIGHTS
13. [PUBLIC] (without the brackets)
14. PUBLIC KEY
15. SECURITY EQUIVALENCE
16. STATION RESTRICTIONS
17. TIME RESTRICTIONS
18. TRUSTEE RIGHTS
19. TTS
20. UNIQUE PASSWORDS

Chapter 12: IntranetWare Configuration

ANSWERS TO QUIZZES

Q12-1

The most common wrong answer is 25. If the problem had been, "What is the smallest number I must pick in order to be sure of getting at least two socks of *different* colors," then the correct answer would have been 25. But the problem calls for at least two socks of the *same* color, so the correct answer is three. If I pick three socks, then either they are all of the same color (in which case I certainly have at least two of the same color), or else two are of one color and the third is of the other color — so, I have two of the same color.

Q12-2

J.

Q12-3

The bear must be white — it must be a polar bear. The usual answer is that the bear must have been standing at the North Pole. Well, this is indeed one possibility, but it's not the only one. From the North Pole, all directions are south, so if the bear is standing at the North Pole and the man is 100 yards south of him and walks 100 yards east, then when he faces north, he will be facing the North Pole again. I'll buy that.

But, there are many more alternative solutions. It could be, for example, that the man is very close to the South Pole on a spot where the Polar circle passing through that spot has a circumference of exactly 100 yards, and the bear is standing 100 yards north of him. Then if the man walks east 100 yards, he would walk right around that circle and be right back at the point he from which he started.

In addition, the man could be a little closer to the South Pole at a point where the polar circle has a circumference of exactly 50 yards, so if he walked east 100 yards, he would walk around that little circle twice and be back where he started. You get the idea.

Of course, in any of these solutions, the bear is sufficiently close to either the North Pole or the South Pole to qualify as a polar bear. There is, of course, the remote possibility that some mischievous human being deliberately transported a brown bear to the North Pole just to spite us — who's paranoid?

Q12-4

Cerebrum

Q12-5

1. The biologist is not Catherine and not from Canada. Therefore, she belongs to C house (she must have one C).

2. If Catherine were the doctor, then she would have to come from Brazil (we know she's not from Australia), and if she were the doctor, she couldn't be from Denmark. Therefore, the doctor is from Brazil — but we are told the doctor is not from Brazil. Therefore, Catherine is not the doctor. Therefore, she must be the author.

3. The biologist is not from Australia and not from Canada. Therefore, she must be from Denmark.

4. Since the biologist is from C house and from Denmark, she must be Alice.

5. Therefore, the doctor is not Alice, and the doctor is not Catherine. Therefore, the doctor is Brett, and Deirdre must be the cartoonist.

6. Since the doctor is Brett, she is not from B house. Therefore, the doctor is from A house (the only alternative left). Therefore, the doctor is from Canada.

7. Since the cartoonist is Deirdre, she cannot be from D house. Therefore, she is from B house. Therefore, the cartoonist is from Australia.

8. Therefore, Catherine, the author, is from Brazil and was in D house.

Complete solution:

Alice	Biologist	C	Denmark
Brett	Doctor	A	Canada
Catherine	Author	D	Brazil
Deirdre	Cartoonist	B	Australia

Q12-6

Here's what was going on inside the cerebrum of "C." If anyone were to see two red and two black, he would know that he was white. If anyone were to see two red, one black, and one white, he would know that he could not be black. If he were, the man with the white disc would see two red and two black and would know that he was white. Similarly, if anyone were to see one red, two black, and two white.

If anyone were to see one red, one black, and two white, he would know that he could not be black. If he were, either of the men wearing white would see one red, two black, and one white, and would argue as above. If anyone were to see two red and two white, he would argue that he could not be black. If he were, someone would see two red, one black, and one white and would argue as above.

If anyone were to see one red and three white, he would argue that he could not be black. If he were, someone would see one red, one black, and two white and would argue as above; similarly, he would know that he could not be red. Therefore, if anyone sees me wearing red or black, he can deduce his color. Therefore, I must be white.

C really needs to get a life.

Q12-7

Ensign Chekov

CASE STUDY: CONFIGURING ACME'S LOGIN SCRIPTS

1. Create the Container login script for the PR Organizational Unit. (If you already did this step, proceed to Step 2.)

   a. Log in as the Admin user and run MS Windows. Switch to the first network drive on the server by typing **F:** and pressing Enter. Log in to the network as the Admin user by typing **LOGIN .ADMIN.ACME** and pressing Enter. Run MS Windows by typing WIN and pressing Enter.

b. Execute the NetWare Administrator utility.

1) Locate the Program Group icon containing the NetWare Tools, and double-click on it. Then, double-click on the NetWare Administrator Program Item icon to run the NetWare Administrator utility.

2) Double-click on the NORAD Organizational Unit using the right mouse button. A menu should be displayed. Select the Details option from the menu and press Enter.

3) Use the scroll bar along the right edge of the screen to display the Login Script button and click on it. Next, single click in the upper-right corner of the window located in the center of the screen.

c. Create the System (Container) login script for the Public Relations department.

1) Key in the appropriate statements for the Public Relations department Container login script using the clues in the Chapter 12 case study. (If you need help with what each script should look like, see Figures C12.1 and C12.2.)

2. Make the FDR user a member of the PRMGRS-Profile login script. (The PRMGRS-Profile login script is located in the ACME container.)

a. Identify PRMGRS-Profile as the name of the Profile Login Script object in the Profile login script field of the FDR's User's login script screen (see Figure C12.3).

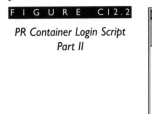

FIGURE C12.1

PR Container Login Script
Part I

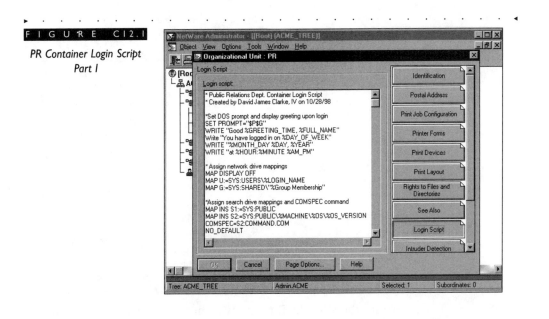

FIGURE C12.2

PR Container Login Script
Part II

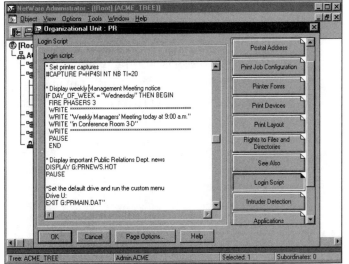

F I G U R E   C I 2 . 3

*Adding FDR to the
PRMGRS-Profile Login
Script Object*

b. Grant the User the R property right to the Login Script property of
the Profile. Also, make sure that the B right to the Profile Login
Script object that was granted by default to [Public] at the [Root]
has not been blocked by an IRF.

3. Login as the FDR user by typing LOGIN .FDR.PR.RIO.ACME and
pressing Enter. Watch as the Container and Profile login scripts are
automatically executed. Fix any errors that occur.

CASE STUDY: CONFIGURING THE ACME MENU SYSTEM

1. Create a custom menu:

```
; PR Main Menu
; Created by David James Clarke, IV on 10/28/99
MENU 01,Public Relations Main Menu
        ITEM   ^AApplications
               SHOW 10
        ITEM   ^EE-Mail
               EXEC WIN WMAIL
        ITEM   ^NNetWare Commands
               SHOW 20
        ITEM   ^LLog off the network
               EXEC LOGOUT
MENU 10,Applications
        ITEM   Database
               EXEC DB
        ITEM   Spreadsheet
               EXEC SS
        ITEM   Word Processing
               EXEC WP
MENU 20,NetWare Utilities
        ITEM   File Management
               EXEC FILER
        ITEM   NCOPY
               GETP Enter Source File(s): { }80,,{}
               GETP Enter Destination File(s): { }80,,{}
               EXEC NCOPY %1 %2
        ITEM   NLIST
               GETO Enter Class Name and Option: { }25,USER/A,{}
               EXEC NLIST
        ITEM   User Tools
               EXEC WIN NWUSER
        ITEM   WHOAMI
               EXEC WHOAMI
```

2. Compile and execute the custom menu (and debug any problems):

```
MENUMAKE PRMAIN.SRC <Enter>
```

```
NMENU PRMAIN.DAT <Enter>
```

(See Figure C12.4 for a sample of what the PR Main Menu should look like.)

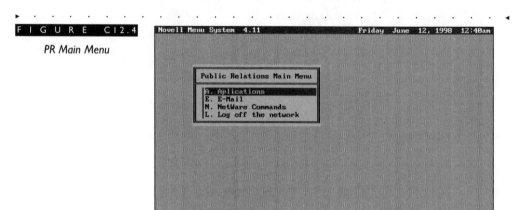

FIGURE   C12.4

PR Main Menu

EXERCISE 12-2: INTRANETWARE CHILDHOOD

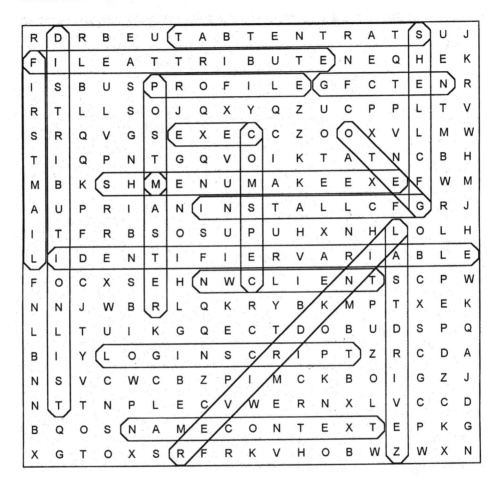

1. COMSPEC
2. DISTRIBUTION LIST
3. EXEC
4. FILE ATTRIBUTE
5. FIRST MAIL
6. GETO
7. IDENTIFIER VARIABLE
8. INSTALL.CFG
9. LASTDRIVE=Z
10. LINK DRIVER

11. LOGIN SCRIPT
12. MENUMAKE.EXE
13. MHS
14. NAME CONTEXT
15. NET.CFG
16. NWCLIENT
17. POSTMASTER
18. PROFILE
19. SHELL.CFG
20. STARTNET.BAT

▶ . . . . ◀

Chapter 13: IntranetWare Management

ANSWERS TO QUIZZES

Q13-1
Actually, the two trains will be at the *same* distance from Boston when they meet.

Q13-2
The answer is a quarter and a nickel. One of them (namely the quarter) is not a nickel.

Q13-3
Thanks — it's 3:31 p.m.

The only times that the hands of a watch are at right angles at an exact minute are 3:00 and 9:00. Since it was afternoon, we must be talking about 3:00 p.m. At 3:00 p.m., it was 30 minutes "before the half-hour." Also, at the next minute, it will be 60 seconds (twice as many seconds) after the same half-hour. Therefore, it's 3:31 p.m.

Q13-4
DAISY

Q13-5
Nice try. Roosters don't lay eggs.

Q13-6
Silence, Wedding Ring, Hole, Debt.

Q13-7
TYPEWRITER

Q13-8
Fools rush in where angels fear to tread. Which one are you?

CASE STUDY: SERVER MANAGEMENT AT ACME

1. VLM /U

    IPXODI /U

    NE2000 /U (or appropriate LAN driver)

    LSL /U

2. VLM /?

3. VLM /4

4. v1.20 (answers will vary)

5. Extended Memory (XMS)

6. CONN.VLM; NETX.VLM

7. The file server console prompt is displayed

8. A message is displayed indicating that a remote (RCONSOLE) connection has been granted. This is important to know in case unauthorized personnel (or worse yet, a hacker) have gained access to your file server console through the RMF utility.

9. AUTOEXEC.NCF; STARTUP.NCF

10. Single (that is, Single Reference)

11. 802.2

12. .2 percent (Answers will vary from .2 to 2 percent.)

13. No, this disk is not mirrored.

14. 64 KB. This default block size was assigned by the operating system

during the installation of IntranetWare on the server based on a hard disk size of 2+ GB. Your block size may vary. On the SYS: volume file compression and block suballocation are turned ON and data migration is turned OFF.

15. 25 (Answers will vary.)

16. If you wanted to create Client installation directories on the server or create client diskettes, you would choose Product options. Otherwise, you would load the IntranetWare /NetWare 4.11 Operating System CD-ROM and run INSTALL.BAT install.

17. 10 days, 2 hours, 6 minutes, and 34 seconds (answers will vary). The elapsed time since the server was last restarted is represented in the format DD:HH:MM:SS, where DD = number of days, HH = number of hours, MM = number of minutes, and SS = number of seconds. Current server utilization is at 8 percent (answers will vary). The total number of cache buffers currently being used would be the number of Original Cache Buffers (7,563) minus the Total Cache Buffers (6,131) (answers will vary). The number of current service processes in use is 5 (answers will vary). Twenty-three licensed connections are available at the moment (25 minus 2 in use).

18. Normal; no. (Answers may vary.)

19. IPX

20. DS.NLM; 677,208 bytes. (Size may vary.)

21. Idle loop (that is, polling)

22. Processor Uptime (called Server Up Time in MONITOR.NLM), Processor Utilization (called Utilization in MONITOR.NLM), Server Processes (called Current Service Processes in MONITOR.NLM), and Logged-in Users (called Current Licensed Connections in MONITOR.NLM).

23. SET command

24. Alt+F3; Alt+F1

25. The Transfer Files to Server option in SERVMAN performs a similar function to the Copy Files option in INSTALL.NLM. The difference between the two is that the RCONSOLE option copies the SYSTEM and PUBLIC files from the workstation's drive rather than the server's.

26. TRACK ON; ACME_TREE; answers will vary regarding the IPX internal network number of other server; AUTOEXEC.NCF in INSTALL.NLM, and CONFIG console command.

27. BROADCAST or SEND. You can acknowledge an incoming BROADCAST or SEND message displayed on the screen by pressing Ctrl+Enter. You can turn off receipt of incoming messages from other users by typing SEND /A=N at the workstation prompt after you exit RCONSOLE. (**Note:** You can also type **SEND /A=C** to receive SEND or BROADCAST messages from the server console only.)

28. DOS name space

29. HELP ALL

30. MODULES; SERVMAN.NLM

EXERCISE 13-1: INTRANETWARE ADULTHOOD

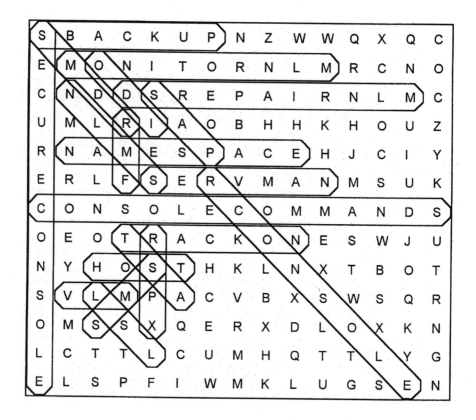

```
S  B  A  C  K  U  P  N  Z  W  W  Q  X  Q  C
E  M  O  N  I  T  O  R  N  L  M  R  C  N  O
C  N  D  D  S  R  E  P  A  I  R  N  L  M  C
U  M  L  R  I  A  O  B  H  H  K  H  O  U  Z
R  N  A  M  E  S  P  A  C  E  H  J  C  I  Y
E  R  L  F  S  E  R  V  M  A  N  M  S  U  K
C  O  N  S  O  L  E  C  O  M  M  A  N  D  S
O  E  O  T  R  A  C  K  O  N  E  S  W  J  U
N  Y  H  O  S  T  H  K  L  N  X  T  B  O  T
S  V  L  M  P  A  C  V  B  X  S  W  S  Q  R
O  M  S  S  X  Q  E  R  X  D  L  O  X  K  N
L  C  T  T  L  C  U  M  H  Q  T  T  L  Y  G
E  L  S  P  F  I  W  M  K  L  U  G  S  E  N
```

1.	CONSOLE COMMANDS	11.	RSPX
2.	DSREPAIR.NLM	12.	SAP
3.	HOST	13.	SBACKUP
4.	LSL	14.	SECURE CONSOLE
5.	MONITOR.NLM	15.	SERVMAN
6.	NAME SPACE	16.	SMDR
7.	NLMS	17.	SMS
8.	ODI	18.	TRACK ON
9.	RCONSOLE	19.	TSA
10.	RMF	20.	VLM

Chapter 14: IntranetWare Printing

ANSWERS TO QUIZZES

Q14-1

There were 12 friends in the group.

Q14-2

QUEUE — pretty sneaky, huh?

Q14-3

V (vowel) 1 = A, and so on
C (consonant) 1 = B, and so on
"Well done! Message successfully decoded."

Q14-4

Like so many puzzles of its type, this looks much more complicated than it really is. In fact, it has a beautifully simple solution. The trick is to first work out how long it takes the man to walk home. You know that the dog has been running for all this time at its given constant speed, so it is then simply a matter of working out how many miles the dog has covered during this period.

In this case, the man walks for 7 miles at 3 m.p.h., which means he takes 2 1/3 hours or 2 hours 20 minutes. Therefore, the dog is running for 2 1/3 hours at 8 m.p.h., which means it covers 18 2/3 miles.

Q14-5

This was a tough one. If you figured it out, you're definitely IntranetWare sleuth material. As a matter of fact, printing is a breeze compared to this brain puzzler.

7	13	4	10
2	12	5	15
9	3	14	8
16	6	11	1

CASE STUDY: BUILDING ACME'S PRINTING SYSTEM

Queue Creation

5. The user that created the queue (.Admin.ACME) and the container where the queue was created (.WHITE.CRIME.TOKYO.ACME) — because all users in the container usually need access.

6. There is a QUEUES directory off the root.

7. One or more.

Printer Creation

6. The print job owner disappears as the person to be notified.

7. The print job owner re-appears as the person to be notified.

Creating the Print Server

6. The context where the print server was created (.WHITE.CRIME.TOKYO.ACME) — because everyone in the container usually has access.

8. .Admin.ACME, because that is the user that created this print server.

10. Because the print server hasn't been loaded yet. It isn't yet running.

11. The print server is down.

Finding the Printer

9. The result of the search is CANONBJ-P1.WHITE.CRIME.TOKYO.ACME.

Loading the Print Server

4. It asks for a password.

5. Enter the password Secret.

7. The status is "waiting for a job; out of paper".

11. The CANONBJ-P1 printer is unloaded as well as the WHITE-SRV1 print server.

CASE STUDY: USING ACME'S PRINTING SYSTEM

3. Capturing is not currently active on LPT1, LPT2, or LPT3. In other words, they are all set to local ports.

4. An error will be displayed indicating that the default print job configuration cannot be found.

5. CX .WHITE.CRIME.TOKYO.ACME

6. CAPTURE Q=CANONBJ-PQ1

7. CAPTURE ENDCAP

13. Settings are: Form Feed, Auto Endcap, Enable Banner, First Banner Name=SHolmes, Second Banner Name=LPT1:, Copies 1.

17. Access not authorized. The only user authorized during print queue creation was the Admin.ACME user.

18. Use NetWare Administrator or PCONSOLE to assign SHolmes or his parent container as a print queue user.

19. Use CAPTURE (DOS), NetWare User Tools (Windows 3.1x) or the Printers icon in the Windows 95 Control Panel.

22. Double-click on the print queue and choose Job List to see the print job you just created when you did the print of the browser screen.

23. CAPTURE /SH

24. Use the DOS PRINT command. PRINT DOSFIL.TXT.

25. CAPTURE Endcap

26. Right mouse-click on the container WHITE.CRIME.TOKYO.ACME and choose Details. Next, choose Print Job Configuration, choose New, then choose the CANONBJ-PQ1 as the queue. Save the new configuration.

27. Choose the print queue by double-clicking. Choose Users. Add the context WHITE.CRIME.TOKYO.ACME to the list of allowed users.

29. CAPTURE still doesn't automatically set you up.

33. The workstation is captured with the settings of the default print job configuration for the .WHITE.CRIME.TOKYO.ACME container.

34. They match the settings in the "Main" print job configuration.

CASE STUDY: MANAGING ACME'S PRINTING SYSTEM

3. The value in the status field changes from "waiting for job" to "stopped".

4. Click on the Cancel button to return to the main NetWare Administrator browser screen. Use Ctrl+Esc to switch in the Windows Program Manager, then go ahead and execute the NetWare User Tools utility. In User Tools, use the "drag and drop" method to capture the

LPT1: port to the CANONBJ-PQ1 print queue, then click on the Exit button to leave the utility. Finally, use the Ctrl+Esc method to return to the NetWare Administrator utility, then select the Print option from the Object menu twice to generate two print jobs.

5. Two jobs submitted.

7. Print job shows user hold.

9. The second job now prints on the printer — the first is still held.

11. Double-click on the CANONBJ-P1 printer and then click on the Printer Status page button. The status will be shown as "offline."

12. The status field shows the percentage of the print job completed as it prints.

14. Each shows a status that indicates that is operational, namely: WHITE-PS1 shows "Running on NetWare server WHITE-SRV1," CANONBJ-P1 shows "Waiting for Job," and CANONBJ-PQ1 shows "Currently Being Serviced."

15. The print server unloads automatically.

16. The print server has an exclamation point next to it. This means the server is not available.

17. The print server should show that it's down.

18. Return to the main NetWare Administrator browser screen, then select the Print option from the Object menu to submit a new print job.

20. The jobs have reordered themselves to place the job just modified at the top of the queue.

EXERCISE 14-4: THE GREAT CHALLENGE

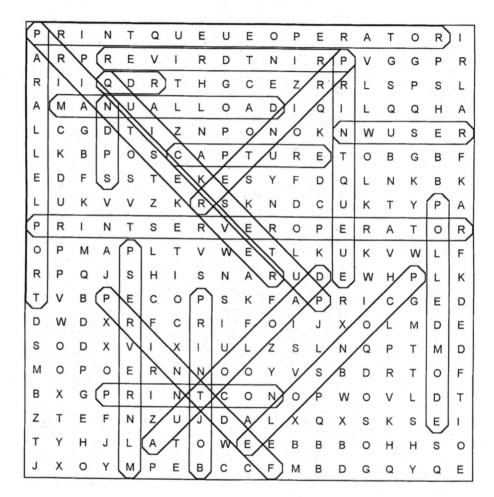

1. AUTO LOAD
2. CAPTURE
3. MANUAL LOAD
4. NDPS
5. NWUSER
6. PARALLEL PORT
7. PCONSOLE
8. POLLED MODE
9. PRINT DRIVER
10. PRINT JOB

11. PRINT QUEUE OPERATOR
12. PRINT QUEUE
13. PRINT SERVER OPERATOR
14. PRINT SERVER
15. PRINTCON
16. PRINTDEF
17. PRINTER
18. PSERVER.NLM
19. QDR
20. QUICK SETUP

Chapter 15: IntranetWare Optimization

ANSWERS TO QUIZZES

Q15-1
Tom, John, Bill, Pat, Kevin

Q15-2
None of them can be a Truthteller. The first man's statement cannot be true. If the second says something to indicate the first man is truthful, he is a Liar. The first man cannot be right. The second man is a Liar, as demonstrated, so the third man, who says the second man is telling the truth, must be a Liar. It is possible that the second man is a Truthteller, but he can't really be because the third man says the second is telling the truth, and he is a proven liar. Therefore, the second man is also lying. Check each one's statements against the others. Good monitoring! You have a future yet.

Q15-3
24198!!

Q15-4
5.5 - 5 × 55 × (5 — 5/5)
or
555/5 — 55/55

Q15-5
It contains the numbers 1 to 9 in alphabetical order.

EXERCISE 15-1: THE FINAL FRONTIER

```
G  A  R  B  A  G  E  C  O  L  L  E  C  T  I  O  N  F
F  I  L  E  C  A  C  H  I  N  G  M  K  U  Y  G  G  Y
I  A  J  N  I  N  O  P  T  I  M  I  Z  A  T  I  O  N
L  U  T  U  R  B  O  F  A  T  L  B  V  K  W  E  S  Q
E  U  P  V  X  J  E  Y  O  C  T  W  S  D  X  L  G  E
S  B  I  W  O  G  B  P  A  C  K  E  T  B  U  R  S  T
E  G  H  B  L  O  C  K  S  I  Z  E  S  Y  K  X  G  E
R  W  G  N  I  H  S  A  H  Y  R  O  T  C  E  R  I  D
V  D  I  R  T  Y  C  A  C  H  E  B  U  F  F  E  R  S
E  V  E  N  T  C  O  N  T  R  O  L  B  L  O  C  K  N
R  R  Q  T  J  L  V  V  Y  M  Q  Q  D  G  R  U  E  B
P  L  O  O  P  Y  R  O  M  E  M  Y  E  R  Y  C  N  R
R  D  J  M  N  K  C  T  N  E  B  O  I  H  H  I  B  P
O  D  S  K  C  E  N  E  L  T  T  O  B  O  G  L  L  G
C  A  C  H  E  U  T  I  L  I  Z  A  T  I  O  N  K  L
E  F  E  O  P  D  S  T  I  H  E  H  C  A  C  O  E  Q
S  U  G  E  Q  X  Q  P  S  W  J  Y  H  J  U  J  F  M
S  R  E  F  F  U  B  E  H  C  A  L  A  T  O  T  E
```

1.	BLOCK SIZE	11.	FILE SERVER PROCESS
2.	BOTTLENECKS	12.	GARBAGE COLLECTION
3.	CACHE HITS	13.	LIP
4.	CACHE UTILIZATION	14.	MEMORY POOL
5.	DET	15.	OPTIMIZATION
6.	DIRECTORY HASHING	16.	PACKET
7.	DIRTY CACHE BUFFERS	17.	PACKET BURST
8.	EVENT CONTROL BLOCK	18.	SET
9.	FAT	19.	TOTAL CACHE BUFFERS
10.	FILE CACHING	20.	TURBO FAT

Part IV: IntranetWare Management

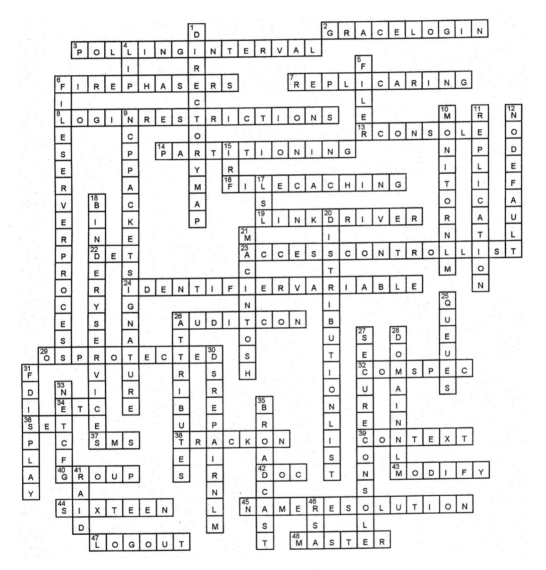

For More Information
and Help

Whenever a product becomes as popular and as widely used as NetWare and IntranetWare, an entire support industry crops up around it. If you are looking for more information about IntranetWare, you're in luck. There is a wide variety of places you can go for help, advice, information, or even just camaraderie.

NetWare and IntranetWare information is as local as your bookstore or local user group, and as international as the Internet forums that focus on Novell products. It can be as informal as articles in a magazine, or as structured as a college course. Best of all, it's easy to tap into most of these resources, wherever you may happen to be on the planet.

There is no point in trudging along through problems by yourself, when there is such a vast array of helpful people and tools at your fingertips.

 ZEN

"Worrying is like standing in a mud hole; it gives you something to do, but it doesn't get you anywhere."

Texas Bix Bender, *Laughing Stock, A Cow's Guide to Life*

This chapter describes the following ways you can get more information or technical support for NetWare. With a little digging, you can probably turn up even more resources than these, but these will get you started.

- ▸ General Novell product information

- ▸ *The Novell Buyer's Guide*

- ▸ Novell on the Internet

- ▸ Novell technical support

- ▸ *Novell's Support Connection*

- ▸ *Novell Application Notes*

- ▸ NetWare Users International (NUI)

- ▸ Novell Press books and other publications

- World Wire

- CyberState University

- *The Clarke Tests v3.0*

General Novell Product Information

The main Novell information number, 1-800-NETWARE, can be your inroad to all types of information about Novell and its products. By calling this number, you can obtain information about Novell products, the locations of your nearest resellers, pricing information, and so on.

The Novell Buyer's Guide

If you are responsible for helping find networking solutions for your organization, you may want to get a copy of the *Novell Buyer's Guide*. This guide is a complete book on everything you could possibly want to buy from Novell.

The *Novell Buyer's Guide* explains all the products Novell is currently offering, complete with rundowns on the technical specifications, features, and benefits of those products.

The *Guide* is available in a variety of formats, too. It is available on-line through Novell's on-line service on the Internet (www.novell.com) and through CompuServe (Go Netwire).

The *Novell Buyer's Guide* also comes on CD-ROM with the Novell's Support Connection (formerly NSEPro) which is explained later in this chapter. If you prefer the written version, you can order the Novell Buyer's Guide by calling one of the following phone numbers (which are all toll-free in Canada and the USA):

- 1-800-NETWARE

- 1-800-544-4446

- 1-800-346-6855

There may be a small charge to purchase the printed version of the *Buyer's Guide*.

▶ . . . . ◀

Novell on the Internet

A tremendous amount of information about Novell and NetWare products (both official and unofficial) is on the Internet. Officially, you can obtain the latest information about Novell from Novell's home page on the Internet, as well as from the Novell forums on CompuServe. Unofficially, there are several active user forums that deal specifically with Novell products, or generally with computers.

Novell's on-line forums offer you access to a wide variety of information and files dealing with IntranetWare and other Novell products (such as GroupWise, LAN Workplace, IntranetWare and ManageWise). You can receive information such as technical advice from sysops (system operators) and other users, updated files and drivers, and the latest patches and workarounds for known problems in Novell products.

ZEN

"Though a program be but three lines long, some day it will have to be maintained."

Geoffrey James, *The Zen of Programming*

Novell's on-line sites also provide a database of technical information from the Novell Technical Support division, as well as information about programs such as Novell Education classes and NetWare Users International (NUI). In addition, you can find marketing and sales information about the various products that Novell produces.

Novell's Internet and CompuServe sites are very dynamic, well-done, and packed with information. They are frequently updated with new information about products, education programs, promotions, and the like. In fact, the technical support features of NetWire on the Internet even garnered a place on the "What's Cool" list of Internet sites from Netscape.

Novell's Internet site is managed by Novell employees and by sysops who have extensive knowledge about NetWare and IntranetWare. Public forums can be quite active, with many knowledgeable users offering advice to those who experience problems.

TIP

To get technical help with a problem, post a message and address the message to the sysops. (But don't send the sysops a personal e-mail message asking for help — the public forums are the approved avenue for help.)

To access the Novell forums on CompuServe, you need a CompuServe account. There is no additional monthly fee for using the Novell forums, although you are charged the connection fee (on an hourly rate) for accessing the service. To get to the Novell forums, use GO NETWIRE. There, you will find information for new users, telling you how the forums are set up, how to get technical help, and so on.

If you have a connection to the Internet, you can access Novell's Internet site in one of the following ways:

▶ **World Wide Web:** http://www.novell.com

▶ **Gopher:** gopher.novell.com

▶ **File Transfer Protocol (FTP):** anonymous FTP to ftp.novell.com

(Users in Europe should replace .com with .de.)
To get to the Novell site on the Microsoft Network, use GO NETWIRE.

Novell Technical Support

If you encounter a problem with your network that you can't solve on your own, there are several places you can go for immediate technical help.

ZEN

"When you find yourself in over your head, don't open your mouth. Swim!"

Texas Bix Bender, *Laughing Stock, A Cow's Guide to Life*

Try some of the following resources:

▸ Try calling your reseller or consultant.

▸ Go on-line, and check out the Technical Support areas of Novell's Internet site. There, you will find postings and databases of problems and solutions. Someone else may have already found and solved your problem for you.

▸ While you're on-line, see if anyone in the on-line forums or Usenet forums knows about the problem or can offer a solution. The knowledge of people in those forums is broad and deep. Don't hesitate to take advantage of it, and don't forget to return the favor if you know some tidbit that might help others.

▸ Call Novell Technical Support. You may want to reserve this for a last resort, simply because Novell Technical Support charges a fee for each incident (an "incident" may involve more than one phone call, if necessary). The fee depends on the product for which you're requesting support.

When you call Technical Support, make sure you have all the necessary information ready (such as the versions of NetWare and any utility or application you're using, the type of hardware you're using, network or node addresses and hardware settings for any workstations or other machines being affected, and so on). You'll also need a major credit card.

To get to Novell's Technical Support, call 1-800-858-4000 (or 1-801-861-4000 outside of the U.S.).

Novell's Support Connection

A subscription to *Novell's Support Connection* formerly known as the *Novell Support Encyclopedia Professional Volume* (NSEPro), can update you every month with the latest technical information about Novell products. *Novell's Support Connection* is two CD-ROMs containing technical information such as:

▸ Novell technical information documents

- ▶ Novell Labs hardware and software test bulletins

- ▶ On-line product manuals

- ▶ *Novell Application Notes*

- ▶ All available NetWare patches, fixes, and drivers

- ▶ The *Novell Buyer's Guide*

- ▶ Novell corporate information (such as event calendars and press releases)

Novell's Support Connection includes Folio information-retrieval software that allows you to access and search easily through the *Novell's Support Connection* information from your workstation using DOS, Macintosh, or Microsoft Windows.

ZEN

"If computers get too powerful, we can organize them into a committee — that will do them in."

from "Bradley's Bromide"

To subscribe to *Novell's Support Connection*, contact your Novell Authorized Reseller or Novell directly at 1-800-377-4136 (in the United States and Canada) or 1-303-297-2725. Also, please find a complete copy of *Novell's Support Connection* on the two CD-ROMs bound in this book. We give, because we care!

Novell Application Notes

Novell's Research department produces a monthly publication called the *Novell Application Notes*. Each issue of *Novell Application Notes* contains research reports and articles on a wide range of topics. The articles delve into topics such as network design, implementation, administration, and integration.

A year's subscription costs $95 ($135 outside the United States), which includes access to the *Novell Application Notes* in their electronic form on Compu-Serve. An electronic-only subscription costs $35 (plus access charges).

To order a subscription, call 1-800-377-4136 or 1-303-297-2725. You can also fax an order to 1-303-294-0930.

NetWare Users International (NUI)

IntranetWare Users International (NUI) is a nonprofit association for networking professionals. With more than 250 affiliated groups worldwide, NUI provides a forum for networking professionals to meet face-to-face, to learn from each other, to trade recommendations, or just to share "war stories."

ZEN

"I believe in computer dating, but only if the computers are truly in love."

Groucho Marx

By joining the NetWare user group in your area, you can take advantage of the following benefits:

- Local user groups that hold regularly scheduled meetings.

- *NetWare Connection*, a bimonthly magazine that provides feature articles on new technologies, network management tips, product reviews, NUI news, and other helpful information.

- A discount on Novell Press books through the *IntranetWare Connection* magazine and also at NUI shows.

- NUInet, NUI's home page on the World Wide Web (available through Novell's home site, under "Programs," or directly at http://www.nuinet.com), which provides NetWare 3 and IntranetWare technical information, a calendar of NUI events, and links to local user group home pages.

▸ Regional NUI conferences, held in different major cities throughout the year (with a 15 percent discount for members).

The best news is, there's usually no fee or only a very low fee for joining an NUI user group.

For more information or to join an NUI user group, call 1-800-228-4NUI or send a fax to 1-801-228-4577.

For a free subscription to *IntranetWare Connection*, fax your name, address, and request for a subscription to 1-801-228-4576. You can also mail NUI a request at:

NetWare Connection
P.O. Box 1928
Orem, UT 84059-1928
USA

REAL WORLD

You don't even have to officially join NUI to get a subscription to *IntranetWare Connection*, but don't let that stop you from joining. "Networking" with other NetWare and IntranetWare administrators can help you in ways you probably can't even think of yet.

Novell Press Books and Other Publications

Every year, more and more books are being published about NetWare and IntranetWare and about networking in general. Whatever topic you can think up, someone's probably written a book about it.

Novell Press itself has an extensive selection of books written about NetWare and IntranetWare and other Novell products. For an up-to-date Novell Press catalog, you can send an e-mail to Novell Press at novellpress@novell.com.

You can also peruse the selection of books on-line. From Novell's main Internet site (http://www.novell.com), you can get to the Novell Press area (located under "Programs"). You can also get to the same location by going directly to http://corp.novell.com/programs/press.

In addition to books, there are a wide variety of magazines that are geared specifically toward networking and general computing professionals, such as *Network News*, *IntranetWare Connection* (from NUI), *LAN Times*, *PCWeek*, and so on.

World Wire

World Wire is an on-line service that gives you incredible new educational avenues for learning about NetWare. It provides you with technical support, technical information, Internet access, testing, and other benefits.

In addition, World Wire gives you access to actual, on-line IntranetWare, NetWare 4.1, and NetWare 3 LANs so that you can get some hands-on experience in the safety of a practice environment, rather than in your real, production environment.

For more information, call 1-510-253-TREK.

CyberState University

CyberState University is the world leader in on-line network certification training. They were the first organization in the world to develop and deliver complete certification training via the Internet. They offer complete CNA, CNE, MCSE, and other programs for a fraction of cost of traditional courses. All of this is made possible because of their proprietary *Synergy Learning System*. Let's take a closer look.

THE SYNERGY LEARNING SYSTEM

CyberState University has developed the Synergy Learning System (SLS) to reduce a student's total study time by accelerating retention and improving recall of course material. The SLS accomplishes these goals by combining multiple teaching mediums into a structured learning environment. These mediums incorporate visual, auditory, and kinesthetic sensory inputs into the educational process. Typically, a student will use one of these inputs as the primary method of learning, and then rely on the other two for reinforcement. The result is quicker absorption and easier recall of complex course material.

Here's a quick list of the many different media used at CyberState University:

▸ Study Guides from #1 best-selling authors (including this book).

▸ Video tapes which focus on "how to do it."

▸ On-line lectures to direct study efforts.

▸ On-line review sessions to reinforce key concepts.

▸ On-line assignments in a live, network Practice Lab. This anchors the course material with "hands-on" experience.

▸ Multimedia skills assessment to focus on critical study strengths and weaknesses.

▸ Multimedia testing to measure proficiency with the course material.

▸ On-line interaction with student from all over the world via "chat forums."

▸ On-line support from instructors via CyberState University's e-mail system.

▸ SmartLinks to related study material anywhere on the Internet.

It's the interactive combination of the complementary teaching media that makes up the SLS. By accelerating retention and improving recall, this innovative on-line curriculum reduces the total number of study hours you need to become a CNA, CNE, or MCSE.

THE CURRICULUM

CyberState University offers a variety of programs for Novell or Microsoft certification training. All of them use the SLS and cost 60 to 75 percent less than traditional courses. Here's a list of the most popular on-line programs and some benefits of CyberState's approach:

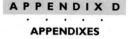

▸ *Novell CNE* — Choose from three programs: CNE-3, CNE-4, and IntranetWare CNE. Each program takes approximately 25 weeks and includes 6 required courses and 1 elective.

▸ *Novell CNE-3/CNE-4* — Combine the CNE-3 and CNE-4 tracks into a single, valuable dual certification. It only takes a few extra weeks.

▸ *Novell CNA* — Choose from three programs: CNA-3, CNA-4, and IntranetWare CNA. Each program takes approximately six weeks and provides a clear upgrade path to the CNE.

▸ *Microsoft MCSE* — Custom tailor your certification from a list of several required and elective courses. Most programs last 30 weeks and cover a total of 6 courses.

▸ *Microsoft MCP* — Choose from several MCP-certification programs, each covering one Microsoft course. Combine MCP certificates to provide the most comprehensive coverage.

▸ *Novell CNE/Microsoft MCSE* — the ultimate certification. This combined Novell and Microsoft certification lasts approximately 50 weeks and covers 13 courses. It provides the greatest prize in the network arena. Students who complete this program will be head-and-shoulders above everybody else in the highly competitive networking job market.

▸ CyberState University has enjoyed a 100 percent certification rate for students who complete the curriculum. That means that every student who finishes becomes a CNE — hundreds of them.

▸ Study any time from anywhere with 24-hour Internet access. You also enjoy unlimited access to campus facilities, including a virtual student union, practice lab, classrooms, and more.

▸ Log in, with Supervisory access, to several servers in the CyberState University practice lab. This gives you the "hands-on" experience with Novell, Microsoft, and third-party products you need to pass Simulation-based and Performance-based certification exams.

▶ Completion of the certification exams is incorporated into the course schedule. Also, you have guaranteed support resources throughout the curriculum. A real person is always there to help you succeed.

▶ Study time is paced to three to four hours per week. In addition, your course length may be adjusted to meet individual needs. CyberState University is very flexible and understanding. Their goal is your goal: Get certified!

FOR MORE INFORMATION ...

CyberState University is behind you every step of the way. Becoming a CNE or MCSE has never been easier, or more fun. If you need a little more help:

▶ Surf the Web at http://www.cyberstateu.com.

▶ Fax us at 1-510-254-9349.

▶ If you'd like to speak to a "real" person, call 1-888-GET-EDUC or 1-510-253-8753 (*internationally*).

Good Luck, and thanks for learning with us.

The Clarke Tests v3.0

Welcome to *The Clarke Tests v3.0*! It is unlike anything you have ever seen. It is more than just sample test questions — this is an Interactive Learning System for CNEs.

The CD-ROM included with this book contains a special Novell Press edition of *The Clarke Tests v3.0* for CNEs. Here's a more detailed look at this wonderful, multimedia learning system.

ZEN

"The Teacher is like the candle which lights others in consuming itself!"

Giovanni Ruffini

FOUR STUDY MODULES TO CHOOSE FROM

Let us help you become a CNA or CNE! The entire *Clarke Tests* collection includes 12 courses, nearly 100 tests, and more than 4,000 study sessions on an interactive CD-ROM. Each test teaches you specific CNE objectives within a subsection of a required CNE course. *The Clarke Tests v3.0* offers four different study modules covering four major Novell certifications — NetWare 4.11 Certified Novell Engineer (CNE-4), NetWare 3.12 CNE (CNE-3), and both Certified Novell Administrators (CNA-4 and CNA-3). Here's a breakdown of the four *Clarke Tests* modules and their corresponding certifications:

- ▸ NetWare 4.11 CNE Target Courses — *part 1 of CNE-4*

- ▸ NetWare 3.12 CNE Target Courses — *part 1 of CNE-3*

- ▸ Core Technologies and Electives — *part 2 of CNE-4/CNE-3*

- ▸ NetWare 3.12 and 4.11 CNA — *covers CNA-4/CNA-3*

THE INTERACTIVE LEARNING SYSTEM

The Clarke Tests v3.0 uses a multimedia, Windows-based interface to maximize your learning potential. This interface closely resembles the software used by Sylvan Prometric and Drake Technologies for actual CNE certification. The goal is to prepare you for the entire testing experience, not just the test objectives. In addition, LearningWare has enhanced the interface to create a complete Interactive Learning System. Here's how it works.

The Tests

Each CNE course is divided into Study and Certification tests. *Study Tests* cover specific CNE objectives within a subsection of a required CNE course. They encompass 35 to 120 questions with the help of a proprietary Navigator. The Navigator allows you to answer questions in any order and return to previously answered questions for review. In addition, we've provided actual CNE *Certification Tests* for adaptive, form, simulation, and performance-based courses. Use the Study Tests to learn and the Certification Tests to prepare.

The Questions

Questions in *The Clarke Tests v3.0* are more than simple, one-dimensional brain teasers; they are complete interactive *Study Sessions*. They include a variety of learning tools to keep things interesting and make learning fun. Each of the following study session types presents the CNE study material in a slightly different way. This forces you to "truly" understand the testing objectives:

▶ *Hot Spots* — "Real life" graphical exhibits that test your hands-on knowledge.

▶ *Performance-based* — A *new* Novell testing strategy for Service and Support and NetWare 4.11 material. These questions test your ability to solve NetWare-related problems.

▶ *Traditional Multiple Choice* — One or more correct answers per question.

▶ *Matching* — Combine many NetWare topics in one interactive study session.

▶ *Fill-In* — Require tough "open-ended" answers.

In addition, many study sessions include graphical exhibits. These exhibits enhance your learning experience by providing screen shots, 3-D graphics, and professional case studies. Finally, if your stuck along the way, *The Clarke Tests v3.0* offers interactive Clues in a separate window. These clues allow you to continue studying without divulging the complete answer. We are with you every step of the way!

Interactive Answers

These are the real stars of the show. Each study session includes a full page or more of explanation and CNE study material. Instead of just displaying the answer, we explain it in detail. In addition, each Interactive Answer includes page references to Novell Authorized courseware, the CyberState University on-line CNE program, *Novell's CNE Study Guide*, *Novell's CNE Study Guide for NetWare 4.1*, *Novell's CNE Study Guide for Core Technologies*, *Novell's CNA Study Guide for NetWare 4.1*, NetWare documentation, and the "So You Wanna Be A CNE?!" video series.

Tracker Scoring

The Clarke Tests v3.0 includes an exciting *new* interactive scoring system called *The Tracker*. The Tracker is a separate module that gathers detailed information about your performance on individual CNE tests. It classifies your results according to key testing objectives and presents them in a table format. Here's how it works:

- ▸ *Certification Scoring* — All actual CNE certification exams are scored on an 800 scale. In order to pass, you must exceed a specific threshold for each course. *The Clarke Tests v3.0* uses the same 800 scale and built-in thresholds as the actual exams. This allows you to accurately assess your chances of passing any given CNE exam.

- ▸ *Prescription Reports* — A series of detailed testing objectives are included with each exam. Your performance in each study area is tracked to help you identify your strengths and weaknesses. *The Clarke Tests v3.0* also includes comprehensive Prescription Reports to help you isolate specific areas of study and track testing improvement.

- ▸ *Database Analysis* — The Tracker data can be exported to numerous database and spreadsheet programs for further graphical analysis. This is a great way to chart your CNE progress.

Tracker scoring is a great way to build custom CNE study sessions. You can trust that when the Clarke Professor says your ready for the real CNE exam. . . . you're ready! Good Luck, and let us help you become a CNE!

 ZEN

"I'll never take another CNE exam without first taking The Clarke Tests!"

Bill King

INSTALLING *THE CLARKE TESTS V3.0*

To install *The Clarke Tests v3.0*, insert the CD-ROM into your CD drive (drive D:, for example).

1 • If you are using Microsoft Windows 95, select Start and Run. Type **D:\CLARKE95\SETUP** in the input window and click OK. (Remember that drive D: is the CD-ROM drive.)

2 • If you are using Microsoft Windows 3.1, select File and Run. Type **D:\CLARKE31\SETUP** in the input window and click OK. (Remember that drive D: is the CD-ROM drive.)

3 • *The Clarke Tests v3.0* Setup will install the Delivery Module ("Clarke!!"), Tracker, and Administrator. By default, *all* tests will be highlighted. Click on any tests you do not want to install and the system will deselect them.

4 • As each test is installed, Setup will ask for a test directory. We recommend that you separate courses into different subdirectories and only install the tests on which you are currently working. In addition, *The Clarke Tests v3.0* includes a "Save" feature that allows you to exit a test without losing your place.

5 • Have Fun!

USING *THE CLARKE TESTS V3.0*

Once *The Clarke Tests v3.0* have been installed correctly, you will notice three icons in The Clarke Test program group. The "Clarke!" icon runs the interactive learning system, the "Admin Maker" is for test administration, and "Tracker" monitors your progress and prints Prescription Reports. Here are a few tips on using *The Clarke Tests v3.0*:

▸ *In the Beginning* — To begin *The Clarke Tests*, select "Clarke!" from the Start menu in Windows 95, or double click on the "Clarke!" icon within Windows 3.1. Next, choose a test and enter your name. Let the tests begin.

▸ *Navigation* — To navigate questions, simply click on the question number or use the arrows at the bottom right-hand corner of the screen. Indicate your desired response by clicking on the appropriate radio button, or by entering text into the fill-in or matching spaces provided. The radio button is the white circle or square to the left of a selection.

. . . . . .

▸ *Clues* — The "Help" button provides clues to guide you in the right direction. Don't worry, they don't give away the answer. When you are finished viewing the Clue, click the Done button to return to the question.

▸ *Interactive Answers* — The Info button provides a detailed answer for each question, including page references to numerous study aids. This is the Interactive Answer. When you are finished viewing the study material, click the Done button to return to the question.

▸ *Scoring* — Once you have completed a question, move to the next one. The Professor will automatically score your response. Correct answers will appear in green, while incorrect responses turn red. Look for lots of green!

▸ *Custom Reports* — Each test includes a detailed Prescription Report. The report helps you identify your strengths and weaknesses by comparing your results against actual CNA and CNE testing objectives. Also, the Professor will allow you to generate sophisticated custom reports using the Tracker Module. With all this help, you are just moments away from an exciting new life as a NetWare or IntranetWare CNA or CNE.

FOR MORE INFORMATION . . .

The Clarke Tests Professor is behind you every step of the way. Becoming a CNA or CNE has never been easier, or more fun. If you need a little more help:

▸ Try *The Clarke Tests* Tutorial — It's a great start!

▸ Check out the "README.CLK" file on the CD-ROM for installation instructions and last-minute changes or suggestions.

▸ Surf the Web at http://www.cyberstateu.com/clarke.htm.

▸ Fax us at 1-801-423-2367.

▸ If you must speak to a "real" person call **1-800-684-8858** for orders and technical support.

Index

INDEX

IDG BOOKS WORLDWIDE, INC.—END-USER LICENSE AGREEMENT

Novell's CNE® Study Guide for Core Technologies

by David James. Clarke, IV

The ideal preparation guide for the two non-NetWare specific exams required for CNE® certification: Service and Support (801) and Networking Technologies (200). This study guide contains real-world case studies, sample test questions and other valuable information. You'll also receive the exclusive Novell NetWire Starter Kit, the ClarkTests v.2 and MICROHOUSE I/O Card Encyclopedia demo.

932 pp plus CD-ROM
$74.99 USA
$104.99 Canada
0-7645-4501-9

Novell's CNA℠ Study Guide for IntranetWare™

by David James Clarke, IV and Kelley J.P. Lindberg

A must for system managers studying for their CNA℠ credential. Organized and easy-to-read, this resource covers all CNA course material including NetWare 2.2 and NetWare 3.1x with real-world scenarios, sample tests and a live on-line NetWare lab. The accompanying Novell Advantage CD contains Novell exclusive software.

700 pp plus CD-ROM
$69.99 USA
$96.99 Canada
0-7645-4513-2

Novell's CNE® Study Guide for IntranetWare™

by David James Clarke, IV

Learn all aspects of Novell's IntranetWare CNE program as well as NDS design and implementation. Covers certification courses 520, 525, 526, 532 and 804. Includes a free Novell Support Connection CD plus hundreds of CNE test questions.

1600 pp plus CD-ROM
$89.99 USA
$124.99 Canada
0-7645-4512-4

Novell's Four Principles of NDS™ Design

by Jeffrey F. Hughes and Blair W. Thomas

Take full advantage of the powerful new features of the NetWare 4 operating system with this clearly illustrated reference guide zeroing in on four essential Novell Directory Services (NDS) design principles: physical infrastructure, organizational structure, optimal partition size and minimum replicas placements, and time synchronization.

343 pp
$39.99 USA
$54.99 Canada
0-7645-4522-1

SMART BOOKS™
from the Novell Experts

IDG BOOKS WORLDWIDE REGISTRATION CARD

Title of this book: Novell's CNE® Study Guide—IntranetWare™: NetWare® 4.11

My overall rating of this book: ❏ Very good [1]   ❏ Good [2]   ❏ Satisfactory [3]   ❏ Fair [4]   ❏ Poor [5]

How I first heard about this book:

❏ Found in bookstore; name: [6] _____

❏ Advertisement: [8]

❏ Word of mouth; heard about book from friend, co-worker, etc.: [10]

❏ Book review: [7]

❏ Catalog: [9]

❏ Other: [11]

What I liked most about this book:

_____
_____
_____

What I would change, add, delete, etc., in future editions of this book:

_____
_____
_____

Other comments:

_____

Number of computer books I purchase in a year: ❏ 1 [12]   ❏ 2-5 [13]   ❏ 6-10 [14]   ❏ More than 10 [15]

I would characterize my computer skills as: ❏ Beginner [16] ❏ Intermediate [17] ❏ Advanced [18] ❏ Professional [19]

I use ❏ DOS [20] ❏ Windows [21] ❏ OS/2 [22] ❏ Unix [23] ❏ Macintosh [24] ❏ Other: [25]_____

(please specify)

I would be interested in new books on the following subjects:

(please check all that apply, and use the spaces provided to identify specific software)

❏ Word processing: [26]

❏ Data bases: [28]

❏ File Utilities: [30]

❏ Networking: [32]

❏ Other: [34]

❏ Spreadsheets: [27]

❏ Desktop publishing: [29]

❏ Money management: [31]

❏ Programming languages: [33]

I use a PC at (please check all that apply): ❏ home [35] ❏ work [36] ❏ school [37] ❏ other: [38] _____

The disks I prefer to use are ❏ 5.25 [39] ❏ 3.5 [40] ❏ other: [41] _____

I have a CD ROM: ❏ yes [42]   ❏ no [43]

I plan to buy or upgrade computer hardware this year: ❏ yes [44]   ❏ no [45]

I plan to buy or upgrade computer software this year: ❏ yes [46]   ❏ no [47]

Name: _____   Business title: [48] _____   Type of Business: [49] _____

Address (❏ home [50] ❏ work [51]/Company name: _____)

Street/Suite#

City [52]/State [53]/Zipcode [54]: _____   Country [55] _____

❏ **I liked this book!** You may quote me by name in future IDG Books Worldwide promotional materials.

My daytime phone number is _____

IDG BOOKS

THE WORLD OF COMPUTER KNOWLEDGE

❑ YES!

Please keep me informed about IDG's World of Computer Knowledge.
Send me the latest IDG Books catalog.